Praise for *Eisenhower in War and Peace*

"Crisply written and meticulous . . . absorbing. . . . [Jean Edward Smith] makes a convincing argument, obliterating earlier arguments by historians that Eisenhower's was a dull, torpid presidency marked by mediocrity and go-along-to-get-along policy . . . Smith has written a biography worthy of his subject."

— *The Christian Science Monitor*

"Too often we forget, even after having had half a century to think about it, that, as Jean Edward Smith puts it in this fine new biography, Eisenhower was 'the only president in the twentieth century to preside over eight years of peace and prosperity.'"

—*The Washington Post*

"The greatest strength of this graceful, well-written and splendidly paced biography is the objectivity that leaps from the pages. Often, biographers lean toward hagiography, gushing profusely about their subject. Smith doesn't do this. . . . Those who don't want to wait for the textbook version of this story can read Smith's candidly refreshing biography and come away not only impressed with the author's pen, but with a new measure of why, even with his flaws, so many people liked Ike."

—*The Washington Independent Review of Books*

"Presidencies, like good wines, improve with age. . . . There is no more powerful example of growing-better-with-age theory of presidential history than Dwight D. Eisenhower's two terms in the Oval Office. . . . Smith's highly readable one-volume biography [is] clearly designed to enhance Ike's claim to greatness."

—*The Wall Street Journal*

"Dwight David Eisenhower's story is told in fascinating and copious detail by historian and master storyteller Jean Edward Smith."

—*The Orange County Register*

# EISENHOWER

★ ★ ★ ★ ★

## IN WAR AND PEACE

# EISENHOWER

## IN WAR AND PEACE

*Jean Edward Smith*

RANDOM HOUSE TRADE PAPERBACKS   NEW YORK

2013 Random House Trade Paperback Edition

Copyright © 2012 by Jean Edward Smith
Maps copyright © 2012 by Mapping Specialists

Published in the United States by Random House Trade Paperbacks,
an imprint of The Random House Publishing Group,
a division of Random House, Inc., New York.

RANDOM HOUSE TRADE PAPERBACKS and colophon are trademarks
of Random House, Inc.

Originally published in hardcover in the United States by Random House,
an imprint of The Random House Publishing Group,
a division of Random House, Inc., in 2012.

LIBRARY OF CONGRESS CATALOGING-IN-PUBLICATION DATA

Smith, Jean Edward.
Eisenhower in war and peace / by Jean Edward Smith.
p. cm.
Includes bibliographical references and index.
ISBN 978-0-8129-8288-6
eISBN 978-0-679-64429-3
1. Eisenhower, Dwight D. (Dwight David), 1890–1969.
2. Presidents—United States—Biography 3. Generals—United States—
Biography. 4. United States—Politics and government—1953–1961.
5. United States. Army—Biography. I. Title.
E836.S56 2012      973.921092—dc22      2011008605
[B]

Printed in the United States of America

www.atrandom.com

8 9 7

Book design by Christopher M. Zucker

*For Christine*

I hate war as only a
soldier who has lived it can.

—DWIGHT D. EISENHOWER

# *Preface*

DWIGHT EISENHOWER REMAINS an enigma. For the majority of Americans he is a benign fatherly figure looming indistinctly out of the mists of the past—a high-ranking general who directed the Allied armies to victory in Europe, and a caretaker president who presided over eight years of international calm and domestic tranquility. To those who knew him, Ike was a tireless taskmaster who worked with incredible subtlety to move events in the direction he wished them to go. Most would agree he was a man of principle, decency, and common sense, whom the country could count on to do what was right. In both war and peace he gave the world confidence in American leadership.

Ike's generalship has often been disparaged. Some have suggested he lacked strategic vision, that he was a mere administrator, a hail-fellow-well-met who simply kept everyone content and in harness while working toward a common goal. It is easy to understand how such misconceptions could arise. Eisenhower made victory appear inevitable. He did not posture or pose for the press, he issued no grandiloquent communiqués, and he did not pit himself against high command or political authority. He got on with the job with a minimum of fuss. He was parsimonious with the lives of the troops entrusted to his command, evenhanded toward his allies, and ready to take responsibility for whatever occurred. He was a military leader in the time-honored tradition of Washington and Grant, a man who symbolized American democracy: the ideal commander for a citizen army of draftees.

Eisenhower's job was not easy. Topside were Churchill, Roosevelt, and de Gaulle, each with his own ideas about how the war should be fought. The chain of command ran through the Combined Chiefs of Staff, principally General George Marshall and Field Marshal Sir Alan Brooke, who were often at odds over what course to follow. Ike handled his command relationships with what appeared to be effortless aplomb. In fact, he did it so well that one rarely considered the complexities involved.

The task he faced was daunting. Eisenhower commanded the largest multinational force ever assembled, mounted an unprecedented cross-Channel invasion of Europe, mastered logistical problems on a scale never before encountered, and came to grips with a battle-tested German Army fighting on familiar terrain. Dealing with fractious but gifted subordinates such as George Patton and Bernard Montgomery seemed relatively simple by comparison.

Like Grant and Pershing, Eisenhower commanded on the spot. He did not dodge difficult decisions, he did not pass the buck to staff conferences or subordinate commanders, and he always knew that if he did not measure up, he would be summarily relieved. Supreme commanders do not enjoy job security. "At any moment a necessity might arise for my relief and consequent demotion," Ike wrote his son John in 1943. When the war ended, Eisenhower's accomplishment in leading the Western powers to victory was fully recognized, yet today it has largely receded from our understanding.

Eisenhower's presidential years appear equally remote. Yet with the exception of Franklin Roosevelt, Dwight Eisenhower was the most successful president of the twentieth century. He ended a three-year, no-win war in Korea with honor and dignity; resisted calls for preventive war against the Soviet Union and China; deployed the Seventh Fleet to protect Formosa from invasion; faced down Khrushchev over Berlin; and restored stability in Lebanon when sectarian violence threatened to pull the country apart. On the home front, Ike punctured the Roosevelt coalition, weaned the Republican party from its isolationist past, restored the nation's sanity after the McCarthyite binge of Communist witch-hunting, and proved unbeatable at the polls. During his two terms in the White House, his monthly approval rating averaged 64 percent, a figure never equaled since World War II.

Eisenhower believed that the United States should not go to war unless national survival was at stake. "There is no alternative to peace," he famously said. He dismissed the necessity of conflict beneath the nuclear threshold and refused to engage American troops in brushfire wars for political abstractions. After Ike made peace in Korea, not a single American died in combat for the next eight years.

When the National Security Council—Dulles, Nixon, and the chairman of the Joint Chiefs of Staff—recommended intervention (including the use of nuclear weapons) at Dien Bien Phu to rescue the beleaguered French garrison, Eisenhower summarily rejected the proposal. "You boys must be crazy," he told his national security assistant, Robert Cutler. "We can't use those awful things against Asians for the second time in less than ten years. My God." Five years later, when China threatened force against Taiwan, the Joint Chiefs recommended an immediate nuclear response, and once again Eisenhower rejected the idea.

When Britain, France, and Israel invaded Egypt to seize the Suez Canal in 1956, Eisenhower forced them to withdraw, toppling Anthony Eden's government in London, undercutting the Fourth Republic in France, and threatening financial sanctions against Israel. That repudiation of what Ike called "old fashioned gunboat diplomacy" not only kept the peace but enhanced American prestige throughout the world.

Domestically, Eisenhower tamed inflation, slashed defense spending, balanced the federal budget, and worked easily with a Democratic Congress. Two of his appointees to the Supreme Court, Chief Justice Earl Warren and William Brennan, launched a judicial revolution. Presidents cannot control the decisions of their appointees, and Ike was disappointed in some of the rulings of the Warren Court, but the advances Americans have experienced in civil liberty and social justice during the past fifty years are in some very large measure attributable to Warren and Brennan.

It was also Eisenhower who began the practice of submitting the names of potential judicial nominees to the American Bar Association for preliminary vetting (a practice discontinued in 2001 by the Bush administration but resumed under President Obama). His appointees to the lower federal courts, moderate Republicans including John Minor Wisdom in Louisiana and Elbert P. Tuttle in Georgia, were the judicial heroes of the civil rights struggle, and Ike's Justice Department backed them to the hilt.

Eisenhower held a textbook view of presidential power. As more than one scholar has observed, he may have been the last president to actually believe in the Constitution. For Ike, Congress made policy and the president carried it out. He took his constitutional responsibility to "take care that the laws be faithfully executed" at face value. In 1957, when a United States District Court in Little Rock, Arkansas, ordered the desegregation of Central High, Eisenhower dispatched the 101st Airborne Division from Fort Campbell, Kentucky, to enforce the court's order. If he had not acted, and if he had not used overwhelming force to ensure compliance with the district court's order, desegregation in the South would have been set back at least a generation. "Sending in the troops was the hardest decision I had had to make since D-Day," Eisenhower said afterward. "But Goddamn it, it was the only thing I could do."

Eisenhower was a progressive conservative. He believed traditional American values encompassed change and progress. He looked to the future, not the past, and his presidency provided a buffered transition from FDR's New Deal and the Fair Deal of Harry Truman into the modern era. "Should any political party attempt to abolish social security and eliminate labor laws and farm programs, you would never hear of that party again," Ike wrote his brother Edgar. "There is a tiny splinter group that believes you can do these things. Among them are H. L. Hunt [and] a few other Texas millionaires. But their number is negligible and they are stupid."

When the economy turned down after the Korean War, Eisenhower initiated the interstate highway program and constructed the

St. Lawrence Seaway, not only revolutionizing the American transportation system, but opening the Great Lakes to ocean traffic. Neither program affected the federal budget. The interstate system—the cost of which eventually exceeded the total expenditures of the New Deal from 1933 to 1941—was funded entirely by increased gasoline taxes, and the seaway through the sale of interest-bearing revenue bonds issued by the U.S.-Canadian Seaway Development Corporation. The National Defense Education Act, which Eisenhower signed into law in 1958, broke the long-standing taboo against direct federal aid to education and has done more to change the face of American universities than any measure since enactment of the GI Bill during World War II.

As president, Eisenhower restored stability to the nation. His levelheaded leadership ensured that the United States would move forward in measured steps under the rule of law at home and collective security abroad. His sensible admonition upon leaving office to be wary of the military-industrial complex was the heartfelt sentiment of a president who recognized the perils of world leadership. Eisenhower gave the country eight years of peace and prosperity. No other president in the twentieth century can make that claim.

As with FDR, politics came naturally to Eisenhower. Bismarck once observed that political judgment was the ability to hear the distant hoofbeats of the horse of history. Ike possessed that talent in abundance. As historian Garry Wills put it, Ike was a political genius. "It is no mere accident that he remained, year after year, the most respected man in America." Veteran political scientist Samuel Lubell said, "It would be difficult to cite any president, including both Roosevelts, who has been more adept in giving the people what they want." Unlike FDR, however, Eisenhower went to great lengths to conceal his political acumen. That too was deliberate. All of his life Eisenhower had managed crises without overreacting. He made every task he undertook look easy. Ike's military experience taught him that an outward display of casualness inspired confidence, and he took that lesson into the White House. Liberal columnist Murray Kempton, who penetrated the façade, noted with grudging admiration that Eisenhower was "the president most superbly equipped for consequential decisions we may ever have had . . . as calm when he was demonstrating the wisdom of leaving a bad situation alone as when he was moving to meet it on those occasions when he absolutely had to."

Eisenhower was one of the few presidents who had achieved national prominence before entering the White House. He was a revered figure on the world stage and moved easily among foreign leaders. Ike had no need to prove himself. That sense of self added stature to the presidency—much as Roosevelt did after 1933.

Dwight Eisenhower was the product of the peacetime professional Army. He had endured the stagnation, the endless wait for promotion, the woeful lack of equipment and manpower that characterized the United States Army between World War I and World War II. Advancement from one rank to the next was based strictly on seniority. The hidden virtue in Ike's case was that a promotion system based on seniority permitted an exceptional independence of thought and action. A junior officer was not required to flatter his commander's whims in order to obtain that outstanding efficiency report upon which meritorious promotions now hinge. There were no meritorious promotions. There was no rapid advancement. Everyone stood in line, at least to the rank of colonel. And while that meant inordinate delay for men such as Eisenhower to reach the top (Ike served in the rank of major for sixteen years), it also ensured that their independence of thought was still intact when they got there. As a result, Eisenhower had supreme confidence in his own judgment.[*]

Contrary to conventional wisdom, Eisenhower was not runner-up to George C. Marshall to command OVERLORD—the Allied invasion of Europe. FDR recognized that Marshall, who was performing superbly as Army chief of staff, had clashed too often with the British on matters of global strategy to be fully effective as supreme commander. The president had taken Eisenhower's measure in North Africa and Sicily, observed his easy manner with the British and French, his fairness and patience dealing with Allied commanders,

---

[*] I am indebted to General Lucius D. Clay for that observation. "Efficiency reports had no bearing whatever on when you would be promoted," said Clay. "They helped determine your next assignment, but unless someone was manifestly unfit you knew exactly the order in which you would be promoted." Clay, interview, Columbia Oral History Project, Columbia University (COHP).

and concluded he was best suited to lead a multinational force across the Channel. The job was Marshall's if he wanted it, but with characteristic self-discipline, the chief of staff deferred to Roosevelt's judgment. FDR's decision proved correct, and despite the inevitable friction of coalition warfare, Ike waged a masterful campaign that left no ally disappointed. As the French military historian Olivier Wieviorka has written, "Eisenhower was the right man at the right place at the right time."

The Army of Eisenhower's day valued understatement. With rare exceptions generals did not decorate themselves like Christmas trees. Action spoke for itself. Nothing did that more eloquently than the simple soldier's funeral of the nation's thirty-fourth president. On April 2, 1969, in Abilene, Kansas, Eisenhower was laid to rest in the presence of his family. He was buried in a government-issue, eighty-dollar pine coffin, wearing his famous Ike jacket with no medals or decorations other than his insignia of rank.

JEAN EDWARD SMITH

# Contents

# EISENHOWER

★   ★   ★   ★   ★

## IN WAR AND PEACE

# ONE

# *Just Folks*

I'm just folks. I come from the people,
the ordinary people.
— DWIGHT D. EISENHOWER

DWIGHT D. EISENHOWER was born in Denison, Texas, on October 14, 1890.[1] He was the third of seven sons born to David and Ida Eisenhower, and the only one born in Texas. The Eisenhowers lived in Denison from October 1888 to March 1892, and it was the economic low point of their married life. David worked for ten dollars a week as an engine wiper for the Missouri, Kansas, and Texas (Katy) Railroad, and the family lived in a soot-encrusted shanty near the tracks.

David's bout with poverty was self-inflicted. His Eisenhower ancestors had been prosperous farmers, first in the Odenwald region of Germany, south of Frankfurt, then in Pennsylvania, then Kansas. The first Eisenhower to arrive in America was Hans Nicholas, who landed in Philadelphia in 1741, part of the wave of Protestant emigration from Europe to the Quaker colony of Pennsylvania. The family flourished amid the fertile soil of the Susquehanna Valley. Originally Lutheran, they married into the River Brethren, a doctrinaire offshoot of the Mennonites, embraced the faith, and quickly emerged as leaders of the flock.[*] Jacob, David's father (and Ike's

---

[*] The River Brethren, several hundred strong, derived their name from their residence along the Susquehanna. Like their nonconformist Mennonite forebears they

grandfather), became the preacher and a patriarch of the sect, attracting large audiences to his sermons, which he delivered in German—
the *plattdeutsch* vernacular that was still spoken in most households.

In 1878, the River Brethren sold their holdings along the Susquehanna and moved to Kansas, lured by the promise of cheap land,
deep soil, and the opportunity to plant their community in the vir-
gin countryside. They took the train from Harrisburg, filling fifteen
freight cars with their farm equipment and belongings, including a
dozen heavy-duty eight-horse wagons new to the prairie. They also
brought a half-million dollars in cash (roughly $9 million in current
dollars), the product of a thrifty lifestyle and successful land sales in
a rising eastern market.[2] That combination of thrift and capital, of
diligence and experience, plus a generous helping of communal support, ensured success where others failed. As an early Kansas history
put it, the River Brethren were "one of the most complete and perfectly organized [colonies] that ever entered a new country."[3]

The colony settled in Dickinson County along the fertile banks of
Smoky Hill River, smack in the middle of Kansas and twenty miles
west of the geographic center of the United States, an area that would
become one of the most productive agricultural regions in the world.[4]
Jacob purchased a quarter section (160 acres) of prime farmland and
erected a large house that also served as a Sunday meeting place for
the brethren. He built a huge barn reminiscent of the Dutch barns

---

rejected infant baptism and the authority of the established church, and believed
the Bible to be the true word of God. They distinguished themselves from the
Mennonite faith by their insistence on baptism by trine immersion and their emphasis on the literal interpretation of the scriptures. The River Brethren, subsequently organized as the Church of the Brethren in Christ, dressed plainly and
stressed the Spartan virtues of self-reliance and self-denial. They rejected violence,
military service, alcohol, tobacco, and other worldly pleasures in obedience to
God's will. On the other hand, the accumulation of property was almost an act of
piety. Prosperity was considered an expression of God's favor. In a sense, the River
Brethren were early evangelicals. The phrase "born again" was not in common
usage at the time, but it would describe their belief that salvation through Christ
is received by personal faith and repentance. For an extensive treatment of the
River Brethren and their beliefs, see Laban T. Brechbill, *History of the Old Order
River Brethren* 5–22 (Lancaster, Pa.: Brechbill and Stricker, 1972). Also see Kenneth S. Davis, *Soldier of Democracy: A Biography of Dwight Eisenhower* 10–13 (Garden City, N.Y.: Doubleday, 1945).

in Pennsylvania, added to his dairy herd, and constructed a wooden windmill.

The River Brethren thrived in their new setting. Jacob acquired more land, helped found a successful local creamery, and established a bank in the nearby village of Hope. When his children married, he provided each with a quarter section of tillable land as a homestead and two thousand dollars in cash, more than enough to get started if they wished to follow in his footsteps.

David Eisenhower was fifteen when his parents moved to Kansas. Unlike his siblings he had no interest in farming and secured his father's permission to study engineering and mechanics at Lane College, a fledgling educational institution founded by the United Brethren in Christ in nearby Lecompton. With a faculty of ten part-time instructors and two hundred students, the school had a modest curriculum emphasizing religious studies and vocational training with a smattering of the liberal arts. David enrolled in September 1883, at the age of twenty, and the following year met a captivating young woman from Virginia, Ida Stover, who had entered Lane to study music.

Ida's background was similar to David's. Her ancestors had emigrated from Swabia (near Stuttgart) a decade before the Eisenhowers, settled initially in Pennsylvania, then in the Shenandoah Valley of Virginia. Among the first Germans to reach the Shenandoah, they prospered tilling the soil and soon accumulated substantial land holdings. Ida was born at Mount Sidney in 1862, one of eleven children, and was baptized in the Lutheran faith. Her parents died when she was young, and she was raised by her maternal grandparents. Blessed with boundless confidence, she left home to attend high school in Staunton, and then taught for two years in a one-room schoolhouse near Mount Sidney. When she turned twenty-one, Ida came into an inheritance of a thousand dollars left by her father. Several of her brothers had already moved to Kansas, and she used part of the money to join them. In June 1883, she settled in Lecompton with her brother William, a successful local minister. That autumn she entered Lane.[5]

Ida and David made an attractive couple, but in many ways they could not have been more different. She was optimistic, perky, and,

David Eisenhower and Ida Stover on their wedding
day, September 23, 1885.

in the words of one biographer, "as bright as the Kansas sunshine."[6]
He was solemn, introverted, and stubborn—as humorless and
self-absorbed as Ida was vivacious and outgoing. They were married
on September 23, 1885, David's twenty-second birthday, and Ida
spent the last of her inheritance, some $600 (roughly $10,000 today),
on a new ebony piano built by Hallett and Cumston in Boston, a
possession she treasured for the rest of her life.

Neither David nor Ida completed their studies at Lane. With his
father's support, David opened a general store in Hope, using the
proceeds from his wedding present as capital.[7] The village of Hope,
located twenty-eight miles southeast of Abilene, was the commercial
center for the River Brethren. The main line of the Topeka, Salina,
and Western Railroad had just reached the settlement, and the opportunity for growth appeared assured. Because David had no busi-

ness experience, he formed a partnership with Milton Good, a young man roughly the same age who was a clothing salesman in Abilene and who was familiar with the retail trade. There were two apartments above the store. David and Ida lived in one, and the Goods in the other.

According to Eisenhower legend, Milton Good was a scoundrel who absconded with the firm's cash, leaving David helpless to pay the store's bills. The business failed, and David was forced to travel to Denison to find work. That is the account David and Ida told, and which the Eisenhower sons dutifully passed on.[8]

That is not what happened. Milton Good did not abscond with the money, and the store did not fail. It had been a rocky partnership from the beginning—the partners were temperamentally mismatched, and David was far from easy to work with. After eighteen months they dissolved the partnership and David bought out Good. He borrowed $3,500 from his father, pledged the store's inventory as collateral, and used the money to purchase Good's share of the business. Three days later Jacob Eisenhower canceled the mortgage, in effect converting the loan into a gift.[9]

Milton Good's place in the store was taken by David's younger brother, Abraham Lincoln Eisenhower, and the firm was rechristened Eisenhower Brothers. Abraham was a River Brethren preacher and practicing veterinarian, and was as genial as David was somber. With Abraham's spark the business continued, although David grew increasingly dissatisfied. He lost interest in the store and walked away from it in October 1888. The business was renamed A. L. Eisenhower & Company, and David drifted off to Denison, leaving Ida, who was six months pregnant, and their two-year-old son, Arthur, in Abraham's care.[10]

David's decision to quit the store and abandon his pregnant wife is incomprehensible. He had no job lined up or profession on which to fall back, and he disdained the farm life at which the Eisenhowers excelled. In fact, the decision is so inexplicable that David could never own up to it, and neither parent ever revealed the truth to their children. Out of pity for David, those who knew the truth—the Eisenhower family and others—also kept the secret to themselves, complicit, as it were, in a myth that had no substance. As a result,

Ike and his brothers died believing the family's straitened circum-stances were due to Milton Good's treachery rather than their father's instability.[11]

Ida remained in Hope with Abraham until her second son—christened Edgar, for Edgar Allan Poe—was born, and in April 1889 moved the family to join David in Denison. Eighteen months later Dwight was born. By this time, the family had hit rock bottom. David was twenty-seven, Ida a year older. Of his own volition, David had squandered a substantial inheritance. The Eisenhowers lived in what was little more than a shack beside the tracks. Aside from Ida's piano (which had been left in Hope), they had no assets other than their clothes and a few household possessions, and absolutely no prospect of doing better.

The family came to the rescue. In 1891, after the death of his wife, Jacob Eisenhower visited his eldest son in Denison and was visibly shaken by the poverty in which he and Ida were living.[12] The Belle Springs Creamery, which Jacob had helped found, and which had become one of the largest and most successful enterprises in Dickin-son County, had recently built a new plant in Abilene.[13] Chris Musser, David's brother-in-law (he had married David's sister Amanda), was the manager of the plant, and Jacob prevailed upon him to find a position for David. Musser offered him a job as a refrig-eration mechanic at "less than $50 a month."[14] That is essentially what David was earning in Denison, but the job was a considerable step up from scrubbing the grime from Katy locomotives, and he would be back in the bosom of the family. At Ida's urging, he ac-cepted immediately. In March 1892, after three and a half years of self-imposed exile, David and Ida returned to Abilene. His total as-sets, which he carried in his pocket, amounted to $24.15.

David and Ida rented a small frame house a few blocks from the creamery. It had no plumbing or electricity, and sat tight by the neighbors with no yard or garden. The Eisenhowers remained there for seven years while three more sons were born: Roy in 1892; Paul in 1894 (he died in infancy); and Earl in 1898. Five boys in a cramped house made life nearly impossible. Again the family came to the rescue. In 1898, David's brother Abraham sold his veterinary prac-tice (he had sold the store several years earlier) and moved west as a

Abilene, Kansas, circa 1900.

religious missionary. Abraham owned a large two-story frame house set on a three-acre lot, complete with a barn and fruit orchard. He agreed to sell the property to David for a thousand dollars. Jacob advanced the money, and the title was put in Ida's name—evidently a precaution against a recurrence of David's wanderlust.[15] That is the house in which the Eisenhower boys grew to maturity, and which is now the focal point of the Eisenhower Presidential Library and Museum in Abilene.

The Abilene of 1898 was not the Abilene of Wild Bill Hickok and the Chisholm Trail.* The famous cow town of the 1860s and '70s

---

* "Hell is now in session in Abilene," proclaimed the *Topeka Sentinel* in July 1867. After the Civil War, the tiny hamlet of Abilene found itself the western terminus of the Kansas Pacific Railroad, and the northern terminus of the Chisholm Trail. Cattlemen from Texas, eager to sell their range-fattened longhorns on the eastern market, drove their cattle 1,200 to 1,500 miles up the Chisholm Trail to the railroad at Abilene, where they would be loaded onto cattle cars and shipped to meat packers in Kansas City and Chicago. In Texas the cattle sold for two dollars to five dollars a head; in Abilene they brought ten and sometimes twenty times that much. Between 1867 and 1872 more than two million cattle were shipped from Abilene. In the peak year of 1871, six hundred thousand made the journey. In

had faded into a sleepy Kansas backwater. The streets were still unpaved, the sidewalks still made of wooden planks, and the scent of
horse apples still lay over the main street. But the saloons and dance
halls were gone. Abilene had but one policeman, who patrolled not
for local crime, of which there was none, but for transient hustlers
and others of ill repute. Churches, hymn singing, and picnics by the
riverbank provided the town's excitement. Abilene had become a
citadel of Protestant fundamentalism, the Kansas cradle of Prohibition. It was one of many buckles on the Bible Belt: a wholesome
town of 3,500 where respectable citizens did not profane the Sabbath
with baseball or football. The politics were populist, but the lifestyle
was as staid and proper as on Boston's Beacon Hill. It was the American heartland.

Eisenhower was eight when the family moved to their new home.
"I have found out later we were very poor," he recalled, "but we
didn't know it at the time."[16] David worked twelve hours a day, six
days a week at the creamery, but his meager salary scarcely covered
basic necessities. Ida ran the household, assigned chores to the children, and managed what became a three-acre garden plot. There
were two cows to provide milk, a flock of chickens for eggs, ducks,
pigs, and a horse to plow the garden and pull the family wagon. Ex-

---

1872, when the rail lines pushed south and west to Wichita and Dodge City,
Abilene ceased to be a shipping point for Texas cattle.

During its cattle heyday from 1867 to 1872, Abilene was America's sin city.
The typical herd consisted of 2,500 cattle. It required ten to twelve cowboys to
move the herd on its long journey, and when they reached Abilene their work was
done. They would be paid off, and after several months on the trail were eager to
celebrate. In 1870, Abilene, with a permanent population of less than a thousand,
offered seventeen saloons, six hotels, and a dozen dance halls. The local boot factory employed twenty bootmakers to keep up with cowboy demand; the Alamo
saloon, Abilene's largest and most famous, kept four bartenders busy pouring
drinks. Drunken cowboys wandered the streets and shootings were commonplace.
A pair of frontier marshals, Tom Smith and James Butler Hickok, brought a sem-
blance of order to Abilene, but it was not until the railhead moved west to Dodge
and Wichita that peace was restored.

Samuel Eliot Morison, *The Oxford History of the American People* 756–57 (New
York: Oxford University Press, 1965); Peter Lyon, *The Wild, Wild West* 75–76
(New York: Funk and Wagnalls, 1969); Larry D. Underwood, *Abilene Lawmen*
1–195 (Lincoln, Neb.: Dageforde Publishing, 1999).

cept for flour, sugar, salt, and kerosene for their lamps, the Eisenhowers were largely self-sufficient. The boys wore hand-me-downs, performed odd jobs around town for spending money, and grew to manhood unencumbered by the complexities of urban life.

Religion loomed large in the Eisenhower household. The day began with David reading scripture to the family, there were prayers before each meal, and after supper the family gathered again to pass the Bible from hand to hand as each boy read a passage out loud. "This was a good way to get us to read the Bible," said Ike's younger brother Milton (who was born in 1899). "I am not sure it was a good way to help us understand it."[17]

None of the Eisenhower brothers shared their parents' religious ardor. By the time Ike left for West Point he had read the Bible through twice. He was familiar with it and often quoted passages from memory, but he rarely took it literally. His vocabulary was punctuated with profanity that would make a mule skinner blush, and throughout his military service he never joined a church or attended Sunday service.[18] As president he allowed himself to be convinced that the United States was a Christian country, joined Mamie in the Presbyterian faith, and urged that the words "under God" be inserted in the pledge of allegiance.[19]* Like FDR, a nominal Episcopalian, Eisenhower appreciated religion's political resonance.

For their part, David and Ida left the River Brethren and began the search for religious certainty in more personal terms. David found it in the Great Pyramid of Giza, which he reproduced in a six-by-ten-foot scale drawing and which he believed corroborated the prophecies in the Bible. Ida turned to a more austere and primitive sect known as Bible Students, which in 1931 adopted the name "Jehovah's Witnesses."[20] Ike's brother Edgar remembers meetings in their house. "Everyone made his own interpretation of the Scripture

---

* When he assumed office in January 1953, Eisenhower made headlines when he announced that he was beginning cabinet sessions with a moment of silent prayer. (The suggestion had been made by Agriculture Secretary Ezra Taft Benson, one of the Twelve Apostles of the Mormon Church.) "I know that without God's help we cannot succeed," said Benson. "With his help we cannot fail" (quoting Lincoln's farewell remarks in Springfield in 1861).

lessons. Mother played the piano, and they sang hymns before and after each meeting. It was a real old time prayer meeting. They talked to God, read Scriptures, and everyone got a chance to state his relationship with Him."[21] David attended Bible Students meetings with Ida for a number of years and then dropped out, retreating into personal mysticism.

After his misadventure in Denison, David was chastened and bitter. He became ever more sullen and introspective—something of a stranger to his children, with a quick and fearful temper. David never played with his sons, never took them hunting or fishing, did not swim with them, showed no interest in who their friends were, and rarely inquired about their activities. "He was an inflexible man with a stern code," said Edgar. "Life to him was a very serious proposition, and that's the way he lived it, soberly and with due reflection."[22]

The Eisenhower household revolved around David's needs. Ida accepted his decisions, boosted his ego, and bowed to his whims. "I never heard a cross word pass between them," Ike remembered.[23] The boys took turns getting up before daylight to build a fire in the cookstove to prepare David's breakfast. They carried his hot lunch to him every day at the creamery, and Ida had dinner prepared when he got home in the evening. David lived in his own world. As Ike's oldest brother, Arthur, put it, their father was absent even when he was there.[24]

Ida took up the slack. "Mother was by far the greatest personal influence on our lives," said Ike.[25] She was there for them when David was not, a constant presence who organized their lives, soothed their hurts, and praised their accomplishments. Despite the near penury in which they lived, Ida could usually see the humorous side of any predicament. Milton said, "She always had a song in her heart."[26] Of all the boys, it was commonly agreed that Ike was the one who resembled his mother most.

The Eisenhower brothers may not have known that they were poor, but they knew they did not want the menial life their father led. As soon as they could, they put Abilene behind them. Arthur was the first to leave, quitting high school after two years to seek his fortune in Kansas City, where he found employment as a bank mes-

The Eisenhower family, 1902. *Front:* David, Milton, and Ida; *back:* Dwight, Edgar, Arthur, Earl, and Roy.

senger.* Beginning at a salary of five dollars a week, Arthur rose through the ranks to become executive vice president and a director of the Commerce Trust, one of the largest banks west of the Mississippi. He became a national expert in the grain trade and, in a fifty-year career with the bank, never missed a day because of ill health.[27] "Arthur was a trail blazer for the rest of us," said Edgar. "He pointed the way upward by being the first to break away to find a job."[28]

Edgar dropped out of school for two years, worked at a series of unskilled jobs at the Belle Springs Creamery, and then returned to graduate from high school with Ike in 1909. He worked his way through Michigan Law School,[29] founded his own firm in Tacoma, Washington (Eisenhower, Hunter, Ramsdell, and Duncan), and was

---

* In Kansas City, Arthur roomed originally in a boardinghouse kept by a Mrs. Trow on Troost Avenue. Another young boarder was Harry Truman, from Independence. "Harry and I had only a dollar a week left over for riotous living," Arthur recalled. David McCullough, *Truman* 72–73 (New York: Simon and Schuster, 1992).

the most financially successful of the brothers. Edgar was also the most combative and avuncular, and the most outspokenly conservative. He admired Chief Justice John Marshall, despised Franklin Roosevelt and the New Deal, and deplored the progressive drift of his brother's presidency.

Roy, the fourth brother, worked equally hard to succeed as a pharmacist, first in Ellsworth, then in Junction City, Kansas, where he owned his own store. Roy traveled the least distance from Abilene, but his store did a thriving business (Fort Riley was nearby), and he became a fixture in local civic organizations. The most social and outgoing of the brothers—a born joiner and glad-hander—he died of a heart condition in 1942 at the age of fifty.

Earl, a successful engineer and newspaperman, also left Abilene after high school and joined Edgar in Tacoma. With Edgar's help he graduated from the University of Washington in 1923 with a degree in electrical engineering, traveled the Far East as an engineer on the passenger liner *President Grant,* and settled in western Pennsylvania with a public utility company. Later he worked as general manager for *Suburban Life,* a biweekly newspaper in La Grange, Illinois, and served one term (1964–66) as a Republican member of the Illinois legislature.

Milton, nine years younger than Ike, was the scholar in the family. Trained in journalism at Kansas State, he entered government service in 1926 after attaining the highest score on that year's civil service examination. He rose rapidly in Washington, and by the early 1930s was the principal assistant to Henry Wallace at the Department of Agriculture. In February 1942, when the Army interned Japanese Americans living on the Pacific coast, FDR named Milton to head the War Relocation Authority to handle their resettlement.[30] Three months later he became deputy director of the newly established Office of War Information. Milton left government in 1943 to become president of Kansas State University, was named president of Penn State in 1950, and six years later became president of Johns Hopkins.

If Ike shared his brothers' urgency to succeed it was not immediately evident. After coasting through high school, he worked for two years at the Belle Springs Creamery, first as an ice puller hoisting

DAVID DWIGHT
EISENHOWER

Senior photo of Dwight from the Abilene
High School yearbook, 1909. Ike's classmates
voted him most likely to become a history professor at Yale.

three-hundred-pound slabs of ice from the freezing unit, then as a
fireman stoking furnaces, and finally as the night superintendent of
the plant. His salary of ninety dollars a month was essentially the
same as his father's, who had been employed at the creamery for
eighteen years.

In high school Eisenhower made good grades with minimal effort.
He had a logical mind, a retentive memory, and a natural gift for
writing clear, effective prose. His best grades were in English and
history. Classmates, in their senior yearbook, predicted that he would
become a professor of history at Yale. That may seem outrageous
academic optimism for a high school on the Great Plains that produced fewer than thirty graduates a year, but the school's rigorous

emphasis on fundamentals was not misplaced. In 1950, three pre–World War I graduates of tiny Abilene High were presidents of major American universities: Dwight Eisenhower at Columbia; Milton at Penn State; and Deane Malott at Cornell.

As a student, Ike engaged in the usual pranks, enjoyed team sports—especially baseball and football—and suffered the customary bumps and bruises. "He was just another average chap," Orin Snider, his high school coach, said later. "He was a capable player, but just another player."[31]

Eisenhower discovered West Point by chance. Some young men, often from military families—men such as Douglas MacArthur and George Patton—grow up thinking of nothing but West Point. Others, such as Ulysses Grant and John J. Pershing, go to the academy for a professional education at the government's expense. And for others attendance is accidental. In Eisenhower's case it was a combination of accidental discovery and the recognition that West Point would provide a free college education that he might not otherwise acquire.

In the summer of 1910, after he had put in a year at the creamery, Eisenhower happened to renew his friendship with an old high school chum, Everett "Swede" Hazlett. Swede was the son of a prosperous Abilene physician who had entered high school with Ike, but soon transferred to a prep school in Wisconsin. He was spending the summer tending a gaslight-fixture store his father owned near the creamery, and had already received a congressional appointment to the United States Naval Academy at Annapolis. Unfortunately, he failed the mathematics portion of the entrance examination and was in Abilene to study for a retake. Ike and Swede became lifelong friends. Their correspondence, which continued until Swede's death in 1958, is remarkably intimate—as introspective and revealing as any Ike ever wrote, explaining his actions, trying out ideas, and using Swede as a sounding board.[32]

In the course of the summer, Swede convinced Ike that the service academies offered the best ticket out of Abilene. "It was not difficult to persuade me this was a good move," Eisenhower wrote later.[33] There is no evidence he fretted about his parents' pacifist convictions. To the contrary, he worked diligently that summer to secure an appointment. His first choice was to accompany Swede to Annapolis, and if that were not possible, to go to West Point.[34]

At Swede's suggestion, Ike wrote Senator Joseph L. Bristow, who had recently been elected to the United States Senate; he was from Salina—just twenty-five miles west of Abilene. Bristow (whose campaign had been directed by his close friend William Allen White of *The Emporia Gazette*) was a reform Republican, an enemy of the spoils system, and the first Kansas senator to be elected by popular vote instead of by the state legislature. Unlike most members of Congress, he was holding a competitive examination for his academy appointments. For Eisenhower, it was a lucky break. His family had no political connections, and he would have been out of the running for a patronage appointment.

On August 20, 1910, Eisenhower wrote the Sunflower State's junior senator:

> Dear Sir:
>
> I would very much like to enter either the school at Annapolis, or the one at West Point. . . .
>
> I have graduated from high school and will be nineteen years of age this fall.
>
> If you find it possible to appoint me to one of these schools, your kindness will certainly be appreciated by me.
>
> *Respectfully yours,*
> DWIGHT EISENHOWER[35]

To enter the Naval Academy an applicant could not be older than nineteen (West Point set the maximum age at twenty-two). Ike was already nineteen when he wrote, and would turn twenty on October 14, 1910. That would have made him ineligible for Annapolis. So he fudged his birth date. In a time before birth certificates were required, his action was not uncommon. Lucius Clay (West Point Class of 1918) lied about his age as well. In Clay's case he thought he was too young, so he added a year. "Everybody knows your birthday—

family and whatnot," said Clay. "So it was much easier to change the year."[36]*

Senator Bristow did not reply, but in early September the *Abilene Daily Reflector* printed a notice from the senator's office announcing that a competitive examination for West Point and Annapolis would be held in Topeka on October 4 and 5, 1910. Ike wrote immediately to inquire whether he might take the exam, and the senator replied that he was welcome to do so.[37]

Eisenhower was one of eight applicants to appear for the examination on October 4. Four, including Ike, indicated they would accept an appointment to either West Point or Annapolis. The other four sought West Point only. After a grueling two days the grades were tallied and Eisenhower finished second overall, and first among those who indicated they would accept either appointment. His scores ranged from 99 in English to 73 in American history, with a final average of 87.5. George Pulsifer of Fort Leavenworth, who finished first overall with an average score of 89.5, was awarded a presidential at-large appointment to West Point, and Ike was named to the senatorial vacancy.[38]

On October 24, Senator Bristow wrote Eisenhower to inform him of his selection. Bristow said that to complete the War Department nomination form, he needed "a statement of your exact age, years and months, and a statement as to how long you have been an actual resident of Kansas."[39]

Eisenhower replied the following day. "I am just nineteen years

---

* Eisenhower was within West Point's requirements and so when he entered in June 1911 he provided his true birth date. In Clay's case, the incorrect date (1897, not 1898) became part of his military record. I discovered the discrepancy in 1970 while researching Clay's biography, and it is the only time I (or probably anyone else) ever saw General Clay flustered. "I hate to put anything like that on the record," he said, "because it is so tied up with my whole legal existence—retirement, Social Security, the whole works." I suggested I could not very well write his biography if I was not candid about his birth date, and he acquiesced. Before Clay died in 1978, he wrote the inscription for his tombstone at West Point and left blank the line where the date of his birth would normally have been inscribed. Several years later the official date was added by his son, Major General Frank Clay. Jean Edward Smith, *Lucius D. Clay: An American Life* 25–26 (New York: Henry Holt, 1990).

and eleven days of age, and have been a resident of Abilene, Kans. for eighteen years."[40] For the second time Ike misstated his age, although at twenty he was fully eligible for the Military Academy.

Armed with a senatorial appointment, Ike cleared the final hurdle on January 13, 1911, when he passed the West Point entrance exam and physical at Jefferson Barracks in Missouri. In March, he received orders from the secretary of war to report to West Point on June 14, 1911, where he would join the Class of 1915. Eisenhower left Abilene on the night train for Kansas City on June 8. His mother saw him off from the front porch. "It is your choice," she said, and waved good-bye as he headed to the station. After he was gone she returned to her room. Milton later told Ike it was the first time anyone had ever heard her cry.[41]

In June 1911 the corps of cadets numbered 650 men divided into four classes: most in the fourth (plebe) year, least in the first, attrition taking a heavy toll. At the age of twenty, Eisenhower was older and more mature than most of his classmates and, having done two years of manual labor, was better prepared for the harsh plebe summer, the relentless spit and polish, and the painstaking attention to detail. "The discipline was not so much harsh as inexorable," he recalled.[42] Like Ulysses Grant, who could not tell one tune from another, Ike had trouble marching in step.* "For days I was assigned to the Awkward Squad until I could coordinate my feet with the beat."[43]

Two hundred and sixty-four young men took the oath of allegiance with Eisenhower on June 14, 1911. There were no women in Ike's class, no blacks, no Hispanics, very few Catholics, and only three young men of the Jewish faith. Most were from white, Protestant, middle-class America. "There weren't many boys from poverty classes," a contemporary of Eisenhower remembered, "and the richer boys went to prep schools that sent them to Harvard or Yale."[44]

Despite the fact that West Point offered a free professional education, its academic reputation was in serious decline when Ike entered. Once a leader in some fields, especially engineering and the

---

* Grant famously said he knew only two tunes: "One was Yankee Doodle. The other wasn't." Horace Porter, *Campaigning with Grant* 83 (New York: Century, 1897).

natural sciences, the academy had secluded itself from the changing currents in higher education. Rote memorization masqueraded as creative thought. Instructors, almost all of whom were recent academy graduates, routinely graded a cadet's daily performance but rarely explained the material or encouraged critical discussion. With but four or five exceptions, the curriculum was identical to that established by Sylvanus Thayer more than a century before. "West Point is not a subject for reform," wrote Superintendent Hugh Scott. "It goes forward on its majestic course from year to year toward the fulfillment of its destiny, moving serenely under its traditions of 'honor, duty, country' . . . without need of radical alteration."[45]

The outbreak of war in 1914 made little impact. While the armies of Europe bled to death in front of Passchendaele and in the marshes of East Prussia, West Point's department of military art concentrated on Gettysburg, Vicksburg, and the Shenandoah. Instructors emphasized the romantic élan of cavalry encounters rather than the grim reality of trench warfare. "The Military Academy is forty years behind the times," Army chief of staff Peyton March complained, but to little effect.[46] President Charles Eliot of Harvard, a member of West Point's board of visitors and a leader in the field of academic reform, lamented the mischievous effect of the "red tape methods" in which the cadets were drilled day after day.[47] Marshal Henri-Philippe Pétain, the hero of Verdun, was shocked when he visited West Point after the war.

> I do not think that young men who are being prepared for the duties of an officer should be required to repeat the same gestures every day during four years. This seems to be too long, and I fear that this monotony must result in fixing the graduate's mind into a groove so rigid that elasticity becomes impaired.
>
> He comes out a well-instructed and obedient subaltern and a first rate drill-master, but outside of a small category that have exceptional force of character, he has got to pass considerable time before he can break the rigid forms into

which his nature has become crystallized and regain his mental vigor.[48]

Douglas MacArthur, who was appointed superintendent shortly after Pétain's visit, did his utmost to bring the academy into the modern era—but that was long after Eisenhower graduated. "How long are we going to continue preparing for the War of 1812?" Mac-Arthur asked his staff upon assuming command.[49]

It is often suggested that the friendships made at West Point contribute to the effectiveness of the officer corps in time of war—that they enable officers who serve together to know more about one another and to have more, or less, confidence in one another, as the case might be. The benefit is more apparent than real. As one of Ike's contemporaries noted, "Of course you know whether you like them or not. But the later development of some of the members of my own class did not indicate that my judgment was any too accurate. I just don't think you have enough maturity of judgment for that to have much value."[50]

Like many another cadet, Eisenhower had little patience with the excessive memorization that posed as academic effort. "They had a course called Military History," he said.

> One of the things we had to study was the battle of Gettysburg. We were required to remember the name of every general officer or acting general officer in the entire opposing forces. You also had to learn what the officer commanded—the exact character of the command. Then you had to remember the situation or the position of each of these commands at such and such an hour on such and such a day. I always did hate memory tests, although I have a pretty good memory. But this wasn't the kind of thing that interested me, so I didn't pay any attention and I almost got "found" [failed] in military history.[51]

If Eisenhower was indifferent to academic requirements, his conduct as a cadet bordered on reckless.

My success in compiling a staggering catalogue of demerits was largely due to a lack of motivation . . . except for
the simple and stark resolve to get a college education.
Class standing was of small moment to me. I enjoyed life
at the Academy, and had a good time with my pals, and
was far from disturbed by an additional demerit or two. I
didn't think of myself as either a scholar whose position
would depend on the knowledge he had acquired in
school, or as a military figure whose professional career
might be seriously affected by his academic or disciplinary
record. I probably looked with distaste on classmates
whose days and nights were haunted by fear of demerits or
low grades.[52]

Eisenhower's principal vices were cigarette smoking and poker—
both of which were forbidden. Ike learned serious poker in Abilene,
and called it his "favorite indoor sport." During his first two years at
the academy he played incessantly and kept a book in which he recorded his classmates' IOUs to be paid after graduation. In his junior
year he learned contract bridge and quickly became addicted. "We
started playing in November 1913," his friend William Britton recalled. "We played every night, except Saturday, until April. Ike and
his partner beat us consistently."[53] With almost total recall and an
uncanny ability to focus on the game, Eisenhower was formidable at
both bridge and poker. Later he stopped playing poker because many
of those with whom he played could not afford to lose and resented
their losses.

It was also in his junior year that Ike took up smoking—a source
of infinite demerits. Cadets were permitted to smoke pipes and ci-
gars, but cigarettes—which were considered déclassé—were strictly
against the rules. "So I started smoking cigarettes. These could not
be purchased at the cadet store but loose Bull Durham tobacco was
available and I became a 'roll your own' smoker."[54] Eisenhower continued smoking throughout his military career, often two or three
packs a day. Journalist John Gunther remembered lunching with Ike
in Washington, "and between 12:45 and 3:00 p.m. he smoked at
least fifteen cigarettes. He smoked like a furnace. I asked him what

brand of cigarettes he liked and he replied it didn't matter in the slightest—he smoked anything."[55]*

Despite Eisenhower's eagerness to live at the edge, the West Point tactical department evidently recognized his latent leadership qualities. The fact that he was two to three years older than most of his classmates may have helped. Being a middle child in a brood of six may also have been an advantage, providing Ike with valuable experience dealing with those both older and younger. After his plebe year Eisenhower was promoted to corporal (he ranked eleventh out of the thirty-six promoted) but was soon busted back to the ranks for an unseemly prank and required to walk the area for a month. In his junior year he was promoted to supply sergeant of his company but was even more quickly reduced to private for "improper dancing" with the daughter of a Spanish instructor. That apparently did not dissuade authorities from naming him color sergeant his senior (first-class) year—affording him the honor of carrying the academy's colors at formations and parades of the corps of cadets.

Had it not been for athletics it is questionable whether Eisenhower would have completed his four years at West Point. Just as Grant resisted conformity by reading literature and painting in the studio of the academy's art instructor, Eisenhower found relief on the playing field. "Ike was the first cadet on the field for football practice and the very last to leave," said longtime Army trainer Marty Maher. "I used to curse him because he would practice so late that I would be collecting footballs he kicked away in the darkness."[56]

Eisenhower's enthusiasm for the game exceeded his ability. "Ike talked a grand game," said classmate Alexander "Babe" Weyand, a varsity standout and Olympic wrestler, but he always came up a bit short. Eisenhower went out for baseball in 1912 but failed to make the team. When he went out for football his plebe year, he was judged too small and too light. (He weighed 155 pounds.) He played junior varsity that year and beefed up to a muscular 175 pounds. He

* Asking Ike what brand he smoked might have been like asking the 1850s Grant what brand of whiskey he drank. Eisenhower went cold turkey in November 1949 while president of Columbia. Asked by Clare Booth Luce how he accomplished it, Eisenhower reportedly said, "I simply gave myself an order." Quoted in Merle Miller, *Ike the Soldier* 40 (New York: G. P. Putnam's Sons, 1987).

Eisenhower, *second from right,* color sergeant at West Point. Ike carries the academy colors.

made the varsity his sophomore year, started in five games (including Army's 27–6 loss to Pop Warner's Carlisle Indians), and suffered a career-ending knee injury against Tufts late in the season. "I couldn't get up, so they took me off the field, and I never got back on as a player again."[57]

During his last two years at the academy, Ike coached the junior varsity to successful seasons and became head cheerleader at Army football games. (Franklin D. Roosevelt served in the same capacity at Harvard.) He also took up gymnastics and learned to chin himself five times using only his right hand, and three times with only his left. He also perfected the technique of standing stiffly erect, hands at his side, and then falling face-first to the floor, breaking the fall at the very last second before his nose hit the deck.*

---

* In 1945, at a wedding party in Berlin, Eisenhower inveigled Marshal Georgy Zhukov, General Vassily Sokolovsky, and General Lucius D. Clay into a contest of falling to the floor. "Here we were, the four of us, in dress uniforms, crashing down and desperately trying not to break our noses—which was not the easiest thing to do." Clay, interview, COHP.

For Ike, West Point meant athletics. Although he was never a player of the first rank, he made up in dedication and enthusiasm what he lacked in size and talent. Competitiveness, teamwork, and the pursuit of a common goal were imprinted as indelibly on Eisenhower's character as was the warrior ethic on men such as Patton and MacArthur. If the Duke of Wellington believed the Battle of Waterloo had been won on the playing fields of Eton, Ike attributed similar virtues to athletic life at West Point. Looking back on his time as supreme commander, he wrote, "I noted with real satisfaction, how well ex-footballers seemed to have leadership qualifications. I think this was more than a coincidence. I believe that football, almost more than any other sport, tends to instill in men the feeling that victory comes through hard work—almost slavish—work, team play, self-confidence, and an enthusiasm that amounts to dedication."[58]

Eisenhower was popular among his classmates. His full-throated renditions while showering of "My Darling Clementine" and "Bury Me Not on the Lone Prairie" became cadet legends. "In those days, Ike affected a tough breezy western manner," remembered one classmate.[59] "Everyone liked him and apparently he liked everyone in turn," said another. "If there is such a thing as a magnetic personality, he had it. He had the priceless ability to make anyone he met feel that he had a genuine interest in him and in his ideas."[60]

At graduation, the tactical department summed up their assessment of Ike. "We saw in Eisenhower a not uncommon type, a man who would thoroughly enjoy his Army life, giving both to duty and recreation their fair values. We did not see in him a man who would throw himself into his job so completely that nothing else would matter."[61] Recognizing Ike's devil-may-care attitude, West Point's commandant of cadets suggested that he "be assigned to an organization under [a] strict commanding officer."[62]

Eisenhower finished 61st in a graduating class of 164. The attrition had been 38 percent. One hundred and one young men who entered with Ike in 1911 had, for one reason or another, failed to complete the program. Without extending himself, Eisenhower ranked 57th in military engineering, 45th in law, 72nd in Spanish, 27th in drill regulations and hippology, 82nd in gunnery, and 125th in conduct. More important than class standing, though, Ike had learned the profession of a soldier. He knew how to march, how to handle a weapon, how to ride, and how to write an order. He knew the customs and traditions of the service, the organization, and the importance of teamwork and discipline. He was not thirsting for glory, but he understood the career he had embarked upon.

Whether Eisenhower would be called to active duty was far from guaranteed. The Army had not begun to mobilize for war—the Wilson administration stoutly opposed any increase in appropriations; the officer corps numbered fewer than five thousand, and there was no shortage of second lieutenants.[63] Considerable care was taken not to commission anyone with a physical disability—something that might cause early retirement and the payment of a disability pension—and Ike's injured football knee posed a problem. When Colonel Henry Alden Shaw, West Point's chief medical officer, initially indicated that he might not make the cut, Ike took the news calmly. "I said that was all right with me. I had always had a curious ambition to go to the Argentine (I was curious about the gauchos and Argentina sounded to me like the Old West), and I might go there and see the place, maybe even live there for two or three years."[64]

Colonel Shaw was struck by Ike's detachment. Several days later he called Eisenhower back and suggested that it might be possible to commission him in the coast artillery—the most sedentary of the combat branches.

"Colonel, I do not want a commission in the coast artillery," Ike replied. Aside from keeping its equipment in readiness for an unlikely enemy invasion, the coast artillery provided "a numbing series of routine chores and a minimum of excitement," in Eisenhower's view. Given the choice, he preferred Argentina, and he assumed his military career had come to an end. "I wrote for travel literature and costs," he recalled.[65]

Colonel Shaw evidently took a liking to Ike. (General Omar Bradley said later, "Ike liked people and it is awfully hard for them not to like him in return.")[66] Shaw rejected the finding of his medical board, which had voted unanimously against awarding Ike a commission, and took the case to the War Department's surgeon general, who ultimately agreed that Eisenhower "would be a good gamble."[67]

Shaw recalled Ike for a third interview. "Mr. Eisenhower," he said, "if you will not ask for mounted service, I will recommend to the Academic Board that you be commissioned." Ike replied that his ambition was to serve in the infantry, and Shaw accepted that. Not until he was chief of staff thirty-one years later did Eisenhower learn that Colonel Shaw (a former coast artilleryman himself) had overridden his medical board and taken Ike's case to Washington.[68]

Human events, Machiavelli noted, are half determined by *fortuna,* and from the beginning, fortune smiled on Ike. If Senator Bristow had not departed from congressional tradition and required competitive examinations for West Point and Annapolis, Eisenhower could not have attended. If Colonel Shaw had not gone to bat for him, he would not have been commissioned. Ike was confident in his ability when he graduated, but he had been given two valuable assists along the way.

When the Class of 1915 was called upon in World War II, it met the challenge. Of the 115 men still on active duty, 60 became general officers. Aside from Eisenhower and Bradley, who became five-star generals of the Army, there were 2 full generals, 7 lieutenant generals, 24 major generals (15 of whom commanded divisions in combat), and 25 brigadier generals. The Class of 1915 is called "the class the stars fell on." Yet they were no different from the West Point classes two or three years before and after. The Military Academy, for all of its shortcomings, trained officers for command responsibility. It fell to the Class of 1915 to lead the way.

# TWO

# The Great War

I suppose we'll spend the rest of our lives
explaining why we didn't get into this war.
—DWIGHT D. EISENHOWER,
*November 11, 1918*

AT GRADUATION, Eisenhower requested assignment to the Philippines—the only member of his class to ask for duty in the Far East. Instead, he was posted to the 19th Infantry—the famed "Rock of Chickamauga" regiment—stationed at Fort Sam Houston in San Antonio.[1] Trouble brewed on the Mexican border, and the War Department was bringing its forces in the region to full strength.

In 1911, Mexico's longtime president, Porfirio Díaz, was overthrown in a revolutionary uprising. A period of instability ensued, culminating in the seizure of power by General Victoriano Huerta in early 1912. The Taft administration maintained a hands-off policy, and was on the verge of recognizing the Huerta regime when it left office. But President Woodrow Wilson had other ideas. A former Princeton politics professor, Wilson was determined "to teach the Latin American republics to elect good men."[2] He withheld diplomatic recognition, and the situation remained in limbo until a minor incident at Tampico in April 1914 provided a pretext for the United States to intervene.[*] Congress granted Wilson authority to take mil-

---

[*] On April 9, 1914, local authorities in Tampico seized a U.S. Navy whaleboat that was loading supplies at the wharf and took the crew into custody. When the

itary action, and on April 21, 1914, U.S. Marines seized the port of Veracruz, choked off Huerta's supplies, and forced him to flee the country three months later. Huerta was succeeded by the constitutionally elected General Venustiano Carranza, whom Wilson eventually recognized as Mexico's de facto government. But Carranza encountered stiff resistance from rebel forces led by General Francisco ("Pancho") Villa in the north, and Emiliano Zapata in the south. The War Department was concerned lest further intervention become necessary, and Congress's authorization to use force continued in effect.

After a final summer in Abilene, Eisenhower reported for duty in September 1915. He was assigned to F Company, 2nd Battalion, 19th Infantry—one of two new West Point second lieutenants to join the regiment.[3] His salary was $141.67 a month, plus modest allowances for subsistence and housing. Other lieutenants in the 19th Infantry—an exceptional group of gifted, ambitious officers—included five future full generals and one lieutenant general. Carl "Tooey" Spaatz commanded American air forces in North Africa, Sicily, and Europe, and later became the first Air Force chief of staff; Jacob L. "Jakie" Devers commanded Ike's Sixth Army Group; and Walton H. Walker, Class of 1912, commanded Eighth Army during the Korean War.[4] Wade Haislip commanded XV Corps in Normandy, then Seventh Army, and finally served as Army vice chief of staff. Leonard T. "Gee" Gerow, a graduate of the Virginia Military Institute, commanded V Corps on D-Day and later Fifteenth Army; and Robert Eichelberger commanded Eighth Army for MacArthur in the Pacific.

---

error was recognized, the crew was immediately released and the Mexican commander sent an apology to Admiral Henry T. Mayo for the incident. Mayo, commanding the Navy's Fifth Division, was not satisfied with the Mexican apology, and demanded that by way of retribution the American flag be hoisted at Tampico and rendered a twenty-one-gun salute. The Mexican government considered its apology sufficient and regarded Mayo's demand as excessive. It considered the matter closed, "unless the United States is looking for an excuse to start trouble." *The New York Times,* April 12, 1914.

Of course, that was exactly what Wilson was looking for, and Mexico's failure to hoist and salute the flag by way of apology provided him with a reason (picayune though it may appear) to intervene.

Fort Sam Houston, founded in 1845 during the period of Texas independence, was the largest troop cantonment in the United States, and was considered a choice assignment. The winters were mild, San Antonio provided diversion, quarters were among the best in the Army, and the possibility of action along the Mexican border was always in the offing. The post was commanded by Major General "Fighting Fred" Funston, who headed the Army's Southern Department. The shortest (five feet five inches tall), youngest (fifty), and most aggressive general on active duty, Funston enjoyed a legendary reputation as the nation's preeminent combat commander. He had distinguished himself as a colonel of Kansas volunteers in Cuba, fought three years in the Philippines, and in 1901 had been awarded the Congressional Medal of Honor and commissioned a brigadier general in the Regular Army for his role in the defeat and capture of Emilio Aguinaldo, leader of the Philippine insurrection. Most recently, Funston had commanded the Army's follow-on occupation of Veracruz, and it was widely assumed that should the United States become involved in further hostilities, Funston would command the forces.

Eisenhower's reputation as coach of West Point's junior varsity preceded him to San Antonio. Shortly after he arrived he was approached by the headmaster of a local prep school, the Peacock Military Academy, to coach the school's football team for the princely salary of $150. "Munificence itself," said Ike in retrospect.[5] But Eisenhower was at his first duty station and unfamiliar with Army routine. Assuming his duties would be round-the-clock, he politely declined the offer. The fact is the Army started its workday early and usually finished training by noon. Afternoons were devoted to maintenance, horse and motor stables, administration, and athletics, all of which were supervised by the unit's noncommissioned officers (NCOs). Officers traditionally had afternoons to themselves. Ironically, Ike's reluctance to coach brought him to the attention of General Funston, an old friend of the headmaster's. With calculated informality, Funston walked into the officers' club shortly afterward, headed for the bar, and asked to no one in particular, "Is Mr. Eisenhower in the room?" Ike acknowledged his presence and Fighting Fred, to the consternation of the post's junior officers, invited him for a beer.

Eisenhower, *first row, left,* as coach of the Peacock Academy football team in San Antonio, 1915.

"Mr. Peabody tells me he would like you to coach his team at the academy," said Funston.

"Yes, sir," Eisenhower replied.

"It would please me and be good for the Army if you would accept his offer."

"Yes, sir."[6]

That fall Ike coached Peacock Academy to a winning season. The next year, 1916, he shifted to St. Louis College, a Catholic preparatory school that had not won a game in five years. Under Ike the school tied its first game, won its next five, and narrowly lost the city championship. Eisenhower's coaching reputation was established. For the next ten years orders to coach various Army football teams would follow him from post to post.

In October 1915, less than a month after reporting to Fort Sam Houston, Eisenhower met and immediately fell in love with nineteen-year-old Mary Geneva Doud, better known as Mamie, the second of four attractive daughters of John and Elivera Doud of Denver, Colorado. Like a number of affluent Coloradans, the Douds wintered in San Antonio, were well acquainted with the military community, and often attended social events on post. Like Ike, Mamie was a total extrovert: full of life, frivolous, flirtatious, and the center of attention at any social gathering. The attraction was mutual. Mamie thought Eisenhower, who was six years older, was "just about the handsomest male I had ever seen."[7] Ike found Mamie's outgoing personality and delicate looks enchanting. "I was intrigued by her appearance."[8]

The Douds inhabited an entirely different world from that with which Eisenhower was familiar. John Sheldon Doud's ancestors landed in America in 1639, were among the founders of Guilford, Connecticut, were uniformly well educated, and prospered commercially. John's father (Mamie's grandfather) established a successful meatpacking firm in Chicago in the 1870s and made a fortune. John graduated from the University of Chicago with a degree in mathematics, founded his own meatpacking firm in Boone, Iowa, and made an even larger fortune. In Boone he married sixteen-year-old Elivera Carlson, daughter of affluent Swedish immigrants, and established a substantial household. "It was a very comfortable life," Mamie's younger sister Mabel ("Mike") recalled. "We had a cook, a nurse, and a yardman. We also had a houseman. He worked inside, but sometimes if the yardman didn't come, he worked outside. And he drove for us."[9]

In 1902, when Mamie was six years old, John Doud decided to retire and move to Colorado. He had accumulated over a million dollars ($20 million currently), and, with no income tax to contend with, believed he had more than enough to live prosperously. After initially sampling life in Pueblo and Colorado Springs, the Douds moved to Denver, where John purchased a fashionable mansion in the affluent Capitol Hill section, just east of the statehouse. There were six bedrooms, white Corinthian columns, broad verandas, and a paneled billiard room in the basement. After Ike was elected president, the Doud house at 750 Lafayette Street became the summer White House.

Unlike the men in the Doud family, Mamie received only a sketchy education. Her father preferred ladylike accomplishments to formal learning. Mamie graduated from the eighth grade and

Mamie as a Denver debutante, 1914–15.

briefly attended Denver's East High, but soon dropped out. She took piano and dance lessons, traveled extensively with the family, and enjoyed the services of the personal maid that John Doud provided for his daughters. In 1914 she enrolled at Miss Wolcott's socially correct finishing school, where young ladies from Denver's finest families were taught the polite graces but few domestic skills. "Most people are raised to do something," Mamie once said. "I wasn't."[10]

Eisenhower was swept off his feet. Not just by Mamie, but by the whole Doud family. John and Elivera treated Ike like the son they never had, and Mamie's sisters rhapsodized about his charms. A whirlwind romance ensued, and on Valentine's Day 1916, Ike proposed and Mamie accepted. John fretted briefly over whether his indulged daughter could adjust to life as an Army wife, but acquiesced and soon provided Mamie a monthly

$100 allowance (slightly more than $1,600 currently) to help make ends meet.[*]

Mamie set the wedding date for November 14, 1916, her twentieth birthday. But events intervened. On March 9, Pancho Villa, evidently hoping to provoke war between the United States and Mexico, crossed the border in strength and mounted a surprise assault against American forces in Columbus, New Mexico. Nine civilians and eight troopers of the 13th Cavalry were killed before Villa (who suffered much heavier casualties) was driven off. Washington responded by ordering General Funston to organize a punitive expedition under Brigadier General John J. Pershing to capture Villa and disperse his forces.[11] All leaves were canceled, and the Southern Department was placed on a war footing. Meanwhile, the conflict in Europe raged unabated. At Verdun, the French narrowly averted disaster at the cost of 350,000 dead. British losses on the Somme in the spring of 1916 exceeded 400,000. Pressure for the United States to intervene mounted daily. State militias were federalized, and war appeared inevitable. At Ike's suggestion, Mamie agreed to advance their wedding to July 1, 1916, provided he could get leave to come to Denver for the ceremony.

Eisenhower requested twenty days' emergency leave ("It seemed to me that imminent marriage was just that"), but was turned down.[12] His colonel did, however, agree to pass Ike's request to the department commander.

Eisenhower approached General Funston's headquarters with trepidation. Funston's adjutant suggested it was a poor time for second lieutenants to be getting married. The chief of staff offered no encouragement. Finally, Ike was ushered into Fighting Fred's office.

"I understand you want to get married," said the general.

Eisenhower affirmed he did, and at that point Funston recalled their earlier encounter. "Oh yes, Mr. Eisenhower. I remember you

---

* Mamie's monthly allowance was not unique among Army wives. Two contemporaries of Ike's, George Patton and Lucius Clay, also married women from wealthy families who received monthly stipends from their parents. This enabled Clay and Patton and Ike to live somewhat better than their contemporaries (much better in Patton's case), and did not pass unnoticed by their fellow officers. Martin Blumenson, 1 *The Patton Papers* 201 (Boston: Houghton Mifflin, 1972); Jean Edward Smith, *Lucius D. Clay* 77.

Ike and Mamie's wedding photo, July 1, 1916.

very well." He asked Ike what the hurry was, and Eisenhower explained as best he could.

"All right, you may have ten days. I am not sure that this is what the War Department had in mind [when it said emergency leaves only], but I'll take the responsibility."[13]

The wedding took place at twelve noon on July 1, 1916—the same day the Army promoted Ike to first lieutenant—in the gladiola-filled music room of the Douds' home. The short Presbyterian service was attended only by the family. Mamie said later that the wedding was the only time she ever saw her husband nervous.[14] After the ceremony, the Douds' chauffeur drove the couple to Eldorado Springs, a thermal resort in the foothills between Denver and Boulder, for a two-day honeymoon. They returned briefly to the Doud house to retrieve their belongings, and then took the train to Abilene so Mamie could meet Ike's family.

They arrived about four o'clock in the morning and found Ida and David waiting on the platform. Mamie was astonished that David was in his shirtsleeves and not wearing a jacket. When they got to the modest Eisenhower home, she was even more surprised that there were no servants and that Ida did all of the cooking and cleaning herself. She was also disconcerted by the Eisenhowers' lack of worldliness. They did not permit drinking, smoking, or card playing, and did not appear to enjoy life as the Douds did. Nevertheless, in the few hours they spent in Abilene, Mamie hit it off with Ida and adored Ike's younger brothers Earl and Milton. David she never warmed to. In future years, Ike and Mamie spent little time in Abilene, and much preferred visiting with the Douds in Denver.[15]

Back at Fort Sam Houston, with no married quarters available, Mamie moved into Ike's two-room suite in the bachelor officers' quarters (BOQ). As a sympathetic biographer observed, "He concentrated on his work; she concentrated on him."[16] Mamie used money from her father's generous wedding check to buy carpets and curtains for Ike's quarters, and rented a piano for five dollars a month. Later, John Doud purchased a used Pullman six-wheeler for Eisenhower to drive—he was one of the very few first lieutenants on active duty to have a car.* Although she could not cook, resented cleaning, and had no clear idea how to make a bed properly, Mamie converted Ike's suite into a gathering place for the post's junior officers and their wives. Sunday night buffet suppers (mostly cooked by Ike) became an Eisenhower ritual. The china, crystal, and silver Mamie received as wedding presents set the scene, and her joie de vivre won the hearts of Ike's contemporaries. As Maureen Clark, General Mark Clark's wife, wrote, "A wife plays a big part in her husband's career," and from the beginning Mamie did her share.[17]

By the end of 1916 the situation on the Mexican border had stabilized. Cross-border raids ceased, and a modicum of order was

---

* The remarkable York Pullman automobile was manufactured in York, Pennsylvania, from 1903 to 1917. It had six wheels, three on each side mounted one behind the other, with the power train flowing to the two middle wheels. The six-wheel concept soon soured, and the few cars that have survived are genuine curiosities. William H. Shank, *History of the York Pullman Automobile, 1903–1917* (York, Pa.: Historical Society of York County, 1985).

restored in Mexico. Pershing failed to catch Villa, and after a humiliating defeat of units from the famed 10th Cavalry (the all-black regiment known to history as "buffalo soldiers")[*] at Carrizal, ninety miles south of El Paso, American enthusiasm for the punitive expedition faded. War with Mexico was averted—due in part to the sagacity of the Carranza government—and Pershing was ordered back to the United States on January 27, 1917. In retrospect, the sole accomplishment of the ten-month exercise was to provide valuable field training that helped prepare the Army for what lay ahead.

The Wilson administration was eager to clear the table of the Mexican problem. The war in Europe was going badly, and American intervention seemed ever more likely. The western front remained intact, but Allied lines were stretched perilously thin. Imperial Russia was on the verge of collapse, revolution loomed, and on February 1, 1917, Germany declared unrestricted submarine warfare, hoping to force Britain from the war. Two days later, following the sinking of the American liner *Housatonic,* President Wilson broke diplomatic relations with Berlin. U-boat sinkings of American vessels continued, and on April 2, Wilson asked Congress for a declaration of war: "The world must be made safe for Democracy."[18] The president requested authorization to draft five hundred thousand men for the Army and bring the Navy to combat readiness. Wilson had favored Funston to command the American forces, but Fighting Fred suffered a fatal heart attack on February 17 and the mantle fell to Pershing.

To accommodate the draftee influx, Regular Army units were cannibalized to provide the framework for new formations. This was in deliberate contrast to the Civil War, during which volunteers were organized in freestanding, self-contained units (for example, the 2nd Iowa), while the Army's regulars fought in the Brigade of Regulars—an elite formation similar to the Brigade of Guards in the British Army. The Civil War pattern initially deprived the Union Army's

---

[*] The origin of the term "buffalo soldiers" is often disputed, but the most compelling explanation relates to the heavy coats made of buffalo hides the soldiers wore during the harsh winters on the western plains. Clad in buffalo skins, the mounted black troopers of the 10th Cavalry from a distance appeared to the Plains Indians to resemble the buffaloes that roamed the countryside.

new volunteer units of the experience and professionalism of the regulars and may have contributed to early Union reverses. In 1917, the War Department hoped to avoid that by parceling out the regulars as cadre.[*]

Eisenhower, along with a dozen other officers and a larger complement of NCOs from the 19th Infantry, was selected as cadre for the new 57th Infantry Regiment, which was to be formed at Leon Springs, Texas, a government preserve twenty miles north of San Antonio. Eisenhower was designated regimental supply officer and shortly afterward was promoted to captain. There was nothing particularly meritorious in the promotion. As the Army expanded, all members of the Class of 1915 were assigned increased responsibility, and all were promoted to captain in early May 1917. What may be more noteworthy is that Eisenhower's first wartime assignment was in logistics. Grant too, during the Mexican War, began his service as a regimental supply officer. Grant and Eisenhower not only learned the importance of keeping the troops supplied, but how to do so. In Grant's case, his experience as a supply officer with Winfield Scott in Mexico afforded him the confidence at Vicksburg to cut loose from his Memphis base and live off the land. For Ike, the logistical buildup before D-Day not only left nothing to be desired, but provided an abundance of everything the Allies needed to take them to Berlin.

Eisenhower assumed that when the 57th was trained and equipped it would ship out for the battlefield in France. "We were sure that we were one of the best outfits in the whole Army and were confident that we were destined for overseas duty."[19] Instead, he was detached from the 57th in September and ordered to Fort Oglethorpe in Georgia to train newly commissioned reserve officers. Ike's final efficiency report with the 57th, written by the regimental commander, called him "an energetic officer; well grounded in his profession and of above average capacity; has executive ability and considerable initiative."[20]

On September 24, 1917, four days after Eisenhower departed for

---

[*] It should be noted that by using regulars as cadre for new formations, promotion was more easily attained. In the Civil War the regulars serving in the Brigade of Regulars were denied promotion and continued to serve in their prewar ranks. That was a sore spot in the professional Army.

Fort Oglethorpe, Mamie gave birth to their first child, a boy she named Doud Dwight Eisenhower, and whom she called "Little Ike," or "Ikey." Fortunately, Mamie's mother, Elivera, was on hand to assist, and the baby was delivered in the post infirmary. "Fort Sam Houston had no maternity facilities," Mamie recalled. "They had to fashion a hopelessly primitive, makeshift delivery room that was little better than a broom closet."[21]

Eisenhower was in the field when Elivera's telegram announcing Little Ike's birth arrived. "You could have knocked me over with a feather," he wrote Mamie that evening. "I've sent you 100,483,491,342 kisses since I've been gone. Please teach *our* son to like 'Sheltering Palms.' Millions of kisses and lots of love to you and [mother]. Your lover—*YOU BET,* Ike."[22]

Ike remained at Fort Oglethorpe until mid-December, constantly in the field, wet, cold, and miserable. The training for new officers was tough—designed to weed out the weak and inept as well as to instruct. "I get up at 5:15 a.m. and go all day long," Eisenhower wrote Mamie. "It is pretty hard to handle this thing, and it keeps a fellow busy until 9:00 p.m."[23] The Army closed the Oglethorpe facility in December and transferred officer training to Fort Leavenworth. Ike was given a brief Christmas leave to visit Mamie and Little Ike, who were now living off post in San Antonio with the Douds. His final efficiency report rated him average in all categories and noted that his performance of duty had been "satisfactory." In the time-tested argot of Army efficiency reports, Colonel T. M. Anderson, the infantry officer commanding, said he would be satisfied to have Eisenhower serve under him, but had no special desire to have him.[24] Separated from Mamie and their young son, removed from his regiment, and disappointed at not going overseas, Ike may have been at the low point of his military career at Fort Oglethorpe.

At Leavenworth, Eisenhower supervised the physical training, calisthenics, and bayonet drill of the new officers. The winter was severe, but Ike found his responsibilities challenging and relished the physical exertion. "Our new captain is one of the most efficient and best Army officers in the country," one of his charges wrote his mother in Worcester, Massachusetts.

He is a corker and has put more fight into us in three days
than we got in all the previous time we were here. He is a
giant for build and at West Point was a noted football
player and physical culture fiend. He knows his job, is
enthusiastic, can tell us what he wants us to do, and is
pretty human, though wickedly harsh and abrupt. He has
given us wonderful bayonet drills. He gets the fellows'
imaginations worked up and hollers and yells and makes
us shout and stomp until we go tearing into the air as if
we meant business.[25]

Another young officer, Princeton's F. Scott Fitzgerald, took a more
jaundiced view of the training at Leavenworth. Despite his tailored
Brooks Brothers uniforms, Scott considered himself "the worst second lieutenant in the United States Army." He was convinced he
would be killed in action, and devoted much of his time at Leavenworth to completing his first novel, "The Romantic Egotist," major
portions of which he wrote in class concealed within a copy of *Small
Problems for Infantry.*[26]

While he was at Leavenworth, Eisenhower found time to take a
course in the Army's first tank school, and in February 1918 was rewarded with orders to report to Camp Meade, Maryland, to join the
65th Engineers, the parent unit of the 301st Heavy Tank Battalion,
slated to ship to France in June. His final efficiency report, a notch
up from Oglethorpe, called him a good all-around officer, painstaking and intelligent, with good military bearing and a pleasing personality.[27]

The tank corps opened a window of opportunity for Ike. He was
thrilled at the possibility of combat and overjoyed at being among
the first in a new branch of service. The tank, though still in its infancy, would revolutionize battlefield tactics, and Eisenhower appreciated that he was in on the ground floor. George Patton, who was
already in the field with the American Expeditionary Force (AEF)
tank corps in France, was also among the first to recognize the tank's
possibilities, as were Charles de Gaulle, Heinz Guderian, and J. F. C.
Fuller.

The early tanks, based on the Holt Caterpillar Tractor, were developed initially by the British to breach the German trench line and open a path for the cavalry to pour through. (At the Somme, Field Marshal Sir Douglas Haig kept tens of thousands of cavalrymen and their mounts in readiness behind British lines waiting in vain for the breakthrough that never came.) These primitive behemoths, which bear as much similarity to modern battle tanks as Eddie Ricken-backer's biplane does to a jet fighter, weighed about thirty tons, moved at two miles an hour (somewhat slower than a combat infan-tryman could walk), and were armed with a six-pounder gun inside a small turret and four machine guns.[28] Aside from poor reliability, the early tanks were not ventilated, fumes inside were suffocating, and the vehicles were stupefyingly noisy. The armor plate would de-flect German machine-gun bullets, but vision was severely restricted and a tank commander transmitted his order to the driver through a series of well-placed kicks to the driver's back and shoulders.

The French developed an alternative light tank manufactured by Renault that was smaller and faster than the British model. With a two-man crew, the Renault tank, rather than opening a gap in enemy lines, was designed to replace horse cavalry entirely and could travel rapidly cross-country once a breakthrough had occurred. It was, as one British observer remarked, "an armored, mechanical horse," and could be deployed in mass formations.[29] At the beginning of 1918, when Eisenhower was assigned to Camp Meade, the United States did not have an operational tank of its own. The War Department had arranged for the British and French tanks to be shipped to the United States for evaluation, but as yet none had arrived.

Ike's task at Camp Meade was to organize and prepare the 301st for combat, a remarkable assignment considering that no tanks were available. The men were all volunteers, morale was high, and Eisen-hower threw himself into his job with enthusiasm. "We were differ-ent," Ike remembered. "The men dreamed of overwhelming assault on enemy lines, rolling effortlessly over wire entanglements and trenches, demolishing gun nests with their fire, and terrorizing the foe into quick and abject surrender."[30]

In mid-March 1918, Eisenhower was informed that the 301st would ship out for France shortly, and that he would command it. British Mark VI tanks, known as "Big Willies," would be provided once the unit arrived. "As a regular officer, I had to preserve the sedate demeanor of one for whom the summons to battle is no novelty. But my exuberance, I'm sure, was shown in every word and gesture to the battalion."[31]

To ensure there were no hitches, Ike rushed to the port of embarkation in New York to iron out the final details of shipment. "Too much depended on our walking up that gangplank for me to take a chance on a slipup anywhere. The port authorities may have thought me a worrywart, but I worked my head off."[32]

When Eisenhower returned to Camp Meade he found his orders had been changed. The War Department had terminated the Corps of Engineers' responsibility for the tankers and established the tank corps as an independent branch of the Army, similar to the infantry, cavalry, and field artillery. Colonel Ira C. Welborn, a canny Mississippian (West Point Class of 1898) who had won the Congressional Medal of Honor with the 9th Infantry at Santiago, Cuba, was named director, and stateside strength was set at 16,660 officers and men.[33] Welborn's office was in the War Department. The tank corps itself would be formed and trained at Camp Colt, an abandoned post on the site of the Gettysburg battlefield, with Captain Eisenhower in command. It was another daunting assignment. Less than three years out of West Point, Eisenhower was charged with organizing the tank corps' first stateside training facility. He would soon be in command of thousands of men, all volunteers, and working with the Army's weapon of the future. There were no training manuals, no experienced officers or NCOs, and no tanks. Ike had been chosen by Welborn because of his organizational ability. Eisenhower, on the other hand, was dismayed that he was unable to take the 301st to France. "My mood was black," he remembered. "Whenever I convinced myself that my superiors . . . had doomed me to run-of-the-mill assignments, I found no better cure than to blow off steam in private and then settle down to do the job at hand."[34]

Once again, fortune smiled on Ike. As he quickly discovered, organizing the tank corps at Camp Colt was scarcely a run-of-the-mill assignment. He arrived in Gettysburg on March 24, 1918, with a handful of cadre. "I was very much on my own. There were no precedents except in basic training and I was the only regular officer in the command. Now I really began to learn about responsibility."[35]

Eisenhower reported to Colonel Welborn in Washington twice a week. Otherwise, the training of the tank corps was in his hands.

> My orders were specific, indeed rigid. I was required to take in volunteers, equip, organize, and instruct them and have them ready for overseas shipment when called upon. The orders warned that my camp was not only a point of mobilization but of embarkation. This meant that the troops sent from Gettysburg would go directly to a port without any intermediate stops.[36]

Working with whatever material he could find, Eisenhower transformed the old battlefield into a first-class Army camp. He obtained tents, food, and uniforms for his men, taught them to drill, and got them in shape. When a freak blizzard hit Gettysburg in April, he bought every available stove in the region. And when no tanks arrived, he organized telegraph and motor schools to maintain morale.

By summer, ten thousand men and six hundred officers were at Camp Colt under Eisenhower's command. He was promoted to major on June 17, 1918, along with most of his infantry classmates. The engineers, all of whom stood higher in the Class of 1915, had been promoted several months earlier, and the artillerymen would be promoted in July. Except for the branch differential, promotions in Ike's class thus far had been strictly in order of class standing at West Point.

Mamie and Little Ike arrived at Gettysburg in late April 1918, after a grueling four-day trip from San Antonio in a railroad day coach. Military quarters were nonexistent, and the Eisenhowers moved three times in the next six months, ending up in the unused Sigma Alpha Epsilon fraternity house on the campus of Gettysburg College. The house had a gigantic ballroom that would have been perfect for entertaining except there was no kitchen. Cooking was done on an electric hot plate with two burners, and the dishes were washed in the bathtub. When time permitted, Ike enjoyed roaming the Gettysburg battlefield, and Mamie—who was supremely uninterested in the location of Union brigades—often accompanied him. "He knew every rock on that battlefield," she said later, which was not necessarily a compliment.[37]

Without tanks, the early training at Camp Colt was rudimentary. Ike eventually obtained some .30-caliber machine guns, mounted them on flatbed trucks, and taught the men to fire from moving platforms. "The only satisfactory place for firing was Big Round Top," he remembered. "Its base made a perfect backstop. The firing might even have been heavier than during the great battle fifty-five years earlier."[38]

As the size of Camp Colt increased, Ike doubled his efforts to stay on top of the situation. "Eisenhower was a strict disciplinarian," Sergeant Major Claude J. Harris recalled.

> He was an inborn soldier, but most human and considerate. Despite his youth, he possessed a high understanding of organization, the ability to place an estimate on a man and fit him into a position where he would "click." In the event his judgment proved erroneous the man would be called in, his errors pointed out, and adjustments made to suit the situation. This principle built for him high admiration and loyalty from his officers perhaps unequaled by few commanding officers.[39]

The first tank—a seven-ton French Renault—arrived at Camp Colt on June 6, 1918. The *Gettysburg Times* reported that the troops "were as happy as a playground full of children with a new toy."[40] Two additional Renaults arrived later in the summer, accompanied by two British tank corps officers as advisers. In 1943, one of the British officers, Lieutenant Colonel Franklin Summers (retired), wrote Eisenhower reminding him of the summer of 1918 at Camp Colt, and asking that he write the introduction to a book on armor the British were publishing. Eisenhower had just completed the Sicily campaign, and he replied immediately.

> No message that I have received in recent months has pleased me more than yours. I have often wondered where you were and what you were doing.

Eisenhower poses with the first Renault tank delivered to Camp Colt, 1918.

I assure you that I could not have attempted to write a forward for your book, except for my very great feeling of indebtedness for the advice and counsel you so kindly gave me years ago in the little town of Gettysburg. I hope I have profited somewhat of it.[41]

In September 1918, Camp Colt was hit by the "Spanish flu" epidemic ravaging the country. More than 548,000 Americans succumbed to the virus, and an estimated 50 to 100 million persons worldwide. The true number that perished will never be known, but before the epidemic was brought under control, the average life expectancy in the United States had dropped by an unbelievable twelve years.[42]

The virus entered the United States through the port of Boston, and the first case was reported at Fort Devens, Massachusetts, on September 8, 1918. Shortly thereafter, 124 men were transferred from Devens to Camp Colt, and the virus came with them. Initially, camp doctors believed the men were suffering the aftereffects of inoculations they had received before shipment, but within twenty-four hours Spanish flu was recognized. Lieutenant Colonel Thomas Scott, the camp's chief surgeon, immediately isolated the patients. "We put up every kind of tent with makeshift bedding and any man with the slightest symptom was isolated from the others," said Ike. "No more than four men were allowed in any tent; three wherever we had room. Each [man] who had been directly exposed to the disease was, whenever possible, put into a tent by himself."[43]

Eisenhower and Scott moved aggressively to contain the disease. On Ike's order, Colt was quarantined. MPs were posted to prevent soldiers without medical passes from leaving camp, restaurants in Gettysburg were ordered not to serve soldiers, and the town's churches were placed off-limits lest an infected soldier inadvertently spread the virus. On clear days, tents were opened and the bedding aired in the sun. Floors were scrubbed daily with Lysol and kerosene. And every soldier in camp was given a daily medical examination.

When the virus struck, there were 10,605 men under Eisenhower's command at Camp Colt. Between September 15 and October 5, 427 soldiers were admitted to post hospitals, 321 suffering from Spanish flu. Of those, 175 died from the disease. By mid-October the worst was over. On October 24, the *Gettysburg Times* reported that Camp Colt was "practically free of influenza." Eisenhower issued a statement thanking the people of Gettysburg for their timely assistance. Later he wrote that "Lieutenant Colonel Scott is another of those men to whom I will always feel obligated."[44]

The 175 deaths at Camp Colt compared favorably to most Army posts. The combination of Spanish flu and pneumonia killed 52,019 American servicemen in 1918, slightly fewer than the 53,402 who were killed in combat.[45] In fact, so effective had Ike and Colonel Scott been in halting the spread of the disease that when Camp Colt's record came to the attention of the War Department, Eisenhower was ordered to detail thirty members of his medical staff to other posts to show exactly what measures had been taken.

On October 14, 1918, Ike's twenty-eighth birthday, he received orders from the War Department promoting him to lieutenant colonel. This time he was not in lockstep with his West Point classmates. Only ten members of the Class of 1915 were promoted to lieutenant colonel during World War I, and Ike was the second.[46] Colonel Welborn rated Eisenhower "superior" (the highest category) in initiative, attention to duty, and capacity for command. "I regard this officer as one of the most efficient young officers I have known. He had the duties and responsibilities commensurate with the rank of brigadier general and he performed those duties under trying conditions in a highly credible manner."[47]

Two weeks after his promotion to lieutenant colonel, Ike received another set of orders from the War Department. He could scarcely contain his enthusiasm as he showed them to Mamie. "My orders for France have come. I go November eighteenth."[48] Eisenhower was to lead the November contingent of troops from Camp Colt to the embarkation depot at Fort Dix, New Jersey, and then overseas. Once in France he would assume command of an armored regiment. Marshal Ferdinand Foch, the Allied supreme commander, was preparing a gigantic spring offensive, and Ike envisioned himself commanding the tanks that would lead the breakthrough on the western front.

Colonel Welborn, who had initially approved Eisenhower's request to go overseas, now had second thoughts about losing the commander of Camp Colt. He summoned Ike to Washington and offered to recommend his immediate promotion to full colonel if he would remain at Gettysburg. Eisenhower respectfully declined. He told Welborn that rather than stay in the States, he would prefer a reduction in rank if necessary to go overseas.[49]

Eisenhower readied the troops at Colt for a mid-November departure. Mamie and Little Ike would return to Denver and stay with the Douds while he was overseas. Before he could put Mamie and Little Ike on the train, however, a telegram from Elivera arrived with sad tidings. Mamie's beloved younger sister Eda Mae ("Buster") had died suddenly of a kidney infection at the age of seventeen. "This was a terrible blow for both of us," Eisenhower wrote. "The two girls had been close and I had deeply loved 'Buster.' She was a favorite of the entire family."[50]

On the morning of November 10, 1918, Ike and Mamie said a tearful good-bye on the Pennsylvania Railroad platform at Harrisburg. "Our parting was the most trying we had encountered in three years of married life."[51] Rumors were already in the air that an armistice on the western front was imminent. By the time Ike returned to Gettysburg, the news was out that a delegation from the German government had crossed the French lines on the way to Foch's headquarters at Compiègne.* At 5:10 a.m., November 11 (11:10 p.m. on the tenth in Gettysburg), the Germans signed the armistice agreement. The guns would go silent at 11 a.m. That would be the eleventh hour of the eleventh day of the eleventh month of 1918.

Eisenhower was sitting in his headquarters with his classmate Major Norman Randolph when the news was announced. "I suppose we'll spend the rest of our lives explaining why we didn't get into this war," Ike moaned. "By God, from now on I am cutting myself a swath that will make up for this."[52]

Eisenhower was morose. He had missed out on the greatest war in history. For a professional soldier, nothing could be more humiliating. Although it was no fault of his own, Eisenhower was embarrassed that he had not seen combat. During World War II, Ike's detractors, particularly in British circles, often pointed out that he had never commanded troops in battle. And it is true that he did not experience the horror of trench warfare on the western front. Yet that may have been just as well. Unlike many British senior commanders, Eisenhower had not been shocked into excessive caution by the futile slaughter of World War I. He was ready for a war of maneuver, and his early experience with America's nascent tank corps perhaps prepared him far better than a year in the trenches would have done.

When the war ended, Colonel Welborn recommended Eisenhower for the Distinguished Service Medal, the Army's highest peacetime decoration. "While commanding Officer of the Tank Corps Training Center," the citation read, "he displayed unusual zeal, foresight, and marked administrative ability in the organization, training, and preparation for overseas service of the tank corps."[53]

---

* On November 9, 1918, William II abdicated and was replaced by a republican government headed by Majority Socialist Friedrich Ebert. The armistice was signed on behalf of the new government by Vice Chancellor Matthias Erzberger, who was assassinated in August 1921 by German nationalists for having done so. Sir John W. Wheeler-Bennett, *The Nemesis of Power: The German Army in Politics, 1918–1945* 19–31 (London: Macmillan, 1964).

## THREE

# The Peacetime Army

No human enterprise goes flat so instantly as an
Army training camp when war ends.

— DWIGHT D. EISENHOWER

INSTEAD OF GOING OVERSEAS, Eisenhower was ordered to
dismantle Camp Colt. "Nothing at West Point or in the forty months
since graduation had prepared me for helping to collapse an Army
from millions to a peacetime core," Ike wrote. "As quickly as possible, we were to clear the site we had occupied for nine months, complete our records, then move to Fort Dix where we would await final
orders."[1]

Eisenhower arrived at Fort Dix in mid-December, 1918, with six
thousand men and three Renault tanks. From there he was ordered
with the remnant of the American tank corps to Fort Benning, Georgia. After discharges, separations, and transfers, only three hundred
of the original six thousand remained. The eight-hundred-mile trip
from New Jersey to Georgia by low-priority Army troop train took
four days and, as Ike recalled, each day seemed like a year: There was
no heat in the passenger cars, no electricity, no hot water, and field
rations were cooked on camp stoves in the baggage car.

Ike brooded about his career. "I was older than my classmates, was
still bothered on occasion by a bad knee, and saw myself in the years
ahead putting on weight in a meaningless chair-bound assignment,
shuffling papers and filling out forms. If not depressed, I was mad,
disappointed, and resented the fact that the war had passed me by."[2]

Eisenhower briefly considered an offer from an Indiana businessman, a former junior officer at Camp Colt, to join his manufacturing firm in Muncie at a salary considerably higher than his lieutenant colonel's pay. But he decided against it, as he would other offers for civilian employment that came to him over the next twenty years. "A lot of his classmates were getting out," Mamie remembered. "I said to him—it was about only twice that I really interfered—and this time I said, 'Well, Ike, I don't think you'd be happy. This is your life and you know it and you like it.' "3

Fort Benning, home of the United States infantry, provided a brief holding pattern for Eisenhower. The infantry had little interest in tanks, and as Ike wrote later, "I had too much time on my hands."4 After several months of indecision, the War Department selected Camp Meade, Maryland, midway between Washington and Baltimore, as the permanent home of the tank corps.

Shortly after Eisenhower arrived at Camp Meade, the War Department announced plans to send a truck convoy across the country from the East Coast to the West Coast. As with most such expeditions the purpose was part publicity and part training, and above all to demonstrate the need for better highways. In 1919 most long-distance travel in the United States was done by rail. There was no highway network, no maps, and drivers often were compelled to navigate by compass. The few vehicular bridges that existed were rickety and ill-constructed; roads were mostly unpaved, little improved since the first settlers moved west in covered wagons, and all but impassable in bad weather. Motor vehicles were uncomfortable, slow and unreliable, prone to breakdowns, and certain to experience one or more tire punctures every hundred miles. A cross-country motor march had never been attempted before, and the Army was not at all certain that it could be done.5

To ensure that the lessons of the convoy were disseminated throughout the service, the War Department asked for volunteers from various branches to accompany it. Eisenhower, not yet integrated into the routine at Camp Meade, was among the first to volunteer. "I wanted to go along partly for a lark and partly to learn."6

On July 7, 1919, the transcontinental motor convoy departed from the Ellipse in Washington, D.C., bound for San Francisco—

3,251 miles away. The expedition was eighty-one vehicles long, including various mobile repair shops, engineer bridging equipment, a wrecker, and requisite fuel and water trucks, plus a Renault tank lashed to a flatbed trailer. In march column the convoy stretched more than two miles. There were 24 officers and 258 enlisted men, plus some two dozen War Department observers. Sixty-two days later, only five days behind schedule, the convoy arrived in San Francisco. Average speed had varied between ten and fifteen miles an hour, and the column managed slightly less than sixty miles a day, marred by repeated breakdowns, rain that turned dirt roads into gumbo, dust that fouled carburetors, searing heat that caused radiators to boil over, collapsed bridges, deeply rutted roadways, and the absence in places of any roadbed whatever. Wyoming was particularly difficult. Most bridges were too light and had to be replaced or reinforced, and a few roads had to be constructed from scratch. In Nevada, deep desert sand delayed the convoy for several days as heavily loaded vehicles sank above their wheel wells and had to be laboriously excavated. An estimated 3.25 million people, roughly three of every one hundred Americans, saw the column as it passed. It aroused great interest in better roads, and several states adopted large bond issues for highway construction.

The convoy followed the planned Lincoln Highway, a right-of-way that eventually became U.S. Highway 30 and in places Interstate 80. In the absence of accurate maps and reliable road signs, a detachment of cavalry scouts mounted on motorcycles pioneered the convoy's route.

Eisenhower had no responsibilities on the motor march other than to prepare a report for the tank corps. The drivers and vehicles had been hastily assembled, and march discipline was initially poor. "The Expedition Train Commander," he advised, "should pay more attention to disciplinary drills for officers and men, and all should be intelligent, snappy soldiers."[7] Ike's solemnity belies the devil-may-care pranksterism he resorted to on the journey. "We were a troupe of traveling clowns," he confessed fifty years later. "Perhaps our finest hour was in western Wyoming." Eisenhower and a companion convinced the convoy that an Indian attack was imminent. Sentinels were posted that evening, while Ike and his friend took concealed

The Army's first transcontinental motor convoy, Washington, D.C., to San Francisco, 1919.

positions outside the perimeter and exchanged warrior yelps in the best tradition of the Old West. They were sufficiently convincing to induce a young officer on guard not only to discharge his weapon but report the encounter with hostile Indians to the War Department.

"Faster than any vehicle in the convoy," Eisenhower recalled, "we shot off in all directions to find the man who was carrying that message to the telegraph office. We found him, took the story to the commanding officer, and pointed out that if such news reached the Adjutant General, he was unlikely to understand our brand of humor. The commanding officer went along with the gag, crossed out the Indian part of the telegram, [and] thereby a number of us were saved lengthy explanations in original and three or more carbons."[8]

All along the route the convoy was greeted by well-wishers. In Akron, Ohio, tire manufacturer Harvey Firestone welcomed the troops to his estate and staged a lavish picnic. From Fort Wayne, Indiana, Ike dropped Mamie a postcard with a picture of the convoy. "Dearest, I'm not in this picture—but I thought you'd like to see it. Love you heaps and heaps. Your lover. Ike."[9]

When the column reached Boone, Iowa, Mamie's aunt and uncle

gave Eisenhower a personal welcome. In North Platte, Nebraska, the midpoint of the journey, Ike was joined by Mamie and her father, John, who had driven two hundred miles over prairie trails from Denver. Mamie had not seen her husband since their parting at Harrisburg in November. "Quarters or no quarters," she said, she was going to join him at Camp Meade, "if I have to live in a tent."[10] Eisenhower agreed, provided she left Ikey in Denver with the Douds until they found suitable housing. Mamie and her father followed the convoy until it reached Laramie, Wyoming, at which point they turned back to Denver.

For Eisenhower, who thirty-seven years later would sign the interstate highway act into law, the firsthand knowledge of the condition of the nation's roads stayed with him. "When we finally secured the necessary congressional approval, we started the 41,000 miles of super highways that are already proving their worth," he wrote after the bill had passed. "The old convoy had started me thinking about good two-lane highways, but Germany had made me see the wisdom of broader ribbons across our land."[11]

When Eisenhower returned to Camp Meade in the autumn of 1919, he found the AEF tank corps back from Europe. The augmented corps was now commanded by Brigadier General Samuel D. Rockenbach, a hard-bitten Virginian (VMI, 1889) who had led American armor in France, and who was several years senior to Colonel Welborn. Rockenbach integrated the returning troops with those from Camp Colt and formed two brigades: a light brigade (the 304th) equipped with French Renaults, and a heavy brigade (the 305th) deploying new American-made Mark VIIIs that had come off the assembly line too late for service in France. Colonel George Patton, fresh from the battlefield, commanded the light brigade; Eisenhower became executive officer of the heavies and later assumed command. From the beginning, Eisenhower and Patton were a mismatched pair. Patton was monumentally egotistical, flamboyant, and unpredictable. Eisenhower was self-effacing and steady. Yet they formed an enduring friendship that lasted until shortly before Patton's death in 1945.

George Patton, five years older than Eisenhower, six years his senior in the Regular Army (Patton was Class of 1909), was born on the family ranch near Pasadena, California, on November 11, 1885. His maternal ancestors had been among the first American settlers to reach California, owned a vast Spanish land grant, and donated the acreage on which the city of Pasadena now stands to encourage immigration to the region. His paternal forebears hailed from Virginia and traced their lineage to English nobility, including sixteen barons who signed the Magna Carta.[12] Patton's grandfather, a colonel of Confederate infantry, was killed facing Philip Sheridan at Cedar Creek. His father attended VMI, moved to California, undertook the practice of law, and became a successful member of the bar and district attorney of Los Angeles County. The Pattons had a housekeeper, a dozen Mexican servants, a European cook, and a governess. They raised purebred cattle and blooded horses, owned a vacation house on fashionable Catalina Island, and counted themselves among California's established aristocracy. George went to private schools and attended VMI for a year before receiving a senatorial appointment to West Point. Ike won his appointment through competitive examination; Patton benefited from family influence.[*]

Throughout his military career Patton traveled with his own stable of horses (at Leavenworth's Command and General Staff School he was excused from the course on equitation so he could exercise his mounts), and drove the finest cars. His uniforms and civilian clothes were tailored on London's Savile Row and his boots came from Ugo Ferrini in Rome. Ike drove a Model T, his uniforms were made in the United States, and he bought his civilian clothes off the rack. Patton's pistols were custom-made Colt .45s with ivory grips; Eisenhower's sidearm was standard government issue.

Unlike Ike, Patton was a loner: highly opinionated, ultraconservative, bigoted, and racist. Eisenhower was more nuanced. He tended to qualify his statements and had no particularly strong views on race or politics.[13] Both married into money, but whereas the Douds were merely wealthy, Patton's wife, Beatrice Ayer, was heiress to an

---

[*] The fact that Patton did not enter West Point through the competitive process should not belie his academic credentials. In 1903 he took the entrance examination for Princeton and was admitted to the Class of 1907, although he chose to attend VMI instead. Blumenson, 1 *Patton Papers* 57.

immense textile fortune that derived from her father's ownership of the American Woolen Company. For Patton, his Army income was incidental; for Eisenhower, it was essential. More significantly, Patton—who won the Distinguished Service Cross for valor in France and who had been seriously wounded leading his men during the Meuse-Argonne campaign—was already a legend in the tank corps. His contemporaries believed there was no limit to the heights he might attain. Eisenhower missed the war and fretted about his future. No one assumed he would rise to the top. Perhaps Eisenhower should have envied Patton, but there is no evidence that he did so.[14]

"From the beginning he and I got along famously," Ike said. "Both of us were students of current military doctrine. Part of our passion was a strong belief in tanks—a belief derided at the time by others."

> George and I and a group of young officers . . . believed that tanks could have a more valuable and spectacular role. We believed they should attack by surprise and in mass. We wanted speed, reliability, and firepower. We wanted armor that would be proof against machine guns and light field guns, but not so heavy as to damage mobility.[15]

Eisenhower and Patton spent weeks and months at Camp Meade testing their theories in the field. "George was not only a believer, he became a flaming apostle," remembered Ike.[16] Both published articles in their respective service journals touting their findings. Writing in the *Infantry Journal* ("Tanks in Future Wars"), Patton brashly called for armor to act independently on the battlefield. "The tank corps grafted on Infantry, cavalry, artillery, or engineers will be like the third leg to a duck, worthless for control, for combat impotent."[17] Eisenhower, writing more circumspectly for the *Infantry Journal* ("A Tank Discussion"), spoke of tanks "as a profitable adjunct to the Infantry." He spelled out the merits of the tank in close combat and noted the deficiencies of existing models. But he did not advocate massing tanks as Patton had done. "The clumsy, awkward and snail-like progress of the old tanks must be forgotten, and in their place we must picture this speedy, reliable and efficient engine of destruction."[18] The articles, both of which challenged existing doctrine, brought down the wrath of the Army establishment. Eisenhower was summoned to Washington by the chief of infantry, Major General Charles S. Farnsworth. "I was told my ideas were not only wrong but dangerous and that henceforth I would keep them to myself. Particularly, I was not to publish anything incompatible with solid infantry doctrine. If I did, I would be hauled before a court-martial. George, I think, was given the same message."[19]

Eisenhower and Patton spent many hours together riding and hunting. Both relished sports. Eisenhower coached the Camp Meade football team; Patton led the equestrian and pistol teams.* When the Eighteenth Amendment mandating Prohibition became law, Ike distilled gin in the bathtub and Patton brewed beer. When they wanted excitement they would arm themselves like modern vigilantes, climb into Patton's Pierce-Arrow, and drive slowly down dark country roads hoping to be waylaid by bandits. "We wanted to see what a fellow's face looked like when he's looking into the other end of a gun," said Ike.[20] But they never encountered any bandits.

Unlike their husbands, who forged an abiding friendship, Mamie Eisenhower and Beatrice Patton were never close. A noted sportswoman who excelled at riding and sailing, Beatrice had been educated in Europe, spoke flawless French, wrote music and poetry, and published two books about Hawaii, one of which was written in French.[21] She traveled widely, moved easily in society, and was considered a gifted conversationalist. Mamie's interests were more restricted. She loathed outdoor activity and had little patience for abstract discussion. A more typical Army wife, Mamie dwelled on the surface of popular culture. She enjoyed cards and mah-jongg, hit tunes, Hollywood fashions, and pulp fiction. Mamie and Beatrice lived in different realms, united only in their determination to further their husbands' careers.

Mamie returned with Ike to Camp Meade following the motor

---

* Patton finished fifth in the modern pentathlon at the 1912 Summer Olympics in Stockholm. The five events included pistol (25 m), swimming (300 m), fencing, mounted steeplechase (5,000 m), and a distance run (4,000 m). The Stockholm Olympics (the Fifth Olympiad) were attended by four thousand athletes, including the first women, representing twenty-eight countries.

march in September 1919. Because no quarters were available, they lived for a time in a furnished room in nearby Laurel, Maryland, and Ike commuted. Ikey was left with the Douds in Denver. After less than a month, Mamie had had enough. "Ike, I can't live my life this way," she said.[22] Eisenhower begged her to stay, but Mamie packed up and took the train back to Denver. "I threw in the sponge," she said later.[23]

While she was away, Mamie wrote rarely. In desperation, Ike wrote to Mrs. Doud, his mother-in-law:

> Dear Mother:
>
> I hear from Mamie so infrequently that I have no idea how you are getting along. . . . Would you mind, when you have time, writing me about Ikey and Daddy, and yourself. I try to be patient and cheerful—but I do like to be with people I love.
>
> *Devotedly,*
> YOUR SON[24]

Mamie did not return to Camp Meade until May 1920, after the Army agreed to convert some abandoned barracks into family quarters. Ike and Patton were assigned adjacent sets. The quarters were rough and required considerable renovation. This time Ikey was left with Mamie's aunt in Boone, Iowa, until work was complete. "For her trouble and his keep, we paid her $100," Eisenhower remembered.[25]

Ikey was three years old in the autumn of 1920 when he finally joined his parents at Camp Meade. Eisenhower doted on the child, determined to be the father David had never been. According to a friend, Ike would lie on the floor pretending to be a kitten, or growl like a bulldog, playing the clown to make him laugh.[26] "For a little boy just getting interested in the outside world, few places could have been more exciting than Meade," said Eisenhower. "Deafening noises of the tanks enthralled him. A football scrimmage was pure delight. And a parade with martial music set him aglow."[27]

To help with Ikey and the household chores, the Eisenhowers hired a young woman from the area who seemed both pleasant and

Little Ikey, the Eisenhowers' first son, one
year before his death from scarlet fever.

efficient. "When she accepted the job, a chain of circumstances
began, linking us to a tragedy from which we never recovered," Ike
recalled.[28] Unknown to the Eisenhowers, the young woman had just
recovered from an attack of scarlet fever. She exhibited no evidence
of the disease, yet she still harbored the bacteria.

Just before Christmas, Ikey came down with a fever. He was placed
in bed, and the post doctor assumed it was simply the flu. When the
temperature did not subside, Ikey was hospitalized. A specialist from
nearby Johns Hopkins was consulted, and the verdict was scarlet
fever. "We have no cure for this," said the doctor. "Either they get
well or you lose them."[29] Ikey was quarantined. "The doctors did not
allow me into his room," Eisenhower remembered. "But there was a
porch on which I was allowed to sit and I could look into the room
and wave to him. Occasionally, they would let me come to the door

just to speak to Ikey. I haunted the halls of the hospital. Hour after hour, Mamie and I could only hope and pray."[30]

Ikey held out for ten days. But the scarlet fever turned into meningitis, and he died in the early morning hours of January 2, 1921. "I have never known such a blow," Eisenhower wrote long afterward. "I didn't know what to do. I blamed myself because I had often taken his presence for granted."

> This was the greatest disappointment and disaster in my life, the one I have never been able to forget completely. Today when I think of it, even now as I write about it, the keenness of our loss comes back to me as fresh and terrible as it was in that long dark day soon after Christmas, 1920.[31]

Mamie said, "For a long time, it was as if a shining light had gone out of Ike's life. Throughout all the years that followed, the memory of those bleak days was a deep inner pain that never seemed to diminish much."[32]

Ikey's death left a permanent scar. Eisenhower, for the rest of his life, sent Mamie a bouquet of yellow roses every year on Ikey's birthday. Yellow had been Ikey's favorite color. But the marriage was no longer the same. The youthful romance was gone. Instead of drawing closer together, each retreated into a private world of sorrow. Eisenhower threw himself into his work and was rarely home.[33] Mamie tried not to think about the child. Ike blamed himself for hiring the maid; Mamie initially blamed herself. Privately they blamed each other.[34] "Half a century later," wrote Julie Nixon Eisenhower, "Mamie was still unwilling to say much about how Ikey's death changed her relationship with Ike. The pain is too deep. But there is no doubt that the loss of their beloved son closed a chapter in the marriage. It could never again be unblemished first love."[35]

On June 2, 1920, Congress passed the National Defense Act of 1920, one of the most far-reaching pieces of legislation in American history.[36] The Army's authorized strength was set at 288,000 (compared to 2.4 million when the war ended). Subsequent legislation reduced that strength still further. By 1922, fewer than 150,000 men remained on active duty. The United States became a third-rate military power. Army appropriations, which hit $9 billion in 1919, dropped to $400 million—a figure that would remain relatively constant until the late 1930s.[37] Officers reverted to their permanent peacetime ranks. On June 30, 1920, Eisenhower and Patton became captains again. In August, after the adjutant general sorted things out, they were promoted to major. Patton's date of rank was set at July 1, 1920; Eisenhower's one day later—an important distinction. Eisenhower would remain in the grade of major for the next sixteen years; Patton for fourteen. "There was no reason to get excited," said Lucius D. Clay, who was also demoted. "It happened to everyone." What was important is that salaries were not reduced. Eisenhower, Patton, and Clay continued to draw the pay and allowances of their previous ranks.[38]

The National Defense Act also established separate branches for the air service, the chemical corps, and the finance department. The tank corps was abolished and returned to the infantry. During hearings on the bill, Secretary of War Newton D. Baker and the Army's chief of staff, General Peyton March, advocated retaining the tank corps as an independent branch. But when General Pershing testified a week later, he suggested that it "ought to be placed under the Chief of Infantry as an adjunct of that arm."[39] Not surprisingly, Congress took Pershing's word. The animosity between Pershing and Wilson's War Department was palpable (Pershing and March were not on speaking terms) and Pershing—the only person to hold the rank of "General of the Armies"—was considered the nation's military oracle.[40] When the tank corps was abolished, Patton decided to return to the cavalry and became executive officer of the 3rd Cavalry at Fort Myer, across the Potomac from Washington. Eisenhower chose to remain with the infantry.

Before Patton left for Fort Myer, he and Beatrice hosted a Sunday dinner party for Brigadier General Fox Conner, to which Ike and Mamie were invited. Conner was already a gray eminence—a military thinker and strategist who wielded vast power under a cloak of general staff anonymity. Many considered him the most influential officer in the Army. During the war he served as Pershing's chief of operations (Lieutenant Colonel George Marshall was one of his as-

General Fox Conner, Ike's mentor and deputy chief
of staff.

sistants), and had masterminded the first American offensive at
Saint-Mihiel, and then the sudden northwestward thrust in the
Meuse-Argonne.[41] Currently he was Pershing's chief of staff in Wash-
ington while "Black Jack" marked time until he would succeed
March at the Army's head.\*

Fox Conner was understatement personified: self-possessed,
soft-spoken, eminently formal, and polite—a general who loved
reading, a profound student of history, and a keen judge of military
talent. Born to a wealthy planter family in the flatwoods of Calhoun

---

\* Because of the animosity between Pershing and March, Secretary Baker, with
congressional approval, had retained the AEF headquarters as an independent entity in Washington with Pershing in command. That permitted Pershing to continue on active duty without having to report to March, and it relieved March of
the burden of issuing orders to a general who outranked him.

County, Mississippi (his nephew Martin Sennet Conner served as governor of Mississippi from 1932 to 1936), he graduated from West Point in 1898, spoke fluent French (acquired during a tour of duty with the French Army in 1911–12), served with Pershing during the punitive expedition against Pancho Villa (where he met George Patton), and married the daughter of a millionaire father who had made a fortune manufacturing patent medicine. In 1930, he was on a short list of two to become Army chief of staff. Pershing backed Conner, but Hoover chose Douglas MacArthur instead. When MacArthur's term expired in 1935, FDR offered the post to Conner (who was then commanding the I Corps Area), but Conner declined. Eisenhower told biographer Stephen Ambrose that "Fox Conner was the ablest man I ever knew. . . . In a lifetime of association with great and good men, he is the one to whom I owe an incalculable debt."[42]

Conner had come to Meade that Sunday purposely to meet Eisenhower, whom Patton had recommended effusively.[43] After a midday dinner, he asked Patton and Eisenhower to show him their tank park and explain their ideas about the future of the weapon. Patton and Ike were tickled. Conner was the most senior officer thus far to show an interest in armored warfare. (It had been Conner, at AEF headquarters, who originally urged Patton to go into the tank corps.)[44] As Eisenhower remembered, "General Conner went down to the shops with us, found a chair to sit in, and then began to ask questions. Some could be answered briefly, while others required long explanations. By the time he had finished, it was almost dark and he was ready to go home. He said little except that it was interesting. He thanked us, and that was that."[45]

It was shortly after the dinner with Conner that Ike ran afoul of *Army Regulations* and the inspector general. Eisenhower was charged with improperly drawing a quarters allowance for Ikey during the period he was residing in Boone, Iowa, with Mamie's aunt. The 1921 Army was an army that looked after the nickels and dimes, and Ike had received $250.76 to which he was not entitled.* Even more im-

---

* The old Army's concern for a precise accounting of every expenditure paid enormous dividends in World War II and Korea, where there was scarcely an incident

portant, he had signed a false official statement—a hanging offense in the Regular Army. Eisenhower claimed he was unfamiliar with the regulations and offered to repay the money, but the War Department was adamant. "The Certificate which this officer filed with his pay vouchers for the months of May to August 1920 were on their face false and untrue. . . . And the result of this investigation leads me to the conclusion that Major Dwight D. Eisenhower, Inf., be brought to trial upon charges based on the facts as developed," wrote the Army's adjutant general on June 21, 1921.[46]

The matter was turned over to the inspector general, Brigadier General Eli A. Helmick (USMA, 1888), for further action. Colonel Rockenbach and the III Corps Area commander, Brigadier General H. F. Hodges, attempted to head off the proceedings by delivering oral reprimands to Ike (the money had been repaid), but Helmick was not dissuaded. On November 1, 1921, he wrote the adjutant general: "Major Eisenhower is a graduate of the Military Academy, of six years' commissioned service. That he should have knowingly attempted to defraud the government in this matter, or, as he contends, that he was ignorant of the laws governing commutation for dependents, are alike inexplicable."[47]

Helmick had Ike squarely in his sights and was about to pull the trigger. Once again, *fortuna* intervened. John J. Pershing had succeeded Peyton March as Army chief of staff; Fox Conner was given command of the 20th Infantry Brigade in the Panama Canal Zone, and Conner wanted Ike to be his executive officer. Eisenhower does not mention the pending court-martial in his memoirs (nor did the first generation of biographers), and simply notes that orders came "out of the blue" transferring him to the Canal Zone. "The red tape was torn to pieces."[48]

What happened was that Helmick was reined in. No one was closer to Pershing than Fox Conner.* When Conner told Pershing

---

of financial malfeasance or excess profits. As a young artillery lieutenant during the Korean conflict, I remember well my battalion executive officer, Major Ejner J. Fulsang, reminding me: "Smith, if you take care of the nickels and dimes, the dollars will take care of themselves."

* When Pershing returned to the United States in 1919, and following a round of gala receptions in Washington and New York, he spent three weeks of vacation

that he wanted Ike in Panama,[49] Pershing made it happen. Helmick, a classmate of Peyton March's, recognized the new alignment of forces in the War Department and gave way. On December 14, 1921, he wrote the adjutant general that while Eisenhower's offenses were "of the gravest character for which he might not only be dismissed from the service but imprisoned," he did not recommend that Ike be brought to trial, and suggested a formal reprimand be placed in his 201 file instead. The reprimand was administered by Brigadier General J. H. McRae, the assistant chief of staff (and a close friend of Conner's), and became part of Eisenhower's permanent Army record.[50] The bottom line is that Ike avoided trial and was off to the Canal Zone.

Eisenhower served at Camp Meade for almost three years. His efficiency reports were consistently above average, and occasionally superior. Rockenbach called him "a most excellent officer and a valuable assistant." His final report, dated January 6, 1922, enclosed a copy of General McRae's reprimand and noted somewhat critically that "having had independence of command for so long a time, his personal views influence his cooperation." Nevertheless, Ike was described as "an enthusiastic young officer of greatest value to tank organizations."[51]

After a rough passage on the Army troopship *St. Mihiel,* Eisenhower and Mamie arrived in Panama on January 7, 1922. The 20th Infantry Brigade was stationed at Camp Gaillard, near the famous Culebra Cut, toward the Pacific end of the canal. The Eisenhowers were assigned quarters adjacent to the Conners', among a row of elaborate frame dwellings put up by the French for upper-echelon engineers during Ferdinand de Lesseps's ill-fated efforts to construct a canal thirty years earlier. Built on stilts with screened verandas on all four sides, the squarish houses resembled substantial seaside cottages on the Carolina coast that had fallen into serious disrepair. The Conners had restored their house (including a tennis court and a

---

in isolation with the Conners at the twenty-seven-thousand-acre Adirondack retreat that belonged to Mrs. Conner's family. Frank E. Vandiver, 2 *Black Jack: The Life and Times of John J. Pershing* 1044–45 (College Station: Texas A&M University Press, 1977); Gene Smith, *Until the Last Trumpet Sounds: The Life of General of the Armies John J. Pershing* 233–35 (New York: Wiley, 1998).

swimming pool) to its earlier splendor, and Ike took the dilapidated houses in stride. But Mamie was appalled. "She made no bones about how mad she was that they had been ordered to such a post," Virginia Conner recalled.[52]

From the beginning, Mamie, who was in the early stages of pregnancy, hated their ramshackle quarters, Ike's duty with the brigade, and Panama itself. "The marriage was clearly in danger," said Mrs. Conner. "They were two young people who were drifting apart. Ike was spending less and less time with Mamie, and there was no warmth between them. They seemed like two people moving in different directions."[53]

For his part, Eisenhower considered his service in Panama the "most interesting and constructive of my life."

> The main reason was the presence of one man, General Fox Conner. [He] was a practical officer, down to earth, equally at home in the company of the most important people in the region and with any of the men in the regiment. He never put on airs of any kind, and he was as open and honest as any man I have ever known. . . . I served as his brigadier exec for three years in Panama and never enjoyed any other three year period as much. He has held a place in my affections for many years that no other, not even a relative, could obtain.[54]

Under Conner's tutelage Eisenhower became a student of military history. Conner had an extraordinary library (the Conners loved books; his nephew Sennet was reputed to possess the finest legal library in Mississippi), which he made available to Eisenhower. Starting with historical novels, he drew Ike in to more serious works of history. Eisenhower studied the Civil War, followed Napoléon's campaigns, and familiarized himself with Frederick the Great's victories. From there he moved to the classics: Tacitus, Plato, and Shakespeare. At Conner's direction, Ike read Clausewitz's *On War* three times. "Those German sentences. I tell you, it's trouble. He'd quiz me. You know Clausewitz has those maxims. He'd make me tell what each one meant."[55]

Reflecting his experience at Pershing's AEF headquarters, Conner taught Ike about coalition warfare.

> He laid great stress in his instruction to me on what he called "the art of persuasion." Since no foreigner could be given outright administrative command of troops of another nation, they would have to be coordinated very closely and this needed persuasion. He would get out a book of applied psychology and we would talk it over. How do you get allies of different nations to march and think as a nation? There is no question of his molding my thinking on this from the time I was thirty-one. I would not say that his views had any *specific* influence on my conduct of SHAEF [Supreme Headquarters, Allied Expeditionary Force], but his forcing me to think about these things gave me a preparation that was unusual in the Army at that time.[56]

Eisenhower considered Conner a storehouse of axiomatic advice.

> He was the man who first remarked to me, "Always take your job seriously, never yourself." He was the man who taught me that splendid line from the French, "All generalities are false, including this one." He often quoted Shakespeare at length and he could relate his works to wars under discussion. Our conversations continued throughout the three years I served with him at Camp Gaillard. It is clear now that life with General Conner was a sort of graduate school in military affairs and the humanities, leavened by the comments and discourses of a man who was experienced in his knowledge of men and their conduct.[57]

In the meantime, Mamie became increasingly depressed and dissatisfied. Aside from the occasional afternoon of bridge, or Saturday night dances at the officers' club, there was little social life at Gaillard, and Mamie resisted the usual round of tennis, swimming, and horseback riding that filled the days of most military dependents. She spoke no Spanish, was too timid to venture into nearby Panama City, and confined her shopping excursions to the post exchange and commissary. The Douds visited in June 1922 and were shocked by the situation they found. They insisted that Mamie return to Denver with them for the birth of her baby. At Camp Meade, when Mamie found conditions not to her liking, she had retreated to the comfort of her parents' home, and once again she readily agreed.

This time Ike and Mamie stayed in touch by writing frequently, and when the baby was born on August 3, 1922, Eisenhower was present, having obtained three weeks' leave from a sympathetic General Conner. Christened John Sheldon Doud Eisenhower in honor of Mamie's father, the baby brought momentary joy to the Eisenhowers. "John did much to fill the gap that we felt so poignantly and so deeply every day of our lives since the death of our first son," Ike later recalled. "While his arrival did not, of course, eliminate the grief we still felt, he was precious in his own right and he did much to take our minds off the tragedy. Living in the present with a healthy, bouncing baby boy can take parents' minds off almost anything."[58]

Eisenhower remained in Denver briefly and then returned to Panama. Mamie stayed another several months. When she returned to Gaillard in the autumn of 1922, she brought a nurse, Katherine Herrick, from Denver General Hospital, to take care of the baby. John Doud paid Ms. Herrick's salary and expenses, and she remained with the family for the next four years. That autumn, Virginia Conner observed a difference in the Eisenhowers. "After Johnny was born and Mamie felt better, she began to change. I had the delight of seeing a rather callow young woman turn into the person to whom everyone turned. I have seen her, with her gay laugh and personality, smooth out Ike's occasional irritability."[59]

But the reconciliation between Ike and Mamie was soon tested. Eisenhower's round-the-clock commitment to Conner and the 20th Infantry Brigade began to take its toll. Mamie became despondent, and her health deteriorated. "I was down to skin and bones and hollow-eyed," she later recalled. "My health and vitality seemed to ebb away. I don't know how I existed."[60]

Once again Mamie fled to Denver, taking the baby and Katherine

Herrick with her. Ike begged her to stay, but she refused. According to their granddaughter Susan, Mamie's return to Denver was a defining moment in her life. "From the vantage of 750 Lafayette Street she was able to take stock of her marriage and the life she had led for nearly eight years."

> Under the watchful eye of her parents, Mamie's health improved and she started to see old friends and classmates again. She could not help but notice how her girlfriends were living: theirs were lives she could understand. These women had husbands who quit working at dinnertime and spent the evenings with their families. They were bankers, lawyers, and doctors who led predictable lives in clean, safe places.
>
> But as Mamie began to feel better, she was able to take a harder look at the men themselves. As secure and stable as their lives seemed to be, Mamie realized she would not want to be married to any of them—she missed Ike. And she had also finally outgrown home.[61]

Mamie made peace with the Army, and with Ike's career. The first great crisis of their married life had been weathered. Mamie returned to Panama and committed herself to tough it out. "I knew almost from the day I married Ike that he would be a great soldier," she said. "Nothing came before his duty. I was forced to match his spirit of personal sacrifice as best I could."[62]

Eisenhower's efficiency reports in Panama were consistently superior. Conner called him "one of the most capable, efficient, and loyal officers I have ever met," and recommended that he be sent to the Command and General Staff School (CGSS) at Fort Leavenworth.[63] Mrs. Conner said, "I never saw two men more congenial than Ike Eisenhower and my husband."[64] Fox Conner was truly Eisenhower's guardian angel. He had saved him from possible court-martial in 1922 when he asked for Ike in Panama. Now, in the summer of 1924, as Conner prepared to leave the Canal Zone (he would become the Army's assistant chief of staff for logistics, G-4), Conner arranged for Eisenhower to be awarded the Distinguished Service Medal for which he had been recommended at Camp Colt, but that had been twice denied. On the parade ground at Gaillard, with the 20th Infantry Brigade drawn up to pass in review, Fox Conner presented Ike with the Army's DSM "for exceptionally meritorious and distinguished services" at Camp Colt in 1918. Conner had recommended to Pershing that the award be conferred, and Pershing habitually accepted Conner's advice.

Eisenhower's tour in Panama ended in September 1924. With General Conner's encouragement he had requested assignment to the CGSS at Fort Leavenworth. Instead, he was ordered back to Camp Meade as an assistant coach of the III Corps Area football team. "Why, three months ahead of schedule I was moved thousands of miles from Panama to Chesapeake Bay to join three other officers in a football coaching assignment is still a cosmic top-secret wonder to me," wrote Eisenhower some forty years later.[65] War Department brass evidently thought a successful season for the local football team would provide valuable publicity for the Army, and they assembled a top-flight coaching staff at Meade. But the coaches did not have the players to work with. Eisenhower's team won only one game that season and lost the final to the Marines 20–0.

Before the season ended Eisenhower received orders for a permanent change of station to Fort Benning, where he was to command the 15th Light Tank Battalion—"the same old tanks I had commanded several years earlier."[66] As Ike saw it, his career had stalled. Without attendance at Leavenworth, there was little prospect of high command. Dismayed at the prospect, Eisenhower went to the War Department to plead his case to the chief of infantry, a post still occupied by Major General Charles S. Farnsworth. Ike should have known better. "Carry out your orders," said Farnsworth, without listening to Eisenhower's reclama. That was Army tradition. Junior officers, even field-grade officers, had no business questioning their assignments.

The chances are that Eisenhower would have been selected by the infantry to attend Leavenworth, if not in the next class, then in the one thereafter. Three years of superior efficiency ratings in Panama placed him in the top 10 percent of all majors on active duty, and his assignment to command a battalion at Benning (a rarity in the Army

Eisenhower family reunion on the front porch in Abilene, 1925. *From left,*
Roy, Arthur, Earl, Edgar, David, Ike, Milton, and Ida.

of 1924) scarcely suggested he was in official disfavor. But Eisenhower was impatient. Contrary to Fox Conner's dictum, he appears
to have taken himself too seriously. On his way out of the old State,
War, and Navy Building on Pennsylvania Avenue he stopped by to
see General Conner, whose office was down the hall from Farnsworth's. There is no record of their conversation, but several days
later Ike received a cryptic telegram:

NO MATTER WHAT ORDERS YOU RECEIVE FROM THE
WAR DEPARTMENT, MAKE NO PROTEST. ACCEPT THEM
WITHOUT QUESTION. SIGNED CONNER.[67]

Conner was sympathetic to Ike's plight, and used his influence to
circumvent the chief of infantry. Eisenhower was abruptly transferred to the adjutant general corps and assigned to Fort Logan, Colorado, on recruiting duty—normally a tombstone appointment for
officers who had been passed over for promotion. "Had anyone else

suggested [such a move] I would have been outraged," said Ike, "but with my solid belief in Fox Conner I kept my temper."[68] For Mamie, the move to Fort Logan could not have been more welcome—a fact that Conner had also considered. Fort Logan is on the outskirts of Denver, roughly seven miles from the Doud home on Lafayette Street, and for the first time in years she and Ike and baby John were able to spend time with her family. Eisenhower went through the motions of a peacetime Army recruiter, and in April 1925, more or less on schedule, orders arrived notifying him that he had been selected by the adjutant general to attend the Command and General Staff School with the class entering in August 1925. "I was ready to fly," said Eisenhower. "And I needed no airplane."[69]*

Once he was accepted for Leavenworth, Ike began to worry whether he was qualified. He had not attended the Infantry School at Fort Benning, normally a prerequisite for line officers, and CGSS had the reputation of being hypercompetitive. Leavenworth was the Army's eye of the needle. Those who did well usually went on to higher command; those who did poorly fell by the wayside. As doubt got the better of him, Eisenhower wrote Fox Conner to ask how he could best prepare for the ordeal.

Conner reassured him. "You may not know it," he wrote Ike, "but because of your three years' work in Panama, you are far better trained and ready for Leavenworth than anybody I know. You will feel no sense of inferiority."[70] Armed with Conner's encouragement, Ike asked George Patton for his notes from his year at CGSS—Patton stood 25th of 248 officers in the Class of 1923–24. According to Mamie, "He studied them to tatters."[71] Eisenhower also obtained copies of lesson plans and problems from previous years and worked through them, checking his answers against the approved solutions.

---

* Eisenhower attended Leavenworth on the adjutant general's quota, although the record indicates there had been no need for Conner to circumvent the chief of infantry. In January 1925, before Ike's transfer to the AG corps, the chief of infantry had recommended forty-seven officers to attend the 1925–26 CGSS course. Eisenhower was listed twenty-sixth. Recommendation by the chief of infantry was tantamount to selection. Of course, Eisenhower did not know that, and no one in the chief's office thought it necessary to inform him. Carlo D'Este, *Eisenhower: A Soldier's Life* 177–78 (New York: Henry Holt, 2002).

After a month of intense effort, Ike discovered that Conner was right. The work came easily and he enjoyed it.[72]

Eisenhower reported to Leavenworth in August 1925—one of 245 field-grade officers selected by the War Department to attend an eleven-month course on the problems of military command. Because he was senior to most of his classmates (his date of rank reflected his prior service as a lieutenant colonel), he and Mamie were assigned a spacious four-bedroom apartment in what eventually became the post's VIP quarters rather than in the cramped accommodations provided for most student families. Mamie flourished in that environment, and although Ike was busy around the clock, the earlier marital tensions disappeared. Mamie had matured since Panama, and as Susan Eisenhower put it, "She had now passed muster as a real army wife."[73]

The Command and General Staff School at Fort Leavenworth was one of the first postgraduate schools in America to employ the case method, and the curriculum was designed to discover not only who had mastered the material, but who could function and survive under severe stress. In battle, exhausted men are required to think and act under extreme pressure, and Leavenworth replicated that. Classes began at eight-thirty and lasted until noon. Afternoons were devoted to solving hypothetical problems. The problems were the core of the curriculum, and a clear head was essential. "If you are mentally fatigued or too stuffed up with facts and figures, it is almost certain a poor mark will result," Eisenhower wrote.[74] "I established a routine that limited my night study to two hours and a half; from seven to nine-thirty. Mamie was charged with the duty of seeing that I got to bed on time."[75]

Students were encouraged to form study groups and most did. Eisenhower thought group study too cumbersome and time-consuming, and chose instead to work through the problems with an old friend from the 19th Infantry at Fort Sam Houston, Leonard Gerow. Gerow shared Eisenhower's intensity. He had finished first in his class at the Infantry School, and his wife and Mamie were close friends of long standing. Evening after evening Ike and Gerow met in the upstairs war room Eisenhower had established in his apartment and gamed their way through the next day's exercise. When the course ended in June 1926, Eisenhower finished first and Gerow second, separated by two-tenths of a percentage point.

"Congratulations," wrote George Patton. "You are kind to think my notes helped you, though I feel sure that you would have done as well without them. If a man thinks war long enough it is bound to affect him in a good way."[76]

Shortly after he graduated from Leavenworth, Eisenhower summarized his impressions for the adjutant general. The essay was subsequently published anonymously in the *Infantry Journal*.[77] Ike sought to demystify the Command and General Staff School and provide advice for future students: Use common sense; don't magnify the importance of insignificant details; don't worry about bygones; and keep it simple. "Remember that Napoleon's battle plans are among the simplest that history records." Focus, common sense, simplicity, and attitude—the recipe for Ike's success.

# FOUR

# With Pershing in Paris

No man can make a successful career on his own.
He needs help.

—MAMIE EISENHOWER

WHEN EISENHOWER COMPLETED the course at the Command and General Staff School, he was pulled three ways. The adjutant general proposed to send him to a major university as the professor of military science and tactics, heading the ROTC program. In addition, it was arranged that Ike would coach the university's football team at a salary of $3,500—roughly doubling his take-home pay. The commandant at CGSS wanted him to remain at Leavenworth on the faculty, a sure ticket to an eventual general staff billet. And the chief of infantry thought Ike needed more troop duty. The chief of infantry prevailed. Eisenhower was appointed executive officer of the 24th Infantry Regiment at Fort Benning.

In retrospect, it is evident that the office of the chief of infantry resented Eisenhower's end run around it to attend the CGSS. Political correctness aside, assignment to the 24th Infantry—the Old Deuce-Four—was scarcely a career-enhancing move. Like the 10th Cavalry, the 24th was an all-black regiment commanded by white officers, few of whom relished their posting. This was the segregated Army, and black units, despite a glorious heritage tracing to the Civil War, were regarded as second-class. The 24th had been founded in 1866, fought with distinction at San Juan Hill and in the Philippines, and marched with Pershing against Pancho Villa. But it sat out World War I, had not been ordered to France, and was currently employed as support troops for the Infantry School at Fort Benning. It was the infantry's Siberia.* In his memoirs Eisenhower does not

---

* During World War II, the 24th was relegated to policing up pockets of holdout Japanese troops after the main fighting was over. It took part in the occupation of Japan and was one of the first units ordered into Korea in 1950. But like many units ordered from Japan into Korea, the 24th initially fought badly—so badly, in fact, that it became the subject of a derisive ditty, "The Bugout Boogie": "When them Chinese mortars begin to thud, the Old Deuce-Four begin to bug."

According to a study of the regiment published in 1996 by the Department of the Army (William T. Bowers, William M. Hammond, and George L. MacGarrigle, *Black Soldier, White Army: The 24th Infantry Regiment in Korea* [Washington, D.C.: Center of Military History, U.S. Army, 1996]), the soldiers of the 24th considered it "a 'penal' regiment for white officers who had 'screwed up.' " (The quotation appears on page 58.)

Ironically, the poor performance of the 24th in Korea played a decisive role in the desegregation of the Army. President Truman had ordered the desegregation of the armed services on July 26, 1948 (Executive Order 9981). The following day, General Omar Bradley, Army chief of staff and Truman's fellow Missourian, took exception to the president's order. "The Army is not out to make any social reforms," said Bradley. "The Army will put men of different races in different companies. It will change that policy when the nation as a whole changes it" (*The New York Times,* July 30, 1948).

Executive Order 9981 provided that desegregation take place as rapidly as possible, "having due regard to the time required to effectuate any necessary changes without impairing efficiency or morale," and Bradley's demurrer was taken in that context. He repeated the Army's reluctance to move before society had done so in a prepared statement to the President's Committee on Equality in the Armed Forces, March 28, 1949, and that is where the issue rested until the Korean War. The Army remained segregated despite the president's order.

It was the poor showing of the 24th in Korea that broke the logjam. In September 1950, two months after the war began, Major General William B. Kean, commander of the 25th Infantry Division, requested that the Eighth Army disband the all-black 24th Infantry Regiment because of its poor performance. General Matthew Ridgway, commanding the Eighth Army, had long opposed segregation. "It has always seemed to me both un-American and un-Christian for free citizens to be taught to downgrade themselves this way as if they were unfit to associate with their fellows or to accept leadership themselves." Ridgway's efforts to desegregate the Eighth Army were stymied temporarily by MacArthur's headquarters in Tokyo and the Department of the Army. But when he succeeded MacArthur as supreme commander in the spring of 1951, Ridgway forced the issue and ordered the desegregation of the troops in the theater, beginning with the 24th Infantry. This time no one in Washington objected.

Morris J. MacGregor, Jr., *Integration of the Armed Forces, 1940–1965* 436–47

mention that the 24th Infantry was a black unit, and his early biographers apparently were unaware of the fact. Nevertheless, it is manifest that Ike was unhappy with the assignment and used his influence to wriggle out. A permanent change of station in the peacetime Army normally involved a three-year posting. Ike stayed at Benning less than five months.

Once again, Fox Conner rode to the rescue. In 1921, Conner had saved Ike from a possible court-martial. In 1924, he circumvented the chief of infantry to send him to Leavenworth. And in 1926 he intervened once more to transfer Ike out of the 24th Infantry. On December 15, 1926, orders arrived from the War Department assigning Eisenhower to the American Battle Monuments Commission—a free-standing, independent government agency in Washington headed by General of the Armies John J. Pershing. Conner was now the Army's deputy chief of staff—the number two military man in the War Department. He appreciated Ike's talent and recognized it was not being properly utilized. To assign the honor graduate of the Command and General Staff School as executive officer of a unit of support troops at Fort Benning made no sense whatever. If not punitive, it was certainly myopic. "No man can make a successful career on his own," Mamie Eisenhower once said. "He needs help. And Ike was fortunate to have sponsors such as Fox Conner and later MacArthur and General Marshall who pushed him ahead."[1]

The Battle Monuments Commission was charged with compiling and organizing the record of American participation in World War I. To some extent it was established as a sinecure for General Pershing. A General of the Armies is never retired from active duty, and the commission provided a post for Pershing outside the War Department chain of command. He continued to be the ranking officer in the Army, and his office remained in the ornate State, War, and Navy Building adjacent to the White House, but his responsibilities were confined to memorializing the American war effort in France.

---

(Washington, D.C.: Center of Military History, U.S. Army 1981); Matthew B. Ridgway, *The Korean War: How We Met the Challenge* 192–93 (Garden City, N.Y.: Doubleday, 1967).

The general needed help preparing a guide to the American battle-fields, and Conner suggested that Eisenhower was the person for the job.

Ike and Mamie moved to Washington in January 1927. Calvin Coolidge was in the White House, the Republicans controlled both houses of Congress, and the nation basked in pre-Depression prosperity. "The business of America is business," President Coolidge told the American Society of Newspaper Editors. The Washington of 1927 was a slow-paced city of southern charm, genteel civility, and white supremacy. Schools, restaurants, hotels, and the federal civil service were strictly segregated; an isolationist Congress had recently enacted the National Origins Act of 1924, effectively closing off most immigration to the United States; and the remarkable Washington Senators, relying on the arm of Walter "Big Train" Johnson, won back-to-back American League pennants and the 1924 World Series. Prohibition notwithstanding, Capitol Hill was awash in booze, and there were few legislative problems that House Speaker Nicholas Longworth and minority leader John Nance Garner could not resolve over a bottle of bootleg bourbon in the Speaker's chambers.

Since no military quarters were available for Ike and Mamie, they took an apartment in the Wyoming, a gracious dowager from Washington's belle epoque at the corner of Connecticut Avenue and Columbia Road. Because of its spacious apartments, soaring ceilings, and marble corridors, the Wyoming was home to a legion of upper- and midlevel officials, including a United States senator, several members of Congress, the surgeon general, and a dozen or more field-grade and general officers. Chief Justice William Howard Taft lived around the corner; Justices Louis Brandeis and George Sutherland down the street. The Eisenhowers had a two-bedroom apartment with a large living room, a separate dining room, a study, and a cavernous kitchen. For this they paid $130 a month—roughly three times the average rent in Washington. Ike's take-home pay was $391 a month, Mamie received an additional $100 from her father, and the cost of living was remarkably low. Bread was 10¢ a loaf, milk cost 9¢ a quart, and Ike's cigarettes were a dollar a carton. Other prices were equally low. A man's tailored three-piece suit sold for less

than $30. A gallon of gas cost 15¢, and a new Chevrolet, Ford, or
Plymouth could be had for $600 to $800. The Eisenhowers had a
full-time maid who also cooked, and a new automobile. They were
members of the Army-Navy town club and the Army-Navy Country
Club, and they entertained frequently at the Willard Hotel—
Washington's leading hostelry. As the wife of an Army contemporary
remarked, "We never lived that well again."[2]

Eisenhower's task with the Battle Monuments Commission was to
sort through the unit histories and official records of the AEF and
prepare a narrative of the American effort in France. Appended to
the narrative history was a description of the battle monuments that
had been erected and the locations of the various cemeteries where
American war dead were buried. The purpose was to provide an easily accessible reference work for Americans who might visit France,
and Eisenhower was given a six-month deadline.

To call *A Guide to the American Battle Fields in Europe* simply a tour-
ist guidebook trivializes the undertaking.[3] It is a guidebook. But
more important, it is a complete history, battle by battle, of the
American war on the western front. Of the 282 pages, roughly a
third are devoted to describing the battlefield monuments; the remaining two hundred pages provide a concise summary of the fighting, beginning with Château-Thierry and Belleau Wood in June
1918 and concluding with the armistice in November. The book is
written from the vantage point of Pershing's headquarters, and in
describing the fighting Eisenhower presents the details with remarkable clarity. Ike had not served in France, but like any good historian
he assimilated the facts and described the battlefront as though he
had taken part. Anyone who reads the *Guide* will be struck by its
completeness. The *Encyclopaedia Britannica* called it "an excellent reference work on World War I." Republished in 1992 by the Army's
Center of Military History,[4] it remains one of the best references to
the American effort in World War I. Ike's prose lacks the eloquence
of Grant's *Memoirs,* but it would be fair to say that when the project
was complete, Eisenhower was the best-informed officer in the Army
on the strategy and battle tactics Pershing employed, apart from
Pershing himself and Fox Conner (who directed the operations of the
AEF).

Writing the history of the western front gave Eisenhower a feel for the geography and an understanding of the problems involved in coordinating the Allied armies. He treats the logistical problems of the AEF exhaustively. It is difficult to imagine a more useful assignment for a future supreme commander than to write a history of the analogous American effort in World War I. In 1927 a second war in Europe was scarcely on the horizon, and Eisenhower often chafed under the tight deadlines Pershing imposed. But the substantive knowledge of the war in France that he derived from the exercise surely stood him in good stead when he commanded the Allied effort seventeen years later.

The Eisenhowers settled in easily at the Wyoming. The building was so congenial that they lived there—off and on—a total of nine years. Ike could take the Connecticut Avenue streetcar (five cents) to work, or walk in good weather. Mamie delighted in Washington's department stores, and bought all of Eisenhower's clothes. Army officers assigned to Washington during the interwar years wore mufti, and as Mamie recalled, "he wouldn't go into a shop and purchase them."[5]

Eisenhower went to work early and stayed at his desk until six. When he came home he wanted to relax. "Ike was the sort of man that when he finished his day's work, he left his work at the office," said Mamie. "When he came home, he was home and we didn't discuss what his big problems were. He kept them to himself. That was the way we managed our lives. That's the way we've kept it. So many people say to me, 'Didn't General Eisenhower used to talk over some of his problems with you?' And I'd say, 'Well, no.' And I didn't say to him, 'The dishwasher didn't work today.' He wouldn't have been interested."[6]

Young Johnny was five when the Eisenhowers moved to Washington. He was enrolled first in a Montessori school, and then when he turned six in the nearby public school. There was little or no homework in those days, but according to Mamie, Ike always reviewed the day's activities with him before he was sent to bed. "If Ike and I were delaying our dinner for some reason, or if we were going out to a party, Johnny would sit down to dinner with candles, and silver candelabra, and his finger bowl, and everything just as if we were at the table. He was even served and he had everything done perfectly."[7]

Shortly before Eisenhower finished his assignment, he was informed that he had been selected for the next class at the Army War College, then located at Washington Barracks (now Fort McNair), in southwest Washington, D.C. Again, the hand of Fox Conner is evident. Unlike the Command and General Staff School, whose purpose was to prepare field-grade officers for the general staff, the War College curriculum was designed to teach future generals an overview of war—how armies were mobilized, supplied, and deployed; relations with allies; and grand strategy.[8] Ike was the youngest member of his class, and one of the youngest ever admitted to the War College.[9]

On August 15, 1927, when Eisenhower's assignment with the Battle Monuments Commission ended, General Pershing expressed his appreciation in a letter to the chief of infantry:

> The detail of Major Dwight D. Eisenhower, who has been assisting the American Battle Monuments Commission in preparing the guide book, expires today. I wish to take this occasion to express my appreciation of the splendid service he has rendered since being with us.
>
> In the discharge of his duties, which were most difficult, and which were rendered even more difficult by reason of the short time available for their completion, he has shown superior ability not only in visualizing his work as a whole but in executing its many details in an efficient and timely manner. What he has done was accomplished only by the exercise of unusual intelligence and constant devotion to duty.
>
> With kindest regards, I am
>
> *Sincerely yours,*
> JOHN J. PERSHING[10]

Pershing's letter of commendation established a watershed in Eisenhower's career. Before that, he was merely a gifted protégé of Fox Conner's, still subject to whatever roughhouse the infantry establishment might choose to inflict. After Pershing's commendation, he was admitted to the ranks of the chosen few. Pershing was parsimonious with praise, and the glowing recommendation he gave Ike made the chief of infantry take notice. Eisenhower's path to the top was not guaranteed. But from that point on his assignments were certain to be commensurate with his ability. If he failed to perform, he would be left by the wayside. But if he continued to excel, he could shoot for the stars.

Eisenhower's sojourn at the War College was a leisurely respite from his hectic days at Leavenworth and the Battle Monuments Commission. There were no tests, no grades, and no final examinations. Students were required to write an original research paper, and Eisenhower chose to address the neglected problem of mobilization. Congress had reduced the Regular Army to fewer than 120,000 men; the National Guard was at half strength; and graduates of the various reserve officer programs numbered about a hundred thousand. But there were virtually no troops for them to command. Eisenhower advocated the creation of an enlisted reserve force, staffed by veterans whose service tour had expired.[11] The report was seventeen pages long, and Eisenhower—contrary to the national mood of pacifist isolation—structured the nation's military needs to meet a possible overseas crisis. When Ike graduated at the end of June 1928, he was given an overall rating of "superior" (students were not ranked for class standing). General William D. Connor, the school commandant, said Eisenhower's theoretical training for high command was superior; his suitability for the War Department General Staff was superior; and his academic accomplishment was superior—in short, he was "a young officer of great promise."[12] Ike was thirty-seven years old.

Along with most of his classmates, Eisenhower was assigned to the War Department General Staff—another choice assignment.[13] But General Pershing, who had moved the Battle Monuments Commission to Paris, set out to redo the guidebook, and wanted Eisenhower for the job. That would necessitate Ike's transfer to Paris, and would enable him to visit the battlefields firsthand. When Pershing inquired, Eisenhower jumped at the opportunity. "This was my first chance to get to know a European country. I saw Paris for the first time. The job now took on new interest. It involved travel, all the way from the Vosges in the southeast of France to the English Channel."[14] The fact that Mamie wanted to go to Paris made the decision easy. On December 16, 1927, "By order of the President," Ike was instructed to join the Battle Monuments Commission in Paris when his course at the War College was complete.[15]

The Eisenhowers sailed for France on July 31, 1928, aboard the recently refitted SS *America,* formerly the SS *Amerika* of the Hamburg-Amerika Line.[*] They were joined by Mamie's parents, and experienced a smooth nine-day crossing, arriving in Cherbourg in the early morning hours of August 9, 1928. They boarded the boat train for Paris and found temporary hotel accommodations. While Ike reported for duty with Pershing, Mamie began the quest to find a suitable apartment. She was assisted by several resident Army wives and an exceptionally favorable exchange rate. The American dollar, normally worth five francs, now bought at least twenty-five, and occasionally as many as forty or fifty. There was little inflation in France; the prices Frenchmen paid had changed little since the war, but the French franc had fallen out of bed on the international exchange market. According to the 1928 *Guide Michelin,* a superior room at world-class hotels such as the Ritz, the Crillon, or the Plaza Athénée cost 250 to 300 francs a night. For Americans that translated into ten to twelve dollars. (Today, the cheapest room at one of these hotels is well in excess of $700.) Prices at less famous establishments were substantially lower. Ernest Hemingway, writing for the *Toronto Star,* said, "Paris in winter is rainy, cold, beautiful and cheap. It is also noisy, jostling, crowded and cheap. It is anything you want—and cheap."[16]

Within a week Mamie had found an elegant furnished apartment in the fashionable sixteenth arrondissement, on the Right Bank,

---

* The SS *America* was built in 1905 at the Harland and Wolff shipyard in Belfast for the Hamburg-Amerika Line. At 22,225 tons, it was the largest ship of the period, and carried 386 persons in first class, 150 in second, 222 in third, and 1,750 in steerage. When war broke out in August 1914, the *Amerika* was in port in Boston. It remained there until the United States entered the war in April 1917, whereupon it was seized, renamed the *America,* and converted to a troopship. After the war it became American property pursuant to the reparations provisions of the Versailles Treaty and was given to the United States Lines, which converted it into a two-class passenger ship. It was seriously damaged by fire while undergoing repairs at Newport News, Virginia, in 1927, and had just been refitted when the Eisenhowers boarded. After service as a troopship in World War II, it was scrapped in January 1957.

about a mile downstream from the Trocadéro and the Eiffel Tower, and close by the Bois de Boulogne. Located on the *premier étage* at 68 Quai d'Auteuil, overlooking the Seine and Pont Mirabeau, the apartment was within easy walking distance of Pershing's headquarters at 20 rue Molitor.[17]

The apartment belonged to the Comtesse de Villefranche, the doyenne of one of France's most distinguished families, and rented for five thousand francs a month—a price that would have been unaffordable for the Eisenhowers except for the exchange rate. It was furnished with fin de siècle elegance: walls paneled in brocade; windows framed by satin draperies cinched with ropes of twisted silk; exquisite Aubusson carpets covering the floors; crystal chandeliers suspended from ornate ceilings; rooms crowded with gilt and brocade chairs and sofas, inlaid desks and armoires, and innumerable small tables laden with Sèvres figurines and bibelots. Mamie said the difference between the Comtesse de Villefranche's apartment and typical Army quarters was "as far as Peary and Amundsen when they reached their respective poles."[18] There was a large vestibule, two drawing rooms, a dining room, three bedrooms, and an immense kitchen, and quarters for the help in the attic. The Eisenhowers employed a live-in maid and a full-time cook, and enjoyed off-street parking for their car, which had been shipped over from the United States.

Eisenhower initially relished his posting to Paris. He and Mamie commenced daily French lessons, and Ike set out to explore Paris on foot. After three months of daily instruction, Eisenhower became proficient at reading and writing French, but the spoken word eluded him. "Major," said his teacher, "you are one of the best readers of French and translators of the written language that I have among my students, but you are the worst candidate as a French linguist I have ever tried to teach."[19] Ike persevered for a year, but his effort to speak French proved hopeless. Mamie, for her part, began enthusiastically but soon lost patience. Unaccustomed to rigorous study, she learned no French at all during their fourteen months in Paris and used a pocket dictionary to communicate. What Mamie did enjoy was shopping. According to Ike, she became "a specialist in the shops that ranged from the flea market and sidewalk stands to the *grands magasins.*"[20] When the Eisenhowers left the White House for Gettysburg in 1961, Mamie's closets were still filled with gowns and dresses and shoes she had purchased during their Paris years.[21]

Paris of the 1920s was a mecca for a generation of Americans. Aside from the favorable exchange rate and the absence of Prohibition, the City of Light had regained its role as the world's great international metropolis. France as a whole had suffered dreadfully during the war. War damage was extensive in the north and east of the country, and casualties were proportionately higher than in any other nation—1.3 million dead, with more than three million wounded and disabled. One in ten Paris conscripts never returned from the fighting.[22] But the city itself had avoided significant damage. The economy flourished, national averages surpassed prewar levels, and the birthrate had turned positive. "I feel as if I was biting into a utopian fruit," said the writer Anaïs Nin about life in the city: "Something velvety and lustrous and rich and vivid."[23]

No other city lived the frantic twenties with greater energy, imagination, and indulgence.[24] Cabaret star Josephine Baker dominated the entertainment scene with her quirky singing and exotic dancing. Anglophone writers, freed from conventional restraints, spawned some of the masterpieces of literary modernism and often wrote of their Paris years. James Joyce, Henry Miller, John Dos Passos, Edith Wharton, E. E. Cummings, Cole Porter, George Gershwin, Gertrude Stein, Archibald MacLeish, Allen Tate, F. Scott Fitzgerald, William Carlos Williams, and Hart Crane shared Ike's time in Paris. There is no evidence their paths crossed, but the Paris they wrote about was the same. Crane captured its essence: "Dinners, soirées, poets, erratic millionaires, painters, translations, lobsters, absinthe, music, promenades, oysters, sherry, aspirin, pictures, sapphic, heiresses, editors, books, sailors. *And How!*"[25]

Two English-language dailies, James Gordon Bennett's venerable *Paris Herald* (daily circulation thirty-nine thousand) and Colonel Robert R. McCormick's upstart *Paris Tribune,* a successor of the *Chicago Tribune*'s Army edition published for the AEF, not only kept the expatriate community informed, but provided employment for a generation of fledgling journalists, including William L. Shirer, Waverley Root, and James Thurber.

Mamie in Paris, 1929.

Eisenhower and his colleagues at Pershing's Battle Monuments Commission paid little attention to the city's artistic community, traditionally drawn to Paris by the combination of cheap rents and available studio space. Picasso, Modigliani, Miro, Chagall, Max Ernst, and the American sculptor Alexander Calder flourished in Montparnasse and the Latin Quarter. What did make an impression, at least among Army wives, was the great Paris exposition of decorative arts shortly before the Eisenhowers' arrival, which launched Art Deco as a new international style.

Many years later Ike and Mamie agreed that the fourteen months they spent in Paris was the most idyllic period in their marriage. "We had a nice life and a nice group of friends. Our son, John, was going to a good school, and we had lots of fun and lots of company."[26] Mamie was at her best. Naturally gregarious and fun-loving, she entertained generously in their spacious apartment, so much so that

68 Quai d'Auteuil was soon christened Club Eisenhower, a home away from home for the American military in Paris. "The apartment became a sort of informal, junior-size American Express for friends who were visiting Paris," said Ike. "Mamie and I were drawn into their trips. In time we both became small-scale authorities on what should not be missed and what should be avoided."[27] When the Eisenhowers entertained formally, it was at the elegant officers' club, the Cercle de l'Union Interalliée, on the Faubourg Saint-Honoré, near the Palais de l'Élysée.[28]

Eisenhower trooped the battlefields relentlessly, not only those on which the AEF fought, but the entire front from the Swiss border to the English Channel. Often away from Paris for days at a time, he immersed himself in mapping, cataloging, and taking notes about every aspect of the battles, tracing trench lines and terrain features. "In this way I came to see the small towns of France and to meet the sound and friendly people working in the fields and along the roads." Captain George Horkan, a colleague on the Battle Monuments Commission who later served as Ike's quartermaster general, believed that the experience gave Eisenhower "a grasp of the military terrain of northern Europe that was absolutely invaluable."[29]

Ike was not all business. "Whenever possible," he recalled, "I stopped along the road to join groups of road workers who were eating their noonday lunch. They were invariably relaxed and hospitable. When my chauffeur (he was always my interpreter) and I would ask if we could join them, their custom was to offer something from their lunchboxes. I developed a habit of carrying a bottle of Evian and an extra bottle of *vin rouge* . . . which was always welcome. Whenever I could find no group along the road, I would save my lunch, look for a little *auberge,* and eat there to mingle with the people."[30]

In the spring of 1929 Ike began to take Mamie and young John on his battlefield trips. "Verdun was a forbidding place," John remembered. "A large portion of the town lay in ruins. Its most frightening place was a strong point named Fort Douaumont. Nearby we visited the Trench of Bayonets, where a squad of Frenchmen, preparing to go over the top, had been buried alive by the impact of a nearby German shell. By some miracle the bayonets had remained sticking out of the ground, and the bodies of the victims had been left unmolested by the French as a national monument."[31]

Eisenhower followed French politics as best he could. The *Herald* and the *Tribune* provided satisfactory summaries in English, and to improve his French he consulted the Paris press. He was dismayed at the multiplicity of parties, the doctrinaire extremism of the Left and the Right, and the absence of a democratic consensus. Unlike Americans, the French did not agree on the rules of the game. Since 1789 there had been three republics, three separate monarchical regimes, two empires, a provisional government, and the Paris Commune.[*] The French Revolution was not so much a revolution as a civil war—and the outcome was still being contested. The radical Right and the church rejected the republic, and the republic rejected Christianity and the church. The principal party of the Third Republic was the Radical-Socialists, which was neither radical nor socialist but a middle-class party dedicated to the secularization of France. The issues were intractable, and Eisenhower soon concluded that France was inherently ungovernable. That realization—which Ike came to during his fourteen months in Paris—helps explain his undisguised admiration and support for Charles de Gaulle fifteen years later. The last thing Eisenhower wanted in 1944 was for his head-

---

[*] Following the fall of the Bastille on July 14, 1789, France experimented for three years with a constitutional monarchy. Louis XVI remained on the throne with his powers curtailed. But in 1792 he was deposed and executed, and the First Republic was established. Napoléon seized power in 1799 and proclaimed the first French Empire. Historians often assert that Napoléon "interrupted" the work of the revolution and left the outcome in doubt. In 1814 the Bourbon monarchy was restored, only to be overthrown in 1830 in favor of the constitutional monarchy of Louis-Philippe, the duc d'Orléans. The Revolution of 1848 toppled the Orleanist monarchy and established the Second Republic, which ruled France until 1852, when Louis-Napoléon Bonaparte (Napoléon's nephew) mounted a coup and established the Second Empire. Napoléon III (as he was styled) ruled France until Germany's 1870 victory in the Franco-Prussian War. A period of instability ensued, marked by the tumultuous episode of the Paris Commune of 1871, a legendary benchmark for the Marxist Left, and the provisional government of Adolphe Thiers. The Third Republic was ushered in in 1875 with little prospect of survival but remarkably had endured, always under attack from the monarchist Right (divided into Bourbon and Orleanist factions), the authoritarian Right (successors to the imperial tradition), and the antidemocratic Left, heirs to the spirit of the Commune.

quarters to be saddled with governing liberated France. De Gaulle and his Free French movement were eager to take on that responsibility, and Eisenhower—despite the entrenched opposition of FDR and the U.S. State Department—was only too happy to turn the problem over to him.

De Gaulle, for his part, always appreciated what Eisenhower had done. The mutual admiration between the two was remarkable.[32] They were almost exactly the same age, shared similar military careers, and possessed extraordinary political instincts. "He knew how to be adroit and supple," wrote de Gaulle about Ike in his *Memoirs*, "but he was also capable of great daring." Later, when de Gaulle was president of the Fifth Republic during the final years of Ike's presidency, the two old soldiers, now heads of state, not only found common ground, but also discovered that they enjoyed each other's company. Eisenhower invited de Gaulle to the farm in Gettysburg, and de Gaulle welcomed Ike to overnight at his summer residence, the Château de Rambouillet.[33] (De Gaulle, incidentally, spoke flawless English, but reserved it for those with whom he felt a special affection.)

On March 20, 1929, Marshal Ferdinand Foch, the Allied commander in chief during the final year of the war, died following a brief illness. General Pershing was an honorary pallbearer, and the officers of the Battle Monuments Commission marched in the funeral procession from the Arc de Triomphe, down the Champs-Élysées, to the cathedral of Notre Dame. For Eisenhower, it was the greatest spectacle of his career. Three million Frenchmen lined the parade route. In addition to the military units and the procession of *anciens combatants* that stretched for half a mile, the cardinals of Paris and Rouen marched behind the catafalque in full panoply of office, marking their first participation in a civic ceremony since the separation of church and state fifty years earlier.[34]

Duty with the Battle Monuments Commission was pleasant enough. While Eisenhower worked at revising the guidebook, General Pershing undertook to write his memoirs.[35] The general's work habits were rigid, but somewhat Churchillian. He rarely came to the office until early afternoon and worked until well past midnight. Pershing appreciated Eisenhower's way with words, and soon drew

Eisenhower, *fifth from right,* marching with Pershing's staff at the Paris funeral of Marshal Ferdinand Foch, March 26, 1929.

him into the project. "I'm unhappy about the description of Saint Mihiel . . . and also about the Argonne," he told Ike. "Read the parts of the book that cover these two periods and let me know what you think."[36]

Pershing's account hewed closely to his wartime diary. Eisenhower read the chapters and suggested that a strong narrative, interspersed with diary entries, would be easier for the reader to follow. Pershing responded enthusiastically and asked Ike to redraft the material. "With considerable effort I produced two chapters and left them with the General," Eisenhower recalled. "After reading them over, he said he was happy with them." Pershing said that before making a final decision, however, he wanted to show the chapters to his former aide, Colonel George C. Marshall. In such matters, he told Ike, he always turned to Marshall for final advice.[37]

Eisenhower had not met George Marshall, but several days later he arrived in Paris and spent several hours with Pershing. He read Ike's chapters and found them interesting. "Nevertheless," he told Eisenhower, "I've advised General Pershing to stick with his original idea. I think to break up the format at the climax of the war would be a mistake." Colonel Marshall rarely explained why he decided anything, and his explanation to Eisenhower suggests he respected the effort Ike had put in.

"I said there was some virtue in continuity," Eisenhower replied, "although I still thought that the battles should be treated as a single narrative, with the proper annotations to give it authenticity.

"He [Marshall] remarked, rather kindly, that my idea was a good one. Nevertheless he thought General Pershing would be happier if he stayed with the original scheme."[38] Eisenhower would not see Marshall again for ten years. But evidently he had made an impression.

After a year in Paris, Eisenhower became anxious about his assignment. He enjoyed the relaxed life he and Mamie led and welcomed the opportunity to travel, but fretted about his career. In many respects the Battle Monuments Commission was a cul-de-sac. Two more years of revising the Army's guidebook for American tourists seemed a frivolous waste of time. Eisenhower was impatient and, as he did whenever he felt stymied, he contacted Fox Conner. Conner was no longer in Washington but was commanding the Hawaiian Division at Schofield Barracks in Honolulu. Once again, he lent a sympathetic ear. On August 10, 1929, Eisenhower received orders from the War Department to report to Washington, where he was to assume the duties of military assistant to the assistant secretary of war. As at Fort Benning three years earlier, his tour was being curtailed—a highly unusual move where an overseas assignment was involved.

Eisenhower's associates at the Battle Monuments Commission were stunned. Major Xenophon Price, Pershing's executive officer, thought Ike was passing up a shining future. "Every officer attached to the Commission is going to be known as a man of special merit," said Price.[39]

Eisenhower disagreed. Price responded by giving him an exceptionally low efficiency report for his last four and a half months in Paris. Price had previously rated Eisenhower four times over a period of three years, and each rating had been "superior." His final rating was "satisfactory." Price acknowledged that Ike possessed a "fine command of the English language," and that he was "an excellent officer of great natural ability." But he was stung by Eisenhower's decision to return to Washington. Price said Ike was "not especially versitile [Price's spelling] in adjusting to changed conditions" and that he "had difficulty adjusting to Paris." It was Eisenhower's lowest rating since he served as a young lieutenant at Fort Oglethorpe in 1917. Its impact on Eisenhower's career, however, was negligible.[*]

On September 17, 1929, the Eisenhowers sailed from Cherbourg on the United States Lines' SS *Leviathan*—the largest (54,282 tons) and fastest (twenty-six knots) liner afloat. Built in 1913 as the SS *Vaterland* for the Hamburg-Amerika Line, the ship had been in New York when World War I began and, like the *Amerika,* had been seized and converted into a troopship by the United States in 1917. The Eisenhowers' cabin was crammed with flowers and presents from their friends in Paris, but no champagne—a jolting reminder they were back in the land of Prohibition.

[*] When Eisenhower returned to Washington as chief of staff in 1946, he inquired what had happened to Xenophon Price. A search of War Department records revealed that he was on active duty with the Corps of Engineers in the rank of lieutenant colonel. Since Price was a year senior in the prewar Army, Eisenhower was shocked. "Why was he only a lieutenant colonel?" he asked. "Bad judgment," came the reply. "Hell, he's not that bad," said Ike, and he ordered Price promoted to colonel. Letter, John S. D. Eisenhower to JES, March 10, 2008.

# FIVE

# With MacArthur in Washington

This officer has no superior of his age and grade.
— GENERAL DOUGLAS MACARTHUR
ON EISENHOWER'S EFFICIENCY REPORT,
*June 30, 1933*

AFTER A MONTH'S LEAVE, during which he and Mamie visited Denver and Abilene, Eisenhower reported for duty at the War Department on November 9, 1929. The Army's general staff, to which he had been appointed, numbered fewer than a hundred officers, most of whom had been handpicked for their assignments—and Ike was no exception. His job was executive assistant to Major General George Van Horn Moseley, the principal military adviser to the assistant secretary of war. George Moseley and Fox Conner were old friends, a year apart at West Point—Conner from Mississippi, Moseley from Alabama—and each was regarded as a thinking man's general. They had served together in the Philippines, and both rode with Pershing against Pancho Villa. During the war, Conner had been Pershing's operations officer (G-3); Moseley was his chief of supply (G-4). When Ike sent a distress call to Conner from Paris in 1929, it is not surprising that he would land on Moseley's War Department doorstep.[1]

Under the National Defense Act of 1920,[2] the assistant secretary of war was responsible for the Army's procurement and supply, paralleling Franklin Roosevelt's task in the Navy Department when he was assistant secretary under Woodrow Wilson. In World War II, the Army post (elevated to undersecretary) would be held by Judge Robert Patterson, who proved to be a production wizard and presided over an unprecedented procurement program virtually without a taint of scandal or cost overrun.

In 1929, the post was held by Frederick H. Payne, a self-made New England millionaire and old-line Hoover Republican, dedicated to fiscal responsibility and enthralled with the social side of official life in Washington.[3] Payne's dilemma was that there was essentially no military procurement in 1929. Working under severe budgetary restraint, the Army had been reduced to 119,000 men, and there was a surfeit of equipment left over from the war. That led Moseley to look to the future. What the Army had on hand would scarcely be adequate in the event of another war. Consequently, at his direction the office of the assistant secretary began to frame an industrial mobilization plan, and Ike was charged with drafting it.

"I am particularly pleased with this detail," Eisenhower wrote in the diary he had begun to keep. "I am looking forward to the opportunity of learning something about the economic and industrial conditions that will probably prevail in this country in the event of a major war."[4]

Eisenhower worked on the project for almost a year. He interviewed industrialists and financiers (including Bernard Baruch), and made an extensive field survey of the possibility of producing synthetic rubber from the guayule bush that grew abundantly in the desert of northern Mexico.[5] The resulting 180-page mobilization plan, subsequently known as the M-Day Plan, was comprehensive, surprisingly well-written, and went largely unread.[6] It gathered dust on the shelves of the War Department until 1940, and then was bypassed by events.

Nevertheless, Payne and General Moseley were impressed by Ike's efforts, and Moseley put his appreciation on record. As he wrote Eisenhower afterward, "You possess one of those exceptional minds which enables you to assemble and to analyze a set of facts, always drawing sound conclusions and, equally important, you have the ability to express those conclusions in clear and convincing form. Many officers can take the first two steps of a problem, but few have

General George Van Horn Moseley, Ike's sponsor on the army general staff in the early 1930s.

your ability of expression."[7]* Moseley had become a surrogate for Fox
Conner. In his eyes, Ike could do no wrong.

Eisenhower, for his part, was captivated by Moseley. As he wrote
in his diary, "Among the senior officers in the Army, he [Moseley]
has been my most intimate friend and the one for whom I have great
admiration and esteem. [He is] a wonderful officer—a splendid gentleman and a true friend. Mentally honest and with great moral
courage he is well equipped for any task this gov't can possibly give
him."[8]

---

* Eisenhower wrote superb declaratory prose, but his talent should not be confused with that of Ulysses Grant—one of the finest wordsmiths in the English
language. In Eisenhower's case, given the bureaucratic style of conventional military writing, his use of active verbs and short sentences made him a standout. "In
the land of the blind, the one-eyed man is king."

In his professional capacity, Moseley was unquestionably an outstanding officer. He had done an exemplary job handling the logistics of the AEF, had helped Charles G. Dawes establish the Bureau of the Budget in 1921, and was highly regarded not only by those for whom he worked, but by those who worked for him as well. George Marshall was one of Moseley's most ardent admirers, believed him to be an unusually perceptive judge of military talent, and consulted him regularly during the war on personnel matters.[9] Douglas MacArthur prized Moseley's organizational ability and considered him one of a handful of close personal friends.[10] Eisenhower, writing in retirement, recalled that Moseley "was always delving into new ideas, and he was an inspiration to the rest of us. He was always quick with praise and was ready to take responsibility for any little error or criticism that came our way from outside."[11]

But there was a dark side to Moseley. In an Army notorious for its ethnocentrism, George Van Horn Moseley stood out as the exemplar of racist xenophobia, white supremacy, anti-Semitism, and political repression. Indeed, George Patton at his most vitriolic resembled an Episcopal choirboy when compared to Moseley. In the fall of 1930, Moseley officially recommended that the War Department round up all radicals and ship them off to Russia.[12] Several years later, speaking to a meeting of reserve medical officers in New Orleans, he castigated the Roosevelt administration's efforts to provide sanctuary for German and Austrian Jews fleeing Hitler and insisted that the refugees should be accepted "with the distinct understanding that they all be sterilized before being permitted to embark. Only that way can we properly protect our future."[13] Moseley was commanding Third Army at the time, and his knuckles were rapped by the War Department. After he retired in 1938 he became a bitter critic of FDR and the New Deal, saw the possibility of war with Germany as a Jewish conspiracy launched by the great investment banks (which in his view were controlled by Jews), and ultimately came to believe that the Jews of Europe "were receiving their just punishment for the crucifixion of Christ."[14]*

---

* Moseley's anti-Semitic views were shared by a generation of senior officers in the late twenties and early thirties, but none were as outspoken as Moseley, or as ex-

Eisenhower was certainly aware of Moseley's sentiments. In 1934, after Moseley had left the War Department to assume command of the IV Corps Area in Atlanta, Ike wrote:

> I miss the talks we used to have on such subjects as "the state of the nation"—and all included matters. So much is happening that is going to be of the utmost significance to our country for generations to come that I would like very much to discuss with you the motives, purposes and methods of some of the actors now occupying the national stage.[15]

Eisenhower did not share Moseley's racist dogmatism, and in his subsequent correspondence he ignored the general's anti-Semitic rants.[16] Yet he never took issue with Moseley's views, and in his memoirs suggested the general had been the victim of bad press coverage. "Many who did not know the man himself may have thought him a reactionary or a militarist. The impression he created was a distortion, I am sure; he was a patriotic American unafraid to disagree with a consensus."[17]

As they had done during their previous tour in Washington, the Eisenhowers took up residence at the Wyoming, this time in a spacious two-bedroom suite on the third floor. John attended nearby John Quincy Adams public school, and Mamie reassembled Club Eisenhower in their apartment. An enthusiastic hostess to all who came calling, Mamie was never regarded as a great beauty, recalled her friend Kate Hughes, but "men were very attracted to her. She was direct, honest, sincere, but also flirtatious and lively."[18] In addition to the many visitors passing through Washington, the Eisenhowers' circle of friends included the Wade Haislips and "Gee" Gerows from the old 19th Infantry at San Antonio, Ike's brother Milton and his wife, Helen (Milton was a rising star at the Agricul-

---

treme. The racist theology of eugenicist Charles Davenport was a standard feature of the curriculum at the Army War College, and nations were ranked according to their Nordic homogeneity. For a thorough analysis of the prewar Army's anti-Semitism, see Joseph W. Bendersky, *The "Jewish Threat": Anti-Semitic Politics of the U.S. Army* (New York: Basic Books, 2000).

ture Department), Ruth and Harry Butcher, who ran the local CBS affiliate WJSV (known to old-time Washingtonians as "When Jesus Saved Virginia"), and the George Pattons. Patton was initially with the office of the chief of cavalry in the War Department, and later with the 3rd Cavalry at Fort Myer.

In addition to the usual Army-Navy Club affairs, the Eisenhowers were members of the Willard Hotel's Saturday Night Dinner Dance Club, and entertained regularly in the hotel's posh dining room (where they received a discount). Ike was eager to promote his career, and though still only a major, he and Mamie first invited Assistant Secretary and Mrs. Payne for dinner at the Willard, then the secretary of war, Patrick J. Hurley. As Mamie recalled, "They had been wonderfully kind to us, so we couldn't see why we shouldn't return their hospitality."[19]

Official Washington was much smaller and more intimate in the twenties and thirties, and Ike's invitations to Hurley and Payne would not have been considered out of line. Major George Patton, who was equally assiduous in promoting his career, offered the use of his stable of horses and squash court to Henry L. Stimson when Stimson returned to Washington as secretary of state in 1929. "My dear Mr. Secretary," Patton wrote on March 29. "Knowing, by previous experience, your fondness for exercise and riding, I am taking the liberty of offering you the use of my horses and squash court, at any time and as often as you may find convenient. The court and the horses are situated at 3000 Cathedral Avenue (the old Newlands Place), not far from the Wardman Park Hotel [where Stimson was staying]." Secretary Stimson graciously accepted the offer. "My dear Major Patton," he wrote on April 6. "Many thanks for the kind offer. . . . I had a delightful ride on Gaylord yesterday." (Gaylord was Patton's favorite jumper.)[20]

The Eisenhowers' private life was a mix of starchy formality and casual relaxation. One Sunday a month Ike donned formal morning dress and he and Mamie paid social calls on the ranking officers of the War Department, left the requisite visiting cards, nibbled dainty cucumber sandwiches, and drank tea—all as prescribed by Washington's rigid protocol. Other Sundays he and James Ulio, the Army's future adjutant general, would strike out for the Old Soldiers' Home and a round of golf.²¹ At home, Mamie's maid wore a de rigueur blue-and-white striped uniform in the morning and changed to black for the afternoon and evening.²² Despite the formality, Ike and young Johnnie shared a morning tub of bathwater. John would bathe first while Eisenhower was shaving, then Ike would climb into the bathwater after his son had finished. Evidently it was a way to express the intimacy of childhood that Ike remembered from Abilene, or perhaps to save time by not refilling the bathtub.²³

On November 21, 1930, Douglas MacArthur succeeded Charles Summerall as the Army's chief of staff, and a wave of change swept through the War Department. George Moseley became MacArthur's deputy chief of staff, and within a year all of the principal general staff officers had been replaced.²⁴ MacArthur had come to the War Department from the Philippines, and his first impression was that the Army's staff divisions were "entirely too self-contained."²⁵ To remedy that he established a general council of the general staff and appointed Moseley as president. As MacArthur's deputy, Moseley presided over the Army general staff and coordinated its functions. And Eisenhower came with him. Fifteen months earlier Ike had been tromping across overgrown battlefields in France, far from the military mainstream. Now he was at the center of the Army's command structure.

When Moseley's appointment as deputy chief of staff was announced, Assistant Secretary Payne insisted he wanted Eisenhower to replace him as his principal adviser, and that Ike be promoted immediately to brigadier general should that be required. Moseley explained it was absolutely impossible to catapult Eisenhower from major to brigadier general,* but he noted Payne's desire on Ike's ef-

---

* On September 20, 1906, President Theodore Roosevelt promoted Captain John J. Pershing to brigadier general, jumping 257 captains who were senior to him, 364 majors, 131 lieutenant colonels, and 110 colonels. TR had great affection for Pershing, whose black 10th Cavalry had led the way up San Juan Hill. The fact that Pershing was the son-in-law of Wyoming senator Francis Warren, chairman of the Senate Military Affairs Committee, was scarcely an impediment to his advancement. Pershing's promotion unleashed a firestorm of criticism, and no president since TR has tampered so drastically with the Army's promotion roster. Vandiver, 1 *Black Jack* 205, 390–91; Gene Smith, *Until the Last Trumpet Sounds* 54, 92; Donald Smythe, *Guerrilla Warrior: The Early Life of John J. Pershing* 53 (New York: Scribner, 1973).

ficiency report and then invited Eisenhower to his home to explain what he had done.[26]

Shortly before MacArthur became chief of staff, Congress passed a joint resolution creating a War Policies Commission "to study and consider amending the Constitution, so that, should there be a war, its burden would fall equally on everyone and it would be profitable for no one."[27] The commission was a response to the growing popular conviction that the United States had been duped into World War I by a consortium of powerful industrialists ("merchants of death") who profited from American involvement. The commission was chaired by the secretary of war, Patrick J. Hurley, and included five additional cabinet officers, four senators, and four members of the House of Representatives.[28] Eisenhower was assigned to work with the commission. He described his duties as "sort of a 'working' Secretary but with no official title or authority," although he became, in effect, the commission's executive secretary.[29]

The commission held hearings through May 1931. Eisenhower prepped many of the witnesses before they testified, and prepared the official War Department statement delivered by General MacArthur on May 13. "I worked for 10 days (and nights) getting it ready," Ike recorded in his diary. "Everything went off splendidly. Gen. MacA. said the paper was 'masterly'—and it seemed to make a great hit. We summarized it in a press release—and Gen. MacA. is to make a short movie-tone synopsis."[30]

Afterward MacArthur sent Ike a letter of commendation, which Mamie had framed.

> My dear Major,
>
> I desire to place on official record this special commendation for excellent work of a highly important nature which you have just completed under my personal direction. You not only accepted this assignment willingly—an assignment which involved much hard work—performing it in addition to your regular duties in the office of The Assistant Secretary of War, but you gave me a most acceptable solution within a minimum of time.
>
> This is not the first occasion when you have been called

upon to perform a special task of this nature. In each case
you have registered successful accomplishment in the
highest degree.

I write you this special commendation so that you may
fully realize that your outstanding talents and your ability
to perform these highly important missions are fully appreciated.

*Sincerely yours,*
DOUGLAS MACARTHUR,
General,
Chief of Staff.[31]

The commission rendered its report to President Hoover on March
5, 1932. The final version, which was also written by Eisenhower,
recommended a constitutional amendment clarifying Congress's authority "to prevent profiteering and to stabilize prices in time of
war."[32] Pending adoption of such an amendment, Congress should
empower a wartime president to stabilize prices, eliminate cost-plus
defense contracts, and tax excess profits at the rate of 95 percent.[*]
Public response was overwhelmingly favorable, and the Hoover administration announced its support for the report, although President Hoover personally disapproved of the commission's work and
did nothing to put the recommendations into effect. "It came back
from one of his staff," Eisenhower remembered, "saying the Presi-

---

* Report of the War Policies Commission, March 5, 1932, National Archives and
Records Administration. During World War II the emergency powers of the president were fleshed out by congressional legislation rather than constitutional
amendment. The Second War Powers Act (56 Stat. 176), passed in early 1942,
authorized the president to allocate facilities and materials, and furnished the statutory basis for consumer rationing. The Emergency Price Control Act (56 Stat. 23)
provided for price controls on almost all commodities, and the Renegotiation Act
(56 Stat. 984) permitted the War Department to recapture excess profits from
defense contractors. Only the latter was seriously challenged on constitutional
grounds, and was upheld. "The constitutionality of the conscription of manpower
for military service is beyond question," said Justice Harold Burton for the Supreme Court. "The constitutional power of Congress to support the armed forces
with equipment and supplies is no less clear and sweeping. The mandatory renegotiation of contracts is valid, *a fortiori.*" *Lichter v. United States,* 334 U.S. 742
(1948).

dent was far too busy to read such drivel: 'that the Government is not thinking of a future war and has no intention of doing so.' "[33] Using the notes he had taken as executive secretary, Eisenhower published an article in the *Cavalry Journal* detailing the commission's work.[34] The article summarized the testimony given and provided readers with an overview of the Army's mobilization plans.

Eisenhower was now wearing three hats. He was officially assigned to the office of the assistant secretary but was working directly for Moseley and occasionally for MacArthur. The strain began to show. "Lots of trouble with my insides lately," Ike wrote in his diary in the spring of 1931. "Have been bothered for 5–6 years with something that seems to border upon dysentery. Doctors have come to the conclusion that it is a result of nervousness, lack of exercise, etc. Am taking some medicine at the moment that for a day or so seemed to be exactly right—but now am apparently no different from usual."[35]

A month later he wrote, "Doctors report, after long X-ray exam, that they can find nothing wrong with my insides."[36] Eisenhower continued to be bothered by health problems throughout the 1930s: acute gastroenteritis, chronic colitis, hemorrhoids, mild arthritis, and, worst of all, severe back pain. Orthopedic surgeons at Walter Reed Army Medical Center noted mild lumbar arthritis, but no evidence of herniated disc or leg atrophy. For his back pain, Ike was instructed to sleep on a hard bed, undergo diathermy, massage, hyperextension exercises, and to take salicylates.[37] Tension from overwork in a demanding job appears to have been the culprit. Ike worked six days a week, often until eight or nine in the evening, and occasionally on Sunday as well. Payne and Moseley relied on him for every writing task that came their way, and MacArthur had begun to do the same.

At the end of 1931, Eisenhower laid plans for his next assignment. His normal three-year tour in Washington would conclude the next summer and he was long overdue for troop duty. At Mamie's urging, he requested the chief of infantry to send him back to the 19th Infantry at Fort Sam Houston. "Made up my mind to do so only after a long struggle as I hate the heat," Ike confided to his diary on December 20. "Family so insistent thought it the best thing to do. Mamie is concerned chiefly with getting a post where servants are good—cheap—plentiful. I'd like a place that offers some interesting outdoor work. Dad, Mother [John and Elivera Doud], and Mamie have talked about San Antonio until it's apparent that they're going to be all down in the mouth with any other selection. So I *asked* for it."[38]

Other offers came Eisenhower's way. General William D. Connor, who commanded the Army War College, had been appointed superintendent of the U.S. Military Academy and asked Ike if he wanted to accompany him as West Point's athletic director. This was not a trifling proposition in the peacetime Army. Major Philip B. Fleming, whom Ike was to replace, would become Harry Hopkins's deputy in the Works Progress Administration (WPA) and later succeeded Hopkins as director when Hopkins became secretary of commerce. Another offer came from General Stuart Heintzelman, who was leaving Washington to become commandant of the Command and General Staff School at Leavenworth. He suggested that Ike join the faculty at CGSS and assume command of the infantry battalion stationed there.

Before Eisenhower could decide, MacArthur intervened. Neither he nor Moseley was eager to see Ike leave. "On Saturday Gen. MacArthur called me to his office for a short conference relative to my prospective transfer," Ike recorded.

> He called attention to the fact that though I would be due for duty with troops this summer I will not have completed a 4-year detail in this city until September 1933. He suggested that I . . . stay here for 4 years. Gave me until today [February 15, 1932] to think it over—and also informed me that at the end of 4 year detail he would give me Fort Washington [home of the 12th Infantry] to command.
>
> Gen. MacA. was very nice to me—and after all I know of no greater compliment the bosses can give you than I want you hanging around.[39]

Eisenhower discussed MacArthur's proposal with Mamie and General Moseley, and had little difficulty accepting. "To say that we were surprised is putting it mildly," Ike wrote John Doud in Denver.

We had no prior hint that such a thing was even considered. Of course we were flattered that he liked my work well enough to want to keep us, and had interested himself personally in seeing how it could be done. . . . All in all there was nothing else to do. It is an opportunity that comes rarely, and when Gen. Moseley, the adjutant general, and Gen. MacA.'s aide all told me that they knew he really *wanted* us to stay—why I just marched back in to his office and said, "O.K. General."[40]

MacArthur moved quickly to take advantage of Eisenhower's talent. Ike was installed in an office between Moseley and the chief of staff, with direct access to both. He remained on the Army's rolls as an assistant to Secretary Payne, but for all practical purposes he became MacArthur's military secretary. When Payne left the government in March 1933, Eisenhower was officially transferred to the chief of staff's office, but was never given a job title. His efficiency reports simply identify him as "On duty in Office [of the] Chief of Staff." MacArthur, who was fifty-two at the time, had been a general officer for the past fourteen years. Ike, who was forty-two, had been a major almost as long.

MacArthur was the antithesis of Eisenhower—much like the difference between Winfield Scott ("Old Fuss and Feathers") and Zachary Taylor ("Old Rough and Ready") during the Mexican War. Scott, in Ulysses Grant's words, "wore all the uniform the law allowed," affected a rhetorical style designed for the benefit of future historians, and often referred to himself in the third person.[41] Taylor, by contrast, preferred blue denim trousers and a cotton duster, mingled easily with the troops under his command, and expressed himself "in the fewest well-chosen words rather than high-sounding sentences."[42] Both Scott and Taylor were brilliant practitioners of the military profession and both were eminently successful in battle. But their manner and style could not have been more different.

Like Scott, Douglas MacArthur was a military aristocrat. His father, Arthur MacArthur, won the Congressional Medal of Honor leading the 24th Wisconsin ("On, Wisconsin") at Missionary Ridge during the Civil War; fought brilliantly in the Philippines; served as military governor during the occupation; and in 1906 became the Army's ranking general officer, though he was never appointed chief of staff. Douglas often said he grew up to the sound of bugle calls. He graduated first in his class at West Point in 1903, where, like Robert E. Lee and John J. Pershing, he became first captain of the corps of cadets. Three years after graduation he was appointed aide-de-camp to President Theodore Roosevelt. During World War I he commanded the 42nd (Rainbow) Division in combat, was wounded and gassed, and was decorated nine times for heroism. After the war he served as a reform-minded superintendent of West Point, married the exceedingly wealthy Louise Cromwell Brooks in 1922, and was exiled by Pershing to the Philippines as a consequence. (Pershing, a widower, had been very fond of Louise Brooks.)[43]

As chief of staff, MacArthur initially kept a low profile, avoided the cocktail and dinner circuit, and was seldom mentioned in the society pages of the Washington press. Yet his vanity was common knowledge. He installed a fifteen-foot-high mirror behind his chair to heighten his image, and often sat at his desk wearing a Japanese ceremonial kimono. Eisenhower, very much in awe, called him "essentially a romantic figure. He is impulsive—able, even brilliant—quick—tenacious in his views and extremely self-confident. [He] has assured me that as long as he stays in the Army I am one of the people earmarked as his 'gang.' "[44]

Ike thought MacArthur had no political ambitions. "His interests are almost exclusively military. He has a reserved dignity—but is most animated in conversations on subjects interesting him. I do not expect to see him ever prominently mentioned for office outside the War Department."[45]

Those were the words of an impressionable forty-two-year-old major. With the benefit of hindsight, Eisenhower altered that assessment. Writing his memoirs thirty-five years later, Ike said, "Most of the senior officers I had known always drew a clean-cut line between the military and the political. But if General MacArthur ever recognized the existence of that line, he usually chose to ignore it."[*]

---

[*] Eisenhower's postpresidential reflections on his 1930s relations with MacArthur have to be taken with a large pinch of salt. Considering that Ike's mentor at the

I called myself his good man Friday. My office was next to his; only a slatted door separated us. He called me to his office by raising his voice. On any subject he chose to discuss, his knowledge poured out in a great torrent of words. "Discuss" is hardly the correct word; discussion suggests dialogue and the General's conversations were usually monologues.[46]

Because General MacArthur kept unusual hours, including luncheons from two to four hours [MacArthur habitually returned to Quarters One at Fort Myer for lunch with his mother] and then stayed on in his office until 8:00, my hours became picturesque. But if occasion came up for me to take a week's leave, all I had to do was tell him I was going away for a few days and he would make no objection.[47]

Eisenhower had returned from Paris to Washington just after the stock market crash in 1929. It was now three years later and the country was in the depths of the Great Depression. One-third of the nation was unemployed. The stock market had lost 90 percent of its pre-1929 value. In Iowa, a bushel of corn was selling for less than a package of chewing gum. Forty-six percent of the nation's farms faced foreclosure. An even larger number of urban home owners could not make their mortgage payments, and new home construction was at a standstill. Factories were idle, businesses were closing their doors, and the banking system teetered on the brink of collapse.

The Hoover administration watched from the sidelines, convinced that natural forces would set things straight. "If we depart from the principles of local responsibility and self-help," Hoover told the nation, "we have struck at the roots of self-government."[48] With no relief in sight, desperate men selling apples appeared on urban street corners, bread lines stretched block after block, and "Hoovervilles"— little settlements of tin shacks, abandoned autos, and discarded packing crates—sprang up in city dumps and railroad yards across

---

time was George Moseley, it is scarcely credible that the senior officers he knew "always drew a clean-cut line between the military and the political."

the country. Children went hungry in every corner of the land. In the coal-mining areas of West Virginia and Kentucky, more than 90 percent of the inhabitants suffered from malnutrition.[49]

Throughout the spring and summer of 1932 unemployed veterans of World War I flocked to Washington to protest the government's inaction and demand payment of wartime bonuses that were not due until 1945. Few groups were better organized or politically more potent than America's veterans. Roughly one-quarter of the federal budget in 1932 was devoted to an elaborate array of entitlements that had been enacted for veterans since World War I, and none of those entitlements aroused greater fervor than the so-called bonuses that were intended to correct the wartime disparity between civilian income and the pay that America's soldiers and sailors had received.[50]

In 1924, Congress enacted legislation providing "adjusted compensation" for the 3.3 million servicemen of World War I.[51] Under the act, each veteran was authorized an additional $1.00 for each day of home service, and $1.25 a day for overseas service. Payment was made in the form of a twenty-one-year endowment life insurance policy that was payable at death or in 1945, whichever came first. The policies would earn 4 percent interest, and the average payout totaled about $1,000 (roughly $13,000 in current dollars).

It was evident from the outset that these were life insurance policies, but as the nation sank deeper into depression that understanding became clouded. The policies were a bonus for wartime service, and for many unemployed veterans it was the only asset they possessed. By 1930 veterans were agitating for prepayment of their "bonuses," and by 1932 legislation to that effect was pending in Congress.[52] Introduced by Representative Wright Patman of Texas, a two-term populist firebrand from one of the poorest districts in the nation (*Time* magazine reported that less than 1 percent of his constituents made enough money to pay income taxes),[53] and a former veteran himself, Patman's bill provided for the immediate cash payment of the face value of each insurance policy, to be financed by the government borrowing the $3.3 billion that would be required.[54] Patman's bill was pigeonholed in the House Ways and Means Committee, and veterans organizations across the country urged a march on Washington to lobby for its passage.

The first contingents, known as the Bonus Expeditionary Force (BEF), or simply the Bonus Army, arrived in late May. They set up a shantytown on the banks of the Anacostia River in southeast Washington and, when space there ran out, occupied several vacant government buildings scheduled for demolition on Pennsylvania Avenue. By mid-June, the BEF numbered more than twenty thousand men.[55] Washington officials coped as best they could. Police chief Pelham Glassford did his utmost to provide tents and bedding for the veterans, furnished medicine, and assisted with food and sanitation. Maintaining order was never a problem. The men were camped illegally, but Glassford (who was a year behind MacArthur at West Point and who had been the youngest brigadier general in the AEF) chose to treat them simply as old soldiers who had fallen on hard times.[56]

The War Department saw it differently. For Secretary Hurley, MacArthur, and George Moseley, the Bonus Army was a ragtag assortment of radicals, aliens, criminals, and social misfits led by a Bolshevik cadre intent on storming the American equivalent of the Winter Palace. For the Army's high command, overthrow of the government lay just around the corner.[57]

On May 24, 1932, as contingents of the Bonus Army snaked their way across the country, MacArthur met with Moseley and the Army's chief of intelligence (G-2) to consider the military's response. Moseley stressed the danger of incipient revolt. He told MacArthur that the Army should be prepared to meet any emergency that might arise.[58] MacArthur was not convinced. But after an evening's reflection, he walked into Moseley's office and put the wheels in motion. "George, you were right yesterday. Go ahead with the preparations you suggested."[59]

Moseley dusted off "Plan White," the general staff's battle plan to defend Washington in the case of domestic insurrection.* He trans-

---

* During and after World War I, the Army general staff developed a rainbow of battle plans to meet any possible contingency: Red—Canada and Great Britain; Green—Mexico; Gold—France and the French islands in the Caribbean; Black—Germany; Orange—Japan; Maroon—Italy; Pink—Russia; Yellow—China; Tan—intervention in Cuba; Brown—Philippine insurrection; Purple—Central America; and White—domestic insurrection. Henry G. Gole, *The Road to Rainbow: Army*

ferred a detachment of tanks from Fort Meade to Fort Myer, just across the Potomac from downtown Washington; augmented the trucks available at both Fort Meade and Fort Washington (some twelve miles downriver) so that those garrisons could be transported quickly into the city; and placed the 3rd Cavalry at Fort Myer and the 12th Infantry at Fort Washington on full alert. Leaves were canceled and the troops were confined to the post. Soldiers received riot control instruction and bayonet drill; horses were practiced to move against crowds.[60] Command of the operation was entrusted to Brigadier General Perry L. Miles from Fort Myer. Moseley coordinated the protection of the White House and the Treasury with the Secret Service, and made arrangements "to put a small force at a moment's notice in the White House grounds."[61]

In early June, MacArthur queried the nine corps area commanders as to the presence of "communistic elements and names of leaders of any known communist leanings" among the Bonus Army units passing through their areas.[62] Most corps commanders filed negative reports, although VIII Corps, headquartered at Fort Sam Houston, reported Jewish Communists financed by Metro-Goldwyn-Mayer among the California contingent.[63] J. Edgar Hoover, leading the Justice Department's Bureau of Investigation (BOI), advised military intelligence that some of the marchers were alleged to have "dynamite in a plan to blow up the White House."[64] Moseley received a letter from a reserve officer in Detroit saying that Communists from that city planned to seize a government building in Washington, "raise a red flag from the flagstaff, and declare a government of the Soviet Union of the United States."[65] Such reports, based entirely on rumor and hearsay, contributed to an air of crisis in the War Department, although subsequent investigation found no evidence of Communist leadership in the Bonus Army.[66]

The presence of the BEF in Washington energized debate on the Patman bill. A discharge petition to pry the measure out of the Ways and Means Committee received the required 218 signatures, but under House rules the bill could not be introduced until June 13,

---

*Planning for Global War, 1934–1940* 166 (Annapolis, Md.: Naval Institute Press, 2003).

1932. Congress was scheduled to adjourn on June 10 so that Republican members could attend the GOP presidential nominating convention in Chicago. But Speaker John Nance Garner of Texas kept the House in session, and on June 15 the measure carried 211 to 176. Fifty-seven Republicans crossed party lines to vote in favor; 51 conservative Democrats, mostly from the South, voted against.

The Senate considered the measure on June 17. Still controlled by the GOP, it voted 44–26 to table the Patman bill, thus killing it for the remainder of the Seventy-second Congress. After the Senate vote, about half of the veterans returned home. Roughly twelve thousand remained in Washington. Some had no place to go, others waited for instructions, others hoped their continued presence would goad the government into action.

The Hoover administration viewed the continued presence of the veterans with alarm. At the War Department, Hurley, MacArthur, and Moseley convinced themselves that revolution was in the offing. Random intelligence reports fed the Army's hysteria.[*] By the third week in July, the president, the District of Columbia commissioners, and the War Department were agreed that the veterans should be dispatched from Washington as soon as possible.[67]

There is no reason to believe that Eisenhower dissented from the War Department consensus. His subsequent report for Secretary Hurley showed little empathy for the BEF:

> After it became apparent that Congress would not favorably consider the bonus project there was of course no lon-

---

[*] On July 5, 1932, Conrad H. Lanza, an Army intelligence agent in upstate New York, notified the adjutant general that the BEF intended to occupy the Capitol permanently, provoke an armed clash with authorities, and instigate fighting in the streets, which would be a signal for Communist uprisings in all of the nation's major cities. Lanza further advised that "at least part of the Marine Corps garrison in Washington would side with the revolutionaries"—which perhaps explains why units at the Marine barracks, some eight blocks from the Capitol, were never called upon in the days ahead.

Lanza's memo was closely guarded by the Army and was not declassified until 1991—some fifty-nine years after the event. It is reproduced in Paul Dickson and Thomas B. Allen, *The Bonus Army: An American Epic* 142–43, 321 (New York: Walker, 2004).

ger any legitimate excuse for the marchers to continue endangering the health of the whole District population by their continued [presence]. From another viewpoint also the concentration in one city of so many destitute persons was exceedingly unwise and undesirable.

Eisenhower noted that after many of the veterans had returned home, "an influx of newcomers occurred, in many instances later arrivals being of radical tendencies and intent upon capitalizing on the situation to embarrass the Government." He maintained that the aid provided to the Bonus Army by District of Columbia police was interpreted "as an indication of timidity rather than sympathy" and that some of the marchers "were ready to take advantage of this supposed weakness whenever it might become expedient to do so."[68] There is no evidence to support any of these assertions. Eisenhower wrote to justify what the Army had done. He believed the case made by his superiors was correct, and he did his utmost to support that.[69]

The fact is that it was not the BEF that sought a confrontation with the government, it was the government that provoked a confrontation with the BEF. Rather than allow time for the veterans to drift away, as police chief Glassford recommended, the Hoover administration chose to force the issue. On July 28, under prodding from the White House, the District of Columbia commissioners ordered Glassford to clear the abandoned buildings along Pennsylvania Avenue in which the veterans were camping. Brief resistance followed, shots rang out, and two veterans were killed. At that point the district commissioners asked the White House for federal troops to maintain order. Hoover passed the request to Hurley, who instructed MacArthur to take the appropriate action.[70]

At 1:40 p.m. MacArthur ordered General Miles to assemble his forces on the Ellipse, immediately south of the White House. Within the hour, troopers of the 3rd Cavalry, led by the regimental executive officer, Major George Patton, clattered across Memorial Bridge into Washington. "We moved in column of fours," Patton wrote. "The tanks on trucks followed by themselves at [a distance of] one mile."[71] The 12th Infantry from Fort Washington came upriver by steamer and arrived about an hour later. Altogether, the troops involved numbered about eight hundred, plus two hundred horses and five Renault light tanks.

When MacArthur received the order to intervene from Hurley, he sent an orderly to Fort Myer to retrieve his uniform and instructed Ike to get into uniform as well.[*] In his memoirs, Eisenhower asserts that he warned MacArthur against doing so. "I told him that the matter could easily become a riot and I thought it highly inappropriate for the Chief of Staff of the Army to be involved in anything like a local or street-corner embroilment. . . . General MacArthur disagreed, saying that it was a question of federal authority in the District of Columbia, and because of his belief that there was 'incipient revolution in the air' as he called it, he paid no attention to my dissent."[72]

Eisenhower's account is self-serving, and there is little likelihood he made such a reclama to MacArthur at the time. When Ike wrote his postpresidential memoirs in 1965, it was abundantly clear that MacArthur had made a colossal mistake in taking the field that day. Eisenhower may well have believed that he warned the chief of staff against it. But memories often blend fact and fiction, and there is no evidence that Ike objected at the time.[†] His diary, in which he regularly confided his innermost thoughts, makes no mention of his having cautioned MacArthur. Ike was a junior officer who had been

---

[*] Most accounts of the Bonus Army eviction report that MacArthur appeared in dress uniform festooned with medals and decorations. That is incorrect. The Army's dress uniform in 1932 was blue. MacArthur wore a Class A service uniform ("pinks and greens"), which was standard garrison attire at every post in the country. The ribbons he wore were customary on that uniform and reflected his wartime service. His boots and Sam Browne belt were polished, but that, too, was customary. MacArthur's judgment would prove flawed that day, but the uniform he wore was the correct one.

[†] An analogous incident involved John Foster Dulles, Eisenhower's secretary of state, who in 1947 vigorously advocated detaching the Ruhr from Germany. Later he became a staunch supporter of keeping Germany intact. As General Lucius Clay recalled, "Foster and I were sitting beside one another at a Lincoln Day Republican dinner, and he leaned over to me and said, 'Lucius, do you remember how you and I fought to keep them from detaching the Ruhr from Germany?' And he really believed it. As Secretary of State his thinking had so changed that he couldn't realize, or couldn't remember, that he'd been the principal advocate in 1947 of detaching the Ruhr from Germany." Jean Edward Smith, *Lucius D. Clay* 418.

A young Major Eisenhower accompanies General MacArthur to supervise the rout of the Bonus Army from downtown Washington in July 1932.

plucked from obscurity by the chief of staff and had been on the job less than five months. His affection for his boss bordered on hero worship. The vast difference in rank between the four-star MacArthur and Eisenhower, reinforced by MacArthur's imperious style, makes it all but certain that Ike offered no rebuke. Indeed, his official report of the Bonus Army affair suggests that he was fully in sympathy with what MacArthur did. Geoffrey Perret, an earlier biographer, wrote that "the chances that Eisenhower told the Chief of Staff to his face that he was making a serious mistake are close to zero," and the weight of evidence supports Perret.[73]

At 4 p.m. General Miles reported to MacArthur that the troops were assembled and ready to move. MacArthur informed Miles that he would accompany the troops "not with a view of commanding the troops but to be on hand as things progressed, so that he could issue necessary instructions on the ground."[74] MacArthur said it was President Hoover's idea. "I'm here to take the rap if there should be any unfavorable or critical repercussions."[75] Eisenhower and Captain T. J. Davis, MacArthur's aide, were at his side.

By five o'clock Army units had surrounded the buildings on Pennsylvania Avenue occupied by the veterans. Cavalrymen drew sabers and cleared the streets while the infantrymen from Fort Washington fixed bayonets and emptied the buildings. The air was saturated with tear gas. Prodded by horses and tanks, the veterans fell back to their encampment on the Anacostia Flats. As evening fell, the Army troops paused short of the bridge across the Anacostia to allow the women and children to be evacuated from the veterans' camp. Twice that evening President Hoover sent instructions to MacArthur not to cross the Anacostia bridge. The first message was carried by General Moseley, the second by Colonel Clement B. Wright, secretary of the Army general staff.[*] MacArthur ignored both messages. Shortly after 9 p.m. he instructed General Miles to cross the bridge and evict the Bonus Army from its encampment. After a tear gas barrage, the

---

* According to Moseley, "Mr. Hurley directed me to inform General MacArthur that the President did not wish the troops to cross the bridge that night. I left my office, contacted General MacArthur, and as we walked away, alone, from the others, I delivered that message to him and discussed it with him. He was very much annoyed in having his plans interfered with in any way until they were executed completely. After assuring myself that he understood the message . . . I returned to my office. Later, I was asked from the White House if I had delivered the message, and stated that I had. Still later, I was instructed to repeat the message and assure myself that General MacArthur received it before he crossed the Anacostia Bridge. I sent Colonel Wright . . . to repeat the message to MacArthur, and explain the situation as I had it from the White House. Colonel Wright contacted General MacArthur immediately, and explained the situation to him fully. As I now recall, Colonel Wright reported to me that the troops had not crossed the Anacostia Bridge but were advancing on the bridge."

After Colonel Wright departed, MacArthur exhibited his displeasure. He told Eisenhower he did not want to be "bothered by people coming down and pretending to bring orders."

General Moseley's comments are from volume two of his unpublished manuscript "One Soldier's Journey" at pages 144–45, Moseley Papers, Library of Congress. Eisenhower's are in *At Ease: Stories I Tell to Friends* 217 (Garden City, N.Y.: Doubleday, 1967).

The Bonus Army's encampment on the Anacostia Flats after being torched
by MacArthur's soldiers.

cavalry swept the camp, followed by infantrymen who systematically
set fire to the veterans' tents and shanties, lest anyone return. Cough-
ing, choking, and vomiting, the veterans and their families fled up
Good Hope Road into Maryland and safety.

An elated MacArthur returned to a triumphal press conference at
the War Department.[76] "That was a bad looking mob," he told the
assembled reporters. "It was animated by the essence of revolution.
Had the President not acted today, he would have been faced with a
grave situation. Had he let it go on another week, I believe the institutions of our government would have been threatened."[77]

Eisenhower wrote in his after-action report that the mob "showed
a surly and obstinate temper, and gave no immediate signs of retreating." The "most efficacious of all weapons in such circumstances is
the tear gas bomb. In the hands of well trained infantry, advancing
with an evident determination, this harmless instrument quickly
saps the will to resist of unorganized and unprepared bodies. Its
small smoke cloud is visible from some distance, and its moral sua-
sion thus extends over a far greater area than does its actual effects."[78]

George Patton, who was in the thick of the action, shared the euphoria of the Army's high command. In his diary, Patton wrote, "In spite of faulty methods the high training and discipline of the soldiers and officers secured a complete and bloodless (mostly) triumph, which by its success, prevented a war and insured the election of a Democrat."[79] Captain Lucian Truscott, who commanded the 3rd Division during the Sicily campaign and later succeeded Patton at the head of Third Army, led a troop of cavalry that day. "Cavalry training and special training for riot duty paid off," he noted in his diary. "The unruly mob had been dispersed . . . with comparatively little trouble."[80]

The nation's press took a different view. Virtually without exception they lambasted Hoover and the War Department for excessive force. "What a pitiful spectacle," said the normally Republican *Washington Daily News*. "The mightiest government in the world chasing unarmed men, women, and children with Army tanks. If the Army must be called out to make war on unarmed citizens, this is no longer America."[81]

The Army's treatment of the BEF was a shabby business, and in the years ahead Eisenhower tried relentlessly to separate himself from what had happened. Yet except for his own long-after-the-fact testimony, there is no evidence to substantiate any disagreement he might have had with War Department policy, or with what MacArthur did. To the contrary: As Ike saw it, it was not MacArthur but the press who were at fault. "A lot of furor has been stirred up by the incident," he confided to his diary on August 10, 1932, "but mostly to make political capital."

Later, when Washington journalists Drew Pearson and Robert Allen devoted a series of columns to MacArthur's mishandling of the crisis, Eisenhower castigated their coverage. "There seems to be no logical reason for their continued outpouring of innuendo, insinuation and even falsehood against a man who has never injured them," Ike wrote. "It appears probable that one of two theories may apply. First, that their assault is inspired [by Steve Early, press secretary in the Roosevelt White House]. The second theory is simply that the two men are innately cowards (which they are) and are giving expression to an inferiority complex by ceaseless attempts to belittle a man recognized as courageous, if nothing else."[82]*

Eisenhower did not vote in the 1932 election. "No one in the Army was voting," said a contemporary of Ike's. "Most of us had lost home identity, had never registered, and seldom stayed long enough anywhere to register. We seldom had the interest in local affairs which encourages registration. These were the reasons, rather than any principle. But we could generate as much nonvoting excitement as anyone else."[83] If Eisenhower generated any nonvoting excitement in 1932, there is no record of it. Three weeks after the election he noted in his diary that while he had "no definite leanings toward any political party I believe it is a good thing the Democrats won—and particularly that one party will have such overwhelming superiority in Congress."[84] (The Democrats won control of the Senate 60–35, and increased their majority in the House to 310–117.)

For the remainder of his tour in Washington, Eisenhower rooted for Roosevelt to pull the country out of the Depression. Ike shared the Regular Army officers' animosity to "socialism" (a remarkable paradox for men who usually lived in government housing, drew subsistence rations from the quartermaster, shopped at the subsidized commissary, and enjoyed free medical and dental care), but he welcomed a strong hand at the tiller. "For two years I've been called 'Dictator Ike' because I believe that virtual dictatorship must be exercised by our President," Ike wrote on the eve of FDR's inauguration. "Things are not going to take an upturn until more power is centered in one man's hands. Only in that way will confidence be inspired; will it be possible to do some

---

* MacArthur brought a libel action against Pearson and Allen, claiming they had wrongly described his treatment of the Bonus Army as "unwarranted, unnecessary, arbitrary, harsh, and brutal," and had generally depicted him as "dictatorial, insubordinate, disloyal, mutinous, and disrespectful of his superiors." He asked $1.75 million in damages. MacArthur withdrew the suit when Pearson threatened to publish the fact that MacArthur had brought a stunning Eurasian concubine from Manila and installed her in an apartment at the fashionable Chastleton, on Sixteenth Street, ten blocks north of the White House. MacArthur apparently did not wish his mother, "Pinky," to learn of the affair. William Manchester, *American Caesar: Douglas MacArthur, 1880–1964* 156 (Boston: Little, Brown, 1978).

of the obvious things for speeding recovery, and we will be freed from the pernicious influence of noisy and selfish minorities."[85]

Along with almost everyone in Washington, Eisenhower was soon caught up in the excitement of the New Deal. When Congress passed the banking bill on March 9, 1933, giving Roosevelt unprecedented authority over the nation's banking system, Eisenhower rejoiced. "Yesterday Congress met and gave the President extraordinary power over banking. Now if they'll just do the same with respect to law enforcement, federal expenditures, transportation systems, there will be such a revival of confidence that things will begin to move."[86]

It was during this period that Ike turned increasingly to his brother Milton for advice and counsel. Milton was a holdover Republican appointee in the Department of Agriculture, but his superb performance as director of information made him indispensable to the incoming Henry Wallace and Rex Tugwell. "Ike and I seldom disagreed," said Milton. "During this period we were together three nights a week. Since it was an intimate relationship, it was also a beautiful human relationship."[87]

Eisenhower's political education was as yet incomplete, his perspective still unformed by experience. When FDR took the United States off the gold standard, Ike deplored Roosevelt's desire to increase foreign trade. "Seems to me that the President is definitely choosing the road toward internationalism rather than nationalism," he wrote on April 20. "I still believe that our best way to get out of trouble is to deal within ourselves—adjust our own production to our own consumption and cease worrying about foreign markets."[88]

Civil libertarians would deplore Ike's diary entry of October 29, 1933:

> I believe that unity of action is essential to success in the current struggle. I believe that individual right must be subordinate to public good, and that the public good can be served only by unanimous adherence to an authoritative plan. We *must* conform to the President's program regardless of the consequences. Otherwise, dissention, confusion and partisan politics will ruin us.[89]

Eisenhower modified these views. As he saw more of the world, as he dealt with policy issues himself, he learned to appreciate a diversity of viewpoints and to value the intrinsic individuality of Western society. His views in 1933 differed little from those of his Regular Army contemporaries. What set him apart was his ability to absorb the lessons around him and broaden his outlook.

# SIX

# *Manila*

I gather I have reason for a divorce,
if I want one.

DOUGLAS MACARTHUR'S FOUR-YEAR term as chief of staff expired in November 1934. The two leading candidates to succeed him, both recommended by John J. Pershing (to whom Roosevelt habitually turned for such advice), were Fox Conner, who was commanding the I Corps Area in Boston, and George Moseley, at IV Corps in Atlanta. FDR offered the post to Conner while on an inspection tour through New England in the summer of 1934, but Conner declined.[1] And the president wanted no part of Moseley, whose antagonism to the New Deal was scarcely a secret.[2]

The Army chief of staff served a four-year term. By tradition no one was appointed to the post who had less than four years to serve before retirement—which was mandatory at sixty-four. Moseley barely fit in since he was scheduled to retire in 1938. But rather than pass over Moseley, who had many supporters within the military,[3] FDR resorted to a subterfuge. MacArthur had requested an extension of his term, and FDR agreed. "I am doing this," the president told his press conference on December 12, 1934, "in order to obtain the benefit of General MacArthur's experience in handling War Department legislation in the coming [congressional] session." MacArthur was to serve "until his successor has been appointed,"[4] and when his tenure stretched well into 1935, Moseley became ineligible.[5]*

For Eisenhower, the extension of MacArthur's term meant another year in Washington. Ike had become a fixture in the chief of staff's office, and MacArthur found him increasingly indispensable. Mamie also welcomed the extension because she couldn't bear to break up their comfortable apartment at the Wyoming—their first real home, which she had renovated and decorated at considerable expense.[6]

It was already agreed that when his tour as chief of staff ended, MacArthur would go to the Philippines. In 1934, Congress passed the Tydings-McDuffie Act, granting commonwealth status (limited self-government) to the Philippines and providing for absolute independence in 1946.[7] Shortly after he signed the Tydings-McDuffie bill into law, FDR invited MacArthur to Hyde Park for a private luncheon. This was an extraordinary invitation, and over lunch Roosevelt suggested to MacArthur that he become the first American high commissioner to the Philippines Commonwealth. MacArthur was thrilled at the prospect, but when he returned to Washington he was advised by the judge advocate general that if he accepted the post, he would have to resign his commission. MacArthur reluctantly wrote the president that he was "somewhat dismayed and nonplussed" to discover there were legal impediments that would prevent him from taking the position.[8] Two weeks later orders were cut appointing MacArthur military adviser to the Philippine government—a post incoming Philippine president Manuel Quezon had long urged him to take.[9]

In his new post MacArthur would remain on active duty while at the same time serving as the principal military adviser to the Philippine government. By an act of the Philippine legislature he also be-

---

* Major General George Simonds, who became deputy chief of staff in April 1935, was MacArthur's candidate for the post, but was the same age as Moseley and equally objectionable for his anti–New Deal remarks. Major General Hugh Drum, who had succeeded Moseley as deputy chief of staff, was also a contender (James Farley, FDR's postmaster general and political confidant, backed him), but was passed over because of his lack of command experience. When MacArthur stayed on, Simonds, like Moseley, became ineligible. James A. Farley, *Jim Farley's Story: The Roosevelt Years* 55 (New York: Whittlesey House, 1948).

came commander of the Philippine Army. His headquarters in Manila was freestanding and was not part of the Philippine Department of the United States Army. The Philippine government provided MacArthur with a rent-free, seven-room penthouse suite in the sumptuous Manila Hotel (one of the jewels of the Orient), and a monthly stipend of $3,000 (roughly $40,000 currently)—which he would draw in addition to his monthly pay of $667 ($8,772 currently) as a general officer in the American Army.[10]

From the time it became clear that he was going to the Philippines, MacArthur insisted that Eisenhower accompany him. "He said that he and I had worked together for a long time and he didn't want to bring in somebody new."[11] Despite his later regrets, Ike was delighted to be going to the Philippines. He had requested assignment to the islands when he graduated from West Point, and again when he submitted his assignment preferences in 1919. And as the assistant military adviser to the Philippine government (his new job title) he would draw an additional stipend of $980 monthly (roughly $13,000 currently), plus a smaller suite at the Manila Hotel. Eisenhower does not mention the additional emolument in his memoirs, but it was more than double his salary as major and made him the second highest paid officer in the Army (MacArthur being first).[12]

Ike assumed that wherever he went, Mamie would accompany him. Unfortunately, Mamie thought otherwise. Remembering her unhappiness in Panama, she wanted no part of the Philippines. Under no circumstances, she said, was she prepared to leave her comfortable surroundings at the Wyoming and venture into the tropical unknown. Initially she hoped Ike's job would not pan out, or that his back would "play up" and he would request a transfer. "Whatever the reasons," wrote Susan Eisenhower, "Mamie was doggedly stubborn about staying behind, at least for a year, and there was little Ike could do about her decision."[13]

Ike, for his part, yielded gracefully. "I hate the whole thought of being separated," he wrote Mamie's mother in Denver. "I know that I am going to be miserable. On the other hand, Mamie is so badly frightened at the prospect of going out there, that I simply cannot urge her to go. My thought is that either I will be able to send her favorable reports as to the conditions of health, education, etc. that she will be willing to come next June, or that I will come home within a reasonably short time."[14] Young Johnnie had another year before he finished school at John Quincy Adams, and that provided a plausible reason to explain Mamie's absence from Manila. She was remaining at home until he completed the next school year and was ready for high school.

A saving feature for Eisenhower was that MacArthur permitted him to select a fellow officer for the mission, and Ike chose his old friend and classmate Major James B. Ord. Ord—whose grandfather had commanded a corps for Grant at Vicksburg—fought with Pershing in Mexico, where he won the Distinguished Service Cross for valor. He also studied at the École de Guerre in Paris, later served as assistant military attaché to France, and spoke French and Spanish fluently. He was currently an instructor at the War College. Ord was accompanied by his wife and two young children and, like Ike, was thrilled at the opportunity.[15]

Before leaving Washington, MacArthur wrote Ike a special letter of commendation.

> My dear Major Eisenhower,
>
> My high official opinion of the services you have rendered during your period of duty under me in the War Department is duly recorded in regular efficiency reports. Nevertheless, upon relinquishing the position of Chief of Staff, I want to leave a written record of my appreciation of certain important considerations connected with your work which have not been easy to describe in normal reports.
>
> You were retained by the Secretary of War, and later by myself, on critically important duties in the Department long past the duration of ordinary staff tours, solely because of your success in performing difficult tasks whose accomplishment required a comprehensive grasp of the military profession in all its principal phases, as well as analytical thought and forceful expression. In this connection, I should like to point out to you that your unusual experience in the Department will be of no less future

value to you as a commander than as a staff officer, since all problems presented to you were necessarily solved from the viewpoint of the High Command.

The numbers of personal requests for your services brought to me by heads of many of the Army's principal activities during the past few years furnish convincing proof of the reputation you have established as an outstanding soldier. I can say no more than that this reputation coincides exactly with my own judgment.

*With personal regard,*
*Sincerely,*
DOUGLAS MACARTHUR[16]

On October 1, 1935, MacArthur and his party departed Washington's Union Station for San Francisco, where they would board the *President Hoover* for the three-week crossing to Manila. In addition to Eisenhower and Ord, MacArthur was accompanied by his eighty-four-year-old mother, Mrs. Arthur MacArthur, his sister-in-law, and his longtime aide, Captain T. J. Davis. MacArthur still wore four stars as chief of staff. His War Department orders stated that he would continue in that post "until relieved from duty as of December 15, 1935."[17] MacArthur believed it was important that he arrive in Manila as chief of staff, and then step down to assume his duties with the Philippine Army. He instructed the adjutant general to cut his orders accordingly. FDR, who had been advised of MacArthur's wishes by Secretary of War George Dern, agreed. On July 18, almost three months before, he notified Dern: "I see no reason why you should not tell General MacArthur that the plan meets with my approval so that he can make his plans accordingly."[18]

Two days out of Washington, as the Union Pacific rumbled into Cheyenne, Wyoming, MacArthur received a telegram from acting secretary of war Harry H. Woodring. "The President has just informed me," Woodring wired, "that he has appointed Malin Craig Chief of Staff, effective this date."[19] MacArthur was stunned. He was not only instantly reduced in rank from four stars to two (his permanent rank of major general), but Craig, a former cavalry officer, was a longtime rival and a favorite of what MacArthur regarded as the

MacArthur's arrival ceremony in Manila. Eisenhower stands in the second row.

Pershing clique in the Army.[*] If FDR wanted to signal a change from the MacArthur era at the War Department, he could scarcely have found a better way to do so.

MacArthur recognized that Roosevelt had outfoxed him. According to Eisenhower, he erupted into "an explosive denunciation of politics, bad manners, bad judgment, broken promises, arrogance, unconstitutionality, insensitivity, and the way the world had gone to hell."[20] After blowing off steam, MacArthur recovered his composure. He telegraphed the president that Craig's appointment was "not only admirable but timely." To Craig he wired, "The entire Army will look forward with keen anticipation to what cannot fail to be a successful tenure of office."[21] MacArthur needed the support of

---

* Craig, five years older than MacArthur, graduated from West Point in 1898 and fought with the 4th Cavalry in Cuba, and with the 6th Cavalry in the 1900 Peking Relief Expedition and the Philippine Insurrection (1900–1904). During the war he was chief of staff to General Hunter Liggett at I Corps, commanded the Army War College, the cavalry school at Fort Riley, and the Panama Department, and from 1930 to 1935 headed the IX Corps Area at San Francisco.

Craig and FDR in the Philippines, and he groveled accordingly. For Eisenhower, it was an unforgettable insight into the nature of Washington politics at the highest level.

MacArthur's party landed in Manila on October 26, 1935, to a rapturous reception. President-elect Quezon and the entire leadership of the new Philippine government were at the dock, as was much of the American expatriate community. To complement the lavish living quarters that had been provided, the mission was soon established in the headquarters of the old Spanish garrison in the fortress wall of the city—a seventeenth-century relic whose massive stone balustrades and high ceilings provided natural insulation from the tropic heat. MacArthur occupied the spacious office of the former commandant, with majestic views overlooking Manila Bay on one side and the city on the other. Eisenhower and Ord had smaller offices, and Captain Davis, who in addition to serving as MacArthur's aide performed the duties of adjutant, sat in a large outer office with a sergeant major and a few clerks.[22] Later they would be joined by Navy lieutenant Sidney Huff, who served as MacArthur's naval aide. With Ike as chief of staff and Ord as operations officer, the mission ran with remarkable harmony. Davis, a relaxed, even-tempered South Carolinian, provided a useful buffer for the mercurial MacArthur and became one of Ike's closest friends. Between them, Davis and Eisenhower would work for MacArthur for a total of eighteen years in the 1930s and developed the capacity to communicate instinctively, often with a nod or gesture.[*]

MacArthur delegated day-to-day operations to Eisenhower and Ord. Although he was the titular commander of the Philippine Army, the actual command was exercised by Filipino officers. "We didn't attempt to command them from our office," said Lucius D. Clay, who served with MacArthur in Manila from 1937 to 1938.[†]

* In World War II, Eisenhower made Davis his adjutant general both in North Africa and at SHAEF. Davis accompanied Ike to Russia in 1945, and served as the Army's assistant adjutant general from 1946 until his retirement in 1953.
† In 1937, MacArthur arranged with General Edward Markham, the chief of engineers, for two engineer officers to come to the Philippines for a year and conduct a hydroelectric survey of the islands. In addition to their Army salary, each officer was to be paid $10,000 (roughly $125,000 currently), receive an apartment at the

Instead, the mission focused on developing policy for the Army. MacArthur established the guidelines and left it to Ike to fill in the details. "General MacArthur never came to the office but about an hour a day," Clay recalled. "He would come down about one o'clock and stay until about two. The rest of the time he wasn't in the office at all. I don't mean that he wasn't thinking, planning, or whatnot over in his hotel suite. The fact is he did most of his work at home. Every once in a while, he'd call me up and we would go to a prize fight. He loved prize fights. Except for that, we didn't see very much of him. No one did. He simply didn't socialize at that point in his career."[23]

MacArthur believed that given sufficient time to prepare, plus a modicum of American support, the Philippines could defend themselves. Eisenhower shared that view. As he wrote in the introduction to the handwritten Philippine diary he began to keep, "If the Filipino people can be, within the next ten years, thoroughly prepared for their own defense . . . they should continue to flourish as a product of Western civilization and contribute to stability and peaceful relationships in the Asiatic area."[24]

War Department opinion had fluctuated. In 1924 the Joint Army and Navy Basic War Plan Orange, the planning document for war in the Pacific, emphasized the need for immediate reinforcements to be rushed to Manila in the event of war.[25] By 1928 the euphoria growing out of World War I had receded and Washington became more realistic. That year's revision of War Plan Orange drew America's defensive perimeter in the Pacific from Alaska to Hawaii to Panama, and recognized that the Philippines would likely fall before reinforcements could arrive. "We must plan on conditions as they are in reality and not as we would wish them to be," said military planners.[26]

---

Manila Hotel, and be given a generous expense allowance. General Markham offered the job to Clay, whose tour in the chief's office was coming to a close, and Clay leapt at the opportunity. He selected Captain Pat Casey, his West Point roommate, then with the Corps in Vicksburg, to accompany him. Clay spent a year in Manila, and in late 1938 returned to build the Denison Dam, on the Red River in Texas. Casey remained with MacArthur and became his chief engineer during World War II. Jean Edward Smith, *Lucius D. Clay* 76–82.

When he became chief of staff in 1930, MacArthur—who had just returned from the Philippines—set aside the revised War Plan Orange and told President Hoover that in the event of war, he would immediately dispatch two of America's stateside divisions to Manila via the Suez Canal.[27] Washington rewrote Plan Orange in 1933 to accommodate MacArthur's views. The Army undertook the immediate commitment of two divisions, some fifty-six thousand men, to defense of the Philippines.[28] But with MacArthur's departure as chief of staff, military planners reverted to hemispheric defense. The 1936 War Plan Orange made no mention of a Philippine relief force.[29] By 1938, with war in Europe looming, the Army made it explicit. The military would protect the continental United States, Alaska, Oahu, and Panama, "but the defense of the Philippines would be left to the garrison and whatever local forces could be raised."[30]

The shift in War Department priorities undercut MacArthur and Eisenhower. They went to the Philippines expecting quick reinforcement from the United States. With that in the offing, it was possible that the Philippine Army could mount an effective defense of the islands, particularly if the U.S. Navy interdicted Japanese shipping. The mission's efforts in 1936 and 1937 have to be appraised in that context. An active defense of the islands by a reinforced Philippine Army was not just a pipe dream.

Eisenhower and Ord moved quickly to lay the groundwork. But the difficulties were enormous. Stateside planning suggested that an annual budget of $24 million was the bare minimum to get the Philippine Army off the ground. Budget imperatives in Manila cut that figure to $8 million. Weapons were antiquated, ammunition was in short supply, there were no training camps or cantonments, and the officer corps, which was taken over from the old constabulary, was insufficient to train the recruits that would be enlisted. Even worse was the attitude Ike and Ord encountered. "We have learned to expect from the Filipinos with whom we deal," wrote Eisenhower, "a minimum of performance from a maximum of promise. When any detail is under discussion, they seem to grasp the essentials of the problem, and readily agree to undertake accomplishment of whatever decision is arrived at. But thereafter it is quite likely that nothing will be done."[31]

Even obtaining obsolescent Enfield rifles from the United States proved particularly complicated. When the mission's routine request for the surplus weapons was submitted to the War Department, the Army's general staff deemed it a political issue that required a presidential decision. "We are at a loss to determine what the question of policy may be," Eisenhower recorded in his diary on January 20, 1936. Ike speculated that it might relate to pacifist opinion in the United States, neutrality legislation pending in Congress, or fear that the weapons might fall into the hands of rebels who would use them against the central government. "We must never forget that every question is settled in Washington today on the basis of getting votes in November. To decide the matter completely in our favor would gain no votes. While to disapprove the request and give the matter some publicity might be considered as a vote getting proposition among the pacifists and other misguided elements of the American electorate."[32]

For FDR the matter was small potatoes. He had no interest in fanning neutralist sentiment and discounted a possible insurrection. Roosevelt referred the question back to Frank Murphy, the U.S. high commissioner in Manila, and upon Murphy's recommendation approved the immediate sale of 100,000 Enfield rifles with an additional 300,000 to be made available over the next eight years.[33]

Meanwhile, Ike's relations with MacArthur, which had bordered on hero worship, began to fray. "It is rapidly becoming apparent that either here or somewhere else it will be advisable for me to keep some notes that I cannot, with propriety dictate," he recorded in his diary at the end of January.

> The General is more and more indulging in a habit of damning everybody who disagrees with him over any detail, in extravagant, sometimes almost hysterical fashion. I've seen him do this, second hand, in the past, but now he seems to consider that the combined use of his rank, a stream of generalizations that are studded with malapropos, and a refusal to permit the presentation of opposing

opinion will, by silencing his subordinates, establish the validity of his contentions.[34]*

The size of the Philippine Army proved a major source of discord. Ike and Ord believed that the budget would eventually support one regular division and ten reserve divisions. "We want to train 20–25,000 men yearly for a minimum period of 10½ months." By contrast, MacArthur insisted on an immediate goal of thirty divisions. "After days of wrangling and arguing on the subject he gave J. [James Ord] and me a ridiculous lecture on 'sufficiency in strength' in armies. He makes nasty cracks about 'technicians' and 'small-minded people' when we try to show that we are simply arguing from the standpoint of the amount of money available."[35]

From the beginning, Eisenhower and Ord urged MacArthur to spend more time cultivating President Quezon. "Things happen, and we know nothing of them," Ike confided to his diary on May 29, 1936. "We're constantly wondering whether the President will approve or disapprove. We ought to *know*. We could if the general would take the trouble to see Q[uezon] weekly—but apparently he thinks it would not be in keeping with his rank and position for him to do so!!!!!"

A lighter issue involved MacArthur's determination to assume the rank of field marshal in the Philippine Army. The origins of the idea are obscure. MacArthur insisted the proposal came from Quezon. Quezon later told Ike it had originated with MacArthur, who still chafed over having been reduced from four stars to two.[36] Included in the proposal was the suggestion that Eisenhower and Ord be commissioned brigadier generals in the Philippine Army, and that Davis

* Brigadier General John S. D. Eisenhower was initially reluctant to make his father's Philippine diary available, but eventually yielded. "In some ways the diary is useful for researchers," he wrote, "but on the whole I wish that the staff [at the Eisenhower Library] had followed Ike's orders and destroyed it. Ike was articulate, especially with the written word, and he suffered from a violent temper. Forced to suppress that temper in his dealings with others, he committed his frustrations to paper. I do not believe that everything he said in these pages represents his lifetime views of Douglas MacArthur." John S. D. Eisenhower, *General Ike: A Personal Reminiscence* 28 (New York: Free Press, 2003).

assume the rank of colonel. Ike was appalled. "To any such idea I have been unalterably opposed from the start," he noted in his diary on February 15, 1936. "I have gone so far as to inform the General that I personally would decline to accept any such appointment in the event it were tendered to me." Davis agreed, and so did Ord, "though in somewhat less positive fashion." Ike said that he and Davis also "strongly advised General MacArthur to decline . . . the acceptance of the title tendered him as Field Marshal."[37]

The discussion became heated. Years later it was still fresh in Eisenhower's mind. "I said, 'General, you have been a four-star general. This is a proud thing. There's only been a few who had it. Why in the hell do you want a banana country giving you a field-marshalship?' Oh, Jesus! He just gave me hell."[38]

Ike suppressed his anger and did not respond. As he turned to leave the room, MacArthur reached out and put his hand on Eisenhower's shoulder. "Ike, it's worthwhile to argue with you sometimes just to see that Dutch temper of yours." According to John Eisenhower, his father was charmed. "But he did not change his views."[39]

Eisenhower's disapproval evidently caused MacArthur second thoughts, but he eventually yielded and accepted the field marshalship. "The General feels that he could not decline without giving offense to the President," Ike wrote in his diary on July 1, 1936. "Anyway, he is tickled pink, and feels that he's made a lot of 'face' locally."[40] That same day, his twentieth wedding anniversary, Eisenhower was promoted to lieutenant colonel.[41]

Ike rekindled his love for flying in Manila. At Fort Sam Houston in 1916 he flirted with joining the aviation section of the Army Signal Corps. But John Doud, who was less than enthusiastic about a potential military son-in-law, insisted that Eisenhower give up the idea of flying if he wished to marry Mamie. In the Philippines, with Mamie in Washington, Ike decided to learn to fly.

"In the beginning of 1936," Eisenhower recalled, "we fixed up a field outside the city limits, selected a few students, and started a miniature air force."

> The students learned rapidly and I decided to take flying
> lessons from Captain Lewis and Lieutenant William Lee,

Ike poses with members of the fledgling Philippine Air Force, 1939.

the American instructors. Because I was learning to fly at the age of forty-six, my reflexes were slower than those of younger men. Training me must have been a trial for Lewis and Lee.

Little more than thirty years had passed since Kitty Hawk and our planes were rather primitive. One had to react alertly to changes in sound or wind or temperature. The engines were good but the pilot who asked too much of one, in a steep climb, for example, learned that the roaring monster could retreat into silent surrender.[42]

Lee said that Ike's flying was fair, "but not as smooth as it could be."[43] Lieutenant Hugh ("Lefty") Parker, another instructor, said, "The biggest trouble I had with Colonel Eisenhower was eyesight. He was farsighted.* When he got around to just takeoffs and landings, he never had a bit of trouble with takeoffs. But the first lesson or two in landings he could not find the ground, which is not abnormal at all. A lot of people are ground shy on their first few landings."[44]

Ike's enthusiasm compensated for his awkwardness. He was regularly at the field at six-thirty in the morning and took his lesson be-

---

* Eisenhower's 1936 annual physical exam reported his distant vision as twenty-twenty, but his near vision was poor. "Compound Hyperoptic Astigmatism, Bilateral," recorded Dr. Howard J. Hutter of the Army Medical Corps on January 6, 1936. EL.

fore going into the office at 1 Calle Victoria in the old Spanish quarter, Cuartel de España.[45] Lieutenant Jesus Villamor, a Filipino instructor with whom Ike flew occasionally, recalled that one day Eisenhower could not do anything right. "I grabbed the controls and landed the plane myself."

"Tell me, Colonel," Villamor asked, "surely you don't expect the plane to do things perfectly when you don't follow the proper procedure, do you?" When Eisenhower did not reply, Villamor repeated the question. "Damn it, Colonel, what the hell is your excuse?"

"No excuse, Lieutenant," said Ike.

"The simplicity of his response stunned me," said Villamor. "His bearing, his manners, his attitude, made me feel completely ashamed of myself. He could very easily have pulled rank on me. Instead, he waited patiently, and at the right moment, brought me down to reality in simple man-to-man fashion."[46]

Eisenhower received his private pilot's license on July 5, 1939, having logged 350 hours of flight time. Shortly before, he wrote about his flying to Lieutenant Parker, who had returned to the United States. "My flying is very intermittent these days," wrote Ike. "Jew Lewis [Captain Mark K. Lewis] says that I did *not* fall off in coordination . . . but as far as I am concerned I haven't had the same confidence in landings."*

> Jew took me on my first blind flying about a week ago!
> You will remember that you gave me a book on the stuff,
> and at the time I memorized the essential paragraphs. But
> Lordy, Lordy, it took me only about 4 minutes to get into
> a steep diving spiral. I tried everything I could think of
> except throwing the stick out of the cockpit. I've had 3

---

* Captain Mark K. Lewis flaunted his Jewishness. A 1927 graduate of the U.S. Military Academy, Lewis was West Point's star goalie in soccer, hockey, and lacrosse for four years. In 1927 he captained the hockey team from the crease. His semiofficial West Point nickname was "the Jew Boy," and he was known as Jew Lewis throughout his military career. There are two personal letters from Lewis to Ike in the correspondence files at the Eisenhower Library, both of which are signed "Jew." Major Lewis was killed December 9, 1941, when his B-26 crashed on take-off.

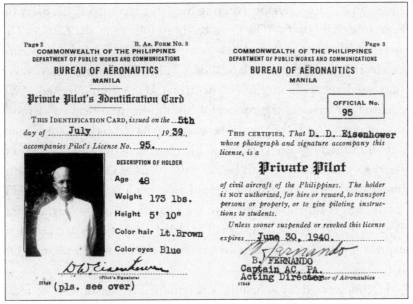

Eisenhower's pilot's license.

lessons [in blind flying] now—and I've gotten to the point where I mess along in an approximate fashion—but, so far as I'm concerned, that's one feature of flying that is plain hard work!

But I have a lot of fun—and even better than that—I think I furnish a lot of fun for the others out at the field, because I often see them grinning at me.[47]

Eisenhower's relations with MacArthur continued to fluctuate. When General William D. Connor, the superintendent at West Point, asked MacArthur whether Ike was available to become commandant of cadets, MacArthur abruptly refused, asserting that Ike was engaged in "duties of the gravest importance. He could not adequately be replaced."[48] Eisenhower was not consulted, but in any case he would have declined the post. "I wanted no part of that," he wrote to a friend at West Point many years later. "The Commandant was merely [in charge of discipline] and I had no ambition to get into that kind of business."[49]

The fact that MacArthur considered Eisenhower indispensable did not shelter him from the general's temper tantrums. "TJ [Davis] and I came in for a terrible bawling out," Ike recorded in his diary on September 26, 1936. "The Gen. has been following the *Literary Digest* [presidential] poll, and has convinced himself that Landon is to be elected, probably in a landslide." When Davis and Eisenhower suggested the poll might be incorrect, MacArthur erupted. "We couldn't understand the reason for his almost hysterical condemnation of our STUPIDITY until he suddenly let drop that he had gone out and urged Q[uezon] to shape his plans for going to the U.S. on the theory that Landon will be elected." Neither Davis nor Ike could understand why MacArthur should take such a risk. "But WHY should he get sore just because we say 'Don't be so d——— certain????' Both of us are 'fearful and small minded people who are afraid to express judgments that are obvious from the evidence at hand.' Oh hell."[*]

Eisenhower's daily schedule was remarkably constant. Like most in the military he arose early, and left the Manila Hotel for the airfield shortly after six. The combination of a low wage scale for native Filipinos and his own generous salary permitted him to employ a local driver who also served as a valet and personal assistant. Ike was at his desk well before eight and worked until one or two in the afternoon. If MacArthur came to the office, Eisenhower usually rode back to the Manila Hotel with the general in his limousine. After lunch and a short nap, Eisenhower joined members of the American expatriate community for bridge in a formal room off the hotel lobby. Other afternoons he would head for the golf course at the Army-Navy Club. Evenings he dined in the hotel's opulent dining room. Later, when Mamie joined him, they dined there together every evening. Bedtime was early—except when social obligations intervened. Ma-

---

[*] When Roosevelt was reelected in the greatest presidential landslide since James Monroe trounced John Quincy Adams with an all-but-unanimous sweep of the electoral college in 1820 (one New Hampshire elector defected to Adams), MacArthur ate crow. "Boy did the General back pedal rapidly," Eisenhower wrote in his diary on November 15, 1936. "I hear he went out to see Q[uezon] on the first or second and 'took back' what he had said. Accused the *Literary Digest* of 'crookedness.' . . . But he's never expressed to TJ or to me any regret for his awful bawling out of a couple of months ago." DDE, Philippine diary, in *Eisenhower: The Prewar Diaries and Selected Papers* 328–29, Daniel D. Holt and James W. Leyerzapf, eds. (Baltimore: Johns Hopkins University Press, 1998).

nila enjoyed a reputation as the liveliest, most social city in the Orient. As one journalist wrote, "Parties are wetter and held oftener; are bigger, showier, more lavish, and last longer, than any other place in the world. Durability is required of the guests."[50] Eisenhower, as a stand-in for MacArthur, ranked high on every guest list.

Ike became a favorite of President Quezon's. He was given an office at the presidential palace, where he handled the mission's business on MacArthur's behalf, and became a regular at the president's all-night bridge and poker games. (Quezon, like Eisenhower, was an expert at bridge and poker.) Weekends were often spent on the presidential yacht, the *Cassiano,* where the games continued nonstop. Another favorite partner for Ike was Marian Huff, the comely wife of Lieutenant Sidney Huff, MacArthur's naval aide. Mrs. Huff was not only young and perky, but also played excellent bridge and a superb game of golf. Whether there was anything more than golf and bridge between Ike and Marian Huff is a matter of conjecture. Mamie certainly saw her as a rival for Ike's affections, but Lieutenant Huff "did not seem in the least bit concerned."[51]

Mamie, for her part, had no intention of becoming a recluse while Ike was in Manila. The social swirl of Club Eisenhower did not continue as such, but Mamie entertained frequently and was frequently entertained in return. "Throughout the winter and spring, Mamie had no shortage of activities to occupy her, no lack of friends to see or escorts to lend their arms," wrote Susan Eisenhower. "Whatever her deepest feelings, Mamie made a life for herself during Ike's absence, and word of her apparent independence and resourcefulness no doubt made its way to Manila."[52]

Eisenhower's letters to his wife became less frequent and, according to Mamie, were "far from cheerful." She wondered if he still cared. "I haven't had a letter from Ike in over two weeks," she wrote her parents on March 31, 1936. "You know he always acts queer in the tropics and if he's not coming home I feel I should go out there—altho I don't think he's very keen about it. . . . He's never told me how much extra pay he's drawing or what rank he is holding."[53]

Mamie finally realized that if she wished to stay married to Ike, she would have to go to the Philippines. In the fall she closed the apartment at the Wyoming, put their furniture in storage, and with Johnnie in tow boarded the Army transport *President Grant* for Manila. Ike was at the dock when they arrived. The reception was chilly.[54] On their way to the Manila Hotel, Ike said tersely, "I gather I have reason for a divorce, if I want one." Eisenhower family legend holds that Ike's comment referred to the fact that Mamie had not sat at home during her time in Washington. "There has never been a suggestion that he was accusing her of violating her wedding vows."[55]

The Eisenhowers moved temporarily into Ike's suite in the Manila Hotel, and Ike laid on a full complement of servants. Nevertheless, their reunion lacked the warmth of earlier years. Deep down, Eisenhower resented Mamie's failure to accompany him to Manila originally; Mamie resented being there at all. Ike was angry about the vibrant social life Mamie had led in Washington; Mamie seethed at Ike's bridge games and golf outings with Marian Huff. "It didn't seem to occur to her," wrote Susan Eisenhower, "that she had been escorted around Washington by a number of male friends during her year alone. But jealousy knows no logic nor does it respect reciprocity."[56]

Soon the Eisenhowers moved into larger, more elegant quarters in the air-conditioned wing of the Manila Hotel, and their adjustment became easier. Never again would they enjoy the happy intimacy of Paris or the Washington years at the Wyoming, but they were soon caught up in the tempo of Manila's throbbing social life. Mamie's letters home tell of an intense schedule of afternoon card parties and evening soirees. MacArthur's young wife, Jean Faircloth, from Murfreesboro, Tennessee, and Marjorie Clay, the wealthy wife of Captain Lucius Clay, became regular shopping and luncheon companions. "We've been financially on easy street for the first time in our married life," Mamie wrote her parents in early 1938. "We're having pretty near anything we wish."[57]

While Mamie shopped and socialized, Eisenhower was spending more and more time at the Malacañan Palace with President Quezon. And as Ike became more involved in Philippine affairs, his early assessments moderated. "Although I've been here for a year and a half," he wrote General George Moseley, "I am not one of those who attempt to ascribe to the Filipino any racial defect which would make it impossible for him ever to become a good officer. Genghis Khan produced one of the finest military machines the World has ever seen, and the only material he had was nomadic tribesmen in Central Asia."[58] Writing to John Doud he challenged the conventional wisdom about Philippine independence.

> A certain group of Americans and Europeans habitually sneer at the Filipino—challenging his sincerity, integrity and ability—and claiming this whole situation [that is, the desire for independence] is the result of the crooked scheming of politicians to get more personal power. But possibly a lot of other reforms have grown out of the same source. In any event, they've started something, and it is most interesting to be here watching the early stages of a development that is certain to have far reaching effects in the coming years.[59]

MacArthur's insistence on a thirty-division Army was a continuing source of friction. According to the figures prepared by Ike and Ord, it would exceed Philippine budget projections by $25 million. They recommended the plan be scaled back, but MacArthur refused. "We urged a budgetary basis for all planning, and he grew furious, accusing us of 'arguing technicalities' to defeat the conceptions of high command," Ike recorded on October 8, 1937.

President Quezon eventually learned of the cost overrun and asked MacArthur for an explanation. At that point MacArthur backed down. The plan was not his, he told Quezon, but had been prepared by Eisenhower and Ord without his approval. Ike could scarcely believe it. "Every scrap of evidence furnishes ample proof that he is again executing one of his amazing 'about faces,' " wrote Eisenhower. "I've got to decide soon whether I can go much further with a person who, either consciously or unconsciously, deceives his boss, his subordinates, and himself (probably) so incessantly as he does. I wonder whether egotism, exclusive devotion to one's own interests (in this case, a $33,000 salary, plus penthouse and expenses) can completely eliminate a person's perception of honest, straight-forwardness and responsibility.

"When irritated at the Pres., I've heard him curse that worthy as a 'conceited little monkey,' and I've heard him, in turn use even worse language with respect to every prominent officer in the U.S. Army, and officials in Washington," Ike continued.

> But sometimes I think that, in his mind, there is nothing ridiculous, absurd, or even unusual in his attitude. He was raised in the conception of Douglas MacArthur superiority. Actually he has become only pathetic. . . . He gets frantic in the face of difficulty, even if the difficulty is only an imaginary one and displays an exaggeration of glee when he believes things are shaping up to glorify his name, or increase his income.
>
> I shall never forget the time in Washington when receipt of instructions to report to the President [Herbert Hoover] led him to conclude, in the greatest seriousness, that he was to be invited to be the President's running mate in the succeeding [1932] election.

Ike had remained in Manila despite MacArthur's capriciousness. "But now I am at a cross road. If the Marshal is to persist in his arbitrary methods, and is going to make things unpleasant, if not impossible, then I'm for home. Right now I'm disgusted and in something of a temper, a bad state of mind in which to make any decisions."

Eisenhower stayed on the job. But MacArthur's assignment in the Philippines was coming to a close. The standard overseas tour for a general officer in the 1930s was two years. As MacArthur approached the end of his second year in Manila, he received a letter from Chief of Staff Malin Craig advising him that upon completion of his two years abroad he would be ordered home. "There will be made available to you, if practicable, any command for which you may express a preference."[60] Craig's letter was a bolt out of the blue. For the second time MacArthur felt he had been double-crossed by the War Department, FDR, and anyone else in Washington who might have had a hand in it. "The last week has been one of the most trying ones I've had in the Philippines," wrote Eisenhower in his diary on August 25, 1937. "There have been an unusually large number of dif-

ficult administrative problems to handle with the [Philippine] Army
staff. . . . But the cause for special perturbation was the receipt by
the Gen. of a letter from the Chief of Staff informing him that he
would be relieved and ordered home on the October transport!"

> From the start T.J. [Davis] and I counseled moderation—
> and at least *initial* dependence on Mr. Quezon's efforts to
> have the order revoked. He [Quezon] agreed to send any
> radio [message] proposed by the Gen. to accomplish such
> revocation, and we got up one worded as strongly as it
> could possibly be. But we had no sooner submitted the
> draft of that radio to the Pres. when a hundred other
> schemes were proposed. . . . We wrote drafts (under in-
> structions) of radios requesting retirement, of others pro-
> testing the "unjust and arbitrary" procedures of the War
> Department while listening for hours on end to hypothe-
> ses and deductions as to what had occasioned the order.
> Gradually it percolated into the Gen.'s head that the the-
> ory lending the greatest hopes for a successful outcome
> was one that held the C of S solely and exclusively respon-
> sible for the action.

As MacArthur saw it, Craig's motivation involved "jealousy; fear of
the growing stature of Gen. MacA. as a world figure; egotism; revenge by the 'Chaumont crowd';[*] and the hopes of pleasing the 'pacifist, subversive element that surrounds the President.' "

> The defense that T.J. and I put up was simply that we
> should give credit to the C of S for being an honorable
> person. . . . We emphasized that we'd done what we could
> when we prepared the telegram for Mr. Quezon's signa-
> ture. We insisted on waiting for an answer before making
> another move, since his wire was addressed to the Presi-

---

[*] The "Chaumont crowd" was MacArthur's shorthand expression for what he considered the Pershing clique in the Army, Chaumont having been the site of Pershing's headquarters in France.

dent of the U.S. Finally, the old habit of accusing every assistant who did not concur without reservation to hysterical theories and arguments with being a blockhead, an ingrate, a stupid dolt and so on manifested itself, so T.J. and I perforce stopped arguing.[61]

Impatient with waiting for a reply to Quezon's message, MacArthur fired off a protest to the War Department. "Your letter has amazed me," he wired Craig. "The action suggested would constitute my summary relief. . . . Considering rank and position it can only be interpreted as constituting disciplinary action."[62] General Craig was unmoved. The action was ordered by the president, he told MacArthur. "In view of world conditions, the President has decided that a soldier of your stature should be in the United States." But he agreed to delay MacArthur's reassignment until February.[63]

Eisenhower seemed relieved. "I hope the subject will now cease to be a topic of conversation. I'm worn out. Every time one of these 'tempests in a teapot' sweeps the office I find myself, sooner or later, bearing the brunt of the General's displeasure, *which always manifests itself against anyone who fails to agree en tote with his theories and hypotheses,* no matter how astounding they may be."[64]

MacArthur thought about Craig's reply until mid-September, and then requested retirement. "I find the thought repugnant of resuming to a subordinate command after having been military head of the Army. . . . It would be as though President Roosevelt were required to go back to his functions as Assistant Secretary of the Navy. It would not only be unsatisfactory to me but the reaction would be such to make me an unsatisfactory subordinate commander."[65] MacArthur's request to retire was approved, effective December 31, 1937. The War Department announced that he would retire with the rank of full general—an exceptional accolade. President Roosevelt wrote MacArthur that he had approved the retirement "with great reluctance and regret."[66]

MacArthur remained in Manila as field marshal of the Philippine Army, freed from the shackles of the War Department chain of command. He continued to enjoy his penthouse in the Manila Hotel, his stipend, and his expense allowance. His retirement pension as a full general differed little from his major general's salary. Eisenhower remained as chief of staff and became the ranking U.S. Army officer on active duty with the mission.

On December 31, 1937, MacArthur wrote Eisenhower's final efficiency report. This would be the last efficiency report MacArthur would prepare on an American officer until he was recalled to active duty by President Roosevelt in June 1941. Despite their occasional differences, he considered Eisenhower indispensable. He rated Ike "superior" in all categories. "A brilliant officer," said MacArthur. "[He] is performing duties which in scope and responsibility are comparable to those of a general officer of the War Department General Staff. . . . In time of war this officer should be promoted to General rank immediately. His general value to the service is 'Superior.' "[67]

Eisenhower, for his part, accepted MacArthur's peculiarities as part of the job. "From the beginning Jim [Ord] and I have been practically isolated in thought, attitude, and intention," he wrote at the end of 1937.

> We did not want to come to the Philippines but were willing to do so because we thought we'd have a wonderful professional opportunity. Once on the job we've concerned ourselves with trying to develop for this government and country the best possible army with the means at hand. We have been beset on all sides by difficulties arising from personal ambition, personal glorification, personal selfishness of the hot shot ($33,000 a year and a penthouse) etc. etc. When we have objected strenuously to measures which we believe unwise such as the Field Marshal–ship . . . we've been told to shut up. In spite of it all, I believe we've done fairly well under the conditions.[68]

As friction with MacArthur continued, Ike's digestive problems resurfaced. In January 1938 he was hospitalized with what his doctors described as "a dangerous stoppage of the bowel"—a forerunner of the intestinal ailment he suffered in the White House. Just as he was about to be anesthetized for surgery, the blockage passed and the operation was canceled. But the pain had been excruciating. Later Ike recalled the ordeal as "the tortures of the damned."[69]

While Eisenhower was recovering in the hospital, he received word that James Ord had been killed in a freak airplane accident. Ord had flown to Baguio, in central Luzon—the site of the new Philippine military academy—for a conference with the commandant. Before landing, he decided to drop a note in the garden of a friend to notify him of his arrival. As the pilot reduced speed and swooped low over the house, Ord leaned out of the open cockpit. The engine failed, and the plane crashed into a nearby hillside. Had Ord not been leaning out of the aircraft to drop the message, he would likely have survived.[70] Ord's death deprived Eisenhower of his closest friend and most intimate associate. "I've lost my right hand," he wrote in his diary shortly afterward. "He was my partner on a tough job, who furnished most of the inspiration needed to keep me plugging away. With him gone much of the zest has departed from a job that we always tackled as a team, never as two individuals."[71]

Despite his occasional differences with MacArthur, Eisenhower relished his work with the Philippine Army as well as the lifestyle he and Mamie were enjoying. Normally, his three-year tour of duty in Manila would have expired in October 1938. But at the request of both President Quezon and MacArthur, he asked for a one-year extension.* MacArthur, who was becoming increasingly remote, recognized that Ike would be difficult to replace, and Quezon considered him essential.

"President Quezon seemed to ask for my advice more and more," said Eisenhower. "He invited me to his office frequently. Because I was the senior active duty officer, my friendship with the President became closer. Our conversations became broader and deeper. They were no longer confined to defense problems. Taxes, education, hon-

---

* The overseas tour of general officers was set by the War Department at two years. For all other military personnel the normal tour was three years. Because MacArthur had retired, Eisenhower's request was submitted to Washington by Major General John H. Hughes, the commander of the Philippine Department, on March 3, 1938. The War Department signaled its approval on March 8. DDE 201 file, EL.

esty in government, and other subjects entered the discussions and he seemed to enjoy them. I certainly did."[72]

This time Mamie did not object to the extension. "You know I'm pretty level-headed about what I know is right," she wrote her parents. "I made a terrible mistake in not coming out here with Ike. It's up to me to rectify lots of things." Mamie said she realized John and Elivera would be disappointed, "but what can I do? You know Ike. I told him the other day that it has taken me 22 years to find out that the only way I can get along with him is to give him his own way *constantly.* Luckily John is very happy in his school."[73]

Mamie now saw herself as a full-fledged participant in Ike's career. "Unlike the picture of a bedridden wife painted by virtually every Eisenhower biographer," wrote Susan Eisenhower, "Mamie stayed remarkably active. She entertained and fulfilled the social obligations beneficial for her husband; it was a question not only of physical strength but also of mental fortitude. Mamie looked after herself by taking siestas and resting when she could, but at the back of her mind was always her concern about 'keeping up' with her husband."[74]

Eisenhower's extension was coupled with approval for him and Mamie to return to the United States for three months, almost two of which would be consumed by travel. Mamie required gynecological surgery, which would be performed by the Doud family doctor in Denver, and Ike would attend to the needs of the Philippine Army with the War Department. But Eisenhower's first order of business before leaving for the States was to replace James Ord, and he turned to another old friend, Major Richard K. Sutherland, then with the 15th Infantry in Tientsin. Ike and Mamie knew the Sutherlands from the Wyoming when Sutherland had been with the operations (G-3) section of the War Department. "He is an excellent officer," Ike wrote in his diary in April 14, 1938, "and I expect him to take a huge burden off my shoulders."

The choice was less than felicitous. Sutherland was undoubtedly capable. But he was ruthlessly ambitious and immediately set about to undermine Eisenhower with MacArthur. The son of West Virginia senator Howard Sutherland, he graduated from Yale in 1916, served in the Connecticut National Guard, and was commissioned a captain in the Regular Army after World War I. Unlike the genial

Ord, Sutherland was brusque, abrasive, and humorless. "A brittle, hard man," said Charles Willoughby, MacArthur's wartime intelligence officer.[75] George Kenney, who commanded Allied air forces in the southwest Pacific during World War II, described Sutherland as someone "who always rubbed people the wrong way."[76] Philippine newspaper editor and Pulitzer Prize–winning correspondent (1942) Carlos Romulo called him "a martinet."[77] Like many authoritarian personalities, Sutherland displayed a streak of obsequiousness when dealing with high command. Eisenhower and Ord had often challenged MacArthur; Sutherland stroked his ego.[78]

The Eisenhowers sailed from Manila on June 26, 1938. Ike left on a high note. "The General has been extraordinarily sympathetic," he wrote just before leaving.

> At one time it seemed almost impossible to discuss with him any point in which there was the slightest difference of opinion, but for the past few months this has not been so. It is difficult to believe that Jimmy's [Ord] loss should have occasioned this change, but the fact is, that ever since then he has grown progressively more mellow. . . . The atmosphere has cleared to such an extent that this job, at long last, has become personally agreeable as well as professionally interesting.[79]

Eisenhower threw himself into his task in Washington with enthusiasm. "I wanted to ask the War Department for more help. At first they were unsympathetic. As long as the Philippines insisted on being independent, the War Department's attitude was that they could jolly well look out for their own defenses." To overcome the general staff's resistance, Ike went directly to General Craig.

> I told him my story, adding that General MacArthur's view was that a friendly Philippines was vital to U.S. interests. General Craig agreed and in short order the word seeped down to the staff. Doors that had been tightly closed began to open and we secured much assistance. The War Department put us in touch with manufacturers who

were ready to do business, and the Army provided obsolete but useful equipment.

After begging or borrowing everything I could from Signal, Quartermaster, Ordnance, and Medical groups, I went to Wichita, bought several planes [from Stearman Aircraft], then to the Winchester Arms Company in Connecticut. With what I had "liberated" and bought, I went back to Manila.[80]

Ike and Mamie sailed from Vancouver aboard the Canadian Pacific's *Empress of Japan* on October 14. Before leaving, the Eisenhowers stopped off at Fort Lewis, Washington, to visit Lieutenant Colonel Mark Clark and his wife, Maurine. Clark, who was two years behind Eisenhower at West Point, had served with Ike in Washington and was now operations officer (G-3) of the 3rd Infantry Division. In 1938 there were only three infantry divisions in the United States. Eisenhower had not been with troops since his brief assignment to the 24th Infantry in 1926, and he discussed with Clark the possibility of his joining the 3rd Division when his tour in the Philippines concluded. According to Clark, there was no urgency in Ike's query, and he voiced no displeasure toward MacArthur.[81]

Eisenhower returned to Manila confident that his trip to Washington had been a success. But the ground had shifted beneath him. During his absence, Sutherland, recently promoted to lieutenant colonel, had poisoned MacArthur's mind against him. "I was familiar with the details," said Lucius D. Clay, who enjoyed the confidence of both Eisenhower and MacArthur.[82]

A group in the Philippine legislature decided that Eisenhower was doing all the work and that he was being paid only $10,000 a year, whereas MacArthur was being given a beautiful penthouse apartment in the Manila Hotel and being paid a much more substantial sum. This little group of Filipino congressmen prepared to introduce a bill that would abolish the top job—MacArthur's job—and leave Eisenhower in charge.

When Eisenhower heard about it, he went to them and

told them that if they ever introduced that bill he would immediately ask to be returned to the United States. That under no circumstances would he be a party to it.

But General MacArthur found out about it. From that moment he had no more use for Eisenhower. And it was absolutely unfounded, although I am sure there were people [for example, Richard Sutherland] who deliberately tried to convince MacArthur that Eisenhower was trying to knife him in the back. But I know this was not true. MacArthur's dislike for Eisenhower was based on the fact that he was either given completely false information, or that he misinterpreted it himself. I suspect it was a little of both.[83]

MacArthur's response was to reorganize the mission. He made Sutherland his chief of staff (a post he would hold throughout World War II), and reduced Ike to operations officer—the post previously held by Ord. That, despite the fact that Eisenhower was senior to Sutherland. Ike was also stripped of any responsibility for dealing with President Quezon and the Philippine government. Eisenhower was not consulted. He learned of the changes upon his arrival back in Manila, and he was furious. His diary entry of November 10, 1938, smokes with anger.

> Why the man [MacArthur] should so patently exhibit a jealousy of a subordinate is beyond me. . . . Of course, he has accomplished one thing he wanted to do, that is, make certain that I'd get out as soon as I decently can. On the surface, all is lovely. I will not give him the satisfaction of showing any resentment. But my usefulness is so curtailed as to rob the job of much of its interest, so I'm going at the earliest possible moment. If the d—— fool had only sent me his plan while I was in the States I would not have returned.

Ike said he regretted working on MacArthur's behalf in Washington.

> But I must say it is almost incomprehensible that after 8 years of working for him, writing every word he publishes,

keeping his secrets, preventing him from making too much of an ass of himself, trying to advance his interests while keeping myself in the background, he should suddenly turn on me. He'd like to occupy a throne room surrounded by experts in flattery; while in a dungeon beneath, unknown to the world, would be a bunch of able slaves doing his work and producing the things that, to the public, would represent the brilliant accomplishment of his mind. He's a fool, but worse he is a puking baby.

My fury is academic. But it is discouraging to have hammered home all the time that he is as stupid as he is crooked. T.J. [Davis] is no higher in his estimation than I. His confidence in our integrity and gentlemanly instincts must be high, because I cannot believe he'd deliberately make enemies of anyone that he feared might in the future reveal the true story of his black and tan affair [a reference to Rosario Cooper, MacArthur's Eurasian mistress]; the circumstances surrounding the withdrawal of his libel suit; the names he's called (in private) President Q[uezon]; his machinations to keep himself on as chief of staff; his speculations on his chances to be *Vice President* of the U.S.; his chiseling to increase the emoluments he's getting from the Phil. Gov't.; his abject fear that he will do anything that might jeopardize his job (rather his salary of $33,000 *and* all expenses). Oh hell—what's the use. Now that I've jotted all this down I hope that it never again comes, even momentarily, to my mind.

The next day Eisenhower dispatched two letters: one to Mark Clark, the other to his old friend James Ulio, now executive officer to the adjutant general. He asked both to do what they could to get him assigned to the 3rd Division as soon as possible, preferably as a battalion commander. Eisenhower, like George Patton, was never shy about pulling strings to advance his career. In 1925, he sought Fox Conner's assistance to gain an appointment to the Command and General Staff School. In 1926, he petitioned Conner to arrange a transfer out of the 24th Infantry. In 1929, when he felt he was in a military backwater with Pershing in Paris, he appealed once again to Conner, who introduced him to George Moseley. Conner and Moseley were retired in 1938, so Ike directed his quest for a new assignment to old friends who were in positions to help. Clark was the favorite of Major General Walter C. Sweeney, the commander of the 3rd Division, and a friend of George C. Marshall, the incoming chief of staff. Ulio was at the personnel switchboard in the adjutant general's office.

While Eisenhower awaited orders, another opportunity arose. After Kristallnacht (November 10, 1938), when Nazi storm troopers smashed shop windows, burned synagogues, and looted Jewish stores in Germany, debate about Hitler's policy toward the Jews became more frequent. At social functions in Manila, the grandees of the Spanish community, most of whom were loyal to Franco, as well as some anti-Semitic American expatriates, expressed admiration for Hitler. Eisenhower took exception, and the arguments often became heated. "There was a considerable Jewish community in the city," wrote Eisenhower, "and I had good friends among them." As a result, in early 1939 Ike received what he called an unusual offer. "Through several friends, I was asked to take a job seeking in China, Southeast Asia, Indonesia, and every other country where they might be acceptable, a haven for Jewish refugees from Nazi Germany. The pay would be $60,000 a year [roughly $775,000 currently] with expenses. The first five years' salary would be placed in escrow to be delivered to me if I should be separated from the new job for any cause whatever." Eisenhower said the offer was appealing for several reasons. He sympathized with the plight of the refugees, and the salary was very attractive. "But I had become so committed to my profession that I declined."[84]

On May 27, 1939, Ike received orders assigning him to the 15th Infantry at Fort Lewis.[85] James Ulio wrote subsequently that the chief of infantry had slated him to be the second-ranking officer in the 15th, virtually assuring Eisenhower of a battalion command. Ulio also said that the adjutant general had taken the question of Ike's reassignment date directly to General Marshall (who had assumed the duties of chief of staff on July 1) and that Marshall decided to terminate Eisenhower's tour at the earliest date to which the Philippine government would agree.[86]

"I cannot tell you how anxiously we are looking forward to our return to the States," Ike wrote Mark Clark on September 23. "I feel like a boy who has been promised an electric train for Christmas."

The date for Eisenhower's departure was fixed at December 13, 1939. President Quezon implored Ike to stay, and offered him a blank contract for his services. "We'll tear up the old contract," he said. "I've already signed this one and it is filled in—except for what you want as your emoluments for remaining. You will write that in." Eisenhower thanked Quezon but declined. "No amount of money can make me change my mind."[87]

Formalities were observed. At a farewell luncheon at the Malaca-ñan Palace, President Quezon awarded Eisenhower the Philippine Distinguished Service Star. MacArthur wrote an affectionate farewell letter. "I cannot tell you how deeply I regret your leaving," he told Ike. "Your distinguished service has been characterized at all times by superior professional ability, unswerving loyalty and unselfish devotion to duty." MacArthur said he would miss Eisenhower, but would "follow with keen interest the brilliant career which unquestionably lies ahead of you."[88]

Eisenhower said later, "I got out *clean*—and that's that."[89]

# SEVEN

# Louisiana Maneuvers

Have you learned to tie your own shoes again
since coming back, Eisenhower?
—GENERAL MARSHALL TO EISENHOWER,
*January 1940*

EISENHOWER ENJOYED AN exemplary reputation as a staff officer. For eighteen years he had amassed an uninterrupted string of "superior" ratings in jobs of increasing complexity. First with Fox Conner in Panama, then with Pershing, then George Moseley, and finally with MacArthur, he had demonstrated an exceptional capacity to produce under pressure. His knowledge of procedure, his mastery of nuance, his political sensitivity, and his capacity to translate the decisions of his superiors into action were unexcelled.

The size of the officer corps had held steady during the interwar years, and most officers of the same rank were acquainted, particularly with members of their own branch.* Ike's reputation for com-

---

* Between 1923 and 1939, the Army maintained an average strength of 14,000 officers and 130,000 enlisted men. By contrast, the German Reichswehr was limited by the Versailles Treaty to 100,000 men, of whom no more than 4,000 could be officers. (Peacemakers wanted the German Army large enough to suppress domestic violence, but not so large as to menace Germany's neighbors.)

These comparative figures suggest that the U.S. Army contained far too many officers for its overall strength, and one of General Marshall's first tasks when he became chief of staff was to prune the deadwood. One of the rationales for the excess of officers in the American Army was their potential employment as cadre

mon sense, his dedication, his sense of humor—and his temper—had become legendary. But except for several months with the 24th Infantry in 1926, he had not been with troops since he commanded the 301st Heavy Tank Battalion at Fort Meade in 1921. If Eisenhower was to rise above the rank of colonel (and in the peacetime Army promotion to colonel was strictly by seniority), he needed command responsibility with an infantry regiment.

For that reason, a posting to the 15th Infantry at Fort Lewis was a plum assignment. But in December 1939, as the Eisenhowers stood on the pier in San Francisco awaiting their luggage, that prospect was put on hold. "A very military looking sergeant came down the line paging Colonel Eisenhower, in a voice that indicated he thought I was still in Hawaii," Ike recalled. "Upon acknowledging, unwillingly, my identity (I could smell trouble), I was handed an order to report to Fourth Army headquarters [at the Presidio of San Francisco] for temporary duty."[1] Lieutenant General John L. DeWitt, commanding Fourth Army, had plucked Ike from the 15th Infantry to help his staff prepare for the summer maneuvers General Marshall had laid on.[2]

"That order blew up a sizeable typhoon in the family," Eisenhower said later. "At first I thought it was the old, old story that once more I was to start a tour of 'staff' duty instead of getting to troops."[3] Mamie was concerned about their quarters at Fort Lewis, and John was eager to enroll for his final semester of high school. When Ike indicated his desire to return to troops as soon as possible, DeWitt assured him the assignment was temporary. He needed someone to do the "pick and shovel work" of drafting orders to assemble the far-flung units of Fourth Army at the maneuver areas. By the end of January, he told Ike, he could proceed to Fort Lewis. Eisenhower and Mamie spent the next month at the Drisko Hotel in San Francisco, and John went on to stay with his uncle Edgar in Tacoma, where he enrolled at Stadium High School.[4]

Eisenhower reported to the 15th Infantry on February 5, 1940. As the senior lieutenant colonel he became regimental executive officer

---

should the Army ever need to expand. Yet the German Army under Hitler expanded rapidly without difficulty and with far fewer officers.

and assumed command of the 1st Battalion. The 15th Infantry, another of the Army's old-line regiments, had only recently returned to Fort Lewis. From 1912 to 1938 it had been stationed in Tientsin, China, guarding American commercial interests in accord with the protocols imposed on China in 1901 after its defeat in the Boxer Rebellion. The regiment had been withdrawn by the Roosevelt administration following the Japanese attack on the gunboat USS *Panay.* The continued presence of American forces in China appeared unnecessarily provocative in the face of the Sino-Japanese conflict, and the withdrawal of the 15th Infantry was a sop to isolationist sentiment in a congressional election year. The regiment's motto was "Can Do," pidgin English reflecting its long service in China, and a posting to the 15th was one of the Army's most sought-after assignments. George C. Marshall served as regimental executive officer from 1924 to 1926—the same job that Ike now held.

In early 1940 the Army was still organized in the ponderous "square" divisions of World War I, a 28,000-man behemoth devised in 1917 for trench warfare on the western front.[*] The troops were regulars—Congress would not enact the draft until September—and many in the 15th Infantry had seen service in China. But the War Department was already cannibalizing existing units to form new cadres. The authorized strength of the regiment was 2,961, but it was 400 men short. It also lacked mortars, machine guns, and automatic rifles.[5] Eisenhower's battalion, which normally would have had two majors and seven captains in addition to a full complement of lieutenants, had only lieutenants. Ike was the only officer above that rank.[6]

"I've been with this regiment about five months, and am having

---

[*] The term "square" pertained to the four regiments in the division. The division was typically deployed with all four regiments on line, with battalions in a column within each regiment. The infantry was essentially cannon fodder. Following a rolling barrage, successive waves of infantry hurled themselves against the enemy trenches. Stacking the infantry battalions in tandem reflected the tactics of Napoléon at Waterloo and Beauregard at Shiloh, and for reasons that are less than obvious fascinated the department of military strategy and tactics at West Point. By 1918 such tactics were obsolescent and by 1939 wholly anachronistic. See especially Christopher R. Gabel, *The U.S. Army GHQ Maneuvers of 1941* 9–11 (Washington, D.C.: Center of Military History, U.S. Army, 1992).

the time of my life," Eisenhower wrote Omar Bradley on July 1, 1940. "Like everyone else in the Army, we're up to our necks in work, but this work is fun. I could not conceive of a better job; except, of course, having one's own regiment, which is out of the question because of rank."[7]

The Fourth Army maneuvers took place in August. For five days and nights Ike led his battalion across the cut-over timberland of Washington State. "Actually it would have made good stage-setting for a play in Hades," he wrote his old friend Leonard Gerow. "Stumps, slashings, fallen logs, tangled brush, holes, hummocks and hills. Through the day I sweated and accumulated a grime of caked dust. At night, we froze. My youngsters kept on going and delivering handsomely after five days of almost no sleep! I was certainly proud of that gang."[8] Looking back on the Fourth Army maneuvers twenty-five years later, Ike wrote, "The experience fortified my conviction that I belonged with troops; with them I was always happy."[9]

Eisenhower's spirits were lifted even higher when he received a letter in September from George Patton, who had left the 3rd Cavalry at Fort Myer to assume command of the newly established 2nd Armored Brigade at Fort Benning. Patton was full of himself. "It seems highly probable that I will get one of the next two armored divisions," he wrote Ike. "If I do, I shall ask for you either as Chief of Staff, which I should prefer, or as a regimental commander. You can tell me which you want. Hoping we are together in a long and BLOODY war."[10]

Eisenhower was enthusiastic. "It would be great to be in the tanks once more, and even better to be associated with you again," he replied. "I suppose it's too much to hope that I could have a regiment in your division, because I'm still almost three years away from my colonelcy. But *I think* I could do a damn good job of commanding a regiment."[11]

Patton, who was in the field, answered as soon as he returned to post. He urged Ike to apply "for a transfer to the Armored Corps NOW. If you have any pull . . . use it for there will be 10 new generals in this corps pretty damn soon."[12]

Eisenhower wrote immediately to Mark Clark, who had been ordered to Washington by General Marshall. Would Clark please let the chief of infantry know how much he wanted to command one of the new armored regiments? Ike asked. "They will probably think me a conceited individual, but I see no objection to setting your sights high. Actually, I will be delighted to serve in the Armored Corps in almost any capacity, but I do hope to avoid Staff and to stay on troop duty for some time to come."[13]

Ike wrote a similar letter to T. J. Davis, his Manila compatriot who was now in the office of the adjutant general: "My ambition is to go, eventually, to the armored outfit," he told Davis. "George Patton has told me that at least two new armored divisions are to be formed early next year, and if he is assigned to command one of them he intends to ask for me, possibly as one of his regimental commanders. That would be a swell job and I only hope that the War Department won't consider me too junior in rank to get a regiment."[14]

Eisenhower's concern about his lack of seniority was justified. Davis replied promptly that General Walter Krueger, who had just assumed command of VIII Corps at Fort Sam Houston, had asked for Ike to be his chief of staff (a colonel's billet) but had been turned down by the War Department because Eisenhower was too junior. Ike was thrilled that Krueger had requested him, but was not displeased to have avoided another staff assignment. "The only job that would really tempt me to leave the 15th Infantry would be to obtain command of an armored regiment," he wrote Davis.

> In view of the fact that the War Department thinks I am too junior to be a chief of staff of the corps, it seems evident that they will consider me too junior for commanding a regiment.
>
> It strikes me that this business of being so particular about the details of rank is, to say the least, somewhat amusing under existing circumstances. When a man has reached the age of fifty years, and has been graduated more than twenty-five, and is some two and one-half years away from his eagles, it seems that the matter of rank could be so adjusted that the War Department could put a man wherever they wanted to.[15]

For the next several weeks Ike dreamed of commanding an armored regiment under George Patton. "But the roof fell in on me shortly after the middle of November."[16] Eisenhower received a telegram from Leonard Gerow, who was now a brigadier general and chief of the War Plans Division in the War Department.

> I NEED YOU IN WAR PLANS DIVISION. DO YOU SERI-
> OUSLY OBJECT TO BEING DETAILED ON THE WAR DEPT
> GENERAL STAFF AND ASSIGNED HERE? PLEASE REPLY
> IMMEDIATELY.

Ike was stunned. He immediately suffered his first and only attack of shingles, a painful skin disease often associated with extreme nervousness or anxiety. Lying flat on his back, he wrote Gerow a three-page, single-spaced letter wrestling with his desire to remain with troops but not wishing to turn down an opportunity to be at the center of action in Washington. Eisenhower believed the letter to be the most important he had ever written,[17] and in the end he left the decision to Gerow.[18]

As the attack of shingles suggests, Ike was torn. With the possibility of war on the horizon, he would have liked nothing better than to be in War Plans. He was confident of his ability to lead troops, but War Department policy explicitly required longer service with his regiment if he was to be considered for promotion to general officer. Gerow understood.

> AFTER CAREFUL CONSIDERATION OF CONTENTS OF
> YOUR LETTER, I HAVE WITHDRAWN MY REQUEST FOR
> YOUR DETAIL TO WAR PLANS DIVISION. REGRET OUR
> SERVICE TOGETHER MUST BE POSTPONED.[19]

Eisenhower took Gerow's decision philosophically. "I'd hate to think that, in trying to explain to you a situation that has been tossed in my teeth more than once, all I accomplished was to pass up something I *wanted* to do, in favor of something I thought I *ought* to do," he replied.[20]

Mamie, of course, was brokenhearted when she learned the opportunity to go to Washington had fallen through. "I didn't know this in advance," Ike wrote Mark Clark, "or I might have given up my struggle to stay with the regiment"—a remarkable admission that speaks volumes about the lack of intimacy that apparently characterized the Eisenhowers' domestic life. Ike told Clark that he had an ulterior motive in wanting to stay with the 15th Infantry, "and that is my hope that I may get one of the armored regiments next spring. I realize this is a very slim possibility and I'm not counting on it at all, but I still think it is a good thing for me to get in at least one year of regimental duty. That year will not be up until the middle of February."[21]

Ike said much the same to his friend Everett Hughes.[*] "I am delighted to stay with troops for two reasons. (1) I like it. (2) I want to convince the most ritualistic-minded guy in the whole d—— Army that I get along with John Soldier."[22]

As Eisenhower's comment suggests, it was still business as usual for many in the Army. Despite the fall of France in June and the ongoing Battle of Britain, the possibility of war seemed remote. "The mass of officers and men lacked any sense of urgency," Ike recalled. "Athletics, recreation, and entertainment took precedence in most units. Some of the officers, in the long years of peace, had worn for themselves deep ruts of professional routine within which they were sheltered from vexing new ideas and troublesome problems. Urgent directives from above could not eliminate an apathy that had its roots in comfort, blindness, and wishful thinking."[23]

In Washington, it was anything but business as usual. In June, on the eve of the Republican convention, President Roosevelt dumped Harry Woodring and Charles Edison, his somnambulant secretaries of war and Navy, and added Republicans Henry L. Stimson and Frank Knox to the cabinet—not only reaching across party lines, but bringing in two of the nation's leading advocates of preparedness.

---

* Everett S. Hughes (USMA, 1908), a charter member of Club Eisenhower at the Wyoming, was an ordnance officer on the War Department General Staff. When Ike assumed command in North Africa, Hughes accompanied him as his deputy chief of staff. In 1945, Hughes became the Army's inspector general, and later served as chief of ordnance.

Stimson, who had been secretary of state under Herbert Hoover and secretary of war under William Howard Taft, was the principal spokesman of the GOP's eastern establishment. Knox, publisher of the *Chicago Daily News,* had been Alf Landon's running mate in 1936 and was a vigorous supporter of a peacetime draft for the armed services.

Stimson brought a new broom to Washington. His assistants, Judge Robert Patterson of the United States Court of Appeals; John J. McCloy, managing partner of the Wall Street law firm of Cravath, Swaine, and Moore; and Robert Lovett, senior partner at the investment house of Brown Brothers Harriman, were dedicated Republicans who had never voted for Franklin Roosevelt. But they were hard-driving administrators who revitalized the War Department—a building Lovett characterized as "so full of dead wood that it was an absolute firetrap."[24]

General Marshall, who had been installed as chief of staff nine months earlier, was already trimming deadwood root and branch. His first target was the bloated square division of World War I.[25] As early as 1920, General Pershing had urged the square division be scrapped in favor of a 15,000-man "triangular" structure of three regiments, which he believed would be easier to control and more suitable to open, mobile warfare.[*] Military traditionalists such as Lieutenant General Hugh Drum, the senior officer on active service, fought the change tooth and nail,[26] but General Marshall pressed ahead. By October 1, 1940, the Army's nine regular divisions had been converted to the triangular structure, and the remaining National Guard divisions followed a few months later.[27]

The Army's equipment was equally antiquated. Like the square division, most of the stocks on hand dated from World War I. The basic infantry weapon was the 1903 bolt-action Springfield, a rifle of re-

---

[*] Unlike the square division, which was designed for the attrition of head-on frontal assault, the triangular division (devised by the Germans) emphasized maneuver and flexibility. Every echelon within the triangular division, from the rifle company to the battalion, the regiment, and the division itself, possessed three maneuver elements, plus a means of fire support. One of the maneuver elements could fix the enemy, a second could find his flank, while a third remained in reserve.

markable accuracy but little sustained firepower. Its replacement, the semiautomatic Garand M1, would not become widely available until 1942. The artillery still relied on a modified version of the French 75 mm as its basic fieldpiece; vehicles were in short supply; and the United States did not have a heavy tank, even on the drawing board. From 1936 to 1939, the Army high command had systematically reduced the War Department's meager development funds, preferring "proven" World War I models to "needless expenditures for unessential research."[28] General J. O. Mauborgne, the Army's chief signal officer, complained that it took twenty-seven months just to complete the paperwork for a new item of equipment—and six years to get it into production.[29] Marshall, aided by Judge Patterson as undersecretary, took Army procurement in hand. Military purchasing officers, many of whom were temperamentally incapable of moving with the speed that mobilization required, were replaced, and Major General Brehon Somervell—an officer of unrelenting purposefulness—was brought in by Marshall as the Army's chief logistics officer (G-4) to impart a sense of urgency.[*]

But it was the Army's personnel system that required the greatest overhaul. In August 1940, Congress authorized the War Department to call up the nation's 300,000 national guardsmen and reservists for twelve months of federal service. On September 16, the first peacetime draft in American history became law. Sixteen million men between the ages of twenty-one and thirty-five were registered, and they were inducted into the service at the rate of 50,000 a month. The Army, which had numbered 189,839 when Eisenhower returned from Manila, would top 1.4 million by mid-1941.[30]

To find competent officers for an expanding Army, and to separate from the service those who were not competent, was one of Mar-

* Somervell, a career engineer officer, had served in Mexico with Pershing and won a Distinguished Service Cross for gallantry in France. In 1935 he took charge of the massive, highly combustible WPA program in New York City and ran it successfully for four years. His no-nonsense dedication and abrasive straightforwardness earned the respect of radicals and reactionaries alike as well as the lifelong confidence of Harry Hopkins. Lieutenant General Henry Aurand, one of Somervell's key subordinates in World War II, called him "a man without a drop of human kindness." Jean Edward Smith, *Lucius D. Clay* 111.

shall's biggest problems. Initially his hands were tied. The Army's seniority-based promotion system had been put in place by statute and could only be changed by legislative action. In June 1940, under prodding from Marshall and Stimson, Congress agreed to promote all officers one rank, based on time in grade. Eisenhower received his promotion to colonel on March 6, 1941—roughly two years ahead of schedule. In October 1940, Congress authorized additional temporary promotions to general officer. But it was not until the summer of 1941 that Marshall received authority from Congress to retire officers who had outlived their usefulness and to promote junior officers of exceptional ability without regard to seniority.[31] Even at that late date, the seniority system had staunch defenders on Capitol Hill. The measure that gave Marshall the authority to circumvent it was concealed as a rider to the Army's annual appropriation bill.[32]

The influx of guardsmen and draftees brought new life to Fort Lewis. On November 30, 1940, Eisenhower was appointed chief of staff of the 3rd Infantry Division—the 15th Infantry's parent unit. Ike's personnel designation was "General Staff with Troops," which kept the clock running on his required troop duty. Three months later he was named chief of staff of IX Corps, also at Fort Lewis. The assignment was identical to the posting that General Krueger had sought for Ike six months earlier. This time, rather than holding that he was too junior for such a position, the War Department promoted Eisenhower to colonel instead.

"It is a grand compliment," Mamie wrote her parents on March 11, 1941. "We knew a week ago when Gen. Joyce [Major General Kenyon A. Joyce, commanding IX Corps] sent a telegram to Washington and have been sitting on needles and pins. It was so very secret. It may mean that we have to move up in the circle where the General's house is. . . . I'm so glad for Ike. Am on my way to play Ma-Jong with Mrs. Joyce. Just wanted to let you know."[33]

Kenyon A. Joyce, who assumed command of IX Corps in the spring of 1941, was one of the last legendary cavalry commanders in the United States Army. He had enlisted as a private during the Spanish-American War, fought with the 3rd Cavalry in the Philippines, and had been severely wounded in France. From 1933 to 1937 he commanded the 3rd Cavalry at Fort Myer (George Patton was his

Eisenhower as IX Corps chief of staff, 1940.

executive officer), and before arriving at Fort Lewis had commanded the 1st Cavalry Division at Fort Bliss, Texas. Joyce personified the panache of the horse cavalry. He was a superb leader of troops, a shrewd judge of character, and a commander who kept his eye on the big picture and did not fret the details. "I am finding this job most intriguing and interesting," Ike wrote after his first month as chief of staff. "General Joyce is a swell commander and a fine person to work for."[34]

Eisenhower served with Joyce less than four months. But he witnessed firsthand the art of direct command. "The commanding General's method of operation is to announce policies and major decisions in definite terms and then to require his Chief of Staff to see to their execution," Ike wrote in a memo to his successor. "Daily you will find that the General spends long periods with the troops. General

Joyce does not read long directives, regulations and circulars. He expects his Chief of Staff to absorb the essentials and to keep him informed." Ike added that Joyce was always interested in uniforms, saluting, and the conduct of the troops in public. "These subjects are important to him as outward signs of real discipline; and he insists that our big job is to inculcate in all ranks a conception and practice of fundamental discipline."[35]

In an intellectual sense, Fox Conner had been Ike's role model. But when it came to the actual command of troops, it was Kenyon Joyce. When General Joyce reached the mandatory retirement age in 1943, Eisenhower brought him to the European Theater and appointed him president of the Allied Control Council for Italy—a post Joyce held for the remainder of the war. When Joyce died in January 1960, President Eisenhower and Mamie attended his funeral service at Fort Myer.

In June 1941, the course of the war changed dramatically. On June 22, Hitler launched Operation BARBAROSSA—the invasion of the Soviet Union. At the time, Eisenhower was on maneuvers with IX Corps at the Hunter Liggett military reservation, south of Monterey. The German attack made little impact. But two days later, as Ike and General Joyce were standing on a hillside awaiting a report from one of the divisions, a messenger told Joyce that the War Department wanted him on the telephone. After taking the call, Joyce called Ike to his side. "Start packing," he said. "Go back to Fort Lewis for orders, which will direct you to go to San Antonio as chief of staff, Third Army."[36]

Eisenhower could scarcely believe it. The United States was divided into four tactical army areas. Third Army (Southern Command) stretched from Florida to New Mexico with a present-for-duty strength of 270,000 men. Lieutenant General Walter Krueger had recently assumed command (moving up from VIII Corps), and once again he wanted Ike to be his chief of staff—a position that called for a brigadier general. This time Krueger bypassed the chief of infantry and wrote directly to his old friend and comrade George Marshall.*

---

* In 1901, Marshall and Krueger served together as young lieutenants in G Company of the 30th Infantry in the Philippines, and later (1908–10) were the only

Krueger told Marshall that he wanted a chief of staff "possessing broad vision, progressive ideas, a thorough grasp of the magnitude of the problems involved in handling an army, and lots of initiative and resourcefulness. Lieutenant Colonel Dwight D. Eisenhower, Infantry, is such a man." Marshall agreed. Whatever objections the adjutant general or the chief of infantry might have had were ignored or overruled.[37]

Ike reported for duty at Fort Sam Houston on July 1, 1941. It was his and Mamie's twenty-fifth wedding anniversary, and they were back at the post where their married life had begun. Instead of a two-room suite in Ike's BOQ, they moved into one of the grand five-bedroom brick houses on Artillery Row. For their anniversary, Ike gave Mamie an elegant platinum watch encrusted in diamonds that he had ordered from Tiffany—and which he paid for from money earned in the Philippines.[38] Mamie wore the watch for the rest of her life. That same day their son John, joined by some 550 equally bewildered classmates, entered his plebe year at West Point. John had won a competitive senatorial appointment from Kansas, and, as he recalled, the ethnic and racial composition of his class was virtually identical to that of his father's thirty years earlier.[39]

As Third Army chief of staff, Eisenhower was entitled to an executive assistant and an orderly. As his executive assistant—military nomenclature for a gofer, aide, and man Friday—Ike retained Captain Ernest R. Lee, known to everyone as "Tex." Lee, a former Metropolitan Life insurance salesman and sales manager for a Chevrolet dealership in San Antonio, was already working at Third Army headquarters. Eisenhower quizzed him for several days, liked his responses, and kept him on. Lee had a breezy, unflappable style, lacked "attitude," and was profoundly loyal to those with whom he worked. He was also a go-getter. Ike and Lee hit it off, and "Tex" became the first member of Eisenhower's personal staff.[40]

The second member of Ike's official "family" was his orderly, Pri-

---

two lieutenants on the faculty of the Command and General Staff School at Leavenworth. Krueger served as the Army's assistant chief of staff for operations (G-3) from 1936 to 1938, when he was succeeded by Marshall. Their friendship ran deep, and they shared a mutual respect. See Forrest C. Pogue, 1 *George C. Marshall* 82–83, 107 (New York: Viking Press, 1963).

In World War II, General Walter Krueger commanded Sixth Army in the Pacific.

vate First Class Michael J. "Mickey" McKeogh—who responded to a help-wanted notice Mamie had posted on the Fort Sam Houston bulletin board. A young draftee from Corona on Long Island, Mickey had worked as a bellhop at New York's posh Plaza hotel for seven years and was wise beyond his years in the ways of the world. His parents were Irish immigrants, and his father had risen to the rank of sergeant in the New York Police Department before his death in 1935. An orderly's job, Mickey thought, was "right down his alley," and like Lee he remained with Ike throughout the war.[41]

Mickey was loyal beyond the call of duty. In December 1943, Eisenhower decided to make a quick visit to the Tunisian front, and instructed Mickey (by then a sergeant) to bring an overnight bag for him to the airfield. "Flying conditions were deplorable," Ike recalled, and he told Mickey there was no need for him to make the flight. Mickey insisted on going. "Sir," he said, "my mother wrote me that my job in this war was to take care of you. 'If General Eisenhower doesn't come back from this war, don't you dare come back.' "[42]

Lieutenant General Walter Krueger, Eisenhower's new commander, was an amalgam of Fox Conner and Kenyon Joyce—a military intellectual who relished leading troops in the field. Universally regarded as "a soldier's soldier," Krueger was a combat infantryman at heart. He was also widely respected as one of the Army's best educated and most perceptive officers, had taught at both the Army and the Navy war colleges, spoke three foreign languages, and as a young officer had translated into English the leading German military texts of the period.[43]

Born into a military family in Prussia, Krueger was nine years older than Ike and at the top of his game. His widowed mother had immigrated to St. Louis when Krueger was eight years old. He enlisted in the Army at seventeen, served with distinction in Cuba, and fought in the Philippine insurrection, with Pershing in Mexico, and in the tank corps during World War I. Although he still spoke with a trace of a German accent, he would be the first officer in American history to rise through the ranks from private soldier to four-star general—a rank he achieved commanding Sixth Army in the Pacific. Eisenhower wrote in retrospect that few officers were physically tougher or more active. "Relentlessly driving himself, he had little need of driving others—they were quick to follow his example."[44]

Krueger was also self-effacing and shunned the limelight. His stern Prussian presence was often intimidating, yet he possessed a robust sense of humor. When he was commanding the 6th Infantry Regiment at Jefferson Barracks in 1933, his adjutant scribbled a covering note to a stack of court-martial proceedings stating that "a crime wave" appeared to have broken out in Missouri. Krueger wrote back, "Captain Wheatley, I do not expect to get all the virtues of mankind for thirty dollars a month."[45]

Krueger's concern for his troops was legendary. Once, during a rainstorm on Leyte in 1945, Krueger found the sentry guarding his command post wet to the skin, cold, and shivering. He ordered the soldier inside and told him to towel off and change into one of Krueger's dry uniforms. When a subordinate asked why, Krueger said, "Son, I've walked many an hour on sentry duty—wet and cold. I know how he felt out there."[46]

The relationship between a commanding general and his chief of staff is a crucial ingredient in military success. The commanding general must have confidence that his chief of staff will translate his decisions into action, and the chief of staff must not burden the commander with excessive detail.* The borderline between their responsibilities is fluid and will always depend on the personalities involved. Eisenhower and Joyce worked seamlessly together, and Ike and Krueger proved to be an even better fit. Krueger had commanded every unit in the Army from a rifle squad during the Spanish-American War to a division, a corps, and now a field army. He was equally experienced at the highest staff level, having been the Army's chief of operations (G-3) from 1936 to 1938. More than most of his contemporaries, he knew the requirements of modern war, had studied German military developments relentlessly, and possessed the gift of an experienced commander to motivate men to action.

Eisenhower's high-level staff experience proved a perfect complement. "Luckily I've spent most of my life in large headquarters, so am not overpowered by the mass of detail," he wrote George Moseley. Ike's approachable nature bridged another gap for Krueger. "Everyone comes [into my office] to discuss his troubles," he told Moseley. "I'm often astonished how much better they seem to work after they have had a chance to recite their woes."[47]

And there were plenty of woes to go around. Aside from the Army's overall expansion, General Marshall had laid on a string of large-scale

* As a reader of military history, I have always been struck by the relations between Field Marshal Gerd von Rundstedt and Erich von Manstein, his chief of staff—the team that planned the German breakthrough in the Ardennes in 1940 and then led Army Group A to victory. Manstein writes that patience was not one of von Rundstedt's virtues. Their headquarters was awash in paperwork but "thanks to a very proper unwritten law in the German Army that the general commanding be kept free of all minor detail, v. Rundstedt was hardly affected and was able to take a long walk every morning on the Rhein promenade. On returning to his desk to await the oral reports which he daily received from myself and other members of the staff, he would fill the time by reading a detective thriller. Like many other prominent people, he found welcome distraction in such literature, but since he was rather shy about this taste of his, he regularly read the novel in an open drawer [of his desk] which could be quickly closed whenever anyone came in to see him." Field Marshal Erich von Manstein, *Lost Victories* 69–70, Anthony G. Powell, ed. and trans. (Novato, Calif.: Presidio Press, 1982).

maneuvers at the division, corps, and field army level to test the nation's military preparedness. Worse perhaps, the summer of 1941 was a bleak one for the Allies. German panzer divisions pressed eastward toward Leningrad, Moscow, and Kiev; Erwin Rommel's Afrika Korps stood at the Egyptian border; the Battle of the Atlantic was going badly; and the situation in the Pacific continued to deteriorate. On July 23, Japanese forces completed their occupation of Indochina, acquiring the use of eight strategic airfields and the naval bases at Saigon and Cam Rahn Bay. Three days later President Roosevelt froze all Japanese assets in the United States, ordered the Philippine Army placed under U.S. command, and recalled Douglas MacArthur to active duty as the overall commander of American forces in the Far East.[48]

"Last night's paper carried the news of General MacArthur's appointment to command all Philippine Forces," Eisenhower wrote his old friend Wade Haislip, who was now the Army's assistant chief of staff for personnel (G-1) in Washington.

> In many ways I was a thorn in his side. I hope and believe he'll never ever consider submitting my name as one of his prospective assistants. However, no one can ever tell which way he is going to jump, and it would not surprise me in the slightest to learn that he had turned in my name to the Department. In any such unlikely event I want you to argue and prove that I'm *positively indispensable* here.
>
> I worked for him long enough! I put in four hard years out there, to say nothing of the War Department tour. If General MacArthur keeps [Richard K.] Sutherland, he'll never mention my name, because my opinion of that buckaroo went lower and lower the longer I knew him.

Ike asked Haislip to confirm the paperwork pertaining to his position at Third Army. "In the meantime, don't send me back to guguland, no matter how wonderful the possibilities may *appear* to be. . . . P.S. I'm *not* a Filipino."[49]*

---

* Haislip replied by return mail that MacArthur had made Sutherland his chief of staff and had not asked for Ike. "I'm happy the 'Field Marshal' didn't recall my

The great Louisiana maneuvers of 1941 were the largest ever conducted on American soil. In the end, nearly five hundred thousand men participated—almost half of the Army's combat strength. "I want the mistakes made down in Louisiana, not over in Europe," General Marshall told doubting members of Congress.[50] Marshall had witnessed firsthand how ill-prepared American officers had been in World War I, how unfamiliar they were with commanding large troop formations in combat, how lacking the coordination had been between different branches and services, and how amateurish U.S. efforts had been initially. Large-scale maneuvers, Marshall believed, were a "combat college for troop leading," and he was determined to bring the Army to readiness as quickly as possible. Among other things, the maneuvers were designed to test new equipment and doctrine, to perfect techniques of supply and support, and above all to give commanders experience in handling large bodies of troops under simulated battle conditions. It was a means, Marshall believed, to identify younger officers capable of increased responsibility, and to eliminate commanders who were manifestly unfit.[51]

The United States was a latecomer to full-blown army maneuvers. As early as the era of Frederick the Great the nations of Europe regularly assembled their armies for large-scale maneuvers, not to train individual soldiers (who, for the most part, were regulars and already highly trained), but to familiarize division, corps, and army commanders and their staffs with the techniques of command and control. After the Franco-Prussian War, the maneuvers became annual events. The Austrian archduke Franz Ferdinand, heir presumptive to the Hapsburg throne, happened to visit Sarajevo in June 1914 while observing the summer maneuvers of the Austrian Army nearby.

During the interwar years the United States experimented with summer encampments for National Guard and reserve divisions, but the emphasis was on individual instruction rather than realistic simulation of major engagements.[52] General Marshall ordered the first round of corps and army maneuvers in the summer of 1940. In 1941, he escalated the exercise to culminate in the clash of two field armies,

---

name," said Eisenhower. "While I felt reasonably certain he would not make a request for me, I didn't want to take chances." DDE to Haislip, August 1941, EL.

pitting one against the other in the pine barrens and bayous of Louisiana. Second Army, commanded by General Ben Lear, would take on General Krueger's Third Army in an area that stretched from Shreveport south to Lake Charles, and from Jasper, Texas, east to the Mississippi River—some thirty thousand square miles that for two weeks would become home to 472,000 troops—the densest concentration of military force in United States history.[53]

The clash of armies was preceded by maneuvers at the corps level. Krueger and Eisenhower left Fort Sam Houston for Lake Charles on August 11, 1941. Corps maneuvers commenced on the seventeenth. "All the oldtimers here say that we are going into a God-awful spot, to live with mud, malaria, mosquitoes and misery," Eisenhower wrote Gerow in Washington. "But I like to go to the field, so I'm not much concerned about it."[54]

The battle between the Second and Third armies kicked off at 0500 hours on September 15, 1941. Lear's Second (Red) Army, some eight divisions, including the nation's only two armored divisions, was arrayed east of the Red River. Its instructions were to cross the river and destroy the Third (Blue) Army, which was assembled in the vicinity of Lake Charles. Krueger's instructions were essentially the opposite. Blue Army (ten divisions but no armor) was to advance toward the Red River, destroy the invading army, and push into enemy territory.

From the beginning, Lear mishandled his forces, particularly his armor. An old horse cavalryman (Lear had won a bronze medal as a member of the United States' three-day-event team at the 1912 Olympics), he used his tanks as infantry support, was slow getting his troops across the Red River, and was unprepared for the speed with which Krueger moved forward. On the third day of battle, the greater part of Second Army was still east of the river and had not made contact with the enemy. Krueger, on the other hand, had advanced with nine divisions (three corps) on line, wheeled right, and rolled over the units of Second Army that had crossed the river. "We're attacking all along the line," Ike wrote General Joyce.[55]

Krueger exercised fingertip control of his troops, shifting divisions to exploit gaps in Second Army's front. Lear's armor was rendered impotent, partially because of the antitank weapons Krueger brought to bear, but even more because of Second Army's failure to use them aggressively. After four days of battle, with Lear's forces nearly surrounded, the umpires brought the first phase of the exercise to a halt.

Phase two began a week later, with the roles reversed. George Patton's 2nd Armored Division was transferred to Third Army, and Krueger was ordered to advance on Shreveport and capture it. Lear was told to defend the city. Krueger now enjoyed numerical superiority, but Lear had the advantage of fighting on the defensive. He did not have to defeat Third Army, but simply prevent it from taking Shreveport within the five days that had been allotted.

Just as the exercise was about to begin, the tail end of a category two hurricane hit the maneuver area. The eye of the storm—with winds exceeding one hundred miles per hour—passed over Houston, Texas, and poor weather persisted throughout the following week. "The Army got a good drenching," Ike wrote Gerow on September 25, 1941. "Yet when the problem started at noon yesterday, everybody was full of vim and ready to go. I do not know how long this problem will last, but I can assure you that in Armies of about a quarter of a million you don't do things in a hurry."[56]

Krueger's Blue Army pressed north, again three corps on line, his right flank anchored on the Red River, his left flank on the Sabine, and Shreveport one hundred miles away. This time Lear's caution worked to Second Army's advantage. He fell back in an orderly manner and declined to give battle, while his engineers blew every bridge and culvert in Krueger's path. High water slowed Third Army's advance to a crawl. On the third day, still more than sixty miles from Shreveport, and still not having made contact with Lear's main force, Krueger launched his armor, cavalry, and mounted infantry on a three-hundred-mile end run around Second Army's flank. Spearheaded by Patton's 2nd Armored Division, the troops from the Blue Army crossed the Sabine into Texas and headed north. Patton covered two hundred miles in twenty-four hours, recrossed the Sabine above Shreveport the following day, and was driving virtually unopposed on the city from the north.[*] "Had it been real war," wrote Hanson Baldwin for *The New York Times,* "Lear's force would have been annihilated."[57] Third Army's main force was still twenty-five miles south of Shreveport, but with Patton already on the city's northern outskirts, General Leslie McNair, the chief umpire, terminated the exercise.[58]

Krueger outgeneraled Lear throughout both phases of the Louisiana maneuvers. His grasp of the strategic requirements, and the command and control he exercised over Third Army, were nearly flawless. The aggressive, offensive-style defense that he waged in phase one, and the use of his armor and mobile forces to flank Lear out of his position in phase two, ran counter to the received wisdom of conventional Army thinking. Eisenhower's role has been exaggerated. He performed ably as Third Army's chief of staff, but command responsibility rested with Krueger. To credit Ike with Third Army's success, as many commentators have done, is like crediting Walter Bedell Smith (Eisenhower's highly efficient chief of staff) with D-Day, or Erich von Manstein rather than von Rundstedt with the 1940 German breakthrough in the Ardennes.

In his memoirs, Ike acknowledged that the credit belonged to Krueger.[59] His son John agreed. "Why Dad got so much credit for Third Army's performance . . . I do not understand, because he was not the commanding general. But Krueger had a tendency to take a back seat, and I guess Dad had more visibility. Dad was not one that tried to shove himself in front . . . but he received much of the credit anyway."[60] In retrospect, that is not difficult to understand. Partially it is a case of *post hoc, ergo propter hoc.* After Ike achieved fame as supreme commander in Europe, it was natural for writers and biographers to embellish his accomplishments in Louisiana. Also, while Krueger exercised hands-on command of Third Army, it fell to Eisenhower to conduct the twice-daily briefings for the press. To the journalists covering the maneuvers, Ike became the face of Third Army. Newsmen such as Hanson Baldwin, Richard C. Hottelet, and

---

[*] During the long motor march, Patton refueled his vehicles at commercial filling stations, paying for the gas out of his own pocket. Carlo D'Este, *Patton: A Genius for War* 396 (New York: HarperCollins, 1995).

Eric Sevareid remembered Eisenhower and had no hesitation about touting his talent.

Insofar as doctrine is concerned, the maneuvers were a mixed bag. Traditionalists continued to believe that firepower trumped mobility, while armor advocates pointed to Patton's whirlwind flanking movement as the future way of battle.[61] In terms of logistics and supply, the maneuvers helped put in place the wartime coordination that distinguished the United States Army in every theater. Lieutenant Colonel LeRoy Lutes, who handled the supply effort of Third Army, became the Army's chief of distribution during World War II and was ultimately promoted to lieutenant general. Lutes ensured that American forces always had more of everything than they might possibly need.[62] The major accomplishment of the great Louisiana maneuvers, aside from the experience it provided for high command, was in the field of personnel. Of the forty-two division, corps, and army commanders who took part in the exercise, thirty-one were relieved or shunted aside.[63] On the positive side, officers who performed well—Patton, Omar Bradley, Terry Allen, William H. Simpson, Eisenhower, and Lutes—were tapped for greater responsibility.

The final critique of the maneuver was conducted by Mark Clark, the deputy chief umpire. As he spoke he was handed a telegram from the War Department listing the names submitted by President Roosevelt to the Senate for promotion to general officer. "I scanned the list," said Clark, "and Eisenhower was number three. I read out the names, but when I came to Ike's name I deliberately skipped it. I tell you, you could hear a pin drop." Clark dismissed the audience, and Eisenhower was obviously crestfallen. As the officers filed from the room, Clark called them to order once more. "I forgot one name—Dwight D. Eisenhower." Amid the general laughter, Clark recalls that Ike broke into a broad smile. "I'll get you for this, you sonofabitch."[64]

Mamie remembers that Ike's promotion to general was the greatest thrill of their married life.[65] Back at Fort Sam Houston, with Mamie and her parents present, Krueger pinned the single stars of a brigadier general on Eisenhower's epaulets. Ike had reached a goal he never expected to attain.[66] "The nicest part of all," he wrote to a friend, "is to be assured by friends that the War Department was not too d—— dumb in making the selection."[67]

Eisenhower said later that the Louisiana maneuvers

> provided me with lessons and experience that I appreciated more and more as subsequent months rolled by. . . . October and November were as busy as the months preceding the maneuvers. Measures to correct defects revealed in Louisiana were begun at unit level; in many cases the return movement offered an immediate opportunity. Some officers had of necessity to be relieved from command; controversies and rumors, following on this step, required quick action to prevent injury to morale.[68]

On Sunday, December 7, 1941, Ike went to his office early to catch up on his paperwork. He returned to his quarters about noon, had lunch with Mamie, and went upstairs for a short nap. Scarcely had he gone to sleep before the phone rang with an urgent call from Tex Lee. The Japanese had attacked Pearl Harbor, said Lee, and America's Pacific Fleet had been destroyed.

"Within an hour," Ike recalled, "orders began pouring into Third Army headquarters from the War Department." Antiaircraft batteries were dispatched to the West Coast; antisabotage orders were put in place; border patrols and port security were reinforced; and major troop formations were alerted for possible movement should the Japanese attack the Pacific mainland. "Immediacy of movement was the keynote. Normal channels of administration were abandoned. A single telephone call would start an infantry regiment across the country."[69]

On December 8, President Roosevelt went to Capitol Hill to ask for a declaration of war against Japan. "December seventh," said the president, is "a date which will live in infamy."[70] On December 11, Germany and Italy declared war on the United States. The following day, the phone on Ike's desk that connected Third Army directly to the War Department began to ring.

"Is that you, Ike?" asked Bedell Smith, secretary of the general staff.

"Yes."

"The Chief [General Marshall] says for you to hop a plane and get up here right away. Tell your boss that formal orders will come through later."[71] Eisenhower was being summoned to Washington to join the War Plans Division of the Army general staff.

Eisenhower had been with troops almost two years. His ratings were consistently "superior." Colonel Jesse Ladd, commanding the 15th Infantry, called Ike "an enthusiastic, aggressive officer of the highest type. One of the few Army officers whom I consider deserves a straight rating of superior."[72] Major General Charles Thompson, commanding the 3rd Infantry Division, said Eisenhower was "affable, energetic, dynamic, zealous, original, loyal, capable, dependable, and outstanding."[73] Kenyon Joyce believed that Ike was "one of the ablest officers in the Army. *This officer is thoroughly qualified for division command at this time.*" (At the time Eisenhower was a colonel; a division is commanded by a major general.)[74] General Krueger, on Ike's final report, rated him second among the 170 general officers with whom he was acquainted.[75]

# EIGHT

# With Marshall in Washington

Tempers are short! There are lots of amateur
strategists on the job—and prima donnas
everywhere. I'd give anything to be back in
the field.

—DWIGHT D. EISENHOWER,
*January 4, 1942*

GENERAL MARSHALL KNEW Eisenhower by reputation. They
had met three times, but only briefly: first in Paris, where they discussed Pershing's memoirs; then in January 1940 during California
maneuvers; and most recently in Louisiana. It was in Louisiana that
Marshall first began to consider Ike as a possible chief of the Army's
War Plans Division. "Toward the end of the Louisiana maneuvers,"
General Walter Krueger recalled, "General Marshall asked me whom
I regarded as best fitted to head the War Plans Division, which I had
headed several years before, and I named Eisenhower, though I was
loath to lose him."[1] Marshall and Krueger had served together for
forty years, and Marshall trusted Krueger's judgment. But before
turning War Plans over to Ike, he wanted to see for himself. When
Eisenhower reported for duty at the War Department on Sunday
morning, December 14, 1941, he was assigned a desk well down the
War Plans pecking order and told that General Marshall wanted to see
him immediately.

"It was the first time in my life that I talked to him for more than
two minutes at a time," Ike remembered.[2] Marshall made no effort to

put him at ease. There was no salutation and no small talk. Marshall outlined the grim situation in the Pacific. America's battleship fleet would be out of action for many months; the Navy's carriers (which had been at sea at the time of the Japanese attack on Pearl Harbor) lacked sufficient escort vessels; Hawaii lay open to attack. The two remaining Allied battleships in the western Pacific, the Royal Navy's *Prince of Wales* and *Repulse,* had been sunk near Singapore by Japanese airplanes. Japan's Army had landed in strength in Malaya and the Dutch East Indies, and was marching from Indochina into Burma. In the Philippines, what limited air strength there was had been caught on the ground and badly damaged by Japanese bombers; the naval facility at Cavite, just outside Manila, was a mass of rubble; and the total strength of the American garrison numbered fewer than thirty-two thousand. The Philippine Army, poorly trained and badly equipped, totaled one hundred thousand, most of whom were reservists recently called to active duty. Marshall said the evidence indicated that the Japanese intended to overrun the Philippines as rapidly as possible.[3]

"What should be our general line of action?" he asked Eisenhower. Ike had spent four years in Manila with MacArthur, and knew the situation on the ground. Marshall was testing him. As one biographer has written, "Marshall wanted to know who could do the job for him and who could not, and he wanted to know it immediately." Eisenhower's answer would tell Marshall whether he was up to the challenge.[4]

Ike was stunned. "I thought for a second and, hoping I was showing a poker face, answered, 'Give me a few hours.' "

"All right," said Marshall.[5]

Eisenhower recognized the enormity of the problem—as well as the fact that he was under scrutiny. "If I was to be of any service to General Marshall, I would have to earn his confidence. My first answer would have to be unimpeachable, and the answer would have to be prompt. [It] should be short, emphatic, and based on reasoning in which I honestly believed. No oratory or glittering generality."[6]

Three hours later, Ike marched back for a second interview. His thoughts were contained in a three-page triple-spaced memorandum that he had typed out but kept in his pocket.[7] Marshall preferred his briefings conducted without notes. That compelled briefing officers to be concise, and Ike was.

General, it will be a long time before major reinforcements can go to the Philippines, longer than the garrison
can hold out with any driblet of assistance, if the enemy
commits major forces to their reduction. The people of
China, of the Philippines, of the Dutch East Indies will be
watching us. They may excuse failure but they will not
excuse abandonment. We must do what we can. Our base
must be Australia, and we must start at once to expand it
and to secure our communications to it. We must take
great risks and spend any amount of money required.[8]

Marshall appeared satisfied. "Eisenhower," he said, "this Department
is filled with able men who analyze their problems well but feel compelled to always bring them to me for final solution. I must have
assistants who will solve their own problems and tell me later what
they have done. The Philippines are your responsibility. Do your
best to save them."[9]

As Eisenhower recalled, "I resolved then and there to do my own
work to the best of my ability and report to the General only situations of obvious necessity or when he personally sent for me."[10] Three
days before, Ike had been chief of staff of Third Army in San Antonio. He was now Marshall's deputy overseeing America's military
effort in the Philippines. Eisenhower stepped up to the responsibility. He and Brehon Somervell, the Army's chief of supply, became a
two-man team working against time. "I met with Somervell every
day," Ike recalled, "in a desperate hope of uncovering some new
method of approach to a problem that defied solution. General Marshall maintained an intensive interest in everything we did and frequently initiated measures calculated to give us some help. In the
final result all our efforts proved feeble enough, but I do not yet see
what more could have been done."[11]

Eisenhower's ability to act without consulting him impressed
Marshall. Ike's deployment of the Cunard liner *Queen Mary* is an example. The British had converted the eighty-thousand-ton luxury
vessel—as well as her sister ship, the *Queen Elizabeth*—into troop-
ships, each capable of carrying fourteen thousand men. When the
*Queen Mary* arrived in New York in January 1942, Eisenhower loaded

the better part of an infantry division aboard and dispatched the ship without escort to Australia. The *Queen Mary* sailed at a cruising speed of almost thirty knots, which Ike believed provided a margin of safety from possible U-boat attack.[*]

The voyage was a long one, and the *Queen* put in to Rio de Janeiro to refuel. It was spotted by an Italian agent who radioed Rome that the vessel, "with about 15,000 soldiers aboard," had left port and was steaming eastward across the Atlantic. "For the next week we lived in terror," said Ike.[12] When the ship arrived safely in Melbourne, the War Plans Division breathed a collective sigh of relief. "This was the kind of thing we kept from General Marshall. There was no use burdening his mind with the worries that we were forced to carry to bed with us. He had enough of his own."[13]

Eisenhower assumed General Marshall was unaware of the risk he had run. But when he informed him that the *Queen Mary* had arrived safely in Australia, Marshall said, "I received that radio intercept [from Rio] the same time you did. I was hoping you might not see it and so I said nothing to you until I knew the outcome."[14]

Eisenhower brought a unique set of skills to War Plans. In addition to his recent experience in the Philippines, he had served directly with the Army's senior leadership for the past twenty years. For six years he had worked with Fox Conner and George Moseley, the intellectual kingpins of the interwar Army. He was with Pershing for two years, and had served with MacArthur for seven. Most recently he had worked for two of the most gifted troop commanders on active duty, Kenyon Joyce and Walter Krueger. He understood the nuance of command at the highest level, as well as the reality of

---

[*] Churchill had offered the use of the *Queen Mary* and the *Queen Elizabeth* to Marshall at the ARCADIA conference in December. When General Marshall asked how many troops the ships could carry, Churchill replied that they could take 8,000 men with access to lifeboats, or 14,000 if one ignored the safety precautions. During five years of war, the *Queen Mary* and *Queen Elizabeth* safely transported more than 300,000 troops. All of the crossings were made without escorts, the vessels were fully loaded on each crossing, and never once did the ships encounter an enemy U-boat. Michael Korda, *Ike: An American Hero* 258n (New York: HarperCollins, 2007). Also see United States Department of State, *Foreign Relations of the United States: Conferences at Washington, 1941–1942, and Casablanca, 1943* 102, 192–95, 201 (Washington, D.C.: U.S. Government Printing Office, 1968).

translating orders into action in the field. Above all, he had learned to look at problems from the standpoint of high command.

Working with Marshall was a special challenge. Years before, Fox Conner had told Ike that he should try for an assignment under Marshall. "In the next war we will have to fight beside allies and George Marshall knows more about the techniques of arranging allied commands than any man I know. He is nothing short of a genius."[15]

On the surface, Ike and Marshall could not have been more different. Eisenhower made everyone feel at ease in his presence. Almost no one felt at ease in Marshall's presence. Eisenhower's grin was infectious, Marshall's visage was intimidating. Everyone (except Marshall) called Eisenhower "Ike"; no one, not even President Roosevelt, called Marshall "George." Eisenhower never forgot the name of anyone he met; Marshall had difficulty remembering the names of those closest to him. His longtime aide, Frank McCarthy, was always Frank McCart*ney*; his secretary, Miss Nason, was Miss Mason; and his second wife, Katherine, was often "Lily"—which had been his first wife's nickname.[16] Both men had terrible tempers, and Ike blew his stack frequently. Despite his anger, Marshall remained calm on the surface. Rarely, if ever, did he betray the slightest emotion. When informed at his quarters early on the morning of June 6, 1944, that the Allies had landed in France, he hung up the phone with a curt "Thank you." When Mrs. Marshall inquired whether he had asked how things were going, Marshall said he had not. "At this distance, don't you think that is Eisenhower's problem?"[17]

George Catlett Marshall was born in Uniontown, Pennsylvania, on the last day of December 1880. Like MacArthur, he was ten years older than Ike. All three men were raised by stern fathers and strong, adoring mothers who had lasting influences on their lives. Marshall had gone to the Virginia Military Institute, not West Point, and, like MacArthur, had been first captain of cadets. He was commissioned a second lieutenant of infantry in 1901, fought in the Philippines, was the honor graduate (like Eisenhower) at Leavenworth, and later taught there. In World War I, Marshall served as Fox Conner's deputy at Pershing's headquarters. When Pershing became chief of staff in 1921, Marshall became his principal military assistant. After four years with Pershing he went to China with the 15th Infantry,

General George C. Marshall.

taught at the Army War College, and served as assistant commandant and chief academic officer at the Infantry School at Fort Benning. In 1933 he assumed command of the 8th Infantry at Fort
Moultrie, South Carolina, and also became the commanding officer
of District F of the Civilian Conservation Corps (CCC), responsible
for organizing nineteen CCC camps in Florida, Georgia, and South
Carolina.

It seemed clear that Marshall was destined for high command.
But late in 1933, General MacArthur, always resentful of "the Per-
shing clique" in the Army, abruptly transferred him to what ap-
peared to be a tombstone assignment as senior adviser to the Illinois
National Guard. Marshall was fifty-three years old and still a colonel.
If not promoted to general officer shortly, he would face mandatory
retirement. Marshall's career was rescued by Pershing and Malin
Craig, who succeeded MacArthur as chief of staff. In September 1936

a new promotion board advanced Marshall to brigadier general, and in 1938 Craig brought him to Washington to head the Army's War Plans Division. Later that year Craig advanced him to deputy chief of staff. When Craig's own term as chief of staff expired in 1939, President Roosevelt, at the urging of Pershing and Harry Hopkins, reached down the Army seniority roster and appointed Marshall chief of staff, jumping thirty-three officers who were senior to him.

Despite the apparent dissimilarity, Marshall and Eisenhower were also very much alike. For twenty years the Army had been the center of each man's existence—a twenty-four-hour job, seven days a week, that made heavy demands on normal family life. Marshall's only diversion was his horses. He rode for an hour each morning before reveille. It was recreation as well as exercise, and it cleared his head for the day's work. Ike's recourse was to bridge and golf, a convivial contrast that served the same purpose.

Both men were exacting taskmasters. "General Eisenhower was not the easiest person in the world to work for," said Lucius D. Clay. "He would give you a job, and when you completed it he would give you another. The more you did, the more he asked. And if you did not measure up, you were gone. He had no tolerance for failure."[18] The same could be said for General Marshall, who was even more demanding. With Ike, there was the occasional burst of humor to lighten the load; with Marshall it was all business, all the time.

The men were also similar in bearing and appearance. They wore neatly tailored uniforms with a minimum of ornamentation. Both were six feet tall, slender but muscular, with the loping stride of former athletes. Both were chain smokers. Both knew how to delegate. When they assigned a task, they stepped aside. Subordinates were free to follow whatever course they wished to get the job done. It was the old Army at its best. General Grant would tell a division commander what he wanted done. He would not tell him how to do it. Both Marshall and Eisenhower demanded team players, rejected exhibitionists, and preferred people who could solve problems rather than create them. They expected subordinates to take responsibility, and then backed them to the hilt when they did.

From the beginning, Marshall and Eisenhower developed a

father-son relationship. But it was a very formal one. They were never "pals." To Eisenhower, Marshall was always "General." Marshall never addressed anyone by his first name.[*] Nevertheless, they shared enormous respect for each other. Eisenhower saw Marshall as remote and austere but said he was also "quick, tough, tireless, and decisive. He accepts responsibility automatically and never goes back on a subordinate."[19] Marshall's opinion of Eisenhower is reflected in the increasing responsibility he assigned to him.

For the first two months in Washington, Eisenhower lived out of a suitcase. Fortunately his brother Milton, who was head of the Department of Agriculture's Office of Land Use Coordination, had a house just outside Washington in Falls Church, Virginia, and Ike boarded with him and his wife, Helen. "Every night when I reached their house, something around midnight, both would be waiting up for me with a snack of midnight supper and a pot of coffee. I cannot remember ever seeing their house in daylight during all the months in Washington."[20]

Back in San Antonio, Mamie waited anxiously. She spent Christmas with John at West Point, and in late December received word that Ike's stint in Washington would be permanent. After only six months at Fort Sam Houston, it was another change of station. Harry Butcher, who still ran the CBS affiliate in Washington, found a one-bedroom apartment for them at the Wardman Park Hotel—no easy task in wartime Washington, which had mushroomed to twice its size almost overnight. "I can't tell you how I hate to dismantle this lovely house you and I fixed up so lovingly," Mamie wrote her mother on January 15, 1942. "Every time I go onto the little porch room I could weep."[21]

Packing the accumulated household treasures of twenty-five years of marriage—including more than sixty crates of china—was an arduous process. Several boxes were sent to the Wardman Park, but most were put in storage and would not be retrieved until Ike and Mamie bought their farm in Gettysburg almost fifteen years later. "I

---

[*] Some have suggested that General Marshall occasionally called George Patton "Georgie," though the evidence is sketchy.

feel like a football—kicked from place to place," Mamie said in February when she moved into their new apartment. "Now that the break is made, I am glad to be here, and poor Ike seems so pleased to have me—even if the apartment is small."[22]

When Eisenhower learned his assignment in Washington would be permanent, he wrote General Krueger. "Up to yesterday," said Ike, "I was determinedly clinging to the hope that I could return to your headquarters at a reasonably early date. That hope went glimmering when I found out last night that my transfer had been made permanent. I was not consulted and naturally I have never been asked as to any personal preference. This, of course, is exactly as it should be, but it does not prevent my telling you how bitterly disappointed I am to have to leave you, particularly at this time."[23]

Krueger replied instantly. "I had little hope of keeping you with the Third Army for long, but scarcely expected that you would be taken away this early in the game. However, I am sure that your new position offers a wider field for your abilities, and is in the best interests of the service."[24]

Eisenhower excelled under the pressure of wartime Washington. "Every day is the same—7:45 a.m. to 11:45 p.m.," he noted in his diary. To LeRoy Lutes, the logistics specialist from the Louisiana maneuvers whom Marshall was also about to pluck from Third Army, Ike wrote:

> Dear Roy:
>    Just to give you an inkling of the kind of mad house you are getting into—it is now eight o'clock New Year's Eve. I have a couple hours' work ahead of me, and tomorrow will be no different from today. I have been here about three weeks and this noon I had my first luncheon outside of the office. Usually it is a hot dog sandwich and a glass of milk. I have had one evening meal the whole period.[25]

As point man for the War Department's oversight of the war in the Philippines, Eisenhower handled a variety of tasks. When former secretary Patrick J. Hurley (a colonel in the reserves) offered his services to FDR, Roosevelt sent him to Marshall, who sent him to Ike.[*] "At that moment we were in search of a man to invigorate our filibustering attempts out of Australia," said Eisenhower. "We needed someone to organize blockade runners for MacArthur, and Hurley was perfect for the job." An old-fashioned buccaneer in politics, the former secretary had the energy and decisiveness the War Department needed. And having originally appointed MacArthur chief of staff, he was devoted to the cause of saving the Philippines.[26]

"When can you report for duty?" asked Ike.

"Now," Hurley replied.

Eisenhower told him to return at midnight prepared for extended field duty. Hurley was promoted to brigadier general on the spot. Ike and Leonard Gerow, who headed War Plans, each donated a star for the ex-secretary's epaulets, and Hurley boarded the night flight to Australia armed with $10 million in cash (slightly more than $120 million currently) to buy whatever supplies and charter as many ships as he could to run the Japanese blockade.[27]

In late December 1941, Prime Minister Churchill, accompanied by the British military leadership, arrived in Washington for their first wartime conference with FDR and the American chiefs of staff.[†] Christened ARCADIA by Churchill, the three-week Washington conference (December 22, 1941–January 14, 1942) proved to be the most important of the war in framing Allied strategy. Roosevelt and Churchill created the Combined Chiefs of Staff—a joint Anglo-American undertaking—to direct Allied military efforts; established the Combined Munitions Assignment Board (another joint undertaking) to allocate supplies among the Allies; agreed to the

---

[*] Eisenhower had served directly under Hurley in the War Department during the last three years of the Hoover administration.

[†] Roosevelt and Churchill, and their staffs, had met previously in Placentia Bay, off the coast of Newfoundland, in early August 1941. At that meeting, FDR and Churchill agreed on a "Hitler first" strategy, and Roosevelt undertook to expedite lend-lease shipments to Britain and Russia, and provide American escorts for British convoys. The meeting concluded with the promulgation of the Atlantic Charter, loosely defining Allied war aims. Jean Edward Smith, *FDR* 498–502, and the sources cited therein (New York: Random House, 2007).

invasion of North Africa (GYMNAST) in the autumn of 1942; and reaffirmed the decision FDR and Churchill had taken at the Atlantic conference in August to defeat Hitler before turning to Japan. Eisenhower was too junior to participate in the discussions, but he attended various meetings of the military chiefs as Marshall's assistant, and accompanied Secretary Stimson when he met privately with Churchill to discuss the situation in the Philippines.[28]

The establishment of the Combined Chiefs of Staff (CCS) was an unprecedented achievement in coalition warfare, and reflected the extraordinary ability of Roosevelt and Churchill to find common ground. Composed of the three British chiefs of staff—General Sir Alan Brooke, chief of the imperial general staff; Admiral Sir Dudley Pound, first sea lord; and Air Chief Marshal Sir Charles Portal—and their American counterparts, George C. Marshall, Admiral Ernest R. King, and General H. H. ("Hap") Arnold, the CCS became the final military authority for the conduct of the war. At FDR's insistence, the CCS was headquartered in Washington, where its work was directed by Field Marshal Sir John Dill, who was Churchill's personal representative. In July, Dill was joined by Admiral William D. Leahy, who had been recalled from retirement by FDR and who became, in effect, the chairman of the American chiefs of staff.[*]

After the top-level command structure was established, Marshall insisted that the war in each theater be fought under a single supreme commander. This was an even greater breakthrough since the Army and Navy, not only in the United States, but in Great Britain as well, jealously guarded their command prerogatives and had never before taken orders from a different service. Marshall presented his proposal when the Combined Chiefs met on the afternoon of Christmas Day. "I am convinced," he said, "that there must be one man in command of the entire theater—air, ground, and ships. We cannot manage by cooperation. Human frailties are such that there would be emphatic unwillingness to place portions of troops under another

---

[*] The statutory basis of the U.S. Joint Chiefs of Staff (and an independent Air Force) was not established until passage of the Defense Reorganization Act of 1947. World War II was fought on an ad hoc basis, but the American element of the Combined Chiefs of Staff (Marshall, King, and Arnold, with Leahy as chairman) became the model for the act.

service. If we can make a plan for unified command now, it will solve nine-tenths of our troubles. . . . I favor one man being in control, but operating under a directive from here."[29]

To secure British approval, Marshall suggested that the first combined command be established in the southwest Pacific, and that General Sir Archibald Wavell, the British commander in chief in India and Burma, be appointed supreme commander. But there was no immediate agreement. When the CCS meeting ended at 5:20 p.m., Marshall turned to Ike: "Eisenhower, draft a letter of instruction for a supreme commander in the Southwest Pacific."[30] Although it was the evening of Christmas Day, Ike returned to his desk at the War Department and hammered out a five-page draft. He finished shortly before midnight. The document specified the mission, defined the authority of the supreme commander, and provided safeguards for each nation in matters affecting national sovereignty. Eisenhower was writing on a blank slate. There were no precedents.

Marshall read Ike's draft the following morning, made one minor change,[31] and gave it to Secretary Stimson. Stimson was delighted. At 10 a.m. he and Marshall presented Eisenhower's draft to the president, who was also enthusiastic.[32] Bringing the British chiefs on board proved to be easier than convincing the U.S. Navy, but Admiral King eventually agreed. That left Churchill. On December 28, 1941, Marshall met with the prime minister, who initially resisted the concept. Secretary Stimson credited Marshall with gaining Churchill's approval, and it was Stimson who suggested that the example of a supreme commander in the southwest Pacific be followed elsewhere.[33] Eisenhower's draft, which established the principle of unity of command, became the model for the instructions issued to each supreme commander throughout the war—including Ike himself less than six months later.

Eisenhower's ability to draft the first set of orders for a supreme commander convinced Marshall that Ike was ready to take over War Plans (G-3). Leonard Gerow was eased out. On February 14, 1942, Gerow was promoted to major general and given command of the 29th Division. Ike moved up two days later. Both men were delighted. "Well," said Gerow, "I got Pearl Harbor on the books; lost the Philippines, Singapore, Sumatra, and all of the Dutch East Indies north of the barrier. Let's see what you can do."[34]

One of the perquisites of the director of War Plans was to sit behind the desk General Philip H. Sheridan used when he was the Army's commanding general in the 1880s. Sheridan's desk, a massive walnut behemoth, was known throughout the War Department as "Sheridan's throne."[35] In Sheridan's day it was adorned with a horseshoe from the great Morgan horse Winchester (née Rienzi) that carried Little Phil on his famous 1864 ride to save the day at Cedar Creek. Sheridan used the horseshoe as a paperweight. Winchester, stuffed and mounted, is on permanent display at the Smithsonian National Museum of American History, but the horseshoe has gone missing.

In addition to Sheridan's desk, Ike was issued new quarters on generals' row at Fort Myer. As the Army's G-3, Eisenhower fell heir to Quarters 7, a handsome redbrick mansion with a panoramic view of Washington, just down the street from Marshall's home at Quarters 1. It was a huge house, built at a time when servants were plentiful and general officers (or their wives) were independently wealthy. Ike and Mamie were thrilled at the move, but Eisenhower's schedule left little time to appreciate their new quarters.

Eisenhower's promotion to head War Plans coincided with General Marshall's reorganization of the War Department. Many of the Army's institutions dated from the Civil War. The general staff had been created in 1903, but in the intervening years had become bloated and calcified—poorly organized to provide timely response to the problems of global war. At least sixty officers, including the various branch and bureau chiefs, had access to the chief of staff, and thirty major commands reported directly to him. Marshall called the War Department "the poorest command post in the Army."[36]

General Marshall unveiled the changes on March 2, 1942. Instead of the numerous bureaus and commands that had previously reported to the chief of staff, the Army was reorganized into three commands: Army Air Forces, under General Hap Arnold; Army Ground Forces, under General Leslie McNair; and the Services of Supply, under General Brehon Somervell. That freed Marshall to concentrate on fighting the war. The old chiefs of infantry, cavalry, and artillery were abolished; the general staff was drastically reduced in size; and the War Plans Division, rechristened the Operations Division (OPD), became Marshall's command post. As chief of OPD, Eisenhower was not just the War Department's chief planner. He became Marshall's deputy for the day-to-day conduct of the war.

Three weeks later Marshall promoted Ike to major general, catapulting him ahead of 162 brigadiers more senior.[37] Eisenhower was "not really a staff officer," Marshall told FDR, but rather his "subordinate commander" who was responsible for "all dispositions of Army forces on a global scale." Marshall said that Ike "had to be able to function without constantly referring problems to him."[38]

"I was made a major general yesterday," Ike wrote in his diary on March 28. "Still a lieutenant colonel [in the Regular Army] but the promotion is just as satisfactory as if a permanent one.[*] This should assure that when I finally get back to troops, I'll get a division."[39]

Two weeks before Eisenhower was promoted, his father, David, died in Abilene. Mamie received the message at home. "One of the hardest things I had to do was telephone Ike and tell him. He is a wonder. People said he worked right on and no one could have known. Guess it was his salvation (work). Poor fellow. I've felt so sorry for him."[40]

Ike's stoicism masked his feelings. "I have felt terribly," he recorded on his office notepad that evening. "I should like so much to be with my Mother these few days, but we are at war, and war is not soft. It was no time to indulge even in the deepest and most sacred emotions. I'm quitting work now, 7:30 p.m. I haven't the heart to go on tonight."[41]

David Eisenhower was buried in Abilene on March 12, 1942, and Ike and Mamie ordered a blanket of red roses and Easter lilies for the casket. At the War Department, Eisenhower closed his door for half an hour to reflect upon his father. "He was not quite 79 years old, but for the last year he had been extremely old physically. Hardened arteries, kidney trouble, etc. He was undemonstrative, quiet, modest,

---

[*] Although soon promoted to lieutenant general and then full general, Eisenhower retained the permanent rank of lieutenant colonel until after the Sicily campaign, when he was promoted to major general in the Regular Army.

and of exemplary habits—he never used alcohol or tobacco. . . . My only regret is that it was always so difficult to let him know the great depth of my affection for him."[42]

As chief of OPD, it fell to Eisenhower to translate FDR's "Hitler first" strategy into a battle plan. The prevailing wisdom—on both sides of the Atlantic—was that a cross-Channel attack would be sheer madness. "Even among those who thought a direct assault by land forces would eventually become necessary," said Ike, "the majority believed that definite signs of cracking German morale would have to appear before it would be practicable to attempt such an enterprise."[43]

As Eisenhower recalled, he was one of the "very few, initially a very, very few," who thought otherwise.[44] As Ike saw it, all other possibilities offered scant hope of success. To deploy American forces on the Russian front was out of the question; an attack through Norway or the Iberian Peninsula would merely nibble at the edges of Nazi power; and to move against Germany from the Mediterranean would involve enormous problems of logistics and terrain. Shipping difficulties alone would make such an endeavor unfeasible, to say nothing of the distance between the Balkans or the boot of Italy and Berlin. In Eisenhower's view, the only scheme that made sense was to attack the Continent from across the Channel. American and British forces could be massed there more easily; the transatlantic journey from New York was the shortest; and there was no natural barrier between the coast of northwest Europe and Germany itself.

Eisenhower made four assumptions crucial to a successful cross-Channel attack. First, the Allies must have overwhelming air superiority. This was essential not only to protect the invasion force, but to isolate the battlefield and prevent the Germans from sending reinforcements. Second, the U-boat menace would have to be eliminated. Convoys crossing the Atlantic must have clear sailing. Third, supporting naval vessels should be present in sufficient strength to batter down coastal defenses; and fourth, specialized landing craft must be available in such numbers that a large army could be poured ashore rapidly, exploiting any initial breach in enemy defenses.[45]

Ike set to work with a small team of dedicated believers—Thomas Handy, Robert Crawford, John Hull, and Albert Wedemeyer—to flesh out plans for the invasion.* According to Eisenhower, "Not many officers were really aware of the existence of the project, nor had they heard any of the great arguments pro and con that went into its making. Many with whom we had to consult were always ready to express doubts of the blackest character."[46]

Eisenhower presented his planning draft to General Marshall on February 28, 1942.[47] "The burden of proof was on us," Ike recalled, and the presentation was lengthy. Marshall quizzed the OPD team relentlessly. At the end he said, "This is it. I approve."[48] Eisenhower was instructed to refine the draft for presentation to the president and the Combined Chiefs of Staff.

The following week the British appeared to draw back from their "Hitler first" commitment. Churchill was badly shaken by the fall of Singapore ("the Gibraltar of the Pacific"), and fretted about the fate of Australia and New Zealand. In a series of cables to Washington, he suggested that the Allied buildup in Europe be postponed.[49] That triggered a strategy session with FDR at the White House on March 5. Stimson and Marshall asserted that it was essential to concentrate American efforts in Europe, that Russia needed urgent support, and that the Pacific theater was secondary. Admiral King pressed the case for war in the Pacific. The next day Marshall met with Stimson to review the discussion. Marshall told the secretary that the War Plans Division was drawing up specific plans for an invasion of Europe, and sent Ike to brief him.

Stimson recorded the meeting in his diary.

> I told Eisenhower that I wanted to reserve my own opin-
> ions on the subject and simply to hear his study, and that
> he was to talk to me not as if I was Secretary of War but as

---

* Brigadier General Thomas T. Handy succeeded Ike as director of OPD (G-3), and later commanded American forces in Europe (1949–53). Brigadier General Crawford served later as Eisenhower's supply officer (G-4) at SHAEF and deputy commanding general of the Services of Supply in Europe. Colonel John Hull became the Army's G-3 after Handy, and finished his career as commander in chief of UN forces in the Far East (1953–55). Colonel Albert C. Wedemeyer, who had attended the German Kriegsakademie in Berlin (1936–38), replaced Stilwell in China, later served as the Army's G-3, and commanded Sixth Army (1948–51).

an ordinary citizen seeking enlightenment. We then stood up in front of my big map of the world and he laid out the main problems as he saw them. When he got through, I found that they coincided almost exactly with what I had expressed in the White House conference the day before, although he had not heard through Marshall of what I had said.[50]

Ike's unusual ability to think like his superiors paid dividends. On March 25 he presented the finished proposal to Marshall.[51] Code-named BOLERO, the plan was stripped to its essentials: Great Britain must be kept secure; Russia must be kept fighting; and the Middle East must be defended. "All other operations must be considered in the highly desirable rather than in the mandatory class."

Eisenhower argued that the principal target for the Allies' first offensive should be Germany, "to be attacked through western Europe." Shipping routes were shortest; an early buildup of forces in Britain would compel Germany to withdraw troops from the Russian front; there were abundant airfields in Britain from which the air force could operate; use of British combat forces would be maximized ("If a large scale attack is made in any other region, a large portion of the British Forces will necessarily be held at home"); and, from the standpoint of an invading force, the highway and railroad networks of western Europe were superior to those found in any other area. After briefly detailing the requisites for a successful cross-Channel attack, he concluded with a dash of rhetorical saber rattling. "The War Plans Division believes that, unless this plan is adopted as the central aim of all our efforts, we must turn our *backs* upon the Eastern Atlantic and go, full out, as quickly as possible, against Japan."[52]

Marshall and Stimson reviewed Ike's plan for a cross-Channel attack that morning, and then presented it to FDR at a meeting at the White House. The luncheon meeting, which was also attended by Navy Secretary Frank Knox, Admiral King, General Arnold, and Harry Hopkins, turned into a full-scale review of American military strategy. Roosevelt played devil's advocate, suggesting, as Churchill might have done, a half dozen alternatives to a cross-Channel attack.[53] When Marshall stood his ground, FDR—who evidently was probing for weaknesses in Ike's plan—gave his approval to the proposal and instructed Marshall to work out the details.

Time became the driving force. Relying on his knowledge of French geography, Eisenhower and his planners worked quickly to come up with an order-of-battle invasion plan (ROUNDUP). D-Day was set for April 1, 1943. By that time, the United States and Great Britain were to have assembled a force of forty-eight divisions (thirty American, eighteen British and Canadian), 5,800 combat aircraft, and 7,000 landing craft. The initial landing would be made on a six-division front between Calais and Le Havre, north of the Seine. British and American paratroops would drop behind enemy lines and prevent reinforcements from reaching the battlefield. As soon as the beachhead was secured, nine armored divisions would be "rushed in to break German resistance," and spearhead a drive toward the Belgian port of Antwerp.[54]

Eisenhower submitted the plan to General Marshall on April 1. Marshall and Stimson made two minor textual revisions, and carried the plan to the White House that afternoon. Once again the discussion was lengthy. Roosevelt examined the plan paragraph by paragraph. No minutes were kept, but in his diary Stimson said that Marshall "set the course while Hopkins and I held the laboring oar."[55]* When FDR gave his final approval, Stimson noted that it would mark April 1, 1942, as one of the memorable dates in the war.[56] Roosevelt agreed that speed was essential. He directed Marshall and Hopkins to fly to London at once and present the plan to Churchill and the British chiefs of staff.

Marshall, Stimson, Hopkins (and Eisenhower) felt that a milestone had been reached. A cross-Channel attack seemed in the offing. Hopkins cabled Churchill, "Will be seeing you soon so please start the fire [a reference to the frigid temperatures that prevailed inside the prime minister's country house, Chequers]." FDR told Churchill

---

* Remarkable as it may seem to a contemporary audience, FDR did not allow minutes or notes to be taken at meetings. As a consequence, the after-meeting diary entries of Stimson, Hopkins, Treasury Secretary Henry Morgenthau, and Marshall are the only records that exist. FDR Library to JES, December 9, 2008.

that he had "reached certain conclusions of such vital importance" that he was sending Marshall and Hopkins to explain them and to seek "your approval thereon. All of it is dependent on the complete cooperation of our two countries."[57]

Marshall and Hopkins arrived in Britain on April 8, 1942. After a week of intensive discussions with Churchill and the British chiefs of staff, Eisenhower's plan for a 1943 cross-Channel assault was approved. "I have read with earnest attention your masterly document about the future of the war and the great operations proposed," Churchill cabled FDR on April 12. "I am in entire agreement in principle with all you propose, and so are the Chiefs of Staff."[58]

Roosevelt replied shortly. "Marshall and Hopkins have told me of the unanimity of opinion relative to our proposals, and I greatly appreciate the message you have sent me confirming this. I believe the results of this decision will be very disheartening to Hitler. It may well be the wedge by which we shall accomplish his downfall."[59]

Marshall, who had done most of the heavy lifting in London, shared the general enthusiasm but recognized the pitfalls that lay ahead. "Virtually everyone agrees with us in principle," he told Army deputy chief of staff Joseph McNarney, "but many if not most hold reservations regarding this or that."[60] Eisenhower took the agreement at face value. "I hope that at long last, after months of struggle by this division, we are all definitely committed to one concept of fighting. If we can agree on major purposes and objectives, our efforts will begin to fall in line and we won't be thrashing around in the dark."[61]

Marshall's concern about the future of BOLERO was justified. At the end of April, President Roosevelt abruptly announced that he was increasing the size of American forces in Australia to 100,000 men and 1,000 combat aircraft.[62] The War Department was caught off guard. FDR was responding to pressure from the governments of Australia and New Zealand as well as from the U.S. Navy, but neither Marshall nor Stimson had been informed. Marshall instructed Eisenhower to prepare a reclama pointing out that any dilution of the forces earmarked for BOLERO would seriously impede the possibility of landing in Europe.[63] Marshall told Roosevelt that he would have to choose between BOLERO and Australia. "If BOLERO is not to be our primary consideration, I would recommend its complete abandonment." And since the British were a part of the scheme, they "should be formally notified that the recent London agreement should be canceled."[64]

FDR was sometimes too quick off the mark, and this time he recognized that he had overstepped. As he often did when caught out, he dissembled. "I did not issue any directive to increase our forces in Australia," he wrote Marshall. Roosevelt said he merely "wanted to know if it were possible to do so. I do not want BOLERO slowed down."[65]

The American buildup in Great Britain was saved for the moment.[66] But for Eisenhower it was a rude awakening. "BOLERO is *supposed* to have the approval of the President and Prime Minister. But the struggle to get everyone behind it, and to keep the highest authority from wrecking it by making additional commitments elsewhere is never ending. The actual fact is that not one man in twenty in the Government realizes what a grisly, dirty, tough business we are in."[67]

While Marshall was in London he took the measure of the American Army's command structure in Britain and found it wanting. The senior American commander, Major General James E. Chaney (USMA, 1908), an air corps officer who had been sent originally to observe the Battle of Britain, seemed out of touch with the unfolding situation, and his headquarters remained wedded to peacetime routine. Officers wore civilian clothes to work, put in an eight-hour day, and always took weekends off. Little effort was made to coordinate with British military staffs, and the headquarters itself seemed to be operating in a vacuum. Marshall told Eisenhower to fly to London and assess the situation. With BOLERO about to begin, General Marshall wanted the Army's command structure capable of handling it. "I'm taking off on the 23rd with General Arnold and others for a trip to England," Ike wrote in his diary on May 21. "My own particular reason for going is an uneasy feeling that either we do not understand our own commanding general and staff in England or they don't understand us. Our planning for BOLERO is not progressing."[68]

Marshall's purpose in sending Eisenhower was twofold. He wanted a second opinion about Chaney, but he also wanted to expose Ike to the British. It was widely assumed that when the invasion of Europe was launched, Marshall would command it. He was grooming Eisenhower to be his chief of staff, and Ike's ability to get on with the British would be important.[69]*

Eisenhower requested that Mark Clark, who was now chief of staff of Army Ground Forces, accompany the mission. "I felt that Clark's observations regarding the suitability of the United Kingdom as a training and staging ground would prove valuable."[70] Eisenhower and Clark, both of whom had been lieutenant colonels a year before, were newly minted major generals, Ike the senior by three weeks.

After a much delayed and rerouted flight across the Atlantic, Eisenhower and Clark rolled into Paddington Station on the morning of May 26, 1942. They were met by a smartly uniformed driver from Britain's Motor Transport Corps (MTC), Kay Summersby. The MTC was a unit of volunteers originally formed by British post-debutantes that had done heroic service driving ambulances in London's East End during the Blitz. They bought their own uniforms and initially received no pay for their services. The drivers were uniformly bright, attractive, upper-class, and knowledgeable about everything in which visiting dignitaries might be interested. Summersby was no exception. A former model for Worth, the Paris house of haute couture, she was recently separated from her husband, a wealthy London publisher, and linked romantically to a dashing young Army captain, Richard Arnold (USMA, 1932), who, like Summersby, was also still married.

---

* On May 11, 1942, Eisenhower prepared a memorandum for Marshall pertaining to the organization of BOLERO and detailing the requirements for the *"type of officer to serve as Commanding General,* United States Forces" in Britain. "If BOLERO develops as planned, there will come a time when United States Forces' activity in that region will become so great as to make it the critical point in our war effort. When this comes about, it is easily possible that the *President may direct the Chief of Staff {Marshall}, himself, to proceed to London and take over command.* The officer previously serving as Commander should be one who could fit in as a Deputy or a Chief of Staff. This will insure continuity in planning and execution, and in understanding." Eisenhower to Marshall, May 11, 1942, in *The Papers of Dwight David Eisenhower,* vol. 1, *The War Years* 292–93, Alfred D. Chandler, Jr., ed. (Baltimore: Johns Hopkins Press, 1970), hereafter 1 *War Years* (Eisenhower's emphasis).

Kay Summersby as she appeared when Ike met her in
1942.

Eisenhower and Clark remained in Britain for ten days, and Summersby was their driver throughout. The two Americans met repeatedly with the British chiefs of staff, and traveled extensively to examine possible staging areas. Ike and Clark were not pleased with what they saw. In their view Chaney and his staff were decidedly "in a back eddy, from which they could scarcely emerge except through a return to the United States." That is how Eisenhower expressed it in his memoirs. At the time he said the whole outfit should be relieved and shipped back to the United States "on a slow boat, without destroyer escort," a likely death sentence given the prevalence of Nazi U-boats at the time.[71]

Among the sites Ike and Clark visited was a major training area in Kent and Sussex to witness a field exercise testing a new organizational structure for infantry divisions. The exercise was directed by

Lieutenant General Sir Bernard L. Montgomery, the British Army commander in southwest England. Montgomery arrived very late for the briefing. "I have been directed to take time from my busy life to brief you gentlemen," he tartly announced, scarcely endearing himself to Eisenhower or Clark.[72]

As Montgomery made his way to the map board and picked up his pointer, Ike lit a cigarette. Montgomery sniffed the air without looking around and briskly asked: "Who's smoking?"

"I am," said Ike.

"Stop it. I don't permit smoking in my office."[73]

Eisenhower put out the cigarette, but his anger smoldered. In his diary, Ike said simply, "General Montgomery is a decisive type who appears to be extremely energetic and professionally able."[74] Riding back to London in the car with Clark, he said, "That son of a bitch." Kay Summersby remembered looking in the rearview mirror and saw that Eisenhower's "face was flaming red and the veins in his forehead looked like worms. He was furious . . . really steaming mad."[75]

Ike and Clark appreciated being chauffeured by someone as knowledgeable and attractive as Kay Summersby. On sightseeing excursions they would occasionally stop at an English pub for a pint of ale or a round of gin and tonics. Once they ignored the barriers of rank and invited Kay for lunch at the Connaught, one of London's most elegant hotels, much to the consternation of neighboring diners. "We were three people," Kay remembered. "Not two generals and a driver."[76] It was at the Connaught that Ike began calling her Kay instead of Miss Summersby. Kay did not yet call Eisenhower "Ike," but she was smitten nonetheless. As one biographer has written, "Sitting opposite him for the first time, she remarked on his 'brilliant blue eyes, sandy hair—but not very much of it—fair and ruddy complexion.' " Kay thought Ike had a strong face, not conventionally handsome, but "very American, certainly very appealing. I succumbed immediately to that grin that was to become so famous."[77]

Toward the end of their stay, Ike and Clark were offered the opportunity to tour Windsor Castle, the country residence of the royal family. The King and Queen, they were told, had been informed of their visit and would remain in their apartment to avoid embarrassing their guests. But King George forgot. It was a beautiful spring day, and when Clark and Eisenhower arrived the royal family was taking tea in the garden. The garden was surrounded by a hedge, and when the King heard the voice of the Royal Constable approaching with the two guests he realized his error. "This is terrible," he told the others. "We must not be seen." The King and Queen of England, and the two young princesses, Elizabeth and Margaret, got down on all fours and crawled on their hands and knees back to the castle door before Ike and Clark entered the garden.[78]

On the evening before their departure, Eisenhower, Clark, and Hap Arnold had dinner at their hotel and compared notes. All agreed that Chaney had to be replaced. The question was with whom. According to Arnold, "We agreed it had to be someone who was fully acquainted with our War Department plans. He must have the confidence of General Marshall and the Secretary of War. We also agreed that he should get to London as soon as possible."[79]

Eisenhower went to bed early, and Clark and Arnold continued talking. As Arnold remembered, "The two of us came to the conclusion that it should be Ike. Clark thought that since I knew Marshall better than he, I should present Eisenhower's name after the three of us told the Chief of Staff of our conclusion that a change should be made at once."[80]

When the time for departure came, Kay Summersby drove Eisenhower and Clark to Northholt air base, outside London. At the field, Ike gave Summersby a "priceless" box of chocolates for her efforts—a gift that only visiting Americans could have come by in war-rationed England. "If I'm ever back this way, I hope you'll drive me again," he said.

"I'd like that, sir," Summersby replied.[81]

Eisenhower reported to Marshall on June 3, thoroughly dissatisfied with what he had seen in Britain. If the buildup for the invasion (BOLERO) had any hope of success, there must be an immediate change of command. Marshall told Ike to put it in writing. Eisenhower's memorandum of June 3, 1942, is a remarkable example of his ability to offer candid advice. "During my visit in England, I gave a great deal of study to the identity of the individual who should now be commanding our Forces in England," he told Marshall. "I was very hopeful that my conclusions would favor the present incumbent. For a variety of reasons, some of which I intimated to you this morning, I believe that a change should be made." Ike said his classmate General Joseph McNarney, who was the Army's deputy chief of staff, was best fitted for the post. McNarney was thoroughly familiar with the planning for BOLERO, enjoyed Marshall's confidence, and understood the complex British command structure. "I believe that General McNarney has the strength of character, the independence of thought, and the ability to fulfill satisfactorily the requirements of this difficult task." Eisenhower also recommended that Mark Clark be appointed to command the initial assault force.[82]

Two days later, Eisenhower sent a second memo to Marshall recommending that whoever was designated to command American forces in England should be promoted immediately to three-star rank. Regardless of whether Chaney was retained, said Ike, the British did not take major generals seriously. "While, in other circumstances, the question of promotion might appear trivial, it would, in this case, have a definite effect upon orderly progress in getting ready for the attack." Eisenhower repeated his recommendation that McNarney be named to the post.[83]

Marshall accepted the second memo without comment. He told Eisenhower to draft a directive specifying the duties and responsibilities of a commanding general for a European theater of operations (ETO). This was the second time Eisenhower had been called upon to prepare the directive for a theater commander. The document, which Ike later referred to as "The Bible," gave the theater commander absolute control of all American forces in the ETO, regardless of branch or service. "The mission of the commanding general, European theater, will be to prepare for and carry on military operations in the European theater against the Axis powers under the strategic directives of the combined U.S.-British Chiefs of Staff as communicated to him by the Chief of Staff U.S. Army."[84] The directive was not as concise as Grant's 1864 orders to Meade ("Lee's army will be your objective. Where Lee goes there you will go also"), but the chain of command was clear. The Combined Chiefs of Staff would set policy, but the European theater commander reported to General Marshall.[85]

Eisenhower presented the directive to Marshall on June 8. By this time Marshall had already decided he wanted Ike to command the European theater. In addition to the recommendations of Arnold and Clark, Vice Admiral Lord Louis Mountbatten, head of British combined operations, who was in Washington for a conference, had put in a strong word on Eisenhower's behalf. His colleagues, he told Marshall, were quite ready to work with Ike as the senior American officer in Britain.[86] Field Marshal Sir John Dill, the representative of the British chiefs in Washington, seconded Mountbatten's appraisal.[87]* But it was Marshall himself who cast the deciding vote. Marshall believed that when the invasion of Europe came, he would command it. And he wanted Eisenhower to prepare the ground as ETO commander.

When Eisenhower handed the draft directive to Marshall, he asked the chief to study it carefully because it could be an important document for the further waging of the war.

"Does the directive suit you?" Marshall asked. "Are you satisfied with it?"

"Yes, sir," Eisenhower replied, "but you may have some suggestions."

"I'm glad it suits you," said Marshall, "because these are the orders you are going to operate under."

"Me?" asked Eisenhower.

"You. You are in command of the European theater. Whom would you like to take with you?"

Eisenhower was briefly flustered. He had no combat experience, and his only command position in the past twenty years had been an infantry battalion at Fort Lewis. But he recovered quickly.

"I'd like to take Mark Clark with me," he told Marshall.

"You can have him. When can you leave?"

"I'd like to talk with Clark before I tell you when we can leave," said Eisenhower.[88]

---

* In 1956, Marshall told Forrest C. Pogue, his biographer, "I sent Eisenhower and some others over so the British could have a look at them and then I asked Churchill what he thought of them. He was extravagant in his estimation of them, so I went ahead with my decision on Eisenhower." Churchill did not meet Eisenhower on this trip, but he evidently heard about him from the British chiefs. Pogue, 2 *Marshall* 339, 474.

Later that day, Ike recorded his thoughts on his notepad. "The C/S told me this morning that it's *possible* I may go to England in command. It's a big job—if U.S. and U.K. stay squarely behind BOLERO and go after it tooth and nail, it will be the biggest American job of the war. Of course command now does not necessarily mean command in the operation—but the job before the battle begins will still be the biggest outside of that of C/S himself."[89]

Marshall cleared Eisenhower's name with Stimson and FDR, and on June 11 Ike's appointment to command the European theater was announced.[90] Three weeks later he was promoted to lieutenant general, leapfrogging sixty-six major generals (including George Patton and Jacob Devers) who were considerably senior. With the promotion, Eisenhower ranked eighteenth among all officers on active duty.[91] His rise had been meteoric. In little more than ten weeks, dating from his promotion from brigadier to major general, Ike had moved ahead of 228 general officers with greater seniority.

Patton wrote immediately to congratulate him. "I particularly appreciate it," Eisenhower replied, "because you and I both know you should have been wearing additional stars long ago. It is entirely possible that I will need you sorely: and when the time comes I will have to battle my diffidence over requesting the services of a man so much senior and so much more able than myself. As I have often told you, you are my idea of a battle commander. . . . I would certainly want you as the lead horse in the team."[92]

Before leaving for London, Eisenhower decided it would be prudent to call on Admiral Ernest King, the crusty chief of naval operations. The Navy had never served under an Army officer, and the senior American sailor in Britain was Harold Stark, a full admiral and King's predecessor as CNO. Would Stark serve under Ike as theater commander?* King saw no problem. "He assured me that he would do everything within his power to sustain my status of actual 'commander' of American forces assigned to me."[93] If King was on

---

* Eisenhower's apprehension about Stark proved unnecessary. As soon as Ike arrived in London, Stark called on him and promised his support. "You may call on me at any hour, day or night, for anything you wish," said Stark. "And when you do, call me 'Betty,' a nickname I've always had in the service." Dwight D. Eisenhower, *Crusade in Europe* 54 (Garden City, N.Y.: Doubleday, 1948).

board, the Navy was on board. FDR said that Admiral King shaved every morning with a blowtorch. He was not as gifted intellectually as Marshall or Leahy or Arnold, but his powerful command presence was precisely what the Navy needed after the defeat at Pearl Harbor.[94]

Eisenhower also had a personal request for King. He wanted his CBS friend Harry Butcher, a lieutenant commander in the U.S. Naval Reserve (USNR), to go to London with him as his naval aide. "I've got to have someone I can relax with," he told King. "Someone I can trust absolutely. Someone who isn't subservient. Someone who will talk back."[95] The fact that Butcher was an excellent bridge player and well versed in the black arts of public relations went unsaid. Again, King saw no problem. In addition to Butcher, Sergeant Mickey McKeogh, and Major Tex Lee, Eisenhower snatched Colonel T. J. Davis from the adjutant general's office to be his own AG. Ike and Davis had shared eight years in MacArthur's headquarters and trusted each other instinctively. Nothing is more important for a commanding general than to have an adjutant who is on the same wavelength. John Rawlins served Grant in that capacity, and few would question that he was a valuable contributor to Grant's success.

Three days before Eisenhower departed, he received a surprise visit from Philippine president Manuel Quezon. Quezon had been evacuated from Corregidor by submarine and was in Washington to plead the cause of the now-occupied Philippines. The president-in-exile presented Ike with a citation for his service in Manila, and offered him an honorarium, evidently exceeding $100,000 ($1.1 million currently). Eisenhower accepted the citation but declined the emolument. To accept the money, he told Quezon, "might operate to destroy whatever usefulness I may have to the allied cause in the present war."[96] Eisenhower's attitude contrasts sharply with that of Douglas MacArthur, who four months earlier had accepted $500,000 ($5.5 million) in cash from Quezon prior to the president's departure from the Philippines. Major General Richard Sutherland, MacArthur's chief of staff, received $75,000 ($830,000), with lesser amounts given to others on MacArthur's staff.[97]

Ike's last letter was to General Kenyon Joyce. "I cannot leave the United States without making acknowledgement to you once again of my deep sense of obligation to your inspiring example of leadership. I am keenly sensible of the enormity of the task I am now undertaking. If hard work will win—we'll do the job. But I'll never fail to realize that it is something bigger than one individual that is responsible for any success I may attain."[98]

Eisenhower departed from Bolling Field at 9 a.m. on June 23, 1942, accompanied by Clark and his personal staff. For Mamie, Ike's appointment to command the European theater was a mixed blessing. Not only would she be separated from her husband for an indefinite period, but she was unceremoniously ordered to clear their quarters at Fort Myer within the week. "It's a lovely way the Army has," said Lucius D. Clay. "When your difficulties start, they make it more difficult."[99]

This was Mamie's fourth move in less than a year. Her parents urged her to come to Denver, but she preferred to remain in Washington, surrounded by old Army friends and closer to John at West Point. Initially, she and Ruth Butcher, Harry's wife, shared an apartment at the Wardman Park. Later she found a two-bedroom apartment there for herself, where she remained for the duration. Eisenhower, who was perpetually shy about any display of affection, asked Mamie not to come to the airfield to see him off, but to stand by the flagpole at Fort Myer so he could see her as the plane made its ascent over the Potomac.

# NINE

# TORCH

I am searching the Army to find the most
capable Chaplain we have in an effort to assure
a fairly decent break in the weather when the
big day comes.

— EISENHOWER TO PATTON,
*September 5, 1942*

EISENHOWER ARRIVED IN LONDON on the evening of June 24, 1942, armed with the plenary powers of a theater commander. He was met at the airfield by Lord Louis Mountbatten and members of the American headquarters staff, and then whisked off to Claridge's— London's most opulent hotel—where a lavish VIP suite awaited. The colonel in charge of arrangements said similar accommodations had been laid on for Mark Clark, and suggested that Sergeant McKeogh, Ike's orderly, might find a bed at the enlisted barracks on Green Street, about two blocks away.

"My sergeant has had a long and trying trip like the rest of us," Eisenhower replied. "I prefer to have him stay here at the hotel for at least a couple of days, until he's had a chance to rest."[1]

Eisenhower, who was solicitous about the welfare of his staff, was not pleased with the gilt-edge accommodations at Claridge's. They were far too elegant for his tastes. The liveried footmen seemed especially out of place in wartime Britain, the ornate lobby struck him as ostentatious, and the red-and-gold Chinese wallpaper in his bedroom resembled a New Orleans bordello. "I think I'm living in sin," he told Harry Butcher.[2]

Within the week Ike moved to less pretentious quarters at the Dorchester, across Park Lane from Hyde Park, another of London's first-class hotels but one whose elegance was understated. Eisenhower's suite, which overlooked Hyde Park, had three large rooms: a generous bedroom for him, another for Butcher, and a stately sitting room with a fireplace. "The General loved an open fire," said Mickey McKeogh, "not so much for the warmth as to look at. He loves to sit in front of a fire and just look into it, and it is handy to throw his cigarette butts into. He always throws them into a fireplace if there's one around." Eisenhower was smoking three to four packs a day, and as Mickey recalled, he did not have much use for ashtrays. "He knocks the ash off his cigarettes by tapping his hand against something—the arm of a chair, the edge of his desk—and he believes that cigarette ashes are good for carpets."[3] The Dorchester would remain Ike's London residence for the duration of the war. It was a short walk to his headquarters on Grosvenor Square, and a quick drive to Whitehall and 10 Downing Street.

"I cannot tell you how much I miss you," Ike wrote Mamie shortly after his arrival. "An assignment like this is not the same as an absence from home on maneuvers. In a tent, surrounded by soldiers, it seems natural to have to get along alone. But when living in an apartment, under city conditions, I constantly find myself wondering, 'why isn't Mamie here?' You've certainly become most necessary to me."[4] Eisenhower wrote 319 letters to Mamie while he was overseas, roughly two each week. And every letter was handwritten, though he sometimes complained about the time that this required. Mamie wrote to Ike just as frequently, and she saved all of his letters to her. For whatever reason, Eisenhower apparently did not keep those he received from Mamie.[5]*

---

* In a curious coincidence, FDR retained all of Eleanor's letters to him, but ER destroyed Franklin's to her, finding his youthful avowals of love too painful to reread. To judge from Ike's replies to Mamie, it would appear that she often raised questions he also preferred to forget. Jean Edward Smith, *FDR* 37 (New York: Random House, 2007).

General John C. H. Lee, a religious zealot
often referred to as "Jesus Christ Himself Lee,"
who proved to be a logistics virtuoso and in
many ways was the unsung hero of the Allied
victory in Europe.

Eisenhower's first order of business was to establish the command
structure for the European theater, and he followed the model General Marshall had established at the War Department. Mark Clark,
who headed II Corps, became the commander of Army ground
troops; Major General Carl "Tooey" Spaatz, who led Eighth Air
Force, became Ike's air commander; and Major General John C. H.
Lee would assume a post similar to Brehon Somervell's as the commander of American service forces in the theater. Spaatz, who was a
year ahead of Eisenhower at West Point, had been one of the pioneers
in Army aviation. He had won the Distinguished Flying Cross for
gallantry during World War I, and in 1929 set the world flight en-
durance record commanding a Fokker trimotor transport that stayed

aloft for 150 hours—refueling in the air thirty-seven times.* A member of the Army general staff like Eisenhower, he had spent the last months of 1940 observing the Battle of Britain. When the United States entered the war, Spaatz was given command of Eighth Air Force and returned to London in March 1942.[6]

Major General John C. H. Lee, a 1909 classmate of George Patton's at West Point, had been born in Junction City, Kansas, in 1887. A career officer in the Corps of Engineers, Lee had been aide-de-camp to General Leonard Wood when Wood was Army chief of staff, had fought in France, and was district engineer in Vicksburg during the great flood of 1927. When war began he commanded the 2nd Infantry Division in California. Like Somervell, Lee was an inveterate empire builder who could be relied upon to provide an army with everything from safety pins and condoms to main battle tanks. Unlike Somervell, he was an evangelical Christian who carried a Bible with him at all times, frequently quoted scripture, and earned the nickname J[esus] C[hrist] H[imself] Lee because of his sanctimoniousness. Eisenhower called Lee his "Cromwell," and considered him "one of the best officers in the Army."[7] And to Lee's credit, he not only got the Allies across the Channel in 1944, he melded the various service branches—ordnance, quartermaster, transportation, signal, engineers, chemical, military police, medical, dental, adjutant general, judge advocate general, and finance—into an effective supply service that freed Eisenhower from logistical concerns and allowed him to concentrate on fighting the enemy. Lee and Spaatz outranked Eisenhower in the prewar Army, just as Sherman, Meade, and Thomas had outranked Grant. It is a reflection of the professionalism of the Regular Army that this made no difference whatever. Just as Sherman, Meade, and Thomas followed Grant's orders to the letter, Lee and Spaatz worked easily under Ike.

Before leaving Washington, Eisenhower had asked Marshall for

---

* Spaatz's plane, the *Question Mark,* was crewed by Captain Ira Eaker, Lieutenant Elwood Quesada, and Lieutenant Harry Halverson. Eaker succeeded Spaatz as commander of Eighth Air Force in December 1942; Quesada commanded the Tactical Air Command and in 1959 was appointed by President Eisenhower to be the first head of the Federal Aviation Administration; and Halverson led the great bombing raid on the Ploesti oil fields in Romania.

Walter Bedell Smith when appointed as Ike's chief of staff.

Bedell Smith as his chief of staff. At the time, Smith was secretary of the Army general staff and Marshall's principal assistant. Smith and Marshall had first met at the Infantry School at Fort Benning in the late twenties when Marshall had been assistant commandant and Smith was the school's secretary. A former enlisted man, Smith was abrasive, bad-tempered, foulmouthed, and addicted to duty. Perhaps because his grandfather had been an enlisted man in the Prussian Army, he had a passion for order and discipline. Forrest Pogue, Marshall's biographer, said, "Those who worked under Smith dreaded both his tongue and his exactions. In an Army where Marshall depended on officers like Eisenhower and Bradley to do their jobs quietly, to conciliate, and to persuade, he required others like Smith who could hack a path through red tape and perform hatchet jobs."[8] Eisenhower needed Smith in precisely that capacity. As Drew Middleton of *The New York Times* put it, "Smith had a mind like a steel trap and was just naturally mean. He was Ike's sonofabitch."[9] Marshall initially did not want to release Smith, but eventually relented, and Beetle (as he preferred to be called) reported to London in September.

The long relationship between Eisenhower and Smith never became anything other than professional. Unlike Patton, Clark, and Bradley, with whom Ike felt kinship, he and Smith were never close. Smith played chess; Eisenhower preferred bridge. Smith read history and biography, leavened by Joseph Conrad and Ford Madox Ford; Eisenhower (like von Rundstedt) chose lighter fare. Eisenhower enjoyed singing hit tunes loudly and off-key; no one ever heard Smith sing. Ike smiled habitually. Smith never did.[10] Like Hindenburg and Ludendorff (who were also distant personally), Eisenhower and Smith made a perfect pair. Smith did everything that was expected of a chief of staff, and relieved Eisenhower from headquarters routine. Ike said later that Smith was like a crutch to a one-legged man. "Remember, Beetle is a Prussian and one must make allowances for it."[11]

After putting his command structure in place, Eisenhower turned to theater headquarters. "Now that everyone here is at liberty to talk to me freely," he wrote Marshall on June 26, 1942, "it becomes abundantly clear that some change was necessary."[12] Eisenhower immediately put the Army on a seven-day week. He was shocked when on his first Sunday several division heads sauntered into their Grosvenor Square offices at ten o'clock. He was even more surprised when he found that many at headquarters routinely left work before he did. "I've served on general staffs probably longer than any officer in the Army," he told Butcher, "and I never left headquarters until my 'Old Man' departed."[13] Eisenhower did not belong to the "counsel and correct" school of military leadership. If an officer underperformed, he was summarily relieved and sent back to the United States. "Colonel Summers requested today that I revoke his orders for returning to the states," Ike recorded in his diary on June 27. "I declined but told him I would carry him over for a month to avoid the implication that I relieved him immediately upon arrival."[14]

High on Eisenhower's personal agenda was to engage Kay Summersby as his driver. He assigned the task of locating her to Tex Lee, but Lee, who evidently did not give it the priority Ike desired, had little success. Eventually Summersby was located driving for Tooey Spaatz. "Kay, where have you been?" asked Eisenhower. "I've been looking all over London for you."

He said to Spaatz, "Tooey, you've been hiding her in the Air Force."

"Now don't take Kay away from me," Spaatz replied. "She's the only driver who knows her way around." Two days later Summersby was driving for Ike.[15]

While Eisenhower established himself as theater commander, Harry Butcher renewed his friendship with the CBS contingent in London: Edward R. Murrow, Robert Trout, and Charles Collingwood, as well as Ray Daniell of *The New York Times* and Quentin Reynolds of *Collier's*. "I trained Bob [Trout] from a pup at WJSV," Butcher recorded.[16] The press corps, most of whom had been in London during the Blitz, were far better informed about the conduct of the war than most officers at Eisenhower's headquarters. Daniell and Murrow were often briefed by Churchill himself, and all had contacts at the highest level in Whitehall. For Butcher, it was a two-way street. The journalists provided a back channel that kept Ike informed, and Eisenhower enjoyed favorable press coverage from the beginning.

As the commander of all American forces in the European theater, Eisenhower met daily with one or more of the British chiefs of staff, or with Lieutenant General Sir Hastings ("Pug") Ismay, Churchill's personal chief of staff. He saw Churchill several times a week, often at a private lunch, and was occasionally invited to spend the weekend at Chequers, the prime minister's country estate. Early on, Ike sensed the British were not happy with a cross-Channel attack, certainly not in 1942. "There seems to be some confusion of thought as to the extent of the British commitment," he alerted Marshall on June 30, 1942.[17]

What Eisenhower sensed was a fundamental resistance, particularly on Churchill's part, to crossing the Channel under fire. Although the British had agreed "in principle" to an invasion of the Continent in the spring of 1943 (ROUNDUP), Churchill was never fully convinced. His doubts surfaced in mid-June following a visit by Soviet foreign minister Vyacheslav Molotov to Washington. At the conclusion of Molotov's visit, the White House and the Kremlin announced in a joint communiqué that "full understanding was reached with regard to the urgent tasks of creating a Second Front in Europe in 1942."[18]

Washington's announcement of a second front in 1942 galvanized Churchill. To cross the Channel in 1943 might be feasible; 1942 was out of the question. The last thing the British government wanted was a premature cross-Channel attack. The enormous battlefield losses of World War I, Churchill's own unfortunate experience with the amphibious landing at Gallipoli in 1915, plus an awareness of how ill-prepared the Allies, particularly the United States, were to take on a battle-tested German Army, caused the British government to rethink its earlier commitment. Scarcely before the ink was dry on the Washington-Moscow communiqué, Churchill boarded a plane for the United States determined to dissuade Roosevelt from any thought of a second front in 1942, and possibly in 1943 as well.

Churchill spent two days cloistered with FDR at Hyde Park. Whenever the two Allied leaders were alone together, policy makers down the line became nervous. "The President was always willing to do any sideshow, and Churchill was always prodding him," said Marshall.[19] Stimson said, "It looks as if the President is going to jump the traces."[20] The fact is, Churchill's arguments against a 1942 cross-Channel attack were remarkably sound. There was a severe shortage of landing craft, the Luftwaffe held a six to one advantage in tactical air, Britain's forces were too thinly spread, America's were unproven, and the time to prepare was too short. "No responsible British military authority has so far been able to make a plan which has any chance of success unless the Germans become utterly demoralized, of which there is no likelihood," said Churchill. The prime minister conceded that the Western Allies could not remain idle "during the whole of 1942," and suggested they redirect their efforts toward landing in North Africa (GYMNAST).[21]

Roosevelt was impressed by Churchill's arguments. Returning with the prime minister to Washington, he summoned Marshall and King to the White House. When Churchill held forth on the advantages of invading North Africa, Marshall and King just as vigorously defended a cross-Channel attack. Marshall argued that GYMNAST was an unnecessary diversion, a pinprick at the periphery that would inevitably postpone the invasion of Europe. King doubted if the British would ever agree to invade the Continent. Tempers rose. At one point, Marshall and King suggested that if Britain persisted in its opposition to a cross-Channel attack, the United States should abandon the "Germany first" strategy agreed to at Placentia Bay and strike decisively against Japan.[22] Roosevelt came down hard. The chiefs' suggestion, he said, was "a little like taking up your dishes and going away."[23]

The president's principal concern was to bring U.S. ground troops into action against the German Army as soon as possible. American public opinion was clamoring for vengeance against Japan. To keep the nation's strategic priorities straight, it was essential to join the battle against Hitler as soon as possible, regardless of the location. There was also the need to assist Russia, which could not be done so long as American forces sat on the sidelines. Finally, congressional midterm elections were set for November. It was inevitable that the Democrats would lose seats, the question was how many? If the United States had not mounted an offensive by then, the loss might be catastrophic.

The June conference in Washington (ARGONAUT) failed to find a solution. Meanwhile, the military situation continued to deteriorate.[24] The British garrison in the Libyan port city of Tobruk surrendered, opening the door for Rommel to move on Alexandria, Cairo, and the Suez Canal. In Russia, the German Army had crossed the Don and was approaching Stalingrad on the Volga; the Crimean fortress of Sevastopol had fallen; and the oil fields of the Caucasus appeared within Hitler's reach. The Chinese war effort had all but collapsed, the fighting on Guadalcanal hung in the balance, four of America's seven aircraft carriers had been sunk, and two were in dry dock for repairs. In the Atlantic, German U-boats prowled virtually unmolested. A thirty-three-ship convoy bound for Archangel lost twenty-four vessels en route, causing shipments to the Soviet Union's Arctic ports to be suspended indefinitely.[25]

An agreement on an offensive strategy was urgently required. On July 16, FDR dispatched Hopkins, Marshall, and King to London to settle the matter. "It is of the highest importance that U.S. ground troops be brought into action against the enemy in 1942," said the president.[26] Eisenhower, who had not been privy to the discussions thus far, met Marshall upon his arrival in London. At the chief of staff's direction, he prepared what amounted to a legal brief detailing the advantages of a cross-Channel assault in 1942 and negating any benefit that might accrue from landing in North Africa—which Marshall considered "completely out of the question."[27]

Ike did not participate in the conference with the British chiefs, but the meetings were tense and sometimes acrimonious. Marshall continued to press for crossing the Channel, but he was fighting a losing battle. On July 22, the British announced that the matter had been submitted to the war cabinet, which had voted unanimously against any cross-Channel operation in 1942.[28] For all practical purposes that decided the issue. When Eisenhower learned of the decision, he told Butcher, "July 22, 1942 could well go down as the 'blackest day' in history"—a silly overreaction he later regretted.[29]

After the British made it clear that they would not cross the Channel in 1942, Hopkins asked Roosevelt for instructions. The president said he was not surprised at the British refusal. He repeated his insistence on coming to grips with the Germans as soon as possible, and suggested that North Africa was the best place to do so.[30] Marshall and King grudgingly acknowledged the president's wishes but remained skeptical. At their final meeting on July 25, the CCS tentatively agreed to a largely American-led landing in North Africa in October, and repledged themselves to a cross-Channel attack in the summer of 1943.

The following day, Marshall told Eisenhower that he would command the North African expedition, which had been rechristened TORCH for security reasons. "General Marshall added that my appointment was not yet official, but that written orders would come through at an early date. In the meantime, he said that I should get started on the planning."[31] Marshall did not tell him of the War Department's skepticism about what it believed was a North African sideshow.

FDR was delighted with the outcome of the London discussions. "I cannot help feeling that last week represented a turning point in the whole war," he cabled Churchill on July 27.[32] Despite the president's clearly stated preference, Marshall and King continued to resist landing in North Africa. Their opposition surfaced at a meeting of the Combined Chiefs of Staff in Washington on July 30. The meeting was chaired by Admiral William D. Leahy, who had recently assumed his duties as chief of staff to the president. When the issue of North Africa arose, Marshall said he did not agree that a final decision had been made; King added that it was "his impression that the President and Prime Minister had not yet reached an agreement."[33] When Admiral Leahy reported the discussion to FDR, the president was furious. Marshall and King were ordered to the White House at eight-thirty that evening, and Roosevelt took the chiefs to the woodshed. As reported afterward by the War Department: "The PRESIDENT stated very definitely that he, as Commander-in-Chief, had made the decision that TORCH would be undertaken at the earliest possible date. He considered that this operation was now our principal objective and the assembling of means to carry it out should take precedence over other operations."[34]

For the first—but not the last—time during the war, Roosevelt asserted his constitutional prerogative as commander in chief and overruled his senior military and naval commanders.[*] FDR's command decision to invade North Africa rather than attempt a cross-Channel attack in 1942 was the most far-reaching American strategic decision of the war. According to Pulitzer Prize–winning historian Rick Atkinson, Roosevelt had "cast his lot with the British . . . repudiated an American military tradition of annihilation . . . and based his fiat on instinct and a political calculation that the time was ripe." His decision saved the United States from what would have been a military disaster.[35] As the ill-fated amphibious

---

[*] The second occasion in which the president asserted his authority was in March 1943, when FDR gave Admiral King a direct order to transfer sixty B-24 Liberator bombers from the Pacific theater to the Atlantic to combat German U-boats. Until that time, the Navy had resisted the transfer and the U-boats had gone largely unchallenged. After the transfer, the Battle of the Atlantic was quickly won. FDR to COMINCH [King], March 18, 1943, FDRL. Also see David Kennedy, *Freedom from Fear* 589 (New York: Oxford University Press, 1999); John Keegan, *The Second World War* 120 (New York: Viking, 1989).

assault by British and Canadian commandos on the French port of Dieppe in August 1942 proved, Hitler's West Wall was a tough nut to crack. Of the 6,000 men who took part in the Dieppe attack, 3,600 were killed, wounded, or captured. Even more compelling was the lackluster performance of the American Army during the early stages of the North African campaign. War Department euphoria notwithstanding, the U.S. Army was not yet battleworthy (in Churchill's words). Certainly it was not ready to take on the Wehrmacht, which would be fighting from behind prepared positions on the French coast.

Uncharacteristically, General Marshall continued to throw sand in the gearbox. In this instance, Marshall's determination served the nation poorly, and his recalcitrance delayed the North African landing by almost a month. Eisenhower, supported by the British, advocated landing on the Mediterranean coast of Algeria, as far east as possible, within striking distance of Tunisia. Both saw the swift occupation of Tunisia as the most crucial element in the invasion—vital to prevent Axis reinforcements coming from Sicily, and essential to trap Rommel's Afrika Korps in Libya. By contrast, General Marshall and the War Department insisted on landing on the Atlantic coast of Morocco, some thousand miles to the west. Marshall argued that it was too chancy to risk passage through the Strait of Gibraltar. Having been aggressive to the point of recklessness when advocating a 1942 cross-Channel attack, Marshall was now consumed with caution. His opposition to sending troop convoys through the strait was either a red herring or the result of a faulty knowledge of geography.[*] At its narrowest point the strait is eight miles wide (scarcely a bottleneck) and it was completely controlled by the Royal Navy and the Royal Air Force. There was also little risk of Spanish intervention to

---

[*] Probably a red herring. As Marshall's official biographer wrote: "On no other issue did the Secretary of War and the Chief of Staff differ so completely with the Commander-in-Chief. Their distrust of his military judgment, their doubts about the Prime Minister's advice, and their deep conviction that TORCH was fundamentally unsound persisted throughout August. With the same kind of tenacity that Churchill used in 1944 in the hope of scuttling the landings in Southern France, they continued by a fine splitting of hairs to insist that the final decision for TORCH had yet to be made." Pogue, 2 *Marshall* 349.

prevent passage since Generalissimo Francisco Franco was now hedging his bets. By contrast, a landing on Morocco's Atlantic coast, given the unusually high surf that prevailed, was a far more hazardous undertaking. It would also render the early occupation of Tunisia virtually impossible. General Marshall's stubborn refusal to consider landing in Algeria, combined with his continued preference for hitting the beaches in distant Morocco, caused British military leadership to question Marshall's strategic ability and contributed to the friction that bedeviled the Combined Chiefs of Staff.[36]

Ultimately Roosevelt and Churchill intervened in what Eisenhower called a "transatlantic essay contest," and a compromise was reached.[37] Allied troops would go ashore at three points: near Casablanca, in French Morocco, and close by the port cities of Oran and Algiers, in Algeria. Eisenhower set the date for November 8, 1942, barely two months away but five days after U.S. congressional elections.[*]

"Hurray!" FDR cabled Churchill on September 5.

"Okay full blast," Churchill replied.[38]

Eisenhower shared that sentiment. "The past six weeks have been the most trying of my life," he wrote George Patton. "You can well imagine that my feelings at the moment are those of great relief that a final decision now seems assured."[39]

Privately, Eisenhower confessed doubts. "We are undertaking something of a quite desperate nature," he wrote in his diary in early September. "In a way it is like the return of Napoleon from Elba—if the guess as to psychological reaction is correct, we may gain a tremendous advantage; if the guess is wrong, we will gain nothing and will lose a lot. . . . [W]e are sailing in a dangerous political sea, and this particular sea is one in which military skill and ability can do little in charting a safe course."[40]

Ike kept that sentiment to himself. To his staff he said TORCH was an order from the commander in chief and the prime minister, and that he was going to carry it out "if I have to go alone in a rowboat."[41]

---

[*] The election was a disaster for the Democrats, who lost eight seats in the Senate and fifty in the House, reducing their majorities to twenty-one and ten respectively.

Not until well after the war did General Marshall acknowledge that Roosevelt had been right and he had been wrong. Even then his acknowledgment was halfhearted. "We failed to see that the leader in a democracy has to keep the people entertained," Marshall told Forrest Pogue. "That may sound like the wrong word, but it conveys the thought. The people demand action. We couldn't wait."[42] Ike was more circumspect. "Later developments convinced me," he wrote shortly after the war, "that those who held the [1942 cross-Channel] operation unwise were correct."[43]

To head the planning for TORCH, Eisenhower prevailed upon General Walter Krueger to release Colonel Alfred Gruenther, who had been the operations officer for Third Army on the Louisiana maneuvers.[44] Planning was shifted from American headquarters on Grosvenor Square to Norfolk House on St. James's Square (the birthplace of George III), and Butcher located a suburban hideaway where Ike could relax—something that was long overdue. "He was not the cheerful man I remembered," said Gruenther upon his arrival in London. "He had aged ten years."[45]

Telegraph Cottage, the retreat Butcher found for Ike, was a picture-postcard English country house, situated on ten acres of dense woods and cultivated lawns, with a winding drive and high hedges that assured absolute privacy. Located between Coombe Hill and Little Coombe golf courses in Kingston, Surrey, the cottage was in the heart of what was known jokingly as London's stockbroker belt, and was roughly thirty minutes from Eisenhower's headquarters on Grosvenor Square. The cottage had five bedrooms, only one bathroom, and no central heating, but a massive fireplace in the living room and an old-fashioned coal stove in the kitchen kept the house comfortable most of the time. The only telephone was a direct line laid by the signal corps to headquarters on Grosvenor Square. At Churchill's insistence, a bomb shelter was dug in the garden before Ike moved in.

Initially, Eisenhower went to the cottage only on weekends. But the atmosphere proved so congenial that he was soon spending four to five nights a week there. "Our cottage is a godsend," Ike wrote Mamie on September 13. "Butch says I'm human again. When the day comes that all this business is over and I come back, you'd better

Ike's rendering of Telegraph Cottage. Eisenhower painted this while president and presented it to Sergeant Moaney with the following inscription: "I helped plan both TORCH 1942 (the Invasion of North Africa) and OVERLORD (1944) D-Day—Telegraph Cottage—15 miles South of London. DDE."

'figger' where we'll go and how we'll live. Possibly a shack, but at least we should be free as air. With a few pigs and chickens we can be as happy as a pair of Georgia crackers with a good still."[46]

Eisenhower shared Telegraph Cottage with Butcher and T. J. Davis, his adjutant general. Mickey McKeogh took charge of housekeeping details, Sergeant John Hunt did the cooking, and Sergeant John Alton Moaney was Ike's batman and valet. Hunt was from Petersburg, Virginia; Moaney, from Maryland's eastern shore. Both were black, and both remained with Eisenhower throughout the war. Moaney stayed until the general's death. Rounding out Ike's unofficial family was Kay Summersby, who initially began as Eisenhower's driver but was almost immediately integrated into off-duty activities. When opportunity permitted, Ike loved to play bridge in the evening, and it was usually he and Kay against Butcher and T.J. When fortune smiled, General Gruenther, recently promoted, who was recognized as one of the nation's outstanding bridge players, would take a hand.

At the time, Summersby was engaged to Richard Arnold, the young West Point officer in the Corps of Engineers who had been in Britain for over a year. Pert, bright, well-bred, and outgoing, Kay's pedigree made her invaluable to her American bosses, who were painfully unfamiliar with English social customs. Summersby could tell them who should sit next to whom at dinner parties, the order in which dinner partners addressed one another, when to light up and when not,[*] when it was permissible to leave a gathering (after royalty departed), and such other details that English hosts took seriously.

The fact is Kay Summersby proved a perfect interlocutor, buffering the transition for Ike's unofficial family into English life. She was thirty-four, one of five children of a retired lieutenant colonel in the Royal Munster Fusiliers—an Irish regiment of distinguished lineage. She was raised on the family estate, Inish Beg, a small island in the Ilen River in County Cork, and lived what she described as a sheltered life of privilege. "There was a succession of governesses, hunts, spatting parents, riding in the fields . . . the usual pattern of that obsolete world. The only tragedy which could becloud life in those days was a sudden Irish thunderstorm—because it might spoil my lovely tennis party."[47] As the daughter of an Army officer living in the country, she grew up around horses, was a fearless rider, and often rode to the hounds. She was also an accomplished bridge player, knew how to pour tea correctly, was well read, articulate, and, having been born into the propertied class, was less intimidated than most by Britain's social stratification.

"Kay was very beautiful in those days," said Anthea Saxe, a fellow member of the Motor Transport Corps. "She was charming and gra-

---

* At a time when smoking was more common, it was considered impermissible to light one's cigarette at the table before the toast to the Crown, usually rendered close to the end of the meal. As a young American professor at the University of Toronto in the early 1960s, I was introduced to the custom, which I considered a quaint relic of colonialism. For Eisenhower, who was a nicotine addict, the rule was oppressive, and when hosts learned of his habit, the toast to the Crown was regularly given after the first course was served.

Telek on the boss's desk.

cious, and she was gay and witty. She had a lot of energy and drive. She was also extremely capable and perhaps more important was very closed mouthed. She never blabbered about anything."[48]

Ike was smitten. "Dad was attracted to vital women, like Marian Huff in the Philippines and Kay," said John Eisenhower, "but these were friendships, not torrid affairs."[49]

To complete the unofficial family, Eisenhower decided they needed a dog. "Would you like to have a dog, Kay?" he asked. "I think I can manage that. I'd like to do something for you for working all these crazy hours and everything."[50] Ike had never owned a dog during his military career, and he delegated the task of finding one to Summersby and Bedell Smith, a knowledgeable dog lover. "I'm going to get a dog," he told Butcher, with a grin "as wide as a watermelon."[51]

Beetle and Kay narrowed the search to two Scotties, and Ike made the final choice and picked the dog's name: T-E-L-E-K. When asked, Eisenhower said the origin of the Scottie's name was "a military secret." To Kay he said, "It's a combination of Telegraph Cottage and Kay, two parts of my life that make me very happy."[52]

Michael Korda, Eisenhower's most recent biographer, suggests

that the selection of a Scottie was not surprising since Fala, FDR's
beloved companion, was probably the most famous dog in the
English-speaking world. "But the name Telek was yet another indication that Ike's feelings for Kay were hardly the normal ones of a
three-star general for his driver."[53]

To Mamie, Ike wrote, "I'm trying to get me a little dog—Scottie
by preference. You can't talk war to a dog, and I'd like to have someone or something to talk to, occasionally, that does not know what
the word means! A dog is my only hope."[54] Eisenhower evidently
saw no incongruity between his growing affection for Summersby
and his love for his wife.

Ike's selection to be supreme commander reflected circumstance
more than choice—another example of the *fortuna* that followed him
throughout his military career. He had gone to England in June
1942 as a stand-in for General Marshall to prepare for the cross-
Channel attack that Marshall would command. When that was
aborted and North Africa was selected as a substitute, neither Marshall nor Admiral King nor Secretary Stimson believed the new operation would ever take place. Certainly they were determined to
prevent it. In that context there was little risk in selecting Eisenhower to command. The fact that he had no combat experience, virtually no command time, and was the most junior lieutenant general
in the United States Army was of no consequence if the operation
was never mounted.

But events took control. Or more accurately, Churchill and Roosevelt took control. Despite the American military's objection to
landing in North Africa, the prime minister and the president ordered the invasion to take place. In addition, FDR insisted that the
United States play the major role. The president, who considered
himself an expert on French politics, was convinced the French had
soured on Great Britain, believing the British had left them in the
lurch by a premature evacuation at Dunkirk. To make matters worse,
the Royal Navy had proceeded to sink much of the French fleet at
Mers el-Kébir in July 1940 to prevent it from falling into German
hands. Roosevelt assumed the French held no such animosity toward
the United States. "I am reasonably sure a simultaneous landing by
British and Americans would result in full resistance by all French in

Africa," the president cabled Churchill on August 30. But "an initial American landing without British ground forces offers a real chance that there would be no French resistance or only a token resistance."[55] If the United States was to provide most of the troops for the invasion of North Africa, it was logical that the operation should be commanded by an American. Eisenhower was in London, he was manifestly American, and he had impressed the British with his openness, his fairness, and his determination. With no alternative candidate in the wings, his selection was foreordained.

What may be most surprising is how Eisenhower rose to the occasion. At the time, the invasion of North Africa in November 1942 was the greatest amphibious operation that had ever been attempted. Unlike the 1944 D-Day landing in Normandy, for which the Allies had three years to prepare, TORCH was mounted in two months, with sketchy intelligence about landing sites, improvised shipping arrangements, and an Army that had never seen combat. Two great armadas totaling more than 400 ships, protected by 300-plus naval vessels, would carry 116,000 men (three-quarters of whom were American) to the invasion beaches. One fleet would sail 2,800 miles from Great Britain through the Strait of Gibraltar to the Algerian coast. A second would sail 4,500 miles from Hampton Roads, Virginia, to Morocco. The troops would be at sea for two weeks. They would land on a potentially hostile shore without benefit of off-loading and regrouping. And no one knew what their reception would be. Eisenhower may have been overwhelmed by the responsibility, but his marching orders to his command were concise. "The object of the operation as a whole is to occupy French Morocco and Algeria with a view to the earliest possible subsequent occupation of Tunisia."[56]

Eisenhower recognized, as did most military planners, that French reaction to the Allied landing would be the single most important factor in guaranteeing early success. And here, FDR's self-assurance about French politics proved misplaced. French North Africa—Algeria, Morocco, and Tunisia—was not occupied by the Germans, and remained under the sovereign control of the French government in Vichy. TORCH, simply put, involved the invasion of the territory of a neutral nation without a declaration of war. The French Army in

North Africa, well officered but poorly equipped, numbered 120,000 men—roughly the size of the invasion force. If the French high command chose to resist the landings, it would not only become a public relations embarrassment but could well result in military defeat.

Allied relations with Vichy were complicated. France, under the terms of the June 1940 armistice with Germany, had been split in two. Northern France, including Paris, was occupied by the Germans. Southern France remained unoccupied, the government located in the provincial resort town of Vichy, headed by eighty-six-year-old Marshal Henri-Philippe Pétain, the hero of Verdun. The Vichy government was collaborationist. But it also reflected the aspirations of that element of French society who rejected the secular, egalitarian principles of the French Revolution. Instead of the democratic ideals of *Liberté, égalité, Fraternité,* the Vichy regime embraced the old-fashioned virtues of *Travail, Famille, Patrie* (Work, Family, Country). It was supported by those who in the 1930s had rallied to the slogan "Hitler rather than Blum"— Socialist Léon Blum, leader of France's Popular Front government. Primarily Catholic, ultraconservative, anti-Semitic, often the descendants of French nobility, and members of the officer corps and the high civil service, those loyal to Vichy accepted an alliance with Hitler as a means of preserving traditional values.

The United States recognized the Vichy regime as the legitimate government of France. Great Britain did not. FDR dispatched Admiral Leahy as American ambassador to Pétain in 1940; Churchill, on the other hand, embraced Charles de Gaulle as the "core of French resistance and the flame of French honour."[57] Roosevelt believed the Allies could do business with Vichy; Churchill took the position that the collaborationist scum should be relegated to the dustbin of history and that France should be reconstituted under de Gaulle's Free French leadership.

FDR's position was not simply a personal whim. Secretary of State Cordell Hull, the Foreign Service, and Admiral Leahy especially espoused the cause of Vichy as the legitimate government of France. Eisenhower was caught in the middle. At this point in the war it was unlikely the French officer corps would accept de Gaulle, who many believed had foresworn his oath of allegiance and was engaged in a treasonous enterprise. It was equally unlikely that the Vichy government would change sides and support the Allies. With both alternatives ruled out, Washington adopted a deus ex machina scheme hatched in the State Department and spearheaded by career diplomat Robert Murphy, a longtime savant of French affairs and since 1940 the senior American official in North Africa. Murphy believed that if the invasion was placed under the command of a ranking French general, one ostensibly loyal to Pétain, the whole of North Africa "would flame into revolt."[58] Local military authorities would accept the incoming general as their superior officer, order a cease-fire, and embrace the Anglo-American forces as liberators and allies. Ambassador Murphy did not use the phrase "dancing in the streets," but he might as well have done so.

There was little evidence to support Murphy's hypothesis. A conservative Catholic—conservative even by the Paleolithic standards of the Foreign Service—Murphy considered de Gaulle's Free French movement dangerously radical and found little to criticize in Vichy's domestic policies.[*] He was awed by the skill with which French administrators kept North Africa's Muslim population under control, and was convinced the Allies would have to retain the existing administrative structure to maintain order.[59] His French friends were largely aristocrats and senior officials who welcomed the stability Pétain provided. De Gaulle said that Murphy was "long familiar with the best society and apparently rather inclined to believe that France consisted of the people he dined with in town."[60]

---

[*] After August 1940, Vichy France became a one-party state. Labor unions were dissolved, free secondary education was abolished, divorce was made more difficult, and married women were denied employment in the public sector. The Jewish Statutes of October 1940 and June 1941 excluded Jews from the civil service and most professions. A Commissariat Général aux Questions Juives was established to enforce anti-Jewish regulations. Thousands of Jews were deported to Nazi concentration camps, and all Jews were persecuted.

Roosevelt's approval of the Pétain government, like his order to evacuate Japanese Americans from their homes along the Pacific coast, and arguably his failure to disrupt German concentration camps, reveals a side of the president's personality that is difficult to explain. Jean Edward Smith, *FDR* 549–53, 610–13. Also see Michael R. Marrus and Robert O. Paxton, *Vichy France and the Jews* 121–76 (New York: Basic Books, 1981); Robert O. Paxton, *Vichy France: Old Guard and New Order, 1940–1944* 51–233 (New York: Knopf, 1972); and David Thomson, *Democracy in France Since 1870* 222–24 (New York: Oxford University Press, 1964).

Murphy was also glib, personable, extremely confident, and exuded Irish charm with a well-honed gift for telling important people what they wanted to hear. Butcher wrote that he "talked more like an American businessman canvassing the ins and outs of a proposed merger than either a diplomat or a soldier."[61] Roosevelt, who usually saw through such people, was utterly charmed by Murphy, and made him his personal representative in North Africa. More than anyone else's, Murphy's views colored FDR's perception of the region and lay at the root of the plan the United States now put in place.

Murphy's candidate to rally the French Army in North Africa was General Henri Giraud, a four-star general who had commanded the French Seventh and Ninth armies in northern France in 1940, was captured by the Germans at Wassigny, had escaped from German captivity, and was living quietly in the Loire. Although he was not on active duty, his rank as a full general made him senior to the military governors in North Africa, and as a supporter of the Pétain government he had not stepped across the line into mutiny. Giraud would become an idée fixe with FDR as the French alternative to de Gaulle, but the fact is he had no place in the command structure of the Army, no popular following, no organization, no program, no interest in politics, and little administrative ability.[62] Simply put, he was an American puppet invented by FDR and the State Department to avoid having to deal with Charles de Gaulle.[63]* None of this was known to Eisenhower, and none of it bothered Murphy, who was confident that a great many Frenchmen in North Africa would rally to Giraud's support.[64]

With the utmost secrecy, Murphy arrived in England on September 16, 1942, and was spirited to Telegraph Cottage, where he briefed Ike on the plan. After an all-night session, Eisenhower cabled Marshall that he had the utmost confidence in Murphy's "judgment and discretion and I know that I will be able to work with him in perfect harmony."[65] Nevertheless, Ike was troubled by the wording of Murphy's mandate from FDR, which was vague about his place in

---

* For the genesis of the Giraud gambit, involving Murphy, H. Freeman Matthews, and various operatives of the Office of Strategic Services (forerunner of the CIA), see William L. Langer, *Our Vichy Gamble* 276–85, 305–35 (New York: Knopf, 1947).

the chain of command. "Since I am responsible for the success of the operations," he told Marshall, "I feel that it is essential that final authority in all matters in this theater rest with me." Marshall agreed. On September 22, Murphy's orders were revised by FDR clarifying that as the president's personal representative, he was still subordinate to Eisenhower.[66]

Murphy believed that prior to the invasion a ranking American officer should go to Algeria and meet clandestinely with senior French officers to secure their support. Mark Clark, now Ike's deputy, volunteered for the mission, and was landed by a British submarine on the Algerian coast in mid-October. Clark met with Murphy and Major General Charles E. Mast, chief of staff of the French XIX Corps. The results were inconclusive. Mast commanded no troops and spoke only for himself, and the meeting was disrupted by the local police. Clark fled, and in the process lost his trousers in the heavy surf reboarding the submarine. The disrupted meeting should have alerted Eisenhower, and certainly Clark, that Murphy's rosy assessment of French cooperation was unlikely to be realized.[67]

Under Gruenther's direction, planning for TORCH took shape. The assault troops were divided into three task forces—one for each target area. The western task force, some thirty-six thousand men commanded by George Patton, would hit the beaches at three points in the vicinity of Casablanca. These troops were drawn entirely from the United States.[68] They would sail from Hampton Roads on October 24, 1942, and would land in the early morning hours of November 8. The Atlantic swarmed with German U-boats, and the mammoth surf on the Moroccan coast might prevent landing for several days, but Patton was undeterred. "I will leave the beaches either a conqueror or a corpse," he told FDR on the eve of departure.[69]

"Don't scare the Navy, George," Marshall cautioned, "they are already afraid of you."[70]

The center task force, thirty-nine thousand troops commanded by Major General Lloyd Fredendall, would land at three sites near the Algerian port of Oran, capture the city in a pincer movement, and secure the port and airfield. Eisenhower had wanted the center task force commanded by Major General Russell ("Scrappy") Hartle, an old friend who commanded V Corps in Northern Ireland, but Marshall objected. Rarely did the chief of staff question a theater commander's judgment pertaining to personnel. But in this instance he asked Ike to consider Clark or "practically anyone you name" from a list of eight corps commanders Marshall provided rather than Hartle.[71] At Clark's suggestion, Eisenhower chose fifty-nine-year-old Lloyd Fredendall, known throughout the service as one of Marshall's men. Anglophobic, short-tempered, "unencumbered with charisma" in the words of historian Rick Atkinson, Fredendall enjoyed a reputation as an effective trainer of troops but would soon prove a military disaster. Both Marshall and Eisenhower can be faulted: Marshall for pushing someone utterly unfit for combat command, and Eisenhower for selecting someone he did not know.[*]

Both the western and center task forces were composed entirely of American troops. The eastern task force, which was to take Algiers, consisted of twenty-eight thousand British and thirteen thousand American troops. The initial assault would be commanded by Major General Charles "Doc" Ryder, Ike's West Point classmate. After the city was secure, command would revert to British lieutenant general Sir Kenneth Anderson, a dour Scot whose American code name was GROUCH. (The British called him "Sunshine.") Blunt to the point of rudeness, Anderson was an aggressive commander who led his men with the rugged determination of a Highland Scot. "He was not a popular type," said Eisenhower, "but I had real respect for his fighting heart."[72]

The eastern and center task forces sailed from the Firth of Clyde on October 26, 1942, under the command of Admiral Sir Andrew Cunningham, who subsequently became Eisenhower's naval commander in chief, and in 1943 succeeded Sir Dudley Pound as Britain's first sea lord. Ike called Cunningham a real sea dog—an admiral in the mode of Nelson who "believed that ships went to sea in order to find and destroy the enemy."[73][†]

---

[*] "My original selection of General Hartle for the Center Task Force was based upon the conviction that he would do a workmanlike job," Eisenhower cabled Marshall on October 3, 1942. "As agreed in subsequent telegrams, I am substituting Fredendall for him and will leave Hartle here in London as my deputy." DDE, 1 *War Years* 590–92.

[†] In late 1943, Eisenhower asked Cunningham to send the British battle fleet,

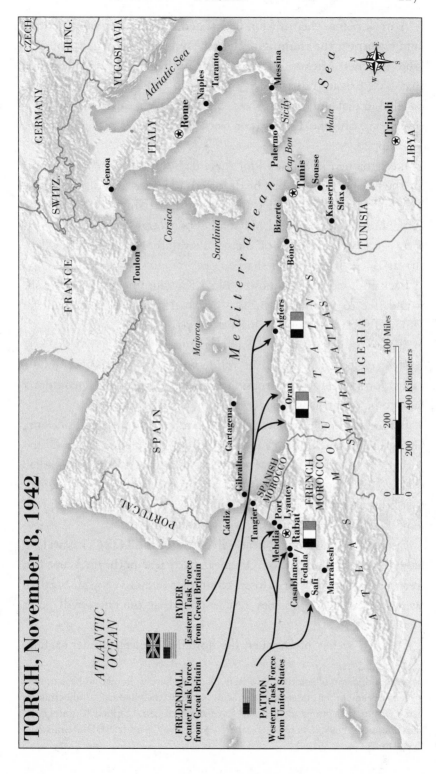

**TORCH, November 8, 1942**

A week before the invasion fleet sailed, Eisenhower went to Scotland to inspect the training of the 1st Division, the Army's Big Red One. Butcher, Mickey, and Kay went with him. Kay remembered that Ike's private railroad car, the *Bayonet*, was quite plush. It was paneled in teak and had a private office, sleeping quarters, and a sitting room. She and Eisenhower worked awhile, then played bridge and napped.[74]

Ike remained in Scotland for three days, and his visit was a tonic for the troops' morale. But he departed downcast and disappointed. "We are short on experience and trained leadership below battalion commander," he informed Marshall. The troops "did not know exactly what was expected of them." Privately, Ike said, "They'll be sitting ducks if they don't sharpen up."[75]

Back in London, Eisenhower asked Kay Summersby whether she would like to accompany him to North Africa—an assignment far removed from the Motor Transport Corps.

"I'd give anything to go," Summersby replied.

"It's settled then. You'll be following us. It will probably be a month or so before the situation is stabilized. And Kay, you don't have to be told this is top secret. Not a word to anyone."[76]

Before leaving, Eisenhower paid a farewell courtesy call on King George VI at Buckingham Palace. Clark accompanied him. "Didn't you get stranded on the beach without your pants?" the King asked Clark.[77] Eisenhower had worried about the protocol requirement that he not turn his back on the King when leaving. "It was no problem," said Ike. "He came right to the door with us."[78]

Eisenhower was now upbeat. "Everything for TORCH is well in hand," he told Marshall on October 29. "I fear nothing except bad weather and possibly large losses to submarines. Given a fair break in these two matters, you may rest assured that the entry will go as planned."[79]

On the last day of October, Ike hosted a farewell dinner at Tele-

---

carrying a division of soldiers, into Italy's Taranto harbor, known to be saturated with mines and other underwater obstacles—an extremely hazardous undertaking that many naval commanders would have avoided. "Sir," replied Cunningham, "His Majesty's Fleet is here to go wherever you may send it." DDE, *Crusade in Europe* 89.

graph Cottage for his family: Butcher, Clark, Davis, Beetle, and Kay. "The eve of battle is an eerie time," Summersby remembered. "There were a few toasts drunk to a successful operation, but no one felt like talking. We did not even play bridge, but simply sat around the living room making remarks now and then, almost like courteous strangers in a waiting room."[80]*

The following day, Robert Murphy threw a spanner in the works (as the British would say). With the invasion armadas already on the high seas, he radioed Ike asking that the landings be postponed for two weeks. General Giraud, it seems, was unable to leave home until November 20, 1942. Eisenhower exploded. "It is inconceivable that [Murphy] can recommend such a delay," he cabled Marshall. "Recommend the President advise [Murphy] immediately that his suggested action is utterly impossible."[81] Roosevelt, who was spending the weekend at Hyde Park, wasted no time. "I fully concur in General Eisenhower's recommendation," he told Marshall. "Please inform him to that effect at once."[82] The invasion was on.

To screen Eisenhower's departure from London, the Army devised the cover story that he was returning to Washington for consultation. The story was widely circulated and Mamie made preparations to receive her husband at their apartment. To maintain security, there was no way Eisenhower could inform her that he would not be coming. Being in transit and headed for battle, there was also no way for him to know when he could write next. His final act in London was to send his wife a postdated letter. "By the time you read this your newspapers will probably have told you where I am and you will understand why your birthday letter had to be written some time in advance." Mamie's forty-sixth birthday was November 14, 1942.

"I'd like to be there to help you celebrate, and to kiss you 46 times (multiplied by any number you care to pick). I will be thinking with the deepest gratitude of the many happy hours and years you have given me. . . . I've never wanted any other wife—you're mine, and for that reason I've been luckier than any other man."[83]

---

* Butcher, in recording the dinner in his diary, neglected to include Summersby when listing those present. Harry C. Butcher, *My Three Years with Eisenhower: The Personal Diary of Captain Harry C. Butcher, USNR, Naval Aide to General Eisenhower, 1942 to 1945* 160 (New York: Simon and Schuster, 1946).

TEN

# Baptism by Fire

At any moment, it is possible that a necessity
might arise for my relief and consequent
demotion.

—DWIGHT D. EISENHOWER,
*February 19, 1943*

EISENHOWER ARRIVED ON Gibraltar on November 5, 1942.
"All of us are well," he cabled Beetle Smith, "although I must say
that the trip by bomber is not something to be taken on your honeymoon. . . . Please find out from Kay how Telek is and include a short
statement in any American message to me—such as Telek O.K. or
Telek very sick, or whatever is applicable. I am quite anxious about
the little black imp!"[1][*]

The Rock of Gibraltar, three square miles of Jurassic limestone, a

---

[*] Eisenhower received an unsigned cable shortly afterward from London reporting "Telek is fine." On November 11, he wired Beetle, "You would scarcely believe
me if I should tell you how much the good news about Telek meant to me. The
little black imp has a real personality that appeals to me tremendously. While I
think this is the one thing in which I did not accept your advice (I mean the choice
of the two dogs), I am delighted I took him on 'love at first sight.' "

Telek accompanied Ike throughout the war. When Eisenhower returned to
Washington to become chief of staff in November 1945, Telek remained with Kay
and died in New York in 1959 at the age of seventeen. *The Papers of Dwight David
Eisenhower,* vol. 2, *The War Years* 693–95, cited subsequently as 2 *War Years;* Kay
Summersby Morgan, *Past Forgetting: My Love Affair with Dwight D. Eisenhower* 281
(New York: Simon and Schuster, 1976).

British colony since 1704, was the only territory on the continent of Europe still occupied by the Western Allies. Until the troops were safely ashore in North Africa, it became the temporary headquarters of the supreme commander. Ike and his staff had flown eight hours from London in five B-17 Flying Fortresses, often through execrable weather, at an average altitude of five hundred feet to evade enemy fighters. As the formation approached the Rock, Major Paul Tibbets, Eisenhower's pilot, said, "This is the first time I've ever had to climb to get into the landing pattern."[2] (Tibbets, who was widely regarded as one of the nation's most accomplished pilots, later flew the *Enola Gay*, which dropped the atomic bomb on Hiroshima.)

Gibraltar had all the earmarks of a beleaguered fortress. Honey-combed with thirty miles of tunnels, the surface crosshatched with water catchment ditches running into underground cisterns, and with an airfield capable of holding six hundred planes, wingtip to wingtip, the Rock would not only provide air cover for the landings, but also afforded Ike a command center from which to communicate with the task forces. Supreme headquarters was six hundred feet deep inside the Rock, ventilated by a few ineffective fans of unknown vintage, dimly lit, rodent infested, and constantly damp from condensation dripping from the ceiling. Eisenhower referred to the setting as "the most dismal we occupied during the war."[3]

To make matters worse, General Henri Giraud, who had been spirited out of France by Murphy's operatives, arrived on Gibraltar on the afternoon of November 7, ready to assume overall command of the invasion. Murphy, it appears, had assured Giraud that if he would put himself at the disposal of the Allies, he would supersede Eisenhower as supreme commander. The unhappy task of disillusioning the general fell to Ike, who called it "my most distressing interview of the war."[4]

For four hours, Eisenhower and Giraud had at it. "I could understand General Giraud's French fairly well," Ike recalled, "but I insisted on using an interpreter to avoid any chance of misunderstanding."[5] After the first hour, they were reduced to repeating themselves. Giraud reminded Eisenhower that he was a four-star general and Ike only a three-star. Eisenhower assured Giraud that the Allies were eager for him to assume command of the French forces in

North Africa and to head civil affairs for the region, but that anything else was out of the question. Giraud saw no point in landing in North Africa, and insisted the troops should be redirected to land in southern France. He also said that since they would be fighting on French soil, he could not possibly subordinate himself to the Combined Chiefs of Staff.[6] With all the delicacy he could muster, Eisenhower explained why Giraud's demands were impossible. Giraud was unmoved. When they broke for dinner—Giraud at Government House, Ike at the British admiralty mess—Giraud told Eisenhower: "General Giraud cannot accept a subordinate position in this command. His countrymen would not understand and his honor as a soldier would be tarnished."[7] Like Charles de Gaulle and Douglas MacArthur, Giraud habitually referred to himself in the third person.

During the dinner break, Eisenhower consulted with his diplomatic advisers, H. Freeman Matthews from the State Department and William H. B. Mack of the British Foreign Office. They suggested placing Giraud in nominal command, with Eisenhower retaining operational control as Giraud's deputy. Eisenhower rejected the proposal.[8] Mark Clark and Admiral Cunningham agreed. Cunningham called Giraud's demands "preposterous and unreasonable."[9]

When the meeting resumed at 10:30 p.m., Giraud remained adamant. After two unproductive hours the discussions broke off. "Giraud will be a spectator in this affair," the French general announced with a shrug.[10] Eisenhower bid him good night, and then informed Marshall he thought Giraud was playing for time. "He realizes that he can do nothing with respect to the landing itself and can gain no credit for it, no matter how successful. Consequently he is choosing to wait to see what happens. If we are generally successful tonight, I will not be surprised to find him more conciliatory tomorrow."[11]*

---

* Eisenhower's assessment of Giraud's motives proved correct. After a night's sleep, Giraud capitulated. "Have just concluded gentleman's agreement with KINGPIN [Giraud's code name] that is entirely acceptable," Ike cabled Marshall on November 8, 1942. "The basis of the agreement is exactly what I offered KINGPIN throughout the long conference of yesterday." Eisenhower to Marshall, November 8, 1942, in 2 *War Years* 675–76.

Marshall replied that Ike had been absolutely correct in the stance he took. "Our only regret is that you have been forced to devote so much of your time to this purpose."[12]

Shortly after 2 a.m. on November 8, 1942, the troops of the western (Patton), center (Fredendall), and eastern (Ryder) task forces debarked from their transports and headed toward the North African shoreline for a hazardous night landing. The surf on the Moroccan coast was unprecedentedly benign (less than four feet), and Patton's men got ashore with no more than the usual number of mishaps. Fredendall's troops misread their maps and landed four miles off target, but for the most part the initial phase of TORCH went as planned. "Information from the task forces is meager," Ike reported to Marshall at 9:30 a.m., "but we do know that we are fairly solidly ashore at eastern and central points and that western attack began as scheduled."[13]

As the troops made their way inland, the fighting intensified. The French were standing their ground. The battle was heaviest at the ports of Algiers and Oran. In the port of Algiers, French coastal batteries sunk an American destroyer, and there was fierce fighting in the harbor itself. At Oran, the planned pincer movement failed to materialize. The airfield and port remained in French hands, and two British destroyers were sunk by naval gunfire. The stubborn resistance of the French, combined with the slowness of inexperienced troops coming under fire for the first time, created increasing anxiety at Eisenhower's headquarters.[14] That anxiety was intensified by the lack of information from Patton in Morocco. Gibraltar had lost radio contact with the western task force, and the last information indicated that a ferocious battle had been joined all along the line.[15]

Isolated from the fighting, and with no ability to influence the outcome, Eisenhower became introspective. At the Wilderness, Grant had passed the time whittling sticks. Eisenhower chose to put his thoughts on paper. "Worries of a Commander," he scribbled at the top of a sheet of government-issue foolscap. In short order, Ike ticked off ten potential problems: Spain was ominously quiet; Giraud was difficult to deal with; Giraud wanted planes; Giraud was impossible.

No news from Task Forces. Reports few and unsatisfactory. Defensive fighting, which seemed halfhearted this morning, has blazed up, and in many places resistance is stubborn.

- We are slowed up in eastern sector when we should be getting toward Bône-Bizerte [in Tunisia] at once.
- We don't know whereabouts or conditions of airborne force. [The planes had been scattered by bad weather and the airborne attacks were unsuccessful.]
- We cannot find out anything.[16]

Alone, and with nothing to do but wait, Ike dispatched a cable to Beetle Smith in London. Could he send a "skeletonized Wack [WAC, Women's Army Corps] Company of fifteen or twenty secretaries and stenographers essential to the headquarters' effective operation?"[17] Eisenhower had evidently planned this beforehand, and it was his way of bringing Kay Summersby and others to North Africa.*

Beetle immediately put the wheels in motion. "I cannot tell you how delighted I am that you have got the Wack business all buttoned up," Ike replied on November 11. "When we get to our own headquarters and can run our own establishment according to our own likes and dislikes, a gang of friends around

---

* On October 27, 1942, Brigadier General Everett Hughes, working as deputy chief of staff at Eisenhower's London headquarters, wrote in his diary, "I suspect from the females that Ike is taking that Butch [Commander Harry C. Butcher] has his eye on a bit of **** for the C[ommanding] G[eneral]."

General Hughes was an old friend of the Eisenhowers from their days at the Wyoming in Washington and the Army general staff. A charter member of Club Eisenhower, he was called "Uncle Everett" by young John. Hughes remained with Eisenhower throughout the war, and was widely regarded as Ike's "eyes and ears." Simply put, Everett Hughes was one of Eisenhower's closest friends. His assessment was that of someone who had known Ike and Mamie for over twenty years. Everett Hughes diary (handwritten), Manuscript Division, Library of Congress. Also see John S. D. Eisenhower, *Strictly Personal* 7 (Garden City, N.Y.: Doubleday, 1974).

with whom we can have an hour's conversation a day will be a God-send."[18]

Eisenhower missed the presence of women. Throughout his military career, Mamie (with few exceptions) had always accompanied him. And the first year in the Philippines when she had not, he had struck up an abiding friendship with Marian Huff. "I think I have learned more about the value of feminine companionship in the last month than I ever knew in my life," Ike wrote Mamie's sister Mike on December 4, 1942. "If a gang of men are off on an expedition of golf or hunting, their sense of loss on this score would not be so noticeable. The difficulty is that all of us live under the highest pressure of responsibility and strain and our only companionship, even at meal time, is ourselves. The result is that finally one feels a bit bewildered but there is nothing to do about it."[19] Eisenhower found the needed companionship with Kay Summersby. Beetle, who suffered from ulcers, developed a relationship with his nurse, Ethel Westermann, sometimes described as "the most beautiful nurse in the whole European theater."[20] Ike's friend Everett Hughes found solace with Rosalind Prismal, a young British widow who worked as his secretary. Butcher had a variety of female friends but eventually was attracted to Molly Jacobs, a young Red Cross worker. George Patton traveled with his "niece." It was not out of the ordinary for the senior commanders of World War II to move with a retinue of female support staff. In the Pacific, MacArthur's wife, Jean, was in residence, and his senior staff became notorious for their dalliances with headquarters personnel. General Marshall kept an edgy eye on what was happening but chose not to intervene.

While Eisenhower reflected on the problems he confronted, the battle hung in the balance. But as French resistance stiffened, *fortuna* intervened once again on Ike's behalf. Admiral Jean-Louis Darlan, the deputy head of the Vichy regime and commander in chief of French armed forces, was in Algiers visiting his son Alain, who had recently contracted polio. Darlan's presence was unexpected. Of more immediate import, General Alphonse Juin, the overall commander of the French Army in North Africa, was also in Algiers.

Juin was subordinate to Darlan, but unlike the admiral, he was decidedly anti-German.[*] By noon on November 8, Juin concluded that it was absurd for the French Army to be fighting the Allies. On his own authority, with Darlan's reluctant acquiescence, Juin sought out General Ryder to arrange an armistice in Algiers.[21]

"Are you the senior commander?" Juin asked Ryder.

"I am."

"Will you assume responsibility for keeping law and order if Algiers is surrendered to you?"

"Yes," Ryder replied, "provided I may have the services of the French gendarmes acting under my orders."

"When will you be ready to do this?"

"Immediately."

"Will you permit French troops to retain their weapons?"

"Yes, provided the troops are assembled in their barracks."[22]

At Juin's order, the French garrison in Algiers ceased fighting and returned to its barracks. Ryder's forces entered the city at 8 p.m. With Algiers in Allied hands, Eisenhower immediately dispatched Clark and Giraud to the city to negotiate a general cease-fire. Except for the surrender of Algiers, the military situation remained uncertain. Fredendall's forces were stymied outside Oran (Fredendall had yet to set foot on shore), and the trickle of news from Morocco portended disaster. "Disturbing report (garbled) was to the effect that at one beach [Patton] was re-embarking under a flag of truce," Eisenhower cabled Bedell Smith. "That I do *not* believe. Unless my opin-

---

* General Juin, who lost the use of his right arm in World War I, had been a classmate of Charles de Gaulle's at Saint-Cyr, the French military academy. In 1940, he commanded the 15th Motorized Infantry Division, whose heroic defense of Lille provided time for the British evacuation at Dunkirk. Despite the senior position he held under Vichy, his sympathy for the Allies was well known. Later, as head of the French Expeditionary Corps fighting as part of Fifth Army in Italy, he asked to be reduced in rank from full general to lieutenant general so as not to outrank Mark Clark. After the war Juin became French chief of staff, represented France at the San Francisco conference that established the United Nations, commanded allied ground forces under NATO, and was made a marshal of France in 1952—the last person invested with that office. He is entombed in Les Invalides. Anthony Clayton, *Three Marshals of France: Leadership After Trauma* 10–38, 65–92, 165–97 (London: Brassey's, 1992).

ion of Georgie is 100% wrong, he wouldn't re-embark anything, including himself."[23]

Ike hoped that Giraud's arrival in Algiers would signal the end of French resistance. But that did not happen. "General Giraud's cold reception by the French in Africa was a terrible blow to our expectations," Eisenhower wrote later. "He was completely ignored. He made a broadcast, announcing assumption of leadership of French North Africa and directing French forces to cease fighting against Allies, but his speech had no effect whatsoever."[24]

With Giraud unexpectedly out of the picture, Clark and Eisenhower recognized that Admiral Darlan, and only Admiral Darlan, could order French forces to end their resistance. But Darlan declined to do so. The situation in Algiers, precipitated by General Juin, was an anomaly. Marshal Pétain had ordered that North Africa be defended, and Darlan, as Pétain's deputy, told Clark that he had no alternative but to do so. "All of my associates and I feel hostilities are useless," said Darlan. "I can simply obey the orders of Pétain."[25]

Sixty-one-year-old Admiral Jean François Darlan was (along with Pierre Laval) the most formidable member of the Pétain government. His anticlericalism set him apart from most in Vichy, but he embraced Pétain's appeal to hierarchy, order, and discipline. Short, thick, energetic, and cynical—he was reputed to have the worldly deviousness of a Renaissance cardinal—Darlan had been the principal architect of Vichy's military cooperation with the Third Reich. Unlike Laval, Darlan was not so much pro-Nazi as he was pro-German and anti-British. As head of the French Navy since 1937, he believed that France might return to glory on Hitler's coattails. Churchill called him "a bad man with a narrow outlook and an evil eye."[26]

At midnight on November 10, as the fighting at Oran and in Morocco continued, Hitler renounced the terms of the German armistice with Vichy and ordered troops into unoccupied France. Ten German and six Italian divisions spilled across the frontiers and by dawn had snuffed out what little autonomy Pétain enjoyed. That gave the French leadership in North Africa an excuse to renounce their oath of allegiance to the marshal. A day of tough bargaining ensued and by nightfall an armistice with the Allies had been declared. French forces in North Africa were ordered to stop fighting.

The three-day battle cost dearly. On the French side, three thousand men had been killed or wounded; twenty-one ships, including the battleship *Jean Bart* and the cruiser *Primauguet,* were sunk; and 135 of the 168 planes based in Algeria and Morocco had been destroyed. Allied losses were similar: three thousand killed, wounded, or missing; more than a dozen ships, including the battleship *Massachusetts* and the cruisers *Wichita* and *Brooklyn,* sunk or heavily damaged; and seventy planes shot down.[27]

The battle for Algeria and Morocco was over. But the terms and conditions of what was to follow had yet to be ironed out. For the next two days, General Clark, Ambassador Murphy, Admiral Darlan, and General Juin hammered out what came to be known as the Clark-Darlan Agreement, specifying Allied rights in North Africa and confirming the continuation of French sovereignty.[*] Under the terms of the agreement the Allies were granted control of all airports, harbor and port facilities, fortifications, arsenals, and military communication networks. The agreement also recognized extraterritorial status for Allied personnel and granted wide emergency powers in case of domestic disorder. In return the Allies guaranteed the preservation of the status quo ante bellum—in effect leaving the Vichy administration of North Africa intact. French military and naval forces remained under French command, independent of the supreme commander. Nowhere in the agreement was there any requirement to remove fascist elements from the governmental structure, to repeal Vichy's anti-Semitic regulations and restrictions, or to liquidate the North African version of the SS. Darlan became high commissioner of North Africa, Giraud assumed direction of French armed forces, and Juin was given command of the Army.[28]

Eisenhower was delighted. "I approve of everything you have done," he cabled Clark on November 12.[29] The following day, Friday the thirteenth, Ike flew to Algiers to put his seal of approval on the document. He was greeted like a conquering hero. According to one observer, Eisenhower was "a living dynamo of energy, good humor,

---

* The Clark-Darlan Agreement, some twenty-one articles, is reprinted in United States Department of State, 2 *Foreign Relations of the United States, 1942: Europe* 453–57 (Washington, D.C.: U.S. Government Printing Office, 1962).

amazing memory for details, and amazing courage for the future."[30] After a celebratory lunch at the Hotel St. Georges, he pinned a third star on Mark Clark's shoulders and flew back triumphantly to Gibraltar.

For Eisenhower, the agreement with Darlan was essential to permit the Allies to shift their focus to Tunisia (where arguably it should have been from the beginning). For Clark, the admiral was a man you could do business with.[31] For Murphy, Darlan was the man of the hour. His appointment as high commissioner would ensure that experienced representatives of the Vichy regime would continue to administer Algeria and Morocco—where the specter of Arab revolt was a continuing concern. In that context, Murphy saw Vichy's anti-Semitic stance as a tactical advantage because it resonated with the indigenous Muslim population. Murphy also believed that the continuity Darlan represented would prevent the dispatch of Gaullist Free French figures from London—men such as Jean Monnet, Maurice Schumann, François Mitterrand, and Michel Debré—whom he considered dangerously radical. "We had no thought," Murphy wrote later, "that a 'Darlan deal' would not be acceptable in Washington."[32]

The euphoria was short-lived. When news of the Clark-Darlan Agreement arrived in London, a firestorm erupted. The British war cabinet was appalled. Foreign Secretary Anthony Eden said the deal smacked of Munich. Churchill's friends in Parliament asked, "Is this then what we have been fighting for?"[33] Public opinion followed suit. Edward R. Murrow, in his daily broadcast to the United States from London, asked: "Are we fighting Nazis or sleeping with them? Why this play with traitors? Don't we see that we could lose this war by winning it?"[34]

The British did not object to the military cease-fire. What they protested was the commitment to keep the Vichy regime in place. Churchill, Eden, and British public sentiment strongly supported Charles de Gaulle's Free French movement as the rallying point for France's liberation. Headquartered in London, the Free French embodied antifascist sentiment in France, spanned the political spectrum from left to right, was in close contact with the Resistance, and transcended the ancient division between the republic and its enemies.* At Washington's insistence, de Gaulle had not been informed of the landings in North Africa in advance, and it appeared from the accord that had been concluded with Darlan that the future of France had been returned to Vichy's control. That was a bitter pill for the British to swallow.

"It is a strategic error to place oneself in a situation contradictory to the moral character of this war," de Gaulle reminded Churchill. "We are no longer in the eighteenth century when Frederick the Great paid the courtiers of Vienna in order to take Silesia, nor in the Italian Renaissance when one hired the myrmidons of Milan or the mercenaries of Florence. If France one day discovers that because of the British and the Americans her liberation consists of Darlan, you perhaps can win the war from a military point of view but you will lose it morally."[35]

The furor in Britain spilled over into the United States, and the administration was caught with its pants down. Roosevelt had initially approved the Clark-Darlan Agreement, but in the face of the public outcry he quickly backed away. On November 17, FDR issued a public statement rapping Ike's knuckles. "I have accepted General Eisenhower's political arrangements made for the time being in North Africa and West Africa. [But] no permanent arrangement should be made with Admiral Darlan. The present temporary arrangement in North and West Africa is only a temporary expedient, justified solely by the stress of battle. *No one in our Army has any authority to discuss the future government of France or the French Empire.*"[36]

Privately, the president cabled Eisenhower:

MARSHALL HAS SHOWN ME YOUR DISPATCH GIVING YOUR REASONS FOR PLACING DARLAN IN CHARGE OF CIVIL ADMINISTRATION OF NORTH AFRICA.† I WANT YOU TO KNOW THAT I

---

* As the symbol of the Free French movement, de Gaulle chose the tricolor flag of the republic with the cross of Lorraine superimposed, reflecting for the first time in French history the union of Christianity and the republic.

† Alerted by Beetle Smith in London and by Marshall that a storm was brewing over the Darlan deal, Eisenhower dispatched a lengthy justification to the Combined Chiefs of Staff that acknowledged that the situation in North Africa "does not repeat not agree even remotely with some of prior calculations." He pointed out that the end of French resistance had come about from Darlan's orders, not

APPRECIATE FULLY THE DIFFICULTIES OF YOUR MILITARY SITU-
ATION. I AM THEREFORE NOT DISPOSED TO IN ANY WAY QUES-
TION THE ACTION YOU HAVE TAKEN. . . .

HOWEVER, I THINK YOU SHOULD KNOW AND HAVE IN MIND
THE FOLLOWING POLICIES OF THIS GOVERNMENT:

1. THAT WE DO NOT TRUST DARLAN.
2. THAT IT IS IMPOSSIBLE TO KEEP A COLLABORATOR OF HIT-
   LER AND ONE WHOM WE BELIEVE TO BE A FASCIST IN CIVIL
   POWER ANY LONGER THAN IS ABSOLUTELY NECESSARY.
3. HIS MOVEMENTS SHOULD BE WATCHED CAREFULLY AND HIS
   COMMUNICATIONS SUPERVISED.[37]

Eisenhower accepted responsibility for the Darlan decision, and he suffered the consequences. At any moment it was possible that Washington might cut him loose. "From what I hear of what has been appearing in the newspapers," Ike wrote his son John, "you are learning that it is easy enough for a man to be a newspaper hero one day and a bum the next."[38]

Eisenhower had been badly served by Robert Murphy, whose assessment of the North African situation reflected his ultraconservative, pro-Vichy bias. But Ike was also culpable. He had not been catapulted over the heads of 345 generals more senior—to say nothing of their British counterparts—because he was a proven combat leader. Nor had he spent the interwar years on remote Army posts doing squads left and squads right. Eisenhower had served seven years with MacArthur at the highest command level in Washington and Manila. He had become Marshall's alter ego at the War Department during the first six months of the war, and in London he had dealt on the most intimate terms with Churchill and the British

---

because the Allies had prevailed in battle, and that if they did not cooperate with Darlan additional trouble might ensue. "I realize there may be a feeling at home that we have been sold a bill of goods, but I assure you that these arrangements have been arrived at only after incessant examination of the important factors and with the determination of getting on with the military objectives in winning the war." Eisenhower made no mention of the political aspects of the agreement. DDE to CCS, November 14, 1942, 2 *War Years* 707–11.

high command. With the exception of Marshall and MacArthur, Eisenhower had more political experience than any officer in the American Army. He was chosen to be supreme commander precisely because of his political sensitivity. Yet he muffed the decision concerning Darlan—not the cease-fire but the perpetuation of the Vichy regime—because he ignored everything he had learned about the fractious nature of French politics during his year in Paris with Pershing. He concentrated exclusively on the military aspect of the situation and overlooked the political consequences. "It was a callow, clumsy army that had arrived in North Africa with little notion how to act as a world power," wrote one recent historian.[39]

Roosevelt's emphasis on the temporary nature of the Darlan accord failed to quell the public outcry. On November 26, 1942, Churchill's national unity government confronted a motion in the House of Commons placing the House on record that "our relations with Admiral Darlan and his kind are inconsistent with the ideals for which we are fighting this war."[40] So great was the opposition in the House that Churchill felt compelled to convene a rare secret session. "I hold no brief for Admiral Darlan," he told the members. "I must however say that personally I consider that in the circumstances prevailing, General Eisenhower was right; *and even if he was not quite right* I should have been very reluctant to hamper or impede his action when so many lives hung in the balance."[41]*

Churchill and FDR gave Eisenhower the benefit of the doubt. But their tepid endorsement was scarcely reassuring. In early December, Roosevelt sent Milton Eisenhower, now deputy director of the Office of War Information, to North Africa to assess the situation. Milton's message from Washington was clear. "Heads must roll, Murphy! Heads must roll," meaning that Vichyites like Darlan had to be dis-

---

* Stalin also came to Ike's support. On December 13, 1942, he wrote FDR that, "in my opinion, as well as that of my colleagues, Eisenhower's policy with regard to Darlan is perfectly correct. I think it is a great achievement that you have succeeded in bringing Darlan and others into the orbit of the Allies fighting Hitler." USSR Ministry of Foreign Affairs, 2 *Correspondence Between the Chairman of the Council of Ministers of the USSR and the Presidents of the United States and the Prime Ministers of Great Britain During the Great Patriotic War* 44 (New York: E. P. Dutton, 1958).

missed.[42] Churchill took his own remedial action. He immediately assigned Harold Macmillan, a British minister of state, to be Eisenhower's political adviser for civil affairs, hoping to counterbalance whatever influence Murphy might have. Eisenhower was chastened. Later he told the president, "I believe in a theatre commander doing these things without referring them back to his home Government and then waiting for approval. If a mere General makes a mistake, he can be repudiated and kicked out and disgraced. But a Government cannot repudiate and kick out and disgrace itself—not, at any rate, in wartime."[43]

Meanwhile, on November 11, British general Sir Kenneth Anderson assumed command of the eastern task force and set out for Tunis, 540 road miles away. Eisenhower (as well as military planners in Washington and London) assumed it would be a cakewalk. The distance from Algiers to Tunis was roughly that between Washington and Cincinnati, the French were coming on board, and Allied intelligence had predicted that it would take at least two weeks for Axis soldiers to reach Tunisia in strength. Even when they did, the troops would be "low category and without motor transport."[44]

Once again, preinvasion estimates proved worthless. Within hours of learning of the Allied landings, Hitler had ordered frontline German troops into Tunisia. "To give up Africa means to give up the Mediterranean," he declared. "It would mean not only the ruin of our revolutions, but also the ruin of our people's future."[45] On the morning of November 9, as the forces of Patton and Fredendall fought their way inland, the first Luftwaffe fighter planes touched down at airfields north of Tunis. Dive-bombers and military transports followed in their wake. By evening, almost one hundred planes were in place, the airfields ringed by paratroopers from the Hermann Göring Division. French response was ambivalent. Initially undecided, the French Navy and Air Force chose not to resist the German arrival. In Tunis, Army commander General Georges Barré, pursuant to orders from General Juin, evacuated the city and marched his division (almost ten thousand men) westward into the mountains to await the Allies. Not one French weapon was discharged to prevent the German landing. There were no casualties, no vehicles destroyed, and no planes shot down. The German takeover of the principal cities of

Field Marshal Albert "Smiling Albert" Kesselring.

Tunis and Bizerte was as bloodless as the 1940 capture of Copenha-
gen. In Tunis, the German high command established its headquarters in the abandoned American consulate.

By November 15, more than fifteen thousand veteran German
soldiers had arrived, including the 10th Panzer Division, some battalions recently equipped with new Tiger tanks armed with a powerful 88mm gun. One week later, German strength exceeded thirty-five
thousand, including a second panzer division and twenty squadrons
of Stukas and Messerschmitts. Overall command was entrusted to
Field Marshal Albert Kesselring, a former Luftwaffe chief of staff,
who was Hitler's commander in chief, south, and one of Germany's
most able military leaders. An eternal optimist—he was nicknamed
"Smiling Albert"—he had risen through the ranks of the field artillery, was transferred against his wishes to the Air Ministry in 1931,

learned to fly at the age of forty-eight, and had been shot down five times on the Polish and Russian fronts. He had commanded air fleets in close-support roles during the Polish and Dutch campaigns, orchestrated much of the Battle of Britain, and achieved air supremacy for the Third Reich in the first year of the Russian campaign. Of all of Germany's senior commanders, including Rommel and von Rundstedt, few were more eager to attack than Kesselring, and none had his ability to combine air and ground operations. Kesselring recognized that the Allies had achieved strategic surprise. Yet he wondered why they had not landed in Tunisia, which was the key to control of the Mediterranean.[46] As soon as the cities of Bizerte and Tunis were secure, he ordered his commanders on the ground to move westward against the oncoming Anderson and drive the Allies back into Algeria.

Anderson's advance guard reached the crest of the Dorsal range of the Atlas Mountains on November 17. Tunis lay less than thirty miles in the distance, its towers and rooftops visible to the naked eye. Remarkable as it appears in retrospect, it required another six months for the Allies to dislodge Kesselring's forces—due largely to faulty preinvasion planning, poor performance, and inferior equipment, not to mention inexperienced leadership, including that of the supreme commander. "Had we struck out boldly and landed our forces far to the east, even in Tunisia," Mark Clark wrote subsequently, "we would almost certainly have been successful."[47]

When Anderson moved out from Algiers to take Tunis, his army numbered fewer than twelve thousand men—barely one-tenth of the Allied invasion force. His armor consisted exclusively of light tanks: British Valentines and American M-3 General Stuarts. The Valentine was armed with a minuscule 40mm (two pounder) principal weapon. The General Stuart was even more lightly armed with a 37mm "squirrel gun," a turret that had to be manually rotated, and an engine that was hand cranked.[48] Neither came close to matching the main German battle tank, the Mark IV. When Eisenhower sought to reinforce Anderson with the medium tanks that had landed with Patton in Morocco, the vehicles proved too wide to fit through the narrow tunnels on the only rail line available—a fact that easily could have been ascertained had Allied planners consulted the dozens of Free French officers in London who had spent the bulk of their careers in North Africa.

In the air it was a similar mismatch. Kesselring's forces possessed seven all-weather airfields in Tunisia plus nearby support bases in Sicily and Sardinia. By contrast, Allied aircraft operated from crude dirt fields at such a distance from the front that they could rarely stay more than ten minutes over the battlefield. German pilots and the Luftwaffe command structure were battle-tested. The Allied air command was poorly coordinated and rent by national rivalry. The German planes—ME-109s, Stuka dive-bombers, and Junker 88s—proved far more reliable than American P-38s and P-40s. By late November, only half of the Allied planes in North Africa were still airworthy. American pilots lost twice as many planes from crashes and other accidents as from combat.[49] The Germans not only gained air superiority, but air supremacy. Allied planes were destroyed on the ground, troop positions were bombed and strafed relentlessly, and the harbor at Bône—the closest Allied port to the fighting—was reduced to rubble. On one day alone in November, five Allied supply ships were sunk by German aircraft. Not one German ship on the Tunis run was sunk by Allied planes during the entire month.

By the third week in November, Anderson had reached the end of his tether. His forces had managed to link up with General Barré's French troops, who were holding firm on his southern flank, but his army was overextended. Troops faced constant bombardment from the air, resupply from Algiers was hampered by lack of transportation, and units were too thin on the ground. Rather than thrust directly toward Tunis, Anderson had divided his forces and advanced along a broad front. That was the preference of Eisenhower's headquarters, and it was consistent with American battle doctrine since the time of Ulysses Grant. Lieutenant colonels at Leavenworth continue to debate whether a pointed drive would have served Anderson better than a broad-front advance. A more pertinent question is why land thirty-five thousand troops under George Patton in Morocco, one thousand miles from the objective?

For the first two weeks of the Allied advance, Eisenhower remained on Gibraltar—far from the battlefield itself. Before the invasion he had neglected to prepare for the political implications of landing on French soil. Stung by that failure, he now devoted far too much attention to the consequences of the Darlan deal. "Since this operation started, three quarters of my time, both night and day, has been necessarily occupied in difficult political maneuvers in attempting to explain to people, far from the scene of action, the basic elements of the local situation," he reported to Beetle on November 18.[50] Eisenhower stayed on the Rock because the communications with Washington and London there were superior to anything available in Algiers. But the result was that he lost contact with the front. Shortly after writing Beetle, he advised London that he hoped "to complete the occupation of Tunisia by mid-December."[51] If Ike had seen what Anderson confronted, he would scarcely have made so optimistic an assessment.

Eisenhower did not move his headquarters to Algiers until November 23, 1942, and even then he showed no inclination to travel to the front.[52] Not until November 28—five days after he arrived—did he and Clark go forward to meet General Anderson. They traveled by armored car with escorts fore and aft, did not cross into Tunisia, and were never remotely close to the fighting. Eisenhower's preoccupation with political issues served the military cause poorly. Churchill cabled as early as November 22 that he hoped Ike was not "too much preoccupied with the political aspect."[53] But Churchill's warning had little effect. As Rick Atkinson observed in *An Army at Dawn,* Eisenhower had yet to learn the art of command. "But a quarter-century as a staff officer, with a staff officer's meticulous attention to detail and instinctive concern for pleasing his superiors, did not slough away easily."[54]

Even after he arrived in Algiers, Ike remained fixated on the domestic situation in North Africa. "We sit on a boiling kettle," he wrote Mamie on November 27.[55] Unfortunately, Eisenhower's perception of the North African situation was filtered through Murphy's eyes. The French colons—the establishment class—were thoroughgoing reactionaries who found it easy to side with Nazi Germany. With their approval, Vichy had installed like-minded men to administer the country, who, in turn, appointed a larger number of fascist petty functionaries—mayors, police chiefs, postmasters—who were less than enthusiastic about an Allied victory.[56] A much larger group of Frenchmen were vigorously anti-Nazi and supported the Allies wholeheartedly. But the Darlan deal retained the Vichyites in power on the flimsy supposition that only they could keep the native population in check. Eisenhower supported that arrangement. "We did not come here to interfere in someone else's business," he reminded Patton on Thanksgiving Day.[57]

By the first week of December the initiative in Tunisia had shifted to the Germans, who had increased their forces much more rapidly than the Allies. Anderson's men were dug in along a line that roughly paralleled the Dorsal range, from Cape Serrat, on the Mediterranean, to El Guettar, three hundred miles to the south. Superior German firepower, plus almost total air supremacy, had compelled Anderson to assume a defensive posture. Battle losses had not been made good, fuel and ammunition were running low, and Anderson's five-hundred-mile supply line was stretched to the breaking point. The destruction of the port facilities at Bône had deprived the Allies of the only deepwater harbor available, which meant that everything shipped forward went over roads that had seen little improvement since the time of the Caesars. Even worse from an offensive standpoint, the weather had turned against the Allies. Tunisia receives sixteen inches of rain per year, almost all of which falls from December to February. The army was mired in a sea of mud that rendered any movement all but impossible.

In their postwar memoirs, Eisenhower and Clark imply that General Anderson was to blame for the failure to take Tunis because he did not strike out boldly. Yet the primary responsibility rested with Ike. Churchill complained that Eisenhower's army was "all tail and no teeth"—a reflection of the fact that less than one-tenth of the forces available were engaged in Tunisia.[58] General Sir Bernard Montgomery, whose Eighth Army was slowly driving Rommel back across the Libyan desert toward Tripoli, looked on the failure to take Tunis with disgust. "The party in Tunisia is a complete dog's breakfast," he cabled London, concerned that Kesselring's forces might defeat "the Western Army" and join forces with Rommel at the Libyan border.[59]

George Patton, whom Ike sent to the front for a look-see, blamed Eisenhower for not taking personal command. "Ike is not well and is

Field Marshal Sir Bernard Montgomery.

very querulous and keeps saying how hard it is to be so high and never to have heard a hostile shot. He could correct that very easily if he wanted to."[60] At the front, Patton found that he was the only general officer the troops had seen since the battle began three weeks earlier. "I think this is true, and it is a sad commentary on our idea of leadership." When he returned to Algiers, Patton found Ike and Clark discussing what to do next. "Neither had been to the front, so showed great lack of decision. They are on the way out, I think. They have no knowledge of men or war."[61]

No one was more critical of Ike's handling of the assault on Tunis than General Sir Alan Brooke, chief of the imperial general staff. "Eisenhower seemed unable to grasp the urgency of pushing on to Tunis before the Germans built up their resistance there," he wrote in his diary in late November 1942. Echoing Patton's complaint, Brooke wrote: "It must be remembered that Eisenhower had never even commanded a battalion in action when he found himself commanding a group of armies in North Africa. No wonder he was at a loss as to what to do. . . . I had little confidence in his having the ability to handle the military situation confronting him, and he caused me great anxiety."[62]*

General Marshall offered last-ditch advice. "I think you should delegate your diplomatic problems to your subordinates and give your complete attention to the battle in Tunisia," he instructed Ike on December 22. "I want you to feel you can do this and depend on us to protect your interests and that you do not have to give your time to making lengthy explanations to us to justify your position." Marshall said he wanted Eisenhower "to feel free to give your exclusive attention to the battle, particularly as German intentions against your right flank seem evident."[63]

Stung by Marshall's admonition, Ike immediately set out for the front, uncertain what to expect. Because the Luftwaffe controlled the skies, he and Butcher traveled in a five-car motorcade to Anderson's headquarters, five hundred miles away. Driving through steady rain, they arrived a day and a half later—midafternoon on Christmas Eve. Anderson had assembled his corps and division commanders for Ike's benefit, and their message was uniformly grim. The winter rains would continue until February. Until the ground dried, no offensive action could be considered. The troops were taking a pounding from German artillery, and the lack of air cover was becoming a serious morale factor, but the weather affected the Germans just as much. They, too, were unlikely to mount any large-scale attack.

The news was scarcely what Ike was hoping for. Nevertheless, his long-overdue visit to the front was salutary. Had he remained in Algiers, he might well have ordered Anderson forward—just as Grant had ordered George Thomas to advance against John Bell Hood from Nashville during an incredible ice storm in December 1864. Neither movement was possible. Grant had been unaware of the problem

---

* Later, Brooke wrote that Eisenhower "was blessed with a wonderful charm that carried him far; *perhaps his greatest asset was a greater share of luck than most of us receive in life.* However, if Ike had rather more than his share of luck we, as allies, were certainly extremely fortunate to have such an exceptionally charming individual. As Supreme Commander what he may have lacked in military ability he greatly made up for by the charm of his personality." Arthur Bryant, *The Turn of the Tide: A History of the War Years Based on the Diaries of Field-Marshal Lord Alanbrooke, Chief of the Imperial General Staff* 430–31n (Garden City, N.Y.: Doubleday, 1957). (Emphasis added.)

Thomas confronted, but Ike saw firsthand that a stalemate had settled in along the Tunisian front.

"The continued rains have made impossible any decisive attack in the near future," Eisenhower informed Marshall. "The abandonment for the time being of our plan for a full-out effort has been the severest disappointment I have suffered to date. However, the evidence is complete, in my opinion, that any attempt to make a major attack under current conditions in northern Tunisia would be merely to court disaster."[64] Sensing Eisenhower's disappointment, Anderson offered to resign, but Ike dismissed the proposal.[65]

As Eisenhower sat down to enjoy a Christmas Eve dinner with Anderson and General Juin, he received an urgent phone call from Clark asking him to return to Algiers immediately. Clark spoke in guarded terms, but from the message Ike understood that Darlan had been assassinated.[66] At two-thirty that afternoon a twenty-year-old Frenchman, Fernand Bonnier de la Chapelle, had entered the summer palace in Algiers where Darlan had his office. He waited in an anteroom for Darlan to appear, and then shot him twice at close range. Darlan died an hour later on a hospital operating table. Bonnier was arrested, tried summarily, and executed by firing squad, all in less than thirty-six hours. To this day, his motivation remains a mystery, and the plot is unsolved. Immediate speculation was that Bonnier de la Chapelle was a monarchist who by assassinating Darlan hoped to aid the cause of the Comte de Paris, pretender to the French throne.

In Washington, White House officials, principally Admiral Leahy, disseminated a story alleging the assassin was a Gaullist.[67] What is known is that Bonnier was a member of the Corps Franc d'Afrique, a paramilitary formation being trained west of Algiers under the direction of Carleton S. Coon, sometime professor of anthropology at Harvard, and the resident OSS official in the area. Coon was near the palace when the assassination occurred, and the weapon Bonnier used was a Colt Woodsman pistol, identical to one owned by Coon.[68] Professor Coon and the Office of Strategic Services were never tied to the plot, and Coon was immediately transferred to a British Special Operations Executive (SOE) unit in Tunisia. Bonnier was executed before any investigation could be conducted. The fact that Admiral

Leahy immediately dispatched a cable to Eisenhower authorizing him to appoint Giraud as Darlan's successor,[69] and that Ike immediately understood from Clark's cryptic phone message that Darlan had been assassinated, is enough to suggest that the United States may at the very least have had prior warning.[*]

Eisenhower returned to Algiers in the late afternoon on Christmas Day. He was delighted to find that the WAC detachment, including Kay Summersby, had arrived safely, following a harrowing sea voyage from Scotland. Rather than chance a flight through Luftwaffe-infested airspace, Beetle had sent the WACs by troopship, only to have the vessel sunk by a German submarine off the Algerian coast. The women spent a nervous night bobbing in a lifeboat, and were rescued the next morning by a British destroyer that landed them in Oran. Ike's plane fetched them to headquarters, and the evening of

---

[*] Charles de Gaulle puts the proposition with droll understatement in the second volume of his *Memoirs*.

> The man who killed [Darlan], Fernand Bonnier de la Chapelle, had made himself the instrument of the aggravated passions that had fired the souls around him to the boiling point but behind which, perhaps, moved a policy determined to liquidate a "temporary expedient" after having made use of him. . . . He believed, moreover, as he repeatedly said until the moment of his execution, that an intervention would be made in his behalf by some outside source so high and powerful that the North African authorities could not refuse to obey it. Of course no individual has the right to kill save on the field of battle. Moreover, Darlan's behavior, as a governor and as a leader, was answerable to national justice, not certainly, to that of a group or an individual. Yet how could we fail to recognize the nature of the intentions that inspired this juvenile fury? That is why the strange, brutal and summary way the investigation was conducted in Algiers, the hasty and abbreviated trial before a military tribunal convened at night and in private session, the immediate and secret execution of Fernand Bonnier de la Chapelle, the orders given to the censors that not even his name should be known—all these led to the suspicion that someone wanted to conceal at any price the origin of his decision and constituted a kind of defiance of those circumstances which, without justifying the drama, explained and, to a certain degree, excused it.

Charles de Gaulle, *War Memoirs* 74–75 (New York: Simon and Schuster, 1959).

Christmas Day, Beetle hosted a grand dinner party for everyone at his villa. George Patton had shipped two live turkeys from Morocco, and the festive atmosphere revived Ike's sagging spirits.[*] During the duty day, Smith exhibited all of the warmth of an SS general, Summersby recalled, but off duty he was charming, witty, thoughtful, and a perfect host.[70]

For Eisenhower, the stalemate at the front, the fallout from the Darlan assassination, and the growing criticism from London were more than enough for him to deal with. But Kay's arrival softened the impact. "We've got a lot of bridge to play," he told Summersby, and they soon settled into a nightly routine.[71]

"Sat around with Ike after the party broke up," Everett Hughes recorded in his diary. "Discussed Kay. I don't know whether Ike is alibiing or not. Says he likes her. Wants to hold her hand. Doesn't sleep with her. He doth protest too much, especially in view of the gal's reputation in London."[72]

If Eisenhower was infatuated with Summersby, he retained his love for Mamie. At the same time that Hughes was recording Ike's confidences in his diary, the supreme commander was writing to his wife.

> Sometimes I get to missing you so that I simply don't know what to do. As pressure mounts and strain increases everyone begins to show weaknesses in his makeup. It is up to the Commander to conceal his. . . . When the strain is long continued the commander gets to feeling more and more alone and lonesome, and his mind instinctively turns to something or someone that can help. . . . No one else could ever fill your place with me—and that is the reason I need you. Maybe a simpler explanation is merely I LOVE you!! Which I do always.[73]

---

[*] Patton's virtues as a hell-for-leather combat commander have obscured the savoir faire he brought to the table. A well-traveled member of the horsey set, Patton admired French civilization, spoke the language easily, and was as much at home with first-growth Bordeaux as with bourbon and branch water. He related easily to the sultan of Morocco, and unlike Clark and Ike (who were culturally limited), quickly established a harmonious working relationship with French civil and military officials in Morocco.

The next day, New Year's Eve, he wrote a follow-up: "In my time I've been intrigued momentarily—I've never *been in love with anyone but you!* I never will."[74]

While Ike attempted to reconcile his love of his wife with his growing affection for Kay, Churchill fretted about the situation at the front. "I am most anxious about the military situation," he cabled Roosevelt on December 31, 1942. "If [the Germans] can get enough transport—a big if—they might bring off the same kind of attack along the sea flank that Alexander and Montgomery did at Alamein with the disastrous results to all our forces that befell the Italians."[75] To Eisenhower, Churchill was more direct. "I am deeply concerned about the unfavorable turn in Tunisia, and our staffs take an even more serious view."[76]

Eisenhower's response was to order Fredendall's center task force, now designated II Corps, into position on the right flank of Anderson's First Army. If the bulk of Anderson's forces were bogged down, Ike believed that Fredendall could punch through to the coast and drive a wedge between Rommel's Afrika Korps and the German forces in the north. The plan was christened Operation SATIN, and Ike's staff put it together during the first two weeks in January. Fredendall's attack was scheduled for January 24—a date when "General Mud" still commanded the battlefield in the north.

On January 14, 1943, Roosevelt and Churchill met at Casablanca for their first overseas conference since their shipboard meeting off Newfoundland in the summer of 1941. Marshal Stalin had been invited, but with the Red Army fully engaged all along the eastern front, he decided that he should remain in Moscow. The purpose of the meeting was to discuss military strategy, and the two leaders were accompanied by their military staffs. As Allied supreme commander in North Africa, Eisenhower was not a member of the conference, although he was invited to brief the Combined Chiefs at 2 p.m. on January 15. This was the third session of the chiefs at Casablanca, and they wanted to hear Ike's assessment of the Tunisian campaign and his plan for Operation SATIN.[77]

Eisenhower spoke without notes. He recounted how most of Anderson's First Army would be mired in mud until mid-March, and explained that the Allies could regain the offensive by sending Fredendall forward farther south where the ground was harder. II Corps' goal was to capture of the port city of Sfax, which would cut Tunisia in two.[78]

General Brooke was skeptical. The German Fifth Panzer Army in the north, now commanded by Colonel-General Hans-Jürgen von Arnim, a battle-scarred veteran of the Russian front whom Hitler had handpicked to defend Tunis, had 85,000 troops available; Rommel's Afrika Korps was estimated to number 80,000. Rather than drive a wedge between the two armies, wasn't it more likely that II Corps would be ground up between them? Anderson could not prevent von Arnim from moving troops south, and Montgomery was in no position to prevent Rommel from striking north. The 30,000 men of Fredendall's corps would be defeated by superior forces attacking from both sides before any assistance could arrive.[79]

Eisenhower was stunned. Sir Alan Brooke had been cited for gallantry six times in World War I, and had managed the British evacuation from Dunkirk in 1940. His battlefield credentials were unassailable. Ike's plan was something that he and Leonard Gerow might have cooked up as students at Leavenworth, or that Gruenther might have devised for the Louisiana maneuvers. It looked good on paper but failed the test of combat worthiness.

Eisenhower attempted a rebuttal, but his balloon had been punctured. General Marshall sat as silent witness to the demolition of Operation SATIN, as did Hap Arnold and Admiral King. They recognized that Brooke was correct. The entire episode lasted less than twenty minutes. As Atkinson put it, "Eisenhower saluted and left the room with the grim look of a man in full retreat."[80] Brooke said later that Ike's plan "was a real bad one"—and the subsequent performance of II Corps under Fredendall at Kasserine Pass suggests he knew what he was talking about.[81]

Later that afternoon, at the president's request, Eisenhower called on FDR at his villa. "Ike seems jittery," Roosevelt told Hopkins, and it was easy to understand why.[82] "His neck is in a noose, and he knows it," said Butcher.[83] Roosevelt quizzed Eisenhower about the Tunisian campaign. "How long is it going to take to finish the job?"

"With any kind of break in the weather, sir, we'll have them all either in the bag or in the sea by late spring."

"What's late spring? June?"

Eisenhower nodded. "Maybe as early as the middle of May. June at the latest."[84]

Roosevelt accepted Ike's assessment, but the delay in Tunisia made any cross-Channel attack in 1943 virtually impossible. FDR showed his displeasure later in the conference when Marshall recommended that Eisenhower be promoted to the rank of a full four-star general. Ike's principal subordinates, Admiral Sir Andrew Cunningham and Air Chief Marshal Sir Arthur Tedder, held that rank, and Marshall claimed it would simplify the command structure if Eisenhower were promoted as well. Roosevelt refused. "The President told General Marshall that he would not promote Eisenhower until there was some damn good reason to do it," Harry Hopkins recorded. "The President said he was going to make it a rule that promotions should go to people who had done some fighting, and that while Eisenhower had done a good job, he hasn't knocked the Germans out of Tunisia."[85]

For his own part, Marshall was disappointed with Ike's limp showing before the Combined Chiefs.[86] Taking Eisenhower aside, he suggested that it might be prudent to appoint George Patton as deputy commander to oversee the fighting while Ike handled the politics. Later that evening, Eisenhower put the possibility to Patton.

"He and I talked until about 0130," Patton recalled. "He thinks his thread is about to be cut. I told him he had to go 'to the front.' He feels he cannot, due to politics." When Ike suggested that Patton become his deputy, George was skeptical. "I doubt if it comes out and am not sure I want the job.[87]*

Eisenhower's position as supreme commander was never in jeopardy. His executive ability was unquestioned and his dexterity in

---

* Patton's doubts about accepting the post may have been well founded. In May 1862, before the Battle of Corinth, General Henry W. Halleck took Grant away from troops and made him deputy commander of the Union Army in the West. Like Patton, Grant was a troop commander par excellence, not a paper pusher, and he became despondent in his new role. Sherman found Grant packing to leave the Army and return to St. Louis, and it was with the greatest difficulty that he convinced Grant to remain. Jean Edward Smith, *Grant* 208–10 (New York: Simon and Schuster, 2001).

General George S. Patton.

keeping all of the balls of an international coalition in the air was truly remarkable. General Sir Alan Brooke, while disparaging of Ike's strategic understanding, thought that he "possessed an exceptional ability to handle Allied forces, to treat them all with strict impartiality, and to get the best out of an inter-Allied force."[88] Tedder and Cunningham agreed, and Cunningham's opinion always carried great weight with Churchill and Roosevelt. Churchill, for his part, repeatedly proclaimed his admiration and affection for Eisenhower, and Roosevelt—buttressed by Marshall's persistent faith in Ike—was unwilling to consider any change.[89]

What was at stake was the control of the ground war in Tunisia, and even Marshall had to concede that Ike was in over his head. When the Combined Chiefs met on January 20, 1943, Brooke proposed that when Montgomery's Eighth Army reached Tunisia, it be placed under Ike's command, and that "General {Sir Harold} Alexander should come in as Deputy Commander-in-Chief under General Eisenhower with the primary task of commanding the group of armies on the Tunisian front."[90] Alexander, the third son of the Earl of Caledon, had been the youngest general in the British Army, and had an impeccable combat record stretching more than thirty years. Commanding the 1st Division of the British Expeditionary Force at Dunkirk in 1940, he was literally the last Englishman to leave France. Utterly unflappable, he was Montgomery's superior as head of the British Near East Command.[*] Brooke's proposal meant that Ike would be retained as supreme commander but that he would have three deputies who would exercise the actual command of the fighting forces: Admiral Cunningham at sea, Air Chief Marshal Tedder in the air, and General Alexander on the ground. Brooke also suggested that Eisenhower assume responsibility for whatever subsequent operation (Sicily or elsewhere) was to be undertaken, again with Alexander as his deputy. Consensus came quickly. Marshall was pleased with the arrangement because it left Eisenhower in supreme command, and the British were delighted to have Alexander control the ground war. Eisenhower was not consulted. When Ike told Marshall that he intended to name Patton as his deputy, Marshall told him to hold off. "Alexander will be your man when British Eighth Army joins you after Tripoli."[91]

That evening, Brooke summarized the agreement in his diary.

> By bringing Alexander over from the Middle East and appointing him Deputy to Eisenhower, we are carrying out a move which could not help flattering and pleasing the Americans insofar as we were placing our senior and experienced commander to function under their commander who had no war experience. . . . We are pushing Eisenhower up into the stratosphere and rarified atmosphere of a Supreme Commander, where he would be free to devote

---

[*] Rudyard Kipling, the historian of the Irish Guards Regiment in World War I, said of Alexander, "At the worst crises he was both inventive and cordial and . . . would somehow contrive to dress the affair in high comedy." Richard Doherty, *Irish Generals: Irish Generals in the British Army in the Second World War* 32 (Belfast: Appletree, 1993).

his time to the political and inter-allied problems, whilst
we inserted under him one of our own commanders to deal
with the military situations and to restore the necessary
drive and coordination which had been so seriously lacking.[92]

Eisenhower announced the new command setup at a press conference
in Algiers on February 10, and praised his British deputies as "three
of England's stars." But in truth, Butcher reported, Ike was burning
inside. His years of high-level staff duty had given him impeccable
instincts about power relationships, and it was obvious that he had
been kicked upstairs.[93] Whatever hurt Eisenhower felt, however, was
quickly assuaged when on February 11 he received notice that FDR
had approved his promotion to full general. If Ike was to be supreme
commander with three British deputies, Roosevelt recognized that
he needed the rank to go with it.

With that promotion, Eisenhower became the twelfth four-star
general in American history, Ulysses S. Grant having been the first.
That evening, Ike broke out the champagne and hosted an impromptu celebration for his unofficial family. "I'll never forget the
sheer pleasure that radiated from him," Summersby remembered.
"The General was always very charming, always had that grin at the
ready, but underneath it all he was a very serious and lonely man who
worried, worried, worried. I used to feel it was a real achievement
whenever we were able to divert him so that he forgot his problems
for a little while and was able to have fun."[94]

Butcher had located another hideaway for Eisenhower, similar to
Telegraph Cottage, where the general and his personal staff could
retreat from the daily cares of office. It was a white stucco villa with
a red-tiled roof, perched on a cliff overlooking the Mediterranean,
about fifteen miles from the city of Algiers. There were stables and
tennis courts, and Butcher arranged for three Arabian stallions to be
put at Ike's disposal. "We would leave the office in the middle of the
afternoon several days a week," said Kay, "ride for a couple of hours,
shower, have a drink and supper, and then drive back to Algiers. The
Army had cleared the area and there were guards posted, so we felt
quite safe. We also felt as if we were on parade. There was always a

security man riding discreetly behind us, in addition to the sharp-shooter guards. It is an eerie feeling knowing that your every move is being watched. Ike often complained about it, not only while riding, but as it affected every phase of his life."[95]

Elspeth Duncan, an attractive Scottish colleague of Kay's on Eisenhower's clerical staff, complained to Everett Hughes that she resented being used as cover for Ike and Kay. (Duncan was often included in their outings.) "She foresees a scandal. Wants to quit. I tell her to stick around. Maybe Kay will help Ike win the war."[96]

Eisenhower's weekly letters to Mamie continued to profess his love. "I just want to say that you're the greatest gal in the world," he wrote on February 20, 1943. "I'll never be in love with anyone but you! So, please be *sure* of that—and I hope it really means as much to you as ever."[97]

On February 22, Eisenhower's professions of love were sorely tested. Margaret Bourke-White, the noted photojournalist, published an article in *Life* magazine detailing the travails of the WAC detachment when their troopship had been torpedoed. Bourke-White had been on board. Entitled "Women in Lifeboats," the article featured Elspeth Duncan, "the best rower of all," and "the irrepressible Kay Summersby, Eisenhower's pretty Irish driver." Bourke-White reported there had been seventeen lifeboats, each carrying between fifty-five and one hundred passengers. She was in the boat with Kay, Elspeth, and Ethel Westermann, who was on her way to be chief nurse at the headquarters dispensary. There were pictures galore, including two of "the beauteous Kay."[98]

Mamie saw the article, as did most Army wives in Washington—and those who did not soon learned of it. "Army cats of the worst sort surrounded her," wrote Kevin McCann, a postwar aide to Ike, "relaying to her—in the most affectionately sympathetic manner—and enlarging viciously on it, the latest bit of scandalous gossip leaked through censorship."[99] Mamie was hurt and embarrassed by the article. Her letter to Eisenhower has apparently been destroyed, but from Ike's reply it is clear that she put him on the spot.

"So *Life* says my old London driver came down," Eisenhower answered on March 2, 1943.

So she did—but the big reason she wanted to serve in this theater is that she is terribly in love with a young American Colonel [Richard Arnold] and is to be married to him come June—assuming both are alive. I doubt if *Life* told that. But I tell you only so that if anyone is banal and foolish enough to lift an eyebrow at an old duffer such as I am [Eisenhower was fifty-two] in connection with WACS—Red Cross workers—nurses and drivers—you will know that I've no emotional involvements and will have none. . . . You are all that any man could ask as a *partner and a sweetheart.*[100]

The day after receiving notice of his promotion, Eisenhower slipped out of Algiers for a quick tour of the southern end of the front held by II Corps. Fredendall's troops were spread thin, but Ike was confident no enemy attack was in the offing. "Axis cannot risk at this moment to embark on an operation which might mean heavy losses of men and equipment," he informed the War Department on February 13.[101] Eisenhower was distressed that the frontline units had made little effort to fortify their positions, but he thought the disposition of the forces was "as good as could be made pending the development of an actual attack and in view of the great value of holding the forward regions."[102]

Scarcely had Eisenhower returned to II Corps headquarters when disaster struck. At 0630 on Sunday, February 14, tanks of the 10th and 21st Panzer divisions crashed out of the Eastern Dorsals and began to roll up the front line of II Corps, which Fredendall had deployed in penny packets on the valley floor. The 21st Panzer came on from the south, the 10th Panzer from the north, and by 1700 the two had completed a double envelopment, sending the remnants of the American 1st Armored Division in headlong retreat. Of the fifty-two Sherman medium tanks the 1st Armored had deployed, only six survived.

At II Corps headquarters Eisenhower, who had received preliminary reports of the rout, whistled in the dark. "I really believe that the fighting of today will show that our troops are giving a very fine

Field Marshal Erwin Rommel.

account of themselves even though we must give up part of our extended line," he informed General Marshall.[103] The fact is the green American troops were no match for the German veterans. The 10th Panzer Division had led von Rundstedt's breakout in the Ardennes in 1940, and the 21st—the first German division in Africa—was in the words of one military historian "perhaps the most experienced desert fighters on earth."[104] Some American troops fought well, but they were the exception. Battalion after battalion was surrounded, overrun, or simply disintegrated.

For the next day and a half the Allied high command remained in denial. Eyewitness testimony of the rout had little impact. Combat Command A (CCA) of the 1st Armored reported that it had lost 1,600 men, nearly 100 tanks, 57 half-tracks, and 29 artillery pieces, but the belief persisted that the German onslaught was less than real. Reality dawned on February 16 when tanks from Rommel's

Afrika Korps joined the assault. Three German armored columns slammed through collapsing American defenses, heading in the general direction of Kasserine Pass. Panic built slowly, but by the evening of the seventeenth the remnants of II Corps were racing to the rear. Fredendall suffered a nervous collapse. Eisenhower reached back to Morocco and summoned Major General Ernest Harmon, commanding the 2nd Armored Division, to rally II Corps, and on the nineteenth General Sir Harold Alexander took command of the front. Two British divisions from Anderson's First Army moved south to close off the German penetration, and by February 23 the breakthrough had been contained.

Eisenhower waited two weeks before relieving Fredendall, and despite his performance, recommended his promotion to lieutenant general and a cushy stateside training command. Ike offered the embattled II Corps to Mark Clark, who now headed Fifth Army in Morocco, and Clark declined—a black mark that Eisenhower never forgot. Ike then turned to Patton, who welcomed the opportunity. Patton was slated to command Seventh Army and was preparing for the invasion of Sicily, but he was delighted to lead troops in battle. He commanded II Corps for six weeks, whipped it into shape, and turned it over to Omar Bradley when he resumed planning for Sicily.

After Kasserine, British planners began referring to American troops as "our Italians." Tommies called GIs "Alice." General Alexander told Montgomery that after taking command in Tunisia he found "no policy, no plan, no reserves, no training, and no building up for the future." The American troops were "mentally and physically soft, and very green. It was the old story: lack of proper training, allied to no experience in war, and linked with too high a standard of living. They were going through their early days, just as we had to go through ours. We had been at war a long time and our mistakes lay mostly behind us."[105]*

---

* "My main anxiety is the poor fighting value of the Americans," Alexander cabled London on February 25. "They simply do not know their job as soldiers and this is the case from the highest to the lowest. . . . Perhaps the weakest link of all is the junior leader, who just does not lead, with the result that their men don't really fight." Quoted in Rick Atkinson, *An Army at Dawn: The War in North Africa, 1942–1943* 377 (New York: Henry Holt, 2002).

The Fifth Panzer Army and the Afrika Korps, which were now linked under von Arnim's command (Rommel had been recalled to Germany), gradually withdrew to the northeast corner of Tunisia with their backs to the Bay of Tunis. For the next three months, Alexander methodically tightened the vice. Primary responsibility was assigned to Anderson's First Army, in the north, and Montgomery's Eighth Army moving up from the south. The two British armies were separated by the French XIX Corps, under General Louis-Marie Koeltz. The U.S. II Corps, now under Omar Bradley, served under Anderson's command.

The Germans did not lose the battle of North Africa so much as they were overwhelmed. Hitler's war machine was no match for America's assembly line. Despite the heavy losses sustained in November and December, by February the Allies had four times as many planes in North Africa as the Luftwaffe. By the end of March, the Allies were flying over a thousand sorties a day. The Germans averaged sixty.[106] Allied air superiority choked off the German supply route. Von Arnim's Fifth Panzer Army had received 187 replacement tanks in November, and 191 in December. By February the number had dropped to 52, and in March to 20. By contrast, at Kasserine Pass the U.S. II Corps lost more tanks (235) than the Germans had deployed at the outset of the battle (228). Yet within two weeks II Corps had been supplied with replacements.[107] "Supplies shattering. Ammunition for 1–2 days. Fuel situation similar," von Armin signaled Berlin in late March.[108]

For the Allies, it was just the opposite. In late January, Eisenhower asked Washington for more trucks. Three weeks later a convoy of twenty ships sailed from American ports with 5,000 two-and-a-half-ton trucks, 2,000 cargo trailers, 400 dump trucks,

---

As a young lieutenant serving with the 6th Infantry Regiment in Berlin in the 1950s, I once accompanied our commander on a visit to the Black Watch. We arrived in the early afternoon, and no officers were present. My colonel asked the Scottish sergeant major where the officers were. "They are not here, sir," he replied. It was during the duty day, and my colonel was surprised.

"Not here?" he asked. "It's only two o'clock. What do the officers do?"

"They show us how to die, sir," said the sergeant major, standing rigidly at attention. That effectively ended the conversation.

and 80 fighter planes. From late February to late March, 130 ships crossed the Atlantic with 84,000 soldiers, 24,000 vehicles, and a million tons of cargo. When Patton demanded new shoes for his troops, 80,000 pairs arrived almost overnight. By April, the Allies could put 1,400 tanks in the field. The Germans could muster only 80. Tunis fell on May 8, 1943, and the last German units surrendered on the thirteenth. Axis losses in Tunisia totaled 290,000 killed or captured—an Allied victory in some respects comparable to the Russian triumph at Stalingrad.

Brute force prevailed. As General Lucius D. Clay, who headed all U.S. military procurement in World War II, noted: "We were never able to build a tank as good as the German tank. But we made so many of them that it didn't really matter."[109] Rommel made a similar observation. "The battle is fought and decided by the quartermaster before the shooting begins."[110]

# ELEVEN

# *Sicily*

I realize I did my duty in a very tactless way, but
so long as my method pleased the God of
Battles, I am content.

— GEORGE S. PATTON,
*September 21, 1943*

AMERICAN PERFORMANCE IN North Africa was abysmal. An
army must learn to crawl before it can walk, Omar Bradley famously
said, and it was in Tunisia that the American Army first learned to
crawl. "The proud and cocky Americans today stand humiliated by
one of the greatest defeats in our history," Commander Harry Butcher
wrote in his diary after Kasserine.[1] Censorship kept the home front
ignorant of the extent of American losses, but the Army had been
driven back eighty-five miles in less than a week—a rout that, if
measured in miles alone, exceeded that of the Battle of the Bulge two
years later. Ike was saved because of German logistical problems:
Rommel ran short of fuel and ammunition. Speaking off the record
to newsmen, Eisenhower assumed full responsibility for the defeat,
and later acknowledged that he had erred by pressing II Corps too far
forward. "Had I been willing to pass to the defensive, no attack
against us could have achieved even temporary success."[2]

Few figures in public life have proved more adept at making a silk
purse out of a sow's ear than Dwight Eisenhower. His official report
to the Combined Chiefs of Staff on the North African campaign proclaimed that the battle of Kasserine Pass, rather than being a mili-

tary disaster, was, in reality, the turning point of the war. According to Ike, the "sands were running out" for Rommel, "and the turn of the tide at KASSERINE proved actually to be the turn of the tide in all of TUNISIA as well."[3] With positive thinking like that it is no wonder that Eisenhower was so popular with Churchill and Roosevelt, or why Patton persisted in referring to him as "Divine Destiny" rather than Dwight David.[4]

Eisenhower radiated the certitude of victory. "I have caught up with myself and have things on a fairly even keel," he wrote Marshall in early March 1943.[5] Alexander's timely arrival had rescued the ground war, and John C. H. Lee's supply services had ensured that everything required to finish the job was always at hand.

Ike's optimism was contagious. He recognized that a few compelling ideas, preached relentlessly, would propel his forces forward.[6] The foremost of those ideas was Allied unity. His problems were not so much with the British, who had been accustomed to fighting alongside allies for centuries, but with his American compatriots, who were notoriously insular. Mark Clark and Omar Bradley were viciously xenophobic, and George Patton, who got along famously with the French, despised the British with a particular passion. Ike's chief contribution at this point in the war was to ride herd on his countrymen and keep them working in harness with the British, who were still doing the lion's share of the fighting. Seventy-five percent of Allied ground forces in the theater were British, as were four out of every five naval vessels and half the air forces. As far as casualties, the British had lost eight times as many men since El Alamein as the Americans.[7] "We are establishing a pattern for complete unity in Allied effort that will stand the Allied nations in good stead throughout the remainder of the war," Ike advised the War Department in early April.[8]

Eisenhower studied his mistakes. "We are learning something every day, and in general do not make the same mistake twice."[9] Ike learned to be tougher with subordinates such as Fredendall. "Officers that fail must be ruthlessly weeded out," Eisenhower wrote his old friend Leonard Gerow. "Considerations of friendship, family, kindness, and nice personality have nothing to do with the problem. . . . You must be tough."[10] He learned the importance of training and

discipline, and how to deploy airpower and massed armor, particularly when confronting Germany's superior panzer formations. One lesson he did not learn was the need for a proper replacement system, and here he betrayed an unwillingness to challenge official doctrine. The United States, unlike the British, the French, or the Germans, treated soldiers as interchangeable parts. As parts wore out, new parts were shipped in to keep units at full strength. These replacements were invariably green, and unit cohesion suffered from the dribble of new men constantly coming in. The British, French, and Germans, by contrast, operated on a unit basis. When a regiment wore out, it was replaced in the line with a fresh regiment and sent to the rear to refit—usually with replacements from the same region. The American system reflected the assembly line attitude that worked well producing tanks and airplanes, but fell woefully short when it came to maintaining unit morale. A product of World War I, it was vigorously embraced by General Marshall. Ike and his field commanders knew it worked poorly, but they never challenged the system.

Above all, it was in North Africa that Eisenhower made the transition from staff officer to senior commander. By the end of the Tunisian campaign he no longer felt that he had to keep Marshall and the War Department informed of his every move. He had confidence in his subordinates—Alexander, Cunningham, Tedder, and Lee—and they gave him their confidence in return. "The only man who could have made things work was Ike," said Churchill's chief of staff, General Sir Hastings Ismay.[11] "He was utterly fair in his dealings," said Alexander. "I envied the clarity of his mind, and his power of accepting responsibility."[12] Harold Macmillan, Ike's political adviser, noted that Eisenhower was "wholly uneducated in any normal sense of the word. Yet compared with the wooden heads and desiccated hearts of many British soldiers I see here, he is a jewel of broadmindedness and wisdom."[13]

At Casablanca, Churchill and Roosevelt agreed that after North Africa was liberated, the Allies should invade Sicily. The extended fighting in Tunisia made a cross-Channel attack all but impossible in 1943, and Eisenhower's forces could not sit idle for the remainder of the year. The island of Sicily, ninety miles north of Tunisia and sepa-

rated from Italy by the narrow Strait of Messina, offered the best opportunity. An invasion could be mounted quickly, the occupation of the island would render Mediterranean shipping lanes more secure, and the invasion of Italy (which the British pressed relentlessly) would be facilitated. The operation was code-named HUSKY, and Eisenhower was instructed to prepare for a landing in early July.[14]

Planning was delayed by the Tunisian campaign, but by May 12, 1943, the final order of battle was fixed. Thirteen Allied divisions—six British, six American, and one Canadian—were committed to HUSKY. The British and Canadian divisions would be commanded by Montgomery and his Eighth Army headquarters. The American divisions would comprise a newly created Seventh Army commanded by Patton. Both armies would be under Alexander's overall command at Fifteenth Army Group.

Because of the marginal performance of American troops in Tunisia, primary responsibility was assigned to Montgomery's Eighth Army. The British would land on the southeast coast of Sicily, press north along the coastal road, capture the port cities of Syracuse, Catania, and Taormina, and take Messina, closing off the escape route for Axis forces on the island. Patton's troops would land west of Eighth Army on Sicily's southern coast and cover Montgomery's left flank as he drove north. D-Day was set for July 10, 1943.

Allied intelligence estimated the number of enemy troops on the island at three hundred thousand: mostly Italian, but including two top-of-the-line German panzer divisions. Sicily was roughly the size of the state of Vermont, and the mountainous terrain tilted the odds heavily in favor of the defenders. Mount Etna, one of Europe's four active volcanoes, stood directly in the path of Montgomery's advance—a ten-thousand-foot obstacle that was twenty miles in diameter.* On the other hand, the Allies would have complete air supremacy, and the Italian Navy—six antiquated battleships and eleven cruisers—would be no match for Cunningham's combined fleet should it choose to do battle, which was highly unlikely.

Eisenhower continued to juggle his obligation to Mamie with his affection for Kay. Summersby was now working as Ike's personal as-

---

* The other three active volcanoes were Vesuvius, Stromboli, and Santorini.

sistant, as well as driving him when the occasion arose.* "I was spending more time than ever with Ike," she recalled. "Even in London with our seven day weeks, I occasionally visited Mummy, lunched with friends, went to the odd cocktail party. But now I trod a very narrow path. From breakfast to the final nightcap, I went where Ike went. Once when Omar Bradley was coming to dinner, Ike and I were a bit late. When we walked in, Brad said, 'Here they are, Ike and his shadow.' "[15]

Omar Bradley, one of the few senior American commanders without a wartime sweetheart, said that Kay's influence over Ike

> was greater than is generally recognized. . . . Their close relationship is quite accurately portrayed, so far as my personal knowledge extends, in Kay's second book, *Past Forgetting.* Ike's son John published his father's personal letters to Mamie, in part to refute Kay's allegation that she and Ike were deeply in love. Many of these letters are obviously Ike's replies to probing letters from Mamie about his relationship with Kay. To my mind, Ike protests too much, thus defeating John's purpose.[16†]

* Since October 1942, Ike's principal driver had been Sergeant Leonard D. Dry. Summersby drove only when Ike asked her. Dry served with Eisenhower throughout the North African campaign and later in England and on the Continent. Dry remained Ike's driver after the war, and as a master sergeant drove for Mamie during the presidential years. After his retirement from the Army, he continued to drive for the Eisenhowers at Gettysburg. Lester David and Irene David, *Ike and Mamie: The Story of the General and His Lady* 149 (New York: G. P. Putnam's Sons, 1981).

† General Bradley's skepticism is well taken. When *Letters to Mamie* was published in 1978, John stated that Eisenhower "apparently destroyed all the letters [Mamie] wrote him." By publishing only Ike's letters, John gives his father the last word and deprives Mamie of any opportunity to make her case.

After publishing Eisenhower's letters, John sold the originals to a private party for what officials at the Eisenhower Library call "a substantial sum." The Eisenhower Library has photocopies, but the originals are in private hands. Perhaps Mamie's are too.

DDE, *Letters to Mamie* 12, John S. D. Eisenhower, ed. (Garden City, N.Y.: Doubleday, 1978).

On June 6, 1943, Colonel Richard Arnold, Kay's fiancé, was killed instantly when a fellow officer set off a trip wire during a mine-clearing operation. Kay was stunned, but her grief passed quickly. "Ours had been a wartime romance," she wrote in retrospect. "There had been weeks and months when we had not seen each other. Each time we met it had been as exciting as a first date, and probably for that very reason our knowledge of each other had not progressed much beyond the first-date stage. Ike knew more about me and had seen more of my family than Dick ever had. . . . Now when I tried to mourn him, I discovered that I did not really know the man I was grieving for."[17]

Mamie and Ike had not seen each other for almost a year. Ensconced in a two-bedroom apartment at Washington's fashionable Wardman Park Hotel, Mamie found herself increasingly alone. She loathed public appearances and the limelight, preferring the company of Army wives, where she now cut a wide swath. She spent her evenings reading pulp fiction, slept late, and either went shopping downtown or played cards and mah-jongg most afternoons with her contemporaries. Always delicate, her weight plummeted to 112 pounds.

Mamie had little interest in politics. To the extent she followed national and international affairs, it was through the eyes of her ultraconservative parents in Denver. When Eleanor Roosevelt invited her for a private luncheon at the White House, Mamie declined—a social gaffe the Roosevelts never forgot. Mrs. Roosevelt attributed Mamie's refusal to alcoholism, a rap that followed her for the rest of her life.[18] When Ike paid a lightning visit to Washington six months later, FDR invited him for dinner at the White House. Mamie was not invited.*

The fact is, Mamie missed her husband and was alone for the first time in her life. She fretted about the continued presence of Kay Summersby at Eisenhower's headquarters. Why did Ike keep her

---

* What goes around comes around. When Eisenhower was inaugurated president in January 1953, Eleanor Roosevelt was serving as a U.S. delegate to the United Nations. Like all diplomatic appointees, she routinely submitted her resignation to the new administration when Ike took office. She was surprised when Eisenhower accepted it. Joseph P. Lash, *A World of Love: Eleanor Roosevelt and Her Friends, 1943–1962* 385 (Garden City, N.Y.: Doubleday, 1984).

around if he knew it made Mamie uncomfortable? Susan Eisenhower, in her biography of her grandmother, puts the matter in perspective. Mamie understood Ike's need for female companionship, wrote Susan. "She had firsthand knowledge that when ambition, rank-pulling, and rivalry were part and parcel of the daily environment, a sympathetic and trustworthy listener was of inestimable value. From the earliest days of their marriage, Mamie herself had created a stress-free after-work environment for Ike—which included having friends in, playing cards, or 'just loafing.' " Mamie worried that Kay had become her surrogate by providing that atmosphere for Ike in Algiers.[19]

Mamie evidently expressed her feelings to Ike in early June. She also included Army gossip about Dick Arnold's messy stateside divorce. Eisenhower received the letter just after Arnold's death, and was not amused. On June 11 he replied to Mamie.

> A very strange coincidence occurred this morning. I had two letters from you . . . and in one of them you mentioned my driver, and a story you'd heard about the former marital difficulties of her fiancé. You said it was a "not pretty" story. Your letter gave me my first intimation that there was any story whatever. In any event, whatever guilt attached to him has been paid in full. At the same moment that your letter arrived I received a report that he was killed. . . . So what young Arnold did, I do not know. But here we considered him a valuable officer and a fine person. I'm saddened by his death.

Ike concluded by reassuring Mamie of his love. "You never quite seem to comprehend how deeply I depend upon you and need you. So when you're lonely, try to remember that I'd rather be by your side than anywhere else in the world."[20]

After Colonel Arnold's death, Eisenhower became especially solicitous of Kay. When he ordered two new Class A uniforms from the finest French tailor in Algiers, he insisted that Kay be measured for two as well.

"How can I ever thank you?" asked Kay.

"Kay, you are someone very special to me," he replied.

> He laid his hand over mine. And he smiled. This was not
> the famous Eisenhower grin. This was a tender, almost
> tremulous smile. And full of love. We just sat there and
> looked at each other. We were both silent, serious, eyes
> searching eyes. It was a communion, a pledging, an avowal
> of love. For over a year, Ike and I had spent more time
> with each other than with anyone else. We had worked,
> worried and played together. Love had grown so naturally
> that it was part of our lives.[21]

Later that day, Ike had second thoughts. "I'm sorry about this morning, Kay. That shouldn't have happened. Please forget it."[22]

And later still, more second thoughts. "Goddamnit, can't you tell I'm crazy about you."

> It was like an explosion. We were suddenly in each other's
> arms. His kisses absolutely unraveled me. Hungry, strong,
> demanding. And I responded every bit as passionately. He
> stopped, took my face between his hands. "Goddamnit, I
> love you."
>
> Ike put his hands on my shoulders. "We have to be very
> careful," he said. "I don't want you to be hurt. I don't want
> people to gossip about you. God, I wish things were dif-
> ferent."[23]

Summersby later recalled,

> The acknowledgement of our love heightened the plea-
> sure of every moment Ike and I spent together—and
> heightened the frustrations as well. As long as we were in
> Algiers, all we could hope for would be a few stolen mo-
> ments of privacy—to talk. No more mad embraces. That
> initial passionate encounter could not be repeated. Love

Eisenhower welcomes King George VI to Algiers.

made no visible change in our lives; the change was all within. We picked up the threads of routine as if they had never been broken.[24]

. . . The cocktail hour was often a time we could count on for ourselves. In Algiers we would sit on the high-backed sofa in the living room, listen to records, have a few drinks, smoke a few cigarettes and steal a few kisses—always conscious that someone would walk in at any moment. We were more like teen-agers than a woman in her thirties and a man in his fifties. We were certainly a curiously innocent couple—or perhaps it was simply the circumstances in which we found ourselves.[25]

On June 11, 1943, the Allies captured the tiny island of Pantelleria, thirty miles off the Tunisian coast, and directly in the path of military convoys sailing for Sicily. The operation, code-named CORK-SCREW, marks the first occasion in which Eisenhower asserted his authority as supreme commander contrary to the advice of his subordinates.

The Isola di Pantelleria, sometimes known as the caper capital of the Mediterranean, was a fifty-two-square-mile volcanic outcropping that had been fortified by Mussolini in the mid-1930s as counterpoise to the British base at Malta. Axis propaganda touted it as the Gibraltar of the central Mediterranean, and because of its rocky coastline with no beaches and only one small harbor less than three hundred yards wide, most military authorities considered it unassailable. Eisenhower nevertheless believed that if left in enemy hands, the island would be a serious menace. Its elaborate network of radio direction finders played havoc with Allied aircraft, and its airfield, though heavily bombed, was still capable of launching aerial assaults against nearby ships.

Eisenhower's deputies—Alexander, Cunningham, and Tedder—stoutly opposed the operation. Alexander, in particular, with memories of Dunkirk fresh in his mind, resisted landing on the island, which he believed would result in "unthinkable casualties." Cunningham initially agreed that it was too risky, as did Tedder. But Eisenhower persisted. Taking advantage of Allied air supremacy, he ordered a bombing campaign to pulverize the island's defenses. In three weeks, Allied planes flew five thousand sorties against Pantelleria, dropped 6,400 tons of bombs, and left the defenders in a state of shock. Tedder and Cunningham now agreed that Italian morale was so low they would not put up much of a fight, but Alexander held firm in his opposition. Eisenhower overruled him and ordered the invasion to proceed. If Bradley, Clark, and Patton believed that Ike was merely a front man for his British deputies (as they did), Pantelleria clearly established who was in command.

In the face of Alexander's continued opposition, Eisenhower decided it would be prudent to make a personal reconnaissance of the island. Three days before the scheduled assault, he boarded Admiral Cunningham's flagship, the HMS *Aurora,* which was to lead a naval task force of cruisers and destroyers in a final bombardment of the island. This would be Ike's first exposure to hostile fire, and *Aurora* moved at flank speed (twenty-eight knots). Cunningham told Eisenhower that the whole area was mined except for a narrow channel that had been swept.

"Are there no floating mines about?" asked Ike.

"Oh yes," Cunningham replied. "But at this speed the bow wave will throw them away from the ship. It would be just bad luck if we should strike one."[26]

The naval bombardment lasted several hours, and Italian shore batteries remained mostly silent. Awed by the destruction, Eisenhower told Cunningham, "Andrew, if you and I got into a small boat, we could capture the place ourselves."[27]

On June 11, 1943, the Italian garrison of eleven thousand men surrendered before the first assault troops went ashore. Pantelleria was in Allied hands, the only casualty a British enlisted man who had been bitten by a mule. "I'm afraid this telegram sounds a bit gloating," Eisenhower confessed in reporting the success to Marshall. "Today marks the completion of my twenty-eighth year of commissioned service and I believe that I am now legally eligible for promotion to colonel [in the Regular Army]."[28]* If Ike were gloating, the gloating was justified. CORKSCREW had been his plan from the beginning. Despite the doubts of his senior commanders, all of whom were more experienced than he, Eisenhower had insisted upon taking the island, and had successfully done so. For Ike, Pantelleria was a watershed. In his mind, it confirmed his strategic judgment and gave him the confidence he needed for the future. The stakes had been trivial, but the outcome could not have been more significant.[29]

At the same time the Allies were taking Pantelleria, the political situation in Algeria began to sort itself out. To the consternation of Robert Murphy, the American State Department, Admiral Leahy, and FDR, Charles de Gaulle emerged as undisputed leader of the French war effort. On May 27, the National Council of the Resistance, meeting clandestinely in Paris, recognized de Gaulle as the leader of the Resistance and demanded that he be installed as presi-

---

* Eisenhower held the permanent rank of lieutenant colonel. On August 30, 1943, he was promoted to major general in the Regular Army, skipping the ranks of colonel and brigadier general.

dent of the provisional government of France in Algeria.[30] On May 30, de Gaulle arrived in Algiers. On June 3, the French Committee of National Liberation (FCNL) was formed with de Gaulle and Giraud as copresidents. The committee proclaimed itself "the central French power. It directs the French war effort. It exercises French sovereignty."[31] De Gaulle's presence in Algiers triggered a wave of popular demonstrations by Frenchmen of all classes and political persuasions. Giraud, though not personally tainted by Vichy, stood for the old order. De Gaulle represented the future. Churchill and the British government made it clear they supported de Gaulle. Eisenhower—with HUSKY about to be launched—was most concerned that French North Africa be unified behind whatever leader might emerge. And Roosevelt was determined that de Gaulle be defeated. "I am fed up with de Gaulle," the president cabled Churchill on June 17. "The time has arrived when we must break him."[32]

FDR's attitude toward de Gaulle was personal and petulant. He dug in his heels and ignored the plethora of evidence that de Gaulle, and only de Gaulle, spoke for the French nation. The president's attitude was analogous to the combination of hubris and obstinacy he displayed in 1937 when he sought to pack the Supreme Court, and in 1938 when he attempted to purge four Democratic senators in their state primaries. Eisenhower, who was now more adept at reading the political situation on the ground, stood aside and let the drama unfold.

In July, Roosevelt invited Giraud to the United States for what he believed would be a ceremonial laying on of hands. Giraud was received politely but unenthusiastically by the North American audience, and by the time he returned to Algiers at the end of the month, de Gaulle had solidified his position as the sole president of the FCNL, which had become the de facto government of France in exile. Giraud retreated to a figurehead position as head of the armed forces, and retired the following year. De Gaulle captured the change as he described his triumphant visit to Casablanca in August 1943. "Six months before, I had had to reside on the city's outskirts, constrained by secrecy and surrounded with barbed wire and American sentry posts. Today my presence served as a symbol and a center of French authority."[33]

Eisenhower understood de Gaulle better than any other Allied leader did. They were the same age, born within a month of each other in 1890. Both came from large families, both attended their country's military academy, and both spent their early careers working with tanks. Both read assiduously, wrote well, and possessed a remarkable command of their respective languages. Both identified with their country's heritage, and in many respects exemplified its virtues and vices. De Gaulle's war record was exceptional, and Eisenhower respected it. Wounded three times on the western front in World War I, he was left for dead on the field at Verdun, only to be rescued and healed by the Germans.

De Gaulle, for his part, understood and appreciated the position in which Eisenhower had been placed. "If occasionally he went so far as to support the pretexts which tended to keep us in obscurity, I can affirm that he did so without conviction. I even saw him submit to my intervention in his own strategy whenever national interest led me to do so. At heart this great soldier felt, in his turn, that mysterious sympathy which for almost two centuries had brought his country and mine together in the world's great dramas."[34]

On July 7, three days before Allied forces were scheduled to land in Sicily, Eisenhower flew from Algiers to Malta, the operational command post for HUSKY, and less than sixty miles from where Patton's troops would go ashore. Ike said he felt "as if my stomach was a clenched fist."[35] This time, unlike TORCH, Eisenhower did not have direct operational responsibility. The ground forces were commanded by Alexander, the air by Tedder, and the naval forces by Cunningham. Ike presided over the three, ready to settle any dispute that might arise, but he did not control day-to-day operations. After the battle plan had been agreed to, the only major decision left in his hands was to give the final go-ahead.

The invasion of Sicily was the largest amphibious assault ever attempted. One hundred and seventy-five thousand troops—seven divisions, two more than would go ashore in Normandy—would land simultaneously on twenty-six beaches along a front that stretched for 105 miles. Within two days, almost five hundred thousand men would be ashore. The invasion armada, which was already at sea, stretched for sixty miles in a mile-wide corridor and comprised more than three thousand vessels, including eight battleships and two carriers. In addition to the landing force, the fleet carried more than two hundred thousand tons of supplies, half of which were munitions. John C. H. Lee, it was said, always doubled whatever his staff thought the Army needed "just in case."[36]

On July 9—D-Day minus one—the weather turned foul. By late afternoon the winds had reached a gale-force thirty knots—Force 7 on the Beaufort scale. "We could barely stand on deck," wrote war correspondent Ernie Pyle aboard the *Biscayne*.[37] Patton's men in flat-bottomed landing craft fared even worse. By 6 p.m. the winds had picked up to thirty-seven knots, then forty knots, churning twelve-foot seas. Marshall, who was following the weather reports hourly, cabled to ask if the invasion was on or off. "My reaction was that I wish I knew," said Ike.[38]

Weather forecasters on Malta predicted the storm had peaked and would soon pass. So, too, did Cunningham, who had sailed the Mediterranean for almost half a century. Staff officers calculated that if the invasion were postponed, it would take two to three weeks to remount it, by which time the element of surprise would have been lost. Whatever Ike's limitations as a strategist, he was never reluctant to make the tough calls. "Let's go," he told Cunningham. To Marshall he radioed, "The operation will proceed as scheduled in spite of an unfortunate westerly wind."[39]

After the decision was made, Eisenhower and his deputies broke for dinner and hoped for the best. "To be perfectly honest," said Admiral Lord Louis Mountbatten, "it doesn't look too good."[40] Tedder observed that it was curious to be invading Italy from the south. "Even Hannibal had the sense to come in with his elephants over the Alps."[41]

The troops were slated to go ashore at 0300 hours. As he waited, Ike broke the tension with a letter to Mamie. "In circumstances such as these, men do almost anything to keep themselves from going slightly mad. I can stand it better than most, but there is no use denying that I feel the strain. . . . Everybody is doing his best. The answer is in the lap of the Gods."[42]

When the first troops went ashore at 0335 hours, a bare half hour late, the storm had subsided. The surf was high on the American beaches, but the landings were largely unopposed, marred only by the usual map-reading fiascos and occasional poor helmsmanship by undertrained landing craft operators. The exception was the 504th Parachute Infantry Regiment of Matthew Ridgway's 82nd Airborne, which was decimated by friendly fire. As the troop-carrying C-47s flew over the invasion fleet on their way to the drop zone, trigger-happy antiaircraft gunners opened fire. Of the 144 planes that took off from Tunisia, 23 were shot down and 37 were badly damaged.[43] Fourteen hundred of the 5,300 paratroopers in the regiment were killed or missing—one of the worst friendly fire episodes in modern warfare.[44]

By nightfall on the tenth, the invasion force was four miles inland and the beachheads were secure. Panzers from the Hermann Göring Division launched a vigorous assault against the landing zone of the 1st Division, but were eventually repulsed by American artillery fire. Italian foot soldiers and coastal defense units surrendered by the thousands. More enemy soldiers were captured during the first week of fighting on Sicily than had surrendered to the U.S. Army in all of World War I.[45] Others simply peeled off their uniforms and joined the hordes of refugees streaming inland—"self-demobilization," in the terminology of the Axis high command.

As the Italian Army melted away, Field Marshal Kesselring— whose skilled defense of Tunisia had delayed the Allies for six months—arrived on the scene, bringing with him two additional German divisions, the 29th Panzer Grenadiers and the 1st Parachute Division, to reinforce the two already on the island. With Allied forces on Sicily already numbering close to five hundred thousand, Kesselring understood that defeat was inevitable. But he was determined to "win time and defend," and recognized that Sicily's geography afforded an exceptional opportunity to build a defensive bastion along the slopes of Mount Etna and the Messina Peninsula.

Once again, Allied planners underestimated German resiliency, minimized the topographic impediments, and overestimated American and British capacity. Two days after the landing, Eisenhower spent a day touring the beachheads and told newsmen that assuming everything proceeded satisfactorily, "We should have Sicily in two weeks."[46] Those two weeks turned into six. Eisenhower played little role in the battle. Alexander, commanding the ground war, had two scorpions in a bottle: Patton and Montgomery, who sometimes appeared more intent on watching each other than chasing Kesselring. When Eighth Army's advance bogged down on the slopes of Mount Etna, Patton struck out on his own toward Palermo, in western Sicily. The military logic was dubious. Alexander let Patton have his way, but the Germans were mystified. Kesselring found it difficult to believe that the strong Allied forces advancing along the coast "had been dispersed to the western parts of Sicily, where the Americans just marched and captured unimportant terrain, instead of fighting at the wing where a major decision had to be reached."[47]

After reaching Palermo, Patton turned east and began attacking along the north coast toward Messina. German resistance was fierce, and Patton pushed his men to the limit. On August 17, 1943, the troops of Seventh Army beat the British to Messina by a number of hours. As in North Africa, brute force had prevailed. The outstanding performance of Seventh Army under Patton was the only bright spot in the fight. Kesselring, with sixty thousand troops, had held back two Allied armies for thirty-eight days, inflicting twenty thousand casualties at a cost of twelve thousand.[48] And all four German divisions, the 15th and 29th Panzer Grenadiers, the 1st Parachute, and the Hermann Göring, were evacuated intact across the Strait of Messina, along with 70,000 Italian troops, 10,000 trucks, and 47 tanks. The withdrawal, one of the most successful in military history, went largely uncontested. Eisenhower's headquarters had made no plans for severing the strait when HUSKY began, nor did any such plan emerge as the campaign reached a climax. Not once did the senior Allied commanders confer on how to prevent Kesselring's escape.[49] The coordination of the air, ground, and naval forces was Ike's responsibility, and in this instance he dropped the ball. An after-action report of the British War Office called Sicily a "chaotic and deplorable example of everything that planning should not be."[50] Montgomery put it more directly. "The truth of the matter is that there was no plan" to prevent the German evacuation.[51]

Allied euphoria over the capture of Sicily temporarily obscured the damage that had been done by permitting the German Army to escape. Like most Americans, Eisenhower rejoiced that Patton's Sev-

enth Army had beaten Montgomery to Messina, and privately relished Monty's discomfiture. But that joy was short-lived. Within
hours after Patton had taken possession of the city at a hastily improvised ceremony in front of city hall, Eisenhower found himself closeted with Brigadier General Frederick A. Blessé, the theater surgeon
general, listening to Blessé's confidential report about Patton's incomprehensible conduct the week before when he had struck and
verbally abused two enlisted men in the hospital.

On August 4, Patton, who was relentlessly pressing his troops
forward, visited a frontline hospital, where he toured the wards and
spoke with the wounded. When he discovered a soldier with no apparent wounds, Patton lost his self-control, slapped the man twice,
and called him "a Goddamn coward." He repeated the episode a
week later at another field hospital, where he called another soldier,
whom he thought was a malingerer, a disgrace to the Army who
ought to be shot, and then pulled his pistol from its holster and
threatened to do it himself. Patton then struck the man with such
force that his helmet liner was knocked off.[*] "I won't have these cow-
ardly bastards hanging around our hospitals," he told the surgeon in
charge. "We'll probably have to shoot them sometime anyway, or
we'll raise a breed of morons."[52] (Patton had struck an enlisted man
before. At the beginning of the Meuse-Argonne campaign in September 1918, Patton, then a lieutenant colonel, hit a skulking soldier on the head with a shovel and wrote to his wife that he thought
he had killed him.)[53]

Eisenhower's initial response was to minimize the episode. "If this
thing ever gets out they'll be howling for Patton's scalp, and that
will be the end of Georgie's service in the war. I simply cannot let

---

[*] The two soldiers involved were Private Charles H. Kuhl, Company F, 26th Infantry, and Private Paul G. Bennett, C Battery, 17th Field Artillery. Kuhl had been
hospitalized for "psychoneurotic anxiety," ran a fever of 102.3, and had suffered
diarrhea for the past month, having as many as ten to twelve stools a day. He was
ultimately diagnosed as suffering from chronic dysentery and malaria. Bennett, a
veteran of four years in the Regular Army, had been evacuated from his unit
against his will with symptoms of "dehydration, listlessness, and confusion." Report of Lieutenant Colonel Perrin H. Long, Medical Corps, to the Surgeon General, NATOUSA, August 16, 1943, reprinted in Blumenson, 2 *Patton Papers*
330–31.

that happen. Patton is *indispensable* to the war effort—one of the guarantors of our victory."[54] Ike instructed Blessé to conduct a confidential investigation, and then wrote in longhand a personal letter to Patton, enclosing the surgeon general's report, and asking for an explanation. Eisenhower's letter was hand delivered, and he assured Patton that the affair would be kept confidential. "In Allied Headquarters there is no record of the attached report or my letter to you, except in my own secret files." Patton was instructed to reply "personally and secretly."[55] In short, there would be no official reprimand, and Patton's service record would remain unblemished.[56]

"No letter that I have been called upon to write in my military career has caused me more anguish than this one," Eisenhower wrote Patton. "In the two cases in the attached report, it is *not* my present intention to institute any formal investigation. . . . [N]evertheless if there is a very considerable element of truth in the allegations accompanying this letter, I must so seriously question your good judgment and your self-discipline as to raise serious doubts in my mind as to your future usefulness. . . . I assure you that conduct such as that described in the accompanying report will *not* be tolerated in this theater no matter who the offender may be."[57]

Eisenhower instructed Patton to apologize to the men involved as well as to the doctors and nurses who had witnessed the episode. Later, Patton was instructed to apologize to all of the men under his command. Patton did so grudgingly, and did not fully grasp the seriousness of his offense. "It is a commentary on justice when an Army commander has to soft-soap a skulker to placate the timidity of those above," he recorded in his diary on August 21, 1943.

Eisenhower did his utmost to keep the two incidents under wraps. He did not inform Marshall or the War Department, and when a delegation of newsmen flew from Sicily to Algiers to confront Ike with the results of their own investigation, Eisenhower charmed them into suppressing the story. "Patton's emotional tenseness and his impulsiveness are the very qualities that make him such a remarkable leader," Ike told the reporters. "The more he drives his men the more he will save their lives. He must be indifferent to fatigue and ruthless in demanding the last atom of physical energy."[58]

Patton did not escape unscathed. A week after the capture of Messina, Eisenhower sent Marshall a report on his subordinates that the chief of staff might use in selecting his commanders for the invasion of France. It was widely assumed that Marshall would command the invasion and that Ike would either become his deputy or return to Washington as acting chief of staff.

Patton's ability spoke for itself, said Eisenhower. "He has conducted a campaign where the brilliant successes scored must be attributed directly to his energy, determination and unflagging aggressiveness. He is an army commander that you can use with certainty that the troops will not be stopped by ordinary obstacles." But Patton brought some unfortunate baggage with him. Despite his success, he "continues to exhibit some of those unfortunate personal traits of which you and I have always known and which during this campaign caused me some most uncomfortable days. . . . Personally, I believe that he is cured—because fundamentally he is so avid for recognition as a great military commander that he will ruthlessly suppress any habit that will jeopardize it. Aside from this one thing, he has qualities that we can't afford to lose unless he ruins himself."[59]

Eisenhower told Marshall that Bradley was running absolutely true to form. "He has brains, a fine capacity for leadership and a thorough understanding of the requirements of modern battle. He has never caused me one moment of worry." Mark Clark, in Ike's view, was the best of the three at planning, organizing, and training, but had not been in battle. "He will shortly have a chance to prove his worth."[60]

Marshall pressed Eisenhower for a specific recommendation. Which of the three would be best to head up preinvasion planning in England and later command American ground troops? Ike recommended Bradley. He was the best rounded of the three, "and he has the great characteristic of never giving his commander one moment of worry." Patton, said Eisenhower, was primarily a combat commander. "Many people fail to realize that the first thing that usually slows up operations is an element of caution, fatigue or doubt on the part of a higher commander. Patton is never affected by these and, consequently, his troops are not affected."[61]

A week later, discussing the Army promotion list, Eisenhower wrote Marshall stressing again that he believed Bradley was "the best rounded combat leader I have met in the service. While he probably lacks some of the extraordinary and ruthless driving power that Patton can exert at critical moments, he still has such force and determination that even in this characteristic he is among our best."[62]

Eisenhower, who had decided it was best to keep the slapping incidents confidential within the theater, still did not inform Marshall. Yet he elliptically noted that in Sicily, Patton had "indulged his temper in certain instances toward individual subordinates who in General Patton's opinion of the moment were guilty of malingering. I took immediate and drastic measures, and I am quite certain this sort of thing will never happen again."[63]

Following Eisenhower's recommendations, Marshall chose Bradley to go to England, catapulting him ahead of Patton, who might otherwise have gotten the nod. Bradley had commanded II Corps in Patton's Seventh Army, and like Ike had been five years junior to Patton in the Regular Army. It is possible that Marshall might have chosen Bradley over Patton in any event, but the slapping incidents effectively ruled Patton out. Eisenhower did not have to recite the details; his reference to Patton's occasional lack of self-control was sufficient.

Aside from having been passed over to lead the cross-Channel attack, Patton appeared to have weathered the storm. Inevitably, however, word of the slappings filtered back to the United States. On November 21, 1943, Washington investigative journalist Drew Pearson, who in 1934 had revealed Douglas MacArthur's escapade with Rosario Cooper, his young Eurasian paramour, told his Sunday evening NBC radio audience that Patton had slapped "a battle weary soldier," that he had been reprimanded by Eisenhower, and that he would never have another important wartime assignment.* The story

---

* At a time when journalists were more deferential to authority, Pearson's Washington Merry-Go-Round column in *The Washington Post* was a lively source of political muckraking. His column was carried by 650 newspapers—more than twice as many as any other journalist. In addition to the MacArthur–Rosario Cooper affair, Pearson exposed the Sherman Adams–Bernard Goldfine payola scandal during the Eisenhower administration, forcing Adams's resignation; the kickbacks of House of Representatives employees to Congressman J. Parnell Thomas, resulting in Thomas's conviction for tax evasion; and was the first to disclose that Attorney General Robert Kennedy had authorized the FBI's electronic surveillance of Dr.

was picked up by the wire services, and most of the nation's newspapers carried articles about Patton the following day. When it was discovered that one of the soldiers was Jewish, the outrage intensified. "These are American soldiers, not Germans," said an American Legion spokesman. "If our boys are going to be mistreated, let's import Hitler and do it right."[64]

Pearson's broadcast was picked up by Army monitoring stations in Algiers, and Eisenhower's headquarters was immediately informed. Ike's initial response was to hunker down and wait for the storm to pass. Hoping to minimize his involvement, he dispatched Bedell Smith to meet the press and answer their questions.* But instead of controlling the blaze, Smith inadvertently added fuel to the fire. Asked by newsmen whether Eisenhower had reprimanded Patton, Smith replied that no official reprimand had been administered. To be fair, Smith may not have known of Ike's private letter to Patton, but his answer was scarcely what the reporters wanted to hear. According to *The New York Times,* Smith's statement "disgusted everyone who heard it."[65]†

As Eisenhower wrote later, "The damage was done."[66] Within minutes, the news that Patton had not been officially reprimanded was flashed to the United States. Members of Congress demanded an investigation, and Marshall cabled for an explanation. What were the facts, he asked, and what had Ike done about the incident?[67]

---

Martin Luther King, Jr. Perhaps Pearson was wrong as often as he was right, but in Patton's case his facts were correct. He stated clearly that Eisenhower had informally reprimanded Patton. *Time,* December 2, 1943.

* "I had been expecting something like this to happen," Patton recorded in his diary on November 22, 1943. "I am sure it would have been much better to have admitted the whole thing to start with, particularly in view of the fact that I was right [in what I did]." Blumenson, 2 *Patton Papers* 374.

† On November 23, *The New York Times* reported that "Allied Force Headquarters denied tonight that Lieut. Gen. George S. Patton had been reprimanded by Gen. Dwight D. Eisenhower and stated that General Patton is still in command of Seventh Army."

The article quoted Smith even more damagingly: "General Patton has never been reprimanded at any time by General Eisenhower or by anyone else in this theater."

Eisenhower replied on November 24. Ike's literary ability to convert defeat into victory was sorely tested, but he rose to the occasion. Patton had been the mainspring in Seventh Army's drive for Messina, he told Marshall. "His absolute refusal to accept any excuses for delay or procrastination resulted in the rapid advance of that army and had much to do with the early collapse of resistance in Sicily. In the campaign he drove himself as hard as he did the members of his army and, as a result, he became almost ruthless in his demands upon individual men." Eisenhower briefly described the slapping incidents, stressing that the men were "unwounded repeat unwounded." He had personally reprimanded Patton, "expressing my extreme displeasure and informing him that any repetition would result in his immediate relief." Ike said he had put nothing official in Patton's 201 file, but had forced Patton to apologize not only to the men involved, but to all of the doctors, nurses, and others who had witnessed the incidents. Those apologies had been accepted.

"To sum up: It is true that General Patton was guilty of reprehensible conduct with respect to two enlisted men. They were suffering from a nervous disorder and in one case the man had a temperature. After exhaustive investigations, including a personal visit to Sicily, I decided that the corrective action as described above was adequate and suitable for the circumstances. I still believe that this decision is sound."[68]

In Washington, Secretary Stimson and Marshall rallied to Eisenhower's defense. "Drew Pearson has spilled the beans," Stimson confided to his diary. "The incident was not a pretty one, but I fully agree with Eisenhower's view that Patton's services must not be lost."[69]

After dispatching a stern letter to Patton, whom he regarded as the Army's "problem child," Stimson deployed his vast influence on Capitol Hill to quiet the furor.* Writing to Senator Robert R.

---

* Stimson had known Patton on a personal basis for many years, and he expressed his disappointment that "so brilliant an officer should so far have offended against his own traditions." According to Patton's most uncritical biographer, "It was Stimson's letter more than anything else that brought home to Patton the true seriousness of the situation. Until its receipt . . . he was inclined to dismiss the incident with a shrug. But the Stimson letter was a hard blow. For the first time

Reynolds of North Carolina, chairman of the Senate Committee on Military Affairs, Stimson emphasized the War Department's determination to gain victory as quickly as possible, with as little loss of life as possible. Eisenhower, he said, had weighed Patton's indefensible conduct against his outstanding service in both world wars and had decided that the country could not afford to lose Patton for the fighting still to come. Stimson observed that Ike had been "obliged to consider this matter from a military viewpoint rather than that of what is termed 'public relations.' " Patton's removal, Stimson cautioned, would deny the United States "the services of a battle-tested Army commander, and also afford aid and comfort to the enemy."[70]

After his return from the Teheran conference, FDR was asked at his White House press conference whether he would comment on General Patton. Roosevelt told the newsmen they might, without attributing the story to him, remember

> a former President who had a good deal of trouble finding a successful commander for the armies of the United States. And one of them turned up one day and he was very successful.
>
> And some very good citizens went to the President. "You can't keep this man. He drinks."
>
> "It must be a good brand of liquor," the President replied.[71]

As Eisenhower anticipated, the storm passed. On December 1, 1943, he wrote Patton, "I think I took the right decision and I will stand by it. You don't need to be afraid of my weakening on the proposition in spite of the fact that I was more than a little annoyed with you."[72] To Kay Summersby, Ike said, "Georgie is one of the best generals I have. But he's just like a time bomb. You never know when he's going to go off. All you can be sure of is that it will probably be in the wrong place at the wrong time."[73]

---

during the 'hullabaloo' he became remorseful and conscience-smitten." Ladislas Farago, *Patton: Ordeal and Triumph* 357 (New York: Ivan Obolensky, 1963).

By striking an enlisted man, Patton had committed a court-martial offense.* In Patton's case, because of his rank, it would have been a general court-martial. Eisenhower accepted responsibility and brushed the affair under the rug. Ike said later that he would never promote Patton above the rank of an army commander, but that on the battlefield he was irreplaceable.

* Article 95 (section 2, number 8) of the *Articles of War* states, "Striking a soldier as a punishment for a dereliction of duty is an offense against military law punishable under this, or the 96th (General Article) according to the seriousness of the case."

Article 96 reads, "Though not mentioned in these articles, all disorders and neglects to the prejudice of good order and military discipline, all conduct of a nature to bring discredit upon the military service, and all crimes or offenses not capital, of which persons subject to military law may be guilty, shall be taken cognizance of by a general or special or summary court-martial, according to the nature of and degree of the offense, and punished at the discretion of such court."

*The Articles of War, Annotated by Lee S. Tillotson* (Harrisburg, Pa.: Military Service Publishing, 1943).

# TWELVE

# Supreme Commander

Won't you come back here, Child,
and have lunch with a dull old man?
— FDR TO KAY SUMMERSBY,
*November 21, 1943*

EISENHOWER PLAYED NO DIRECT ROLE in the battle for Sicily. "I am the Chairman of a Board," he told Lord Louis Mountbatten.[1] Alexander, with his headquarters close to the fighting in Sicily, controlled the ground war. Cunningham, at the Royal Navy's base on Malta, directed the war at sea. And Tedder waged the air war from Tunis. Ike remained at Allied Forces Headquarters (AFHQ) in Algiers and was primarily concerned with keeping London and Washington abreast of the fighting while overseeing civil affairs in French North Africa and coordinating the work of his deputies. But as the escape of the German Army across the Strait of Messina demonstrated, the commanders in chief were too widely separated to be coordinated easily, and at the close of the Sicilian campaign Eisenhower ordered them back to Algiers.

Ike was pampered. Even before the return of Alexander, Cunningham, Tedder, and their staffs to Algiers, AFHQ numbered more than four thousand officers, most with John C. H. Lee's Services of Supply, although Bedell Smith shared Lee's preference for redundancy, and the necessity to commingle British and American officers sometimes doubled the normal staff complement.[*]

The sheer size of Allied Forces Headquarters meant that Ike's personal preferences could be accommodated easily. He lived in a spacious seven-bedroom villa overlooking the Mediterranean, enjoyed a country retreat near Carthage, and had a personal staff (his "family") that catered to his needs. Sergeant Mickey McKeogh supervised the household; his valet, Sergeant John Moaney, dressed him each morning; and Tex Lee and Harry Butcher ran whatever errands were required. The duty day began at seven with cigarettes and countless cups of scalding black coffee, and continued until about four, when Eisenhower headed for his country place, went riding with Kay when weather permitted, and returned for cocktails about six. Dinner was informal, unless visiting dignitaries were present, and was inevitably followed by a rubber of bridge with Ike and Kay taking on Butcher and whoever else might be available, usually T. J. Davis, the theater adjutant general. Kay made Eisenhower's off-duty moments as pleasant as she could, and often attended top-level meetings as his personal assistant and confidant. "We have no secrets from Kay," Ike was quoted as saying.[2] Curious about their relationship, General James Gavin of the 82nd Airborne asked veteran correspondent John "Beaver" Thompson of the *Chicago Tribune* if the rumors they were having an affair were true. "Well," Thompson replied, "I have never before seen a chauffeur get out of a car and kiss the General good morning when he comes from his office."[3]

Eisenhower's executive ability—his capacity to delegate while assuming ultimate responsibility—was exceptional. After the war, Omar Bradley said that Ike "did not know how to manage a battlefield," but as a theater commander he proved uniquely gifted. Mont-

---

[*] Bedell Smith was initially concerned that Alexander had too few Americans on his staff at Fifteenth Army Group. Harold Macmillan told Smith that the quality of the American officers previously provided was poor and "quite frankly that he must supply some better American officers if they were to be taken seriously." Smith got the message and dispatched Lyman Lemnitzer to be Alexander's deputy. (Lemnitzer served as chairman of the U.S. Joint Chiefs of Staff from 1960 to 1962.) Harold Macmillan, *The Blast of War: 1939–1945* 304 (New York: Harper and Row, 1968).

gomery concurred. He would not class Eisenhower as a great soldier, said Monty, "but he was a great Supreme Commander—a military statesman."[4]* No other general officer, British or American, could have dealt as effectively with Washington and London, kept headstrong subordinates working in harmony, and (with the help of John C. H. Lee) amassed the matériel that ensured ultimate victory. In a sense, Ike was like a giant umbrella. He absorbed what was coming down from above, shielded his commanders from higher authority, and allowed them to fight the war without excessive second-guessing.

But the pressures took a toll. Harold Macmillan, whom Churchill had dispatched to provide political guidance, noted in his diary during the Sicily campaign that Ike

> was getting pretty harassed. Telegrams (private, personal and most immediate) pour in upon him from the following sources:
>
> (i)    Combined Chiefs of Staff (Washington), his official masters.
> (ii)   General Marshall, Chief of U.S. Army, his immediate superior.
> (iii)  The President.
> (iv)  The Secretary of State.
> (v)   Our Prime Minister (direct).
> (vi)  Our Prime Minister (through me).
> (vii) The Foreign Minister (through me).

"All these instructions are naturally contradictory and conflicting," said Macmillan, and it was like a parlor game to juggle them and get things right.[5]

Eisenhower described his job in a lengthy letter to Admiral Louis Mountbatten in mid-September 1943. Mountbatten had recently

---

* After conceding Eisenhower's executive ability, Monty wrote Field Marshal Sir Alan Brooke, chief of the imperial general staff, that Ike "knows nothing whatever about how to make war or fight battles; he should be kept away from all that business if we want to win this war." Montgomery to Brooke, April 4, 1943, Montgomery Papers, Imperial War Museum, London.

been named supreme Allied commander for Southeast Asia, and wrote to ask Ike's advice. Eisenhower stressed the importance of personal relationships. Allied unity "involves the human equation and must be met day by day. Patience, tolerance, frankness, absolute honesty in all dealings, particularly with persons of the opposite nationality, is absolutely essential." Ike said the three commanders in chief (air, ground, and sea) must be given broad authority. "Without a great degree of decentralization no allied command can be made to work."

Eisenhower told Mountbatten that mutual respect and confidence among the senior commanders was the most important ingredient in achieving allied unity.

> All of us are human and we like to be favorably noticed by those above us and even by the public. An Allied Commander-in-Chief, among all others practicing the art of war, must more sternly than any other individual repress such notions. He must be self-effacing, quick to give credit, ready to meet the other fellow more than half way, must seek and absorb advice and must learn to decentralize. On the other hand, when the time comes that he feels he must make a decision, he must make it in a clean-cut fashion and on his own responsibility and take full blame for anything that goes wrong; in fact he must be quick to take the blame for anything that goes wrong whether or not it results from his mistake or from an error on the part of a subordinate.

Ike said that while clear-cut lines of authority were important, in the last analysis "your personality and your good sense *must* make it work. Otherwise *Allied* action in any theater will be impossible."[6]

It was during the Sicily campaign that Mussolini fell from office and Italy sued for peace. On July 19, 1943, Allied bombers hit Rome for the first time. More than five hundred bombers from bases in North Africa and Pantelleria struck at the sprawling Littorio rail yards in the center of the city. Historic sites and the Vatican were spared, although a single thousand-pound bomb ripped through the roof of the Basilica of San Lorenzo, built in the fourth century and considered one of Rome's finest churches. Estimates of the dead ranged from seven hundred to three thousand, with many more injured.[7]

The bombing of Rome, combined with the reverses in North Africa and Sicily, meant that Mussolini's days were numbered. On July 25 the Grand Council of Fascism (which had not met since 1939) voted no confidence in Il Duce. King Victor Emmanuel relieved him of office that evening, and Mussolini was placed in protective custody. News of the dictator's fall triggered massive celebrations in the streets of Rome, and Victor Emmanuel, instead of naming a Fascist replacement, turned to Italy's most distinguished soldier, Marshal Pietro Badoglio. "Fascism fell like a rotten pear," said Badoglio later.[8]

In 1936, Badoglio had turned the Italian debacle in Ethiopia into victory, and subsequently served as chief of the Supreme General Staff (Commando Supremo) until December 1940, when he broke with Mussolini over the invasion of Greece. As soon as he was installed in office, Badoglio assured Hitler of Italy's continued loyalty. He then initiated secret discussions with the Allies, first in Madrid, then Lisbon. Eisenhower's headquarters was represented by Bedell Smith and British brigadier Kenneth Strong, and after considerable to-ing and fro-ing an armistice was set to take effect the evening of September 8.[9] "The House of Savoy," a Free French newspaper observed, "never finished a war on the same side it started, unless the war lasted long enough to change sides twice."[10]

The Italian surrender had little practical effect. Badoglio and the King fled to Brindisi (on the heel of the Italian boot), the Germans occupied Rome, and the Italian Army was disarmed and demobilized. The principal gain was that the Italian fleet sailed from its bases in La Spezia and Taranto to Malta to be interned. Ike and Admiral Cunningham watched from the deck of the destroyer HMS *Hambledon* as the Taranto squadron sailed into St. Paul's harbor, flags aloft, sailors manning the rails. "When they replied to our bosun's whistle," Butcher remembered, "I swear theirs had an operatic trill."[11] By mid-September, six battleships, eight cruisers, thirty-three destroyers, and one hundred merchant ships had surrendered to the Allies.[12]

Meanwhile, Roosevelt and Churchill met with the Combined Chiefs of Staff at Quebec (QUADRANT) to plan the invasion of Europe. Despite Churchill's misgivings, it was agreed that Allied forces would cross the Channel in May 1944. It was further agreed that seven divisions, three British and four American, would be withdrawn from the Mediterranean and shipped to Great Britain to take part in the landings. But to satisfy Churchill's desire to pursue a Mediterranean strategy and hit Germany through what he persistently referred to as Europe's "soft underbelly," it was also agreed to land in Italy following the fall of Sicily. In effect, QUADRANT gave something to everyone. Roosevelt and Marshall obtained Britain's commitment to land in France in 1944, and Churchill got American approval to invade Italy, although with fewer forces than he would have liked.

Most significantly, Roosevelt insisted that the invasion of France (code name OVERLORD) be commanded by an American. By 1944, the United States would be furnishing the greater number of troops, said FDR, and the American public would demand an American supreme commander. Churchill yielded gracefully, although he had previously promised the position to General Sir Alan Brooke.[*] No one was named to the post, but it was widely assumed that it would go to Marshall and that Eisenhower would return to Washington as chief of staff.

QUADRANT also approved rearming the French. Following a recommendation from Eisenhower, it was agreed that the United States would provide the equipment to outfit eleven French divisions—four armored and seven infantry—to be raised in North Africa. The divisions would be earmarked for the invasion of southern France (ANVIL), which would be coordinated with OVER-

---

[*] "It was a crashing blow to hear from him [Churchill] that he was now handing over this appointment to the Americans," Brooke recorded in his diary entry of August 15, 1943. "Not for one moment did he realize what this meant to me. He offered no sympathy, no regrets at having had to change his mind and dealt with the matter as if it were one of minor importance." Field Marshal Lord Alanbrooke, *War Diaries, 1939–1945* 441–42, Alex Danchev and Daniel Todman, eds. (Berkeley and Los Angeles: University of California Press, 2001). When Field Marshal Sir Alan Brooke was elevated to the peerage, he adopted the name Alanbrooke.

LORD.[13] Britain and the United States also accepted the French Committee of National Liberation as the responsible French authority for the conduct of the war, although FDR remained adamant against formal diplomatic recognition. Roosevelt said he wanted "a sheet anchor out against the machinations of de Gaulle" and that he would not "give de Gaulle a white horse on which he could ride into France and make himself the master of the government there."[14]

When the time came, the invasion of Italy was mishandled as badly as the invasion of North Africa had been. Instead of landing in one location with overwhelming force as Eisenhower had insisted on doing in Sicily, the Allies once again landed piecemeal. On September 3, 1943, Montgomery crossed the Strait of Messina with two veteran divisions from Eighth Army, landed on the toe of the Italian boot, and secured the adjacent coastline to protect Allied shipping (BAYTOWN). Six days later, three divisions from Mark Clark's Fifth Army landed at Salerno, three hundred miles north of Montgomery, and less than fifty miles below Naples (AVALANCHE). No effort was made to coordinate the landings, and by dividing his forces, Eisenhower not only weakened the landing at Salerno, but deprived AVALANCHE of the battle-tested troops of Eighth Army.[*]

Eisenhower, his AFHQ staff, and his commanders in chief overestimated the impact of Italy's surrender, underestimated Kesselring's ability to mount a spirited defense, and again failed to comprehend the topographic impediments that an army would encounter pressing north. The uninterrupted strand of beaches at Salerno provided a favorable landing site. But they were ringed by low-lying mountains from which German mortars and artillery could blast the troops coming ashore. As one Navy planner put it, "The landing site was

---

* Montgomery's orders instructed him "to secure a bridgehead on the toe of Italy, to enable our naval forces to operate through the Straits of Messina." No effort was made to coordinate his efforts with the Fifth Army, and it was not anticipated that the Eighth Army would move north beyond the neck of Catanzaro, the ankle of the Italian boot. Alexander to Montgomery, August 20, 1943, Montgomery Papers, Imperial War Museum, London. Also see *The Memoirs of Field-Marshal the Viscount Montgomery of Alamein* 173 (Cleveland: World Publishing, 1958); Nigel Hamilton, *Master of the Battlefield: Monty's War Years, 1942–1944* 386–87 (New York: McGraw-Hill, 1983).

like the inside of a coffee cup."[15] And although Salerno appeared on small-scale planning maps to be just south of Naples, it was separated from the city by the Vesuvian massif, a barrier just as formidable as Mount Etna had proved to be in Sicily. Eisenhower assumed that Naples would be in Allied hands within the week and planned to move his headquarters there later in the month. Clark shared Ike's optimism. "You don't have to worry about this operation," he told an old Army friend. "This will be a pursuit, not a battle."[16] The fact is Clark's troops did not enter Naples until October 1, 1943, after three weeks of some of the most difficult fighting of the war.

In the south, Montgomery encountered little opposition. Kesselring chose not to defend every inch of Italian territory, and with Sicily already in Allied hands, southern Calabria was of little strategic value. But at Salerno it was a different story. Fifth Army came within an eyelash of being driven back into the sea. Eisenhower ultimately deployed every bomber in the theater and every warship Cunningham could muster to protect the beachhead, and eventually the German counterattack was turned back. But it was truly the most dangerous moment of the war in Europe for the Western Allies. An entire field army of two corps and four divisions was on the verge of annihilation.[17]

Eisenhower had gambled that the Italian surrender would change the nature of the war and that Clark would face little opposition. The fact is, both he and Marshal Badoglio were playing a double game. Ike and Bedell Smith led Badoglio and his representatives to believe that the Allies would land at various points along the Italian coast with no fewer than twelve divisions. Assuming that so many American and British troops would be coming ashore so quickly, Badoglio pledged that the Italian Army would switch sides and assist the Allies. Eisenhower and his staff became so enthralled with the possibility of Italian support that they devised a last-minute scheme to land an airborne division in Rome (almost two hundred miles north of Salerno) to protect the Badoglio government and "stiffen the Italian formations" (GIANT II).

Four days before Fifth Army was scheduled to land at Salerno, Ike snatched the 82nd Airborne from Clark and ordered it to drop on the Eternal City at the same time Clark's men went ashore. Eisenhower assured Matthew Ridgway, the division commander, that the Italians would prepare the way. Ridgway was skeptical. Having lost a quarter of his division on the way to Sicily because of faulty Allied planning, he was reluctant to take Ike's word for it. At Ridgway's insistence Brigadier General Maxwell D. Taylor, who commanded the 82nd Airborne Division's artillery, and who spoke Italian fluently,[*] was smuggled clandestinely into Rome to reconnoiter the situation.[18] Twenty-four hours after arriving, Taylor radioed back that there was no hope whatsoever of receiving Italian support and that any landing in Rome was doomed to failure. At the last moment, with the troop-carrying planes on the runway and some already in the air, GIANT II was canceled. For years afterward Eisenhower believed that the airdrop on Rome had been feasible, and Bedell Smith to his dying day thought Taylor a coward.[19] To their credit, Ridgway and Taylor resisted the quixotic, dangerously ill-conceived plan of the high command and saved their division from catastrophe. At Chattanooga in 1863, George Thomas refused Grant's order to attack until he was resupplied with draft horses to pull his artillery. Grant was furious, but Thomas was right and, by refusing to attack prematurely, he probably saved Grant's career. Ridgway and Taylor were also correct, and may well have saved Ike from certain disaster.[†]

At 0200 on September 9, 1943, the men of the assault wave of Fifth Army clambered into their landing craft and headed toward the Italian shoreline. Instead of the seven divisions that went ashore in Sicily, Clark would hit the beaches with only three, one of which—

---

* In addition to having been first captain of the corps of cadets (USMA, 1922), Taylor was a gifted linguist who had taught French and Spanish at the academy.
† "When the time comes that I must meet my Maker," wrote Ridgway in his memoirs, "the source of most humble pride to me will not be accomplishments in battle, but the fact that I was guided to make the decision to oppose this thing [GIANT II]. I deeply and sincerely believe that by taking the stand I took we saved the lives of thousands of brave men.

"The hard decisions," Ridgway added, "are not the ones you make in the heat of battle. Far harder to make are those involved in speaking your mind about some hare-brained scheme, which proposes to commit troops to action under conditions where failure is almost certain, and the only results will be the needless sacrifice of priceless lives." *Soldier: The Memoirs of Matthew B. Ridgway, as Told to Harold H. Martin* 82–83 (New York: Harper, 1956).

the 36th Infantry—was a Texas National Guard unit that had never seen combat. In Sicily, the Allies had put a half million men ashore by D-Day plus two. Clark would command fewer than sixty thousand. Eisenhower believed that with Italy out of the war, the Germans would not make a stand at Salerno but would fall back to a defensive line north of Rome along the Arno River, roughly from Pisa to Rimini, and protect the Po Valley. Alexander and Clark shared that view. Montgomery objected, but his reclama had little impact.[20] The fact is, after Mussolini's ouster, Hitler had rushed fourteen divisions into Italy, in addition to the four evacuated from Sicily. Six of those divisions, including three fully refitted panzer divisions, were within two days' march of Salerno. And Kesselring had no intention of withdrawing.

To complicate matters further, the news that Italy had surrendered was announced shortly before the troops boarded their landing craft. Many believed the beaches would not be defended. Admiral Henry Hewitt, commanding the naval task force, noted with alarm that Fifth Army's "keen fighting edge" had been dulled.[21] Incredible as it seems in retrospect, the 36th Division elected to forgo a preparatory naval barrage to soften enemy defenses. "I see no point to killing a lot of peaceful Italians and destroying their homes," said Major General Fred L. Walker, the division commander.[22] Clark supported that decision. As a consequence, German artillery and mortar fire pummeled the beaches at will. Allied planners had assumed Fifth Army would be four thousand yards inland by daylight. Instead, by midmorning the beachhead scarcely extended four hundred yards.[23] At that point the destroyers and cruisers accompanying the invasion force moved close to shore and began to shell the German positions on Monte Soprano. The Germans pulled back, and by nightfall the beachhead was secure.

By Sunday, September 12, Fifth Army had pushed inland to an average depth of six miles along a thirty-five-mile front. "Combat efficiency of all units excellent," Clark reported. "Ready to march toward Naples."[24] It was another pipe dream. Rather than withdrawing, General Heinrich von Vietinghoff, Kesselring's field commander, had been concentrating his forces and now had five divisions, including the Hermann Göring and 16th Panzer, ready to counterattack. With six hundred tanks and self-propelled guns he struck Clark's lines at dawn on September 13—"Black Monday"—intent on driving Fifth Army back into the sea. Vietinghoff concentrated his attack along the seam between Clark's two corps, and by evening of the thirteenth, Fifth Army was on the ropes. Clark ordered the 82nd Airborne (which had been restored to his command) to drop inside the beachhead, and at the same time commenced contingency planning to evacuate, beginning with his own headquarters (Operation BRASS RAIL).

When Eisenhower learned that Clark contemplated evacuation, he was thunderstruck. Had he made a mistake in giving Fifth Army to Clark? he asked Butcher. Should he have selected Patton, who at least "would prefer to die fighting"? A commanding general should stay with his men to give them confidence, said Ike. "He should show the spirit of a naval captain and, if necessary, go down with his ship."[25] Eisenhower told Butcher that "if the Salerno battle ended in disaster, he would probably be out."[26]

Faced with impending doom, Eisenhower sprang into action, determined, as he put it, "to move heaven and earth to save Fifth Army." Tedder was ordered to deploy the full strength of the Allied air force—including B-17 strategic bombers—to protect the beachhead; Cunningham rushed the main battle fleet to the Gulf of Salerno; Alexander was dispatched to bolster Clark's resolve; and Montgomery was ordered to hasten his advance from Calabria. "An evacuation from Salerno," Cunningham wrote later, "would have resulted in a reverse of the first magnitude—an Allied defeat which would have completely offset the Italian surrender."[27]

The battle at Salerno lasted four days. Allied bombers dropped almost a thousand tons of high explosives per square mile, annihilating intersections, rail lines, and whole villages.[28] Cunningham's fleet delivered more than eleven thousand tons of highly accurate five- and six-inch shells in direct support of Clark's troops. "The attack this morning had to endure naval gunfire from at least 16 to 18 battleships, cruisers and large destroyers," Vietinghoff informed Kesselring on September 14. "With astonishing precision and freedom of maneuver, these ships shot at every recognized target with overwhelming effect."[29]

By the evening of September 16 the crisis was over. Elements of Eighth Army had made contact with Clark's forces forty miles south of Salerno, and Kesselring ordered Vietinghoff to pull back to a defensive position on the Volturno River north of Naples. Allied casualties totaled about nine thousand, of whom twelve hundred were killed in action. Total German losses numbered roughly thirty-five hundred, including six hundred dead.[30] Once again overwhelming Allied firepower saved the day.

In postwar interviews, as well as in their memoirs, Eisenhower, Clark, and Bedell Smith planted the idea that much of Fifth Army's problem at Salerno was attributable to Montgomery's failure to move up from Messina more rapidly.[31] It is another illustration of Ike's ability to reshape the record. Not only did the initial orders given Montgomery not contemplate his direct support of AVALANCHE, but Eighth Army was not provided sufficient transport to move beyond Calabria. When he was belatedly ordered to rush to Clark's support, additional transport was provided and Montgomery closed the gap in three days. For Monty it was old hat. In February he had been asked by Alexander to hasten his advance into Tunisia to ease the pressure on Fredendall at Kasserine Pass. Now he was hustling to assist Clark.[*]

The blame for the setback at Salerno rests squarely with Eisenhower and Clark and the rosy scenario they painted as to what would follow Italy's surrender. As a consequence, too few troops were deployed, Montgomery's Eighth Army veterans were dispatched on a wild-goose chase three hundred miles south of the main battle area, naval and air support were initially haphazard, and the quality of tactical leadership was manifestly inadequate. As General Rudolf Sieckenius, commanding the 16th Panzer, put it, the Americans and

---

[*] Could Eighth Army have reached Salerno more quickly? The U.S. Army's official history of the Salerno campaign, written by the distinguished military historian Martin Blumenson, states that the "unequivocal answer is impossible." After describing the difficulties Eighth Army surmounted, Blumenson quotes Mark Clark's note to Montgomery while the battle was still in progress: "Please accept my deep appreciation for assistance your Eighth Army has provided Fifth Army by your skillful and rapid advance." Clark to Montgomery, September 15, 1943, in Martin Blumenson, *Salerno to Cassino* 140–41 (Washington, D.C.: Office of the Chief of Military History, U.S. Army, 1969).

British were "devoid of offensive spirit, excessively dependent on artillery support, and reluctant to close with the enemy."[32]

Eisenhower learned from the crisis at Salerno, and the mistakes were not repeated at Normandy. Whether Clark learned anything continues to be a matter of debate. What is clear is that a foul-up as significant as Salerno required a scapegoat, and the victim was Major General Ernest J. Dawley, who commanded Clark's VI Corps. Dawley's performance was no worse than any other general officer's at Salerno. Yet he quarreled repeatedly with Clark (Dawley vehemently objected to evacuating the beachhead), and Clark convinced Ike that Dawley was unstable. Eisenhower, with some misgiving, reduced Dawley to his permanent peacetime rank of colonel and sent him back to the United States, where he was assigned to a training command.[33] "It was just as well," Dawley said later. "I couldn't work with Clark. He made decisions off the top of his head."[34] Dawley regained one star almost immediately, returned to the European theater in 1945, and retired as a major general two years later. "He is being promoted," Marshall told Texas senator Tom Connally, "as a reward for keeping his mouth shut."[35]

On September 22, 1943, Churchill—who was deeply committed to the invasion of Italy—praised Ike for the outcome at Salerno. "I congratulate you on the victorious landing and deployment northwards of our armies," he cabled. "As the Duke of Wellington said of the battle of Waterloo, 'It was a damned close-run thing,' but your policy of running risks has been vindicated."[36]

Marshall did not share Churchill's enthusiasm. The following day he chastised Eisenhower for launching Montgomery in Calabria before Clark hit the beach at Salerno. "Quite evidently you and Alexander had a different view but at long range it would seem that you gave the enemy too much time to prepare and eventually find yourself up against very stiff resistance."[37]

Marshall said he and Field Marshal Sir John Dill, head of the British mission in Washington, feared that Eisenhower was about to repeat the same mistake. If he took the time to develop a secure position around Naples, said Marshall, "you will afford the other fellow so much time that he will be in a position to make things much more difficult in the matter of an advance to Rome." Marshall asked Eisenhower if he had considered halting the advance on Naples and making a dash for Rome, perhaps by amphibious means.[38]

According to Butcher, Marshall's letter "took the starch out of Ike."[39] Accustomed to nothing but praise from his mentor in Washington, Eisenhower had been pulled up short. He fretted over a reply for a day, and then sent Marshall a whine reminiscent of George McClellan's frequent responses to Lincoln in 1862. "I do not see how any individual could possibly be devoting more thought and energy to speeding up operations or to attacking boldly and with admitted risk than I do."[40] Eisenhower said there was no way that the landing at Salerno "could have logically preceded BAYTOWN [Montgomery's landing in Calabria]." This reply was less than candid. Before BAYTOWN was launched, Montgomery told Eisenhower and Alexander that it was a mistake to send Eighth Army across the Strait of Messina and that everything should be concentrated at Salerno. But neither Ike nor Alexander listened. As one military historian has put it: "Instead of keeping Eighth Army concentrated for landing further north, Eisenhower committed himself to one of the most senseless assaults of the war, and then blamed Montgomery for being slow."[41]

Marshall's rebuke disconcerted Eisenhower. While Churchill had applauded his willingness to take risks, Marshall and Dill, from their global perspective in Washington, questioned his judgment.[42] It was the beginning of Ike's autumn of discontent. The battle for Italy was not the cakewalk he had anticipated. Allied troops would not enter Rome for another nine months; the Germans now had twenty-four divisions south of the Alps; winter was approaching, and the mountainous hinterland north of Naples scarcely suggested a "soft underbelly." The rivers in Italy flow east and west, and each provided a defense line for the ever resourceful Kesselring. Even worse, Italy was now a secondary theater. The Allies' main tent was OVERLORD, and Eisenhower had already lost seven divisions and three strategic bombing groups to the buildup in Britain. His requests for men and matériel often went unheeded, and he was losing many of his best officers (such as Bradley) to the cross-Channel attack.

Ike was also growing irritable and testy. Late that fall, after a tiring inspection trip to Italy, he asked Bedell Smith to join him for dinner. Smith was evidently just as weary as Ike, and said he would rather not. Eisenhower hit the roof. He accused Smith of being disrespectful. No subordinate, Eisenhower shouted, could abruptly decline his commanding officer's invitation to dinner. Smith said he would ask for a transfer. Ike said that was OK with him. Both men sulked, and Smith finally calmed down and apologized. Eisenhower did, too, and the incident passed.[43]

Eisenhower biographers uniformly attribute Ike's funk in the fall of 1943 to his despair at the prospect of returning to Washington to replace Marshall as chief of staff. That possibility undoubtedly affected his mood. But he was also concerned that he might be trapped in a military sideshow. The battle for Italy would be long, hard, and thankless, and Ike despaired at finding a way out.

In 1925, when Eisenhower believed he had been passed over for the Command and General Staff School at Leavenworth, Fox Conner had executed an end run around the chief of infantry and Ike secured an appointment. When Eisenhower was stuck in the all-black 24th Infantry at Fort Benning, Conner intervened to have him assigned to Pershing's Battle Monument Commission. And when duty with Pershing in Paris appeared to be a dead end, Conner arranged Ike's transfer to the office of the assistant secretary of war in Washington. But Fox Conner had long retired and Eisenhower was stuck.

George Patton often referred to Ike as "Divine Destiny." The British—Brooke, Alexander, and Montgomery—never thought much of Eisenhower's generalship but always welcomed his good luck. Napoléon also preferred lucky generals, and it was not long until *fortuna* came to Ike's relief. On November 17, 1943, Prime Minister Churchill, accompanied by the British high command, stopped off in Malta for a preliminary conference with Eisenhower before meeting with FDR in Cairo, and then with Stalin in Teheran. Churchill pressed his Mediterranean strategy on Ike and confessed that the idea of crossing the English Channel left him cold. "We must take care that the tides do not run red with the blood of American and British youth, or the beaches be choked with their bodies."[44]

Both Churchill and Eisenhower were suffering from severe respiratory infections, and in the course of commiserating, Churchill hinted that the command of OVERLORD was not firmly fixed. He told Ike he was disappointed that the job would not go to Brooke, and that the final decision was in the president's hands. "We British will be glad to accept either you or Marshall."[45] Whether Eisenhower was being actively considered is doubtful.[*] Churchill was simply stating a fact. The British could accept either Marshall or Ike. There was nothing in the prime minister's statement to suggest that the nod would not go to Marshall. Nevertheless, this was the first inkling Eisenhower had that the matter was undecided, and the message was clear.[46] It was Roosevelt's call.

Two days after meeting with Churchill, Eisenhower stood on the pier of the great French naval base at Mers el-Kébir, six miles west of Oran, awaiting the arrival of the president. Standing with Ike were Admiral Cunningham and FDR's sons Elliott and Franklin, Jr., who were stationed nearby. In the harbor, the USS *Iowa,* the latest of a new class of battleships, rode at anchor following a 3,800-mile passage from Hampton Roads.[47] In addition to the president, the *Iowa*'s passengers included Harry Hopkins, Roosevelt's White House aides, the Joint Chiefs of Staff, and a full complement of military planners. The eight-day crossing had allowed the president time to review plans for the war in Europe with his military chiefs before meeting Churchill and Stalin. "The sea voyage had done Father good," Elliott recalled. "He looked fit and he was filled with excited anticipation of the days ahead."[48]

---

* On October 30, 1943, FDR cabled Churchill that it was important for a commander of OVERLORD to be appointed quickly, but, "as you know I cannot make Marshall available immediately." The president asked Churchill if he could appoint a British deputy supreme commander "who in receipt of precisely the same measure of support as will eventually be accorded Marshall could well carry the work forward."

Churchill replied the following day. "Can you give me a firm date when Marshall will be available, as I see great difficulties in the various stop gap arrangements proposed?" Warren F. Kimball, ed. 2 *Churchill and Roosevelt: The Complete Correspondence* 571, 573 (Princeton, N.J.: Princeton University Press, 1984). Also see Winston S. Churchill, *Closing the Ring* 304–6 (Boston: Houghton Mifflin, 1951).

Roosevelt had initially planned to spend only one day, Saturday, November 20, 1943, in French North Africa, but ended up spending two. He and Ike had met briefly twice before, once in the White House in June 1942, before Eisenhower left for London, and again at Casablanca in January.[49] But they did not know each other well. FDR anticipated a series of perfunctory briefings in Tunis, and would then leave by plane for Cairo the next morning.

"A night flight, Sunday night, would be better," said Ike.

"A night flight? Why?" asked the president.

Daylight flights were too risky, Eisenhower explained. "We don't want to have to run fighter escort all the way to Cairo. It would just be asking for trouble."

"Okay, Ike. You're the boss. But I get something in return."

"What's that, Sir?"

"If you're going to make me stay over at Carthage all Sunday, you've got to take me on a personally conducted tour of the battlefields—ancient and modern."

"That's a bargain, Sir."[50]

The one-day briefing turned into a two-day lovefest. FDR and Ike were both engaging extroverts, and they hit it off from the beginning. Roosevelt was accustomed to being the center of attention; Eisenhower was equally accustomed to dealing with celebrities such as Churchill and MacArthur, and knew instinctively how to make them comfortable.

"Where is Miss Summersby?" the president asked as soon as he was settled in Ike's quarters. Eisenhower sent for Kay, and introduced her.

"Mr. President, this is Miss Kay Summersby, the British girl you asked about."

"I've heard quite a bit about you," FDR told Kay. "Why didn't you drive me from the plane? I'd been looking forward to it."

"Mr. President, your Secret Service wouldn't let me drive."

"Would you like to drive me from now on?" Roosevelt asked.

"It would be a privilege, Sir."

"Very well. You shall drive me then. I'm going on an inspection trip soon."[51]

At dinner that evening Kay sat one place from the president.* "I was exposed to the fabled F.D.R. charm," she remembered. "He had it on full, with all stops out." Roosevelt took his leave at ten-thirty. "See you tomorrow, Child," he said to Summersby, in a tone she had not heard since she was a girl.[52]

The next morning Roosevelt, his son Franklin, Eisenhower, and Summersby, joined by Telek, the Scottie Ike and Kay shared, set out in Ike's staff car to tour the battlefields. According to Franklin, his father grilled Ike closely, not only about the recent battles but also those of ancient Carthage. "The fact that Ike knew the details of each conflict pleased Father hugely: it showed that Ike, like Father, had a bent for history, and a love for knowledge."[53]

Scarcely had the tour begun when Telek jumped onto the president's lap. Nothing could have been better calculated to put FDR at ease. "The President played with him as one who knows and loves dogs," said Summersby. Roosevelt talked about Fala, and asked whether Telek was British or American. Eisenhower allowed as how he was British, but had an American wife. "I guess I think as much of him, Mr. President, as you do of Fala."[54]

A little after noon, Roosevelt spotted a rare eucalyptus grove, an oasis in the desert landscape. "That's an awfully nice place. Could you pull up there, Child, for our little picnic?" When the car came to a stop, surrounded by squads of GIs with fixed bayonets, Kay opened the picnic basket.

"No, let me do that, Kay, I'm very good at passing sandwiches around," said Ike.

Eisenhower got out of the car, went to the front passenger seat, and selected a chicken sandwich for the president.[55] Ike claimed he

---

* The dinner guests, in addition to FDR and Kay Summersby, included Eisenhower, Admiral Leahy, General Spaatz, Air Chief Marshal Tedder, Elliott Roosevelt, Franklin Roosevelt, Jr., and Miss Nancy Gatch, a Red Cross worker who was Butcher's latest girlfriend. Lieutenant Junior Grade William Rigdon, who kept the president's logbook, decorously listed Summersby and Gatch as the guests of Franklin, Jr., and Elliott. U.S. Department of State, *Foreign Relations of the United States: The Conferences at Cairo and Tehran, 1943* 287 (Washington, D.C.: U.S. Government Printing Office, 1961).

Ike and FDR review the troops in Algiers.

knew his chicken sandwiches because of all the Sunday-school picnics he had gone to as a child.[56]

Before biting in, Roosevelt turned to Kay. He patted the empty
seat beside him and said, "Won't you come back here, Child, and
have lunch with a dull old man?"[57]

"Roosevelt enjoyed himself immensely," Summersby recalled.
"He had a gift of putting a person completely at ease, and I soon got
over my awe of him and was chatting away as if I had known him all
my life."[58]*

No one appreciated a picnic more than FDR. When he was at
Hyde Park, whenever he could escape from matters of state, he loved
to go off for long picnics with his cousin Margaret ("Daisy") Suckley,

---

* In the course of the conversation, FDR asked Summersby whether she would
like to join the Women's Army Corps (WACs). Kay replied she would like nothing
better, but she wasn't an American citizen and therefore was not eligible. "Well,
who knows?" Roosevelt replied. "Stranger things have happened."

By order of the president, Kay Summersby was commissioned a second lieutenant in the WACs in October 1944. Korda, *Ike* 422.

or with Eleanor and her friends at Val-Kill. Roosevelt relished the company of pretty, attentive women, and flirting with them was one of his favorite pastimes. The brief sojourn with Kay in the desert was no exception.[59]

When they returned to Eisenhower's quarters late that afternoon, FDR was beaming. He leaned over and put his hand on Ike's arm. "You know, Ike—I'm afraid I'm going to have to do something you won't like.

"I know what Harry Butcher is to you [but] I may have to take him away." The president explained that Elmer Davis was leaving his post as director of the Office of War Information, and had recommended Butcher as his successor. "What would you say if I drafted 'Butch' to take over the job?" asked Roosevelt.

"Well, Mr. President, I won't pretend it wouldn't be tough. But if you need him, if you give the word, the answer is, sure, go ahead."

According to Franklin junior, "Father paused, with a very satisfied look on his face. It was the sort of answer he liked, and he was bound to like Eisenhower the more for it, especially inasmuch as he knew what losing Butcher would mean to the General."[60]

That evening after dinner, Eisenhower accompanied FDR to the airport. Just before the president boarded the plane, he mentioned the command of OVERLORD—which evidently he had been thinking about.

> Ike, you and I know who was the Chief of Staff during the last years of the Civil War but practically no one else knows, although the names of the field generals—Grant, of course, and Lee, and Jackson, Sherman, Sheridan and the others—every schoolboy knows them. I hate to think that 50 years from now practically nobody will know who George Marshall was. That is one of the reasons why I want George to have the Big Command—he is entitled to establish his place in history as a great General.[61]

FDR went on to say that he dreaded the thought of losing Marshall from Washington. "It is dangerous to monkey with a winning team."[62]

Roosevelt was thinking out loud. Marshall was the logical choice to command OVERLORD, and it was generally assumed that he would do so.* Stimson and Hopkins vigorously endorsed the chief of staff, and both Churchill and Stalin believed it was only a matter of time until Roosevelt announced the choice.

But FDR was having second thoughts. General John J. Pershing, who knew both Marshall and Eisenhower, had written from his sickbed at Walter Reed Army Medical Center to caution the president against sending Marshall to London. The command structures in Washington and overseas were working well, said Pershing. "It would be a fundamental and very grave error in our military policy to break up working relationships at both levels."[63]

Marshall's colleagues on the Joint Chiefs also voiced concern. Leahy, King, and Arnold believed it essential to retain Marshall as a member of the Combined Chiefs of Staff, where he could fight for American interests. "None of us, least of all myself, wanted to deny Marshall the thing he wanted most," wrote Leahy. "On the other hand, he was a tower of strength to Roosevelt and to the high command."[64]

FDR was also concerned about recent press criticism suggesting that Marshall's transfer to Europe was a left-wing plot to elevate General Brehon Somervell to chief of staff and possibly position him as a running mate in 1944. Somervell, who had headed the WPA in New York under Hopkins, was considered an ardent New Dealer (which surely would have astonished Somervell), and more in sympathy with FDR's domestic agenda than Marshall. Above all, however, there was the problem of dealing with Congress, which after the 1942 midterm election had become increasingly difficult. Most members of Congress believed George Marshall could do no wrong,

---

* Marshall, although he consistently refused to express any opinion on the appointment, evidently assumed he would be named to the post. Mrs. Marshall had begun moving the family's personal belongings out of Quarters 1 at Fort Myer to their home in Leesburg, Virginia, and Marshall had had his desk, the behemoth used by General Pershing (and now used by the secretary of defense), crated for shipment to London. Katherine Tupper Marshall, *Together: Annals of an Army Wife* 156–57 (New York: Tupper and Love, 1946); David Eisenhower, *Eisenhower at War, 1943–1945* 42–43 (New York: Random House, 1986).

and FDR wondered whether a new chief of staff would enjoy similar credibility on Capitol Hill.[65]

On the other side of the ledger, Roosevelt had just subjected Eisenhower to the most searching scrutiny and liked what he saw. Unlike Lincoln, who was prone to error until he found Grant in 1863, FDR was exceptionally able at selecting military commanders (Marshall, MacArthur, Leahy, King), and he believed Ike would be a good fit to head the cross-Channel attack. The job was Marshall's if he wanted it, but Eisenhower seemed to have all the necessary qualifications. He had proven his ability to command large multinational coalitions, he worked well with the British high command in London, and he had demonstrated a particular ability to underplay American special interests for the benefit of the common cause—an essential attribute that Marshall may have lacked. Roosevelt was not a friend of detail and did not pursue matters to the third decimal place. The landings in North Africa, Sicily, and at Salerno may not have been textbook examples of military precision, but Ike had prevailed. (Shiloh and the Wilderness were not pretty, either.) As a result of those landings, Eisenhower had a firsthand knowledge of amphibious operations that Marshall did not have.

FDR also liked Ike. Not only was he easy to get along with, but he exhibited none of the posturing that often accompanied high rank in the military. Ike might just be the man for the job, Roosevelt thought as he boarded his plane for Cairo. But he wanted a second look. He ordered Eisenhower to join the conference in Cairo "in two or three days" and report on the situation in the Mediterranean.[66]

Eisenhower took off for Cairo on Tuesday evening, November 23. As a thoughtful gesture, he invited the president's son Colonel Elliott Roosevelt and FDR's son-in-law, Major John Boettiger, to accompany him. Elliott commanded the theater's photo reconnaissance group, and Boettiger, former publisher of the *Seattle Post-Intelligencer,* was attached to Allied military government in Italy. He and his wife, Anna, had been friends of the Eisenhowers since Ike was stationed at Fort Lewis in 1940. In addition to Elliott and Boettiger, Eisenhower's party included Kay Summersby, his personal staff, and the theater commanders in chief.

The Cairo conference (SEXTANT) was the most acrimonious wartime meeting of the Allied chiefs. Despite the agreement at Quebec, Churchill had become increasingly opposed to a cross-Channel attack and was obsessed with taking the island of Rhodes. Turkey, he argued, could be induced to join the Allies, and the key to Turkish participation was the capture of Rhodes. "I can control him [Churchill] no more," General Sir Alan Brooke lamented in his diary. "He has worked himself into a frenzy over the Rhodes attack, so that he can no longer see anything else and has set his heart on capturing the island even at the expense of endangering his relations with the President and the Americans."[67]

The issue exploded at the meeting of the Combined Chiefs of Staff attended by Roosevelt and Churchill on November 24, 1943. The prime minister and Marshall went head-to-head. As Marshall recalled, "It got hotter and hotter. Finally Churchill grabbed his lapels, his spit curls hung down, and he said, 'His Majesty's Government can't have its troops standing idle. Muskets must flame.' "

"God forbid if I should try to dictate," Marshall replied. "But not one American soldier is going to die on that goddamned beach."[68]

The meeting was stunned. Marshall carried the point, but Churchill never completely forgave him.[69] When Elliott called on his father later that morning, he found FDR still musing about the exchange. "I think Winston is beginning not to like George Marshall very much."[70]

"I wouldn't envy anybody the job of standing up to the P.M.," said Elliott.

"Well, I'll tell you one man who deserves a medal for being able to get along with Winston. And that's Ike Eisenhower."

Elliott asked his father if he was serious about giving Eisenhower a medal.

"Sure I am. But he won't take one. At the same time MacArthur was given the Medal of Honor, it was offered to Ike, and he turned it down. Said it was for valor, and he hadn't done anything valorous."[*]

---

[*] FDR's memory failed him, or perhaps the wish was father to the thought, as sometimes happened with the president. MacArthur was awarded the Medal of Honor in March 1942 after his escape from the Philippines. At that time Eisenhower headed the War Plans Division in the War Department and certainly would not have been recommended for the Medal of Honor. Eisenhower had opposed the

Elliott replied that Bedell Smith had told him that Eisenhower would really like to have the Legion of Merit. It was a medal that anyone could get, even an Army cook, but Ike had never received one.

"Could we keep it a secret?" asked FDR.

"I don't know why not."

"Good. Get a message to Smith. Have him draw up a citation—North African campaign, Sicilian campaign. If he can get a medal here in time, I'll pin it on Ike myself, before we leave for Teheran."[71]

A report from Eisenhower was not on the original agenda drawn up by the Combined Chiefs, but since he was in Cairo they asked him to report at their final session on November 26. Minutes before the meeting Ike was summoned to the president's villa. The medal had arrived from Smith in Algiers, and FDR wanted to award it. "It was just the kind of surprise he loved to spring," Elliott recalled.

In the brief ceremony, which came as a total surprise to Eisenhower, the president glowed with admiration. "You deserve this, and much more, Ike."

Eisenhower's eyes filled with tears. "It is the happiest moment of my life, Sir. I appreciate this decoration more than any other you could give me."[72]

Eisenhower's presentation to the Combined Chiefs that afternoon was a measured assessment of the military situation in Italy. If the CCS provided the resources necessary, he said he could reach the Po River by spring. But that would delay OVERLORD by several months. Without additional resources, he could take Rome, but then would have to assume a defensive posture. Unlike his sophomoric presentation to the Combined Chiefs at Casablanca, where he lost points by recommending an unfeasible war games solution to the problem in Tunisia, Eisenhower demonstrated a firm grasp of the strategic situation and appeared realistic about the possibilities. Asked by Brooke about the situation in Yugoslavia, Ike said that Allied propaganda to the contrary, all possible equipment "should be sent to Tito, since Mihailovic's forces were of very little value."[73]

---

award of the medal to MacArthur, which FDR may have remembered. Manchester, *American Caesar* 275–76.

FDR presents Ike with the Legion of Merit in Cairo.

The chiefs were impressed with Eisenhower's presentation.[74] But Marshall noticed Ike looked tired. He was working too hard and needed to take some time off. Eisenhower said there was too much work waiting for him back in Algiers. "Look, Eisenhower," Marshall replied, "everything is going well. Just let someone else run that war up there for a couple of days. If your subordinates can't do it for you, you haven't organized them properly."[75]

Given what was in essence an order, Eisenhower had no choice. At the suggestion of Air Chief Marshal Tedder, he flew up the Nile to Luxor to visit the Valley of the Kings, the Pyramids, and the great temple at Karnak. "General Ike was happy as a kid," Kay Summersby remembered, "making no attempt to hide his natural enjoyment, protesting frequently that we moved along too quickly."[76] From Egypt, Ike and Kay, accompanied by Tex Lee and several WACs, flew to Palestine, lunched at the King David Hotel in Jerusalem, visited Bethlehem, and walked in the Garden of Gethsemane. According to Summersby, "a stroll in the Garden of Gethsemane was the high point of the visit. None of the Christ's long ago agony communicated itself to us; it seemed, rather, more peaceful than the other religious landmarks we visited, a place where meditation seemed natural."[77]

Eisenhower's affection for Kay had become increasingly evident. Years later Churchill remembered how miffed Ike had been when Summersby was not included among the dinner guests slated to dine with him at the British embassy in Cairo.[78] And when FDR returned to Washington after Teheran, he told his daughter, Anna, that he thought Ike was sleeping with Kay.[*] Eisenhower also left a discreet paper trail. Whether he and Kay were intimate remains a matter of conjecture. But there is no question they were in love. On the return night flight to Algiers he presented Kay with a postcard of the Garden of Gethsemane inscribed, *"Good night! There are lots of things I could say—you know them. Good night."*[79]

At Teheran it was apparent that FDR was having second thoughts about naming Marshall supreme commander. It was the first meeting of the Big Three, and Roosevelt had gone to Teheran determined to strike up a working relationship with Marshal Stalin. "He is not going to allow anything to interfere with that purpose," said Harry Hopkins, who had become Roosevelt's principal diplomatic troubleshooter. "He has spent his life managing men, and Stalin at bottom could not be so very much different from other people."[80]

The first meeting of the Big Three convened at 4 p.m., Sunday, November 28, 1943, in the conference room of the Soviet embassy, which had been especially fitted with a large round table to preempt any question of who would sit at its head. As the only head of state, Roosevelt presided, and would continue to do so throughout the conference. Informality prevailed. There was no formal agenda, and

---

[*] In a lengthy letter to her husband postmarked December 19, 1943, Anna described FDR's return to the White House. "LL [Little Lady, Eleanor Roosevelt] is now in N.Y., so OM [Old Man, FDR] and I are having the Norwegians [Princess Martha] for tea, and then OM, the big kids and I will swim. . . . OM and I had a good talk about Elliott. During the discussion, you'll be amused to know that he suspects that the man you first wrote to about going into the Army [Eisenhower], is sleeping with his attractive driver!" Anna Roosevelt Boettiger to John Boettiger, Franklin D. Roosevelt Library, Hyde Park.

Roosevelt carried no briefing books or position papers. The issues he wanted to discuss were political, and the president steered his own course.

The principal issue at Teheran was the second front. Stalin pressed the point. "If we are here to discuss military matters, Russia is only interested in OVERLORD."[81] Churchill dissembled. Unwilling to accept the reality of a cross-Channel attack, the prime minister extolled the advantages of alternative approaches—Italy, Turkey, Rhodes—and the shortage of landing craft, which was indeed a problem. Roosevelt came down hard on Stalin's side. "We are all agreed that OVERLORD is the dominating operation, and that any operation that might delay OVERLORD cannot be considered by us."[82] The president said he favored sticking to the original date agreed on at Quebec, early May 1944. Stalin replied that he didn't care whether it was May 1 or May 15 or May 20. "But a definite date is important."[83]

Stalin then turned to FDR. "Who will command OVERLORD?" Roosevelt was caught off guard. "That old Bolshevik is trying to force me to give him a name," the president whispered to Admiral Leahy, "but I can't tell him because I haven't made up my mind."[84]

After the translation of Stalin's remarks, Roosevelt replied that the matter was not yet decided. "Then nothing will come out of these operations," said Stalin. The Soviet Union had learned that in military matters decisions could not be made by committee. "One man must be responsible and one man must make decisions."[85] Stalin said the Soviet Union did not presume that it would take part in the selection of a supreme commander, but merely wanted to know who this officer would be and felt strongly that he should be appointed as soon as possible. Churchill said he thought the choice should be made "within a fortnight," to which Roosevelt agreed.

When the conference ended on December 2, 1943, FDR still had not reached a decision. He recognized Marshall was entitled to the post, and understood his obligation to the chief of staff. But he had increasingly come to believe that Eisenhower might be a better choice, and he was truly reluctant to lose Marshall from Washington. What did Marshall want? Back in Cairo, Roosevelt delegated Hopkins to find out. When Hopkins called on Marshall, the chief of staff declined to state his opinion. "I will wholeheartedly accept whatever decision the President makes," said Marshall.[86]

The following day, Sunday, December 5, FDR sent for Marshall shortly before lunch. "I was determined," Marshall said later, "that I should not embarrass the President one way or the other—that he must be able to deal in this matter with a perfectly free hand in whatever he felt was the best interest of the country."[87]

After a few brief formalities, Roosevelt asked Marshall directly what he wanted to do. "Evidently it was left up to me," Marshall recalled. "I repeated again in as convincing language as I could that I wanted him to feel free to act in whatever way he felt was to the best interest of the country and to his satisfaction and not in any way to consider my feelings."[88]

"Then it will be Eisenhower," said Roosevelt. "I don't think I could sleep at night with you out of the country."[89]*

---

* The British were delighted that Roosevelt chose Eisenhower rather than Marshall. After leaving Teheran, FDR told Elliott, "It's absolutely clear that Winston will refuse absolutely to let Marshall take over. It's not that [Marshall] argued too often with the P.M. on military matters, it's just that he's won too often."

In his memoirs, Churchill insisted it was the president's decision, but when informed by Roosevelt that it would be Eisenhower, he replied that he had the "warmest regard for General Eisenhower, and would trust our fortunes to his direction with hearty good will."

General Sir Alan Brooke, who was often critical of Eisenhower, called the decision "a good one. Eisenhower had now a certain amount of experience as a Commander and was beginning to find his feet. The combination of Eisenhower and Bedell Smith had much to be said for it. On the other hand Marshall had never commanded anything in war except, I believe, a company in the First World War."

Elliott Roosevelt, *As He Saw It* 209 (New York: Duell, Sloan, and Pearce, 1946); Winston S. Churchill, *Closing the Ring* 418; Lord Alanbrooke, *War Diaries* 491.

# THIRTEEN

# D-Day

You will enter the continent of Europe, and
undertake operations aimed at the heart of
Germany and the destruction of her armed
forces.

—COMBINED CHIEFS OF STAFF
TO EISENHOWER,
*February 12, 1944*

"WELL, IKE, YOU'D BETTER START PACKING," said FDR
when he landed in Tunis on his return to Washington. "You are
going to command OVERLORD."[1] Roosevelt said the official announcement would be made later in December, but the matter was
settled and that Eisenhower should wind up his affairs in North Africa and be in London by the beginning of January.

"The General was so happy I thought he would burst," Kay Summersby recalled. "That grin never left his face."[2]

Roosevelt was scheduled to remain in Tunis only one day. But his
plane developed hydraulic trouble and he again stayed for two. FDR
said that if a legitimate reason for the delay had not been found, he
would have invented one because he wanted to spend more time
with Ike. When Eisenhower expressed surprise that the president
could not determine his own travel schedule, Roosevelt replied, "You
haven't had to argue with the Secret Service."[3]

According to Butcher, "The President discussed all sorts of problems, ideas, and ambitions with Ike. These were not confined to mil-

itary subjects [and] Ike felt complimented by the President's frankness and indications of complete confidence in him."[4]

Because Eisenhower would command OVERLORD, it was understood that his successor in the Mediterranean would be British, and Churchill, at the recommendation of Brooke, chose General Sir Henry Maitland "Jumbo" Wilson. Wilson was then Allied commander in chief in the Middle East and had a proven track record dealing with explosive situations in Palestine, Syria, Jordan, and Iraq. Churchill also wanted Bedell Smith to remain in Algiers as chief of staff to Wilson, but Eisenhower insisted that Smith accompany him to London. Ike also wanted Alexander as his deputy and ground commander, but the British said no. Churchill, who continued to believe the war might be won in Italy, wanted Alexander to remain there, and Brooke, who did not share the prime minister's high regard for Alexander, thought him entirely too pliable for OVERLORD. "Ike knew he could handle Alex," wrote Brooke, but "I would have had little confidence in Alex running that show."[5]

The obvious choice to direct the landings in France was Montgomery. As Churchill saw it, Monty was a national hero in Britain "and will give confidence among our people."[6] For Brooke, it was a matter of competence. No one could argue that Montgomery was not qualified. He might be difficult, and Ike was not fond of him, but in Brooke's opinion Montgomery would add the necessary battlefield experience to the command structure. Eisenhower accepted the inevitable. In his memoirs, Ike conceded that no one was better at winning the affection of the enlisted men serving with him than Montgomery, and when it came to fighting set-piece battles, Monty had no peer.[7] Eisenhower was tickled pink to be named supreme commander, and if Churchill and the British war cabinet wanted Montgomery to be the ground commander for OVERLORD, he would make it work.

But he did not want Montgomery as his deputy. Instead, Eisenhower secured the Combined Chiefs' approval to take Air Chief Marshal Sir Arthur Tedder to London. Ike and Tedder worked well together, and were equally committed to the principle of "allied"— rather than national—command.[8] Tedder was an advocate of close air-ground support, and the term "Tedder's carpet" derived from a bombing technique he devised to clear a path for ground troops through enemy defenses.*

Eisenhower intended that Tedder wear two hats: one as his deputy and a second as commander of the air force for OVERLORD. But the Combined Chiefs decided otherwise. Without consulting Ike, Air Chief Marshal Sir Trafford Leigh-Mallory, who led RAF Fighter Command, was assigned to head the air arm. Eisenhower did not know Leigh-Mallory, had never worked with him, and was not pleased. "I understand Mallory is a fighter commander of the very highest quality," Ike wrote Marshall, "but this tendency to freeze organization so that a commander may not use trusted and superior subordinates [that is, Tedder] in their proper spheres disturbs me very much indeed."[9]

Ike's reservations were well founded. Tedder's talents were wasted in a position whose duties were never defined, and Leigh-Mallory, who did not work well with others, became a source of friction between Ike and the strategic air commanders. He grew excessively pessimistic as D-Day approached, was eased out of his position in October 1944, and died in a plane crash the following month.

To command the naval forces for OVERLORD, Eisenhower would have preferred Andrew Cunningham, but in October, Cunningham had been recalled to London to succeed Sir Dudley Pound as first sea lord. (Pound had been fatally stricken with cancer.) Instead, he selected Admiral Sir Bertram Ramsay, who had been Cunningham's deputy. Ramsay, born in 1883, had retired in 1938, but was recalled when war began and had almost single-handedly put together the fleet of small ships that evacuated the British Expeditionary Force from Dunkirk. Because Ramsay was on the retired list and only temporarily on active duty, the Admiralty had given the Mediterranean

---

* According to a Luftwaffe intelligence report: "Tedder is on good terms with Eisenhower to whom he is superior in both intelligence and energy. He regards the Air Force as a 'spearhead artillery' rendering the enemy vulnerable to an attack. His tactics in North Africa, Sicily and Italy, based on this theory, provided air support for the advance of even the smallest Army unit." Luftwaffe Academy lecture, February 7, 1944, British Air Ministry files, quoted in Forrest C. Pogue, *The Supreme Command* 61 (Washington, D.C.: Office of the Chief of Military History, Department of the Army, 1954).

fleet to Cunningham and made Ramsay his deputy. The arrangement
had worked well, and despite his age, Ramsay was indefatigable. He
also liked Americans. "All of us knew him to be helpful and compan-
ionable," wrote Eisenhower, "even though we sometimes laughed
among ourselves at the care with which he guarded the 'senior service' position of the British Navy."[10]

An additional appointment, one that Eisenhower insisted upon
from the beginning, was that of John C. H. Lee to head the logistics
effort. Despite his grandiose manner, indeed, perhaps because of it,
Lee had no equal in amassing the supplies that an army needed to
move forward—and crossing the Channel would pose an unprecedented logistical challenge. Eisenhower installed Lee as deputy theater commander and commanding general of Army Service Forces.[11]*
"I hope that General Lee is big enough for this job," Ike cabled Marshall, "but I assure you it is one that takes a world of ability, not only
in technical matters, but in coordinating and cooperating with Allies."[12]

With the exception of Bedell Smith as his chief of staff, and Lee in
charge of logistics, all of Eisenhower's principal deputies were once
again British. When they were in place, Ike turned to the American
component of OVERLORD. The British side would be Monty's responsibility. On December 17, Ike suggested to Marshall that he
would like Bradley as his senior army group commander, and Tooey
Spaatz to command the strategic air force. He also said he wanted
Patton to command one of the American armies.[13] Marshall was in
Australia visiting MacArthur, and a brief period of confusion followed. Exactly when Marshall received Eisenhower's cable is unclear,
but on December 21 the chief of staff informed Ike that he thought
General Leslie McNair, who was commanding Army Ground Forces,
should be his senior ground commander, and that the armies should
be commanded by Jacob Devers (who had taken Ike's place in London) and Bradley, or Bradley and Courtney Hodges, who was then
commanding Third Army at Fort Sam Houston. "Hodges is exactly

* On March 12, 1943, the U.S. Army's Services of Supply (commanded by Bre-
hon Somervell) was rechristened Army Service Forces to parallel the Army Ground
Forces (commanded by Leslie McNair) and Army Air Forces (commanded by
H. H. Arnold).

the same class of man as Bradley in practically every respect," said Marshall. "Wonderful shot, great hunter, quiet, self-effacing, thorough understanding of ground fighting, DSC [Distinguished Service Cross], etc." No mention was made of Patton, and instead of Spaatz, Marshall thought Ira Eaker should command the air force. Both Devers and Eaker were already in England, and Marshall gently chided Ike for wanting to strip the Mediterranean of its senior officers.[14]

Marshall's cable created considerable consternation at AFHQ, but Eisenhower stuck to his guns. He wanted commanders with recent battle experience, he told Marshall, and since McNair and Devers had none, that meant Bradley and Patton. Hodges would be acceptable, said Ike, but Devers should be assigned to command American forces in the Mediterranean, and Eaker should replace Spaatz there. "I regret that you found anything disturbing in the recommendations I made but, frankly, they are the best I could evolve considering the jobs to be filled."[15] As delicately as he could, Eisenhower was reminding Marshall that OVERLORD was now his responsibility and he wanted to choose his own subordinates.

Marshall returned to Washington shortly after Christmas and quickly set matters straight. "It appears that we have gotten into complete confusion regarding future assignments," he cabled Eisenhower. Marshall said he had been "following a confused trail in the Pacific" and was just now able to digest what Ike was recommending. One of the chief of staff's greatest strengths was his ability to delegate. It was, of course, Eisenhower's responsibility, said Marshall, and whoever he wanted would be approved. "I think the foregoing should clarify things and leave you free to proceed."[16]

As Butcher recorded, "Marshall's message was like the sun breaking through the fog. When Ike received the good news . . . his whole demeanor changed."[17] In effect, Marshall had given Eisenhower carte blanche: The supreme commander would be the supreme commander.

With his team in place, Eisenhower turned to the plan for OVERLORD. At the Casablanca conference in January 1943, the Combined Chiefs had established a planning group (COSSAC) under Major General Sir Frederick Morgan to put together the framework for the cross-Channel attack. "Well, there it is," Brooke told Morgan when he was assigned the task. "It won't work, but you must bloody well make it."[18]

The planners got some things right. The Allies would land in Normandy, not the Pas-de-Calais, the closest point across the Channel from Britain, where the Germans were ready and waiting. The beaches were selected, the times fixed, and the tides were right. But because of the shortage of landing craft, COSSAC planned for only three divisions in the initial assault. The landings would be limited to a narrow front; troops from Britain, Canada, and the United States would be intermingled; and the follow-on forces would funnel through a single beachhead. When Eisenhower examined the plan he was struck by the similarity to Salerno. "Not enough wallop in the initial attack," he told Butcher.[19]

Montgomery, who was shown a copy of the plan by Churchill, was absolutely appalled. Monty was one of the few British leaders who believed in OVERLORD, but he told Churchill the plan developed by COSSAC "would never do." For the prime minister's benefit, Montgomery spelled out the changes he thought necessary.

- The initial landings must be made on the widest possible front.
- Each corps must have a separate beach, and other corps must not land through those beaches.
- Because of differences in organization and equipment, the British and American landing areas must be kept separate.
- After landing, the first order of business must be to secure a good port through which supplies can be unloaded.

Above all, said Montgomery, "the air battle must be won before the operation is launched. We must then aim at success in the land battle by the speed and violence of our operations."[20]

From the beginning, Eisenhower and Montgomery were on the same page. COSSAC's plan was a useful starting point, but drastic revisions were required. The basic problem, said Monty, was that the plan had been drawn up as an intellectual exercise by staff officers with little battlefield experience. Churchill needed no convincing.

Always skeptical of a cross-Channel attack, he was won over by Montgomery's enthusiasm. "Grip the show," he encouraged Monty. "Grip the show." Afterward, Churchill wrote, "I felt a strong reassurance that all would be well."[21]

Before Eisenhower could leave for London, the politics of North Africa erupted. On December 21, 1943, the French Committee of National Liberation accelerated its purge of former Darlan officials and ordered the arrest of the three most prominent Vichyites who had assisted the Allies.[*] Ike was blindsided, Churchill was shocked, and FDR was livid. "Please inform the French Committee as follows," he instructed Eisenhower: "In view of assistance given to the Allied Armies during the campaign in Africa by Boisson, Peyrouton and Flandin, you are directed to take no action against these individuals at the present time."[22]

FDR then vented his dislike for de Gaulle to Churchill. "It seems to me that this is the proper time effectively to eliminate the Jeanne d'Arc complex and to return to realism," he cabled the prime minister. "I too am shocked by the high handed arrests at this time."[23]

Roosevelt had overreacted. Contrary to the president's assumption, North Africa was not occupied territory, and there was no way the United States could issue a peremptory order to the French. Eisenhower was caught in the middle. If he delivered the message as the president instructed, the FCNL would regard it as an ultimatum, and Ike had no doubt that de Gaulle would reject it. That, in turn, would be a direct slap at the president that the United States could not accept, and matters would escalate from there. French rearmament would be halted, the use of French troops would be thrown into question, and the all-important support of the Resistance in France would be rendered doubtful.

Rather than deliver the message, AFHQ sat on the president's cable. Bedell Smith went to see Churchill, who was convalescing in Morocco, and explained the problem. Churchill cabled FDR suggesting that Eisenhower inform de Gaulle of their concern orally,[24] and Roosevelt, having blown off steam, acquiesced. On December 26 he instructed Eisenhower to pursue the matter informally. In-

---

[*] Pierre Boisson, Marcel Peyrouton, and Pierre-Étienne Flandin.

stead of "directing" the FCNL, Ike was merely to inform de Gaulle that the United States "views with alarm" the arrest of the former Vichyites.[25]*

Roosevelt's change of heart coincided with Eisenhower's desire to secure de Gaulle's support for OVERLORD. Having spent more than a year dealing with the political problems of North Africa, Ike was convinced that de Gaulle was the only person who could rally the French against Hitler.[26] In keeping with de Gaulle's position as provisional president of France (whether the United States recognized it or not), Eisenhower requested an appointment and called on the French leader.

"You were originally described to me in an unfavorable sense," said Ike. "Today, I realize that judgment was in error. For the coming battle, I shall need not only the co-operation of your forces, but still more the assistance of your officials and the moral support of the French people. I must have your assistance, and I have come to ask for it."

"Splendid," de Gaulle replied. "You are a man! For you know how to say, 'I was wrong.' "[27]

Ike told Butcher that from that point on the meeting became "a love fest."[28] De Gaulle was concerned that the liberation of Paris be done by French troops. Eisenhower said he would try to arrange it. Ike was concerned about the fate of Boisson, Peyrouton, and Flandin. De Gaulle promised to delay their trial until after France was liberated and a properly constituted national assembly could determine their fate. In the interim they would be housed in comfortable quarters in Algiers.[29] When Eisenhower took his leave, he told de Gaulle that he did not know what "theoretical position" Washington would take, but "I will not recognize any other authority in France than yours."[30] From that point on, Ike became de Gaulle's best friend in the Allied camp, and de Gaulle, for his part, spared Eisenhower the necessity of having to govern a liberated France.

Eisenhower had intended to go from Algiers directly to London,

* Roosevelt believed the arrests had been triggered by de Gaulle's desire for revenge. But according to British intelligence, the impetus came from newly chosen members of the FCNL who represented the Resistance movement in France. Kimball, 2 *Churchill and Roosevelt* 634.

but on December 28 Marshall suggested he first report to Washington to consult the War Department, "see your family, and get at least a bit of rest" before assuming his position as supreme commander.[31] Ike declined. "With regard to my visit home," he told Marshall, "I feel that for the moment it is an impossibility. I truly hope that February or early March will afford me such an opportunity."[32]

Marshall would have none of it. He might delegate to Eisenhower the choice of American generals for OVERLORD, but rest and attention to family were not negotiable. "You will be under terrific strain from now on," he told Ike. "I am interested that you are fully prepared to bear the strain and I am not interested in the usual rejoinder that you can take it. It is of vast importance that you be fresh mentally and you certainly will not be if you go straight from one great problem to another. Now come on home and see your wife and trust somebody else for 20 minutes in England."[33]

Eisenhower recognized that Marshall was not joking. "I will be on my way within twenty-four hours," he cabled on December 30. "I earnestly request that you keep this visit as secret as possible."[34]

"Delighted," said Marshall. "Will arrange for any trip or travel you desire and will make tentative preparations on basis of complete secrecy."[35]

Shortly after noon on New Year's Eve, Summersby drove Ike to the airport in Algiers. "Two weeks seems like a long time," she said. "Especially when you are going to be so far away."

"Twelve days," Ike replied. "You'll be with me all the time." At the airport a small crowd had gathered. Eisenhower shook hands with his staff, and Summersby was last. He retrieved a slip of paper from his pocket and passed it to her. "Kay, can you take care of this for me?" he asked.

"Certainly, General. Have a safe trip." Ike boarded the plane, the cabin door closed, and Kay read the note. *Think of me,* Ike had written. *You know what I will be thinking.*[36]*

---

* The brief note on plain paper was among those auctioned by Sotheby's in New York on June 13, 1991. It was purchased by the Forbes Collection, which resold it in 2002. Its present provenance is unknown. See William Safire, "Indeed a Very Dear Friend," *The New York Times,* June 6, 1991.

Eisenhower, Churchill, and General Maitland "Jumbo" Wilson in Marrakesh, French Morocco, January 1944, with Air Chief Marshal Sir Arthur Tedder (*second row left*); Admiral Andrew Cunningham (*second row, second from left*); General Sir Harold Alexander (*second row, center*); and General Walter Bedell Smith (*second row, right*).

Eisenhower's plane took off for Marrakesh, in French Morocco, where Churchill was still recuperating from a nasty bout of pneumonia. Ike wanted to pay his respects to the prime minister before heading to Washington, as well as lay the groundwork for the handover of authority in the Mediterranean to Jumbo Wilson. By chance, Montgomery had also stopped off in Marrakesh on his way to London, and in a brief meeting he and Ike compared notes on OVERLORD. Both agreed on the major revisions that were required, and Eisenhower deputized Monty to go to London and work them out. "I was to analyze and revise the plan and have it ready for him on his arrival in England about the middle of January," Montgomery recorded in his diary.[37]

From Marrakesh Ike flew to the Azores, then to Bermuda, and arrived in Washington in the early morning hours of January 2, 1944. The flight, including the visit to Churchill and lengthy refueling stops in the Azores and Bermuda, had taken a day and a half.

It was after one in the morning when Ike and Butcher drove up in an unmarked car to the Wardman Park. Marshall had alerted Mamie of Eisenhower's return, and she waited up. But the reunion was less than rapturous. Ike and Butcher had brought two puppies, the offspring of Telek and his "American wife," as gifts for Ruth Butcher and Mamie. After being released from the crate in which they had been confined, the puppies proceeded to relieve themselves on the Eisenhowers' carpet, and then repeated the performance at the Butchers'. Neither Mamie nor Ruth was amused. The puppies were reminders of the life Ike and Butcher led overseas, and were quickly dispatched to foster homes.

At a more substantive level, Ike and Mamie had changed, and the divide between them was greater than ever. They had not seen each other for eighteen months. Eisenhower had grown in stature and was accustomed to command. He had become the confidant of Churchill and Roosevelt, moved easily in the highest circles of government, and held the fate of armies in his hands. He spoke abruptly, rationed his time, and had little patience for small talk. Above all, he had come to Washington under duress and was eager to return to his command.

Mamie's position had changed as well. No segment of society is more rank-conscious than Army wives, and Mamie was now First Lady of the coven of military dependents living in northwest Washington. She, too, was accustomed to being deferred to, and her concerns were everyday matters that confronted women whose husbands were abroad. A quintessential Army wife, Mamie's perspective was limited to family matters, wartime shortages, and military gossip. "How difficult it was for men to come home and live in a home, and how hard it was for us to have a man around the house," Mamie recalled years later.[38]

At 6 a.m. Eisenhower was cooking his own bacon and eggs in the kitchen, and then was off to the War Department for a day of conferences with Marshall, Stimson, King, and Somervell. Mamie, as was her habit, rose later. The War Department had moved from the cramped temporary quarters it had occupied on the Washington Mall since World War I, and was now installed in the Pentagon, the world's largest office building, located on the south shore of the Po-

tomac on the former grounds of old Fort Hunt and Hoover Airport.*
Eisenhower expressed his concern to Marshall that the strategic
bombers based in Britain be placed under his command, and Marshall pledged his support.[39] Ike was less successful with Admiral
King, who declined to transfer landing craft from the Pacific theater
to Europe.

The next day Eisenhower went to the White House to see the
president. Roosevelt, like Churchill, was suffering from a respiratory
infection and was propped up in bed, supported by a pile of pillows.
Eisenhower sought to soften FDR's hostility to de Gaulle, but found
the president intransigent. Roosevelt insisted the French people
would never submit to the authority of the FCNL, and that any attempt to impose de Gaulle could lead to civil war. As best he could,
Eisenhower tried to suggest the president's position was unrealistic,
but FDR was adamant—another example of the Dutch stubbornness
that sometimes got the better of him. Eisenhower said later that the
difficulties imposed by Washington's desire to ignore de Gaulle
caused him one of the "most acutely annoying problems" he had to
face before D-Day.[40]

On the third day Ike and Mamie boarded the chief of staff's private Pullman car for a rendezvous with their son John at West Point.
They stayed for lunch and dinner, and John noticed his father was
preoccupied and appeared "impatient to get on with his new job of
planning the invasion." When Mamie complained of her husband's
abrupt manner, Ike responded, "Hell, I'm going back to my theater
where I can do what I want." Eisenhower grinned, but his words
were harsh.[41]

Back in Washington the next day, January 5, 1944, Eisenhower
again called on the president, who showed him a cable from Churchill

* With five sides, five floors, and five concentric rings, the Pentagon provides
more than 3.6 million square feet of office space and has 17.5 miles of corridors.
Construction began in September 1941 and was completed in sixteen months at a
cost of $83 million. Colonel Leslie Groves, who later commanded the Manhattan
Engineer District, which developed the atomic bomb, was in charge of construction. Because of the wartime shortage of steel, the building is primarily a reinforced concrete structure with a limestone façade. It spans 28.7 acres and houses a
workforce of some 25,000. Steve Vogel, *The Pentagon: A History* (New York: Random House, 2007).

suggesting that Jumbo Wilson assume command in the Mediterranean on January 8—three days away. Eisenhower quickly agreed, and fired off a cable to Bedell Smith saying he would go from Washington directly to London. "However, I would like to come back to [Algiers] purely as a visitor within a week or ten days merely to say goodbye."[42] Smith suggested otherwise. "It is not repeat not pleasant to be the guest where you have been the master."[43] Eisenhower followed Bedell's advice.

From Washington, Ike and Mamie went on Marshall's orders to the Greenbrier in White Sulphur Springs—acidly described by biographer Geoffrey Perret as "a stuffy resort in West Virginia favored by the haute bourgeoisie."[44] The Army had taken over the Greenbrier to use as a hospital and convalescent facility, and the cottages on the grounds were set aside for family visits. The enforced sojourn suited neither Ike nor Mamie, and after two days Eisenhower flew to Fort Riley, Kansas, for a family reunion. ("I kept calling her Kay," Ike told Summersby afterward. "Every time I opened my mouth to say something to Mamie, I'd call her Kay. She was furious.")[45]

From Fort Riley, Ike was driven to his brother Milton's home in Manhattan—Milton was now president of Kansas State University—where he was joined by his older brother Arthur, his mother, Ida, now eighty-one, and the Douds, who drove in from Denver. "Why it's Dwight," exclaimed Ida, as she embraced him. Ida did not believe Ike had changed, but his brothers were impressed by his confidence and self-control. "Though he seemed as friendly as ever, he never let himself go 'all out'—as though he was keeping a good deal of himself in reserve for emergency use."[46]

Eisenhower flew back to the Greenbrier for an additional two days, and then he and Mamie returned to Washington, where Ike met with Marshall and had a final session on Wednesday evening, January 12, with the president. "I was so provoked to think that Mr. Roosevelt, knowing that I hadn't seen this man in so long, would demand that he come to the White House and spend the whole evening, when I thought the time belonged to me," Mamie said later.[47]

Eisenhower again tried to talk to Roosevelt about de Gaulle, but the president was already focused on postwar Germany and the zones of occupation. FDR had taken to calling Eisenhower "Ike," and Mrs.

Roosevelt came in briefly to be introduced. The president wanted to know how Ike liked his new title "supreme commander." Eisenhower agreed it had a ring of importance. "Something like Sultan."[48]

As the meeting concluded, well after 10 p.m., FDR asked Ike about Kay. He said he remembered their picnic at Carthage, and had promised her a photograph. "Give her my very best wishes," Roosevelt said, as he inscribed a photo of himself for Eisenhower to take back.[49]

Eisenhower left for London the following evening, having spent the day at the Pentagon. "If my personal staff [which had been in Algiers] has reached London before my arrival," he cabled Omar Bradley, "please tell Colonel ["Tex"] Lee to make proper arrangements for my driver to meet me at the station."[50]

Meanwhile, Montgomery had hit London with the intensity of "Christ cleansing the temple," in the words of one military historian.[51] Montgomery was commander in chief of the ground forces for OVERLORD. Armed with written authorization as Ike's surrogate, with Bedell Smith at his side and Churchill at his back, Montgomery sent COSSAC planners back to their drawing boards. Instead of three divisions in the initial assault, Monty wanted five. Instead of five follow-on divisions, it should be nine. Instead of one landing site, Montgomery wanted five—three British and two American—spanning a front of sixty miles. And the landing sites should be protected by the simultaneous drop of three airborne divisions behind German lines to isolate the battlefield. Montgomery's decisiveness was like a breath of fresh air, said one American planner.[52] "Now that the great Montgomery was in command, I think we all experienced a kind of relief," said another. "At least we no longer carried our dreadful burden of responsibility."[53]

As it finally evolved, the plan for the D-Day landing (NEPTUNE) reflected Montgomery's wishes. The American First Army, commanded by Omar Bradley, would land on the two westernmost beaches, Utah and Omaha. The British Second Army, commanded by General Sir Miles "Bimbo" Dempsey, would send troops ashore at Gold, Juno, and Sword beaches. Each beach would constitute a corps area. The U.S. VII Corps under J. Lawton "Lightning Joe" Collins would land at Utah beach; the U.S. V Corps, under Ike's old friend

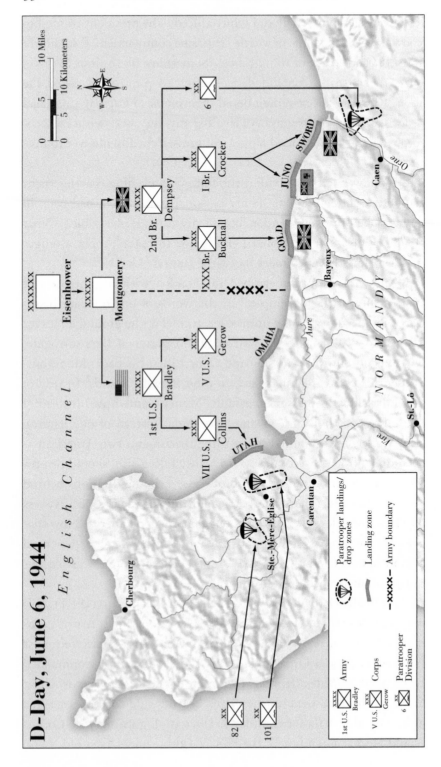

**D-Day, June 6, 1944**

Gee Gerow, would land at Omaha. The 82nd and 101st Airborne divisions would drop inland on the right flank of VII Corps. The British 6th Airborne Division would land on the left flank of the British I Corps.

As soon as it was ashore, VII Corps would slice across the Cotentin Peninsula, then wheel right and capture the port of Cherbourg. Until the harbor was cleared, Allied forces would be supplied through two temporary harbors (MULBERRYs) assembled in England and towed across the Channel. Fuel would be pumped through a flexible pipeline (PLUTO) laid on the Channel floor. The entire operation would be commanded by Twenty-first Army Group under Montgomery.

As the beachheads expanded, the First Canadian Army under General Henry Crerar and the U.S. Third Army under Patton would funnel through. At that point, Montgomery and the Twenty-first Army Group would assume command of the British and Canadian armies, and Bradley would establish the Twelfth Army Group headquarters to control the U.S. First and Third armies. Courtney Hodges would move up to succeed Bradley at the head of First Army, and Ike would assume overall command of the ground forces.

When Eisenhower returned to Britain, the outlines of OVERLORD had been roughed in. But vital issues awaited his attention. Aside from the manifold problems of assembling the men and matériel, there were barely enough landing craft for a three-division assault, much less five, to say nothing of the nine follow-on divisions Monty wanted. The strategic bombers based in Britain—RAF Bomber Command and U.S. Strategic Air Forces—were still operating independently. And Eisenhower had yet to find a way to insinuate de Gaulle into France in order to avoid saddling SHAEF (Supreme Headquarters, Allied Expeditionary Force) with the responsibility for governing liberated territory.

Eisenhower and Butcher arrived in London by special train from Prestwick, Scotland, shortly after 11 p.m. on January 15, 1944. They were met at the station by Summersby and Colonel James Gault of the Scots Guards, Ike's British military aide. Gault, later Sir James Gault, was an investment banker in private life and a peacetime denizen of the upper reaches of English society. Using his connections, he had secured for Ike an elegantly furnished town house off Berkeley Square in fashionable Mayfair, within walking distance of Allied headquarters.

Eisenhower examined his new quarters with the enthusiasm of a schoolboy. "I don't need a big place like this," he told Summersby, "but it's very pleasant. Very pleasant. Still and all, I think I would rather be back at Telegraph Cottage."[54]

Eisenhower and Summersby relaxed over a few drinks, and then Ike gave Kay the photo FDR had autographed. After a few more drinks they embraced, kissed, and tried those things lovers do. Summersby reports this was one of two times Ike was impotent.[55] As David Eisenhower, the general's grandson noted, "However far it went, they [Ike and Kay] were attached. Eisenhower was under tremendous pressure and in need of company. Beyond this, the truth was known only by them, and both are gone."[56]

Eisenhower's immediate problem was the acute shortage of landing craft. The Navy's Bureau of Yards and Docks, which was the responsible agency, preferred to build carriers and battleships, and the landing craft program got short shrift. Late in 1943, General Somervell took over the program and, in Marshall's words, "swept the cobwebs out of their pants."[*] But Admiral King continued to divert two-thirds of the landing craft produced to the island-hopping war in the Pacific. The poorly executed landing at Anzio—which rivaled Salerno in its ineptitude—had drawn off others.

The problem was exacerbated by the plan to land a second invasion force on the Mediterranean coast of France simultaneously with the cross-Channel attack. At Teheran, the Combined Chiefs of Staff had promised the Russians that the Allies would supplement OVERLORD with a landing near Marseilles (code name ANVIL) to seize the vital French port, draw off additional German troops, and press

---

* "We had found by bitter experience that we could make successful landings if we had the appropriate number of landing craft to go in," said General Lucius D. Clay, who was in charge of all military procurement. "It was almost mathematical. But the Navy didn't believe in it. So Somervell became the prime pusher. It was his impetuosity and initiative that forced the program. And if he hadn't I don't know whether we would ever have landed in France." Jean Edward Smith, *Lucius D. Clay* 110.

north. Eisenhower was strongly in favor of ANVIL. It might make OVERLORD easier, and was the only way a significant number of French troops could be brought into the war. The nine French divisions that had been raised in North Africa were composed primarily of African troops, and for racial reasons the British did not want them billeted in the United Kingdom. That precluded their participation in OVERLORD, but it did not rule out their landing on the Riviera. The British were lukewarm to ANVIL and would have preferred to reinforce the Allied effort in Italy, but Eisenhower, backed by Marshall and de Gaulle, insisted the landing take place.

Nevertheless, it soon became apparent that OVERLORD and ANVIL could not be mounted simultaneously. It was also apparent that even OVERLORD could not be launched as scheduled in early May because of the shortage of landing craft. Ike trimmed his sails. He ordered OVERLORD pushed back to early June and, with the approval of the Combined Chiefs, reset the landing on the Riviera (rechristened DRAGOON) for mid-August. That would permit all available landing craft to be committed to the cross-Channel attack, and then redeployed to the Mediterranean.*

The struggle for control of the strategic bombers based in Britain was not so easily resolved. But for Eisenhower, remembering his unhappy experience at Salerno, command was essential: "When a battle needs the last ounce of available force, the commander must not be in the position of depending upon request and negotiation to get it. It was vital that the entire sum of our assault power, including the two Strategic Air Forces, be available for use during the critical stages of the attack."57

The problem was part doctrinal, part political, and part personal. At the doctrinal level, Air Chief Marshal Sir Arthur ("Bomber") Harris, who commanded RAF Bomber Command, and Lieutenant General Tooey Spaatz, who commanded the U.S. Strategic Air Forces,

---

* When it was launched on August 15, 1944, DRAGOON was under the control of Seventh Army, commanded by Lieutenant General Alexander Patch. For the landing, Seventh Army was composed of the U.S. VI Corps, commanded by Lucian Truscott, and two French corps under General Jean de Lattre de Tassigny. Once ashore, the two French corps, some 256,000 men, were formed into the First French Army.

were committed to the concept that the war could be won by strategic bombing alone, rendering OVERLORD unnecessary. For Harris, sometimes described as a propeller-driven version of William Tecumseh Sherman, Germany would be brought to her knees by the relentless bombing of populated areas: the thousand-bomber raids he launched against Berlin, Cologne, and Hamburg (and later Dresden) to sap civilian morale. The fact that the Luftwaffe's attacks on London and Coventry had precisely the opposite effect on British morale failed to enter Harris's calculations. For Spaatz, who like Harris had been weaned on the airpower theories of Giulio Douhet and Billy Mitchell,[*] the primary target was Germany's oil refineries, which, if destroyed from the air, would make further resistance by the Wehrmacht impossible. Neither Harris nor Spaatz was prepared to target the transportation net in France to disrupt Hitler's ability to rush reinforcements to Normandy, nor were they willing to render the preinvasion bombardment that Eisenhower deemed essential.[58] Harris and Spaatz assumed it would be easy to get ashore and stay ashore. Eisenhower knew he needed all the help he could get.

The political problem involved Churchill's reluctance to surrender control of Bomber Command to SHAEF. On February 29, 1944, the prime minister told Ike that the Bomber, Fighter, and Coastal commands had the primary function of defending the British Isles, and he was unwilling to turn them over to the supreme commander of a task force that happened to be operating from British soil. They would cooperate with OVERLORD, but would remain under the control of the Combined Chiefs of Staff.[59] A second political problem

---

[*] Giulio Douhet's *The Command of the Air* (1921), which posed the possibility of victory through airpower alone, became the bible for many airmen during the interwar years. Douhet, a World War I Italian military pilot, argued that the infliction of heavy damage on civilian targets would shatter morale and unravel the social basis of resistance. Like Billy Mitchell, he was court-martialed for his advocacy of airpower and resigned from the service after the war.

Spaatz served with Mitchell, the patron saint of an independent air force, in France during World War I and afterward in Washington, and was one of the first defense witnesses called at Mitchell's 1925 court-martial.

For the influence of Douhet and Mitchell on Spaatz, see Richard G. Davis, *Carl A. Spaatz and the Air War in Europe* 16–21 (Washington, D.C.: Center for Air Force History, 1993).

pertained to the collateral damage that would be done should the strategic air forces attack targets in France. Some estimates put the number of French casualties as high as eighty thousand. Churchill and the British war cabinet found that figure unacceptable. "Postwar France must be our friend," said Churchill. "It is not alone a question of humanitarianism. It is also a question of high state policy."[60]

The number of possible French casualties was worrisome. But de Gaulle saw no problem, nor did General Pierre Koenig, the hero of the Battle of Bir Hakeim, who commanded the French Forces of the Interior (FFI) under de Gaulle. "This is War," Koenig told Bedell Smith. "It must be expected that people will be killed. We will take the anticipated loss to be rid of the Germans."[61] When Churchill took his case to the president, FDR came down hard on Eisenhower's side. "However regrettable the loss of civilian life is," Roosevelt cabled Churchill, "I am not prepared to impose from this distance any restriction on military action by the responsible commanders that in their opinion might militate against the success of OVERLORD or cause additional loss of life to our Allied forces of invasion."[62]

The most serious problem, however, was the personal. Harris and Spaatz detested Leigh-Mallory, Ike's commander in chief for air, and refused to place their commands under his control. "This came as somewhat of a surprise to me," said Eisenhower, "since I understood that he [Leigh-Mallory] had been especially selected by the British themselves for this post."[63]

When Eisenhower decided he was fighting a losing battle, he told Churchill he would "simply have to go home."[64] Ike's threat precipitated a compromise. Rather than place Harris and Spaatz under Leigh-Mallory, it was agreed that Ike's deputy, Air Chief Marshal Tedder, would assume "direction" of RAF Bomber Command and U.S. Strategic Air Forces, as well as the tactical air units already assigned to OVERLORD, in effect putting Harris, Spaatz, and Leigh-Mallory on the same level. And when the British war cabinet continued to resist bombing French targets, Eisenhower simply ordered Harris and Spaatz to commence the attack.[65] The order was obeyed, and the war cabinet made no protest. By D-Day, American and British heavy bombers had dropped 76,000 tons of bombs on rail marshaling yards, bridges, and tunnels, cutting French rail traffic in half. The Seine bridges north of Paris remained out of commission until late June.[66] Normandy was sealed off, and the Germans were unable to rush reinforcements to the beachheads. The Allies lost almost 2,000 planes and 12,000 men. French casualties numbered fewer than 10,000.[67]

The problem of inserting de Gaulle into liberated France over Roosevelt's objections required considerable maneuvering. When Ike arrived in London in January, he was informed by Smith that the State Department had instructed SHAEF to have no dealings with the FCNL or de Gaulle pertaining to civil affairs in France. Eisenhower was dumbfounded. As he saw it, there was no alternative to de Gaulle, and he had already committed himself.

Ike decided to challenge the directive head-on. "It is essential that immediate crystallization of plans relating to civil affairs in Metropolitan France be accomplished," he cabled Marshall on January 19, 1944. "I therefore request that General de Gaulle be asked to designate an individual or group of individuals with whom I can enter into immediate negotiations. The need for prompt action cannot be overemphasized."[68]

Eisenhower's cable found a receptive audience at the War Department. Assistant Secretary John J. McCloy, who often handled delicate issues with the president, was dispatched to convince FDR of Ike's need for de Gaulle. McCloy, former managing partner of the prestigious New York law firm of Cravath, Swaine, and Moore, had come to Washington with Henry Stimson in 1940. The warmth of his personality and the clarity of his intellect convinced many in the capital that he could put any deal across. He was a favorite of Roosevelt's, and he took Ike's cable with him to the White House. After a half hour of subtle advocacy, mixing flattery with fact, McCloy brought FDR around to the point that the president authorized the War Department to tell Eisenhower "informally" that he should feel entirely free in making decisions about French civil affairs, "even if it involved dealing with representatives of the French Committee."[69]

McCloy kept at it, and two months later Roosevelt approved a War Department directive that empowered the supreme commander to decide "where, when, and how the Civil Administration in France" should be exercised. Eisenhower was given explicit authority to consult with the FCNL and allow it to select and install civil officers, providing this did not constitute official recognition of the committee as the government of France.[70] On April 9, Secretary of State Cordell Hull expanded FDR's instructions when he announced in a radio address, "The President and I are disposed to see the French Committee of National Liberation exercise leadership to establish law and order under the supervision of the Allied Commander in Chief."[71] Hull's statement did not satisfy de Gaulle, but Eisenhower believed it gave him sufficient room to operate.* "The whole matter has been thrown back in my lap," he recorded, "and I [may] deal with any French body that seems capable of assisting us."[72] The solution was not perfect, but Ike was accustomed to dealing with ambiguity.

"The current stage of preparation is a replica of the others I have been through," Eisenhower wrote Somervell in early April. "As the big day approaches tension grows and everybody gets more and more on edge. This time, because of the stakes involved, the atmosphere is probably more electric than ever before. A sense of humor and a great faith, or else a complete lack of imagination, are essential to sanity."[73]

Eisenhower wrote regularly to Mamie, sometimes in response to her questions, more often of his own volition. On March 11, 1944, he wrote, "I desperately miss you. Why we have to have wars to separate families and cause all the anguish that they do is sometimes impossible for me to understand."

Ike's sense of humor was sorely tested later in April when George Patton found himself in the headlines again. Patton, who was playing decoy in East Anglia (decrypted German cable traffic indicated the Wehrmacht assumed Patton would lead the invasion force), had been invited to speak at the opening of a club for American servicemen in the village of Knutsford. Patton spoke on Anglo-American

---

* "The President's intentions seemed to me on the same order as Alice's adventures in Wonderland," wrote de Gaulle. "In North Africa, Roosevelt had already ventured on a political enterprise analogous to the one he was now contemplating for France. Yet of that attempt nothing remained. That the failure of his policy in Africa had not been able to dispel Roosevelt's illusions was a situation I regretted for him and for our relations." De Gaulle, 2 *War Memoirs* 240–41.

Mamie insisted that Ike write in longhand.

unity. After quoting Bernard Shaw to the effect that the British and Americans were two peoples separated by a common language, Patton said: "Since it seems to be the evident destiny of the British and Americans to rule the world, the better we know each other the better the job we will do."[74]* The idea that Britain and the United States would rule the world sent shock waves through the alliance. A local newsman quoted Patton in his report of the club opening, the wire services picked up the report, newspapers in the United States

---

* Patton's words have been variously quoted. Some writers render his remarks to include the Russians as well as the British and Americans. But there is no doubt that Patton did not include the Russians in his original statement. Commander Harry C. Butcher reports in his diary entry of April 28, 1944, that "our PRO [Public Relations Officer—Colonel R. Ernest Dupuy] has been busy on his own getting Russia included and to some extent has succeeded."

Eisenhower, in his report to Marshall of April 29, quoted Patton as speaking of "the destiny of America, Britain, and Russia to rule the world," but Forrest C. Pogue, George Marshall's official biographer, states that Ike "appears to have been misled by staff members of his own headquarters."

Pogue, Stephen Ambrose, John S. D. Eisenhower, and David Eisenhower agree that Patton did not include the Russians in his statement, and I have adopted their conclusion. Butcher, *My Three Years with Eisenhower* 531; Pogue, *Marshall* 384, 647; Stephen E. Ambrose, *The Supreme Commander: The War Years of General Dwight D. Eisenhower* 342 (Garden City, N.Y.: Doubleday, 1970); John S. D. Eisenhower, *General Ike* 58; David Eisenhower, *Eisenhower at War* 219.

Cf. Blumenson, *Patton Papers* 441; Merle Miller, *Ike the Soldier* 593; D'Este, *Patton* 586; Mark Perry, *Partners in Command: George Marshall and Dwight Eisenhower in War and Peace* 290 (New York: Penguin Press, 2007).

and Britain carried banner headlines, and Patton was again in hot water.

"We were just about to get [Senate] confirmation of the permanent [Regular Army] promotion list," Marshall cabled Eisenhower on April 26, "but this I fear has killed them all."[75] (Patton had been on the list, moving from the permanent peacetime rank of colonel to major general.)

Eisenhower was in the field observing maneuvers when Marshall's cable arrived. "Your cable," he told the chief of staff, "was my first intimation that Patton had broken out again. Apparently he is unable to use reasonably good sense in all those matters where senior commanders must appreciate the effect of their actions upon public opinion and this raises doubts as to the wisdom of retaining him in high command despite his demonstrated capacity in battle leadership." Eisenhower suggested Patton might have been misquoted, and told Marshall he would delay taking any action until he could gauge the situation better. If it turned out that Patton's action diminished public confidence in the War Department, he would relieve him.[76]

"You carry the burden of responsibility for OVERLORD," Marshall replied. "If you feel that the operation can be carried out with the same assurance of success with Hodges in command instead of Patton, all well and good. If you doubt it, then between us we can bear the burden of the present unfortunate reaction."[77]

On April 30, Eisenhower instructed Smith to have Patton report to headquarters. He then cabled Marshall that unless Patton could provide a satisfactory explanation, "I will relieve him of command and send him home. After a year and a half of working with him it appears hopeless to expect that he will ever completely overcome his lifelong habit of posing and self-dramatization which causes him to break out in these extraordinary ways."[78]

Marshall reiterated his support. "The decision is exclusively yours," he told Eisenhower on May 2. "Send him home if you see fit, and in grade, or hold him there as surplus if you desire, or continue him in command if that promises best for OVERLORD. Consider only OVERLORD and your own heavy responsibility for its success. Everything else is of minor importance." Marshall evidently was having second thoughts about relieving Patton. He told Ike that he might have overemphasized the editorial fallout in Washington, and that "no one has called for Patton's removal."[79]

Marshall's cable provided Eisenhower the guidance he needed. With obvious relief he radioed Marshall: "Because your telegram leaves the decision exclusively in my hands, to be decided solely upon my convictions as the effect on OVERLORD, I have decided to retain him in command." Eisenhower said Patton's demonstrated ability as an army commander in battle, as well as his ability to get "the utmost out of soldiers in offensive operations," rendered him invaluable.[80]

Patton was yet to be informed of Eisenhower's decision, and Ike kept him sweating. "After an interval I sent for him, told him I had decided to keep him on, and said that he had to learn to keep his mouth shut on political issues."

> When I gave him the verdict, tears streamed down his face and he tried to assure me of his gratitude. He put his head on my shoulder as he said it, and this caused his helmet to fall off—a gleaming helmet I sometimes thought he wore while in bed. . . . Here was George Patton telling me how sorry he was he had caused me distress and anguish, and swearing by all our many years of friendship that he would never again offend, while his helmet bounced across the floor into a corner.
>
> George could recover from emotion as quickly as he fell into it. Without apology and without embarrassment, he walked over, picked up his helmet, adjusted it, saluted, and said, "Sir, could I now go back to my headquarters?"
>
> "Yes," I said, "after you have lunch with me in about an hour."[81]

Eisenhower continued to juggle his affection for Kay with his love for Mamie. "I never forget that 28 years ago I brought out the West Point Class Ring to 1216 McCullough [in San Antonio], proud as a peacock," he wrote his wife on Valentine's Day.[82] Ike wrote superb letters, and he continued almost weekly to tell Mamie how much he missed her. From his letters it is apparent that Mamie often chided him. "I know that people at home always think of an army in the field as living a life of night clubs, gayety and loose morals," Eisenhower replied shortly before D-Day.

> So far as I can see the American forces here are living cleaner and more nearly normal lives than they did in Louisiana—California—etc. In the larger cities, such as London, there are undoubtedly numbers of officers and men that are living loosely; but it is also true that the pictures painted by gossips are grossly exaggerated. So far as the group around me is concerned, I know that the principal concern is work—and that their habits are above reproach.[83]

As D-Day approached, Eisenhower smoked more and slept less. He moved from Mayfair to Telegraph Cottage, and then in April to an advance headquarters in the woods outside Portsmouth, on Britain's south coast—the principal embarkation point for OVERLORD. From February 1 to June 1, Ike visited twenty-six divisions, twenty-four airfields, and countless depots, hospitals, and other installations, his grin always at the ready. "Soldiers like to see the men who are directing operations," wrote Eisenhower. "Diffidence or modesty must never blind the commander to his duty of showing himself to his men, of speaking to them, of mingling with them to the extent of physical limitations."[84]

Montgomery knew this even better than Ike. "Even Eisenhower with all his engaging ease could never stir American troops to the rapture with which Monty was welcomed by his," Omar Bradley remembered.[85] Montgomery visited every unit going ashore on D-Day, American as well as British and Canadian, encouraging the men to break ranks and gather around while he told them what an honor it was to command them. "General Eisenhower is the captain of the team, and I am proud to serve under him," said Monty. By his own reckoning, Montgomery estimated that he had inspected, "and been inspected by," well over one million men.[86] Bedell Smith reported afterward that the confidence of the troops in the high command was without parallel, thanks to Monty. "They thought he was a friendly, genuine person without any traces of pomposity."[87]*

Whatever their later quarrels, Eisenhower and Montgomery were on good terms as D-Day approached. Ike had given Montgomery free rein to plan, prepare, and rehearse the invasion without hindrance, and Monty, for his part, believed Eisenhower had grown in stature during the lead-up. "Eisenhower is just the right man for the job," Monty confided to his diary after dining with Ike on June 2, 1944. "He is really a big man and is in every way an Allied commander. I like him immensely; he has a generous and lovable character and I would trust him to the last gasp."[88]

On May 15, Eisenhower gathered his OVERLORD commanders for a final review at St. Paul's School in London—the headquarters of Montgomery's Twenty-first Army Group.† Formal invitations were extended to the King, Churchill, the war cabinet, and the British chiefs of staff, as well as some four dozen senior commanders and staff officers. "Eisenhower was quite excellent," Montgomery noted in his diary. "He spoke very little, but what he said was good and high level."[89] But it was Monty who stole the show. "I have no clear recollection of his actual words," wrote General Sir Hastings Ismay, Churchill's chief of staff, "but the impression left on my mind is still vivid."

> Plans and preparations are now complete in every detail.
> All difficulties have been foreseen and provided against.
> Nothing has been left to chance. Every man knew exactly

---

* On June 22, 1944 (D-Day plus sixteen), Smith wrote Montgomery that, "having spent my life with American soldiers, and knowing too well their innate distrust of everything foreign, I can appreciate far better than you can what a triumph of leadership you accomplished in inspiring such feeling and confidence." Reprinted in Montgomery, *Memoirs* 201–2.

† Founded in 1509 by the dean of St. Paul's Cathedral, St. Paul's was one of nine original English public schools recognized by Parliament in 1868. The students were evacuated during the Blitz, and Montgomery, an Old Pauline, took it over as his headquarters in January 1944. "My office was located in the room of the High Master," Monty wrote in his memoirs. "Although I had been a school prefect, captain of the 1st XV [rugby]; in the cricket XI and on the swimming team, I had never entered that room before." Montgomery, *Memoirs* 192.

what he had to do. Their equipment left nothing to be desired. If there was anyone who had doubts, he would prefer his room to his company. It reminded me of King Henry's speech before Agincourt in Shakespeare's *Henry V:*

> . . . he that has no stomach to this fight,
> Let him depart; his passport should be made,
> And crowns for every convoy put into his purse.[90]

After Montgomery spoke, Churchill addressed the audience. "Gentlemen, I am hardening toward this enterprise. I repeat, I am *now* hardening toward this enterprise. Let us not expect all to go according to plan. Flexibility of mind will be one of the deciding factors. We must not have another Anzio. Risks must be taken."[91] King George VI spoke last, a brief hortatory speech, much like Nelson's message to the fleet at Trafalgar. Eisenhower recalled many years later that "the smell of victory was in the air."[92]

Despite what appeared to be a White House go-ahead to deal with de Gaulle, Roosevelt began to hedge his commitment. On May 11, Eisenhower advised the Combined Chiefs that it was increasingly urgent to resolve a host of issues pertaining to the upcoming situation in liberated France. "The most effective means of doing so," he said, "would be for General de Gaulle himself to come to London. I would then be able to deal with him direct on the most immediate and pressing problem of the initial approach to the French people and their organized resistance groups."[93] Churchill agreed, but Roosevelt vetoed any discussion of political issues. "We must always remember," said the president, "that the French population is quite naturally shell shocked. It will take some time for them quietly and normally to think through the matters pertaining to their political future. We as liberators have no 'right' to color their views or give any group the sole right to impose one side of a case on them."[94]

Eisenhower, who was taken aback by FDR's resistance, recharted his course. On May 16 he assured Roosevelt that he would "carefully avoid anything that could be interpreted as an effort to influence the character of the future government of France. *However,* I think I should tell you that so far as I am able to determine from information given to me through agents and through escaped prisoners of war, there exists in France today only two major groups, of which one is the Vichy gang, and the other seems almost idolatrous in its worship of de Gaulle." Eisenhower told FDR that once ashore he expected to find "a universal desire to adhere to the de Gaullist group."

Ike was counting on Roosevelt's ultimate willingness to defer to the commander in the field. But to build a backstop against presidential caprice, he reminded FDR that SHAEF was an Allied command. "I hope that your desires on this subject of which I am already aware, can eventually come to me as a joint directive of the two governments."[95] By suggesting that Roosevelt needed Churchill's concurrence, Eisenhower hoped to find the wiggle room he needed to deal with de Gaulle.

And deal with de Gaulle he must. "We were depending on considerable assistance from the Resistance in France, and an open clash with de Gaulle would hurt us immeasurably," wrote Eisenhower in his memoirs. Roosevelt's objections were "academic." As Ike saw it, in the initial stages of OVERLORD "de Gaulle would represent the only authority that could produce any kind of French co-ordination and unification, and no harm would result from giving him the kind of recognition he sought. He would merely be placed on notice that once the country was liberated the freely expressed will of the French people would determine their own government."[96]

Eisenhower thought it essential to retain de Gaulle's goodwill. On May 23, 1944, he wrote the French leader (who was still in Algiers) to congratulate him on the performance of French troops fighting in Italy. De Gaulle's response was precisely what Ike hoped for: "I assure you again that the French government is very happy to have a place in your army under your supreme command . . . and has the fullest confidence that you will conduct the armies of liberation to a rapid victory."[97]

As D-Day neared, Eisenhower and Churchill became apprehensive about conditions in France and de Gaulle's continued absence. "It is very difficult to cut the French out of the liberation of France," Churchill cabled FDR on May 26.[98] With Roosevelt's grudging approval, Churchill sent his personal plane to fetch de Gaulle, who arrived in London on June 4. The prime minister immediately whisked

Churchill escorts de Gaulle to Eisenhower's headquarters on June 4, 1944.

him off to Ike's field headquarters near Portsmouth, where, Churchill told Roosevelt, "Generals Eisenhower and Bedell Smith went to the utmost limit in their endeavor to conciliate him, making it clear that in practice events would probably mean that the Committee [FCNL] would be the natural authority with whom the Supreme Commander would deal."[99] Deftly, Churchill was preparing FDR for what would become the new reality in France.

Eisenhower gave de Gaulle a half-hour briefing on OVERLORD. "He explained to us, with great clarity and self-command, the plan for the landing and the state of preparations to date," wrote de Gaulle.[100] "The ships were ready to leave port at any moment. The planes could take off at the first signal. The troops had been entrained for several days. The great machinery of the embarkation, the crossing and landing of eight divisions and the matériel which formed the first echelon was prepared down to the minutest detail." It was quickly agreed that General Pierre Koenig, who commanded the French Forces of the Interior, would fold the Resistance into the French Army and would report to Ike.

Eisenhower told de Gaulle he was worried about the weather, and had at most twenty-four hours in which to decide whether to go or not. "What do you think I should do?"

De Gaulle, who was flattered to be asked, insisted the decision was Eisenhower's alone. "Whatever decision you make, I approve in advance and without reservation. I will only tell you that in your place I should not delay."[101]

When the briefing concluded, Eisenhower, with evident embarrassment, gave de Gaulle the copy of a speech SHAEF wished him to deliver to the French people after the troops had landed. As Ike anticipated, de Gaulle refused. Aside from the limp military prose (which would have been reason enough to decline), de Gaulle rejected the idea that as head of the provisional government of France, his words should be written by the Allies. Instead, he wrote his own message—a masterpiece of subtle phrasing that implied he was broadcasting as president of France (though he did not say so), and that urged all Frenchmen to follow precisely the orders of the supreme commander (though he did not use that terminology).* "General de Gaulle and his chief of staff are anxious to assist every possible way and to have the lodgment effected as soon as possible," Eisenhower cabled the Combined Chiefs after the meeting.[102]

Future generals might find it useful to reflect upon the fact that on the eve of battle Eisenhower was cognizant of the responsibility he bore to preserve Europe's historic shrines and symbols. "Bomber" Harris and Spaatz were not under Ike's direct command, and he could not prevent the bombing of German cities even if he had wanted to. But to his own commanders—Montgomery, Bradley, Ramsay, and Leigh-Mallory—he issued an explicit order to preserve historic shrines whenever possible. Military necessity would inevitably require that some sites be destroyed. "But there are many cir-

---

* "The supreme battle has been joined," said de Gaulle in his broadcast on the morning of June 6, 1944. "It is, of course, the Battle of France, and the battle for France! For the sons of France, wherever they are, whatever they are, the simple and sacred duty is to fight the enemy by every means in their power. *The orders given by the French government and by the leaders which it has recognized must be followed precisely.* From behind the cloud so heavy with our blood and our tears, the sun of our greatness is now appearing." De Gaulle, *War Memoirs* 256. (Emphasis added.)

cumstances in which damage and destruction are not necessary and cannot be justified. In such cases, through the exercise of restraint and discipline, commanders will preserve centers and objects of historical and cultural significance."[103]

On D-Day minus seven, with the battle plan set, Air Chief Marshal Leigh-Mallory questioned the wisdom of dropping the 82nd and 101st Airborne divisions behind enemy lines on the Cherbourg Peninsula. Leigh-Mallory had always been skeptical of the plan, and recent aerial photos of German defenses convinced him that the divisions would lose 70 percent of their gliders and 50 percent of their paratroop strength to antiaircraft fire. Eisenhower was shaken. The airborne landings were essential to seize the causeways that would allow VII Corps to move inland from Utah beach and seize the port of Cherbourg. Without Cherbourg the invasion would be imperiled. "The whole operation suddenly acquired a degree of risk, even foolhardiness that presaged a gigantic failure, possibly Allied defeat in Europe," wrote Eisenhower.[104]

Leigh-Mallory was Ike's commander in chief for air, and to protect him in case his advice was disregarded, Eisenhower instructed him to put his objections on paper. "I went to my tent alone and sat down to think. I took the problem to no one else. I realized that if I disregarded the advice of my technical expert and his predictions should prove accurate, then I would carry to my grave the unbearable burden of a conscience justly accusing me of the stupid, blind sacrifice of thousands of the flower of our youth."

After thinking the problem through, Eisenhower decided the drops would go forward. "Leigh-Mallory's estimate was just an estimate, and our experience in Sicily and Italy did not support his degree of pessimism. I telephoned him that the attack would go as planned and that I would confirm this at once in writing."*

Unexpected problems continued to arise. No sooner had Ike re-

---

* Of the 805 C-47s airlifting the 82nd and 101st, only 20 were lost, and all but 4 gliders made it through safely. Contrary to Leigh-Mallory's fears there had been little flak and no fighter opposition. Chester Wilmot, *The Struggle for Europe* 244 (New York: Harper and Row, 1952). Also see S.L.A. Marshall, *Night Drop: The American Airborne Invasion of Normandy* (Boston: Little, Brown, 1962).

plied to Leigh-Mallory than he received a phone call from Admiral Ramsay, his naval commander in chief, stating that Churchill intended to observe the invasion from the deck of the cruiser HMS *Belfast.* When Eisenhower objected, Churchill asserted that as Britain's minister of defense it was his prerogative to participate, and that he was not subject to the orders of the supreme commander.[*] Technically, Churchill was correct, but the last thing Eisenhower wanted was to have the prime minister aboard one of the ships bombarding the French coast.

Churchill had previously discussed his plan with the King, and George VI initially embraced the idea, telling Churchill he would like to come along. The King said he "had not been under fire since the Battle of Jutland, and eagerly welcomed the prospect of renewing the experiences of his youth."[105] But George VI soon had second thoughts. On May 31, 1944, he wrote Churchill that it would be a severe setback to the Allied cause "if at this juncture a chance bomb, torpedo, or even mine, should remove you from the scene; equally a change of Sovereign at this moment would be a serious matter for the country and Empire. We should both, I know, love to be there, but in all seriousness I would ask you to reconsider your plan."[106]

Churchill was not dissuaded, and at that point Eisenhower recognized the seriousness of the problem. At Ike's direction, Bedell Smith contacted the King's staff at Buckingham Palace, who then prompted His Majesty to write a second, more urgent, letter to Churchill. "I am a younger man than you, I am a sailor, and there is nothing I would like better than to go to sea," said the King. "But I have agreed to stay home. Is it fair that you should then do exactly what I should have liked to do myself? . . . If the King cannot do this, it does not seem to me right that his Prime Minister should take his place."[107]

Churchill yielded, but was always resentful. "Since Your Majesty does me the honor to be so much concerned about my personal safety, I must defer to Your Majesty's wishes, and indeed commands."[108] Later Churchill wrote,

---

[*] Churchill served simultaneously as prime minister and minister of defense in the war cabinet.

A man who has to play an effective part in taking grave and terrible decisions of war may need the refreshment of adventure. He may need also the comfort that when sending so many others to their death he may share in some small way their risks. No one was more careful of his personal safety than I was, but I thought my view was sufficiently important and authoritative to entitle me to full freedom of judgment as to how I discharged my task in such a personal matter.[109]

Eisenhower's lonely decision to drop the 82nd and 101st Airborne was preamble to an even lonelier choice: whether to buck the weather and attempt a Channel crossing, or postpone the invasion for two weeks. SHAEF planners had determined that the proper confluence of tides, moon, hours of daylight, and weather would occur from June 5 to June 7, 1944. The next opportunity would be June 19, when tidal conditions would again be favorable. D-Day had been set for June 5, but on June 3 the weather reports took a turn for the worse. By June 4, they were menacing. Group Captain J. M. Stagg, the unflappable Scot who headed SHAEF's meteorological team, predicted low clouds, high winds, and formidable wave action on the French coast for the morning of June 5. Air support would be impossible, naval gunfire would be inefficient, and the handling of landing craft would be hazardous. The vast invasion armada was already at sea, and to stand down carried problems of its own. Eisenhower polled his commanders. Montgomery, concerned about the disadvantages of delay, thought the attack should go forward on schedule. Ramsay thought the landing could be managed, but said it would be difficult to adjust the naval gunfire. Tedder and Leigh-Mallory, the two airmen, were flatly opposed. Eisenhower, who deemed close-in air support essential, ordered a twenty-four-hour postponement.[110]

The meeting reconvened at 10 p.m. on June 4, with still no break in the weather. Eisenhower set another meeting for 0400—six hours later—the last possible moment to order an assault on June 6. When the commanders assembled at Admiral Ramsay's Portsmouth headquarters, the winds had reached gale proportions and the rain pelted down in horizontal streaks. Group Captain Stagg said the same conditions prevailed in Normandy, meaning that if the invasion had gone forward on the fifth, it would have been a disaster. Yet as Bedell Smith recalled, "There was the ghost of a smile on the tired face of Group Captain Stagg."

"I think we have found a gleam of hope for you, sir," Stagg told Eisenhower. "The mass of weather coming in from the Atlantic is moving faster than we anticipated. We predict there will be rather fair conditions beginning late on June 5 and lasting until the next morning, June 6." But the weather would close in again on the evening of the sixth, said Stagg, and conditions would turn foul. How long the bad weather would last, he could not say. But there was a window of about twenty-four hours when conditions would be tolerable.[111]

Again, Eisenhower polled his commanders. Admiral Ramsay said whatever was decided, the signal had to be flashed to the fleet within the next half hour. He asked Stagg about the seas and the wind velocity, and said he was satisfied. Leigh-Mallory and Tedder thought it was "chancy." Montgomery said, "Go!"[112]

After everyone had spoken, Eisenhower sat quietly. Smith remembered the silence lasted for five full minutes. "I never realized before the loneliness and isolation of a commander at a time when such a momentous decision has to be taken, with the full knowledge that failure or success rests on his judgment alone."[113]

When Ike looked up, he was somber but not troubled.

"OK, we'll go."[114] With those words, Eisenhower launched the D-Day invasion of Europe, an enterprise without precedent in the history of warfare.

The decision to launch the invasion having been made, events passed from Eisenhower's control. That afternoon he scribbled a note on a plain sheet of paper and tucked it into his wallet. It was reminiscent of the private note Lincoln penned anticipating defeat in the 1864 election.[*] Said Ike:

---

[*] On August 23, 1864, Lincoln wrote: "This morning, as for some days past, it seems exceedingly probable that this Administration will not be re-elected. Then it will be my duty to cooperate with the President-elect to save the Union between the election and the inauguration; as he will have secured his election on such ground that he cannot possibly save it afterward." Roy F. Basler, ed., 7 *The Collected*

Eisenhower visits troops of the 101st Airborne on the eve of D-Day.

Our landings in the Cherbourg-Havre area have failed to gain a satisfactory foothold and I have withdrawn the troops. My decision to attack at this time and place was based upon the best information available. The troops, the air, and the Navy did all that bravery and devotion to duty could do. If any blame or fault attaches to the attempt it is mine alone.—June 5.[115]

Late on the evening of June 5, Eisenhower paid an emotional visit to the American airborne regiments near Newbury, Wiltshire, about twenty-five miles south of Oxford. They would be the last units to leave England and the first to land in France. "There was no military pomp about his visit," Summersby remembered. "Ike got out and just started walking among the men. He went from group to group and shook hands with as many men as he could. He spoke a few words to every man and he looked the man in the eye as he wished

*Works of Abraham Lincoln* 514 (New Brunswick, N.J.: Rutgers University Press, 1955).

him success. 'It's very hard really to look a soldier in the eye,' he told me later, 'when you fear you are sending him to his death.' "[116]

Eisenhower and Summersby returned to his camp outside Portsmouth.

> We just sat in the trailer waiting for reports. Every once in a while, I would stand behind Ike and massage his shoulders, but in those predawn hours, no matter how much strength I used, I could not undo the knots at the base of his neck. His eyes were bloodshot, and he was so tired that his hand shook when he lit a cigarette.
>
> It meant a lot to me that I was the person he chose to be with in those crucial hours. If Ike had wished, he could have been surrounded by top brass, by Churchill and de Gaulle, by any of the important personages who were gathered just a few miles away in Portsmouth. But he preferred to wait in solitude. And I was the one he permitted to share his solitude.*[117]

---

* "I was startled to learn," wrote General James Gavin of the 82nd Airborne, "that after General Eisenhower's visit to the airborne troops, before they took off for Normandy on the night of June 5, he chose to spend the night in a caravan with Miss Summersby." James M. Gavin, *On to Berlin: Battles of an Airborne Commander, 1943–1946* (New York: Viking, 1978) 142.

# FOURTEEN

# The Liberation of France

Make peace, you idiots!

—VON RUNDSTEDT TO KEITEL,
*July 3, 1944*

SHORTLY AFTER MIDNIGHT on June 6, 1944, paratroopers
from three airborne divisions began dropping on the flanks of the
invasion beaches to seize vital bridges and causeways. At 3 a.m. British and American planes commenced their bombing runs over German coastal defenses, the first of almost thirteen thousand sorties
Allied aircraft would fly that day. When the preliminary air bombardment ceased, the guns of Admiral Ramsay's combined fleet
opened up. Of the 1,213 warships covering the landing, almost 80
percent were British or Canadian, the remainder from the United
States (16 percent), the Netherlands, Norway, and France. Fifty-nine
convoys, formed into five invasion fleets—a total of 6,483 ships—
steamed toward the beaches. For Admiral Ramsay it was a remarkable achievement. Four years earlier, almost to the day, Ramsay had
patched together the fleet of small ships that rescued the British Expeditionary Force at Dunkirk. Now he was commanding the greatest
naval armada ever assembled to return to the Continent.

At 0630 hours, the American First Army under Omar Bradley
came ashore at Omaha and Utah beaches. An hour later, because of
the tides, the British Second Army landed at Gold, Juno, and Sword.
Of the 132,000 troops who came ashore on June 6, 1944, 75,000
were British and Canadian; 57,000 were American. The landings

went according to plan at Utah, Gold, Juno, and Sword beaches, and by evening the lodgments were secure. But at Omaha, the American V Corps hung by a thread.[1]

Weather, bad luck, and a series of glaringly inept command decisions contributed to the crisis at Omaha. The sea was choppy, although not so rough as at the British beaches. But there was close-in cloud cover at Omaha that precluded low-level air support. Misfortune intervened to the extent that Allied intelligence failed to notice that the German 352nd Infantry Division, a veteran unit back from the Russian front, had taken up position directly athwart Omaha.[*] First Army planners had assumed V Corps would encounter a heavily fortified but lightly manned coastline. Instead they found it both heavily fortified and strongly garrisoned.

Aside from weather and bad luck, faulty command decisions ensured that the landing at Omaha would be difficult. Rather than order a preliminary naval bombardment of at least four hours with the heaviest guns in the fleet, as was customary in the Pacific, Bradley sent the troops ashore at Omaha with a "shoe string bombardment fleet" and allowed the ships only forty minutes to attack German fortifications that had been years in the making.[2]

Instead of lowering assault craft from their mother ships seven miles offshore, as was common practice in the Royal Navy, Bradley and Major General Gee Gerow, commanding V Corps, ordered the debarkation twelve miles out. While this minimized the possibility that any of the transports would be hit by coastal shelling, the three-hour passage not only increased the danger of swamping and the possibility of navigation errors, but guaranteed that the troops would be thoroughly groggy and seasick when they tumbled onto the beach.[†] To compound the problem, Gerow disregarded the les-

---

[*] The failure of Allied intelligence to properly locate the 352nd Infantry Division, and the subsequent cover-up, is treated as a case study in historiography by Professors Jacques Barzun and Henry Graff in *The Modern Researcher* 140–41, 6th ed. (Belmont, Calif.: Wadsworth, 2004).

[†] American GIs were grotesquely overloaded. In addition to his weapon, each soldier carried 68 pounds of military impedimenta, whereas the British and Canadian troops going ashore at Sword, Juno, and Gold carried between 15 and 20 pounds. Max Hastings, *Overlord: D-Day and the Battle for Normandy* 90 (New York: Simon and Schuster, 1984).

# OVERLORD
## Order of Battle

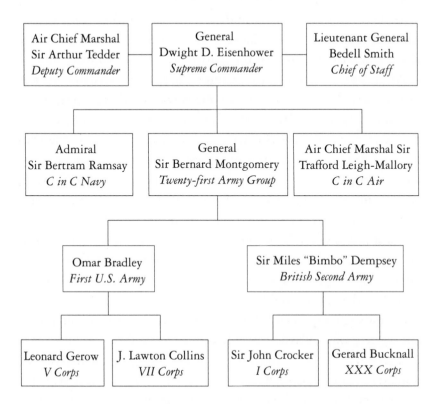

sons of North Africa, Sicily, and Salerno, and launched his attack frontally at German strong points rather than assaulting them from the flank or rear. That was the head-on doctrine preferred by General Marshall and which was taught in the Army's advanced schools. Gallantry, it was believed, would carry the day. Finally, Gerow made no effort to equip his troops with the latest armored equipment developed by the British to breach minefields, neutralize fortifications, and surmount obstacles.* As a consequence, those troops who made

---

* During the run-up to OVERLORD, Britain's Major General Sir Percy Hobart developed a veritable menagerie of tanks to assist the landing. One variety, labeled "Crabs," flailed steel chains in front and alongside to clear minefields. Another, called "Crocodiles," were simply armored flamethrowers that could approach an

it to shore found themselves pinned down and unable to move through the elaborate minefields the Germans had laid.[3]

By noon on June 6, the assault regiments were clinging to barely a hundred yards of beach. At midafternoon Bradley was ready to give up on Omaha, and asked Montgomery whether the remainder of V Corps could funnel through the British beaches. The answer was no: Gold, Sword, and Juno were crammed to capacity. As Bradley and Gerow sweated, the situation at Omaha stabilized. The veteran 1st Division took hold. "Two kinds of people are staying on this beach," shouted Colonel George A. Taylor as he rallied his troops in the 18th Infantry Regiment, "the dead and those who are going to die. Now let's get the hell out of here."[4] Eventually the line inched forward, and by nightfall the beachhead was almost a mile deep along a four-mile front. As one military historian put it, "The failures and errors of judgment of high command had been redeemed by the men on the sand."[5] Said another, "This success was principally due to the unquenchable spirit and drive of the 1st Division. Without 'The Big Red One' the battle would have been lost."[6]

Gerow's refusal to bend textbook tactics to the reality of amphibious warfare was a classic example of military hubris. Eisenhower is partially to blame. On December 23, 1943, Ike told Marshall that he wanted only generals with combat experience for OVERLORD. Yet he assigned V Corps to his old friend Gee Gerow despite the fact that Gerow had none. And Gerow proceeded to make the mistakes of a greenhorn.[*] Overall, Allied casualties on D-Day, including airborne

---

enemy pillbox undamaged and then destroy the occupants. Duplex drive (DD) tanks were amphibious vehicles. AVREs (armored vehicle, Royal Engineers) were tanks with a blade mounted in front, in effect armored bulldozers for demolishing fortifications. Bradley and Gerow were given demonstrations of the vehicles, but Bradley took only the DDs, and when they were launched so far offshore by V Corps, virtually all sank to the floor of the Bay of the Seine. Wilmot, *Struggle for Europe* 265–66; David Eisenhower, *Eisenhower at War* 269.

* VII Corps, which landed on Utah beach, was commanded by J. Lawton "Lightning Joe" Collins, who had commanded the 25th "Tropic Lightning" Division on Guadalcanal, and who was well versed in amphibious assault. VII Corps quickly surmounted the beach defenses and lost only 197 men on D-Day even though the spearhead 4th Division had never seen combat. Omar Bradley and Clay Blair, *A General's Life: An Autobiography* 224, 249 (New York: Simon and Schuster, 1983).

losses, totaled about ten thousand, of whom six thousand were American, mostly at Omaha.[7]

The Germans were caught flatfooted. German meteorologists had observed the same weather front as Group Captain Stagg, but they did not notice the brief window of opportunity that Stagg discovered. "There can be no invasion within the next fortnight," chief meteorologist Major Heinz Lettau reported on June 4.[8] On the strength of Lettau's forecast, Field Marshal Erwin Rommel, commanding Army Group B, left Paris in the early morning of June 5 for his home near Ulm to celebrate his wife's birthday. Before leaving, Rommel reported to Field Marshal von Rundstedt, the commander in chief west, that Allied preparations indicated an invasion would be forthcoming, and that the *Schwerpunkt* (main focus) would likely be between Dunkirk and Dieppe in the Pas-de-Calais. But in Rommel's view it was not imminent. "Air reconnaissance showed no great increase of landing craft in Dover area. Other harbours on England's south coast NOT visited by reconnaissance aircraft." Rommel requested that reconnaissance planes be dispatched to cover the south coast, but the weather on June 5 kept the Luftwaffe grounded. The Kriegsmarine (German Navy) patrols of the Channel were also suspended on June 5 because of the weather. And on the evening of the fifth, the Allies jammed all German radar sites between Cherbourg and Le Havre. Miraculous as it appears in retrospect, Ramsay's invasion fleet of more than six thousand ships went undetected by the Germans.

When airborne troops began landing shortly after midnight, both Rommel's headquarters at Château de La Roche Guyon and von Rundstedt's in Saint-Germain-en-Laye dismissed the landings as little more than local incursions. No alert was ordered. At 0230 hours, as the size of the airdrops became manifest, von Rundstedt notified the German high command (OKW) in Berlin, and also Hitler, who was at Berchtesgaden, but took no further action, waiting for the situation to develop. The commander in chief west was perplexed that the drops were to the south in Calvados, not the Pas-de-Calais.

By 0430, as the fighting intensified, von Rundstedt became convinced the airdrops were a prelude to a landing at dawn on the Cal-

# GERMAN ORDER OF BATTLE
## June 6, 1944

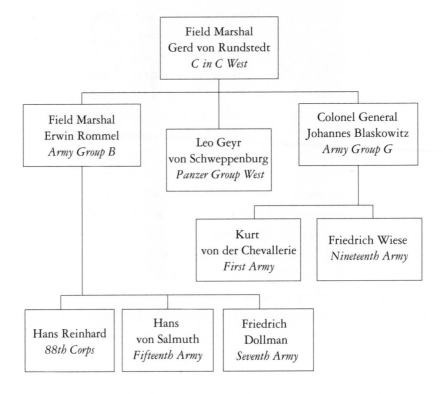

vados coast. The Germans held five panzer divisions in reserve, waiting for the Allied invasion. But they could not be deployed without Hitler's express consent. On his own authority, von Rundstedt ordered two of the five divisions to move toward Caen, the midpoint between the American and British drops.[9] Field Marshal Gerd von Rundstedt, at sixty-eight, was not only the oldest, but the most senior commander in the Wehrmacht.[*] Known as the "Black

---

[*] Gerd von Rundstedt, the son of a military officer, was born in Aschersleben on December 12, 1875. That made him five years older than Marshall and MacArthur, and fifteen years older than Eisenhower. He joined the Army as an officer cadet at the age of sixteen, fought with the German contingent of the international force that suppressed the Boxer Rebellion in China in 1900, served in the infantry

Field Marshal Gerd von Rundstedt.

during World War I, was decorated for gallantry (Iron Cross, first class) in 1914, and was a major when the war ended. Selected as one of four thousand officers for the 100,000-man Reichswehr, he rose steadily through the ranks and was promoted to general officer in 1927.

Von Rundstedt exuded the courtly demeanor of old Prussian nobility, spoke French and English fluently, and was one of Germany's five representatives at the state funeral of George V in 1936. When Hitler sought to appoint Walther von Reichenau, an outspoken pro-Nazi officer, to be the Army's commander in chief, von Rundstedt stepped in to block the appointment. When General Werner von Fritsch, the Army's chief of staff from 1934 to 1938, was falsely accused of homosexual behavior by the Gestapo, von Rundstedt intervened with Hitler and demanded a court-martial on Fritsch's behalf at which he was acquitted. (Hitler had asked von Rundstedt to come to the back door of the Chancellery in the evening wearing civilian clothes.) Shortly after the Fritsch verdict, von Rundstedt was placed on the retired list. He was recalled to active duty in 1939 to command Army Group South in the invasion of Poland. Charles Messenger, *The Last Prussian: A Biography of Field Marshal Gerd von Rundstedt, 1875–1953* (London:

Knight" (*Schwarzer Ritter*), he had led the invasion of Poland in 1939, the breakthrough in the Ardennes in 1940, and the capture of Kiev in 1941. Relieved by Hitler in November 1941 because of his insistence on withdrawing to a defensive line on the Russian front, he was nevertheless recalled four months later and entrusted with overall command in the west. As his former chief of staff Erich von Manstein noted, von Rundstedt never shied from accepting responsibility. In the early morning hours of June 6 he acted to meet the invasion threat, assumed Hitler's approval, and reported his action to Berchtesgaden.

Fortunately for the Allies, von Rundstedt was not the final authority. At 0630 hours, Colonel General Alfred Jodl, OKW's chief of operations, who was with the Führer, called Saint-Germain and ordered von Rundstedt to halt the panzer divisions in place. Hitler was still asleep, said Jodl, but it was clear the airdrops were merely a feint. The panzer divisions must be held back to meet the real landing that was coming in the Pas-de-Calais. Von Rundstedt erupted with a string of expletives about the "imbeciles" in command, but declined to place a personal call to Hitler to protest OKW's decision. It was not deference on von Rundstedt's part so much as contempt for the man he habitually referred to as "that Bohemian corporal."[10] He would not beg Hitler's permission. Not until midafternoon, ten hours later, did the Führer release the panzer divisions to von Rundstedt, and by then there was no hope they could arrive at the beachhead until the following day. To add to the German misfortune, the Luftwaffe put less than a hundred fighters in the air on D-Day, and mounted only twenty-two sorties against Ramsay's fleet.[11]

Eisenhower spent D-Day nervously awaiting news, but reports from Normandy were slow to trickle in. "I have as yet no information concerning the actual landings nor of our progress through beach obstacles," Ike cabled Marshall that morning. "All preliminary reports are satisfactory. Airborne formations apparently landed in good order. Preliminary bombings by air went off as scheduled. Navy reports sweeping some mines, but so far as is known channels

Brassey's, 1991); Günther Blumentritt, *Von Rundstedt: The Soldier and the Man* (London: Odhams Press, 1952).

are clear and operation proceeding as planned. I will keep you informed."[12]

News of the crisis at Omaha reached Eisenhower at 1:30 p.m. through the Navy, which had observers at the scene. There was little Ike could do other than authorize Leigh-Mallory to deploy his tactical bombers to drop their payloads through the cloud cover, risking the possibility of short rounds falling on American positions.[13] By evening it was clear the landings were a success. Eisenhower, Tedder, Leigh-Mallory, and Ramsay met again at Ramsay's fleet headquarters in Portsmouth to review the day's action (Montgomery had departed for Normandy). In Tedder's view the Allies had achieved tactical surprise, but needed to link up the beachheads quickly. The next ninety-six hours would be crucial. Omaha, in the center of the invasion front, was still perilous. V Corps held but a sliver of territory, and was separated by ten miles from the British at Gold beach, and by seven miles from VII Corps at Utah. Montgomery was on the scene and in command, but Ike was restless and decided to cross the Channel himself for a look-see the following morning.

After breakfast on June 7, Eisenhower boarded the British minelayer *Apollo* to visit the beachheads. He arrived off Omaha shortly after eleven, and by that time Montgomery and Bradley had already moved to consolidate the landings. Collins was ordered to turn VII Corps away from Cherbourg and link up with Gerow's forces as soon as possible, and the British 50th Division at Gold was instructed to do the same. The change of plans would delay the capture of the port of Cherbourg, but would deny Rommel and von Rundstedt the opportunity to exploit the separation between Allied lodgments. "I briefed Ike as fully as I was able," Bradley recalled. "I also told him of the modification in the battle plan Monty and I had agreed to earlier in the day. Ike had little to say. On the whole, Ike's visit had been perhaps necessary for his own personal satisfaction, but from my point of view it was a pointless interruption and annoyance."[14]

Kay Summersby remembered that Eisenhower suffered a terrible letdown after D-Day. It was "as if he had run out of steam. And he was very much depressed." Montgomery was running the ground war, Tedder and Leigh-Mallory handled what there was of an air war, and Ramsay controlled the fighting at sea. "Most of the time we simply sat in the trailer in the woods waiting," said Summersby. "We stayed late every night waiting for just one more report to come through. I would call up the mess and have them send sandwiches over for supper, and I would boil water on the little spirit stove for Ike's powdered coffee. He would sit there and smoke and worry. Every time the telephone would ring he would grab it."[15]

Eisenhower's mood improved the following week when his son John, newly commissioned at West Point, arrived to spend his post-graduation leave with his father. "John will be in soon," Ike wrote Mamie on June 13. "I'm really as excited as a bride—but luckily I have so much to do I haven't time to get nervous."[16]

Like Summersby, John noted that his father was unusually fretful, "like a football player sitting on the bench, anxious to get in the game."[17] Despite their obvious affection, John was always conscious of their respective positions—as was Ike. "There existed a certain military wall between us," said John.

> Had I ever, for example, even in later years, pre-empted the right rear seat of a car or walked on the Boss's right, I knew he would have been annoyed, even though he might have said nothing. . . .[18]
>
> On practically the first evening I had arrived in London, Dad and I were walking together at SHAEF, and I asked in all earnestness: "If we meet an officer who ranks above me but below you, how do we handle this? Should I salute first and when they return my salute do you return theirs?" Dad's annoyed reaction was short: "John, there isn't an officer in this theater who doesn't rank above you and below me."[19]

Summersby, who had the opportunity to observe father and son at close range, thought "Ike was not a particularly doting father. He loved John very much and he was proud of him, but he was also critical. John took it all very good naturedly. No matter how sharply Ike criticized him, it was obvious he adored this son of his."[20]

In Normandy, the Allies profited from Hitler's assumption that the D-Day landings were a diversion and that the principal attack was still to come in the Pas-de-Calais. As a consequence, the German Fifteenth Army, some nineteen divisions with eight hundred tanks, remained idle north of the Seine awaiting an invasion that would never come.[*] To meet the threat in Calvados, Rommel was forced to rely on the seven infantry divisions available to Seventh Army, plus the panzer reserve Hitler had belatedly released.[21] And his troops were stretched too thin. By the night of June 7 (D-Day plus one), the British Second Army held a solid lodgment twenty-two miles wide and five to ten miles deep; the U.S. VII Corps held a zone eight miles deep and nine miles wide; and the U.S. V Corps, now solidly ashore, moved inland rapidly against light opposition. British commandos linked up with Gerow's forces on D-Day plus two, and four days later VII Corps joined, giving the Allies a continuous beachhead across the whole front.

Both sides were plagued by a shortage of supplies. The Allies had an abundance of shipping but found it difficult to off-load matériel across the beaches, and the two MULBERRYs, while ingenious, could not accommodate the thousands of tons of food and ammunition that were required daily. At the end of the first week, less than 50 percent of the scheduled supplies had been landed; and at Omaha, less than 25 percent. The Germans, for their part, were hampered by Allied air supremacy, which prevented their use of the roads during daylight, plus the fact that the strategic bombing campaign conducted by Harris and Spaatz had effectively isolated the Normandy battlefields, rendering rail traffic impossible. In addition, the Resistance, now organized under the French Forces of the Interior, proved effective in hindering the transport of supplies forward. As early as June 10, the German Seventh Army found itself in serious straits for both fuel and ammunition.

---

[*] By the evening of June 7, 1944, both von Rundstedt and Rommel were convinced that the landings in Normandy represented an all-out effort by the Allies but were unable to convince either Hitler or OKW in Berlin to deploy Fifteenth Army south of the Seine. According to ULTRA code intercepts, this brought both von Rundstedt and Rommel to the brink of tendering their resignations. Hans-Adolf Jacobsen and Jürgen Rohwer, eds., *Decisive Battles of World War II: The German View* 337 (New York: G. P. Putnam's Sons, 1965); Frederick William Winterbotham, *The Ultra Secret* 137 (New York: Harper and Row, 1974).

With the front in Normandy consolidated, Montgomery turned to the next stage: the capture of the vital port of Cherbourg, and the breakout of the American First Army from the hedgerow country of Calvados to the plain beyond. Monty's strategy was straightforward: to pull the bulk of the German forces, particularly the panzer divisions, onto Dempsey's Second British Army while Bradley took Cherbourg, wheeled east, and broke into the open against reduced resistance.[22] Ike and Bedell Smith never fully understood Montgomery's concept. Reared on the continuous-attack-all-along-the-line strategy espoused by Pershing and Marshall, they failed to understand why the British Second Army did not go all out to capture the city of Caen. Like Pershing and Marshall, Ike and Smith subscribed to the doctrine of attrition. For Montgomery, given the horrendous British losses in the trench warfare of World War I, attrition was unthinkable. Instead, he preferred to keep the enemy off balance by maneuvering and then deliver a concentrated blow at a single point. Rather than conduct a broad-front offensive, Monty sought to breach the enemy line and exploit the breakthrough. "It is clear that Ike is *quite* unsuited for the post of Supreme Commander as far as running the strategy of the war is concerned," Field Marshal Alan Brooke, chief of the imperial general staff, wrote in despair.[23]

But Bradley understood Montgomery's concept, Patton understood it as well, and so did Rommel and von Rundstedt. The British Second Army sat astride the direct route to Paris and the Ruhr beyond, and Dempsey's troops had to be contained at all costs. By mid-June, the British Second Army confronted seven of the eight panzer divisions available to Rommel, all deployed in a defensive posture. Monty had tied the German armor down and deprived Rommel of the ability to mount a large-scale counterattack. As a consequence, Bradley would not necessarily have clear sailing, but he would have few panzer formations to contend with.

"Was up forward again yesterday," Rommel wrote his wife on June 14. "The situation does not improve. We must be prepared for grave events. The troops are fighting with the utmost courage, but the balance of strength tips more heavily against us every day. It appears dubious whether the gravity of the situation is realized up above, and whether the proper conclusions are being drawn."[24]

The destruction of Caen.

After the war, Eisenhower and Smith muddied the historical account of the Normandy breakout by asserting that Montgomery's failure to capture Caen caused them to change plans and order Bradley to break out on the right instead.[25] It is another example of Ike's ability to spin the record, similar to his reshaping of his role under MacArthur at the time of the Bonus Army marchers in 1932. Bradley is harsh in his criticism. "I have never been able to understand why Ike and Bedell made those statements," he wrote. "They were both intimately acquainted with the OVERLORD ground strategy formulated months before. That called for Monty not to 'break out' but to hold and draw the Germans to his sector, while I 'broke out' in my sector and wheeled east. We adhered to that basic concept throughout the Normandy campaign with no major changes in strategy or tactics."[26] In effect, by adopting Montgomery's breakout strategy and attacking on a narrow front, Bradley was disregarding classic American military doctrine.

As Bradley suggests, the ground war unfolded methodically under Montgomery's direction. With the bulk of the German armor deployed against the British Second Army at Caen, Collins's VII Corps sliced across the Cotentin Peninsula and reached the sea on June 18, isolating the port of Cherbourg and its defenders. Collins turned north and a week later Cherbourg capitulated, sending 39,042 German troops into Allied captivity. Add to that the number killed or missing, and the Germans had lost the equivalent of four infantry divisions that could not be replaced. By contrast, on June 26, when Cherbourg fell, there were twenty-five Allied divisions in Normandy, plus fifteen in Britain awaiting shipment to the front. "I am being bled white," Rommel complained to von Rundstedt, "and have nothing to show for it."[27]

With the capture of Cherbourg, the Allies gained a port that could sustain the invasion force until Marseilles was liberated in August. Cherbourg had been badly damaged by the Germans, but was soon operating full tilt. By the first week in July, the Allies had landed more than a million men in Normandy, almost 200,000 vehicles, and a half-million tons of supplies. By the end of the month, there were 1,566,000 troops ashore, 333,000 vehicles, and 1.6 million tons of food, equipment, and ammunition.[28]

Eisenhower may not have been fully cognizant of the ground strategy Montgomery was pursuing, but no one could have handled the political pressures that rained down on the supreme commander better than he. On June 13, the first V-1 rockets landed in Britain. The V-1,[*] developed under Wernher von Braun at the German research station at Peenemünde on the Baltic, was an unguided, jet-powered, flying bomb that flew at 420 miles per hour and delivered a payload of 1,875 pounds of high explosives that exploded upon impact. Between June 13 and the end of September 1944, the Germans launched more than 8,000 V-1s against Britain, killing more than 6,000 persons and injuring another 20,000. Its successor, the V-2, was a guided ballistic missile with a larger payload that reached an altitude of sixty miles traveling at a speed of 2,500 miles per hour. The V-1 had a maximum range of 125 miles; the V-2, which was far more deadly, could reach targets 200 miles away.[29]

The rocket blitz had a pronounced effect on British morale, and

---

[*] Short for *Vergeltungswaffe-1*—Retaliation Weapon 1.

large numbers of people were evacuated from London. "Had the Germans perfected the rockets six months earlier," said Ike, "and had they targeted the assembly areas in Portsmouth and Southampton, OVERLORD might have been written off."[30] Churchill asked Eisenhower to give priority to bombing the launch sites and Ike agreed, although subsequent studies showed the bombings had little effect.[31] But when the prime minister suggested that the Allies destroy specific German cities in a tit-for-tat reprisal, Eisenhower refused.[32] A week later, when the British chiefs of staff proposed using poison gas against the launch sites, Ike blew his stack. "Let's for God's sake, keep our eye on the ball and use some sense," he told Air Chief Marshal Sir Arthur Tedder.[33]

Dealing with de Gaulle brought out the best in Eisenhower. FDR and Secretary of State Hull, buttressed by Admiral Leahy and Robert Murphy, insisted that contact with de Gaulle be restricted to military matters. For Eisenhower, who was soon to be saddled with the problem of civil affairs in France, that was patently foolish. Fortunately Ike could count on the sympathy of the War Department—particularly Secretary Stimson and John McCloy, both of whom recognized his problem, and who were ably supported by Jean Monnet, the representative of the FCNL in Washington. The upshot was that Eisenhower paid lip service to the nonrecognition policy Roosevelt insisted upon, but for all practical purposes dealt with de Gaulle as France's legitimate head of state.

On June 14, little more than a week after the Allies had landed, de Gaulle returned to French soil with a lightning visit to the ancient Norman city of Bayeux, site of a majestic thirteenth-century cathedral and home of the world-famous Bayeux Tapestry.* Bayeux was the first French town liberated by the Allies. The British war cabinet, with Eisenhower's approval, authorized de Gaulle's visit, and Admiral Ramsay placed the Free French destroyer *La Combattante* at his disposal for the Channel crossing. June 14, as fate would have it, was the day the Germans had marched into Paris in 1940.

---

* The Bayeux Tapestry, eighty-four square yards of fabric, was embroidered by the ladies of the court of William the Conqueror to commemorate the conquest in 1066.

De Gaulle enters Bayeux, the first town liberated in France, June 12, 1944.

"That was a mistake," quipped de Gaulle when reminded of the fact.[34]

At the entrance to Bayeux, de Gaulle dismounted from his vehicle and proceeded on foot to the town hall. He was immediately surrounded by vast cheering crowds. "We walked on together," de Gaulle remembered, "all overwhelmed by comradeship, feeling of national joy, pride and hope rise again from the depths of the abyss."[35] At the town hall, where the portrait of Marshal Pétain had been removed moments before, the Vichy-appointed prefect pledged his support, as did all civil officials, as well as the bishop of Bayeux and Lisieux, who was the first caller to pay his respects. That symbolic union of the church and the republic, which had eluded France since 1789, was a vital component of the Gaullist appeal. De Gaulle later visited two nearby towns, received similar receptions, and departed that evening firmly in control. Whatever doubts Washington may have harbored about de Gaulle's support had been crisply dispelled. SHAEF civil affairs officers threw their occupation manuals in the wastebasket and commenced working with de Gaulle's appointees.

For all practical purposes, Bayeux had become the temporary capital of Free France.[36]

When he returned to Algiers on June 16, de Gaulle addressed the French Consultative Assembly (the temporary stand-in for the National Assembly); informed them of what had been achieved; and paid tribute to Eisenhower, "in whom the French Government has complete confidence for the victorious conduct of the common military operations."[37] As de Gaulle recognized, Ike was largely responsible for the swift transition de Gaulle had made from being a controversial pretender to the unquestioned leader of France. Eisenhower had ignored Washington's wishes and relied on his own judgment. As a recent biographer has written,

> Ike has received precious little credit for this, but it is a perfect example of what a quick learner he was. He had suffered through the chaos brought about by American policies in North Africa, when he had paid too much attention to Robert Murphy and the wishes of the president, and he was not about to let that happen again. No other American general, except perhaps Douglas MacArthur in his treatment of Japan at the end of the war, took on such heavy responsibilities or made such far reaching decisions on his own initiative.[38]

Because of Ike's unstinting support for de Gaulle, liberated France was spared the civil war Washington feared. And although de Gaulle did not always march in step with Allied policy, he could be relied on to keep France united. That was no small blessing.

Eisenhower's most serious problem, and the one that caused him the most anguish, was to ensure that the landings on the southern coast of France near Marseilles (DRAGOON) took place on schedule. Although the landings had been agreed to at Teheran, Churchill and the British chiefs of staff continued to oppose the operation. It was, said Eisenhower, "one of the longest-sustained arguments that I had with Prime Minister Churchill throughout the period of the war."[39] In Churchill's view, the Riviera landing was "bleak and sterile," and would have no effect on OVERLORD for many months.[40]

Instead, he proposed to reinforce the campaign in Italy, mount a landing on the Istria Peninsula in the Adriatic, capture Trieste, and move through the Ljubljana gap into Austria and Hungary.

Eisenhower objected strenuously. He told Marshall that the Combined Chiefs had "long ago decided to make Western Europe the base from which to conduct decisive operations against Germany," and that "to contemplate wandering off overland via Trieste to Ljubljana is to engage in conjecture to an unwarranted degree. We must concentrate our forces to the greatest possible degree and put them into battle in the decisive theater."[41] When the Joint Chiefs supported Ike, Churchill carried his case to the president, and was again rebuffed. "I am impressed by Eisenhower's statement that [DRAGOON] is of transcendent importance," said FDR. "Since the agreement was made at Teheran to mount [DRAGOON], I cannot accept, without consultation with Stalin, any course of action which abandons this operation." In his own hand, Roosevelt added a paragraph telling Churchill that "for purely political considerations over here I would never survive even a slight setback in OVERLORD if it were known that fairly large forces had been diverted to the Balkans."[42] (The 1944 presidential election was four months away.)

For the British chiefs of staff, Roosevelt's final paragraph tipped the balance. If it was a matter of FDR's reelection, they had no alternative. "Just back from a meeting with Winston," Brooke recorded in his diary on June 30. "I thought at first we might have trouble with him, he looked like he wanted to fight the President. However, in the end we got him to agree to our outlook which is: 'All right, if you insist on being damned fools, sooner than falling out with you, which would be fatal, we shall be damned fools with you, and we shall see that we perform the role of damned fools damned well.' "[43]

Pressed by his chiefs, Churchill yielded grudgingly. "I need scarcely say that we shall do our best to make a success of anything that is undertaken," he cabled Roosevelt.[44]

"I honestly believe that God will be with us," FDR replied. "I always think of my early geometry, 'A straight line is the shortest distance between two points.' "[45]

Churchill had agreed to DRAGOON, but his resentment festered. And like a smoldering volcano, it erupted full force in early

August. On August 4, less than two weeks before the landings were to take place, the prime minister cabled Roosevelt and suggested switching DRAGOON from the Riviera to the coast of Brittany. The next day he visited Ike at his field headquarters in France and cajoled and pleaded for six hours. According to Butcher, "Ike said no, continued saying no all afternoon, and ended by saying no in every form of the English language at his command. He was practically limp when the PM departed."[46]

The following day Eisenhower cabled Marshall that he would "not repeat not under any conditions agree at this moment to a cancellation of DRAGOON."[47] FDR never wavered in his support. On August 8 he told Churchill that it was his considered opinion that DRAGOON "should be launched as planned at the earliest practicable date and I have full confidence that it will be successful and of great assistance to Eisenhower in driving the Huns from France."[48]

"I pray God you may be right," Churchill replied. "We shall, of course, do everything in our power to help you achieve success."[49]

Presumably that should have ended the matter. But when Ike dined with Churchill at No. 10 Downing Street the following day, he was subjected to another harangue in which the prime minister pulled out all the stops, including the threat that he might have to go to the King and "lay down the mantle of my high office."[50] Churchill accused the Americans of bullying the British and refusing to listen to their strategic ideas. Eisenhower later called the meeting with Churchill one of the most difficult sessions he'd had in the entire war. "I have never seen him so obviously stirred, upset, and even despondent," he cabled Marshall.[51]

Churchill departed for the Mediterranean the following day. After visiting British troops in Italy, he embraced the inevitable, donned a flak jacket, and watched the troops of Alexander Patch's Seventh Army clamber ashore east of Toulon from the deck of the destroyer HMS *Kimberly.* "I watched this landing yesterday from afar," the prime minister cabled Ike afterward. "All I have seen there makes me admire the perfect precision with which the landing was arranged and the intimate collaboration of British-American forces."[52]

Eisenhower replied with equal generosity. "I am delighted that you have personally and legally adopted the DRAGOON. I am sure that he will grow fat and prosperous under your watchfulness."[53] To Marshall, Ike confessed that after "all the fighting and mental anguish I went through in order to preserve that operation, I don't know whether to sit down and laugh or to cry."[54]

On the other side of the hill, Rommel and von Rundstedt were at their wits' end trying to defeat the invasion under the limitations Hitler imposed. Not only had the Führer refused to move Fifteenth Army south of the Seine, but he insisted on defending every inch of French soil.[55] Both field marshals considered that absurd.

On June 17 Hitler paid a whirlwind visit to France to buttress his commanders' resolve. He met with von Rundstedt and Rommel near Soissons at a heavily bunkered command post that had been constructed in 1940 for his use during the planned invasion of Britain (SEA LION). The Führer appeared uninterested in what the field marshals had to report and ranted about the V-1 superweapons, which he assured them would bring Britain to its knees. When von Rundstedt suggested the weapons be directed against the embarkation ports in England or against the Allied bridgehead, Hitler declared that the bombardment of London was more important and would make the English "eager for peace."[56] Both von Rundstedt and Rommel stressed the need for air support. When von Rundstedt asked for the infantry divisions in Fifteenth Army so that Rommel's panzer divisions could be relieved from their defensive posture, Hitler refused, just as he dismissed the field marshals' request to pull back beyond the range of Allied naval gunfire. Cherbourg, he insisted, was to be defended at all costs, and Rommel was instructed to retake Bayeux with whatever forces were available.

The meeting lasted four hours. At the end, von Rundstedt and Rommel restated their view that the situation was dire and asked Hitler whether he had considered a political solution.* "Don't concern yourself about the future course of the war," the Führer replied. "Look to your own invasion front."[57] Shortly after the meeting concluded, an errant V-1 destined for London malfunctioned and landed

---

* General Alfred Jodl testified before the Nuremberg War Crimes Tribunal that "no Field Marshal other than von Rundstedt could have told Hitler this." 21 *The Trial of German Major War Criminals: Proceedings of the International Military Tribunal Sitting at Nuremberg, Germany* 129 (London: HMSO, 1949).

in the compound near Hitler's bunker, at which point the Führer hightailed it back to Berchtesgaden. Of the two field marshals, Rommel was more susceptible to Hitler's hypnotic appeal. "I am looking forward to the future with less anxiety than I did a week ago," he wrote his wife the day afterward. "The Führer was very cordial and in good humor. He realizes the gravity of the situation."[58] Von Rundstedt, by contrast, saw the handwriting on the wall. The meeting did little to convince him that the war could be won.[59]

On June 22, 1944, the third anniversary of Hitler's invasion of Russia (BARBAROSSA), Stalin fulfilled the pledge he made at Teheran and launched the Red Army in what would prove to be the greatest Allied offensive of the war. From Leningrad to the Crimea, along a front of eight hundred miles, Russian forces moved against the overextended German line. The principal assault (code-named BAGRATION, for the great Czarist general killed at Borodino in 1812) was directed at Army Group Center, some 700,000 troops who held the midsection of the German front. Marshal Georgy Zhukov, who coordinated the attack, committed 166 Red Army divisions—2.4 million troops, 5,300 aircraft, and 5,200 tanks—twice that of any previous offensive, to overrunning the German position. Army Group Center was no match for the oncoming Russians. By July 5, the front had collapsed. Hitler lost 28 divisions and 350,000 men, almost double the number at Stalingrad. Finland sued for peace, Romania surrendered, the Baltic states were overrun, and the Red Army was on the Vistula, a hair's breadth from the German frontier.

The collapse of Army Group Center in the summer of 1944 marked the beginning of the end of the war on the eastern front. Eisenhower makes no mention of the great Russian offensive in *Crusade in Europe,* but the scope and extent of the Russian victory in less than two weeks dwarfs the narrow front on which the Western Allies were advancing. At the very least it denied Hitler the opportunity to reinforce his armies in France with veteran formations from the eastern front. *Crusade in Europe* was published in 1948 at the height of the Cold War, and Ike evidently thought it best to ignore Russia's contribution to victory in the west.

On June 29, after the fall of Cherbourg, Hitler summoned von Rundstedt and Rommel to Berchtesgaden. The Führer instructed his commanders to confine the Allies to their beachhead, wage a war of attrition, and ultimately force them to withdraw. Von Rundstedt replied that although the German lines were holding, all their reserves had been committed, and an Allied breakthrough was imminent. When it came, it could not be contained. Rommel recommended withdrawing to the Seine and forming a defensive line to the Swiss frontier.[60] Hitler rejected the idea peremptorily. Reichsmarschal Hermann Göring, Admiral Karl Dönitz, and Field Marshal Hugo Sperrle of the Luftwaffe joined the meeting, at which point Hitler commenced a monologue touting the new wonder weapons that would bring victory. Hitler's tirade left Rommel and von Rundstedt depressed. It was clear to both that the Führer had lost touch with reality. Again they raised the matter of peace terms, and again Hitler dismissed the idea. When the meeting concluded, both von Rundstedt and Rommel assumed they would be relieved.[61]

On June 30, 1944, back at Saint-Germain, von Rundstedt received orders from OKW in Berlin instructing him to counterattack the British position at Caen. At the same time, Rommel called and recommended a withdrawal at Caen, lest his troops be encircled. Von Rundstedt agreed, told Rommel to prepare to withdraw, and informed Berlin what he had done. That triggered an immediate reply from OKW ordering him to tell Rommel to hold fast. There could be no withdrawal.[62]

For von Rundstedt that was the last straw. He immediately telephoned Field Marshal Wilhelm Keitel, who was with Hitler at Berchtesgaden.

"What shall we do?" asked Keitel.

"Make peace, you idiots," von Rundstedt replied. "What else can you do? If you doubt what we are doing, get up here and take over this shambles yourself."[63]

When Keitel reported the conversation to Hitler, the Führer chose to take von Rundstedt at his word. He wrote a personal letter by hand relieving him of command because of his health, awarded von Rundstedt Oak Leaves to his Knight's Cross, and appointed Field Marshal Günther von Kluge to replace him. Within a week, von Kluge had come to the same conclusion as Rommel and von Rundstedt. The situation was untenable.

At SHAEF, the precariousness of the German position was not apparent. Von Rundstedt's troops, although outgunned, outmanned, and short of virtually every military necessity, fought with skill and tenacity, while Rommel took advantage of every American and British miscue. By the third week in July, fourteen German divisions, including six panzer divisions, faced the British and Canadians at Caen. Eleven divisions, but only two panzer divisions, confronted Bradley's First Army. The boundaries of the Allied beachhead, some seventy miles long, but no more than ten miles deep at its shallowest point, had changed little during the past month. And with the German lines holding firm, an air of pessimism enveloped Allied headquarters. According to Butcher, Ike was "blue as indigo over Monty's slowdown."[64]

Unlike Montgomery and Bradley, who were on the scene and confident of the strategy they were pursuing, Eisenhower was sitting in Britain looking at lines on a map that were not moving. In some respects it was the mirror image of what Hitler saw at Berchtesgaden, and it suggested stalemate. The situation was analogous to the first week in November 1918. Then as now the Germans were deep inside France and their lines were holding firm. But Hindenburg and Ludendorff knew it was only a matter of time until the Allies broke through, and that when they did they could not be contained. And so out of the blue, as it were, Hindenburg and Ludendorff requested the government to ask for an armistice. In July 1944, Rommel, von Rundstedt, and von Kluge realized they were caught in a similar situation, and Monty and Bradley suspected as much.

But Ike wanted movement. Bedell Smith said, "Ike was up and down the line like a football coach, exhorting everyone to aggressive action."[65] Butcher said, "Ike is like a blind dog in a meathouse—he can smell it, but he can't find it."[66] The problem was exacerbated by a growing impatience in Washington, where Marshall and Stimson were also looking at lines on a map. American press coverage, to which Eisenhower was painfully sensitive, also chimed in, suggesting the Allies had dropped the ball.

For Eisenhower, the culprit was Montgomery, and he took his complaint to Churchill. Lunching with the prime minister on July 26, Ike asked Churchill "to persuade Monty to get off his bicycle and start moving."[67] While Churchill was fond of Ike and sympathized with his impatience, he trusted Montgomery's strategy and supported it fully. To mollify Eisenhower, and perhaps smooth Ike's relations with Montgomery, Churchill arranged a dinner the following evening with Eisenhower, Smith, and Alan Brooke, the British chief of staff. "It did a lot of good," Brooke wrote afterward. "There is no doubt that Ike is all out to do all he can to maintain the best relations between British and Americans, but it is equally clear that he knows nothing about strategy."[68] To Montgomery, Brooke wrote,

> It is quite clear that Ike considers that Dempsey [British Second Army] should be doing more than he does; it is equally clear that Ike has the very vaguest conception of the war! I drew his attention to what your basic strategy had been, i.e. to hold with your left and draw the Germans onto the flank while you pushed with your right. . . . Evidently he has some conception of attacking on the whole front, which must be an American doctrine judging by Mark Clark with Fifth Army in Italy![69]*

On July 26, Montgomery's concept came to fruition as Bradley launched J. Lawton Collins's VII Corps against the German line at Saint-Lô. The attack was preceded by a carpet bombing of unprecedented proportion as 2,500 Allied aircraft plastered the attack area with 4,000 tons of explosives.† Collins attacked on a narrow 7,000-yard front with three veteran divisions abreast, and three more, including the Big Red One and the 2nd and 3rd Armored, following behind. In two days, VII Corps advanced thirty miles against crum-

---

* "I told Ike that if he had any feelings that you were not running operations as he wished, he should most certainly tell you. That it was far better to put his cards on the table. He evidently is a little shy about doing so." Brooke to Montgomery, July 28, 1944, quoted in Arthur Bryant, *Triumph in the West: A History of the War Years Based on the Diaries of Field-Marshal Lord Alanbrooke, Chief of the Imperial General Staff* 192 (Garden City, N.Y.: Doubleday, 1959).

† General Lesley McNair, commander of Army Ground Forces, was visiting the front and was one of 111 American servicemen killed by bombs falling short of the intended impact area.

bling opposition. Patton's Third Army, which had assembled behind Collins's troops, was activated on August 1 and tore through the gap in the German line. VII Corps was attached to Patton, and what had been a breakthrough became a breakout. "The whole Western Front has been ripped open," von Kluge informed Berlin. "The left flank has collapsed."[70]

Patton raced into Brittany virtually unchecked. VII Corps captured the vital town of Mortain, on which Third Army then pivoted and swung east into the plain of southern Normandy, driving on Le Mans and Alençon and the German supply depots behind the battlefield.

"Once a gap appears in the enemy front," Montgomery instructed Bradley, "we must pass into it and through it and beyond it into the enemy rear areas. Everyone must go all out. The broad strategy of the Allied armies is to swing the right flank towards Paris and to force the enemy back to the Seine."[71] In the next three days, Patton advanced one hundred miles, cutting deep into the rear of von Kluge's forces, which now faced encirclement as the Canadian First Army came on from the north.

On August 7, Eisenhower moved his advance command post from Portsmouth across the Channel to the Norman village of Tournières, about twelve miles southwest of Bayeux. Bradley's Twelfth Army Group headquarters was activated, and General Courtney Hodges replaced Bradley at the head of First Army. There were now four Allied armies in France: the First and Third U.S. armies (Hodges and Patton) under Bradley's operational control; and the Second British (Dempsey) and First Canadian (Crerar) reporting to Twenty-first Army Group. But Montgomery, not Ike, retained overall command of the ground war.

The site of Eisenhower's headquarters (SHELLBURST) was a bucolic apple orchard surrounded by hedgerows—a rustic, pastoral retreat where, according to Summersby, "we had our first good nights of sleep in weeks, free of the [German] buzz bombs."[72] A few days after Ike moved in, local farmers presented him with a cow so that he might have fresh milk. "The first morning we had it," said his mess sergeant Marty Snyder, "Moaney, Hunt, and I gathered around the cow and tried to solve how to get milk out of it. Each of us tried, pulling, squeezing, massaging, but we couldn't get a drop."

"What's going on here?" asked Ike.

"We can't get this thing to work," Snyder said.

"Let me sit down," Eisenhower replied. "I'll show you how to do this."

Snyder got up from the stool and Ike sat down. Then, in steady strokes, he began to milk the cow. In a few minutes the bucket was full.

"You city slickers have a lot to learn," said Ike.[73]

Eisenhower's spirits soared. Patton had broken out, the British and Canadians were moving ahead, and it would only be a matter of time until the ports of Brittany were under Allied control. "I am extremely hopeful about the outcome of our current operations," he cabled Marshall on August 11. "If we can destroy a good portion of the enemy's army now in front of us we will have a greater freedom of movement in northern France and I would expect things to move very rapidly."[74]

Once again, Hitler came to the aid of the Allies. Von Kluge and his commanders planned to fall back to a shorter line roughly along the Seine and the Yonne to the Swiss frontier. But Hitler, ever more irrational since the July 20, 1944, attempt on his life, rejected the plan and ordered an all-out counterattack at Mortain, the shoulder of Third Army's breakout. If successful, Patton's armored columns would be cut off. For twenty-four hours, the German attack wedge of four panzer divisions moved forward. But the heroic stand of the U.S. 30th Division outside Mortain, which Collins called "one of the outstanding small-unit actions of World War II"[75]—combined with the round-the-clock bombardment from the air—forced the Germans to fall back. Hitler ordered the attack renewed and forbade any retreat. After a week of some of the most desperate fighting of the war, the remnants of the German Seventh Army and Fifth Panzer Army were almost completely encircled in the Falaise pocket. Von Kluge ordered a retreat without Hitler's permission, and some forty thousand soldiers made their escape before the Allies closed the gap. On August 19, the tanks of the French 2nd Armored

Division, under General Jacques Leclerc,[*] serving with Patton's Third Army, met the oncoming units of the Canadian First Army, trapping more than fifty thousand German troops and ending the battle for Normandy.

The battlefield at Falaise was one of the greatest killing grounds of the war in the West. "Forty-eight hours after the closing of the gap," Eisenhower wrote, "I was conducted through it on foot, to encounter scenes that could only be described by Dante. It was literally possible to walk for hundreds of yards at a time, stepping on nothing but dead and decaying flesh."[76] A veteran officer who had fought in the battles of the Aisne-Marne, Saint-Mihiel, and the Meuse-Argonne in World War I, said,

> None of those compared to what I saw yesterday [at Falaise]. It was as if an avenging angel had swept the area bent on destroying all things German. As far as my eye could see, on every line of sight, there were vehicles, wagons, tanks, guns, prime movers, rolling kitchens, etc., in various stages of destruction. [But] I saw no foxholes or any other type of shelter or field fortifications. The Germans were running and had no place to run. They were

---

[*] Unlike the Free French forces that were fighting in Italy, and the First French Army that would land on the Riviera (DRAGOON), which were primarily African troops, the French 2nd Armored Division was composed of native Frenchmen, a smattering of white legionnaires (Spanish, Italian, Czech, and Polish), plus the Régiment de Marche du Tchad and a battalion of Moroccan Spahis. It was formed especially for OVERLORD and to represent France at the liberation of Paris. The division was transferred from North Africa to Yorkshire in April 1944, and landed in France as part of Patton's Third Army on July 29.

General Jacques Leclerc (raised posthumously to the rank of marshal of France) was the nom de guerre of the Viscount Jacques-Philippe de Hauteclocque, a career French Army officer who had joined de Gaulle in 1940 and had assumed the pseudonym "Leclerc" to protect his family in France. A legendary battlefield commander, Leclerc was most famous for fighting his way north with a Free French force 420 miles from Fort Lamy in Chad to join the British Eighth Army in the Sahara in February 1941. John Keegan, *Six Armies in Normandy: From D-Day to the Liberation of Paris, June 6th –August 25th, 1944* 300–301 (New York: Viking Press, 1982).

probably too exhausted to dig. They were probably too tired even to surrender.[77]

The fighting in Normandy had raged for seventy-five days. The German Army Group B, commanded initially by Rommel, then by von Kluge,[*] had committed two veteran armies, the Seventh and Fifth Panzer, some forty divisions (600,000 men), and 1,500 tanks to the battle. The Allies deployed four armies, also totaling about forty divisions, 600,000 men, and 3,000 tanks. The vital difference was in the air. The Allies brought more than 12,000 aircraft to the battle; the Germans had almost none. When the fighting ended, the Germans had lost almost 500,000 men, killed, wounded, or captured, and virtually all of their equipment. Allied losses totaled almost 200,000, two-thirds of whom were American.[78] The Allied losses were quickly replenished; the German losses were irreplaceable.

As the battle for Normandy wound down, von Kluge was recalled to Berlin, and having been implicated in the July 20 plot on Hitler's life, committed suicide on a side road near Valmy, France, on August 17, 1944. He was succeeded by Field Marshal Walther Model (sometimes known as "Hitler's fireman"), who had successfully restored the German battle line on the eastern front after Operation BAGRATION.

As Model attempted to reestablish a defensive position, Alexander Patch's Seventh U.S. Army and Jean de Lattre de Tassigny's First French Army landed on the Riviera (DRAGOON) and began to move quickly up the Rhône Valley. Both armies were controlled by Sixth Army Group, commanded by General Jacob Devers. The port of Marseilles was captured by the French in undamaged condition, easing the Allies' supply problem, while Patch's Seventh Army, advancing up the Route Napoléon, reached Grenoble on August 20, 1944, aided substantially by the work of the Resistance (FFI), which was at its strongest in the region.

---

* On July 17, 1944, Rommel was seriously injured in an automobile accident after his car had been strafed by Allied aircraft. He returned to Germany to convalesce, and was succeeded by von Kluge, who assumed the command of Army Group B as well as continuing as commander in chief west.

While Sixth Army Group came on from the south, Patton continued his relentless advance toward the Seine. Le Mans, Orléans, and Chartres fell to Third Army as German resistance collapsed. Patton's columns moved so quickly, and his corps were so widely dispersed, that he resorted to flying forward in artillery spotter planes. "This Army covers so much ground that I have to fly in [Piper] Cubs most places," he wrote his wife on August 18. "I don't like it. I feel like a clay pigeon."[79] In Washington, Secretary Stimson chortled that Patton had "set his tanks to run around France like bedbugs in a Georgetown kitchen."[80]

On August 19, the day the gap closed on the Falaise pocket, the 79th Division of Third Army reached the Seine, thirty-five miles west of Paris. There they found an undamaged hydroelectric dam with a footbridge on top, and quickly established a bridgehead on the other side of the river. Patton paid a flying visit and proudly told Bradley, "I pissed in the Seine this morning."[81]

Eisenhower and Montgomery planned to bypass Paris and accelerate the pursuit of the retreating Germans. Patton's Third Army would swing south of the city, cross the Seine at Melum, near Fontainebleau, and move east toward Metz and the German border. Hodges's First Army would pass north of the city heading for Reims, the Ardennes, and Luxembourg. Meanwhile, Twenty-first Army Group would assault the V-1 and V-2 launching sites in the Pas-de-Calais, move into Belgium, and take the port of Antwerp. Eisenhower feared that if the Germans defended Paris, the street fighting would consume the Allies for a month. Casualties would be high and the collateral damage would be unacceptable. Paris was still undamaged. The bridges across the Seine had been spared in the bombing campaign Harris and Spaatz waged to isolate the Normandy battlefield, and the rail yards likewise had not been struck. There was also a serious logistical problem of providing food and fuel for a city of four million people. The primary Allied supply line stretched 250 miles to Cherbourg, and was already overburdened. Until the linkups to Marseilles and Antwerp were achieved, Eisenhower thought it best to leave the Germans saddled with supplying Paris. Fearing a repeat of the premature popular uprising that had just taken place in Warsaw, General Pierre Koenig, commanding the French Forces of the Interior, issued firm instructions to the Resistance to stand down until notified.

But Paris would not wait. On August 12, French railway workers walked off the job, paralyzing the city's transportation net. On the fifteenth, the Paris police force went out on strike. On the eighteenth, the postal service shut down, the Communist newspaper, *L'Humanité,* called for an *insurrection populaire,* and three thousand policemen, armed but wearing civilian clothes, seized the *préfecture de police* and hoisted the *tricolore.* Two days later, a Gaullist group took possession of the Hôtel de Ville, the seat of the city government.

De Gaulle, still in Algiers, monitored the situation closely. On August 15 he advised General Jumbo Wilson, the overall Allied commander in the Mediterranean, that he wished to return to France in the next day or two. (The trip required Allied approval.) Wilson forwarded the request to Ike, who informed the Combined Chiefs that he had no objection, and that he thought de Gaulle wished to be present at the liberation of Paris. Eisenhower pointedly asked whether de Gaulle's "rather premature arrival will in any way embarrass the British or American governments."[82]

At the War Department, Eisenhower's query was fielded by John McCloy, who raised no objection. Neither the White House nor the State Department was consulted.[83] The British were more than eager for de Gaulle to return, and had already begun to worry about a possible Communist insurrection in Paris.[84] With the way cleared, de Gaulle arrived at Eisenhower's headquarters in Tournières on August 20. Ike greeted him warmly.

Eisenhower briefed de Gaulle quickly on the military situation, and explained that he intended to bypass Paris for the moment. De Gaulle expressed concern. "Why cross the Seine everywhere but Paris?" he asked. It was a matter of national importance. The population of Paris was already in revolt, and it was essential to send troops into the city as soon as possible. De Gaulle's concern was twofold: the danger of a Communist takeover (the French Communists constituted the most active element of the Resistance in Paris), and the necessity to preclude a Darlan-type deal that elements of the American government appeared to be negotiating with Pierre Laval, the premier of the Vichy regime.[*] De Gaulle suggested that Leclerc's 2nd Armored Division be ordered to Paris immediately, and gently hinted that if Ike delayed too long, he would order Leclerc to Paris himself. According to de Gaulle, Eisenhower was visibly embarrassed at the delay and agreed that when the time came, he would send Leclerc to Paris to lead the liberation. But he could not set a date.[85]

If the Germans defended Paris, Eisenhower's strategy had merit. Hitler had ordered his new commanders, Field Marshal Model, now the commander in chief west, and General der Infanterie Dietrich von Choltitz, the military governor of Paris, to hold the city at all costs. "The loss of Paris always means the loss of France," the Führer told Model. "Paris must not fall into the hands of the enemy except as a field of ruins."[86] Model was ordered to form his battle line on the Seine, with Paris as the *Schwerpunkt*. Von Choltitz was told "the fighting in and around Paris will be conducted without regard to the destruction of the city." The bridges and monuments were to be wired for demolition, the waterworks and power plants to be destroyed, and the principal industrial sites leveled to the ground.[87]

There was nothing in the military backgrounds of Model or von Choltitz to suggest that Hitler's orders would not be obeyed. Both were hard-bitten combat commanders—muddy boots generals with well-earned reputations for faithfully discharging their duty. If Rommel was Germany's offensive beau ideal, Model had won acclaim as a defensive virtuoso in three years on the Russian front. Choltitz, for his part, had dropped with the first paratroop battalion on Rotterdam in 1940, and led the regiment that stormed the fortress at Sevastopol in 1942. He was appointed military governor of Paris on August 7, 1944, precisely because the OKW told Hitler that Choltitz was "an officer who had never questioned an order no matter how harsh it was."[88]

---

[*] Laval proposed to reconvene the French National Assembly, which had not met since 1940, and officially welcome the Allies to Paris, instituting direct Allied military rule through local Vichy officials and undercutting de Gaulle and the French Committee of National Liberation. Allen Dulles, heading OSS efforts in Bern, Switzerland, was allegedly in contact with Laval's agents. The plot imploded when Laval could find no French notables to cooperate. See de Gaulle, 2 *War Memoirs* 324–33; David Eisenhower, *Eisenhower at War* 415.

Model was the first to recognize that Hitler's orders would lead to the destruction of the German Army in France. Patton was racing across the Seine south and east of Paris, and Montgomery was crossing the river to the west. To hold Paris would mean another encirclement, and would open the door for the Allies to advance into the German heartland. Model told Berlin that he could hold Paris with two hundred thousand more troops and six additional panzer divisions. But without them he was withdrawing north of the city and would try to form a defensive line on the Marne and the Somme. "Tell the Führer that I know what I'm doing," he told an incredulous Jodl in Berlin.[89] On August 20, Model issued orders to the German First Army and Fifth Panzer Army to evacuate their position in front of Paris, cross the Seine using the bridges in the city, and move north. Paris would become von Choltitz's responsibility.

With no battle to be fought in front of Paris, von Choltitz faced a difficult choice. He could carry out his orders and destroy the city, or he could surrender it. For a fourth-generation Prussian officer, married to the daughter of a general of William II, the choice was not easy. "I try always to do my duty," he wrote his wife on August 21, 1944. "I must often ask God to help me find the path on which it lies."[90] To gain time, and to maintain a modicum of order in the city, von Choltitz struck a seventy-two-hour truce with the Resistance. Von Choltitz agreed to recognize the FFI as military combatants, and the Resistance agreed to allow the retreating columns of Army Group B to move through the city without being fired upon. Of one thing von Choltitz could be certain: Although the bridges and monuments of Paris were being wired for demolition, the discipline of the Wehrmacht was such that no one would set them off until he gave the order.

De Gaulle, who was triumphantly touring liberated France, increased his pressure on Eisenhower. On August 21 he wrote Ike from Brittany that serious trouble could arise in Paris at any moment. "I believe it is necessary to have Paris occupied by the French and Allied forces as soon as possible even if it means a certain amount of fighting and a certain amount of damage within the city." If disorder broke out, said de Gaulle, it would be difficult to contain "and might even hinder subsequent military operations."[91]

The Resistance and von Choltitz also mounted appeals. Representatives of the FFI made their way into the American lines on August 22, were shuttled from Patton to Bradley, and made clear that the way to Paris was open. The German Army was moving north, the city was running short of food, and the truce that had been negotiated was about to expire. The Allies must come quickly.

Equally important, Von Choltitz had resolved his dilemma. If a battle were to have been fought at Paris, he could accept its destruction. But he was not willing to go down in history as the man who destroyed Paris wantonly. On August 22 he deputized the Swedish consul general, Raoul Nordling, to inform the Allies of the danger hanging over Paris. Von Choltitz said he would not obey the orders he had been given to destroy it, and he wanted to surrender the city intact. But the Allies must come quickly. Hitler and the OKW were pressing him to commence the demolitions, and it was only a matter of time until he would be relieved of command. "Twenty-four, forty-eight hours are all you have. After that, I cannot promise you what will happen here."[92]*

The converging requests by de Gaulle, the Resistance, and von Choltitz caused Eisenhower to reconsider his strategic decision to bypass Paris. De Gaulle warned of a repeat of the Paris Commune of 1871 if the Allies did not arrive quickly. And after the civil affairs

---

* The day after von Choltitz dispatched Nordling, he was visited at his office in the Hotel Meurice by four SS officers from Berlin. Von Choltitz assumed they had found out about Nordling's mission and had come to arrest him. Instead, they said they had been sent by Heinrich Himmler to take possession of the Bayeux Tapestry and bring it to Germany. The tapestry had been evacuated from Bayeux and for safekeeping was stored in the Louvre.

"*Ach, Kinder,*" said a visibly relieved von Choltitz. "How wonderful of you to help save these valuable objects from destruction. While you are at it, why not take the *Mona Lisa* and *Winged Victory* as well?"

"No, no," the senior SS officer replied. The only thing Himmler and the Führer wanted was the Bayeux Tapestry.

Von Choltitz led the four men to the balcony and showed them the Louvre across the Tuileries Gardens. It was occupied by the Resistance, but if they wished, von Choltitz said he would put an armored car and a squad of soldiers at their disposal. The SS officers saluted and withdrew. They would radio Berlin for instructions. Von Choltitz never saw them again. Larry Collins and Dominique Lapierre, *Is Paris Burning?* 197–99 (New York: Simon and Schuster, 1965).

donnybrook in North Africa, Ike had learned to trust de Gaulle's judgment. The Resistance said the road to Paris was open. If that were the case, could Ike refuse to take it? And then there was the message from von Choltitz.

Eisenhower had lived in Paris for a year and a half. He knew the city better than any British or American general—and better than Churchill or Eden, better than Roosevelt or Stimson. If von Choltitz had refused to destroy Paris, Ike decided he was not going to give Hitler a second chance.

"What the hell, Brad. I guess we'll have to go in. Tell Leclerc to saddle up."[93]

Eisenhower's decision was political and moral, but not military. Every West Point cadet is taught time and again that General George Meade erred in 1863 when he did not pursue Lee after Gettysburg. And by not devoting all of his resources to chasing the broken German Army, Ike was inevitably prolonging the war. His cable to the Combined Chiefs informing them of his decision is one of the most important he ever wrote: a masterpiece of subtlety and insinuation.

Eisenhower rejected making an overt political announcement about Paris because he knew it would carry little weight with the chiefs. And so he couched his decision in purely military terms. On the evening of August 22, Ike cabled Washington that from a logistics standpoint it would be wise to defer the capture of Paris. "I do not believe this is possible. If the enemy tries to hold Paris with any real strength he would be a constant menace to our flank. If he largely evacuates the place, it falls into our hands whether we like it or not." Ike did not explicitly tell the Combined Chiefs he was going to take Paris, but the implication was clear.

The French 2nd Armored Division had just closed the door on the Germans in the Falaise pocket and was 122 miles west of Paris when Leclerc received Bradley's order to move out. With sixteen thousand troops and four thousand vehicles, Leclerc advanced in three columns, overcame scattered German resistance, and arrived at the suburbs of Paris on the evening of August 24, 1944.[94] The church bells of the city tolled his arrival. The next day, August 25, the 2nd Armored, supported by the U.S. 4th Division, entered Paris. For reasons of military honor, the German garrison mounted a token

De Gaulle and General Leclerc at Leclerc's headquarters at the Gare Mont-parnesse.

resistance, and von Choltitz surrendered the city to Leclerc in the early afternoon.[95]* De Gaulle appointed General Pierre Koenig military governor of Paris, and took up residence at the home of the president of France, the Palais de l'Élysée.

On Saturday, August 26, de Gaulle relit the flame at the tomb of the unknown at the Arc de Triomphe, and then on foot, followed by

---

* Dietrich von Choltitz was released from Allied captivity in 1947, and died at Baden-Baden in 1966. In his later years, von Choltitz was shunned by his fellow Wehrmacht officers, but became warm friends with General Pierre Koenig, who attended his funeral together with the ranking military officers of the Fifth Republic in full regalia.

Walther Model commanded Army Group B for the remainder of the war. As the curtain came down in April 1945, he discharged the oldest and youngest soldiers under his command so they could return to their homes. Model then walked into the woods near Duisburg and committed suicide.

Army Group B had three wartime commanders: Rommel, von Kluge, and Model. All three committed suicide.

Place de la Concorde, during the fighting on August 25, 1944.

Generals Juin, Koenig, Leclerc, and the notables of the Resistance, led the 2nd Armored Division down the Champs-Élysées to the Place de la Concorde. Two million Parisians lined the route—"a miracle of national consciousness," in de Gaulle's words, "one of those gestures which sometimes, in the course of centuries, illuminate the history of France."[96] From the Place de la Concorde, de Gaulle went to Notre Dame for the traditional Te Deum. Again, the route was lined with an exuberant tide of spectators, and the cathedral was jammed. At de Gaulle's request, Monsignor Jacques Suhard, the cardinal-archbishop of Paris, a buttress of the Vichy regime, remained in his residence and the service was conducted by Monsignor Paul Brot, the next senior prelate.

Eisenhower stayed away from Paris that day to avoid stealing the limelight from de Gaulle. "I desired that he, as the symbol of French resistance, should make an entrance before I had to go in."[97] But on Sunday, August 27, Ike and Bradley took a whirlwind tour of the city, after which Eisenhower paid a formal call on de Gaulle at the Palais de l'Élysée: the supreme commander of Allied forces paying

De Gaulle leading the victory parade down the Champs-Élysées. General Leclerc is over de Gaulle's left shoulder.

tribute to the president of France. "I did this very deliberately as a kind of de facto recognition of him as the provisional President of France," Eisenhower explained years later. "He was very grateful—he never forgot it—looked upon it as a very definite recognition of his high position. That was of course what he wanted and what Roosevelt had never given him."[98]

On his own authority, Eisenhower initialed a civil affairs agreement "to provide a secure rear area," which effectively transferred civil power in France to de Gaulle.[99] He also said he planned to establish SHAEF headquarters at Versailles, to which de Gaulle readily agreed. "I thought it was advantageous to have the Allied commander in chief not lodged in Paris but useful that he be nearby."[100] De Gaulle asked Ike's help with food and fuel for the city, and said he would like to retain the 2nd Armored for several days to ensure order. He also asked for two American divisions to parade through the city as an additional show of force, to which Ike agreed. The following afternoon, the 28th Infantry Division and the 5th Armored marched down the Champs-Élysées on their way through Paris to engage German forces north of the city. De Gaulle took the review, flanked by Bradley and Leclerc.[101]

In the end, Paris was saved by the actions of five men: Model, who ignored Hitler's order to defend the city and moved Army Group B north to the Marne and the Somme; von Choltitz, who reached out to the Resistance and disobeyed the Führer's instruction to demolish the city; Leclerc, who moved more than a hundred miles in two days and provided a massive show of force that snuffed out any potential Communist insurrection; de Gaulle, who steadfastly exerted every ounce of influence as president of the provisional government to save Paris; and Eisenhower, who rejected textbook military doctrine and let common sense prevail. Ike may not have understood Montgomery's strategy in Normandy, but when confronted with the most important decision of his career to that point, he made it without flinching.[102]

# FIFTEEN

# Germany

It's all so terrible, so awful, that I constantly
wonder how "civilization" can stand war at all.
— DWIGHT D. EISENHOWER,
*November 12, 1944*

EISENHOWER'S DECISION TO liberate Paris marked the end of
his apprenticeship and his entrance onto the world stage. On his own
authority, without seeking the approval of the Combined Chiefs of
Staff, the British war cabinet, or Washington, he had installed a new
government in France, saved Paris from destruction, and received
the adulation of the French people. By providing de Gaulle the opportunity to occupy the Palais de l'Élysée, he outmaneuvered FDR
and the State Department so skillfully that he left no fingerprints.

Eisenhower was still a Kansas original. He talked too loudly, peppered his conversation with sports-page aphorisms, smoked excessively, and made no effort to conceal his relationship with Kay
Summersby. Yet he was no longer just George Marshall's protégé—the
too-young general officer catapulted ahead of 263 more senior soldiers; the inexperienced supreme commander who had never seen
combat; the American interloper shunted ahead of more seasoned
British allies. Like de Gaulle, Eisenhower arrived on the world scene
unheralded. But whereas de Gaulle made his way by forcing his iron
will on others, Ike moved by subtlety and indirection. His amiable
personality and avuncular enthusiasm concealed a calculating political instinct that had been honed to perfection.

Ike's political dexterity stood in marked contrast to his grasp of military strategy. On strategic issues he remained a prisoner of the doughboy dogma of John J. Pershing and George Marshall that all-out-attack-all-along-the-line was the way to win wars. That was the lesson the Americans (but not the British, French, or Germans) took from World War I.[*] It was propagated at Leavenworth and the War College, and Ike was a disciple, as were most American officers.[1] George Patton and Douglas MacArthur were the exceptions. Said differently, no one who wore the uniform of the United States or Great Britain during the Second World War possessed the political acumen of Eisenhower. But Ike's understanding of the battlefield was abstract and academic.

The contrast became evident immediately after the liberation of Paris. On September 1, 1944, Eisenhower assumed direct command of the ground war. Montgomery reverted to command of Twenty-first Army Group (the British Second Army and First Canadian Army); Bradley commanded Twelfth Army Group (the First and Third U.S. armies); and Jacob Devers commanded Sixth Army Group coming up from the south (the First French Army and U.S. Seventh Army). The very qualities that made Eisenhower successful as supreme commander militated against his success on the battlefield. As a military statesman, Ike's emphasis on team play, his willingness to compromise, and his ability to reconcile diverse interests were unique assets. But as a field commander, where decisiveness is essential, Eisenhower's preference for consensus became a liability. A slightly ambiguous directive at the headquarters of an Allied coalition may facilitate agreement; an ambiguous order in the field will lead to confusion and perhaps even disaster.

If Eisenhower had remained above the fray and left the ground war to Montgomery, would the fighting in Europe have ended

* Some commentators suggest the head-on American strategy traces to Ulysses Grant in the Civil War. That is a superficial reading of Grant. When Grant saw the Confederate fortifications at Vicksburg in 1863, he eschewed a frontal attack, broke off from his supply base at Memphis, crossed the Mississippi south of Vicksburg, and besieged the fortress from the east—maneuver, not frontal attack. Similarly, after a fruitless charge at Cold Harbor in 1864 (which Grant always regretted), he broke contact with Lee, stealthily crossed the James River below Richmond, and moved on Petersburg. Indeed, throughout the entire 1864–65 campaign in Virginia, Grant continually sidled to his left to maneuver Lee out of his fortifications. Jean Edward Smith, *Grant* (New York: Simon and Schuster, 2001).

# ALLIED GROUND FORCES COMMAND
## September 1, 1944

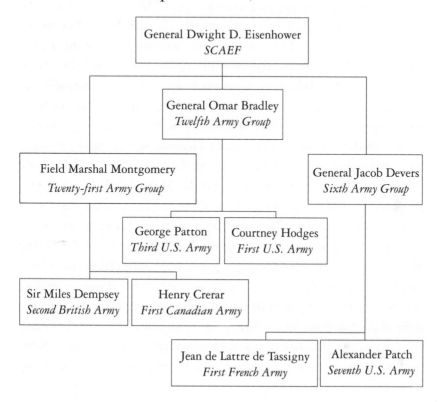

General Dwight D. Eisenhower
*SCAEF*

General Omar Bradley
*Twelfth Army Group*

Field Marshal Montgomery
*Twenty-first Army Group*

General Jacob Devers
*Sixth Army Group*

George Patton
*Third U.S. Army*

Courtney Hodges
*First U.S. Army*

Sir Miles Dempsey
*Second British Army*

Henry Crerar
*First Canadian Army*

Jean de Lattre de Tassigny
*First French Army*

Alexander Patch
*Seventh U.S. Army*

sooner? Would the Western Allies have taken Berlin before the Russians? Field Marshal Sir Alan Brooke, chief of the imperial general staff, certainly thought so. "Eisenhower's decision to assume command in the field is likely to add another 3 to 6 months on to the war," Brooke confided to his diary on August 28. "He [Eisenhower] straight away wants to split his forces, sending an American contingent toward Nancy whilst the British army group moves along the coast. If the Germans were not as beat as they are, this would be a fatal move. As it is, it may not do too much harm."[2] As Brooke suggests, Eisenhower's assumption of command may have made little difference. After the fall of Paris and the rout of the German Army in France, Allied victory was inevitable. It was merely a question of time. A more pertinent question is whether, if Ike had not assumed control of the ground war, would he have received the victor's acclaim that led him to the White House?[*]

The German collapse in France caught SHAEF by surprise. The planning for OVERLORD assumed the Germans would be forced back to a defensive line on the Seine roughly four months after D-Day. At that point the Allies would pause and regroup. But Model's decision to withdraw the German Army created an unanticipated vacuum. "An orderly retreat became impossible," wrote General Hans Speidel, Model's chief of staff. "The Allied motorized armies surrounded the slow and exhausted German foot divisions in separate groups and smashed them up. Weakened remnants of the Fifth Panzer and Seventh Armies reached the Meuse on September 5th. Only a hundred armored vehicles and heavy guns crossed the river."[3]

On the left of the Allied line, Montgomery's Twenty-first Army Group outstripped Patton and advanced two hundred miles in less than a week. While the Canadian First Army mopped up the Channel ports, Bimbo Dempsey's British troops entered Belgium on September 2, 1944, liberated Brussels a day later, and captured the vital port of Antwerp on September 4. To Montgomery's right, Courtney Hodges's First U.S. Army rolled northeast through Soissons to Mons and on to Namur in Belgium. In the center, Patton's Third Army

---

[*] In a postwar interview, Montgomery confirmed his view that Eisenhower and SHAEF had been ill-prepared for running the ground war. "The whole command setup was fundamentally wrong. There was no one who could give his complete and undivided attention to the day-to-day direction of the land battle as a whole. Eisenhower had not the experience, the knowledge or the time. He should have been devoting himself to questions of overall strategy, to political problems, to problems of inter-Allied relations and military government. . . . Instead he insisted on trying to run the land battle himself. Here he was out of his depth and in trying to do this, he neglected his real job on the highest level." "Allied Strategy After the Fall of Paris," Montgomery interview by Wilmot, March 23, 1949, Wilmot Collection, Liddell Hart Papers, cited in D'Este, *Eisenhower* 596. Carlo D'Este, one of a new generation of historians, notes Montgomery's observation was "not without justification." His willingness to consider Montgomery's critique objectively stands in marked contrast to the first generation of American historians of the war in Europe. Official Army historians Forrest Pogue and Martin Blumenson treated Eisenhower and Marshall as demigods, and early biographers such as Kenneth Davis, Stephen Ambrose, and Kevin McCann took their cue from them. All rejected Monty's criticism as sour grapes.

took Reims and then wheeled east through Verdun toward Metz. Another column of Patton's army headed due east and captured Nancy. Farther south, Devers's Sixth Army Group linked up with Third Army at Dijon. Alexander Patch's Seventh Army went into position next to Third Army, while the French First Army held the extreme right of the Allied line from Vesoul in the foothills of the Vosges Mountains to the Swiss frontier.

From the breakout at Saint-Lô on July 26, Allied forces had advanced three hundred miles in little over a month. The greater part of France, Belgium, and Luxembourg had been liberated, and Patton's Third Army stood within eighty miles of the German border.[4] But it was in Belgium that opportunity beckoned most urgently. The British Second Army had halted on the Meuse-Escaut Canal, 280 miles north of the Seine, with Antwerp, the Belgian airfields, and an undamaged rail net securely under their control. A SHAEF intelligence report indicated that the Germans possessed only two weakened panzer divisions and nine badly battered infantry divisions north of the Ardennes.[5] According to Model's own estimate, the Allies held a ten-to-one advantage in tanks, three to one in artillery, and an "almost unlimited" superiority in airpower.[6]

One hundred and thirty miles to the northeast of the British Second Army was the Ruhr—Germany's industrial heartland. The terrain between the Meuse-Escaut Canal and the Ruhr was open and rolling. It was a classic invasion route that had been used (in reverse) by Alfred von Schlieffen and Helmuth von Moltke in planning the German assault in 1914. Beyond the Ruhr, across the unobstructed North German plain, lay Berlin—another two hundred miles away. Rarely in any war has there been such an opportunity.[7]

Montgomery urged Ike to strike quickly. The end of the war in Europe was within reach. The Twenty-first and Twelfth army groups should advance side by side north of the Ardennes—"a solid mass of some forty divisions which would be so strong that it need fear nothing."[8] As Monty wrote later, it was "the German Schlieffen Plan of 1914 in reverse, except that it would be executed against a shattered and disorganized enemy. Its success depended on the concentration of Allied strength on the left wing."[9]

Bradley countered with his own proposal for a single thrust into

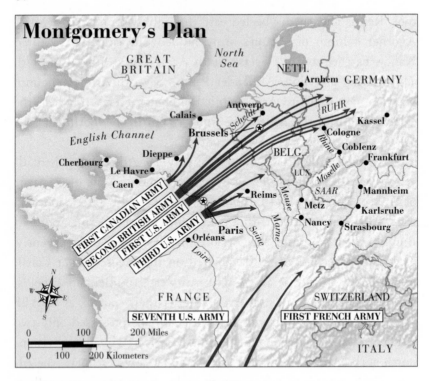

Montgomery's Plan

Germany, except that it would be led by Twelfth Army Group south of the Ardennes, through the Eifel Mountains and Pfälzer Bergland into the Saar. Patton's Third Army would spearhead the drive along the axis Metz-Saarbrücken-Mannheim and on to Frankfurt. Ike had a choice. He could have adopted Montgomery's modified Schlieffen Plan or opted for the assault through the Frankfurt gap. Either would have retained the momentum of the Allied advance, although Monty's plan, given the terrain, was more feasible and would likely have ended the war sooner.

Eisenhower hesitated. Rather than choose between Montgomery and Bradley, Ike's penchant for compromise led him to opt for both. Monty was encouraged to press ahead, and Hodges's First U.S. Army was assigned to protect his right flank. At the same time, Patton was urged to continue his advance. By allowing both attacks to proceed, Eisenhower was adhering to the Marshall-Pershing strategy of maintaining pressure all along the line. That had been Ike's plan before D-Day, and like everyone else at SHAEF he was mentally unprepared

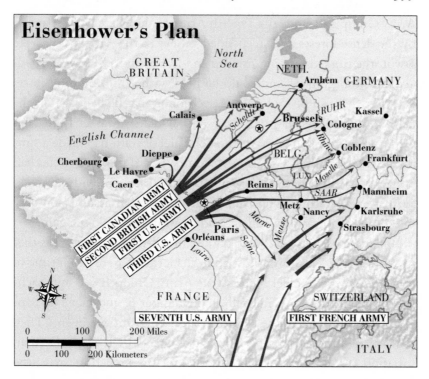

**Eisenhower's Plan**

to exploit the German collapse. Montgomery was critical, and so was Patton. As Monty saw it, Ike's approach of applying pressure all along the line would lead to stalemate all along the line—"just as it had in the First World War."[10] Patton, who was even more critical, called Eisenhower's decision "the most momentous error of the war."[11]

The first problem Eisenhower encountered was that the strained logistics of SHAEF would not support two simultaneous offensives. The pipelines that had been laid across the Channel (PLUTO) were supplying an abundance of fuel, but there was a shortage of transport to ship it forward. And to supply two fronts made it doubly difficult. Second, neither Bradley nor Montgomery was satisfied with the arrangement. Bradley continued to complain about losing Hodges's First Army to Montgomery (though it remained under Twelfth Army Group's command), and Ike soon reversed himself, ordering Hodges south of the Ardennes alongside Patton.

This was a strategic error pregnant with disaster. Not only was the drive on the Ruhr fatally weakened, but Montgomery's Twenty-first

Army Group and Bradley's Twelfth Army Group were now separated by the dense forests and steep-sided valleys of the Ardennes. As Ike saw it, the rugged terrain provided an ideal boundary between Bradley and Montgomery, and could be held with a minimum of force. The best that can be said of Ike's decision is that he had been in the field on maneuvers in June 1940, and evidently was unaware that General Maurice Gamelin, the French chief of staff, had made a similar calculation. The prevailing view in Western military circles had been that the impenetrable terrain of the Ardennes provided a shield against enemy armor. Von Rundstedt proved that assumption false in 1940 with devastating effect, and he would soon do so again.

But the most serious defect in Ike's broad-front strategy was that the Allied momentum was lost and the Germans were given time to recover. General Speidel reports that Army Group B was approaching a total collapse. Namur fell on September 6, and Liège on September 8. The door to the Reich through Belgium was open. "Then something unexpected occurred," wrote Speidel. "It was a German variation of the 'miracle on the Marne' for the French in 1914: the furious advance of the Allies suddenly faded away. There could be no serious supply difficulties with such secure lines of communication. Nor was the 'decreasing strength of the attack' the reason, as new or rested formations were being constantly brought up. *The method of the Allied Supreme Command was the main reason.*" As Speidel saw it, the Allies spread out and refitted rather than pursuing their advantage. "Had the Allies held on grimly to the retreating Germans they could have harried the breath out of every man and beast and ended the war half a year earlier. There were no German forces of any importance that could be thrown in, and next to nothing in the air. The battles in East Prussia and Hungary [on the eastern front] were at their climax and absorbed all available forces."[12]

General Günther Blumentritt, chief of staff of the entire western front until September 5, 1944, agreed with Speidel. A breakthrough northeast to the Ruhr "would have torn in pieces the weak German front and ended the war."[13] General Siegfried Westphal, Blumentritt's successor, concurred. "Not a single bridge over the Rhine had been prepared for demolition," wrote Westphal. "Until the middle of October the enemy could have broken through at any point he liked with ease, and would then have been able to cross the Rhine and thrust deep into Germany almost unhindered."[14]

But SHAEF's window of opportunity was brief. When the Allied advance halted, Hitler asked von Rundstedt to retake control of the western front. Model retained command of Army Group B, and between them they stitched together a defense that would hold the Allies for another six months.

The price the Allies paid for their missed opportunity in September was heavy. Of the 750,000 battle casualties the Western Allies suffered in Europe, two-thirds occurred after their autumn slowdown. The collateral costs were even greater. Millions of men and women on both sides died as a result of the continued fighting—to say nothing of the ongoing barbarism of Nazi concentration camps. The Red Army had not yet penetrated into central Europe in September 1944, and the occupation boundaries in Germany had yet to be drawn. The future of Europe hung in the balance.[15]

"Eisenhower's 'broad front' plan of advance to the Rhine," wrote respected military analyst B. H. Liddell Hart, "would have been a good way to strain and crack the resistance of a strong and still unbeaten enemy. But it was far less suited to the actual situation, where the enemy had already collapsed, and the issue depended on exploiting their collapse so deeply and rapidly that they would have no chance to rally. That called for pursuit without pause."[16]

Writing years later, Omar Bradley put Ike's decision in context. An all-out drive northeast to the Ruhr would have fallen under the control of Montgomery's Twenty-first Army Group. "It would give Monty too large a role in the ground command, in effect upstaging and obscuring Ike," said Bradley. "It was a time of extreme jingoism; the American public demanded its own epic-size war heroes, and it wanted them in command at the kill."[17] Stephen Ambrose, Eisenhower's most assiduous biographer, reached much the same conclusion. "Had Bradley and Patton been on the left, Eisenhower might have given greater consideration to the single-thrust concept, but handling Montgomery was another matter."[18]

The logistical problems Eisenhower encountered after the fall of Paris were by-products of his decision to advance on a broad front. To provide food, fuel, and ammunition for six armies across a front that stretched from the English Channel to the Swiss frontier required significantly more transport than was necessary to supply a single drive. The problem was exacerbated by the distance between Patton's Third Army and the Channel ports, which in many instances exceeded three hundred miles. Add to that the inevitable problems of waste, pilferage, and leakage to the black market. It required 650 tons of supplies a day to keep an American division in action. A German division of equivalent size managed on 200 tons.[19]

Many military commentators have blamed General John C. H. Lee, Ike's logistics chief, for the supply shortfall, and Lee was not without fault. His ill-advised decision to move his bloated COMZ (Communications Zone) headquarters to Paris in September clearly contributed to the problem. While Patton, Bradley, and Montgomery clamored for ammunition and gasoline, Lee commandeered badly needed fuel and shipping facilities to move 8,000 officers and 20,000 enlisted men to the City of Light, where they lived in sybaritic comfort. (The French subsequently complained that the demands of the American Army in Paris greatly exceeded those made by the Germans.)[20] As a consequence, Lee became the scapegoat for the logistics foul-up, and Patton and Bradley demanded his scalp.[21]

Eisenhower initially agreed. On September 20, 1944, he asked Marshall for a replacement for Lee. The War Department suggested several names, including Lucius D. Clay, who was then wearing two hats in Washington, as the nation's deputy director of war mobilization, under James Byrnes, and as the Army's chief of procurement. Ike picked Clay, an old friend who had served with him on MacArthur's staff in the Philippines, and who had earned a well-deserved reputation in Washington for his brisk, efficient management of war production. But when Clay arrived at SHAEF in early October, Ike had changed his mind about relieving Lee. Given time to reflect, Eisenhower concluded that the logistics shortfall was not entirely Lee's fault. Ike told Clay he was sorry, but since victory was in sight, he had decided to stick with Lee. The supply system might not work perfectly, but it worked, and he did not want to swap horses in the middle of the stream. At Ike's request, Clay went briefly to Cherbourg, where he unsnarled the port backup, and then returned to Washington.[22]

By mid-December, three and a half months after the liberation of

Paris, the Allies still had not crossed the Rhine. In the north, Twenty-first Army Group failed at Arnhem; the U.S. First Army ran into a German buzz saw in the Hürtgen Forest; and Patton stubbed his toe at Metz. In the south, Sixth Army Group reached the Rhine near Strasbourg in mid-November and laid on an assault crossing at Rastatt, but Eisenhower ordered Devers to stand down. Ike wanted to wait until Montgomery and Patton had moved up, and then force the river on a broad front, focusing on the Ruhr and the Saar. A crossing on the upper Rhine by Sixth Army Group, which would have outflanked the forces facing Patton, was not in SHAEF's plans.

The German forces facing Devers were stretched thin, and there were few reserves that could have been thrown in. But for the second time in 1944, Ike rejected the possibility of breaking the German line. Once again, personalities intervened. Just as the animus between Ike and Montgomery had precluded the September breakout toward the Ruhr, so the disdain Eisenhower felt for Devers contributed to the supreme commander's decision to halt Sixth Army Group west of the Rhine.[*]

As a result of Ike's insistence on a broad-front approach, the Allies inched forward along a 450-mile front from Basel to Antwerp. The days grew shorter, the cold became bitter, and whenever the ground thawed, men and vehicles were swamped in a sea of mud. Eisenhower described it as

> the dirtiest kind of infantry slugging. Advances were slow and laborious. Gains were ordinarily measured in terms of yards rather than miles. Operations became mainly a matter of artillery and ammunition, and, on the part of the infantry, endurance, stamina, and courage. Infantry losses were high, particularly in rifle platoons. Frostbite, trench foot, and respiratory diseases also took a toll. Because of

---

[*] The strained relations between Eisenhower and Devers, and Ike's decision to forestall Sixth Army Group's advance, is treated in detail in David P. Colley's *Decision at Strasbourg: Ike's Strategic Mistake to Halt the Sixth Army Group at the Rhine in 1944* (Annapolis: Naval Institute Press, 2008). Like Carlo D'Este, Colley represents a new generation of military analysts who question the conventional wisdom pertaining to Western strategy in Europe during World War II.

depletion of their infantry strength, divisions quickly exhausted themselves in action.[23]

Between September and mid-December 1944, Patton's Third Army advanced less than twenty-five miles and suffered 53,182 casualties. The U.S. First Army lost 47,034 men, killed, wounded, and missing during the same period. The U.S. Ninth Army, under General William H. Simpson, which was thrown into the line between Hodges and Montgomery in late October, suffered 10,056 combat losses. The three armies of Twelfth Army Group sustained an additional 113,742 nonbattle casualties, mostly trench foot and combat fatigue, and lost almost a thousand tanks.[24] "To put it candidly," wrote Omar Bradley, "we were mired in a ghastly war of attrition."[25]

Montgomery remained critical of Eisenhower's strategy. "I personally regard the whole thing as dreadful," Monty confided to Field Marshal Sir Alan Brooke. "I think now that if we want the war to end within any reasonable period you will have to get Eisenhower's hand taken off the land battle. He has never commanded anything in his whole career; now, for the first time, he has elected to take direct command of very large-scale operations and he does not know how to do it."[26] Bradley, Devers, and Patton shared Monty's doubts, but kept their opinions to themselves. Brooke, on the other hand, tackled the issue head-on.

Meeting with the British chiefs of staff (BCOS) on November 24, Brooke called for Ike's replacement.

> I put before the Committee my views on the very unsatisfactory state of affairs in France, with no one running the land battle. Eisenhower, though supposed to be doing so, is on the golf links at Reims—entirely detached and taking practically no part in the running of the war. Matters got so bad lately that a deputation of [Major General J. F. M. "Jock"] Whiteley [SHAEF's deputy chief of staff], Bedell Smith and a few others went up to tell him that he must get down to it and RUN the war, which he said he would. Personally, I think he is incapable of running the war even if he tries.[27]

The BCOS agreed that Brooke should take the matter to Churchill and, since there were now twice as many American forces under SHAEF as British and Canadian, suggest that Bradley be named overall ground commander; that Patton succeed Bradley at Twelfth Army Group; and that Ike return to his duties as supreme commander. "It is one of the most difficult problems I have had to tackle," Brooke confided to his diary.[28]

Brooke met with the prime minister on November 28. "The American conception of attacking all along the front, irrespective of the strength available, was sheer madness," he told Churchill. SHAEF was attacking on six army fronts without any reserves anywhere. "We are bogged down and reduced to the trench warfare it has always been our object to avoid."[29] When Brooke suggested that Bradley assume command of the ground war, Churchill said he would prefer Alexander. Since Brooke had little confidence in Alexander, the matter was left in abeyance.

For von Rundstedt, the Allied slowdown was a godsend. The breathing space permitted the old field marshal to restore an element of cohesion to the German front. With a steady professional hand he arrested the disintegration of frontline combat units, placed new formations in position, and withdrew his panzers into a mobile reserve. "I realized when I took over again in September that the situation was very serious," said von Rundstedt.

> I told those about me that if I was not interfered with I believed I could hold the enemy outside the frontier of the Reich for a while. I knew that a war of position was impossible for any length of time, and that [the Allies] could affect a breakthrough at any point they chose to concentrate their forces. I knew there was not a chance of winning the war, but I hoped that if I held out as long as possible some political turn of events might have prevented a complete collapse. A military victory was out of the question. As far as I was concerned the war was ended in September.[30]

Von Rundstedt recognized that the only feasible defensive line was the Rhine. "Stiff resistance should have been offered as long, and as far to the west, as possible in an effort to gain time. The withdrawal of the front behind the Rhine should then have followed voluntarily and at the right moment and not after the almost complete annihilation of all available forward units, merely in order 'to hold every foot of ground.' "[31]

The elderly von Rundstedt was revered by the Army, and in contrast to 1918, the discipline of the Wehrmacht held firm as the troops retreated. "It was a miracle that these brave, battered troops showed little deterioration in their conduct or morale," wrote General Blumentritt. "It is true that the troops were tired, often exhausted, and in many cases apathetic—but they all retained the will to fight."[32] One of the reasons was that German commanders habitually led their troops from the front. In September, von Rundstedt and his deputy, General Siegfried Westphal, were almost captured by tanks of the 5th Armored Division as they witnessed the defense of Trier on the Moselle.[33]

With the notable exception of Patton, Matthew Ridgway, and J. Lawton Collins, most American generals led from the rear. Eisenhower established an advance command post at Reims, but his principal headquarters was at the luxurious Trianon Palace Hotel, set in eight acres of beautiful gardens adjacent to the palace at Versailles.[34] For his residence, he chose the same landmark eighteenth-century villa in nearby Saint-Germain that von Rundstedt had occupied. During his two years in France, von Rundstedt never carried a weapon, had no bodyguards, and regularly took a two-hour stroll through Saint-Germain and the city park. An avid gardener, he refused to allow the villa's lawns to be disturbed to build an air-raid shelter. "One can be killed just as comfortably in bed as in the cellar," he told his aides.[35] Under Ike, the villa and the Trianon Palace Hotel became an armed camp. Von Rundstedt, who before the war had resided in an elegant twelve-room apartment on Berlin's fashionable Hardenbergstrasse near the Tiergarten, took pleasure in the villa's antique furnishings. Ike seemed uncomfortable with them, although he relished the privacy the villa provided.[36]

Eisenhower's office was in a ballroom annex of the hotel. The room was roughly divided by blankets suspended from the ceiling. Summersby, who was now a fixture in Ike's life, occupied the portion nearest the door; Eisenhower, the larger section near the fireplace. "This gave me the shameless opportunity to hear as much as a whisper in his sanctum," Kay recalled. "I thoroughly enjoyed the luxury of eavesdropping on conversations in the Throne Room."[37] On October 14, 1944, thanks to FDR, Summersby was commissioned a second lieutenant in the Women's Army Corps. T. J. Davis, the theater adjutant general, swore her in, and Ike pinned on her gold bars. "It was the highlight of my wartime career," said Summersby. "I could no longer drive the General. As it turned out, I still traveled with Ike almost everywhere he went. I continued to breakfast with him and we still drove to the office together. The only difference was that I now sat in the back seat with him instead of in the front behind the wheel."[38] Shortly afterward, at Eisenhower's request, Churchill awarded Kay the Medal of the British Empire (MBE). When Summersby expressed surprise, Ike reassured her. "I don't think you realize how valuable your services have been. I do. And so does the P.M."[39]

The evident closeness between Eisenhower and Summersby continued to fuel gossip and speculation. When Churchill and Brooke visited SHAEF in mid-November, Brooke expressed surprise that Kay was seated next to the prime minister at dinner. "I was interested to see that she had been promoted to hostess," wrote Brooke. "In so doing Ike produced a lot of undesirable gossip that did him no good."[40]

Rumors of Eisenhower's affection for Kay inevitably made their way to Washington and did little to improve his relations with Mamie. As the wife of the supreme commander, Mamie was always on public view and she bore the strain with remarkable dignity. On occasion, she vented her concern to Ike, and in the autumn of 1944 her anxiety was intensified by the fact that John, who had just finished the platoon leaders course at Fort Benning, had been assigned to the 71st Infantry Division and was soon to ship out for Europe. Evidently Mamie lashed out in a letter to Eisenhower in early November, prompting what granddaughter Susan described as Ike's "testiest" response.[41]

"I fully understand your distress when contemplating [John's] departure," wrote Eisenhower.

But it always depresses me when you talk about "dirty tricks" I've played and what a beating you've taken, apparently because of me. You've always put your own interpretation on every act, look or word of mine, and when you've made yourself unhappy, that has, in turn, made me the same.

It's true we've now been apart for 2½ years, and at a time that made separations painful and hard to bear. Don't forget that I take a beating every day. Entirely aside from my own problems, I constantly receive letters from bereaved mothers, sisters, and wives that are begging me to send their men home, or at least out of the battle zone.

So far as John is concerned, we can do nothing but pray. If I interfered even slightly or indirectly he would be so resentful for the remainder of his life that neither I (nor you, if he thought you had anything to do with it), could be comfortable with him. It's all so terrible, so awful, that I constantly wonder how "civilization" can stand war at all.

I truly love you and I do know that when you blow off steam you don't really think of me as such a black hearted creature as your language implies. I'd rather you didn't mention any of this again.[42]

On December 15, 1944, President Roosevelt nominated Eisenhower for promotion to the five-star rank of General of the Army, along with Marshall, MacArthur, and "Hap" Arnold of the air force. They were joined by Leahy, King, and Chester Nimitz, who were named to the equivalent naval five-star rank of Admiral of the Fleet. Ulysses S. Grant was the first general in American history to wear four stars as a full general. George Washington wore three as a lieutenant general. And John J. Pershing had worn six as General of the Armies. The five-star rank was introduced to place senior American commanders on a par with their British counterparts who were field marshals, air chief marshals, and fleet admirals.

The following day, December 16, 1944, the world of SHAEF turned upside down. Out of the snow and freezing cold of the Ardennes four German armies—two panzer and two infantry—some twenty-eight divisions with more than 300,000 men and close to 1,500 tanks, smashed through the lightly held Allied line in the forest. On D-Day, it was the Germans who had been taken by surprise. Now it was the Americans who were caught napping.

As a result of Ike's broad-front strategy, Allied troops were spread thin, but nowhere so thin as in the Ardennes. No one expected a German attack, and Bradley had deployed just four divisions, two of which were newly arrived, to hold an eighty-five-mile sector of the front. It was the Battle of Kasserine Pass redux. Little had been done to prepare a defensive position: No wire or minefields had been laid; few foxholes had been dug in the frozen ground; and night patrolling had been perfunctory. Green frontline troops bolted at the German approach, and American commanders initially underestimated the magnitude of the onslaught. For two days, Bradley and Simpson, commanding Ninth Army, failed to react, and Hodges at First Army suffered a nervous collapse similar to that sustained by Fredendall at Kasserine.

For the Germans, it was the breakthrough of May 1940 all over again, except that the Wehrmacht of 1944 was a pale copy of the panzer legions loosed against the French. In 1940, von Rundstedt's army group deployed more than three thousand newly minted tanks in perfect running order, the panzer divisions possessed an abundance of fuel and ammunition, and the troops had never known defeat. In December 1944, the German Army was a patchwork of understrength units, battered equipment, and chronic shortages of artillery shells and diesel fuel. von Rundstedt and Model had requested 500 gallons of fuel for each tank; they received 150.

Planning for the Ardennes attack (HERBSTNEBEL, or Autumn Mist) originated with Hitler after the fall of Paris. The Führer wanted to drive a wedge between the British and American armies, recross the Meuse, seize the supply dumps on the other side of the river, capture Brussels and Antwerp, and compel the Western powers to sue for peace. It was the rosiest of rosy scenarios. Hitler hoped to gain time before turning anew against the Russians, and continued to insist that a military victory could be won. Von Rundstedt and

Model, who were kept in the dark about the Führer's plans until November, recognized the strategic brilliance of the attack but saw no hope of capturing Antwerp. Both argued for a more limited operation aimed at temporarily dislocating the Allied advance but were overruled.[43]*

The Battle of the Bulge was Ike's finest hour as a military commander. While Bradley and Simpson dithered, and Hodges took to his bed, Eisenhower assumed control of the front and moved quickly to shore up the shoulders on either side of the German breakthrough. Patton was ordered to dispatch the 10th Armored Division to hold the line south of the penetration, and the 7th Armored of Ninth Army was given the same task to the north. With the width of the breakthrough restricted, Eisenhower turned to his strategic reserve: Matthew Ridgway's XVIII Airborne Corps, which was refitting near Reims. James Gavin's 82nd Airborne Division was rushed by truck to hold the vital road junction at Saint-Vith, and the 101st was sent south to hold a similar road junction at Bastogne: two important choke points essential to the German advance. John C. H. Lee, commanding the Army Service Forces, was ordered to defend the Meuse crossings with whatever engineers he could scrape up, and to prepare the bridges for demolition. The air force, the Allies' most potent weapon, was unable to fly because of bad weather. The size of von Rundstedt's attack was not yet clear. What was apparent was that the Allied front in the Ardennes had given way and that German panzers were heading west.

On December 19, Eisenhower met with Bradley, Devers, Patton, Tedder, and Bedell Smith at Verdun. Montgomery was represented by his chief of staff, Major General Francis de Guingand. The German advance was continuing, although the pace had slowed, and the

---

* "All Hitler wants me to do is to cross a river, capture Brussels, and then go on to take Antwerp," said Nazi general Sepp Dietrich, commanding Sixth SS Panzer Army. "And all this at the worst time of the year through the Ardennes when the snow is waist-deep and there isn't room to deploy four tanks abreast let alone armoured divisions. When it doesn't get light until eight and it's dark again at four and with re-formed divisions made up chiefly of kids and sick old men—and at Christmas." Quoted in Max Hastings, *Armageddon: The Battle for Germany, 1944–1945* 198 (New York: Knopf, 2004).

mood at Verdun was glum. The Allies had been taken by surprise and whipped decisively. Like a football coach whose team was behind with the clock running out, Eisenhower knew that he must rally his commanders. Alone among the downcast group, he exuded optimism. "The present situation is to be regarded as an opportunity, not a disaster," said Ike. The German Army had exposed itself, and once their drive had been blunted, it could be destroyed while still in the open.

"Hell," replied Patton, "let's have the guts to let the sons of bitches go all the way to Paris. Then we'll really cut 'em up."[44]

Patton's quip broke the tension. Ike explained that he wanted the Germans halted before they crossed the Meuse. When they were contained, the Allies would counterattack. "George, I want you to command this move. When can you attack?"

"The morning of December twenty-first, with three divisions," Patton replied. That was two days away. Eisenhower initially thought Patton was grandstanding, but the fact was that George had come to Verdun with three plans for Third Army already prepared, ready to comply with whatever Ike might direct. "This was the sublime moment of his career," wrote biographer Martin Blumenson. Eisenhower told Patton to take another day. He didn't want him to attack piecemeal. "I want your initial blow to be a strong one."[45]

Patton's readiness to attack electrified the meeting. It meant withdrawing his entire army from its eastward assault, turning ninety degrees north, and moving over icy roads to prepare for a major counterattack within seventy-two hours. "Altogether it was an operation that only a master could think of executing," wrote Blumenson.[46] Eisenhower had saved Patton's career twice: first in Sicily after the slapping incident, then in Britain following his remarks in Warwickshire. Now Patton was helping to save his.

It would be three days before Third Army could join the battle. Meanwhile, the German advance continued. Bradley, whose Twelfth Army Group headquarters was in Luxembourg, had lost contact with Hodges and Simpson, who were north of the breakthrough. Veteran units such as VII Corps (Collins) and V Corps (Gerow) were holding their ground, but VIII Corps (Middleton) had been overrun and First Army headquarters had ceased to function due to Hodges's breakdown.* On December 20 Ike turned to Montgomery. Twenty-first Army Group headquarters was in the north, and it seemed logical to put First and Ninth armies under Montgomery's command. It was, as one military historian has written, "a stroke of wisdom of the kind which justified all the Supreme Commander's claims to his authority."[47] The personal relations between Ike and Monty were strained, but with German panzers racing toward the Meuse, Eisenhower knew he could rely on the prickly field marshal to steady the American forces north of the breakthrough. Ike called Bradley to break the news.

Bradley reacted badly. "By God, Ike, I cannot be responsible to the American people if you do this. I resign," he protested.

Eisenhower held firm. "Brad," said Ike calmly, "I—not you—am responsible to the American people. Your resignation means absolutely nothing."

There was a pause. Bradley protested again, but Eisenhower cut him short. "Brad, those are my orders."[48]

In the late afternoon of December 20, Montgomery took command of all troops on the northern flank of the German penetration. Lieutenant General Sir Brian Horrocks's battle-tested British XXX Corps was rushed to a blocking position on the Meuse, and Montgomery paid a lightning visit to Hodges and Simpson. Bradley had not seen them since the attack began. "They seemed delighted to have someone give them firm orders," Monty reported to SHAEF that evening.[49]

With Patton pulling most of Third Army out of the line and mov-

---

* For the disarray at First Army headquarters, see J. D. Morelock, *Generals of the Ardennes: American Leadership in the Battle of the Bulge,* chap. 2, passim (Washington, D.C.: National Defense University Press, 1994); David W. Hogan, Jr., *A Command Post at War: First Army Headquarters in Europe, 1944–1945* 212–15 (Washington, D.C.: Center of Military History, 2000). Brigadier General Thomas J. Betts, SHAEF's deputy G-2, who visited First Army headquarters three days after the attack, said, "I found the place a terrible mess. They just didn't know what was going on. As far as fighting a war was concerned the First Army seemed to have no plan at all for meeting this attack." Betts recommended to Bedell Smith that Hodges be relieved. Betts Oral History, EL. Also see D.K.R. Crosswell, *The Chief of Staff: The Military Career of General Walter Bedell Smith* 284–86 (Westport, Conn.: Greenwood Press, 1991).

ing north, Eisenhower instructed Devers to shorten Sixth Army Group's front and take up the slack. In particular, Seventh Army was to pull back from an exposed salient containing Strasbourg, and re-form at the foot of the Vosges Mountains.[50] When de Gaulle learned of Ike's plan, he protested immediately. Strasbourg was sacred soil, said de Gaulle, the heart of Alsace and a symbol to the French people of their ancient rivalry across the Rhine. To surrender it to the Germans voluntarily would not only imperil the lives of hundreds of thousands of French men and women residing in the region, but would threaten the stability of the government itself. "If we were at *Kriegspiel* [war games]," said de Gaulle, "I would say you are right. But I must consider the matter from another point of view. Retreat in Alsace would yield French territory to the enemy. In the realm of strategy this would only be a maneuver. But for France it would be a national disaster."[51]

The discussion, heated at times, continued for several hours, and eventually de Gaulle prevailed. When pressed on the matter, Ike saw de Gaulle's point. He also realized that Allied supply lines, one from Cherbourg, the other from Marseilles, would be in danger without French support. He could not risk civil unrest or a collapse of the government. In de Gaulle's presence, Eisenhower called Devers and canceled the order to retreat.[52] Churchill, who happened to be visiting Ike at the Trianon Palace Hotel when de Gaulle arrived, said afterward, "I think you've done the wise and proper thing."[53]*

By December 22 the crisis in the Ardennes had passed, although weeks of hard fighting lay ahead. In the north, Montgomery turned tactical control of his American forces over to J. Lawton Collins, who mounted a spirited counterattack against the advancing panzer spearhead of Hasso von Manteuffel's Fifth Panzer Army. In the south,

---

* As was the case with the liberation of Paris, Eisenhower disguised his decision in purely military terms when he reported to Marshall. "I originally looked at the matter merely as a conflict between military and political considerations, and felt completely justified in handling the matter on a purely military basis. However, when I found that execution of the original plan would have such grave consequences in France that all lines of communication and my vast rear areas might become badly involved through loss of service troops and through unrest, it was clearly a military necessity to prevent this." DDE to GCM, January 6, 1945, 4 *War Years* 2399–401.

Eisenhower congratulates Patton for his drive to Bastogne. General Bradley looks on.

Patton's troops made contact with the beleaguered 101st Airborne at Bastogne late in the afternoon of December 26. The weather cleared and Allied airpower entered the battle, pounding German tanks as they advanced. Manteuffel's panzers were less than three miles from the Meuse, but had literally run out of fuel and were annihilated by Collins's oncoming troops from the American 2nd Armored Division. At that point the German generals recognized their advance was spent. Von Rundstedt, Model, and Manteuffel all asked for permission to withdraw, but Hitler refused. "It was Stalingrad No. 2," said von Rundstedt.[54]

The Battle of the Bulge cost the Germans between 80,000 and 100,000 men, plus the bulk of Hitler's armored reserve. The Wehrmacht might continue to fight a defensive war in the west, but it was no longer capable of offensive action. American losses totaled 80,987 (killed, wounded, captured, or missing), making it the most costly battle in American history since Grant's campaign in northern Virginia in 1864.[55]

Grandpa
Ted Leonard
was in the
Battle of The
Bulge. Would
not talk about
it.

## TO DO
## THIS WEEK

- [ ] _____
- [ ] _____
- [ ] _____

**ME**
TO
**WE**

Eisenhower is to blame for the broad-front strategy that stretched Allied lines so thin that German armor had little difficulty breaking through. With a candor that is rare among military commanders, Ike later accepted full responsibility. "If giving him [Hitler] that chance is to be condemned by historians, their condemnations should be directed at me alone."[56] Eisenhower can also be faulted for permitting the enemy to make a measured retreat from the Bulge without attempting to cut them off. Patton and Montgomery battered the Germans relentlessly, but little effort was made to prevent their retreat or to surround them.

By the same token, Eisenhower is entitled to full credit for the victory. From the start of the German offensive, he showed a quicker grasp of the situation than any of his subordinates, and he acted decisively to contain the attack. The width of the breakthrough was restricted; the strategic reserves were quickly deployed at Bastogne and Saint-Vith, and when Bradley lost contact with the First and Ninth armies, Ike turned the American forces over to Montgomery. Perhaps above all, Eisenhower had the nerve to allow the German advance to continue until it ran out of steam, and then deliver massive counterattacks from the south under Patton, and from the north under Montgomery.

Ulysses S. Grant, reflecting on his experience as a young lieutenant during the Mexican War, wrote the following appraisal of his commander General Zachary Taylor—"Old Rough and Ready": "No soldier could face danger or responsibility more calmly than he. These qualities are more rarely found than genius or physical courage."[57]

Patton and Montgomery approached the level of military genius, and their physical courage was beyond doubt. But it was Eisenhower who accepted responsibility. "In all his career as Supreme Commander there was perhaps no other time when Eisenhower revealed so clearly the greatness of his qualities," wrote historian Chester Wilmot, who had covered the Battle of the Bulge as a war correspondent.[58]

Montgomery and Patton were consummate military professionals. Unfortunately, both suffered from terminal infections of foot-in-mouth disease. On January 7, 1945, after stabilizing the northern flank of the German breakthrough, Montgomery called a press conference to announce the fact. Ike, Churchill, and Brooke had approved, and Monty's intent was to praise the American troops who had been placed under his command. "The text was innocuous," said Brigadier Sir Edgar Williams, Monty's intelligence chief. "But the presentation was quite appalling. Disastrous, really."[59]* Despite his best intentions, Montgomery came across as patronizing and condescending. He had rescued the Americans. The Yanks fought well when given strong leadership. Of course they were jolly brave. "It was a very interesting little battle. Possibly one of the most interesting and tricky battles I have ever handled."[60] Press coverage was initially favorable, but Bradley and Patton were disgusted with what they considered Monty's effort to steal the spotlight, and from that point on Eisenhower's senior commanders were virtually at sword point.[61]

The distinguished British military writer Sir Max Hastings draws a compelling contrast between Ike and Monty. Eisenhower was less genial than he appeared, wrote Hastings. "Yet the Abilene boy who grew up in classically humble rural American circumstances, the poker-player who retained a lifelong enthusiasm for dime Western novels, always behaved in public as one of nature's gentlemen. Montgomery, the bishop's son educated at St. Paul's and Sandhurst, never did. He was a cleverer man and far more professional soldier than his Supreme Commander, but his crassness toward his peers was a fatal impediment to greatness."[62]

The original battle line in the Bulge was not restored until January 28, 1945, and it took another month for Allied armies to recover their balance. The British and Americans were still west of the Rhine, the Siegfried line remained largely intact, and manpower losses crippled the effectiveness of many frontline divisions. In the east, the Soviets launched their final winter offensive on January 12.

---

* The full text of Montgomery's notes for his press conference is published in his *Memoirs*. They support Brigadier Williams's recollection. In fact, Monty went out of his way to praise Eisenhower, "who is the captain of our team." Montgomery later regretted holding the press conference. "So great was the feeling against me on the part of the American generals [Bradley and Patton], that whatever I said was bound to be wrong. I should therefore have said nothing. The 'best laid' Press conferences of 'Mice and men gang aft agley.'" Montgomery, *Memoirs*, 278–82.

As the Western Allies struggled to regain the initiative, the army groups of Field Marshals Georgy Zhukov, Ivan Konev, and Konstantin Rokossovsky, some four million men and ten thousand tanks, stormed forward along a two-hundred-mile front from the mountains of Bohemia to the Baltic. In six weeks the Red Army advanced from Warsaw, on the Vistula, to Stettin, Frankfurt, and Breslau, on the Oder. Zhukov's troops established a bridgehead across the Oder on February 2. Berlin lay thirty miles away. The Russian armies paused to regroup and refit, but it was abundantly clear to Ike and everyone else at SHAEF that the Red Army would reach the German capital long before the Allies.

On the eve of the Red Army's attack, Eisenhower dispatched his deputy, Air Chief Marshal Sir Arthur Tedder, to Moscow to consult with Stalin about Russian plans and to establish liaison arrangements to coordinate the eventual linkup of the two sides in Germany. A less obvious purpose was to inform Stalin of Ike's planned broad-front advance and to gain Russian approval before the Combined Chiefs of Staff convened in Malta to review Allied strategy. (The Malta meeting was preparatory to the meeting of the Big Three at Yalta.) By sending Tedder to Moscow, Eisenhower sought to preempt the strategic discussion at Malta since the chiefs could scarcely reject what the Soviets had approved. Just as he had outmaneuvered FDR and the State Department by providing de Gaulle the opportunity to occupy the Palais de l'Élysée, Ike now sought to outmaneuver Brooke and Churchill by dealing directly with Stalin.[63]

Tedder's reception in Moscow was more than Eisenhower could have hoped for. Stalin discussed the Russian offensive in detail, and inquired about the effect of von Rundstedt's attack in the Ardennes on Allied plans for crossing the Rhine. Tedder said the Allies "had no intention of letting up," and then described Ike's plans for a two-pronged crossing of the river, the principal one under Montgomery near Düsseldorf, the other under Bradley near Frankfurt. The Allies would then advance on a broad front and link up with the Russians somewhere near Leipzig. Tedder did not mention Berlin explicitly, but indicated that Eisenhower was uninterested in prestige objectives and would focus on the defeat of the German Army, wherever it stood.

Stalin, who was outspoken in his praise for Eisenhower's policy, was particularly delighted with the two-pronged idea. Red Army doctrine, he said, always emphasized the importance of secondary attacks. "We have no treaty," Stalin told Tedder when he departed, "but we are comrades. It is proper and also sound policy that we should help each other in times of difficulty."[64] Stalin agreed to maintain direct military exchanges with SHAEF, and shortly afterward wrote Eisenhower that the meeting with Tedder had been very useful. The Soviet offensive was proceeding in a satisfactory manner, he said, and would "ease the positions of the Allied troops and will accelerate preparations for your intended offensives."[65]

Eisenhower planned to cross the Rhine on a wide front. Montgomery's Twenty-first Army Group, reinforced by Simpson's Ninth U.S. Army, would attack in the north toward Düsseldorf, Essen, and the Ruhr's industrial heartland. In the center, Hodges's First Army would move on Cologne while Patton continued down the Moselle in the direction of Koblenz and Mainz. In the south, under Devers's Sixth Army Group, Alexander Patch's Seventh Army would advance toward Kaiserslautern and Karlsruhe, and the French First Army toward Mulhouse and Freiburg. Montgomery had a preponderance of men and matériel, and initial plans assumed he would push on to Berlin after the Ruhr had been taken. But Eisenhower successfully resisted pressure from London to concentrate his attack solely in the north.

By the end of February, Ike's broad-front strategy approached fruition. The largest Allied force ever assembled stood poised to launch the final offensive of the war in western Europe. Almost three million U.S., British, French, and Canadian troops—in three army groups, seven armies, twenty-one corps, and seventy-three divisions—struck that portion of the German Army still west of the Rhine. Hitler had transferred the bulk of his remaining panzer divisions to hold the Russians on the Oder, and German resistance to the Allied assault was spotty.

On February 24, 1945, Eisenhower met the press at the Hotel Scribe in Paris—his first press conference since November. More than two hundred reporters crammed into the ballroom for what visiting White House press secretary Steve Early called "the most magnificent performance of any man at a press conference that I have

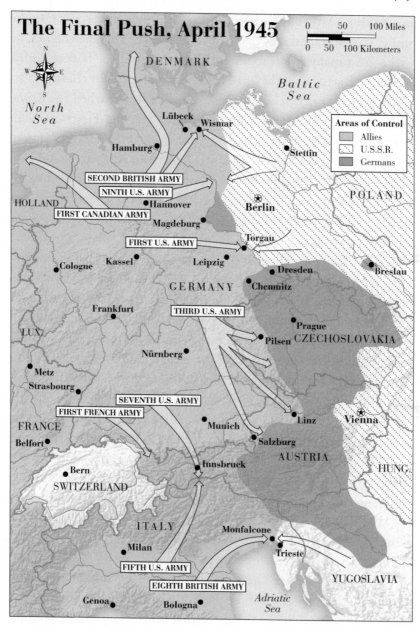

## The Final Push, April 1945

0    50    100 Miles

0    50    100 Kilometers

**Areas of Control**
- Allies
- U.S.S.R.
- Germans

DENMARK

*Baltic Sea*

*North Sea*

Lübeck

Wismar

Hamburg

Stettin

SECOND BRITISH ARMY

NINTH U.S. ARMY

HOLLAND

Hannover

POLAND

FIRST CANADIAN ARMY

Magdeburg

Berlin

FIRST U.S. ARMY

Torgau

Cologne

Kassel

Leipzig

Dresden

Breslau

GERMANY

Chemnitz

Frankfurt

THIRD U.S. ARMY

LUX.

Prague

Pilsen CZECHOSLOVAKIA

Metz

Nürnberg

Strasbourg

SEVENTH U.S. ARMY

FIRST FRENCH ARMY

Munich

Linz

Vienna

FRANCE

Belfort

Salzburg

AUSTRIA

HUNG.

Innsbruck

Bern

SWITZERLAND

ITALY

Monfalcone

Milan

Trieste

FIFTH U.S. ARMY

EIGHTH BRITISH ARMY

*Adriatic Sea*

YUGOSLAVIA

Genoa

Bologna

ever seen."[66] The Allies were advancing all along the front, and Ike had the facts at his fingertips. Reporters' probes about relations between Bradley and Montgomery were diplomatically deflected. Merle Miller, who was attending his first press conference as a correspondent for the European edition of *Yank,* was overwhelmed. "Ike is a master," Miller recorded in his diary, "though for my taste he smiles too much and says too little. Sometimes, when he chooses, he uses a great many words to say nothing at all, but the boys and girls of the press acted as if they had heard Einstein explain relativity."[67]

On March 2, troops of Simpson's Ninth Army reached the Rhine at Düsseldorf. The British Second Army and the First Canadian Army closed to the river a day later, and on the fifth, Hodges's forces arrived at Cologne. SHAEF planners had assumed there would be a fierce battle for Cologne, but on March 7 what was left of the city fell to VII Corps. "We had come well over 600 miles from Utah Beach," said J. Lawton Collins, "and the day before had captured our 140,000th prisoner."[68]

The day Cologne fell, elements of the 9th Armored Division moving into Remagen, south of Bonn, captured the Ludendorff railroad bridge across the Rhine before German sappers could demolish it. A formidable structure more than a thousand feet long, and wide enough for two railroad tracks with pedestrian walkways on either side, the Ludendorff bridge was one of the last escape routes for the retreating Germans west of the river, and the demolition teams had waited until the last moment to destroy it. News of the capture percolated quickly up the chain of command. "When Bradley reported that we had a permanent bridge across the Rhine I could scarcely believe my ears," said Ike. "This was completely unforeseen. The final defeat of the enemy, which we had long calculated would be accomplished in the spring and summer of 1945, was suddenly just around the corner."

"How much have you got in that vicinity that you can throw across the river?" Eisenhower asked Bradley.

"Four divisions," Bradley replied.

"Well, Brad, we expected to have that many divisions tied up around Cologne and now those are free. Go ahead and shove over at least five divisions and anything else that is necessary to make certain of our hold."[69]

Over the next two weeks, nine divisions crossed the Rhine at Remagen. The rugged terrain on the east bank was ill-suited to major offensive action, and did not affect SHAEF's plans for the upcoming crossings by Montgomery and Patton. Nevertheless, the bridgehead constituted a threat to the entire German front on the

Münster, April 1945.

Rhine. (After the capture of the bridge, Hitler relieved von Rundstedt for the last time and replaced him with Albert Kesselring.) By
the time the big railroad bridge finally collapsed on March 17, First
Army had constructed six pontoon bridges across the river and the
bridgehead was twenty miles long and eight miles deep.[70]

As German resistance crumbled, Eisenhower elected to take a
well-earned respite from the daily grind at SHAEF. On March 19, at
the urging of Kay and Bedell, Eisenhower accepted the invitation of
the Dillon family (founders of the Wall Street investment firm Dillon, Reed) to spend a few days at their sumptuous villa on the Riviera. "Today I leave for a five day trip," Ike wrote Mamie. "And I
hope to make three days of them my first 'rest period' of the war."[71]
Eisenhower was accompanied by Kay, Bedell, Bedell's friend Ethel
Westermann, Ike's aide Tex Lee, and WACs Ruth Briggs and Nana
Rae. Bradley joined the group in Cannes the following day. It was
four men and four women taking time off from the war to enjoy what
Kay described as "the most luxurious place I have ever seen. Nothing
that contributed to comfort was lacking. For the first couple of days,
all [Ike] did was sleep. He woke up long enough to eat and move

British troops move through Stadtlohn, April 1945.

from his bedroom to the terrace. He would eat lunch on the terrace, with two or three glasses of wine, and shuffle back to bed again. After forty-eight hours of this he began to look somewhat human.

"As he started to feel better, we would sit on the terrace all day long, looking out over the Mediterranean, chatting lazily, drinking white wine and sunbathing. By the end of the week, he was so much better it was hard to believe what a wreck he had been."[72] On the final day at Cannes, Eisenhower, Bradley, and Smith reviewed the strategy for bringing the war to a close. With German resistance collapsing, Ike wanted to take a fresh look at the plans for Montgomery to press on to Berlin from the Ruhr.

Since the liquidation of the Bulge, and especially after establishing the bridgehead at Remagen, Eisenhower's inclination had been to keep increasing the strength of the attack on Bradley's front. At first the attack by Twelfth Army Group had been intended as a diversion, then as a secondary effort to help Montgomery, then as a possible alternative should Monty bog down. By the time Ike and

Thousands of German POWs marching into captivity after the Allies crossed the Rhine. Note the total absence of any guards.

Bradley conferred on March 21, Bradley's attack had become, in Eisenhower's mind, the main thrust for the Allies' final offensive.[73] Patton would cross the Rhine near Frankfurt, Hodges would push out from Remagen, and the two armies would advance abreast toward Kassel. At that point Simpson's Ninth Army would revert to Bradley's command, and Twelfth Army Group would turn east, meeting the Russians on the Elbe. Montgomery's Twenty-first Army Group (less the U.S. Ninth Army), would move northeast toward Hamburg and Lübeck on the Baltic.

There were sound military reasons for Eisenhower to reconsider taking Berlin. Allied bombing had virtually destroyed the city from the air, and there was nothing of strategic value that could be gained. As he later phrased it, Berlin had become a prestige objective, devoid of military significance. More important, Zhukov's First Belorussian Army Group, almost a million men, stood poised a mere thirty miles east of Berlin, having already established a bridgehead across the Oder analogous to Hodges's at Remagen. Konev's First Ukrainian Army Group, another 750,000 men, was moving on the city from the south. The zones of occupation had been given final approval by the Big Three at Yalta, and Berlin (though it was to be occupied by

Kay, Ike, and Ethel Westermann at Sous le Vent on the Riviera, March 1945.

all four powers)* was well within the Soviet zone. With the zonal boundaries fixed, neither Eisenhower nor Bradley was inclined to engage the Soviets in a race for the city.

"What would it take?" Ike asked Bradley.

"Probably a hundred thousand casualties," Bradley replied. "A pretty steep price for a prestige objective, especially when you've got to fall back and let the other fellow take over."[74]†

Eisenhower, Bradley, and Smith were also concerned about intelligence reports that die-hard Nazis planned to continue a guerrilla war from a national redoubt in the Bavarian Alps. "The evidence was clear that the Nazis intended to make the attempt and I decided to give them no opportunity to carry it out," said Eisenhower.[75] The best way to prevent that was to link up with the Russians as soon as possible and sever the connections between Berlin and Bavaria. The fact that the national redoubt turned out to be a hoax in no way diminishes the seriousness with which SHAEF treated it.

---

* At Churchill's insistence, France was added as an occupying power.

† After the war Bradley wrote, "I could see no political advantage accruing from the capture of Berlin that would offset the need for quick destruction of the German army on our front." Omar Bradley, *A Soldier's Story* 535–36 (New York: Henry Holt, 1951).

Finally, Model's Army Group B, battered but still formidable, stood directly in Montgomery's path. By contrast, a drive by the First, Third, and Ninth armies into central Germany would face mostly home-guard units recently mustered into service.

These were valid military considerations. But there were other reasons perhaps even more important. U.S. troops now outnumbered British and Canadian three to one, and after the rapid advance to the Rhine, public opinion in the United States clamored for additional manifestations of American success. Personalities intervened as well. Bradley had come to loathe Montgomery, and Ike's relations with Brooke had soured. After the Battle of the Bulge, Brooke and the British chiefs of staff resurrected the idea that Alexander should be named overall ground commander at SHAEF and that Ike should revert to his position as supreme commander. Alexander would replace Tedder as Ike's deputy, and Tedder would assume command in the Mediterranean. Eisenhower met the threat with his customary adroitness. He would be delighted to have his "great friend" Alexander as his deputy, he told Brooke, but Alex would have to understand that he would be deputy without portfolio, and would likely be responsible for ensuring the quality of life for people in liberated areas. "There can be no question whatsoever of placing between me and my Army Group Commanders any intermediate headquarters, either official or unofficial in character." Also, if Tedder were reassigned, Ike said he would make Tooey Spaatz his overall air commander.[76] If there was anything the British did not want, it was to place their air forces under Spaatz's command. Churchill, who had signed on to the scheme, recognized they had been outmaneuvered and instructed Brooke to drop the matter. "It would be a waste of Field Marshal Alexander's military gifts and experience," said Churchill.[77] Nothing further was said, but Eisenhower still smoldered over the episode. Montgomery, in this instance, was blameless, but if given the choice, Ike preferred the final drive of the campaign to be under Bradley's command.*

---

* "Dear Brookie," Montgomery wrote the chief of the imperial general staff on March 3, 1945. "Delighted that the Alexander business has been postponed; and I hope this will lead to a cancellation. The change would have upset matters without any doubt. We are now on a very good wicket; Ike has learnt his lesson and he

Unfortunately, Eisenhower neglected to tell Montgomery of his change of plans, and Monty, uncharacteristically, now had the bit between his teeth. On March 27 he informed Eisenhower that Twenty-first Army Group was driving hard for the Elbe. Montgomery said he was moving his headquarters forward, first to Münster, then Hannover—"thence via the AUTOBAHN to Berlin, I hope."[78]

Eisenhower, who had been in Paris for a press conference, did not receive Montgomery's message until his return to Reims on the twenty-eighth.[79] Ike had assumed that Monty would move with his customary deliberateness, and was caught off guard to learn that he was heading for the Elbe and Berlin. Forced with the sudden necessity to bring Montgomery to a halt, Eisenhower elected to play his Moscow trump card once again. Without consulting the Combined Chiefs of Staff, he immediately wrote what David Eisenhower has described as "an unprecedented 'personal' letter to Marshal Stalin."[80]* Ike told Stalin that after eliminating German resistance in the Ruhr, he would concentrate on linking up with Soviet forces in the Erfurt-Leipzig-Dresden area. "I regard it as essential that we coordinate our action and make every effort to perfect the liaison between our advancing forces." By implication, the Western Allies would ignore Berlin, which would relegate Montgomery and Twenty-first Army Group to a secondary role.[81]

After dispatching his letter to Stalin, Eisenhower then replied to Montgomery. Ike told Monty that he was coordinating Allied movements with Stalin, and that as soon as the Germans in the Ruhr had been encircled, he was transferring Simpson's Ninth Army back to Bradley's command. Bradley would then move to link up with the Russians in the Erfurt-Leipzig area. "The mission of your army group will be to protect Bradley's northern flank. . . . Devers will protect Bradley's right [southern] flank."[82] By invoking Stalin, Ike kept Monty and the Combined Chiefs out of the decision. Berlin would be left to the Russians.

---

consults with me before taking any action." Papers of Lord Alanbrooke, quoted in Andrew Roberts, *Masters and Commanders* 560 (New York: HarperCollins, 2009).

* The Combined Chiefs of Staff had authorized Eisenhower to deal directly with the Russians pertaining to the linkup in Germany, but assumed that he would communicate with the Soviet military, not with Marshal Stalin.

Montgomery was stunned. As his most recent biographer reports, "For Monty it was perhaps the biggest shock of the war."[83] Montgomery had been with Churchill, Eisenhower, Brooke, and Bradley three days before when Twenty-first Army Group crossed the Rhine, and no mention had been made of transferring Ninth Army to Bradley or consulting with Stalin. Not only had Eisenhower abandoned Berlin as an objective, but Twenty-first Army Group had been reduced to a supporting role. "All very dirty work, I fear," Monty informed Brooke.[84]

In London, Eisenhower's message to Stalin ignited a firestorm. The British chiefs of staff were enraged that Ike had usurped the authority of the Combined Chiefs to communicate directly with Stalin. They were also concerned that the message was badly written (Brooke called it "unintelligible"), and most important that it represented "a change from all that had been agreed upon."[85] The BCOS registered an immediate protest with Washington "against this procedure and change of plans without any consultation with Combined Chiefs of Staff."[86]

Churchill was even more concerned. Relations between London and Moscow were strained to the breaking point over the Kremlin's refusal to permit free elections in Poland, and by writing to Stalin, Churchill feared Eisenhower was undercutting the Allies' negotiating position. But the prime minister's principal worry was that Ike failed to understand the political significance of Berlin. "The idea of neglecting Berlin and leaving it to the Russians to take at a later stage does not appear to me to be correct," Churchill told the British chiefs. Not only would German resistance be stimulated, but when the city fell, the Soviets would be regarded as the real victors in the war and the liberators of central Europe.[87] To clarify the situation, Churchill cabled Eisenhower at SHAEF to ask for an explanation.

Eisenhower replied on March 30, 1945, restating his intention to advance in the direction of Leipzig with Bradley's Twelfth Army Group "to join hands with the Russians or to attain the general line of the Elbe." Ike added that he had no intention of crossing the Elbe.[88] Insofar as Eisenhower was concerned, he was acting consistent with his authority as supreme commander. As he saw it, he had made a decision based on military considerations.

After Ike replied to Churchill, a message arrived from Marshall that indicated how serious the issue had become. SHAEF was again taken by surprise. Marshall said the British chiefs were concerned about Eisenhower's change of plans and particularly about his moving on Leipzig instead of Berlin.[89] Eisenhower replied testily (and disingenuously) that he had not changed plans. He was concentrating on the destruction of the German armed forces, and the quick linkup with the Russians in the area of Leipzig was the most effective way to accomplish that. Ike said he was "merely following the principle that Field Marshal Brooke has always shouted to me, I am determined to concentrate on one major thrust and all that my plan does is to place the Ninth US Army back under Bradley for that phase of operations involving the advance from Kassel to Leipzig."[90]

At this point in the war, with German resistance collapsing, Eisenhower's standing with the Joint Chiefs could not have been better. They endorsed his decision unreservedly, and briskly informed the British of their support for Ike. "The battle for Germany," said Marshall, "is now at a point when it is up to the Field Commander to judge the measures which should be taken. The single objective should be quick and complete victory."[91] Churchill remained unconvinced. "I do not know why it would be an advantage not to cross the Elbe," he cabled Eisenhower on March 31.

IF THE ENEMY'S RESISTANCE SHOULD WEAKEN, AS YOU EVIDENTLY EXPECT AND WHICH MAY WELL BE FULFILLED, WHY SHOULD WE NOT CROSS THE ELBE AND ADVANCE AS FAR EASTWARD AS POSSIBLE? THIS HAS AN IMPORTANT POLITICAL BEARING. . . .

I DO NOT CONSIDER MYSELF THAT BERLIN HAS LOST ITS MILITARY AND CERTAINLY NOT ITS POLITICAL SIGNIFICANCE. THE FALL OF BERLIN WOULD HAVE A PROFOUND PSYCHOLOGICAL EFFECT ON GERMAN RESISTANCE IN EVERY PART OF THE REICH. WHILE BERLIN HOLDS OUT, GREAT MASSES OF GERMANS WILL FEEL IT THEIR DUTY TO GO DOWN FIGHTING. . . . WHILE BERLIN REMAINS UNDER THE GERMAN FLAG IT CANNOT, IN MY OPINION, FAIL TO BE THE MOST DECISIVE POINT IN GERMANY.[92]

The following day, April 1, 1945, Easter Sunday, Churchill escalated the furor by writing to FDR. "There is only one thing worse than fighting with allies," he told Brooke, "and that is fighting without them."[93] In his message to Roosevelt, Churchill expressed his complete confidence in Eisenhower, but repeated his concern about not pressing on to Berlin. He called FDR's attention to the fact that Ike "has changed the plans that had been agreed upon" by moving on Leipzig and Dresden. "This is surely a matter upon which a reasonable latitude of discussion should be allowed to our two Chiefs of Staff Committees before any final commitment involving the Russians is entered into."[94]

Roosevelt, whose health was failing rapidly, was at Warm Springs when Churchill's message arrived, and the reply (over FDR's name) was evidently written by Marshall. "I do not get the point," said the president. "Leipzig is not far removed from Berlin and is well within" the scope of what had been agreed upon. Why the concern? "I regret that the phrasing of a formal discussion [at Malta] should have so disturbed you but I regret even more that at the moment of great victory by our combined forces we should become involved in such unfortunate reactions."[95] Roosevelt's support for Eisenhower ended the debate. Ike and Churchill exchanged cordial messages backing away from a confrontation. "I regard all this business as smoothing itself down quite satisfactorily," said the prime minister, although he repeated his view that "I deem it highly important that we should shake hands with the Russians as far to the east as possible."[96]

On April 3, 1945, Ike sent Tedder to London to make peace with the British chiefs of staff. The only reason Eisenhower wrote Stalin, Tedder told them, was to forestall Montgomery's advance. Brooke was incredulous. For the BCOS, this was one of the more bizarre episodes of the war. "I said that I was astonished Ike found it necessary to call on Stalin in order to control Montgomery," Brooke noted in his diary. Since the boundaries of Simpson's Ninth Army did not change, the only difference was that Ninth Army was transferred from Monty to Bradley. "Surely Stalin's help need not be called in for such a transfer."[97] Earlier in the war, such an issue would have led to a full-scale debate between the British and American chiefs of staff.

Eisenhower, accompanied by Patton, visits the horror of Buchenwald.

But with Germany's collapse imminent, it scarcely seemed worth the trouble. The British chiefs accepted Tedder's explanation and gave way gracefully.[98]

Churchill ended the contretemps with a final telegram to Roosevelt on April 5. "The changes in the main plan now turn out to be much less than we at first supposed," said the prime minister. "My personal relations with General Eisenhower are of the most friendly character. I regard the matter as closed, and to prove my sincerity I will use one of my very few Latin quotations: *Amantium irae amoris integratio est*"—which Churchill translated as "The wrath of lovers hots up their love."[99]

The decision to bypass Berlin and meet the Russians on the Elbe was the last major issue Eisenhower confronted during the war. President Roosevelt died on April 12, 1945, Hitler committed suicide on April 30, and on May 7 General Jodl formally surrendered the last elements of German resistance to Ike at Reims. In the ceremonial photo taken to mark the occasion, Kay Summersby stands in the second row, directly behind Ike and Smith. In the War Department's official photo Kay has been airbrushed out, just as she was soon to be airbrushed out of Eisenhower's life. As Henry VIII might have ob-

Celebrating the German surrender, May 7, 1945.

served, a passion lasts a thousand days, and with the end of the war, Kay's thousand days were coming to a close.

The broad-front strategy pursued by Eisenhower may well have prolonged the war six months—as many critics have charged. But during those six months Germany's complete defeat became manifest. There was no "stab in the back" myth such as the one that poisoned German history after World War I, and in the midst of the destruction and desolation there was no nostalgia for Hitler or the Nazi regime. In many respects, Germany's total defeat resembled the total defeat of the Confederacy in the American Civil War.

In 1878, on a world tour after his presidency, Ulysses Grant called on Chancellor Bismarck in Berlin. Bismarck commiserated with Grant about the Civil War, and lamented the fact that the war had been so terrible. It had to be terrible, Grant replied. "There had to be an end to slavery. We were fighting an enemy with whom we could not make peace. We had to destroy him. No treaty was possible—only destruction."

"It was a long war," Bismarck observed. "I suppose it means a long peace."

"I believe so," said Grant.[100]

# SIXTEEN

# Chief of Staff

I expressed the hope that we would never have
to use such a thing against any enemy because I
disliked seeing the United States take the lead
in introducing into war something as horrible
and destructive as this new weapon was
described to be.

—EISENHOWER TO HENRY L. STIMSON,

*Potsdam, July 1945*

WHEN HOSTILITIES ENDED, U.S. and British troops were well
within the territory that had been designated as the Soviet zone of
occupation. Eisenhower saw this as a purely military problem, and as
early as April 5, 1945, sought permission from the Combined Chiefs
to allow his army group commanders (Montgomery, Bradley, and
Devers) to work out arrangements with their Russian counterparts
for a withdrawal to the agreed boundaries.[1] The British had objected.
As Churchill and the British Foreign Office saw it, the territory the
Western Allies occupied would provide "a powerful lever to obtain
concessions" from the Russians, and the decision to withdraw should
be made at the governmental level. "There cannot be such a hurry
about our withdrawing from a place we have gained that the few
days necessary for consulting the Governments in Washington and
London cannot be found," said Churchill.[2]

Eisenhower had little sympathy for the British position. He was
concerned about a possible clash with the Soviets as the Red Army

approached and, when he received no instructions from the Combined Chiefs, accepted the responsibility and authorized his field commanders to negotiate directly with their Russian opposites.[3]

"Let's put it this way," Bradley told Simpson. "We would prefer to hold our present line until we can arrange an orderly changeover. But if the Russian insists on going forward to his line of occupation, we're not going to start any trouble. Work it out as best you can and allow him to. We are not going to risk an explosion that might bring a sequel to the war and bring World War III."[4]

Eisenhower's order triggered another row with London. The back-and-forth continued throughout May. Washington backed Ike and insisted the withdrawal be handled at the tactical level; the British were adamant that the matter was political. "I do not quite understand why the Prime Minister has been so determined to intermingle political and military considerations," Eisenhower cabled Marshall. "My original recommendation was a simple one and I thought provided for a very sensible arrangement."[5] Churchill responded with his famous "iron curtain" cable to President Truman.*

---

* "I am profoundly concerned about the European situation," said Churchill. The Western Allies were demobilizing and withdrawing. "Meanwhile what is to happen about Russia? . . . *An iron curtain is drawn down upon their front.* We do not know what is going on behind. There seems to be little doubt that the whole of the regions east of the line Lübeck-Trieste-Corfu will soon be completely in their hands. To this must be added the further enormous area conquered by the American armies between Eisenach and the Elbe, which will, I suppose, in a few weeks be occupied, when the Americans retreat, by the Russian power." Churchill to Truman, May 12, 1945, in Winston S. Churchill, *Triumph and Tragedy* 572–74 (Boston: Houghton Mifflin, 1953). Emphasis added.

Churchill is generally credited for the origin of the term "iron curtain," but as David Reynolds points out, he "probably took the phrase . . . from Nazi propaganda in the dying days of the Third Reich."

Joseph Goebbels, in his diary entry of March 13, 1945, wrote about the Kremlin letting "fall an iron curtain" in Romania "so that they can carry on their fearful bloody work behind it." On March 14, Goebbels wrote, "Storm signals are visible over Finland. Having let down their iron curtain the Soviets are now at work bringing the country ruthlessly under their thumb." And on March 17, "The iron curtain has descended on the fate of Rumania." Goebbels was Nazi propaganda minister at the time.

David Reynolds, *In Command of History: Churchill Fighting and Writing the Second World War* 479 (New York: Random House, 2005); *Final Entries, 1945: The Dia-*

Ike and Churchill having a postwar discussion in London.

"Surely," said the prime minister, "it is vital now to come to an understanding with Russia, or to see where we are with her, before we weaken our armies mortally or retire to the zones of occupation."[6]

Churchill proposed that he and Truman meet to review the situation, but the president declined. "I could see no valid reason for questioning an agreement [on zonal boundaries] on which we were so clearly committed," said Truman. "The only practical thing to do was to stick carefully to our agreement and to try our best to make the Russians carry out their agreements."[7] To accomplish that, the president dispatched Harry Hopkins to Moscow to arrange a postwar Big Three meeting with Stalin. "In the meantime," he told Churchill, "it is my present intention to adhere to our interpretation of the Yalta agreements," which meant that the United States would withdraw to its zonal area.[8]

The Yalta agreements to which President Truman referred not only delineated the zonal boundaries within Germany, but specified

---

*ries of Joseph Goebbels* 122, 133, 160, Hugh Trevor-Roper, ed., and Richard Barry, trans. (New York: G. P. Putnam's Sons, 1978).

that the country would be governed jointly by the United States, Great Britain, the Soviet Union, and France acting through a quadripartite Allied Control Council (ACC). Technically, the four-power occupation of Germany could not legally begin until the Allied Control Council was established, and the ACC could not be established until each power was in control of its own zone. On May 16, 1945, Eisenhower visited Churchill in London to impress on him the urgency of the problem, but he made little headway. As Ike advised Washington afterward, the prime minister "did not appear to be in any real hurry" to have four-power occupation begin.[9]

By late May the problem was becoming critical. It was no longer a tactical question of meeting the Red Army, but the much larger issue of governing postwar Germany. The Allied armies were still holding their battle positions, and Eisenhower was still in supreme command. The issues pertaining to the occupation were not being addressed. On May 23, Eisenhower advised Washington that he "could not carry out his mission much longer" in the absence of four-power government. Ike suggested that SHAEF be abolished and that the withdrawal from the Russian zone begin immediately.[10]

The British continued to oppose any withdrawal, but suggested that the four military commanders in Germany (Eisenhower, Zhukov, Montgomery, and de Lattre de Tassigny) meet in Berlin and establish the Allied Control Council. The ACC, said the British, could discuss the Allied withdrawal from the Russian zone, but until all outstanding issues with the Soviet Union were resolved, American and British forces should stand fast.

After a week of protracted negotiations at the governmental level, it was agreed that the four military commanders would meet in Berlin on June 5, 1945, to complete the paperwork necessary for the creation of the Allied Control Council and the assumption of supreme authority in Germany. But differences between Washington and London persisted. Eisenhower was authorized by the president to work out the withdrawal with Zhukov, but Montgomery was told by the Foreign Office that the continued occupation of large parts of the Russian zone was an "important bargaining counter for obtaining satisfaction from the Soviet government on a number of outstanding questions."[11]

In desperation, Eisenhower again cabled Washington for instructions. The Russians, he said, were certain to raise the question of Allied withdrawal from the Soviet zone, and might even make that a prerequisite for establishing the ACC. Ike asked how he should respond. "Any cause for delay in the establishment of the Control Council due to delay in withdrawal would be attributed to us and might well develop strong public reaction."[12]

Marshall cleared his answer with the White House, and then told Ike on June 3 that the question of withdrawal should not be a prerequisite for establishing the Allied Control Council. "If the Russians raise the point, you should state in substance that the matter of withdrawal is one of the items to be worked out in the Control Council. As to the actual movement of U.S. Forces, you should state that this is primarily a military matter; its timing will be in accordance with U.S. ability to withdraw their forces . . . and the Russian ability to take over."[13]

Churchill, who received a copy of Marshall's message, remained resolute. "I view with profound misgivings the retreat of the American Army to our line of occupation," he cabled Truman. "I hoped this retreat, if it has to be made, would be accompanied by the settlement of many great things which would be the true foundation of world peace. Nothing really important has been settled yet, and you and I will have to bear great responsibility for the future."[14]

Churchill visualized the Cold War, and may even have been contributing to its onset. Eisenhower hoped that the defeat of Nazi Germany would lay the groundwork for a peaceful world in which the victorious Allies would cooperate. If there was going to be conflict with the Soviet Union—hot or cold—Ike was determined that the United States was not going to be responsible for starting it. As he told Butcher in late May, he thought relations with the Russians were about like American relations with the British at the beginning of the war.

> As we dealt with each other, we learned the British ways
> and they learned ours. Now the Russians, who have had
> relatively little contact with the Americans and British,
> do not understand us, nor do we them. The more contact

Eisenhower, Zhukov, and Montgomery celebrating at Ike's Frankfurt headquarters, June 1945.

we have with the Russians, the more they will understand
us and the greater will be the cooperation. It should be
possible to work with Russia if we will follow the same
pattern of friendly co-operation that has resulted in the
great record of Allied unity demonstrated first by AFHQ
[in North Africa and Sicily] and subsequently by SHAEF.
Only now, in peace, the motive for co-operation is the bet-
terment of the lot in life of the common man. If we can
create singleness of purpose on this theme, as we did to
win the war, then peace should be assured.[15]

On June 5, 1945, Eisenhower met with Zhukov, Montgomery, and
de Lattre de Tassigny at Zhukov's headquarters in Berlin. "The cir-
cular conference table was the largest I have ever seen," wrote Eisenhower. "Each national delegation was assigned a ninety-degree
quadrant at the table. The commanders were surrounded by a crowd
of military and political assistants."[16] Eisenhower was accompanied

by General Lucius D. Clay, his deputy for military government, and his political adviser, Robert Murphy. Zhukov was joined by his deputy, Marshal Vassily Sokolovsky, and Andrey Vyshinsky. "The Russians treated us cordially," Eisenhower reported to Marshall. "I gave Zhukov, in the name of the President, the Legion of Merit in the grade of Chief Commander and he reciprocated by awarding me the Order of Victory."[17]

The four military commanders signed the formal declaration assuming total power in Germany.[*] But as Eisenhower anticipated, Zhukov made it clear that any steps to set up control machinery would have to await the Allied withdrawal from the Soviet zone. "There is some justification for Zhukov's position that he is unable to discuss administrative problems in Germany when he still is not in control and hence not familiar with the problems of the zone for which he will eventually be responsible," Ike told Marshall. "As a result of my discussion with Zhukov I am optimistic that the Russians will join in some form of control machinery when the withdrawal is accomplished and will agree to our force entering into Berlin concurrently with our withdrawal from their zone."[18] Murphy subsequently cabled the State Department: "For the Depts secret information, I believe that Gen Eisenhower does not consider that the retention of our forces in the Russian zone is wise or that it will be productive of advantages."[19]

Two days after the conference in Berlin, Harry Hopkins stopped off at Eisenhower's headquarters on his return from Moscow to Washington. Hopkins had arranged with Stalin for the Big Three to meet at Potsdam on July 15, and wanted to discuss the situation in Germany with Ike. Hopkins remained in Frankfurt twenty-four hours, after which he cabled President Truman that he was convinced "the present indeterminate status of date of withdrawal of Allied troops from area assigned to the Russians is certain to be misunderstood by Russia as well as at home."

Hopkins, who had just met with Stalin, and Eisenhower, who had

---

[*] "Declaration Regarding the Defeat of Germany and the Assumption of Supreme Authority." For text, see Beate Ruhm von Oppen, ed., *Documents on Germany Under Occupation, 1945–1954* 29–37 (London: Oxford University Press, 1955).

just seen Zhukov, concurred in their assessment. As Hopkins told Truman, "It is manifest that Allied control machinery cannot be started until Allied troops have withdrawn from territory included in the Russian area of occupation. Any delay in the establishment of control machinery interferes seriously with the development of governmental administrative machinery for Germany and the application of Allied policy in Germany." Hopkins said that a delay of a week or so "would not be disastrous," but that the withdrawal should be accomplished before the July 15 meeting with Stalin at Potsdam. Hopkins, whose health was failing, said the issue was so serious that he would remain in Europe if the president thought it would be helpful.[20]

Hopkins's message broke the logjam. Whereas Eisenhower had not been able to overcome British resistance in the Combined Chiefs of Staff, Hopkins succeeded in driving home to President Truman the importance of withdrawing Allied forces. On June 11, Truman informed Churchill that he was "unable to delay the withdrawal of American troops from the Soviet zone in order to use pressure in the settlement of other problems." The president said that SHAEF should be dissolved immediately, and that separate U.S. and British zones under Eisenhower and Montgomery should begin to function forthwith. American troops, said Truman, would commence their withdrawal from the Soviet zone on June 21.[21]

Churchill yielded gracefully. "Obviously we are obliged to conform to your decision," he cabled the president on June 14. "I sincerely hope that your action will in the long run make for a lasting peace in Europe."[22]

On the personal front, Eisenhower's affection for Kay Summersby crested as the war ended. According to Kay, Ike pledged his love and insisted they go to London, take in a show, and celebrate VE Day. At the theater they were joined in Ike's box by John and his British date; General Bradley; and Kay's mother. It was all very public. When the audience demanded that Eisenhower speak, he told them how happy he was to be back in England. "It's nice," he said, "to be back in a country where I can *almost* speak the language."[23] After the theater they adjourned to Ciro's for dinner and dancing. Again, all very public. "It was hard to tell what step we were doing or what

Ike and Kay at the Prince of Wales Theater in London.

beat Ike was listening to," Kay remembered. "We were sort of hopping around the floor. But I didn't care."[24]

According to General Lucius Clay, who was Ike's deputy at the time, "General Eisenhower was under considerable pressure immediately after the war to take up permanent residence in England. A group of leading citizens, led by Jimmy Gault [Sir James Gault, Eisenhower's British aide], who was very influential in London financial circles, wanted General Eisenhower to live in Britain and had even selected a residence for him."

I asked General Clay if that would have involved Kay Summersby. Clay blushed and did not answer. After a significant pause Clay continued: "General Eisenhower was a General of the Army. That was a lifetime appointment. He would never be required to retire. He would always draw his pay and allowances. So living in England was a real possibility."[25]

President Truman told Merle Miller that "right after the war was over, he [Eisenhower] wrote to General Marshall saying that he wanted to be relieved of duty," so that he could divorce Mamie and marry Kay. According to the former president, Marshall replied harshly that if Ike ever attempted such a thing he would "bust him out of the Army" and make his life miserable. Truman said that before he left office in 1953, he "got those letters from [Eisenhower's] file in the Pentagon and I destroyed them."

When Miller published his interview with President Truman in 1974, the American historical establishment expressed incredulity.[26] The reaction was similar to that following the publication of Fawn Brodie's biography of Thomas Jefferson suggesting that Jefferson and Sally Hemmings had enjoyed a sexual relationship.[27] Like Brodie's book, Truman's story has the ring of reality. Professor Garrett Mattingly, the distinguished Columbia University historian who won the Pulitzer Prize in 1959 for *The Armada,* was stationed in Washington during the war as a junior officer in Naval Intelligence. It was Mattingly's job to read the outgoing cables from the high command for censorship purposes. In the early 1950s, when Ike was president of Columbia University, Professor Mattingly told his history department colleagues that he had seen Marshall's cable to Eisenhower. The only difference between Mattingly's version and Truman's was that Mattingly recalled Marshall saying that he would relieve Eisenhower as supreme commander if he did such a thing. Truman's "bust him out of the Army" is a down-home Missouri embellishment. Professor Mattingly died in 1962—well before Truman's interview with Merle Miller.[*]

It is not unlikely that Eisenhower, as a lifetime General of the Army, with his financial future secure, could have contemplated a life with Kay in Britain. It is certainly conceivable that he could have written to General Marshall in May 1945 to explore the possibility. Should Marshall have replied harshly, and if he had threatened to relieve Eisenhower as supreme commander, with the public humiliation that would have entailed, it is certain that Ike would have dismissed the possibility. Few figures in public life have had Dwight D. Eisenhower's willpower. A lifetime smoker of three to four packs of cigarettes a day, Eisenhower quit cold turkey while president of

---

[*] I am indebted to Professor Henry F. Graff of Columbia for relating Garrett Mattingly's observation.

Columbia and never touched a cigarette again. If, after hearing from Marshall, he decided against pursuing his romance with Kay, there is no doubt he could have turned on a dime. Eisenhower continued to write affectionate letters to Mamie throughout May, and there is no indication in their correspondence that their marriage was in trouble.* If Eisenhower was considering divorce he played his cards close to his chest. That, too, would have been in character.

An additional incident offers tangential corroboration. On June 4, 1945, Eisenhower wrote Marshall to suggest that American officers remaining in Germany on occupation duty be permitted to bring their wives from the States.

> General Bradley has been the only senior officer I know who has been an ardent supporter of some such policy, but I am sure that something of this order will eventually have to be done.
>
> *So far as my own case is concerned, I will admit that the last six weeks have been my hardest of the war. I presume that aside from disappointment in being unable to solve in clean-cut fashion some of the nagging problems that seem to be always with us, part of my trouble is that I just plain miss my family.*[28]

Eisenhower was signaling that his affair with Kay had ended. As Eisenhower biographer Michael Korda has pointed out, the most curious aspect of Ike's letter is that he felt it necessary to write Marshall in the first place. "If Ike had simply told Mamie to pack her bags and join him, it is hard to imagine that anybody would have been shocked or angered."[29] When Clay succeeded Eisenhower as military governor, he authorized dependents to come to Germany without consulting Washington and caused scarcely a ripple.[30]

Eisenhower continued to enjoy Kay's company so long as he remained in Germany. They went horseback riding, played bridge in the evening, and when Ike visited Hitler's retreat at Berchtesgaden,

---

* "Loads of love," Ike wrote Mamie on May 18, 1945. "How I miss you—and it gets worse every day. Don't worry, for Lord's sake, about 'decisions' about our future life. Let's just try to keep a bit of tolerance for fixed habits and a sense of humor and then try to have some fun together. I love you." *Letters to Mamie* 254–55.

Kay accompanied him. They vacationed again at the Dillon estate in Cannes and went on a fishing trip with Bedell Smith and Ethel Westermann. But ambition conquered affection. When Eisenhower returned to Washington to succeed Marshall as chief of staff in November 1945, Kay was the only member of Ike's personal staff who did not join him. There were no teary good-byes. As Kay has written, "A telex came in from Washington saying that Lieutenant Summersby was dropped from the roster of those scheduled to leave for Washington. There was no explanation. No reason given."[31]

Shortly afterward Kay received a typewritten "Dear John" letter from Eisenhower on War Department stationery.

> Dear Kay:
>
> I am terribly distressed, first because it has become impossible longer to keep you as a member of my personal official family, and secondly because I cannot come back and give you a detailed account of the reasons. . . .
>
> In this letter I shall not attempt to express the depth of my appreciation for the unexcelled loyalty and faithfulness with which you have worked for the past three and a half years under my personal direction. . . .
>
> I am sure you understand that I am personally much distressed that an association that has been so valuable to me has to be terminated in this particular fashion but it is by reasons over which I have no control. . . .
>
> Finally, I hope that you will drop me a note from time to time—I will always be interested to know how you are getting along.

In his own hand, Ike added a postscript: "Take care of yourself—and retain your optimism."[32] The postscript notwithstanding, Eisenhower's letter to Kay is cold-blooded and ruthless. FDR would have been incapable of writing such a missive, and George Patton would have said a warmer good-bye to his horse. With his letter Eisenhower closed the book on his relationship with Kay Summersby. Kay would not completely go away, but Ike had taken the necessary step to restore his marriage to Mamie and resume his career. Eisenhower and his son John have been assiduous in their attempt to minimize the role Kay Summersby played in Ike's life.* Kay's wartime diary, for example, which is at the Eisenhower Library in Abilene, is filed under the "Barbara Wyden Papers" (Wyden assisted Kay in writing *Past Forgetting*), not under "Kay Summersby."[33]

A wartime romance is scarcely a deadly sin. In 1941, Franklin Roosevelt resumed his relationship with Lucy Mercer Rutherfurd, and Lucy was with FDR when he died at Warm Springs. For twenty years after the president's death, Roosevelt scholars pooh-poohed the possibility of a presidential romance with Lucy Mercer. "Such rumors," wrote Harvard professor Frank Freidel, "seem preposterous. They reflect more on the teller than FDR."[34] But the truth eventually emerged, and did not adversely affect FDR's reputation. As Arthur Schlesinger, Jr., the dean of Roosevelt biographers, has noted, "If Lucy Mercer in any way helped Franklin Roosevelt sustain the frightful burden of leadership in the Second World War, the nation has good reason to be grateful to her."[35] The same might be said for Kay Summersby. Major General Everett Hughes, a close friend of both Ike and Mamie, and who was regarded as Eisenhower's "eyes and ears" at SHAEF, put it in almost identical terms. "Leave Ike and Kay alone," he once admonished Eisenhower's aide Tex Lee. "She's helping him win the war."[36]

Victory celebrations engulfed Europe. Like the Duke of Wellington after Waterloo, Eisenhower was the hero of the hour. He was feted in the pomp and circumstance of London's Guildhall, and the stately splendor of the Palais de l'Élysée. At the Guildhall, Ike addressed the assembled establishment of Great Britain, was proclaimed an honorary citizen, and was presented with a ceremonial sword bearing the insignia of the Order of Merit, Britain's highest decoration. In Paris, he placed a wreath on the tomb of the unknown in an elaborate ceremony at the Arc de Triomphe, was named a Compagnon de la Libération, and on behalf of the American people received a sword that had belonged to Napoléon. After a state dinner

---

* Ike never apologized for having Kay Summersby on his staff, wrote Susan Eisenhower. He simply "expected everyone to accept his version of events." Susan Eisenhower, *Mrs. Ike* 235.

De Gaulle presents Eisenhower with a sword of Napoléon's for the American people.

at the Élysée and another speech, de Gaulle presented him with a platinum cigarette case embossed with five sapphire stars and engraved in de Gaulle's own handwriting.* There were similar celebrations and decorations bestowed in Belgium, the Netherlands, Luxembourg, Norway, Denmark, Poland, and Czechoslovakia. Eisenhower had become the most popular figure in western Europe, and he bore the acclaim with grace, dignity, and a residual midwestern humility.

On June 16, 1945, Eisenhower left Frankfurt for Washington, his

---

* A month or so later, while stationed in Germany, Eisenhower presented the cigarette case to Kay. "I'd like you to have it, Kay," said Ike. "I'll never be able to give you anything like this, and I'd like to think of you having it. The sapphires match your eyes."

Summersby declined. "Ike, I can't take it. Please. I just can't. I wouldn't be right. I'd love it. But I can't."

When Eisenhower returned to the United States he gave the case to Mamie, who was a heavy smoker. It is on display among Mamie's jewelry at the Eisenhower Museum in Abilene. Morgan, *Past Forgetting* 235.

Ike and Mamie in Washington, June 17, 1945.

first visit home in almost two years. President Truman dispatched the presidential plane, *The Sacred Cow,* for Ike's use, and the party stopped for a day in Bermuda so that Eisenhower might have some time in the sun before embarking on his triumphal tour. In Washington, Ike addressed a joint session of Congress, met with President Truman and Secretary Stimson, and was awarded a second oak leaf cluster for his Distinguished Service Medal. Marshall had furnished Eisenhower a prepared text for his address to Congress, but Ike discarded it and spoke extemporaneously. When Eisenhower talked off the cuff, listeners were always impressed with his warmth and sincerity. When he spoke from a text, he appeared wooden and pedantic.[37] Lawmakers were charmed by Ike's directness and gave him the longest standing ovation in congressional history.[38] Was Eisenhower a Democrat or a Republican? That was a question veteran leaders on both sides of the aisle found themselves asking.

From Washington, Ike flew to New York, where four to five million people—the largest crowd in the city's history—turned out to greet him. At City Hall, Mayor Fiorello La Guardia made Eisenhower an honorary citizen, and Ike responded with another informal address. "At one stretch in our trip this morning the mayor told me there were 450,000 schoolchildren watching. Can the parents and the relatives of those children look ten years ahead and be satisfied with anything less than your best to keep them away from the horrors of the battlefield? It has got to be done."[39]

That evening at a dinner in his honor at the Waldorf Astoria, Eisenhower returned to the theme:

> As I see it, peace is an absolute necessity in this world. I believe that we should let no specious argument of any kind deter us from exploring every direction in which peace can be maintained. I believe we should be strong, but we should be tolerant. We should be ready to defend our rights, but we should be considerate and recognize the rights of others.[40]

On the morning of June 20 Eisenhower went to West Point, where he spoke to the corps of cadets, and then flew to Kansas for a reunion with his mother and brothers. Tiny Abilene (population five thousand) was jammed with twenty thousand well-wishers, and Ike remained for three days, staying with his brother Milton at Kansas State. In Abilene, newsmen had the opportunity to meet with Eisenhower at close range, and they peppered him with questions about his future. Was political office on the horizon?

"I am in the federal service and I take orders from my commander in chief," Ike replied.

> All I want is to be a citizen of the United States, and when the War Department turns me out to pasture that's all I want to be.
>
> I'm a soldier, and I am positive that no one thinks of me as a politician. In the strongest language you can command you can state that I have no political ambitions at all. Make it even stronger than that if you can. I'd like to

go even further than Sherman did in expressing myself on this subject.[41]*

In typical Eisenhower fashion, Ike cited Sherman but did not use Sherman's words—which were absolute. To say "I'd *like* to go even further than Sherman" is not the same as saying categorically that he would not accept if nominated, and would not serve if elected. By appearing to take himself out of contention but not actually doing so, Eisenhower had implicitly announced his availability.†

From Abilene, Ike returned briefly to Washington, and then joined Mamie, John, and the Douds at the Greenbrier in White Sulphur Springs, West Virginia, for ten days of golf, horseback riding, and fly-fishing. Back in Washington on July 5 for another round of conferences, he returned to Germany on July 10. "I truly enjoyed my trip to the U.S.," Ike wrote Mamie from Frankfurt. "If you'd just once understand how exclusively I love you and long for you then you'd realize how much a week at White Sulphur meant. Please don't forget that I love only you—loyal friends and helpers [for example, Kay Summersby] are not involved in the wonderful feelings I have for you."[42]

The Potsdam conference convened on July 15, 1945. Eisenhower was not a member of the American delegation, but flew up frequently from Frankfurt to consult with Marshall, Stimson, and President Truman. One day, following a lengthy lunch, Ike and Bradley took the president on a tour through the ruins of Berlin. According to Bradley, Truman was very much at ease and in a generous mood. He turned to Eisenhower and said, "General, there is nothing that you may want that I won't try to help you get. That definitely and specifically includes the presidency in 1948." Eisenhower and Bradley

* On June 5, 1884, General William Tecumseh Sherman informed the Republican National Convention, "If drafted, I will not run; if nominated, I will not accept; if elected, I will not serve." John Marszalek, "William Tecumseh Sherman," in *Encyclopedia of the American Civil War* 1769 (New York: W. W. Norton, 2002).
† Bedell Smith, when asked by Major General Sir Ian Jacob, Churchill's deputy chief of staff, whether Ike wanted to be president, replied, "Want it! He wants it so bad he can taste it." Jacob, interview by Peter Lyon, cited in Lyon, *Eisenhower: Portrait of the Hero* 348 (Boston: Little, Brown, 1974).

Ida Eisenhower basking in the glow
of Ike's achievements. Asked by a
newsman if she was proud of her
son, Ida responded, "Which one?"

were stunned. "I kept a poker face," Bradley recalled, "wondering
how Ike would reply to that."[43]

Eisenhower laughed heartily and said, "Mr. President, I don't
know who will be your opponent for the presidency, but it will not
be I."[44]

It was while the Potsdam conference was taking place that Eisenhower first learned of the atomic bomb. During a long talk at Ike's
Frankfurt headquarters, Secretary Stimson, who was the cabinet officer responsible for the bomb's development, informed Eisenhower
of the successful test in New Mexico and said the government was
preparing to drop the bomb on Japan unless the Japanese surrendered quickly. This was Ike's first introduction to atomic weapons,
and he was appalled. As Secretary Stimson laid out the facts, Eisenhower recalled that he was overcome by depression.

So I voiced to him my grave misgivings, first on the basis of my belief that Japan was already defeated and that dropping the bomb was completely unnecessary, and secondly because I thought that our country should avoid shocking world opinion by the use of a weapon whose employment was no longer mandatory as a measure to save American lives. . . . I disliked seeing the United States take the lead in introducing into war something as horrible and destructive as this new weapon was described to be.[45]

Eisenhower was the only one at Potsdam who opposed using the bomb. And when Ike expressed his misgivings, Stimson became highly agitated, "almost angrily refuting the reasons I gave for my quick conclusions."[46] Eisenhower was not an original thinker. But he thought for himself and he was blessed with uncommon common sense. Just as he had done when he permitted de Gaulle to occupy the Palais de l'Élysée, he was applying common sense to a complex issue rather than accept the conventional wisdom. Alone among those present at Potsdam, Eisenhower recognized that once the genie was out of the bottle, it could not be put back in. The bomb would increase world tension, just when it seemed possible that it might be controlled.[47]*

As president, Eisenhower would twice be presented with recommendations from his National Security Council and the Joint Chiefs of Staff that the bomb be used; first, in Vietnam to protect the French at Dien Bien Phu, then against China at the time of the Formosa Strait crisis. Both times Eisenhower rejected the recommendations. As a former supreme commander, Eisenhower had the confidence to

---

* "Before the atom bomb was used," Eisenhower later told *Saturday Evening Post* war correspondent Edgar Snow, "I would have said yes, I was sure we could keep peace with Russia. Now I don't know. I had hoped the bomb wouldn't figure in this war. Until now I would have said that we three, Britain with her mighty fleet, America with the strongest air force, and Russia with the strongest land force on the continent, we three could have guaranteed the peace of the world for a long, long time to come. But now, I don't know. People are frightened and disturbed all over. Everyone feels insecure again." Edgar Snow, *Journey to the Beginning* 360–61 (New York: Random House, 1958).

do so, where other presidents might not have. And by rejecting the use of the bomb, there is no question that Eisenhower raised the threshold at which atomic weaponry could be employed—a legacy we continue to enjoy.

On August 11, 1945, Eisenhower undertook a long-delayed visit to Moscow. Stalin had invited him earlier, but the date had conflicted with Ike's scheduled journey to the United States. Eisenhower flew from Berlin in his personal C-54, the *Sunflower,* and was accompanied by Marshal Zhukov—who would be his official host—Lucius Clay, T. J. Davis, and his son John—an intimate group of old friends.[48] Pursuant to Russian practice, Ike's plane flew low, and Ike was impressed by the devastation he saw. "I did not see a house standing between the western borders of the country and the area around Moscow," he wrote. "Through this overrun region, Marshal Zhukov told me, so many women, children, and old men had been killed that the Russian Government would never be able to estimate the total."[49] Eisenhower and Zhukov bonded during the five-hour flight. Sitting to themselves, with Zhukov's urbane interpreter alongside, they reveled in each other's expertise. Zhukov unhooked the high collar of his tunic and inquired about Allied logistics. Had they really laid pipelines under the Channel, and how did the red ball express work—the one-way road net that John C. H. Lee's transportation people devised to speed supplies to the front? Ike was interested in how Zhukov smashed through German minefields with so little loss of armor. It wasn't complicated, Zhukov replied. He sent the infantry through first. "The losses we get from personnel mines we consider only equal to those we would have gotten from machine guns and artillery if the Germans had chosen to defend that particular area with strong bodies of troops instead of with mine fields."[50]*

In Moscow, Eisenhower was treated with extraordinary deference.

---

* Liberal journalist Murray Kempton, in a perceptive appraisal of Eisenhower's presidency, noted that Zhukov's description of moving through German minefields made a lasting impression on Ike. "Keep Nixon and Dulles around for marching through minefields" became one of Eisenhower's operating principles. Murray Kempton, "The Underestimation of Dwight D. Eisenhower," *Esquire* 109, September 1967.

Aside from the customary banquets and receptions, he reviewed the annual Physical Culture Parade in Red Square, standing alongside Stalin on top of Lenin's tomb, the only foreigner ever accorded that honor. One hundred thousand athletes and gymnasts marched past in a five-hour display of synchronized athleticism, while a thousand-man band played continuously. "None of us had ever witnessed anything remotely similar," wrote Eisenhower.[51] Eisenhower and Zhukov attended a soccer game at Moscow's Dynamo Stadium and received a prolonged standing ovation from the eighty thousand spectators. Unable to speak to the crowd in Russian, Ike put his arm around Zhukov's shoulders as a gesture of goodwill. The fans roared their approval. The marshal escorted Ike to a collective farm, an airplane factory, the glittering Moscow subway, and on an extended tour of the Kremlin, another treat rarely offered foreigners.

After a side trip to Leningrad at Eisenhower's request—he wanted to see the site of the nine-hundred-day siege where 350,000 civilians had starved to death—he met with Stalin for a series of extended conversations relating primarily to the occupation of Germany and postwar Allied cooperation. Stalin emphasized how badly the Soviet Union needed American help in recovering from the war. It was not simply money. "We must learn about your scientific achievements in agriculture. We must get your technicians to help us in our engineering and construction problems, and we want to know more about mass production methods in factories. We know that we are behind in these things and we know that you can help us."[52] When Eisenhower responded sympathetically, Stalin expressed his appreciation. Later he told Ambassador W. Averell Harriman that he thought Eisenhower was a great man. "Not only because of his military achievements but because of his human, friendly, kind and frank nature. He is not coarse like most military men."[53]

For his part, Eisenhower was equally impressed, finding Stalin "benign and fatherly." He told Brooks Atkinson, the Moscow correspondent of *The New York Times,* that he felt he was in the hands of friends and sensed "a genuine atmosphere of hospitality." Ike said he was "convinced that Russia and the United States must work together in a spirit of amity" and said he "was eager to help promote that." Asked by Atkinson about U.S. policy in Germany, Eisenhower stressed the importance of providing the Germans with as much freedom and independence as possible. "The thing to be avoided is committing the nation to a dictatorship under which one man has the power to send the people to war."[54] The following day, Ike told a news conference in Moscow, "I see nothing in the future that would prevent Russia and the United States from being the closest possible friends. If we are going to be friends, we must really understand each other a bit."[55]*

Lucius Clay concurred with Ike's assessment of their reception. "There was no tension whatever," he remembered. "Nothing could have been more friendly."[56] With Washington's approval, Eisenhower invited Zhukov to tour the United States, and offered to provide his personal plane for the trip. Zhukov tentatively accepted and asked that Ike or Clay accompany him. But Zhukov, whom Stalin stripped of command in 1946, fearing he was becoming too popular, never received permission to make the trip.[57]

Shortly after Eisenhower returned to Germany from Moscow, he was faced with another Patton eruption. In addition to commanding Third Army, Patton had been made military governor of Bavaria, and in that capacity made no secret of his opposition to the denazification policies the Allies had agreed upon.† During a press confer-

---

* At the press conference, Eisenhower told the Russian correspondents present that they must expect that American publishers would be harshly critical of the Soviet Union. "They will give you the devil," said Ike. "All I suggest is that we all keep our sense of values and not be upset by the lies or propaganda of a few crackpots." *The New York Times,* August 15, 1945.

† On August 11, 1945, Patton complained to Eisenhower that too many trained administrators were being removed from office because of the denazification program and were being replaced by "inexperienced and inefficient people." According to Patton, "It is no more possible for a man to be a civil servant in Germany and not have paid lip service to Nazism than it is for a man to be a postmaster in America and not have paid at least lip service to the Democratic Party or Republican Party when it is in power."

Eisenhower pulled Patton up short. "The United States entered this war as a foe of Nazism," he reminded the Third Army commander. "Victory is not complete until we have eliminated from positions of responsibility and, in appropriate cases properly punished, every active adherent to the Nazi party. . . . The discussional stage of this question is long past. . . . I expect just as loyal service in the execution of this policy . . . as I received during the war."

GSP to DDE, August 11, 1945, in Blumenson, 2 *Patton Papers* 738; DDE to

ence at his headquarters in Bad Tölz on September 22, 1945, Patton was asked by a reporter why reactionaries were still in power in Bavaria. "Reactionaries!" Patton exploded. "Do you want a lot of Communists?" He paused for a moment, considering his response. "I don't know anything about parties," he said. "The Nazi thing is just like a Democratic or Republican election fight."[58]

Patton's remarks caused a sensation. Had American policy in Germany reversed? Was Patton announcing the change, or was he again shooting from the hip? Eisenhower summoned him to Frankfurt. "That man is yet going to drive me to drink," Ike wrote Mamie. "He misses more opportunities to keep his mouth shut than almost anyone I ever knew."[59]

Patton reported to Ike on September 28. "General Eisenhower came in that day looking as though he hadn't slept a wink," Kay Summersby recalled. "I knew at once he had decided to take action against his old friend. He had aged ten years in reaching the decision." Patton and Eisenhower were closeted for over an hour. It was "one of the stormiest sessions ever staged in our headquarters," said Summersby. "It was the first time I ever heard General Eisenhower raise his voice."[60] Patton was relieved as military governor of Bavaria and commander of Third Army, and reassigned to head Fifteenth Army, a paper formation whose purpose was to write the history of the European campaign. Eisenhower later told his son John that they could have survived the tempest Patton had created. "Actually, I'm not moving George for what he's done—just for what he's going to do next."[61] At a more consequential level, Eisenhower's relief of Patton made it abundantly clear that the United States had no intention of backing away from denazification. The most distinguished battle leader in the American Army had been relieved of command. Throughout the American zone, military government detachments in every village and hamlet understood that Eisenhower had made the purge of Nazi officials the immediate purpose of zonal policy.[*]

---

GSP, September 11, 1945, *The Papers of Dwight David Eisenhower,* vol. 6, *Occupation* 351–52.

* On Sunday, December 9, 1945, Patton was involved in a freak automobile accident near Mannheim. His neck was broken, and he died in the hospital on December 21. He is buried alongside his troops in the U.S. Military Cemetery at

By late summer it was obvious that Eisenhower's time in Germany was nearing an end, and that he would be returning to Washington to succeed Marshall as chief of staff. The groundwork had been laid in May, immediately after Germany's surrender. Marshall wanted to retire—he had been on the job for six years rather than the statutory four—but agreed to stay until the war with Japan ended. President Truman, for his part, wanted a senior World War II commander to head the Veterans Administration. Ike, like Marshall, wanted to retire. And Omar Bradley wanted to become chief of staff. The result was a package deal. Bradley would return to the United States immediately to become chief of the Veterans Administration, but would serve only two years and would remain on active duty as a four-star general. When Marshall retired, Eisenhower would succeed him, and would serve two years. And when Ike retired, Bradley would move from the VA to become chief of staff.

Bradley left on schedule for Washington in June, and in August Marshall submitted his resignation to President Truman, recommending Ike as his successor. "There is no position other than Chief of Staff of the Army which is suitable to his present rank and prestige," said Marshall.[62]

"The most 'suitable' position for me is unquestionably a remotely situated cottage in a state of permanent retirement," Eisenhower replied. "Of course, I know that there are still very difficult problems to solve, and . . . I am willing to attempt anything that my superiors may direct."[63]

In late October, President Truman reluctantly accepted Marshall's resignation and set the changeover for November 26, 1945. Eisenhower prepared to leave Germany, but wanted to see Zhukov one last

---

Hamm in Luxembourg. It was War Department policy at the time that servicemen who died overseas be buried overseas. On December 21, Eisenhower cabled Bedell Smith that if Mrs. Patton wished George to be returned for a stateside burial, he would assume responsibility for doing so, and would clear it with higher authority. No request was made.

Neither Eisenhower nor Bedell Smith was listed among the honorary pallbearers at Patton's funeral. Patton's final judgment of Eisenhower was harsh. "I hope he makes a better President than he was a General." Quoted in D'Este, *Patton* 801. DDE to Smith, December 21, 1945, *The Papers of Dwight David Eisenhower,* vol. 7, *Chief of Staff* 673–74. Cited subsequently as 7 *Chief of Staff.*

Eisenhower, General Lucius D. Clay, Zhukov, and Marshal Vassily Sokolovsky at a Berlin reception following the wedding of Clay's son Frank.

time before he departed. On November 7, the twenty-eighth anniversary of the Bolshevik Revolution, Ike went to Berlin to attend the
Soviet reception and spent the evening discussing postwar problems
with Zhukov. "The whole purpose of my long talk with him," Eisenhower told Clay afterward, "was to renew and strengthen the spirit
of understanding that he has seemed to show toward you and me so
cordially and to get certain concrete concessions that I thought
would do much to prove the sincerity of both sides." Nagging problems concerning the air corridors to Berlin were resolved, and when
Zhukov asked that the delivery of reparations designated for Russia
be expedited, Ike agreed. "I hope you will follow these things up
with General Sokolovsky and move instantly to meet them always at
least half way," he instructed Clay.[64]

Later, in 1948, Eisenhower wrote that his time in Germany
marked the high point of U.S.-Soviet cooperation. "We in Berlin saw
no reason why the Soviet system of government and democracy as

practiced by the Western Allies could not live side by side in the world provided each respected the rights, the territory, and the convictions of the other, and each system avoided overt or covert action against the integrity of the other."[65]

Eisenhower left Frankfurt on November 10, 1945, and after stops in Paris, the Azores, and Boston arrived in Washington on the twelfth. The administration's proposals for universal military training (UMT) and for the creation of a single Department of Defense were pending on Capitol Hill, and Ike was rushed off to testify.[66] On November 15, he appeared before the House Military Affairs Committee to support UMT, and the following day went to the Senate to back the merger of the services into a single department. Eisenhower felt strongly about both. He made headlines across the country responding to the questioning of Congressman J. Parnell Thomas, the Red-baiting Republican from Allendale, New Jersey, who later chaired the House Un-American Activities Committee.[*]

Thomas apparently wanted to establish Ike's credentials as a vigilant anti-Communist. He laid out a scenario suggesting the United States was threatened by foreign enemies and that another Pearl Harbor was in the offing. Who were those enemies?

THOMAS: Let us name a couple of names.

EISENHOWER: You name them.

THOMAS: All right. I'll name them, and I'd like to have your views on them. What about Great Britain as a potential aggressor?

EISENHOWER: There will never be a war between Great Britain and the United States. (*Applause.*)

THOMAS: What about Russia as a potential aggressor?

EISENHOWER: Russia has not the slightest thing to gain by a struggle with the United States. There is no one thing, I believe, that guides the policy of Russia more today than to keep friendship with the United States.

---

[*] In 1950, Thomas was indicted and convicted for taking kickbacks from his congressional staff and sentenced to eighteen months in a federal penitentiary. He was pardoned by President Truman on Christmas Eve, 1951.

Frustrated by Ike's response, Thomas turned to nuclear weapons. Wasn't there a danger of espionage? Couldn't the secret be stolen?

EISENHOWER: I am sure that if we could establish through the United Nations Organization a complete interchange of knowledge and free access of every government to every other, you would at least inspire confidence, and thereby you could give such secrets to all nations and it would make no difference.

THOMAS: Should the United States maintain its monopoly of atomic secrets?

EISENHOWER: Let's be realistic. The scientists say other nations will get the secret anyway. There is some point in making a virtue out of necessity.[67]

From the moment he arrived in Washington, Eisenhower was clearly a potential presidential candidate. But his responses to Thomas did little to galvanize political support among hard-core party faithful on the Republican right. On the other hand, it established Eisenhower's credentials as a thoughtful observer of the world scene who could be relied on for evenhanded analysis. Liberal Republicans and Democrats were delighted; the GOP's crackpot brigade felt betrayed. Unlike Douglas MacArthur, Ike was not a man on horseback.

Immediately after testifying, Ike and Mamie visited Mamie's relatives in Boone, Iowa. Both had come down with severe cases of bronchial pneumonia, and were hospitalized until early December. Eisenhower did not assume his duties as chief of staff until December 3, 1945. And he did so reluctantly. "The job I am taking now represents nothing but straight duty," he wrote his childhood friend Swede Hazlett from the hospital.[68]

On his third day in office, Eisenhower penned a personal letter to Zhukov expressing his appreciation for the marshal's friendship and cooperation. "I hope you will always permit me to call you 'friend,' " Ike wrote.

I truly feel that if the same type of association that you and I have experienced over the past several months could be established and maintained between large numbers of

Soviet and American personnel, we would do much in promoting mutual understanding, confidence, and faith between our two peoples. . . .

I should like to request that at any time you feel that I might do anything for you personally or that I might be helpful in promoting the friendships that I feel are so valuable to the world, I will be more than glad to respond to your suggestions, so far as it is in my power to do so.[69]*

For Ike and Mamie, Eisenhower's tour as chief of staff was a period of adjustment. They had been separated for three and a half years. They moved into Quarters 1 at Fort Myer, not necessarily as strangers, but as people who had become independent of each other. Eisenhower was surrounded by a military entourage that catered to his every need: a valet, a cook, and a chauffeur, plus a full assortment of military aides and secretaries. They tended to freeze Mamie out, said John's wife, Barbara. "Mamie could feel herself being nudged to the periphery, and she had to fight for her place."[70] Ike had also changed. He was no longer the Army field-grade officer who came home every evening to share life with his family. The loneliness of command had made Eisenhower emotionally self-sufficient. He was accustomed to issuing orders and having those orders obeyed. He was more abrupt and less tolerant of frivolity and small talk. Grant as the Army's commanding general after the Civil War found the transition from war to peace challenging, but his wife, Julia, had accompanied him during the last two years of the conflict and there was no personal adjustment required. Nor would there have been for MacArthur, whose wife, Jean, was always at his side. But for Eisenhower, he was not just becoming chief of staff of a peacetime Army, his entire pattern of living was changing as well.

Mamie had also become set in her ways. She had lived in the limelight in Washington, making her own social and financial decisions.

---

* Zhukov replied that he regretted that they would not be able to meet as frequently as in the past. "I nevertheless hope that we shall remain good friends as we have been, and therefore I agree beyond all doubt to your calling me your friend, and I trust that you will likewise allow me to call you my friend." *The Papers of Dwight David Eisenhower*, vol. 7; *Chief of Staff* 592n1.

She would now be required to defer to Ike, and that was difficult. Leaving aside the legacy of Ike's affair with Kay Summersby, it was not easy for two dominating personalities to meld themselves into a married couple again.[71] According to Major General Howard Snyder, the Eisenhower family physician, Mamie was reluctant to move into Quarters 1. The Wardman Park apartment had been her sheet anchor during the war, and she was reluctant to give it up. "We almost had to take her physically and transport her to Fort Myer before we could persuade her that she could be happy in the home."[72]

Quarters 1 at Fort Myer aided the transition. The most storied residence in the Army, it had been the home of chiefs of staff since 1910, and its twenty-one rooms easily accommodated the furniture the Eisenhowers had accumulated over the years. Pershing had lived there. So, too, had MacArthur and Marshall. Built in 1899 by the Corps of Engineers as a residence for the commander of Fort Myer, its large formal rooms provided ample space for entertaining, while there was an abundance of family space on the second and third floors. Marshall had kept a flock of chickens in the backyard; Ike turned to raising corn and tomatoes.

Fort Myer itself was a military treasure. Situated on a high ridge with a majestic view of Washington, Arlington Cemetery, and the Potomac, the post had been established during the early days of the Civil War and was considered one of the strongest fortifications protecting the nation's capital. The land had been owned by Martha Washington's family, and descended through marriage to Robert E. Lee, who lost title in a sheriff's foreclosure sale in 1864 for failure to pay property taxes. (The government had previously confiscated it for military purposes.) The post was named for Brigadier General Albert J. Myer, who was the Army's first chief signal officer, and since the time of Phil Sheridan it had been home to the 3rd Cavalry—the Army's showpiece ceremonial regiment. George Patton had commanded the 3rd Cavalry before the war, and the 1,500 horses that were stabled at Fort Myer were an integral part of official life in Washington.*

---

* As a young boy growing up in the capital in the 1930s, I vividly remember being taken by my parents late on Sunday afternoons to watch the retreat cere-

Except for formal dinners and receptions, Ike and Mamie lived mostly on the second floor. The family living room was a glassed-in sunporch in the rear of the house furnished with Mamie's rattan furniture purchased in the Philippines. There was no television in those days, but Ike had a movie projector and screen set up, and enjoyed evenings watching Westerns and detective whodunits. Hopalong Cassidy was a favorite. (William Boyd, who played Cassidy, looked remarkably like Ike.) Next to the sunroom was a small library where Mamie displayed Ike's medals and decorations. On one wall his 1915 commission as a second lieutenant of infantry hung alongside his commission thirty years later as General of the Army.[73] There were two master bedrooms, each with a bath en suite, another small bedroom with bath, and five closets. There was also an elevator, a three-car garage, three stoves, and five refrigerators.[74] At 10,111 square feet, Quarters 1 was large enough for Ike and Mamie to resume their life together without getting on each other's nerves.

Eisenhower had little enthusiasm for presiding over the demobilization of the Army. "This job is as bad as I always thought it would be," Ike wrote in his diary on December 15, 1945. "I'm astounded and appalled at the size and scope of plans the staff sees as necessary to maintain our security position now and in the future. The cost is terrific. We'll be merely tilting at windmills unless we can develop something more in line with financial possibilities."[75]

Having served as MacArthur's senior military assistant when MacArthur was chief of staff, Eisenhower understood the necessity to acquaint Congress and the public with the Army's needs. He delegated most administrative matters to the staff George Marshall had assembled, and took advantage of his enormous popularity to make the case for the Army at home and abroad. Ike disliked the term "public relations," but that quickly became his primary concern.[*]

---

mony of the 3rd Cavalry, at which the Army Band rendered honors. The ceremony was conducted by the flagpole in front of Quarters 1, and General Marshall, sometimes in dress blues, was often there. I am sure Patton was there as well, but he was not so well known that my parents would have recognized him and pointed him out.

[*] In his postpresidential memoirs, Eisenhower noted that public relations had become an essential skill for a military officer. Until World War II, said Ike, the

During his first year as chief of staff, Eisenhower made forty-six major speeches to national audiences, often on university campuses; testified before Congress on fourteen occasions; and visited thirteen foreign countries. In his second year, 1947, he made thirty public speeches, and testified on the Hill twelve times—all of which were heavily covered in the press. By the time he left office in 1948, Eisenhower had spoken in every state of the Union at least once, and his name was as familiar to the American public as any political organizer might have hoped for.[76]

Ike was a keen observer on his trips abroad, and recorded his observations in his diary. "Trouble everywhere," he wrote on his return from Brazil near the end of 1946. "So far as South America is concerned, I feel we're very shortsighted," a reference to the attitude of tutelage that prevailed in administration circles. After stopping in Panama and taking his measure of the political situation, he noted the changes taking place. Ike had been stationed in the Canal Zone for three years in the early 1920s, and was clear-sighted about the future. "Personally I think we ought to get out of Panama, lock, stock, and barrel so far as the military is concerned, and have so recommended."[77]

Eisenhower's relations with President Truman were cordial and correct, but the two were never close. Truman worshipped George Marshall, and Ike may have seemed a pale substitute. The president was also intently aware of Eisenhower's public appeal, and it would have been natural for him to be resentful. When the 35th Division, President Truman's old World War I outfit, held a D-Day anniversary celebration in Kansas City in June 1947, the two flew out on the presidential plane. When the plane landed, reporters mobbed Ike and ignored Truman. It was also Eisenhower who delivered the principal address.[78]

Nevertheless, the president relied on Ike, had confidence in his judgment, and entrusted him with one of the most delicate missions during Truman's first year in office. By the beginning of 1946, President Truman had become disenchanted with James Byrnes as his

---

Army had ignored the public and as a result had become "a budgetary stepchild." DDE, *At Ease* 320.

secretary of state. Byrnes, he felt, was not only too cozy with the Soviets, but failed to show proper deference to the presidency.[*] To replace Byrnes, Truman wanted George Marshall. But Marshall was in China attempting to make peace between the government of Chiang Kai-shek and Chairman Mao's Communist movement. (The day after Marshall stepped down as chief of staff, Patrick Hurley resigned as American ambassador to China, and President Truman had tapped Marshall to replace him.) Truman wanted to know if Marshall would accept the job. He could not inquire through normal diplomatic channels because Byrnes would have been tipped off. So he entrusted the query to Ike. "Tell Marshall that my secretary of state had stomach trouble and I wanted to know if he would take the job when it became vacant."[79]

Eisenhower, ostensibly on an inspection tour of the Far East, arrived in Nanking on May 9, 1946. He lunched with Generalissimo and Madame Chiang, and then met privately with Marshall. When he explained the president's proposal, Marshall broke into a rare smile. "Eisenhower," he said, "I would do almost anything to get out of this place. I'd even enlist in the Army."[80] When Ike informed Truman of Marshall's response, the president was delighted. Although Truman wanted to be rid of Byrnes, he was wary of the South Carolinian's support on Capitol Hill. "This gives me a wonderful ace in the hole," he told Ike.[81] Byrnes submitted his resignation in December, and Marshall's appointment was announced by the White House on January 8, 1947.[82]

Eisenhower's speaking engagements brought him into contact with the leaders of American industry, banking, and commerce. On April 2, 1946, Ike was the featured speaker at ceremonies marking

---

[*] One of the by-products of Truman's displeasure with Byrnes was passage of congressional legislation altering the line of presidential succession. From the time of Grover Cleveland, the order of succession ran from president to vice president to secretary of state, and then around the cabinet by rank. The purpose was to ensure that the party in power remained in power, assuming all members of the president's cabinet would be of the same party. At Truman's urging, Congress inserted the Speaker of the House and the president pro tem of the Senate before the secretary of state. The ostensible reason was that the Speaker and president pro tem held elected office and the secretary of state did not. The underlying reason was Truman's disdain for Byrnes, whom he did not want in a position to succeed him.

the Diamond Jubilee of the Metropolitan Museum of Art in New York City. Thomas J. Watson, the chief executive officer of IBM, was chairman of the board at the Met and Ike's host for the occasion. Watson was also on the board of trustees of Columbia University. Columbia's president of forty-four years, the legendary Nicholas Murray Butler ("Nicholas Miraculous"), was in failing health and on the verge of retirement. Over drinks that evening in Ike's suite at the Waldorf-Astoria, Watson asked Eisenhower if he would consider taking the job. Ike demurred. If Columbia wanted a president, he told Watson, they should consider his brother Milton. No, said Watson. Columbia needed a president of international stature, someone who could step into the shoes of the redoubtable Butler. They did not need an educator. The faculty ran the university. Columbia needed the prestige that Eisenhower would bring to the post. Ike did not turn Watson down. He said that given his responsibilities as chief of staff, he would not be available for two years, and therefore could not consider the possibility at the present time.[83]

Ike's answer was what Watson was hoping for. Butler was still very much a presence in Morningside Heights; various search committees were beating the bushes for a successor, and the time was not ripe. But as Watson recognized, Eisenhower had signaled his availability. Ike, for his part, discussed Watson's suggestion with Milton, but thought no more about it. Thirteen months later the search at Columbia had failed to produce a suitable candidate.* At this point, Watson approached Eisenhower again. Ike was in New York filling in for President Truman as guest speaker at a banquet for insurance underwriters, and Watson again met him for drinks at the Waldorf. "To my chagrin," Eisenhower wrote Milton, "his proposal was that I seriously consider committing myself to take over the job [at Columbia] once I have been relieved as Chief of Staff. He urged the importance of the public service I could perform in that spot."[84] Watson had evidently canvassed his fellow board members, and as

* The fruitless Columbia presidential search is described in detail by Travis Beal Jacobs in *Eisenhower at Columbia* 1–49 (New Brunswick, N.J.: Transaction Publishers, 2001). Offers were made to James Phinney Baxter III, president of Williams, and Robert G. Sproul, president of the University of California, both of whom declined.

Ike told Milton, he was speaking with somewhat more authority than in their earlier conversation. "Mr. Watson pressed me pretty hard to give them an early answer. Actually, I am going to stall along until I see you next week but my final answer is going to be a refusal to tie myself down."[85]

For Eisenhower, the Columbia offer was something he had never contemplated. For the past thirty-six years his assignments had been dictated by the Army. He now faced a monumental career choice with absolutely no experience in making career choices, and he was temporarily at a loss.* How would Mamie react? Could they live in New York? Could he run a great university? Would a lot of entertaining be required? Was he expected to raise money, as Nicholas Murray Butler had done so effectively? These were all questions that bothered Ike. When they met, Milton encouraged him to take the post. Columbia, he told Ike, wanted a symbolic leader, and that would work to Eisenhower's advantage. He would have a national platform from which to speak out on major issues. The appointment would be mutually beneficial. And administering a great university like Columbia, said Milton, was like administering any successful corporation, and certainly less difficult than what Ike had experienced in Europe.

A week later, on June 2, 1947, Eisenhower was the commencement speaker at West Point. Watson and Thomas I. Parkinson, president of Equitable Life and the chairman of the Columbia search committee, drove up from the city to tender an official offer to Ike. They met in the home of the academy's superintendent, General Maxwell D. Taylor. Watson and Parkinson repeated their promise that Eisenhower would not have to concern himself with curriculum or faculty. Ike asked for more time. Watson and Parkinson gave him three weeks.

---

* "It was almost the first decision I ever had to make in my life that was directly concerned with myself," Eisenhower wrote Bedell Smith. "I had to struggle against every instinct I had. . . . I think my real dream was to get a small college of an undergraduate character somewhere in the Virginia or Pennsylvania area or possibly even in the Northwest and live quietly with Mamie in that kind of an atmosphere." DDE to Smith, July 3, 1947, *The Papers of Dwight David Eisenhower,* vol. 8, *Chief of Staff* 1799–800.

When Ike returned to Washington, he went to the White House to discuss the Columbia offer with President Truman. Truman urged him to accept, and said he could release Eisenhower as chief of staff in early 1948.[86] In the meantime, Watson assured Eisenhower that the entertaining would be minimal, that he would not have to bother with academic matters, and that fund-raising would be handled by the trustees—all of whom were gratified that Ike was considering accepting the post.[87]

On June 23, 1947, three weeks to the day after the offer had been made, Eisenhower wrote Thomas Parkinson to indicate his acceptance.

> I am anxious that before the Board meets tomorrow, all its members understand very clearly the general picture that you, Mr. Watson and the others have painted to me of the basic purpose lying behind my selection; to devote my energies in providing internal leadership on broad and liberal lines for the University itself and to promote the basic concepts of education in a democracy with particular emphasis upon the *American* system of democracy. . . . I earnestly hope that you will not be disappointed in your choice.[88]

The following day, June 24, 1947, the board of trustees of Columbia University unanimously elected Eisenhower the thirteenth president of the university.

# SEVENTEEN

# Columbia

Stand Columbia! Alma Mater
Through the storms of Time abide
— GILBERT OAKLEY WARD

EISENHOWER STEPPED DOWN as chief of staff on February 7, 1948, and Omar Bradley was sworn in as his successor. By arrangement with the board of trustees, Ike would assume his duties at Columbia at the end of the academic year, and by agreement with Bradley, he and Mamie would remain at Quarters 1 until he was ready to move to New York.* In the interim, Eisenhower intended to write his memoirs.

Eisenhower had planned to write his memoirs from the time he assumed command of the North African invasion of 1942. Kay Summersby and Harry Butcher had kept diaries for him, Ike occasionally made entries in his own diary, and the staff both at AFHQ and SHAEF had been meticulous in maintaining a record of his activities. Even before the war ended Eisenhower received offers from publishers, but did not take them seriously until toward the end of his tour as chief of staff. "I don't believe that any man on active duty has the right or the time to undertake the writing of a book of this kind."[1]

---

* General Bradley lived down the street from Eisenhower at Fort Myer's Quarters 7. Ike and Bradley worked together harmoniously but did not socialize. Evidently Mamie and Bradley's wife, Mary, did not get along. Bradley and Blair, *General's Life* 463.

What Ike did do was set aside evenings at Quarters 1 to reread the *Memoirs* of Ulysses Grant, which he would use as a model.[2] Grant's lean and elegant prose has often been cited by critics as diverse as Edmund Wilson and Gertrude Stein as the finest nonfiction writing in American literature.[3] Grant was generous in his praise and sparing with his criticism, which also appealed to Ike. "I would not indulge in the kind of personal criticism or disparagement of others that had badly marred many military accounts."[4]

Negotiations began in earnest in December 1947. Ike was approached by Simon and Schuster and by Harper and Brothers, but eventually signed on with Doubleday, acting in conjunction with the *New York Herald Tribune,* who made what Eisenhower considered a preemptive offer. Instead of the customary advance against royalties, Doubleday and the *Trib* proposed to buy all of the rights to Ike's book in a single package. There would be no royalties, but Eisenhower would receive a lump sum payment of $635,000 upon completion of the manuscript.[5][*] It was a handshake deal. Ike said a written contract was not necessary.[6]

Under the arrangement, Eisenhower received roughly the modern equivalent of $6 million, about half of what President Clinton received from Alfred A. Knopf as an advance against royalties for his memoirs. But unlike Clinton's royalties, Ike's lump sum payment in 1948 was treated as a capital gain, not as income. That was standard IRS procedure at the time for onetime authors who received a lump sum payment, and Ike received no special consideration.[7] It meant that instead of paying income tax at the rate of 82.13 percent, which would have been Ike's tax bracket, he paid taxes at the capital gains rate of 25 percent.[8] That left Ike $476,250, or roughly $4.5 million in today's dollars, and it made him financially independent. Some biographers have suggested that Eisenhower would have been better off under a standard royalty arrangement—over a million copies of

---

[*] Ulysses Grant was offered a similar lump sum arrangement by Mark Twain for his memoirs but turned it down in favor of royalties. If Twain did not make money on the book, Grant did not want any. "This was just like Grant," said Twain. "It was absolutely impossible for him to entertain for a moment any proposition which might prosper him at the risk of any other man." Samuel Clemens, 1 *Mark Twain's Autobiography* 40 (New York: Harper and Brothers, 1924).

*Crusade in Europe* have been sold—but the near-confiscatory income tax rates in the 1940s and '50s make that doubtful.

Eisenhower began writing on February 8, 1948. He worked sixteen hours a day, seven days a week. There was no ghost writer. Ike dictated to three stenographers who worked in tandem. When a chapter was typed, Eisenhower edited it lightly and then gave it to a team of staff officers who fact-checked and served as research assistants. "Because I habitually rose at six, it was a tough grind for all of us," Ike recalled, "but in a way it was fun. There were no delays for lack of material. My secretarial help was superb and at times my execrable handwriting provided a reason for a laugh."[9]

After the fact-checking was finished, there was another round of editing and the chapter was sent off to Ike's editors in New York, the legendary Kenneth McCormick, editor in chief of Doubleday, and Joe Barnes, then foreign editor of the *Herald Tribune* and later editor in chief of Simon and Schuster. McCormick and Barnes were awed by Eisenhower's performance. Barnes said that on one occasion he saw Ike dictate, without stopping, five thousand words that required almost no editing. Barnes had "never seen such a performance."[10] Eisenhower listened to the advice he received from McCormick and Barnes, but for the most part he relied on his own instincts for rewriting and correcting, and his determination to get the facts right.[11]

As a result, *Crusade in Europe* remains one of the clearest and least opinionated books to come out of World War II. If Ike had an ax to grind, he avoided doing so in his book. Like Grant's *Memoirs,* it is also free of the petty bitterness that characterized the books of Montgomery and Lord Alanbrooke, and the diaries of George Patton, which were published posthumously. Unlike Churchill's monumental six-volume history of the war, Eisenhower also did not avoid subjects that were embarrassing and did not hesitate to accept responsibility for matters that went wrong. Grant's reputation as one of the finest American writers of nonfiction remains secure, but *Crusade in Europe* is a remarkably complete record of the war in Europe and a reliable reference that will continue to be consulted by future historians. The fact that it is still in print after sixty-five years speaks for itself.

When the manuscript was finished, in mid-April, William Robinson, publisher of the *Herald Tribune,* presented Eisenhower two

checks totaling $625,000, and then whisked Ike and Mamie off for a
two-week vacation at the Augusta National Golf Club. It was Eisenhower's first visit to Augusta, and the club soon became an integral
part of his life.* At Augusta, Robinson introduced Ike to a group of
men who became his lifelong friends. Rich, Republican, and devoted
to golf and bridge, they took it upon themselves to make Eisenhower's leisure time enjoyable and to pick up the expenses. Known
as "the Gang," they included, in addition to Robinson, Clifford Roberts, a New York investment banker who with golfing legend Bobby
Jones had founded the Augusta National; Robert Woodruff, chairman of the board of Coca-Cola; W. Alton ("Pete") Jones, president of
Cities Service Company (a precursor to Citgo); and Ellis Slater, president of Frankfort Distilleries. The sole Democrat in the Gang was
Mississippi's George Allen, one of the country's sharpest legal minds
who hid his talent behind a roly-poly façade as court jester to presidents. The Gang made Eisenhower a member of Augusta, built a
cottage for him near the tenth tee, and put in a fish pond well stocked
with bass for his private use.[12]

Presidential boomlets for Eisenhower erupted spontaneously. A
national Draft Eisenhower league set up shop, and the biweekly polls
conducted by the Gallup and Roper organizations showed Ike to be
running ahead of Governor Dewey and Senator Taft among likely
Republican voters, and ahead of President Truman among Democrats. Eisenhower did nothing to encourage his supporters. But he
also did nothing to discourage them. "I am frequently flayed," he
wrote Bedell Smith in September 1947, "because I insist that I do
not want to have any political office and still will not use the language of Sherman. The two cases are not parallel."[13] A month later
he explained to his brother Milton that he would feel under no obligation to accept the nomination if it came to him as the result of a
deadlocked convention (as it did to Sherman), but a genuine draft
was a different matter. And for that reason he did not want to use

* The Augusta National Golf Club, site of the annual Masters Tournament, is
ranked by golfing aficionados as the finest course in the nation. Membership in the
club is limited to three hundred and is by invitation only. One does not apply. Annual dues are low because of the television earnings from the Masters. Current
members include Bill Gates, Warren Buffett, Jack Welch, and T. Boone Pickens.

Sherman's words. "Every citizen," said Ike, "is required to do his duty for the country no matter what it may be."[14]

The issue came to a head in January 1948. On January 9, a group of New Hampshire Republicans formally entered a slate of delegates pledged to Eisenhower in the upcoming March primary. Leonard Finder, publisher of the Manchester *Union Leader,* wrote to inform Ike of the action and enclosed a front-page editorial from the paper endorsing him. "No man should deny the will of the people in a matter such as this," wrote Finder.[15]

Eisenhower pondered his reply for more than a week. All signs pointed to a Republican victory in the fall. Thomas E. Dewey, the GOP front-runner, was forty-eight; Robert A. Taft was fifty-nine— both young enough to serve two terms. In eight years Ike would be sixty-six, much too old for a man to make his first campaign for the presidency, particularly for someone who was not in politics.[16] If Eisenhower were going to run, he would have to do so now.

Given the choice of whether to fish or cut bait, Eisenhower chose to cut bait. "It is my conviction that the necessary and wise subordination of the military to civil power will best be sustained . . . when lifelong professional soldiers, in the absence of some obvious and overriding reasons, abstain from seeking high political office," he replied to Finder on January 22, 1948. After thanking those who had worked on his behalf, Ike issued the flat denial that seemingly closed the door on the possibility of his becoming president. "My decision to remove myself completely from the political scene is definite and positive. I could not accept nomination even under the remote circumstance that it was tendered to me."[17]

Numerous commentators have speculated that if Eisenhower had been the Republican candidate in 1948 he would have won. That may be so, but it would have been an uphill fight for him to win the nomination. Few states elected their convention delegates by primaries in 1948, and even if Ike had won all of the primaries, he would have gone into the convention far short of the number of delegates required. Dewey and Taft had been campaigning for eight years, and the Republican organization in most states was pledged to one or the other. Regardless of his public support, it is unlikely that Eisenhower could have won the nomination.[18]

Ike arrived on Morningside Heights on May 2, 1948. He and Mamie moved into the president's mansion at 60 Morningside Drive and began to settle in. Nicholas Murray Butler had died in early December, and the house had been completely renovated by Dorothy Draper, one of the nation's best-known interior decorators.[*] Built of brick and Indiana limestone in 1912 by McKim, Mead, and White for Butler, the four-story Italianate house was as close to a ducal palazzo as one might find west of Florence. The two lower floors were designed for formal entertaining, with marble floors, crystal chandeliers, and a dining room that seated thirty comfortably. Butler once estimated that between 2,500 and 3,000 people came to the presidential house for receptions, lunches, and dinners every year.[19] Guests included the King and Queen of England, Cardinal Eugenio Pacelli (later Pope Pius XII), more than a dozen heads of state, and countless Nobel Prize winners.[†] According to *The New Yorker*, an invitation to 60 Morningside Drive was "the most sought after of high cultural invitations, proof that the privileged recipient had arrived in New York society."[20]

The third floor of the mansion was set aside for family living, with guest rooms and servants quarters on the fourth. Draper had converted an old water storage room on the roof into a penthouse solarium for the Eisenhowers. Mamie furnished it with her Philippine rattan furniture, members of the Gang gathered there regularly for bridge, and Ike had a studio for painting. There was a household staff of nine—which Mrs. Butler had trained to perfection—to

[*] Dorothy Draper, considered by many to be the doyenne of the design industry in the twentieth century, is best known as the inventor of "Modern Baroque"—a flamboyant style best suited for large public places where people might come and feel elevated in the presence of great beauty. Her works include New York's Hotel Carlyle and Hampshire House; the Greenbrier in White Sulphur Springs, West Virginia; Washington's Mayflower Hotel; the Drake Hotel in Chicago; and the Palácio Quitandinha in Petrópolis, an hour north of Rio de Janeiro. The restaurant at New York's Metropolitan Museum of Art was once nicknamed the "Dorotheum" because of her design. Carleton Varney, *The Draper Touch: The High Life and High Style of Dorothy Draper* (New York: Prentice Hall, 1988).

[†] Butler himself had won the Nobel Peace Prize in 1931, sharing it with Jane Addams, former president of the Women's International League for Peace and Freedom and founder of Hull House in Chicago.

which were added Sergeant John Moaney, Ike's valet, and Sergeant Leonard Dry, who had been his driver since 1943.

By arrangement with the board of trustees, Eisenhower would assume his official duties as president on June 7, 1948, one week after commencement, with a formal installation ceremony scheduled for the fall. The month's hiatus between his arrival in May and June 7 would give him a chance to become familiar with the university and his responsibilities. Ike had requested that the president's offices in Low Memorial Library be relocated and made more accessible. Butler's office, one floor above the rotunda, could be reached only by a private elevator from the office of the secretary of the university. Eisenhower chose rooms on the main floor, just off the rotunda. "There, I hoped, both students and faculty might have direct and easy access to their President and I would not feel immured in a remote citadel."²¹ The campus regarded the move with satisfaction. Less salubrious was Ike's decision to bring with him from the Pentagon Major Robert L. Schulz as his administrative aide, and Kevin McCann as a special assistant. Schulz and McCann, who knew little about university affairs and nothing about Columbia, organized Eisenhower's office like a military headquarters, kept the faculty at arm's length, and were determined to protect Ike rather than allowing him to be himself. "They didn't have the knowledge of things academic," said historian Harry J. Carman, the beloved dean of Columbia College, and "I put part of the difficulty which President Eisenhower encountered here squarely at their doorstep."²²

Scarcely had he settled in when Eisenhower was confronted with two major challenges pertaining to civil liberty and academic freedom. The spring and early summer of 1948 witnessed the arrival of the Cold War with full intensity. The Russians launched the Berlin blockade in June, and Communist witch-hunting would soon reach epidemic proportions in the United States. State legislature after state legislature enacted loyalty-oath requirements for university faculty, and the great private universities of the Ivy League—Harvard, Princeton, Yale, and Columbia—were not immune from the witch-hunting virus.

At Columbia, the issues involved guest speakers on campus and the use of endowed chairs for faculty appointments. In December

1947, before Ike's arrival, the university had raised no objection when Columbia's Marxist Study Group invited Arnold Johnson, the legislative director of the American Communist Party, to speak on campus in Pupin Hall.* Pupin's daughter had written to question Columbia's policy, and with the arrival of Eisenhower her husband took up the cause. "Will Columbia agree to keep traitors out of Pupin Hall?" he wrote Ike on May 20. "With Kremlin agents . . . among our school and college teachers and administrators, it is now no time for speakers 'explaining Marxism' by attacking all our characteristic institutions."[23]

Eisenhower replied immediately. While he had not been on campus at the time, said Ike, he fully supported the decision Columbia had made to allow Johnson to speak.

> The virtues of our system will never be fully appreciated . . . unless we also understand the essentials of opposing ideologies. . . . I deem it not only unobjectionable but very wise to allow opposing systems to be presented by their proponents. . . . Indeed, I believe that arbitrary refusal to allow students—especially upon their own request—to hear the apostles of these false systems, would create in their minds a justified suspicion that we ourselves fear a real comparison between democracy and dictatorship.[24]

The second issue involved an endowed chair funded by the Polish government for the study of Polish philology, language, and literature. Columbia had accepted the gift in early May, and announced the appointment of Professor Manfred Kridl, an eminent Polish scholar at Smith College, to the post. The Polish-American Congress

---

* Pupin Hall, a National Historic Landmark, was built by McKim, Mead, and White in the late twenties, and is one of the major edifices on the Columbia campus. It was named for Michael I. Pupin, a Serbian American professor of electro-mechanics at Columbia from 1901 to 1935, and houses the physics and astronomy departments. The building is best known as the site where Enrico Fermi first split the atom on January 25, 1939. Its large seminar rooms were often used for public lectures, and at the time were easily accessible from 120th Street and Broadway.

demanded that the university rescind the gift, charging that the Polish government was the tool of Moscow and was engaged in a campaign of "academic infiltration" at Columbia. The press took up the cry. "Coddling Communism at Columbia," said *The San Francisco Examiner* in a lead editorial.[25]

Once again, Eisenhower stood firm. Professor Kridl, said Ike, was a distinguished scholar of Polish literature who had been appointed "solely by Columbia without advice or suggestion from non-University sources." The establishment of the Polish chair, he said, "will make it possible for the students of Columbia to learn more about the language and literature of a country that has suffered so much. A great deal of the trouble in the world today is traceable to a lack of understanding of the culture of various countries. I intend to do all in my power to remedy this situation."[26]

When Eisenhower reported the incident to the trustees on September 20, he said the charges made against Columbia were absurd. "I am certain that none of the professors [involved in filling the Polish chair] is disloyal to our government."[27] At his official installation on October 12, Eisenhower returned to the theme with a spirited defense of academic freedom. "There will be no administrative suppression or distortion of any subject that merits a place in this University's curriculum," said Ike. "The facts of communism, for example, shall be taught here. . . . Ignorance of communism, fascism, or any other police-state philosophy is far more dangerous than ignorance of the most virulent disease. . . . Columbia University will forever be bound by its loyalty to truth and the basic concepts of democratic freedom. No intellectual iron curtain shall screen students from disturbing facts."[28]

Eisenhower's standing on campus could not have been higher. Historian Allan Nevins, writing in *The New York Times,* said, "No one can visit Morningside without feeling great energies vibrating there." With her new president, "Columbia's greatest years lie before her, and she knows that she will share them with a nation which has become the first power on the globe, and a city which has become a world capital."[29]

In late June, Governor Dewey won the Republican nomination on the third ballot and selected Governor Earl Warren of California as

Eisenhower installed as the thirteenth president of Columbia University, October 12, 1948. The mace is carried by English professor John H. H. Lyon.

his running mate. It looked like an unbeatable ticket. In despair, many Democrats turned to Ike. "No one knew whether he was a Democrat or a Republican," wrote *The New Yorker*'s Richard Rovere. "For all anyone knew he might have been a Greenbacker or a Social Credit crank. No one knew whether he knew what he was." What people knew was that "he could win an election."[30]

As the Democratic convention approached, the pressure on Ike intensified. On July 1, 1948, the Eisenhowers celebrated their thirty-second wedding anniversary with the Gang at 60 Morningside Drive. Ellis "Slats" Slater recalled that an enthusiastic throng of two to three hundred persons gathered outside the residence chanting "We Like Ike." Eisenhower went out on the balcony and waved good-naturedly to the crowd.[31] On July 3, a host of Democratic leaders, including New York mayor William O'Dwyer, Senator Lister Hill (Alabama), Governor Chester Bowles (Connecticut), Jacob Arvey (Illinois), Governor J. Strom Thurmond (South Carolina), Congressman James Roosevelt (California), and Minneapolis mayor Hubert H. Humphrey, sent telegrams to all 1,592 Democratic delegates inviting them to attend a caucus in Philadelphia on July 10—two days before the convention would begin. The purpose was to "find the ablest and strongest man available" to lead the party in the coming election. No candidate was mentioned, but it was clearly an effort to dump Truman and draft Ike. At this point Eisenhower recognized that he had to step in. On the evening of July 5, he authorized Robert Harron, Columbia's director of public information, to issue a formal statement to the press restating his January refusal to run. "I shall continue, subject to the pleasure of the University Trustees, to perform the important duties I have undertaken as President of Columbia," said Ike. "I will not, at this time, identify myself with any political party, and could not accept nomination for any public office or participate in a partisan political contest."[32]

As Eisenhower later told journalist Marquis Childs, he thought with that statement he was out of the woods.[33] But the phrase "at this time" encouraged Ike's supporters to believe that he would accept a draft. President Truman evidently thought so as well. At Truman's direction, Secretary of the Army Kenneth Royall called Eisenhower, and over the telephone Ike and Royall drafted a follow-up statement that was then dispatched to James Roosevelt, Senator Claude Pepper (Florida), and Jersey City mayor Frank Hague—all of whom were still beating the drum for Ike. This time Eisenhower was unequivocal. "No matter under what terms, conditions, or premises a proposal might be couched, I would refuse to accept the nomination."[34] So ended the boom for Eisenhower in the Democratic party, although few doubted the nomination would have been his if he had wanted it.

Eisenhower was very much a presence on Columbia's campus in the fall of 1948. He attended home football games at Baker Field, presided over the traditional dinner for freshmen in John Jay Hall, and welcomed the alumni back on a gala Homecoming Day. Ike particularly liked to break off an occasional afternoon and visit Baker Field at 218th Street and Broadway to watch the Columbia football team practice under coaching great Lou Little. A few months before, Little had received an attractive offer from Yale, but to the delight of every Columbia alumnus, Eisenhower had persuaded him to remain

Eisenhower and Columbia coach Lou Little watch football practice at Baker Field.

on Morningside Heights. "You never will, in your entire time as president of the university, do anything which will elicit more universal approval," wrote Joseph Lang (LLB, 1921).[35] Little had been at Columbia since 1930. In 1934, his team had scored a stunning upset over Stanford in the Rose Bowl, and in 1947 had snapped Army's thirty-two-game winning streak with a dramatic fourth-quarter, come-from-behind, 21–20 victory. Ike liked to talk football with Little, and would occasionally reminisce about their first meeting on the football field in 1924, when Eisenhower was coaching the Fort Meade team and Little was at Georgetown. (Georgetown won 7–0.)[36]

Eisenhower also took up painting. Encouraged by Churchill, and inspired by watching Thomas Stephens do a portrait of Mamie, Ike began to paint with oils in his penthouse conservatory. Stephens had supplied the initial paints and brushes, and Ike, after some early hesitation, became an enthusiastic dauber. "My most urgent need at the start was a generous-sized tarpaulin to cover the floor around the easel," wrote Ike years later. "The one thing I could do well from the beginning was to cover hands, clothes, brush handles, chair and floor with more paint than ever reached the canvas."

Eisenhower thought the conservatory at 60 Morningside was an ideal studio. "A professional might have objected to its lack of northern exposure, but privacy and quiet were more important to me than lighting."[37] Gradually, Eisenhower became proficient, although unlike Churchill he never took himself seriously as a painter. "I have nothing whatever of artistic talents," he wrote his childhood friend Swede Hazlett in August 1949. "I simply get a bang out of working with colors and occasionally one of my efforts comes out with sufficient appeal about it to entice some of my friends to steal it and carry it away. Many others find their way to the waste paper basket." Eisenhower not only derived pleasure from painting, but found the quiet time useful for meditating and assembling his thoughts. At Columbia, he usually painted in the evening between eleven and twelve-thirty, but as he warned Hazlett, "if you ever take it up it will consume so many of your vertical hours that you will wonder how they have ever slipped away from you."[38]

Eisenhower took no role in the 1948 election. On election night he was joined at 60 Morningside Drive by George Allen, Bill Robinson, and Cliff Roberts for dinner and bridge. As they played cards and listened to the returns, it became apparent that the election was going to be close and that Truman might win. Roberts said Ike was "just as disappointed as Robinson and I were." Roberts was unable to recall Eisenhower's exact words, but remembered that the general "indicated quite clearly to me that he was having second thoughts about his decision to stay clear of political involvement."[39][*]

With Dewey's defeat, Eisenhower was back in the political spotlight. The GOP nomination in 1952 was now wide open, and Ike moved cautiously to reposition himself. During the fall, Eisenhower

---

[*] Stephen Ambrose, citing an undated interview with John Eisenhower, alleges that November 2 "was the darkest night of Eisenhower's life" because he would be thrust back into the political arena. The quotation does not ring true, given Eisenhower's subsequent activity. As with many of Ambrose's "interviews," his assertion should be taken with a large grain of salt. See Richard Rayner, "Channeling Ike," *The New Yorker*, April 26, 2010.

had been in Washington on several occasions to consult with Defense Secretary James Forrestal and the Joint Chiefs on the Defense Department budget. On November 4, two days after Truman's victory, Ike wrote Forrestal. Without referring to the election, Ike told the secretary that he shared Forrestal's concern over the state of world affairs, and volunteered his assistance. "I can scarcely think of any chore that I would refuse to do whenever people in responsible positions feel that I might be able to help."[40]

Forrestal was delighted. The National Security Act of 1947, which had created the Department of Defense, did not provide for a chairman of the Joint Chiefs of Staff.[*] Forrestal saw Ike's offer as a way to circumvent that omission. "What I have in mind," he wrote Truman on November 9, "was inviting him [Eisenhower] to come down, with your approval, of course, to sit with us for a period of three or four weeks. I should like, if it were possible, to have him named by you to preside over the Joint Chiefs, but if that were impossible an informal basis would be second best."[41]

One hand washed the other. With Dewey defeated, life at Columbia may have looked less attractive to Ike, and with Congress barring the door to the creation of a chairman for the Joint Chiefs, Forrestal saw Eisenhower as an informal substitute. Whether Ike and Forrestal coordinated more closely is unclear, but on November 18, Eisenhower wrote Truman to congratulate him on his reelection. "It seems almost needless for me to reaffirm my loyalty to you as President; or to assure you again that I always stand ready to attempt the performance of any professional duty for which my constitutional superiors believe I might be specially suited."[42]

Ike was fishing and President Truman took the bait. "You didn't have to reaffirm your loyalty to me," he replied on November 26. Resorting to a bit of double entendre, the president told Eisenhower, "I always know exactly where you stand." Nevertheless, he asked Ike

---

[*] Congressman Carl Vinson, a powerful Democrat from Georgia who had chaired the House Naval Affairs Committee and who would chair the new Armed Services Committee, strongly opposed the creation of a post that would resemble a single chief of staff for the armed forces. To gain Vinson's support for the bill when it was before the House, the Truman administration dropped the proposal for a chairman of the Joint Chiefs.

to stop by the White House and see him the next time he was in Washington.[43]

Eisenhower followed a familiar game plan. When stymied in his career, he invariably sought outside assistance. He had appealed to Fox Conner three times—to attend Leavenworth, to escape from the 24th Infantry, and to be rescued from a dead-end assignment with Pershing in Paris. In 1939, when duty in Manila with MacArthur paled, he wrote his friend Mark Clark and was promptly reassigned to the 3rd Infantry Division at Fort Lewis, Washington. For any number of reasons Ike was growing restive at Columbia, and his approach to Forrestal and Truman followed a pattern.

The irony is that in the fall of 1948, Eisenhower had mastered Columbia. "General Eisenhower has taken Columbia the way he took Normandy Beach," said *The New York Times* on November 7. "The entire university population of 35,000—students, professors, officers, trustees, and janitors—has happily surrendered and adores its conqueror."[44]

Eisenhower was also much in demand as a public speaker. The *New York Herald Tribune* began serializing *Crusade in Europe* the Sunday after the election, and the book was released by Doubleday on November 22. Prepublication publicity had been massive, the first pressrun was 150,000 copies, and the book was greeted with critical acclaim on both sides of the Atlantic. Drew Middleton, writing in *The New York Times Book Review,* placed *Crusade* "in the first rank of military memoirs." Robert Sherwood, who had won three Pulitzer Prizes as a playwright and a fourth for his biography *Roosevelt and Hopkins: An Intimate History,* called the book "a heartening demonstration of what we are pleased to call Americanism at its best." Liberal critic Richard Rovere, writing in *Harper's,* considered *Crusade in Europe* "a document that sometimes comes close to splendor." In London, Goronwy Rees, reviewing *Crusade* for *The Spectator,* called Ike "the greatest single architect of the greatest military alliance in history. I don't believe any other man could have achieved what he achieved."[45]

On the Columbia campus, where publish or perish was a way of life, the response was rapturous. Ike might not have had a graduate degree, but he had proved he could hold his own with the nation's best historians. Allan Nevins said he started reading the book as his train was leaving Washington and became so absorbed that he missed his stop at Princeton where he was scheduled to give a lecture and had to take another train back.[46]

Eisenhower also mixed effectively with faculty and students when he chose to do so. When Professor Robert Livingston Schuyler asked him to speak to his graduate class in historiography, Ike not only agreed but "spoke with passion and deep knowledge about two of the college's most illustrious former students, Alexander Hamilton and John Jay."[47] When the history faculty invited Eisenhower to their annual black-tie dinner, Ike stole the show. According to Jacques Barzun, Columbia's brilliant intellectual historian, one of his colleagues quoted Churchill's remark about Europe's "soft underbelly." Eisenhower, according to Barzun, "got quite huffy, and said, 'That is one of the most ignorant remarks made by anybody,' and he proceeded to give us, without prompting, a history of the campaigns, beginning with Thucydides and the Peloponnesian War, that had taken place in the south of Europe which, as we all know, is a mass of mountains, and he went right on to the Austrian War of 1866, the German-Austrian War. It was a masterly performance and with hardly a hesitation for words."[48] Henry Graff, a junior member of the department at the time, recalled that it was "a dazzling talk delivered without notes and with uncommon insight and learning. He spoke of the great captains of history who had preceded him on the battlefields of Europe. Let no one tell you that he was not an historian, that he was not one of us."[49]

Eisenhower also invigorated the administrative side of the university. He instituted organizational reforms advocated by the consulting firm of Booz Allen years earlier, and established a mandatory retirement age of sixty-eight for faculty and administrative staff. Most important, he balanced Columbia's budget for the first time in four years and put in place the first systematic fund-raising structure the university had known. Nicholas Murray Butler had been spectacularly successful as a fund-raiser during his first thirty years as president, but he did so on a strictly personal basis. Unlike Harvard, Princeton, and Yale, Columbia had no fund-raising arm other than Butler himself. The combination of advancing age, the Great Depression, and the progressive income tax caused Columbia's fund-raising to dry up almost completely. Its principal source of income, other than tuition, was the rent on Manhattan real estate, most of which had been let on long-term leases at prices far below 1948 levels. As a result, Columbia was living off its capital. Figures provided by the American Council of Education show that between 1929 and 1939, Columbia's endowment decreased by $3 million ($46 million in current dollars). During the same period, Harvard's endowment increased by $27 million ($416 million currently) and Yale's by $18 million ($278 million). Of the sixteen universities in the council's study, Columbia was the only institution whose endowment had declined.[50]

Columbia's financial problem was exacerbated by a decaying physical plant in which scheduled maintenance had been deferred, and by the influx of thousands of veterans who had to be accommodated. Eisenhower addressed the problem by putting in place a private gifts organization patterned on Princeton's annual alumni campaign, and in October 1948 launched a $210 million fund drive ($1.9 billion currently) to restore the university's solvency. Ike had not anticipated that he would be required to raise money when he accepted Columbia's offer in 1947—Watson and Parkinson had explicitly assured him that he would not—but when confronted with the reality of the university's budgetary shortfall, he moved promptly with the support of the trustees to correct it.

In nonacademic matters, Eisenhower also used his considerable clout to Columbia's advantage. When university maintenance workers threatened to strike over wages and working conditions, Ike negotiated directly with Michael J. Quill, head of the Transport Workers Union of America. (The Columbia employees were members.) Eisenhower and Quill quickly reached a settlement. "Look, General," said Quill, "I'm not going to have any trouble with you. I've got more sense than to be taking on an opponent who is as popular as you seem to be in this city."[51]

A more enduring contribution, for which Columbia faculty and students have been eternally grateful, is that Eisenhower prevailed upon Mayor William O'Dwyer and the New York City Council to close 116th Street between Broadway and Amsterdam Avenue. The

main campus of Columbia, a total of twenty-six acres, stretches from
114th Street to 120th, and is bounded on the east by Amsterdam
Avenue and on the west by Broadway. When the university moved
from midtown to Morningside Heights in 1897, all of the interior
streets were closed off except for 116th, which bisected the campus.
Like all New York streets, it was noisy and crowded with traffic and
parked cars. It made the Columbia campus look like a factory yard,
said more than one observer. Nicholas Murray Butler had sought
repeatedly and without success to have the street closed off. But as
was the case with Mike Quill, no one on the city council wanted to
pick a fight with Ike, and the street was soon closed, bringing the
two halves of the campus together. Located in the midst of Manhattan, Columbia is scarcely a green oasis. Yet thanks to Eisenhower it
now stands as a single entity, giving the campus a unified appearance. A visitor to Columbia today would never suspect that 116th
Street was a through street as recently as the early 1950s.

In his first six months on campus, Eisenhower demonstrated to
the satisfaction of even the greatest skeptic that he was capable of
providing the leadership that Columbia required. But he was not
comfortable. The complexity of Columbia confounded him. Initially
he had assumed—based on his West Point experience—that Columbia was primarily an undergraduate institution with a few professional schools attached. His educational mission, as he saw it, was to
encourage the teaching of civic virtue. In reality, Columbia was an
aggregation of more than two dozen schools and faculties ranging
from law and medicine to education and journalism. Columbia College, the undergraduate body, had but 2,400 students—roughly 8
percent of the total enrolled at the university. And very few (if any)
of the faculty saw their mission as one of teaching the responsibilities
of citizenship.

Dean Carman recalled that Eisenhower invited him for a talk early
that fall and related how he had really wanted to be president of a
small rural college where "he thought he could be useful." But, said
Ike, "in a moment of weakness I listened to the blandishments of a
couple of your Trustees and here I find myself with a gigantic organization on my hands, and I don't know a goddamn thing about
it."[52]

Universities are governed by consensus. Eisenhower was accustomed to a chain of command. Like most who have not served an apprenticeship in academe, he assumed the important people on campus were the deans and department chairmen. They were his corps and divisions commanders. The faculty were the officers and the students the enlisted personnel. In reality, particularly in the supercharged intellectual atmosphere on Morningside Heights, it is the scholars who determine policy. They are the university. And in 1948–49, the faculty at Columbia was one of the most distinguished ever assembled. The roster reads like a who's who of intellectual life in America: Ruth Benedict and Margaret Mead in anthropology; C. Wright Mills, Robert Lynd, Robert Merton, and Paul Lazarsfeld in sociology; Nobel Prize winners Enrico Fermi and Isador Rabi in physics; Harold Urey (another Nobel laureate) in chemistry; Joseph Wood Krutch, Lionel Trilling, and Mark Van Doren in English. The history department represented the core of the discipline in the twentieth century. In addition to Barzun and Graff, the senior scholars included Henry Steele Commager, Dumas Malone, Carlton J. H. Hayes, Lynn Thorndike, Garrett Mattingly, and Allan Nevins. Among the younger members were David Herbert Donald, Richard Hofstadter, and William Leuchtenburg.

By dealing through deans and chairmen and ignoring Columbia's scholars, Eisenhower was moving against the grain. If Ike had dedicated himself full-time to Columbia, he would have soon mastered the nuances of university life. But in late December 1948, he went to Washington, conferred with Forrestal and the president, and agreed to become the senior adviser to the secretary of defense and acting chairman of the Joint Chiefs. Unification of the services was working poorly, the Army and Navy were at loggerheads over the defense budget, and Forrestal's health had begun to deteriorate. Ike assured Columbia's trustees that he could handle both jobs, and began a backbreaking schedule commuting between Washington and Morningside Heights. "We would go up to New York," recalled Major Schulz, "be met by a car, go to Columbia, get a little work done, go downtown to a dinner where the General would speak, over to Penn Station, into a train, and do it all over again. Frankly, there were days that I didn't know whether I was waking up in New York or Washington. And he [Eisenhower] must have been the same way. It was a rat race."[53]

By February it was clear that the situation in the Pentagon would require Ike's full-time presence in Washington. Not only was the budget contentious, but the Navy and the Air Force were at each other's throat over the future of the naval air arm. "Pres. and Mr. F[orrestal] assume that I have some miraculous power to make these warring elements lie down and make peace together," Eisenhower recorded in his diary on February 9, 1949.[54] Ike agreed to assume the duties of chairman of the Joint Chiefs for a period of three months, and the Columbia trustees granted him a leave of absence. "Cognizant of the tradition of public service which has characterized Columbia's long history," said board chairman Frederick Coykendall, the trustees "are happy to give their full approval to President Eisenhower's important work in Washington . . . and are glad the University can make this contribution to the public welfare."[55] No acting president was named, and Columbia's provost, Albert C. Jacobs, assumed operating responsibility in Ike's absence.

Not having to commute eased the pressure on Eisenhower partially, but Forrestal collapsed in late February, Truman accepted his resignation, and Louis Johnson, who became secretary of defense, expected Ike to carry the ball. Eisenhower continued his extensive speaking schedule and returned to New York monthly to meet with the trustees. Mamie remained at 60 Morningside Drive, and Ike lived out of a suitcase at Washington's Statler Hotel. Nevertheless, the infighting at the Pentagon continued. "I am so weary of this inter-service struggle for position, prestige and power that this morning I practically 'blew my top,' " Ike wrote on March 14, 1949. "I would hate to have my doctor take my blood pressure at the moment."[56] Five days later, after a particularly testy meeting with the Joint Chiefs, he began his diary entry with the blunt statement "The situation grows intolerable"—a reference to the Navy's reluctance to cooperate with unification. Even worse, Secretary Johnson informed Eisenhower that he expected him to remain in Washington for the "next six months, *at least.* He says he told Pres. he'd take job only if I stayed on!"[57]

The tension of holding two jobs, even if he was on leave from Columbia, was getting to Ike. On March 21, after a luncheon with the

Motion Picture Association of America, he became ill with a severe stomach disorder and returned to his hotel. Major Schulz recalled that by the time they got Eisenhower to his room, "his stomach was bloated and getting larger. It seemed like a balloon." Dr. Snyder flew down from New York, diagnosed Ike's condition as "a severe case of acute gastroenteritis," and ordered complete rest. "I knew that I was sick," wrote Eisenhower in his memoir. Dr. Snyder "treated me as though I were at the edge of the precipice and teetering a bit. For days, my head was not off the pillow."[58]

Eisenhower, at Truman's recommendation, flew to the naval station at Key West aboard *The Sacred Cow,* where he underwent an extensive battery of tests and was forbidden solid food and cigarettes. After two weeks in Key West, he flew to Augusta, where Mamie joined him. Ike remained at the Augusta National Golf Club for the next month, playing golf and painting. "I feel stronger every day," he wrote Secretary Johnson on April 20, "though I must admit the 'drives' are somewhat short of their expected destination."[59] A week later he wrote Swede Hazlett that he had been miserable for a time but that for the past two weeks "I have been puttering around with a bit of golf every day."[60] There is no evidence, as some have asserted, that Eisenhower suffered a mild heart attack and that Dr. Snyder had covered it up.*

---

* Dr. Thomas Mattingly, a cardiologist at Walter Reed Army Medical Center in Washington, who treated Eisenhower following his heart attack in 1955, suggested that Ike may have suffered a previous attack in 1949, but that it had been covered up by Snyder's "deceptive diagnosis." Mattingly acknowledged, however, that he had no proof. See pages 80–82 of Mattingly's unpublished "Life Health Record of Dwight D. Eisenhower" at the Eisenhower Library. Professor Clarence G. Lasby of the University of Texas examined Mattingly's claim in detail and after ten pages of convincing evidence notes that it points to one conclusion: "Eisenhower did not have a heart attack in 1949." Consider, for example, Ike's letter to his former aide James Stack written on May 16, his first day back at Columbia, which belies the possibility of a heart attack. Ike told Stack that "I have frequently played eighteen holes of golf a day during the past month and on one or two occasions even twenty-seven holes. This did not seem to bother me in spite of the fact that I take a great many more strokes than the average person does in getting around the course." DDE to James Stack, May 16, 1949, *The Papers of Dwight David Eisenhower,* vol. 10, *Columbia* 581; Clarence G. Lasby, *Eisenhower's Heart Attack: How Ike Beat Heart Disease and Held On to the Presidency* 47–50 (Lawrence: University Press

Ike returned to Columbia in mid-May, presided over commencement activities in June, and then went on an extended summer vacation to Wisconsin and Colorado. "I am going to take not less than a total of 10 weeks leave during the year," he wrote his brother Milton at Kansas State. "If I am not able to keep up to this leave schedule, I will simply quit all my jobs except that of helping out in Washington."[61]

Eisenhower was back at Columbia, but the university had become a secondary interest. As the supreme commander of the greatest allied effort in history, and recently exposed to the wrenching problems of military unification, Ike found academic affairs increasingly trivial. At commencement, he declined to host the traditional reception for honorary degree recipients ("He wouldn't even read the citations," said Provost Jacobs), and chose instead to have a private dinner at 60 Morningside with General Lucius D. Clay and his wife, Marjorie. Provost Jacobs held the reception for the university's distinguished guests, including Helen Hayes, Arnold Toynbee, and General Omar Bradley, at the Men's Faculty Club in Ike's stead.[62]*

After two months of fishing and golf in the lake country of Wisconsin and in Denver, Eisenhower was back on Morningside Heights on September 17. He had been appointed president of Columbia twenty-seven months earlier, but of those twenty-seven months, he had spent less than ten on campus. The seeds of discontent were beginning to sprout. Columbia needed a full-time chief executive, and Ike was devoting less and less time to university affairs. Eisenhower had an "auspicious start," Lionel Trilling recalled, but it "gradually and quickly disintegrated. I began to sense he was nowhere in relation to the University."[63] Professor Eli Ginsberg, who had worked with Ike in Washington and who was one of his few acquaintances on the faculty, thought that Eisenhower "never found a way of responding to anything substantive on campus. Nothing gave him a real

---

of Kansas, 1997); compare, Robert H. Ferrell, *Ill-Advised: Presidential Health and Public Trust* 63, 65 (Columbia: University of Missouri Press, 1992).

* The fact that Ike and Mamie chose to dine with Lucius and Marjorie Clay and snub Omar and Mary Bradley not only suggests Eisenhower's disdain for university responsibilities but also reflects the tension in the relationship between Mamie and Mary Bradley.

kick . . . a central focus."[64] Jacques Barzun, who would soon become provost, thought Eisenhower had "a curiously ambivalent feeling about the University, especially the faculty."[65] Trilling, Ginsberg, and Barzun were not only senior scholars, but had devoted their professional lives to Columbia and understood the university intimately. They had no ax to grind.

Eisenhower lacked a sixth sense, an intuitive feel to tell him what was important to the faculty. He declined to preside at meetings of the university council and at various faculty meetings as Butler had done, refused to attend the university's gala celebration for John Dewey on the philosopher's ninetieth birthday, and avoided almost all participation in academic affairs, leading many on Morningside Heights to conclude that he "begrudged the University."[66]

The Eisenhowers, both Ike and Mamie, also had a sense of entitlement that rubbed the faculty the wrong way. The presidential mansion at 60 Morningside Drive was traditionally the social center of the university. Evenings with Nicholas Murray Butler could be "exceedingly stiff and formal," Dean Carman recalled, but those evenings served a useful university purpose.[67] The Eisenhowers never revived those dinners. Ike and Mamie saw 60 Morningside as their private residence. They entertained old Army friends who might be passing through New York and invited the Gang for dinner and bridge several nights a week. In the late evening, Eisenhower would get out his paints and canvas and go to work. On weekends, John and Barbara would come down from West Point with their son David for a visit. But the house no longer brought the Columbia community together. "I don't know of a single instance where any of the Columbia people were ever invited," said Gang member Cliff Roberts.[68]

Ike recognized that he was being pulled in different directions. He was no longer traveling to Washington, but his extensive speaking schedule kept him on the road and away from Columbia. "I believe that if a man were able to give his full or nearly full attention to such a job as this," he wrote Swede Hazlett, "he would find it completely absorbing. . . . Sometimes, however, my loyalties to several different kinds of purposes lead me into a confusing kind of living."[69] For Eisenhower, national politics were never far from the horizon. In November, he met privately with Governor Dewey. The

Columbia Business School had just completed a comprehensive report on the New York State hospital system, and Ike presented it to the governor in a formal ceremony at the Men's Faculty Club. Afterward they adjourned to 60 Morningside. Dewey "remains of the opinion that I must soon enter politics," Ike wrote in his diary on November 25, 1949. "He wants me to run for Gov. of N.Y. in 1950. I said 'No'—but he wants to talk about it once more. Every day this question comes before me in some way or other. I'm worn out trying to explain myself."[70]

By the spring of 1950 the support for Eisenhower at Columbia had all but evaporated. A puff piece by Quentin Reynolds in *Life* magazine ("Mr. President Eisenhower") backfired badly,[71] and the feeling developed on campus that Ike was using the university for his own political purposes. "There is intense hostility toward him on the part of both faculty and the student body," wrote Richard Rovere in *Harper's*. "Columbia's disappointment in Eisenhower stems not so much from any administrative ineptitude as from his inattentiveness to the problems of administration. It isn't so much that he is a bad president as that he hardly ever functions as president."[72] Grayson Kirk, who would succeed Eisenhower as president, said that Ike "had alienated many on the faculty by making speeches about the purpose of education being to develop citizens rather than develop people intellectually."[73]

Kirk's observation is valid. Eisenhower was not an intellectual. But on the other side of the ledger, at a time when many university presidents ran for cover, Ike did not flinch when members of the Columbia faculty came under attack for Communist leanings. On March 8, 1950, Senator Joseph McCarthy, the first-term Republican from Wisconsin, accused Ambassador-at-Large Philip C. Jessup, Hamilton Fish professor of international law and diplomacy at Columbia, of "an unusual affinity for Communist causes." This was one month after McCarthy's dramatic speech in Wheeling, West Virginia, in which he claimed to have a list of 205 Communist sympathizers in government, and he was flying high. Jessup was called to testify before a Senate subcommittee, and Eisenhower—without prompting—wrote a letter on Jessup's behalf that was introduced into the record. "My dear Jessup," wrote Ike. "I am writing to tell you how much your

University deplores the association of your name with the current loyalty investigation in the United States Senate. Your long and distinguished record as a scholar . . . has won for you the respect of your colleagues and of the American people as well. No one who has known you can for a moment question the depth or sincerity of your devotion to the principles of Americanism."[74] Ike's public letter handed McCarthy his first setback. A year later, when he was in France commanding NATO, Eisenhower again came to Jessup's defense.[75]

When North Korea invaded South Korea in June 1950, the Cold War turned hot, and speculation about Eisenhower's future occupied the nation's pundits. American forces were in headlong retreat on the Korean Peninsula, and many wondered how long he would remain on the sidelines. On Friday, October 13, 1950, Governor Dewey called Ike and said he was scheduled to appear on *Meet the Press* on Sunday, and that he planned to endorse Eisenhower for the 1952 Republican nomination. "I merely said I'd say 'No comment,' " Ike recorded in his diary.[76] Governor Dewey followed through, the press picked up the scent, and Eisenhower's hat was in the ring. His official denial of interest, which was issued by the Columbia public information office the next day, was scarcely designed to take him out of the race.* And the fact that Dewey cleared his announcement with Ike beforehand speaks for itself.

---

* Eisenhower's October 16, 1952, statement is reprinted in full below. Compare it to his statement on the eve of the Democratic convention, which is at page 477. Said Ike:

> Any American would be complimented by the knowledge that any other American considered him qualified to fill the most important post in our country. In this case the compliment comes from a man who is Governor of a great State and who has devoted many years of his life to public service. So, of course, I am grateful for Governor Dewey's good opinion of me.
>
> As for myself, my convictions as to the place and methods through which I can best contribute something to the cause of freedom have been often expressed. They have not changed. Here at Columbia University I have a task that would excite the pride and challenge the qualifications and strength of any man—I still believe that it offers to such an individual as myself rich opportunities for serving America. *The Papers of Dwight David Eisenhower,* vol. 11, *Columbia* 1383.

The combination of the Berlin blockade and the fighting in Korea acted as a spur to the United States and the nations of Western Europe to move forward with the North Atlantic Treaty Organization, and to establish a military force under NATO's control. President Truman and the European heads of government believed that only Eisenhower, the supreme commander in World War II, had sufficient credibility to bring those forces into being—and at the same time to be taken seriously by the Soviets. American public opinion was also not convinced that U.S. forces should be sent back to Europe, particularly with the war in Korea, and it would require someone of Ike's stature to make the case.

Discussions began in late October 1950. President Truman caught up with Eisenhower in Chicago—Ike was on a speaking tour to Columbia alumni groups in the Midwest—and in a brief telephone conversation asked him to come to Washington when the tour ended to discuss the possibility of his assuming command of the (still to be created) Atlantic Pact Defense Forces. "I arrived in Washington by military plane about midnight on Friday, the 27th," Eisenhower recorded in his diary. "The situation seems to be about as follows:"

> The American Chiefs of Staff are convinced that the Commander-in-Chief for the Atlantic Pact Forces should be named immediately. Originally, it was the conception that the Commander should not be named until there were actually large forces to command. . . . The opinion finally prevailed that if a commander's prestige was going to do any good, it would be best used . . . while we are trying to get each of the nations involved to put forth maximum effort. I am informed that they unanimously desire that the Commander should be an American and specifically myself.[77]

Eisenhower and Truman sparred briefly over semantics. Ike wanted to be ordered back to active duty; the president wanted to make it a "request." But that was not a sticking point. A more serious problem pertained to German rearmament. The United States and Britain wanted German forces included in NATO; the French were strongly opposed. Ike thought the matter could be gradually resolved with a bit of give-and-take on both sides, but that if it were not, he would have "great doubts" about the wisdom of accepting command. "As of this moment, I would estimate that the chances are about nine out of ten that I will be back in uniform in a short time."[78]

No public announcement was made. Throughout November the matter remained in abeyance, although the *Columbia Spectator,* the campus undergraduate newspaper, reported that Eisenhower's presidential office would make no appointments for him after January 5, 1951.[79] The technicalities were tricky. Truman could not name Ike as supreme commander until requested to do so by the North Atlantic Council, and the council did not meet until December 18. On the morning of the eighteenth in Brussels, they unanimously requested Truman to name Eisenhower, and as soon as he was informed, the president called Ike with the news.[80]

Eisenhower was sitting in a Pullman car outside Tiffin, Ohio, when he was told that the president was trying to reach him. Ike had stopped at Tiffin to speak at Heidelberg College, which was celebrating its centennial year, and was en route to Denver for the Christmas holidays.

"Where can I take the call?" Eisenhower asked.

"Well, there is a little box down the line," he was told. "Maybe an eighth of a mile. You can take the call right there."[81]

Eisenhower tromped down the tracks through a foot of snow and got a connection to the White House, and the president asked him to take the NATO command. As Ike recalled, Truman put it in the form of a request, and he met the president halfway. "I told him I had been a soldier all my life and I would report at any time he said."[82]

The Columbia trustees immediately granted Eisenhower an indefinite leave of absence and named Vice President Grayson Kirk as the university's chief administrative officer in Ike's absence. "It is understood," said board chairman Coykendall, "that General Eisenhower will resume his duties as President of the University immediately upon his military release."[83]

The *Columbia Spectator,* which had been critical of Eisenhower in recent months, praised Ike for having restored Columbia's reputation. "The University must strive to maintain the ideals which its

Eisenhower reports to President Truman on the parlous state of Western Europe's defenses, January 31, 1951.

President has been called upon to defend once again. With General Eisenhower go the hopes of the nation and free world."[84]

Eisenhower, in uniform again, departed for Paris on an exploratory visit on January 6, 1951. He returned to Washington on January 31 and was met by President Truman at National Airport. After briefing the president, he addressed a joint session of Congress and then delivered a radio and television broadcast to the nation. *Time* magazine, which put Ike on its cover for the sixth time, said that he had done what President Truman could not do. According to *Time,* Eisenhower had routed the "calamity-howlers and the super cautious. In the desolate winter of 1951, the Western world heard the first, heart-warming note of spring."[85]

Ike's media blitz was an indication of how controversial the idea of a North Atlantic alliance had become. While Eisenhower and the Truman administration argued that America's borders were no longer on the Atlantic and Pacific coasts, but on the Elbe and the thirty-eighth parallel in Korea, the Republican Old Guard appeared determined to retreat to Fortress America. Former president Herbert

Hoover, emerging from the long eclipse into which FDR had cast him, demanded the withdrawal of all American forces from Europe, and Senator Robert Taft, perhaps the most vocal Republican in the Senate, had not only voted against the NATO treaty but was actively trying to scuttle the plan to build up Western forces in Europe by arguing that the president had no authority to send troops overseas in peacetime without congressional authorization.

Taft was making his fourth bid for the presidency, and with the internationalist wing of the Republican party in disarray following the successive defeats of Wendell Willkie in 1940, and Dewey in 1944 and 1948, was the odds-on favorite to win the GOP nomination in 1952. Eisenhower saw Taft as the key to obtaining a domestic consensus for the idea of collective security. On his own authority, and without discussing the matter with President Truman, Ike invited Taft to the Pentagon for a private chat. If Taft would support American participation in NATO on a bipartisan basis, Eisenhower was prepared to repudiate any efforts to make himself the GOP candidate in 1952. Since Ike was the only person who stood between Taft and the nomination, his refusal to run would cinch the nomination for Taft.

Eisenhower was fully aware of the import of his commitment. As he had done the night before D-Day, he wrote out a note in longhand and put it in his coat pocket. If Taft would come on board and support collective security, Ike planned to issue the statement to the press that evening, dramatically taking himself out of the presidential race. "Having been called back to military duty," he wrote, "I want to announce that my name may not be used by anyone as a candidate for president—and if they do I will repudiate such efforts."[86]

The meeting went poorly. Taft was whisked up to Ike's office clandestinely for what Eisenhower later described as "a long talk." Despite every argument Ike mounted, Taft remained unmoved. NATO, he thought, was more likely to provoke the Soviet Union rather than deter it. Membership in the alliance represented an "interventionist" policy that would involve the United States in the old quarrels of Europe. It would also require money, which would mean higher taxes and might possibly fuel inflation. "Our conversation was friendly," Ike recalled, "but I had no success." When Taft left, Eisenhower called in his aides and tore up the statement he had written.[87] "My disappointment was acute," said Ike. "I concluded that it might be more effective to keep some aura of mystery around my future plans. For the moment I decided to remain silent, not to declare myself out as a potential political factor."[88]

Ike had taken Taft's measure. He did not disagree with the senator on domestic issues, but found his insularity appalling. "He is a very stupid man," Eisenhower subsequently told Cyrus Sulzberger of *The New York Times*. "He has no intellectual ability, nor any comprehension of the world"—a surprisingly harsh assessment from someone who had finished well down in his class at West Point.[89] Taft had been valedictorian at Yale and finished first in his class at Harvard Law, but whereas Ike had grown to assume global responsibility, Taft over the years had become painfully provincial.[90]

On February 8, 1951, Eisenhower met with Columbia's board of trustees. Ike said that after examining the situation in Europe, he could not estimate the length of his assignment. He suggested that his leave commence March 1, and that the president's house be closed during his absence. "You gentlemen cannot long afford to go on under the situation of having an 'absentee' president," said Ike. He told the board they should feel free whenever they found it necessary "to take steps to find my successor. You may consider, accordingly, that you have my resignation before you, to be acted on at any time you desire."[91]

That evening, Ike and Mamie said farewell to three hundred trustees and faculty at a reception at the Faculty Club. "Dr. Butler would have had the reception at 60 Morningside," noted Dean Carl Ackerman of the School of Journalism, "but Mrs. E. has not received any Univ. people in Pres. House." Eisenhower, speaking to the guests assembled, said, "I will always have a warm spot in my heart for Columbia," and that he "hoped to return some day." After a brief vacation in Puerto Rico, he and Mamie departed for Paris on February 15.[92]

University presidents come and go like ships passing in the night. They hope for clear sailing. Those who provide sustained academic leadership are few and far between: Charles Eliot at Harvard, Nicholas Murray Butler, and Robert Hutchins at Chicago are the most notable examples. Eisenhower was far from a failure. He gave Columbia enhanced international prestige, defended academic freedom in a time of uncertainty, broke the cycle of deficit spending, and put the university's fiscal house in order. "He didn't mess things up," said Columbia historian Eric Foner. "That's what one hopes for in a president."[93]

# EIGHTEEN

# *"I Like Ike"*

The fact remains, this was a very simple man in
a lot of ways.

— GENERAL LUCIUS D. CLAY

IKE AND MAMIE arrived in Cherbourg on the *Queen Elizabeth* in
the early morning hours of February 22, 1951. He found the Western Allies in disarray. At that point there were no forces under NATO
control; no headquarters, no command structure, no staff, and no
logistical support. The political situation was equally grim. De
Gaulle had long since relinquished power in France to the Fourth
Republic, and French political life had reverted to its prewar instability. René Pleven was the eighth premier since 1947; the French
Communist Party (PCF) was the second largest party in the National
Assembly; and there would be five more cabinet shuffles before
Eisenhower returned to the United States the following year. Mili-
tarily the United States and Britain each had one division stationed
in Germany, the bulk of the French Army was in Indochina, and the
Germans had not yet begun to rearm. Against this puny force the
Russians could deploy upwards of seventy-five full-strength divi-
sions and an equal number of satellite formations.

At no time did Eisenhower believe the Soviets would attack.[1]
Aside from the preponderant American nuclear arsenal, Russian
losses in World War II had been so severe, and the damage so widespread, that the likelihood of renewed hostilities seemed to him remote. Far more serious was the danger of Communist political

takeovers, and in Ike's view a resolute Atlantic alliance would help deter it. His task, as he saw it, was to provide symbolic leadership and to encourage the eleven European members of NATO to raise the forces that would be necessary to convince the Soviets that Europe was prepared to defend itself. The primary purpose of NATO, in Eisenhower's view, was "the preservation of peace." Its secondary mission was to defend Western Europe should that fail.[2]

In a very real sense, Ike was NATO and NATO was Ike. During his first year in Europe, Eisenhower traveled tirelessly from capital to capital assuring his listeners that the United States was their partner but that in the end Europe would have to be defended by Europeans. "We cannot be a modern Rome guarding the far frontiers of empire with our legions," said Ike.[3] When, shortly after announcing the "Truman Doctrine" of aid to Greece and Turkey, President Truman told Eisenhower that he would support any country against Communism, Ike suggested a more subtle shading. "We should promise support to any country prepared to defend itself. We should not embark on a straight anti-Communist campaign around the world. We must encourage independent nations to fight for their independence against aggression."[4]

Eisenhower officially assumed his duties as supreme Allied commander, Europe (SACEUR), on Monday, April 2, 1951. He and Mamie found temporary lodging in his old quarters at the Trianon Palace Hotel in Versailles, then much more substantial accommodations at the Villa Saint-Pierre—a former residence of the emperor Napoléon III in the village of Marnes-la-Coquette, about ten miles west of Paris. The villa was one of four stately mansions arranged in a palatial parklike setting. General Alfred Gruenther (Ike's chief of staff) and his wife, Grace, lived in the mansion closest to the Eisenhowers; Major General Howard Snyder, Ike's doctor, and his wife lived in another; and the fourth was divided for Eisenhower's longtime aide Colonel Robert Schulz, and his driver, Sergeant Leonard Dry, and their families.

From the outset Eisenhower decided that his headquarters, SHAPE (Supreme Headquarters Allied Powers Europe), which was located at a specially constructed site in the nearby village of Rocquencourt, should be a policy-making body, not an operational command post.

Eisenhower upon hearing the news that President Truman had relieved MacArthur in Korea, April 11, 1951.

Initial staff planning had assumed some 600 officers would be required to operate efficiently, but Ike soon cut the number to 250. Most were American and British, which Eisenhower deplored. He became dependent on other countries for support and most were reluctant at first to assign their best officers to SHAPE. As Ike told Cyrus Sulzberger of *The New York Times,* assignment to NATO for most officers was a "crown of thorns," not a "bed of roses."[5]

There were some familiar faces. Brigadier Sir James Gault of the Scots Guards, his wartime aide, was there once again as an aide. And Field Marshal Montgomery, now Viscount Montgomery of Alamein, fresh from a stint as chief of the imperial general staff (CIGS), was his deputy—an arrangement that pleased both Ike and Monty. As General Gruenther recalled, the two worked together seamlessly and without friction. Montgomery shared Eisenhower's commitment to

NATO, and was highly respected by senior officers throughout the alliance. His proven military skill complemented Ike's political ability perfectly.

Except for his frequent visits to confer with leaders in the various NATO capitals, Eisenhower stayed close to home and office. American officers and their wives were a tight-knit group, sharing dinners, golf, and bridge parties, and they rarely ventured into Paris or the French countryside. They lived not so much in France as at an American base that happened to be located among the French.[6] Eisenhower's lunch and dinner companions were overwhelmingly American—diplomats, military people, members of the press, and visiting political figures from both parties. Members of the Gang flew over frequently for lengthy sessions of golf and bridge, and to discuss politics.

In addition to his NATO duties, Eisenhower kept close watch on the GOP presidential campaign. Whenever asked, he firmly denied any interest in the nomination. That was consistent with his NATO responsibilities, and it was also good politics. "The seeker is never so popular as the sought," he told Gang member Bill Robinson. "People want what they can't get."[7]

General Lucius D. Clay, who was one of Ike's longtime friends and would play a crucial role in the campaign, thought Eisenhower had mixed emotions about seeking the nomination.

> He wasn't being coy, because he knew that the party wasn't going to go out and give him the Republican nomination on a platter. Nobody ever gets it that way, and he knew that. Eisenhower was no fool. I think it was more like this: He knew that he had tremendous standing in America, but that if he entered into a political contest he could lose the nomination, in which case his standing would be greatly lowered. Or he could lose the election, in which case it would be lowered even more. Therefore, in a personal sense, what did he have to gain? On the other hand, he really and truly had the feeling that if there was a chance, you just didn't have the right to say you wouldn't

do it. There was some ambition mixed with this, and there were some other things.* The fact remains, this was a very simple man in a lot of ways. But there is no question in my mind that he was tremendously influenced by the position which he held in public esteem. This sounds like an oversimplification, but I really think these were the things that played on his mind.[8]

It was New York governor Thomas Dewey who initiated the effort to compel Eisenhower to announce his candidacy. Dewey had endorsed Ike before a national television audience on NBC's *Meet the Press* in the autumn of 1950. And as Eisenhower continued to sit on the fence, Dewey fretted that Taft was on the verge of locking up the Republican nomination. Of the 604 delegates required, media reports already credited Taft with more than 400. Equally serious, the key posts at the convention—presiding officer and chairman of the rules, credentials, and platform committees—had gone to Taft supporters. If Ike did not get into the race, Dewey believed that Taft would win by default.[9]

In late September 1951, Dewey invited General Clay to his apartment in the Roosevelt Hotel for dinner. The two had met previously, but were not socially connected. Dewey told Clay that as things now stood Taft was going to be the Republican nominee, and that he could not possibly be elected. The only person who could change that was Eisenhower. Dewey knew that Clay was personally close to Eisenhower, and asked whether he thought Ike would run.[10]

Clay said he did not know. It would require a groundswell of popular demand, an effective campaign organization, and adequate financial support. Clay told Dewey that if he could put those together, "I think it would be the right thing for him to do, and I would be prepared to do everything I could to get him to run." Dewey, who is

---

* Clay's reference to "some other things" pertains to Ike's fears of the viciousness of a presidential campaign. Rumors of his romance with Kay Summersby had already surfaced, and he was aware that his 1945 letter to Marshall might somehow be leaked to the press. He was also concerned that rumors of Mamie's alleged drinking problem might become an issue.

sometimes described even by his most ardent supporters as "cold as a February iceberg," had charmed Clay.[11] On the spot he became an ardent Republican ready to do his utmost to get Ike to announce his candidacy for the GOP nomination.[12]

The intimate relationship between Eisenhower and Clay dated to 1937, when both had served with MacArthur in Manila. Marjorie Clay and Mamie were the closest of friends and had lived in adjacent apartments at the Wardman Park in the closing year of the war. Clay had been Ike's deputy for military government in Germany, and was now chairman and CEO of the Continental Can Company in New York. Later he would become the managing partner of Lehman Brothers.* Eisenhower not only admired Clay's success in the business world but considered him a walking encyclopedia of American politics. Clay's father had been a three-term United States senator from Georgia, and Lucius had grown up on a steady diet of Washington politics. During the New Deal, Clay had been the front man for the Corps of Engineers with Congress; levered the Corps into providing the infrastructure for Harry Hopkins and the WPA; headed all military procurement for the Army and air force during World War II; and was the deputy director of war mobilization under James Byrnes. In Germany, Ike had consulted frequently with Clay about his political plans, and while at Columbia had sought Clay's advice before taking himself out of the New Hampshire primary in 1948.

Clay wrote Eisenhower on September 24, 1951, to inform him of his meeting with Dewey—who was given the code name "Our Friend." Ike replied on the twenty-seventh, noting that his "attitude toward possible future duty should be clear." Which, of course, it was not. Eisenhower then suggested that he would like to talk to Clay personally. "You and I think so much alike on so many problems connected with public service . . . that I think it would do me

---

* I once asked General Clay if it wasn't unusual for an Army officer to head a major American investment bank. "Well," he replied, "I don't know of anyone else on Wall Street who ever conducted a major currency reform. Or for that matter who established a government"—a reference to the introduction of the deutsche mark in 1948 and the formation of the Federal Republic of Germany in 1949. Jean Edward Smith, *Lucius D. Clay* 13.

General Lucius D. Clay.

good just to have a long talk with you one of these days. . . . My very warm regards to Our Friend and to any others of our common friends that you may encounter."[13]

Clay was encouraged. Eisenhower had not said no. Clay followed up with a second letter to Ike on September 29. President Truman, said Clay, "will not run if you run. He has made this statement to two separate and reliable persons. He will run if [Taft] does, and in my opinion would beat [Taft] to a frazzle. The result would be four more years of the very bad government we have today, and it could even mean the downfall in this country of the two-party system." Clay urged Ike to announce his candidacy.[14]*

* Beginning with his letter of September 29, 1951, Clay's letters to Eisenhower, as well as Ike's replies, would be hand-carried by TWA pilots on the Paris–New York route. Subsequent cable messages from Clay to Eisenhower would be addressed to Colonel Robert Schulz, Ike's aide, and signed "Shelley," for Edna Shel-

Eisenhower replied with a lengthy letter on October 5 in which he detailed why he could make no public statement because of his NATO responsibilities. "It has been asserted to me, time and again, that the character of the Washington leadership is more important to this job than the commander on the spot. This is probably true; yet the fact is that I am *now* on a job assigned to me as a duty. This makes it impossible for me to be in the position (no matter how remotely or indirectly) of seeking another post." After that disclaimer, Eisenhower went on to discuss the status of the campaign, making it clear that he was very much interested. "You need not worry that I shall ever disregard Our Friend. I have implicit confidence in his sincerity and in his good faith." Once again, Eisenhower told Clay that he would like to meet with him. "In your job, is there any *obvious* reason for you to make a European trip this fall or winter?"[15]

Clay was unable to find an obvious reason for visiting Europe, but in early November the problems involved in getting NATO off the ground forced Eisenhower to come to Washington. On November 5, he met Clay for breakfast in his suite at the Statler. "At that time NATO was his primary concern," Clay recalled, "and I was very worried that he might say he was not receptive to an invitation to run. We had not yet had time for the movement to really jell."

Despite Clay's urging, Eisenhower continued to keep his own counsel. "The sum and substance of our talk," said Clay, "was that I could say [when I returned to New York] that I had reason to believe that if the movement generated enough public support, that we *might* have a candidate. It wasn't a green light, but it wasn't a red light either. And in my own mind I thought he would run—although he hadn't said that."[16]

Later that afternoon Eisenhower met with President Truman at the White House. Truman was also interested in Ike's plans. After discussing the problems of NATO, the president told Eisenhower that the offer he had made in 1948 was still valid. Truman would bow out if Ike would accept the Democratic nomination in 1952. When Truman pressed the offer, Eisenhower stepped back. Although

---

ley, Clay's secretary at Continental Can. Similarly, Ike's cables to Clay would be addressed to Shelley and signed "Schulz." Smith, *Lucius D. Clay* 589.

he and the president agreed on foreign policy, his differences with the Democrats on domestic issues were too great for him to consider accepting. The two nodded and changed the subject.[17]

Back in New York, Clay informed Dewey of his conversation with Eisenhower and told him to move ahead. General Clay was like that. If he was not explicitly called off, he would do what he thought best. And Ike had not called him off. On November 10, five days after Clay's meeting with Eisenhower, Dewey convened a second meeting in his apartment at the Roosevelt Hotel to set up the campaign. He and Clay were joined by Herbert Brownell, Jr., who had managed Dewey's campaigns in 1940 and 1944; Russell Sprague, the GOP national committeeman from New York; Senator James Duff of Pennsylvania; Harry Darby of Kansas, who was heading a Citizens for Eisenhower movement; Senator Henry Cabot Lodge, Jr., of Massachusetts; and Harold Talbott of Chrysler, who had been the principal fund-raiser for Dewey's campaigns.

Neither Clay nor Dewey thought it advisable that they be publicly identified as heading the Eisenhower campaign. Having lost twice, Dewey was persona non grata with the conservative wing of the Republican party, and as a former military man Clay recognized that it was best to keep a low profile. Herbert Brownell, perhaps the most logical choice, had been tarred with Dewey's brush, and was also unacceptable. The upshot was that Clay and Dewey asked Senator Lodge to be the official campaign chairman. "I was there because they needed a front man," said Lodge. "All of these men knew what to do. Herb Brownell was the planner and thinker. And it was Lucius who called the shots. In those early stages, Clay was the key figure. Except for Lucius, none of us had ever talked to Eisenhower. And Harold Talbott became our fund raiser."[18]

Much to Clay and Dewey's distress, Eisenhower remained tight-lipped. In early December, Clay sent Ike a brief memorandum detailing the state of the campaign and the complications caused by his continuing silence. Clay also pointed out some organizational problems. Senator Duff, he said, was "full of ego and determined to be anointed." Duff did not like Lodge, Lodge "could not stand Duff," Dewey was doubtful about both Duff and Lodge, and no one trusted Harold Stassen, who was suggesting himself as a stalking horse for

Eisenhower. Clay noted the dates of the upcoming state conventions, and the problems they were having attracting delegates because those delegates could not be sure that Ike was a candidate. In 1952, delegates to party conventions were primarily political professionals, and the pros did not want to be kept dangling, said Clay.[19]*

Eisenhower replied on December 19. He told Clay that while he "instinctively agreed" with the points Clay made, his position as the commander of Allied forces in Europe prevented him from taking any action that "would inspire partisan argument in America. To my mind this would be close to disloyalty."

Ike still refused to commit himself. He told Clay that "Our Friend" [Dewey] wanted him to make a positive statement defining his political status by January 15, 1952. "Even to contemplate such a thing makes me extremely uneasy, although I have in the past admitted to Our Friend that my family ties, my own meager voting record [Ike voted for Dewey in 1948], and my own convictions align me fairly closely with what I call the progressive branch of the Republican party."[20]

Eisenhower was walking a tightrope, and the campaign difficulties were mounting daily. Ike wanted greater evidence of a groundswell of public support, but Clay, Dewey, and Brownell needed Eisenhower's public blessing to cause that groundswell to materialize. Four days before Christmas, Clay wrote again to Ike to explain the problem. In effect, Clay told Ike he could not work both sides of the street.

"Your letter has just come across my desk and it disturbs me so much that I am putting everything else aside to answer immediately," Eisenhower replied on December 27. Ike tried to reassure Clay of his interest in the campaign, but he still dodged an outright commitment.

> Only yesterday I was asked to name the personality in the United States who was best acquainted with me and my methods, and who had a wide acquaintanceship with peo-

* Only thirteen states held presidential primaries in 1952. The others chose their delegates in party conventions.

ple of substance at home. [The question had been put to Eisenhower by Gang member William Robinson, publisher of the *New York Herald Tribune.*] Without hesitation I gave your name. This came about in connection with the discussion as to who was best qualified to act as an intermediary between me and the "pros," since direct communication between us could obviously be embarrassing.[21]

To help Clay explain his reluctance to formally announce his candidacy, Eisenhower cited the applicable Army regulation that governed him:

AR 600–10. 18. Election to, and performance of duties of, public office.

a. Members of the Regular Army, while on active duty, may accept nomination for public office, provided such nomination is tendered without direct *or indirect* activity or solicitation on their part. [Eisenhower's emphasis.][22]

The wish may have been father to the thought, but Clay felt reassured that Eisenhower would run. Ike confirmed as much in a letter two days later to Henry Cabot Lodge, in which he gave Clay the equivalent of carte blanche to act on his behalf. "My confidence in General Clay is such, his accuracy in interpretation is so great, and his personal loyalty to me is so complete, that nothing he could ever say about me could be contrary to his belief as to what I would want him to say."[23] Princeton political scientist Fred I. Greenstein has written at length about Eisenhower's indirect but carefully calculated style of political leadership.[*] His use of Clay in his 1951–52 quest for the Republican presidential nomination is an early manifestation of that style.

On December 28, Eisenhower received a handwritten letter from President Truman inquiring about his intent.

---

[*] Fred I. Greenstein, *The Hidden-Hand Presidency: Eisenhower as Leader* (New York: Basis Books, 1982).

The columnists, the slick magazines and all the political people who like to speculate are saying many things about what is to happen in 1952.

As I told you in 1948 and at our luncheon in 1951 [November 5], do what you think is best for the country. My own position is in the balance. If I do what I want to do, I'll go back to Missouri and *maybe* run for the Senate. If you decide to finish the European job (and I don't know who else can) I must keep the isolationists out of the White House. I wish you would let me know what you intend to do. It will be between us and no one else.[24]

Truman's message was clear. If Eisenhower intended to run, he would happily go back to Missouri. But if he did not, then the president would feel compelled to seek reelection against Taft.

Eisenhower replied to the president with a lengthy handwritten letter of his own. "I am deeply touched by the confidence in me you express," wrote Ike, "even more by that implied in the writing of such a letter by the President of the United States." Eisenhower said he, too, would like to live a semiretired life with his family. "But just as you have decided that circumstances may not permit you to do exactly as you please, so I've found that fervent desire may sometimes have to give way to conviction to duty." Eisenhower said he would not seek the presidency, but left the door open to accepting a draft.[25]

In 1952, the New Hampshire primary posed the first test for Eisenhower. Governor Sherman Adams was confident that Ike would carry the state, but to do so he had to be listed on the ballot. That required an affirmation from Eisenhower that he was a Republican, and this he still declined to give. Clay and Dewey were at their wits' end. On January 4, as the filing deadline approached, Clay authorized Lodge to enter Eisenhower in the Republican primary. Lodge wrote the necessary letter to Governor Adams, stating that Eisenhower had voted Republican and was in sympathy with "enlightened Republican doctrine."[26] Two days later Lodge met the press in Washington and formally threw Ike's hat into the ring. Eisenhower would accept the Republican nomination if it were offered, said

Lodge, and reporters could check with him at his headquarters in France. "I know I will not be repudiated."[27]

Lodge assumed that Clay had cleared the announcement with Eisenhower.[28] The fact is, Clay forced the issue—just as he had done many times while military governor of Germany.* Clay simply assumed responsibility and told Lodge to go ahead. If Eisenhower wished to repudiate Lodge he could do so.

Clay telephoned Eisenhower to warn him of Lodge's announcement. As Clay anticipated, Ike accepted the fait accompli. "Your telephone call saying that some personal comment on the matter would be necessary in order to cinch the sincerity of the statements was acceptable but not enjoyable to me," he wrote Clay.[29] Besieged by reporters at Rocquencourt, Eisenhower issued a formal statement on January 7 that Lodge's announcement "gives an accurate account of the general tenor of my political convictions and of my voting record." But Ike's announcement was qualified. "Under no circumstances will I ask for relief from this assignment in order to seek nomination for political office, and I shall not participate in . . . preconvention activities."[30]

Asked at his next press conference about Eisenhower's announcement, President Truman was full of praise. With Ike in the race, Truman was confident that Taft would be beaten and he could return to Missouri. "I'm just as fond of General Eisenhower as I can be," said the president. "I think he is one of the great men produced by World War II [and] I don't want to stand in his way at all. If he wants to get out and have all the mud and rotten eggs thrown at him, that's his business."[31]

The battle lines were drawn. And foreign policy was the decisive issue. On February 7, 1952, former president Herbert Hoover released the names of sixteen prominent Republicans, including Senator Taft, who agreed with him that "American troops [should] be brought home." In Hoover's view, the continental United States

---

* The Berlin airlift, for example, was undertaken by Clay on his own authority. "I never asked permission or approval to begin the airlift," said Clay. "I asked permission to go in on the ground [which was refused], because if we were stopped we'd have to start shooting. I did not ask permission for the airlift." Smith, *Lucius D. Clay* 502–3.

should become the "Gibraltar of freedom."³² Eisenhower was appalled. It was, he wrote Clay, "the false doctrine of isolationism." In the nineteenth century Gibraltar was a truly great stronghold, said Ike. "Today, Gibraltar is one of the weakest military spots in the world. It could be reduced to nothing by a few modern guns posted in the hills and concentrating their fire on it."³³

As for the campaign, Ike said he was trying to be straightforward and aboveboard. "Consequently, I do not intend to do anything that would, to my mind, be clearly 'participation' in a preconvention campaign." Then he backpedaled. "I certainly hope that I am not stiffnecked and unreasonable in trying to carry interpretations to fantastic lengths," he told Clay. Eisenhower said he "would never ignore the rank and file of any organization if the setting could be arranged so as to make it logical and natural. If you have any ideas along this line, you might let me know."³⁴

For Clay, Ike's message was another green light. Eisenhower's question was answered the next day when Dewey's team staged a midnight rally at Madison Square Garden. The Garden was packed with more than thirty thousand eager supporters chanting "We Like Ike" while waving "I Like Ike" banners. The rally lasted until dawn, and was filmed by financier Floyd Odlum and his wife, the famous aviator Jacqueline Cochran. Cochran immediately flew the film to Paris for Eisenhower to see. "I thought it was a lot of damn foolishness," said Clay, "but it did have a real effect in persuading General Eisenhower to announce. When you are at this stage of the game, it doesn't take much to tip the balance."³⁵

Eisenhower and Mamie watched the film with increasing wonder. "As the film went on, Mamie and I were profoundly affected," said Ike. "It was a moving experience to witness the obvious unanimity of such a huge crowd. The incident impressed me more than had all the arguments presented by the individuals who had been plaguing me with political questions for many months."³⁶

When the film ended, Jackie Cochran told Eisenhower that he would have to declare his candidacy and return to the United States. "I'm as sure as I am sitting here and looking at you that Taft will get the nomination if you don't declare yourself."

"Tell General Clay to come over for a talk," Ike replied. "And tell Bill Robinson that I am going to run."[37]

The day after viewing Cochran's film, Eisenhower wrote Clay that for the first time he understood "what it means to be the object of interest to a great section of packed humanity. I told her [Jackie Cochran] that you had said you expected to be over here before the end of the month, and I would not only depend largely on your reasoning, but that you were the real channel through which I learned the opinions of others in the States."

Eisenhower told Clay he was leaving shortly for the funeral of King George VI in London (the King had died on February 6, 1952) and that he planned to spend the weekend at Brigadier Gault's country home, just outside the city. "If you really feel there is any great rush about this business, I can see you over there."[38]

On February 16, Eisenhower met Clay at the home of Brigadier Gault. Both agreed that an unannounced meeting in the English countryside would attract less media attention than a meeting at Ike's headquarters. Clay explained the status of the campaign and emphasized how important it was for Ike to make a public commitment to run and return to the United States as soon as possible. Clay told Eisenhower that winning the nomination would be harder than winning the election, that Taft now had 450 of the 604 votes required, and that another 70 were leaning in his direction.

"I pressed General Eisenhower all I could for a definite answer and he still did not want to give one. In fact, he got quite angry with me for insisting."

"Well," Clay finally told Ike, "there is nothing more I can do." And he rose to leave the room and retrieve his coat.

"Wait," said Eisenhower, and he followed Clay to the cloakroom. "Let's not leave things on this note."

In the privacy of the cloakroom at Sir James Gault's country residence, Eisenhower told Clay that he would run. He agreed to come back to the United States before the Republican convention and to resign his commission at that time. No date was set, but Clay suggested June 1, 1952.[39]

When New Hampshire voters went to the polls on March 11, Eisenhower swept the state with 50.4 percent of the vote to Taft's

38.7 percent. Stassen ran a poor third with 7.1 percent. Ike won all fourteen of the Granite State's convention delegates. The following week in Minnesota, Eisenhower received 108,692 write-in votes while Stassen, running in his home state with his name on the ballot, received 129,706.[40] The bandwagon was rolling, but Eisenhower still declined to set a date for his return.

"When I was a boy, I would go out to the corral in the morning and watch one of the men trying to get a loop over the neck of a horse that he was going to ride for the day," Eisenhower wrote Clay on March 28. "I was always pulling for the horse but he was always caught—no matter how vigorously he ducked and dodged and snorted and stomped. Little did I think, then, that I would ever be in the position of the horse."[41]

"I am delighted you retain your sense of humor," Clay replied. "All I can say is that our country needs you. There is no one else."[42]

The day after Ike wrote to Clay, President Truman announced his decision not to stand for reelection. Speaking to an overflow gathering of Democrats at the annual Jefferson-Jackson Day Dinner in Washington, Truman departed from the text of his prepared speech to state, "I shall not be a candidate for re-election. I have served my country long, and I think efficiently and honestly. I shall not accept a re-nomination."[43]

With Eisenhower still procrastinating about the date of his return, Clay and Dewey devised a stratagem to force his hand. Douglas MacArthur had been selected to give the keynote address to the convention. MacArthur was crisscrossing America, whipping up a rhetorical frenzy over his dismissal by President Truman, and it was possible that in the heat of a deadlocked convention his oratorical skills might propel him forward as a compromise between Eisenhower and Taft. Certainly it was a plausible scenario.

Having served with Ike in Manila, Clay knew the one thing Eisenhower could not tolerate would be for MacArthur to wrest the Republican nomination away from him. Dewey needed no coaxing. On March 30 he wrote to Eisenhower in longhand that unless Ike set a definite date to return, a deadlocked convention was a distinct possibility, and in that case MacArthur might win the day. Clay forwarded Dewey's letter to Eisenhower on the next TWA flight to

Paris. It was hand-carried by the pilot, Captain Robert Nixon, and delivered to Eisenhower's aide Colonel Robert Schulz, when the plane landed at Orly.[44]

On April 1, Republican voters went to the polls in Illinois, Nebraska, and Wisconsin. It was a landslide for Taft. In Illinois, Taft won 74 percent of the vote and took all 60 delegates. Eisenhower was not on the ballot. In Nebraska, Taft trumped Eisenhower with 79,357 votes to Ike's 66,078, and took 13 of the Cornhusker State's 18 delegates. In Wisconsin, where Eisenhower was also not on the ballot, the Taft forces elected 24 of the state's 30 delegates.

The following day, April 2, 1952, Eisenhower wrote President Truman asking to be relieved as supreme commander, allied powers Europe on June 1. "My request contemplates transfer to inactive status on the date that I can make a final report to the proper officials in Washington. In the event that I should be nominated for high political office, my resignation as an officer of the Army will be instantly submitted to you for your approval."[45] Truman replied with a handsome handwritten letter on April 6. "Your resignation makes me rather sad," said the president. "I hope you will be happy in your new role."[46]

Eisenhower was sixty-one years old and in excellent health. He continued to put in twelve- to fourteen-hour days, seven days a week, and according to most observers had never looked better. The foundation for NATO had been laid, the foreign ministers of France, Germany, Italy, and the Benelux countries had just signed the treaty creating the European Defense Community (EDC) paving the way for German rearmament, and Field Marshal Alan Brooke, now Viscount Alanbrooke, put wartime disagreements aside to congratulate Ike upon becoming a candidate. "The future security of the world depends on your now assuming this great office during the critical years to come."[47]

In Washington on June 1, Eisenhower paid a farewell call on the president. After summarizing the condition of NATO, Ike complained to Truman about the nasty campaign the Taft forces were waging. It was not only his romance with Kay Summersby and Mamie's dependence on alcohol that were being bantered about. Gossips now said that Eisenhower was Jewish—"Ike the Kike"; that he had been recently baptized by the pope in Rome and was anti-Semitic; or that he enjoyed carousing with Marshal Zhukov, his "Communist drinking buddy." Truman contemplated Eisenhower's distress with amused detachment. "If that's all it is, Ike, then you can just figure you're lucky."[48]

Eisenhower launched his campaign for the Republican nomination in Abilene on June 4. The homecoming was scheduled to allow Ike to attend the dedication of his boyhood home and lay the cornerstone for the Eisenhower museum. Publicity was massive, national television provided live coverage, and the event was to conclude with a dramatic address by Eisenhower to an overflow crowd of thirty thousand supporters jammed into the high school football stadium.

Nothing went as planned. Torrential rains whipped Abilene all afternoon, the stadium was less than half full when Eisenhower spoke, television cameras panned the empty seats relentlessly, and Ike fumbled his lines and lost his place as he read dyspeptically from a prepared text. Buttoned up in a see-through plastic slicker, with a rain hat on his head, Eisenhower looked every inch like a tired old man doing what he did not want to do. When he took his rain hat off, his few strands of hair blew in the wind, making him seem even more lost and forlorn.[49] The speech was even worse—an amalgam of warmed-over clichés and familiar platitudes about the evils of big government, excessive taxation, and the need for national solvency. It had been cobbled together by Kevin McCann and Ike's personal staff, and wreaked of the amateurism of political outsiders looking in. "It looks like Ike is pretty much for mother, home, and heaven," chortled B. Carroll Reece, longtime Republican member of the House of Representatives from eastern Tennessee.[50]

In New York, Dewey, Clay, and Brownell, who were watching the event on television, were appalled. It was evident that Eisenhower was not ready for political prime time. Invited back to New York, Ike spent the week at 60 Morningside Drive refitting and boning up for the fight ahead. For the first time he began to understand that he might lose the nomination to Senator Taft. The Republican convention was little more than five weeks away, Taft was well ahead in the delegate count, and Ike's Abilene performance had scarcely started a prairie fire, in the words of *The New York Times*.[51]

From New York, Eisenhower moved to Denver and set up headquarters in the Brown Palace Hotel. The problem, it was agreed, was reading from a formal text, which obscured Ike's folksy charisma. Henceforth, he would speak off the cuff. Ten days after his dismal performance in Abilene, Eisenhower roused a Denver audience with a high-voltage display of extemporaneous speechmaking. "The speech was magnificent," Dewey cabled that evening. "I hope you never use a text again."[52]

When the Republican National Convention convened in Chicago on July 6, Taft claimed 525 committed delegates; Eisenhower had roughly 500; California, with 70 delegates, was backing its favorite son, Earl Warren; Minnesota's 28 votes were behind Stassen; a scattering of delegates were uncommitted, and three states—Georgia, Louisiana, and Texas—sent rival delegations to Chicago, another 70 votes. The credentials committee, which was controlled by the Taft forces, voted to seat the Taft delegations from the contested states, and a floor fight loomed. If the Taft delegates were seated, the senator would be perilously close to the 604 votes required for the nomination.

Under the rules of the Republican party that had been in effect since the convention of 1912—the convention that nominated Taft's father after ejecting Theodore Roosevelt's supporters—the delegates from contested states approved by the credentials committee were permitted to vote on the question of the seating of other contested delegations. If this rule were adopted again, the Taft forces would prevail and Ike would be counted out. Herbert Brownell, who was Eisenhower's chief strategist at the convention, focused his efforts on preventing the contested delegations from voting. Working with Dewey's team of lawyers, Brownell devised what was called the "Fair Play Amendment" to the rules: No contested delegate could vote on the seating of other delegates until his own credentials had been approved by the convention.

A bitter battle ensued. Eisenhower delegates draped the hall with banners reading THOU SHALT NOT STEAL, while Taft forces poured invective from the rostrum. Senator Everett Dirksen of Illinois, a leading Taft spokesman, peered down from the platform at the New

York delegation and shook his finger at Governor Dewey. "We followed you before and you took us down the path to defeat."[53] Pandemonium broke out on the floor as the Republican Old Guard vented its hatred for the New York governor. Dewey sat through it unperturbed, which annoyed Taft's supporters even more.

When the vote was finally taken—the question before the convention was a Taft motion to exempt members of the Louisiana delegation from the Fair Play Amendment—the Taft forces lost 548–658. California and Minnesota voted against the motion, and the Fair Play Amendment was then adopted by voice vote. The Eisenhower delegation from Louisiana was seated. Another roll call followed on seating the Georgia delegation, and the Eisenhower slate won 607–531. The Eisenhower delegation from Texas was then seated by voice vote without a roll call. Taft had lost all three votes, and the momentum of the convention shifted in Eisenhower's favor.

The Taft team counted on MacArthur's keynote to help them regain control of the convention. But MacArthur's speech fell flat: an overly long jeremiad of accumulated bitterness that put all but the most committed delegates to sleep. MacArthur was followed by Senator Joe McCarthy, who woke the delegates up with his anti-Communist rant. "One Communist in a defense plant is one Communist too many. One Communist among the American advisers at Yalta was one Communist too many. And even if there were only one Communist in the State Department, that would still be one Communist too many."[54] McCarthy's rabble-rousing roused the rabble, but the momentum of the convention did not change.

Ike watched the proceedings on television from his suite at the Blackstone Hotel, joined by Brownell, Clay, and his brother Milton. Governor Sherman Adams managed the Eisenhower forces on the convention floor, and Governor Dewey had his hands full with the New York delegation, eighteen of whom were leaning toward Taft. As the credentials fight climaxed, Eisenhower suffered what Brownell thought was an ileitis attack. "General Clay and I were the only ones outside of Mrs. Eisenhower and Milton who knew about it. The delegates did not know. General Eisenhower was in extreme pain. But he got up and dressed and went out and had a news conference, and then went back to bed. It was one of the greatest performances I ever saw in my life."[55]*

The balloting for president began at 11 a.m. on Friday, July 11. Five candidates had been nominated—Taft, Eisenhower, Warren, Stassen, and MacArthur. As the roll of the states was called, Brownell and Clay huddled in front of the TV in Eisenhower's suite while Ike watched from a distance. "Eisenhower was certainly the calmest person in the room," said Brownell. "I could never understand how he didn't have some feelings inside of him, but he was either an awfully good actor or else he was awfully calm. Of course, when you're managing a presidential campaign you can't let the candidate know how close it may be. It would be very distracting for him to know all the headaches that you are having dealing with the various state delegations."[56]

Brownell's strategy was to stay even with Taft on the first ballot, keep a few votes in reserve, and then switch those votes to Eisenhower on the second ballot. Hopefully California and Minnesota would follow suit. But when the clerk called New York and Governor Dewey announced that the Empire State was casting 92 votes for Eisenhower and only 4 for Taft, everything changed. Brownell and Clay had assumed that Taft would get 18 votes in New York. Dewey had twisted arms and threatened excommunication to any New York delegate who voted for Taft, and succeeded in delivering an almost unanimous delegation for Ike. "If you think Taft has a steamroller," Dewey told the waverers, "wait until you see my steamroller operate."[57]

The 14 extra votes from New York caused Brownell and Clay to recalculate. Victory appeared in sight. Brownell called Sherman Adams on the floor and told him not to hold anything back. "We were going for broke on the first ballot," said Clay.[58] When the roll of the states was complete, Eisenhower had 595 votes to Taft's 500. Earl Warren had 81, Stassen 20, and MacArthur 10. On the floor,

---

* General Clay did not think Eisenhower's attack was as serious as Brownell suggested. "I'd known General Eisenhower for a long time," said Clay, "and he had some very bad eating habits. Maybe it was a forerunner of the ileitis attack, but I doubt it. Obviously, his nerves were at a very high tension. I think it was just a stomach cramp. That's par for that type and kind of situation." Jean Edward Smith, *Lucius D. Clay* 598.

Warren Burger was frantically waving the Minnesota standard for attention. Speaker Joe Martin, the convention's presiding officer, who had not yet announced the result, recognized Senator Edward Thye, the chairman of the delegation. Over Stassen's objections, Thye switched all of Minnesota's 28 votes to Eisenhower. Ike was over the top.

"That was an awfully close call, wasn't it?" said Eisenhower—who, at least according to Brownell, was totally flabbergasted by the whole process. "He'd never seen anything like it. He didn't know how Clay and I knew what was going to happen."*

As soon as Speaker Martin announced the result, Eisenhower decided to call on Senator Taft as a matter of courtesy. Taft was ensconced with his entourage in the Hilton, just across the street from the Blackstone. Ike's decision was unprecedented, and he phoned Taft to ask his permission. The senator was taken by surprise but immediately agreed. "Senator Taft could not have been more gracious," Clay remembered. "Around the Taft camp there was an air of tremendous disappointment, even some bitterness. But not between Taft and Eisenhower."[59]

With Clay and Brownell in tow, Eisenhower fought his way through a crush of reporters and spectators to Taft's ninth-floor suite in the Hilton. "I'm quite sure that it took ten minutes to get across the street," Eisenhower recalled. There was no police escort because the visit was decided at the last minute, and in 1952 presidential candidates did not have Secret Service protection.

When Eisenhower arrived, Taft asked if his sons could be present, and then spoke gently to Ike, who appeared highly agitated in the excitement of victory. After a minute or so of small talk, Taft ushered Eisenhower outside to face the newsmen. "You'll get used to it," he confided.

There was another mob scene in the corridor, but Taft waved his arms and shouted for attention. "I want to congratulate General Eisenhower. I shall do everything possible in the campaign to secure

---

* In contrast to Eisenhower, Clay and Brownell were worried sick when the balloting concluded. "We got down to Wisconsin on the roll call and we were still not over the top, and we had thrown in all our reserve strength," said Clay. "Then Minnesota switched and everything was fine." Jean Edward Smith, *Lucius D. Clay* 599.

his election and to help in his administration." Taft had failed for the fourth time in his quest for the Republican nomination but seemed totally in control of the situation. Newsmen noted that it was Eisenhower who looked drawn and haggard, his eyes moist with emotion, while Taft seemed poised and dry-eyed. Arthur Krock, writing in *The New York Times,* called it Taft's "finest hour."[60]

That evening over a celebratory dinner in Ike's suite, Brownell and Clay reminded Eisenhower that the convention would select the vice presidential nominee the next day. Had Eisenhower considered whom he wanted as a running mate? asked Brownell.

"Well, I thought that was up to the convention," said Eisenhower. "I didn't realize that that was for me to decide."

Clay and Brownell exchanged glances but concealed their surprise. After digesting Ike's comment, Brownell responded with perfect pitch: "Yes, sir, General, that is true insofar as the balloting is concerned. But I am sure that the delegates will look to you exclusively for guidance."[61] According to Brownell, Eisenhower thought about it and appeared satisfied.

"So I said that if he would give us his choice, I would convey it to the key leaders of the party. We would see that the selection was done smoothly at the Convention.

"So General Eisenhower went over a list of people. He mentioned the people he had confidence in, mostly business people—the president of General Electric [Charles Wilson], the president of American Airlines [C. R. Smith]—that sort of thing. People who General Eisenhower believed had great executive ability."

For old political pros such as Clay and Brownell, it seemed like a visit with Alice in Wonderland. Finally Brownell interrupted. "General, these are all fine men, and I am sure they would make excellent vice presidents, but we really need a name that would be recognizable to the average delegate on the floor—someone they can relate to."

Eisenhower nodded and Brownell continued, suggesting the principles they should consider.

> In view of his [Eisenhower's] age, we wanted a young man. We hopefully wanted someone from the West, someone with political experience to balance the ticket. I went

Eisenhower and Senator Richard Nixon after Nixon's selection as Ike's running mate, Chicago, July 11, 1952.

over the necessary qualifications for a vice president. I said that General Clay, and Governor Dewey and I had talked it over and that, unless he expressed a preference otherwise, we would recommend Senator Nixon of California to him.

General Eisenhower thought it over for a moment, said he had met Senator Nixon, and that he would be guided by our advice. He told us to clear Nixon's name with the other leaders of the party. And that was it.[62]

The choice of Richard Nixon was not a spur-of-the-moment decision. Although Eisenhower was unaware of it, Senator Nixon had played a critical role in the convention strategy that Brownell and Clay devised. California had seventy delegates, all of whom were committed to Earl Warren on the first ballot. No one knew what Governor Warren intended (the relations between Warren and Dewey were strained), and Taft had powerful backers in the California delegation, including Senator William F. Knowland, the state's senior senator. Nixon became Eisenhower's "fifth column" in California, assigned to undermine Warren and lead a second-ballot shift to Ike.

The initial overture to Nixon had been made by Henry Cabot Lodge, Jr., weeks before. "We had some very practical thoughts about Nixon," Lodge recalled. "We needed a counter to Taft in California, and Nixon was it. I approached him on the Senate floor, well before the Convention, and asked him if he would be interested in the vice presidency. 'Who wouldn't?' he said. Not very elegant, but that's what he said."[63]

Lodge reported the encounter to Clay, and at Clay's suggestion Dewey invited Nixon to be the principal speaker at the annual GOP fund-raising dinner in New York on May 8, 1952. Nixon gave a boffo performance and stressed that the GOP must nominate a candidate who would appeal to Democrats and independents. Dewey invited him up to his suite for a nightcap. Clay and Brownell were there as well. When Dewey suggested the vice presidency on an Eisenhower ticket, Nixon said he would be honored to accept. "Make me a promise," Dewey replied. "Don't get fat, don't lose your zeal, and you can be president some day."[64]

"There is no question that Nixon was the man we wanted," said Clay. "He had a fine name among most Republicans as a result of the disclosures in the Alger Hiss–Whittaker Chambers case. He was young, vigorous, and appealing. I was very much for him"[65]

On June 12, 1952, Nixon was nominated by acclamation. Ike and Mamie headed west for a precampaign vacation, and Eisenhower resigned his commission as General of the Army. Forty-one years and one month after taking the oath as a cadet at West Point, Eisenhower severed his connection with the United States Army.

# NINETEEN

# The Great Crusade

I know something of the solemn responsibility
of leading a crusade. I accept your summons. I
will lead this crusade.

—DWIGHT D. EISENHOWER,
*July 11, 1952*

MORAL COMPLACENCY was the hallmark of the Eisenhower years. It reflected the nation's self-satisfaction in the 1950s, it was good politics, and it fit with Ike's starchy sense of propriety. Kay Summersby had no place in that world, and the burnishers of Eisenhower's image have worked overtime to eradicate her from the record. Eisenhower became the exemplar of civic and family virtue. He was fresh, strong, decent, and generous—a model American to whom the country was eager to entrust its future. "The American people took him for what they wanted Americans to be," said Lucius Clay. "I don't think they really cared much about what he stood for."[1]

On July 15, 1952, Ike and Mamie flew from Chicago to Denver, where Eisenhower set up headquarters once more in the Brown Palace Hotel. Two days later, he went off for an extended holiday at the Fraser, Colorado, ranch of the Douds' old friend Aksel Nielsen, longtime president of the Title Guaranty Company of Denver. Before leaving, Eisenhower replied to a handwritten letter from George Marshall congratulating him for his victory in Chicago. Marshall said he had followed the campaign closely but had refrained from writing earlier. "I felt because of the vigorous attacks on me by various Republicans any communication with you might be . . . detrimental to your cause."[2]* Eisenhower thanked Marshall for his support and ignored his reference to the Republican attacks. "I am firm in my belief," said Ike, "that our government cannot stand the excesses that come about through one party domination for too long a time."[3]

Aksel Nielsen's 1,900-acre cattle ranch, on the western slope of the Continental Divide, sixty miles northwest of Denver, was one of Ike's favorite vacation spots. Amid a daily routine of fly-fishing, painting, and outdoor cooking, Eisenhower played host to the Gang and a swarm of visitors, including Richard Nixon—whose lack of aptitude for fly-fishing was painfully recorded by photographers.

While Ike vacationed in Fraser, the Democrats were meeting in Chicago, and on the third ballot nominated Illinois governor Adlai E. Stevenson for president. An eloquent speaker from a patrician background, Stevenson could claim the support of the bare-knuckle Cook County organization of Jake Arvey, while his polished, literate, and often humorous manner had proven unusually successful in appealing to liberal Republican and independent voters. In 1948, Stevenson had been elected governor by a plurality of 572,067 votes—over half a million more than President Truman, who carried Illinois that year by only 33,000. Eisenhower listened to Stevenson's acceptance speech over the radio at Nielsen's ranch. "Don't worry," said Gang member George Allen. "He's too accomplished an orator. He will be easy to beat."[4]

Eisenhower appeared supremely confident. In late July he arranged with Gang member Cliff Roberts for a postelection holiday at the Augusta National. "Tentatively—very tentatively—I make a suggestion that *may* be completely fantastic. It is that you consider the possibility that, if the Republicans are successful, you might

---

* In the postwar period, General George Marshall was the most prominent member of the Roosevelt administration remaining in public life and became a whipping boy for the ultraconservative wing of the Republican party for the loss of Eastern Europe to the Communists. But his biggest failing in their eyes was the subsequent loss of China, where he had served as President Truman's special envoy after he stepped down as chief of staff in November 1945. As Republican critics would have it, Marshall had "sold out" Chiang Kai-shek and the Kuomintang to Chairman Mao and the Communists.

open the club four or five days earlier than is normally done."⁵ Roberts told Ike any time after November 1 would be fine, and then suggested that he consider joining a church. The argument, said Roberts, "is that the church belt (meaning the Evangelistic Protestants in the South) will never support a candidate who does not belong to a church."⁶

Eisenhower was not convinced. Mamie had been baptized a Presbyterian, he told Roberts, but "my brothers and I have always been a little bit 'non-conformist.' " Ike said he and his brothers were all seriously religious—"We could not help being so considering our upbringing"—but the only reason he could see for joining a church would be "the ease it provides in answering questions. It is much easier to say 'I am a Presbyterian' than to say 'I am a Christian but I do not belong to any denomination.' Aside from that I have always sort of treasured my independence."⁷*

Eisenhower returned to Denver on July 28, 1952, and spent most of August assembling his staff and planning the campaign. Dewey, Clay, and Brownell had important jobs that kept them in New York (Brownell was senior partner in the prestigious law firm Lord, Day, and Lord), and Henry Cabot Lodge had his hands full with his own senatorial campaign in Massachusetts against John F. Kennedy. Given the bitterness of Taft's supporters, it also would have been bad politics for any of the four to have been too visible during the campaign.

With his first team unavailable for frontline duty, Ike turned to Sherman Adams, who had done yeoman service at the convention as floor manager of the Eisenhower forces. Governor Adams would become Ike's chief of staff and travel with him throughout the campaign. Arthur Summerfield of Michigan, the new chairman of the Republican National Committee, was named campaign manager, but the real authority rested with Adams. Boston banker Robert Cutler became his deputy. Tom Stephens, who was Dewey's appointments secretary, and James Hagerty, Dewey's press secretary, took

---

* Eisenhower was baptized into the National Presbyterian Church in Washington, D.C., on February 1, 1953. He is the only president who did not belong to a church at the time of his election. *The New York Times,* February 2, 1953.

the same roles with Ike. Emmet J. Hughes, a senior editor at *Life,* was soon added as Eisenhower's principal speechwriter.

As he had done at the time of OVERLORD, Eisenhower assumed control of the broad outlines of the campaign but left the details to others. A presidential campaign is in some respects not unlike a military campaign, and the Republican chain of command was clear from the outset. Eisenhower was in charge. He not only set the tone, but made the major decisions. Dewey had been criticized after the 1948 election for waging a complacent campaign. Eisenhower was determined not to repeat that mistake. First, he elected to go all out, crisscrossing the country giving short, impromptu talks to local audiences from dawn to dusk. Whenever possible, motorcades would be laid on to allow Ike to be seen by as many people as possible. Ultimately, Eisenhower would travel more than fifty thousand miles by rail and air, visit 232 towns and cities, and speak in every state other than Mississippi.

Second, with the exception of Mississippi, Eisenhower chose to carry the Republican campaign to the Solid South. Stevenson would win the cotton states in November, but Ike picked up Tennessee, Texas, Virginia, and Florida, and made it respectable to vote Republican south of the Potomac River. Eisenhower did not crack the Solid South, but he laid the groundwork for a Republican renaissance.

Most important, as with D-Day, Eisenhower determined the timing of the campaign. The politicians wanted to start early, but Ike held back. "I alone had to be the judge of my reserve of physical energy," he said. "I believed I could go at full speed for eight or nine weeks, assuming an average of seven hours sleep daily, with an occasional twenty-four hours reserved for complete rest and catching up." Accordingly, Ike set September 2 for the campaign kickoff. "Right after Labor Day, I'll really start swinging," he told his staff.[8] An additional dividend was that Ike's strenuous eight-week campaign preempted any questions about his age (sixty-two). Anyone who could maintain his schedule was obviously fit enough to be president.

In early August, Eisenhower held his first postconvention press conference in Denver. Murray Kempton of *The New Yorker,* who had covered Ike at Columbia, was on hand and alerted James Hagerty that he intended to ask Eisenhower about Republican criticism of General Marshall.* Eisenhower was forewarned, the stage was set, and Kempton followed through.

"General," Kempton asked, "what do you think of those people who call General Marshall a living lie?"

Eisenhower's face flushed beet red. He jumped from behind his desk and shook his finger at Kempton. His voice was angry and harsh. "How dare anyone say such a thing about General Marshall, who was a perfect example of patriotism and loyal service to the United States. I have no patience with anyone who can find in his record of service for this country anything to criticize."[9]

Eisenhower's response was calculated. Warned in advance, he thundered against Marshall's detractors but never mentioned Jenner or McCarthy by name. Ike was experienced leading coalitions. Jenner and McCarthy were Republicans and by definition members of his coalition. Both were up for reelection, and Indiana and Wisconsin were critical states. Dealing in wartime with de Gaulle, Churchill, and Montgomery had taught Eisenhower one thing: Don't pick fights with members of your own team.†

Eisenhower had no such qualms dealing with President Truman. Shortly after the Democratic National Convention, the president invited both Eisenhower and Stevenson to the White House for a briefing on foreign policy. Truman entrusted the invitation for Eisenhower to General Bradley, who was chairman of the Joint Chiefs of Staff,

---

* On September 15, 1950, Senator William Jenner of Indiana, speaking on the Senate floor during the debate to amend the National Security Act, had called General Marshall "a front man for traitors . . . a living lie . . . an errand boy, a front man, a stooge, or a co-conspirator for this administration's crazy assortment of collectivist cutthroat crackpots and Communist fellow traveling appeasers."

Senator Joseph McCarthy took up the cry, and on June 14, 1951, also on the Senate floor, called Marshall "part of a conspiracy so immense as to dwarf any previous such venture in the history of man, a conspiracy of infamy so black that when it is finally exposed, its principals shall be forever deserving of the maledictions of all honest men."

96 *Congressional Record* 14914–14917, 81st Cong., 2d sess.; 97 *Congressional Record* 6602, 82nd Cong., 1st sess.

† Eisenhower harbored no resentment toward Kempton. After the news conference, when Hagerty led the reporter over for an introduction, Ike beamed his brightest smile and greeted Kempton warmly. Lyon, *Eisenhower* 449.

and Bradley evidently dropped the ball. "Being unfamiliar with political matters it never occurred to me that the timing of the notifica-
tion might become an issue," said Bradley afterward.[10] Not having
received the president's invitation, Eisenhower appeared outraged
when the press reported on August 12 that Governor Stevenson had
visited the White House, where he had been briefed on the international situation by Bradley and CIA director Bedell Smith, among
others. Ike accused Truman of playing politics. In a press statement
later that day, Eisenhower called Stevenson's White House briefing
"an unusual spectacle that implied a decision to involve responsible
nonpolitical officers of our Government who bear heavy responsibilities in our national defense organization into a political campaign in
which they have no part."[11]

Truman had been blindsided by Bradley's lapse, Eisenhower ex-
ploited it, and relations between the two never recovered. The president immediately wrote Eisenhower to extend an invitation to the
White House for a foreign policy briefing, and also for a private
lunch. Ike declined.

> In my current position as standard bearer of the Republi-
> can Party and of other Americans who want to bring about
> a change in the national government, it is my duty to re-
> main free to analyze publicly the policies and acts of the
> present administration. During the present period the
> people are deciding our country's leadership for the next
> four years. The decision rests between the Republican
> nominee and the candidate you and your cabinet are sup-
> porting and with whom you conferred before sending
> your message.

As a consequence, said Eisenhower, he thought it would be unwise
to come to the White House.[12]

Truman replied with a handwritten note on August 19. "I am
sorry if I caused you embarrassment," said the president. "What I
had in mind was and is a continuing foreign policy. You know that
is a fact, because you had a part in outlining it. Partisan politics
should stop at the boundaries of the United States. I am extremely

sorry that you have allowed a bunch of screwballs to come between us." The president, who had a thicker skin than Ike, closed his letter, "From a man who has always been your friend and who always wanted to be."[13] Truman still liked Ike, and it was Eisenhower who was playing politics. His campaign hinged on differentiating himself from the Truman administration, and he feared the president's embrace.

Eisenhower may have been an onlooker at the Republican convention as Brownell, Clay, and Dewey marshaled his forces, but he was now calling the shots. He may not have been familiar with the intricacies of a roll call vote, but he knew the pulse of the American electorate better than anyone. Historian Garry Wills put it best when he wrote that most politicians painted by the numbers. Ike was Renoir. "Eisenhower was not a political sophisticate; he was a political genius."[14] Contrary to President Truman's assertion that "a bunch of screwballs" were coming between them, it was Eisenhower who chose to engineer the break. As the Republican commander, Ike needed to get his troops in line before he could take on the enemy. Taft's disgruntled supporters were sitting in their tents nursing their wounds, and Eisenhower had to bring them into action. Truman's embrace would have been fatal, and so Eisenhower picked a fight with the president.

As for the campaign itself, Eisenhower would not be rushed. When the Scripps Howard chain of newspapers—which had supported him for the nomination—editorialized on August 25, 1952, that "Ike is running like a dry creek," he was not in the least perturbed. Eisenhower's tactical sense had been honed over the years, and he knew never to attack prematurely. He also recognized the damage that might be done to his popular image if he appeared too eager for the job. Zhukov had waited on the Oder for ten weeks before attacking Berlin, just as Eisenhower had waited on the Rhine. So Ike held his fire. He made an occasional speech but waited until Labor Day to launch his attack.

Eisenhower kicked off the campaign with a monster rally in Atlanta on September 2, 1952, where he was welcomed by the city's Democratic mayor, William Hartsfield, and introduced by the state's Democratic governor, Eugene Talmadge. From Atlanta he went to

Jacksonville, Miami,* and Tampa, and then on to Birmingham and Little Rock. On September 9, Ike was in Indianapolis, with a major address scheduled that evening at the Butler University Field House, where an overflow crowd of twenty thousand awaited. Senator William Jenner—he of the "living lie" accusation—would not only be on the platform, but was slated to introduce Eisenhower. Ike was troubled and asked Lucius Clay for advice. Should he appear? "The question came all the way back to us in New York," Clay recalled. "And we—Herb Brownell, Governor Dewey, and I—felt that Eisenhower had to do it. That he had to appear with Jenner. Jenner was the candidate of the Republican party in Indiana and you would really create a chasm if Eisenhower snubbed him."[15]

Distasteful as the appearance was, Eisenhower followed Clay's advice. Ike's speech, delivered in the Republican heartland, was one of his most partisan of the campaign. Eisenhower said he had decided to run because he could not sit by while his country was "the prey of fear-mongers, quack doctors, and bare-faced looters."[16] At every sustained burst of applause, Jenner reached out and held Ike's arm aloft as if designating the winner in a prizefight. When Eisenhower concluded, he asked support for the entire Republican ticket in Indiana "from top to bottom," in effect endorsing Jenner but not by name. The Indiana GOP leadership was disappointed Eisenhower did not mention Jenner, but settled for half a loaf. Jenner leaped up and embraced Ike in a bear hug, flashbulbs recorded the scene for the morning papers, and Ike gritted his teeth. "Charlie, get me out of here," he commanded Congressman Charles Halleck, the Republican whip in the House of Representatives, and they left the platform before anyone knew what had happened. "I felt dirty at the touch of the man," Eisenhower told Emmet Hughes.[17]

Eisenhower's implicit endorsement of Jenner was an important benchmark in putting the Republican party back together after Taft's defeat in Chicago. Far more significant was Ike's meeting with Senator Taft himself on September 12 in New York City. The Co-

---

* In Miami, Eisenhower spoke to a mass rally in Bay Front Park, site of the February 1933 assassination attempt against president-elect Franklin Roosevelt in which Chicago's mayor, Anton Cermak, was killed.

lumbia University trustees had kept the presidential mansion at 60 Morningside Drive available for Eisenhower's use (he was officially "on leave"), and promptly at seven-thirty that Friday morning the senator arrived for a highly publicized breakfast with Ike. Over honeydew melon, scrambled eggs, toast, and coffee, Eisenhower and Taft agreed to an armistice. Taft endorsed Ike enthusiastically, Eisenhower noted his basic agreement with a policy document Taft had drafted, and the two agreed to disagree about foreign policy. "The differences are differences of degree," said Taft afterward.[18]

Liberal commentators characterized Ike's meeting with Taft as the "surrender on Morningside Heights." Stevenson quipped, "Taft lost the nomination and won the nominee."[19] Despite the criticism, Eisenhower was the big winner. The public display of party unity represented by the meeting with Taft was a tonic for the Republican faithful. The Democrats were less of a worry to Eisenhower in September 1952 than the cohesion of his own party. "Until Bob Taft blows the bugle, a lot of us are not going to fight in this Army," said a prominent Republican national committeeman.[20] By coming to 60 Morningside Drive, Taft had blown the bugle and his troops were falling in.

By all accounts, the meeting between Taft and Eisenhower was exceptionally cordial. Taft had furnished a prepared statement of principles for Ike to read beforehand, but Eisenhower simply perused it and noted his general agreement. In Ike's view, the text was not so important as the symbolism of the meeting, and on most domestic matters he really didn't disagree with Taft. When reporters were ushered in after the two-hour session, Ike and Taft were discussing fly-fishing. A newsman asked Eisenhower if he agreed with Senator McCarthy. Ike responded by turning to Taft, shaking his hand, and walking out of the room without comment.[21] Eisenhower left it to Taft to explain their meeting—another masterstroke by a master politician. Taft could put whatever gloss he wished on their encounter, his supporters would be mollified, the party would be united, and Ike could continue the campaign with his coalition intact.

With his battle line formed, Eisenhower marched off to the Great Crusade only to be upended on Thursday, September 18, when the Nixon fund scandal broke. The Great Crusade became the Great

Dodge-the-Bullet, and Ike scrambled to reorganize his forces. SE-
CRET NIXON FUND screamed the banner headline in the *New York
Post,* a left-liberal newspaper decidedly hostile to the Republican
ticket. SECRET RICH MEN'S TRUST FUND KEEPS NIXON IN STYLE FAR
BEYOND HIS SALARY read the header.[22] Nixon was whistle-stopping
in northern California when the story broke, and muffed his opportunity to put it to rest. There was nothing illegal about the fund; no
votes were bought, no favors were given, and the money (roughly
$16,000) went largely for office expenses not covered by Nixon's
senatorial allowance. The fund was administered by a third party,
and Nixon did not know the names of the donors. Such funds were
not uncommon in 1952. Governor Stevenson, it would be revealed
subsequently, had one as well.*

Instead of addressing the issue head-on, Nixon played the Red
card. As his train was pulling out of Marysville, California, Nixon
heard someone in the crowd ask about the fund. "Hold the train,"
said Nixon.

> I heard a question over there. "Tell them about the
> $16,000." You folks know the work I did investigating
> the Communists in the United States. Ever since I have
> done that work, the Communists and the left-wingers
> have been fighting me with every possible smear. When I
> received the nomination for the Vice Presidency I was
> warned that if I continued to attack the Communists in
> the government they would continue to smear me. They
> started it yesterday. They tried to say that I had taken
> $16,000 for my personal use.[23]

Nixon had made a mountain out of a molehill. ("We never comment
on a *New York Post* story," said Jim Hagerty on Ike's campaign
train.)[24] Newspapers across the country picked up the story, and
what could have been explained away was now front-page news.

---

* Stevenson had a fund of $18,150 from a thousand donors—surplus campaign
contributions from his 1948 gubernatorial campaign—that he used as governor to
augment the salaries of state employees. See Arthur Edward Rowse, *Slanted News:
A Case Study of the Nixon and Stevenson Fund Stories* 8 (Boston: Beacon Press, 1957).

Nixon's failure to explain the fund threatened to undermine the moral crusade the Republicans were waging, and Eisenhower moved to control the damage. "What are the facts?" he asked his staff. "Let's find out the facts before I shoot my mouth off." According to Robert Cutler, Ike was "the calmest person in this manufactured hurricane."[25]

Eisenhower instructed Sherman Adams to launch an investigation. Adams turned to Paul Hoffman, president of the Ford Foundation, who had headed the Marshall Plan aid program in Europe, who immediately engaged the accounting firm of Price Waterhouse to audit Nixon's finances, as well as the Los Angeles law firm of Gibson, Dunn, and Crutcher to review the legal implications of the fund. Ike then asked Cutler for a pencil and paper, and retreated to a corner of the car where he composed a personal message to Nixon. Eisenhower wrote that he was being pressed by reporters for a comment, but was unable to do so until he knew the facts.

> I suggest immediate publication by you and Mr. Smith [Dana C. Smith, the fund custodian] of all documentary evidence including amounts received in full, all payments from it, and exact nature of the speeches, letters, addresses and documents for which expenses were met out of fund. The fact that you never received a cent in cash is of the utmost importance and should be made clear in the evidence given the public. Any delay will be interpreted, I think, as reluctance to let the light of day into the case and will arouse additional doubt or suspicion. Could you not consider the advisability, coincidentally with giving the documents to the public, of inviting the Democratic former-chairman of the Committee on Ethics in government [Senator Paul Douglas of Illinois] to examine your complete records and to make his findings public? Such a readiness and announcement on your part would I believe be effective in meeting this charge.
>
> Our train schedules today seemingly prevent a telephone conversation but you know I am ready to consult with you on the matter whenever it is physically possible.[26]

Eisenhower was not going to sweep the matter under the rug. Nor was he going to offer Nixon any support. Not only did he want a full accounting, but he wanted it blessed by Senator Paul Douglas, a Stevenson ally. He also made it clear that he expected Nixon to contact him. Ike's longhand letter was passed to a typist for transcription, and then dispatched to Nixon by telegram.

Speaking off the record to reporters on the train later that day, Eisenhower said he was greatly disturbed. He knew Nixon only slightly but thought he was the sort of young leader the country needed. He did not believe Nixon was involved in anything crooked or unethical, but Nixon must prove it. "Of what avail is it," Ike asked, "for us to carry on this Crusade against this business of what has been going on in Washington if we ourselves aren't as clean as a hound's tooth?"[27] As Eisenhower spoke, Senator William Knowland, the senior senator from California, was hurrying back from a Hawaiian vacation to join the train in St. Louis. He had been summoned by Sherman Adams. If Nixon had to go, Knowland would replace him.

Eisenhower's off-the-record comments were reported almost immediately. So, too, was the word of Knowland's return. This was not accidental. Eisenhower was sending unmistakable signals that he wanted Nixon to step down. Or at least, to offer to step down. On Friday evening the early editions of the *New York Herald Tribune* and *The Washington Post,* both supporting Eisenhower, called for Nixon's resignation. "The proper course of Senator Nixon in the circumstances is to make a formal offer of a withdrawal from the ticket," said the *Trib.* "How this offer is acted on will be determined by an appraisal of all the facts in light of General Eisenhower's unsurpassed fairness of mind." Nixon's departure, said the *Post,* "would provide the Republican Party an unparalleled opportunity to demonstrate the sincerity of its campaign against loose conduct and corruption in government."[28] Like the *Post* and the *Trib,* those closest to Eisenhower on the campaign train, as well as Dewey, Clay, and Brownell, were appalled by Nixon's gaff and wanted him off the ticket. But they did not want Eisenhower to ask for his resignation. Nixon should walk the plank of his own volition.

All day Friday and Saturday Ike kept Nixon at arm's length, waiting for the expected resignation that did not come. In New York,

Clay, Dewey, and Brownell put their heads together. Which one thought of the idea is unclear, but by noon Sunday they had settled on a plan to break the stalemate. Dewey, who had the best relations with Nixon, would call him and suggest that he go on national television, explain the fund, and conclude by offering to step down from the ticket, leaving the final decision to Eisenhower. Clay would inform Ike, and Brownell would take off immediately for St. Louis, meet Eisenhower's train when it arrived, and work out the details.

"I called General Eisenhower," said Clay. "There was no telephone on board his campaign train. We got word to the train somehow, and General Eisenhower got off [in Jefferson City, Missouri] and talked to me from a phone booth. I asked him not to say anything or issue any statement. I said 'Herb Brownell is on his way to St. Louis to sit down with you and dope out the proper strategy.' "[29]

Brownell found that Ike was not easy to convince. Eisenhower felt that Nixon had undermined the Crusade, the report on his finances was not yet in, and he was more than peeved that Nixon had not called and proffered his resignation. "The meeting," said Brownell, "was a long one. It ended somewhere around midnight."[30] Eisenhower at length signed on to the strategy and assumed that Nixon would conclude his speech with an offer to step down. Arthur Summerfield was instructed to provide $75,000 from RNC funds to pay for the television time, and at Brownell's suggestion Ike placed a telephone call to Nixon—who was campaigning in Portland, Oregon—to inform him of the decision. It was shortly after midnight in St. Louis, shortly after ten in Portland.

Eisenhower was not happy that it was he and not Nixon who was initiating the call, and the conversation was frosty. Eisenhower told Nixon he had not made a decision and then paused waiting for Nixon to reply. Nixon remained silent. If Eisenhower wanted to drop him he could do so. But Nixon was not going to volunteer. The phone lay dead for almost a minute. Finally Eisenhower said, "I don't want to be in the position of condemning an innocent man. I think you ought to go on a nationwide television program and tell them everything there is to tell, everything you can remember since the day you entered public life. Tell them about any money you have ever received."[31]

Nixon asked Eisenhower if he planned to endorse him. "This is an awfully hard thing for me to decide," Ike replied. "You are the one who has to decide what to do. After all, if the impression got around that you got off the ticket because I forced you off, it is going to be very bad. On the other hand, if I issue a statement now backing you up, in effect people will accuse me of condoning wrongdoing."

"General," Nixon asked, "do you think after the television program an announcement could then be made one way or another?"

Eisenhower declined to be pinned down. "We will have to wait three or four days after the television show to see what the effect of the program is."

"General, the great trouble here is the indecision. There comes a time in politics when you have to pee or get off the pot."[32]

Nixon had won the first round. He was still on the ticket, and the RNC would purchase thirty minutes of prime-time television for him to address the nation. But the cost was high. Trust between the Eisenhower and Nixon campaign teams was rapidly eroding, and at the personal level Ike saw Nixon as a potential impediment to his own success. Telegrams arriving on Eisenhower's train were running three to one against Nixon, and on Monday the Gang waded in.[33] "My personal view is that Nixon's continuation on the ticket seriously blunts and dilutes the sharp edge of the corruption issue and seriously burdens you with a heavy and unfair handicap," cabled Bill Robinson. "This view is shared by Cliff Roberts."[34] Late Monday, Paul Hoffman reported that Gibson, Dunn, and Crutcher and Price Waterhouse had found no improprieties in the fund, and that there had been "no expenditure that couldn't legitimately be called a campaign expense."[35] Nevertheless, the mood on Eisenhower's train remained grim. Nixon's fund had become, for the moment at least, the main story of the 1952 campaign, and Ike was letting Nixon take the heat. There were no words of support from the head of the ticket: no further phone calls, no telegrams, no intermediaries offering succor.

On Tuesday afternoon, Bill Robinson boarded Eisenhower's train in Columbus, Ohio, en route to Cleveland. Ike and Robinson were closeted in Eisenhower's compartment for the remainder of the trip. When the train arrived in Cleveland, the candidate and his party went immediately to the Carter Hotel, and Eisenhower summoned New York congressman Leonard Hall to his suite. Hall was Dewey's liaison man on the train. Eisenhower instructed Hall to contact Dewey immediately. It was less than three hours before Nixon was to speak. Ike wanted Dewey to call Nixon and convince him to resign from the ticket at the conclusion of his speech, regardless of his defense or the public reaction.[36] Having wrestled with the decision for three days, Eisenhower had bitten the bullet. Nixon must resign, and Dewey, who had been Nixon's original sponsor, would be the messenger. With the matter settled, Ike and Robinson and Sherman Adams went off for a relaxed dinner before the television broadcast.

Leonard Hall had difficulty running Dewey down but eventually contacted him little more than an hour before Nixon was scheduled to speak. Dewey promptly called Nixon at the Ambassador Hotel in Los Angeles and delivered the message. Carefully shielding Eisenhower, Dewey said that a meeting of Ike's top advisers had just taken place and it was their consensus that "at the close of the broadcast tonight you should submit your resignation to Eisenhower."

"What does Eisenhower want me to do?" asked Nixon.

Dewey hedged. He had not spoken directly to Eisenhower, he said, but those who asked him to call had such a close relationship with the general that the request "surely represented Eisenhower's view."

"It's kind of late for them to pass on this kind of recommendation to me now," said Nixon. "I've already prepared my remarks, and it would be very difficult for me to change them now."

Dewey replied that Nixon should continue with his planned defense of the fund but at the conclusion he should announce that he did not want to be a liability to the Eisenhower Crusade, that he was submitting his resignation to Ike, and was insisting that Eisenhower accept it. Dewey added that in his view Nixon should also resign his Senate seat and seek vindication in a special election.

"What shall I tell them you are going to do?" asked Dewey.

Nixon paused before replying. "Just tell them that I haven't the slightest idea what I am going to do. If they want to find out, they'd better listen to the broadcast. And tell them I know something about politics too." With that he slammed the receiver down and terminated the conversation.[37]

Batten, Barton, Durstine, and Osborn (BBDO), the prestigious advertising agency handling the Eisenhower campaign, had knitted together a network of more than 60 NBC television stations, plus some 190 CBS radio stations, and virtually all of Mutual Radio's 500 stations for Nixon's speech, guaranteeing that it would be seen or heard everywhere in the country. The time slot on Tuesday was 9:30 to 10:00 p.m. eastern time, just after the Milton Berle show—one of the most popular television programs of the era. Subsequent reports indicated that Nixon was seen by sixty million people—48.9 percent of the possible viewers—the greatest audience for a single event in the young history of television.[38]

In Cleveland, Eisenhower and his campaign staff gathered in the manager's office of the Cleveland Public Auditorium, three floors above the fifteen thousand persons who had come to hear Ike speak that evening on the topic of inflation. The crowd would watch Nixon on a large screen, and afterward Eisenhower would address them. In the manager's office, Eisenhower sat between Mamie and Bill Robinson, armed with a yellow legal pad and pencil, and fully expecting Nixon to follow orders and take himself out of the race.

Nixon's speech was indescribably maudlin. "A slick production," said *Variety,* the show business weekly. "Nixon parlayed all the schmaltz and human interest of the 'Just Plain Bill'–'Our Gal Sunday' genre of weepers."[39] After describing his humble origins and inventorying in excruciating detail how hard-pressed he and his wife, Pat, were to make ends meet, Nixon plucked the heart strings. "Pat doesn't have a mink coat. But she does have a respectable Republican cloth coat. And I always tell her that she looks good in anything."

The audience in the Cleveland Public Auditorium, as in the rest of America, watched intently, many with tears in their eyes. Mamie dabbed her eyes with her handkerchief, as Eisenhower looked on, impatiently drumming his pencil against his yellow tablet.[40] The emotional high point of the speech came when Nixon aped Franklin D. Roosevelt's famous Fala imagery with a soliloquy about his family dog Checkers. FDR was poking fun at his Republican critics in the

1944 election; Nixon seemed on the verge of weeping.[*] His daughters, Tricia and Julie, had received a cocker spaniel puppy as a gift from a well-wisher in Texas. "And our little girl—Tricia, the six-year-old—named it Checkers. And you know the kids love the dog and I just want to say right now, that regardless of what they say about it, we're going to keep it."

Nixon played offense as well as defense. Having laid bare his own financial status, he challenged Stevenson and his running mate, Senator John Sparkman of Alabama, to do the same. "If they don't it will be an admission that they have something to hide. And I think you will agree with me. Because, remember, a man who's to be President and a man who's to be Vice President must have the confidence of the people."

In Cleveland, while others nodded their approval, Eisenhower stopped tapping with his pencil and jammed it down hard onto the yellow pad. The back of his neck turned red and the signs of anger were evident. Nixon had not mentioned Eisenhower, but the implication could not be missed. All candidates should release their financial records. That meant Ike would have to disclose the favorable tax treatment he had received for *Crusade in Europe.*[†] More tellingly, perhaps, Nixon had turned the tables on Eisenhower. The general had forced him to reveal his finances; now he would compel Ike to do the same.

As Eisenhower's blood pressure rose, Nixon approached his con-

---

[*] On September 23, 1944, Roosevelt kicked off the Democratic presidential campaign with a speech to the Teamsters Union at the Statler Hotel in Washington, D.C. "These Republican leaders have not been content with attacks on me, or my wife, or my sons," said FDR. "No, they now include my little dog, Fala. Well, of course, I don't resent attacks, and my family doesn't resent attacks, but Fala does resent them. You know, Fala is Scotch, and being a Scottie . . . his Scotch soul was furious." The hilarious reception of Roosevelt's remarks drove the Republicans to despair. 13 *Public Papers and Addresses of Franklin D. Roosevelt* 290 (New York: Harper and Brothers, 1950).

[†] When Eisenhower eventually released his financial records they showed that he had earned $888,303.99 since 1942, including $635,000 for *Crusade in Europe,* but his total tax bill had been less than 25 percent. Stevenson, whose ten-year income was almost exactly half a million dollars, had paid 42 percent in taxes. "I am not conscious of any public interest in my personal finances," said Ike testily. *The New York Times,* October 15, 1952.

clusion. "And now, finally, I know that you wonder whether or not I am going to stay on the Republican ticket or resign. Let me say this: I don't believe I ought to quit because I'm not a quitter." Wham! Ike stabbed his pencil down so hard he broke the point.

"The decision, my friends, is not mine," Nixon continued. "I would do nothing that would harm the possibilities of Dwight Eisenhower becoming President of the United States. And for that reason I am submitting to the Republican National Committee tonight, through this television broadcast, the decision which it is theirs to make. . . . Wire or write the Republican National Committee whether you think I should stay or whether I should get off. And whatever their decision is, I will abide by it."[41]

Eisenhower was furious. Nixon had not only defied his instructions and failed to resign, but he had removed the final decision from Eisenhower's hands and placed it in those of the RNC. The Republican National Committee—the party regulars, the hard-nosed, old-school politicians who were generally sympathetic to Nixon— would be the arbiter of his fate and not Ike.

"Well, Arthur," Eisenhower said to Summerfield, "you surely got your seventy-five thousand dollars' worth." In the auditorium below, the audience, which had been worked into a frenzy by Ohio congressman George Bender, a Taft stalwart, was chanting, "We Want Nixon! We Want Nixon!" and shaking the rafters. Eisenhower jettisoned his talk on inflation and marched out to greet the partisan crowd. "I have seen many brave men in tough situations," said Ike, "but I have never seen anyone come through in better fashion than Senator Nixon did tonight."

When the cheering died down, Eisenhower deftly reasserted his authority. "I am not intending to duck any responsibility that falls upon me as the standard bearer of the Republican party," said Ike. The final decision would be his regardless of what Nixon had proposed, and he had not made up his mind. "It is obvious that I have to have something more than a single presentation, necessarily limited to thirty minutes." Eisenhower was responding to Nixon's insubordination, and Ike's spur-of-the-moment performance deserves textbook recognition. The supreme commander was reminding everyone, Nixon included, of the chain of command. "I possibly am now guilty of being a little egotistical. But in critical situations in service to my country I've had to depend on my judgment as to men . . . whether a man was fit to command . . . or whether this man should be saved from the executioner's squad. Except for asking for such divine guidance as I may be granted, I shall make up my own mind, and that will be done as soon as I have had a chance to meet Senator Nixon face-to-face."

The standing room only crowd in the Cleveland Auditorium was now hushed as Eisenhower read to them the telegram he had just sent Nixon:

> YOUR PRESENTATION WAS MAGNIFICENT. WHILE TECH-
> NICALLY NO DECISION RESTS WITH ME, YOU AND I
> KNOW THE REALITIES OF THE SITUATION WILL RE-
> QUIRE A PERSONAL PRONOUNCEMENT, WHICH SO FAR
> AS THE PUBLIC IS CONCERNED WILL BE CONSIDERED
> DECISIVE.
>
> IN VIEW OF YOUR COMPREHENSIVE PRESENTATION,
> MY PERSONAL DECISION IS GOING TO BE BASED ON A
> PERSONAL CONCLUSION. . . . I WOULD BE MOST APPRE-
> CIATIVE IF YOU COULD FLY TO SEE ME AT ONCE. TO-
> MORROW EVENING I SHALL BE IN WHEELING, WEST
> VIRGINIA.[42]

Nixon had been taken to the woodshed. Ike's telegram was tanta-mount to a command, and to make it public, as Eisenhower did, left Nixon little choice. He was to be in Wheeling tomorrow night. Pe-riod. Eisenhower was not only reasserting his authority, but he was doing it visibly for all in the country to see.

Reactions to Nixon's speech varied. "I watched it at home on tele-vision," said Lucius Clay. "I thought it was so corny that it would be an immediate flop. I went downstairs to get a newspaper. I found the elevator man crying and the doorman was crying, and I knew then that I was wrong."[43] Across the nation there was an outpouring of sympathy for Nixon. More than four million telegrams, letters, and calls flooded in. *The New York Times* reported the early messages run-ning two hundred to one in Nixon's favor.[44] Dewey said the speech was "superb"; Senator William Knowland expressed his "full confidence" in Nixon; and Harold Stassen, who had previously urged Nixon to withdraw, wired his support as well.[45]

Nixon momentarily flirted with ignoring Eisenhower's command and resuming his campaign. He made a brief appearance in Missoula, Montana, and then yielded to force majeure and flew to Wheeling. Eisenhower met Nixon's plane when it arrived, bounced up the steps, and embraced the senator. "You're my boy," said Ike, condescending just enough to make it clear who was in charge.

Nixon remained on the ticket, and his speech proved to be an asset for the campaign. With a shrewd, emotional delivery he had gone over Eisenhower's head, forced his hand, and rehabilitated himself.[46] But the episode left permanent scars. From that point on Eisenhower never trusted Nixon.[*] The vice president was never given an office in the West Wing of the White House, he was not consulted on policy issues, and he and Pat were never invited to social functions in the family quarters or to the farm in Gettysburg. Nixon, for his part, never forgave Ike for putting him through the wringer. The relationship between the two, as one Nixon biographer noted, was similar to that between Ahab and the whale: awe and fascination on Nixon's part, "soured with fear and a desire to supplant; along with a knowledge that whatever nobility one may aspire to will come from the attention of the Great One."[47]

Having dodged the bullet over the Nixon fund, the Eisenhower campaign rolled on. On October 3, Ike was whistle-stopping in Wisconsin with a major speech scheduled for Milwaukee that evening. Because of Eisenhower's discomfiture over the Jenner episode in Indianapolis, Dewey and Clay had urged him not to visit Wisconsin, where McCarthy's presence would become an issue.[48] Eisenhower so instructed his staff, but his instructions were apparently overlooked and the campaign train was routed from Illinois to Minnesota, passing through Wisconsin. "This occasioned the sharpest flare-up I can

---

* Despite his public embrace of Nixon in Wheeling, Eisenhower remained skeptical of his running mate's finances. After the emotional rally concluded, Ike invited Dick and Pat back to his railroad car and grilled them harshly about redecorating charges Pat had incurred when decorating the Nixon house. *RN: The Memoirs of Richard Nixon* 107–8 (New York: Grosset and Dunlap, 1978).

**"NAUGHTY NAUGHTY"**
*October 29, 1952*

recall between my staff and [me] during the entire campaign," said Eisenhower.[49]

With a visit to Wisconsin inevitable, Ike decided to stand up for General Marshall "right in McCarthy's back yard," as he put it to his staff before embarking.[50] Eisenhower then wrote out a paragraph that he inserted into the major speech slated for Milwaukee:

> I know that charges of disloyalty have, in the past, been leveled at General George C. Marshall. I have been privileged for thirty-five years to know General Marshall personally. I know him as a man and as a soldier, to be dedicated with singular selflessness and the profoundest patriotism to the service of America. And this episode is a sobering lesson in the way freedom must *not* defend itself.[51]

When Wisconsin Republican leaders, including Governor Walter Kohler, who was up for reelection, saw advance copies of the speech, they pleaded with Eisenhower to delete the paragraph. The reference to Marshall, they said, was unduly provocative and would divide the party, perhaps even throw the state to the Democrats.* Sherman Adams agreed. Eisenhower cut the paragraph, but he always regretted it.[52] The original text of the speech had been distributed to the press, and when Ike omitted the paragraph he was charged with surrendering to McCarthy. Five days later, Governor Stevenson, campaigning in Wisconsin, quipped, "My opponent has been worrying about my funny bone. I'm worrying about his backbone."[53] The damage was done, and Eisenhower had to live with the omission for the remainder of his life.

The 1952 campaign saw the introduction of spot television advertising for political candidates. Pioneered by Rosser Reeves of the Ted Bates agency, the thirty-second political commercial soon set the tone of the Eisenhower campaign. Never one to overestimate the intelligence and attention span of his audience, Reeves sold Eisenhower to the television audience just as he sold soap and aspirin. Eisenhower took a day off from the campaign trail in September to film the spots—"To think that an old soldier should come to this," said Ike—and the GOP ran the advertisements repeatedly in key states with devastating effect.[54]

Stevenson and the Democrats, pursuing a more traditional campaign, derided the spots as Madison Avenue hucksterism. "This is the worst thing I've ever heard of," Stevenson told Lou Cowan of CBS. "Selling the presidency like cereal. How can you talk seriously about issues with half-minute spots?"[55] Liberal journalist Marya Mannes, writing in *The Reporter,* a slick Cold War journal designed to appeal to the intellectual community, mocked the role of Madison Avenue in the election.

> Eisenhower hits the spot.
> One full general, that's a lot.

---

* In November, Eisenhower carried Wisconsin with 61 percent of the vote. McCarthy defeated his opponent, Thomas E. Fairchild, 870,444 to 731,402. *Congressional Quarterly's Guide to U.S. Elections* 509 (Washington, D.C.: Congressional Quarterly Press, 1975).

Feeling sluggish, feeling sick?
Take a dose of Ike and Dick.
Philip Morris, Lucky Strike.
Alka Seltzer, I like Ike.[56]

The Democrats were behind the curve. Stevenson, whose low-key manner played quite well on television, nevertheless detested the medium. David Halberstam suggests it was a class thing. "Many of the people in [Stevenson's] circle refused to admit that they even watched television, let alone owned one."[57] In a sense, Stevenson appealed to the voters' minds while Ike appealed to their hearts. The irony, as Robert J. Donovan of the *Los Angeles Times* put it, was that Stevenson was a warm, friendly man whose eloquence caused him to appear cool and distant. Eisenhower, on the other hand, "is quite a cold man, yet that smile of his, that expression, throws a light over a hall."[58]

The 1952 campaign was also one of the nastiest on record. While Eisenhower took the high road, Nixon, Jenner, and McCarthy took the low road. Not only were there bogus claims of a Communist conspiracy within the Truman administration, but the GOP launched a whispering campaign about the sexual orientation of Governor Stevenson. Stevenson was a bachelor, recently divorced, and his cultured, almost scholarly demeanor made him a potential target.

In 1940, the Republicans had been furnished with documentary evidence pertaining to the homosexual activities of Undersecretary of State Sumner Welles, but they declined to use it.[*] Wendell Willkie was consorting openly with a woman other than his wife (*New York Herald Tribune* book review editor Irita Van Doren). As a result, the GOP chose to ignore Welles's behavior. In 1952, Republicans felt no such constraint. J. Edgar Hoover saw to it that uncorroborated FBI

---

* Welles had represented President Roosevelt at the Jasper, Alabama, funeral of House Speaker William Bankhead in September 1940. On the return trip to Washington by rail, Welles had propositioned each of the porters working in his Pullman car for oral sex. The porters refused and filed affidavits pertaining to Welles's overtures with their employers. Those affidavits were subsequently made available to the Republican National Committee. Jean Edward Smith, *FDR* 473.

field reports were leaked from the agency's raw files, and gossips had a field day. Stevenson was alleged to have been arrested in Illinois and Maryland for homosexual offenses; Stevenson and Bradley University president David B. Owen were "the two best known homosexuals" in the state of Illinois; Stevenson was known to his intimates as "Adeline"; and he was listed in the FBI card file of sexual deviants.[59] Most newspaper editors and national columnists were aware of the allegations and dismissed them as unsubstantiated hearsay. But Senator Joseph McCarthy was less reticent. Preparing for a national broadcast from Chicago (the "McCarthy Broadcast Dinner") on October 27, McCarthy let it be known that he intended to attack the Stevenson campaign as being full of "pinks, punks, and pansies." The Democrats responded with the nuclear option. White House aides let it be known that if McCarthy attacked Stevenson on the basis of sexual orientation, they would leak General Marshall's 1945 letter to Eisenhower harshly critical of Ike's plans to divorce Mamie and marry Kay Summersby.[60] McCarthy backed down, and his broadcast was relatively innocuous.[*]

The election turned into a popularity contest between Eisenhower and Stevenson, waged before a backdrop of twenty years of Democratic rule. The country was ready for a change, and Eisenhower seemed the ideal candidate to provide that. The most successful military commander of World War II, he never romanticized war. And the Korean War, now entering its third year, loomed large in voters' minds. The United States Army in the 1950s was a draftee army. There were no college deferments, and young men from all classes of American life were called into service. As a consequence, the reality

---

[*] As a result of my many interviews with General Clay, President Truman's comment to Merle Miller, the personal wartime observation of Professor Garrett Mattingly that he related to Professor Henry Graff, and the McCarthy incident in the 1952 election, which has been variously reported, I am convinced that Eisenhower wrote to Marshall in the heady aftermath of victory in Europe seeking to divorce Mamie and marry Kay, and that General Marshall stomped on the idea. I also believe that much of the bitterness that developed during the 1952 campaign between Eisenhower and President Truman was attributable less to political partisanship than to Ike's knowledge that he was hostage to the possible release of General Marshall's letter.

of the war struck home, and the country wanted out. In a sense, the 1952 election paralleled the election in 1868, which brought Grant to the White House. In 1868 the American frontier was ablaze with armed conflict as the Indian tribes resisted the settlers' advance. Grant, who had conquered Lee and defeated the rebellion, was seen as the savior of westward expansion, and he carried all of the frontier states handily. In 1952, the issue was Korea, and who better to lead the United States to victory than the man who had defeated Hitler and the Third Reich.

The Republicans framed the issues in the campaign as Korea, Communism, and Corruption—K$^1$ C$^2$ in the formulation of Senator Karl Mundt of South Dakota. But of the three, it was the continuing stalemate in Korea that energized the electorate. Since June 1950, the United States had suffered well over a hundred thousand casualties, including more than twenty-five thousand men killed in action, and the Truman administration appeared to have no plan for ending the conflict. By October the war had become a partisan issue. President Truman, speaking in Hartford, Connecticut, on October 16, challenged Eisenhower to offer a plan for settling the war as a means for saving American lives.[61] Eisenhower responded the following week with a dramatic pledge to go to Korea. Speaking on October 24 at Detroit's Masonic Temple over a nationwide television hookup, Eisenhower said his administration would give top priority to ending the war. "That job requires a personal trip to Korea. I shall make that trip. Only in that way could I learn how best to serve the American people in the cause of peace. I shall go to Korea."[62]

Eisenhower's pledge electrified the nation. "For all practical purposes, the contest ended that night," wrote the Associated Press.[63] Note that Eisenhower had not tipped his hand. He had not said what he would do once he had gone to Korea. Truman responded angrily that if Ike had a plan he should tell him now. "Let's save a lot of lives and not wait. If he can do it after he is elected, we can do it now."[64]

Eisenhower spent election day at 60 Morningside Drive. "When I got there, he was up on the top floor painting," Herbert Brownell recalled. "I had never seen a candidate do that on election day." Eisenhower, who evidently had been thinking about it, asked

Brownell to become White House chief of staff. Brownell declined. "I told him that my principal interest in life was to be a lawyer and I wanted to continue in the law."

"You want to be a lawyer?" asked Ike.

"Yes," Brownell replied.

"How about being Attorney General?"

"I was quite overwhelmed. I went back to my office to see how much money I had. Well, I figured I had just enough to last four years. So I went back up to Columbia and told General Eisenhower I would take it."[65]

The election results were a foregone conclusion. Stevenson conceded shortly after midnight. Quoting Abraham Lincoln, he reminded his supporters of the little boy who had stubbed his toe in the dark. "He said he was too old to cry, but it hurt too much to laugh."[66]

Eisenhower carried all but nine of the forty-eight states, with 442 electoral votes to Stevenson's 89. More than 61 million Americans went to the polls—13 million more than in 1948—and Ike won 55 percent. Final results showed Eisenhower with 33,936,137 votes to Stevenson's 27,314,649. More significantly, Eisenhower had cracked Franklin Roosevelt's Democratic coalition. Catholics, particularly those from Eastern Europe, defected to the GOP in large numbers, as did farmers and many blue-collar workers. And the fast-growing suburbs were rapidly becoming Republican. Stevenson carried only the Deep South, plus Kentucky and West Virginia. In Kentucky, his margin over Ike was 700 out of the almost 1 million votes cast. The election of 1952 was an electoral revolution. After twenty years in the political wilderness, the Republicans—with Eisenhower indisputably in command—had stormed back into power, taking the House of Representatives and the Senate as well on Ike's coattails.[67]

"Congratulations on your overwhelming victory," President Truman wired Ike on Wednesday, November 5. "The *Independence* [the presidential airplane] will be at your disposal if you still desire to go to Korea"—a final partisan jab that Truman could not resist.[68*]

---

* In 1947, Mr. Truman's presidential plane, a Douglas C-54 that Truman called *The Sacred Cow,* was replaced by a larger C-118. Truman yielded to stuffed-shirt criticism and christened the new plane the *Independence,* which supposedly was more in keeping with the dignity of the office. When he became president, Eisen-

"I deeply appreciate your courteous and generous telegram," Eisenhower replied. "I am most appreciative of your offer of the use of the *Independence* but assure you that any suitable transport plane that one of the services could make available will be satisfactory for my planned trip to Korea." Eisenhower said he would arrange the matter with the secretary of defense [Robert Lovett], and departed that evening for a ten-day holiday at the Augusta National.[69]

---

hower replaced the C-118 with a Lockheed Constellation that he called the *Colum-bine,* after the state flower of Colorado.

# TWENTY

# Eight Millionaires and a Plumber

Every gun that is made, every warship launched,
every rocket fired signifies, in the final sense, a
theft from those who hunger and are not fed,
those who are cold and are not clothed.
— DWIGHT D. EISENHOWER,
*April 16, 1953*

DWIGHT D. EISENHOWER is the only president in the twentieth century to preside over eight years of peace and prosperity. When he left office in 1961, his popularity ratings were as high as when he was inaugurated. As with the election campaign, the chain of command during the Eisenhower years was clear. Ike made the final decisions, and he enjoyed doing so. His serene self-confidence combined with his global experience fitted him uniquely to lead the nation into the postwar era. And he remained lucky. On the first ballot in Chicago, for instance, Brownell and Clay went all out and were still nine votes shy of the nomination. Unexpectedly, Minnesota switched from Stassen to Ike and he was over the top: "Divine Destiny"—in the memorable phrase of George Patton.

Like a true professional, Eisenhower made things look easy. He was a master of the essentials. He appeared to be performing less work than he did because he knew instinctively which matters required his attention and which could be delegated to subordinates. His experience as supreme commander taught him to use experts without being intimidated by them. He structured matters so that he always had the last word, and in a curious way that encouraged his subordinates to do their best. The lines of authority were clear, the national interest was broadly defined, and there was no buck passing.

The selection of his cabinet provides a perfect example of Eisenhower's ability to delegate. The morning after the election, before leaving for Augusta, Ike met with Clay and Brownell to consider the matter. He had already decided that Brownell would be his attorney general, but the other positions were unfilled. Brownell and Clay had made the tactical decisions that helped him get elected, and Eisenhower trusted their judgment. They knew the political landscape better than he, and not surprisingly he turned to them for the selection of his cabinet. "We were told to consult with a representative of the Taft forces [Thomas Coleman, Republican national committeeman from Wisconsin]," Clay recalled, "but he wasn't much interested and never showed up. So Brownell and I were a committee of two."[1]

> General Eisenhower didn't give us any instructions. In the Army, you rarely know the people you are assigned to work with beforehand. General Eisenhower was remarkably gifted in bringing people from a variety of backgrounds together and forging them into a successful team. He wanted people who were exceedingly competent and on whom he could rely to run their departments. And he relied on Mr. Brownell and me to assemble them. We didn't go into this extended search in which you have elaborate committees and staff people play such an important role. Brownell and I knew most of these people first-hand.[2]

For secretary of state, Brownell and Clay turned to John Foster Dulles. Contrary to conventional wisdom, Dulles was not a shoo-in. Both Clay and Eisenhower favored their old friend John J. McCloy. But McCloy's Republican credentials were tarnished.* He had served

* McCloy, a card-carrying Republican, came to Washington with Henry L. Stimson in 1940. Before that he had been managing partner of Cravath, Swaine, and

both FDR and Truman as *the* assistant secretary of war (there was only one assistant secretary in those days), and Truman had appointed him to head the World Bank, and then to succeed Clay as American high commissioner in Germany. Brownell, strongly supported by Dewey, urged that McCloy be bypassed at least initially in favor of Dulles. Brownell and Dewey accurately pointed out that Dulles had helped rescue the Republican party from its isolationist past (he had been Dewey's foreign affairs adviser in both the 1944 and 1948 campaigns), and that his service should be rewarded. Later, if Ike wished to appoint McCloy, he could do so. Clay and Eisenhower recognized the wisdom of that argument and chose Dulles.[3]

With Dulles, one took the bitter with the sweet. He was a committed internationalist and an accomplished lawyer (a senior partner at Sullivan and Cromwell) who had helped frame the plank in the 1944 Republican platform calling for an independent Jewish state in Palestine. Both his grandfather John W. Foster and his uncle, Robert Lansing, had served as secretary of state (under Benjamin Harrison and Woodrow Wilson, respectively).

Dulles was also an extremely devout Christian who saw the world through the eyes of an Old Testament prophet. Most who knew him considered him a pompous prig devoid of a sense of humor. "Dull, duller, Dulles," as the British often put it.[*] He was given to sweep-

---

Moore, one of New York's most distinguished law firms, and had supervised the case of *Schechter Poultry Co. v. United States,* 295 U.S. 495 (1935), which overturned the New Deal's National Industrial Recovery Act. Unlike Dulles, McCloy was affable, indefatigable, and brilliant without pretense. He was easy to work with, and Eisenhower and Clay respected his judgment. (Personal disclosure: I interviewed Mr. McCloy in his office at Milbank, Tweed, Hadley, and McCloy, on February 19, 1971, for my biography of Clay, and found him to be the most engaging person I have ever interviewed. He was frank and well-informed, and charmed the socks off me.) For McCloy generally, see Kai Bird, *The Chairman: John J. McCloy: The Making of the American Establishment* (New York: Simon and Schuster, 1992).

* British prime minister Harold Macmillan, after negotiating with Dulles, noted in his diary that "his speech was slow, but it easily kept pace with his thought." Harold Macmillan, *Riding the Storm, 1956–1959* 321 (New York: Harper and Row, 1971).

Dulles finished second in the Princeton Class of 1908, but was never invited to join an eating club. In later years, as a distinguished member of the New York bar, he was invited to join Cottage, a first-rank club, and did so as an alumni

ing pronunciamentos with little footing in reality, and was fiercely determined to roll back the iron curtain by any means available. His advocacy of apocalyptic policies such as massive retaliation and brinkmanship frightened America's allies. Eisenhower was not reckless, and Dulles provided him with a stalking horse behind which to maneuver. As Murray Kempton put it, Ike would not have trusted Dulles "with a stick of dynamite to blow up a duck pond," but found him useful for clearing minefields.[4]

The remaining cabinet positions were also filled while Eisenhower was at Augusta. Clay and Brownell flew down to Georgia on Sunday, November 9, 1952, in a Continental Can plane, and landed at a private airstrip to avoid reporters. Clay was attending the annual meeting of the elite Business Advisory Council at Sea Island, while Brownell joined Ike at the Augusta National. At Sea Island, Clay met informally with his fellow corporate executives and discussed openly the names of possible appointees. "I remember having a drink with Lucius and Sidney Weinberg [of Goldman Sachs]," said Paul Cabot, head of the First Boston Corporation. "Lucius had a definite opinion about everyone. No qualifications whatever. Finally, I blew up. I said, 'Jesus Christ, Lucius, there is a word "maybe" in the English language. Don't you ever use it?' "[5]

After Dulles's selection as secretary of state and Brownell as attorney general, the two principal positions to be filled were Defense and Treasury. Clay seized on two fellow members of the Business Advisory Council who were with him at Sea Island. For secretary of defense, he tapped Charles E. Wilson, the bluff, outspoken head of General Motors who was known as "Engine Charlie" to distinguish him from the other Charles E. Wilson, who headed General Electric ("Electric Charlie"). Wilson was rumored to be the highest-paid executive in the United States with salary and bonuses exceeding $500,000 annually. (The salary of a cabinet officer in 1953 was $22,500.)

As Clay recalled,

---

member. Townsend Hoopes, *The Devil and John Foster Dulles* 18–21 (Boston: Little, Brown, 1973).

I said to President Eisenhower, "If you are going to go to
the business world for the secretary of defense, why not go
to the biggest business we have?" So that's why we went
to Mr. Wilson. We felt that Defense was the most difficult
administrative job in government, and here was a man
with certainly as wide an administrative experience as any
man in the country. As a result of the Defense reorganization [under the National Security Act of 1947], we had
created a huge department, and it seemed to me that its
first need was to be established on a sound administrative
basis. That may not have been the right decision, but in
spite of all the things that happened,[*] I think Mr. Wilson
set up a pretty fair administrative structure in the defense
department.[6]

At Treasury, Clay settled on George M. Humphrey, who was president of M. A. Hanna and Company of Cleveland—a large multinational conglomerate involved in iron and steel production, banking,
and plastics. "Mr. Humphrey may have been suggested by Sidney
Weinberg," said Clay.

Certainly Mr. Weinberg thought highly of him, as did I.
Mr. Humphrey was a man with a great deal of experience
in the financial world. I had met him when I was in Germany. He had been appointed by President Truman [in
1948] to look into the reparations question. And we were
in considerable disagreement at the time. But I formed a
great respect for his fairness and his ability. It was not
because we were operating on the same wave length. We

---

* Clay's reference is to Wilson's refusal to sell his stock in General Motors and his
testimony at his Senate confirmation hearing when asked about a possible conflict
of interest. Wilson replied, "I cannot conceive of a conflict because for years I
thought what was good for our country was good for General Motors, and vice
versa. The difference did not exist. Our country is too big. It goes with the welfare
of the country. Our contribution to the welfare of the nation is considerable." Wilson's remarks were often replayed as "What's good for General Motors is good for
the country," although he did not put it in that order.

were not. He wanted to cancel all reparations. It did not seem to me that was consistent with the commitments we had made [to our allies].[7]

Eisenhower did not hit it off with Wilson, whom he considered narrow and simplistic, but he found Humphrey enormously congenial, and he was the only member of the cabinet with whom Ike formed a close personal relationship. Like Eisenhower, Humphrey exuded a natural warmth. He and Ike were the same age, both abhorred high taxes and deficit spending, and they shared a love for hunting and fly-fishing. At their first meeting, Eisenhower grinned as he greeted the balding Humphrey with, "Well, George, I see you comb your hair just the way I do."[8] According to legend, Humphrey stipulated one condition for his acceptance of the post. "If anyone talks to you about money," he told Ike, "you tell him to go see George."[9] Clay erred in not clearing Humphrey's appointment with Taft—the senior senator from Ohio—but of all the original cabinet appointees, Humphrey proved to be the most successful.[*]

For Interior, Clay and Brownell picked outgoing governor Douglas McKay of Oregon. "Our first choice had been Governor Arthur Langlie of Washington," said Clay, "but he had just been elected to a four-year term, and he declined."

> We recommended Ezra Taft Benson of Utah for Agriculture. We considered both Congressman Clifford Hope of Kansas and Senator Frank Carlson of Kansas, but we wanted someone from further west. Benson was not too partisan and he had a record of agricultural reform. He was also strongly recommended by Senator Taft. Neither Brownell nor I knew him, but we thought it was a good idea to have at least one person recommended by Taft in

---

[*] As the senior senator from Ohio, senatorial courtesy would have suggested that Taft be consulted, or at least informed of the choice. Taft had favored Virginia senator Harry F. Byrd, a nominal Democrat, for secretary of the Treasury. Later Taft grumbled to friends that Eisenhower had appointed an Ohioan without even asking his opinion. James T. Patterson, *Mr. Republican: A Biography of Robert A. Taft* 584 (Boston: Houghton Mifflin, 1972).

the cabinet. Benson was one of the twelve apostles of the Mormon Church, and I think President Eisenhower rather liked that.[10]

Sinclair Weeks, a conservative New England banker, was named secretary of commerce. Weeks anchored the right flank of the Eisenhower administration, and would have felt more at home serving under Calvin Coolidge. Determined to emasculate the federal government, Weeks reduced the budget of the Civil Aeronautics Administration to the point where air safety became a serious national problem. Shortly after the administration took office, Eisenhower complained in his diary that Weeks "seems so completely conservative in his views that at times he seems to be illogical. I hope that I am mistaken or if not that he will become a little more aware of the world as it is today."[11]

For postmaster general, traditionally the gatekeeper of political patronage, Clay and Brownell turned to Arthur Summerfield, a Michigan automobile dealer who had recently become chairman of the Republican National Committee. Much to Summerfield's surprise, Eisenhower insisted he step down as party chairman. Henry Cabot Lodge, Jr., who lost his Senate seat to John F. Kennedy, was named United States ambassador to the United Nations and given cabinet rank. Oveta Culp Hobby, publisher of *The Houston Post,* leader of "Democrats for Eisenhower," and commander of the Women's Army Corps during the war, was named head of the Federal Security Agency (a forerunner of the Department of Health, Education, and Welfare), also with cabinet rank. Joseph Dodge, president of the Detroit Bank, who had headed economic affairs for Clay in Germany, was named director of the Bureau of the Budget, and Sherman Adams became White House chief of staff.

The most difficult position to fill was secretary of labor. "We were thinking about appearances at that point," said Clay, "and we wanted more diversity. If possible, we wanted someone from the AFL. Finally, someone recommended Martin Durkin, who was president of the plumbers and steamfitters union. He was a Democrat and a Catholic. We thought it was a good idea to have a Catholic in the cabinet."[12] Taft disagreed and called Durkin's appointment "incredible," and it proved to be a poor fit. "Eight millionaires and a plumber," crowed *The New Republic,* when the choice was announced.

Eisenhower's cabinet was conservative but not excessively partisan.[13] What is remarkable is that not one of the appointees had prior experience in Washington; none was a professional politician (McKay, like Summerfield, was an automobile dealer—prompting Adlai Stevenson to quip that the New Dealers had been replaced by the car dealers); none had served an apprenticeship in party ranks; and few were known to Eisenhower beforehand.[14] All were highly successful in their trade or profession, and they came to Washington with their intellectual baggage uncluttered with complexity. Thanks to the intimate friendship between Sidney Weinberg and Lucius Clay, the new secretary of the Treasury reflected the suggestion of Goldman Sachs.* *Plus ça change, plus c'est la même chose.*

On November 29, 1952, Eisenhower departed for Korea. He was accompanied by Omar Bradley, Charles Wilson, and Herbert Brownell, and was joined en route by Admiral Arthur Radford, the commander in chief in the Pacific (CINCPAC). Before leaving, Eisenhower was briefed at the Pentagon by the Joint Chiefs of Staff. They saw only two options in Korea—to continue fighting indefinitely along the present battle line, or to seek a military victory by conventional means, which would involve a significantly greater commitment of American forces with a corresponding increase in casualties. Ike dismissed both options.[15]

Eisenhower spent three days in Korea. Once again he was the supreme commander visiting the front, and only incidentally the

---

* "Ike and Lucius were very, very close," said Leonard Hall, who succeeded Arthur Summerfield as chairman of the Republican National Committee. "They understood one another instinctively. Not only had they worked together for many years, but they spoke the same language. Not just Army lingo. They were on the same wavelength. There was an unspoken rapport between them. When Ike had a serious problem, he talked to Lucius. Ike gave him a free hand to pick his cabinet. He trusted Lucius's judgment. And Lucius picked his confreres in the business world. He didn't consult with the [Republican] National Committee. He and Brownell sent the names over to us after the selections had been made, but it was only a courtesy. They didn't ask our advice; they told us these were the cabinet appointees." Leonard Hall, interview by Jean Edward Smith, April 4, 1971, quoted in Smith, *Lucius D. Clay* 614.

Ike eating at the field mess of the 1st Battalion, 15th Infantry in Korea—the same unit he commanded at Fort Lewis in 1940.

president-elect.[16] The overall commander of the UN forces was Mark Clark, who ten years before had served with Ike in North Africa. James Van Fleet, Eisenhower's West Point classmate and a division commander in Europe during the war, commanded the U.S. Eighth Army. Ike knew both intimately. He knew their strengths as well as their weaknesses, and there was no question where they fit in the chain of command.

Eisenhower visited frontline units and talked to senior commanders and their men. Despite the bitter cold, he wanted to see for himself. Bundled in a heavy pile jacket and GI thermal boots, he surveyed the terrain and watched an artillery duel through binoculars. He met his son John, now a major, who was serving at the front, and ate an outdoor meal from a mess kit with the 1st Battalion of the 15th Infantry, the unit he had commanded at Fort Lewis in 1939–40. The high point of the trip was a reconnaissance flight along the length of the front—essentially the thirty-eighth parallel—in an artillery spotter plane. Squeezed behind the pilot in the Army's equivalent of a Piper Cub, Ike thought the terrain below was reminiscent of Tunisia—only worse.[17] It was mountainous, rocky, snow covered, and desolate. The North Koreans and Chinese had developed a formidable defensive position supported with a series of tunnels to shield their artillery. "It was obvious that any frontal attack would present great difficulties," Eisenhower concluded.[18]

Ike met briefly with South Korean president Syngman Rhee, who was full of fierce threats to drive the Communists back to the Yalu and unify Korea. Mark Clark shared the view that a renewed UN offensive would be successful. According to Bradley, "Clark and Van Fleet had cooked up a victory plan [Oplan 8-52] that could only be described as 'MacArthuresque.'"[19] Clark wanted Eighth Army, reinforced by eight divisions, to advance all along the front. At the same time, he would launch air and sea operations against the Chinese mainland. Clark also sought to use Chiang Kai-shek's troops from Formosa (which President Truman and the Joint Chiefs of Staff had rejected), and proposed that "serious consideration" be given to using atomic weapons.[20] Clark kept Ike up until 3 a.m. arguing that victory was possible. When Clark finally ran out of steam, Eisenhower told him to forget it. "I know just how you feel, militarily," said Ike, "but I have a mandate from the people to stop this fighting. That's my decision."[21]

A president-elect without Eisenhower's military experience—Governor Stevenson or Senator Taft, for example—might have been swayed by the determination of the commander on the spot, particularly when his view was enthusiastically reinforced by the local head of state. Eisenhower trusted his own judgment and dismissed what he heard as poppycock. Rhee was a petty despot who would have invaded Japan if given the opportunity, and Clark's military credentials were underwhelming. Eisenhower had been on the verge of relieving him at Salerno, and Clark's subsequent conduct of the Italian campaign was at best lackluster. The war must be ended. "At this time—December 1952," wrote Eisenhower, "it had been tacitly accepted by both sides that we were fighting defensively and would take no risks of turning the conflict into a global war. . . . My conclusion as I left Korea was that we could not stand forever on a static front and continue to accept casualties without any visible results.

Small attacks on small hills would not end this war." It was time to negotiate a settlement.[22]

Eisenhower left Seoul on December 5 headed for Guam, where he boarded the cruiser USS *Helena* bound for Hawaii. He was accompanied by Wilson and Brownell, while Bradley and Admiral Radford flew ahead to Pearl Harbor. At Wake Island, on the seventh, Ike's party was joined by Dulles, Humphrey, Clay, and budget director Joseph Dodge. The week at sea provided a shakedown cruise for the principal members of the cabinet, and gave Eisenhower the opportunity to set the broad outlines of policy before assuming office. "By the time we finished that trip," Humphrey recalled, "we knew each other pretty well and knew pretty well what each of us thought and what each of the others thought about the things we were about to do."[23]

Like FDR's wartime conferences with his staff aboard the *Iowa,* Eisenhower was very much in command, and the shape of the administration for the next four years was charted out. The Korean War would be brought to an end; Europe would remain the focus of American foreign policy; containment would be pursued; and foreign aid would continue. To reduce the budget deficit, conventional forces would be drawn down and nuclear-war capabilities enhanced. Domestically, tax cuts would be deferred until the budget was balanced. Price and wage controls would be terminated, but basic New Deal programs such as Social Security and agricultural price supports would continue. Savings would be achieved by managing the government more efficiently.

Eisenhower's goals fell far short of what the Republican platform had promised. There would be no victory in Korea, no reduction in foreign aid, no shift in emphasis from Europe to Asia, no immediate tax cut, and no end of the New Deal.[24] The changes would be incremental. Eisenhower was a realist, not an ideologue, and his policies would hew to the middle of the road. The difference between the new Republican administration and the Democrats—aside from ending the war in Korea and terminating wage and price controls— would be in more efficient management.[*]

---

[*] The Republicans took office in January 1953 determined to root out waste and inefficiency in government. My mother was a longtime secretary in the office of the

When the *Helena* arrived at Pearl Harbor on December 14, Eisenhower made a brief statement to the press about Korea. "We face an enemy," he said, "whom we cannot hope to impress by words, however eloquent, but only by deeds—executed under circumstances of our own choosing."[25] Eisenhower was laying down a smoke screen. He made no threat to use atomic weapons, but the implication was clear. Unless the Chinese accepted an armistice in Korea, the new administration would escalate the war.

Eisenhower returned to 60 Morningside Drive, met with his prospective cabinet twice in early January at the Commodore Hotel, and departed for Washington by rail on January 19, 1953. He was accompanied by Mamie, his son John, and John's wife, Barbara. Two weeks earlier, President Truman had ordered John back from Korea to attend his father's inauguration. Truman gave the order directly to the Army's adjutant general, bypassing the normal chain of command (neither Bradley nor Army chief of staff J. Lawton Collins was informed), and he intended to keep the origin of the order secret as an unexpected surprise for the Eisenhowers. "I always appreciated Mr. Truman's kind gesture," John wrote later.[26]

Eisenhower messed up badly on inauguration day and allowed personal pettiness to cloud his normal good judgment and common sense. It is customary for the president-elect to call on the president at the White House and ride with him up Pennsylvania Avenue to the Capitol for the ceremony.* It is also customary for the president-elect to dismount from his vehicle and enter the White House to greet the president. In March 1933, Franklin Roosevelt, because he

---

assistant attorney general (Civil Division) in the Department of Justice. Warren Burger, the new Republican assistant attorney general, sought every way possible to save money. The office had a stationery closet with an electric lightbulb that went off when the door closed. According to my mother, Burger was not convinced the light went off. "Mrs. Smith," he said, "I'm going to stand in the closet and I want you to close the door." To Burger's satisfaction, the light went off. I should add that my mother, as a loyal government employee, did not relate this story until after Chief Justice Burger's death.

* There have been three exceptions to the rule. In 1801, John Adams left Washington at dawn to avoid seeing Thomas Jefferson sworn in. His son John Quincy Adams refused to attend Andrew Jackson's inaugural in 1829, and Andrew Johnson avoided Ulysses Grant's in 1869.

Chief Justice Fred M. Vinson administers the presidential oath to Eisenhower, January 20, 1953.

was unable to walk, had remained in the car, but President Hoover was informed beforehand and graciously came out on the north portico while the presidential party assembled. In 1953, instead of observing what normal courtesy required, Eisenhower deliberately snubbed President Truman. When the presidential limousine arrived at the White House, Ike remained seated and waited for the president to appear. Mrs. Truman had laid out coffee, but Eisenhower refused the invitation. The president of the United States would have to join him for the ride to the Capitol.

"It was a shocking moment," remembered CBS correspondent Eric Sevareid, who was on the portico close by. "Truman was gracious and he had just been snubbed. He showed his superiority by what he did."[27]

It is routinely asserted that Eisenhower snubbed Truman because he was offended by the intensity of the president's partisanship during the campaign. That cannot be taken seriously. Eisenhower was not a political babe in the woods. For the past ten years he had been dealing with the likes of Churchill, de Gaulle, Stalin, and Roosevelt—to say nothing of Taft, Stevenson, Montgomery, and MacArthur—and he understood the cut and thrust of politics. It is inconceivable that Truman's partisan criticism would have aroused such animosity. A more plausible explanation is that Eisenhower knew that the White House had threatened to release Marshall's 1945 letter harshly critical of his plans to divorce Mamie and marry Kay, and he took this personally. He resented having been held hostage by the president. Eisenhower, of course, had been the author of his own misfortune, and his behavior on inauguration day was churlish.

The Eisenhowers settled into the White House with little difficulty. After Quarters 1 at Fort Myer, 60 Morningside Drive, and the Villa Saint-Pierre, it was simply institutional living on a larger scale. Ike's personal retainers continued to serve, and Mamie was assisted by a professional White House staff led by veteran chief usher Howell G. Crim and his deputy, J. Bernard West. The Executive Mansion contains 132 rooms and is 1.6 million square feet in area, but the family quarters on the second floor are relatively intimate. The entire structure had been gutted and renovated during the Trumans' tenure, and the finishes and fixtures were all new. Mamie converted the small bedroom in which Eleanor Roosevelt and Bess Truman slept into a dressing room, and made their considerably larger reception room her bedroom, moving in a king-size bed and her personal furniture from 60 Morningside. Mamie wanted the king-size bed, she said, so that "I can reach over and pat Ike on his old bald head anytime I want to."[28]

Mamie customarily slept late, and because Eisenhower habitually rose early, he occupied the same presidential bedroom that FDR and Truman had, with an adjoining sitting room. Ike made his morning coffee with an electric percolator (later a small kitchen was added to the family quarters), and ate breakfast alone in his sitting room while reading the morning papers: the *New York Herald Tribune, The New York Times,* and *The Washington Post.* He then walked over to the West Wing with Colonel Robert Schulz, his military aide, and was in his office by seven-thirty. Eisenhower normally worked at his desk until one, had a business lunch, and returned briefly to the office. Ordinarily his business day ended between three and four. Unlike Truman and FDR, Eisenhower did not take papers back to the family quarters. "After you spend a certain number of hours at work," he told J. B. West, "you pass your peak of efficiency. I function best in my office when I can relax in the evenings."[29] Eisenhower had an unused bedroom (facing north) converted into a painting studio, and continued his regular rounds of golf and bridge with the Gang. Most evenings the Eisenhowers ate alone upstairs in the family dining room. Later, when color television came in, they ate from trays set up in front of the TV set. Several nights a week the Eisenhowers watched movies in the White House theater. Ike was often in bed by nine-thirty; Mamie was a night owl and usually stayed up past midnight.[30]

"My first day at the president's desk," Eisenhower wrote in his diary on January 21, 1953. "Plenty of difficult problems. But such has been my portion for a long time. The result is that this just seems (today) like a continuation of all I've been doing since July, 1941— even before that."[31]

Eisenhower was pleasantly surprised at how smoothly the transition had gone. By the third day in office he had recovered his good judgment and wrote President Truman a gracious letter to express his appreciation.

> The efforts you made to assure the orderly transfer of government are largely a matter of public record, but I am personally aware of the fact that you went to far greater trouble to accomplish this than almost anyone else could have known.
>
> On the personal side, I especially want to thank you for your thoughtfulness in ordering my son home from Korea for the Inauguration; and even more especially for not allowing either him or me to know that you had done so.[32]*

President Truman's conduct had been exemplary. Not only had he quietly ordered John back from Korea, but he had also destroyed the

---

* On the ride up Pennsylvania Avenue to the Capitol, Eisenhower had asked the president who ordered John back from Korea. "I did," Truman replied. The mood remained chilly, and nothing further was said. McCullough, *Truman* 921.

only remaining copy of General Marshall's 1945 letter, which could have been so embarrassing to Eisenhower.[*] But the Trumans would never be invited to the White House during the Eisenhower years, and Truman and Ike did not meet again until General Marshall's funeral in 1959. They did not bury the hatchet until the funeral of President Kennedy in 1963.

When Eisenhower returned to the White House after the inaugural parade—his first entrance into the Executive Mansion as president—he was presented with a teaching opportunity. Howell Crim, the chief usher, handed him a sealed envelope. "Never bring me a sealed envelope," said Ike. "That's what I have a staff for."[33] To Eisenhower, a sealed envelope was concrete proof the White House was badly organized. Letters to the president must be screened, and only those that were essential for him to read should be placed before him. A smoothly functioning staff system was long overdue. Ike was determined to keep routine matters out of the White House, saving his time to deal with those of major importance. Sherman Adams was installed as the first ever White House chief of staff, and Ike left it to Adams to do the rest. Eisenhower never spelled out Adams's exact duties, but both men knew what was expected. "The president does the most important things," Adams told a reporter for *The New York Times*. "I do the next most important things."[34]

Governor Sherman Adams was a crusty paragon of New England frostiness. His frugality was legendary. Adams brought his lunch to the White House in a brown paper bag that had been packed by his wife, Rachel, and it was rumored that some of his suits dated back to his freshman year at Dartmouth thirty years before. He was equally parsimonious with language, and never used a sentence when a single word would do. A flinty silence was even better. Eisenhower liked Adams because he made decisions quickly and always assumed responsibility for them. As one biographer noted, rather than being a softer civilian version of Ike's wartime chief of staff, Bedell Smith,

---

[*] My surmise is that Eisenhower may also have discovered that President Truman had destroyed his correspondence with General Marshall and was writing to express his appreciation. It would have been typical of Ike not to address so delicate an issue directly, but to thank Truman obliquely.

who was famously blunt, decisive, and tactless, "Sherman Adams made Bedell Smith look like an honors graduate of charm school."[35]

Eisenhower expected his cabinet officers to run their departments and not come to him with problems within their purview. They were the equivalent of his Army commanders. If First Army had a problem during the war, Courtney Hodges would have handled it. Third Army's issues had been George Patton's responsibility. Similarly, matters pertaining to the Treasury were for Humphrey to decide, Agriculture was Benson's bailiwick, and Commerce belonged to Weeks. Attorney General Brownell enjoyed far greater latitude to set legal policy than he anticipated. Only when matters were of national importance, or when administration policy was unclear, did Eisenhower expect to be consulted. The exceptions were national security issues—State and Defense—where Ike took a direct interest. And the fact is that Dulles and Wilson required more guidance on policy matters than the other members of the cabinet.

Eisenhower met his cabinet regularly on Friday mornings. Ezra Taft Benson suggested the sessions be opened with a prayer. "The suggestion is made only because of my love for you, members of the Cabinet, and the people of this great Christian nation," said Benson. "I know that without God's help we cannot succeed. With His help we cannot fail."[36] Eisenhower asked Dulles to poll the cabinet, and it was agreed to have a prayer, but the prayer should be a silent one.[37] One Friday morning Eisenhower overlooked the prayer and launched straight into a discussion of the first item on the agenda. Cabinet secretary Max Rabb slipped him a note to remind him of the omission. "Oh, goddamnit," Eisenhower exclaimed, "we forgot the silent prayer."[38]

Neither FDR nor Truman attached much importance to cabinet meetings and preferred to handle major issues in the Oval Office.[*] Eisenhower looked on the cabinet as his principal sounding board.

---

[*] "The cold fact is that on important matters we are seldom called upon for advice," wrote Harold Ickes, FDR's long-serving secretary of the interior. "We never discuss exhaustively any policy of government or question of political strategy. The President makes all of his own decisions and so far as the Cabinet is concerned, without taking counsel with a group of advisers. 1 *The Secret Diaries of Harold L. Ickes* 308 (New York: Simon and Schuster, 1953).

General Jerry Persons, Ike's congressional liaison, said the president enjoyed hitting "those fungoes out there just to see what would happen. He would direct questions to each person around the table, and all members were free to contribute their thoughts on any subject, regardless of their responsibilities."[39]

Eisenhower expected the cabinet to present options and argue with one another about the superiority of one course of action or another—just as Bradley and Montgomery might have done. The one thing they were not permitted to do was raise matters that pertained solely to their own departments. Eisenhower thought that was something for each of them to decide individually.

Charles Wilson talked too much, Dulles pontificated, Durkin felt uncomfortable, and Weeks was back in the Stone Age, but Eisenhower appeared satisfied. "All of my early cabinet meetings have revealed the existence of a spirit of teamwork and friendship that augurs well for the future," he confided to his diary in early February. "Everybody is working hard and doing it with a will." Ike thought the White House staff was also rounding into shape. His problems were on Capitol Hill. "The Republicans have been so long in opposition to the executive that Republican senators are having a hard time getting through their heads that they now belong to a team that includes the White House."[40]

Two weeks after the inauguration, Eisenhower heeded political advice and joined the Presbyterian church. Clare Boothe Luce in particular had pressed Ike to join. It was what the country expected, she said. On February 1, 1953, Ike and Mamie joined the congregation at the National Presbyterian Church at 1764 N Street in Washington. Eisenhower was baptized in a private ceremony beforehand. "We were scarcely home before the fact was being publicized, by the pastor [Dr. Edward Elson], to the hilt," said Eisenhower. "I had been promised, by him, that there was to be no publicity. I feel like changing at once to another church of the same denomination. I shall if he breaks out again."[41]

The cabinet was Eisenhower's sounding board. The National Security Council (NSC) was his instrument of policy. Created by Congress under the National Security Act of 1947, the NSC was designed to fuse the nation's security policies into an integrated whole. It was patterned after the British war cabinet, and to a very large extent arose out of the lack of coordination that contributed to Pearl Harbor. Its statutory members included the secretary of state, the secretary of defense, the chairman of the Joint Chiefs, the director of central intelligence, the director of defense mobilization, and the vice president. The president was chairman. At President Truman's insistence when the act was before Congress, the NSC was made an advisory body only. Unlike the British war cabinet, it had no decision-making authority. Truman insisted that this rested with the president.

Eisenhower saw the NSC as his principal tool for governing. He expanded its regular membership to include the secretary of the Treasury, the director of the Bureau of the Budget, and the director of foreign aid. If trade issues were to be discussed, Weeks was invited; if military matters loomed, the service chiefs came; Brownell was often present for his legal contribution, as was any other senior official whose expertise might be relevant. Robert Cutler, the hardworking Boston banker who had been Ike's deputy chief of staff during the campaign, became his special assistant for national security affairs. Unlike his successors who went to academia for their national security advisers, Eisenhower did not need foreign policy advice.[*] What he wanted was a staff secretary to organize the agenda, prepare the documentation, and record the results. Cutler fit the bill admirably. His credentials included wartime service on the staff of Henry L. Stimson, where he rose to the rank of brigadier general, and a literary flare unique among Boston bankers. He had been class poet of the Harvard Class of 1922 and was the author of two novels.[†] Cutler was also blessed with a winning personality (George Marshall called him

---

[*] The job title was changed from national security *assistant* to national security *adviser* under President John F. Kennedy. Kennedy and Lyndon Johnson employed Harvard dean McGeorge Bundy in that capacity; Nixon went to Harvard for Henry Kissinger; and Carter turned to Columbia for Zbigniew Brzezinski. The pattern continued through George W. Bush, who went to Stanford for Condoleezza Rice. President Obama initially chose Marine Corps general James L. Jones, the first nonacademic to hold the post since the Eisenhower years.

[†] *Louisburg Square* (New York: Macmillan, 1917) and *The Speckled Bird* (New York: Macmillan, 1923).

"a rose among cabbages") and got along well with all of the NSC principals—whom he referred to as "the whales."[42]

Under Truman, the NSC met sporadically, and until the Korean War broke out in 1950 the president rarely attended. Eisenhower scheduled meetings for every Thursday morning and presided personally. Agendas and background documents were distributed beforehand, CIA director Allen Dulles led off with a twenty-minute intelligence briefing, Cutler moved through the agenda briskly, and the meetings adjourned promptly at noon. During the first 115 weeks of the Eisenhower administration, the NSC met 115 times. Of the 343 council meetings between January 29, 1953, and January 12, 1961, Eisenhower presided at 319. Those he missed were because of illness or because he was out of town.[43]

As with the cabinet, Eisenhower presided actively. But unlike the cabinet the issues were more focused and Eisenhower preferred to allow the discussion to proceed until it reached a logical conclusion. Sometimes he announced his decision, often he did not. But the regularity of the meetings, combined with the precise agenda, assured that Eisenhower kept firm control, just as he might have done at staff meetings as supreme commander. "Eisenhower made all the vital decisions and firmly enforced them," said Gordon Gray, who succeeded Cutler as the president's national security assistant. "His reliance on the staff system stopped at the deciding line. His grasp of complex issues was profound, and his exposition of his own views was forceful and clear." The mythical Eisenhower, who left decision making to subordinates, whose mind was "lazy" and who was not very bright, cannot be found in the minutes of the National Security Council, said Gray.[44]

Eisenhower often used NSC meetings to raise the consciousness of his more insular colleagues. When Charles Wilson objected to expanding trade with Eastern Europe, including the sale of low-grade military hardware ("I don't like to sell firearms to the Indians," said Wilson), Eisenhower rebuked him sharply. "The last thing you want to do," said Eisenhower, "is to force all these peripheral countries—the Baltic States, Poland, Czechoslovakia and the rest of them—to depend on Moscow for the rest of their lives."[45] When Humphrey opposed foreign aid to India because he thought the nation was becoming socialist, Eisenhower reined him in. "George," he said, "you don't understand the Indian problem. Their situation isn't like our situation. We can operate a free-enterprise economy, but it depends on a whole lot of underpinnings that the Indians simply don't have. If I were the prime minister of India, I would have to resort to many measures which you would call socialistic. So it's quite a mistaken idea that we should judge the Indian situation or the Indian needs or the Indian policies by criteria which may be relevant for us."[46]

Late in February 1953, Eisenhower prepared for his first presidential visit to the Augusta National. On February 25, the day before leaving, he met the press. Questions pertaining to foreign affairs dominated the session. May Craig, then with the *Portland (Maine) Press Herald,* asked about the wartime agreements with the Soviet Union. Should FDR and Truman have foreseen that the Russians would violate them?

"I have no interest in going back and raking up the ashes of the dead past," Eisenhower replied. "I think it was perfectly right in the past years to try to establish a method of friendship, of finding this thing that Latin scholars call a 'modus vivendi.' Of course we should have sought it."

A follow-up question pertained to Stalin. Robert Clark of the International News Service noted that Stalin had recently said he would look favorably on a face-to-face meeting. "Would you be willing to go out of this country to meet with Stalin?"

"I will meet anybody, anywhere, where I thought there was the slightest chance of doing any good," said Eisenhower. What he meant, he explained, was that defending freedom "is not just one nation's job. I would go to any suitable spot, let's say halfway between, and talk with anybody, and with the full knowledge of our allies and friends as to the kind of things I was talking about."[47]

Eisenhower spent four days in Augusta and returned to the White House on March 2, 1953. On March 3, he met extensively with Prince Faisal al-Saud, the foreign minister and later king of Saudi Arabia, and promised to try to correct deteriorating relations between the United States and the Arab countries. He went to bed early that evening.[48]

At 2 a.m. on March 4, Allen Dulles called Robert Cutler at his home on H Street. "Uncle Joe has had a stroke and is either dead or dying," said Dulles. "Do you think I should wake the Boss?"

"No, Allen, I wouldn't," Cutler replied. "He gets up at six. Why not wait until then. When you call him, why don't you say we will be waiting in his office at seven-thirty?"

When Eisenhower walked into the Oval Office at seven-thirty, Cutler and Dulles were there, along with press secretary James Hagerty and presidential assistant C. D. Jackson, a skilled wordsmith and former publisher of *Fortune.* Ann Whitman, the president's secretary, remembers that Ike was dressed in brown that morning. Brown suit, brown tie, brown shoes. Whenever Eisenhower appeared in brown, according to Whitman, they were in for a hard day.

"What do you think we can do about *this?*"asked Eisenhower.[49]

He was surprised to learn that neither State nor Defense had any contingency plans, but pleased that Cutler and Jackson had each drafted statements for him to issue. For the next two hours Ike worked with Cutler and Jackson to combine the two statements into one, and then went to a regularly scheduled meeting of the NSC.[50] Shortly before noon, the president's message was sent to the press: a carefully crafted, nonincendiary statement that in the Cold War context hit all the right notes. Stalin was neither praised nor vilified (in fact, he was not mentioned by name), but the sympathy of the American people was expressed in unmistakable terms.

> At this moment in history when multitudes of Russians are anxiously concerned because of the illness of the Soviet ruler, the thoughts of America go out to all the people of the U.S.S.R. . . .
>
> Regardless of the identity of government personalities, the prayer of us Americans continues to be that the Almighty will watch over the people of that vast country and bring them, in His wisdom, opportunity to live their

lives in a world where all men and women and children dwell in peace and comradeship.[51]

It was a masterly document designed, as Eisenhower wished, to extend a friendly gesture—an overture for peace, without explicitly doing so. Cold War rhetoric was kept to a minimum, and the references to the Almighty were designed as much for American consumption as for the Soviets. As seen in the Kremlin, the message was unmistakable.[*]

On March 15, 1953, Georgy Malenkov, Stalin's successor as prime minister, responded in a major speech to the Supreme Soviet. Speaking to thirteen hundred delegates in the great hall of the Kremlin, Malenkov announced: "At the present time there is no dispute or unresolved question that cannot be settled peacefully by mutual agreement of the interested countries. This applies to our relations with all states, including the United States of America."[52]

Washington was caught off guard. "Ever since 1946 the experts have been yapping about what would happen when Stalin dies and what we should do about it," Eisenhower told the cabinet. "Well, he's dead. And you can turn the files of our government inside out looking for any plans laid. We have no plans."[53]

Eisenhower stepped into the vacuum. When speechwriter Emmet Hughes entered the Oval Office shortly after Malenkov's address to review some routine matters with the president, Ike said there was a danger of dropping the ball. "I am tired—and I think everyone is tired—of just plain indictments of the Soviet regime. What are *we* ready to do to improve the chances of peace? Malenkov isn't going to be frightened with speeches. What are we trying to achieve?"[54]

Eisenhower got up from his desk and began to pace around the

---

* When Stalin died on March 5, 1953, the official U.S. response was stiff and formal. "The Government of the United States tenders its official condolences to the Government of the U.S.S.R. on the death of Generalissimo Joseph Stalin, Prime Minister of the Soviet Union." Eisenhower made no personal statement. *Public Papers of the Presidents of the United States, Dwight D. Eisenhower, 1953* 91 (Washington, D.C.: National Archives and Records Administration, 1960). Cited subsequently as *Public Papers*.

room. He wheeled abruptly to face Hughes. "Here is what I would like to say:

"The jet plane that roars over your head costs three-quarter of a million dollars. That is more money than a man making ten thousand dollars every year is going to make in his lifetime. What world can afford this sort of thing for long? We are in an armaments race. Where will it lead us? At worst, to atomic warfare. At best, to robbing every people and nation on earth of the fruits of their own toil."

Eisenhower told Hughes he wanted to see the resources of the world used for bread, clothes, homes, hospitals, and schools but not for guns. He did not want to make a speech that included the standard criticism of the Soviet Union. "The past speaks for itself. I am interested in the future. Both their government and ours now have new men in them. The slate is clean. Now let us begin talking to each other. *And let us say what we've got to say so that every person on earth can understand it.*"[55]

Hughes was swept away by Eisenhower's intensity. But he interjected a note of caution. He told the president he had just spoken with Secretary Dulles about the possibility of peace in Korea. According to Hughes, Dulles said he would be sorry to see it until we gave the Chinese "one hell of a licking."[56]

Eisenhower froze in place. He was visibly angry. "All right," he told Hughes. "If Mr. Dulles and all his sophisticated advisers really mean that they can not talk peace seriously, then I am in the wrong pew. For if it's *war* we should be talking about, I know the people who should give me advice on that—and they're not in the State Department. Now either we cut out all this fooling around and make a serious bid for peace—or we forget the whole thing."[57]

On March 27, Eisenhower informed the cabinet that he had begun work on a major foreign policy speech that he intended to give as his keynote address to the annual meeting of the American Society of Newspaper Editors at the Statler Hotel in Washington on April 16. The Soviets, meanwhile, were continuing to send peace signals. Travel restrictions were relaxed in Berlin, the Russian press began to play up the wartime cooperation that had existed with Britain and the United States, and at the United Nations, the Soviet delegation agreed to support Dag Hammarskjöld to succeed Trygve Lie as secretary-general. In Korea, the long stalemate also showed signs of thaw. In late February, Mark Clark, having been so instructed by Washington, had offered to exchange sick and wounded prisoners with the Chinese and North Koreans in accordance with article 109 of the Geneva Convention.* On March 28, General Peng Teh-huai and Marshal Kim Il Sung, the respective Chinese and North Korea commanders, not only replied positively to Clark's offer, but suggested that full-dress peace negotiations—which had been suspended for the last six months—be resumed at Panmunjom.[58] Chinese foreign minister Chou En-lai, back in Beijing after attending Stalin's funeral in Moscow, added his support on March 30. Chou went further and suggested the return of all prisoners who wished to be repatriated, clearly indicating that the Communists would no longer insist on forcible repatriation,[59] which had been a major stumbling block to negotiations.

In Washington, Eisenhower responded favorably. At his press conference on April 2, the president was asked by Merriman Smith of United Press International to comment on the Chinese peace overtures. "We should take at face value every offer that is made to us, until it is proved not to be worthy of being so taken," Eisenhower replied. The president said the quick exchange of sick and wounded prisoners "would be a clear indication that deeds, rather than words, are now coming into fashion."[60]

Eisenhower was in the driver's seat. At a National Security Council meeting on April 9, 1953, John Foster Dulles argued that the Chinese offer to negotiate should be rejected. "It was now quite possible to secure a much more satisfactory settlement in Korea than a mere armistice at the thirty-eighth parallel," said Dulles. Even if there was an armistice, Dulles believed that the United States would have to break it soon in order to achieve the unification of Korea.

Eisenhower pulled Dulles up short. "It will be impossible to call off the armistice and go to war again," he told the secretary. "The

---

* Article 109 provides that "parties to the conflict are bound to send back to their own country . . . seriously wounded and seriously sick prisoners of war, after having cared for them until they are fit to travel." The article also provides that the prisoners will not be repatriated against their will. International Committee of the Red Cross, Geneva Convention Relative to the Treatment of Prisoners of War (third Geneva convention), August 12, 1949.

American people will never stand for such a move."[61] When Charles Wilson piped up to support Dulles, the president shut him down. He had already said he would regard the exchange of sick and wounded prisoners as a test of faith on the part of the Chinese, said Eisenhower. The issue was closed.[62] On April 20, Operation LITTLE SWITCH, the exchange of sick and wounded prisoners, began. Within the week, plenary discussions between the U.S. and Communist negotiators resumed at Panmunjom.

Eisenhower spent much of the first two weeks of April preparing his speech for the newspaper editors. "Every day or two, the president would find a few hours to review with me in detail our latest version," Hughes recalled. "I lost count of these multiplying drafts after the number passed a dozen, but the basic structure never changed."[63] When the speech was finished, Eisenhower titled it "The Chance for Peace," and it remains one of the most important speeches any president has delivered—an epic event that altered the currents of the Cold War. Dulles fought it to the very end. "I know how he feels," Eisenhower told Hughes. "But sometimes Foster is just too worried about being accused of sounding like Truman and Acheson. I think he worries too much about it."[64]

The night before his speech was to be delivered, Eisenhower suffered a severe intestinal attack. He was in intense pain as he mounted the podium at the Statler. "I could concentrate on the text only by extreme effort," Eisenhower recalled. "At times I became so dizzy I feared I would faint."[65] Gripping the lectern to steady himself, the president laid out a new direction of march. "Every gun that is made, every warship launched, every rocket fired," said Eisenhower, "signifies, in the final sense, a theft from those who hunger and are not fed, those who are cold and are not clothed."

"Is there no other way the world may live?" he asked. The new Soviet leadership "has a precious opportunity . . . to help turn the tide of history. A world that begins to witness a rebirth of trust among nations *can* find its way to a peace that is neither partial nor punitive. . . . *The first great step along this way must be the conclusion of an honorable armistice in Korea.*"

Eisenhower went on to propose a reduction in "the burden of armaments" now weighing upon the world. He suggested that the

United States would be prepared to enter "into the most solemn agreements" limiting the size of military forces and restricting weapons production. Atomic energy should be placed under international control "to promote its use for peaceful purposes only and to insure the prohibition of atomic weapons." Other weapons of mass destruction should be banned, with adequate safeguards provided by "a practical system of inspection under the United Nations."

"These proposals spring, without ulterior purpose or political passion, from our calm conviction that the hunger for peace is in the hearts of all people—those of Russia and of China no less than of our own country."[66]

*The New York Times* called the speech "magnificent and deeply moving." The staunchly Democratic *New York Post* said it was "America's voice at its best."[67] Richard Rovere, scarcely an admirer of the Eisenhower administration, called the speech "an immense triumph. It firmly established [Eisenhower's] leadership in America and re-established America's leadership in the world."[68]

The ideas for Eisenhower's speech did not bubble up from the bureaucracy. They did not reflect a cabinet consensus—Dulles and Wilson were opposed; they did not derive from learned professorial research; nor did they represent the work product of policy think tanks. They were pure Eisenhower. Ike believed the country wanted peace, and he was determined to provide it. War was neither a board game nor a seminar exercise for armchair intellectuals. America's two great military presidents—Grant and Eisenhower—both abhorred war. In 1869, Grant overruled Sherman and Sheridan and brought peace to the Great Plains; in 1953, Eisenhower dismissed the objections of Dulles and Wilson, to say nothing of those of Senator Taft and the congressional Republicans, and brought peace to Korea.

The principal obstacle was no longer China and North Korea, but South Korean president Syngman Rhee, who continued to insist on marching to the Yalu. When a full prisoner exchange between the two sides was agreed to, Rhee ordered the gates of the South Korean stockades opened so that the Chinese and North Korean prisoners might escape. When it became fully apparent that the United Nations was going to agree to an armistice along the thirty-eighth parallel, Rhee threatened to withdraw the South Korean Army (ROK) from UN command. Eisenhower was unfazed. Having twice brought de Gaulle to heel under similar circumstances during the war in Europe, Ike understood the exercise. Cut off all Class 3 and Class 5 [fuel and ammunition] supplies for the ROK Army, Mark Clark was instructed. As his supplies dwindled, Rhee recognized he was holding a losing hand.

"Unless you are prepared immediately and unequivocally to accept the authority of the UN Command to conduct the present hostilities and to bring them to a close, it will be necessary to effect another arrangement," Eisenhower informed Rhee on June 18.[69] That "arrangement" would be the total withdrawal of U.S. forces from Korea and the termination of all military and financial assistance.

Rhee held out for another three weeks, hoping that Republican sentiment in Congress would force Eisenhower to relent, but to no avail. On July 12, the South Korean president issued a public statement promising to cooperate.[70]

The armistice was signed at Panmunjom at 10:12 a.m. on July 27, 1953, bringing the Korean War to a close. American casualties totaled 142,091—33,629 killed, 103,284 wounded, and 5,178 missing. Not one American serviceman or woman would die in combat for the next eight years.

It was Sunday, July 26, thirteen hours earlier in Washington, when Eisenhower received the news. He went downstairs to the broadcast room in the White House to tell the nation. "And so at long last the carnage of war is to cease and the negotiations at the conference table to begin. On this Sabbath evening each of us devoutly prays that all nations may come to see the wisdom of composing differences in this fashion before, rather than after, there is a resort to brutal and futile battle."

Eisenhower spoke for less than five minutes. He concluded with Lincoln's famous remarks from his second inaugural: "With malice toward none; with charity for all; with firmness in the right as God gives us to see the right, let us strive on . . . to do all which may achieve and cherish a lasting peace, among ourselves, and with all nations."[71]

When he finished, Eisenhower was asked by a photographer how he felt.

"The war is over," the president said with a smile. "I hope my son is going to come home soon."[72]

# TWENTY-ONE

# First Off the Tee

I just won't get into a pissing contest with that skunk.

— DWIGHT D. EISENHOWER

DWIGHT D. EISENHOWER did not play more golf than any president in American history. Woodrow Wilson, on doctor's orders, played every day—a total of almost sixteen hundred rounds during his eight years in the White House. Wilson was a terrible golfer. He once needed twenty-six strokes, including fifteen putts, to finish the par-4 second hole at the Washington Golf and Country Club. "My right eye is like a horse's," Wilson said. "I can see straight out with it, but not sideways. As a result, I cannot take a full swing because my nose gets in the way and cuts off my view of the ball."[1]

Ike was also not the best golfer to occupy the White House. That distinction goes to John F. Kennedy, who was obsessively secretive about his love for the game. But of the fourteen presidents since William Howard Taft who have played golf while in the White House,[*] Eisenhower was clearly the most dedicated. When Ike took office in 1953, 3.2 million Americans played the game on some five thousand golf courses around the nation.[2] By 1961, the number of golfers had more than doubled, and there were not enough tee times to meet the surging demand. "Whatever remained to be done to remove the last traces of the average man's carefully nurtured prejudice against a

---

[*] Truman, Hoover, and Jimmy Carter did not play.

Golfing greats Byron Nelson and Ben Hogan with Ike and Clifford Roberts at the Augusta National.

game originally linked with the wealthy and aloof was done by President Eisenhower," wrote historian Herbert Warren Wind.[3] Ike made golf accessible, motivating millions of men who were forty and over to try the game for the first time.[4]

Golf was as necessary to Eisenhower's mental health as a good night's sleep. "Without golf," said Major General Howard Snyder, the president's longtime personal physician, "he'd be like a caged lion, with all those tensions building up inside him. If this fellow couldn't play golf, I'd have a nut case on my hands."[5]

Eisenhower played nearly 800 rounds of golf during his time as president, including 210 at the Augusta National. As soon as he awoke each morning, Ike reached for a pitching wedge and started swinging it to warm up his wrists and arms. He carried the club to the West Wing and rested it against a credenza in the Oval Office. Sometimes while dictating he took practice swings with an eight-iron. Most afternoons he would slip on his golf cleats, grab his putter, his wedge, and his eight-iron, and head out to the South Lawn.

His cleat marks were still visible in the wooden floor in the Oval Office until Richard Nixon had the floor replaced in 1969. Eisenhower also had a custom-built putting green (funded by private donations) constructed just outside the French doors of his office. The green had two undersized holes and a small sand trap.[6]

The Democrats initially sought partisan advantage and criticized Ike for his time on the links. Some portrayed him as a full-time golfer who moonlighted as president. "Ben Hogan for President," read a bumper sticker in the 1956 campaign. "If we're going to have a golfer, let's have a good one." Others joked that Ike had a thirty-six-hole workweek, which was literally true since he usually played a round on Wednesday afternoon and another on Saturday morning.[7] It was President Truman—a nongolfer himself—who finally blew the whistle on such criticism. "To criticize the President . . . because he plays a game of golf is unfair and picayunish," said Truman. "He has the same right to relax from the heavy burdens of office as any other man."[8]*

It was clear that Eisenhower needed the relaxation. While Ike might delegate the details, the major decisions—and the responsibility—rested with him. The Republicans in Congress had no intention of giving up their opposition to the federal government just because their party had captured the White House. Eisenhower's principal adversaries throughout his tenure as president were not the Democrats but the calcified wing of the Republican party, which continued to live in the shadow of Calvin Coolidge and to see Communists under every bedstead.

"Yesterday was one of the worst days I have experienced since January 20th," Eisenhower confided to his diary on May 1, 1953. "The difficulty arose at the weekly meeting of the Executive Departments and the leaders of the Republican Party in the Congress." Eisenhower had explained to the GOP leadership how the forthcoming

---

* Eisenhower's brother Edgar sent him a cartoon from the *Chicago Tribune* critical of his golfing. "My only comment," Ike replied, "is that while I may allow my eye to stray from the ball, I am never so careless as to let it stray far enough so as to read the *Chicago Tribune*." DDE to Edgar Newton Eisenhower, June 9, 1953, *The Papers of Dwight David Eisenhower*, vol. 14, *The Presidency* 287. Cited subsequently as 14 *The Presidency*.

budget would reduce expenditures by \$8.4 billion, but could not be cut more because of defense requirements in the Cold War.

> In spite of the apparent satisfaction of most of those present, Senator Taft broke out in a violent objection to everything that had been done. He accused the National Security Council of merely adopting the Truman strategy [and] classed the savings as "puny." . . .
>
> I think that everyone present was astonished at the demagogic nature of his tirade, because not once did he mention the security of the United States. He simply wanted expenditures reduced, regardless. . . . I do not see how he can maintain any reputation for considered judgment when he attempts to discuss weighty, serious, and even critical matters in such an ill-tempered and violent fashion.
>
> The ludicrous part of the affair came when several of my close friends around the table saw that my temper was getting a little out of hand, and they did not want any breech to be brought about that would be completely unbridge-able. So George Humphrey and Joe Dodge in turn jumped into the conversation as quickly as there was the slightest chance to interrupt and held the floor until I cooled down somewhat.

Taft backed down, but Eisenhower doubted if the senator was really on board.

> Of course I am pleased that I did not add any fuel to the flames, even though it is possible I might have done so except for the quick intervention of my devoted friends. If this thing has to be dragged out into the open, we at least have the right to stand firmly on the platform of taking no unnecessary chances with our country's safety. . . . However, I still maintain it does not create any confidence in the reliability and effectiveness of our leadership in one of the important houses of Congress.[9]

It was in the Senate that problems festered. Taft had become majority leader when the Republicans regained control on Ike's coattails, and on most issues he cooperated with the White House. "Taft and I have developed a curious sort of personal friendship," Eisenhower wrote a month later.

> It is not any Damon and Pythias sort of thing that insures compatibility of intellectual viewpoint, nor even, for that matter, complete courtesy in the public discussion of political questions. . . . The real point of difference between us is that he wants to reduce taxes immediately, believing that this is possible if we arbitrarily reduce the security establishment by [an additional] ten billion dollars. And he believes that in no other way can the Republicans be returned to the control of Congress in 1954. I personally agree with none of this. . . .
>
> In the foreign field, Senator Taft never disagrees with me when we discuss such affairs academically or theoretically. However, when we take up each individual problem he easily loses his temper and makes extravagant statements. . . .
>
> The implication of all this is that Senator Taft and I will never completely really agree on policies affecting either the domestic or foreign scene. Moreover, we will never be sufficiently close that we are impelled by mutual friendship to seek ways and means to minimize any evidence of apparent opposition.[10]

Taft, who had not been previously diagnosed, died suddenly of stomach cancer on July 31, 1953, and was succeeded as majority leader by William Knowland, the senior senator from California.[11] But Eisenhower's difficulties did not lessen. Though he often disagreed with Ike, Taft's political and intellectual stature had kept the right wing of the party more or less under control. With him gone, Joseph McCarthy and his cohorts had free rein. McCarthy, who was now chairman of the Senate Committee on Government Operations, saw Ike somewhat contemptuously as an amiable military man who understood little about Washington politics and was at best a dupe for sinister forces in the eastern establishment. Eisenhower, for his part, never forgave McCarthy for his criticism of George Marshall and considered him a bully whose anti-Communist fervor was simply an effort to attain notoriety.

A collision was inevitable, and it came sooner than Eisenhower anticipated. On January 21, 1953, Ike's second day in office, he sent the Senate his nominees for subcabinet posts—the undersecretaries and assistant secretaries who ensure administration control of the executive branch. Like all presidents, he assumed pro forma confirmation. That proved not to be the case. Utilizing the arcane rules of the Senate, McCarthy put an immediate hold on Ike's first nominee: General Walter Bedell Smith to be undersecretary of state, the senior subcabinet position. According to McCarthy, Smith was a possible Communist sympathizer and fellow traveler. As America's postwar ambassador to the Soviet Union, Smith had defended career diplomat John Paton Davies, Jr., a member of his staff in Moscow, against McCarthy's charges of disloyalty, and in McCarthy's eyes that made Smith suspect as well.

Eisenhower hit the ceiling. Not only had Smith served as his wartime chief of staff, but his political views were somewhere to the right of Attila the Hun. (Smith once told Ike that he thought Nelson Rockefeller was a Communist.)[12] In addition to serving as ambassador to Moscow, Smith had been the director of central intelligence. To consider him a fellow traveler was absurd. Eisenhower called Taft and told him to put a stop to the nonsense about Smith immediately. Taft did as Ike asked, McCarthy withdrew his hold, and Smith was confirmed. But the episode left a lasting scar. To question Bedell Smith's loyalty was preposterous. Eisenhower saw firsthand the meaning of McCarthyism. In the words of one biographer, he came to loathe the senator "almost as much as he hated Hitler."[13]

No sooner was Smith confirmed than McCarthy was objecting again. This time it was to Dr. James B. Conant, the distinguished president of Harvard, whom Eisenhower had nominated to succeed John J. McCloy as American high commissioner in Germany. Any president of Harvard would probably have been suspect to McCarthy, but Conant had had the temerity of once stating that there were no Communists on the university's faculty. Obviously he was a pinko fellow traveler. Eisenhower exploded again. This time he dispatched Nixon to call McCarthy off. Confronted with the White House's determination, the senator backed down. McCarthy wrote Ike that he was "much opposed" to Conant but would not carry his opposition to the Senate floor because he did not "want to make a row."[14]

Senate confirmation of Bedell Smith and James B. Conant represented preliminary skirmishes. The first real battle between Eisenhower and McCarthy was joined on February 27, 1953, when Eisenhower nominated Charles E. "Chip" Bohlen to be ambassador to Moscow. A career Foreign Service officer who was fluent in Russian and French, Bohlen was currently serving as counselor in the State Department, the senior professional post. He had previously served in Moscow and was considered an authority on Soviet affairs. Because of his fluency in Russian, he had been FDR's interpreter at Teheran and Yalta, and had served Truman in the same capacity at Potsdam. For McCarthy, that was tantamount to treason.

Dulles warned the president that the nomination might be in trouble and at one point appeared ready to throw Bohlen under the bus, but Eisenhower would have none of it. "I knew Bohlen and had learned to respect and like him," said Ike. "When I was the Allied commander in NATO . . . I had many conversations with him concerning our difficulties with the Soviets. So fully did I believe in his tough, firm but fair attitude . . . that I came to look upon him as one of the ablest Foreign Service officers I had ever met."[15] Eisenhower assumed that if he made his support for Bohlen clear, the Republicans in the Senate would fall into line. That did not happen. Not only was Bohlen tarred for having been an accomplice to the "sell out" to Stalin at Teheran and Yalta, but there was also derogatory information in his FBI security file that had been leaked to McCarthy.*

Eisenhower, who was confident Bohlen would pass muster, over-

---

* In the argot of the 1950s, the damaging information in Bohlen's security file pertained to his "family life," a euphemism for his sexual orientation. The suggestion was that he was homosexual. The accusation, which was unfounded, was based on the fact that once while serving abroad he had rented his house in Washington to a homosexual couple.

"We Have
Documentary Evidence
That This Man
Is Planning
A Trip To Moscow"

3/25/1953

ruled Attorney General Brownell and authorized two senators, one from each party, Taft and Alabama's John Sparkman, to review the file. After reading the file at the Department of Justice, Taft and Sparkman reported that it contained nothing that should stand in the way of Bohlen's confirmation.[16]

Nevertheless, a bitter floor fight followed. In a lengthy Senate speech, McCarthy asserted that Bohlen had been "at Roosevelt's left hand at Teheran and Yalta, and at Truman's left hand at Potsdam," and ranted about his "ugly record of great betrayal." Senator Herman Welker of Idaho said, "Don't send Bohlen to Moscow. Send General Van Fleet [the commander of Eighth Army in Korea] instead." Senator Everett Dirksen piled on. "I reject Yalta, so I reject Yalta men."[17]

Eisenhower supported Bohlen with the full prestige of the presidency. "The reason I sent his name to the Senate, and the reason it stays there, is because I believe he is the best qualified man for the job," he said at a press conference on March 26.[18] The following day the Senate voted to confirm Bohlen 74–13.* The Senate's overwhelm-

---

* Of the thirteen no votes, eleven were Republicans: John Bricker (Ohio), Styles Bridges (New Hampshire), Everett Dirksen (Illinois), Henry Dworshak (Idaho), Barry Goldwater (Arizona), Bourke Hickenlooper (Iowa), George "Molly" Malone (Nevada), Joseph McCarthy (Wisconsin), Karl Mundt (South Dakota), Andrew

ing confirmation of Bohlen represented a major victory for Eisenhower. The president had stood up to the hysteria about loyalty and security that McCarthy and his supporters had fanned, and had obtained Bohlen's confirmation to be his ambassador to Moscow. Bohlen was the only man remaining in public life who could be tied, regardless of how remotely, to the wartime diplomacy of Franklin Roosevelt. It was a remarkable fight, and Ike stood his ground.

"Eleven Republican senators voted against us," Eisenhower wrote in his diary on April 1, 1953.

> I was surprised by the vote of [John W.] Bricker and [Barry] Goldwater. These two seemed to me a bit more intelligent than the others, who sought to defend their position with the most misleading kind of argument.
>
> Senator McCarthy is, of course, so anxious for headlines that he is prepared to go to any extremes in order to secure some mention of his name in the press. I really believe that nothing will be so effective in combating his particular kind of trouble-making as to ignore him. This he cannot stand.[19]

McCarthy had struck out against Ike's diplomatic nominees. The State Department's Voice of America provided easier pickings. In February, the Government Operations Committee set out to purge the VOA's 189 overseas libraries of the works of pro-Communist authors. McCarthy charged that the committee had found more than thirty thousand books by 418 suspect writers, including W. H. Auden, Edna Ferber, John Dewey, Bernard De Voto, and Arthur Schlesinger, Jr.[20] Dashiel Hammett's totally nonpolitical detective classics *The Maltese Falcon* and *The Thin Man* were expunged because Hammett was a "Fifth Amendment Communist," based on his refusal to testify before the House Un-American Activities Committee.[21]

The committee's principal investigators were twenty-six-year-old

Schoeppel (Kansas), and Herman Welker (Idaho). Democrats Pat McCarran of Nevada and Edwin C. Johnson of Colorado also voted no.

Roy Cohn, who McCarthy hired as chief counsel, and G. David Schine, a friend of Cohn's whose father owned a chain of luxury hotels. Cohn's credentials stemmed from a stint in the U.S. Attorney's office in Manhattan, while Schine was simply a nice young man on whom Cohn had a crush. The two romped through the major cities of Western Europe looking for subversive literature on the shelves of American libraries. Cohn's attitude is best illustrated by his comment after visiting the VOA library in Vienna and the Soviet counterpart in the Russian sector of the city. "We discovered that some of the same books—for example, the works of Howard Fast—were stocked by both. One of us—the United States or the Soviet Union—had to be wrong."[22]

Eisenhower struck back on June 14. Slated to give the commencement address at Dartmouth College, Ike found himself on the platform with fellow honorary degree recipients John McCloy; Sherman Adams (Dartmouth, 1920); Lester Pearson, the Canadian minister of external affairs; and Joseph Proskauer, chairman of the New York State Crime Commission. McCloy, who was well connected in Germany after his years as high commissioner, was telling the others how books were being burned in American libraries abroad at the instigation of Senator McCarthy.

"What's this?" asked Eisenhower. "What's this?"

"I was telling about the burning of State Department books abroad," McCloy replied.

"Oh, they're not burning books," said Eisenhower.

"I'm afraid they are, Mr. President. I have the evidence. And the value of those books that are being destroyed was that they were uncensored. They criticize you and me and anyone else in government. The Germans knew they were uncensored and that's why they streamed into our libraries."[23]

Eisenhower sat quietly reflecting on what McCloy had said. When his time came to speak he discarded his prepared text and spoke extemporaneously. "Old soldiers love to reminisce," said Ike, "and they are notoriously garrulous." The graduands guffawed at the unmistakable dig at Douglas MacArthur. Then Eisenhower turned serious. "Don't join the book burners," he said. "Don't think you are going to conceal faults by concealing evidence that they ever existed. Don't be afraid to go in your library and read every book, as long as that document does not offend your own sense of decency. That should be the only censorship. . . . How will we defeat communism unless we know what it is?"[24]

There was little doubt about Eisenhower's target. Telegrams and messages pouring into the White House backed the president ten to one. On Capitol Hill, reaction was mixed. "He couldn't very well have been referring to me," McCarthy deadpanned. "I have burned no books."[25]

Eisenhower's Dartmouth College speech notwithstanding, McCarthy had a pernicious impact throughout the government. Several of Eisenhower's cabinet appointees—Arthur Summerfield and Sinclair Weeks, for example—initially were strong supporters of the senator, as was General Jerry Persons, Ike's congressional aide. The Loyalty Review Board appointed by President Truman worked overtime to discover Communist sympathizers on the federal payroll. American employees of international organizations were caught up in the net. Ralph Bunche of the United Nations, who had won the Nobel Peace Prize in 1950 for negotiating an armistice between Israel and the Arab states, was investigated by the board as a dangerous leftist.

When Eisenhower learned that the FBI was collecting information branding Bunche a Communist, he was appalled. "I am willing to bet he's no more a Communist than I am," Ike told cabinet secretary Max Rabb.

"I feel very strongly about this," said the president. "Bunche is a superior man, a credit to our country. I just can't stand by and permit a man like that to be chopped to pieces because of McCarthy feeling."[26]

Eisenhower asked Bunche how he could help, but Bunche was confident he could handle the matter himself. He was called before the board to answer accusations on several occasions. One hearing was shortened to enable Bunche to keep a dinner appointment. He had been invited to dine at the White House with the president.[27] Eisenhower offered no direct help, but the symbolism was unmistakable. On May 28, 1954, the Loyalty Board unanimously found that Bunche was above suspicion and that his loyalty to the United States was not in doubt.

Eisenhower declined to attack McCarthy publicly. First, he believed that McCarthy was the Senate's problem, and it would do no good for him to become embroiled in an internal Senate dispute.[*] More important, he believed McCarthy only sought notoriety, and if the president attacked him, that would serve the senator's purpose. There was also the possibility that by attacking McCarthy, he would make the senator a hero in the eyes of some. Far better to work behind the scenes. Given enough rope, McCarthy would someday hang himself. "I just won't get into a pissing contest with that skunk," Ike told his brother Milton.[28]

Eisenhower's luck ran true to form. At the end of 1953, McCarthy's approval ratings had reached an all-time high of 50 percent in the Gallup poll.[29] Encouraged by that showing, McCarthy unleashed his committee's investigative team to rout out Communists in the United States Army. Informed by one of his many spotters that an Army dentist at Camp Kilmer, New Jersey, was a member of the American Labor Party (a Trotskyite group on the attorney general's list of subversive organizations), the senator launched a full-scale investigation. The officer in question was Captain Irving Peress, a dentist at Camp Kilmer's reception center for inductees, who had been drafted into the service for two years under the doctor draft law. Peress had refused to sign a loyalty oath, and the Army's adjutant general was preparing his discharge papers. Before the discharge came through, McCarthy interrogated Peress, who invoked the Fifth Amendment and declined to testify. McCarthy demanded that Peress be court-martialed. Peress requested an immediate discharge and the Army complied, routinely promoting him to major in the process—as the doctor draft law required.

McCarthy had his issue. "Who promoted Peress?" The senator called Camp Kilmer's commanding officer, Brigadier General Ralph Zwicker, to testify. Confronting Zwicker in a one-man hearing, McCarthy was at his abusive best. Zwicker, who had been decorated

---

[*] Franklin Roosevelt made a fatal error in 1937 when he intervened in the Democratic caucus to force the election of Alben Barkley (Kentucky) as majority leader instead of Pat Harrison (Mississippi), the Senate's sentimental choice. Many senators, especially those from the South, never forgave the president. Jean Edward Smith, *FDR* 391–92.

for heroism on D-Day, did not flinch. He knew nothing about the matter, he said. The general explained that Peress's promotion was a routine matter dictated by statute. No one was at fault. "You have the brains of a five-year-old child," McCarthy responded. "You are a disgrace to the uniform you wear."[30]

McCarthy had crossed the line. The American Legion and the Veterans of Foreign Wars issued public rebukes, and even the *Chicago Tribune* editorialized that General Zwicker deserved better treatment.[31] On the Senate floor, Republican senator Ralph Flanders of Vermont rose to deliver the sharpest attack yet made on McCarthy by a colleague. "In this battle [against Communism] what is the part played by the junior Senator from Wisconsin? He dons his war paint, he goes into his war dance, he emits his war whoops. He goes forth to battle and proudly returns with the scalp of a pink Army dentist."[32] Flanders, a former president of the Federal Reserve Bank of Boston, enjoyed impeccable Republican credentials. Scarcely had he finished speaking than he received a note from the White House. "I was very much interested in reading the comments you made in the Senate today," wrote Eisenhower. "I think America needs to hear more Republican voices like yours."[33]

That same evening, Edward R. Murrow broke television journalism's self-imposed ban against attacking McCarthy and devoted his entire program *See It Now* to film clips of the senator in action—bullying, blustering, out of control. "The line between investigation and persecution is a very fine one," said Murrow, "and the junior senator from Wisconsin has stepped over it repeatedly."[34] The next day Eisenhower invited Murrow to the White House and congratulated him.[35]

Eisenhower explained his unwillingness to attack McCarthy directly. "This is not namby-pamby," Ike wrote his friend Paul Helms. "It is certainly not Pollyanna-ish. It is just common sense. A leader's job is to get others to go along with him in promoting something. . . . I am quite sure that the people who want me to stand up and publicly label McCarthy with derogatory titles are the most mistaken people that are dealing with this whole problem, even though in many instances they happen to be my warm friends."[36]

Privately, Eisenhower was outspoken. "This guy McCarthy wants to be president," Ike told James Hagerty. "He's the last guy in the world who'll ever get there if I have anything to say."[37] Instead of attacking McCarthy directly, Eisenhower deployed what Princeton politics professor Fred Greenstein called "the hidden hand," and his defeat of McCarthy, culminating in the Senate's vote of condemnation, represents what may well be the most adroit use of the indirect approach by any occupant of the White House.[38]

First off the mark was the Army. Secretary Robert T. Stevens, who had already crossed swords with McCarthy, ordered General Zwicker not to testify further before McCarthy's committee. The order was expanded to include all members of the military. Officers were instructed to ignore whatever summonses they might receive from McCarthy. Eisenhower escalated the response. Writing to Secretary of Defense Charles Wilson, the president extended the ban to all employees of the executive branch. Not only were they not to testify, but they were forbidden to submit any documents or other evidence to the committee. "I direct this action so as to maintain the proper separation of powers between the Executive and Legislative Branches of the Government in accordance with my responsibilities and duties under the Constitution," Eisenhower wrote. "This separation is vital to preclude the exercise of arbitrary power by any branch of the Government."[39] As Ike told Senate majority leader Knowland, "My people are not going to be subpoenaed."[40]

Eisenhower's action was unprecedented. He had expanded the concept of executive privilege far beyond that employed by any of his predecessors. Arthur Schlesinger, Jr., writing in *The Imperial Presidency,* called it "the most absolute assertion of presidential right to withhold information from Congress ever uttered to that day in American history."[41] McCarthy was stymied. Without the power to subpoena government records or employees, his investigations would grind to a halt. McCarthy appealed to government employees to disregard the president's order and report directly to him on "graft, corruption, Communism, and treason."[42] Insofar as Eisenhower was concerned, McCarthy was now beyond the pale. The senator's statement, he told Jim Hagerty, "is the most arrogant invitation to subversion and disloyalty that I have ever heard of. I won't stand for it one minute."[43]

A showdown was in the offing. On March 11, 1954, the Army submitted an official complaint to the Senate's Permanent Investigations Subcommittee charging that McCarthy and Cohn had repeatedly badgered it to obtain preferential treatment for Cohn's friend G. David Schine, who had been drafted in November. Schine was assigned to Fort Dix for basic training, and according to the Army's complaint, Cohn bombarded officials up and down the chain of command with demands on Schine's behalf and threatened to "wreck the Army" unless they were granted. McCarthy responded by charging that the Army was holding Schine hostage to blackmail him into terminating his investigation. Members of the subcommittee voted to hold hearings; McCarthy was compelled by the Senate's leadership to step down as chairman; and when the senator from Wisconsin insisted on retaining his right to vote, Eisenhower skewered him at his weekly press conference. "In America, if a man is a party to a dispute, he does not sit in judgment on his own case."[44]

The hearings began on April 22, and were televised nationally. The Army was represented by Joseph Welch, a gentle, courtly, old-fashioned lawyer from the prestigious Boston firm of Hale and Dorr. McCarthy and Cohn acted as their own counsel. The hearings lasted thirty-five days, and across the country the nation watched, spellbound by the spectacle. (I was in my senior year at Princeton, and classes regularly shut down as we tromped over to Whig Hall to sit before one of the few large-screen television sets on campus. My classmate Donald Rumsfeld ascribes his decision to enter politics partially to the fascination he felt watching the hearings.)[45] The folksy, understated manner of Joseph Welch played well on television. McCarthy and Cohn came across as villainous bullies engulfed in a cloud of darkness.

The high point of the hearings came with Roy Cohn on the witness stand. He was being examined by Welch about a cropped photo of Army Secretary Stevens and Private Schine. Welch wanted to know who had cropped the photo, and Cohn was being evasive. Finally, in exasperation, Welch said, "Surely, Mr. Cohn, you don't suggest it was done by a pixie?"

McCarthy interrupted. "Point of order. Point of order, Mr. Chairman. Will Mr. Welch please tell the Committee what a pixie is?"

Welch savored the moment. Turning to face the senator, Welch said: "Senator, a pixie is a very close relation to a fairy." (In the 1950s, "fairy" was a pejorative term used to identify a man who was gay, and the close relationship between Cohn and G. David Schine was an omnipresent undercurrent in the hearings.)

The committee room erupted in sustained laughter. With that well-aimed quip, Welch torpedoed the terror of McCarthyism. The country was laughing at the senator, not with him.

The final blow was delivered by Welch one week later when McCarthy gratuitously accused a young member of Welch's Boston law firm of having been a member of the National Lawyers Guild, which McCarthy claimed was "the legal bulwark of the Communist party." Welch was dumbstruck. Composing himself carefully, he replied with evident anguish, "Senator, until this moment I never really gauged your cruelty or your recklessness." Welch explained that the young man (Frederick G. Fisher) had briefly belonged to the guild for a few months while a student at Harvard, and was now secretary of the Young Republicans in Newton, Massachusetts. Turning to McCarthy, Welch said, "Little did I dream you could be so reckless and so cruel as to do an injury to that lad. I feel he will always bear a scar needlessly inflicted by you." When McCarthy tried to continue, Welch intervened. "Let us not assassinate this lad further, Senator. Have you no sense of decency?" For McCarthy it was all over. His recklessness had been exposed for all the world to see.

When the hearings ended on June 18, Eisenhower invited Welch to the Oval Office to congratulate him on his presentation of the Army's case. Welch said the only good thing to come out of the hearings was that they had given the country an opportunity to see McCarthy in action.[46] On December 2, 1954, the Senate condemned McCarthy by a vote of 67–22 for conduct unbecoming a senator. Eisenhower's indirect strategy had paid off. Ike always believed that if he had attacked McCarthy directly, the Senate would never have taken action. Later he wrote, "McCarthyism took its toll on many individuals and on the nation. No one was safe from charges recklessly made from inside the walls of congressional immunity. . . . Un-American activity cannot be prevented or routed out by employing un-American methods; to preserve freedom we must use the tools that freedom provides."[47] After the Senate's vote of condemnation, McCarthy began drinking heavily. He died of cirrhosis of the liver on May 2, 1957.

As the battle with McCarthy played out, Eisenhower was engaged on another front with Senate conservatives who sought to amend the Constitution to restrict the power of the president to conclude agreements with foreign countries. The immediate impetus for the drive stemmed from FDR's wartime agreements with the Soviet Union, but the issue was one of long standing.

Article 6 of the Constitution provides that "This Constitution, and the Laws of the United States which shall be made in Pursuance thereof; and all Treaties made, or which shall be made, under the Authority of the United States, shall be the supreme Law of the Land."

This is known as the "supremacy clause." Note that for a law passed by Congress to be the supreme law of the land, it must be made pursuant to the Constitution. But treaties face no such test. A treaty becomes the supreme law of the land as soon as it goes into effect. And, except for the requirement that a treaty cannot violate the express terms of the Constitution, there is no limit to the treaty power.[48] In 1916, the United States government wanted to regulate the hunting of migratory birds on their annual flights in spring and fall, but it lacked authority under the Constitution to do so. So it concluded a treaty with Canada that had the same effect.* And this pertained not only to treaties. Executive agreements made by the president with foreign countries, which unlike treaties do not re-

---

* At the beginning of the twentieth century, naturalists and other environmentalists became concerned that migratory fowl were threatened with extinction because of unregulated hunting during their biannual flights. In 1913, Congress passed legislation to restrict such hunting, but the courts struck it down because there was no provision in the Constitution that gave Congress that authority. The federal government responded by negotiating the Migratory Bird Treaty of 1916 with Great Britain (on Canada's behalf), which accomplished the same purpose. This was upheld by the Supreme Court in 1920 in the leading case of *Missouri v. Holland,* 252 U.S. 416. Said Justice Oliver Wendell Holmes, Jr., speaking for the court: "Acts of Congress are the supreme law of the land only when made in pursuance of the Constitution, while treaties are declared so when made under the authority of the United States."

quire the approval of two-thirds of the Senate, also become the supreme law of the land as soon as they go into effect.[49] And because
both treaties and executive agreements supersede state law, states'
rights advocates since the time of the Migratory Bird Treaty in 1916
have sought to curtail the treaty power. Roosevelt's wartime agreements with Stalin gave the movement a new urgency, and additional
fuel was added to the fire by agreements relating to the United Nations, particularly a proposed "Covenant on Human Rights," which
conservatives charged would impose "socialism by treaty" on the
United States.

When the Eighty-third Congress convened on January 7, 1953,
Senator John Bricker of Ohio, who had been Dewey's running mate
in 1944, stepped forward to introduce a constitutional amendment
to restrict the treaty power. Designated Senate Joint Resolution 1
(S.J. Res. 1), Bricker's amendment would give Congress the power to
regulate all agreements made by the president with foreign countries. It also specified that a treaty would become effective as internal
law in the United States "only through legislation which would be
valid in the absence of a treaty," in effect repealing the Supreme
Court's 1920 decision in the migratory bird case.[50]

The Bricker Amendment was cosponsored by sixty-four senators,
giving it the necessary two-thirds of the Senate required for passage,
even if all ninety-six senators voted. Forty-five of the Senate's
forty-eight Republicans backed the resolution, as did nineteen Democrats. If the amendment cleared the Senate, passage by two-thirds
of the House of Representatives was a foregone conclusion, and in
the political climate of 1953, adoption by three-quarters of the state
legislatures was all but guaranteed. The amendment was endorsed
by a large portion of the American Bar Association, the U.S. Chamber of Commerce, the Daughters of the American Revolution, the
American Legion, the Veterans of Foreign Wars, and a grassroots
organization called Vigilant Women for the Bricker Amendment,
which quickly obtained more than a half million signatures in support. Mail to congressional offices ran nine to one in favor of the
amendment, and with the exception of *The Washington Post* and *The
New York Times,* most of the nation's press supported it as well.[51]

Unlike Joe McCarthy, who was vulgar, disheveled, and repellant, John Bricker was a conservative Midwesterner's beau ideal: an embodiment of the GOP's reactionary Old Guard who continued to believe that entry into World War I was a tragic mistake, that the New Deal was a socialist plot foisted on the United States by Franklin Roosevelt, and that if the country retreated once again to fortress America all would be right with the world. Tall, stately, and handsome, Bricker was blessed with a full head of wavy white hair that was meticulously coiffed. He exuded a moral certitude bordering on arrogance, and struck observers as pompous even among colleagues where pomposity was scarcely unknown. As one wag put it, Bricker walked with a senatorial dignity so profound it was "as if someone was carrying a full-length mirror in front of him."[52]

Initially, Eisenhower sought to conciliate the GOP's Old Guard and avoid a confrontation. "Can't we find a way to avert a head-on collision over this thing?" Ike asked early on.[53] In the case of McCarthy, the president had resisted the temptation to criticize the senator because he believed it would work to McCarthy's advantage. In the case of Bricker, Eisenhower wanted to avoid disclosing the fissure in the Republican party. "I'm so sick of this I could scream," he told his cabinet in early April. "The whole damn thing is senseless and plain damaging to the prestige of the United States. We talk about the French not being able to govern themselves—and we sit here wrestling with the Bricker Amendment."[54]

Eisenhower's primary objection to the Bricker Amendment was that it would curtail the power of the president to conclude agreements with foreign countries. That would include the status-of-forces agreements that the United States was negotiating with the various NATO countries and with which Ike had firsthand familiarity. To give Congress control of those arrangements would add boundless complications. Perhaps equally important, the Bricker Amendment would subject all treaties to continuing review by Congress. That would jeopardize the permanence of treaties because one Congress could nullify the action of a preceding Congress. If that were the case, few foreign countries would feel comfortable negotiating with the United States. America was now the principal power in the Western world and the primary obstacle to Communist expansion. This was no time to be curtailing the power of the president to conduct foreign affairs.

The Bricker Amendment was reported favorably by the Senate Judiciary Committee on June 15, 1953. Eisenhower remained reluctant to go public with his opposition, fearing an irretrievable split in Republican ranks. But within the administration he was caustic. "Bricker seems determined to save the United States from Eleanor Roosevelt," he told the cabinet in July. At that point John Foster Dulles broke in and urged Eisenhower to speak out.

"We just have to make up our minds and stop being fuzzy on this," said Dulles.

"I haven't been fuzzy on this," Eisenhower replied. "There was nothing fuzzy in what I told Bricker. I said we'd go just so far and no further."

"I know, sir," Dulles replied, "but have you told anyone else?"[55]

Eisenhower made it through the first session of the Eighty-third Congress without the Bricker Amendment coming to a vote. The amendment stayed on the front pages of the nation's newspapers but the president declined to make a public statement. Lucius Clay watched from the sidelines. "The White House staff always got a little edgy whenever I got involved, so I tried to be very careful not to get involved."[56]

Late in 1953, Clay received a telephone call from John W. Davis, the distinguished constitutional lawyer (of Davis, Polk, Wardwell, Sunderland, and Kiendl) who had been the Democratic nominee for president in 1924 against Calvin Coolidge. "Davis was held in awe by most of the legal profession," said Clay. "I knew him, but not well."[57]

Davis told Clay how concerned he was about the Bricker Amendment, and how he and Professor Edward S. Corwin at Princeton, the dean of constitutional law scholars, were organizing a committee to fight it: the Committee for Defense of the Constitution. Davis asked Clay if he would join them as cochairman.

> And so I did. We set up a small staff and enlisted a broad cross-section of prominent Americans to help us. People

like former Supreme Court Justice Owen Roberts, Dean Griswold at Harvard Law School, Jack McCloy, Henry Wriston, Averell Harriman, and so on.

Very quickly we recognized that President Eisenhower was the key to this thing. So I arranged for Mr. Davis and Professor Corwin to have a private dinner with General Eisenhower in the family quarters of the White House. And it was a very good meeting. The president held a great respect for John Davis.[58]

Davis and Professor Corwin dined with Eisenhower on January 23, 1954. Two days later, Ike went public. "I am unalterably opposed to the Bricker Amendment," the president wrote Senate majority leader Knowland. "Adoption of the Bricker Amendment by the Senate would be notice to our friends as well as our enemies abroad that our country intends to withdraw from its leadership in world affairs."[59] The battle lines were now drawn: Eisenhower and Senate liberals against the conservative blocs in both parties. Lyndon Johnson, the Senate minority leader, held the key.

Johnson and his fellow New Deal Democrats from the South were caught between a rock and a hard place. They did not want to diminish the authority of the president to conduct foreign policy, but their constituents expected them to vote for the Bricker Amendment. In Johnson's case his major financial backers, Texas millionaires Sid Richardson, Clint Murchison, H. R. Cullen, and H. L. Hunt, insisted that he vote in favor of it.

The strategy Johnson devised was convoluted, even by LBJ's standards. First, he convinced elderly Walter F. George of Georgia, the doyen of the Senate who for many years had chaired the Foreign Relations Committee, to introduce a more benign resolution as a substitute for the Bricker Amendment.[*] Then he convinced his caucus to vote against Bricker's amendment in favor of the George substi-

---

[*] The "George substitute" for the Bricker Amendment deleted the objectionable "which clause"—"A treaty shall become effective as domestic law . . . only through legislation *which would be valid in the absence of treaty*"—as well as the provision that would have subjected executive agreements to congressional review. The text of the George substitute is reprinted in note 60.

tute.[60] The almost solid Democratic phalanx, supported by Eisenhower Republicans, would ensure the defeat of the Bricker Amendment. Finally, and most important, Johnson had to count noses well enough to ensure that he and his southern colleagues could safely vote for the George substitute, but that it would ultimately fail to win the necessary two-thirds for passage. Except for the occasional Medici prince in Renaissance Florence, there were few politicians other than Lyndon Johnson who could have framed such a scheme.

The Senate commenced consideration of the Bricker Amendment on January 27, 1954. For the next month the "Bricker Debate" generated headlines across the country—a no-holds-barred battle pitting the White House and its few Republican supporters against the aroused anger of the party's Old Guard—with most Democrats aligned on Ike's side. White House operatives, including even Sherman Adams—who as a former congressman had access to the floor—besieged the Republican cloakrooms; Johnson worked the Democratic side.

On Friday, February 26, 1954, the Senate began to vote. First, on the Bricker Amendment itself, S.J. Res. 1, which, when initially introduced the year before, had enjoyed 64 cosponsors. As the clerk called the roll, it was evident the amendment was going down. Of the 19 Democrats who had originally signed on in support, 13 voted no. White House pressure caused additional Republicans to defect, and when the tally was announced, the Bricker Amendment was defeated 42 votes to 50. Not only did the amendment fail to receive the necessary two-thirds, it did not receive even a simple majority.[61]

The administration introduced its own resolution, the Knowland-Ferguson Amendment, but the Senate voted overwhelmingly (61–30) to put it aside in favor of the George substitute. Bricker and the Republican Old Guard rallied to support George's amendment as the best that could be worked out, and Vice President Nixon, who was in the chair for the historic vote, ordered the clerk to call the roll. It was a moment of high drama. Johnson and the southern Democrats voted as a bloc in favor of the George substitute; all the while LBJ was nervously following the count. When the roll call concluded, 60 votes were recorded in favor and 30 against, precisely the two-thirds needed for passage. One of Johnson's no votes had failed to answer the roll call. Senator Harley Kilgore of West Virginia, tenth on the Senate's seniority list and a firm opponent of limiting presidential power, was not on the floor. The vote was kept open as Johnson's aides frantically searched for Kilgore. He had fallen asleep on the couch in his office, apparently having lost an afternoon bout with the bottle. As Johnson stalled, Kilgore made it to the floor, pulled himself together, and nodded to the chair.

"The Senator from West Virginia," Nixon said.

"Mr. Kilgore," the clerk intoned.

"No," Kilgore voted, as he walked unsteadily to his seat in the Democratic front row of desks.

"On this roll call," Vice President Nixon announced, "the yeas are sixty, the nays are thirty-one. Two-thirds of the Senators present not having voted in the affirmative, the joint resolution is rejected."[62]

Eisenhower won the Bricker Amendment fight, but his leadership had been hesitant. Not until John W. Davis and Professor Corwin aroused him to the constitutional danger posed by the amendment did he take his opposition public. The true victors in the amendment fight were Davis, who organized the opposition and knew which buttons to press, and Lyndon Johnson, whose Machiavellian dexterity ultimately saved the day.

Eisenhower's battles with McCarthy, Bricker, and the Old Guard of the GOP drove him toward the center—toward the Democrats and the liberal wing of the Republican party. When Chief Justice Fred Vinson died unexpectedly of a massive heart attack on September 8, 1953 (Vinson was sixty-three), it was natural that Ike should look to his left for a replacement. Eisenhower's first instinct was to promote from within. That was the Army's method, and it made imminent sense. There would be no break-in period. The obvious choice was Associate Justice Robert H. Jackson, who had been American chief prosecutor at the Nuremberg war crimes trials. The fact that Jackson was a Democrat did not seem to matter. What ruled him out was the bitter public feud he was conducting with Justice Hugo Black. Brownell warned Ike against taking sides, and also noted that Jackson, as an assistant attorney general, had backed FDR's court-packing effort in 1937. The only Republican on the court was Harold Burton, a former senator from Ohio whom Harry

Truman had appointed in 1945. But Burton was in poor health and probably not up to the job in any case.

With an internal appointment ruled out, Eisenhower looked outside. His first choice was John W. Davis, scarcely a liberal, but whose credentials were unassailable. But Davis, who had been Woodrow Wilson's solicitor general, had been born in 1873 and was far too old for the post. As a matter of courtesy, Ike asked Dulles if he were interested, but the secretary declined. "I'm highly complimented," he told the president, "but my interests lie with the duties of my present post."[63]

That left Earl Warren. During the campaign, Eisenhower had met with Warren on several occasions and discussed the possibility of either a cabinet post or a Supreme Court appointment.[*] In early December, as president-elect, Eisenhower called Warren to tell him that he would not be asked to join the cabinet. "But I want you to know that I intend to offer you the first vacancy on the Supreme Court. That is my personal commitment to you."[64]

After his inauguration, Eisenhower appointed Warren one of four American delegates to the coronation of Queen Elizabeth II in London on June 2, 1953. (Marshall, Omar Bradley, and Fleur Cowles, wife of the publisher of *Look*, were the other delegates.) On his return to California following the ceremony, Warren stopped off in Washington, where Attorney General Brownell suggested that he accept the post of solicitor general prior to joining the court. According to Brownell, it had been some time since Warren had practiced law, and "the President believed that service as Solicitor General would be valuable prior to membership in the Supreme Court."[65] Warren, who was preparing to step down after three terms as governor of California, agreed to

---

[*] Eisenhower was indebted to Warren for his action at the Republican convention, as well as for campaigning vigorously for the ticket. At the convention, California had supported Ike's forces and voted for the "Fair Play Amendment," which led to the seating of the Eisenhower delegations from Georgia, Louisiana, and Texas. Then he had remained in the race as a favorite son, denying California's seventy votes to Taft. Eisenhower always denied he was politically indebted to Warren, but that was often Ike's way. See 14 *The Presidency* 564–70, diary entry October 8, 1953.

think about it. "I meditated long and hard," Warren wrote later. "The position of Solicitor General is probably the most prestigious one in America in the practice of the law. Finally I wired the Attorney General in a sort of self-devised code that he but not others would understand, and notified him that if tendered the position by the President, I would accept."[66] On September 3, Warren held a news conference in Sacramento to announce he would not seek reelection as governor. There was no indication that he would be going to Washington as solicitor general, and Chief Justice Vinson died five days later.

Eisenhower may or may not have assumed that his commitment to Warren included the chief justiceship. In his *Memoirs,* Ike said he did not. Warren assumed it did. In any event, finding himself unable to make an internal appointment, and with Davis and Dulles out of the picture, Eisenhower dispatched Brownell to California to offer the post to Warren. The fall term of the court would begin on October 5, and Ike wanted the vacancy filled before then. A number of important cases were on the calendar—including reargument of the great desegregation case *Brown v. Board of Education*—and it was important to have a full bench.

Brownell flew to California and met clandestinely with Warren at McClellan Air Force Base, ten miles from Sacramento, on Sunday morning, September 27. Brownell made the offer and Warren accepted. The only condition, said Brownell, "is that you take your seat a week from tomorrow." Warren allowed as how that was "a helluva way" to leave the governorship of California after eleven years, but if it was necessary it could be done.[67] At his press conference three days later, Wednesday, September 30, Eisenhower announced Warren's appointment as chief justice of the United States. It was a recess appointment, Congress was not in session, and Warren took the oath of office in the Supreme Court chamber on October 5.[*]

---

[*] According to legend, after he left office Eisenhower is supposed to have said that his great mistake as president was to appoint Earl Warren chief justice of the United States. The legend has acquired the status of revealed truth, and countless writers have cited it as if it were fact. The problem is that Eisenhower never said that. I have found no evidence that he ever made such a statement. To the contrary, there is abundant evidence that he did not. Herbert Brownell, who was also con-

Reaction to Warren's appointment was overwhelmingly favorable. "Warren is honest and highly intelligent," said *The New York Times.* "He is a liberal and humanitarian when basic issues must be faced. If rancor exists on the High Bench—as unhappily it does—there is no person better qualified than Earl Warren to sooth and mollify." Governor Dewey said his former running mate would make "a superb Chief Justice." Adlai Stevenson called it "an excellent appointment."[68] The Far Left and Far Right registered dissents. *The Nation* and *The New Republic* cited Warren's support for the evacuation of Japanese Americans from the West Coast after Pearl Harbor and questioned whether he would be able to protect human rights and civil liberties.[*] The Republican Old Guard deplored Warren's "leftist" attitude as California's governor. Barry Goldwater scolded Eisenhower for appointing someone "who hadn't practiced law in twenty-five years and was a socialist."[69]

Eisenhower's brothers Edgar and Milton both criticized the choice. From his perch on the Far Right, Edgar said Warren's appointment

---

cerned about the allegation, conducted his own detailed investigation and reported that the story was apocryphal.

Myths about presidents and chief justices are plentiful. An analogous canard pertains to Andrew Jackson and Chief Justice John Marshall. After Marshall rendered the decision of the court in the 1832 Cherokee case (*Worcester v. Georgia*, 31 U.S. 515), President Jackson is alleged to have said, "John Marshall has made his decision, now let him enforce it." Again, the problem is that Jackson never said that. It was concocted by Horace Greeley in 1864 and put in Jackson's mouth. (Jackson died in 1845.) The story of Eisenhower and Warren is equally bogus.

See Herbert Brownell and John P. Burke, *Advising Ike: The Memoirs of Attorney General Herbert Brownell* 173 (Lawrence: University Press of Kansas, 1993); Jean Edward Smith, *John Marshall: Definer of a Nation* 518 (New York: Henry Holt, 1996); Horace Greeley, 1 *The American Conflict: A History of the Great Rebellion in the United States of America, 1860–64* 106 (Hartford, Conn.: O. D. Case, 1864).

[*] Curiously, Warren's early support for the internment of Japanese Americans on the Pacific Coast led southern senators such as Walter George and Richard Russell of Georgia to vigorously support his nomination for chief justice, assuming that Warren would naturally support racial segregation. As for the evacuation, Warren later confessed that he had been wrong in 1942. "I have since deeply regretted the removal order and my own testimony advocating it, because it was not in keeping with our American concept of freedom and the rights of citizens. Whenever I thought of the innocent little children who were torn from their home, school, friends, and congenial surroundings, I was conscious-stricken." *The Memoirs of Earl Warren* 149 (Garden City, N.Y.: Doubleday, 1977).

"would be a tragedy" and would cost Ike "a lot of support." Milton, who was now president of Penn State, thought Warren to be dangerously to the right.[70] Eisenhower took time off to reply to both. "What you consider a tragedy, I consider a very splendid and promising development," he wrote Edgar. "I wonder how often you have met and talked seriously with Governor Warren. This I have done on a number of occasions. To my mind, he is a statesman, a man of national stature, of unimpeachable integrity, of middle-of-the-road views, and with a splendid record during his years of active law work."[71]

Ike told Milton he was surprised Milton thought Warren too far to the right, since so far "the only people that opposed the idea of his appointment were of the *Chicago Tribune* stripe."

"I believe we need *statesmanship* on the Supreme Court," said Eisenhower.

> Statesmanship is developed in the hard knocks of general experience, private and public. Naturally, a man occupying the post must be competent in the law—and Warren has had seventeen years of practice in *public law,* during which his record was one of remarkable accomplishment and success, to say nothing of dedication.[*] He has been very definitely a liberal-conservative; he represents the kind of political, economic, and social thinking that I believe we need on the Supreme Court.[72]

When Congress reconvened in January 1954, Eisenhower sent Warren's formal nomination to the Senate. The Republican Old Guard, led this time by William Langer of North Dakota, chairman of the Judiciary Committee, mounted a desperate attempt to derail the nomination in committee. Crackpot organizations of every variety testified that Warren was either a "100 percent Marxist" or an abettor of organized crime. Warren, as was customary at the time, de-

---

[*] Warren served as deputy district attorney of Alameda County, California, from 1920 to 1925; as district attorney from 1925 to 1939; and as attorney general of California from 1939 to 1943.

clined to testify, and Eisenhower fought back with the full force of the administration. "If the Republicans [in the Senate] should try to repudiate him, I shall leave the Republican Party and try to organize an intelligent group of Independents, no matter how small," Ike confided to his diary.[73] Langer eventually found himself outnumbered, the Judiciary Committee voted to confirm Warren 12–3, and Majority Leader Knowland called the nomination to the floor on March 1. Warren was confirmed unanimously by voice vote. "One must hope," said *The New York Times,* "that this kind of circus will not play again in Washington."[74]

Eisenhower's appointment of Earl Warren to be chief justice of the United States, like John Adams's appointment of John Marshall, was one of the major events of his presidency. Ultimately, Ike would appoint five justices to the court, including John Marshall Harlan and William Brennan.[75] His appointees ushered in a judicial revolution in citizenship law, civil liberties, and civil rights. Eisenhower did not always agree with the decisions of the Warren Court, but he accepted his constitutional responsibility to "take care that the laws be faithfully enforced." He was also the first president to submit his judicial nominees to the American Bar Association for formal vetting (a practice discontinued by George W. Bush but resumed by President Obama). His appointees to the lower federal courts, moderate Republicans such as John Minor Wisdom in Louisiana and Elbert P. Tuttle in Georgia, were judicial heroes in the civil rights struggle. Those who would criticize Eisenhower for not moving fast enough on civil rights should remember that it was his judicial nominees who made the revolution possible.

# TWENTY-TWO

# Dien Bien Phu

You boys must be crazy. We can't use those
awful things against Asians for the second time
in less than ten years.

—DWIGHT D. EISENHOWER,

*May 1, 1954*

WHILE EISENHOWER STRUGGLED with Bricker and McCarthy, and sought to make peace in Korea, the French position in Indochina deteriorated. The French had acquired Indochina (Vietnam, Cambodia, and Laos) in the nineteenth century during a period of European colonial expansion. Following the fall of France in 1940, the Japanese occupied the area and remained there until Japan's surrender in August 1945. When the French sought to reassert control, they found themselves in conflict with a wartime resistance coalition of Vietnamese nationalists and Communists under the leadership of Ho Chi Minh. Known as the Viet Minh, the resistance movement had been supported by the United States during the war, and had wrested control of the countryside from the Japanese.

In September 1945, Ho Chi Minh declared independence for the Democratic Republic of Vietnam. At that point the French returned in force, and bitter fighting ensued. The French Army regained control of Vietnam's major cities, but the Viet Minh continued to dominate the countryside. In 1950, Ho again proclaimed independence for the Democratic Republic of Vietnam, and this time was recognized by the Communist governments of China and the Soviet

Union. The battle for Vietnamese independence played out in the context of the Cold War.

For the French, the struggle in Indochina was a colonial war—*"La guerre sale,"* as it was called back in France, "the dirty war"—and the longer it went on, the less popular it became. Just as American public opinion turned against the war in Korea, the French public wanted out of Vietnam. As early as 1950, the National Assembly voted against sending draftees to fight there, and the government kept a tight rein on expenditures. The United States picked up the slack. Even before the outbreak of hostilities in Korea, the Truman administration had begun to finance French forces in Vietnam. By 1953, America had spent more than $2.6 billion ($21.2 billion currently) in military aid and had converted the war into part of the larger struggle of democracy against Communism. When Eisenhower took office, the United States appeared to have more interest in continuing the war than the French did.[1]

The fact is, the French Expeditionary Force in Vietnam, some five hundred thousand men, was swallowed up in rice paddies and jungles fighting a guerrilla war against an elusive enemy who held the initiative. Commanded by the resourceful General Vo Nguyen Giap, the Viet Minh struck the French only when they were vulnerable, usually in well-prepared ambushes, and preferably at night. The cost to the French Army was high. Every year at least a third of the graduating class at Saint-Cyr, the French military academy, were killed in Vietnam. By early 1953 it was clear that France was on the defensive, and that the continued hemorrhaging of French forces could not be sustained.

Into this quagmire the government of the Fourth Republic sent General Henri Navarre with orders to reach a settlement with the Viet Minh. But Navarre was not ready to admit defeat. He switched from defense to offense, determined to lure the Viet Minh into a fixed battle in which French artillery and airpower would prove decisive. On September 28, 1953, *Time* magazine featured Navarre on its cover. "A year ago none of us could see victory," an aide was quoted as saying. "Now we can see it clearly—like light at the end of a tunnel."[2]

The site for Navarre's set-piece battle would be Dien Bien Phu—a small outpost on the Laotian border. General Navarre believed he was setting a trap. The Viet Minh would be lured into attacking the well-fortified French position and would be worn down by superior firepower. There were three problems Navarre failed to anticipate: First, the fighting quality of the Viet Minh, who, like the Chinese veterans the U.S. Army encountered in Korea, were first-class soldiers, well trained, well equipped, and fighting for their country against French colonialism. Second, the ability of General Giap to concentrate his forces. Navarre assumed he would be fighting one Viet Minh division at most. As the battle developed, Giap brought more than fifty thousand soldiers into action supported by an additional one hundred thousand Vietnamese peasants to supply the combat troops. Most important, however, was the location. Dien Bien Phu (which in Vietnamese means "large administrative center on the frontier") was a cluster of villages eight miles long and five miles wide on the floor of a valley surrounded by rough mountainous terrain. It was remote, difficult to resupply except by air, and had no strategic importance. One high-ranking French defense official likened it to a chamber pot (*vase de nuit*), with the French garrison on the bottom and the Viet Minh sitting on the rim above.[3]

In late 1953, when Eisenhower learned of Navarre's plan to lure the enemy into battle at Dien Bien Phu, he was appalled. "You cannot do this," he told Henri Bonnet, the French ambassador in Washington. "The fate of troops invested in an isolated fortress is almost inevitable."[4] Eisenhower instructed both the State and Defense departments to communicate his concern to their French counterparts, but the French took no notice. "We cannot find them [the Viet Minh] in the jungle," Ike was told. "This will draw them out where we can then win."[5]

Eisenhower was caught betwixt and between. On the one hand he saw the fighting in Vietnam as part of the global struggle against Communism. On the other, he deplored France's unwillingness to grant independence to the Vietnamese. "I wholeheartedly agree," he wrote Republican senator Ralph Flanders of Vermont, "that France should announce a firm intention of establishing self-government and independence in the associated states of Indochina [Vietnam, Cambodia, and Laos]. I have personally urged this upon the French authorities and secured their agreement in principle. So far the trouble has been that they have made such announcements only in an obscure and round-about fashion—instead of boldly, forthrightly, and repeatedly."[6]

On March 13, 1954, the siege of Dien Bien Phu began. "Hell in a very small place," French writer Bernard Fall called it.[7] Within two days perimeter strongpoints were overrun and French airstrips immobilized by Viet Minh artillery. General Giap did not deploy his fieldpieces on the reverse slope, as is common practice in the artillery, but placed them in well-entrenched positions on the forward slope firing directly into the French position. It was like shooting fish in a barrel. The battle was over almost before it started. The fifteen-thousand-man French garrison could be supplied only by dropping supplies from aircraft flying at high altitudes, and relief columns were unable to break through. As casualties mounted and supplies dwindled, it was evident that the only hope for Dien Bien Phu—and it was a slender hope at best—was some form of American intervention.

In January the French had asked for twenty-five bombers and four hundred mechanics to maintain them. Eisenhower gave them ten planes and two hundred mechanics. Even then, Congress was skeptical. "First we give them planes, then we send men," Senator John Stennis of Mississippi warned.[8] Richard Russell of Georgia, the ranking Democrat on the Senate Armed Services Committee, voiced similar doubts. Senator Leverett Saltonstall of Massachusetts, who chaired the committee, asked Ike directly: Was another president going to take the country into yet another war by the back door?[9] Eisenhower admitted that he was "frightened about getting ground forces tied up in Indochina" and promised that the mechanics would not be in the combat zone and that he would withdraw them by June 15, 1954.[10]

In late March, as the French position at Dien Bien Phu eroded, General Paul Ely, the French chief of staff, came to Washington to seek additional assistance. Ely was highly regarded in American defense circles and had served as France's representative on the NATO Standing Group when Eisenhower commanded NATO forces. Ike knew Ely well, and during a meeting at the White House agreed to provide additional C-119 Flying Boxcars that could drop napalm, "which would burn out a considerable area and help to reveal enemy artillery positions." But he declined to offer additional support and pressed Ely for a definite statement on Vietnamese independence.[11]

The Joint Chiefs of Staff were more forthcoming than Eisenhower. Meeting with the JCS at the Pentagon, Ely, together with Admiral Arthur Radford, who had succeeded Omar Bradley as chairman, devised a plan for massive American air support for Dien Bien Phu. Known as Operation VULTURE, the JCS plan, which quickly obtained French approval, would involve carpet bombing of the Viet Minh position by 60 B-29 bombers stationed at Clark Field in the Philippines, supported by 150 fighter-bombers from the carriers of the Seventh Fleet (*Essex* and *Boxer*) on station in the Gulf of Tonkin. Three so-called tactical atomic bombs would be used. General Nathan Twining, Air Force chief of staff, thought one would be sufficient. "You could take all day to drop a bomb, make sure you put it in the right place . . . and clean those Commies out of there and the band would play the 'Marseillaise' and the French would come marching out . . . in great shape."[12]

Publicly, Eisenhower kept American options open. As Ike saw it, there was no reason to foreclose U.S. intervention, and that uncertainty might help dissuade China and the Soviet Union from becoming involved. On April 4, Eisenhower wrote Churchill (who was serving his final term as prime minister) seeking British support. "We failed to halt Hirohito, Mussolini and Hitler by not acting in unity and in time," said Eisenhower.[13] Churchill was unimpressed. The British had given up India and were fighting guerrilla wars in Malaya and Kenya. The last thing they wanted was to be involved in another Korean-type conflict on behalf of the French.

Nevertheless, Eisenhower pressed on. At his news conference on April 7, Ike invoked what he called the "falling domino" principle. "You have a row of dominoes set up, you knock over the first one, and what will happen to the last one is the certainty that it will go over very quickly." By implication, if Indochina fell, Burma, Thailand, Malaya, and Indonesia would follow.[14]*

---

* On April 16, 1954, Vice President Nixon, whether speaking on his own or with administration sanction, added to the perception of possible American interven-

Privately, Eisenhower was setting out the conditions for American involvement in such a way so as to ensure that it did not happen. It was typical of Ike at his best. Feint in one direction publicly, move privately in another. First, there must be an ironclad commitment by France to grant independence to the countries of Indochina. Second, the United States must be part of an international coalition, including not only Great Britain, Australia, and New Zealand, but Thailand and the Philippines as well. Third, the allied forces would assume direction of the war and not operate under French command. Finally, and most significantly, the United States would not send ground forces into combat without specific congressional authorization.[15] There was little likelihood that any of these, let alone all four, would occur.

In addition to his own doubts, Eisenhower received reinforcement from the field. General Matthew Ridgway, who had succeeded MacArthur in Korea and was now Army chief of staff, weighed in heavily against intervention. On his own authority, Ridgway dispatched a blue-ribbon team of staff officers to Vietnam to determine what intervention would involve. Their report was devastating: at least five infantry divisions, possibly ten, plus fifty-five engineering companies. (There had been six divisions in Korea.) Altogether, that meant between five hundred thousand and a million men. Draft calls would be far greater than those for Korea. In addition, local political conditions in Vietnam were much worse than in Korea, where the local population had supported American intervention. In Vietnam, because of French colonialism, that would not be the case.[16] As for airpower, Ridgway told the president it was like a high-tech aspirin. It provided some immediate relief but did not cure the underlying problem.[17] Eisenhower respected Ridgway's judgment. In 1943, Ridgway had resisted Ike's order to drop an airborne division on Rome, and Ridgway had been right. There was no reason to believe he was wrong now.

On April 26, Eisenhower wrote to his old friend General Alfred

---

tion when he told the American Society of Newspaper Editors that he "hoped the United States will not have to send troops there [Vietnam], but if this Government cannot avoid it, the Administration must face up to the situation and dispatch forces. I personally would support such a position." *RN* 152–53.

Gruenther, who now held Ike's position at SHAPE. Gruenther had written to warn Ike against intervening in Vietnam. "Your adverse opinion exactly parallels mine," Eisenhower replied. "As you know, you and I started more than three years ago to convince the French that they could *not* win in the Indochina War." Ike told Gruenther that his administration had repeatedly advised the French that no Western power could intervene in Asia except as part of a coalition that included Asian people. "To contemplate anything else is to lay ourselves open to the charge of imperialism and colonialism or—at the very least—of objectionable paternalism. Even if we could by some sudden stroke assure the saving of the Dien Bien Phu garrison, I think that under the conditions proposed by the French, the free world would lose more than it would gain."[18]

Later that day, addressing the annual meeting of the U.S. Chamber of Commerce, Eisenhower spoke of the necessity of achieving a modus vivendi in Vietnam. "We would hope that the logic of today's situation would appeal to all peoples," said Ike, "regardless of their ruthlessness, so that they see the futility of depending upon war, or the threat of war, as a means of settling international difficulty."[19] At his press conference three days later, the president was asked about his use of the term "modus vivendi" in Vietnam. "You are steering a course between two extremes," Eisenhower responded. "One of which, I would say, would be unattainable, and the other unacceptable." A French victory was most likely unattainable, and a total Communist victory would be unacceptable. "The most you can work out is a practical way of getting along." He then referred to the situation in Berlin as an example.[20]

At the meeting of the National Security Council on April 29, 1954, Eisenhower laid down the law. There would be no intervention in Vietnam. Dulles, who was in Geneva, had cabled that strong American leadership was required. Eisenhower rejected that advice. "In spite of the views of the Secretary of State," he told the NSC, for the United States to intervene unilaterally seemed "quite beyond his comprehension." For almost two hours Eisenhower waged a one-man battle against the statutory members of the NSC, all of whom advocated coming to France's rescue. Admiral Radford, Vice President Nixon, Undersecretary of State Bedell Smith (on Dulles's behalf), and Harold Stassen, the director of foreign aid, placed the issue in the Cold War context. As Stassen put it, Congress and the American people would support intervention "if the Commander-in-Chief made it clear to them that it was necessary to save Southeast Asia from Communism."

Eisenhower remained unmoved. "It was all well and good to state that if the French collapsed the United States must move in to save Southeast Asia," he told Stassen. "But if the French indeed collapsed and the United States moved in, we would in the eyes of many Asiatic peoples merely replace French colonialism with American colonialism." The president noted that the Vietnamese people had no interest in fighting for the French, and as a practical matter, where would the United States find the troops to intervene? It would require a general mobilization, said Eisenhower.

Ike then upped the ante. If the United States intervened, China and perhaps the Soviet Union would come in as well. Were his advisers ready for a general war? "To go in unilaterally in Indochina or other areas of the world which were endangered, amounted to an attempt to police the entire world. If we attempted such a course of action, using our armed forces and going into areas whether we were wanted or not, we would lose all our significant support in the free world." Unless we had reliable allies who joined us, said Ike, "the leader is just an adventurer like Genghis Khan."

Nixon and Bedell Smith countered that American air support would encourage the French to fight on. Eisenhower would have none of it. "The cause of the free world could never win, and the United States could never survive, if we frittered away our resources in local engagements." The discussion closed. Eisenhower did not explicitly say that the United States would not intervene, but his decision was obvious.[21]

By the beginning of May it was clear that the French position at Dien Bien Phu was hopeless. The garrison's defensive perimeter had shrunk to an area fifteen hundred yards in diameter and there were fewer than ten thousand men available for duty—against a Viet Minh force five times that size. On May 1, Robert Cutler, the president's national security assistant, presented Eisenhower with the Joint Chiefs' plan for Operation VULTURE. Ike dismissed it out of hand. "I certainly do not think that the atomic bomb can be used by the United States unilaterally," he told Cutler. "You boys must be crazy. We can't use those awful things against Asians for the second time in less than ten years. My God."[22]

Eisenhower had made the final crucial decision. At any time during the last few weeks at Dien Bien Phu he could have ordered an air strike, but he refused to do so. As at D-Day, it was his decision. And in many respects, it was of far greater import. The landing on D-Day was a purely military matter. If not June 6, then sometime later. At Dien Bien Phu it was a matter of war and peace. Eisenhower overruled the highest national security officials in his administration and chose peace.

On May 7, 1954, Dien Bien Phu surrendered. The garrison numbered fewer than five thousand effectives, and the final position had been reduced to the size of a baseball field. French premier Joseph Laniel, barely able to control his voice, broke the news to the National Assembly.[23] That night all French television and radio programming was canceled in favor of the Berlioz "Requiem." Shortly thereafter, meeting at Geneva, the foreign ministers of China, the Soviet Union, the United States, Great Britain, and France worked out a settlement. The French left the scene, and Vietnam was divided. North Vietnam became a Communist state under Ho Chi Minh; in South Vietnam, an anti-Communist state was formed under Ngo Dinh Diem, a Catholic mandarin who had sat out World War II in the United States and was vigorously supported by American officials on the scene. As Eisenhower had hinted in his address to the Chamber of Commerce, the United States preferred partition to free elections. If the Vietnamese had been given a choice, it was clear that Ho Chi Minh would have won decisively.

Writing about Dien Bien Phu years later, Eisenhower said that he had been moved by public opinion, which was clearly opposed to American intervention, but that this factor was not decisive. Far more serious were the consequences that would have resulted from sending the American Army into Vietnam. "The presence of ever more numbers of white men in uniform would have aggravated rather than assuaged Asiatic resentments," Ike wrote. "Among all the powerful nations of the world the United States is the only one

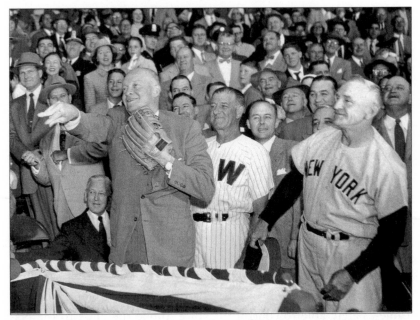

Eisenhower throwing out the first pitch at Griffith Stadium, April 13, 1954, with Bucky Harris and Casey Stengel standing by.

with a tradition of anti-colonialism." That was an asset of incalculable value. "It means our counsel is trusted where that of others may not be. It is essential to our position of leadership in a world wherein the majority of the nations have at some time or another felt the yoke of colonialism." As Ike saw it, "the moral position of the United States was more to be guarded than the Tonkin Delta, indeed than all of Indochina."

Eisenhower wrote those words in 1963 for the chapter on Indochina in his memoir *Mandate for Change.* Whether because of space requirements, or out of deference to the Kennedy-Johnson administration, which was slowly building an American presence in Vietnam, he deleted them from the final version.[24] Unlike his successors, Eisenhower had served four years in the Philippines. He understood the issue of colonialism far better than they—and far better than Dulles, Radford, and Nixon for that matter. He had also seen the terror of war firsthand and was not going to lead the country into another one. "That may not have been bold leadership," one scholar has written, "but it was wisdom."[25]

Eisenhower was less sure-footed when it came to dealing with Iran. In Vietnam, Ike took the lead and kept the United States out of war. In Iran, he listened to the advice that bubbled up from below and authorized the CIA-directed coup that ousted Mohammad Mossadegh, Iran's legitimately elected prime minister, terminating democratic government in Teheran and installing what became the twenty-five-year dictatorship of the shah. That dictatorship spawned the Islamic Revolution of 1979, which brought to power the passionately anti-American Iranian theocracy that has bedeviled world politics since.[26] Eisenhower had served much of his military career in Europe and Asia, and understood the elemental forces at work there. The Middle East was terra incognita, and Ike initially accepted the advice of diplomatic and intelligence professionals who tended to see Communists lurking on every street corner. In Vietnam, the president had refused to bail out French colonialism; in Iran he was only too happy to rescue British commercial interests under the guise of fighting Communism. The Eisenhower administration, and Ike himself, bear heavy responsibility for snuffing out responsible government in Iran.

The issue was oil. In 1933, Mohammad Reza Pahlavi, the shah's father, granted the Anglo-Iranian Oil Company (later British Petroleum—BP) an exclusive sixty-year concession to extract oil from Iran. Under the terms of the concession, Iran would receive 16 percent of the proceeds. Accounting was spotty, Iranian workers lived in deplorable conditions, and payoffs to the royal family were routine. For Britain, on the other hand, the concession proved a bonanza. The British government owned 52 percent of the Anglo-Iranian Oil Company (AIOC), and after World War II effectively balanced its budget through the sale of Iranian oil. By the late 1940s, Iran had become the world's fourth largest oil exporter, supplying 90 percent of Europe's petroleum.[27]

Given the lopsided distribution of benefits, Iranian public opinion clamored for a renegotiation of the 1933 concession, and there were precedents for doing so. In 1948, the Venezuelan government of Romulo Gallegos and Creole Petroleum agreed to a fifty-fifty compromise on profits, and in 1950 the Arabian American Oil Company (ARAMCO) reached a similar accord with the Saudi government. But AIOC refused to negotiate. The oil was theirs for sixty years (until 1993), and the British insisted the agreement was binding.

AIOC's refusal to renegotiate the concession produced growing popular sentiment in Iran to nationalize the company. Led by the elderly European-educated Dr. Mohammad Mossadegh, Iran's most popular political figure, the nationalization movement won overwhelming control of the Iranian parliament (Majlis), and on March 15, 1951, adopted a resolution accepting "the principle that oil should be nationalized throughout Iran." In Britain, Clement Attlee's Labour government appeared ready to compromise. "What argument can I advance against anyone claiming the right to nationalize the resources of their country?" asked Foreign Secretary Ernest Bevin. "We are doing the same thing here in coal, electricity, railways, transport, and steel."[28]

On May 1, 1951, the Iranian Majlis voted unanimously to revoke the 1933 concession and nationalize the Anglo-Iranian Oil Company. On May 6, the shah named Mossadegh prime minister. "Since nationalization is an accomplished fact," Henry Grady, the U.S. ambassador in Teheran, told *The Wall Street Journal,* "it would be wise for Britain to adopt a conciliatory attitude. Mossadegh's National Front Party is the closest thing to a moderate and stable element in the national parliament."[29]

But the British position had hardened. Bevin died in April and had been replaced as foreign minister by Herbert Morrison, one of the leading war hawks in London. Instead of negotiating, Morrison advocated sending the 16th Parachute Brigade, stationed in Cyprus, to retake AIOC's massive Abadan refinery. When British plans for military intervention arrived in Washington, President Truman and Secretary of State Dean Acheson objected strongly. The United States was resolutely opposed to "the use of force or the threat of the use of force" against Iran, Acheson told Sir Oliver Franks, His Majesty's ambassador. Truman said "no situation should be allowed to develop into an armed conflict between British and Persian forces."[30] Confronted with strenuous American objections, the Attlee government backed down.

Throughout the summer of 1951, the Truman administration

pressed the British to negotiate. Acheson told Franks that Mossa-degh represented "a very deep revolution, national in character, which was sweeping not only Iran but the entire Middle East."[31] President Truman wrote Attlee that "negotiations should be entered into at once" to prevent a worsening of "the explosive situation in Iran."[32]

Despite American efforts the British position stiffened further. Churchill, scarcely a friend of decolonialization, defeated Attlee in the October 1951 general election, and his Conservative government was in no mood to compromise with Mossadegh. The British were fighting alongside the United States in Korea, Churchill reminded Truman, and he expected American support in Iran.

When the British protested AIOC's nationalization to the UN Security Council, Mossadegh flew to New York, presented Iran's case, and won a smashing victory when the Security Council agreed it had no jurisdiction. President Truman invited Mossadegh to Washington, installed him in Blair House, across the street from the White House, and attempted to work out a compromise but with no success. On his return to Teheran, Mossadegh stopped in Egypt, re-ceived a hero's welcome, and signed a friendship treaty with the gov-ernment of King Farouk. *Time* magazine chose Mossadegh as its "Man of the Year" for 1951. "The British position in the whole Mid-dle East is hopeless," said *Time*. "They are hated and distrusted every-where. The old colonial relationship is finished."[33]

The situation worsened in 1952. The British imposed an eco-nomic embargo on Iran, attempted a palace coup against Mossadegh, and brought suit in the World Court at The Hague on Anglo-Iranian's behalf. The coup failed, the World Court dismissed Britain's claim, and world opinion, particularly in the Middle East, turned against Britain because of the embargo. On October 16, 1952, Iran broke diplomatic relations with Great Britain and expelled all British dip-lomats. "We tried to get the blockheaded British to have their oil company make a fair deal with Iran," wrote President Truman. "No, no, they couldn't do that. They knew all about how to handle it—we didn't according to them."[34]

Less than three weeks after Iran broke diplomatic relations with Britain, Eisenhower was elected president. The political climate in

Washington changed, and the British were quick to take advantage. Whereas Truman and Acheson had discouraged intervention in Iran, Eisenhower and Dulles proved receptive, particularly if the issue was framed in terms of anti-Communism. In late November, senior British intelligence officials (MI6) visited their counterparts in the CIA and floated their plan to topple Mossadegh. "Not wishing to be accused of trying to use the Americans to pull British chestnuts out of the fire," said senior agent Christopher Montague Woodhouse, "I decided to emphasize the Communist threat to Iran rather than the need to recover control of the oil industry."[35] Iran had a one-thousand-mile border with the Soviet Union, it possessed the world's largest known oil reserves, and had an active Communist (Tudeh) Party. The possibility that Iran might become Communist provided a tailor-made opportunity for the new administration to demonstrate its prowess. Bedell Smith, then director of the CIA, and his deputy Allen Dulles quickly signed on to the British scheme. When Ike took office, Smith moved on to become undersecretary of state, and Allen Dulles succeeded him at the CIA. Smith, Allen Dulles, and John Foster Dulles, the new secretary of state, became the principal advocates in the administration for moving against Mossadegh.

Eisenhower initially took little interest. When he met with President Truman at the White House two weeks after the election, Dean Acheson had mentioned the crisis in Iran and said "both sides were being unreasonable." Acheson told Ike that he was planning to prod the British to hasten a settlement and warned that this might cause "some ill feeling in London."[36] In early January, Eisenhower met with Churchill in New York and pushed him to reach a settlement. "All that he [Churchill] did," Ike confided to his diary, "was to get Mossadegh to accuse us of being a partner of the British in 'browbeating a weak nation.' "

Eisenhower's efforts had little effect. "Winston is trying to relive the days of World War II," Ike lamented.

> In the present international complexities, any hope of establishing such a relationship is completely fatuous. . . . The two strongest Western powers must not appear before the world as a combination of forces to compel adherence

to the status quo. The free world's hope of defeating the Communist aims does not include objecting to national aspirations. . . . Winston does not by any means propose to resort to power politics and disregard legitimate aspirations of weaker peoples. But he does take the rather old-fashioned, paternalistic approach. . . . . I wish that he would turn over leadership of the British Conservative Party to younger men.[37]

Insofar as Iranian national aspirations were concerned, Eisenhower was sympathetic. But he had a blind spot. He worried about the shutoff of Iranian oil to the West. Writing to his childhood friend Swede Hazlett from SHAPE the year before, Ike said the situation in Iran was tragic.

A stream of visitors goes through my office, and some of the individuals concerned consider themselves authorities on the Iranian question. Numbers of them attach as much blame to Western stupidity as to Iranian fanaticism and Communist intrigue in bringing about all the trouble. Frankly, I've gotten to the point that I am concerned primarily, and almost solely, in some scheme or plan that will permit that oil to keep flowing to the westward. We cannot ignore the tremendous importance of 675,000 barrels of oil a day.

Eisenhower told Swede that the West had failed in China. "I most certainly hope that this calamity does not repeat in the case of Iran."[38]

While Eisenhower settled into the White House, Bedell Smith and Allen Dulles stepped up planning for the coup. Kermit Roosevelt, Jr., the grandson of Theodore Roosevelt who headed CIA activities in the Middle East, was given operational control (Operation AJAX), and Dulles turned on the agency's cash spigot to provide whatever funding was required to set events in motion. "Pull up your socks and get going," Smith instructed Roosevelt.[39] Mobs were bought and paid for, and rioting in the streets of Teheran became commonplace. The object was to create an impression of instability.

On March 1, 1953, the CIA provided Eisenhower with a national estimate on Iran suggesting the situation was getting out of hand. "The result has been a steady decrease in the power and influence of the Western democracies and the building up of a situation where a Communist takeover is becoming more and more of a possibility."[40]

At the regular meeting of the National Security Council on March 4, Eisenhower asked plaintively if it wasn't possible "to get some of the people in these downtrodden countries to like us instead of hating us?" Secretary of State Dulles responded with a summary of recent events in Iran. Dulles said that Mossadegh would likely remain in power, but that if he were assassinated "a power vacuum might occur and the Communists might easily take over. Not only would the free world be deprived of the enormous assets represented by Iranian oil production and reserves, but the Russians would secure these assets and thus henceforth be free of any anxiety about their petroleum situation."

Treasury Secretary George Humphrey asked Dulles if he was convinced Russia would ultimately secure Iran. According to the official record of the meeting, "Secretary Dulles replied in the affirmative, and Mr. [Robert] Cutler pointed out that this, of course, meant that with the loss of Iran we would lose the neighboring countries of the Middle East and that loss would be terribly serious."

Eisenhower allowed that if the Soviets did move against Iran, the United States would have to act quickly. "If I had $500,000,000 of money to spend in secret, I would get $100,000,000 of it to Iran right now."[41]

British foreign secretary Anthony Eden arrived in Washington the next day for a series of high-level conferences on the Middle East. When he broached the subject of Iran and the proposed coup, he found everyone supportive except Eisenhower. Ike told Eden he considered Mossadegh "the only hope for the West in Iran," and was greatly concerned about the possibility of a Communist takeover if Mossadegh fell. "I would like to give the guy ten million bucks," said Ike. In the discussions that followed, Eden did his best to discredit Mossadegh, arguing that the longer he stayed in power, the more harm he could do to the West. "We should be better occupied looking for alternatives to Mossadegh rather than trying to buy him off," he told Eisenhower.[42] Later, Eden cabled Churchill, saying that "the President seemed obsessed by the fear of a Communist Iran. [His] experts had told him that a pipeline could be built from Abadan to the Caucasus in a matter of a couple of years."[43]

Eden's intervention evidently shook Eisenhower's resolve. At the next meeting of the National Security Council, on March 11, Defense Secretary Charles Wilson asked whether the United States might not negotiate directly with Iran concerning their oil. Ike replied he had "very real doubts whether . . . we could make a successful deal with Mossadegh. It would not be worth the paper it was written on, and the example might have very grave effects on United States oil concessions in other parts of the world."[44]

As the violence escalated on the streets of Teheran, Eisenhower swung more and more against Mossadegh. By late spring Ike had come to the conclusion that Iran was collapsing and that the collapse could not be prevented so long as Mossadegh remained in power.[45] Eden's suggestion that they find an alternative looked increasingly attractive. As one biographer put it, "Eisenhower and Foster Dulles spent many a cocktail hour together," and over drinks in the evening Ike was brought around to accept a coup, providing America's hand would not be visible. With Eisenhower's tacit approval, the CIA and British MI6 accelerated plans for taking action in Teheran.[46]

On May 28 Mossadegh appealed to Eisenhower for American aid to offset the effects of the British economic embargo. "The Iranian people," said Mossadegh, were "suffering financial hardships and struggling with political intrigues carried on by the former oil company and the British government."[47] Eisenhower did not reply immediately. Instead, on June 14, Allen Dulles went to the White House to brief Ike on Operation AJAX. Sensing that the president did not want to know too much, Dulles gave him what Kermit Roosevelt called only a "broad brush outline of what was proposed." Eisenhower signed on, and shortly afterward Churchill gave his much more enthusiastic approval.[48]

On June 25 Kermit Roosevelt returned to Washington to brief officials on the details of AJAX. The meeting was held in the Foggy Bottom office of Secretary of State Dulles. Eisenhower did not attend. When Roosevelt finished, Dulles asked the others what they thought. Allen Dulles, Bedell Smith, and Defense Secretary Wilson endorsed the plan for the coup without reservation. Loy Henderson, who had succeeded Henry Grady as American ambassador in Teheran, said, "We have no choice." Secretary of State Dulles agreed. "That's that, then. Let's get going."[49]

On June 30, after the coup had been agreed to, Eisenhower dispatched his belated reply to Mossadegh. The president told the Iranian leader that American help would not be forthcoming. Instead, Mossadegh should settle with the British. "There is a strong feeling in the United States," said Ike, "that it would not be fair to the American taxpayers for the United States Government to extend any considerable amount of economic aid to Iran so long as Iran could have access to funds derived from the sale of its oil." American policy toward Iran had undergone a sea change. "I refused to pour more American money into a country in turmoil in order to bail Mossadegh out of troubles rooted in his refusal to work out an agreement with the British," Ike wrote later.[50]

Secretary Dulles monitored the planning for the coup closely. After a high-level meeting on the Middle East in late July, he became concerned when Iran was discussed and no mention was made of AJAX. The next morning he called his brother at the CIA to ask if something had gone wrong. According to Allen Dulles's phone log, "The Secy [JFD] called and said in your talk about Iran yesterday you did not mention the other matter. Is it off? A[llen] W[.] D[ulles] said he doesn't talk about it, *it was cleared directly with the President,* and is still active."[51]

At his press conference the following week, Dulles began to set the stage for American intervention. "Recent developments in Iran, especially the efforts of the illegal Communist party, which appears to be tolerated by the Iranian Government, have caused us concern," said Secretary Dulles. "These developments make it difficult for the United States to give assistance to Iran so long as its government tolerates this sort of activity."[52]

It was a self-fulfilling prophecy. On the one hand, Kermit Roosevelt and his agents in Teheran were fomenting ever higher levels of violence; on the other, Secretary Dulles was criticizing the Iranian government for not arresting the violence Roosevelt was creating.

With the country aflame, Mossadegh chose to hold a referendum, which he thought might solidify his power. The blatantly tainted result showed 99.4 percent for Mossadegh. That convinced Eisenhower that a Communist takeover was imminent. "Iran's downhill course toward Communist-supported dictatorship was picking up momentum," said Ike afterward.[53]

The shah's cooperation was crucial for the coup's success. To make the initial overture to Pahlavi, Allen Dulles dispatched retired major general H. Norman Schwarzkopf, the father of Desert Storm's "Stormin' Norman," to Teheran.* The elder Schwarzkopf had spent most of the 1940s in Iran commanding the constabulary and training the twenty-thousand-man Imperial Iranian Gendarmerie, the country's national police force. The shah was deeply indebted to Schwarzkopf, and had every reason to trust whatever assurances he gave. Schwarzkopf also had many friends among the senior officers of the Iranian Army and police force. He arrived in Teheran on August 1 "armed with a diplomatic passport and a couple of large bags containing millions of dollars."[54] Later that day he called on the shah at the Saad Abad Palace, explained the details of the coup, and assured him that the United States would give him full support if he cooperated. Schwarzkopf then put the shah in contact with Roosevelt and stepped aside.

By mid-August, Roosevelt had his team in place and was ready to strike. Protests and riots organized by his operatives had turned the streets of Teheran into battlegrounds. Newspapers and religious leaders were screaming for Mossadegh's head. According to Donald Wil-

---

* A 1917 graduate of West Point, the senior Schwarzkopf fought at the Second Battle of the Marne in World War I, resigned from the Army in the 1920s, and became the first superintendent of the New Jersey State Police (with the rank of colonel). He acquired celebrity status directing the investigation of the Lindbergh kidnapping and later spent several years as the narrator of the popular weekly radio drama *Gang Busters*. When World War II broke out, Schwarzkopf returned to active duty and was assigned to Iran. See H. Norman Schwarzkopf [Jr.], *It Doesn't Take a Hero: General H. Norman Schwarzkopf, the Autobiography* 1–40 (New York: Bantam Books, 1992).

bur, who headed CIA planning for AJAX in Washington, "anti-government propaganda poured off the Agency's presses and was rushed by air to Teheran."[55]

On August 15, 1953, the coup commenced. By the nineteenth, after a crescendo of street violence, Mossadegh had been removed from office and was under arrest.[*] In his *Memoirs,* Eisenhower hailed the coup as a spontaneous uprising of the shah's supporters against Mossadegh and the Communists.[56] No mention was made of the CIA's involvement or American complicity. A month later in Denver, Eisenhower met privately with Kermit Roosevelt and awarded him the National Security Medal in a closed-door ceremony. In his diary Ike wrote, "The things we did were covert," and he acknowledged that the United States would be embarrassed if the CIA's role ever became known. Eisenhower said that Kermit Roosevelt "worked intelligently, courageously, and tirelessly. I listened to his detailed report and it seemed more like a dime novel than an historical fact."[57][†]

---

[*] Mossadegh was tried before a military tribunal for having resisted the shah's order dismissing him and for "inciting the people to armed insurrection." Mossadegh defended himself, pointing out among other things that the shah lacked the constitutional authority to dismiss a prime minister unless the Majlis had voted no confidence—which it had not done. "My only crime is that I nationalized the Iranian oil industry and removed from this land the network of colonialism . . . of the greatest empire on earth." Mossadegh was convicted and sentenced to three years in prison, followed by house arrest for life. He died on March 5, 1967, at the age of eighty-five. No public funeral was permitted. *Musaddig's Memoirs* 74, Homa Katouzian, ed. (London: JEBHE, 1988).

[†] Eisenhower's diary entry (October 8, 1953) was revealed by Stephen Ambrose in 1984 in the second volume of his biography of Ike. As an associate editor of the *Eisenhower Papers,* Ambrose had access to the diary and saw no reason not to publish what he found. But when the relevant volume of the *Eisenhower Papers* was published by the Johns Hopkins University Press in 1998, all reference to the coup in Iran was deleted from Ike's October 8 diary entry. "The NSC deleted a portion of this document," according to the relevant note. When Robert H. Ferrell published *The Eisenhower Diaries* in 1981, the October 8 entry is omitted in its entirety. The diary entry was not declassified until May 10, 2010. It reads as Ambrose cited it.

Stephen E. Ambrose, 2 *Eisenhower* 129 (New York: Simon and Schuster, 1984); *The Papers of Dwight David Eisenhower,* vol. 14, *The Presidency* 564–73n26; Robert H. Ferrell, ed., *The Eisenhower Diaries* (New York: Norton, 1981); Box 4, DDE Diary Series, EL.

In the coup's aftermath, the United States generously provided the emergency financial aid to Iran that had been denied Mossadegh. The new Iranian government responded by agreeing to a new oil concession with an international consortium, with Iran receiving 50 percent of the proceeds. British Petroleum retained 40 percent of the shares in the consortium, five American companies held another 40 percent, and the remainder were divided between Royal Dutch Shell and the Compagnie Française des Pétroles.[58] The consortium retained the name Mossadegh gave it—the National Iranian Oil Company—to preserve the façade of nationalization, but its books were not opened to Iranian auditors, nor were Iranians allowed to serve on its board of directors.[59]

On March 17, 2000—forty-seven years later—the United States officially acknowledged its involvement in the coup. Secretary of State Madeleine Albright, speaking before the American-Iranian Council in Washington, delivered what amounted to an apology. "In 1953 the United States played a significant role in orchestrating the overthrow of Iran's popular prime minister, Mohammad Mossadegh. The Eisenhower administration believed its actions were justified for strategic reasons. But the coup was clearly a setback for Iran's political development. And it is easy to see now why many Iranians continue to resent this intervention by America in their internal affairs."[60]

The success of Operation AJAX encouraged the Eisenhower administration to intervene elsewhere. Under Eisenhower the Central Intelligence Agency became a major instrument of American foreign policy. Its budget increased exponentially, and the overthrow of objectionable regimes became an accepted tool of statecraft. As one biographer put it, "the CIA offered the President a quick fix for his problems,"[61] and Latin America had many problems that needed to be fixed—at least as the Eisenhower administration saw it.

The first target was Guatemala. In October 1944, the country's fledgling middle class had overthrown the long, brutal dictatorship of General Jorge Ubico, who was closely identified with the United Fruit Company (UFCO), and began an experiment in democracy inspired by Franklin Roosevelt's New Deal.

In Guatemala, the United Fruit Company (known as "El Pulpo,"

Mount Eisenhower, a 9,400-foot massif in the Canadian Rockies, midway between Banff and Lake Louise.

the octopus) played an analogous role to the Anglo-Iranian Oil Company in Iran. It owned 42 percent of the arable land, was exempt from all taxes and duties, controlled the country's only port as well as its electrical and transportation systems, and owned the telephone and telegraph facilities. The company's annual profits amounted to twice the total revenue of the Guatemalan government. Most of its vast acreage was kept idle in order not to flood the market with bananas and bring the price down.[62]

Guatemala's new democratic government soon clashed with United Fruit. The labor reforms instituted by the government, including minimum wage legislation and the right of workers to organize and bargain collectively, most of which were patterned on the New Deal, were predictably assailed by UFCO as "Communistic." Education reforms to combat widespread illiteracy were equally suspect. But the new government struck deep popular roots. In March 1951, when the revolution was seven years old, Jacobo Arbenz Guzmán, the former defense minister, was elected president, winning more than twice the number of votes of all other candidates combined. Arbenz ran on a platform of land reform, and in June 1952, the Guatemalan national assembly enacted legislation providing for the redistribution of idle land held by large landowners.

Owners were compensated with twenty-five-year government bonds at 3 percent interest, the value of the property determined by the owner's own tax declaration for 1952.[63]

In March 1953, the Arbenz government expropriated 234,000 acres of fallow land on the Pacific slope belonging to the United Fruit Company. In February 1954, it took an additional 173,000 acres of idle land from United Fruit on the Caribbean coast. From that point on the days of the Arbenz government were numbered. As Kenneth Redmond, president of United Fruit, put it, "From here on out it's not a matter of the people of Guatemala against the United Fruit Company; the question is going to be Communism against the right of property, the life and security of the Western Hemisphere."[64]

Land reform was a red flag in Washington, and Redmond's prediction fell on fertile ground. Like the reach of the Anglo-Iranian Oil Company in London, the tentacles of United Fruit stretched to the highest levels of American government. Both John Foster Dulles and Allen Dulles had managed the legal affairs of United Fruit at Sullivan and Cromwell.[*] Ann Whitman, Eisenhower's personal secretary, was married to Ed Whitman, the head of United Fruit's public relations department. Robert Cutler, Ike's national security assistant, was United Fruit's banker in Boston. (UFCO was based in Boston.) And Bedell Smith longed to work for the company after he left government service.[65] Most important, however, was Thomas G. Corcoran—"Tommy the Cork"—the legendary Washington insider and FDR confidant who was United Fruit's longtime lobbyist in Washington. E. Howard Hunt, the CIA soldier of fortune who directed the action on the ground inside Guatemala, and who later spent thirty-three months in federal prison for his role in the Watergate break-in, credits Corcoran with winning Eisenhower's support for the coup.[66]

---

[*] In 1936, as executive partner at Sullivan and Cromwell, John Foster Dulles had supervised the drafting of the agreement with the Ubico government of Guatemala that gave the United Fruit Company a tax-free status for ninety-nine years as well as control of the country's only port, Puerto Barrios. Richard H. Immerman, *The CIA in Guatemala: The Foreign Policy of Intervention* 124 (Austin: University of Texas Press, 1982); Thomas McCann, *An American Company: The Tragedy of United Fruit,* Henry Scammell, ed. 13, 56 (New York: Crown Publishers, 1976).

Eisenhower was open to Corcoran's persuasion. In the spring of 1953—shortly after the Arbenz government had expropriated the land of United Fruit—Ike sent his brother Milton to Latin America to report on conditions. Milton Eisenhower did not visit Central America on his ten-nation tour. His report nevertheless alluded to Guatemala, and emphasized the importance of timely American action "to prevent Communism from spreading seriously beyond Guatemala." As Milton put it: "The possible conquest of a Latin American nation today would not be by direct assault. It would come, rather, through the insidious process of infiltration, conspiracy, spreading of lies, and the undermining of free institutions. . . . One [Latin] American nation has succumbed to Communist infiltration."[67]

Milton Eisenhower did not set foot in Guatemala, but he accepted the premise that the land reform of the Arbenz government was the entering wedge of a Communist takeover. Milton's message was reinforced by the Dulles brothers and Bedell Smith. The precise date when Ike signed on to the coup is unclear. But when Kermit Roosevelt made his report to the White House on Operation AJAX in September 1953, planning was already well advanced. Roosevelt reports that Allen Dulles offered him the assignment leading the coup in Guatemala, but he declined.[68]

In one of the early planning sessions, Eisenhower asked Allen Dulles about the chances of success. "Better than forty percent," said Dulles, "but less than even." That was sufficient for Ike. He gave Dulles the go-ahead, but reserved the right to cancel the operation if it did not feel right.[69]

The coup was code-named PBSUCCESS. Howard Hunt was given operational control while Richard Bissell, the CIA director of operations, managed affairs from Washington. The agency enlisted scores of recruits, primarily mercenaries from Guatemala, Honduras, and Nicaragua, while putting together a small air force for what was euphemistically called the "national liberation force." The mercenaries were paid three hundred dollars a month—ten times the going wage for United Fruit workers in Guatemala. Training took place at a CIA camp in Opa-locka, Florida, and in Honduras. As with Operation AJAX, Eisenhower remained officially aloof, discussing the matter casually over cocktails or at the Sunday brunch that Eleanor Dulles hosted for her two brothers each week.[70]

By mid-June 1954, all of the pieces of PBSUCCESS were in place: the mini air force of three planes was ready; additional CIA pilots were standing by in Managua, Nicaragua; a Voice of Liberation radio station was set up in Honduras to broadcast on the rebels' behalf; and a leader, Castillo Armas, stood ready to command the expedition. Armas had been personally selected by Hunt because, among other things, he had "that good Indian look about him . . . which was great for the people."[71]

On June 16, 1954, Eisenhower gave his final approval for the coup. At a breakfast meeting with his principal national security officials in the family quarters of the White House, the president listened intently as Allen Dulles laid out the plan. "Are you sure this is going to succeed?" Ike asked. The Dulles brothers, the Joint Chiefs, Defense Secretary Charles Wilson, and Robert Cutler all agreed that it would.

"I want all of you to be damn good and sure you succeed," said Eisenhower. "I'm prepared to take any steps that are necessary to see that it succeeds. When you commit the flag, you commit it to win."[72]

Operation PBSUCCESS commenced on June 18, 1954, when Castillo Armas's ragtag "national liberation force" of 150 men crossed the border from Honduras and moved six miles into Guatemala. RE-VOLT LAUNCHED IN GUATEMALA: LAND-AIR-SEA INVASION RE-PORTED: RISINGS UNDER WAY IN KEY CITIES, bannered *The New York Times*.[73] The *Times* was reporting from a CIA handout. American journalists were excluded from the area lest they find out how puny the effort was.[74] Armas's men settled down in a local church and waited for the Arbenz regime to collapse, but nothing happened. The Guatemalan Army remained in its barracks, and the capital city showed no sign of unrest despite occasional bombing runs by the liberation air force. Soon two of Armas's three planes were out of action. At an emergency meeting in the White House on June 22, Allen Dulles reported that without additional air support the rebellion would collapse. Dulles said that Nicaragua's Anastasio Somoza had offered to give Armas two P-51 fighter-bombers if the United States agreed to replace them.[75]

"What do you think Castillo's chances would be without the aircraft?" Eisenhower asked Dulles.

"About zero," Dulles replied.

"Suppose we supply the aircraft? What would the chances be then?"

"About twenty percent."

Eisenhower was convinced. Later he wrote that he knew from his experience in Europe "the important psychological impact of even a small amount of air support. . . . My duty was clear to me. We would replace the airplanes."[76]

Eisenhower to Somoza to Armas: The national liberation force got its airplanes. Bombing runs over Guatemala City resumed, CIA pilots stationed at Managua's international airport joined in, the Guatemalan Army continued to remain in its barracks, and by June 27, Arbenz had agreed to resign. He was replaced by a military dictatorship. Aside from the air support, the key to the coup was the CIA's radio station based in Honduras. The agency had jammed the government station and created a fictional war over the airwaves in which liberation troops were relentlessly moving forward. Arbenz's defeat was made to appear inevitable.[77] The CIA snatched victory from the jaws of defeat.

Eisenhower had recognized the problem of French colonialism in Indochina. He was less cognizant of British commercial imperialism in Iran or American in Latin America. The United States was in an apocalyptic struggle with Communism, and the normal rules of fair play did not apply. Iran and Guatemala were not isolated phenomena. The role of the United States in world affairs was changing. As America's international reach and sense of obligation increased, the instinct to adhere to traditional democratic procedures diminished. Eisenhower was a leading player in that process.[78]

Wartime presidents are not perfect. Lincoln suspended the writ of habeas corpus during the Civil War, and Franklin Roosevelt authorized the internment of Japanese Americans after Pearl Harbor. Eisenhower's Cold War use of the CIA to topple the legitimately elected governments of Iran and Guatemala represents a similar reaction.

In Guatemala, Ike listened to the advice of Tommy Corcoran, the

Dulles brothers, Bedell Smith, and Robert Cutler and convinced himself that a full-fledged Communist takeover was in the offing. He would have been better advised to heed the message he received from his old friend William Prescott Allen, Texas publisher of *The Laredo Times,* who visited Guatemala in June 1954. "Yes," Allen cabled Ike, "Guatemala has a very small minority of Communists, but not as many as San Francisco."[79]

# TWENTY-THREE

# *New Look*

Our most valued, our most costly asset is our
young men. Let's don't use them any more than
we have to.

—DWIGHT D. EISENHOWER,
*March 17, 1954*

THE EISENHOWERS, LIKE THE ROOSEVELTS, were accustomed to servants. When Eisenhower got out of bed each morning, Sergeant Moaney held the president's undershorts for him to step into. When Ike took practice shots on the South Lawn, Sergeant Moaney retrieved the balls for him. And when Ike cooked stew for his friends, Sergeant Moaney assembled the ingredients, chopped the meat and vegetables, and stood by like a surgical assistant to hand Eisenhower whatever he required.

Mamie was pampered equally by her personal maid, Rose Woods. Rose rinsed out the First Lady's stockings and underwear in the bathroom every night and dressed her in the late morning. Sergeant Moaney's wife, Delores, served as the Eisenhowers' personal cook and maid in the family quarters of the White House, and Sergeant Leonard Dry drove for Mamie. Elivera Doud, Mamie's mother, lived in the White House, just as Madge Wallace, Bess Truman's mother, had done, and as Marian Robinson, President Obama's mother-in-law, currently does.[1]

Mamie's experience running large household establishments was immediately evident. "She appeared fragile and feminine," said White

Ike and Sergeant Moaney grilling steaks.

House chief usher J. B. West, but "once behind the White House gates she ruled as if she were Queen."[2] Unlike Eleanor Roosevelt, Mamie paid close attention to the White House menu. Although she had never learned to cook herself, she had an instinctive understanding of the compatibility of various dishes, and chided the staff to avoid waste. Every morning she asked for a list of food that had not been eaten the previous day. "Three people turned down second servings of Cornish hen last night," she reminded Charles Ficklin, the White House maître d'. "Please use it in chicken salad today."[3]

Official entertaining at the White House was straitlaced. The food was superior to that served by the Roosevelts, but the drinks were sharply rationed. Cocktails were never served, and butlers poured only American wines at the table with dinner. Alcohol flowed more freely in the family quarters. Eisenhower preferred scotch, and Mamie liked old-fashioneds, although, as J. B. West reports, her consumption was very modest despite rumors to the contrary.[4]

Mamie's particular passion was watching television soap operas, and she rarely missed an episode of CBS's *As the World Turns*. After her private time watching television, Mamie would be joined by her old friends from wartime Washington in the Monroe Room for an afternoon of Bolivia, a form of canasta that she adored. According to West, "The Bolivia players usually took a break for tea at 5:00 p.m., and sometimes they would stay for dinner."* In the evenings the Eisenhowers and their guests would often watch movies in the White House theater. Ike's taste ran predictably to Westerns, most of which he had seen three or four times. Unlike Eleanor Roosevelt and Lady Bird Johnson, Mamie did not take up public causes and rarely ventured outside her role as the president's wife. "I have but one career," she often said, "and its name is Ike."[5]

Once a month Eisenhower would host a stag dinner for sixteen or so guests, bringing together men from various professions whom he had read about and wanted to meet. Dress was usually black tie, and the conversation was free-flowing. "I used these dinners to try to draw from leaders in various sections of American life their views on many domestic and international questions," said Ike. "The stag dinners were, for me, a means of gaining information and intelligent opinion as well as enjoying good company."[6]

Eisenhower's concern for appearances sometimes led him to make fussy decisions. Allegedly to save money he shut down the presidential winter quarters at the Key West Naval Station and got rid of the *Williamsburg,* the presidential yacht on which the Trumans often entertained. "The very word 'yacht' created a symbol of luxury in the public mind," Ike wrote his friend Swede Hazlett.[7] At the same time, Eisenhower permitted Arthur Summerfield, the Michigan GM dealer who served as postmaster general, to repaint the nation's mailboxes and postal trucks from traditional post office green to a car salesman's red, white, and blue—supposedly as a symbol of American patriotism.[8]

* Mamie's Bolivia regulars included Mrs. Everett Hughes, Mrs. Walton Walker, and Mrs. Harry Butcher, all former neighbors from the Wyoming or the Wardman Park, as well as Mrs. George Allen and Mrs. Howard Snyder, the wife of Ike's personal physician. J. B. West and Mary Lynn Kotz, *Upstairs at the White House: My Life with the First Ladies* 161 (New York: Coward, McCann, and Geoghegan, 1973).

"Shangri-La," FDR's rustic retreat in Maryland's Catoctin Mountains, which the WPA had built in the 1930s, also went on the chopping block.[*] But Mamie intervened, insisted that it be updated and redecorated, and used as a weekend getaway until the farm at Gettysburg could be rehabilitated. Like Key West, Shangri-La was maintained by the Navy, and as J. B. West writes, "Soon came the order for the Navy to redecorate Shangri-La, with Mrs. Eisenhower as the consultant, and the rustic lodge soon took on a '1950s modern' look, in greens, yellows, and beiges."[9] When it was finished, Eisenhower renamed it "Camp David" in honor of his five-year-old grandson, evidently hoping to erase the memory of Franklin D. Roosevelt.

The Eisenhowers occasionally used Camp David as a retreat and conference center, but Ike much preferred to accept the hospitality provided by his friends in the Gang, with whom he felt he could best relax. His favorite spot was the Augusta National, and he used his trips to Augusta to unwind, much as FDR had done at Warm Springs.[10] Eisenhower also enjoyed extended fishing vacations at Aksel Nielsen's estate near Fraser, Colorado, and at Denver developer Bal Swan's purebred Hereford ranch on the north fork of the South Platte River.

Above all, Ike and Mamie were soon caught up restoring the farm at Gettysburg they had purchased in 1950. After Eisenhower left the Army, he and Mamie began looking for a place to retire. They wanted a place in the country, preferably with a few acres, and not too far from Washington or New York. Gang member George Allen, a country boy from Mississippi, owned a farm near Gettysburg and recommended the region to Ike. Eisenhower had served two years at

---

* "Shangri-La" is a fictional place described in the 1933 novel *Lost Horizon* by James Hilton—a mythical Himalayan utopia isolated from the outside world. The novel was made into a film of the same name by Frank Capra in 1937 and starred Ronald Colman. FDR was fond both of the novel and the film and named the presidential retreat accordingly. In 1942, when newsmen asked him where the bombers that bombed Tokyo had come from, the president mirthfully said, "Shangri-La," a reference to the Himalayan utopia, not the presidential retreat. James Hilton, *Lost Horizon* (London: Macmillan, 1933). Also see Charles Allen, *The Search for Shangri-La: A Journey into Tibetan History* (London: Little, Brown, 1999); Presidential press conference, April 21, 1942, 19 *Complete Presidential Press Conferences of Franklin D. Roosevelt* 291–92 (New York: Da Capo Press, 1972).

Camp Colt (on the Gettysburg battlefield) during World War I, and had never forgotten the lush rolling countryside. Mamie remembered the friendly townspeople. When Allen told them that a 189-acre farm had been put on the market, Mamie went to inspect it and fell in love with the property.

"I must have this place," she told Ike.

"Well, Mamie, if you like it, buy it."[11]

The property, known as the Allen Redding farm, was adjacent to the battlefield and about three miles from town. During the Battle of Gettysburg the house had served as a dressing station for Confederate wounded. Eisenhower paid a total of $40,000 ($362,000 currently): $24,000 for the farm, and $16,000 for the livestock and equipment. In addition to the two-story brick farmhouse, there was a massive wooden barn (one of the largest in Adams County), thirty-six Holstein dairy cattle, and five hundred white leghorn chickens. It was a working farm. The milk was picked up every morning by a Baltimore dairy, and the eggs (about twenty dozen daily) were marketed through a cooperative in Gettysburg. There were also two tractors and all the machinery necessary to operate the farm.[12]

Eisenhower, who was then president of Columbia, decided to retain the farm as a going concern. An old Army associate, retired brigadier general Arthur Nevins, who had been Ike's deputy G-2 at SHAEF, was talked into becoming the farm's manager, and General Nevins and his wife, Ann, moved into the house in the spring of 1951. The Nevinses and the Eisenhowers had been close friends since their service together in the Philippines.[13]

Ike and Mamie decided to renovate the house after they moved to Washington. Plans were drawn by Penn State architecture professor Milton Osborne, Mamie engaged interior designer Dorothy Draper, and the construction work was handled by Charles Tompkins, one of the largest contractors on the East Coast. Eisenhower insisted on using union labor, which meant that most workers had to drive from Washington or Baltimore, which added considerably to the final cost. On the other hand, Charles Tompkins charged no overhead and billed Ike only for actual expenses, which balanced things out.

When the project was completed in 1955, little remained of the original house. There were now fifteen rooms, eight baths, a thirty-seven-by-twenty-one-foot living room, and an oak-beamed study for Ike. The total cost came to $215,000 ($1.75 million currently), and was paid largely from the receipts Eisenhower realized for *Crusade in Europe*.[14] Shortly afterward, Gang member W. Alton "Pete" Jones (president of Cities Service Company) bought three adjoining farms on which he planted hundreds of strategically sited trees to assure Ike's privacy.[15] The farms were combined and worked under the supervision of General Nevins. Ike raised purebred Angus cattle in partnership with Alton Jones and George Allen, but the venture was primarily a hobby rather than an attempt to turn a profit.[16] Toward the end of his presidency, Eisenhower purchased an adjacent five acres containing an abandoned rural schoolhouse. The schoolhouse was remodeled to provide a home for John, Barbara, and their four children, and a private road was built connecting the two houses. Eisenhower doted on his grandchildren, and could never see enough of them.*

But Ike's time was limited. His first priority as president was to make peace in Korea. His second was to balance the budget. Unlike the Republican party's Old Guard, he ruled out any reduction in social programs. Savings would be achieved through the elimination of government waste and a review of all other programs. National security, the largest budget item, was an obvious target, and when Ike took office, he ordered an immediate review of the nation's military structure.

Eisenhower was critical of existing defense policy for two reasons. First, he believed President Truman had demobilized the armed forces too quickly after World War II, withdrawing from Korea and thus inviting attack. Second, after the Korean War started, the Truman administration quadrupled defense spending without considering the costs. That threw the budget seriously out of kilter. What

---

* Alton Jones was killed in an air accident in 1962. He bequeathed his farms to the United States government as an addition to the Gettysburg National Military Park, subject to Ike's continued use of the property until his death. On November 27, 1967, Eisenhower and Mamie gave their farm to the government as well, with the provision that Mamie could stay until her death. The farm is now maintained by the National Park Service and is open to the public.

Ike and John with David, Susan, and Barbara Ann at Gettysburg.

was required in Ike's view was a defense policy that could be sustained over the long run without sending the country to the poorhouse.

Eisenhower was uniquely qualified to lead the reappraisal. With the possible exception of Ulysses Grant, who confronted different but equally difficult military issues, no president has been better equipped by outlook and experience to deal with matters of national security. Like Grant, Ike was his own military expert, and as with Grant the country trusted him implicitly. Both Grant and Eisenhower twice won elections by massive margins because the electorate had confidence in their abilities to defend the nation. In Grant's case, the danger pertained to Reconstruction and restoring the Union. In Ike's case, it was a Cold War that might turn hot. Here lay Eisenhower's supreme personal expertise, and he tackled the issue with enthusiasm.

In his first State of the Union message, two weeks after assuming office, Eisenhower told Congress that "to amass military power without regard to our economic capacity would be to defend ourselves against one kind of disaster by inviting another."[17] Shortly afterward, he took the issue to the country. Speaking to a national radio and television audience on May 19, 1953, Eisenhower said, "Our defense [policy] must be one we can bear for a long and indefinite period of time. It cannot consist of sudden, blind responses to a series of fire alarm emergencies." The United States could not prepare to meet every contingency, said Ike. That would require a total mobilization that would "devote our whole nation to the grim purposes of the garrison state. This, I firmly believe, is not the way to defend America."[18]

Eisenhower announced that he intended to direct 40 percent of the upcoming defense budget to the Air Force. The Army and Navy would be reduced accordingly. The object was to prevent war, not to fight one. With the war in Korea approaching an end, there was no reason to maintain an Army of twenty divisions. The implication was clear. Under Ike there would be no limited wars, no police actions, no conflicts beneath the nuclear threshold. "Our most valued, our most costly asset is our young men," said the president. "Let's don't use them any more than we have to."

Ike put the matter in personal terms. "For forty years I was in the Army, and I did one thing: study how you can get an infantry platoon out of battle. The most terrible job in warfare is to be a second lieutenant leading a platoon when you are on the battlefield."[19]

The Pentagon pushed back. Omar Bradley, still chairman of the Joint Chiefs, told the National Security Council that the United States had to prepare for both conventional and nuclear war. "The build-up of the military strength of the United States is the keystone and indeed, the very life blood of the free world's strategy to frustrate the Kremlin's designs," wrote Bradley. To cut military spending as the president proposed "would so increase the risk to the United States as to pose a grave threat to the survival of our allies and the security of this nation."[20]

Eisenhower was unswayed. The Joint Chiefs were seeking to fight a war; he was determined to prevent one. And their parochialism was appalling. In a letter to his friend Swede Hazlett, Ike noted that the Joint Chiefs had a lot to learn. "Each of these men must cease regarding himself as the advocate for any particular Service; he must think strictly and solely for the United States. Character rather than intellect, and moral courage rather than mere professional skill, are the dominant qualifications required."[21]

Ike fretted about the chiefs' recalcitrance. "Someday there is going to be a man sitting in my present chair who has not been raised in the military services and who will have little understanding of where slashes in [the Pentagon's] estimates can be made with little or no damage. If that should happen while we still have the state of tension that now exists in the world, I shudder to think of what could happen to this country."

Eisenhower told Swede that his "most frustrating domestic problem" was with the leadership of the armed services.

> I patiently explain over and over again that American strength is a combination of its economic, moral and military force. If we demand too much in taxes in order to build planes and ships, we will tend to dry up the accumulations of capital that are necessary to provide jobs for the millions of new workers that we must absorb each year. . . . I simply must find men who have the breadth of understanding and devotion to their country rather than to a single Service that will bring about better solutions than I get now.[22]

By the end of the summer of 1953, each of the Joint Chiefs had been replaced. Eisenhower did not relieve any, but as their terms expired they were not reappointed. Admiral Radford replaced Bradley as chairman, Matthew Ridgway succeeded J. Lawton Collins as Army chief of staff, Admiral Robert B. Carney replaced William Fechteler as chief of naval operations, and Nathan Twining followed Hoyt Vandenberg as Air Force chief of staff. Ike spoke with each before appointing him, and each assured Eisenhower of his support.

With his military team in place, and after extensive staff studies, Eisenhower was ready to act. At the beginning of December 1953, the president wrote budget director Joseph Dodge that he had instructed Secretary Wilson "to establish personnel ceilings in each service that will place everything on an austerity basis." Ike said the forces in Korea should be kept at full strength, as should the Strategic Air Command and the various interceptor squadrons, but that everything else should be reduced across the board. "We are no longer fighting in Korea, and the Defense establishment should show its appreciation of this fact without wailing about the mission they have to accomplish."[23]

As a result of Eisenhower's directive, the Army was reduced from 1.5 million men in 1953 to 1 million by June 1955. The Navy and Marine Corps shrank from 1 million to 870,000, while the Air Force increased from 950,000 to 970,000.[24] Admiral Radford announced the shift in a speech to the National Press Club on December 14. Radford called the change a "New Look" in defense policy, using a term then in vogue in the fashion industry to describe the lengthening of women's skirts. Journalists labeled it "more bang for the buck."[25]

Eisenhower directed Secretary of State Dulles to put the shift in context. In a major speech to the Council on Foreign Relations on January 14, 1954—a speech that had been carefully vetted by Ike— Dulles explained the strategic significance of the New Look. Paraphrasing Eisenhower's views, Dulles said, "Emergency measures are costly, they are superficial and they imply the enemy has the initiative." The new aim of American policy, he said, was to make collective security more effective and less costly "by placing more reliance on deterrent power, and less dependence on local defensive power." Dulles explained why the shift was necessary. "If the enemy could pick his time and place and method of warfare, then we needed to be ready to fight in the arctic and in the tropics; in Asia, the Near East and in Europe; by sea, by land, and by air; with old weapons and with new weapons." But that was now changed. The United States would deter wars rather than fight them. "The basic decision was to depend primarily upon a capacity to retaliate instantly, by means and at places of our choosing." That sentence had been added by Eisenhower when he reviewed Dulles's original draft. The handmaiden of the military's New Look was instantly dubbed the "doctrine of massive retaliation." Dulles was given credit for the statement, but the words belonged to Ike.[26]

At his press conference the following day, Eisenhower was asked to comment on Dulles's remarks. Not surprisingly, Ike declined. "I think no amplification of the statement is either necessary or wise," said the president. "He was merely stating what, to my mind, is a fundamental truth and really doesn't take much discussion; it is just a fundamental truth."[27]

Other administration figures were less reticent to chime in. Treasury Secretary George Humphrey said the United States had "no business getting into little wars. If a situation comes up where our interests justify intervention, let's intervene decisively with all we have or get out." Nixon said, "Rather than let the Communists nibble us to death all over the world in little wars, we would rely in the future primarily on our massive mobile retaliatory power . . . against the major source of aggression."[28]

But the New Look was not embraced by everyone within the administration. General Matthew Ridgway, although he initially signed on, soon became restive. Testifying before the Senate Appropriations Committee in January 1955, Ridgway criticized the ongoing reduction in Army ground forces. The New Look, he told senators, was forcing the United States into an "all or nothing" posture and would expose the country to a series of future Koreas. "The foot soldier is still the dominant factor in war," said Ridgway, "and weakening our ground forces would be a grievous blow to freedom."[29]

When Eisenhower met with the Senate Republican leadership the next day, he was asked by Senator Styles Bridges of New Hampshire how they should handle Ridgway's testimony. "Ridgway is the Army's chief of staff," said Ike.

> When he is called up on the Hill and asked for his personal convictions, he has got to give them. But we must realize that as commander-in-chief, I have to make the final decisions. I have to consider—which the heads of the services do not—the very delicate balance between the national debt, taxes, and expenditures. Actually, the only thing we fear is an atomic attack delivered by air on our cities. God damn it, it would be perfect rot to talk about shipping troops abroad when fifteen of our cities were in ruins.

That's the trouble with Ridgway. He's talking theory—
I'm trying to talk sound sense. We have to have a sound
base here at home. We have got to restore order and our
productivity before we can do anything else. That's why in
our military thinking we have to put emphasis on two or
three things first. One, we have to maintain a strong striking retaliatory Air Force and secondly, we have to build up
our warning system so that we can receive as much advance notice as possible of any attack.

Press secretary James Hagerty, who was at the meeting, said the senators listened with rapt attention. "You could hear a pin drop in the
room. He [Eisenhower] pounded the table a few times for emphasis,
and everyone in the room realized both the seriousness of the situation and the President's arguments."[30]

When Ridgway's term expired in the summer of 1955 he was not
reappointed. Instead, Eisenhower turned to Maxwell Taylor, with
equally disappointing results. Taylor, a gifted linguist who had commanded the 101st Airborne in World War II and later Eighth Army
in Korea, was considered a serious military thinker and an officer of
keen intellect. Before sending Taylor's name to the Senate, Eisenhower extracted from him a firm commitment to support the New
Look and the nuclear strategy upon which it was based. "Loyalty in
spirit as well as in letter is necessary," he told Taylor.[31]

Like Ridgway, Taylor was soon off the reservation, arguing that
the United States should abandon massive retaliation and the New
Look in favor of what he called Flexible Response. Much to Eisenhower's consternation, Taylor argued that a future war between the
United States and the Soviet Union could be fought with conventional weapons. "That's fatuous," Eisenhower told Radford and Wilson. In Ike's view, any war with Russia would be a nuclear war and
in all probability that was why there was not going to be one. When
Taylor persisted and suggested that the next war would be a limited
one similar to Korea, Eisenhower rejected the idea. "Anything of
Korean proportions would be one for the use of atomics," said the
president.[32]

Taylor served as Army chief of staff for four years. After stepping down in 1959, he continued to press the doctrine of Flexible Response.[33] Academic circles joined the debate. Henry Kissinger established his reputation as a foreign policy expert with the publication of *Nuclear Weapons and Foreign Policy* in 1957—an unrelenting critique of Eisenhower's New Look strategy.[34] In the partisan days of the late 1950s, the Democrats adopted the concept of Flexible Response. John Kennedy anchored his campaign for president on a pledge to jettison the doctrine of massive retaliation. When he was elected, Kennedy undertook an accelerated program to enhance America's conventional war capabilities. Maxwell Taylor was recalled from retirement to advise the president (and was later appointed chairman of the Joint Chiefs), and Army ground forces, particularly special forces, enjoyed a renewed emphasis.

Critics of the Kennedy-Johnson administration and of the subsequent U.S. involvement in Vietnam often fault Kennedy's revival of America's limited war capability. By having the troops available to intervene incrementally, it was easier for the president to intervene incrementally. As Secretary of State Madeleine Albright put it (in a different context), "What's the point of having this superb military if we can't use it?"[35] That was the antithesis of Eisenhower's position. For Ike, war was not a policy alternative. The purpose of military power was to avoid war, not fight one. Soldiers were not paper cutouts, and combat was not a board game.

Eisenhower's emphasis on the New Look and nuclear weapons preserved the peace during the Cold War. But it spawned a variety of side effects, some benign and beneficial, others downright pernicious. Among the pernicious was the arms race that led to the development of thermonuclear weapons, intercontinental ballistic missiles, and the spiral in defense spending that Ike had hoped to avoid. The possibility of mutual assured annihilation scarcely made for restful sleeping. On the other hand, Eisenhower's emphasis on nuclear technology fostered significant scientific and educational advances. Research and development became an integral part of the federal budget. Under Ike, the government funded not only applied research, but generously supported pure research in a variety of scientific disciplines. And to do so, Eisenhower often had to beat down the opposition of Charles Wilson and George Humphrey. "Between the year I entered office and the year I left," wrote Ike, "the federal appropriations for medical research at the National Institutes of Health multiplied nearly ten times, going from $59 million to $560 million [$4.1 billion currently]."[36]

After the Soviets successfully launched the world's first man-made satellite (*Sputnik*) in 1957, Eisenhower created the position of a full-time science adviser to the president, and appointed Dr. James Killian, the president of the Massachusetts Institute of Technology, to the post. Under Killian's direction, the White House established the President's Science Advisory Committee (PSAC), which provided Eisenhower a direct avenue for independent advice from the nation's scientific community. Beginning in 1955, Eisenhower had pressed Congress to provide federal aid to the states for school construction—an unprecedented breakthrough in the relationship between the federal government and the states. The legislation lay dormant for two years on Capitol Hill, but in the aftermath of the Sputnik program, Congress enacted the National Defense Education Act of 1958, providing significant federal aid to education, particularly in the funding of graduate fellowships and improved public school instruction in science, mathematics, and foreign languages. The act followed closely Eisenhower's recommendations in his message to Congress in late January 1957.[37] Ike sold the measure to a reluctant Congress as an emergency measure in the face of Soviet scientific achievements, and the breakthrough in federal funding for education has changed the face of the American educational system.

The Republicans lost control of both the House and the Senate in 1954. In the midterm elections, the Democrats picked up twenty-one House seats and one in the Senate. That gave the Democrats a comfortable (232–203) majority in the House, and a narrow two-vote margin in the Senate with Wayne Morse of Oregon, still an independent, now voting with the Democrats.[38] For Eisenhower, who would face Democratic congressional majorities for his remaining six years in office, it was a blessing in disguise. The Democrats supported Ike down the line in foreign affairs, had little interest in returning to the era of Calvin Coolidge domestically, and were not clamoring to investigate the executive branch.

In the House, Sam Rayburn took up the reins once more as

Speaker, and Lyndon Johnson became Senate majority leader. Rayburn, a bachelor from Bonham, Texas, was a man of few words. But he ruled the House with a discipline rarely seen since the days of "Czar" Joseph Cannon.* He had first been elected Speaker in 1940 following the death of William Bankhead, and was the undisputed leader of House Democrats. In the Senate, Lyndon Johnson, at forty-six, became the youngest majority leader in Senate history, and as Robert Caro explains, was soon the *Master of the Senate.*[39] With Eisenhower in the White House, Sam Rayburn as Speaker, and Lyndon Johnson as majority leader, the country was in the hands of skilled professionals. Ike, LBJ, and "Mr. Sam" did not trust one another completely and they did not see eye to eye on every issue, but they understood one another and had no difficulty working together. Eisenhower continued to meet regularly with the Republican leadership. But his weekly sessions with Rayburn and Johnson, usually in the evening over drinks, were far more productive.[40]

For Johnson and Rayburn, it was shrewd politics to cooperate with Ike. Eisenhower was wildly popular in the country, and his foreign policy was essentially a recognition of America's new role in world affairs. By supporting a Republican president against the Old Guard of his own party, the Democrats hoped to share Ike's popularity. "Eisenhower was so popular," Johnson explained, "whoever was supporting him would be on the popular side."[41]

For Rayburn, it was personal as well. Eisenhower had been born in Denison, Texas, which was in Mr. Sam's district. Rayburn had known Ike for years, and he liked him. "He was a wonderful baby," the Speaker would say with a grin.[42] Rayburn not only admired Eisenhower's wartime leadership, but appreciated his truthfulness whenever he had testified before Congress. The Speaker admired

---

* As a young fellow growing up in Washington, D.C., I frequently held summer jobs on Capitol Hill. Often when work was over, I would go into the visitor's gallery overlooking the House chamber and watch the proceedings. I still remember Speaker Rayburn's command of those proceedings. On occasion he would ask for the yeas and nays. Sometimes the nays would be shouted far louder than the ayes. That did not bother Mr. Sam. The gavel would come down and Rayburn would announce that the ayes had it (or whatever outcome he desired). He was rarely challenged.

truthfulness. He also respected Eisenhower's judgment on national security. "I told President Eisenhower . . . that he should know more about what it took to defend this country than practically anyone and that if he would send up a budget for the amount he thought was necessary to put the country in a position to defend ourselves against attack, I would promise to deliver 95 percent of the Democratic votes in the House."[43] On domestic issues, Rayburn said the Democrats would not oppose just for the sake of opposing. "Any jackass can kick a barn down. But it takes a good carpenter to build one."[44]

Eisenhower, for his part, had often found the Republican leadership testy. Taft had been difficult, and William Knowland was but a slight improvement. In the House, Speaker (later minority leader) Joe Martin and party whip Charles Halleck were scarcely on speaking terms. The GOP majority in the Eighty-third Congress seemed less interested in grappling with the problems of the day than in repudiating the work of Truman and Roosevelt. In the Senate, conservative Republicans had introduced no less than 107 constitutional amendments designed to repeal the New Deal. Several sought to annul the decision at Appomattox by asserting the supremacy of the states over the federal government, while one would have abolished the separation of church and state by inserting the following words in the Constitution: "This nation devoutly recognizes the authority and law of Jesus Christ, Savior and Ruler of Nations through whom are bestowed the blessings of Almighty God."[45] Later in his presidency, Eisenhower found himself so frustrated with the Republican leadership in Congress that he told his secretary Ann Whitman, "I don't know why anyone should be a member of the Republican Party."[46]

With Rayburn and Johnson in charge, Ike's relations with the Hill were much easier. "Speaker Rayburn and I had long maintained friendly contact," Eisenhower recalled. "For many years prior to my inauguration he had called me 'Captain Ike.' "[47] Eisenhower was also on friendly terms with Johnson, and kept a vigil on LBJ's health. Whenever Johnson was in the hospital, Ike was sure to be at his bedside. "I don't see any reason why these people shouldn't be my friends," Eisenhower once told an inquiring reporter. "They have been my friends in the past."[48]

Two of the most significant public works projects in American history—the interstate highway system and the St. Lawrence Seaway—are products of the Eisenhower years. The St. Lawrence Seaway, which opened the Great Lakes to ocean traffic, had been on the drawing board for many years, but it was Eisenhower who got behind it and marshaled the necessary votes to push it through Congress. From the time of Theodore Roosevelt, American presidents had advocated building the seaway, but had been thwarted by the powerful lobbying efforts mounted by American railroads, East and Gulf coast port authorities, coal mine operators in Pennsylvania and West Virginia, and the United Mine Workers, led by the truculent John L. Lewis, all of whom believed they would suffer if the seaway were built. Eisenhower, who believed the project was essential for national security, and who feared the Canadians would go ahead regardless of American participation, stepped out in front of the effort. "It was the only major issue on which my brother and I ever disagreed," said Milton Eisenhower, then president of Penn State.[49]

With Ike's vigorous backing, the measure was passed by the Senate in January 1954, and by the House in May. The vote crossed party lines. In the Senate, a bipartisan coalition of twenty-five Democrats and twenty-five Republicans voted in favor. In the House, the vote was 230–158, with each party also divided. Without Eisenhower's support, the measure would never have been reported out of committee. Ike signed the bill into law on May 13, 1954, and the St. Lawrence Seaway, linking the Gulf of St. Lawrence with Lake Superior, became a reality. "This marks the legislative culmination of an effort that has taken 30 years," said the president.[50] On June 26, 1959, the seaway was officially opened by Eisenhower and Queen Elizabeth II with a short cruise aboard the royal yacht *Britannia*. Since its completion, the seaway has averaged fifty million metric tons of shipping annually, and provides an easy means for the bulk shipping of American grains and minerals from the Midwest to ports abroad.[*]

---

[*] The St. Lawrence Seaway runs from the Gulf of St. Lawrence to Duluth, Minnesota, on the western shore of Lake Superior, a total of 2,275 miles. More than two thousand ships traverse the seaway annually, with the trip from Lake Superior to the Atlantic averaging eight to ten days.

Eisenhower and Queen Elizabeth II at the opening of the St. Lawrence Seaway in Montreal, June 26, 1959.

Eisenhower is personally responsible for the interstate highway system—the largest public works project ever attempted. In the aftermath of the Korean War, defense spending slowed and the nation's economy headed south. The danger signs were evident as early as February 1954. At a cabinet meeting on February 5, Eisenhower stressed the need to develop a public works program so that if needed it could be put into effect immediately. "If we don't move rapidly, we could be in serious trouble," said the president.[51]

Eisenhower favored a highway program. In 1919, Ike had been one of six officers to lead the Army's first transcontinental motor convoy across largely unpaved roads and makeshift bridges from Washington to San Francisco, and he understood from firsthand experience the need for a network of national highways. During the

---

Critics of the seaway were not entirely wrong as to its adverse effect on eastern cities. Buffalo, New York, which had been the eastern terminus for Great Lakes shipping before the seaway, was the fifteenth largest city in the United States in 1950. In 2010, it ranks forty-fifth and its population has declined by half.

war, Eisenhower witnessed the effectiveness of the German auto-bahns.[52]

By the summer of 1954 it was clear that an economic crisis was at hand. Unemployment rose, and a recession seemed just around the corner. Needing to act, and to act quickly, Eisenhower summoned his old friend Lucius Clay to Washington—the only time during his eight years in the White House that Ike turned to Clay. "We had lunch," Clay recalled, "and he asked me if I would head a committee to recommend what should be done. He felt that a highway program was very important. That was the genesis of the President's Advisory Committee on a National Highway Program."

Following his lunch with Eisenhower, Clay put together a five-man high-level committee stacked to recommend a national highway system: Stephen Bechtel of the Bechtel Corporation; William Roberts, head of Allis-Chalmers; Samuel Sloan Colt, president of Bankers Trust; and Dave Beck, president of the Teamsters Union. All had a vested interest. "That's why I picked them," said Clay. "They knew what the highway system was all about."

> It was evident we needed better highways. We needed them for safety, to accommodate more automobiles. We needed them for defense purposes, if that should ever be necessary. And we needed them for the economy. Not just as a public works measure, but for future growth. It was also evident that these new and better highways should be so connected to provide routes from somewhere to somewhere. Therefore, the interstate concept. This idea was already well developed within the old Bureau of Public Roads, and we built on that.[53]

The Clay committee rendered its report to Eisenhower on January 12, 1955. It recommended an expenditure of $101 billion ($823 billion currently) over ten years, and forty-one thousand miles of divided highways linking all U.S. cities with a population of more than fifty thousand. Not only was it the largest public works project ever proposed, but when completed it would provide the United

States with a highway net superior to that in any country, including Germany. Eisenhower, who had followed the work of the Clay committee closely, signed on immediately—with one exception. Clay had recommended the system be funded initially by a $25 billion federal bond issue at 3 percent interest. Ike said he preferred a toll road system. Clay demurred. Toll roads, he told Eisenhower, would work in the heavily populated sections of the East and West coasts, but were not feasible in the remainder of the country. "We have taken the position that a toll road is luxury transportation and is all right in sections of the country where the public have alternative roads to travel. [But] where the interstate highway system is the only road we do not think it should be tolled."[54] Eisenhower accepted Clay's explanation, and on February 22, 1955, sent the National Highway Program to Congress. "Our unity as a nation is sustained by free communication of thought and by easy transportation of people and goods," said the president. "The nation's highway system is a gigantic enterprise. One in every seven Americans gains his livelihood and supports his family out of it. But, in large part, the network is inadequate for the nation's growing needs." Eisenhower asked for speedy approval of the measure.[55]

The Federal-Aid Highway Act sailed through the Senate in May, but lost in the House 123–292. The Democratic majority objected to the bond issue and wanted the money for the interstates to come directly from the Treasury. When the second session of the Eighty-fourth Congress convened in January, a compromise had been reached. Rather than paying for the interstates through a bond issue, or by direct federal expenditures, the federal government would levy a gasoline tax of 4¢ per gallon, the money designated for a highway trust fund. Eisenhower was satisfied the measure would not be a charge on the Treasury, and the Democrats were content with user taxes. The revised measure passed both houses easily, and Eisenhower signed the bill into law on June 29, 1956. Today, the interstate highway system, officially the "Dwight D. Eisenhower National System of Interstate and Defense Highways," stretches 46,876 miles, and contains 55,512 bridges and 14,756 interchanges. The Highway Trust Fund, funded originally by a 4¢ per gallon levy, is now supported by the federal fuel tax of 18.4¢ per gallon, of which 2.86¢ is earmarked for mass transit. Total revenue from the tax exceeds $40 billion annually.

Eisenhower was a fiscal conservative. He believed in a balanced budget, worked hard to attain it, and eventually succeeded.[*] But he was not a movement ideologue and had no interest in dismantling the national government. Federal action, he once said, was sometimes required to "floor over the pit of personal disaster in our complex modern society."[56] The interstate highway system and the St. Lawrence Seaway are enduring examples of Eisenhower's belief in a positive role for government. Less well known is his expansion of Social Security in 1954 to provide coverage for an additional ten million self-employed farmers, doctors, lawyers, dentists, and others; his decision to increase benefits 16 percent for those already enrolled; his raising the minimum wage by a third (from 75¢ to $1 an hour),[†] his decision to provide the funds for Salk polio vaccine for the nation's underprivileged children, and his establishment of the Department of Health, Education, and Welfare. When Ike appointed Oveta Culp Hobby as the first secretary of HEW, he told her he wanted to establish a national system of health care similar to what everyone received in the Army.[57] FDR had made a similar suggestion to Frances Perkins when the Social Security system was on the drawing board in 1935. In both instances the presidential requests fell by the wayside in the day-to-day press of business.[‡]

---

[*] The budget Eisenhower inherited in 1953 showed a deficit of $6.5 billion. That was reduced to $1.2 billion in 1954, and by 1956 the federal budget was $3.9 billion in the black. The arms race plunged the budget back into deficit in 1958, but in 1960, Ike's last year in office, the government ran a surplus of $301 million. Financial Management Service, U.S. Department of the Treasury.

[†] A one-dollar-an-hour minimum wage does not seem like much today. But a dollar in 1955, adjusted for inflation, equals $8.15 currently. Today's minimum wage is only $7.25. In comparative terms, that is 90¢ less than in Ike's day.

[‡] In 1954, the Eisenhower administration introduced a reinsurance plan to backstop private insurance companies against "abnormal loss" if they expanded their coverage to individuals not adequately covered by health insurance. The reinsurance plan, in Ike's view, was a "middle way" between government and private insurance. Despite vigorous administration backing, the plan was opposed by the American Medical Association as the opening wedge to "socialized medicine." On July 13, 1954, it lost in the House of Representatives, 134–238, with 75 Repub-

During Eisenhower's third year in office the nation found itself on the brink of war. Again, it was in the Far East, and again with China. In 1949, when Chiang Kai-shek's Nationalist forces had been driven from the Chinese mainland to Formosa (Taiwan), scattered Nationalist garrisons remained on three offshore island groups: the Tachens, Quemoy, and Matsu. Formosa, roughly 150 miles off the China coast, had been liberated from the Japanese in 1945 by the United States and was an integral part of the American defense perimeter in the Pacific. But the three island groups, much closer to the mainland, were historically a part of China itself and had been under the control of the central government. The Tachens, far to the north, were occupied by fifteen thousand Nationalist troops. The Matsu chain, some nineteen rocky outcroppings less than ten miles from the mainland port of Fuchou, were held by nine thousand of Chiang's soldiers, and the Quemoy group, roughly sixty square miles in area, blocked the port of Xiamen, which was less than two miles away. The Quemoy garrison numbered fifty thousand or so, and was face-to-face with Chinese Communist forces across a few thousand yards of water.

From 1949 to 1954 an uneasy truce had prevailed as the Chinese Communist government consolidated its position on the mainland and Chiang did the same on Formosa. But on September 3, 1954, Communist forces on the mainland launched a sustained artillery barrage against Quemoy, and sporadic shelling continued throughout the fall. "The shelling did not come as a complete surprise," wrote Eisenhower. Chiang Kai-shek had been threatening to attack the mainland "in the not distant future," and Chou En-lai had called for the "liberation of Formosa" in reply. It was almost inevitable that the war of words would escalate. An invasion of Quemoy appeared imminent.[58]

In Washington, the Joint Chiefs of Staff (Ridgway excepted) urged that the United States commit itself to defending the offshore islands and launch air strikes, with tactical nuclear weapons if neces-

---

licans voting no. "The people that voted against this bill just don't understand what are the facts of American life," Eisenhower told his press conference the following day. *Public Papers, 1954* 633.

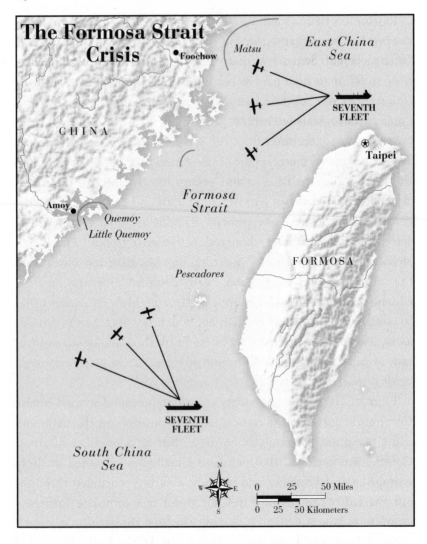

The Formosa Strait Crisis

sary, against the mainland to break up Communist forces assembling there. Eisenhower said no. "We are not talking now about a brush-fire war," Ike told the chiefs. "We're talking about going to the threshold of World War III. If we attack China, we're not going to impose limits on our military actions, as in Korea. [And] if we get into a general war, the logical enemy is Russia, not China, and we'll have to strike there."[59]

Confronted with the possibility of total nuclear war, the Joint

Chiefs cooled their ardor. But on Capitol Hill the "China Lobby" stepped up its demands for the United States to take action on Chiang's behalf. Senator William Knowland, the Republican leader, went so far as to urge preventive war against China and the Soviet Union. "Do you suppose that Knowland would actually carry his thesis to the logical conclusion of presenting a resolution to the Congress aiming at the initiation of such a conflict?" Eisenhower wrote General Gruenther at NATO. "I don't believe this for a second." Knowland's only policy, Ike told Gruenther, was "to develop high blood pressure whenever he says 'Red China.' "[60]

Eisenhower steered a difficult course. On the one hand, he was determined to defend Formosa, and on the other he was equally determined to avoid war with China. The offshore islands were not worth fighting for, but he could not abandon them. Chiang was unwilling to withdraw because of the adverse effect on his Army's morale, but if the Communists wished to take them they could easily do so. Ike was a poker player. It was time to bluff without revealing his hand. China must be made wary of possible U.S. intervention, and Chiang must be restrained from launching any attack against the mainland. "The hard way is to have the courage to be patient," Eisenhower told Senate Republicans.[61]

On January 18, 1955, Communist forces landed on the island of Ichiang, seven miles from the Tachen group, and quickly overwhelmed the defenders. A move on the Tachens—which were two hundred miles from Formosa—appeared inevitable. Eisenhower responded with a two-step. He asked Congress for authorization to defend Formosa and the nearby Pescadores, but suggested that the Tachens be evacuated. Chiang would get a congressional guarantee of American support, but to do so he must relinquish the distant island group. The fate of Quemoy and Matsu was left ambiguous. "I do not suggest that the United States enlarge its defensive obligations beyond Formosa and the Pescadores," Eisenhower told Congress, "but the danger of armed attack directed against that area compels us to take into account closely related localities which, under current conditions, might determine the failure or success of such an attack."[62]

Chiang, who recognized that the Tachens could not be defended without direct American intervention, acquiesced and was rewarded with a mutual defense treaty in which the United States undertook a solemn treaty obligation to defend Formosa and the Pescadores. But the Joint Chiefs initially resisted Ike's strategy. Admiral Carney, the chief of naval operations, argued that because of harbor obstructions evacuating the islands would be more difficult for the Navy than defending them. Eisenhower, with amphibious landings in North Africa, Sicily, and Normandy under his belt, overruled Carney's objection. Admiral Felix Stump, the commander in chief of the Pacific fleet, was ordered to evacuate Nationalist forces from the Tachens, as well as all civilians who wished to leave. Stump was told not to initiate hostilities, but if fired upon he could return fire. One week later the Seventh Fleet successfully evacuated almost fifteen thousand of Chiang's troops and twenty thousand civilians from the Tachens without incident.

On January 29, 1955, the Senate adopted the Formosa resolution Eisenhower had requested, authorizing the president "to employ the armed forces of the United States as he deems necessary for the specific purpose of securing and protecting Formosa and the Pescadores against armed attack." The resolution also gave Ike the discretion to include "such related positions and territories of that area now in friendly hands . . . as he judges to be required or appropriate"—a veiled reference to Quemoy and Matsu without including them explicitly. The vote was 83–3 in the Senate, with Democratic senator Walter George of Georgia, chairman of the Foreign Relations Committee, introducing the resolution on the administration's behalf. In the House, the vote was a lopsided 410–3. In what may seem a curious twist in light of recent history, the opposition in the Senate was mounted by liberal Democrats who argued that the president's inherent powers as commander in chief gave him adequate authority to take action and that the resolution was unnecessary.[63]

With the passage of the Formosa Resolution, Eisenhower had what he wanted. The Chinese Communists were put on notice that the United States would defend Formosa, and the possibility that it might also protect Quemoy and Matsu was left to the president's discretion. In another quid pro quo, Chiang agreed not to attack the mainland without U.S. approval. The situation played out during the spring of 1955. Eisenhower's stance was sufficiently ambiguous to keep the Chinese Communists in check, and the danger that Chiang would upset the apple cart had been eliminated. It was a time of watchful waiting. "Sometimes," Ike told a meeting of legislative leaders on February 16, "I wish those damned little offshore islands would sink."[64]

While both sides held back militarily, the rhetoric escalated. Before his news conference on March 23, press secretary James Hagerty told Eisenhower, "Some of the people in the State Department say that the Formosa Strait situation is so delicate that no matter what question you get on it, you shouldn't say anything at all."

"Don't worry, Jim," Ike replied. "If that question comes up, I'll just confuse them."[65]

Ike was true to his word. Halfway through the president's news conference, Joseph C. Harsch of *The Christian Science Monitor* asked Eisenhower the question the world was waiting for. "If we got into an issue with the Chinese, say over Matsu and Quemoy, that we wanted to keep limited, do you conceive of using this specific kind of [tactical] atomic weapon in that situation or not?"

Eisenhower's answer was a masterpiece of obfuscation.

THE PRESIDENT: Well, Mr. Harsch, I must confess I cannot answer that question in advance.

The only thing I know about war are two things: the most changeable factor in war is human nature in its day-by-day manifestation; but the only unchanging factor in war is human nature.

And the next thing is that every war is going to astonish you in the way it occurred, and in the way it is carried out.

So that for a man to predict, particularly if he has the responsibility for making the decision, to predict what he is going to use, how he is going to do it, would I think exhibit his ignorance of war; that is what I believe.

So I think you just have to wait, and that is the kind of prayerful decision that may some day face a President.

We are trying to establish conditions where he doesn't.[66]

The Chinese evidently deciphered Ike's answer and chose to stand pat. But the Joint Chiefs remained restive. At the end of March, Admiral Carney leaked word to the press alleging that the president and his advisers believed an attack on Quemoy and Matsu was imminent. Eisenhower was furious. Carney was rocking the boat. The last thing Ike wanted was talk of war. The next day, at the president's direction, Hagerty provided his own leak to the White House press corps: "The President did not believe war was upon us." Carney's views were "parochial," said Hagerty, and should not be confused with the facts of the matter.[67]* In his diary, Ike wrote, "I believe hostilities are not so imminent as is indicated by the forebodings of a number of my associates. I have so often been through these periods of strain that I have become accustomed to the fact that most of the calamities that we anticipate really never occur."[68] Several days later, Eisenhower told Sam Rayburn that "the tricky business is to determine whether or not an attack on Quemoy and Matsu, if made, is truly a local operation or a preliminary to a major effort against Formosa."[69]

Eisenhower's cool head defused the crisis. The bellicose rhetoric subsided, the war party in Washington pulled in their horns, and the Chinese flashed an all clear. At the first conference of Asian-African nations meeting at Bandung, Indonesia, on April 23, 1955, Chou En-lai declared the Chinese government was "willing to sit down with the United States government to discuss the question of relaxing tension in the Far East."[70] Eisenhower responded positively. If the Chinese Communists wanted to talk about a cease-fire, the pres-

---

* At his press conference on March 30, 1955, Eisenhower was asked whether Admiral Carney would be reprimanded for his remarks. "Not by me," the president replied—a classic Eisenhower response. Carney's reprimand came from Defense Secretary Wilson, who immediately issued an order directing all military personnel to henceforth submit for clearance all speeches, press releases, and "other information" intended for publication. When Carney's term as CNO expired that summer, he was replaced by Admiral Arleigh "Thirty-one Knot" Burke. (During World War II, Burke mistakenly led his destroyer squadron into a Japanese minefield. Admiral Halsey radioed to ask Burke what he was doing in a Japanese minefield. "Thirty-one knots," Burke replied. Eisenhower advanced Burke over the heads of ninety admirals more senior.) Press conference, March 30, 1955, *Public Papers, 1955* 374.

ident told his news conference on April 27, "we would be glad to meet with them and talk with them."[71]

The shelling of Quemoy and Matsu eased off, and by mid-May it stopped completely. Talks by American and Chinese representatives commenced on August 1, and shortly afterward, the last American prisoners held by the Chinese from the Korean War were quietly released.[72]

Writing about the offshore island crisis years later, Eisenhower summed up the advice he had received. Former British prime minister Clement Attlee had urged him to liquidate Chiang Kai-shek. Anthony Eden advocated neutralizing Quemoy and Matsu. Various Democratic senators had urged the islands be abandoned. Admiral Radford and Senator Knowland wanted to defend the Tachens, blockade the Chinese coast, and bomb the mainland, while Syngman Rhee wanted to launch a "holy war of liberation."[73] Eisenhower charted his own course and emerged from the crisis with almost total victory. War with China had been avoided, Quemoy and Matsu remained in Nationalist hands, and the defense of Formosa was secure.

Congress had given Eisenhower what amounted to a blank check when it adopted the Formosa Resolution, and Ike had delivered. Without excessive saber rattling, he had so confused the Chinese as to whether the United States would use atomic weapons to defend Quemoy and Matsu that they decided not to risk it. Eisenhower's ambiguous public remarks had restored calm to a situation that could easily have triggered World War III. He did not have to use the bomb, he kept the peace, and with the exception of evacuating the Tachens, restored the status quo.

As more than one observer has written, Eisenhower's handling of the Quemoy-Matsu crisis was a tour de force. It was one of the great victories of his career, and the key had been his coolness under pressure—his calculated use of ambiguity and deception. Eisenhower was comfortable wrestling with uncertainty. "The beauty of Eisenhower's policy," wrote historian Robert Divine, "is that to this day no one can be sure whether or not he would have responded militarily to an invasion of the offshore islands, and whether he would have used nuclear weapons."[74] The chances are that Ike himself did not know. As he told Sam Rayburn, the tricky part was to determine what the Chinese were up to. It was a two-way street. The Chinese kept Eisenhower guessing, just as he kept them off balance. One thing stands out: As on D-Day and at Dien Bien Phu, Eisenhower kept the final decision in his own hands.[*]

* In a lengthy letter to General Gruenther, Eisenhower attempted to explain his thought process on the Formosa question.

> We must make a distinction (this is a difficult one) between an attack that has *only* as its objective the capture of an offshore island and one that is *primarily a preliminary movement to an all-out attack on Formosa.* . . . More and more I find myself, in this type of situation—and perhaps it is because of my advancing years—tending to strip each problem down to its simplest possible form. Having gotten the issue well defined in my mind, I try in the next step to determine what answer would best serve the *long term* advantage and welfare of the United States and the free world. I then consider the *immediate problem* and what solution we can get that will best conform to the long term interests of the country and at the same time *can command a sufficient approval in this country so as to secure the necessary Congressional action.*
>
> When I get a problem solved on this rough basis, I merely stick to the *essential* answer and let associates [Dulles? Nixon?] have a field day on words and terminology. . . .
>
> Whatever is now to happen, I know that nothing could be worse than global war.

DDE to Gruenther, February 1, 1955, *The Papers of Dwight David Eisenhower,* vol. 16, *The Presidency* 1539, cited subsequently as 16 *The Presidency.* (Eisenhower's emphasis.)

# TWENTY-FOUR

# Heart Attack

Misfortune, and particularly the misfortune of
illness, brings to all of us an understanding of
how good people are.

—DWIGHT D. EISENHOWER,
*November 11, 1955*

THROUGHOUT THE SPRING and summer of 1955, the thaw in
the Cold War continued. First came an agreement about Austria,
which had been occupied by the Allies since 1945. On April 19, the
Soviet government suggested that the Big Four foreign ministers
(Britain, France, the United States, and the USSR) meet in Vienna
"in the nearest future" to conclude a peace treaty "for the restoration
of an independent, democratic Austria." Eisenhower had said that an
Austrian peace treaty would set an important benchmark in the effort to reduce world tensions, and the new Soviet leadership appeared
willing to cooperate. The quadripartite occupation of Austria ended
on May 15, 1955, with the signing of the Austrian State Treaty.
British, French, American, and Soviet forces withdrew, and the new
Austrian government pledged to remain neutral between East and
West.

The situation in central Europe stabilized further on May 5, 1955,
when the division of Germany was formally accepted. The three
Western powers recognized the Federal Republic, ending the
ten-year occupation. The following day West Germany became a
member of the North Atlantic Treaty Organization. In the East, the

Soviets followed suit. The German Democratic Republic (East Germany) was accorded full sovereignty, and on May 14 in Warsaw the Soviet Union signed a mutual defense treaty with seven nations of Eastern Europe, including the GDR, creating the Warsaw Pact alliance.

Europe was now divided between the member states of NATO and the Warsaw Pact, while Austria, Sweden, Finland, and Switzerland remained neutral. With the boundaries drawn, and the outlines of a modus vivendi taking shape, the time seemed appropriate to dust off Sir Winston Churchill's 1953 suggestion for a Big Four meeting "with a measure of informality and a still greater measure of privacy and seclusion."[1]

Great Britain, France, and the Soviet Union pressed for a summit conference. In Britain, Anthony Eden had succeeded Churchill as prime minister in April and faced a general election at the end of May. Eden believed that the announcement of a meeting of the heads of government would enhance his prestige prior to the election.[2] In France, Edgar Faure, who had been premier of the Fourth Republic since February, shared the view that a summit meeting would redound to his political advantage, and the new Soviet leadership of Marshal Nikolai Bulganin, who had replaced Georgy Malenkov as chairman of the council of ministers, and Nikita Khrushchev, first secretary of the Communist Party of the Soviet Union (CPSU), seemed similarly motivated. In the United States, Dulles and Eisenhower were initially reluctant, but were soon swept up by world opinion, which clamored for a summit. The time seemed ripe to press for a truce in the Cold War. Senator Walter George of Georgia, the influential chairman of the Foreign Relations Committee, added his voice to those urging a meeting, and Eisenhower yielded. "Not wishing to appear senselessly stubborn in my attitude toward a Summit meeting," wrote Ike, "I instructed Secretary Dulles to let it be known through diplomatic channels that if the other powers were genuinely interested in such a meeting we were ready to listen to their reasoning."[3]

On May 8, 1955, the governments of Britain, France, and the United States dispatched identical notes to Moscow suggesting a meeting of the four heads of government "to remove sources of conflict between us."[4] The Soviets accepted one week later, and on June 13 it was announced that the Big Four would meet in Geneva on July 18.

When the meeting was announced, the Republican Old Guard threw a tantrum. Senator Styles Bridges of New Hampshire, evoking images of Munich and Yalta, warned that all international conferences contained seeds of "appeasement, compromise, and weakness."[5] Joe McCarthy, still reeling from the Senate's condemnation, proposed a resolution requiring the president to condition his going to Geneva on Russian agreement to have the conference discuss the satellite nations of Eastern Europe. Senate majority leader Lyndon Johnson sprang to Ike's defense. McCarthy's proposal "placed a loaded gun at the President's head," said LBJ.[6] Johnson immediately recognized the opportunity McCarthy had provided to put the Senate on record supporting Eisenhower and to embarrass the GOP's Old Guard at the same time. With Senator George's cooperation, LBJ kept McCarthy's resolution alive, reported it to the Senate floor with Democratic votes, and let the Republicans squirm. When McCarthy belatedly recognized his error and sought unanimous consent to withdraw his resolution, Johnson objected. The yeas and nays were called, and McCarthy's resolution was defeated 77–4. The vote was a ringing endorsement for Ike and the Geneva summit. Shortly afterward, the president met with congressional leaders to assure them that Geneva would not be another Yalta. No decisions would be made without their approval, said Eisenhower, and there would be no appeasement.[7]

"Personally, I do not expect any spectacular results from the forthcoming 'Big Four' Conference," Ike wrote Swede Hazlett. "Nevertheless, the general world and domestic outlook is better than it was two and a half years ago."[8]

As the date for the conference approached, expectations increased, and Eisenhower was caught up in the spirit. Speaking to a national radio and television audience from the White House less than an hour before his departure for Geneva, Ike said his trip was unprecedented.

> Other Presidents have left the continental limits of our country for the purpose of discharging their duties as

Commander in Chief in time of war, or to participate in conference at the end of a war. But now, for the first time, a President goes to engage in a conference with the heads of other governments in order to prevent wars, in order to see whether in this time of stress and strain we cannot devise measures that will keep from us this terrible scourge that afflicts mankind.[9]

Eisenhower was the last of the Big Four to arrive in Geneva. By a quirk of fate, the Reverend Billy Graham was holding a revival crusade in the city that coincided with the summit. Graham acknowledged that the timing was accidental, although he did not rule out the possibility that Providence may have played a role. Graham told *The New Yorker*'s Richard Rovere that he was much in favor of the summit. "Moses long ago held a parley at the Summit," said Graham, "and had there received a ten-point directive that the heads of government would do well to restudy."[10]

The summit lasted five days.* Little progress was made on the agenda items the Big Four considered—disarmament, European security, and German reunification—but the atmosphere of collegiality provided a refreshing change from the hostile chill that had characterized East-West relations since the imposition of the Berlin blockade in 1948. At Geneva, the Big Four agreed to disagree. As one scholar of the period put it, they implicitly agreed to accept the status quo, and a decision to accept the status quo can be every bit as important, and in certain circumstances, as helpful, as a decision to change things.[11] Anthony Eden said it best when he told Parliament the summit "has given this simple message to the whole world: It has reduced the danger of war."[12] Nikita Khrushchev agreed. "Nei-

---

* Eisenhower insisted that the meeting not be "unduly prolonged." A lengthy meeting, he wrote Eden, "will inevitably lead the public to expect concrete solutions to the specific problems that obviously trouble the world. A meeting of a very few days could logically be accepted by the people as an effort to ease tensions and to outline means and methods of attacking the tough problems we have to face. But a prolonged meeting would lead to expectations which cannot possibly be realized." Eisenhower to Anthony Eden, May 31, 1955, 16 *The Presidency* 1720–21.

ther side wants war," he told the East Germans on his way back to Moscow.[13]

Socially, the delegations mixed easily. Eisenhower held a lengthy private luncheon with his old friend Marshal Zhukov, who had been rescued from the internal exile Stalin had imposed and was now the Soviet minister of defense. In his memoirs, Eisenhower—who had been stung by political criticism of his friendship with Zhukov—was at pains to distance himself from his former comrade, who was "no longer the same man he had been in 1945."[14] But the notes of the luncheon conversation kept by Ambassador Charles Bohlen, who translated for Ike, reveal an animated, wide-ranging two-and-a-half-hour discussion that touched on most issues confronting the two countries. Zhukov insisted the Soviet Union did not want war. Eisenhower said all his experience with Zhukov in Berlin led him to believe his old friend, and he believed him now. Zhukov appealed for détente. Eisenhower replied that fear and distrust flourished on both sides; they were emotions difficult to dispel. And now there was the arms race.[15]

Zhukov suggested that the way to relax tensions would be to curtail the polemic and invective between nations. Ike agreed, but reminded Zhukov that he could not control either Congress or the press. The discussion widened. Ike pressed disarmament. What about inspection to determine the facts? asked the president. Why not? Zhukov responded. And why not reduce the size of the armies? Eisenhower agreed. When Zhukov mentioned the admission of mainland China to the United Nations, and Ike brought up the subject of prisoners of war still held by the Soviet Union, it was clear the conversation had reached its end.

The day after his lunch with Zhukov, Eisenhower stole the spotlight at Geneva when he unveiled his "Open Skies" proposal to throw open the airspace above the United States and the Soviet Union to mutual inspection flights by each country. Ike's proposal was totally unanticipated and caught the world by surprise. But the plan had been carefully crafted by a high-level committee of experts working under Nelson Rockefeller, Ike's special assistant for Cold War strategy, at the Marine base in Quantico, Virginia, just south of Washington. The proposal was then thoroughly vetted at NSC level by

"Pretty Good—How Have Things Been Going With You?"
7/17/1955

Radford, Dulles, Stassen, and Deputy Defense Secretary Robert Anderson, as well as Ike's old friend General Alfred Gruenther and various subcabinet appointees. The administration maintained the utmost secrecy about the plan, but when Ike rose to speak he was scarcely shooting from the hip.

To add drama to the occasion, Eisenhower spoke without notes. "Surprise in presentation I knew might be important," the president observed afterward. Looking directly at the Soviet delegation, Eisenhower said, "I have been searching my heart and mind for something that I could say here that could convince everyone of the great sincerity of the United States in approaching the problem of disarmament." The ornate council chamber of the Palais des Nations (the former home of the League of Nations) was hushed as Eisenhower continued. José-María Serty Badia's massive neo-Baroque murals stared down on the delegates from the walls and ceiling. Outside a torrential rain was falling. Neither Cecil B. DeMille nor Alfred Hitchcock could have devised a more intimidating setting.

Eisenhower told the Soviets that the terrible modern weapons they both possessed posed grave dangers of surprise attack. To minimize that danger, the president suggested that they "give to each other a complete blueprint of our military establishments, from beginning to end, from one end of our countries to the other." The United States was also willing, if the Soviets would reciprocate, to open its skies for aerial photography so that each nation could scrutinize the other to reduce "the possibility of great surprise attack, thus lessening danger and relaxing tension." Eisenhower said that practical progress toward a lasting peace was his fondest hope. "A sound peace—with security, justice, well being, and freedom for the people of the world—*can* be achieved, but only by patiently and thoughtfully following a hard and sure and tested road."[16]

At the precise moment Eisenhower concluded, a tremendous flash of lightning followed by a clap of thunder filled the council chamber. Every light in the building went out. "It was the loudest clap of thunder I have ever heard," said Eisenhower. "For a moment there was stunned silence. Then I remarked that I had not dreamed I was so eloquent as to put the lights out."[17]*

Eisenhower's "Open Skies" proposal captured the world's imagination, even though the Soviets were uninterested. After Stalin's death, the Russian leadership continued to be obsessed with secrecy. Telephone directories and maps were unavailable to most in the Soviet Union, and the Kremlin was not about to introduce an open society. Khrushchev later denounced Eisenhower's proposal as a ploy aimed at penetrating the iron curtain for purposes of espionage.

Elsewhere, Eisenhower was the hero of the hour. "Without being effusive or overreacting," wrote journalist Robert Donovan, "Eisenhower conveyed a sense of decency and dignity which mocked the picture of his country as an immature nation hell-bent for war."

---

* "To this day, the Russians are still trying to figure out how we did it," wrote General Vernon Walters, who served as one of the translators for the American delegation. Vernon A. Walters, *Silent Missions* 289 (Garden City, N.Y.: Doubleday, 1978).

Richard Rovere told readers of *The New Yorker* that "the man has an absolutely unique ability to convince people that he has no talent for duplicity."\* *Le Monde,* then in a robustly anti-American phase, reported that "Eisenhower, whose personality has long been misunderstood, has emerged as the type of leader that humanity needs today."[18] Eisenhower's "Open Skies" proposal was a dramatic moment in the Cold War, and an important attempt to begin the retreat from the danger of a nuclear Armageddon.

The summit concluded on a high note. "This has been an historic meeting," Eisenhower told his departing colleagues. "It is my judgment that the prospects for a lasting peace are brighter. The dangers of the overwhelming tragedy of modern war are less."[19] For Eisenhower, the Geneva summit of 1955 provided a new window through which to view Soviet behavior, much as Ronald Reagan discovered after meeting Mikhail Gorbachev in the Swiss city thirty years later. "There is no doubt in my mind, that in the few days we were there I personally gained insight and understanding that I could never have achieved otherwise," Ike wrote his brother Milton on July 25. "I think, too, that the personal contact—in some cases, the friendships— that were developed there alone made the trip worthwhile."[20]

Eisenhower returned to a rapturous reception. The Gallup poll reported his approval rating at a record 79 percent.[21] James Reston, writing in *The New York Times,* announced that "the popularity of President Eisenhower has got beyond the bounds of reasonable calculation and will have to be put down as a national phenomenon, like baseball. The thing is no longer just a remarkable political fact but a kind of national love affair, which cannot be analyzed satisfac-

---

\* In a 1965 interview, Eisenhower said, "We knew the Soviets wouldn't accept it ["Open Skies"]. We were sure of that." But there is little contemporary evidence to support Ike's assertion. To the contrary, American actions at Geneva indicate they were exceedingly anxious for the Soviets to accept. Also see Eisenhower's letter to General Gruenther, July 25, 1955, in which he extols the possibility of agreement with the Russians. For whatever reason, perhaps because of renewed tension in Berlin or the war in Vietnam, Eisenhower chose to back away from the "Open Skies" proposal. It is another example of Ike's effort to recalibrate history, not unlike his rewriting of his wartime relationship with Kay Summersby. For Eisenhower 's 1965 comments, see Dwight D. Eisenhower, Dulles Oral History, Princeton University. The Gruenther letter is in 16 *The Presidency* 1790–91.

torily by the political scientists and will probably have to be turned over to the head-shrinkers."[22]

Eisenhower worked assiduously to keep the "Spirit of Geneva" alive. "Now that the Four Power Conference has become a part of history," he wrote Bulganin on July 27, "I want you to know how deeply I believe that our combined efforts during the past week produced an effect that will benefit the world. Since last Saturday evening, I have been thinking over your farewell words to me, which were to the effect, 'Things are going to be better; they are going to come out all right.'. . . If we can continue along this line, with earnest efforts to be fair to each other and to achieve understanding of each other's problems, then, eventually, a durable peace based on right and justice will be the monument to the work we have begun."[23]*

The "Spirit of Geneva" seemed to introduce a new, more relaxed phase of the Cold War. From 1948 to the summer of 1955, there were war scares on an almost monthly basis, with major fighting in Korea and Vietnam. For the time being, both sides stepped back from the brink. As British foreign secretary Harold Macmillan put it, the summit had made it clear that "all the great nations who were in the nuclear game now accepted that modern war, that is nuclear war, was quite impossible and could only lead to mutual destruction."[24]

Not everyone was pleased. The thaw in East-West relations was serious enough for J. Edgar Hoover to warn a closed session of a House Appropriations subcommittee that the "Spirit of Geneva" was encouraging American Communists to leave their hiding places and make inroads among naïve fellow citizens. Hoover said that for each of the country's estimated 22,280 Communists, there were ten more Americans being duped.[25]

Following his success at Geneva, Eisenhower found himself

---

* Bulganin replied on August 9, 1955. He agreed with Eisenhower that progress toward peace would be slow. "But the fact that we succeeded in clearing the ground for quests for agreement and in making a beginning toward sincere cooperation is very encouraging. There may be differences in ideological questions, but this must not interfere with our being good neighbors." Bulganin to Eisenhower, August 9, 1955, 16 *The Presidency* 1795n6.

under increasing pressure to announce his candidacy for reelection. With Ike heading the ticket, the GOP would not only retain the White House, but stood a good chance of regaining the House and Senate as well. With anyone other than Ike, the Republicans had no chance whatever. Public opinion polls showed that just about any Democrat could beat just about any Republican except Eisenhower.[26]

As in 1951, the effort to extract a commitment from Ike was led by Lucius Clay. "Clay approached the matter circumspectly and even in roundabout fashion," Eisenhower confided to his diary shortly after the midterm elections. "But when he once got on to the real purpose of his visit, he pursued his usual tactics aimed at overpowering all opposition and settling the matter without further question." Clay told Eisenhower that the recent loss of the House and Senate meant that the Republican party had to be revitalized into an "Eisenhower Republican Party." Although the name troubled him, Ike did not disagree. "The Republican party," he wrote, "must be known as a progressive organization or it is sunk. I believe that so emphatically that I think that far from appeasing or reasoning with the dyed-in-the-wool reactionary fringe, we should completely ignore it and when necessary, repudiate it."[27]

Eisenhower said the Republican party had been led astray by people such as Robert Wood, New Jersey congressman Fred Hartley, "several of our old generals, two of whom are my classmates, Malone, McCarthy, and Bertie McCormick.* The political strength that these people could generate in the United States could not elect a man who was committed to giving away $20 gold pieces to every citizen for every day of the calendar year! But entirely aside from their po-

---

* Robert Wood, the longtime head of Sears, Roebuck, was cochairman of For America, an activist isolationist organization dedicated to keeping the United States free of international commitments. Fred A. Hartley, Jr., was the coauthor of the 1947 Taft-Hartley Act. Eisenhower's classmates were retired generals James Van Fleet and George E. Stratemeyer, both of whom had joined For America. Senators George W. "Molly" Malone (R., Nev.) and Joseph McCarthy (R., Wis.) anchored the right wing of the GOP in the Senate, and Bertie McCormick was Colonel Robert R. McCormick, publisher of the *Chicago Tribune* and with Wood a founder of For America.

litical significance is the fact that their thinking is completely unco-ordinated with the times in which we live."

Eisenhower recognized that Clay was speaking for the group who helped him secure the nomination in 1952.

> Since the men who are associated with Clay both in and out of government are committed to opposing the efforts both of the reactionaries on the one side and the A[mericans for] D[emocratic] A[ction] on the other, it is clear that their efforts would be directed exactly along the lines in which I firmly believe. . . . I tried to make Clay see that what we must all do is to work for this kind of idea. I ad-mitted that it was probably easier to personalize such an effort and therefore to use my name as an adjective in de-scribing it. But I pointed out that if we focused the whole effort on me as an individual, then it would follow that in the event of my disability or death, the whole effort would collapse.
>
> Here is where we parted company. Clay said, "I am ready to work for you at whatever sacrifice to myself be-cause I believe in you. I am not ready to work for anybody else that you can name." He insisted that he did not mean working for me in the personal sense; but he also insisted that he and his friends needed now the assurance that I would not "pull the rug out from under them." This is exactly the phrase they used on me in 1951, and I well know how such a foot in the door can be expanded until someone has taken possession of your whole house.[28]

Eisenhower noted that he was troubled about his age and the need to bring younger men into positions of leadership. The growing com-plexity of the problems the president confronted also bothered him, as did the two-term limit imposed by the Twenty-second Amend-ment. Not that Ike wanted a third term, but the amendment, in his view, made any president a lame duck as soon as his second term began. Eisenhower understood the political advantage he retained by keeping his plans to himself. But he was also genuinely in doubt. Earlier he had written to Milton that if he ever showed signs of wanting a second term, Milton should "call in the psychiatrist—or even better the sheriff."[29]

After meeting with Clay, Eisenhower wrote Swede Hazlett that he was troubled by the Twenty-second Amendment, which Ike thought significantly reduced the influence of a second-term president. "The implication of this is that only the most unusual of circumstances should induce any man to stand a second time for the Presidency."[30]

On July 11, 1955, before Eisenhower's departure for Geneva, fifty-four Republican members of the House issued a formal call urging the president to announce that he would seek reelection. Eisenhower did not reply. Upon his return from Geneva, a delegation of distinguished Republicans from Ohio known as the Bull Elephants Club called on Ike in the White House and presented him with a similar appeal. Eisenhower responded with a rambling, impromptu speech (Ike at his dissembling best) delineating the burdens of the presidency and the need for more young Republicans, but totally avoiding any answer to their request.[31] At his news conference on August 4, Edward Folliard of *The Washington Post* asked the president about his response to the Bull Elephants, and whether the Geneva Big Four meeting had made it more or less likely that he would run in 1956.

Eisenhower, who evidently expected the question, was ready with his answer. "Eddie, if I were such an infallible prophet that I could understand all about the world situation, the domestic situation, and my own situation, including the way I felt, and possibly with the health and everything else, as of that moment, then there would be no great excuse for deferring the decision. I have not that gift of prophecy."[32]

With speculation rife, Eisenhower departed Washington on August 14, 1955, for a lengthy summer vacation in Colorado. Over the next several weeks the president enjoyed the hospitality of Aksel Nielson at his ranch near Fraser, and spent most of his time ensconced in the rambling home of the Douds at 750 Lafayette Street, known to the press as the "Summer White House." A habitual early riser, Ike visited his office at nearby Lowry Air Force Base for an hour or two each morning, and then headed for the golf course at the Cherry Hills Country Club, which was one of his favorites. Friday, September 23, was no exception. Ike was in good spirits. His secretary Ann Whitman noted in her diary, "I have never seen him look or act better."[33] Eisenhower raced through his correspondence and dashed off a quick note to Lyndon Johnson, who had recently suffered a heart attack and was convalescing at his ranch in Texas. "I am delighted to have your encouraging report on your recovery," Ike wrote. "I most earnestly hope that you will not let your natural bent for living life to the hilt make you try to do too much too quickly."[34]

Eisenhower played eighteen holes that morning with the club pro, "Rip" Arnold. The game was interrupted twice by phone calls from Secretary of State Dulles, wanting to discuss matters that Ike thought could have waited. (There were no cell phones in 1955, and Eisenhower had to leave the course and return to the clubhouse to field each call.) Eisenhower was in a foul mood at lunch, wolfed down a hamburger lavishly garnished with raw onions, and decided to play another nine holes with Arnold that afternoon. Again he was interrupted by a phone call from Washington. "At this point his anger was so real that the veins stood out on his forehead like whipcords," an observer noted.[35] The call proved to be a false alarm, no one was calling, and Eisenhower really hit the roof. After eight holes he called it quits, complaining of heartburn, which he attributed to the onions at lunch.[36]

Back at the Doud home, Eisenhower painted for several hours and then was joined for dinner by George Allen and his wife, who were visiting Denver. Ike and Allen passed up their customary predinner drink, and Eisenhower retired about ten o'clock. He was awakened by severe chest pain at about 1:30 a.m., which he again attributed to the onions at lunch. Mamie, who was sleeping in an adjoining bedroom, heard him stirring and asked if he wanted anything. Ike asked for some milk of magnesia, and she found it and gave him a dose. When Mamie turned on the light and looked at her husband, she decided he was seriously ill and immediately called Major General Howard Snyder, the family physician. Snyder, who had accompanied the Eisenhowers to Denver, was staying at the BOQ at Lowry Air Force Base. He arrived at the Doud home a little before 3 a.m.

Dr. Howard McCrum Snyder, seventy-five years old, a career Army doctor, had been Eisenhower's personal physician since 1945. During the war he had treated Mamie at General Marshall's request, and was soon part of the Eisenhowers' personal entourage. Tall, handsome, and energetic, he was a frequent bridge and golfing partner for Ike, and his wife was one of Mamie's canasta regulars. Snyder had accompanied Eisenhower to Columbia, then to NATO, and, like General Gruenther, had become one of Ike's closest friends. When Eisenhower was elected president, Snyder was appointed the personal physician to the president. Dr. Snyder was a surgeon by training, had served on various military posts during the interwar years, and did a stint as the War Department's deputy inspector general. He was devoted to the Eisenhowers, but his medical skills were rusty: "an old-time general practitioner," as one military associate put it.[37] In 1954, Lucius Clay, speaking on behalf of Gang members Cliff Roberts, Bill Robinson, and himself, urged Ike to employ a younger, more proficient presidential physician, but Eisenhower would not consider it.[38] As the president wrote to the Army's adjutant general on Snyder's 1955 efficiency report, "His [Snyder's] devotion to me and to our family is selfless and complete. I hope he continues in his present post for the remainder of my time here."[39]*

When Dr. Snyder examined Eisenhower, he concluded that Ike was suffering from acute indigestion and treated him accordingly. An 8 a.m. press release from the president's office at Lowry announced that Eisenhower had suffered a "digestive upset" during the night, that Dr. Snyder was with him, that the president was still in bed, and that he would not be coming into the office until much later in the day.[40] At 12:15 p.m. that Saturday, deputy White House press secretary Murray Snyder, who handled the press chores in Den-

* Eisenhower's relationship with Dr. Snyder was not unlike that of FDR's with Admiral Ross McIntire, who was Roosevelt's White House physician. Like Snyder, McIntire was a friend of the family and a poker-playing crony of the president. He was an ear, nose, and throat specialist and had been engaged originally because of FDR's chronic respiratory problems. But he had no training in cardiology, and allowed Roosevelt's hypertension to go for years without treatment. Like many physicians at the time, McIntire believed older people needed higher blood pressure to move their blood through narrowing arteries. In both cases. FDR and Eisenhower were poorly served by their doctor friends. Jean Edward Smith, *FDR* 602–6.

ver, met with reporters in the conference room at Lowry and issued the following statement: "I just talked with General Snyder and he tells me that the president is resting. He said that this indigestion is not serious and he says that it is the same type of indigestion that many people have had. It is not serious. He [Eisenhower] is resting in bed now, and I am not going to predict how long it will take him to shake it off."[41]

There was no cover-up. Dr. Snyder genuinely believed that Ike was suffering from indigestion.* Not until roughly 1:15 p.m. did Snyder realize that Eisenhower's symptoms more closely resembled those of someone suffering a heart attack rather than a digestive upset. At that point, he called Fitzsimmons Army Hospital to order an electrocardiogram. The equipment was brought to the Doud home by Dr. Byron Pollock, chief of cardiology at Fitzsimmons, and General Martin Griffin, the hospital commander, dressed (at Snyder's request) in civilian clothes. "At 2:00 p.m.," according to the report filed by James Rowley, the chief of Eisenhower's Secret Service detail, "they announced the cardiograph disclosed a coronary thrombosis condition and they all concluded it would be best to move the president to the hospital where all the necessary equipment was available."[42]

Eisenhower was placed in an oxygen tent at Fitzsimmons, the appropriate medication was administered, and Dr. Paul Dudley White of Massachusetts General, the nation's preeminent heart specialist, assumed responsibility for the president's care. White met the press almost immediately after examining Ike and briefed them completely on his condition. "Tell them everything," Ike instructed him. White noted that coronary thrombosis was "the commonest impor-

---

* The only cover-up was Dr. Snyder's subsequent attempt to conceal the fact that he had misdiagnosed the president. Most early biographers, as well as the Eisenhower family, accepted Dr. Snyder's version of events: namely, that he recognized from the start that Ike had suffered a heart attack and treated him accordingly. Many heart specialists familiar with Eisenhower's case were skeptical of Dr. Snyder's statement, but the full record was not revealed until Professor Clarence G. Lasby of the University of Texas published *Eisenhower's Heart Attack* in 1997. Professor Lasby provides convincing evidence that Dr. Snyder erred in his initial diagnosis, and details Snyder's subsequent attempt to conceal the fact. See especially pages 57–112.

tant illness that besets a middle-age man in this country today." He told reporters that Eisenhower had suffered a "moderate" heart attack—"not a mild one, not a severe one, but something in between." The president was still seriously ill, said White, but there was good reason to believe that he could make a complete recovery.[43] That Eisenhower survived the twelve-hour hiatus between the initial attack and the first accurate diagnosis was a testament to his remarkable constitution. At sixty-four, Ike weighed 172 pounds, only seven pounds more than when he graduated from West Point. His blood pressure was a reasonable 140/80 and his pulse averaged sixty beats per minute. He exercised daily and spent hours out of doors on the golf course. He had the willpower of an ox. And he continued to be just plain lucky. "Divine Destiny," George Patton had often called him, and on September 24, 1955, Eisenhower's luck ran true to form.

If Eisenhower had to have a heart attack, September 1955 was a good time to have one. Congress was in recess, the Geneva Big Four meeting had already taken place, there were no urgent foreign or domestic matters that required his personal attention, and the 1956 election campaign had not begun. On Monday, September 26, the New York Stock Exchange took its worst plunge since the Great Depression, but the encouraging words of Dr. White soon set things straight. In Washington, Vice President Nixon presided over routine meetings of the cabinet and the National Security Council, while John Foster Dulles, as the ranking cabinet officer, handled major policy issues. Sherman Adams and James Hagerty moved their offices to Denver, Attorney General Brownell ruled that no delegation of authority was required, and Ike's cabinet officers continued to run their departments as if nothing had happened. Nixon, for his part, studiously avoided any attempt to assume command in Eisenhower's absence. "The policies and programs of the administration as determined and approved by the President are well established along definite lines and are well known," said a White House press release on September 30. "Coordination of the activities of the several departments . . . will be continued by the full cooperation among the responsible officers of those departments so that the functions of the

Ike at Fitzsimmons Army Hospital in Denver, October 14, 1955.

government will be carried forward in an effective manner during the absence of the President."[44]

In Denver, Eisenhower's recovery moved forward without complication. On October 14, 1955, Ike's sixty-fifth birthday, he was photographed in a wheelchair on the hospital roof looking tanned and healthy. On his shirt pocket, the words MUCH BETTER THANKS had been embroidered. With matters running smoothly in Washington, Eisenhower ruled out any return until he could walk into the White House without assistance. If cabinet officers needed guidance, they flew to Denver, and Adams carried Eisenhower's wishes back to Washington each Friday.

On Veterans Day, November 11, 1955, Eisenhower and his doctors felt he was sufficiently recovered to return. "I leave with my heart unusually filled with gratefulness," the president told the assembled staff at Fitzsimmons. "Misfortune, and particularly the misfortune of illness, brings to all of us an understanding of how good people are."[45]

In Washington, a crowd of five thousand well-wishers greeted the president at National Airport. "The doctors have given me at least a parole if not a pardon," Ike told the happy onlookers. "I expect to be back at my accustomed duties, although they say I must ease into them and not bulldoze my way into them."[46] After a long weekend in the White House, Eisenhower and Mamie drove to Gettysburg for another period of rest and recuperation. He presided over the occasional cabinet meeting at Camp David, and returned to Washington just before Christmas.

As he recovered, Eisenhower fretted about the 1956 election. If the doctors had doubts about his health, the issue would be settled. He would not run. But if they gave him something approaching a clean bill of health, then he would have to decide whether to seek reelection. The Republican convention was scheduled to meet in San Francisco in August, and sooner or later he would have to announce his intentions. As in 1951, Eisenhower was undecided. But he also relished the uncertainty that made him the center of attention, and the longer he could hold off making an announcement, the greater was his clout in the White House. This was particularly important if he should choose not to run again.

Aside from his health, Eisenhower's principal concern was his successor. If he stepped down, who would take his place? The landscape looked barren. In the Republican party, Earl Warren was the most obvious choice, but it was unlikely that he would resign his post as chief justice. Eisenhower was also skeptical of Warren's ability to make crisp decisions. The former governor, in Ike's view, preferred to wrestle with decisions far too long. Richard Nixon was too inexperienced, and Senator William Knowland was "impossible." Both wanted the job, but neither was presidential timber. Eisenhower thought that either Governor Dewey or Herbert Brownell could handle the responsibility, but they were anathema to Republicans in the Midwest and would split the party. Neither could be elected. Treasury Secretary George Humphrey would make an excellent president, and so would Ike's brother Milton, but neither could get the nomination. The same was true of Alfred Gruenther and Lucius Clay.

On the Democratic side the outlook was even bleaker. This was not a partisan judgment. Eisenhower respected Johnson and Rayburn, as well as Governor Frank Lausche of Ohio, and a number of Democrats in the Senate. But none could win the nomination. It was the three Democratic front-runners that bothered Ike most. Adlai Stevenson, Averell Harriman, and Tennessee senator Estes Kefauver simply "did not have the competency to run the office of President." The ill will between Eisenhower and Stevenson was palpable, Kefauver with his coonskin hat was a bad joke, and Harriman was nothing but a "Park Avenue Truman." "I don't want to run, but I may have to," Eisenhower told James Hagerty in early December.[47]

It was shortly after Ike's conversation with Hagerty that Leonard Hall, who had succeeded Arthur Summerfield as chairman of the Republican party, visited Eisenhower in Gettysburg to discuss the nomination. "I chatted with him," Hall recalled, "and he was really low—the way most men are after they have heart attacks."

> Finally I said, "Chief, the Cabinet members have all been up here to see you, and when asked by the newspaper men whether they talked any politics with the president, they were able to say no. If I go out of here and say I haven't talked politics with you, they'll call me a damned liar."
>
> "Len," Eisenhower replied, "you go out and say what you think you should say."
>
> That was the way he operated. Ike was a fellow who could delegate. He would give you tremendous leeway. He wanted you to take the initiative.
>
> So I went out and said to the press that the ticket was going to be Ike and Dick. George Allen told me later that he was with the president when my statement came over the ticker. He said Ike grinned and said, "Dammit, I didn't tell Len to say that." But that was the way Ike worked.[48]

Clay met Eisenhower in Gettysburg the following day. Hall's statement to the press was all he needed. Clay told Eisenhower that he would soon be meeting with various Republican leaders and that he intended to tell them that the president planned to run again, providing his health permitted. "I gave him the opportunity to call me off," said Clay, "but he didn't. So I set the meetings up."[49] First at the Links Club on East Sixty-second Street in New York, then at Attorney General Brownell's home in Washington, Clay assembled the Eisenhower loyalists from 1952. Like a trusted deputy, he spread the word that Ike was running and brought the troops into line.

Eisenhower still made no public statement. That, too, was typical. If he decided not to run, Clay and Hall could be disowned and no damage would be done. On the other hand, if he was running, it would be useful for them to prepare the way. In early February 1956, Eisenhower checked into Walter Reed Army Medical Center in Washington for what amounted to a final physical. Afterward, Dr. Paul Dudley White announced, "Medically the chances are that the President should be able to carry on an active life satisfactorily for another five to ten years." The way was clear for Eisenhower to run. If he did, White said he would vote for him.[50]

Eisenhower continued to keep his own counsel. From Walter Reed he went to George Humphrey's Georgia plantation for two weeks of quail hunting, golf, and fishing. He pushed himself physically, played eighteen holes of golf on two occasions, and tromped through the woods like a veteran hunter. But he still made no announcement about his future plans. The word was out through Clay and Hall that Ike was running, but Eisenhower had not confirmed it.

On February 25, 1956, the president returned to the White House. Three days later he called Clay in New York. "Please come down here for dinner tonight and spend the night with us," said Eisenhower.

"I knew that when he called up personally that something was involved," Clay recalled. "So I said, 'Of course, except we cannot spend the night.'" Clay and his wife, Marjorie, were expected in Houston, Texas, later that evening.

So we went down to the White House, and we had dinner. And after dinner we went up to the family quarters. And he said he was going to make a decision that night as to whether he was going to run again. He said he had waited until his health was all right, and he was satisfied that there were no immediate health problems.

He said, "I can't get Mamie to express herself."

She said, "No, I certainly am not going to say one word. It is your decision. If you don't do it and are unhappy because you didn't do it, it's got to be your unhappiness. If you do it and it breaks your health down, that has to be your decision too."

Finally, he said, "OK. I have to do it. I'll run again. I'm going to run again."

Then we went downstairs and saw a movie. He didn't call me down [to Washington] to help participate in his decision. He had already made his mind up. Because of my closeness to him and the part I had played in his first nomination, he wanted to give me the privilege of being there and knowing what he was going to do before he announced it.[51]

The following day, February 29, 1956, President Eisenhower told a special news conference that he intended to run. "I have reached a decision," he told the press. "If the Republican National Convention asks me to run, my answer will be positive, that is, affirmative."

"How many persons were in on your secret?" asked Edward Folliard of *The Washington Post*.

"Well, since last evening there have probably been a half dozen," Eisenhower replied.

"How about before that, Mr. President?"

"Well, there could have been no one because I didn't know myself."[52]

Eisenhower was peppered at his news conference with questions about his running mate. Would Nixon be on the ticket? Eisenhower declined to answer. "I believe it is traditional that the Vice President is not nominated until after a presidential candidate is nominated; so I think that we will have to wait to see who the Republican Convention nominates [for president]."

CHARLES VON FREMD (CBS): Mr. President, I just wonder if you could clarify that further. Should you be nominated by the convention, would you like to have the Vice President?

THE PRESIDENT: I will say nothing more about it. I have said that my admiration and my respect for Vice President Nixon is unbounded. He has been for me a loyal and dedicated associate, and a successful one. I am very fond of him, but I am going to say no more about it.[53]

Eisenhower's reluctance to endorse Nixon was scarcely a vote of confidence. Earlier he had suggested to Nixon that he might be better off to accept a cabinet post (anything except secretary of state or attorney general), where he could acquire some administrative experience. "The subject came up at five or six of our private conversations," Nixon recalled, "and I always gave the same answer: 'If you believe your own candidacy and your Administration would be better served with me off the ticket, you tell me what you want me to do and I'll do it. I want to do what is best for you.' "

According to Nixon, Eisenhower never faced up to the issue. "He always answered somewhat obliquely saying, 'No, I think we've got to do what's best for you.' "[54] Sherman Adams and James Hagerty urged Ike to dump Nixon—Adams believed the vice president would cost Eisenhower three or four percentage points—and so, too, did his friends in the Gang. But Eisenhower declined to ask Nixon to step down. Better than most perhaps, Eisenhower recognized that Nixon was his principal link to the Republican Old Guard, and he hesitated to sever that connection. And if it were a matter of retaining that tie, he much preferred Nixon as his go-between rather than William Knowland and the other GOP oligarchs on Capitol Hill.[55]

Eisenhower was genuinely conflicted. He would not endorse Nixon, but he would not ask him to step down. The choice was Nixon's. "He has his own way to make," Ike told Jim Hagerty in March. "But there is nothing to be gained politically by ditching him."[56] On the other hand, Eisenhower doubted Nixon's capacity to govern. "I've watched Dick a long time," the president told former speechwriter Emmet Hughes, "and he just hasn't grown. So I just haven't honestly been able to believe that he is presidential timber."[57]

At his press conference on April 25, 1956, Eisenhower was reminded that he had said Nixon must chart his own course. "Had he done this?" asked William Lawrence of *The New York Times.*

"Well," Eisenhower replied, "he hasn't reported back in the terms in which I used the expression . . . no."[58]

That was Nixon's opening. He asked for an appointment with the president the following day. "I would be honored to continue as Vice President under you," he told Eisenhower. "The only reason I waited this long to tell you was that I didn't want to do anything that would make you think I was trying to force my way onto the ticket if you didn't want me."[59] Eisenhower said he was pleased. He called Hagerty and said, "Dick has just told me, he'll stay on the ticket. Why don't you take him out right now and let him tell the reporters himself. And you can tell them that I'm delighted with the news."[60]

# TWENTY-FIVE

# Suez

Foster, you tell them, Goddamnit, that we're
going to apply sanctions, we're going to the
United Nations, we're going to do everything
that there is so we can stop this thing.
— EISENHOWER TO JOHN FOSTER DULLES,
*October 29, 1956*

AS THE DOMESTIC CALDRON BUBBLED, the political situation in the Middle East deteriorated. The armistice that ended Israel's victorious war in 1948 had not been followed by a peace treaty, and the new Egyptian regime, headed since 1954 by Colonel Gamal Abdel Nasser, did nothing to halt the raids by Palestinian Arab guerrillas into Israel from the Egyptian-held Gaza Strip. An Israeli ship, sent to test whether Egypt would allow Israel's commercial vessels passage through the Suez Canal, had been seized by the Egyptians. Allen Dulles warned the National Security Council on March 8, 1956, that "Arab-Israeli hostilities could break out without further warning."[1]

In his diary that evening, Eisenhower lamented his failure to bring the two sides together. "Of course, there can be no change in our basic position, which is that we must be friends with both contestants in that region in order that we can bring them closer together. To take sides could do nothing but to destroy our influence in leading toward a peaceful settlement of one of the most explosive situations in the world today.["2]* With American support, Britain attempted to establish an alliance of Arab states, the "Baghdad Pact," which was designed to impede Soviet penetration of the Middle East. But Nasser balked at joining the pact, which he saw as an effort to perpetuate Western colonialism. Instead, he sought to put Egypt in the forefront of the effort to create a global "third force" that would be independent of the two Cold War blocs.

The Arab-Israeli dispute, which was complicated enough, was exacerbated by the rise of anticolonialism in the region, the decline of British and French power, the growing influence of the Soviet Union, and Western Europe's need for oil—all of which conspired to make an intractable problem all the more intractable. In 1950, the United States, Britain, and France issued the Tripartite Declaration pledging to enforce the existing boundaries between Israel and its neighbors, and agreeing not to supply any state in the region with arms that might be used for offensive purposes.[3] The declaration was hortatory and left the signatories considerable wiggle room. France discovered Israel to be a natural ally against Arab nationalist movements in Algeria, Morocco, and Tunisia, and soon undertook to provide a wide array of weaponry for the Israeli armed forces. Britain, for its part, was stung when Egyptian Army officers overthrew King Farouk in 1952, denounced the 1936 Anglo-Egyptian Treaty of Friendship and Alliance, and ordered British forces out of the country. The governments of Churchill and Eden also saw Israel as an ally against the rising tide of Arab nationalism and quietly began to provide arms for the Israelis. Only the United States held fast to the strict letter of the

---

* Eisenhower was keenly aware of the strategic importance of the Arab states, but he was also mindful of the moral claims of the Jewish people to their newly re-created homeland. In his diary, Ike observed: "The oil of the Arab world has grown increasingly important to all of Europe. The economy of European countries would collapse if those oil supplies were cut off. If the economy of Europe would collapse, the United States would be in a situation of which the difficulty could scarcely be exaggerated. On the other hand, Israel, a tiny country, surrounded by enemies, is nevertheless one we had recognized—and on top of this, that has a very strong position in the heart and emotions of the Western world because of the tragic suffering of the Jews throughout twenty-five hundred years of history." DDE diary, March 13, 1956, *16 The Presidency*, 2668–70.

declaration, and for the most part ignored the growing tension along Israel's frontiers.

On February 28, 1955, an Israeli commando raid into Gaza resulted in heavy Egyptian casualties, and was condemned unanimously by the UN Security Council. Egypt responded with a counterstrike, triggering a wave of raids and reprisals. President Nasser had been assured by the United States and Great Britain that "everything would remain quiet in the region."[4] An American envoy was dispatched to the area and shuttled between Jerusalem and Cairo for two months, failing to calm tensions. With the frontier ablaze, Nasser appealed to the United States for weapons. Egypt was short of everything, said U.S. ambassador Henry Byroade. Her Air Force had only six serviceable planes, tank ammunition would last for only an hour of battle, 60 percent of her tanks were in need of major repairs, and her artillery was in a similar deplorable state.[5] When Eisenhower saw Nasser's request, he was astonished. "Why, this is peanuts," he told Dulles.[6] But no action was taken. The administration hesitated to stir up pro-Zionist sentiment in Congress, and officials at the State and the Defense departments dragged their feet by insisting that Egypt pay for the weapons in cash, contrary to the military aid the United States provided to most nations.[7]

When the weapons negotiations with the United States broke down, Nasser turned to the Soviet Union. Washington officials, from Secretary of State Dulles down, believed Nasser was bluffing and that in any event the Russians had no surplus arms to give him. Even when Nasser told U.S. authorities that he preferred American weapons to those the Soviets would provide, Washington turned a deaf ear. When the truth finally dawned at the State Department that Nasser was indeed serious, Dulles dispatched Kermit Roosevelt to Cairo to dissuade him. Roosevelt, the CIA head in the Middle East who had masterminded the coup in Iran, was a personal friend of Nasser's, but by then it was too late. The deal with the Soviets had been struck. Asked by Nasser how he could soften the blow, Roosevelt suggested half-humorously that he might call it a Czech deal. "Say you are dealing with Prague"—which Nasser did. On September 27, 1955, three days after Eisenhower suffered his heart attack in

Denver, Nasser formally announced the acquisition of Soviet arms from Czechoslovakia. The equipment was estimated to be worth between $90 and $200 million, far more than the $27 million Nasser had requested from the United States. In Washington, Dulles conceded that it was "difficult to be critical" of Egypt for seeking the weapons, which "they sincerely need for defense."[8] When Israel asked the United States for arms to offset those Egypt would receive from the Soviet Union, Eisenhower declined, fearing it would only contribute to the arms race in the Middle East.[9]

Nasser's weapons deal with the Soviet Union caught Washington by surprise. An even greater surprise arrived several days later as rumors spread that the Russians had offered to finance and build the massive Aswan High Dam on the Nile. The Aswan High Dam was an enormous engineering project—U.S. undersecretary of state Herbert Hoover, Jr., called it "the largest single project yet undertaken anywhere in the world"—designed to store and distribute the waters of the Nile for the irrigation of new farmland and provide electric power for industrialization. Feasibility studies undertaken by the World Bank in 1953 and 1954 indicated that the dam was both technologically feasible and within the economic capacity of Egypt to construct, assuming reasonable outside financing arrangements.[10] Confronted with the Soviet offer, Nasser immediately informed Washington that Egypt would much prefer to deal with the United States and the World Bank rather than the Russians.

With Eisenhower recuperating in Denver, Dulles took the lead in shaping the American response. Nasser's desire for Western aid provided an opportunity to close the door on Soviet influence in Cairo, and Dulles quickly signed on. Meeting in Geneva, Dulles and British foreign secretary Harold Macmillan agreed to assist in the construction of the Aswan Dam in return for Egypt's cooperation in arriving at an Arab-Israeli settlement.[11] Quadripartite negotiations involving Great Britain, the United States, the World Bank, and Egypt commenced in Washington on November 21, 1955, and by that time Eisenhower was back in control. "Is there any reason not to go all out for the dam in Egypt?" he asked Dulles.[12]

At the meeting of the National Security Council on December 1, the first one presided over by the president since his heart attack, Eisenhower jettisoned the agenda in order to discuss the Aswan Dam. The case for American support was presented by Dulles and Undersecretary Hoover. Treasury Secretary George Humphrey opposed. The United States was simply "building up a socialized economy in Egypt for all the world to look at." Eisenhower rejected Humphrey's advice. The only way the United States had been able to build the Hoover Dam, the president reminded him, had been "through the instrumentality of the Government and Government financing." Dulles added that implicit in the plan was Egyptian cooperation in reaching an understanding with Israel. The minutes of the meeting noted specifically that the program had "the president's approval."[13]

The Western financial package for the first phase of construction of the Aswan Dam was formalized on December 16, 1955. The World Bank would lend Egypt $200 million, the United States and Great Britain would provide cash grants of $56 million and $14 million, respectively, and would consider later grants of up to $200 million as the work progressed. Total cost of the dam was estimated at $1.3 billion, the balance of which would be handled by Egypt spread over fifteen to eighteen years.

Eugene Black, president of the World Bank, carried the proposal to Cairo for Nasser's approval. "Don't act like a banker," Dulles chided him.[14] By mid-February, Black had reached substantial agreement with Nasser on most points, only to find that American support for the project was fast eroding. Continued skirmishing along the Israeli-Egyptian border made it evident that peace was unlikely to be achieved, and Zionist opposition to the dam had become manifest. As Sherman Adams put it, "Any attempt to give aid to the Arabs always met with opposition behind the scenes in Washington, where members of Congress were acutely aware of the . . . many well-organized pro-Israel lobbies that were always effective and influential in the Capitol."[15] In addition, Truman Democrats who would normally have supported the administration in foreign policy backed off because of Nasser's arms deal with the Soviets, while cotton-state Democrats worried that newly irrigated farmland in the fertile Nile Valley would flood the market with long-staple cotton in competition with American growers.[16]*

As opposition grew, Dulles began to question the wisdom of the proposal. The British were backing off as well,† and Nasser was becoming increasingly influential as a leader of neutralist sentiment throughout the world—along with India's Nehru and Marshal Tito of Yugoslavia. For Dulles, neutralism was heresy in the holy war against Communism. On May 16, 1956, when Nasser recognized mainland China, he moved beyond the pale. As one of Dulles's biographers has written, in the secretary's pantheon of devils, "the Red Chinese represented perhaps the highest and purest evil."[17] For Dulles and many at State, Defense, and in the intelligence community, Nasser was now in the enemy camp. The fact that both Great Britain and Israel had previously recognized the Communist regime in Beijing made no difference.

Eisenhower was more tolerant. At his press conference the week after Nasser's action, the president noted that he was disappointed, "but a single act on the part of another nation does not, in itself, destroy friendship for that nation."

"It's just like your family," Ike told the reporters. "Every difference or spat doesn't mean you're going to the divorce courts. In the same way here, you can't take any one idea or any one act on the part of another government and say, 'That's the end; that's that.' "[18]

Two weeks later the president explicitly accepted neutralism as a viable policy for many countries. Speaking to the press on the twelfth anniversary of D-Day, Eisenhower said, "If you are waging peace, you can't be too particular about the special attitudes that different coun-

---

* Not only did Walter George of Georgia, who was chairman of the Senate Foreign Relations Committee, come from the deep South, but of the twelve Democrats on the Appropriations Committee, ten were from cotton-growing states. *Congressional Directory*, 84th Cong., 1st sess., 207 (Washington, D.C.: Government Printing Office, 1955).

† On March 1, 1956, King Hussein abruptly dismissed Sir John Bagot Glubb (Glubb Pasha) as commander of the famed Arab Legion in Jordan, a move the British (incorrectly) attributed to Nasser. "The world is not big enough to hold both me and Nasser," Anthony Eden was quoted as saying. Anthony Nutting, *No End of a Lesson: The Story of Suez* 18 (New York: Clarkson N. Potter, 1967).

tries take. We were a young country once, and our whole policy for the first 150 years was, we were neutral. We constantly asserted we were neutral in the wars of the world." The United States, he said, should not assume that neutral nations do not deserve assistance. "We must not be parsimonious. . . . As long as we are not shooting, we are not spending one-tenth as much as we would if we were."[19]

The difference between Eisenhower and his secretary of state was evident. When the president's press conference remarks came over the wire, Dulles rushed to the White House to urge Ike to issue a clarification. Eisenhower did so, but his four-paragraph clarification, a genuine fog of words, clarified only that he and Dulles were miles apart on neutralism and how to deal with it.[20]

Two days later Eisenhower suffered a massive ileitis attack requiring major surgery that kept him out of action for the next five weeks. Shortly after midnight on June 8, 1956, Eisenhower suffered what appeared to be a digestive upset. These were not infrequent, and initially Dr. Snyder saw no cause for alarm. But when the pain did not subside, it was clear the president was far sicker than originally thought. Snyder called it "chronic ileitis."[21] At noon, Eisenhower was rushed to Walter Reed and by evening doctors concluded the president had an "obstruction of the intestine in the terminal ileum."* He was operated on at 2 a.m. on June 9, and surgeons pronounced the procedure a success. Eisenhower's life expectancy might even have been enhanced, the doctors said, because they corrected an intestinal condition that had existed for years.[22]

The operation was conducted without incident. But recovery was far more difficult for Eisenhower than his recuperation from the heart attack nine months earlier. Four weeks later he was still wearing a surgical drainage tube and his mood was morose. Ann Whitman described the president as uncomfortable and depressed, unable to concentrate on the issues at hand. Nixon said Eisenhower "looked far worse than he had in 1955. The ileitis was not half as serious [as

---

* On May 10, 1956, less than a month before, Eisenhower underwent a complete physical at Walter Reed, and X-rays revealed "several constricted areas in the terminal ileum." Dr. Snyder chose not to inform Eisenhower because he thought it would cause the president "unnecessary anxiety." No remedial surgery was suggested. "DDE's Ileitis Operation," Snyder Papers, EL.

the heart attack], but he suffered more pain over a longer period of time."[23] The slowness of the president's recovery was never revealed to the public, but for the next four weeks Eisenhower was effectively out of the loop. Meetings with staff members were minimal, and as one scholar has put it, "Foster Dulles was left to his own devices."[24]

Without Eisenhower's restraining hand, Dulles moved discreetly to scuttle the financing for the Aswan Dam. On June 20, Nasser met with Eugene Black in Cairo and resolved all outstanding differences. Black returned to Washington and reported to Dulles on June 25. Everything was set, said Black, and Nasser still preferred to deal with the West rather than the Russians. Dulles was uninterested. When Black cautioned the secretary, "If you call it off I think all hell will break loose," Dulles rose from his seat and walked out of the room, terminating the conversation.[25]

At this point Dulles began to prepare the public for the cancellation of the Aswan project. On July 9, *The New York Times,* reflecting a leak from the top, reported that the State Department was "fundamentally re-examining United States relations with Egypt," including the Aswan Dam.[26] Henry Byroade, who was one of Nasser's most consistent supporters in the State Department, was eased out as American ambassador in Cairo, and congressional leaders were quietly informed that the Aswan Dam was no longer a priority for the administration.

Eisenhower was on the sidelines. Not until five days after Ike's surgery did Dulles travel to Gettysburg for his first substantive conversation with the president. The meeting was short, with numerous items on the agenda, and the Aswan Dam was briefly alluded to at the conclusion. Dulles said simply that the State Department's view of the merits of the matter "had somewhat altered" and let it go at that. Eisenhower did not respond. "For Eisenhower, this discussion of Aswan must have sounded like something happening on another planet," said one biographer. "He had no up-to-date information and did not seek any."[27]

One week later the die was cast. Following a twenty-minute pro forma meeting of the National Security Council on July 19, the first chaired by Ike since his operation, Dulles told the president that relations with Nasser had worsened and that the State Department believed the American offer to support the Aswan Dam should be withdrawn. Eisenhower, who had not followed the developments, did not object. Dulles showed the president a draft statement he intended to release. Eisenhower read it cursorily and nodded his approval.[28] Four hours later Dulles briskly informed Egypt's ambassador in Washington that the United States no longer found the Aswan Dam economically feasible. It was canceling its offer of support.[29]* One week later, on July 26, 1956, Nasser announced that Egypt was nationalizing the Suez Canal. "The fat was in the fire," Eisenhower wrote later in his memoirs.[30]

The cancellation of the Aswan Dam was the greatest diplomatic debacle of the Eisenhower era, and the West was totally unprepared to respond to Nasser's action.[†] Britain and France feverishly organized military forces to retake the canal, and Dulles was away from Washington attending conferences in Latin America. Eisenhower, who was still recovering from his operation, was thrust back into command. It was a blessing in disguise. With the president back on the bridge, the American ship of state resumed its steady course. Ike refused to panic. What authority did Nasser have to seize the canal? he asked Herbert Brownell. "The entire length of the Canal lay within Egyptian territory," the attorney general answered.[31] It was a matter of eminent domain. From that point on, Eisenhower's policy was clear. "Egypt was within its rights," he told Dulles, "and until

* The Soviets followed through on their offer to build the Aswan Dam. The money was provided in 1958, and construction began in 1960. The dam was designed by the Soviet Hydroproject Institute in Moscow, and employed more than twenty-five thousand Egyptian engineers and workers. It was completed on July 21, 1970, and the reservoir, Lake Nasser, reached capacity in 1976. The Aswan Dam is 4,189 yards long, 1,072 yards wide at its base, and 365 feet tall. Lake Nasser, which was formed by the dam, is 342 miles long, 22 miles wide, and holds nearly 90 million acre-feet of water. Irrigation from the Aswan Dam increased Egypt's arable land by 500 percent, and when opened, the dam produced half of Egypt's electricity.

† Maurice Couve de Murville, the veteran diplomat who was France's ambassador in Washington, and who had served two years in Cairo, explicitly warned the State Department several days earlier that if the United States reneged on financing the Aswan Dam, Nasser would most likely seize the Suez Canal. His warning was ignored by Dulles. Herman Finer, *Dulles over Suez: The Theory and Practice of His Diplomacy* 47 (Chicago: Quadrangle Books, 1964).

its operation of the Canal proves incompetent, there is nothing to do."[32]*

Eisenhower immediately wrote Prime Minister Anthony Eden to emphasize "the unwisdom *even of contemplating* the use of military force at the moment."[33] When Britain and France persisted with plans to intervene, Dulles, the Joint Chiefs, and the congressional leadership, particularly Lyndon Johnson, argued that America's allies deserved moral and economic support. Eisenhower rejected the argument. When Dulles suggested an international consortium to operate the canal, Eisenhower would have no part of it. "How would we like an international consortium running the Panama Canal?" asked the president.[34] Admiral Arleigh Burke said the Joint Chiefs agreed that "Nasser must be broken." Eisenhower disagreed. "Nasser embodies the emotional demands of the people of the area for independence and for 'slapping the White Man down.' " Unless we were careful, said the president, Muslim solidarity could "array the world from Dakar to the Philippine Islands against us."[35]

Eisenhower was back to working seven days a week. He had temporarily averted war over Suez, the British and French stood down, and the Republican National Convention was due to convene at the Cow Palace in San Francisco on August 20, 1956. The Democrats, meeting in Chicago, had renominated Adlai Stevenson for president, and Estes Kefauver had secured the vice presidential nomination after a bruising floor fight with Senator John F. Kennedy. The Republican convention held no surprises. Eisenhower was renominated by acclamation on the first ballot, as was Nixon. A brief boomlet led by Harold Stassen to replace the vice president with Congressman

---

* The Suez Canal, conceived and constructed under the direction of Ferdinand de Lesseps, was opened to traffic on November 17, 1869. (Giuseppe Verdi wrote the opera *Aida* to commemorate the opening.) One hundred and one miles long and two hundred feet wide at its narrowest point, the canal was owned by the Compagnie Universelle du Canal Maritime de Suez, a private stock company. Of the company's 32 directors, 16 were French, 9 British, 5 Egyptian, 1 Dutch, and 1 American. The British government held 44 percent of the stock, another 44 percent was held by assorted French institutions, and the balance was held by individuals of various nationalities. In 1955, 14,666 ships passed through the canal, of which roughly one-third were British. Most of those were oil tankers. Two-thirds of Britain's crude oil imports passed through the canal. Lyon, *Eisenhower* 693.

Eisenhower and Mamie at the farm in Gettysburg.

Christian A. Herter of Massachusetts collapsed when Leonard Hall made it clear that such a move would disrupt party unity.[36] In his acceptance speech, which critics believe was one of Eisenhower's best, Ike did not mention Suez or the crisis in the Middle East. "The Republican Party is the Party of the Future," said Ike, "because it is the party through which many of the things that still need doing will soonest be done."[37]

The autumn of 1956 was the lull before the storm. Eisenhower took a leaf from Grant's book in 1872 and campaigned sparingly. (Grant did not campaign at all.) Except for intensified cross-border skirmishing, the Middle East remained calm, and Eden took pains to assure Ike that Great Britain preferred a negotiated settlement concerning Suez. In reality, Britain, France, and Israel were organizing to retake the canal by force. On October 24, 1956, at Sèvres, outside Paris, Israeli prime minister David Ben-Gurion signed a secret protocol with Britain and France putting the plan in motion. Israeli troops would invade the Sinai Peninsula on October 29 and advance toward the Suez Canal. Britain and France would issue an ultimatum to Israel and Egypt to cease hostilities and accept Anglo-French occupation of the Canal Zone. Egypt presumably would refuse, at which point Britain and France would launch their own invasion of

Suez. With American voters going to the polls on November 6, planners in London, Paris, and Tel Aviv assumed the American government could not respond until after the seizure of the canal was a fait accompli.

When the Israelis struck on October 29, Eisenhower was campaigning in Richmond, Virginia. Ike felt he had been betrayed by Eden and was furious. To compound the problem, American intelligence had failed to anticipate the Israeli attack. The president flew back to Washington and angrily ordered Dulles to fire off a message to Tel Aviv. "Foster, you tell them, Goddamnit, that we're going to apply sanctions, we're going to the United Nations, we're going to do everything that there is so we can stop this thing."[38] At a hastily convened meeting in the Oval Office, Ike reminded those present that the 1950 Tripartite Declaration pledged the signatories to "support any victim of aggression in the Middle East." When Dulles suggested that the British and French believed we had to support them, Ike hit the ceiling. "What would they think if we were to go in to aid Egypt to fulfill our pledge?" he asked angrily. "Nothing justifies double-crossing us. I don't care whether I'm re-elected or not. We must make good on our word, otherwise we are a nation without honor."[39]

A good night's sleep did nothing to improve Ike's temper. "The French and British do not have adequate cause for war," he told Dulles and Sherman Adams the next morning. "Egyptian action in nationalizing the Canal is not enough to justify this."[40] At Eisenhower's direction, Henry Cabot Lodge introduced a motion in the UN Security Council calling for an immediate cease-fire and the withdrawal of Israeli forces. When the vote was taken that afternoon, Britain and France cast vetoes—their first in the history of the United Nations. A follow-on Soviet motion to the same effect was also vetoed. The British and French vetoes upset Ike. Later that afternoon, when Defense Mobilization Director Arthur Flemming warned Eisenhower that the Israeli attack imperiled Western Europe's oil supply, the president barked back that "those who began this operation should be left to work out their own oil problems—to boil in their own oil." The United States would not provide assistance.[41] Lodge was instructed to appeal the cease-fire resolution to the UN

General Assembly—a procedure that had not been used since the beginning of the Korean War in 1950—and Treasury Secretary George Humphrey was told to look at the financial implications of the invasion for Britain and France. "This cost of war was not irrelevant," said Eisenhower.[42]

On October 30, as planned, Britain and France issued ultimatums to Egypt and Israel to stop fighting, withdraw from the canal, and permit Anglo-French occupation of the Canal Zone to ensure canal traffic would not be interrupted. If they did not, Britain and France would take the canal by force. Dulles told Eisenhower the ultimatums were "about as crude and brutal as anything he had ever seen."[43] The Israelis announced their readiness to comply, the Egyptians ignored the ultimatums, and twelve hours later Britain and French planes commenced attacks on targets in Cairo, Port Said, and Alexandria. *The New York Times* reported sightings of "the largest naval concentration seen in the eastern Mediterranean since World War II."[44] Nasser responded by sinking a 320-foot freighter loaded with cement at the narrowest point of the canal, effectively blocking transit.[45]

On November 1, Admiral Burke ordered the Sixth Fleet in the Mediterranean to stay near the Egyptian coast and be ready for any contingency.

"Who's the enemy?" asked Vice Admiral Charles R. ("Cat") Brown, commanding.

"I don't know," Burke replied. "We are still having that discussion."[46]

Later that afternoon, at Eisenhower's direction, Dulles presented the United States' cease-fire resolution to the UN General Assembly. Dulles also issued a sharply worded statement pertaining to sanctions against Israel if the fighting continued. At the same time, Eisenhower moved quietly to tighten the screws on Britain and France. "You are not going to get a cease-fire by saying everybody please stop," he told Dulles.[47] The administration pigeonholed plans to supply Western Europe with oil in the event supplies from the Middle East were cut off, and the Treasury Department moved to reduce British access to dollar accounts in the United States.[48] The pound sterling was already under siege on world markets, and Eisenhower wanted nothing done to ease the pressure. Also on November

1, Syrian Army engineers destroyed three pumping stations of the pipeline carrying Iraqi oil to the Mediterranean. Those pipelines had a capacity of five hundred thousand barrels a day. With the pipelines shut down, the Suez Canal blocked, and the United States not shipping any oil, Europe's supply of petroleum was dwindling rapidly.

That evening Eisenhower spoke to a Republican rally in Philadelphia's Convention Hall—his final speech of the campaign.

> We cannot and will not condone armed aggression—no matter who the attacker, and no matter who the victim.
>
> We cannot—in the world, any more than in our own nation—subscribe to one law for the weak, another law for the strong; one law for those opposing us, another for those allied with us.

Eisenhower did not mention Britain or France by name, and did not refer to the resolution pending in the General Assembly, but the thrust of his remarks was clear. "We believe humanity must cease preying upon itself. We believe that the power of modern weapons makes war not only perilous—but preposterous—and the only way to win World War III is to prevent it."[49]

Eisenhower did not have wine with dinner that evening on the train back from Philadelphia, but he drank two tall scotches before the meal and three after.[50] The presidential party arrived back in Washington shortly after midnight. Four hours later Dulles reported from New York that the General Assembly had approved the U.S. cease-fire resolution 64–5, with only Australia and New Zealand joining Britain, France, and Israel voting against. Following passage of the resolution, Canada's Lester Pearson proposed that a UN police force be organized and deployed between the combatants to ensure the effectiveness of the cease-fire.*

"Life gets more difficult by the minute," Ike wrote Alfred Gruenther. "I could really use a good bridge game."[51] To Swede Hazlett he wrote,

---

* In 1957, Lester Pearson was awarded the Nobel Peace Prize for his work organizing the peacekeeping UN Emergency Force.

The Middle East is a terrible mess. I think that France and Britain have made a terrible mistake. Of course, nothing in the region would be so difficult to solve except for the underlying cause of the unrest that exists there—that is the Arab-Israel quarrel. This quarrel seems to have no limit. Everybody in the Moslem and Jewish worlds are affected by it. It is so intense that the second any action is taken against one Arab state, all the other Arab and Moslem states seem to regard it as a Jewish plot and react violently.[52]

By the weekend, Israeli troops had taken most of the Sinai Peninsula and the Gaza Strip; the aerial bombardment of Egyptian targets continued, but British and French forces had yet to come ashore. In Washington, Dulles was rushed to Walter Reed for emergency surgery. What doctors initially assumed to be a kidney stone turned out to be a cancerous tumor in the colon. The operation to remove it was successful, but the secretary would be out of action for at least a month.

The fighting in Egypt was upstaged early on Sunday, November 4, when Eisenhower learned that the Soviet Union had intervened with massive military force to snuff out Hungary's brief experiment in democracy.[*] Premier Imre Nagy fled to the Yugoslav embassy, and a new Hungarian government led by János Kádár was installed by the Soviets. Hungarian "freedom fighters" resisted briefly, and asked

---

* Following publication of Nikita Khrushchev's "secret speech" to the Twentieth Party Congress detailing the horrors of the Stalin era, riots in Poland swept out the Soviet-dominated government and installed Wladyslaw Gomulka as premier. Gomulka announced that "there is more than one road to socialism," and warned that the Polish people "would defend themselves with all means." On October 22, 1956, the successful Polish action triggered widespread rioting in Hungary, demanding among other things that Imre Nagy, who had been deposed by the Russians in 1955, be returned to power. Nagy was installed as premier on October 23, and order was briefly restored. The leadership of the Soviet Union apparently was at a loss how to proceed. Initially they announced that Soviet troops would be withdrawn, but evidently had a change of heart. On November 4, two hundred thousand troops of the Red Army supported by four thousand tanks converged on Budapest.

for U.S. support. Over the years, John Foster Dulles, Radio Free Europe, and the Voice of America had repeatedly spoken of liberation, and to many this seemed the time to follow through. Ambassador Clare Boothe Luce cabled Eisenhower directly from Rome. "Ask not for whom the bell tolls in Hungary today," she said. "It tolls for us if freedom's holy light is extinguished in blood and iron over there."[53]

For Eisenhower it was not that simple. The president recognized the precariousness of the situation, the possible escalation of the crisis into nuclear war, and the fact that Hungary was surrounded by Soviet-bloc and neutral nations. It was, as he later phrased it, "as inaccessible as Tibet."[54] When the CIA sought approval to air-drop arms to the Hungarians, Eisenhower said no. "We have never asked for a people to rise up against a ruthless military force," he told his press conference shortly afterward. "We simply insist upon the right of all people to be free to live under governments of their own choosing."[55] Eisenhower dispatched a sharp letter to Bulganin asking that Soviet troops be withdrawn from Hungary, but with the Middle East on fire, chose not to press the issue further.[56]

On Monday, November 5, the British and French armada finally arrived off the Egyptian coast: some two hundred ships including five aircraft carriers, six battleships, a dozen cruisers, and an assortment of lighter craft. What followed was a textbook World War II amphibious landing. Paratroopers jumped before dawn; commandos went ashore at first light, and by noon most of Port Said, at the mouth of the Suez Canal, was in the hands of British and French forces. To minimize damage on shore, Lord Louis Mountbatten, Britain's first sea lord, had restricted the preinvasion bombardment to guns of 4.5 inches or less. Mountbatten had argued strongly in Whitehall against the invasion, and better than the politicians of the Eden government, he knew the enormous destruction that would be caused by the fleet's 15- and 16-inch guns. With the British and French ashore, the issue was now a military problem, and Eisenhower instinctively assumed command. "If we could have for the next two or three days a period of relative calm while your troops did nothing but land," he told Eden, "we might much more swiftly develop a solution that would be acceptable to both sides and to the world."[57]

Ike's solution unfolded quickly. At 10 a.m. the markets in New York opened and the pound came under unprecedented pressure. In 1956, currency exchange rates were fixed, and the British pound was pegged at $2.78. To maintain its value, the British government was forced to liquidate much of its gold and dollar reserves. That afternoon Deputy Prime Minister Rab Butler placed an urgent call to his friend George Humphrey and pleaded for a loan. Humphrey had anticipated the call and was ready with an offer: a $1.5 billion loan with the interest payments deferred. It was available, said Humphrey, as soon as the British ceased firing and withdrew their troops from Suez.[58] Meanwhile in Britain motorists queued at petrol stations and tens of thousands of demonstrators crammed into Trafalgar Square to protest the Suez policy of the Eden government. The British press, without exception, blasted what *The Manchester Guardian* called "Eden's war."

On Monday afternoon the stakes were raised when Soviet premier Nikolai Bulganin fired off messages to Eden, Mollet, and Ben-Gurion announcing that Russia was prepared to use force to restore peace in the Middle East and suggesting the situation might escalate. The use of nuclear weapons was implicit.[59] Bulganin also dispatched a letter to Eisenhower suggesting that the United States and Soviet Union join forces to restore peace and tranquility in the Middle East. "If this war is not stopped," said Bulganin, "it is fraught with danger and can grow into a third world war."[60]

Eisenhower remained calm. He assumed Bulganin's message was most likely an attempt to divert attention from the situation in Hungary, but the United States could take no chances. "Those boys are both furious and scared," he told a meeting of senior officials in the Oval Office. "Just as with Hitler, that makes for the most dangerous possible state of mind. And we better be damn sure that every Intelligence point and every outpost of our armed forces is absolutely right on their toes. . . . If those fellows start something, we may have to hit them—and, if necessary, with *everything* in the bucket."[61] Eisenhower instructed Allen Dulles to send U-2 reconnaissance flights over Syria and Israel, but not over Russia. If the U-2s discovered Soviet planes at Syrian air bases, that would create a serious problem. But Ike thought the Russians were bluffing. "Look at the map," he told those present.[62]

Rather than answer Bulganin's letter, Eisenhower chose to issue a White House press release, a more effective way, in his view, of making his point without threatening the Soviet leader directly. It was "unthinkable" that the United States join military forces with the Soviets in Egypt, said the White House. Moreover, "Neither the Soviet or any other military forces should now enter the Middle East area except under United Nations mandate." If they did, the United States would "oppose any such effort." The message was a clear warning to the Russians to stay out.

Tuesday, November 6, 1956, was election day. At 9 a.m. Eisenhower and Mamie drove to Gettysburg to vote, and then returned to Washington by helicopter. They arrived about noon. Ike was informed that the U-2s had found no evidence of Russian planes in Syria, nor were any moving into Egypt. But the best was yet to come. At 12:30 Washington time, Eden announced that Great Britain was ready to accept a cease-fire.

American financial pressure had done the trick. On Tuesday morning the British government had requested the International Monetary Fund to make available the dollar funds the British had on deposit. The U.S. Treasury Department, as was its prerogative under IMF rules, blocked the transfer. At that point, Harold Macmillan, who was now chancellor of the exchequer, told an emergency meeting of the British cabinet that he could "not any more be responsible for Her Majesty's exchequer" unless a cease-fire was ordered. Eden had no choice.[*]

When he learned of the decision of the British cabinet, Eisenhower placed an immediate call to Eden.

---

[*] In their post-Suez memoirs, numerous British officials indicated that they thought the U.S. government had engineered the run on the pound in New York. Harold Macmillan explicitly accused the New York Federal Reserve of selling pounds at a rate that was "far above what was necessary to protect the value of their holdings." Macmillan, *Riding the Storm* 163–64; Diane B. Kunz, *The Economic Diplomacy of the Suez Crisis* 131–33 (Chapel Hill: University of North Carolina Press, 1991). Also see *Full Circle: The Memoirs of Anthony Eden* 623 (Boston: Houghton Mifflin, 1960).

"Anthony," said Ike, "I can't tell you how pleased we are that you found it possible to accept the cease-fire."

"We are going to cease firing tonight," Eden replied.

"Without conditions?" asked the president.

"We cease firing tonight at midnight unless attacked."

Eisenhower pressed Eden to withdraw quickly. Eden was evasive. Perhaps the British would remain as part of the peacekeeping force, or to help clear the canal. Eisenhower—who still held the trump hand—rejected the idea. "I would like to see none of the great nations in it," he replied. "I am afraid the Red boy is going to demand the lion's share. I would rather make it no troops from the big five"—a reference to the five permanent members of the UN Security Council.[63]

When Eden continued to evade a commitment, Eisenhower got tough. "If you don't get out of Port Said tomorrow, I'll cause a run on the pound and drive it down to zero," said Ike.[64] Eden capitulated. France followed suit. Israel did not agree to withdraw until the following day, and did not complete the movement until January 1957, after receiving American assurance of its right of free passage through the Gulf of Aqaba. Eden stepped down as prime minister and was succeeded by Harold Macmillan. Guy Mollet survived for another seven months, and in Israel the war was viewed as a success. The state had demonstrated its military prowess, and henceforth would be a power to be reckoned with.

In the closing days of the campaign, Governor Stevenson, Eleanor Roosevelt, and former president Truman excoriated Eisenhower for turning his back on Israel and America's allies. Their criticism may have ensured that most of the Jewish vote remained in the Democratic column.[65] But at a time of international crisis, the overwhelming majority of Americans preferred to keep Eisenhower in the White House. When the votes were tabulated on election night, Eisenhower swamped Stevenson 35 million to 26 million—the largest presidential majority since FDR routed Alf Landon in 1936. Ike carried forty-one states to Stevenson's seven.*

---

* Stevenson carried six states in the Deep South, plus Missouri. His majority in Missouri was a minuscule 3,984 out of almost 2 million votes cast (50.1 percent to 49.9 percent). *Congressional Quarterly's Guide to U.S. Elections* 295.

# TWENTY-SIX

# Little Rock

A most interesting subject for detailed study
would be Eisenhower's role in connection with
the segregation storm in the South, his part in
bringing about that storm, in subtly promoting
its increased violence, and in steering it towards
the ultimate objective of his Communist bosses
who planned the whole thing far in advance.

— ROBERT WELCH,
FOUNDER, THE JOHN BIRCH SOCIETY

NEVER IN THE POSTWAR ERA was American prestige higher
than in the aftermath of Suez. Small nations could scarcely believe
the United States would support Egypt, a Third World country, in a
fight against two of America's oldest allies, or that it would come to
the aid of a Muslim state resisting Israeli aggression. "Never has
there been such a tremendous acclaim for the President's policy,"
Henry Cabot Lodge reported from the United Nations. "It has been
absolutely spectacular."[1]

More than any Western statesman, Eisenhower recognized that
the age of imperial rule had passed. Both at Dien Bien Phu and during the Suez crisis he urged his European allies to bury the corpse of
colonialism and move on. In his memoirs, Eisenhower wrote that the
three weeks of the Suez affair were "the most demanding three weeks
of my entire presidency."[2] In the midst of a contentious election campaign, Ike had reined in his wartime partners in the face of fierce

Democratic criticism; deterred the Soviets from intervening during the Suez crisis; avoided needless provocation at the time of the Hungarian uprising; and preserved the peace. Any misstep could have triggered a chain of events leading to nuclear war. Throughout these crises Eisenhower had exercised personal control. American policy was not set in the State Department or the Department of Defense or by White House assistants, but by the president himself. Even more than on D-Day or at the time of the Battle of the Bulge, Eisenhower assumed direct command.

Domestically, Eisenhower's record was no less impressive. By 1956 he had balanced the federal budget, and when unemployment rose and recession threatened in the aftermath of the Korean War, he had nipped it in the bud with the interstate highway program—the mother of all stimulus programs. But the most serious domestic challenge Ike faced—and the most intractable—was the question of civil rights and equality for African Americans.

The Fourteenth Amendment to the Constitution, adopted after the Civil War, states unequivocally, "No State shall . . . deny to any person within its jurisdiction the equal protection of the laws." So long as Grant was president, and federal troops remained in the South, the amendment was enforced, and former slaves were guaranteed equality, particularly the right to vote. But after the disputed election of Rutherford B. Hayes in 1876, the United States Army was withdrawn from the South (part of a quid pro quo in which Democrats agreed not to challenge Hayes's election), and from that point on African Americans suffered systematic discrimination at the hands of a white southern society that, like the Bourbons of France after the revolution, had "learned nothing and forgotten nothing."

The first casualty was the right to vote. Southern states adopted literacy tests, the poll tax, and property qualifications (all with "grandfather clauses" insulating poor whites) that stripped blacks from the voting rolls.* When that was insufficient, violence and in-

---

* The term "grandfather clause" arises out of the Black Codes enacted after Reconstruction. A would-be voter had to prove he could read and write, "unless his grandfather had voted." Since the grandfathers of African Americans had been slaves, they had not voted and so the literacy requirement was applied to them. It was assumed that the grandfathers of white folks had voted and so they were ex-

timidation followed. Lynchings became commonplace. The resulting all-white legislatures enacted Black Codes—codes of laws
pertaining to African Americans—that legalized racial segregation.
The constitutionality of these "Jim Crow" statutes was open to question, given the equal protection clause of the Fourteenth Amendment.[*] The issue reached the U.S. Supreme Court in 1896 in the
landmark case of *Plessy v. Ferguson,* testing the legality of a Louisiana
law requiring blacks and whites to ride in separate railroad coaches.[3]
This was an era when reconciliation with the white South was at the
top of the nation's agenda, and the Supreme Court, by a vote of 7–1,
upheld racial segregation as constitutionally permissible. The equal
protection clause, said the court, required equality; it did not mandate a "commingling" of the races. "If one race be inferior to the
other socially, the Constitution of the United States cannot put them
on the same plane." The resulting doctrine, known as "separate but
equal," became the law of the land for the next fifty-eight years. The
United States was a racially segregated society, and the Supreme
Court had given that segregation a constitutional blessing.[4][†] "Sepa-

---

empt. Not until 1915 were grandfather clauses intended to keep blacks from voting declared unconstitutional. *Guinn v. United States,* 238 U.S. 347 (1915).

[*] The term "Jim Crow" derives from a pre–Civil War minstrel song sung by
Thomas D. "Daddy" Rice, a white actor in blackface. Rice ended every performance with his trademark song and dance:

> Wheel about and turn about and do just so. Ev'vy time I wheel about
> I jump Jim Crow.

By the late 1830s, "Jim Crow" had become a pejorative term to describe African Americans.

[†] The lone dissenter in *Plessy v. Ferguson* was Justice John Marshall Harlan of Kentucky—who knew firsthand the pernicious effects of racial segregation and whose
dissent is perhaps the most memorable in the long history of the Supreme Court.
"But in the view of the Constitution, in the eyes of the law, there is in this country
no superior, dominant ruling class of citizens. There is no caste here," said Harlan.
"Our Constitution is color blind, and neither knows nor tolerates classes among
citizens. In respect of civil rights, all citizens are equal before the law. The hum-
blest is the peer of the most powerful." Justice Harlan went on to predict that the
court's decision in *Plessy* would "prove to be quite as pernicious as the decision
made by this tribunal in the *Dred Scott* case" just prior to the Civil War. 163 U.S.
537 (1896) at 544.

rate but equal," of course, was a myth. Facilities were segregated, but they were rarely equal, and African Americans suffered accordingly.

This was the world to which Eisenhower was accustomed. There were virtually no blacks in Kansas when he grew up, none at West Point, and the Army was strictly segregated, with the few black units, such as the 10th Cavalry and the 24th and 25th Infantry regiments, commanded by white officers. Eisenhower himself had briefly served as executive officer of the 24th Infantry at Fort Benning in the 1920s. The assignment had been a punitive one inflicted by the chief of infantry, and Ike quickly managed a transfer. World War II was fought with segregated units, black soldiers were most often assigned as support troops, and segregation was accepted as a fact of American life. Whether it involved restaurants, hotels, restrooms, athletic events, water fountains, parks, schools, or swimming pools, Americans for the most part lived in a segregated world. Eisenhower's friends were white and many were from the South. At the professional level he did not encounter African Americans. That is not to say Ike was racially prejudiced. He simply did not question racial segregation—a situation to which the Supreme Court of the United States had given its seal of approval.

In the few cases that had come before the court in the 1930s and '40s testing the doctrine of separate but equal, the court had ruled that states were required to provide comparable professional and graduate educations for blacks and whites. But these decisions did not challenge the basic holding in *Plessy*, and indeed reinforced it.[5]

That changed in 1954 when the Supreme Court, in a decision written by Chief Justice Earl Warren, reversed the holding in *Plessy v. Ferguson* and held that racial segregation, in and of itself, was a denial of the equal protection of the laws. The decision of the Warren Court was unanimous, and the case, *Brown v. Board of Education,* involving the desegregation of public schools in Topeka, Kansas, introduced a new era of racial equality.[6] But the decision in *Brown,* while it enunciated a new principle of law, bound only the litigants to the case. The struggle to attain equality engulfed the nation for the next two decades, and Eisenhower's leadership would prove critical.

Legal scholars have sometimes criticized Chief Justice Warren's epic decision in *Brown* because it relied on contemporary evidence and argued broad principles at the expense of judicial precedent. That criticism overlooks the fact that the great constitutional decisions of Chief Justice John Marshall—decisions that defined the very nature of the American system of government—were also based on principle, not precedent. Like *Brown,* the decisions of the Marshall Court in *Marbury v. Madison,* the cornerstone of the Supreme Court's constitutional authority; *McCulloch v. Maryland,* upholding the broad legislative powers of Congress; and *Gibbons v. Ogden,* defining the commerce power, are innocent of legal precedent.[7] Like in *Brown,* the argument of the chief justice was so convincing that precedent was unnecessary. Like in *Brown,* the issues were so fundamental that precedent was beside the point. And like in *Brown,* the decisions in *Marbury, McCulloch,* and *Gibbons* were unanimous. Earl Warren and John Marshall understood that when dealing with the nation's fundamental structure, the court must speak with one voice. A unanimous court leaves no doubt about the law of the land.

The decision in *Brown* came down on May 17, 1954, near the end of the court's 1954 term. With one blow, the Supreme Court deprived racial segregation of its constitutional legitimacy. The Eisenhower administration had filed an amicus curiae brief in *Brown* arguing that *Plessy v. Ferguson* be overturned, and at the invitation of the court Assistant Attorney General J. Lee Rankin presented oral argument. Asked by the justices whether the Eisenhower administration thought school segregation was constitutional, Rankin replied that it did not.[8]

While Eisenhower accepted segregation as a fact of life, he personally had no patience with racial discrimination. But as president he recognized how divisive the issue was in the South, and he wanted to move forward cautiously. Ike's goal was to keep the country united under the rule of law. Unlike Presidents Kennedy and Johnson, who spearheaded the fight for racial equality, Eisenhower sought to stake out a nonpartisan position grounded in the president's constitutional responsibility to take care that the laws be faithfully enforced. He eschewed the bully pulpit and preferred to remind the nation of its duty to obey the law. Eisenhower recognized the need for change, but wanted to achieve it with the cooperation of the white South if possible. That was consistent with Ike's instinct to build coalitions based on consensus and was in many ways exactly what the country needed to buffer a change that was so fundamental. In retrospect, it is difficult to say that he was wrong.

But there is no doubt where Eisenhower stood. In his first State of the Union message in February 1953, Ike said, "I propose to use whatever authority exists in the office of the President to end segregation in the District of Columbia, including the Federal Government, and any segregation in the Armed Forces."⁹* When Representative Adam Clayton Powell, the prominent black congressman from Harlem, called Eisenhower's attention to the fact that despite President Truman's order to integrate, two-thirds of the units in the Army were still segregated, Ike moved swiftly. Where Truman had tried to convince the Army to desegregate, Eisenhower ordered it to do so. "Wherever Federal funds are expended," he told his news conference on March 19, 1953, "I do not see how any American can justify a discrimination in the expenditure of those funds."¹⁰ Military officers (such as General Omar Bradley) who had found dozens of reasons why desegregation was premature were not willing to resist a direct order from the commander in chief. On October 24, 1954, Defense Secretary Charles Wilson announced that the last racially segregated unit in the armed forces had been abolished.¹¹

Schools on military bases posed an additional problem. Those in the South were segregated, and many were operated by local school boards. Eisenhower ordered those to desegregate as well—fifteen months before the court's decision in *Brown.* Where local boards refused, the federal government simply assumed control of the schools and desegregated them. By the beginning of the 1955 school year, all schools on military posts were operating on a racially integrated basis. Hospitals run by the Veterans Administration were desegregated by order of the president in September 1953.

Navy yards in the South, employing thousands of civilian workers, proved particularly difficult to desegregate. "The Navy must recognize the customs and usages prevailing in certain geographic

---

* It may be difficult for a contemporary audience to realize that Washington, D.C., the nation's capital, was still a segregated city in the 1950s. Public transportation was not segregated in Washington, but schools, hotels, restaurants, and movie theaters were.

areas of our country which the Navy had no part in creating," said Robert Anderson, Eisenhower's first secretary of the Navy, on May 28, 1953.[12] Ike overruled him. Eisenhower told Congressman Powell that he would not permit the desegregation of federal facilities to be obstructed by his subordinates. "We have not taken and we shall not take a single backward step," the president said. "There must be no second class citizens in this country."[13] The Navy yard in Charleston, South Carolina, was the last holdout. "Not even President Truman deemed [desegregation] necessary at such installations," Governor James Byrnes wrote Eisenhower in August 1953.[14] Despite his affection for Byrnes, Ike was unmoved. On January 14, 1954, the Charleston yard reported that the last vestige of segregation had been eliminated.[15] Eisenhower successfully integrated the armed forces, the VA hospitals, Navy yards in the South, and the schools on military bases well before the Supreme Court held "separate but equal" unconstitutional. Adam Clayton Powell—scarcely anyone's Uncle Tom—put it best in a speech to his constituents on February 28, 1954. "The Honorable Dwight D. Eisenhower has done more to eliminate discrimination and to restore the Negro to the status of first-class citizenship than any President since Abraham Lincoln," he said.[16]

When the decision in *Brown* was announced, Eisenhower immediately ordered the schools in the District of Columbia desegregated.[17] Washington's schools, he told the D.C. commissioners, should be "a model for the nation."[18]* But the court left open how desegregation was to be achieved elsewhere. Unless local school boards acted on

---

* I attended an inner-city white high school in Washington, McKinley Tech, that was located adjacent to a large black community. Under the leadership of its principal, Dr. Charles E. Bish, McKinley became a model for desegregation. Within a year of the president's order, McKinley was almost half black and half white, and integration proceeded without incident. It was the first white high school in Washington to enroll black students, and one of the first in the country. As a white high school, McKinley was always a contender for the city championship (white) in football and basketball. As an integrated high school, McKinley continued to be a contender for the city's premier athletic championships. Today, McKinley Technological High School is still an inner-city school but with a largely black enrollment. As a charter school, it is ranked among the best in the nation and sends 94 percent of its graduates on to college.

their own initiative, the issue remained in limbo. Not until a year later did the court hand down a second decision (*Brown II*) providing guidance as to how integration should proceed. In another unanimous decision, also written by the chief justice, the Supreme Court entrusted desegregation to the local school boards, supervised by the ninety United States District Courts scattered across the country. The Supreme Court set no timetable, except to say that desegregation should proceed "with all deliberate speed."[19]* As the court decreed, integration would be achieved through legal process at the local level, not by sweeping judicial fiat or executive intervention.

In the hiatus between *Brown* and *Brown II,* Justice Robert Jackson died, creating a Supreme Court vacancy for Eisenhower to fill. To replace Jackson, the president nominated Judge John Marshall Harlan II of the United States Court of Appeals for the Second Circuit. Harlan had replaced the legendary Learned Hand on the second circuit, and now Eisenhower was tapping him for the Supreme Court. Harlan was the grandson and namesake of Justice John Marshall Harlan, the great dissenter in *Plessy-Ferguson,* and no appointment could have been better calculated to indicate where Ike's sympathies lay.[20] Eisenhower would make three more appointments to the Supreme Court, William Brennan (1956), Charles Whittaker (1957), and Potter Stewart (1958). If Eisenhower had been skeptical of the holding in *Brown,* he could easily have appointed southerners who might have challenged the decision. But he did not. Harlan, Brennan, Whittaker, and Stewart supported the holding in *Brown* that "separate but equal" was unconstitutional, and became part of the continuing unanimity of the Warren Court on racial issues.

Eisenhower's judicial appointees to lower courts in the Deep South were equally opposed to segregation. Ordinarily, the appointment of federal judges involves significant senatorial input. But the senators from the South were wedded to segregation, and their judicial nom-

---

* The phrase "with all deliberate speed" originated with Eisenhower. While reviewing the government's brief in *Brown II,* Ike penciled the phrase in the margin. It was incorporated into the brief, Solicitor General J. Lee Rankin used it in oral argument, and Chief Justice Warren carried it over into his decision of the court. Herbert Brownell interview, cited in David Eisenhower and Julie Nixon Eisenhower, *Going Home to Glory* 104 (New York: Simon and Schuster, 2010).

inees invariably shared that view. The senators were also Democrats. Party affiliation afforded Eisenhower sufficient reason to ignore their preferences, and the Department of Justice under Herbert Brownell habitually recommended judges for the Fifth Circuit (Alabama, Florida, Georgia, Louisiana, Mississippi, and Texas) without senatorial endorsement. That enabled Eisenhower to appoint supporters of desegregation who did yeoman service to make the decision in *Brown* a reality. Elbert Tuttle of Georgia, John Minor Wisdom of Louisiana, and John Brown of Nebraska were appointed to the United States Court of Appeals for the Fifth Circuit, where they joined Richard Taylor Rives, a Truman appointee, to form a solid phalanx determined to enforce desegregation.\* At the district court level, Eisenhower appointed Frank M. Johnson, Jr., in Alabama; in 1956 he struck down segregated seating on Montgomery's buses after Rosa Parks's refusal to give up her seat had triggered a citywide black boycott of the city buses. It was also Johnson who ordered the teaching staffs of Montgomery's schools desegregated—a monumental step on the road to racial integration.

Resistance to the ruling in *Brown* was immediate. Throughout the South, White Citizens Councils sprang up, composed of outraged citizens determined to preserve white supremacy at the local level. The Citizens Councils did not wear sheets and did not burn crosses, but their tactics of bullying and intimidation were often as vicious as the Klan's. ("The Ku Klux Klan in business suits," in the words of one social historian.)[21] There was also vociferous opposition in Congress. On March 10, 1956, Senator J. Strom Thurmond of South Carolina announced the "Southern Manifesto," a document signed by 101 members of Congress pledging themselves "to use all lawful means to bring about a reversal of this decision [*Brown v. Board of Education*] which is contrary to the Constitution." The document was

---

\* "Those four judges, I think, have made as much of an imprint on American society and American law as any four judges below the Supreme Court have ever done on any court," said Burke Marshall, assistant attorney general for civil rights in the Kennedy administration. "If it had not been for judges like that on the Fifth Circuit, I think *Brown* would have failed in the end." David A. Nichols, *A Matter of Justice: Eisenhower and the Beginning of the Civil Rights Revolution* 84 (New York: Simon and Schuster, 2007).

signed by every member of the congressional delegations from Alabama, Arkansas, Georgia, Louisiana, Mississippi, South Carolina, and Virginia, plus a sprinkling from other states. In what has become a hackneyed refrain, the signatories said, "We regard the decision of the Supreme Court in the school cases as a clear abuse of judicial power. It climaxes a trend in the federal judiciary undertaking to legislate . . . and encroach upon the reserved rights of the States and the people."[22]

At his press conference four days later, Eisenhower was asked by ABC's Edward P. Morgan to comment on the "manifesto," particularly insofar as the president's responsibility was concerned. Ike typically replied with a carrot and a stick. He commended the signers for pledging to use legal means to resist the court's decision. But he coupled that with a clear warning. If they were thinking about nullification, there would be serious trouble. In words that Andrew Jackson might have used, Ike said, "I am sworn to defend and uphold the Constitution of the United States and I can never abandon or refuse to carry out my own duty."

Eisenhower pleaded for patience and moderation. He reminded the press that because segregation had been constitutional for almost sixty years, it was going to take time and effort to bring about change. "I have never yet given up my belief that the American people, faced with a great problem like this, will approach it intelligently and with patience and understanding, and we will get somewhere."[23] Eisenhower worked behind the scenes, hoping to enlist the South's religious leaders to ease the way. A week after his press conference, he met with evangelist Billy Graham for almost an hour in the White House. Graham said later that Ike "felt strongly that the church could make a tremendous contribution toward the bettering of race relations" in the South.[24]

Eisenhower followed up his meeting with Graham with a lengthy letter. "Ministers know that peacemakers are blessed," he told the evangelist. "They should also know that the most effective peacemaker is one who prevents a quarrel from developing." Ike suggested to Graham that more qualified blacks be elected to local offices in the South, that entrance to graduate school be strictly on the basis of merit without regard to race, and that public transportation be fully integrated. "It appears to me that things like this could be properly mentioned in a pulpit." Eisenhower also suggested that Graham might find an opportunity to commend the Reverend Joseph Francis Rummel, the longtime Catholic archbishop of New Orleans, who had desegregated the city's parochial schools on his own authority. In a pastoral letter, Rummel warned Catholics they faced "automatic excommunication" if they supported segregation for parochial schools.[25]

Outside of the Catholic schools in New Orleans, however, desegregation in the South was minimal. According to the NAACP, no public schools had been desegregated in eight southern states in 1955, and the economic intimidation of blacks was on the increase. In Mississippi, a state whose population included 900,000 blacks, the number of African Americans on the voting rolls had declined from 22,000 to 8,000 during the year. Racial violence also spiked upward. No lynchings had been recorded in the Magnolia State during the five years from 1950 through 1954. In 1955, there were three.[26] And it was not just in the South. Fiery crosses were burned in the front yards of Supreme Court justices in Washington, and kerosene was dumped under the windows of Attorney General Brownell's house in the District.[27]

The decisive battle in the struggle to desegregate the schools in the South was fought at Little Rock in 1957. Following the decision in *Brown II,* the Little Rock school board adopted a plan for the gradual integration of the city's schools over a seven-year period. The first step was the admission of a handful of carefully selected black students to Central High School in September 1957. But in late August a group of white parents (the Mothers' League of Little Rock Central High) brought suit in state court to block the school board's plan and appealed to Governor Orval Faubus to intervene. Faubus testified in court that gun sales in Little Rock had increased rapidly, and he feared violence when school opened. Based on the governor's testimony, Judge Murray Reed of the Pulaski County Chancery Court issued an injunction on August 29 to delay the integration of Central High. At that point Thurgood Marshall, the NAACP's legal counsel who had argued both *Brown* cases before the Supreme Court, rushed to Little Rock to place the issue before the federal court.

After a brief hearing on August 30, Judge Ronald N. Davies of the U.S. District Court for the Eastern District of Arkansas ruled that the state chancery court had no jurisdiction and ordered desegregation to proceed as planned. Schools in Little Rock were scheduled to open on Tuesday, September 3. On Monday, Governor Faubus ordered the Arkansas National Guard to active duty in Little Rock. "The purpose of the state militia," said Faubus, "is to maintain or restore order and protect the lives and property of citizens."[28]* The following day, Central High was ringed by 250 guardsmen in battle dress, and an even larger crowd of white demonstrators determined to prevent the black students from entering. But the nine black students who had been selected to attend Central High did not appear. Rather than confront the angry mob, NAACP officials and the school board chose to return to federal court for further instructions. When they did, Judge Davies ordered the school board to proceed with integration. "This is an obligation from which I shall not shrink," said the judge.[29]

On Wednesday, September 4, the nine black students attempted to enter Central High. The Arkansas National Guard blocked their way while an unruly mob of more than five hundred white demonstrators shouted obscenities. Judge Davies responded by requesting the Justice Department to investigate Faubus's claim that an imminent threat of violence justified his use of the Guard to thwart integration. Davies's request landed on Herbert Brownell's desk at the Justice Department on Wednesday afternoon. The attorney general, who had been following events in Little Rock closely, immediately dispatched a team of FBI agents and federal marshals to Little Rock pursuant to the judge's request. The following day Governor Faubus sent an angry telegram to Eisenhower protesting the intervention of

---

* Governor Faubus's order to General Sherman T. Clinger, the commander of the Arkansas National Guard, stated: "You are directed to place off limits to white students those schools for colored students and to place off limits to colored students those schools heretofore operated and recently set up for white students. This order will remain in effect until the demobilization of the Guard or until further orders." Opinion of the Attorney General [Brownell] to the President on Little Rock School Desegregation, in Brownell, *Advising Ike: The Memoirs of Herbert Brownell* 368 [Appendix I] (Lawrence: University Press of Kansas, 1993).

federal authorities. Faubus said the government agents were plotting to arrest him, claimed his telephone was being tapped, and blamed federal authorities for any future violence at Central High. Eisenhower backed Brownell to the hilt. "When I became President," Ike fired back, "I took an oath to support and defend the Constitution of the United States. The only assurance I can give you," he told Faubus, "is that the Federal Constitution will be upheld by me by every legal means at my command."[30]*

Orval Faubus was not a racist, in the sense of Mississippi's Theodore G. Bilbo or Eugene Talmadge in Georgia. He was more of an opportunist, akin to Louisiana's Huey Long, a southern populist from what one knowledgeable observer called the "Snopes school of politics." Shrewd and earthy, Faubus was determined to win a third term as governor in a state where third terms were rare. And in 1957 it was clear that the path to electoral victory lay in opposing desegregation.

On September 9, federal agents in Little Rock reported to the court that there had been no increase in the sale of guns in Little Rock, and that Faubus's orders to the Guard were designed to prevent the black students from entering the school building. Upon receiving the report, Judge Davies asked the Justice Department to enter the case and file a request for a preliminary injunction against the deployment of the Arkansas National Guard at Central High. Brownell did so on September 10. Judge Davies set the hearing on the government's motion for September 20, and ordered Faubus to appear in court and defend his actions.[31] The battle was joined. As Eisenhower wrote later, "The United States government and the Governor of Arkansas were now heading toward a collision."[32]

Faubus recognized he had overreached. His popularity among Arkansas's white voters stood at an all-time high, but he faced a possible contempt citation from Judge Davies and all the consequences that might entail. As Brownell observed, "The governor's action rep-

---

* Eisenhower also told Faubus, "There is no basis of fact to the statements you made in your telegram that Federal authorities have been considering taking you into custody or that telephone lines to your Executive Mansion have been tapped by any agency of the Federal Government." DDE to Faubus, September 5, 1957, EL.

resented an attempt to nullify the Constitution and the laws of the United States and to disregard the orders of the federal court."[33]

Eisenhower, who was summering at the naval base in Newport, Rhode Island, was determined that whatever the district court in Little Rock ruled, that decision would be enforced. At the same time, he wanted to give Faubus the opportunity to make "an orderly retreat."[34] When Representative Brooks Hays of Arkansas, the long-time liberal congressman from Little Rock, suggested that the president meet with Faubus at Newport to work out a peaceful settlement, Eisenhower was initially reluctant. The president, said Sherman Adams, would not meet "with a state governor who was standing in open defiance of the Constitution." When Hays persisted and said Faubus "realizes he has made a mistake and is looking for a way out," Eisenhower agreed to meet with the governor, providing that Faubus announce beforehand his willingness to comply with the orders of the district court. That statement should be "crystal clear," the president told Brownell.[35] Adams and Hays drafted a statement for Faubus that was consistent with Ike's wishes, and assumed they had an agreement. But when Faubus released the text in Little Rock, he added a proviso. He would comply with the court order "consistent with my responsibility under the Arkansas constitution," in effect negating his commitment. Brownell told Eisenhower that this was typical of Faubus and that it was pointless to meet with him, but Ike chose to do so anyway.

Faubus arrived in Newport on September 14. He and Eisenhower met privately for twenty minutes, and then were joined by Brownell, Sherman Adams, and Congressman Hays. At their private meeting, Eisenhower offered Faubus a face-saving solution. Keep the Arkansas National Guard in place at Central High, but change their orders. Instead of preventing the black students from entering, instruct the Guard to continue to preserve order and allow the children to attend school. "You should take this action promptly," said Ike. No one would benefit from a trial of strength between the president and a governor, he told Faubus. "Where the federal government has assumed jurisdiction and this is upheld by the Supreme Court, there can only be one outcome: the state will lose. I don't want to see any governor humiliated."[36]

As Eisenhower recalled, Faubus "seemed to be very appreciative of this attitude. I definitely got the understanding that he was going back to Arkansas and would act within a matter of hours to revoke his orders to the Guard to prevent re-entry of the Negro children into the school."[37] At the subsequent meeting with Brownell, Adams, and Hays, Eisenhower said that Faubus had agreed that the black children would be admitted to Central High, and Faubus did not dispute the president's statement. "I knew Eisenhower was a persuasive person," said Brownell later, "but I was incredulous at Faubus's ostensible capitulation and the seemingly abrupt end of a constitutional crisis of such impact."[38]

Brownell's skepticism proved correct, and Ike was wrong. When Faubus returned to Arkansas, nothing happened. The governor remained silent and the Arkansas National Guard stayed at Central High preventing the black students from entering. Eisenhower was furious. "Faubus broke his word," the president told Brownell. According to Brownell, Ike's voice was tense. "He was acting as a military commander-in-chief, dealing with Faubus as a subordinate who had let him down in the midst of battle."[39] Eisenhower wanted to issue a statement immediately denouncing Faubus. Brownell and Adams urged Ike to hold his fire. Faubus was due to appear in court before Judge Davies on Friday, September 20. There was little doubt that Davies would order Faubus to admit the black students, and it was equally clear that the governor would refuse. Let Faubus overplay his hand. Once he was in defiance of a court order, Eisenhower would be justified to use whatever means were necessary to compel compliance.

On September 20, Judge Davies called his court to order for the hearing on Civil Case 3113, a motion by the United States for a preliminary injunction enjoining "all persons" from interfering with the integration of Central High. Faubus was represented by lawyers from the state attorney general's office in Little Rock, who immediately moved that Judge Davies disqualify himself because of prejudice. The judge denied the motion, at which point Faubus's lawyers packed up their brief cases and walked out. Judge Davies said the hearing would continue without them.

The Justice Department lawyers presented a convincing case. The mayor of Little Rock, the chief of police, and members of the school board presented unchallenged testimony concerning Little Rock's history of peaceful race relations for the past twenty-five years. "Jim Crow" seating on the city's buses had been discontinued in January without incident. The witnesses were unanimous that there had been no evidence that the desegregation of Central High would produce disorder. The mayor and the chief of police also testified that Faubus had not asked for a police report on the possibility of danger before he mobilized the Guard. It was also their view that the Little Rock police department had been fully capable of maintaining order.

When the government concluded its case, Judge Davies spoke in measured tones. "It is very clear to this court," said the judge, "that the plan of integration adopted by the Little Rock school board and approved by this court and the Court of Appeals for the Eighth Circuit has been thwarted by the Governor of Arkansas. It is equally demonstrable from the testimony here today that there would have been no violence in carrying out the plan of integration and that there has been no violence." Judge Davies thereupon granted the injunction and ordered Faubus and the commander of the Arkansas National Guard to cease further interference with the court's orders.[40]

Three hours after receiving the court's ruling, Faubus removed the National Guard from Central High. That evening he went on statewide television to announce his compliance with the injunction. He said the court's order would be appealed with the Eighth Circuit, and in the meantime he asked black parents not to send their children to the high school until tempers cooled. Faubus thereupon departed Little Rock for the Southern Governors' Conference in Sea Island, Georgia. *Aprés moi le déluge.*

On Saturday, September 21, Eisenhower issued a brief statement announcing that Faubus had withdrawn the Arkansas National Guard from Central High. He did not praise Faubus's action, he simply announced it. But he did praise the nine black children who had been denied admission by the Guard. "They and their parents have conducted themselves with dignity and restraint. I am confident that the citizens of the City of Little Rock and the State of Arkansas will welcome this opportunity to demonstrate that in their city and in their state proper orders of a United States Court will be executed promptly and without disorder."[41]

But that did not happen. When school opened on Monday, Central High was ringed by a mob of well over a thousand angry white protestors determined to prevent the black students from entering. Police barricades initially kept the crowd at bay, and the black students entered unseen through a side door. But the crowd continued to grow and was in an ugly mood. Out-of-state newsmen were assaulted, and by eleven-thirty the police lines had been breached. Demonstrators stormed into the school, and Gene Smith, Little Rock's deputy police chief, decided to remove the black students for their own protection. They left the school under police escort, were placed in police cars, and driven home. The rioting continued. Virgil Blossom, the superintendent of schools, called the Department of Justice to request federal assistance. The crowd had grown to more than fifteen hundred, said Blossom, and local authorities could no longer contain it. An hour later, Mayor Woodrow Wilson Mann sent an urgent telegram to Eisenhower in Newport. "The mob that gathered was no spontaneous assembly," Mann told the president. "It was agitated, aroused, and assembled by a concerted plan of action." Mann said that allies of Faubus had organized the mob, and that "Governor Faubus was at least cognizant of what was going to take place."[42]

Eisenhower, who had been apprised of the situation by Brownell, acted promptly. Secretary of the Army Wilbur Brucker was alerted that military force might be required in Little Rock, and at Eisenhower's direction, Army chief of staff Maxwell Taylor was ordered to prepare the 101st Airborne at Fort Campbell, Kentucky, for possible movement. "In my career I have learned," the president told Brownell, "that if you have to use force, use overwhelming force and save lives thereby."[43]

At 4:45 p.m. Eisenhower assumed direct command of the situation in Little Rock with a formal statement putting the demonstrators on notice. "The Federal law and the orders of a United States District Court implementing that law cannot be flouted with impunity by any individual or any mob of extremists. I will use the full power of the United States including whatever force may be necessary to prevent any obstruction of the law and to carry out the orders of the Federal Court." There were no weasel words or conditional offers in Ike's statement.[44] Judge Davies's order would be enforced and the black students would be admitted to Central High using whatever force might be necessary. An hour later the White House issued an official proclamation signed by the president calling on the demonstrators to disperse. After briefly detailing the obstruction of justice in Little Rock, and citing the relevant legal authority, the key sentence read:

> Now, THEREFORE, I, Dwight D. Eisenhower, President of the United States, under and by virtue of the authority vested in me by the Constitution . . . do command all persons engaged in such obstruction of justice to cease and desist therefrom, and to disperse forthwith.[45]

Under the relevant federal statutes, issuance of the proclamation was a prerequisite before the president could employ military force to suppress domestic violence.[46] When Ike signed the proclamation, the deck was cleared for action. And to be sure the import of the proclamation registered in Little Rock, the document noted President Washington's use of federal troops to suppress the Whiskey Rebellion in 1794, and President Cleveland's similar action to enforce a federal court injunction during the Pullman strike in 1894.*

Despite the deliberate effort of the White House to telegraph its intention to intervene, the situation in Little Rock continued to deteriorate. Racial fighting broke out on Main Street, bricks and bottles were hurled through shop windows, and hundreds of cars packed with gun-toting hoodlums cruised ominously through black neighborhoods.

By Tuesday morning it was evident that federal troops would be

---

* In upholding President Cleveland's action, the Supreme Court stated, "The entire strength of the nation may be used to enforce in any part of the land the full and free exercise of all national powers and the security of all rights entrusted by the Constitution to its care. . . . If the emergency arises, the army of the Nation, and all its militia, are at the service of the Nation to compel obedience to its laws." *In re Debs,* 158 U.S. 564 (1895).

required. The question was no longer whether to intervene, wrote Eisenhower, "but what force I should use to insure execution of the court's order."[47] Ike placed a call to Maxwell Taylor at the Pentagon. Taylor suggested using the Arkansas National Guard before ordering federal troops to the scene. Eisenhower was dubious. He told Taylor he was concerned about pitting "brother against brother." If they used the Guard, said the president, the units should come from elsewhere in the state, not from Little Rock.

Before a decision was reached, another emergency telegram arrived in Newport from Mayor Mann. "The immediate need for federal troops is urgent," said the mayor. "The mob is much larger in number at 8 AM than at any time yesterday. People are converging on the scene from all directions. Mob is armed and engaging in fisticuffs and other acts of violence. Situation is out of control and police cannot dispense the mob." Mann asked the president to send the necessary troops as soon as possible.[48]

Eisenhower placed another call to Taylor in Washington. The Arkansas Guard, he told the Army's chief of staff, could not muster soon enough to defuse the crisis. The 101st Airborne Division, which had already been alerted, was ready for action. Eisenhower instructed Taylor to send the 101st to Little Rock immediately. He also said he was issuing an Executive Order (no. 10730) calling the Arkansas National Guard into federal service. That would deprive Faubus of their use. Taylor put the wheels in motion. By midafternoon on Tuesday, an armada of C-130s was carrying the troops from Fort Campbell to Little Rock.* John Chancellor of NBC News was on the scene when the first contingent of five hundred men of the 101st Airborne arrived. "As they marched in, the clean, sharp sound of their boots clacking on the street was a reminder of their profession-

---

* At the insistence of the Department of Justice, Major General Thomas L. Sherburne, commanding the 101st Airborne, was instructed to prune the units going into Little Rock of all black soldiers. The division chain of command was surprised, but complied. Not until a month later were the black soldiers of the 101st integrated back into their units in Little Rock, and it occurred without incident.

I am indebted to my classmate Martin Hoffmann, former secretary of the Army, for this information. In 1957, Hoffmann was an aide to General Sherburne, and in that capacity organized the division's compliance.

alism," Chancellor recalled. The young journalist (Chancellor was thirty at the time) said he'd never thought much about the Constitution before, but he realized that day he was watching the Constitution in action. "There was something majestic about the scene: it was a moment at once thrilling and somehow frightening as well."[49]

As soon as the 101st was aloft, Eisenhower left Newport for Washington. "Meet me at the White House," he instructed Brownell. "I am going to address the nation on TV."[50] Eisenhower chose to return to Washington to emphasize the gravity of the situation in Little Rock. He drafted his remarks on the flight from Newport, and worked over them with Brownell in the Oval Office. At 9 p.m. he faced the nation. Ike wore a somber three-piece gray suit, and spoke directly into the camera. He did not use a teleprompter, and only rarely consulted the text in front of him. "For a few minutes this evening I want to speak to you about the serious situation that has arisen in Little Rock," said the president. "In that city, under the leadership of demagogic extremists, disorderly mobs have deliberately prevented the carrying out of proper orders from a Federal Court."

Eisenhower recounted the events in Little Rock leading up to his decision to send troops to the scene. "The very basis of our individual rights and freedoms depends upon the certainty that the President will enforce the decisions of the courts," said Ike. "Unless the President did so, anarchy would result. . . . Mob rule cannot be allowed to override the decisions of our courts. . . . A foundation of our American way of life is our national respect for the law." Eisenhower emphasized that the Army was not in Little Rock to take over the school system or to supplant local authority. "The troops are there solely for the purpose of preventing interference with the orders of the Court."

Mindful of the need to tamp down the crisis, Ike reached out for southern support. The Supreme Court had decided that separate educational facilities based on race are inherently unequal and therefore unconstitutional, said the president. "Our personal opinions about the decision have no bearing on the matter of enforcement; the responsibility and authority of the Supreme Court are very clear." Eisenhower said he knew the South and had many friends there. "I know that the overwhelming majority of the people of the

Soldiers of the 101st Airborne Division escorting members of the Little Rock Nine into Central High School, September 24, 1957.

South—including those of Arkansas and of Little Rock—are of good will, united in their efforts to preserve and respect the law even when they disagree with it." Liberal commentators have often criticized Eisenhower for these remarks, but the president was on firm ground. He wanted to defuse the crisis and pave the way for integration with as few side effects as possible. His conciliatory tone went a long way in doing so.

At Dulles's suggestion, Eisenhower spoke about the pernicious impact of the situation in Little Rock on American foreign relations. "Our enemies are gloating over this incident and using it everywhere to misrepresent our whole nation." The president made it clear that the law would be enforced and called upon the people of Arkansas to assist. "Thus will be restored the image of America and of all its parts as one nation, indivisible, with liberty and justice for all."[51]

It was a powerful speech, powerfully delivered. The next morning in Little Rock the mob again tried to assemble at Central High only to find the way blocked by the soldiers of the 101st Airborne. The troops had established barriers a block away from the school, and systematically dispersed the crowd. When scattered bands of protestors persisted, the troops moved forward, elbow to elbow, bayonets fixed. A scuffle or two ensued, but by 9 a.m. the area had been cleared. The nine black children assembled, as they habitually did, at the home of Daisy Bates, the local head of the NAACP, waiting for instructions. An Army officer appeared at the door and saluted. "Mrs. Bates, we're ready for the children," he said. "We will return them to your home at three-thirty." It was, said Minniejean Brown, one of the black students, an exhilarating experience. "For the first time in my life I felt like an American citizen."[52]

Eisenhower returned to Newport that same day. As he often did, he gave a ride on *Columbine II* to a member of the White House press pool, this time John L. Steele of *Time* magazine. Sitting next to the president, Steele coaxed Ike into a candid off-the-record discussion about his decision to intervene.* Sending in the troops, said Eisenhower, was the hardest decision he'd ever had to make, save possibly for D-Day. "But Goddamn it, it was the only thing I could do." Eisenhower emphasized that the issue as he saw it was not segregation. "It isn't even the maintenance of public order. It is a question of upholding the law—otherwise you have people shooting people." Simply put, said Ike, it was to enforce the law of the land. "This thing is going to go on and on and on in other places. These damned hooligans . . . I was trying to speak last night to the reasonable people, the decent people of the South." Eisenhower told Steele he thought his speech might have struck the right tone. But the ordeal had taken a toll. "It has been nagging me day and night."[53]

Public reaction to Eisenhower's speech was overwhelmingly favorable. A Trendex poll published on September 26 indicated 68.4 percent of the country (77.5 percent outside the South) approved the president's decision to send troops to Little Rock. The following week, the Gallup poll showed two-thirds of the public believed Ike had done the "right thing."[54]

A flood of responses rolled into the White House. "Thank you for your masterful statement," wired Harry Ashmore, editor of *The Arkansas Gazette.*[55] Jazz legend Louis Armstrong telegraphed the president, "Daddy, if and when you decide to take those little Negro

---

* Steele did not publish the interview, but prepared a confidential memorandum dated September 25, 1957, which is on file at the Eisenhower Library.

children personally into Central High School along with your marvelous troops, take me along. . . . You have a good heart."[56]

"Please accept my congratulations," Jackie Robinson wired. "I should have known you would do the right thing at the crucial time."[57] Texas oil barons Sid Richardson and Monty Moncrief telegraphed their support. "The overwhelming majority of the American people are in full accord with the determined action you have taken," said Moncrief.[58]

Martin Luther King, Jr., who had been critical of Eisenhower earlier, wrote, "The overwhelming majority of southerners, Negro and white, stand firmly behind your resolute action to restore law and order in Little Rock."[59] In Little Rock itself, the Reverend Robert Raymond Brown, the Episcopal bishop of Arkansas, telephoned to say that the church leaders of the city supported the president's action and offered to do anything they could to ameliorate the crisis.[60] Leading business and civic leaders in Little Rock signed a petition to urge their fellow citizens to remain calm and show respect for the tradition of law and order. "I think your action to be in the finest tradition of American citizenship," Eisenhower replied. "I cannot help but believe that under this kind of leadership, the City of Little Rock may rapidly return to normal patterns of peaceful living."[61]

Southern officeholders, elected by an all-white electorate, were not so kind. Congressman Carl Elliott of Alabama called Eisenhower's action illegal, unwarranted, and unwise. "There are not enough troops to occupy every high school campus in the South," said Elliott.[62] The hardest blow was delivered by Senator Richard Russell of Georgia, chairman of the Armed Forces Committee and normally a supporter of Ike's policies. Russell protested what he called "the high-handed and illegal methods being employed by the armed forces of the United States under your command who are carrying out your orders to mix the races in the public schools of Little Rock, Arkansas." Russell described incidents of alleged brutality, and accused the Army of "disregarding and overriding the elementary rights of American citizens by applying tactics which must have been copied from the manual issued [to] the officers of Hitler's storm troopers."[63]

According to Sherman Adams, Eisenhower hit the roof when he

read Russell's telegram. The fact that Russell released it to the press before the White House received it made Ike furious. He wrote out a reply in longhand. "I must say that I completely fail to comprehend your comparison of our troops to Hitler's storm troopers," said the president. "In one case military power was used to further the ambitious and purposes of a ruthless dictator, in the other to preserve the institutions of free government." The action was necessary, Eisenhower told Russell, because the state of Arkansas had misused the National Guard, encouraged "mobs of extremists to flout the orders of a Federal Court," and had failed to protect "persons who are peaceably exercising their right under the Constitution." Eisenhower said that "failure to act in such a case would be tantamount to acquiescence in anarchy and the dissolution of the union."[64]

Elements of the 101st Airborne remained in Little Rock until Thanksgiving, and were gradually replaced by units from the Arkansas National Guard. On May 8, 1958, Eisenhower announced that he would release the Guard at the end of the school year. Of the original nine black students, eight went on to graduate from Central High and one, Ernest Green, became an assistant secretary of labor in the cabinet of Jimmy Carter. Orval Faubus gained what he wanted from the showdown in Little Rock. He portrayed himself as the champion of states' rights, overwhelmed by massive federal power. For many white citizens of Arkansas, Faubus symbolized resistance to racial integration. His reelection to a third term in 1958—which had seemed unlikely before Little Rock—was guaranteed. Faubus won the Democratic primary (equivalent to election in Arkansas at the time) with twice as many votes as his opponents combined. Faubus easily won a fourth term, then a fifth, and finally a sixth. His twelve years as governor of Arkansas stands as a record in the Razorback State.

Eisenhower's moderation in the crisis has often been misunderstood. He was determined to enforce the court order, but with as little bluster as possible. Like Theodore Roosevelt, Ike preferred to walk softly and carry a big stick. Rather than emphasize integration, Eisenhower preferred to stress the rule of law. His deployment of the 101st Airborne Division—one of the legendary units in the United States Army—sent an unmistakable message to the South: The decision of the Supreme Court that segregation was unconstitutional was the law of the land. Desegregation would proceed at the local level with all deliberate speed, as determined by local school boards under the supervision of the United States District Courts. But it would proceed. And the full force of the federal government stood ready to enforce it.[*] Eisenhower took the most divisive issue to confront American society since the Civil War and moved it toward a solution with as little rancor as possible. At the time, that satisfied neither those who sought immediate integration everywhere, nor those rabid segregationists who opposed any change anywhere. In the long run, Ike's course proved correct. His moderation carried the day. Had he not acted, had he not sent the 101st to Little Rock, every white racist from Manassas to Vicksburg would have understood: The way to block integration is to take to the streets. Appear in sufficient numbers, and be sufficiently menacing, and desegregation will not happen. It is thanks to Eisenhower that integration proceeded and the rule of law prevailed.

Ike said it best in a letter to Swede Hazlett when the crisis in Little Rock began.

> The plan of the Supreme Court to accomplish integration gradually and sensibly seems to me to provide the only possible answer if we are to consider on the one hand the customs and fears of a great section of our population, and on the other the binding effect that Supreme Court decisions must have on all of us if our form of government is to survive and prosper. . . . [65]

---

[*] In 1958, General Alfred Gruenther, then head of the American Red Cross, informed Eisenhower of the Red Cross's problem of supplying blood to the South. The state of Louisiana had a statute requiring that blood from black donors and white donors be segregated. Eisenhower told him to ignore it—that he should make no differentiation between blood. Ike told Gruenther that in early 1942 when he had been chief of operations in the War Department, Australia needed troops desperately and he assigned three divisions to go there. He was immediately visited by the Australian ambassador, who said there was a law in Australia prohibiting blacks from entering the country. Eisenhower said he told the ambassador, "All right. No troops." The next morning Ike said he had a flood of cables from Australia saying everything would be all right. Ike told Gruenther to stand his ground in Louisiana. Ann Whitman diary, November 23, 1958, EL.

There must be respect for the Constitution—which means the Supreme Court's interpretation of the Constitution—or we shall have chaos. We cannot possibly imagine a successful form of government in which every individual citizen would have the right to interpret the Constitution according to his own convictions, beliefs, and prejudices. Chaos would develop. This I believe with all my heart—and shall always act accordingly.[66*]

* In 1984, Stephen Ambrose published the first of several biographies of Eisenhower. In it he stated that "Eisenhower personally wished that the Court had upheld *Plessy v. Ferguson.*" The allegation is repeated by Ambrose in his subsequent works. Because of Ambrose's position as an associate editor of the *Eisenhower Papers,* a generation of historians have accepted his version of Ike's views. Ambrose provides no documentation, no references, and cites only "private" conversations. The fact is Ambrose cut the allegation from whole cloth. There is no evidence whatsoever to sustain Ambrose's claim. David A. Nichols, in his definitive study of Eisenhower and civil rights, writes that "there is no credible evidence" for Ambrose's assertion; Blanche Wiesen Cook, one of the earliest researchers in the archives of the Eisenhower Library, found none, nor have I. In the April 26, 2010, issue of *The New Yorker* magazine, Richard Rayner reports that Ambrose's alleged interviews with Eisenhower never took place. The record does not sustain that he ever met privately with Ike. Timothy D. Rives, deputy director of the Eisenhower Presidential Library, provided chapter and verse sustaining Rayner's conclusions in a subsequent article appearing online on George Mason University's History News Network, May 17, 2010.

Ambrose sometimes twisted the facts to fit his portrait of Ike, but never with such pernicious effect as in Eisenhower's views of civil rights. I did not know Ambrose, and I have no personal animosity toward him. To the contrary, I have always felt indebted to him for his very generous review of my biography of Lucius Clay in *The New York Times Book Review* in 1990.

Ambrose, 2 *Eisenhower* 190; Ambrose, *Eisenhower: Soldier and President* 367; Nichols, *Matter of Justice* 279; Rayner, "Channeling Ike," 20–21; Timothy D. Rives, "Ambrose and Eisenhower: A View from the Stacks," HNN, May 17, 2010.

# TWENTY-SEVEN

# Military-Industrial Complex

In the councils of government, we must guard
against the acquisition of unwarranted influence,
whether sought or unsought, by the military-
industrial complex.

— DWIGHT D. EISENHOWER,
*January 17, 1961*

ON OCTOBER 4, 1957, with the news that the Soviet Union had successfully launched the world's first man-made satellite, the nation's attention shifted abruptly from Little Rock and civil rights to outer space and the arms race. The Russians called the satellite *Sputnik,* a word artfully translated as "fellow traveler." It was a small aluminum alloy sphere, 22.8 inches in diameter, weighing 184 pounds, and equipped with two radio transmitters sending continuous signals back to earth. *Sputnik* orbited the earth, 560 miles up, traveling at a speed of eighteen thousand miles an hour. Shortly afterward came *Sputnik II,* launched on November 3, six times larger than its predecessor, with an orbit even higher.

Neither *Sputnik* nor *Sputnik II* had any direct military application. They carried no weapons systems or scientific equipment. But the technological breakthrough represented by the launch and the size of the thrust required to propel the satellites into orbit caught the world by surprise. American reaction varied between measured anxiety and total hysteria. The Joint Chiefs clamored for massive increases in the defense budget, civil defense officials mounted an urgent drive to construct bomb shelters nationwide, the academic community pressed for more funds for scientific research, and the Democrats—believing that they had found a chink in Ike's armor—ballyhooed the missile gap and America's unpreparedness.

Eisenhower refused to panic. As at Little Rock, he responded calmly and deliberately, and kept the issue in perspective. Ike was peppered at his news conference on October 9 about the Soviet launch. Charles von Fremd of CBS wanted to know whether the Strategic Air Command was now a museum piece, as Nikita Khrushchev claimed. Absolutely not, Eisenhower replied. Any change in weapons systems would be evolutionary over a long period of time. Robert Clark of the International News Service asked whether we had made a mistake in not recognizing we were in a race with Russians. No, said Ike, the satellite program is a scientific program unrelated to national security. "I don't know why our scientists should have come in and urged that we do this before anybody else." May Craig wanted to know whether the Soviets could launch rockets from the satellites. "Not at this time," Ike replied. They might be able to transmit photographic data back to earth, but that was still under development. Eisenhower carefully distinguished between launching a satellite and firing an intercontinental ballistic missile, where accuracy and guidance were of paramount importance. There was no reason to assume the Russians had any advantage in that respect.

The key question was put to Eisenhower by Hazel Markel of NBC:

Q: Mr. President, in light of the great faith which the American people have in your military knowledge and leadership, are you saying at this time with the Russian satellite whirling about the world, you are not more concerned nor overly concerned about our nation's security?

EISENHOWER: So far as the satellite itself is concerned, that does not raise my apprehensions, not one iota. I see nothing at this moment, at this stage of development that is significant in that development as far as security is concerned.[1]

Eisenhower's resolute assurance calmed the nation's jitters. His manner that afternoon exuded confidence. It was not bravado on Ike's part, nor was he playacting. His assurance rested on iron-clad evidence provided by extensive CIA surveillance flights over the Soviet Union mounted by the agency's U-2 spy planes. When Eisenhower assumed office in 1953, he was troubled by the lack of accurate information about Soviet military activity. The possibility of surprise attack loomed large. Russian secrecy also contributed to American anxiety, ratcheting up the pressure to spend more and more on potentially useless weapons systems. Aerial surveillance seemed the answer. Eisenhower had pressed for "Open Skies" at Geneva, but the Soviets were uninterested. When MIT president James Killian, who was Ike's science adviser, and Edwin Land, the inventor of the Polaroid camera, suggested development of a plane that could overfly Soviet airspace at altitudes above Russian antiaircraft defenses and produce highly accurate photographs of the ground below, Eisenhower signed on immediately. His one stipulation was that he did not want uniformed Air Force pilots violating Soviet airspace. That meant it would be a CIA project.[2]

The resulting U-2 surveillance aircraft, designed by America's most talented airplane designer, Kelly Johnson, was built in a super-secret area (the Skunk Works) at Lockheed's sprawling Burbank, California, facility in 1955–56. Based originally on the Air Force's F-104 but longer, lower, and lighter, with a wingspan of eighty feet, the U-2 was more of a glider than a jet and could stay aloft for eleven hours with a range of 4,750 miles. It flew at 70,000 feet (soon 80,000), and its cameras could capture the smallest objects on the ground some fourteen miles below. The first reconnaissance flights were made from England in July 1956. They flew over Eastern Europe, and Eisenhower was shown photographs from the missions. Ike was stunned at the clarity of the photos. You could see not only a parking lot fourteen miles below, but you could even see "the lines marking the parking areas for individual cars."[3] In terms of intelligence work, the U-2 was a breakthrough of gigantic proportions. As one high-ranking CIA official put it, "Photography became to the Fifties what code-breaking was to the Forties."[4]

On July 4, 1957, the first flight into Soviet airspace took off from a West German airfield, crossed Eastern Europe, flew over Russian Air Force bases in the Ukraine, then up to Leningrad. The next day a second flight crossed southern Ukraine and went on to Moscow. Eisenhower was shown the photos several days later and was again astounded at the clarity. The photos also depicted Soviet fighters rising to challenge the U-2 but flaming out at 50,000 feet and tumbling back to earth until the pilots could restart their engines.[5]

On July 10, the Soviet Union filed a formal diplomatic protest pertaining to the overflights, including an accurate description of what the U-2s had done and where they had gone. The State Department rejected the allegations. John Foster Dulles personally wrote out the reply that no *military* plane had violated Soviet airspace.[6] The Russians, for their part, chose not to go public with their protests about the U-2 flights because they did not want to admit to the world that their military was powerless to stop them. Eisenhower recognized that each U-2 flight was a provocation and insisted on approving the flights personally. The risk was small—Allen Dulles had assured the president that if the Soviets ever did shoot down a U-2, the pilot could not survive the crash—but Eisenhower demanded direct control. A former pilot himself, Ike often plotted the routes for the U-2 on flight maps with CIA deputy director Richard Bissell.[7]

The U-2 photographs not only provided convincing evidence that there was no missile gap, but that the Soviets had yet to launch an intercontinental ballistic missile. During the *Sputnik* crisis, John Foster Dulles urged the president to tell the country about the U-2 flights to reassure the public that the United States retained the strategic edge over the Soviets. Eisenhower declined to do so. If he revealed the flights, Ike believed he would come under intense Soviet pressure to halt them. Moscow might even declare that the next flight would be considered an act of war. Rather than take that risk, Eisenhower kept the flights secret, so important was the information they obtained.

The crises over Little Rock and *Sputnik* took a toll. In both instances Eisenhower's steady hand reassured a nation in doubt. But the emotional cost was high. Ike kept his personal feelings bottled up—as he always did—but he suffered for doing so. On Monday, November 25, 1957, Eisenhower welcomed King Mohammed V of Morocco to Washington in a brief ceremony at National Airport, then returned to the White House for a light lunch and a brief nap. Returning to his office in the early afternoon, he suddenly felt dizzy. He had difficulty reading the papers in front of him, could not pick up his pen, and slumped in his chair, unable to get up. He buzzed his secretary Ann Whitman. When Whitman came into the room, Eisenhower tried to tell her what had happened, only to discover that he could not speak intelligibly. His words were slurred and jumbled. "It was impossible for me to express any coherent thought whatsoever. I began to feel truly helpless."[8]

Ann Whitman was alarmed to find the president talking gibberish and immediately summoned General Andrew Goodpaster, Eisenhower's staff secretary, who occupied the adjacent office. Goodpaster assessed the situation quickly and concluded Ike had suffered a slight seizure. "Mr. President, I think we should get you to bed."[9] Eisenhower had no difficulty walking with Goodpaster's support, nor did he feel any pain. Goodpaster helped Ike undress and got him into bed. Dr. Snyder arrived shortly afterward. "Having resigned myself to bed, I spent no time worrying about the source of my trouble," Eisenhower recalled. "I just turned over to take a nap."

When the president awoke, two of the nation's leading neurological surgeons conducted an extensive examination and concluded that Eisenhower had experienced a minor spasm in one of the small capillaries of his brain. The problem was temporary, the doctors agreed, and they predicted a full recovery in a matter of days.[10]

Encouraged by the doctors' prognosis, Eisenhower got up and began to dress for the state dinner that evening honoring King Mohammed. Mamie, John, and Dr. Snyder objected strenuously. Vice President Nixon had already been tapped to substitute for the president, and they insisted that Ike remain in bed. The discussion became heated. Finally, Mamie said that if Eisenhower insisted on going to the dinner, she would not. "It soon appeared to me that a retirement in good order was called for," said Ike. "I went back to bed."[11]

The following morning Eisenhower was much improved but not yet fully recovered. He was unable to identify a famous William Turner watercolor hanging on his bedroom wall (*The Smugglers*), one of his favorite pictures, and his words were still slightly garbled.

After two additional days of bed rest, the doctors pronounced Eisenhower fully recovered. He and Mamie attended church services in Washington on Thanksgiving, and then drove to Gettysburg for the weekend.

The doctors were satisfied, but Eisenhower was unsure. This was his third serious illness in three years, and he did not want to cling to office if he was incapable of fulfilling his duties. The memory of Woodrow Wilson's last year as president troubled Ike, and he was especially sensitive to the possibility that he might not recognize his own disability. Against much high level advice, Eisenhower decided to test himself. The NATO conference of heads of government was due to convene in Paris in mid-December. Dulles suggested that Nixon attend in Ike's place, but Eisenhower saw it as a test. "If I could carry out this program successfully and without noticeable damage to myself, then I would continue in my duties. If I felt the results to be less than satisfactory, then I would resign."[12]

The trip was a complete success. The president's motorcade from Orly Airport was greeted by thousands of cheering Parisians, Eisenhower stood in an open car for almost an hour acknowledging their welcome, and his introductory remarks at the Palais de Chaillot went off without a hitch. Ike paid an unscheduled visit to his old NATO headquarters and spoke extemporaneously to the assembled staff and their families. "The talk was short, but to me it represented another milestone. I felt that my recovery was progressing satisfactorily."[13] For three days Eisenhower participated in the NATO meetings with no apparent loss for words. On the flight back to Washington, Dr. Snyder confided to Ike that he was much improved. "As he spoke, I realized that I already had abandoned my doubt concerning my physical capacity to continue my duties; during the remaining three years of my Presidency no question of the kind again occurred to me."[14]

One of the aftereffects of Ike's stroke was a little known undertaking by him to step down in the event of any future incapacity. In an exchange of letters revealed for the first time with the publication of his memoirs in 1965, Eisenhower carefully laid out for Nixon the circumstances under which the vice president would assume the power and duties of the presidency. If he were disabled, and aware of

Eisenhower at his easel.

it, Ike said he would inform Nixon and Nixon would take over. But if he were disabled and unaware of it, Nixon would be exclusively responsible for determining when he should take over. "You will decide. . . . The decision will be yours only." Eisenhower said that if medical experts agreed that his disability was permanent, he would immediately resign. By the same token, "I will be the one to determine if and when it is proper for me to resume the powers and duties of the Presidency."[15] Eisenhower's undertaking was almost a decade before the ratification of the Twenty-fifth Amendment to the Constitution, which provides for presidential disability.

As Eisenhower's second term progressed, his principal assistants fell by the wayside. Like a football team with a comfortable lead in the fourth quarter, the starters came off the field. Treasury Secretary George Humphrey, perhaps the most powerful member of the cabinet, resigned on July 28, 1957. Defense Secretary Charles Wilson left on October 8, and Herbert Brownell, in many ways Ike's most trusted adviser, departed after Little Rock. John Foster Dulles was crippled with cancer, and though he briefly returned to office, he resigned the following year. The loss of the four was a serious setback for Eisenhower. Humphrey, Wilson, Brownell, and Dulles were powerful figures of independent judgment. They were intensely loyal to the president, but could be counted on to speak forcefully when they disagreed. But the most serious loss Ike suffered in his second term was that of Sherman Adams. Adams was by no stretch of the imagination the deputy president. But as White House chief of staff he kept the administration in step and coordinated—just as Bedell Smith had done at SHAEF during the war.

The parallel between Sherman Adams and Bedell Smith is striking. Both were brusque, austere administrators capable of making on-the-spot decisions that freed Eisenhower of countless details. When generals in Europe were disappointed in decisions made at SHAEF, they usually blamed Bedell rather than Ike. So, too, in Washington. Politicians of both parties focused their ire on Sherman Adams when their requests were denied by the White House. Both Smith and Adams were scrupulously honest. Yet both had curious blind spots. In 1945, as the Allies overran Germany, the German gold hoard fell into American hands. Bedell Smith suggested that part of it be used to strike gold medals for the victorious generals. Eisenhower and Clay dismissed Smith's suggestion out of hand, yet Smith had meant well. He simply failed to understand why it was inappropriate.[16] Sherman Adams's difficulty was much the same.

Adams's problem arose out of his long friendship with New England industrialist Bernard Goldfine. The friendship between the Adams and Goldfine families dated to the early 1940s, when Adams had been Speaker of the New Hampshire General Court (the state legislature) and Goldfine had played an active role in financing textile mills in the state. The families sometimes vacationed together and often exchanged small presents on festive occasions. Goldfine retained an apartment in a downtown Boston hotel that was often used by visiting friends and business associates. When Adams went to Washington in 1953, Goldfine invited him to stay in the apartment whenever he was in Boston, and to sign Goldfine's name on hotel bills for room service and other incidentals. Goldfine also gave Adams a vicuña coat from one of his mills, and loaned him an oriental rug for his Washington home. Adams, for his part, once gave Goldfine a gold watch, and Rachel, Adams's wife, had given him a painting—all of which seemed innocent enough among old friends.

The Adams-Goldfine relationship surfaced in June 1958 during a congressional investigation into Goldfine's financial dealings. The hotel bills signed by Adams were discovered among Goldfine's records, and legislators assumed there had been a quid pro quo. On his own initiative Adams asked to testify. There was no subpoena, but he wanted to set the record straight. Adams had made two routine phone calls to the Securities and Exchange Commission to obtain information on Goldfine's behalf, but there had been no effort to influence the commission. Like Bedell Smith and the German gold, Sherman Adams failed to perceive how a phone call from the White House would be interpreted. Adams said that in retrospect he should have acted more prudently, but insisted he had done nothing wrong. The public perception was otherwise.

At his news conference the following day Eisenhower undertook a staunch defense of Adams. "Anyone who knows Sherman Adams has never had any doubt of his personal integrity and honesty," said the president. Perhaps mindful of the largess he had often received from his friends in the Gang, Ike told the newsmen that "a gift is not a bribe. One is evil, the other is a tangible expression of friendship." Eisenhower acknowledged that Adams might have acted imprudently, but "I believe with my whole heart that he is an invaluable public servant doing a difficult job efficiently, honestly, and tirelessly."[17]

On August 13, 1958, the House of Representatives cited Goldfine for contempt of Congress because of his refusal to answer some twenty-two questions during his testimony. Democrats were prepared to give Adams a pass, but congressional Republicans clamored for his scalp. It was an election year, and the GOP campaign committees viewed Adams as an anchor who would pull down Republican candidates nationwide. The appearance of influence peddling, valid or not, was an unnecessary burden in what was shaping up as a vintage year for the Democrats.

Eisenhower initially stood by Adams. "Completely convinced of his innocence, I refused to ask for his resignation."[18] As the White House hunkered down, the calls for Adams's resignation on Capitol Hill mounted daily. Nixon reported that the vast majority of Republicans in the House and Senate thought Adams should go. Meade Alcorn, the RNC chairman, repeated the message, as did Winthrop Aldrich, a friend of Adams whom Ike consulted.

The state of Maine always holds its statewide and congressional elections in September, six weeks or so before the rest of the nation goes to the polls. When the results in Maine were tabulated in 1958, the Republicans lost in a landslide—which many attributed to the negative publicity pertaining to Adams's relations with Goldfine. At that point Eisenhower realized that whether justified or not, Adams had become too much of a liability to retain. "How dreadful it is that cheap politicians can so pillory an honorable man," the president told Ann Whitman.[19] On September 17, Eisenhower asked for Adams's resignation. The chief of staff stepped down the following week, but it was too late to reverse the headwind blowing against the Republicans.[20] In the November elections, the Democrats picked up fifty seats in the House and fifteen in the Senate. Adams was replaced as White House chief of staff by his deputy, retired major general Wilton B. "Jerry" Persons, an old friend of Ike's. At Treasury, Humphrey was succeeded by Robert B. Anderson; Neil H. McElroy replaced Wilson at Defense; William P. Rogers, Nixon's old friend and associate, took Brownell's place as attorney general; and former congressman Christian A. Herter of Massachusetts became secretary of state. Persons, Anderson, McElroy, Rogers, and Herter were competent executives, but scarcely of the caliber of the cabinet officers they replaced.

In the summer of 1958, Eisenhower's attention was drawn once more to the Middle East. In the aftermath of the Suez affair, Eisenhower had asked Congress for blanket authorization to use military force to preserve the independence of the countries of the region if requested to do so. As with the Formosa Resolution, which Congress had adopted in 1955, the administration's proposal left the final decision to the president and was deliberately vague as to the circumstances that might trigger it. Known subsequently as the Eisenhower

Doctrine, the proposal was approved in March 1957.[21] "The existing vacuum in the Middle East must be filled by the United States before it is filled by Russia," Eisenhower told members of Congress.[22]

The Eisenhower Doctrine was framed in the Cold War context and had little immediate application. Like the Formosa Resolution, it was hortatory, designed to dissuade the Soviets rather than a call to action. Nevertheless it was a blank check, and in the summer of 1958 Eisenhower chose to cash it—not in relation to the Soviets, nor to combat Communist expansion, but to maintain stability in Lebanon.

Lebanon was nominally an Arab country and a member of the Arab League, although a slim majority of its people were Maronite Catholic. The president and the Army commander were traditionally Christian, while the prime minister and speaker of the legislature were Muslim.[23] This uneasy equilibrium was threatened in the aftermath of the Suez War by the influx of thousands of Arab refugees from Palestine. There was brief street fighting in the spring of 1958, although order was quickly restored. But on July 14, 1958, the situation changed dramatically following the violent overthrow of the British-installed monarchy in Iraq by radical Iraqi nationalists. The royal houses of Jordan and Saudi Arabia were threatened, and in Lebanon, President Camille Chamoun immediately asked Eisenhower for American troops to maintain order. The fear was revolutionary Arab nationalism, a decidedly secular movement sponsored by Egypt and Syria, not to be confused with Muslim religious fundamentalism. Eisenhower responded on July 15 with the dispatch of three battalions of Marines from the Sixth Fleet, followed by two airborne battle groups from Germany, a total of some fourteen thousand men. "You are doing a Suez on me," joked British prime minister Harold Macmillan, who sent a battalion of paratroopers to Amman to bolster the regime of King Hussein.[24]

The Marines landed without incident; there was no fighting of any kind and no casualties. The troops were withdrawn four months later. The intervention in Lebanon was the only time during Eisenhower's eight years in the White House that American troops were dispatched to a foreign country, and as in Little Rock, Ike chose to use overwhelming force. The reason for doing so, which Eisenhower never doubted, was to ensure the stability of regimes in the Middle East favorable to the United States, and to demonstrate Washington's ability to deploy troops in the area on a moment's notice. The whole affair, Eisenhower noted in his memoirs, brought about "a definite change in Nasser's attitude toward the United States."[25]

No sooner had the crisis in Lebanon eased, than the uneasy standoff in the Formosa Strait fell apart. Against Washington's advice, Chiang Kai-shek had recently deployed more than one hundred thousand troops—over a third of his army—on the islands of Quemoy and Matsu. Beijing considered the move provocative and demanded the troops be withdrawn. When Chiang refused, the Chinese commenced a sustained shelling of the islands. Eisenhower was momentarily caught in a dilemma. On the one hand, there was no possibility that Chiang's forces could mount an invasion of the mainland, and his increase in the size of the garrisons had been unquestionably provocative. On the other, Chiang was America's ally and the United States was committed to the defense of Formosa and the offshore islands as well in certain circumstances. What Eisenhower worried about was that Chiang might escalate the crisis to draw the United States into a war with mainland China. "The Orientals can be very devious," he told Deputy Secretary of Defense Donald Quarles. "If we give Chiang our full support he would then call the tune."[26]

Eisenhower dispatched two additional carriers to the region and ordered the Seventh Fleet to convoy Chiang's supply ships on the high seas, but not within the three-mile coastal limit. The mainland Chinese responded by holding their fire until the Nationalist vessels came close to shore. As resupply problems for Quemoy and Matsu mounted, Dulles and the Joint Chiefs suggested that the commander of the Seventh Fleet be authorized to use tactical atomic weapons against the Chinese without reference to Washington. Eisenhower refused. An attack on the mainland "could be ordered only with my approval,"[27] said the president. The crisis simmered into early September. On September 4, 1958, Dulles issued a statement reaffirming the intention of the United States to protect the offshore islands, but including a thinly veiled offer to negotiate, which Eisenhower insisted upon.[28] Two days later, Chou En-lai responded positively. Shortly thereafter U.S. and Chinese diplomats resumed discussions over the conference table in Warsaw, discussions that had broken off the year before. The Joint Chiefs also revised their position. On September 11, Secretary of Defense Neil McElroy told Eisenhower that the chiefs had concluded that the offshore islands were not necessary for the defense of Formosa and should be vacated. That evening Eisenhower went on national television to address the crisis. "There is not going to be any appeasement," said Ike, but "I believe there is not going to be any war."[29] Both sides got the message. Chiang accepted in principle the need to reduce the garrisons on the offshore islands, and the Chinese announced that they would fire on the Nationalist convoys only on the odd days of the month, permitting resupply on the even days. "I wondered if we were in a Gilbert and Sullivan war," Eisenhower later noted in his memoirs.[30] The crisis passed. Quemoy and Matsu remained in Nationalist hands, the size of the garrisons was reduced, though not nearly so much as Eisenhower wished, and the firing ceased. Ike had remained cool throughout the crisis and once again war was avoided.

The most serious foreign policy issue Eisenhower confronted in 1958 concerned Berlin. The city of Berlin, still technically under four-power occupation from World War II, was located 110 miles within what had been the Soviet zone of occupation, now the German Democratic Republic (GDR). The three western sectors of the city (British, French, and American) were consolidated and governed as "West Berlin"; the Soviet sector—"East Berlin"—was integrated into the GDR. Simply put, West Berlin was part of the democratic West and NATO; East Berlin was part of the Communist East and the Warsaw Pact. This uneasy situation had prevailed for over a decade. West Berlin was linked to West Germany by three air corridors, three autobahns, and three rail lines. The Russians had attempted to block access in 1948 during the Berlin blockade, but the Allied airlift had kept West Berlin supplied, and the Russians eventually backed down. A tacit understanding pertaining to access gradually evolved and was no longer at issue. What was at issue in 1958 was the precarious state of the German Democratic Republic and the desperate Soviet need to ensure its survival.

The military boundary between NATO and the Warsaw Pact was for all practical purposes the boundary between the two Germanies.

It was heavily fortified and impenetrable. Churchill called it an "iron curtain." No commerce passed through; there was no civilian traffic or access of any kind—save for the corridors to West Berlin. The situation in Berlin was entirely different. Although divided between East and West for governmental purposes, and possessing different currencies, movement within the city was unimpeded. There were no border controls between East Berlin and West Berlin, streets ran through, as did the U-Bahn, the S-Bahn, and city buses. One could travel freely anywhere in the city. West Berlin was cordoned off from East Germany, but not from East Berlin. And East Berlin opened into East Germany. There were no border controls since East Berlin was the capital of the GDR.

That was at the root of the problem in 1958. Disaffected East Germans could travel freely to East Berlin, and then simply cross over to West Berlin, ask for political asylum, and be flown out and resettled in West Germany. What had begun as a trickle of refugees in the early postwar years had reached mammoth proportions by 1958. The population of the former Soviet zone (now the GDR), which numbered close to twenty million in 1945, had shrunk to seventeen million by 1958, and those who were leaving often represented the most productive elements of East German society.[31] This extraordinary emigration of professionals and skilled workers was more than the Communist regime of East Germany could endure.

The most obvious way to halt the population drain was to plug the escape route in Berlin. At the end of October 1958, Walter Ulbricht, the head of the East German government, commenced the effort by charging that the continued presence of Allied forces in Berlin was illegal. According to Ulbricht—and with patent disregard for the relevant quadripartite agreements—all of Berlin belonged to the GDR.[32] One month later the theme was picked up by Nikita Khrushchev. In separate notes to the United States, Britain, and France, Khrushchev demanded that the Allied occupation of Berlin be terminated and that West Berlin be converted into a demilitarized "free city." Khrushchev gave the Western powers a six-month ultimatum. If the Allies had not accepted his proposal within that time, the Soviet Union would conclude its own agreement with the GDR and end the occupation unilaterally.[33]

Khrushchev's ultimatum hit the West like a bombshell. In West Berlin, Mayor Willy Brandt pointed out that Berlin was only part of the larger struggle between East and West and that there was "no isolated solution."[34] Eisenhower, who was taking time off for a much needed rest at the Augusta National, issued a terse statement dismissing the Soviet note out of hand.* At Ike's direction, General Henry I. Hodes, the commander of American forces in Europe (USAREUR), paid a highly publicized visit to Berlin to demonstrate U.S. resolve, and German chancellor Konrad Adenauer made one of his rare trips to the city. West Berlin elections were scheduled for the following week, and in an unusual display of unity Brandt and Adenauer campaigned together. "The clouds have darkened over this city," said Adenauer, "but we shall not be frightened."[35] Brandt was reelected handily, and the Communists' high hopes were dashed when they received just 31,500 votes out of the 1.7 million votes cast.

Buoyed by the West Berlin election results, the Western powers girded to hold their ground. Dulles, joined by his British and French counterparts, issued a formal statement announcing the intention of their governments to remain in Berlin, the NATO Council stated it would not yield to threats, and in Washington the government issued a lengthy document spelling out the legal status of Berlin.[36] At the end of the year the United States, Britain, and France delivered their official replies to the Soviet demand. In identical notes the three governments told Moscow that they had no intention of relinquishing their rights in Berlin, and that they continued to hold the Soviet Union responsible under the relevant wartime agreements. The Russian proposal to convert West Berlin into a "free city" was unacceptable. Eisenhower, ably supported by Macmillan and de Gaulle, was determined to hold firm. Ike also recognized the need to give Khrushchev a way to back down gracefully. At his suggestion, the Allied replies noted that Berlin was simply a part of the larger

---

* "The United States will not enter into any arrangement or embark on any course of conduct which will have the effect of abandoning the responsibilities which the United States, with Great Britain and France, has formally assumed for the freedom and security of the people of West Berlin," said Eisenhower. White House Press Release, November 30, 1958, EL.

question of Germany, and offered to commence negotiations on that subject. Those negotiations, of course, could not take place under threat of an ultimatum.[37] It was Eisenhower at his best: a carrot and a stick.

Khrushchev got the message. On a whirlwind unofficial visit to the United States, Soviet deputy premier Anastas Mikoyan said his government's six-month ultimatum related only to the beginning of discussions, not to a settlement of the dispute. Khrushchev told the East Germans much the same. Speaking to the Ninth All-German Workers Conference in Leipzig on March 7, Khrushchev told the East Germans not to hurry. "The wind does not blow in your face. The conditions are not ripe as yet for a new scheme of things. Each fruit has its season."[38]

On May 27, 1959, Khrushchev's ultimatum came and went. Nothing happened. In Berlin it was business as usual.* Thanks to Eisenhower's determination the crisis eased. Two years later, as East Germany continued to hemorrhage, Khrushchev took the measure of another American president and decided to risk it. After meeting John F. Kennedy in Vienna in June 1961, Khrushchev flashed Ulbricht the signal to go ahead. On August 13, 1961, the East Germans closed the border between East and West Berlin and began construction of the Berlin Wall—action they had declined to take with Ike in the White House. Kennedy affirmed America's commitment to West Berlin; Eisenhower defended the quadripartive status of the entire city.

In the early summer of 1959, Khrushchev let it be known that he would like to visit the United States. Eisenhower thought it would be a good idea. "This will take the crisis edge off the Berlin situation," Ike wrote Harold Macmillan.[39] After a brief exchange of notes it was agreed that Khrushchev would come to the United States in mid-September, with Eisenhower paying a return visit to the Soviet

---

* I was stationed in Berlin at the time as a junior officer in the 6th Infantry Regiment. Throughout the entire six-month crisis I do not remember that we did anything out of the ordinary. Never for a moment did we think anything would happen—although we were prepared to meet every contingency. As I look back on it, I believe the fact that we did not do anything out of the ordinary provided great reassurance to the Berliners.

Union the following year. Before receiving Khrushchev, Eisenhower thought it best to visit Europe and touch base with Macmillan, Adenauer, and de Gaulle—all of whom were understandably nervous about a one-on-one meeting between the American and Soviet leaders.

Ike's meeting with de Gaulle was memorable. Recalled in 1958 from the political wilderness to handle the crisis in Algeria, de Gaulle had been the last premier of the Fourth Republic, the author of the constitution of the Fifth Republic, the first president of France under the new regime, and the exemplar of national reconciliation, bridging the historic divide between Left and Right. In 1959, de Gaulle was at the height of his power. "I at once sensed important changes since I had last seen him," said Eisenhower. "He now appeared a more benign, less forbidding individual than the fiery division commander who had made himself the symbol of French resistance in World War II."[40]

De Gaulle for his part was effusive in welcoming Eisenhower to France. "Whatever may come in the future, whatever may happen in the years ahead, you will for us forever be the generalissimo of the armies of freedom."[41] On the second evening, after the formal program concluded at the Château de Rambouillet, the summer residence of the presidents of France, the two heads of state, who were spending the night at Rambouillet, sat before the fireplace in Ike's apartment in their bathrobes and began to reminisce. "Isn't it curious," observed de Gaulle, "that we are two old generals who have written our memoirs and we have never carped or recriminated at the other. Roosevelt thought that I took myself for Joan of Arc. He was wrong. I simply took myself for General de Gaulle."[42]

The discussion that evening was wide-ranging, covering the major issues confronting the West, including France's effort to develop its own nuclear weapons program—which de Gaulle put in perspective. "You, Eisenhower, would go to nuclear war for Europe because you know what is at stake. But as the Soviet Union develops the capability to strike the cities of North America, one of your successors [may not]. When that comes, I or my successor must have in hand the nuclear means to turn what the Soviets may want to be a conventional war into a nuclear war."[43] It was precisely that perception of

Eisenhower—that he would not flinch from launching a nuclear war if necessary to protect the West—that made the United States so formidable.

As for Khrushchev, Eisenhower had indicated that in addition to the public tour, he wanted to meet privately with the Soviet leader at Camp David. This threw the Kremlin into a tizzy. What and where was Camp David? Was it an internment facility? Perhaps a quarantine station? Was the Russian leadership to be held hostage? Frantic messages to and from the Soviet embassy in Washington soon clarified that Camp David was an American version of a Russian dacha that Roosevelt had built as a weekend retreat. An invitation there was a signal of honor. "We never told anyone at the time about not knowing what Camp David was," Khrushchev confessed in his memoirs. "I can laugh about it now, but I'm a little bit ashamed. It shows how ignorant we were in some respects."[44]

Khrushchev arrived in Washington on September 15, 1959, stayed thirteen days, and visited seven cities. The trip was a media circus, and Khrushchev made good copy, whether he was sparring with hecklers at banquets, hurling ears of corn at reporters on the Iowa farm of Roswell Garst, or giving his wristwatch to a worker on an assembly line in Pittsburgh. He was accompanied throughout by the urbane Henry Cabot Lodge, for whom Khrushchev developed a fondness. Lodge had a sense of humor, which Khrushchev appreciated. "He was a pleasant companion to pass the time with during the many hours we spent on planes and trains. We tried to avoid talking business if possible. There was no need to get ourselves all worked up talking politics."[45]

Eisenhower and Khrushchev met for three days at Camp David. Ike also took the Soviet leader to the farm at Gettysburg and presented him with a young Angus bull that Khrushchev had admired. When Khrushchev returned to Moscow he reciprocated by sending Ike a small forest of birch trees to be planted on the farm. In the evenings they watched Westerns, which Khrushchev also enjoyed.[*]

---

[*] According to Khrushchev, Stalin liked Westerns as well. "When the movie ended, Stalin always denounced it for its ideological content. But the very next day we'd be back in the movie theater watching another Western." *Khrushchev Remembers: The Last Testament* 407, Strobe Talbott, ed. and trans. (Boston: Little, Brown,

9/15/59

The talks between Eisenhower and Khrushchev were substantive, covering the full range of issues, but ultimately unproductive. No solutions were forthcoming, but the fact that the meetings were held helped lower the temperature in East-West relations. In effect, Ike and Khrushchev agreed to disagree, and found they had more in common than met the eye.

At one point Eisenhower asked Khrushchev about military expenditures. "Tell me, Mr. Khrushchev, how do you decide on funds for the military?" Before Khrushchev could answer, Ike volunteered to tell him how it was in the United States. "My military leaders come to me and say, 'Mr. President, we need such and such a sum for such and such a program. If we don't get the funds we need, we'll fall behind the Soviet Union.' So I invariably give in. That's how they wring money out of me. Now tell me, how is it with you?"

"It's just the same," Khrushchev replied. "Some people from our

---

1974). Also see *Khrushchev Remembers* 297–98, Strobe Talbott, ed. and trans. (Boston: Little, Brown, 1970).

military department come and say, 'Comrade Khrushchev, look at this! The Americans are developing such and such a system. We could develop the same system but it would cost such and such.' I tell them there's no money. So they say, 'If we don't get the money we need and if there's a war, then the enemy will have superiority over us.' So we talk about it some more, I mull over their request and finally come to the conclusion that the military should be supported with whatever funds they need."

"That's what I thought," said Eisenhower. "You know, we really should come to some sort of an agreement in order to stop this fruitless, really wasteful rivalry."[46]

On Berlin, the meetings at Camp David cleared the air. Eisenhower and Khrushchev discussed the issue at length on September 26, with no one present except their interpreters. Eisenhower pointed out that Berlin was simply a part of the larger problem of a divided Germany and said the Soviet ultimatum had created a very difficult situation. Khrushchev replied that "the Soviet Union did not want to take any unilateral action and that he wanted to solve the German problem together with the United States in the friendliest manner possible."[47] As Eisenhower wrote later, Khrushchev "realized he had a bear by the tail on the Berlin issue and was relieved to have found a way out with reasonable dignity."[48]

Khrushchev's explicit withdrawal of his Berlin ultimatum at Camp David paved the way for the Paris summit. The issues on the agenda were Germany and disarmament. Eisenhower, Khrushchev, Macmillan, and de Gaulle agreed to meet in Paris on May 16, 1960. De Gaulle would be host. An agreement banning nuclear testing appeared in the offing, and the Berlin issue had moved to a back burner. Both Eisenhower and Khrushchev wanted to reduce military expenditures, and Macmillan and de Gaulle wanted to participate in the process. "Never in the Cold War did agreement seem closer," wrote one historian of the period.[49] Eisenhower planned to visit the Soviet Union after the summit, and an itinerary had been worked out with the Soviet ambassador in Washington, Mikhail Menshikov. For Eisenhower, as the end of his presidency approached, the world appeared far safer than eight years before. The Cold War was not over, but U.S.–Soviet relations had rarely been better. Domestically,

America had never enjoyed greater prosperity. Ike's final budget would be balanced; the national debt, which stood at 100 percent of the nation's GDP when Eisenhower took office, had been reduced to 56 percent; unemployment had shrunk to little more than 5 percent; and desegregation in the South was proceeding "with all deliberate speed." Everything seemed to be coming nicely to fruition as Ike contemplated another trip to Paris.

On May 1, 1960, Eisenhower's proverbial luck ran out. Russian surface-to-air missiles (SAMs) finally succeeded in shooting down an American U-2 spy plane, this time 1,200 miles inside the Soviet Union near Sverdlovsk (formerly known as Yekaterinburg). And it happened on May Day—the most festive day on the Communist calendar. For the next two weeks the world was treated to a comedy of errors as Washington attempted to cover up, while the Soviets released the evidence piece by piece. Khrushchev and his colleagues may not have known where or what Camp David was, but they surely knew how to exploit an American miscue.

By 1960 it had become clear that the U-2 was fast becoming obsolete. Soviet missiles were improving in range and accuracy, and it was only a matter of time before a plane would be shot down. The United States had developed a highly secret satellite program (Corona) to replace the U-2, but it was not yet operational. And so in the early spring of 1960, the intelligence community requested permission to mount several additional U-2 flights to fill in "gaps" in the coverage. Eisenhower was reluctant. Khrushchev, the president said, had outlined Soviet missile capability at Camp David, and "every bit of information I have seen from the overflights corroborates what Khrushchev told me." According to the notes of the White House meeting kept by General Goodpaster, "The President said that he has one tremendous asset in a Summit meeting [and] that is his reputation for honesty. If one of these aircraft were lost when we were engaged in apparently sincere deliberations, it could be put on display in Moscow and ruin the President's effectiveness."[50]

Despite his initial reluctance, Eisenhower granted the CIA permission to launch a flight on April 9, 1960. The flight took place without incident, and photographs revealed no new missile sites. The CIA asked for another flight. Eisenhower agreed, providing it took place within the next two weeks. Weather intervened and Allen Dulles asked the president for an extension. Again, Eisenhower agreed, this time for one more week. "After checking with the President," wrote General Goodpaster, "I informed Mr. Bissell that one additional operation may be undertaken, provided it is carried out by May 1. No operation is to be carried out after May 1."[51]

On the morning of May 1, the weather cleared and Francis Gary Powers, a veteran U-2 pilot who had flown missions over the Soviet Union for the past four years, took off from Peshawar, Pakistan, heading for Bodø, Norway. The flight would require nine hours and would cover 3,800 miles, passing over suspected Russian missile sites en route. Ironically, it was to have been the last flight of the U-2.

Moscow initially made no announcement of having shot down the plane. Late in the afternoon of May 1, Goodpaster informed Eisenhower that the U-2 was missing, but that triggered no alarm since it was assumed that the plane would be destroyed on impact and the pilot would be dead. Additional reports that day indicated that Powers had spoken of an engine flameout, but that, too, caused no upset. Eisenhower thought it best to ignore the incident, hoping that Khrushchev might do the same in the interest of harmony at the summit. Those hopes were dashed on May 5 when Khrushchev, in a lengthy speech to the Supreme Soviet, announced they had shot down an American spy plane deep inside the Soviet Union. Khrushchev blamed "Pentagon militarists" for the act. Eisenhower was not mentioned nor was the fact that Francis Gary Powers was in Soviet custody. "I went out of my way not to accuse the President," Khrushchev wrote later.[52]

In Washington the cover-up began. NASA issued a press release that one of its U-2 meteorological research planes had been missing since May 1, "when its pilot reported he was having oxygen difficulties over the Lake Van, Turkey area." Presumably the plane had strayed off course and been shot down by the Soviets. The State Department issued a similar denial. "It is entirely possible that having failure in the oxygen equipment, which could result in the pilot losing consciousness, the plane continued on automatic pilot for a considerable distance and accidentally violated Soviet airspace."[53]

Two days later Khrushchev sprang the trap. Speaking once again to the Supreme Soviet, the chairman announced that he not only had the wreckage of the plane, but the pilot and the film. "The pilot's name is Francis Gary Powers. He is thirty years old and works for the CIA." Khrushchev then displayed some of the photos showing Soviet air bases with fighters lined up on the runway. "The whole world knows that Allen Dulles is no weatherman," said Khrushchev.[54]

In Washington, Eisenhower exploded. For years he had been assured by Allen Dulles that no U-2 pilot would fall into Soviet hands alive. Now Khrushchev had irrefutable proof that the United States had systematically violated Soviet airspace. Nevertheless, the cover-up continued. "As a result of the inquiry ordered by the President," said a State Department press release, "it has been established that insofar as the authorities in Washington are concerned, there was no such authorization for any such flight as described by Mr. Khrushchev."[55] The story did not hold water. The press was skeptical and Eisenhower himself soon had second thoughts. After attending Sunday service in Gettysburg on May 8, the president telephoned Secretary Herter and instructed him to issue a new statement acknowledging that for the past four years U-2s had regularly been sent into the Soviet Union under orders from the president to obtain knowledge of the Soviet military-industrial complex.[56] Milton Eisenhower, now president of Johns Hopkins, told his brother that he must not take the rap for the U-2. Ike disagreed. He said he would not blame subordinates for his decisions. It would be a "glaring and permanent injustice." John suggested his father fire Allen Dulles. Again Ike said no. "I am not going to shift the blame to my underlings."[57] The following day, Monday, May 9, Eisenhower told a meeting of top officials in the Oval Office, "We will now just have to endure the storm," meaning that he personally would be the one who did the enduring.[58]

Eisenhower's decision to accept personal responsibility for the U-2 flights may have been the finest hour of his presidency. Rather than force Allen Dulles and Richard Bissell to walk the plank for reasons of state, Eisenhower acknowledged his own culpability. FDR would not have done so; Ronald Reagan was shielded from Iran-Contra, and nobody knows what Reagan's successors might have done. John F.

Kennedy announced his personal liability for the Bay of Pigs fiasco, but except for dimming the luster of the New Frontier, little damage was done. In Eisenhower's case the president, by taking direct responsibility, doomed the Paris summit, scuttled an impending nuclear test ban treaty, blew the chance to reduce defense expenditures, and forfeited the possibility of progress on the German question. "I had longed to give the United States and the world a lasting peace," Eisenhower said later. "I was able only to contribute to a stalemate."[59]

Ike was always his own harshest critic. In May 1960, his essential decency and personal sense of responsibility had carried the day. "He had this thing about honesty," said Undersecretary of State Douglas Dillon. "That was the military tradition."[60]* Cynics would argue that such sentiment is out of place in the Oval Office. But it was not out of place for Eisenhower. Ike knew the difference between right and wrong, and tried to apply that knowledge to politics and diplomacy. That is why the country always trusted him.

The Paris summit convened on May 16, 1960, in the high-ceilinged conference room of the Palais de l'Élysée, only a few rooms removed from de Gaulle's own office. As host, the French president presided. After calling the conference to order, de Gaulle recognized Eisenhower to speak first. Since he was the only head of state (other than de Gaulle), it was strictly protocol that Ike should speak first. Khrushchev heatedly objected. All delegation chairmen were equal, he insisted, and he demanded to speak first. De Gaulle shot a glance toward Eisenhower, Ike shrugged, and de Gaulle recognized Khrushchev. For the next forty-five minutes Khrushchev lambasted the United States and the U-2 overflights as though haranguing a party rally in Red Square. At one point Ike passed a mordant note to Christian Herter: "I think I'm going to take up smoking again."[61] When

---

* Eisenhower put it somewhat differently. Speaking later to Gang member Ellis Slater, Ike said it was absolutely essential to create a feeling of confidence and trust among people working for government. "His [Eisenhower's] philosophy is that by cajoling, by assurances, by backing up and by sharing responsibility, he can insure people staying in government service. . . . Hence, if errors had been made in the U-2 or other cases, honest mistakes, unavoidable perhaps—he felt that D[wight] E[isenhower] should assume responsibility." Ellis D. Slater, *The Ike I Knew* 229 (Ellis D. Slater Trust, 1980).

Khrushchev, having lashed himself into an oratorical frenzy, pointed to the ceiling and shouted, "I have been overflown!" de Gaulle had had enough. "I too have been overflown," the French president interrupted.

"By your American allies?" asked Khrushchev.

"No, by you," de Gaulle replied drily. "That satellite you launched just before you left Moscow to impress us overflew the sky of France eighteen times without my permission. How do I know you do not have cameras aboard which are taking pictures of my country?"

"You don't think I would do a thing like that?" asked Khrushchev.

"Well," replied de Gaulle, "how did you take those pictures of the far side of the moon?"

"That one had cameras."

"Ah," said de Gaulle, "that one had cameras. Pray continue."[62]

Khrushchev resumed reading his prepared text with increasing venom. He closed by announcing that unless Eisenhower personally apologized for the overflights, the conference could not continue. Almost as an afterthought, Khrushchev rescinded the invitation for Eisenhower to visit the Soviet Union. "How can I invite as a dear guest the leader of a country which has committed an aggressive act against us?"[63]

Eisenhower replied briefly, pointing out that the U-2 flights involved no aggressive intent, were only gathering information to guard against surprise attacks, and in any event had been permanently discontinued.[64] At that point the Soviet delegation rose and left the conference room. The other delegations looked at one another. De Gaulle said he would stay in touch with the Russians, and everyone got up to leave. De Gaulle walked over to Eisenhower and took him by the arm. "I do not know what Khrushchev is going to do, nor what is going to happen, but whatever he does, or whatever happens, I want you to know that I am with you to the end."[65]

Eisenhower was deeply moved. As he walked down the stairs of the Palais de l'Élysée he turned to Colonel Vernon Walters, who had overheard de Gaulle's remarks. "That de Gaulle is really quite a guy," said Ike.[66]

Eisenhower played only a minor role in the 1960 election. He declined to endorse any candidate prior to the GOP convention, briefly tried to coax Robert Anderson, then Oveta Culp Hobby, into running, and accepted Nixon's nomination as inevitable. Nixon had served Ike loyally for the past eight years, yet Eisenhower was still not ready to concede that his vice president was capable of taking command. If the alternative was Nelson Rockefeller, Ike preferred Nixon. But it was a Hobson's choice. When Eisenhower addressed the Republican National Convention in Chicago on July 26, he devoted his entire speech to the accomplishments of the past eight years and never once mentioned Nixon, although Nixon by that point was the only candidate in the race.[67]*

Nixon, for his part, wanted to prove that he could win in his own right and was content to keep Ike in the background. Perhaps the president could put in a good word or two at his press conferences, but Nixon did not want Eisenhower barnstorming the country. The press conference strategy proved a disaster. Asked on August 10 whether he intended to give Nixon a greater voice in the administration "in view of his responsibilities as the nominee of the Republican Party," Eisenhower replied that he alone would make the decisions. He would continue to consult Nixon, said Ike, but "I'm going to decide according to my judgment." Charles Bartlett of the *Chattanooga Daily Times* asked if there were any differences between Nixon and the president on nuclear testing. "Well," Eisenhower responded, "I can't recall what he has ever said specifically about nuclear underground testing."[68]

It got worse. At Ike's next news conference, Sarah McClendon asked Eisenhower to "tell us some of the big decisions that Mr. Nixon has participated in . . . as Vice President?" The president was almost gruff in his reply. "No one participates in the decisions. . . . No one can make a decision except me. . . . I have all sorts of advisers, and one of the principal ones is Mr. Nixon. . . . When you talk about other people sharing a decision, how can they? No one can, because then who is going to be responsible?"

---

* Arizona nominated Barry Goldwater, but Goldwater immediately withdrew. He received ten votes from Louisiana on the first ballot, and then Nixon was nominated by acclamation.

Charles Mohr of *Time* wanted to know more. Nixon's experience had become an issue in the campaign, he said. The Republicans claimed that Nixon "has had a great deal of practice at being President." In light of the president's answer to Ms. McClendon, asked Mohr, "would it be fair to assume that what you mean is that he has been primarily an observer and not a participant in the executive branch of the Government?" Eisenhower, whose command of the English language was always impeccable, particularly at news conferences, and especially when he wanted to evade a question, tried to work his way out. "I said he was not part of the decision-making. That has to be in the mind and heart of one man." But every leader has to consult, said Ike. And for the past eight years the vice president has participated in every consultative meeting that has been held "and has never hesitated to express his opinion."

MR. MOHR: We understand that the power of the decision is entirely yours, Mr. President. I just wondered if you could give us an example of a major idea of his that you had adopted in that role, as the decider and final—

THE PRESIDENT: If you give me a week, I might think of one. I don't remember.

"Thank you, Mr. President," said Jack Bell of the Associated Press, terminating the news conference.[69]

Not surprisingly, relations between Eisenhower and Nixon, which were tepid to begin with, cooled further as the campaign progressed. Eisenhower believed that Nixon was becoming too partisan and was driving away independents and conservative Democrats who had voted for Ike in droves; Nixon chafed under Eisenhower's shadow and resented playing second fiddle. At the end of August, Eisenhower paid a highly publicized visit to Nixon at Walter Reed—Nixon was in the hospital with an infected knee. Afterward, Ike told Ann Whitman, there was "some lack of warmth." According to Whitman's notes, "He [Eisenhower] mentioned again, as he has several times, the fact that the Vice President has very few personal friends." As Whitman saw it, the difference between Ike and Nixon was all too obvious. "The president is a man of integrity and sincere in his

1960 Herblock Cartoon, copyright by The Herb Block Foundation

**"SELDOM HAS A CANDIDATE HAD SO MUCH
EXPERIENCE AT NOT BEING RESPONSIBLE
FOR DECISIONS"**

*August 25, 1960*

every action. He radiates this, everybody knows it, and everybody loves and trusts him. But the Vice President sometimes seems like a man who is acting like a nice man rather than being one."[70]

Nixon insisted on making all of the important campaign decisions himself. Ike's advice was not sought, and when offered was rarely heeded. Eisenhower suggested Nixon not debate Kennedy on television because Nixon was much better known, and there was no reason to give Kennedy so much free exposure. Nixon rejected the advice on the grounds that he was a much better debater than Kennedy. The first debate was an unmitigated catastrophe. As Ted Rogers, Nixon's television adviser said, Nixon's eight years of experience as vice president was "wiped out in a single evening."[71]

The election was a cliffhanger. With a 64.5 percent turnout, Kennedy received 34,221,463 votes to Nixon's 34,108,582—a difference of 112,881 out of the more than 68 million ballots cast.* In the electoral college, Kennedy carried twenty-three states with 303 electoral votes; Nixon carried twenty-six states with 219 votes. (Mississippi cast its electoral vote for Senator Harry F. Byrd of Virginia.) A shift of only 4,500 votes in Illinois and 28,000 in Texas would have given Nixon the election.[72]

As Eisenhower's term drew to a close, Norman Cousins, the longtime editor in chief of *Saturday Review,* suggested to Ike that he give a "farewell address" to the nation—a parting testament after fifty years of public service. Eisenhower at the time was the oldest president to occupy the White House, and would be the last to be born in the nineteenth century. John F. Kennedy, at forty-three, was the youngest ever to be elected. Eisenhower liked Cousins's suggestion. George Washington had warned the country against entangling alliances; Ike wanted to warn against the perils of ever-increasing defense expenditures and the garrison state.[73]

Eisenhower worked on the speech for more than a month, aided by his brother Milton and speechwriter Malcolm Moos, a young political science professor on leave from Johns Hopkins. At eight-thirty on the evening of January 17, 1961, Ike spoke to the country from the Oval Office. After briefly sketching the larger issues of war and peace, Eisenhower warmed to his theme. "Our military organization bears little relation to that known by any of my predecessors in peacetime." Until World War II, "the United States had no armaments industry. American makers of plowshares could . . . make swords as well." But now, because of the Cold War, "we have been compelled to create a permanent armaments industry of vast proportions. Added to this, three and a half million men and women are directly engaged in the defense establishment. We annually spend more on military security than the net income of all United States corporations."

* American voter turnout is always reported as a percentage of the population twenty-one years and older. In Canada, Great Britain, and in western Europe, turnout figures are reported as a percentage of registered voters. That is why European and Canadian turnout figures are always so much higher. It's apples and oranges.

Eisenhower's voice continued with somber intonation. "This conjunction of an immense military establishment and a large arms industry is new to the American experience. The total influence—economic, political, even spiritual—is felt in every city, every State house, every office of the Federal government." Then, in the most widely quoted passage, Ike said: "In the councils of government, we must guard against the acquisition of unwarranted influence, whether sought or unsought, by the military-industrial complex. The potential for the disastrous rise of misplaced power exists and will persist."

Eisenhower's fear of the garrison state also manifested itself in his warning against excessive government influence in the world of scholarship. "The free university, historically the fountainhead of free ideas and scientific discovery, has experienced a revolution in the conduct of research. Because of the huge costs involved, a government contract becomes virtually a substitute for intellectual curiosity." Eisenhower cautioned against "the domination of the nation's scholars" by the power of federal money, which he said was a danger "to be gravely regarded."*

Then, in a timeless warning for the future, Eisenhower said America "must avoid becoming a community of dreadful fear and hate, and be, instead, a proud confederation of mutual trust and respect."[74]

---

* Eisenhower also warned against the growing power of a "scientific-technological elite." Herbert F. York, an academic physicist who served Eisenhower as director of defense research and engineering, explained that Ike had in mind what had happened during the forty months from the launching of *Sputnik* to the end of his administration: "The people who irritated him were the hard-sell technologists who tried to exploit Sputnik and the missile gap psychosis it engendered. . . . They invented all sorts of technological threats to our safety and offered a thousand and one technical delights for confronting them." Eisenhower understood both "the necessity of having a military-industrial complex and . . . the problems and dangers it brought with it." Herbert F. York, *Making Weapons, Talking Peace: A Physicist's Odyssey from Hiroshima to Geneva* 126 (New York: Basic Books, 1987).

# TWENTY-EIGHT

# *Taps*

Lower the shades. Pull me up. Higher. I want to
go. God take me.

— DWIGHT D. EISENHOWER,
*March 28, 1969*

EISENHOWER AND MAMIE departed Washington immediately
after John F. Kennedy's inaugural ceremony on January 20, 1961.
They drove to Gettysburg in the 1955 Chrysler Imperial that Mamie
had given Ike on his sixty-fifth birthday, followed by a lone Secret
Service car. At the entrance to the farm the car honked, and the
agents waved and made a U-turn to head back to Washington. In
1961, ex-presidents were not entitled to Secret Service protection.

Eisenhower settled in easily to Gettysburg. He taught himself to
drive again, passed the Pennsylvania test for a driver's license, and
learned to use a dial telephone. He was given an office at Gettysburg
College, and his classified papers were housed in a vault at Fort Det-
rick, in Frederick, Maryland.

Before leaving Washington, Eisenhower let it be known that he
would like to be restored to his five-star rank as General of the Army,
an action that required congressional legislation.[*] President Ken-

---

[*] On March 4, 1885, former president Ulysses S. Grant, in dire financial circumstances, was restored to his rank of four-star general by unanimous vote of both
houses of Congress. The legislation had been originally introduced by Joseph E.
Johnston, the former Confederate general who now represented Virginia's Third
Congressional District.

nedy was mystified. Why would Ike want to relinquish the title of "Mr. President" to be called "General"? he asked his military assistant, Brigadier General Ted Clifton. As best he could, Clifton explained to Kennedy that Eisenhower was a military man at heart. The term "Mr. President" applied to Herbert Hoover, Harry Truman, and Kennedy himself, but General of the Army was an independent title, something Ike had worked for all of his life. "Besides, if he is a five-star general, he needs no favors from you or the White House."[1] Kennedy saw the point, and the bill was passed unanimously in March 1961.

Eisenhower devoted himself to writing his presidential memoirs—a two-volume collection commendable for its completeness and documentation but scarcely bedtime reading for the uninitiated. Unlike *Crusade in Europe,* which was written personally by Ike in twelve-to-sixteen-hour days, *Mandate for Change* and *Waging Peace,* dealing with his first and second terms, were initially drafted by his son John and former White House speechwriter William Ewald. Eisenhower reviewed the drafts and retooled the manuscripts, and the prose is serviceable. But the books, which have set the tone for subsequent presidential memoirs, lack the elegance of Grant's memoirs or the feistiness of Harry Truman's. Ike eschewed high drama in the interest of historical accuracy. He is circumspect, befitting an elder statesman, and more than evenhanded when dealing with adversaries such as Joe McCarthy. The books received mixed reviews. As Eisenhower wished, they provide an indispensible guide to his eight years in the White House and are essential for scholars of the period. Later, Ike wrote the commendable *At Ease: Stories I Tell to Friends,* an informal, almost random, look at the events of his life before the presidency. Eisenhower dictated these reminiscences in the evenings at Gettysburg, and his portraits of old associates such as Fox Conner, Douglas MacArthur, and George Patton are frank and uninhibited.

---

In Grant's day, former presidents did not receive pensions, but as a general his salary would be restored. Eisenhower did not benefit financially by regaining his rank, but as a General of the Army he was permitted to retain the servies of his driver, Leonard Dry; his valet, Sergeant Moaney; and his aide, Colonel Robert Schulz.

For Grant, see Jean Edward Smith, *Grant* 622–25.

Ike at leisure in Gettysburg.

Eisenhower's daily schedule at Gettysburg varied little from his time in the White House. He rose at six or so, read the daily papers as he ate breakfast, and was in his office by seven-thirty. He returned home for lunch at noon, took a short nap, and then either returned to the office or headed for the golf course. Back home at five, he showered and changed clothes, enjoyed a scotch before dinner, and invariably ate alongside Mamie on trays set up in front of the television set. If a quorum could be mustered, there was often a bridge game. He was usually in bed well before ten.

In the fall of 1961 Eisenhower and Mamie took up winter residence at the Eldorado Country Club in California's Coachella Valley, midway between Palm Desert and Indian Wells. For the next seven years they would spend five months a year at Eldorado, Ike finding the dry desert air more agreeable than the humidity at Augusta, and the company just as exclusive. After sending troops to Little Rock in

1957, Eisenhower's welcome at Augusta was also not as warm as it had once been. At Eldorado, the Eisenhowers lived in a home on the eleventh fairway recently constructed by Texas oil baron Robert McCulloch for their exclusive use. Ike established his office at the Cochran Ranch in nearby Indio, and found the seclusion at Eldorado much to his liking. Unlike Gettysburg, where the Eisenhowers lived on a place open to the public, Eldorado was a gated, heavily protected community for the cream of society in the California desert.

Other than writing his memoirs, Eisenhower played little role in national politics. He supported Nixon for governor of California in 1962, never warmed to Barry Goldwater's presidential bid in 1964, and strongly endorsed Nixon's effort four years later. In his role as elder statesman, he buttressed Kennedy at the time of the Cuban missile crisis, and refrained from criticizing Lyndon Johnson over Vietnam.[2]

At the state funeral of President Kennedy, he and Harry Truman once again found common ground. Protocol dictated that as former presidents the two would ride in the same limousine from Blair House to Arlington National Cemetery. Making a virtue of necessity, the two decided to share a glass of whiskey at Blair House before leaving. Perhaps the whiskey had a mellowing effect, after the saying *in vino veritas.* The two former presidents forgot their past animosity and began to chat affably, trading observations and stories about former colleagues. Among other things, they agreed that their actions as president sometimes had a rationale that few others would understand. Perhaps it was best left that way. "We know what we did," said Truman.

"We surely do," Ike replied.[3]

It was after President Kennedy's funeral that Congress passed legislation to provide full Secret Service protection to former presidents. In the summer of 1965 a detail of agents returned to Gettysburg and staked out the positions they had used when Eisenhower was president. Ike was ambivalent about the protection. "Life for me personally would be much happier if I had less of this so-called 'protection,' " Eisenhower wrote his son John. Ike said one man with a six-shooter—"possibly reinforced by one in my own pocket"—should be sufficient for his own security, but he worried about "cranks" targeting the family, particularly the grandchildren.[4]

Eisenhower was seventy-five. His health was failing. At the Augusta National in November 1965 he suffered a second near-fatal heart attack. He began to lose weight, and his interest in the farm diminished. The Angus herd was disbursed in 1966. Nevertheless his hold on American public opinion continued unabated. In January 1968, with disaster looming in Vietnam, the Gallup poll named Eisenhower the man most admired by the American people—an honor he had previously won in 1950 and 1952.[5] Ike and Mamie went to California as usual, and Eisenhower spent as much time on the links as possible. On February 6, 1968, he presented the Eisenhower Trophy to the winner of the Bob Hope Classic—his good friend Arnold Palmer. The following day he shot a hole-in-one at the Seven Lakes Country Club—the first he had ever shot, climaxing, as it were, his lifetime devotion to the game.[6]

On Monday, April 20, 1968, Ike was again on the course at Seven Lakes but quit after nine holes complaining of chest pains. He went home, but was soon rushed to the hospital with what doctors initially diagnosed as a mild heart attack. He was placed in intensive care at nearby March Air Force Base, but failed to respond to treatment. After four weeks he was flown to Washington and installed in the presidential suite at Walter Reed. Mamie moved in next door. For the next ten months, from May 1968 to March 1969, Eisenhower remained hospitalized, gradually losing ground to a series of follow-on heart attacks. On March 27, Ike instructed his son John to remove him from the life support system to which he had been attached. "I've had enough, John. Tell them to let me go."[7]

At 12:35 p.m. the following day, Dwight David Eisenhower died, surrounded by his family and the doctors who had treated him. Eisenhower's body lay in state in the Capitol Rotunda, resting in a standard-issue eighty-dollar Army coffin, clad in his Ike jacket, unadorned with metals or decorations other than his insignia of rank. After the ceremony his flag-draped casket was placed in a railroad car of a funeral train for the trip back to Abilene. Forty hours later Eisenhower was laid to rest on the grounds of the home in

De Gaulle renders a final salute, in the rotunda of the Capitol.

which he grew up. It was a simple ceremony, closed to all but family and friends.[8]

Several years later, a young David Eisenhower asked his grandmother Mamie whether she felt she had really known Dwight David Eisenhower.

"I'm not sure anyone did," Mamie replied.[9]

# Acknowledgments

Once again my principal indebtedness is to Rhonda Frye in the office of the president at Marshall University. I write in longhand with a ballpoint pen on yellow legal pads. As with *FDR,* Mrs. Frye reads what I have written, transfers it to typescript, and presents me with clean copy every morning. She has typed at least a dozen drafts of every chapter, and does so faultlessly and without complaint. I have been privileged to work with her.

I am also deeply indebted to Professor Sanford Lakoff of the University of California, San Diego, and Professor John Seaman of the University of the Pacific. Sandy, a former colleague at the University of Toronto, has read the drafts of every biography I have written. His erudition and vast knowledge of the literature has saved me from countless errors. John, a 1954 classmate of mine at Princeton, has read every word in the manuscripts of every book I have written, beginning with *The Defense of Berlin* in 1964. If the prose now flows smoothly, it is in no small measure attributable to his influence.

My research assistant, Elizabeth Williams, deserves special recognition. Ms. Williams, former chief paralegal at Ashland Oil and now a graduate student at Marshall, not only prepared the bibliography, but ran down and verified each of the citations in the notes. Her assistance has been invaluable. Rick Haye of Marshall University served as illustrations editor. No one is better at tweaking photos than Rick, and I am deeply indebted.

To others who have read the manuscript of *Eisenhower in War and Peace* and offered suggestions, I am eternally grateful. Each reader brings a different perspective, and their individual criticism has been especially helpful. They include Tom Berquist, Steven Canby, Paul Ehrlich, Bennett Feigenbaum, Ellen Feldman, Alan Gould, Henry Graff, Harry Moul, William Nelson, Kristen Pack, Kelly and David Vaziri, Judge Frank Williams, and Jack Zeiler.

Dr. Sonya Vaziri of the Harvard Medical School provided professional advice pertaining to Ike's heart condition, just as she did for FDR's hypertension.

The archivists and librarians at the Eisenhower Presidential Library have been especially helpful: Timothy Rives, Kathy Struss, Chalsea Millner, and Catherine Cain. I am also indebted to Jocelyn Wilk at the Manuscript Library of Columbia University.

The title, *Eisenhower in War and Peace,* was suggested by Victoria Coates in the office of Donald Rumsfeld.

To the "Eisenhower Irregulars" at Marshall University—my students over the past several years—I am also indebted. They have read chapters in the manuscript, offered suggestions, and kept me apprised of contemporary attitudes. I would especially like to commend Jessica Elliott, Matthew Newlon, and Yasmine Zeid.

At Random House I am especially indebted to Dennis Ambrose, Jonathan Jao, and Ben Steinberg. My agent was Elizabeth Kaplan. The index was prepared by Judith Hancock and Melvin Hancock. Copyediting was done by Michelle Daniel. Ms. Daniel deserves special commendation. She is the best of the best, and I am eternally grateful.

My final debt is to my editor at Random House, the legendary Robert Loomis. Bob retired last year after fifty-four years at Random House, and this was one of his last books. Bob was a pleasure to work with. He reads every word of every manuscript submitted to him, and offers gentle but always insightful suggestions. His example is an inspiration to every author who has had the privilege of working with him.

# *Notes*

The initial epigraph is from General Eisenhower's speech to the Canadian Club, Ottawa, Canada, January 10, 1946. The preface is written without endnotes. The quotations appear elsewhere in the text and are fully cited at that point.

## ABBREVIATIONS

| | |
|---|---|
| AG | Adjutant General |
| CCS | Combined Chiefs of Staff |
| COHP | Columbia Oral History Project, Columbia University |
| DDE | Dwight D. Eisenhower |
| EL | Eisenhower Library |
| FDR | Franklin Delano Roosevelt |
| FDRL | Franklin D. Roosevelt Library |
| *FRUS* | *Foreign Relations of the United States* |
| GCM | George C. Marshall |
| GSP | George S. Patton |
| HST | Harry S. Truman |
| JCS | Joint Chiefs of Staff |
| JFD | John Foster Dulles |
| LDC | Lucius D. Clay |
| MDE | Mamie Doud Eisenhower |

MMBA  MacArthur Memorial Bureau of Archives
NARA  National Archives and Records Administration
TR    Theodore Roosevelt
WSC   Winston S. Churchill

CHAPTER ONE: JUST FOLKS

The epigraph is a quote from General Eisenhower reminiscing about the difference between his heritage and that of the "aristocrat" Douglas MacArthur. Quoted in John Gunther, *Eisenhower: The Man and the Symbol* 50 (New York: Harper and Row, 1952).

1. Birth certificates were not issued in Grayson County, Tex., when Eisenhower was born. His mother recorded his name in the family Bible as "D. Dwight Eisenhower," the "D" for David, his father's name. "Dwight" was for the noted evangelist Dwight Lyman Moody, whom Ida admired. Eisenhower was always called Dwight, not David, and when he entered school his name was officially entered as Dwight D. Eisenhower, reversing the order of his two given names.

2. Jacob Eisenhower sold his farm in Pennsylvania for $175 an acre. In Kansas, his quarter section cost $7.50 an acre. Dwight D. Eisenhower, *At Ease: Stories I Tell to Friends* 62 (Garden City, N.Y.: Doubleday, 1967).

3. A. T. Andreas, *History of the State of Kansas Containing a Full Account of Its Growth from an Uninhabited Territory to a Wealthy and Important State* 686 (Chicago: A. T. Andreas, 1883). Currency conversions are based on the calculations of Robert C. Sahr, Political Science Department, Oregon State University.

4. The River Brethren chose Dickinson County after an extensive survey of Kansas property. Except for annual rainfall, the climate was similar to Pennsylvania's, with winter temperatures averaging from 41 to 44 degrees. The fertile topsoil, similar to that of the Susquehanna Valley, was an astounding twelve feet deep. For an extensive comparison between Dickinson County and Lancaster County, Pennsylvania, see John R. Hertzler, "The 1879 Brethren in Christ [River Brethren] Migration from Southeastern Pennsylvania to Dickinson County, Kansas," *Pennsylvania Mennonite Heritage* 11–18, January 1980.

5. Carlo D'Este, *Eisenhower: A Soldier's Life* 15–16 (New York: Henry Holt, 2002).

6. Stephen E. Ambrose, 1 *Eisenhower* 16 (New York: Simon and Schuster, 1983).

7. Instead of giving David a quarter section of farmland, Jacob mortgaged it to his son-in-law Chris Musser for $2,000, which he presented to David. That, plus Jacob's standard gift of $2,000, allowed David to construct a store on the main street of Hope and stock it with merchandise. The Eisenhower Building, as it was called, was the largest structure on Hope's main street. Thomas Branigar, "No Villains—No Heroes," *Kansas History* 170, Autumn 1990.

8. DDE, *At Ease* 31. Also see Edgar Eisenhower's statement recorded in Edgar Newton Eisenhower and John McCallum, *Six Roads from Abilene: Some Personal Recollections of Edgar Eisenhower* 18 (Seattle: Wood and Reber, 1960). Earl Eisenhower is quoted to the same effect in Bela Kornitzer, *The Great American Heritage: The Story of the Five Eisenhower Brothers* 11–12 (New York: Farrar, Straus, and Cudahy, 1955). Early biographers repeated the Eisenhower version. See, for example, Kenneth S. Davis, *Soldier of Democracy: A Biography of Dwight Eisenhower* 36–37 (Garden City, N.Y.: Doubleday, 1946); Ambrose, 1 *Eisenhower* 17.

9. Chattel Mortgage Record Book O, page 74, Archives Division, Dickinson County Historical Society. On November 4, 1886, *The Hope Dispatch* published the following notice signed by David Eisenhower: "This is to certify that I have this day bought all the interest in the late firm of Good & Eisenhower, thereby releasing M. D. Good from all responsibilities of the late firm."

10. *The Hope Dispatch,* November 5, 19, 1886. Unlike David Eisenhower, Milton Good was well-liked by the community. He not only did not flee, but after the partnership was dissolved the *Dispatch* encouraged him "to spend the remainder of his natural days" in Hope, regardless of the type of business he chose to pursue. Ibid.

11. The exhaustive primary research into David's early failure was conducted by Thomas Branigar of the Eisenhower Library and published in 1990 in *Kansas History* 168–79 under the title "No Villains—No Heroes: The David Eisenhower–Milton Good Controversy." According to Branigar, at page 179,

> When historians began studying the Eisenhower family history after David's death, the older Eisenhower generation, even those who may have known the truth, probably repeated David's stories out of loyalty to his memory. The younger generation, represented by the President and his brothers, who were not alive at the time of the partnership, could only repeat what they had been told by their elders. . . . By relying solely on Eisenhower family tradition, historians obtained and perpetuated a distorted view of the Good–Eisenhower partnership.

12. D'Este, *Eisenhower* 22.

13. By the late 1890s, the Belle Springs Creamery was producing well over two million pounds of butter annually. It had established milk-buying stations in twenty-nine Kansas locations and processing plants in Abilene and Salina, and employed fifty persons full-time. See Hertzler, "1879 Brethren in Christ Migration" 15–17.

14. Peter Lyon, *Eisenhower: Portrait of the Hero* 36 (Boston: Little, Brown, 1974). Musser was concerned about David's stability. After advancing the money for train tickets for the family's return to Abilene, he gave David a contract that specified he would receive a salary of $340 a year: $25 a month for six

months, $30 a month for four months, and $35 a month for two months. In addition, the contract specified that "at the end of each month 12% of the salary is retained until the end of the year when the full amount is paid." Musser wanted to be doubly certain David did not bolt from the job. Merle Miller, *Ike the Soldier* 60 (New York: G. P. Putnam's Sons, 1987).

15. Whether by prior agreement or not, in 1908, ten years later, Ida transferred the title to David. Geoffrey Perret, *Eisenhower* 15 (New York: Random House, 1999).

16. Kornitzer, *Great American Heritage* 26.

17. Ibid. 32–33.

18. When they were serving together in the 1930s, General MacArthur rebuked Eisenhower for never attending church. "I've gone to West Point Chapel so goddamn often," said Ike, "I'm never going inside a church again." William Clark to Stewart Alsop, March 3, 1954, Alsops' Papers, Library of Congress. Cited in Piers Brendon, *Ike: His Life and Times* 9 (New York: Harper and Row, 1986).

19. Eisenhower signed the legislation adding the words "under God" to the pledge on Flag Day ( June 14) 1954. "From this day forward," said the president, "the millions of our school children will daily proclaim in every city and town, every village and rural school house, the dedication of our nation and our people to the Almighty." *Public Papers of the Presidents: Dwight D. Eisenhower, 1954* 141 (Washington, D.C.: National Archives and Records Service, 1960).

20. Jerry Bergman, "Steeped in Religion: President Eisenhower and the Influence of the Jehovah's Witnesses," *Kansas History* 148–67, Autumn 1998. When Ike graduated from West Point in 1915, Ida gave him a standard Watchtower Bible, in which the word "Jehovah" is substituted throughout for the word "God." Eisenhower used this Bible when he was sworn in for his second presidential term in 1957, but in his quotation from it, "Blessed is the nation whose God is Jehovah," he substituted "Lord" for "Jehovah." N. H. Knorr, "Conspiracy Against Jehovah's Name," 78 *Watchtower* 323–24 ( June 1, 1957).

    After Ida's death in 1946, Milton, then president of Kansas State University, quietly disposed of her fifty-year collection of *Watchtower,* the monthly publication of the Jehovah's Witnesses, lest there be any unfavorable publicity. Presumably, David's pyramid diagram was removed at the same time. Jack Anderson, Washington Merry-Go-Round, *The Washington Post,* September 23, 1956; Merle Miller, *Ike the Soldier* 79.

21. Edgar Newton Eisenhower and McCallum, *Six Roads from Abilene* 21.

22. Ibid. 31–32.

23. DDE, *At Ease* 31.

24. Perret, *Eisenhower* 11.

25. DDE, *At Ease* 37. "Our love for our father was based on respect," said Edgar. "Our love for our mother was based on something more." Edgar Newton Eisenhower and McCallum, *Six Roads from Abilene* 35.

26. Milton Eisenhower, interview by Stephen Ambrose, in Ambrose, 1 *Eisenhower* 21.

27. "From my present position as a banker," Arthur once said, "I can grasp our early economic situation better than I could while I was a youngster. Indeed, were it not for the three-acre garden patch behind the house, we might have faced real want at times." Kornitzer, *Great American Heritage* 63.

28. Edgar Newton Eisenhower and McCallum, *Six Roads from Abilene* 92–93.

29. With characteristic rigidity, David agreed to support Edgar if he would attend medical school at the University of Kansas but not if he wanted to study law. With equally characteristic stubbornness, Edgar refused and was partially supported at Michigan by his uncle, Chris Musser, who countersigned Edgar's notes at the Farmers National Bank of Abilene. Neither Edgar nor Chris Musser ever informed David of the arrangement. Ibid.

30. "I had nothing to do with the decision to move Japanese nationals and Japanese-Americans from the Pacific coast," Milton told Bela Kornitzer. "When the decision was made, I was asked by the President to establish an agency that would be responsible for bringing about the movement of some hundred and twenty thousand men, women, and children in about three months." Later Milton wrote, "I have brooded over this episode on and off for the past three decades. It need not have happened." Kornitzer, *Great American Heritage* 232.

31. Lyon, *Eisenhower* 38.

32. Dwight D. Eisenhower, *Ike's Letters to a Friend: 1941–1958,* Robert Griffith, ed. (Lawrence: University of Kansas Press, 1984).

33. DDE, *At Ease* 104.

34. Kenneth S. Davis, one of the earliest biographers of Eisenhower, postulated that Ike spent the summer of 1910 worrying about attending one of the service academies given his mother's faith. Numerous biographers have followed Davis's lead, but there is not a shred of evidence to substantiate his assertion. At a presidential press conference on July 7, 1954, Eisenhower said the stories of his parents' objections were totally incorrect. "She [Ida] never said one single word to me." *The New York Times,* July 8, 1954. Compare Kenneth S. Davis, *Soldier of Democracy* 107–8.

35. DDE to Bristow, August 20, 1910, in Dwight D. Eisenhower, *Eisenhower: The Prewar Diaries and Selected Papers, 1905–1941* 8, Daniel D. Holt and James W. Leyerzapf, eds. (Baltimore: Johns Hopkins University Press, 1998).

36. Jean Edward Smith, *Lucius D. Clay: An American Life* 26 (New York: Henry Holt, 1990).

37. DDE, *Eisenhower: Prewar Diaries* 8.

38. Pulsifer joined Ike in the Class of 1915, graduated 116th of 164 (Eisenhower ranked 61st), and retired from the Army because of a disability in 1920 with the rank of major. Merle Miller, *Ike the Soldier* 116.

39. Bristow to DDE, October 24, 1910, Joseph L. Bristow Papers, Kansas State Historical Society Archives.

40. DDE to Bristow, October 25, 1910, ibid.

41. DDE, *At Ease* 108.

42. Ibid. 8.

43. Ibid. 5.

44. Jean Edward Smith, *Lucius D. Clay* 34.

45. General Hugh Scott, *Some Memories of a Soldier* 420 (New York: Century, 1928).

46. Quoted in Edward M. Coffman, *The Hilt of the Sword: The Career of Peyton C. March* 186 (Madison: University of Wisconsin Press, 1966).

47. "The graduates of West Point," wrote Eliot, "did not escape, with few exceptions, from the methods they had been taught and drilled in during peace. The methods of fighting were in the main new, and the methods of supply and accounting ought to have been new. The red tape methods [of the peacetime Army] were very mischievous all through the actual fighting and remain a serious impediment to the efficiency of the War Department to this day." *The New York Times,* May 9, 1920.

48. Quoted in T. Bentley Mott, "West Point: A Criticism," *Harpers* 478–79, March 1934.

49. William Manchester, *American Caesar: Douglas MacArthur, 1880–1964* 121 (Boston: Little, Brown, 1978). "I am not the most rabid worshipper of MacArthur that there is in this world," said Lucius D. Clay. "But I give him a tremendous amount of credit for recognizing the need for change at the Military Academy to meet the change in the whole national outlook and environment. He knew it had to be changed, and he changed it—against a good deal of opposition from members of his own faculty." Jean Edward Smith, *Lucius D. Clay* 39.

50. Ibid. Eisenhower inclined to the more conventional view. "One thing that has struck me very forcibly . . . is the frequency with which one finds the older officer of today [January 31, 1944] to be merely a more mature edition of the kid [we] knew as a Cadet. This is not always so and sometimes the exceptions are so glaring as to prove the rule. . . . Frequently, I get a lot of fun checking up my present impressions of people with the impressions I had of them when they were very young and I am amazed to find how often these impressions are identical." Quoted in Merle Miller, *Ike the Soldier* 45.

51. DDE, interview by Edgar F. Puryear, Jr., May 2, 1963, quoted in Puryear, *19 Stars: A Study in Military Character and Leadership* 13 (Orange, Va.: Green Publishers, 1971).

52. DDE, *At Ease* 10, 12. During World War II, Eisenhower expressed incredulity when he learned one of his classmates had been promoted to brigadier general. "Christ," he said, "he's always been afraid to break a regulation." Ambrose, 1 *Eisenhower* 48.

53. Quoted in Merle Miller, *Ike the Soldier* 29.

54. DDE, *At Ease* 16–17.

55. Gunther, *Eisenhower* 29.

56. Marty Maher, *Bringing Up the Brass* 177 (New York: McKay, 1951).

57. Dwight D. Eisenhower, *In Review: Pictures I've Kept; A Concise Pictorial "Auto-biography"* 14 (Garden City, N.Y.: Doubleday, 1969).

58. DDE, *At Ease* 16. Omar Bradley, a classmate of Ike's and a member of both the varsity baseball and football teams, said much the same. "No extracurricular endeavor I know of could better prepare a soldier for the battlefield." Omar N. Bradley and Clay Blair, *A General's Life: An Autobiography* 34 (New York: Simon and Schuster, 1983).

59. Alexander M. "Babe" Weyand, "The Athletic Cadet Eisenhower," *Assembly* 11, Spring 1968.

60. Brigadier General Carl C. Bank to Edgar F. Puryear, Jr., January 13, 1963, in Puryear, *19 Stars* 19.

61. Francis T. Miller, *Eisenhower: Man and Soldier* 149–50 (Philadelphia: John C. Winston, 1944).

62. Lieutenant Colonel Morton F. Smith, Commandant of Cadets, 1915 USMA Efficiency Report, DDE Personnel File, Eisenhower Library (EL), Abilene, Kansas.

63. In 1915 the Army totaled 106,764 men, of whom 4,948 were officers. Expenditures totaled $115,410,000. Those figures did not increase significantly until 1917. United States Department of the Army, *The Army Almanac* 692 (Washington, D.C.: U.S. Government Printing Office, 1950); United States Bureau of the Census, *The Statistical History of the United States from Colonial Times to the Present* 736 (Stamford, Conn.: Fairfield Publishers, 1965).

64. DDE, *At Ease* 24.

65. Ibid. 25.

66. Quoted in Merle Miller, *Ike the Soldier* 43.

67. Colonel Herman Beukema to DDE, April 1946, EL.

68. Ibid.

## CHAPTER TWO: THE GREAT WAR

The epigraph is a comment made by Lieutenant Colonel Eisenhower to his classmate Major Norman Randolph upon learning of the armistice on the western front, November 11, 1918. Randolph to DDE, June 20, 1945, EL.

1. On September 19–20, 1863, the 19th Infantry held the center of George Thomas's line at Chickamauga, earning for itself and General Thomas the epithet "Rock of Chickamauga." When the fighting ended, the regiment, still holding its position, had but forty men and four officers remaining, and was commanded by a second lieutenant.

2. R. S. Baker, 4 *Woodrow Wilson: Life and Letters* 289 (Garden City, N.Y.: Doubleday, 1931). The best recent survey of Wilson's intervention in Mexico is John S. D. Eisenhower's *Intervention! The United States Involvement in the Mexican Revolution, 1913–1917* (New York: W. W. Norton, 1993). His earlier *So Far from God: The United States War with Mexico, 1846–1848* (New York: Random House, 1989) is an equally good assessment of the Mexican War under Polk.

3. Eisenhower was joined in the 19th Infantry by his classmate Thomas F. Tay-

lor, who was soon posted to the 16th Infantry at Del Rio, along the Mexican border.

4. Lieutenant General Walker was killed in a vehicle accident in Korea and did not attain the rank of full general.

5. DDE, *At Ease* 121.

6. Ibid. 122.

7. Vivian Cadden, "Mamie and Ike Talk About Fifty Years of Marriage," *McCall's,* September 1966; Steve Neal, *The Eisenhowers: Reluctant Dynasty* 35 (Garden City, N.Y.: Doubleday, 1978).

8. DDE, *At Ease* 113.

9. Mabel Frances [Doud] Moore, interview by Merle Miller, quoted in Miller, *Ike the Soldier* 141.

10. Mamie Doud Eisenhower Oral History, EL. Quoted in Marilyn Irvin Holt, *Mamie Doud Eisenhower: The General's First Lady* 6 (Lawrence: University Press of Kansas, 2007).

11. Funston was the area commander, but the War Department took the unusual step of prescribing to him who should command the expedition. It did so because General Hugh Scott, Army chief of staff, believed Pershing less volatile than Funston, and more capable of handling a situation that required diplomacy. American forces were violating Mexican sovereignty, and the Wilson administration wanted to avoid a war if possible. John S. D. Eisenhower, *Intervention* 235.

12. DDE, *At Ease* 121.

13. Ibid. 122.

14. Merle Miller, *Ike the Soldier* 149. Fifty years later, celebrating his wedding anniversary with Mamie, Eisenhower was asked the secret of their marital success. He attributed it to a sense of humor, "and not insist[ing] on being right. Being right all the time is perhaps the most tiresome quality anyone can have." Cadden, "Mamie and Ike Talk About 50 Years of Marriage."

15. Years later Mamie said, "I got out of [Abilene] in a hurry, I'll tell you, every time I got the chance." MDE Oral History, EL.

16. Ambrose, 1 *Eisenhower* 59.

17. Maureen Clark, *Captain's Bride, General's Lady* 24 (New York: McGraw-Hill, 1956).

18. For the text of Wilson's speech, see *The New York Times,* April 3, 1917.

19. DDE, *At Ease* 131.

20. DDE efficiency report, December 2, 1917, EL. Ironically, the 57th Infantry never made it overseas and spent the war on garrison duty at Fort Sam Houston.

21. Susan Eisenhower, *Mrs. Ike: Memories and Reflections on the Life of Mamie Eisenhower* 43 (New York: Farrar, Straus and Giroux, 1996).

22. DDE to MDE, September 25, 1917, in DDE, *Eisenhower: Prewar Diaries* 13–14. (Eisenhower's emphasis.) Ike's reference to "Sheltering Palms" is to the hit song "Down Among the Sheltering Palms," published in 1914. Music by Abe Olman; lyrics by James Brockman.

23. DDE to MDE, September 26, 1917, in DDE, *Eisenhower: Prewar Diaries* 15.

24. DDE efficiency report, February 22, 1917, to November 26, 1917, EL.

25. Lieutenant Edward C. Thayer to his mother, January 1918, Presidential Papers, EL.

26. Fitzgerald twice submitted "The Romantic Egotist" to Scribner's and both times it was rejected. Major portions later appeared in *This Side of Paradise.* Arthur Mizener, *The Far Side of Paradise: A Biography of F. Scott Fitzgerald* 75–77 (Boston: Houghton Mifflin, 1965). Also see Fitzgerald to Edmund Wilson, January 10, 1918, in *The Letters of F. Scott Fitzgerald* 321–24, Andrew Turnbull, ed. (New York: Scribner, 1963).

27. DDE efficiency report, December 15, 1917, to January 3, 1918, EL.

28. British artillery was classified by the weight of the projectile, in this case six pounds, or 2.7 kilograms, and the gun had a muzzle velocity of 720 meters per second. In World War II, twin six pounders were a standard British coast artillery weapon.

29. Quoted in Michael Korda, *Ike: An American Hero* 137 (New York: Harper-Collins, 2007).

30. DDE, *At Ease* 136.

31. Ibid. 137.

32. Ibid.

33. A separate tank corps was established in France under the command of Brigadier General Samuel D. Rockenbach with an authorized strength of 14,827 officers and men. Merle Miller, *Ike the Soldier* 168.

34. DDE, *At Ease* 137, 135.

35. Ibid. 138.

36. Ibid.

37. Neal, *Eisenhowers* 45.

38. DDE, *At Ease* 140.

39. Francis T. Miller, *Eisenhower* 172.

40. *Gettysburg Times,* June 7, 1918.

41. DDE to Lieutenant Colonel F. Summers, August 26, 1943, EL. Eisenhower's foreword, also written on August 26, stated:

> More than a quarter of a century ago, the tank made its debut upon the battlefield as a clumsy, belly-crawling monster whose weakness in locomotion and whose structural frailties were so glaring as to drive from the ranks of its adherents all except men of vision, of faith, and of fortitude. To those that were able to see in early failures only challenge to greater effort, we are indebted for the hastening of the German defeat in 1918.
>
> But more than this, imbued with a conviction that modern science stood ready to offer to armies speed of movement in battle with protection against the inevitable hail of small arms fire, they urged that there was thus presented an opportunity through which the wise would prosper and the ignorant would meet disaster. Their number was all too few, but, fortunately, they persisted. Among them, none was more eloquent nor more farseeing than

those distinguished soldiers that have contributed to this book. In a very marked sense, we owe to them the overwhelming nature of the Allied Tunisian victory—to say nothing of the triumphal odyssey of the British Eighth Army that began at El Alamein and has already reached Catania.

42. The estimates are from Gina Kolata, *Flu: The Story of the Great Influenza Pandemic of 1918 and the Search for the Virus That Caused It* 6–21 (New York: Farrar, Straus and Giroux, 1999). The term "Spanish flu" derives from the fact that it was first detected in San Sebastián, Spain, in the winter of 1918.

43. DDE, *At Ease* 149.

44. Ibid. 150.

45. U.S. Bureau of the Census, *Statistical History of the United States* 735.

46. Ernest F. Miller (Corps of Engineers), who graduated fourth in the Class of 1915, was promoted to lieutenant colonel on September 28, 1918—two weeks before Eisenhower.

47. DDE efficiency report, March 15, 1918, to November 15, 1918, EL.

48. Quoted in Alden Hatch, *Red Carpet for Mamie* 116 (New York: Henry Holt, 1954).

49. DDE, *At Ease* 151.

50. Ibid.

51. Ibid.

52. Randolph to DDE, June 20, 1945, EL.

53. Citation, DSM, EL. Although Welborn recommended Eisenhower for the Distinguished Service Medal immediately after the war, he did not receive it until 1924. James B. Ord, Class of 1915, received the DSM for service with Pershing in Mexico, and four of Ike's classmates were awarded the Distinguished Service Cross for valor in France: Charles W. Ryder, Sidney C. Graves, John W. Leonard, and Harry Harvey (posthumously).

## CHAPTER THREE: THE PEACETIME ARMY

The epigraph is an observation made by Eisenhower discussing demobilization after World War I. DDE, *At Ease* 152.

1. DDE, *At Ease* 151–52.

2. Ibid. 155.

3. MDE Oral History, EL.

4. DDE, *At Ease* 156. Also see John E. Wickman, "Ike and the Great Truck Train—1919," *Kansas History* 139–47, Autumn 1990.

5. Vaughn Smartt, "1919: The Interstate Expedition," 55 *Constructor* 18–25 (August 1973).

6. DDE, *At Ease* 157.

7. Dwight D. Eisenhower, "Report on Transcontinental Trip," November 3, 1919, EL.

8. DDE, *At Ease* 163–65.

9. Susan Eisenhower, *Mrs. Ike* 59.

10. Dorothy Barrett Brandon, *Mamie Doud Eisenhower: A Portrait of a First Lady* 106–8 (New York: Scribner, 1954).

11. DDE, *At Ease* 166–67.

12. Martin Blumenson, 1 *The Patton Papers* 24 (Boston: Houghton Mifflin, 1972).

13. Ambrose, 1 *Eisenhower* 70.

14. As Mark Clark put it, "Ike was not an envious man." Mark Clark, interview by Merle Miller, quoted in Miller, *Ike the Soldier* 184.

15. DDE, *At Ease* 169–70.

16. Dwight D. Eisenhower, unpublished assessments of World War II personalities, Post-Presidential Papers, EL.

17. George S. Patton, "Tanks in Future Wars," 16 *Infantry Journal* (May 1920).

18. Dwight D. Eisenhower, "A Tank Discussion," 17 *Infantry Journal* 453–58 (November 1920).

19. DDE, *At Ease* 173.

20. John Eisenhower, interview by Merle Miller, quoted in Miller, *Ike the Soldier* 186.

21. Beatrice Patton's books included *Légendes Hawaiiennes,* a compilation of Hawaiian lore that she wrote in French; *Blood of a Shark,* a historic novel set in Hawaii, and *Reminiscences of Frederick Ayer,* about her father. She also translated French Army manuals into English for the War Department and wrote the stirring "Second Armored Division March." George commanded the 2nd Armored in North Africa in 1943.

22. Julie Nixon Eisenhower, *Special People* 199–200 (New York: Simon and Schuster, 1977).

23. MDE Oral History, EL.

24. DDE to Elivera Doud, November 16, 1919, in Susan Eisenhower, *Mrs. Ike* 61.

25. DDE, *At Ease* 176.

26. Kevin McCann, quoted in Merle Miller, *Ike the Soldier* 191.

27. DDE, *At Ease* 180.

28. Ibid. 180–81.

29. Susan Eisenhower, *Mrs. Ike* 67.

30. DDE, *At Ease* 181.

31. Ibid.

32. Neal, *Eisenhowers* 64–65.

33. D'Este, *Eisenhower* 156.

34. Ambrose, 1 *Eisenhower* 75.

35. Julie Nixon Eisenhower, *Special People* 198–99.

36. Blumenson, 1 *Patton Papers* 738. *U.S. Statutes at Large,* ch. 227, 66th Cong., 2d sess., 1920.

37. U.S. Bureau of the Census, *Statistical History of the United States* 736.

38. Jean Edward Smith, *Lucius D. Clay* 49.

39. George F. Hofmann, "The Demise of the U.S. Tank Corps," *Military Affairs,* February 1973.

40. Pershing's date of rank as General of the Armies (a six-star rank) was Septem-

ber 2, 1919. Marshall, MacArthur, Eisenhower, Arnold, and Bradley were five-star Generals of the Army.

41. "No commander had an abler Chief of Operations," Pershing later said of Conner. "I could have spared any other man in the A.E.F. better than you." Quoted in Michael E. Bigelow, "Brigadier General Fox Conner and the American Military Forces" (master's thesis, Temple University, 1984).

42. DDE, interview by Stephen Ambrose, quoted in Ambrose, 1 *Eisenhower* 75.

43. Merle Miller, *Ike the Soldier* 187. Eisenhower would later note that perhaps the greatest reward of his friendship with George Patton was meeting Conner that Sunday afternoon in the autumn of 1920. Carlo D'Este, *Patton: A Genius for War* 294 (New York: HarperCollins, 1995).

44. Blumenson, 1 *Patton Papers* 474.

45. DDE, *At Ease* 178.

46. The documents pertaining to the misappropriated $250.76 are in Eisenhower's Army 201 file. Lengthy excerpts are reprinted in Merle Miller, *Ike the Soldier* 196–206.

47. Ibid. 202.

48. DDE, *At Ease* 182.

49. Conner to Pershing, n.d., reproduced in Merle Miller, *Ike the Soldier* 202.

50. General McRae's reprimand stated:

> The Secretary of War directs:
>
> 1st. That a letter, substantially as follows be sent to Major Dwight D. Eisenhower, Infantry, through the Chief of Infantry.
>
> With respect to the charges preferred against you for violation of the 94th and 98th Articles of War, in that you did draw commutation of quarters, heat and light for a dependent son while your lawful wife was resident with you at Camp Meade, Md. and did, with you, during the period for which commutation was drawn for your son, actually occupy public quarters, heated and lighted from public funds, the decision of the Secretary of War is that you not be brought to trial on those charges but be reprimanded instead. In arriving at this decision, due weight has been given to your disclaimer of any intent to defraud the Government and to the fact that you voluntarily subjected yourself to investigation nearly a year after the commutation was drawn by you. Your admitted ignorance of the law, however, is to your discredit, and your failure to take ordinary precautions to obtain from proper authority a decision as to the validity of your claims, is in an officer of your grade, likewise to your discredit. Opinions of the Judge Advocate General and decisions of the Comptroller General are appropriately published for the guidance of all officers. A failure to conform to these opinions and decisions has, in the present case, led to these grave charges being properly preferred against you.
>
> A copy of this letter will be filed with your record.

2nd. That all accompanying papers then be returned to the Office of the Inspector General for file.

51. DDE efficiency reports, March 31, 1921, and January 6, 1922, EL.
52. Quoted in Merle Miller, *Ike the Soldier* 208.
53. Lester David and Irene David, *Ike and Mamie: The Story of a General and His Lady* 90 (New York: G. P. Putnam's Sons, 1981).
54. DDE, *At Ease* 185; DDE, diary entry (1933) quoted in Merle Miller, *Ike the Soldier* 208.
55. DDE, interview by Charles H. Brown, quoted in Brown, "Fox Conner: A General's General," John Ray Skates, ed., *Journal of Mississippi History* 205, August 1987.
56. Ibid. 209.
57. DDE, *At Ease* 187.
58. Ibid. 194.
59. Virginia Conner, *What Father Forbad* 120–21 (Philadelphia: Dorrance, 1951).
60. Quoted in Susan Eisenhower, *Mrs. Ike* 83.
61. Ibid.
62. Ibid. 85.
63. DDE efficiency reports, June 30, 1922, June 30, 1923, June 30, 1924, and August 31, 1924, EL.
64. Conner, *What Father Forbad* 120.
65. Eisenhower was not normally caustic in his memoirs, yet he was unforgiving when describing his assignment to Meade in 1924:

> The whole thing may have started in a heavy think session of staff officers as an attempt to (what is now called) "improve the image" of the Army. On the other hand, it may all have come about because some bright young junior officer, relaxing with his seniors after a golf game, remarked for lack of anything more constructive to say, "Wouldn't it be dandy to get an Army team together that could play an undefeated, untied season and smear the Marines?"
>
> Such a casual question, if dimly comprehended by a senior officer who nods his head in silent acquiescence as the easiest way of being good company, can result in an amazing amount of activity. A younger man, loaded with energy, interprets the nod as official approval to start things moving. In no time at all, a Big Project is under way. The initiator simply announces that the General wants it. The same thing, I am sure, happens in other human organizations. But I suspect that it happened most easily in the Army of forty years ago when hot lines of communications were unknown and a hint that the old man wanted something done was a peremptory summons to action.
>
> DDE, *At Ease* 196.

66. Ibid. 198.
67. Ibid. 199.
68. Ibid.
69. Ibid. 200.
70. Quoted in ibid. 201.
71. Hatch, *Red Carpet for Mamie* 141.
72. Ambrose, 1 *Eisenhower* 79.
73. Susan Eisenhower, *Mrs. Ike* 89.
74. Dwight D. Eisenhower, "On the Command and General Staff School," August 1926, in DDE, *Eisenhower: Prewar Diaries* 43–58.
75. DDE, *At Ease* 202.
76. GSP to DDE, July 6, 1926, reproduced in Blumenson, 1 *Patton Papers* 801. Patton was then G-1 of the Pacific Division at Schofield Barracks in Hawaii.
77. A Young Graduate, "The Leavenworth Course," *Infantry Journal* 60, June 1922.

### CHAPTER FOUR: WITH PERSHING IN PARIS
The epigraph is a comment by Mamie Eisenhower to Dr. John Wickman, MDE Oral History, EL.

1. MDE, interview by John Wickman, EL.
2. Ibid. The comment is by Marjorie Clay, wife of General Lucius D. Clay, who was subsequently CEO of Continental Can Corporation and then the managing partner of Lehman Brothers—scarcely a stranger to an affluent lifestyle. Jean Edward Smith, *Lucius D. Clay* 72.
3. American Battle Monuments Commission, *A Guide to the American Battle Fields in Europe* (Washington, D.C.: Government Printing Office, 1927). The *Guide* was sold by the Superintendent of Documents for 75 cents.
4. United States Army, Center of Military History, *American Armies and the Battlefields of Europe* (Washington, D.C.: Government Printing Office, 1992).
5. MDE, interview by John Wickman, EL.
6. Ibid.
7. Ibid.
8. D'Este, *Eisenhower* 192.
9. Perret, *Eisenhower* 99.
10. Pershing to Major General Robert H. Allen, August 15, 1927, DDE 201 File, EL.
11. Dwight D. Eisenhower, Memorandum for the Assistant Commandant, Army War College, Subject: An Enlisted Reserve for the Regular Army, March 15, 1928. Reprinted in DDE, *Eisenhower: Prewar Diaries* 62–79. Also see Benjamin Franklin Conkling, "Dwight D. Eisenhower at the Army War College, 1927–1928," 1 *Parameters* 26–31 (1975).
12. DDE efficiency report, June 30, 1928, EL.
13. War Department Special Orders 284, November 30, 1927, EL.
14. DDE, *At Ease* 205.

15. War Department Special Orders 298, December 16, 1927, EL. The styling of Eisenhower's orders, "By order of the President," was not customary and suggests Pershing applied his influence outside the chain of command to have Ike join him.

16. Ernest Hemingway, "Living on $1,000 a Year in Paris," *Dateline, Toronto: The Complete Toronto Star Dispatches, 1920–1924* 88, William White, ed. (New York: Scribner's, 1985).

17. *Premier étage* should not be translated as "first floor." The ground (first) floor of most European apartment buildings is occupied by the *portier* and his or her family, plus various tradespeople. The next floor up, the *premier étage* (or *piano nobile* in Italian), is the preferred floor in the building, usually with higher ceilings, larger windows, and greater ornamentation.

18. Quoted in Hatch, *Red Carpet for Mamie* 150.

19. Quoted in Merle Miller, *Ike the Soldier* 241.

20. DDE, *At Ease* 206.

21. Susan Eisenhower, *Mrs. Ike* 94.

22. Colin Jones, *Paris: The Biography of a City* 385 (New York: Viking, 2005).

23. T. Gerald Kennedy, *Imagining Paris: Exile, Writing, and American Identity* 12 (New Haven, Conn.: Yale University Press, 1993).

24. Jones, *Paris* 388.

25. Hart Crane, postcard to Samuel Loveman, in *Americans in Paris: A Literary Anthology* 335, Adam Gopnik, ed. (New York: Library of America, 2004). *Americans in Paris* includes a delightful collection of Paris articles by noted American authors ranging from Benjamin Franklin and Thomas Jefferson to Art Buchwald, James Baldwin, A. J. Liebling, and Jack Kerouac.

26. Rosalind Massow, "Ike and Mamie Talk About 50 Years of Marriage," *Parade,* June 26, 1966.

27. DDE, *At Ease* 206.

28. On May 11, 1929, the *Paris Tribune* noted that "Major and Mrs. Dwight D. Eisenhower entertained a few friends [sixteen couples] yesterday evening, commencing with a cocktail party at their home in the Quai d'Auteuil taking their party later to the dinner dance at the Union Interalliée." The *Paris Herald* carried a similar report. Susan Eisenhower, *Mrs. Ike* 98.

29. George A. Horkan, Jr., interview, EL.

30. DDE, *At Ease* 205.

31. John S. D. Eisenhower, *Strictly Personal* 304 (Garden City, N.Y.: Doubleday, 1974).

32. John S. D. Eisenhower, *General Ike: A Personal Reminiscence* 143–75 (New York: Free Press, 2003).

33. Vernon A. Walters, *Silent Missions* 489–91 (Garden City, N.Y.: Doubleday, 1978).

34. Janet Flanner, *Paris Was Yesterday* 52–54 (New York: Viking Press, 1972).

35. John J. Pershing, *My Experiences in the World War,* 2 vols. (New York: Frederick A. Stokes, 1931).

36. DDE, *At Ease* 208.

37. Ibid.
38. Ibid. 208–9.
39. Ibid. 205.

## CHAPTER FIVE:
## WITH MACARTHUR IN WASHINGTON

The epigraph is General MacArthur's comment on Eisenhower's efficiency report, June 30, 1933, EL. MacArthur always wrote Ike's efficiency reports in longhand.

1. On February 18, 1933, Major General George Van Horn Moseley wrote Ike: "Over three years ago when I arrived here and found myself in need of expert assistance you, a stranger to me, were recommended and I had you brought to the Office of The Assistant Secretary of War. What a great blessing you have been!" EL. Also see Moseley to DDE, September 26, 1935, and D' Este, *Eisenhower* 203.

2. National Defense Act, June 4, 1920, 41 Stat. 759.

3. According to Eisenhower, Payne "attends every tea-dance and reception to which he is invited. Likes also to appear at conventions, dinners, etc., where he is invited to speak but cares very little what material appears in the speech. His thrill comes from the invitation itself." DDE diary, labeled as "Chief of Staff Diary," EL.

4. Ibid., November 9, 1929.

5. DDE to Assistant Secretary of War, "Report of Inspection of Guayule Rubber Industry," June 6, 1930, in DDE, *Eisenhower: Prewar Diaries* 126–38.

6. The original of the 1930 Plan for Mobilization is at the Hoover Presidential Library in West Branch, Iowa. A copy is at the EL. For a useful analysis of Ike's role, see Kerry E. Irish, "Apt Pupil: Dwight Eisenhower and the 1930 Industrial Mobilization Plan," 70 *Journal of Military History* 31–61 (January 2006). By 1940 the plan was dreadfully outdated. "I don't recall ever looking at it," said General Lucius D. Clay, who was in charge of all military procurement in World War II. Clay, interview, Columbia Oral History Project, Columbia University (COHP).

7. Moseley to DDE, February 18, 1933, EL. On Ike's efficiency report dated December 30, 1930, Moseley described him as "a powerfully built fellow—a strong body supporting an unusually fine mind. An outstanding personality in any group, and one of the coming men in the Army." EL.

8. DDE diary, June 14–August 10, 1932, in DDE, *Eisenhower: Prewar Diaries* 225–26.

9. When Moseley retired in 1938, Marshall wrote, "I know you will leave behind a host of younger men who have a loyal devotion to you and for what you have stood for. I am one of that company, and it makes me very sad to think that I cannot serve with you and under you again." Marshall to Moseley, September 9, 1938, in 3 *The Papers of George Catlett Marshall* 626, Larry I. Bland, ed. (Baltimore: Johns Hopkins University Press, 1986). Also see Forrest C. Pogue, 2 *George C. Marshall* 12–13 (New York: Viking, 1986); Ed

Cray, *General of the Army: George C. Marshall, Soldier and Statesman* 6–7, 118, 479 (New York: Norton, 1990).

10. D. Clayton James, 1 *The Years of MacArthur* 383–84 (Boston: Houghton Mifflin, 1970).

11. DDE, *At Ease* 213.

12. Moseley to Payne, October 9, 1930, Moseley Papers, Library of Congress.

13. Moseley to General Malin Craig, May 18, 1938, ibid. Also see *New York Herald Tribune,* May 14, 1938; *Atlanta Constitution,* May 24, 1938.

14. Moseley's rancid views are captured in unexpurgated form in his unpublished four-volume memoir, "One Soldier's Journey," among the Moseley papers at the Library of Congress. The quotation is from volume four, pages 215–19. Also see Moseley's speech to the National Defense Meeting in Philadelphia, March 28, 1939, published by the Pelley Publishers of Asheville, N.C.

15. DDE to Moseley, January 24, 1934, in DDE, *Eisenhower: Prewar Papers* 261–62.

16. DDE to Moseley, August 27, 1942, EL. For a remarkable survey of anti-Semitism in the Army, see Joseph W. Bendersky's *The "Jewish Threat": Anti-Semitism of the U.S. Army* (New York: Basic Books, 2000). I am indebted to Professor Bendersky for his analysis of Ike's relations with General Moseley.

17. DDE, *At Ease* 213. Moseley, for his part, later recognized that he was a liability for Ike. As he wrote on September 29, 1943:

> You must always keep me far in the background and unknown as far as our friendship is concerned. As you know, I spoke over the country in '38 and '39, attacking the subversive and un-American elements and attempting to show how peace could be maintained. I made many enemies. Thus, I am a liability and must not be mentioned in any way in connection with your brilliant career.

On October 7, Eisenhower generously replied, "Never doubt my pride in our friendship that has endured so many years." EL.

18. Kate Hughes, interview by Barbara Thompson Eisenhower, quoted in Susan Eisenhower, *Mrs. Ike* 110.

19. Neal, *Eisenhowers* 78.

20. Blumenson, 1 *Patton Papers* 857.

21. John S. D. Eisenhower, *Strictly Personal* 8.

22. Susan Eisenhower, *Mrs. Ike* 111.

23. John S. D. Eisenhower, *Strictly Personal* 6.

24. Department of the Army, *Army Almanac* 52–62.

25. James, 1 *Years of MacArthur* 366.

26. Moseley wrote: "When the undersigned was selected for Deputy Chief of Staff, The Assistant Secretary of War, Mr. Payne, after going over the situation carefully, stated that Major Eisenhower was his first choice for my place. Only the fact that Major Eisenhower was a major and could not be jumped

to a grade appropriate to the position, prevented him from having the place."
DDE efficiency report, December 20, 1930, EL. Also see Eisenhower's diary
entry of November 24, 1930, in DDE, *Eisenhower: Prewar Diaries* 146.

27. Public Resolution Number 98, 71st Cong., 2d sess., H.J. Res. 251.

28. In addition to the secretary of war, the commission included Secretary of the
Navy Charles Francis Adams, Secretary of Agriculture Arthur M. Hyde, At-
torney General William D. Mitchell, Secretary of Commerce Robert P.
Lamont, and Secretary of Labor William N. Doak; Senators David A. Reed
(R., Pa.), Arthur Vandenberg (R., Mich.), Joseph Robinson (D., Ark.), and
Claude A. Swanson (D., Va.); Representatives John J. McSwain (D., S.C.),
Ross Collins (D., Miss.), William P. Holaday (R., Ill.), and Lindley H. Had-
ley (R., Wash.).

29. DDE diary, March 13, 1931, in DDE, *Eisenhower: Prewar Diaries* 168.

30. Ibid., May 18, 1931, page 171. Said MacArthur:

> The [War] Department holds to the belief that a reasonable prepa-
> ration for defense is one of the best guarantees of peace. In our at-
> tempts to equalize the burdens of, and remove the profits from,
> war, we must guard against the tendency to over-emphasize ad-
> ministrative efficiency and underemphasize national effective-
> ness. . . . It is conceivable that war might be conducted with such
> regard for individual justice and administrative efficiency as to
> make impossible those evils whose existence in past wars inspired
> the drafting of Public Resolution 98. . . . It is also conceivable that
> the outcome of such a war would be defeat.

May 13, 1931, Records of the Secretary of War, National Archives and Records Administration (NARA).

31. MacArthur to DDE, November 4, 1931, EL.

32. Eisenhower provided Senator Arthur Vandenberg with the text of a proposed
amendment to the "taking clause" of the Fifth Amendment (which prevents
the government from taking private property for public use without just
compensation).

> Change the period to a semi-colon and add the following:
> Provided, however, that in time of war Congress may regulate
> or provide for the regulation of prices, rent, or compensation to be
> exacted or paid by any person in respect of the sale, rent or use of
> any real or personal property, tangible or otherwise, without re-
> gard to any limitation contained in this Article or any other Arti-
> cle of the Constitution.

Memorandum for Senator Arthur Vandenberg, March 7, 1932, in DDE,
*Eisenhower: Prewar Diaries* 220–21.

33. DDE, interview by Raymond Henle, July 13, 1967, Herbert Hoover Presidential Library.

34. Dwight D. Eisenhower, "War Policies," 40 *Cavalry Journal* 25–29 (1931).

35. DDE diary, March 28, 1931, EL.

36. Ibid. April 27, 1931.

37. Report of Lieutenant Colonel M. A. Dailey, Assistant Chief of Medical Service, Walter Reed General Hospital, August 25, 1934, EL.

38. DDE diary, December 20, 1931 (Eisenhower's emphasis).

39. Ibid. February 15, 1932.

40. DDE to John Doud, undated, in DDE, *Eisenhower: Prewar Diaries* 212–13. (Eisenhower's emphasis.)

41. 1 *Personal Memoirs of U. S. Grant* 138 (New York: Charles L. Webster, 1885).

42. Ibid. 139.

43. Manchester, *American Caesar* 129–30; cf. James, 1 *Years of MacArthur* 291–92. Professor James cites journalist Robert Considine, who quotes Louise after her wedding night that MacArthur "may be a general in the Army, but he's a buck private in the boudoir," 669n38. Biographer Geoffrey Perret believed Louise's comment was a compliment, suggesting that MacArthur made love with reckless abandon. *Old Soldiers Never Die: The Life of Douglas MacArthur* 127 (New York: Random House, 1996). Professor Carol Morris Petillo, in *Douglas MacArthur: The Philippine Years,* states that although MacArthur was already past forty when he married, "there is little evidence to suggest that he had ever known a woman intimately, and considerable reason to believe that he had not." At page 140 (Bloomington: Indiana University Press, 1981). Douglas and Louise were divorced in 1929.

44. DDE diary, June 15, 1932, in DDE, *Eisenhower: Prewar Diaries* 230.

45. Ibid.

46. Quoted in Merle Miller, *Ike the Soldier* 258–59.

47. DDE, *At Ease* 213–15.

48. Herbert Hoover, 3 *Memoirs* 55–56 (New York: Macmillan, 1952).

49. 113 *Literary Digest* 6 (November 12, 1932).

50. Ernest Lindley, *The Roosevelt Revolution: First Phase* 87–89 (New York: Viking Press, 1933).

51. World War Adjusted Compensation Act, May 19, 1924, 43 Stat. 121.

52. The most complete coverage of the Bonus Army affair is provided by Paul Dickson and Thomas B. Allen in their superb book *The Bonus Army: An American Epic* (New York: Walker, 2004), to which I am deeply indebted.

53. *Time,* April 11, 1932. The Patman papers are at the LBJ Presidential Library in Austin, Tex. For Patman's role in the bonus fight, see Nancy Beck Young, "Wright Patman's Entrepreneurial Leadership in Congress," in *Franklin D. Roosevelt and Congress: The New Deal and Its Aftermath* 79–97, Thomas P. Wolf, William D. Pederson, and Byron W. Daynes, eds. (Armonk, N.Y.: M. E. Sharpe, 2001).

54. 72nd Cong., 2d sess., H.J.R. 1, 1932.

55. Dickson and Allen, *Bonus Army* 317.

56. Fleta Campbell Springer, "Glassford and the Siege of Washington," 145 *Harper's* 641–55 (1932). Also see John Dos Passos, "The Veterans Come

Home to Roost," 71 *The New Republic* 177 (1932); Donald J. Lisio, *The President and Protest: Hoover, MacArthur, and the Bonus Riot* (New York: Fordham University Press, 1994).

57. Reflecting on the episode in his *Reminiscences,* MacArthur wrote, "The [bonus] movement was actually far deeper and more dangerous than an effort to secure funds from a nearly depleted federal treasury. The American Communist Party planned a riot of such proportions that it was hoped the United States Army, in its effort to maintain peace, would have to fire on the marchers. Red organizers infiltrated the veteran groups and presently took command of their unwitting leaders." Douglas MacArthur, *Reminiscences* 93 (New York: McGraw-Hill, 1964). The record does not support General MacArthur's contention. The quotation is reprinted to illustrate MacArthur's mind-set.

58. Moseley, 2 "One Soldier's Journey" 557–64, unpublished memoir, Manuscripts Division, Library of Congress. Later that day Moseley wrote his bleak estimate of the situation to his friend Herbert Corey.

> Intensive investigations of the past months have disclosed that we are harboring a very large group of drifters, dope fiends, unfortunates and degenerates of all kinds, that had become "a distinct menace" to the nation. For years we have been breeding and accumulating a mass of inferior people, still a minority it is true, but tools ready at hand for those seeking to strike at the very vitals of our institutions. Liberty is a sacred thing, but it ceases to be liberty when under its banner minorities force their will on the majority.

59. Moseley to MacArthur, November 3, 1942, quoted in James, 1 *Years of MacArthur* 679. Also see Moseley 2 "One Soldier's Journey" 138–39.

60. Blumenson, 1 *Patton Papers* 895.

61. James F. and Jean H. Vivian, "The Bonus March of 1932: The Role of General George Van Horn Moseley," *Wisconsin Magazine of History* 31, Autumn 1967.

62. Secretary of War to All Corps Area Commanders (in code), June 10, 1932. Adjutant general's files, 1926–1939, Bonus Marchers, RRG 94, NARA.

63. Joan M. Jensen, *Army Surveillance in America, 1775–1980* 203 (New Haven, Conn.: Yale University Press, 1991). Also see Colonel James Totten to AG, June 27, 1932, in Adjutant General's files, supra.

64. J. Edgar Hoover to Colonel William H. Wilson, Military Intelligence Division, General Staff, July 11, 1932.

65. Harry C. Lar to Moseley, June 4, 1932, quoted in *U.S. Military Intelligence Reports: Surveillance of Radicals in the U.S., 1917–1941,* Randolph Boehm, ed. (Frederick, Md.: University Publications of America, 1984).

66. Lisio, *President and Protest* 90–111, 194–225, 310–11. Also see Dickson and Allen, *Bonus Army* 124ff.

67. James, 1 *Years of MacArthur* 394. Illustrative of the Army's paranoia, Major

General Courtney Whitney wrote that the BEF ranks were swollen with "a heavy percentage of criminals, men with prison records for such crimes as murder, manslaughter, rape, robbery, burglary, blackmail and assault. A secret document which was captured later disclosed that the Communist plan covered even such details as the public trial and hanging in front of the Capitol of high government officials. At the very top of the list was the name of Army Chief of Staff MacArthur." There was no such document, except in Army lore handed down to Whitney. Courtney Whitney, *MacArthur: His Rendezvous with History* 513 (New York: Knopf, 1955).

68. Report to the Secretary of War, August 15, 1932, in DDE, *Eisenhower: Prewar Diaries* 234–35. The report was written by Ike for MacArthur's signature. "A lot of furor has been stirred up," wrote Eisenhower, "but mostly to make political capital. I wrote the General's report, which is as accurate as I could make it."

69. DDE diary, August 10, 1932, in DDE, *Eisenhower: Prewar Diaries* 233.

70. The text of Hurley's order to MacArthur, reprinted in *The New York Times,* July 29, 1932, reads as follows:

TO: General Douglas MacArthur, Chief of Staff, U.S. Army.

The President has just informed me that the civil government of the District of Columbia has reported to him that it is unable to maintain law and order in the District.

You will have United States troops proceed immediately to the scene of disorder. Cooperate fully with the District of Columbia police force which is now in charge. Surround the affected area and clear it without delay.

Turn over all prisoners to the civil authorities.

In your orders insist that any women and children who may be in the affected area be accorded every consideration and kindness. Use all humanity consistent with the due execution of this order.

PATRICK J. HURLEY
*Secretary of War*

71. Blumenson, 1 *Patton Papers* 895.

72. DDE, *At Ease* 216.

73. Perret, *Eisenhower* 112–13. Other recent biographers are equally skeptical. See Brendon, *Ike* 63–64; Merle Miller, *Ike the Soldier* 266–67; D'Este, *Eisenhower* 223–24.

74. Miles to MacArthur, August 4, 1932, quoted in James, 1 *Years of MacArthur* 398–99. In the after-action report Eisenhower wrote for MacArthur's signature, Ike said, "I accompanied the troops in person, anticipating the possibility of such a serious situation arising that necessary decisions might lie beyond the purview of responsibility of any subordinate commander, and with the purpose of obtaining a personal familiarity with every phase of the troops' activities." DDE, *Eisenhower: Prewar Diaries* 238.

75. Perry L. Miles, *Fallen Leaves: Memories of an Old Solider* 307 (Berkeley, Calif.:

Wureth, 1964). In his *Reminiscences,* MacArthur said he went with the troops "in accordance with the President's request." At page 95.

76. Before meeting the press, MacArthur and Hurley went to the White House to brief President Hoover on what had occurred. There is no record of the meeting, but Hoover later told F. Trubee Davison, the assistant secretary of war for air, that he was furious with MacArthur and had "upbraided" him for disobeying orders. F. Trubee Davison, interview, Oral History Collection, Herbert Hoover Presidential Library.

77. *The New York Times,* July 29, 1932.

78. MacArthur for Hurley (written entirely by DDE), July 1930, reprinted in DDE, *Eisenhower: Prewar Diaries* 233–47. In *At Ease,* Eisenhower writes somewhat more sympathetically of the veterans than he did at the time. He further suggests that he recommended that MacArthur not speak to the press, but this, too, seems unlikely. Eisenhower concludes his treatment of the affair by noting that some accounts call it "one of the darkest blots on the MacArthur reputation. This, I feel, is unfortunate." At pages 216–18.

79. Blumenson, 1 *Patton Papers* 900.

80. Lucian K. Truscott, Jr., *The Twilight of the U.S. Cavalry: Life in the Old Army, 1917–1942* 130, Colonel Lucian K. Truscott III, ed. (Lawrence: University Press of Kansas, 1989).

81. *The Washington Daily News,* July 29, 1932.

82. DDE diary, April 26, 1934, in DDE, *Eisenhower: Prewar Diaries* 268–69.

83. General Lucius D. Clay, in Jean Edward Smith, *Lucius D. Clay* 57.

84. DDE diary, November 30, 1932, in DDE, *Eisenhower: Prewar Diaries* 247.

85. Ibid. 247–48, February 28, 1933.

86. Ibid. 249, March 10, 1933.

87. Milton Eisenhower, quoted in Neal, *Eisenhowers* 94.

88. DDE diary, April 20, 1933, in DDE, *Eisenhower: Prewar Diaries* 251–52.

89. Ibid. 253–54, October 29, 1933. (Eisenhower's emphasis.)

## CHAPTER SIX: MANILA

The epigraph, a family legend, is reported by Susan Eisenhower in *Mrs. Ike* 143.

1. Charles H. Brown, "Fox Conner: A General's General," John Ray Skates, ed., *Journal of Mississippi History* 208, August 1987.

2. "General Moseley hates the President," wrote Colonel Herman Bukema to Professor William Myers, September 28, 1934. Quoted in Bendersky, *"Jewish Threat"* 468.

3. "I hear your name mentioned [for the position] possibly more frequently and more favorably than anyone else's," Eisenhower wrote Moseley on September 24, 1934, "but I honestly think that no one but the President knows exactly what is to be done and he will make his announcement in his own good time." DDE, *Eisenhower: Prewar Diaries* 276.

4. Press Conference 164, December 12, 1934. 4 *Complete Presidential Press Conferences of Franklin D. Roosevelt* 268–69 (New York: Da Capo Press, 1972). For

MacArthur's desire for an extension, see Eisenhower memo in DDE, *Eisenhower: Prewar Diaries* 97.

5. William Manchester states that FDR extended MacArthur's term for a year to pass over General George Simonds. Simonds was born in 1874, as was Moseley. But FDR's primary aim was to short-circuit Moseley's chances. Manchester, *American Caesar* 159.

6. Susan Eisenhower, *Mrs. Ike* 133–38.

7. 48 Stat. 456, PL 73–127 (1934).

8. MacArthur to FDR, September 9, 1935. Also see FDR to MacArthur, August 31, 1935; MacArthur to FDR, September 2, 1935. Franklin D. Roosevelt Library (FDRL).

9. War Department Special Orders 220, September 18, 1935.

10. One of the best reports of arrangements leading to MacArthur's appointment was written by Eisenhower ("Philippine diary") in November 1935, and is reprinted in DDE, *Eisenhower: Prewar Diaries* 286–93. Geoffrey Perret, citing "Memorandum of the Terms of Agreement Between the President of the Philippine Commonwealth and General MacArthur," notes that MacArthur would also receive .46 of 1 percent of Philippine defense spending through 1941. That translates into an additional $23,000 annually, given a budget of $8 million. *Old Soldiers Never Die* 188.

11. DDE, *At Ease* 219–20.

12. DDE, *Eisenhower: Prewar Diaries* 284.

13. Susan Eisenhower, *Mrs. Ike* 133–34.

14. DDE to Elivera Doud, August 8, 1935, in DDE, *Eisenhower: Prewar Diaries* 281–82.

15. DDE, *At Ease* 221.

16. MacArthur to DDE, September 30, 1935, DDE 201 file, EL.

17. War Department Special Orders 220, September 18, 1935.

18. FDR to Secretary of War, July 18, 1935, FDRL.

19. Woodring to MacArthur, October 2, 1935, MacArthur Memorial Bureau of Archives (MMBA), Norfolk, Virginia.

20. DDE, *At Ease* 223.

21. MacArthur to FDR, October 2, 1935, FDRL; MacArthur to Craig, October 2, 1935, MMBA.

22. Jean Edward Smith, *Lucius D. Clay* 77.

23. Ibid. 78.

24. DDE Philippine diary, December 1935, in DDE, *Eisenhower: Prewar Diaries* 292.

25. Joint Army and Navy Basic War Plan Orange, August 1924, Record Group 165, NARA.

26. War Plan Orange, March 1929, Record Group 407, NARA.

27. MacArthur to Bonner Fellers, June 1, 1939, MMBA; Moseley, 2 "One Soldier's Story" 153.

28. War Plan Orange, June 13, 1933, Record Group 407, NARA. According to marginal notes on the plan, "Genl MacA" stated his belief that such rein-

forcement was possible because the Japanese would not seek to capture the Philippines so long as the U.S. fleet stood guard. MacArthur predicted "that war would be declared (if at all) by the enemy and initiated by a surprise attack on our fleet if surprise were possible." Quoted in Brian McAllister Linn, *Guardians of Empire: The U.S. Army and the Pacific, 1902–1940* 176 (Chapel Hill: University of North Carolina Press, 1997).

29. Current Estimate, War Plan Orange, 1936, Record Group 407, NARA.
30. War Plan Orange, 1939, Record Group 407, NARA. Quoted in Linn, *Guardians of Empire* 182.
31. DDE Philippine diary, December 27, 1935, in DDE, *Eisenhower: Prewar Diaries.*
32. Ibid., January 20, 1936.
33. Ibid., February 6, 1936.
34. Ibid., January 20, 1936.
35. Ibid.
36. James, 1 *Years of MacArthur* 506. On April 5, 1939, Eisenhower reported a three-hour conversation with President Quezon at the presidential palace. The conversation was at Quezon's request.

> He said he bitterly opposed the appointment [of MacArthur as field marshal], although he did *not* say he opposed it openly to General MacA. He did say that the incident made his government look ridiculous! I was astounded, since General MacA's account of the same affair was exactly the opposite. . . . Somebody certainly has lied. The Gen. said he accepted the appointment with *great reluctance* and only because refusal would have mortally offended the Pres!! Wow!!
> (DDE Philippine diary, in DDE, *Eisenhower: Prewar Diaries.*)

37. DDE Philippine diary, February 15, 1936.
38. DDE, interview by Peter Lyon, August 1967, quoted in Lyon, *Eisenhower* 78.
39. John S. D. Eisenhower, *General Ike* 27–28.
40. DDE Philippine diary, July 1, 1936, in DDE, *Eisenhower: Prewar Diaries.*
41. War Department Special Order, July 1, 1936.
42. DDE, *At Ease* 280.
43. William L. Lee, interview, EL.
44. Brigadier General Hugh A. Parker, interview, EL.
45. John S. D. Eisenhower, *General Ike* 26.
46. Jesus A. Villamor, "He Knew How to Take It," *The American Legion Magazine* 14–15, 42–43, September 1960.
47. DDE to Hugh A. Parker, February 4, 1936, in DDE, *Eisenhower: Prewar Diaries* 420–22.
48. MacArthur to Major General William D. Connor, September 15, 1936, EL.
49. DDE to Colonel George A. Lincoln, September 6, 1967, EL.
50. W. B. Courtney, "Can We Hold the Richest Land on Earth?" *Collier's* 12–13, 54–56, July 1, 1939.

51. Susan Eisenhower, *Mrs. Ike* 144–45.

52. Ibid. 137.

53. MDE to the Douds, March 31, 1936, EL.

54. D'Este, *Eisenhower* 241.

55. Susan Eisenhower, *Mrs. Ike* 143.

56. Ibid. 145.

57. MDE to the Douds, February 8, 1938, EL.

58. DDE to Moseley, April 26, 1937, EL.

59. DDE to John Doud, April 29, 1937, EL.

60. Craig to MacArthur, August 16, 1937, MMBA.

61. DDE Philippine diary, August 25, 1937, in DDE, *Eisenhower: Prewar Diaries*.

62. MacArthur to Craig, August 22, 1937, MMBA.

63. Craig to MacArthur, August 24, 1937, MMBA.

64. "These comic opera wars never center about any problem incident to the 'job,' " Eisenhower continued. "They invariably involve something personal to the Gen. I too could be the fair-haired boy if I'd only yes, yes, yes!!" DDE Philippine diary, August 25, 1937, in DDE, *Eisenhower: Prewar Diaries*. (Eisenhower's emphasis.)

65. MacArthur to Craig, September 10, 1937; MacArthur to the Adjutant General, September 16, 1937, MMBA.

66. FDR to MacArthur, October 11, 1937, FDRL. "The other day we got the Gen.'s order for retirement," Ike wrote in his diary on October 15, 1937. "The Pres. of the U.S. sent him a flowery telegram which was, of course, promptly released to the press. His retirement, to take effect on Dec. 31, will leave him a free agent so that he can continue to live in the Penthouse, draw his munificent salary—do no work—and be protected against possible transfer to another station."

67. DDE efficiency report, December 31, 1937, EL.

68. DDE Philippine diary, December 21, 1937, in DDE, *Eisenhower: Prewar Diaries*. When the Philippine government sought to increase Ike's per diem allowance, MacArthur blocked it. Eisenhower took it personally.

> He [MacArthur] knows we *know* he had prevaricated in his administration of the defense plan, for the sole purpose of assuring his hold on $33,000 *and* a penthouse, *and* all expenses. He has come to regard us as a menace to him and his soft berth. . . . The popular notion of his great ability as a soldier and leader, is, of course, not difficult to explain to those who know how wartime citations were often secured. These, plus direct intervention of Sec[retary of War Newton D.] Baker to give him his first star (Regular) have been parlayed . . . to a reputation of wisdom, brilliance and magnificent leadership.

69. Quoted in D'Este, *Eisenhower* 247.

70. In *At Ease,* Eisenhower attributed the crash to the inexperienced Filipino

pilot. But in the letter he wrote to Mrs. Ord immediately afterward, Ike exonerated the pilot: "Lieut Cruz, a very fine flyer with whom many of us ride regularly." His subsequent diary entry blamed the crash on "a combination of unfortunate circumstances, rather than of any one particular thing." *At Ease* 227–28. Compare DDE to Emily Ord, January 31, 1938, and Philippine diary, February 15, 1938, both in DDE, *Eisenhower: Prewar Diaries* 373–76.

71. DDE Philippine diary, February 15, 1938, in DDE, *Eisenhower: Prewar Diaries*.

72. DDE, *At Ease* 228.

73. MDE to the Douds, March 9, 1938, EL. (Mamie's emphasis.)

74. Susan Eisenhower, *Mrs. Ike* 154.

75. Charles A. Willoughby and John Chamberlain, *MacArthur: 1941–1951* 35 (New York: McGraw-Hill, 1954).

76. George C. Kenney, *General Kenney Reports* 151–52 (New York: Duell, Sloan, and Pearce, 1949).

77. Romulo to William Manchester, October 18, 1977, cited in Manchester, *American Caesar* 184.

78. D'Este, *Eisenhower* 248.

79. DDE Philippine diary, June 18, 1938, in DDE, *Eisenhower: Prewar Diaries*.

80. DDE, *At Ease* 228–29.

81. Daniel D. Holt, "An Unlikely Partnership and Service: Dwight Eisenhower, Mark Clark, and the Philippines," 13 *Kansas History* 149, 157 (Autumn 1990).

82. Jean Edward Smith, *Lucius D. Clay* 80.

83. Ibid. 80–81.

84. DDE, *At Ease* 229–30.

85. DDE to Mark Clark, May 27, 1939, in DDE, *Eisenhower: Prewar Diaries* 434–35.

86. DDE Philippine diary, July 16, 1939, in ibid.

87. DDE, *At Ease* 231. "The President, and his Malacañan assistants *appear* to be genuinely sorry that I am going," Ike wrote in his diary on November 15, 1939. "I hope they are sincere, but the Malay mind is still a sealed book to me. They may be secretly delighted. However, I'm tempted to believe them."

88. MacArthur to DDE, December 9, 1939, EL.

89. DDE to Colonel Norman Randolph, October 6, 1941, in DDE, *Eisenhower: Prewar Diaries* 547–48.

## CHAPTER SEVEN: LOUISIANA MANEUVERS

The epigraph is a question directed at Eisenhower by General Marshall during a chance meeting while the chief of staff was attending Fourth Army maneuvers south of Monterey, California, in January 1940. It was the second occasion on which Marshall and Eisenhower met, the first being in Paris in 1929. DDE, *At Ease* 236.

1. DDE to Captain Hugh A. ("Lefty") Parker, December 13, 1940, in DDE, *Eisenhower: Prewar Diaries* 515.

2. General DeWitt was still the senior Army commander on the West Coast at the time of Pearl Harbor and was the prime mover behind the War Department's recommendation to FDR that Japanese Americans living in the Pacific war zone be relocated inland. "The Japanese race is an enemy race and while many second and third generation Japanese born on United States soil have become Americanized the racial strain is undiluted." DeWitt to War Department, February 14, 1942. Also see Greg Robinson, *By Order of the President: FDR and the Internment of Japanese Americans* 85 (Cambridge: Harvard University Press, 2001); Jean Edward Smith, *FDR* 549–52, 773–74 (New York: Random House, 2007).

3. DDE Philippine diary, January 25, 1940, in DDE, *Eisenhower: Prewar Diaries*. Although Eisenhower was back in the United States, he continued to write his impressions in his Philippine diary.

4. Ibid.; John S. D. Eisenhower, *Strictly Personal* 28–29; Susan Eisenhower, *Mrs. Ike* 160–61.

5. DDE to Leonard T. Gerow, August 23, 1940, DDE, *Eisenhower: Prewar Diaries* 489–90. By the end of September, the regiment would be 1,300 men understrength as troops were constantly being transferred to staff new units. DDE, Fort Lewis diary, September 26, 1940, in DDE, *Eisenhower: Prewar Diaries* 493–95.

6. DDE to Everett Hughes, November 26, 1940, EL.

7. DDE to Omar Bradley, July 1, 1940, EL.

8. DDE to Gerow, August 23, 1940, in DDE, *Eisenhower: Prewar Diaries* 489–90; DDE, *At Ease* 237; DDE to Hughes, November 26, 1940, EL.

9. DDE, *At Ease* 237.

10. GSP to DDE, October 1, 1940, in Blumenthal, 2 *The Patton Papers* 15.

11. DDE to GSP, September 17, 1940, EL. (Eisenhower's emphasis.)

12. GSP to DDE, November 1, 1940, EL.

13. DDE to Mark Clark, October 31, 1940, EL.

14. DDE to T. J. Davis, October 31, 1940, EL. Eisenhower also wrote to James Ulio on the adjutant general's staff, but that letter has been lost.

15. DDE to T. J. Davis, November 14, 1940, EL.

16. DDE, *At Ease* 238.

17. Lyon, *Eisenhower* 82.

18. Eisenhower's letter to Gerow, November 18, 1940, is reprinted in DDE, *Eisenhower: Prewar Diaries* 503–5.

19. For Gerow's telegram, see DDE, *Eisenhower: Prewar Diaries* 508n1.

20. DDE to Gerow, November 25, 1940, EL.

21. DDE to Mark Clark, November 28, 1940, EL.

22. DDE to Hughes, November 26, 1940, EL.

23. Dwight D. Eisenhower, *Crusade in Europe* 7–8 (Garden City, N.Y.: Doubleday, 1948).

24. Robert Lovett, interview by Jean Edward Smith, March 30, 1971, COHP.

25. Russell F. Weigley, *Eisenhower's Lieutenants: The Campaign of France and Germany, 1944–1945* 22–28 (Bloomington: Indiana University Press, 1981).

26. Jean R. Moenk, *A History of Large-Scale Army Maneuvers in the United States, 1935–1964* 25, 39 (Fort Monroe, Va.: Continental Army Command, 1969). In 1939, Hugh Drum was the candidate of the Army's Old Guard to succeed Malin Craig as chief of staff, but Roosevelt passed over him to name Marshall. "I'm tired of hearing Drum beat the drum for Drum," FDR told Harry Hopkins. After Pearl Harbor, Secretary Stimson and Marshall offered Drum the position of chief of staff to Generalissimo Chiang Kai-shek, heading the American effort in the China theater. Drum, who saw himself as Pershing's successor in Europe, declined in a stormy scene with Marshall. Having overplayed his hand, Drum was retired without fanfare in 1943, when he reached the mandatory retirement age. After the row with Drum, Marshall selected Joseph Stilwell for the China post. Pogue, 2 *Marshall* 356–60; Noel F. Bush, "General Drum," *Life* 96, June 16, 1941.

27. Kent Roberts Greenfield, Robert R. Palmer, and Bell I. Wiley, *The Organization of Ground Combat Troops* 12, 271–76 (Washington, D.C.: Center of Military History, U.S. Army, 2004).

28. AC of S (G-4) [General George R. Spalding] to C of S [General Malin Craig], October 30, 1936, subject: Research and Development for FY 1939, NARA.

29. Chief Signal Officer to C of S [Marshall], February 20, 1940, NARA.

30. U.S. Bureau of the Census, *Statistical History of the United States* 736.

31. Public Law 190, July 29, 1941. To ensure fairness in the elimination of unfit officers, Marshall entrusted the final decision to a board of six retired officers, headed by former chief of staff Malin Craig. In 1941, the board discharged 31 colonels, 117 lieutenant colonels, 31 majors, and 16 captains. During the war years, Marshall sacked almost 500 full colonels as unfit to command. Mark Skinner Watson, *Chief of Staff: Prewar Plans and Preparations* 241–47 (Washington, D.C.: Historical Division, Department of the Army, 1950).

32. Pogue, 2 *Marshall* 98; James F. Byrnes, *All in One Lifetime* 113–14 (New York: Harper, 1958). Another of Marshall's reforms was to break the autocratic hold on assignments exercised by the chief of infantry, the chief of cavalry, and the chief of artillery. Those offices were abolished when Marshall reorganized the War Department on March 9, 1942. The assignment and promotion authority moved to Marshall and the adjutant general's office.

33. MDE to the Douds, March 11, 1941, quoted in Susan Eisenhower, *Mrs. Ike* 167.

34. DDE Fort Lewis diary, April 4, 1941, in DDE, *Eisenhower: Prewar Diaries* 516.

35. DDE to Colonel Charles H. Corlett, June 1941, ibid. 517–20.

36. DDE to Gerow, July 18, 1941, EL.

37. Krueger to Marshall, June 11, 1941; Marshall to Krueger, June 13, 1941. Also see Pogue, 2 *Marshall* 163; Kevin C. Holzimmer, *General Walter Krueger: Unsung Hero of the Pacific War* 71 (Lawrence: University Press of Kansas, 2007).

38. Brigadier General John S. D. Eisenhower, who is the executor of his parents'

estates, has deposited their complete financial records at the Eisenhower Library, but has refused to open them for inspection. (The financial records of FDR, Eleanor, and Sara are fully available at the Roosevelt Library at Hyde Park.) When the National Archives and Records Administration prepared to open Ike's financial records in 2010, John threatened to bring suit to keep them closed. Nevertheless, it would appear that Ike returned to the United States with roughly $10,000 ($130,000 in current dollars) in his account at Washington's Riggs National Bank. DDE Philippine diary, November 15, 1939, EL.

39. John S. D. Eisenhower, *Strictly Personal* 35. According to John, one member of the class was Asian.

40. Kenneth S. Davis, *Soldier of Democracy* 267–68.

41. Ibid. 268–69.

42. DDE, *Crusade in Europe* 133–34.

43. Friedrich Immanuel, *The Regimental War Game,* Walter Krueger, trans. (Kansas City, Mo.: Hudson Press, 1907); General Julius K. L. Merteus, *Tactics and Techniques of River Crossings,* Walter Krueger, trans. (New York: D. Van Nostrand, 1918); and William Balck, *Tactics,* 2 vols., Walter Krueger, trans. (Fort Leavenworth: U.S. Cavalry Association, 1911). Krueger's World War II memoir, *From Down Under to Nippon: The Story of Sixth Army in World War II* (Washington, D.C.: Combat Forces Press, 1953), is a remarkable, rancor-free account of Sixth Army's ground war in the Pacific.

44. DDE, *Crusade in Europe* 11.

45. Krueger Papers, United States Military Academy. Quoted in D'Este, *Eisenhower* 274–75.

46. Ibid. 275.

47. DDE to George Van Horn Moseley, August 28, 1941, EL.

48. The details of MacArthur's recall remain murky. The most complete account is that provided by Watson in *Chief of Staff* 434–38. Also see Manchester, *American Caesar* 188–90; Pogue, 2 *Marshall* 181, 466.

49. DDE to Brigadier General Wade Haislip, July 28, 1941, EL. (Eisenhower's emphasis.)

50. Pogue, 2 *Marshall* 89. The approximate cost of the Louisiana maneuvers was $28.6 million (roughly $350 million currently). Christopher R. Gabel, *The U.S. Army GHQ Maneuvers of 1941* 50 (Washington, D.C.: Center of Military History, U.S. Army, 1992).

51. George C. Marshall, Speech to the National Guard Association of the United States, October 27, 1939, in 2 *Papers of George Catlett Marshall* 94–99.

52. Gabel, *GHQ Maneuvers of 1941* 4.

53. Ibid. 59.

54. DDE to Gerow, August 5, 1941, EL.

55. DDE to Joyce, September 15, 1941, EL.

56. DDE to Gerow, September 26, 1941, EL.

57. *The New York Times,* September 29, 1941.

58. Gabel, *GHQ Maneuvers of 1941* 111.

59. DDE, *At Ease* 244.

60. John S. D. Eisenhower Oral History, EL, quoted in D'Este, *Eisenhower* 280. Colonel D'Este explores the reaction of General Krueger to the fame that Ike acquired at pages 280–81.

61. Gabel, *GHQ Maneuvers of 1941* 115–25.

62. "General Krueger didn't have a thing to do with logistics and neither did Ike," said Lutes. "Ike said, 'You handle it.' And Krueger said, 'You handle it.' And I couldn't take a single question to them. They didn't want it. All they wanted to know was how I did it." Lutes Oral History, EL. After the maneuvers, Lutes was promoted by General Marshall directly to the rank of brigadier general, skipping the intermediate step of colonel. DDE to Lutes, December 5, 1941, EL.

63. Gabel, *GHQ Maneuvers of 1941* 187.

64. Mark Clark, *Calculated Risk* 16 (New York: Harper, 1950); Clark, interview by Merle Miller, cited in Miller, *Ike the Soldier* 328–29.

65. MDE Oral History, EL.

66. D'Este, *Eisenhower* 281.

67. Ibid.

68. Eisenhower, *Crusade in Europe* 12–13.

69. Ibid. 13–14.

70. Ibid.

71. Ibid.

72. DDE efficiency report, June 30, 1940, EL.

73. Ibid., March 5, 1941, EL.

74. Ibid., June 21, 1941, EL. (Joyce's emphasis.)

75. Ibid., December 19, 1941, EL.

## CHAPTER EIGHT:
## WITH MARSHALL IN WASHINGTON

During his tour in War Plans, Eisenhower jotted down his thoughts on a notepad he kept on his desk. The epigraph was written by Ike on January 4, 1942. It is reprinted in *The Papers of Dwight David Eisenhower,* vol. 1, *The War Years* 39, Alfred D. Chandler, Jr., ed. (Baltimore: Johns Hopkins Press, 1970). Cited subsequently as 1 *War Years.*

1. Krueger, *From Down Under to Nippon* 4.

2. DDE, *Crusade in Europe* 16.

3. Pogue, 2 *Marshall* 238. Also see Louis Morton, *The Fall of the Philippines* 30 (Washington, D.C.: Office of the Chief of Military History, Department of the Army, 1953).

4. Stephen E. Ambrose, *The Supreme Commander: The War Years of Dwight D. Eisenhower* 4 (Garden City, N.Y.: Doubleday, 1970).

5. DDE, *Crusade in Europe* 18.

6. Ibid.

7. Eisenhower's December 14, 1941, memo, "Assistance to Far East," is in 1 *War Years* 5–6.

8. DDE, *Crusade in Europe* 21–22.

9. Pogue, 2 *Marshall* 239.

10. Dwight D. Eisenhower, in *Addresses Delivered at the Dedication Ceremonies of the George C. Marshall Research Library,* May 24, 1964, 14.

11. DDE, *Crusade in Europe* 22–24.

12. Ibid. 30.

13. Ibid.

14. DDE, in *Addresses Delivered at Dedication* 14–15.

15. DDE, *At Ease* 195.

16. Merle Miller, *Ike the Soldier* 338–39.

17. Katherine Marshall, interview by Vernon Waters, quoted in ibid. 340.

18. Lucius D. Clay (LDC), interview, COHP.

19. DDE to S. A. Akin, June 19, 1942, EL.

20. DDE, *Crusade in Europe* 24.

21. Quoted in Susan Eisenhower, *Mrs. Ike* 175.

22. MDE to the Douds, February 7, 1942, EL.

23. DDE to Krueger, December 20, 1941, 1 *War Years* 16–17.

24. Krueger to DDE, December 23, 1941, EL.

25. DDE to Lutes, December 31, 1941, 1 *War Years* 33.

26. Pogue, 2 *Marshall* 244; DDE, *Crusade in Europe* 25. Also see Russell D. Buhite, *Patrick J. Hurley and American Foreign Policy* 101–2 (Ithaca, N.Y.: Cornell University Press, 1973).

27. Ibid. Also see DDE, memo pad entry, January 17, 1942, 1 *War Years* 61–62.

28. United States Department of State, *Foreign Relations of the United States: Conferences at Washington, 1941–1942, and Casablanca, 1943* 81–82 (Washington, D.C.: U.S. Government Printing Office, 1968). Cited subsequently as *FRUS: Washington and Casablanca.*

29. Meeting of the U.S.-British chiefs of staff, December 25, 1941, ibid. 93.

30. Pogue, 2 *Marshall* 276–77.

31. Eisenhower's draft letter of instructions for the supreme commander, Southwestern Pacific Theater, December 26, 1941, is at 1 *War Years* 28–31. For Marshall's change, see 30–31n3.

32. Pogue, 2 *Marshall* 278.

33. Stimson diary, December 29, 1941, Yale University.

34. DDE diary, February 16, 1942, in 1 *War Years* 109. In his final efficiency report on Ike, Gerow said he considered Eisenhower "the best officer of his rank in the entire Army," and that in wartime he should be entrusted with "the highest command." DDE efficiency report, February 14, 1942, EL.

35. DDE to Lieutenant Colonel William Lee, February 24, 1942, EL.

36. Pogue, 2 *Marshall* 289, 290.

37. Adjutant General's Office, *Official Army Register, January 1, 1942* 4–5 (Washington, D.C.: Government Printing Office, 1942).

38. DDE, *At Ease* 249–50.

39. DDE diary, March 28, March 30, 1942, in DDE, *The Eisenhower Diaries,* Robert H. Ferrell, ed., 52–53 (New York: Norton, 1981).

40. MDE to the Douds, March 13, 1942, EL.

41. DDE diary, March 11, 1942, in DDE, *Eisenhower Diaries* 51.

42. Ibid., March 12, 1942. Upon his return from the Philippines in December 1939, Eisenhower commenced sending his parents $20 monthly (approximately $250 currently). This continued until his mother's death. DDE to Edgar N. Eisenhower, April 13, May 1, 1942, EL.

43. DDE, *Crusade in Europe* 46.

44. Ibid. "Tom Handy and I stick to our idea that we must win in Europe," Ike wrote in his diary on January 27, 1942. "We can't win by sitting on our fannies giving our stuff in driblets all over the world."

45. DDE, *Crusade in Europe* 46.

46. Ibid.

47. Memorandum for the Chief of Staff, February 28, 1942, DDE, 1 *War Years* 149–55.

48. DDE, *Crusade in Europe* 47.

49. Winston S. Churchill, *The Hinge of Fate* 189–94 (Boston: Houghton Mifflin, 1950).

50. Stimson diary, March 6, 1942, Yale University. Secretary Stimson went on to say that the main problem was the U.S. Navy, which was "getting wedded to fighting in the Pacific where they had the lead. Eisenhower was quite strong to the effect that Admiral King's proposition of a slow step by step creeping movement through the Island of New Caledonia, New Britain, etc., would not get anywhere in solving the big situation as it is being fought out in Europe."

51. Memorandum for the Chief of Staff, "Critical Points in the Development of Coordinated Viewpoint as to Major Tasks of War," March 25, 1942, 1 *War Years* 205–7.

52. Ibid. (Eisenhower's emphasis.)

53. Pogue, 2 *Marshall* 305–6; Stimson diary, March 25, 1942, Yale University; Ray S. Cline, *Washington Command Post: The Operations Division* 155–58 (Washington, D.C.: Center of Military History, U.S. Army, 2003).

54. OPD Exec. 10, Item 30 A, in Cline, *Washington Command Post* 157–58. In addition to ROUNDUP, Ike and his staff prepared an ancillary plan (SLEDGEHAMMER) for an immediate but smaller landing in 1942, should it be necessary to stave off a Russian collapse. Also see Maurice Matloff and Edwin C. Snell, *Strategic Planning for Coalition Warfare, 1941–1942* 183–87 (Washington, D.C.: Office of the Chief of Military History, U.S. Army, 1953).

55. Stimson diary, April 1, 1942, Yale University. Also see Henry Harley Arnold, *Global Mission* 305 (New York: Harper, 1949).

56. Stimson diary, April 1, 1942, Yale University.

57. Former Naval Person from the President, April 1, 1942, Walter F. Kimball, ed., 1 *Churchill and Roosevelt: The Complete Correspondence* 437 (Princeton, N.J.: Princeton University Press, 1984). The Hopkins and Roosevelt cables are also reprinted in Robert E. Sherwood's *Roosevelt and Hopkins: An Intimate History* 521 (New York: Harper, 1948).

58. WSC to FDR, April 12, 1942, Kimball, 1 *Churchill and Roosevelt* 448–49.

59. FDR to WSC, April 21, 1942, ibid. 466–67.

60. Marshall to McNarney, April 13, 1942, in Pogue, 2 *Marshall* 318.

61. DDE diary, April 20, 1942, EL.

62. Memo, Captain John L. McCrea [FDR's naval aide] to JCS [Joint Chiefs of Staff], May 1, 1942, in Snell and Matloff, *Strategic Planning* 217.

63. Eisenhower's memo (signed Marshall), May 4, 1942, is at 1 *War Years* 276–77.

64. Marshall to FDR, May 6, 1942, "Pacific Theater versus BOLERO," in Snell and Matloff, *Strategic Planning* 218–19. Marshall's letter was written by Eisenhower.

65. FDR to Marshall, May 6, 1942, Snell and Matloff, *Strategic Planning* 219.

66. Roosevelt sent memorandums on May 6, 1942, to the secretaries of war and Navy, the three chiefs of staff, and Hopkins, emphasizing his basic strategy of holding in the Pacific and taking the offensive against Germany. COS TS Decimal File, 1941–43, 381, Sec. 1.

67. DDE diary, May 5, 1942, EL. (Eisenhower's emphasis.)

68. Ibid., May 21, 1942.

69. Pogue, 2 *Marshall* 339.

70. DDE, *Crusade in Europe* 49.

71. Ibid. 50; Kay Summersby, *Eisenhower Was My Boss* 16 (New York: Prentice-Hall, 1948).

72. Quoted in Martin Blumenson, *Mark Clark* 57 (New York: Congdon and Weed, 1984).

73. Mark Clark, *Calculated Risk* 19.

74. DDE diary, May 27, 1942, EL.

75. Kay Summersby Morgan, *Past Forgetting: My Love Affair with Dwight D. Eisenhower* 28 (New York: Simon and Schuster, 1976).

76. Summersby, *Eisenhower Was My Boss* 4; Kay Summersby Morgan, *Past Forgetting* 31–32.

77. Korda, *Ike* 272; Kay Summersby Morgan, *Past Forgetting* 31.

78. "When the King told me this story, he laughed uproariously." DDE, *At Ease* 277–78. Also see Harry C. Butcher, *My Three Years with Eisenhower: The Personal Diary of Captain Harry C. Butcher, USNR, Naval Aide to General Eisenhower, 1942 to 1945* 17–18 (New York: Simon and Schuster, 1946).

79. Arnold, *Global Mission* 315.

80. Ibid.

81. Summersby, *Eisenhower Was My Boss* 10; Kay Summersby Morgan, *Past Forgetting* 37.

82. DDE to GCM, "Command arrangements for BOLERO," June 3, 1942, 1 *War Years* 327–28. Eisenhower recommended that Major General Robert L. Eichelberger replace McNarney as deputy chief of staff.

83. DDE to GCM, "Command in England," June 6, 1942, 1 *War Years* 331–32.

84. Directive for the Commanding General, ETO, June 8, 1942, ibid. 334–35.

85. The directive explicitly specified that "the commanding general, European theater, will keep the Chief of Staff U.S. Army fully advised of all that concerns his command and will communicate his recommendations freely and directly to the War Department." Ibid.

86. Lyon, *Eisenhower* 124; Clark, *Calculated Risk* 20.

87. Pogue, 2 *Marshall* 339, 476n52.

88. Kenneth S. Davis, *Soldier of Democracy* 299–300.

89. DDE diary, June 8, 1942, EL. (Eisenhower's emphasis.)

90. DDE, 1 *War Years* 337.

91. Adjutant General's Office, *Official Army Register, 1942*, 4.

92. DDE to GSP, July 20, 1942, EL.

93. DDE, *Crusade in Europe* 51.

94. Jean Edward Smith, *FDR* 546–47n.

95. Kenneth S. Davis, *Soldier of Democracy* 302–3.

96. Eisenhower diary, June 20, 1942, EL.

97. Carol M. Petillo, "Douglas MacArthur and Manuel Quezon: A Note on an Imperial Bond," 48 *Pacific Historical Review* 107–17 (1979). Professor Petillo discovered the payments while working in the Richard K. Sutherland papers at the Library of Congress. The payments were made while the decision was pending on whether to evacuate Quezon and his family from Corregidor by submarine, and the paperwork was backdated to January 3, 1942. Stimson and FDR appear to have been aware of the payments and made no objection. Under the terms of MacArthur's 1935 appointment as military adviser to the Philippine government, the payments would have been permissible. But on July 26, 1941, the military adviser's office was abolished and MacArthur returned to active duty as commander of U.S. Army forces in the Philippines. From that date onward, he and his staff were bound by Army regulations, which explicitly prohibit such gifts, loans, or emoluments. (Army Regulations 600–10, Par. 2e [9], December 6, 1938.) Also see Paul P. Rogers, "MacArthur, Quezon, and Executive Order Number One—Another View," 52 *Pacific Historical Review* 93–102 (1983); Petillo, *Douglas MacArthur* 208–13; Perret, *Old Soldiers Never Die* 271–72.

98. DDE to Kenyon Joyce, June 22, 1942, EL.

99. Jean Edward Smith, *Lucius D. Clay* 219.

### CHAPTER NINE: TORCH

The epigraph is from a letter from DDE to GSP, September 5, 1942, in 1 *War Years* 541–42.

1. Michael J. McKeogh and Richard Lockridge, *Sgt. Mickey and General Ike* 29 (New York: G. P. Putnam's Sons, 1946).

2. Quoted in Kenneth S. Davis, *Soldier of Democracy* 314; also see Butcher, *My Three Years with Eisenhower* 5–6.

3. McKeogh and Lockridge, *Sgt. Mickey* 39.

4. DDE to MDE, June 26, 1942, in DDE, *Letters to Mamie* 23–24, John S. D. Eisenhower, ed. (Garden City, N.Y.: Doubleday, 1978).

5. DDE, *Letters to Mamie* 12.

6. Richard G. Davis, *Carl A. Spaatz and the Air War in Europe* 3–89 (Washington, D.C.: Center for Air Force History, 1992).

7. DDE diary, June 29, 1942, EL.

8. Pogue, 2 *Marshall* 408. Smith's maternal grandfather served in the cavalry during the Franco-Prussian War, and his spiked helmet was prominently displayed in the Smith home. D. K. R. Crosswell, *The Chief of Staff: The Military Career of General Walter Bedell Smith* 4 (Westport, Conn.: Greenwood Press, 1991).

9. Drew Middleton, interview by Merle Miller, quoted in Miller, *Ike the Soldier* 394. George Patton, who had to work with Smith, considered him "an s.o.b. of the finest type: selfish, dishonest, and very swell-headed." GSP diary, November 11, 1943, Library of Congress.

10. Merle Miller, *Ike the Soldier* 393.

11. Quoted in ibid. 394. According to Smith's biographer, "Although their relationship remained friendly, their personalities were not compatible." Crosswell, *Chief of Staff* 139.

12. DDE to GCM, June 26, 1942, 1 *War Years* 359–61.

13. Butcher, *My Three Years with Eisenhower* 12.

14. DDE diary, June 27, 1942, in DDE, *Eisenhower Diaries* 67. The reference is presumably to Colonel Iverson B. Summers, Eisenhower's West Point classmate and a member of the adjutant general's division.

15. Kay Summersby Morgan, *Past Forgetting* 41–42.

16. Butcher, *My Three Years with Eisenhower* 21.

17. DDE to GCM, June 30, 1942, 1 *War Years* 366–67.

18. *The New York Times,* June 12, 1942.

19. Pogue, 2 *Marshall* 329.

20. Stimson diary, June 17, 1942, Yale University.

21. WSC to FDR, June 20, 1942, quoted in Winston S. Churchill, *Hinge of Fate* 381–82. The full text of the memo is reprinted in Kimball, 1 *Churchill and Roosevelt* 515–16.

22. Mark A. Stoler, *The Politics of the Second Front: American Military Planning and Diplomacy in Coalition Warfare, 1941–1943* 55 (Westport, Conn.: Greenwood Press, 1977).

23. Quoted in Henry L. Stimson and McGeorge Bundy, *On Active Service in Peace and War* 425 (New York: Harper and Brothers, 1948). Also see Sherwood, *Roosevelt and Hopkins* 600–601.

24. For documents and minutes pertaining to ARGONAUT, see *FRUS: Washington and Casablanca* 419–86.

25. Williamson Murray and Allan R. Millett, *A War to Be Won: Fighting the Second World War, 1937–1945* 273–78 (Cambridge, Mass.: Belknap Press of Harvard University Press, 2000). The carriers *Lexington, Yorktown, Wasp,* and *Hornet* had been sunk; *Saratoga* and *Enterprise* were badly damaged and out of service. Only the *Ranger,* in the Atlantic, was ready for duty.

26. FDR to Hopkins, Marshall, and King, July 16, 1942, reprinted in full in Sherwood, *Roosevelt and Hopkins* 603–5.

27. DDE to GCM, July 17, 19, 21, 1942, in 1 *War Years* 388–404.

28. Pogue, 2 *Marshall* 345.

29. Butcher, *My Three Years with Eisenhower* 29.

30. Sherwood, *Roosevelt and Hopkins* 610–11.

31. DDE to Major General Orlando Ward, April 15, 1951, in Matloff and Snell, *Strategic Planning for Coalition Warfare* 286. Eisenhower's orders from the Combined Chiefs of Staff designating him supreme commander were dated August 13, 1942. Ibid. 287n74.

32. FDR to WSC, July 27, 1942, in Kimball 1 *Churchill and Roosevelt* 543–44.

33. Minutes, 34th meeting of the Combined Chiefs of Staff, July 30, 1942, cited in Matloff and Snell, *Strategic Planning for Coalition Warfare* 282–83.

34. Memo, Gen. [Walter Bedell] Smith for JCS, 1 August 1942, sub: Notes of Conf Held at White House, 8:30 p.m., July 30, 1942, quoted in Matloff and Snell, *Strategic Planning for Coalition Warfare* 283–84.

35. Rick Atkinson, *An Army at Dawn: The War in North Africa, 1942–1943* 16 (New York: Henry Holt, 2002).

36. For General Sir Alan Brooke's opinion of Marshall, see Arthur Bryant, *The Turn of the Tide: A History of the War Years Based on the Diaries of Field-Marshal Lord Alanbrooke, Chief of the Imperial General Staff* 290 (Garden City, N.Y.: Doubleday, 1957).

37. Eisenhower's remark is quoted in Arthur L. Funk, *The Politics of TORCH: The Allied Landings and the Algiers Putsch, 1942* 100 (Lawrence: University Press of Kansas, 1974).

38. FDR to WSC, September 5, 1942, and WSC to FDR, September 6, 1942, in Kimball, 1 *Churchill and Roosevelt* 592.

39. DDE to GSP, September 5, 1942, 1 *War Years* 541–42.

40. DDE diary entry, September 2, 1942, 1 *War Years* 524–27.

41. Quoted in Butcher, *My Three Years with Eisenhower* 50.

42. Marshall, interview by Forrest C. Pogue, November 15, 1956, quoted in Pogue, 2 *Marshall* 330.

43. DDE, *Crusade in Europe* 71.

44. "I cannot tell you how much I appreciate your making [Gruenther] available for duty in this theater," Ike wrote Krueger on July 30, 1942. "When I talked to General Marshall about Gruenther I told him that you had voluntarily called me just before I left Washington and stated that you stood ready to make available the very best men in your command in order that they might be placed where their talents are badly needed. He seemed highly pleased and it was because of your assurance that I had the nerve to put down Gruenther's name." In 1953, General Gruenther succeeded Eisenhower as supreme Allied commander in Europe. 1 *War Years* 400.

45. Quoted in Merle Miller, *Ike the Soldier* 388.

46. DDE, *Letters to Mamie* 40–41.

47. Summersby, *Eisenhower Was My Boss* 6–7.

48. Susan Eisenhower, *Mrs. Ike* 206.

49. Quoted in Merle Miller, *Ike the Soldier* 378.

50. Kay Summersby Morgan, *Past Forgetting* 65–66. Also see Summersby, *Eisenhower Was My Boss* 30–32.

51. Butcher, *My Three Years with Eisenhower* 137. Butcher recommended a Dandie Dinmont, but Eisenhower preferred "the attitude of independence struck by a strutting Scottie."

52. Kay Summersby Morgan, *Past Forgetting* 77.

53. Korda, *Ike* 286–87.

54. DDE to MDE, October 13, 1942, *Letters to Mamie* 45–46.

55. FDR to WSC, August 30, 1942, Kimball, 1 *Churchill and Roosevelt* 583–84.

56. DDE, Directive to Naval Task Force Commander, Western Task Force [Rear Admiral Henry K. Hewitt], October 13, 1942, 1 *War Years* 611–12.

57. Winston S. Churchill, *Hinge of Fate* 628.

58. Quoted in Korda, *Ike* 316.

59. Ambrose, *Supreme Commander* 99.

60. Charles de Gaulle, 1 *War Memoirs* (New York: Simon and Schuster) 10.

61. Butcher, *My Three Years with Eisenhower* 106. Washington columnist Walter Lippmann characterized Murphy as "a most agreeable and ingratiating man whose warm heart causes him to form passionate, personal, and partisan attachments rather than cool and detached judgments." *New York Herald Tribune,* January 19, 1943.

62. Arthur L. Funk, *Charles de Gaulle: The Crucial Years, 1943–1944* 34–35 (Norman: University of Oklahoma Press, 1959).

63. Jean Edward Smith, *FDR* 566.

64. Ambrose, *Supreme Commander* 100.

65. DDE to GCM, September 19, 1942, 1 *War Years* 562–63.

66. Ibid.

67. Blumenson, *Mark Clark* 78–89. Clark's *Calculated Risk* 67–89 presents a meretricious account of the meeting.

68. Patton's hastily assembled force was composed of the 2nd Armored Division, and the 3rd and 9th Infantry divisions. The divisions were brought to full strength by ransacking eight other stateside divisions for the necessary personnel. Atkinson, *Army at Dawn* 36.

69. Ladislas Farago, *Patton: Ordeal and Triumph* 195 (New York: Ivan Obolensky, 1963).

70. GSP diary, October 23, 1942, Library of Congress.

71. Marshall's September 26, 1942, message objecting to Hartle was evidently hand-carried to Eisenhower by Clark, 1 *War Years* 593n1. Marshall's list included Courtney Hodges, William H. Simpson, and John P. Lucas as possible alternatives. 3 *Papers of George Catlett Marshall* 367–68; Pogue, 2 *Marshall* 407.

72. DDE, *Crusade in Europe* 83. General Anderson spent much of his prewar career with the Seaforth Highlanders.

73. Ibid. 89.

74. Kay Summersby Morgan, *Past Forgetting* 91. In *My Three Years with Eisenhower,* Butcher fails to list Kay among those who accompanied Ike. (At page 147.)

75. Ibid 80. "The exercises that I witnessed had both encouraging and discouraging aspects," Eisenhower told Marshall. "The men looked fine and were earnest in trying to do the right thing. Their greatest weakness is uncertainty." DDE to GCM, October 20, 1942, 1 *War Years* 626–28.

76. Kay Summersby Morgan, *Past Forgetting* 78.

77. Clark, *Calculated Risk* 90.

78. Summersby, *Eisenhower Was My Boss* 36. Also see Butcher, *My Three Years with Eisenhower* 158.

79. DDE to GCM, October 29, 1942, 1 *War Years* 639–43.

80. Kay Summersby Morgan, *Past Forgetting* 81–82. Also see Summersby, *Eisenhower Was My Boss* 37–38. Butcher mentions the dinner in his diary but once again neglects to list Summersby among the attendees. *My Three Years with Eisenhower* 160.

81. DDE to GCM, November 1, 1942, 1 *War Years* 651.

82. FDR to Secretary of War, November 2, 1942, 1 *War Years* 651n6. On behalf of the Combined Chiefs of Staff, Admiral Leahy wired Murphy, "The decision of the President is that the operation will be carried out as now planned and that you will do your utmost to secure understanding and cooperation of the French officials with whom you are in contact." Quoted in Langer, *Our Vichy Gamble* 335–36 (New York: Knopf, 1947).

83. DDE, *Letters to Mamie* 50–52.

## CHAPTER TEN: BAPTISM BY FIRE

The epigraph is from a letter that Eisenhower wrote to his son John, February 19, 1943, in *The Papers of Dwight David Eisenhower*, vol. 2, *The War Years* 967–68. Cited subsequently as 2 *War Years*.

1. DDE to Smith, November 6, 1942, in 1 *War Years* 658–59.

2. Quoted in DDE, *Crusade in Europe* 97.

3. Ibid. 95.

4. Ibid. 99. The text of Murphy's offer to Giraud, November 2, 1942, is reprinted in Langer, *Our Vichy Gamble* 333–34. Murphy, as Professor Langer points out, was shooting from the hip. The State Department did not receive a copy of Murphy's letter until the spring of 1943.

5. DDE, *Crusade in Europe* 101.

6. DDE to GCM, November 8, 1942, 2 *War Years* 669–72.

7. DDE, *Crusade in Europe* 100.

8. Ibid.

9. DDE to GCM, November 8, 1942, 2 *War Years* 669–72.

10. DDE, *Crusade in Europe* 181.

11. DDE to GCM, November 8, 1942, 2 *War Years* 669–72.

12. GCM to DDE, November 8, 1942, ibid., note 6.

13. DDE to GCM, November 8, 1942, ibid. 673–74.

14. Korda, *Ike* 324.

15. DDE to Smith, November 9, 1942, 2 *War Years* 677–78.

16. DDE, "Worries of a Commander," November 8, 1942, ibid. 675.

17. DDE to Smith, November 9, 1942, EL.

18. DDE to Smith, November 11, 1942, 2 *War Years* 693–95.

19. DDE to Mabel Frances ["Mike"] Moore, December 4, 1942, ibid. 796–98.

20. Kay Summersby Morgan, *Past Forgetting* 92.

21. De Gaulle, 1 *War Memoirs* 49.

22. Charles W. Ryder, Oral History, March 1949, U.S. Army Military History Institute, Carlisle, Pa.

23. DDE to Smith, November 9, 1942, 2 *War Years* 677–78. (Eisenhower's emphasis.)

24. DDE, *Crusade in Europe* 104. In his postpresidential memoirs, Ike wrote that Giraud "proved wholly incapable of influencing anyone." DDE, *At Ease* 258.

25. Clark, *Calculated Risk* 109.

26. Quoted in Richard Lamb, *Churchill as War Leader* 211 (New York: Carroll and Graf, 1993).

27. De Gaulle, 1 *War Memoirs* 49–50. Rick Atkinson, in his elegant account of the North African landings, states that "sixty years after TORCH, a precise count of Allied casualties remains elusive," and then cites ballpark figures similar to those above. *Army at Dawn* 159.

28. George S. Paxton, *Vichy France: Old Guard and New Order, 1940–1944* 282–84 (New York: Knopf, 1972); Funk, *Charles de Gaulle* 40–41.

29. DDE to Clark, November 12, 1942, 2 *War Years* 698.

30. Kenneth Pendar, *Adventure in Diplomacy: The Emergence of General de Gaulle in North Africa* 119 (London: Cassell, 1966).

31. Ambrose, *Supreme Commander* 125–26.

32. Robert Murphy, *Diplomat Among Warriors* 118 (Garden City, N.Y.: Doubleday, 1964).

33. Winston S. Churchill, *Hinge of Fate* 637.

34. Quoted in Milton S. Eisenhower, *The President Is Calling* 137 (Garden City, N.Y.: Doubleday, 1974). Also see Ambrose, *Supreme Commander* 130.

35. De Gaulle, 1 *War Memoirs* 57.

36. 12 *The Public Papers and Addresses of Franklin D. Roosevelt with Special Material and Explanatory Notes by Samuel I. Rosenman* 479–82 (New York: Harper and Brothers, 1950). (Emphasis added.)

37. FDR's message to Eisenhower was first published in Sherwood, *Roosevelt and Hopkins* 654.

38. DDE to John S. D. Eisenhower, December 20, 1942, 2 *War Years* 855–56.

39. Atkinson, *Army at Dawn* 159.

40. Quoted in Langer, *Our Vichy Gamble* 372.

41. Murphy, *Diplomat Among Warriors* 150–51.

42. Winston S. Churchill, *Hinge of Fate* 641.

43. Sherwood, *Roosevelt and Hopkins* 651.

44. F. H. Hinsley, 2 *British Intelligence in the Second World War: Its Influence on Strategy and Operations* 466–67 (New York: Cambridge University Press, 1981).

45. Anthony Martienssen, *Hitler and His Admirals* 147 (New York: E. P. Dutton, 1949).

46. Atkinson, *Army at Dawn* 167.

47. Clark, *Calculated Risk* 134–35.

48. Atkinson, *Army at Dawn* 187.

49. Ibid. 184.

50. DDE to Smith, November 18, 1942, 2 *War Years* 732–34.

51. DDE to British War Office, November 22, 1942, ibid. 761–64.

52. Atkinson, *Army at Dawn* 191.

53. WSC to DDE, November 22, 1942, 2 *War Years* 767n2.

54. Atkinson, *Army at Dawn* 197.

55. DDE to MDE, November 27, 1942, *Letters to Mamie* 66.

56. Lyon, *Eisenhower* 185.

57. DDE to GSP, November 26, 1942, 2 *War Years* 774–75.

58. Quoted in Korda, *Ike* 353.

59. Nigel Hamilton, *Master of the Battlefield: Monty's War Years, 1942–1944* 145 (London: Hamish Hamilton, 1983).

60. Blumenson, 2 *Patton Papers* 135. Patton went on to say he almost thought Ike was "timid. When he goes out, a peep [jeep?] full of armed men precedes and follows his armed limousine."

61. Ibid. 137–38 (December 10, 1942).

62. Bryant, *Turn of the Tide* 430.

63. GCM to DDE, December 22, 1942, 3 *Papers of George Catlett Marshall* 488.

64. DDE to GCM, December 26, 1942, 2 *War Years* 867–68.

65. Atkinson, *Army at Dawn* 249.

66. Butcher, *My Three Years with Eisenhower* 228–29.

67. Funk, *Charles de Gaulle* 48–51.

68. Robin W. Winks, *Cloak and Gown: Scholars in the Secret War, 1939–1961* 183–84 (New York: William Morrow, 1987). Professor Winks, the Randolph W. Townsend, Jr., Professor of History at Yale, was afforded access to Professor Coon's papers at the University of Pennsylvania (they are restricted), and discusses Coon's view of the efficacy of political assassinations at some length. Also see Carleton S. Coon, *A North Africa Story: The Anthropologist as OSS Agent, 1941–1943* (Ipswich, Mass.: Gambit, 1980). Stephen Ambrose and Richard Immerman relate the story in *Ike's Spies: Eisenhower and the Intelligence Establishment* 48–56 (Garden City, N.Y.: Doubleday, 1981). Neither Murphy nor Professor Coon was willing to be interviewed by Ambrose.

69. Leahy to DDE, December 25, 1942, EL.

70. Kay Summersby Morgan, *Past Forgetting* 98–99.

71. Ibid. 101.

72. Major General Everett J. Hughes diary, December 30, 1942, Manuscript Division, Library of Congress. The reference to Summersby's reputation in London pertains to the fact that she took up with Captain Richard ("Dick") Arnold of the U.S. Corps of Engineers while her divorce from Mr. Summersby was still pending. Arnold was also married at the time.

73. DDE to MDE, December 30, 1942, *Letters to Mamie* 74–75.

74. DDE to MDE, December 31, 1942, ibid. 76. (Eisenhower's emphasis.)

75. WSC to FDR, December 31, 1942, Kimball, 2 *Churchill and Roosevelt* 98–99.

76. WSC to DDE, December 31, 1942, 2 *War Years* 883n2. Also see Martin Gilbert, 7 *Winston S. Churchill* 286 (London: Heinemann, 1986).

77. For the proceedings of the Casablanca conference, see *FRUS: Washington and*

*Casablanca.* Eisenhower's presentation to the third session of the Combined Chiefs is at pages 567–69.

78. Ibid. 567.
79. Ibid. 568–69.
80. Atkinson, *Army at Dawn* 283.
81. Bryant, *Turn of the Tide* 448.
82. Sherwood, *Roosevelt and Hopkins* 676.
83. Butcher, *My Three Years with Eisenhower* 243.
84. Quoted in Elliott Roosevelt, *As He Saw It* 79 (New York: Duell, Sloan, and Pearce, 1946).
85. Sherwood, *Roosevelt and Hopkins* 689.
86. Atkinson, *Army at Dawn* 286.
87. Blumenson, 2 *Patton Papers* 154–55.
88. Bryant, *Turn of the Tide* 430–31.
89. Sherwood, *Roosevelt and Hopkins* 677.
90. *FRUS: Washington and Casablanca* 660.
91. DDE to GCM, January 17, 1943, and GCM to DDE, January 18, 1943, 2 *War Years* 908–11. The fact that Marshall told Ike about the appointment of Alexander two days before Brooke made the formal proposal suggests they had discussed it beforehand.
92. Quoted in Bryant, *Turn of the Tide* 454–55.
93. Butcher, *My Three Years with Eisenhower* 258–59.
94. Kay Summersby Morgan, *Past Forgetting* 110.
95. Ibid. 107–8.
96. Hughes diary, February 12, 1943, Manuscript Division, Library of Congress
97. DDE to MDE, February 20, 1943, *Letters to Mamie* 97. (Eisenhower's emphasis.)
98. Margaret Bourke-White, "Women in Lifeboats: Torpedoed on an African-bound Troopship, a *Life* Photographer Finds Them as Brave in War as Men," *Life* 48–54, February 22, 1943.
99. Quoted in Susan Eisenhower, *Mrs. Ike* 204–5.
100. DDE to MDE, March 2, 1943, *Letters to Mamie* 104–5. (Eisenhower's emphasis.)
101. DDE to AGWAR [Adjutant General, War Department], 1013 hrs, February 13, 1943, quoted in Atkinson, *Army at Dawn* 337.
102. DDE to GCM, February 15, 1942, 2 *War Years* 955–57. II Corps' operations log contained the entry "General disposition of forces was satisfactory to General Eisenhower on February 13." Atkinson, *Army at Dawn* 332.
103. DDE to GCM, February 15, 1942, 2 *War Years* 956.
104. Atkinson, *Army at Dawn* 346.
105. Bernard Law Montgomery, *The Memoirs of Field-Marshal the Viscount Montgomery of Alamein* 142 (Cleveland: World Publishing, 1958).
106. John Ellis, *Brute Force: Allied Strategy and Tactics in the Second World War* 304 (New York: Viking, 1990).
107. Ibid. 298

108. Ibid. 304.

109. LDC interview, COHP.

110. Martin Van Creveld, *Supplying War: Logistics from Wallenstein to Patton* 201 (Cambridge: Cambridge University Press, 1977).

## CHAPTER ELEVEN: SICILY

The epigraph was recorded by George S. Patton in his diary, September 21, 1943, Manuscript Division, Library of Congress. The comment pertains to the "slapping incidents" in Sicily.

1. Butcher, *My Three Years with Eisenhower* 268.

2. Ibid. 265; DDE, *Crusade in Europe* 147.

3. Allied Force Headquarters, Commander-in-Chief's Dispatch, "North African Campaign, 1942, 1943," 37, Army War College, Carlisle, Pa.

4. GSP diary, January 28, 1943, et seq.

5. DDE to GCM, March 3, 1943, 1 *War Years* 860–61.

6. Atkinson, *Army at Dawn* 412–13.

7. John S. D. Eisenhower, *Allies: Pearl Harbor to D-Day* 304 (Garden City, N.Y.: Doubleday, 1982).

8. DDE to Major General Alexander Day Surles, April 6, 1943, 2 *War Years* 1080–81.

9. DDE to Charles Moreau Harger, publisher of the *Abilene Reflector,* April 23, 1943, ibid. 1099–1100.

10. DDE to Leonard Gerow, February 24, 1933, ibid. 985–87.

11. Quoted in Rick Atkinson, *The Day of Battle: The War in Sicily and Italy, 1943–1944* 49 (New York: Henry Holt, 2007).

12. D. Clayton James and Anne Sharp Wells, *A Time for Giants: Politics of the American High Command in World War II* 95 (New York: Franklin Watts, 1987).

13. Harold Macmillan, *War Diaries: Politics and War in the Mediterranean* 260 (New York: St. Martin's Press, 1984).

14. *FRUS: Washington and Casablanca* 711–16.

15. Kay Summersby Morgan, *Past Forgetting* 123–24.

16. Bradley and Blair, *A General's Life* 133, 133n.

17. Kay Summersby Morgan, *Past Forgetting* 118.

18. Holt, *Mamie Doud Eisenhower* 56.

19. Susan Eisenhower, *Mrs. Ike* 205.

20. DDE to MDE, June 11, 1943, DDE, *Letters to Mamie* 127–28.

21. Kay Summersby Morgan, *Past Forgetting* 128.

22. Ibid. 131.

23. Ibid. 132.

24. Ibid. 133–34.

25. Ibid. 137.

26. DDE, *Crusade in Europe* 166.

27. DDE, *At Ease* 265.

28. DDE to GCM, June 11, 1943, 2 *War Years* 1185–86.

29. Ambrose, 1 *Eisenhower* 247–48.

30. For the text of the statement of the National Council of the Resistance, see de Gaulle, 2 *War Memoirs* 112–13.

31. Ibid. 120–21.

32. FDR to WSC, June 17, 1943, in Kimball, 2 *Churchill and Roosevelt* 255.

33. De Gaulle, 2 *War Memoirs* 143.

34. Ibid. 132–33.

35. Harry C. Butcher diary, July 8, 1943, EL.

36. Quoted in Atkinson, *Day of Battle* 58.

37. Ernie Pyle, *Brave Men* 13 (New York: Henry Holt, 1944).

38. DDE, *Crusade in Europe* 172.

39. DDE to GCM, July 9, 1943, 2 *War Years* 1247.

40. Butcher, *My Three Years with Eisenhower* 348.

41. Quoted in Vincent Orange, *Tedder: Quietly in Command* 225 (London: Frank Cass, 2004).

42. DDE to MDE, July 9, 1943, DDE, *Letters to Mamie* 134–35.

43. Albert N. Garland and Howard McGaw Smyth, *Sicily and the Surrender of Italy* 181 (Washington, D.C.: Office of the Chief of Military History, Department of the Army, 1965).

44. Atkinson, *Day of Battle* 109–10. Wartime censorship prevented the losses from being known until well after the end of the hostilities.

45. Ibid. 115.

46. Butcher, *My Three Years with Eisenhower* 363.

47. Quoted in Hanson Baldwin, *Battles Lost and Won: Great Campaigns of World War II* 460–61 (New York: Harper and Row, 1966).

48. Ambrose, 1 *Eisenhower* 250.

49. Atkinson, *Day of Battle* 168.

50. Hugh Pond, *Sicily* 220 (London: W. Kimber, 1962).

51. Quoted in Ralph Bennett, *ULTRA and the Mediterranean Strategy* 234–35 (New York: William Morrow, 1989).

52. Quoted in Merle Miller, *Ike the Soldier* 531–32. Also see Bradley and Blair, *General's Life* 197–98.

53. Letter, GSP to his wife, Beatrice, September 28, 1918, in Blumenson, 2 *Patton Papers* 616–17.

54. Ambrose, *Supreme Commander* 229. (Eisenhower's emphasis.)

55. DDE to GSP, August 17, 1943, 2 *War Years* 1340–41.

56. Ambrose, *Supreme Commander* 230.

57. DDE to GSP, August 17, 1943, 2 *War Years* 1340–41. (Eisenhower's emphasis.)

58. Ladislas Farago, *Patton* 346.

59. DDE to GCM, August 24, 1943, 2 *War Years* 1353.

60. Ibid. 1353–54.

61. DDE to GCM, August 27, 1943, 2 *War Years* 1357–58.

62. DDE to GCM, September 6, 1943, ibid. 1387–90.

63. Ibid.

64. Quoted in Merle Miller, *Ike the Soldier* 541.

65. Ibid. Also see Crosswell, *Chief of Staff* 201.

66. DDE, *Crusade in Europe* 182.

67. In September, Colonel Herbert S. Clarkson, the theater inspector general, after conducting a full investigation, recommended that Marshall be notified of the incidents in case the matter should become public and the War Department embarrassed. There is no record that Marshall was informed, but the Army's informal system of communication makes it highly likely that he was generally aware of the incident. Like many senior officials, Marshall was accomplished in not letting it be known that he knew what he was not supposed to know. Marshall's message to Ike, November 23, 1943, is reported at *The Papers of Dwight David Eisenhower*, vol. 3, *The War Years* 1573n1. Cited subsequently as 3 *War Years*.

68. DDE to GCM, November 24, 1943, 3 *War Years* 1571–72.

69. Stimson and Bundy, *On Active Service* 499.

70. Stimson to Reynolds, December 3, 1943, in 89 *Congressional Record* 10567, 78th Cong., 1st sess.

71. 22 *Complete Presidential Press Conferences of Franklin D. Roosevelt* 227–28.

72. DDE to GSP, December 1, 1943, 3 *War Years* 1576.

73. Kay Summersby Morgan, *Past Forgetting* 145.

## CHAPTER TWELVE: SUPREME COMMANDER

The epigraph is a comment President Roosevelt made to Kay Summersby when she and Ike and FDR stopped for a picnic lunch near Carthage, in Tunisia, November 21, 1943. Summersby, *Eisenhower Was My Boss* 94.

1. DDE to Mountbatten, September 14, 1943, 3 *War Years* 1423.

2. Merle Miller, *Ike the Soldier* 639.

3. James M. Gavin, *On to Berlin: Battles of an Airborne Commander, 1943–1946* 142 (New York: Viking, 1978).

4. Bradley and Blair, *General's Life* 151; Montgomery, *Memoirs* 484.

5. Harold Macmillan, *The Blast of War, 1939–1945* 308 (New York: Harper and Row, 1968).

6. DDE to Mountbatten, September 14, 1943, 3 *War Years* 1420–23. (Eisenhower's emphasis.)

7. Atkinson, *Day of Battle* 140.

8. Pietro Badoglio, *Italy in the Second World War: Memories and Documents* 46 (Westport, Conn.: Greenwood Press, 1976).

9. The intricate negotiations leading to the Italian surrender are superbly chronicled in Garland and Smyth, *Sicily and the Surrender of Italy* 435–55.

10. Peter Tomkins, *Italy Betrayed* 271 (New York: Simon and Schuster, 1966).

11. Butcher, *My Three Years with Eisenhower* 415.

12. Atkinson, *Day of Battle* 243–44.

13. The QUADRANT conference is fully reported in United States Department of State, *Foreign Relations of the United States: Conferences at Washington and Quebec, 1943* (Washington, D.C.: U.S. Government Printing Office, 1970). The agreement to rearm the French is at pages 939–40. Also see Marcel

Vigneras, *Rearming the French* 91–98 (Washington, D.C.: Office of the Chief of Military History, Department of the Army, 1957).

14. Quoted in Funk, *Charles de Gaulle* 158.
15. "Reminiscences of George C. Dyer" 330, United States Naval Institute, Oral History Department, Annapolis, Md.
16. Clark's comment was to Major General Lucian Truscott. Quoted in Atkinson, *Day of Battle* 182.
17. Ambrose, *Supreme Commander* 270.
18. Maxwell Taylor, interview by Nigel Hamilton, October 17, 1981, quoted in Hamilton, *Master of the Battlefield* 400.
19. Bedell Smith, interview by H. M. Smyth, May 13, 1947; Eisenhower, interview by Smyth, October 27, 1947. Both in Office of the Chief of Military History Collection, Military History Institute, Carlisle, Pa.
20. "Alexander was very optimistic and was obviously prepared to think that the Italians would do all they said," Montgomery recorded in his diary on September 5, 1943.

> I took him aside for a talk. I told him my opinion was that when the Germans found out what was going on, they would stomp on the Italians. The Italian soldiers were quite useless and would never face up to the Germans.
>
> I said he should impress on all senior commanders that we must make our plans so that it would make no difference if the Italians failed us, as they most certainly would.
>
> The Germans were in great strength in Italy and we were very weak. We must watch our step very carefully, do nothing foolish. I said the Germans could concentrate against AVALANCHE quicker than we could build up; that the operation would need careful watching. (Montgomery, *Memoirs* 175–76.)

21. Henry Kent Hewitt Papers, Naval Historical Center, Washington, D.C., quoted in Atkinson, *Day of Battle* 200.
22. Quoted in ibid. 199.
23. Ibid. 207.
24. Clark to Alexander, September 12, 1943, Army Center of Military History, Fort McNair, Washington, D.C.
25. Butcher diary, September 15, 1943, EL. When Butcher published his diary in 1946 as *My Three Years with Eisenhower,* he omitted Ike's chilling criticism of Clark.
26. Butcher, *My Three Years with Eisenhower* 420.
27. Andrew Browne Cunningham, *A Sailor's Odyssey: The Autobiography of Admiral of the Fleet, Viscount Cunningham of Hyndhope* 570 (London: Hutchinson, 1951).
28. Wesley Frank Craven and James Lea Cate, eds., 2 *The Army Air Forces in World War II* 350–55 (Chicago: University of Chicago Press, 1949).
29. Samuel Eliot Morison, *The Two Ocean War: A Short History of the United States Navy in the Second World War* 356 (Boston: Little, Brown, 1963).

30. Blumenson, *Salerno to Casino* 144 (Washington, D.C.: Office of the Chief of Military History, U.S. Army, 1969).

31. Eisenhower, interview by H. M. Smyth, February 2, 1949, Office of the Chief of Military History Collection, Military History Institute, Carlisle, Pa. Bedell Smith, interview by Smyth, May 13, 1947, ibid; Clark, interview by Smyth, October 29, 1947, ibid. Also see Butcher, *My Three Years with Eisenhower;* and Mark Clark, *Calculated Risk* 199–200.

32. Quoted in Atkinson, *Day of Battle* 236.

33. See especially DDE to Dawley, September 22, 1943. "I want you to know, definitely, that your relief from VI Corps does not reflect in the slightest degree upon your character, your loyalty, or your sincere devotion to duty," wrote Ike. 3 *War Years* 1447–48.

34. Alan Williamson, "Dawley Was Shafted" 10, typewritten manuscript, Texas Military Forces Museum, Austin, Tex.

35. Ibid. Also see Atkinson, *Day of Battle* 235.

36. WSC to DDE, September 22, 1943, 3 *War Years* 1283n; also see Butcher, *My Three Years with Eisenhower* 423.

37. GCM to DDE, September 22, 1943, *Papers of George Catlett Marshall* 136.

38. Ibid.

39. Butcher, *My Three Years with Eisenhower* 423.

40. DDE to GCM, September 24, 1943, 3 *War Years* 1452–54.

41. Montgomery, *Memoirs* 171–76; Nigel Hamilton, *Master of the Battlefield* 393. According to Hamilton, "Eisenhower, for all his political panache, utterly failed to see the absurdity of 'Baytown'—for to his inexperienced eye, frustrated by desk-soldiering, the mainland across the Straits of Messina simply *demanded* Allied occupation." (Hamilton's emphasis.)

42. Butcher, *My Three Years with Eisenhower* 424–25.

43. Crosswell, *Chief of Staff* 202.

44. DDE, *Crusade in Europe* 194.

45. Ibid. 197.

46. John S. D. Eisenhower, *Allies* 388.

47. The 58,000-ton *Iowa* was a sister ship of the *New Jersey,* the *Wisconsin,* and the *Missouri.* The vessels were 888 feet long, 108 feet wide, and armed with nine 16-inch guns. The ships had a top speed of 33.5 knots, and a crew of 2,636 men. *Iowa* was commanded by Captain John L. McCrea, the president's first naval aide in the White House.

48. Elliott Roosevelt, *As He Saw It* 133.

49. Sherwood, *Roosevelt and Hopkins* 676–77.

50. Elliott Roosevelt, *As He Saw It* 136–37.

51. Kay Summersby Morgan, *Eisenhower Was My Boss* 89.

52. Ibid. 91.

53. Elliott Roosevelt, *As He Saw It* 137.

54. Kay Summersby Morgan, *Eisenhower Was My Boss* 93.

55. Korda, *Ike* 421.

56. Kay Summersby Morgan, *Past Forgetting* 152.

57. Summersby, *Eisenhower Was My Boss* 94.

58. Kay Summersby Morgan, *Past Forgetting* 152.

59. Korda, *Ike* 422.

60. Elliott Roosevelt, *As He Saw It* 137–38.

61. Sherwood, *Roosevelt and Hopkins* 770.

62. DDE, *Crusade in Europe* 197.

63. General Pershing's letter to FDR and the president's reply are published in Katherine Tupper Marshall, *Together: Annals of an Army Wife* 156–57 (New York: Tupper and Love, 1946).

64. William D. Leahy, *I Was There: The Personal Story of the Chief of Staff to Presidents Roosevelt and Truman: Based on His Notes and Diaries Made at the Time* 192 (New York: Whittlesey House, 1950).

65. On September 15, 1943, Republican senators Warren Austin (Vt.), Styles Bridges (N.H.), and Chan Gurney (S.Dak.) called on Stimson at his home to remind the secretary that they relied heavily on Marshall to win support from their colleagues for controversial measures to aid the Army. Austin, Bridges, and Gurney were the ranking Republican members of the Senate Military Affairs Committee. The intense Washington lobbying to retain Marshall as chief of staff is covered extensively in Pogue, 3 *Marshall* 263–78.

66. DDE, *Crusade in Europe* 197.

67. Field Marshal Lord Alanbrooke, *War Diaries, 1939–1945* 459, Alex Dencher and Daniel Todman, eds. (Berkeley and Los Angeles: University of California Press, 2001).

68. Pogue, 3 *Marshall* 307. The official minutes of the November 24, 1943, session, which are not verbatim, omit the exchange between Marshall and Churchill. United States Department of State, *Foreign Relations of the United States, The Conferences at Cairo and Tehran, 1943* 329–34 (Washington, D.C.: U.S. Government Printing Office, 1961). Cited subsequently as *FRUS: Cairo and Tehran.*

69. Marshall told Forrest Pogue, his official biographer, that Lord Ismay had to stay up with Churchill all night to calm him down. Pogue, 3 *Marshall* 307.

70. Elliott Roosevelt, *As He Saw It* 144.

71. Ibid. 144–45.

72. Ibid. 166.

73. *FRUS: Cairo and Tehran* 361. Colonel Dragoljub Mihajlović, leader of the Chetniks, a Serbian resistance group, initially enjoyed the support of the Yugoslav government in exile. But following Ike's presentation at Cairo, combined with growing British skepticism, the Allies withdrew their support in December 1943, and from that point on Mihajlović's forces limited their role. Tito's partisans gained the upper hand, and in 1946 Mihajlović was executed for treason and war crimes.

74. Ambrose, *Supreme Commander* 305.

75. DDE, *At Ease* 266.

76. Kay Summersby Morgan, *Eisenhower Was My Boss* 102–3.

77. Kay Summersby Morgan, *Past Forgetting* 160.

78. Korda, *Ike* 393; cf. Kay Summersby Morgan, *Past Forgetting* 147–48.

79. A photograph of the card from Ike appears in Kay Summersby Morgan's *Past Forgetting* at page 161.

80. Hopkins's remarks were made in Teheran to Lord Moran, Churchill's personal physician. Charles McMoran Wilson Moran, *Churchill: The Struggle for Survival, 1940–1965, Taken from the Diaries of Lord Moran* 143 (Boston: Houghton Mifflin, 1966).

81. *FRUS: Cairo and Tehran* 535–37; Sherwood, *Roosevelt and Hopkins* 788–89; Moran, *Churchill* 147.

82. Moran, *Churchill* 147.

83. Ibid.

84. Leahy, *I Was There* 208.

85. Charles E. Bohlen, *Witness to History, 1929–1969* 148 (New York: Norton, 1973).

86. *FRUS: Cairo and Tehran* 542.

87. Sherwood, *Roosevelt and Hopkins* 803; Forrest C. Pogue, *The Supreme Command* 32 (Washington, D.C.: Office of the Chief of Military History, Department of the Army, 1954).

88. Pogue, 3 *Marshall* 321.

89. Ibid. 321–22.

## CHAPTER THIRTEEN: D-DAY

The epigraph is from the directive issued to Eisenhower by the Combined Chiefs of Staff, February 12, 1944. Pogue, *Supreme Command* 53.

1. John S. D. Eisenhower, *Allies* 424.

2. Kay Summersby Morgan, *Past Forgetting* 163.

3. DDE, *Crusade in Europe* 207.

4. Butcher, *My Three Years with Eisenhower* 455. Also see Sherwood, *Roosevelt and Hopkins* 803.

5. Lord Alanbrooke, *War Diaries* 496.

6. WSC to FDR, December 19, 1943, Kimball, 2 *Churchill and Roosevelt* 622–24. Churchill, who was apprehensive that FDR might balk at Montgomery, followed up with a second message on December 22: "I hope to see Eisenhower on the 23rd and will discuss the matter with him. He would prefer Alexander for OVERLORD but War Cabinet consider that the public confidence would be better sustained by the inclusion of the well known and famous name of Montgomery and I agree with them as the operations will be to many people heart shaking." Ibid. 627.

7. DDE, *Crusade in Europe* 211.

8. Ibid. 210.

9. DDE to GCM, December 31, 1943, 3 *War Years* 1648–49.

10. DDE, *Crusade in Europe* 211.

11. Butcher, *My Three Years with Eisenhower* 456.

12. DDE to GCM, December 28, 1943, 3 *War Years* 1626–27.

13. DDE to GCM, December 17, 1943, ibid. 1604–6.

14. GCM to DDE, December 21, 1943, 4 *Papers of George Catlett Marshall* 184–86.
15. DDE to GCM, December 25, 1943, 3 *War Years* 1611–14. Also see DDE to GCM, December 23, 1943, ibid. 1609–10.
16. GCM to DDE, December 28, 1943, 4 *Papers of George Catlett Marshall* 210.
17. Butcher diary, December 29, 1943, EL.
18. Sir Frederick Morgan, *Overture to Overlord* 15 (Garden City, N.Y.: Doubleday, 1950). The acronym "COSSAC" stood for chief of staff, supreme Allied commander.
19. Butcher diary, EL.
20. First Impression of Operation OVERLORD, made at the request of the Prime Minister by General Montgomery, 1.1.44. Montgomery Papers, British War Museum, London.
21. Winston S. Churchill, *Closing the Ring* 445 (Boston: Houghton Mifflin, 1950).
22. FDR to DDE, December 22, 1943, United States Department of State, *Foreign Relations of the United States, 1943,* vol. 2, *Europe* 195 (Washington, D.C.: U.S. Government Printing Office, 1964). Cited subsequently as 2 *FRUS, 1943.*
23. FDR to WSC, December 22, 1943, Kimball, 2 *Churchill and Roosevelt* 626.
24. Colonel Warden [WSC] to FDR, December 23, 1943, ibid. 630.
25. FDR to DDE, December 26, 1943, 2 *FRUS, 1943* 197.
26. John S. D. Eisenhower, *General Ike* 157.
27. Charles de Gaulle, 2 *War Memoirs* 241.
28. Butcher, *My Three Years with Eisenhower* 473.
29. "Please convey to the President my earnest recommendation that this assurance be accepted as satisfactory," Eisenhower cabled Marshall on December 31, 1943. The next day, Admiral Leahy replied that "the assurances given by De Gaulle are acceptable to the president as satisfactory," 3 *War Years* 1644–45.
30. De Gaulle, 2 *War Memoirs* 241.
31. GCM to DDE, December 28, 1943, 4 *Papers of George Catlett Marshall* 210.
32. DDE to GCM, December 29, 1943, 3 *War Years* 1632.
33. GCM to DDE, December 29, 1943, 4 *Papers of George Catlett Marshall* 215.
34. DDE to GCM, December 30, 1943, 3 *War Years* 1641–42.
35. GCM to DDE, December 30, 1943, 4 *Papers of George Catlett Marshall* 220–21.
36. Kay Summersby Morgan, *Past Forgetting* 166.
37. Montgomery, *Memoirs* 189. Also see DDE, *Crusade in Europe* 217; 3 *War Years* 1653.
38. MDE interview, EL, quoted in D'Este, *Eisenhower* 478.
39. Butcher, *My Three Years with Eisenhower* 467.
40. Ambrose, 1 *Eisenhower* 280.
41. John S. D. Eisenhower, *Strictly Personal* 51.
42. DDE to W. B. Smith, January 5, 1944, 3 *War Years* 1651.
43. W. B. Smith to DDE, January 11, 1944, W-9869, *War Years* 1651n3.

44. Perret, *Eisenhower* 253.

45. Kay Summersby Morgan, *Past Forgetting* 176; Perret, *Eisenhower* 253; Korda, *Ike* 443; Ambrose, 1 *Eisenhower* 278. When Ike discussed the matter with Kay back in London, she said she was sorry. "It must have been a bit upsetting for her. And for you too."

"Jesus Christ! You have no idea," Eisenhower replied.

46. Kenneth S. Davis, *Soldier of Democracy* 456–57.

47. MDE interview, August 15, 1972, EL, quoted in Susan Eisenhower, *Mrs. Ike* 217–18.

48. DDE, *At Ease* 268.

49. Kay Summersby Morgan, *Past Forgetting* 171. Also see David Eisenhower, *Eisenhower at War, 1943–1945* 63–64 (New York: Random House, 1986).

50. DDE to Omar Bradley, January 13, 1944, 3 *War Years* 1656.

51. John S. D. Eisenhower, *Allies* 434.

52. The remark is that of Major General Kenneth G. McLean, chief of the planning section of SHAEF G-3. Interview by Forrest C. Pogue, October 16, 1946, quoted in Nigel Hamilton, *Master of the Battlefield* 497.

53. Quoted in ibid.

54. Kay Summersby Morgan, *Past Forgetting* 170.

55. Ibid. 172.

56. David Eisenhower, *Eisenhower at War* 198.

57. DDE, *Crusade in Europe* 222.

58. Korda, *Ike* 454.

59. John S. D. Eisenhower, *Allies* 445–46.

60. WSC to DDE, April 5, 1944, quoted in DDE, *Crusade in Europe* 232.

61. Bedell Smith to Marshall, May 17, 1944, quoted in Crosswell, *Chief of Staff* 231. At Bir Hakeim, west of Tobruk, in May–June 1942, the 1st Free French Brigade under Koenig held off Rommel's Afrika Korps for more than two weeks until ordered to withdraw. Bir Hakeim did much to establish the Free French as a fighting force. (As a young lieutenant stationed in postwar Berlin, I noted that the French garrison's officers club on Tegelsee was christened "Bir Hakeim.")

62. FDR to WSC, April 11, 1944, quoted in WSC, *Closing the Ring* 530.

63. Memorandum for the Record, March 22, 1944, 3 *War Years* 1782–85.

64. Ambrose, *Supreme Commander* 369. In his March 22 "Memorandum for the Record," Eisenhower wrote, "If a satisfactory answer is not reached I am going to inform the Combined Chiefs of Staff that unless the matter is settled at once I will request relief from this Command." 3 *War Years* 1782–85.

65. John S. D. Eisenhower, *Allies* 442.

66. Ambrose, *Supreme Commander* 375.

67. Korda, *Ike* 458.

68. DDE to GCM, January 19, 1944, 3 *War Years* 1667–68.

69. McCloy to DDE, January 25, 1944, 3 *War Years* 1668n2.

70. McCloy to DDE, April 15, 1944, 3 *War Years* 1785–86. For the text of the directive, see Harry L. Coles and Albert K. Weinberg, *Civil Affairs: Soldiers*

*Become Governors* 667–68 (Washington, D.C.: Center of Military History, U.S. Army, 2004).

71. Quoted in Pogue, *Supreme Command* 146.
72. DDE, Memorandum for Record, March 22, 1944, 3 *War Years* 1783–84.
73. DDE to Somervell, April 4, 1944, 3 *War Years* 1806–7.
74. Quoted in Pogue, 3 *Marshall* 384.
75. GCM to DDE, April 26, 1944, 3 *War Years* 1838n.
76. DDE to GCM, April 29, 1944, ibid. 1837–38.
77. GCM to DDE, April 29, 1944, in Pogue, 3 *Marshall* 385.
78. DDE to GCM, April 30, 1944, 3 *War Years* 1840–41.
79. GCM to DDE, May 2, 1944, in Pogue, 3 *Marshall* 385–86.
80. DDE to GCM, May 3, 1944, 3 *War Years* 1846.
81. DDE, *At Ease* 270–71.
82. DDE to MDE, February 14, 1944, DDE, *Letters to Mamie* 168.
83. DDE to MDE, May 12, 1944, ibid. 179.
84. DDE, *Crusade in Europe* 238.
85. Omar N. Bradley, *A Soldier's Story* 209 (New York: Henry Holt, 1951).
86. Max Hastings, *Overlord: D-Day and the Battle for Normandy* 58 (New York: Simon and Schuster, 1984); Montgomery, *Memoirs* 201.
87. Ambrose, *Supreme Commander* 347.
88. Montgomery Papers, Imperial War Museum, London.
89. Quoted in Nigel Hamilton, *Master of the Battlefield* 581. Alan Brooke did not share Montgomery's assessment of Ike. "The main impression I gathered was that Eisenhower was a swinger and no real director of thought, plans, energy or direction," he recorded in his diary that evening. "Just a coordinator—a good mixer, a champion of inter-allied cooperation, and in those respects few can hold a candle to him. But is that enough?" Lord Alanbrooke, *War Diaries* 546–47.
90. *The Memoirs of General Lord Ismay* 351 (New York: Viking, 1960). There is no transcript of Montgomery's remarks. His extensive notes are reprinted unedited in Nigel Hamilton, *Master of the Battlefield* 582–89.
91. Allied Expeditionary Air Force, Historical Record, quoted in D'Este, *Eisenhower* 502. (Churchill's emphasis.)
92. DDE, *At Ease* 275. ("England expects every man to do his duty," Nelson famously signaled the fleet as it sailed into battle.)
93. DDE to CCS, May 11, 1944, 3 *War Years* 1857–58.
94. WSC to FDR, May 12, 1944, Kimball, 3 *Churchill and Roosevelt* 129–30; FDR to WSC, May 12, 1944, ibid. 130; FDR to DDE, May 13, 1944, 3 *War Years* 1867–68.
95. DDE to GCM (for FDR), May 16, 1944, 3 *War Years* 1866–67. (Emphasis added.)
96. DDE, *Crusade in Europe* 248.
97. DDE to de Gaulle, May 23, 1944; de Gaulle to DDE, May 27, 1944, 3 *War Years* 1886.
98. WSC to FDR, May 26, 1944, Kimball, 3 *Churchill and Roosevelt* 145.

99. WSC to FDR, June 7, 1944, ibid. 171–72.

100. De Gaulle, 2 *War Memoirs* 253.

101. Ibid. 254.

102. DDE to CCS, June 4, 1944, 3 *War Years* 1906–7.

103. DDE to Montgomery, Bradley, Ramsay, and Leigh-Mallory, May 26, 1944, ibid. 1890–91.

104. DDE, *Crusade in Europe* 246–47. For Eisenhower's letter to Leigh-Mallory, May 30, 1944, see 3 *War Years* 1894–95.

105. WSC, *Closing the Ring* 620.

106. George VI to WSC, May 31, 1944, reproduced in ibid.

107. George VI to WSC, June 2, 1944, ibid. 622.

108. WSC to George VI, June 3, 1944, ibid. 623–24.

109. Ibid. 624.

110. DDE, *Crusade in Europe* 249; Pogue, *Supreme Command* 169.

111. Walter Bedell Smith, *Eisenhower's Six Great Decisions: Europe 1944–1945* 53–54 (New York: Longmans, Green, 1956).

112. Pogue, *Supreme Command* 170.

113. Walter Bedell Smith, *Eisenhower's Six Great Decisions: Europe 1944–1945* (New York: Lingmans, Green, 1956) 55. Smith's time estimate is on the high side. Eisenhower thought it was less than a minute. Others present put it at two to three to four minutes. Whatever the time, Eisenhower made the decision only after considerable reflection.

114. John S. D. Eisenhower, *Allies* 469.

115. Eisenhower's undated note is in the Eisenhower Library at Abilene. It is quoted in Stephen E. Ambrose, *Eisenhower: Soldier and President* 140 (New York: Simon and Schuster, 1990).

116. Kay Summersby Morgan, *Past Forgetting* 190.

117. Ibid. 191–92.

## CHAPTER FOURTEEN:
## THE LIBERATION OF FRANCE

The epigraph is Field Marshal von Rundstedt's reply to Wilhelm Keitel's query, "What shall we do now?" Keitel was chief of the Wehrmacht Supreme Command (OKW). Charles Messinger, *The Last Prussian: A Biography of Field Marshal Gerd von Rundstedt, 1875–1953* 197 (London: Brassey's, 1991).

1. The figures cited in the preceding two paragraphs are from Gordon A. Harrison, *Cross-Channel Attack* (Washington, D.C.: Center of Military History, U.S. Army, 2002); Hastings, *Overlord;* Chester Wilmot, *The Struggle for Europe* (New York: Harper and Row, 1952); I. C. B. Dear, ed., *The Oxford Companion to World War II* (New York: Oxford University Press, 1995).

2. In the attack on Kwajalein Atoll in the Marshall Islands in January 1944, the naval fire support for the Army's 7th Division consisted of seven battleships, three heavy cruisers, and eighteen destroyers for a period of almost six hours. At Omaha, the bombardment fleet consisted of two vintage battleships (*Arkansas* and *Texas*), four light cruisers (HMS *Bellona,* HMS *Glasgow,*

*Georges Leygues* [French], and *Montcalm* [French]), and twelve destroyers for a much shorter period. Adrian R. Lewis, *Omaha Beach: A Flawed Victory* 227–31 (Chapel Hill: University of North Carolina Press, 2001); Murray, *A War to Be Won: Fighting the Second World War, 1937–1945* (Cambridge, Mass.: Belknap Press of Harvard University Press, 2000) 419.

3. In his final report to the Combined Chiefs, Eisenhower tacitly acknowledged the error in not employing the British armored equipment at Omaha. In Ike's words, "Apart from the factor of tactical surprise, the comparatively light casualties we sustained on all beaches, except Omaha, were in large measure due to the success of the novel mechanical contrivances which we employed and to the staggering moral and material effect of the armour landed in the leading waves of the assault." Dwight D. Eisenhower, *Report by the Supreme Commander to the Combined Chiefs of Staff on the Operations in Europe of the Allied Expeditionary Force, 6 June 1944 to 8 May 1945* 30 (London: HMSO, 1946).

4. Wilmot, *Struggle for Europe* 263.

5. Hastings, *Overlord* 101.

6. Wilmot, *Struggle for Europe* 261; Hastings, *Overlord* 98.

7. Dear, *Oxford Companion to World War II* 667. Carlo D'Este lists American casualties at 6,577, comprising 1,465 killed, 3,184 wounded, and 1,928 missing in action (D'Este, *Eisenhower* 534).

8. Wilmot, *Struggle for Europe* 229.

9. These were the 12th SS Panzer Division, which was sixty-five miles from Caen, and the Panzer Lehr division, eighty-five miles away. Bradley and Blair, *General's Life* 253.

10. Antony Beevor, *D-Day: The Battle for Normandy* 35 (New York: Viking, 2009); Cornelius Ryan, *The Longest Day* 231–32 (New York: Simon and Schuster, 1959). The term "that Bohemian corporal" was initially used by Hindenburg and was well known in the Reichswehr. Hans Speidel, *We Defended Normandy* 89, Ian Colvin, trans. (London: Herbert Jenkins, 1951).

11. Hastings, *Overlord* 122. Günther Blumentritt, von Rundstedt's chief of staff in France, reports that von Rundstedt and Hitler never spoke on the telephone, and communicated through Keitel or Jodl. Blumentritt, *Von Rundstedt: The Soldier and the Man* 95 (London: Odhams Press, 1952).

12. DDE to GCM, June 6, 1944, 3 *War Years* 1914–15.

13. David Eisenhower, *Eisenhower at War* 271.

14. Bradley and Blair, *General's Life* 257.

15. Kay Summersby Morgan, *Past Forgetting* 194.

16. DDE to MDE, June 13, 1944, *Letters to Mamie* 190.

17. John S. D. Eisenhower, *Strictly Personal* 57.

18. Ibid. 63–64.

19. Ibid. 63.

20. Kay Summersby Morgan, *Past Forgetting* 195–97.

21. Pogue, *Supreme Command* 179. An additional seven divisions, five infantry and two parachute, were available to Seventh Army in Brittany, but the combination of Allied air superiority and fear of second landings near Brest

rendered them unavailable initially. For the deployment of German forces on D-Day, see the map in Messinger, *Last Prussian* 187.

22. Montgomery to Brooke, June 11, 1944, in Ambrose, *Supreme Commander* 428.

23. Lord Alanbrooke, *War Diaries* 575. (Brooke's emphasis.)

24. *The Rommel Papers* 491, B. H. Liddell Hart, ed. (New York: Harcourt, Brace, 1953).

25. DDE, *Report by the Supreme Commander to the Combined Chiefs* 41; Walter Bedell Smith, *Eisenhower's Six Great Decisions* 73. The misinterpretation of Montgomery's strategy by Eisenhower and Smith is treated at length by Chester Wilmot in *Struggle for Europe* 336–41.

26. Bradley and Blair, *General's Life* 265.

27. Quoted in Wilmot, *Struggle for Europe* 319.

28. Jacobsen and Rohwer, *Decisive Battles of World War II* 336.

29. Dear, *Oxford Companion to World War II* 978–80.

30. DDE, *Crusade in Europe* 260.

31. DDE to Tedder, June 8, 1944, 3 *War Years* 1933. For the results of the bombing campaign, see Craven and Cate, 3 *Army Air Forces in World War II* 541.

32. "As I have before indicated, I am opposed to retaliation as a method of stopping this business—at least until every other method has been tried and failed," Eisenhower wrote Tedder on July 5, 1944. 3 *War Years* 1975.

33. *With Prejudice: The War Memoirs of Marshal of the Royal Air Force, Lord Tedder* 582 (London: Cassell, 1966).

34. Robert Aron, *Histoire de la libération de la France, juin 1944–mai 1945* 78 (Paris: A. Fayard, 1959).

35. De Gaulle, 2 *War Memoirs* 260.

36. Beevor, *D-Day* 200.

37. De Gaulle, 1 *Discours et Messages* 444 (Paris: Plon, 1974), quoted in Pogue, *Supreme Command* 234.

38. I am indebted to Michael Korda for these observations. *Ike* 497.

39. DDE, *Crusade in Europe* 281.

40. WSC to FDR, June 28, 1944, Kimball 3 *Churchill and Roosevelt* 214–20.

41. DDE to GCM, June 20, 1944, 3 *War Years* 1938.

42. FDR to WSC, June 29, 1944, Kimball, 3 *Churchill and Roosevelt* 221–23.

43. Lord Alanbrooke, *War Diaries* 565.

44. WSC to FDR, July 1, 1944, Kimball, 3 *Churchill and Roosevelt* 227–29.

45. FDR to WSC, July 1, 1944, ibid. 232.

46. Butcher, *My Three Years with Eisenhower* 634–35.

47. DDE to GCM, August 5, 1944, *The Papers of Dwight David Eisenhower,* vol. 4, *The War Years* 2055. Cited subsequently as 4 *War Years.*

48. FDR to WSC, August 8, 1944, Kimball, 3 *Churchill and Roosevelt* 267.

49. WSC to FDR, August 8, 1944, ibid.

50. Butcher, *My Three Years with Eisenhower* 639.

51. DDE to GCM, August 11, 1944, 4 *War Years* 2066–67.

52. WSC to DDE, August 18, 1944, in Pogue, *Supreme Command* 228. "Have just returned from watching the assault from considerable distance," Churchill cabled Roosevelt. "Everything seems to be working like clockwork here, and there have been few casualties so far." WSC to FDR, August 16, 1944, Kimball, 3 *Churchill and Roosevelt* 278. To George VI, Churchill wrote, "Your Majesty knows my opinion about the strategy, but the perfect execution of the plan was deeply interesting." WSC to George VI, August 16, 1944, in Gilbert, 7 *Winston S. Churchill* 899.

53. DDE to WSC, August 24, 1944, 4 *War Years* 2095. "If you can guarantee that your presence at all such operations will have the same effect that it did in this wonderful show I will make sure that in any future operations in this theater you are given a fleet of your own," Ike told Churchill.

54. DDE to GCM, August 24, 1944, ibid. 2092–94.

55. On June 10, 1944, Hitler issued his famous stand-fast order: "Every man shall fight and fall where he stands." Wilmot, *Struggle for Europe* 323.

56. Testimony of General Alfred Jodl at Nuremberg, 15 *The Trial of German Major War Criminals: Proceedings of the International Military Tribunal Sitting at Nuremberg, Germany* 354 (London: HMSO, 1948).

57. Speidel, *We Defended Normandy* 105–11.

58. Rommel to his wife, June 18, 1944, *Rommel Papers* 492.

59. Messenger, *Last Prussian* 194.

60. Wilmot, *Struggle for Europe* 346.

61. *Rommel Papers* 479–80; Blumentritt, *Von Rundstedt* 238–39; Messenger, *Last Prussian* 196–97.

62. Messenger, *Last Prussian* 197; L. F. Ellis, 1 *Victory in the West* 320–21 (London: HMSO, 1962).

63. Messenger, *Last Prussian* 197; Hastings, *Overlord* 175.

64. Butcher, *My Three Years with Eisenhower* 618.

65. Walter Bedell Smith, *Eisenhower's Six Great Decisions* 75.

66. Butcher, *My Three Years with Eisenhower* 618.

67. Arthur Bryant, *Triumph in the West: A History of the War Years Based on the Diaries of Field-Marshal Lord Alanbrooke, Chief of the Imperial General Staff* 180 (Garden City, N.Y.: Doubleday, 1959).

68. Lord Alanbrooke, *War Diaries* 575.

69. Quoted in Bryant, *Triumph in the West* 183.

70. Quoted in Wilmot, *Struggle for Europe* 394–95.

71. Montgomery to Bradley, August 4, 1944, ibid. 400.

72. Summersby, *Eisenhower Was My Boss* 171.

73. Merle Miller, *Ike the Soldier* 671.

74. DDE to GCM, August 11, 1944, 4 *War Years* 2066–67.

75. Quoted in D'Este, *Eisenhower* 568. Each of the four company commanders of the 2nd Battalion, 120th Infantry, 30th Division, which bore the brunt of the German attack, were awarded the Distinguished Service Cross for valor.

76. DDE, *Crusade in Europe* 279. Ike's sentiment reflects General Ulysses Grant's comment at Shiloh after surveying the scene at the Hornet's Nest. According

to Grant, the ground was "so covered with dead that it would have been possible to walk across, in any direction, stepping on dead bodies, without a foot touching the ground." 1 *Personal Memoirs* 356.

77. Quoted in Martin Blumenson, *Breakout and Pursuit* 558 (Washington, D.C.: Office of the Chief of Military History, Department of the Army, 1961).

78. Bradley and Blair, *General's Life* 304.

79. Blumenson, 2 *Patton Papers* 517.

80. Stimson and Bundy, *On Active Service* 659–60. It is more likely that Stimson, knowing Georgetown, said "roaches," and Bundy euphemized it to "bedbugs."

81. Blumenson, 2 *Patton Papers* 521.

82. DDE to CCS, August 15, 1944, 4 *War Years* 2069–70.

83. FACS 58, OPD TS Message File, ibid., note 2. Also see Larry Collins and Dominique Lapierre, *Is Paris Burning?* 90–91 (New York: Simon and Schuster, 1965).

84. *The Reckoning: The Memoirs of Anthony Eden, Earl of Avon* 544 (Boston: Houghton Mifflin, 1965).

85. De Gaulle, 2 *War Memoirs* 332–33. De Gaulle believed Eisenhower's hands were tied by some "summit-level intrigue" under way at the White House. General Juin, who had been dealing with the general staff at SHAEF, came to the same conclusion.

De Gaulle's suspicions were not unfounded. According to Robert Murphy, FDR in the summer of 1944 was still "perfectly prepared to accept any viable alternative to de Gaulle—providing one could be found." Quoted in Collins and Lapierre, *Is Paris Burning?* 23.

86. Hitler's order is quoted in full in Dietrich von Choltitz, *Soldat unter Soldaten* 255–59 (Zurich: Europa Verlag, 1960). For an extract, see Blumenson, *Breakout and Pursuit* 598.

87. Cited in Blumenson, *Breakout and Pursuit* 598.

88. Collins and Lapierre, *Is Paris Burning?* 31. When Choltitz mounted the final attack on the fortress at Sevastopol on July 27, 1942, his regiment contained 4,800 men. When the battle ended, 347 were left, and Choltitz had been seriously wounded in the right arm.

89. Ibid. 222.

90. Dietrich von Choltitz to Uberta von Choltitz, August 21, 1944, Collins and Lapierre, *Is Paris Burning?* 154.

91. De Gaulle to DDE, August 21, 1944, in Jean Lacouture, *De Gaulle: The Rebel, 1890–1944* 564, Patrick O. Brian, trans. (New York: Norton, 1990).

92. DDE to CCS, August 22, 1944, 4 *War Years* 2087–89.

93. Collins and Lapierre, *Is Paris Burning?* 194.

94. Courtney Hodges, Commanding the First U.S. Army, to which the French 2nd Armored had been attached, withdrew several artillery battalions from the division before the march. "I don't want them to get the idea they can beat up Paris with a howitzer every time a machine gun gets in their way." Quoted in ibid.

95. The casualties in Paris during the fighting of August 24–25, 1944, were not

inconsequential. The 2nd Armored lost 28 officers and 600 enlisted men. German casualties amounted to 3,200, plus 14,800 taken prisoner. Among the prisoners was my future father-in-law, Johannes Zinsel, a forty-one-year-old private soldier who had been drafted the year before and was one of the defenders of the Palais du Luxembourg—the last German stronghold to surrender. That evening he wrote his family, courtesy of the Red Cross: "I have been taken prisoner. So far I am all right." Mr. Zinsel was a teacher at the Hindenburg Gymnasium in Berlin and was fluent in English and French; he became the prison camp interpreter and was given an early release from captivity in November 1945.

96. De Gaulle, 2 *War Memoirs* 350.
97. DDE, *Crusade in Europe* 297.
98. Quoted in D'Este, *Eisenhower* 576.
99. David Eisenhower, *Eisenhower at War* 425.
100. De Gaulle, 2 *War Memoirs* 358.
101. DDE, *Crusade in Europe* 298. "Because this ceremonial march coincided exactly with the local battle plan it became possibly the only instance in history of troops marching in parade through the capital of a great country to participate in a pitched battle the next day."
102. The only discordant note in the liberation of Paris was sounded by Major General Gee Gerow, commanding V Corps. Because of the demarcation line between the First and Third armies (Hodges and Patton), Leclerc's division was temporarily taken from Patton and assigned to First Army's V Corps. Gerow, whom Patton considered "the poorest corps commander in France," proceeded to display a political ignorance exceeded only by his military obtuseness at Omaha. For whatever reason, Gerow assumed that he, not Leclerc, was to liberate Paris. He established himself as military governor, was miffed that von Choltitz surrendered to Leclerc, and then on August 26 explicitly ordered Leclerc and his division not to participate in the victory parade down the Champs-Élysées.

"You are operating under my direct command and will not accept orders from any other source," Gerow wrote Leclerc. "I understand you have been directed by General de Gaulle to parade your troops this afternoon at 1400 hours. You will disregard those orders and continue on the present mission assigned you of clearing up all resistance in Paris and environs within your zone of action."

Leclerc, on de Gaulle's instructions, ignored Gerow's order. When Ike called on de Gaulle, it was apparent to him that Gerow had been out of bounds. Gerow was ordered out of the city that afternoon, and gratuitously informed General Koenig that he was turning Paris over to him. Koenig replied icily that he had been military governor of Paris since August 25, 1944, when the first troops arrived.

Gerow was one of "Marshall's men," a number of senior officers, including Hodges and Bedell Smith, who had not graduated from West Point and with whom the chief of staff felt a comradeship. After the war, when Marshall appointed Gerow head of the Command and General Staff School at Leavenworth, Patton wrote his wife that it was a joke. GSP to Beatrice Patton, August 18, 1945, in Blumenson, 2 *Patton Papers* 739, 740. Also see de Gaulle, 2 *War Memoirs* 358; cf. DDE to GCM, August 31, 1944, 4 *War Years* 2107–8.

## CHAPTER FIFTEEN: GERMANY

The epigraph is from a letter Ike wrote to Mamie, November 12, 1944. DDE, *Letters to Mamie* 219–20.

1. For an authoritative statement of the American head-on doctrine, see *FM 100–5, Field Service Regulations, 1939* para. 91. Also see Crosswell, *Chief of Staff* 252–53; Martin van Creveld, *Fighting Power: German and U.S. Army Performance, 1939–1945* 30–34 (Westport, Conn.: Greenwood Press, 1982). A useful contrast between American and German strategic thinking and a critique of the head-on doctrine is provided by Professor Russell F. Weigley in *Eisenhower's Lieutenants* 4–7.

2. Lord Alanbrooke, *War Diaries* 587. For Eisenhower's proposal, see DDE to GCM, August 22, 1944, 4 *War Years* 2087–89.

3. Speidel, *We Defended Normandy* 152.

4. Vincent J. Esposito, ed., 2 *The West Point Atlas of American Wars* map 56 (New York: Praeger, 1967); D'Este, *Eisenhower* 585.

5. The SHAEF report is quoted in Montgomery, *Memoirs* 238–39.

6. Model to von Rundstedt, September 27, 1944, in *German Army Documents, Dealing with the War in the Western Front from June to October, 1944*, U.S. Army Military History Institute, Carlisle Barracks, Pa.

7. B. H. Liddell Hart, *History of the Second World War* 558 (London: Cassell, 1970).

8. Montgomery to Brooke, August 18, 1944, in Nigel Hamilton, *Master of the Battlefield* 798. "I entirely agree," Brooke replied the following day. Ibid. 799.

9. Montgomery, *Memoirs* 239.

10. Crosswell, *Chief of Staff* 257.

11. Quoted in Liddell Hart, *History of the Second World War* 562. The chronology of Eisenhower's broad-front decision is laid out in commendable detail by Nigel Hamilton in chap. 16 of *Master of the Battlefield* 806–18.

12. Speidel, *We Defended Normandy* 152–53. (Emphasis added.) Speidel's reference to "beast" reflects the fact that by 1944 well over half of the Wehrmacht's transportation was horse-drawn.

13. Blumentritt's comment was made after the war to Liddell Hart and is reported in Liddell Hart's *The Other Side of the Hill: Germany's Generals, Their Rise and Fall, with Their Own Account of Military Events, 1939–1945* 428 (London: Cassell, 1951). Blumentritt also believed Patton's drive on Metz was unnecessary and that "a swerve northward in the direction of Luxemburg and Bitburg would have met with great success." Ibid.

14. Siegfried Westphal, *The German Army in the West* 172–74 (London: Cassell, 1951).

15. Liddell Hart, *History of the Second World War* 561.

16. Ibid. 566.

17. Bradley and Blair, *General's Life* 311.

18. Ambrose, *Supreme Commander* 529.

19. A German panzer grenadier division (armored infantry) had an authorized strength of 14,446 men versus 14,037 for the standard American infantry division. Van Creveld, *Fighting Power* 54–55. For usage figures, see Max Hastings, *Armageddon: The Battle for Germany, 1944–1945* (New York: Knopf, 2004) 23–24.

20. Pogue, *Supreme Command* 322–23.

21. See DDE to John C. H. Lee, September 16, 1944, 4 *War Years* 2153–54.

22. Jean Edward Smith, *Lucius D. Clay* 182–84.

23. DDE, *Crusade in Europe* 332–33.

24. Hastings, *Armageddon* 196.

25. Bradley and Blair, *General's Life* 343.

26. Montgomery to Brooke, December 7, 1944, in Nigel Hamilton, *Monty: Final Years of the Field-Marshal, 1944–1976* 162 (New York: McGraw-Hill, 1987); Bryant, *Triumph in the West* 252.

27. Bryant, *Triumph in the West* 257. When Bryant published *Triumph in the West* he omitted the last sentence. It is printed in the 2001 edition of Alanbrooke's *War Diaries,* published by the University of California Press, at page 628.

28. Bryant, *Triumph in the West* 256. On December 15, 1944, there were 3.24 million men under Eisenhower's command: 1,965,000 American; 810,584 British; 293,411 French; and 116,411 Canadian. Hastings, *Armageddon* 380.

29. Bryant, *Triumph in the West* 258.

30. War Office interrogation of Field Marshal von Rundstedt, July 1945, quoted in Milton Shulman, *Defeat in the West* 205–6 (New York: E. P. Dutton, 1948).

31. Ibid. 247.

32. Quoted in Blumentritt, *Von Rundstedt* 246.

33. Westphal, *German Army in the West* 174.

34. Korda, *Ike* 542.

35. Blumentritt, *Von Rundstedt* 211. At Hitler's order, the Todt Organization constructed a shelter while von Rundstedt was on leave and then carefully restored the garden. Ibid. 212.

36. Summersby, *Eisenhower Was My Boss* 184.

37. Ibid.

38. Kay Summersby Morgan, *Past Forgetting* 214–15.

39. Quoted ibid.

40. Lord Alanbrooke, "Notes from My Life," November 14, 1944, quoted in D'Este, *Eisenhower* 631.

41. Susan Eisenhower, *Mrs. Ike* 225.

42. DDE, *Letters to Mamie* 219–20.

43. "I was staggered," said von Rundstedt after the war. "Hitler had not consulted me. It was obvious that the available forces were far too small for such

an ambitious plan. Model took the same view as I did. But I knew by now it was useless to protest to Hitler about the possibility of anything. After consultation with Model and [General Hasso von] Manteuffel I felt the only hope was to wean Hitler from this fantastic aim by putting forward an alternative proposal that might appeal to him. This was for a limited offensive with the aim of pinching off the Allies' salient around Aachen." Liddell Hart, *Other Side of the Hill* 447.

44. D'Este, *Eisenhower: A Soldier's Life* 644.
45. Blumenson, 2 *Patton Papers* 599.
46. Ibid. 600.
47. Hastings, *Armageddon* 220.
48. Quoted in Ambrose, *Eisenhower: Soldier and President* 174.
49. Message 383, 2255 hrs, December 20, 1944, quoted in Nigel Hamilton, *Monty* 213. This was four days after the battle had begun. Montgomery reported that morale was low at the First and Ninth armies, and questioned Hodges's capacity, but a day later reported that he seemed to have recovered. Because Hodges was American, Montgomery chose not to relieve him.
50. Weigley, *Eisenhower's Lieutenants* 552. Also see DDE to GCM, January 1, 1945, 4 *War Years* 2390–91.
51. De Gaulle, 3 *War Memoirs* 169–70.
52. David Eisenhower, *Eisenhower at War* 604.
53. DDE, *Crusade in Europe* 363.
54. Liddell Hart, *Other Side of the Hill* 464.
55. The battle statistics are from Hastings, *Armageddon* 235. Cf. Pogue, *Supreme Command* 396–97.
56. DDE, *Crusade in Europe* 341.
57. Grant, 1 *Personal Memoirs* 100.
58. Wilmot, *Struggle for Europe* 614. Field Marshal Sir Alan Brooke concurred. "Calamity acted on Ike as a restorative," said Brooke. "It brought out all the greatness in his character." Quoted in Bradley and Blair, *General's Life* 323.
59. Sir Edgar Williams, interview by Nigel Hamilton, December 12, 1979, quoted in Hamilton, *Monty* 303–4.
60. Quoted in Hastings, *Armageddon* 231. Also see Nigel Hamilton, *Monty* 303–4.
61. "No handsomer tribute was ever paid to the American soldier than that of Field Marshal Montgomery," reported *The New York Times* on January 9, 1945. As for Bradley and Patton's reaction, Eisenhower wrote: "I doubt that Montgomery ever came to realize how deeply resentful some American commanders were. They believed he had belittled them—and were not slow to voice reciprocal scorn and contempt." DDE, *Crusade in Europe* 356.
62. Hastings, *Armageddon* 232.
63. For Eisenhower's intent, see especially David Eisenhower, *Eisenhower at War* 608–20.
64. Memorandum of Conference with Marshal Stalin, January 15, 1945, EL.
65. Quoted in Merle Miller, *Ike the Soldier* 748–49.
66. Butcher, *My Three Years with Eisenhower* 763.
67. Merle Miller diary, February 26, 1945, quoted in *Ike the Soldier* 752. Miller

went on to write that Eisenhower was particularly vague when discussing Montgomery. "He took about five minutes to say absolutely nothing."

68. Ibid. 753.

69. DDE, *Crusade in Europe* 379–80. Also see Bradley and Blair, *General's Life* 406–7. For the German critique, see Shulman, *Defeat in the West* 273–75. Shulman quotes Göring to the effect that the capture of the Remagen bridge "made a long defense of the Rhine impossible and upset our entire defense scheme along the river." Also see Westphal, *German Army in the West* 193–97.

70. Ambrose, *Eisenhower: Soldier and President* 186.

71. DDE to MDE, March 19, 1945, DDE, *Letters to Mamie* 244–45.

72. Kay Summersby Morgan, *Past Forgetting* 217. For the composition of Ike's party, I have consulted Summersby's *Eisenhower Was My Boss* 226; Ambrose, *Eisenhower: Soldier and President* 187; and Bradley and Blair, *General's Life* 411.

73. Ambrose, *Supreme Commander* 625.

74. Bradley, *Soldier's Story* 535.

75. DDE, *Crusade in Europe* 397. In reality, the national redoubt existed only in the propaganda disseminated by the Nazis. But it was not until after the war that the ruse was exposed. "It grew into so exaggerated a scheme that I am astonished we could have believed it as innocently as we did," wrote Bradley in *Soldier's Story* 536.

76. DDE to Alan Brooke, February 16, 1945, 4 *War Years* 2480–82.

77. WSC to DDE, February 22, 1945, ibid. 2494n1. Eisenhower's reply to Churchill is at page 2494 as well.

78. M562, March 27, 1945, reprinted in ibid. 440.

79. The full text of Eisenhower's March 27, 1945, press conference at the Scribe Hotel in Paris is reprinted in Butcher, *My Three Years with Eisenhower* 779–90.

80. David Eisenhower, *Eisenhower at War* 740.

81. DDE to Stalin, March 28, 1945, 4 *War Years* 2551. David Eisenhower, who had unlimited family cooperation when writing about his grandfather, states explicitly that Ike's purpose in writing to Stalin was twofold: "to bid for quick Soviet approval to seal the issue of Berlin; [and] to display the scope of his authority over American and British forces so that the Soviets would refer all military questions to SHAEF" and not the Combined Chiefs of Staff. *Eisenhower at War* 741.

82. DDE to Montgomery, March 28, 1945, 4 *War Years* 2552. Eisenhower dispatched a final cable to Marshall that day informing the chief of staff of his message to Stalin but not mentioning the message to Montgomery or the change of plans entailed. DDE to GCM, March 28, 1945, ibid. 2552–53.

83. Nigel Hamilton, *Monty* 442.

84. Montgomery to Brooke, April 8, 1945, quoted in ibid. 443.

85. Lord Alanbrooke, *War Diaries* 679, March 29, 1945.

86. Diary of Admiral Lord Cunningham, First Sea Lord, March 30, 1945, quoted in Andrew Roberts, *Masters and Commanders* (New York: HarperCollins, 2009) 563.

87. Prime Minister's Personal Minute, March 31, 1945, in Gilbert, 7 *Winston S. Churchill* 1273–74.
88. DDE to WSC, March 30, 1945, 4 *War Years* 2562–63.
89. GCM to DDE, March 29, 1945, W-60507, ibid. 2559n1.
90. DDE to GCM, March 30, 1945, ibid. 2559–62.
91. Memorandum by the U.S. Chief of Staff, March 30, 1945, 5 *Papers of George Catlett Marshall* 106–7.
92. WSC to DDE, March 31, 1945, WSC, *Triumph and Tragedy* 463 (Boston: Houghton Mifflin, 1953).
93. Lord Alanbrooke, *War Diaries* 680, April 1, 1945.
94. WSC to FDR, April 1, 1945, Kimball, 3 *Churchill and Roosevelt* 603–4.
95. FDR [Marshall] to WSC, April 4, 1945, ibid. 607–9.
96. WSC to DDE, April 2, 1945, WSC in *Triumph and Tragedy* 467.
97. Lord Alanbrooke, *War Diaries* 680–81, April 3, 1945. Also see Tedder's *With Prejudice* 681.
98. Roberts, *Masters and Commanders* 564–65.
99. Gilbert, 7 *Winston S. Churchill* 1296. The official U.S. translation rendered Churchill's words as "Lovers' quarrels always go with true love." Kimball, 3 *Churchill and Roosevelt* 612.
100. John Russell Young, 1 *Around the World with General Grant* 416–17 (New York: American News Company, 1879).

## CHAPTER SIXTEEN: CHIEF OF STAFF

The epigraph is Eisenhower's recollection of his reaction when Secretary Stimson informed him of the successful test of the atomic bomb in July 1945. *Crusade in Europe* 443. Also see Dwight D. Eisenhower, *Mandate for Change: 1953–1956, the White House Years* 312–13 (Garden City, N.Y.: Doubleday, 1963).

1. DDE to CCS, April 5, 1945, 4 *War Years* 2583.
2. WSC to Lord Ismay for BCOS, April 7, 1945, in WSC, *Triumph and Tragedy* 512–13.
3. David Eisenhower, *Eisenhower at War* 755–56.
4. Bradley, *Soldier's Story* 544.
5. DDE to GCM, April 23, 1945. Earlier, Eisenhower told Marshall, "Frankly, if I should have forces *in the Russian occupational zone* and be faced with an order or 'request' to retire so that they may advance, I can see no recourse except to comply. To do otherwise would probably provoke an incident, with the logic of the situation all on the side of the Soviets. I cannot see exactly what the British have in mind for me to do. It is a bridge that I will have to cross when I come to it." 4 *War Years* 2640–41, 2614–16. (Eisenhower's emphasis.)
6. WSC to HST, May 12, 1945, in WSC, *Triumph and Tragedy* 572–74.
7. Harry S. Truman, 1 *Memoirs* 214 (Garden City, N.Y.: Doubleday, 1955).
8. Ibid. 219.
9. Quoted in ibid. 300.
10. Eisenhower's cable to Washington of May 23, 1945, is discussed in Herbert

Feis, *Between War and Peace: The Potsdam Conference* 77 (Princeton, N.J.: Princeton University Press, 1960). For whatever reason, Alfred Chandler and Stephen Ambrose, editors of *The Papers of Dwight D. Eisenhower*, omitted the cable in volume six of the *Papers*, which deals with this period.

11. Montgomery's instructions are summarized in his *Memoirs* 338.

12. DDE to CCS, June 2, 1945, *The Papers of Dwight D. Eisenhower*, vol. 6, *Occupation* 125. Cited subsequently as 6 *Occupation*. This cable was drafted by General Lucius D. Clay, Eisenhower's deputy for military government. See 1 *The Papers of General Lucius D. Clay: Germany, 1945–1949* 16–17, Jean Edward Smith, ed. (Bloomington: Indiana University Press, 1974). Cited subsequently as 1 *Clay Papers*.

13. JCS to DDE, June 3, 1945, in Truman, 1 *Memoirs* 301. Also see 1 *Clay Papers* 17; 6 *Occupation* 125n1.

14. WSC to HST, June 4, 1945, WSC, *Triumph and Tragedy* 603. In the message, Churchill again used the "iron curtain" metaphor to describe the situation in eastern Europe.

15. Butcher, *My Three Years with Eisenhower* 855.

16. DDE, *Crusade in Europe* 436.

17. DDE [Clay] to JCS, June 6, 1945, 6 *Occupation* 135–36; 1 *Clay Papers* 18–20. Montgomery also received the Order of Victory from Zhukov, and de Lattre de Tassigny a lesser decoration. According to Ike, it was the first time the Russian Order of Victory had been awarded to foreigners. DDE, *Crusade in Europe* 437.

18. DDE [Clay] to JCS, June 6, 1945, 6 *Occupation* 135–36.

19. United States Department of State, 3 *Foreign Relations of the United States, 1945* 330–32 (Washington, D.C.: U.S. Government Printing Office, 1964).

20. Harry Hopkins's June 8, 1945, cable to President Truman was drafted by General Clay and submitted through military channels by Eisenhower. For text, see 1 *Clay Papers* 21–22. Hopkins's notes pertaining to his visit with Eisenhower are reprinted in Sherwood, *Roosevelt and Hopkins* 913–14. For Hopkins's visit to Moscow, see United States Department of State, *The Conference of Berlin: The Potsdam Conference, 1945* 24–62 (Washington, D.C.: U.S. Government Printing Office, 1960).

21. HST, 1 *Memoirs* 303.

22. WSC, *Triumph and Tragedy* 605–6.

23. Kay Summersby Morgan, *Past Forgetting* 222–24. (Emphasis in original.)

24. Ibid. 225.

25. My interviews with General Clay, some ninety hours' worth, were conducted in his New York apartment in 1969–70, and were preliminary to my biography of Clay (*Lucius D. Clay: An American Life*), which was published by Henry Holt in 1990. The rank of General of the Army was established by an Act of Congress, December 14, 1944, Public Law 482. Eisenhower, along with Arnold, Marshall, and MacArthur, was appointed to that rank on February 15, 1945. Sir James Gault, a graduate of Eton and Trinity College, Cambridge, was a member of the Scots Guards and a charter member of the British establishment. Eventually through Gault's efforts a twelve-room

apartment was made available for Eisenhower on the top floor of Culzean Castle on the Firth of Clyde in Scotland courtesy of the National Trust for Scotland.

26. Merle Miller, *Plain Speaking: An Oral Biography of Harry S. Truman* 339–40 (New York: Berkeley, 1974).

27. Fawn Brodie, *Thomas Jefferson: An Intimate History* (New York: W. W. Norton, 1974).

28. DDE to GCM, June 4, 1945, 6 *Occupation* 126–27. (Emphasis added.) Eisenhower went on to ask Marshall whether, in the event no general policy could be adopted, he might still bring Mamie over. Would there be any resentment to

> my arranging to bring my own wife here? This is something that of course I cannot fully determine, but my real feeling is that most people would understand that after three years of continued separation at my age, and with no opportunity to engage, except on extraordinary occasions, in normal social activities, they would be sympathetic about the matter.
>
> I should like very much to have your frank reaction because while I am perfectly willing to carry on in this assignment as long as the War Department may decide I should do so, I really would like to make it a bit easier on myself from the personal view point.

29. Korda, *Ike* 589. Stephen Ambrose is also curious why Ike felt it necessary to write Marshall. 1 *Eisenhower* 415.

30. Jean Edward Smith, *Lucius D. Clay* 325–26. "I don't believe in keeping families separated too long," said Clay. They'd been separated, many of these people, for quite a long time already. Perhaps I was carried away by my own feelings. I wanted my family with me."

31. Kay Summersby Morgan, *Past Forgetting* 242.

32. DDE to Kathleen McCarthy-Morrogh Summersby, November 22, 1945, 6 *Occupation* 546–47.

33. Bradley and Blair, *General's Life* 133n. According to Bradley, the "close relationship: between Ike and Kay is quite accurately portrayed as far as my personal knowledge extends, in Kay's second book, *Past Forgetting*."

34. Frank Freidel, *Franklin D. Roosevelt*, vol. 1, *The Apprenticeship* 320n (Boston: Little, Brown, 1952).

35. Arthur Schlesinger, Jr., in Ellen Feldman, *Lucy: A Novel* 1 (New York: W. W. Norton, 2003).

36. Everett Hughes diary, Manuscript Division, Library of Congress. Also see Ambrose, 1 *Eisenhower* 418.

37. Brendon, *Ike* 191.

38. Ambrose, 1 *Eisenhower* 412; also see Butcher, *My Three Years with Eisenhower* 870.

39. Quoted in Kenneth S. Davis, *Soldier of Democracy* 547.

40. Ibid.

41. *The New York Times,* June 22, 1945.

42. DDE to MDE, July 13 or 14, 1945, DDE, *Letters to Mamie* 263–64. On July 18, Eisenhower repeated his assurance, "I *love you, only!*" (DDE's emphasis.) Ibid. 265.

43. Bradley and Blair, *General's Life* 444–45.

44. DDE, *Crusade in Europe* 444.

45. DDE, *Mandate for Change* 312–13; DDE, *Crusade in Europe* 443.

46. DDE, *Mandate for Change* 313. Also see John S. D. Eisenhower, *Strictly Personal* 97.

47. I am indebted to Michael Korda for this observation. Korda, *Ike* 596.

48. "I suppose I was invited," said Clay, "because I knew Zhukov better than anyone else. . . . They were very, very friendly. There was no tension whatever." Jean Edward Smith, *Lucius D. Clay* 263.

49. DDE, *Crusade in Europe* 469.

50. Ibid. 468. Also see John S. D. Eisenhower, *Strictly Personal* 100–107.

51. DDE, *Crusade in Europe* 460–61; John S. D. Eisenhower, *Strictly Personal* 102–4; Jean Edward Smith, *Lucius D. Clay* 263.

52. DDE, *Crusade in Europe* 461–62.

53. Quoted in Ambrose, 1 *Eisenhower* 430.

54. *The New York Times,* August 14, 1945.

55. Ibid., August 15, 1945.

56. Jean Edward Smith, *Lucius D. Clay* 263.

57. For the arrangements for Zhukov's visit to the United States, see DDE to GCM, September 28, 1945, 6 *Occupation* 354–55.

58. Quoted in Lyon, *Eisenhower* 361. Also see Ambrose, 1 *Eisenhower* 424. Contemporary news coverage makes it abundantly clear that the words were entirely Patton's and were not put into his mouth by a reporter. See *The New York Times,* September 20 to September 30, 1945. The unofficial transcript of the press conference is reprinted in Blumenson, 2 *Patton Papers* 770–72, 775.

59. DDE to MDE, September 24, 1945, DDE, *Letters to Mamie* 272.

60. Summersby, *Eisenhower Was My Boss* 278. Major General Clarence Adcock, Clay's deputy for military government, and Professor Walter Dorn, then of Ohio State University, joined the meeting, which is described in detail in Stanley P. Hirshson, *General Patton: A Soldier's Life* 666–70 (New York: HarperCollins, 2002). Hirshson's account relies on the notes of the meeting taken by Professor Dorn. Dorn wrote subsequently that the "impact of the Patton affair upon the administration of the U.S. zone can scarcely be exaggerated. Henceforth, a new atmosphere prevailed. Dorn, "Unfinished Purge," chap. 8, 28, box 13, Dorn Papers, Columbia University.

61. John S. D. Eisenhower, *Strictly Personal* 114. Also see John S. D. Eisenhower, *General Ike* 71–73.

62. GCM to HST, August 20, 1945, 6 *Occupation* 310n1.

63. DDE to GCM, August 27, 1945, ibid. 309–10.

64. DDE to LDC, November 8, 1945, ibid. 521–27. On December 2, 1945, Clay wrote Eisenhower that "we were able to give Zhukov the [manufacturing] plants he desired, which pleased him immensely as it evidenced your good faith." Ibid., note 9.

65. DDE, *Crusade in Europe* 475. Eisenhower devotes the final chapter of *Crusade in Europe* (twenty-one pages) to relations with Russia.

66. See DDE to GCM, November 10, 1945, 6 *Occupations* 534–35. Ike told Marshall that it would be impossible for him to give a formal presentation but that he would study the briefing documents and speak informally. "For each committee I should like to have prepared one or two good solid paragraphs setting forth, without argument and without explanation the general scheme we propose and the general advantages we expect to result therefrom."

67. House Committee on Military Affairs, *Hearings on H.R. 515* 77–78, 79th Cong., 1st sess., 1945.

68. DDE, *Ike's Letters to Friend* 27–31.

69. DDE to Zhukov, December 6, 1945, *The Papers of Dwight David Eisenhower,* vol. 7, *Chief of Staff* 591–92. Cited subsequently as 7 *Chief of Staff.*

70. Susan Eisenhower, *Mrs. Ike* 235.

71. Susan Eisenhower's treatment of this period, seen through the eyes of her mother, is exemplary. Ibid. 234–49.

72. Snyder Papers, EL, quoted in Travis Beal Jacobs, *Eisenhower at Columbia* 9 (New Brunswick, N.J.: Transaction Publishers, 2001).

73. Hatch, *Red Carpet for Mamie* 204–5.

74. United States Department of the Interior, National Park Service, "National Survey of Historic Sites and Buildings: Quarters 1. Fort Myer Historic District."

75. DDE, *Eisenhower Diaries* 136.

76. Ambrose, 1 *Eisenhower* 435; Korda, *Ike* 697.

77. DDE, *Eisenhower Diaries* 137, November 1, 1946.

78. Ambrose, 1 *Eisenhower* 443–44.

79. Truman, 1 *Memoirs* 553.

80. DDE, *Mandate for Change* 81.

81. DDE to GCM, May 28, 1946, 7 *Chief of Staff* 1085.

82. Pogue, 4 *Marshall* 141.

83. Ambrose, 1 *Eisenhower* 470.

84. DDE to Milton S. Eisenhower, May 29, 1947, *The Papers of Dwight David Eisenhower,* vol. 8, *Chief of Staff* 1737–38. Cited subsequently as 8 *Chief of Staff.*

85. Ibid.

86. DDE to Thomas J. Watson, June 14, 1947, ibid. 1757–58.

87. Michael Rosenthal, *Nicholas Miraculous: The Amazing Career of the Redoubtable Dr. Nicholas Murray Butler* 453–54 (New York: Farrar, Straus and Giroux, 2006). Also see DDE to Milton S. Eisenhower, June 14, 1947, 8 *Chief of Staff* 1759–60.

88. DDE to Thomas I. Parkinson, June 23, 1947, ibid. 1775–76. (Eisenhower's emphasis.)

## CHAPTER SEVENTEEN: COLUMBIA

The epigraph is from the anthem of Columbia University, written by Gilbert Oakley Ward of the Class of 1902.

1. DDE, *At Ease* 325. Also see Perret, *Eisenhower* 377–79.
2. Grant, *Personal Memoirs.*
3. Jean Edward Smith, *Grant* 627.
4. DDE, *At Ease* 328.
5. Doubleday would pay $500,000; the *New York Herald Tribune* would pay $135,000 to serialize the book.
6. Douglas Black (publisher of Doubleday), interview by Travis Beal Jacobs, June 6, 1973, quoted in Jacobs, *Eisenhower at Columbia* 71.
7. "The Treasury Department informs me that the capital gains treatment of a sale such as we have in mind where the entire bundle of rights are involved is absolutely applicable," Ike wrote William Edward Robinson of the *Herald Tribune* on December 20, 1947. Eisenhower had previously written to Treasury Undersecretary Archibald Lee Manning Wiggins, who referred the question to George J. Schoeneman, the commissioner of the Internal Revenue Service. DDE's letter and Schoeneman's reply are in the Presidential Papers, Official File, at the EL. DDE to Robinson, December 20, 1947, *The Papers of Dwight David Eisenhower,* vol. 9, *Chief of Staff* 2153. Cited subsequently as 9 *Chief of Staff.*
8. For 1948 tax brackets, see Internal Revenue Service, "Personal Exemptions and Individual Income Tax Rates, 1913–2002."
9. DDE, *At Ease* 327.
10. Eli Ginsberg, interview by Travis Beal Jacobs, December 11, 1990, quoted in Jacobs, *Eisenhower at Columbia* 71.
11. Korda, *Ike* 614.
12. Ambrose, 1 *Eisenhower* 476–78. Eisenhower used Cliff Roberts as his financial adviser, and gave Roberts his check for *Crusade in Europe* to invest.
13. DDE to Bedell Smith, September 18, 1947, 9 *Chief of Staff* 1933–34.
14. DDE to Milton Eisenhower, October 16, 1947, ibid. 1986–87.
15. Leonard Finder to DDE, January 12, 1948, ibid. 2193n.
16. Lyon, *Eisenhower* 379.
17. DDE to Leonard V. Finder, January 22, 1948, 9 *Chief of Staff* 2191–93. Eisenhower added the qualifying phrase "in the absence of some obvious and overriding reasons" to avoid any suggestion that he was also ruling out MacArthur as a candidate.
18. Ambrose, 1 *Eisenhower* 464.
19. Rosenthal, *Nicholas Miraculous* 248.
20. Alva Johnson, "Nicholas Murray Butler," *The New Yorker* 233, November 15, 1930.
21. DDE, *At Ease* 342.
22. Dean Harry J. Carmen, interview by Travis Beal Jacobs, December 1, 1961, quoted in Jacobs, *Eisenhower at Columbia* 319.
23. Louis Graham Smith to DDE, May 20, 1948, *The Papers of Dwight David Eisenhower,* vol. 10, *Columbia* 86n. Cited subsequently as 10 *Columbia.*

24. DDE to Louis Graham Smith, May 25, 1948, ibid. 84–87. The university mailed copies of Eisenhower's letter to all Columbia alumni.

25. DDE to Henry Steele Commager, July 29, 1948, ibid. 170–71n1.

26. DDE to Arthur Prudden Coleman, July 12, 1948, ibid. 139–40. Coleman, a twenty-year assistant professor in Columbia's Department of Slavic Languages, had resigned in protest of the chair. Eisenhower accepted his resignation.

27. DDE to Columbia Trustees, September 20, 1948, quoted in ibid. 167n2.

28. Text of Installation Address, *The New York Times,* October 13, 1948.

29. *The New York Times,* June 6, 1944.

30. Richard H. Rovere, "The Second Eisenhower Boom," *Harper's* 31–39, May 1950.

31. Ellis Slater, interview by Travis Beal Jacobs, September 1, 1972, quoted in Jacobs, *Eisenhower at Columbia* 92.

32. DDE to Donald Harron, July 5, 1948, 10 *Columbia* 124–25.

33. DDE to Marquis Childs, July 8, 1948, ibid. 128–29.

34. DDE to James Roosevelt, July 8, 1948, ibid. 129–31. The same letter was sent to Pepper and Hague. On July 9, Senator Pepper replied, "I reluctantly bow to your determination."

35. Joseph Lang to DDE, October 11, 1948, ibid. 252n2.

36. Jacobs, *Eisenhower at Columbia* 110.

37. DDE, *At Ease* 341.

38. DDE, *Ike's Letters to a Friend* 61–62.

39. Clifford Roberts, interview, September 12, 29, 1968, COHP.

40. DDE to Forrestal, November 4, 1948, 10 *Columbia* 283. "I know that you understand you can call on me at anytime for anything," said Ike.

41. Forrestal to HST, November 9, 1948, ibid. 284n3.

42. DDE to HST, November 18, 1948, ibid. 310.

43. HST to DDE, November 26, 1948, ibid. 311n4.

44. Ira Henry Freeman, "Eisenhower of Columbia," *The New York Times Magazine,* November 7, 1948.

45. Drew Middleton, *The New York Times Book Review,* November 21, 1948; Robert E. Sherwood, *New York Herald Tribune,* November 21, 1948; Richard Rovere, *Harper's,* November 1948; Goronwy Rees, *The Spectator,* January 7, 1949. In addition to *Roosevelt and Hopkins,* Sherwood won Pulitzers for *Idiot's Delight* (1936), *Abe Lincoln in Illinois* (1939), and *There Shall Be No Night* (1941).

46. Kevin McCann, interview by Travis Beal Jacobs, July 25, 1972, quoted in Jacobs, *Eisenhower at Columbia* 133–39.

47. R. Gordon Hoxie, interview by Travis Beal Jacobs, June 9, 1995, quoted in ibid. 126.

48. Jacques Barzun, interview by Travis Beal Jacobs, April 5, 1979, quoted in ibid. 144.

49. Henry F. Graff, letter to the editor, 25 *Presidential Studies Quarterly* 862–63 (Fall 1995).

50. Rosenthal, *Nicholas Miraculous* 411.

51. DDE, *At Ease* 356.

52. Harry J. Carman, interview by Travis Beal Jacobs, December 1, 1961, quoted in Jacobs, *Eisenhower at Columbia* 87.

53. Robert L. Schulz, interview, COHP, quoted in ibid. 156.

54. DDE diary, February 9, 1949, in *Eisenhower Diaries* 157.

55. DDE, 10 *Columbia* 479n4.

56. DDE to H. H. Arnold, March 14, 1949, ibid. 544–45.

57. DDE diary, March 19, 1949, in *Eisenhower Diaries* 158. (Eisenhower's emphasis.)

58. DDE, *At Ease* 354.

59. DDE to Louis Johnson, April 20, 1949, 10 *Columbia* 560.

60. DDE to Everett Hazlett, April 27, 1949, DDE, *Ike's Letters to a Friend* 53–54.

61. DDE to Milton Eisenhower, May 13, 1949, 10 *Columbia* 580–81.

62. Albert C. Jacobs, interview by Travis Beal Jacobs, February 5, 1965, quoted in Travis Beal Jacobs, *Eisenhower at Columbia* 172.

63. Lionel Trilling, interview, February 4, 1958, COHP.

64. Eli Ginsberg, interview by Travis Beal Jacobs, December 11, 1990, quoted in Jacobs, *Eisenhower at Columbia* 205.

65. Jacques Barzun, interview, April 5, 1979, COHP.

66. David B. Truman, interview by Travis Beal Jacobs, February 4, 1958, quoted in Jacobs, *Eisenhower at Columbia* 199.

67. Harry J. Carman, interview, December 1, 1961, COHP.

68. Cliff Roberts, interview, September 12, 1968, COHP.

69. DDE to Hazlett, February 24, 1950, DDE, *Ike's Letters to a Friend* 68–76.

70. DDE diary, November 25, 1949, 10 *Columbia* 839–41.

71. Quentin Reynolds, "Mr. President Eisenhower," *Life* 144–60, April 17, 1950.

72. Richard H. Rovere, "The Second Eisenhower Boom," *Harper's* 31–39, May 1950. Ike noted the article in his diary. "This week another article came out—this time in *Harper's* which castigated me, on the ground that here the students and faculties hate me—and I return the sentiment with interest." Diary, May 2, 1950, *The Papers of Dwight David Eisenhower*, vol. 11, *Columbia* 1096–97. Cited subsequently as 11 *Columbia*.

73. Grayson Kirk, interview, July 22, 1987, COHP.

74. DDE to Philip C. Jessup, March 18, 1950, 11 *Columbia* 1014.

75. Jacobs, *Eisenhower at Columbia* 229.

76. DDE diary, October 13, 1950, 11 *Columbia* 1382–83.

77. DDE diary, October 28, 1950, ibid. 1388–92.

78. Ibid.

79. *Columbia Spectator*, November 10, 1950.

80. HST, 2 *Memoirs* 258. The unanimous request of the foreign ministers of the North Atlantic Treaty nations, meeting in Brussels on December 18, was flashed to the White House by Secretary of State Dean Acheson. United States Department of State, 3 *Foreign Relations of the United States: 1950 West-*

*ern Europe* 594–95 (Washington, D.C.: U.S. Government Printing Office, 1950).

81. John Krout, interview by Travis Beal Jacobs, July 22, 1963, April 27, 1977, quoted in Jacobs, *Eisenhower at Columbia* 251–52.
82. DDE, *At Ease* 361.
83. Jacobs, *Eisenhower at Columbia* 252.
84. *Columbia Spectator,* December 20, 1950.
85. *Time,* February 12, 1951.
86. DDE, *At Ease* 372.
87. Ibid.
88. DDE, *Mandate for Change* 14.
89. C. L. Sulzberger, *A Long Row of Candles: Memoirs and Diaries, 1934–1954* 702 (New York: Macmillan, 1969).
90. James T. Patterson, *Mr. Republican: A Biography of Robert A. Taft* 30 (Boston: Houghton Mifflin, 1972).
91. Minutes, Columbia Board of Trustees, February 8, 1951.
92. Carl W. Ackerman manuscript collection, Library of Congress.
93. Eric Foner, interview by Jean Edward Smith, April 20, 2010.

## CHAPTER EIGHTEEN: "I LIKE IKE"

The epigraph is General Clay's comment pertaining to Ike's indecision over whether to seek the GOP nomination in 1952. Jean Edward Smith, *Lucius D. Clay* 591.

1. DDE, *Mandate for Change* 14.
2. Sulzberger, *Long Row of Candles* 614.
3. Quoted in Korda, *Ike* 631.
4. Sulzberger, *Long Row of Candles* 686.
5. Of the 250 Allied officers at SHAPE, 150 were either British or American. Ibid.
6. Lyon, *Eisenhower* 424.
7. Quoted in David Halberstam, *The Fifties* 209 (New York: Villard Books, 1993).
8. Jean Edward Smith, *Lucius D. Clay* 591–92.
9. Richard Norton Smith, *Thomas E. Dewey and His Times* 578 (New York: Simon and Schuster, 1982).
10. Jean Edward Smith, *Lucius D. Clay* 584.
11. The sentiment was that of Ruth McCormick Simms, one of Dewey's aides at the 1940 Republican National Convention. Charles Peters, *Five Days in Philadelphia* 19 (New York: Public Affairs, 2005).
12. Jean Edward Smith, *Lucius D. Clay* 584.
13. DDE to LDC, September 27, 1951, *The Papers of Dwight D. Eisenhower,* vol. 12, *NATO and the Campaign of 1952* 580. Cited subsequently as 12 *NATO*.
14. LDC to DDE, September 29, 1951, ibid. 607n5.
15. DDE to LDC, October 5, 1951, ibid. 605–7. (Eisenhower's emphasis.)

16. Jean Edward Smith, *Lucius D. Clay* 586.

17. The story of President Truman's offer to Eisenhower was first reported by Arthur Krock in *The New York Times,* November 8, 1951, and subsequently mentioned in Krock's *Memoirs: Sixty Years on the Firing Line* 267–69 (New York: Funk and Wagnalls, 1968).

18. Henry Cabot Lodge, Jr., interview by Jean Edward Smith, May 5, 1971. "Lucius's father and my grandfather served together in the United States Senate," said Lodge, "and Lucius became absorbed in politics at a very early age. Lucius can be extremely blunt. In a rough-and-tumble political fight . . . a man like Clay can be extremely useful. He scared some people to death." Smith, *Lucius D. Clay* 585.

19. LDC to DDE, December 7, 1951, DDE Personal File, EL. Also see LDC to DDE, December 13, 1951, ibid.

20. DDE to LDC, December 19, 1951, 12 *NATO* 796–97.

21. DDE to LDC, December 27, 1951, ibid. 817–18.

22. Ibid.

23. DDE to Henry Cabot Lodge, Jr., December 29, 1951, ibid. 829.

24. HST to DDE, handwritten, December 18, 1951, in David McCullough, *Truman* 888 (New York: Simon and Schuster, 1992). Mr. Truman's letter was not delivered to Eisenhower until December 28, 1951.

25. DDE to HST, January 1, 1952, 12 *NATO* 830–31.

26. For the text of Lodge's letter to Adams, see *The New York Times,* January 7, 1952.

27. Ibid.

28. Henry Cabot Lodge, Jr., interview by Jean Edward Smith, May 5, 1971.

29. DDE to LDC, January 8, 1952, *The Papers of Dwight David Eisenhower,* vol. 13, *NATO* 860–61. Cited subsequently as 13 *NATO.*

30. For the text of Eisenhower's statement, see *The New York Times,* January 8, 1952.

31. The transcript of President Truman's press conference is in *The New York Times,* January 11 1952. Truman sent Eisenhower a recording of his remarks. "I am grateful for your thoughtfulness," Eisenhower replied on January 23. "It is difficult to understand why any individual should want to produce irritation or mutual resentment between us. . . . I deeply appreciate your determination to avoid any such thing—a purpose which does and will govern my own conduct." DDE to HST, January 23, 1952, 13 *NATO* 907–8.

32. *The New York Times,* February 8, 1952. Hoover's "Gibraltar of freedom" metaphor derived from a speech he made to a national television and radio audience on January 27. For the text, see *The New York Times,* January 28, 1952.

33. DDE to LDC, February 9, 1952, 13 *NATO* 962–64.

34. Ibid.

35. Jean Edward Smith, *Lucius D. Clay* 593.

36. DDE, *Mandate for Change* 20.

37. Jacqueline Cochran, interview, EL.

38. DDE to LDC, February 12, 1952, 13 *NATO* 974–75.

39. Jean Edward Smith, *Lucius D. Clay* 591.

40. All primary figures are from *Congressional Quarterly's Guide to U.S. Elections* 334–35 (Washington, D.C.: Congressional Quarterly Press, 1975).

41. DDE to LDC, March 28, 1952, 13 *NATO* 1139–41.

42. LDC to DDE, March 29, 1952, ibid. 1141n1.

43. HST, 2 *Memoirs* 492. George Allen, a close friend of both the president's and Ike's had confided to Truman that Eisenhower intended to run.

44. Jean Edward Smith, *Lucius D. Clay* 595. Also see Richard N. Smith, *Thomas E. Dewey* 582.

45. DDE to HST, April 2, 1952, 13 *NATO* 1154–56. Also see DDE to Secretary of Defense Robert Lovett, April 2, 1952, ibid. 1157–59. Eisenhower was placed on the Army's retired list on May 31, 1952 (ibid. 1238).

46. HST to DDE, April 6, 1952, ibid. 1156n10.

47. Lord Alanbrooke to DDE, May 17, 1952, EL.

48. Marquis William Childs, *Eisenhower: Captive Hero* 134 (New York: Harcourt, Brace, 1958).

49. Halberstam, *Fifties* 211.

50. *The New York Times,* June 5, 1952.

51. Ibid. June 15, 1952.

52. Richard N. Smith, *Thomas E. Dewey* 586.

53. Ibid. 593.

54. Thomas C. Reeves, *The Life and Times of Joe McCarthy* 426 (New York: Stein and Day, 1982).

55. Herbert Brownell, interview by Jean Edward Smith, April 7, 1971, quoted in Smith, *Lucius D. Clay* 597–98.

56. Ibid. 599.

57. Richard N. Smith, *Thomas E. Dewey* 590.

58. Jean Edward Smith, *Lucius D. Clay* 599.

59. Ibid.

60. *The New York Times,* July 12, 1952. Also see Patterson, *Mr. Republican* 563.

61. Herbert Brownell, interview by Jean Edward Smith, April 7, 1971.

62. Ibid.

63. Henry Cabot Lodge, Jr., interview by Jean Edward Smith, May 5, 1971.

64. Quoted in Halberstam, *Fifties* 213. Also see Jean Edward Smith, *Lucius D. Clay* 602.

65. Ibid.

## CHAPTER NINETEEN: THE GREAT CRUSADE

The epigraph is from Eisenhower's acceptance speech to the Republican National Convention, July 11, 1952. George L. Hart, *Official Report of the Proceedings of the Twenty-fifth Republican National Convention* 432 (Washington, D.C.: Republican National Committee, 1952).

1. Jean Edward Smith, *Lucius D. Clay* 603.

2. GCM to DDE, July 12, 1952, EL.

3. DDE to GCM, July 17, 1952, 13 *NATO* 1277–78.

4. DDE, *Mandate for Change* 50.

5. DDE to Cliff Roberts, July 29, 1952, 13 *NATO* 1283–85. (Eisenhower's emphasis.)

6. Roberts to DDE, ibid, note 7.

7. DDE to Roberts, July 29, 1952, ibid. 1283–85.

8. DDE, *Mandate for Change* 54–55. Labor Day in 1952 fell on September 1.

9. DDE, *Mandate for Change* 318n. Also see Lyon, *Eisenhower* 448–49.

10. *The New York Times,* August 15, 1952. I have reported the official Democratic explanation of why Eisenhower was not invited to the White House. It is conceivable that Truman messed up, did not think to invite Eisenhower, and Bradley took the fall.

11. Ibid. August 13, 1952.

12. DDE to HST, August 14, 1952, 13 *NATO* 1322–23.

13. HST to DDE, August 16, 1952, 13 *NATO* 1327n1.

14. Gary Wills, *Nixon Agonistes: The Crises of the Self-Made Man* 118 (Boston: Houghton Mifflin, 1970).

15. Jean Edward Smith, *Lucius D. Clay* 603–4.

16. *The New York Times,* September 10, 1952.

17. Herbert S. Parmet, *Eisenhower and the American Crusades* 128 (New York: Macmillan, 1972); Emmet John Hughes, *The Ordeal of Power: A Political Memoir of the Eisenhower Years* 41 (New York: Atheneum, 1963).

18. DDE, *Mandate for Change* 64.

19. *The New York Times,* September 16, 1952.

20. Lyon, *Eisenhower* 449.

21. Parmet, *Eisenhower and the American Crusades* 129.

22. *New York Post,* September 18, 1952.

23. Quoted in Wills, *Nixon Agonistes* 95–96.

24. Quoted in Earl Mazo, *Richard Nixon: A Political and Personal Portrait* 101 (New York: Harper and Brothers, 1959).

25. Robert Cutler, *No Time for Rest* 284–85 (Boston: Little, Brown, 1966). Also see Milton S. Eisenhower, *The President Is Calling* 251–52.

26. Roger Morris, *Richard Milhous Nixon: The Rise of an American Politician* 770–71 (New York: Henry Holt, 1990). The document is also reprinted in vol. 13 of the *Papers of Dwight David Eisenhower* at page 1358. The editor of the *Papers* suggests the message was not sent. I have gone with Morris, who as Nixon's biographer was in a better position to know.

27. Lyon, *Eisenhower* 456.

28. *New York Herald Tribune, The Washington Post,* September 20, 1952. The early editions of the Saturday papers were available Friday evening, September 19, 1952.

29. Jean Edward Smith, *Lucius D. Clay* 605.

30. Ibid. 606.

31. Wills, *Nixon Agonistes* 102.

32. Lyon, *Eisenhower* 457–58. Nixon's side of the conversation was monitored by Murray Chotiner, his campaign manager; James Bassett, his press secretary; and William P. Rogers, his close friend and later secretary of state.

33. Morris, *Richard Milhous Nixon* 816.

34. William Robinson to DDE, September 22, 1952, Robinson Papers, EL.

35. Paul Hoffman Papers, Truman Presidential Library, quoted in Morris, *Richard Milhous Nixon* 816.

36. Morris, *Richard Milhous Nixon* 818; Richard Norton Smith, *Thomas E. Dewey and His Times* 601–2. Herbert Browell, interview by Jean Edward Smith, April 7, 1971, COHP.

37. Morris, *Richard Milhous Nixon* 822–23; Richard Norton Smith, *Thomas E. Dewey and His Times* 601–2.

38. Morris, *Richard Milhous Nixon* 827.

39. *Variety,* September 14, 1952.

40. Parmet, *Eisenhower and the American Crusades* 138.

41. For the text of Nixon's speech see *The New York Times,* September 24, 1952.

42. Ibid.

43. Jean Edward Smith, *Lucius D. Clay* 606.

44. Ibid.

45. For Dewey's comments, see *The New York Times,* September 26, 1952. For Knowland and Stassen, see Morris, *Richard Milhous Nixon* 845.

46. Halberstam, *Fifties* 242.

47. Wills, *Nixon Agonistes* 117.

48. Perret, *Eisenhower* 416.

49. DDE, *Mandate for Change* 317.

50. Hughes, *Ordeal of Power* 42.

51. Ibid. (Eisenhower's emphasis.)

52. DDE, *Mandate for Change* 318.

53. *The New York Times,* October 9, 1952.

54. Halberstam, *Fifties* 230.

55. Lou Cowan, interview by David Halberstam, quoted in ibid. 232.

56. David Halberstam, *The Powers That Be* 236 (New York: Knopf, 1979).

57. Halberstam, *Fifties* 232.

58. Robert J. Donovan Oral History, EL.

59. Informal Memo, New York SAC Edward Scheidt to FBI Director Hoover, April 17, 1952; Informal Memo, FBI Assistant Director Milton Ladd to FBI Director, June 24, 1952; Informal Memo, FBI Supervisor Milton Jones to Assistant FBI Director Louis Nichols, July 24, 1952; Memo, FBI Assistant Director Milton Ladd to FBI Director Hoover, August 15, 1952. All reprinted in Athan Theoharis, *From the Secret Files of J. Edgar Hoover* 284–86 (Chicago: Ivan R. Dee, 1991).

60. David K. Johnson, *The Lavender Scare: The Cold War Persecution of Gays and Lesbians in the Federal Government* 122–23 (Chicago: University of Chicago Press, 2004); Curt Gentry, *J. Edgar Hoover: The Man and the Secrets* 402–3 (New York: Norton, 1991); Marquis William Childs, *Witness to Power* 67–68 (New York: McGraw-Hill, 1975).

61. *The New York Times,* October 17, 1952.

62. Ibid., October 25, 1952. In his memoirs, General Bradley dismissed Eisenhower's pledge as "pure showbiz. Ike was well informed on all aspects of the

Korean War and the delicacy of the armistice negotiations. He knew very well that he could achieve nothing by going to Korea." Bradley and Blair, *General's Life* 656.

63. Quoted in Sherman Adams, *Firsthand Report: The Story of the Eisenhower Administration* 43–44 (New York: Harper and Brothers, 1961).

64. Quoted in McCullough, *Truman* 912.

65. Herbert Brownell, interview by Jean Edward Smith, April 7, 1971, COHP.

66. *The New York Times,* November 5, 1952.

67. *Congressional Quarterly's Guide to U.S. Elections* 294. The Republicans won the House 221–211, and the Senate 48–47–1, the one independent being Wayne Morse of Oregon, who voted with the GOP to organize the Senate. In Kentucky, Stevenson received 495,729 votes to Ike's 495,029—less than one-tenth of one percentage point separating them.

68. HST to DDE, November 5, 1952, in 13 *NATO* 1412–13, notes.

69. DDE to HST, November 5, 1952, ibid. 1412.

CHAPTER TWENTY:
EIGHT MILLIONAIRES AND A PLUMBER

The epigraph is from Eisenhower's speech "The Chance for Peace," delivered to the American Society of Newspaper Editors, April 16, 1953. *Public Papers of the Presidents: Dwight D. Eisenhower, 1953* 179–88. Cited subsequently as *Public Papers.*

1. Jean Edward Smith, *Lucius D. Clay* 606–7.

2. Ibid. 607.

3. Ibid. 609.

4. Murray Kempton, "The Underestimation of Dwight D. Eisenhower," *Esquire,* 108–9, September 1967.

5. Paul Cabot, interview by Jean Edward Smith, December 12, 1970.

6. Jean Edward Smith, *Lucius D. Clay* 610–11. Clay was on the board of directors of General Motors.

7. Ibid.

8. Childs, *Eisenhower* 167.

9. Ibid.

10. Jean Edward Smith, *Lucius D. Clay* 612.

11. DDE diary, February 7, 1953, *Eisenhower Diaries* 227.

12. Jean Edward Smith, *Lucius D. Clay* 612.

13. *The New Republic,* December 15, 1952.

14. For Stevenson's comment, see Alden Whitman and *The New York Times, Portrait: Adlai E. Stevenson: Politician, Diplomat, Friend* 108 (New York: Harper and Row, 1965).

15. Carl M. Brauer, *Presidential Transitions: Eisenhower Through Reagan* 22 (New York: Oxford University Press, 1986).

16. Lyon, *Eisenhower* 470.

17. Korda, *Ike* 658.

18. DDE, *Mandate for Change* 95.

19. Bradley and Blair, *General's Life* 658.

20. James F. Schnabel and Robert J. Watson, *History of the Joint Chiefs of Staff,* vol. 3, *The Korean War* 932–34 (Wilmington, Del.: Glazer, 1979).

21. Mark Clark Oral History, COHP. In his memoirs, *From the Danube to the Yalu* 233 (New York: Harper, 1954), Clark inexplicably says he was not given an opportunity to present his plan to Eisenhower. I have adopted Clark's version in his oral history.

22. DDE, *Mandate for Change* 95.

23. Quoted in Brauer, *Presidential Transitions* 23.

24. I am indebted to Stephen Ambrose for this summary of the *Helena* voyage. Ambrose, 2 *Eisenhower* 34.

25. *The New York Times,* December 15, 1952.

26. John S. D. Eisenhower, *Strictly Personal* 156. News reports at the time suggested that both John and Ike were offended that John was ordered back. That was not the case.

27. Quoted in McCullough, *Truman* 921.

28. J. B. West and Mary Lynn Kotz, *Upstairs at the White House: My Life with the First Ladies* (New York: Coward, McCann, and Geoghegan, 1973).

29. Ibid. 137.

30. David and David, *Ike and Mamie* 195–97.

31. DDE diary, January 21, 1953, *Eisenhower Diaries* 225.

32. DDE to HST, January 23, 1953, *The Papers of Dwight David Eisenhower,* vol. 14, *The Presidency* 9. Cited subsequently as 14 *The Presidency.*

33. Brauer, *Presidential Transitions* 33.

34. Richard Strout, "The Administration's Abominable No Man," *The New York Times Magazine,* June 3, 1956.

35. Perret, *Eisenhower* 440.

36. Ezra Taft Benson to DDE, January 28, 1953, EL.

37. DDE to Dulles, February 3, 1952, 14 *The Presidency* 22. Nine members favored a silent prayer; five preferred an oral one. Parmet, *Eisenhower and the American Crusades* 176.

38. Parmet, *Eisenhower and the American Crusades* 176.

39. Ibid.

40. DDE diary, February 7, 1953, *Eisenhower Diaries* 227.

41. DDE diary, February 1, 1953, ibid. 226. Across the nation, Eisenhower's decision to join the National Presbyterian Church made front-page news. See *The New York Times, New York Herald Tribune,* and *The Washington Post,* February 2, 1953.

42. Cutler, *No Time for Rest* 241.

43. Ibid. 295–395.

44. Quoted in Krock, *Memoirs* 281.

45. Quoted in Robert J. Donovan, *Eisenhower: The Inside Story* 10–11 (New York: Harper and Brothers, 1956).

46. Quoted in Parmet, *Eisenhower and the American Crusades* 192. Professor Parmet cites a "confidential source," who evidently was George Humphrey.

47. Press Conference, February 25, 1953, *Public Papers, 1953* 58–70.

48. Donovan, *Eisenhower* 40.

49. Cutler, *No Time for Rest* 320–21. (Eisenhower's emphasis.)

50. Lyon, *Eisenhower* 531.

51. Statement of the President Concerning the Illness of Joseph Stalin, March 4, 1953, *Public Papers, 1953* 75.

52. Quoted in Lyon, *Eisenhower* 531.

53. Quoted in Hughes, *Ordeal of Power* 101.

54. Ibid. 103. (Eisenhower's emphasis.)

55. Ibid. 103–4. (Eisenhower's emphasis.)

56. Ibid. 105.

57. Ibid.

58. Clark, *From the Danube to the Yalu* 240–42.

59. Ibid. 244.

60. Press Conference, April 2, 1953, *Public Papers, 1953* 147–48.

61. NCS notes, April 9, 1953, quoted in Ambrose, *Eisenhower: Soldier and President* 327.

62. See DDE to Dulles, April 2, 1953, 14 *The Presidency* 146–47.

63. Hughes, *Ordeal of Power* 107.

64. Ibid. 112.

65. DDE, *Mandate for Change* 147.

66. "The Chance for Peace," April 16, 1953, *Public Papers, 1953* 179–88. (Emphasis added.)

67. *The New York Times, New York Post,* April 17, 1953.

68. *The New Yorker,* May 2, 1953.

69. DDE to Syngman Rhee, June 18, 1953, 14 *The Presidency* 309–10.

70. DDE, *Mandate for Change* 187.

71. Radio and Television Address Announcing the Signing of the Korean Armistice, July 26, 1953, *Public Papers, 1953* 520–22.

72. Donovan, *Eisenhower* 128–29.

## CHAPTER TWENTY-ONE: FIRST OFF THE TEE

The chapter title is from Don Van Natta, Jr.'s book of the same name (New York: PublicAffairs, 2003.) The epigraph is from Eisenhower's comment to his brother Milton, quoted in Ambrose, *Eisenhower* 57. Also see Milton S. Eisenhower, *The President Is Calling* 318.

1. Don Van Natta, Jr., *First Off the Tee: The Presidential Hackers, Duffers, and Cheaters from Taft to Bush* 138 (New York: PublicAffairs, 2003).

2. Arthur Daley, "3,265,000 Reasons for Playing Golf," *The New York Times Magazine,* May 31, 1953.

3. Herbert Warren Wind, *The Story of American Golf: Its Champions and Its Championships* 58 (New York: Farrar, Straus, 1962).

4. Van Natta, *First Off the Tee* 57.

5. Quoted in ibid. 58.

6. The information in these paragraphs is drawn from Van Natta's marvelous *First Off the Tee,* which documents the golfing skills (and lack thereof) of the

presidents. His portion dealing with Taft, Wilson, Coolidge, and Reagan ("Worst Off the Tee") is priceless. The Eisenhower material I have used is on pages 56–60.

7. Ibid. 64–65.
8. Quoted in ibid. 67.
9. DDE diary, May 1, 1953, 14 *The Presidency* 195–97. Also see Patterson, *Mr. Republican* 599–600.
10. DDE diary, June 1, 1953, 14 *The Presidency* 265–67.
11. Patterson, *Mr. Republican* 611–14.
12. Ambrose, 2 *Eisenhower* 56.
13. Ibid. 57.
14. Ibid. 59.
15. DDE, *Mandate for Change* 212. By contrast, after Senate criticism, Dulles asked Bohlen if he intended to step down, and he insisted they ride in separate cars to Capitol Hill so as to avoid being photographed together. Walter Isaacson and Evan Thomas, *The Wise Men: Six Friends and the World They Made* 568 (New York: Simon and Schuster, 1986).
16. *Congressional Record* 2277–81, 83rd Cong., 1st sess.
17. Ibid. 2282–83, 2285, 2291–92.
18. Press Conference, March 26, 1953, *Public Papers, 1953* 130.
19. 14 *The Presidency* 136.
20. Parmet, *Eisenhower and the American Crusades* 261.
21. Fred Greenstein, *The Hidden-Hand Presidency: Eisenhower as Leader* 175 (New York: Basic Books, 1982).
22. Roy Cohn, *McCarthy* 88 (New York: New American Library, 1968).
23. Quoted in Kai Bird, *The Chairman: John J. McCloy; The Making of the American Establishment* 468 (New York: Simon and Schuster, 1992).
24. Remarks at Dartmouth College Commencement Exercises, June 14, 1953, *Public Papers, 1953* 411–15.
25. *The New York Times,* June 17, 1953.
26. Max Rabb, interview by Herbert Parmet, January 12, 1970, quoted in Parmet, *Eisenhower and the American Crusades* 254–55.
27. Ralph Bunche, interview by Herbert Parmet, January 31, 1970, quoted in ibid. 255.
28. Milton S. Eisenhower, *The President Is Calling* 318; Ambrose, 2 *Eisenhower* 57.
29. Gallup poll, January 15, 1954. Cited in Parmet, *Eisenhower and the American Crusades* 266.
30. Greenstein, *Hidden-Hand Presidency* 184–85; Parmet, *Eisenhower and the American Crusades* 346.
31. *Chicago Tribune,* February 25, 1954.
32. *The New York Times,* March 10, 1954.
33. DDE to Ralph Flanders, March 9, 1954, Flanders Papers, Syracuse University Library.
34. *In Search of Light: The Broadcasts of Edward R. Murrow, 1938–1961* 247–48, Edward Bliss, Jr., ed. (New York: Knopf, 1967).
35. Perret, *Eisenhower* 502.

36. DDE to Paul Hoy Helms, March 9, 1954, *The Papers of Dwight David Eisenhower,* vol. 15, *The Presidency* 937–39. Cited subsequently as 15 *The Presidency.*

37. James Hagerty diary, February 25, 1954, EL.

38. In his scholarly account of the Eisenhower presidency, *The Hidden-Hand Presidency,* Professor Greenstein provides one primary case study: "The Joe McCarthy Case," pages 155–227.

39. DDE to Charles Wilson, May 17, 1954, *Public Papers, 1954* 483–84.

40. James Hagerty diary, March 28, 1954, EL.

41. Arthur M. Schlesinger, Jr., *The Imperial Presidency* 156 (Boston: Houghton Mifflin, 1973).

42. Quoted in Ambrose, 2 *Eisenhower* 188.

43. James Hagerty diary, March 28, 1954, EL.

44. Press Conference, March 24, 1954, *Public Papers, 1954* 339.

45. Donald Rumsfeld, *Known and Unknown: A Memoir* 50 (New York: Sentinel, 2011).

46. David M. Oshinsky, *A Conspiracy So Immense: The World of Joe McCarthy* 471 (New York: Free Press, 1983).

47. DDE, *Mandate for Change* 330–31.

48. The rule was enunciated clearly by Justice Field in the case of *Geofroy v. Riggs,* 133 U.S. 258 (1890):

> The treaty power, as expressed in the Constitution, is in terms unlimited except by those restraints which are found in that instrument. . . . But with these exceptions, it is not perceived that there is any limit to the questions which can be adjusted touching any matter which is properly the subject of negotiations with a foreign country.

49. In the leading cases of *United States v. Belmont,* 301 U.S. 324 (1937) and *United States v. Pink,* 315 U.S. 203 (1942), the Supreme Court elevated executive agreements to the same constitutional status as treaties. As Justice Douglas said for the court in *Pink,* an executive agreement is "a modest implied power of the President who is the 'sole organ of the Federal Government in the field of international relations.' "

50. The operative portions of the Bricker Amendment read as follows:

> Senate Joint Resolution 1
> 83rd Congress, 1st Session
>
> Section 1. A provision of a treaty which conflicts with this Constitution shall not be of any force or effect.
>
> Section 2. A treaty shall become effective as internal law in the United States only through legislation which would be valid in the absence of treaty.

Section 3. Congress shall have power to regulate all Executive and other agreements with any foreign power or international organization. All such agreements shall be subject to the limitations imposed on treaties by this article.

Section 4. The Congress shall have power to enforce this article by appropriate legislation.

Section 5. This article shall be inoperative unless it shall have been ratified as an amendment to the Constitution by the legislatures of three-fourths of the several States within seven years of the date of its submission.

51. Robert A. Caro, *Master of the Senate* 528 (New York: Knopf, 2002).
52. The remark is generally attributed to *New York Herald Tribune* television critic John Crosby.
53. Quoted in Hughes, *Ordeal of Power* 143.
54. Cabinet minutes, April 3, 1953 EL.
55. Ibid. July 17, 1953.
56. Jean Edward Smith, *Lucius D. Clay* 616.
57. Ibid.
58. Ibid. 616–17.
59. 15 *The Presidency* 848–49.
60. George substitute for the Bricker Amendment:

Sec. 1. A provision of a treaty or other international agreement which conflicts with this Constitution shall not be of any force or effect.

Sec. 2. An international agreement other than a treaty shall become effective as internal law in the United States only by an act of the Congress.

Sec. 3. On the question of advising and consenting to the ratification of a treaty the vote shall be determined by yeas and nays, and the names of the persons voting for and against shall be entered on the Journal of the Senate.

Sec. 4. This article shall be inoperative unless it shall have been ratified as an amendment to the Constitution by the legislatures of three-fourths of the several States within 7 years from the date of its submission.

61. Caro, *Master of the Senate* 536.
62. Ibid. 539. Also see Robert F. Maddox, *The Senatorial Career of Harley Martin*

*Kilgore* 317 (New York: Garland, 1981); Duane Tananbaum, *The Bricker Amendment Controversy: A Test of Eisenhower's Political Leadership* 179–80 (Ithaca, N.Y.: Cornell University Press, 1988).

63. DDE, *Mandate for Change* 227.

64. *The Memoirs of Earl Warren* 260 (Garden City, N.Y.: Doubleday, 1977).

65. Herbert Brownell, interview, Earl Warren Oral History Project, Bancroft Library, University of California.

66. *Memoirs of Earl Warren* 269.

67. Ibid. 270–71. Also see Bernard Schwartz, *Super Chief: Earl Warren and His Supreme Court* 5–7 (New York: New York University Press, 1983); Jack Harrison Pollack, *Earl Warren: The Judge Who Changed America* 152–57 (Englewood Cliffs, N.J.: Prentice Hall, 1979).

68. *The New York Times,* October 1, 1953.

69. Quoted in Pollack, *Earl Warren* 160–61.

70. Edgar Eisenhower to DDE, September 28, 1953, 14 *The Presidency* 552n1; Milton Eisenhower to DDE, undated, ibid. 578n1.

71. DDE to Edgar Eisenhower, October 1, 1953, ibid. 551–52.

72. DDE to Milton Eisenhower, October 9, 1953, ibid. 576–78. (Eisenhower's emphasis.)

73. DDE diary, October 8, 1953, ibid. 564–70.

74. *The New York Times,* February 26, 1954.

75. In addition to Warren, Harlan, and Brennan, Eisenhower also appointed Charles E. Whittaker and Potter Stewart to the Supreme Court. Observers of the Eisenhower era have often expressed surprise that Ike appointed William Brennan to the court. According to Herbert Brownell, following the resignation of Sherman Minton in October 1956, Eisenhower told Brownell that he wanted to appoint a Democrat, and preferably an Irish Catholic. Eisenhower had apparently been impressed by John F. Kennedy's campaign for the Democratic vice presidential nomination in 1956, and told Brownell he thought the court needed an Irish Catholic. Brennan, a well-known judge on the New Jersey Supreme Court, was the obvious choice. Brennan was the first state supreme court justice appointed to the court since Hoover appointed Benjamin Cardozo in 1932. Herbert Brownell and John P. Burke, *Advising Ike: The Memoirs of Attorney General Herbert Brownell* 179–80 (Lawrence: University Press of Kansas, 1993); Professor Henry F. Graff, interview by Jean Edward Smith, September 6, 2010.

## CHAPTER TWENTY-TWO: DIEN BIEN PHU

The epigraph is a comment by DDE to Robert Cutler, his national security assistant, May 1, 1954. The source is an interview of DDE by Stephen Ambrose cited in Ambrose's 2 *Eisenhower* 184, 688. The quotation has often been reprinted, but as Richard Rayner has pointed out, Ambrose's citations to interviews with DDE must be approached skeptically. To my mind, this one rings true. See Richard Rayner, "Channeling Ike," *The New Yorker* 21–22, April 26, 2010.

1. Halberstam, *Fifties* 398–99; Parmet, *Eisenhower and the American Crusades* 353–55; Chester L. Cooper, *The Lost Crusade: America in Vietnam* 62–72 (New York: Dodd, Mead, 1970).

2. *Time,* September 28, 1953.

3. Deputy War Minister Pierre de Chevigné, quoted in Halberstam, *Fifties* 403.

4. DDE, *Mandate for Change* 339, 351.

5. Ibid. 351.

6. DDE to Flanders, July 7, 1953, 14 *The Presidency* 371–73.

7. Bernard Fall, *Hell in a Very Small Place: The Siege of Dien Bien Phu* (Philadelphia: Lippincott, 1967). (Fall was on the faculty at Howard University in Washington, D.C.)

8. Quoted in Halberstam, *Fifties* 404.

9. Minutes, Legislative Leaders Meeting, February 8, 1954, EL.

10. Ibid.

11. Ambrose, 2 *Eisenhower* 177.

12. John Prados, *The Sky Would Fall: Operation Vulture, the U.S. Bombing Mission in Indochina, 1954* 92 (New York: Dial Press, 1983).

13. DDE to WSC, April 4, 1954, *The Papers of Dwight David Eisenhower,* vol. 15, *The Presidency* 1002–4. Cited subsequently as 15 *The Presidency.* "I have known many reverses," Churchill told Admiral Radford. "I have not given in. I have suffered Singapore, Hong-Kong, Tobruk; the French will have Dien Bien Phu." *From Pearl Harbor to Vietnam: The Memoirs of Admiral Arthur W. Radford* 408–9, Stephen Jurika, Jr., ed. (Stanford, Calif.: Hoover Institution Press, 1980).

14. Press Conference, April 7, 1954, *Public Papers, 1954* 381–83.

15. DDE, *Mandate for Change* 345.

16. Matthew Ridgway, *Soldier: The Memoirs of Matthew B. Ridgway as Told to Harold H. Martin* 275–78 (New York: Harper, 1956).

17. General Ridgway, interview by David Halberstam, quoted in Halberstam, *Fifties* 407. In a memorandum to Defense Secretary Wilson, April 22, 1954, Ridgway said intervention in Vietnam was "a dangerous strategic diversion of limited United States military capabilities in a non-decisive theater to the attainment of non-decisive objectives." Memo, Ridgway to JCS, April 6, 1954. Quoted in George C. Herring and Richard H. Immerman, "Eisenhower, Dulles and Dien Bien Phu: 'The Day We Didn't Go to War' Revisited," 71 *Journal of American History* 354–55 (September 1984).

18. DDE to Gruenther, April 26, 1954, 14 *The Presidency* 1033–35. (Eisenhower's emphasis.)

19. Remarks to the 42nd Annual Meeting of the United States Chamber of Commerce, April 26, 1954, *Public Papers, 1954* 421–24.

20. Press Conference, April 29, 1954, *Public Papers, 1954* 427–28.

21. Memorandum of Discussion at the 194th Meeting of the National Security Council, April 29, 1954, United States Department of State, 13 *Foreign Relations of the United States, 1952–1954: Indochina* 1431–45 (Washington, D.C.: U.S. Government Printing Office, 1982).

22. Ambrose, 1 *Eisenhower* 184.

23. Halberstam, *Fifties* 408.

24. Eisenhower's draft was retained by White House staffer William Bragg Ewald, Jr., and published for the first time in Ewald's *Eisenhower the President: Crucial Days, 1951–1960* 118–20 (Englewood Cliffs, N.J.: Prentice Hall, 1981).

25. Melanie Billings-Yun, *Decision Against War: Eisenhower and Dien Bien Phu, 1954* 160 (New York: Columbia University Press, 1988).

26. Stephen Kinzer, *All the Shah's Men: An American Coup and the Roots of Middle East Terror* preface (Hoboken, N.J.: John Wiley and Sons, 2003).

27. Ibid. 94.

28. Ibid. 89.

29. *The Wall Street Journal,* June 9, 1951.

30. Franks to F[oreign] O[ffice] 371/91534, quoted in Mostafa Elm, *Oil, Power, and Principle: Iran's Oil Nationalization and Its Aftermath* 158 (Syracuse, N.Y.: Syracuse University Press, 1992). In his *Memoirs,* Clement Attlee wrote that choosing Morrison to replace Bevin was "the worst appointment I ever made." Clement R. Attlee, *As It Happened* 246–47 (New York: Viking, 1954); Kenneth Harris, *Attlee* 472 (London: Weidenfeld and Nicolson, 1983).

31. James Chace, *Acheson: The Secretary of State Who Created the American World* 353 (New York: Simon and Schuster, 1998).

32. HST to Attlee, United States Department of State, 10 *Foreign Relations of the United States 1952–1954: Iran* 59–63 (Washington, D.C.: U.S. Government Printing Office, 1989). Cited subsequently as 10 *FRUS: Iran 1952–1954.*

33. *Time,* January 7, 1952.

34. HST to Henry Grady, Henry Grady Papers, Truman Presidential Library, Independence, Mo.

35. C. M. Woodhouse, *Something Ventured* 117 (London: Granada, 1982). Woodhouse, later a Tory MP, was elevated to the peerage as Lord Terrington and became editor in chief of Penguin Books.

36. "Memorandum by the Secretary of State of a Meeting at the White House Between the President and General Eisenhower," November 18, 1952, United States Department of State, 1 *Foreign Relations of the United States, 1952–1954: General: Economic and Political Matters* 25–26 (Washington, D.C.: U.S. Government Printing Office, 1983). Also see Donovan, *Eisenhower* 15–16.

37. DDE diary, January 6, 1953, 13 *NATO* 1481–83.

38. DDE to Hazlett, June 21, 1951, DDE, *Ike's Letters to a Friend* 84–88.

39. Kermit Roosevelt, *Countercoup: The Struggle for the Control of Iran* 115–16 (New York: McGraw-Hill, 1979).

40. Memorandum, Office of National Estimates, Central Intelligence Agency, for the President, March 1, 1953, 10 *FRUS: Iran, 1952–1954* 689–91.

41. Memorandum of Discussion, 135th Meeting of the National Security Council, March 4, 1953, ibid. 692–701.

42. Foreign Office 371/104614, Ministerial Visit to the U.S.: Record of meeting

with President Eisenhower, March 6, 1953, EL. Also see *Full Circle: The Memoirs of Anthony Eden* 236 (Boston: Houghton Mifflin, 1960).

43. Eden to WSC, March 6, 1953, Eden, *Full Circle* 235.

44. Memorandum of Discussion, 136th Meeting of the National Security Council, March 11, 1953, *10 FRUS: Iran, 1952–1954* 711–14.

45. Kinzer, *All the Shah's Men* 160.

46. Ambrose, 2 *Eisenhower* 111–12.

47. Mossadegh's letter of May 28, 1951, is reprinted in DDE, *Mandate for Change* 161–62.

48. Kinzer, *All the Shah's Men* 161; John Prados, *Presidents' Secret Wars: CIA and Pentagon Secret Operations Since World War II* 95 (New York: William Morrow, 1986); Elm, *Oil, Power, and Principle* 297.

49. Kermit Roosevelt, *Countercoup* 18; Elm, *Oil, Power, and Principle* 299.

50. DDE, *Mandate for Change* 162.

51. Memorandum of Telephone Conversation, by the Secretary of State, July 24, 1953, 10:55 a.m., *10 FRUS: Iran, 1952–1954* 737. (Emphasis added.)

52. Department of State *Bulletin* 178, August 10, 1953.

53. DDE, *Mandate for Change* 163.

54. Kermit Roosevelt, *Countercoup* 147–49. Also see Elm, *Oil, Power, and Principle* 301–2.

55. Donald N. Wilber, *Adventures in the Middle East: Excursion and Incursions* 188–89 (Pennington, N.J.: Darwin, 1986).

56. DDE, *Mandate for Change* 162–65.

57. Ambrose, 2 *Eisenhower* 129.

58. The American companies were Standard Oil of New Jersey, Standard Oil of California, Socony-Vacuum, Texaco, and Gulf. Later, to comply with U.S. antitrust requirements, independent oil producers were given 5 percent, which reduced the share of each of the majors to 7 percent. Shell held 14 percent, and Compagnie Française 6 percent.

59. Kinzer, *All the Shah's Men* 195–96.

60. *The New York Times,* March 18, 2000.

61. Ambrose, *Eisenhower: Soldier and President* 333.

62. Blanche Wiesen Cook, *The Declassified Eisenhower: A Divided Legacy of Peace and Political Warfare* 220–21 (Garden City, N.Y.: Doubleday, 1981); Halberstam, *Fifties* 377–79.

63. Cook, *Declassified Eisenhower* 224.

64. Quoted in Lyon, *Eisenhower* 590. The government's confiscation left United Fruit with 162,000 acres, only 50,000 of which were under cultivation. Ambrose and Immerman, *Ike's Spies* 221.

65. Halberstam, *Fifties* 375. When Smith left the State Department in 1955, he joined the board of the United Fruit Company.

66. E. Howard Hunt, *Undercover: Memoirs of an American Secret Agent* 96–97 (New York: Berkley Publishing, 1974).

67. Milton Eisenhower, "Report to the President," quoted in Richard H. Immerman, *The CIA in Guatemala: The Foreign Policy of Intervention* 18 (Austin: University of Texas Press, 1982).

68. Kermit Roosevelt, *Countercoup* 209–10; Kermit Roosevelt, interview by David Halberstam, cited in Halberstam, *Fifties* 371.

69. Halberstam, *Fifties* 376.

70. Eleanor Dulles, interview by Richard Immerman, October 9, 1979, cited in Immerman, *CIA in Guatemala* 134. Also see Halberstam, *Fifties* 381.

71. E. Howard Hunt, interview by Stephen Ambrose, cited in Ambrose and Immerman, *Ike's Spies* 226.

72. Quoted in David Wise and Thomas B. Ross, *The Invisible Government* 176 (New York: Random House, 1964). Also see *Newsweek,* March 4, 1963.

73. *The New York Times,* June 19, 1954.

74. The *New York Times's* correspondent Sydney Gruson and his wife, Flora Lewis, were expelled from Guatemala prior to the coup to prevent them from reporting on it. For Gruson's account, see Halberstam, *Fifties* 381–83.

75. Ambrose, 2 *Eisenhower* 195.

76. DDE, *Mandate for Change* 425–26.

77. Halberstam, *Fifties* 385.

78. Ibid. 371.

79. Allen to DDE, June 24, 1954, EL.

## CHAPTER TWENTY-THREE: NEW LOOK

The epigraph is part of Eisenhower's response to a question about defense policy at his news conference, March 17, 1954. *Public Papers, 1954* 330.

1. West and Kotz, *Upstairs at the White House* 140–41.

2. Ibid. 132.

3. Ibid. 146.

4. Ibid. 160.

5. Ibid. 141.

6. DDE, *Mandate for Change* 264–65.

7. DDE, *Ike's Letters to a Friend* 111.

8. After World War I, mailboxes and postal trucks were painted green as an economy measure, utilizing the War Department's surplus olive drab paint. It was scarcely a money-saving gesture to repaint them red, white, and blue. Historian, United States Postal Service.

9. West and Kotz, *Upstairs at the White House* 160.

10. The cottage at the Augusta National, one of seven, is known as "Mamie's Cabin," and is a spacious three-story white frame structure with green shutters that looks remarkably like FDR's cottage at Warm Springs. It cost $150,000 ($1.222 million currently) and was paid for by the Gang. Perret, *Eisenhower* 555; Van Natta, *First Off the Tee* 75.

11. David and David, *Ike and Mamie* 216.

12. Stanley R. Wolf and Audrey (Wolf) Weiland, *Ike: Gettysburg's Gentleman Farmer* 28–29 (Privately published, 2008).

13. For Arthur Nevins's account, see Nevins, *Gettysburg's Five-Star Farmer* (New York: Carlton Press, 1977). General Nevins is the brother of Columbia history professor Allan Nevins.

14. DDE, *At Ease* 360; Holt, *Mamie Dowd Eisenhower* 64. Holt cites the Elizabeth {Dorothy} Draper Papers for cost figures.

Eisenhower gave his aide Colonel Schulz precise instructions as to how his study should be arranged. One entire wall, said Ike, should be fitted with bookshelves.

The top shelf should be approximately six feet from the floor. I think the shelves should be 12 inches high and about 12 inches deep. Books should be divided as follows:

    a. Encyclopedia and reference works
    b. Professional military books of all kinds
    c. Histories
    d. Biographies
    e. Art, including technical books on the art of painting.
    f. Classics in literature
    g. Fiction
       1. Historical novels
       2. General popular fiction
       3. Anything that I keep that could be classed as Westerns
    h. Miscellaneous

Eisenhower to Colonel Robert L. Schulz, May 13, 1955, *The Papers of Dwight David Eisenhower,* vol. 16, *The Presidency* 1710–11. Cited subsequently as 16 *The Presidency.*

15. Perret, *Eisenhower* 602.
16. Wolf and Weiland, *Ike* 66–80.
17. DDE, State of the Union Address, February 2, 1953, *Public Papers, 1953* 17.
18. Radio-Television Address on National Security and Its Costs, May 19, 1953, *Public Papers, 1953* 306–16.
19. Press Conference, March 16, 1954, *Public Papers, 1954* 56–57.
20. Bradley to Secretary of Defense Wilson, March 19, 1953, quoted in Robert R. Bowie and Richard H. Immerman, *Waging Peace: How Eisenhower Shaped an Enduring Cold War Strategy* 102 (New York: Oxford University Press, 1998).
21. DDE to Hazlett, November 14, 1951, DDE, *Ike's Letters to a Friend* 93.
22. DDE to Hazlett, August 20, 1956, ibid. 167–69.
23. DDE to Joseph Dodge, December 1, 1953, 15 *The Presidency* 710–12.
24. DDE, *Mandate for Change* 452.
25. Stephen Jurika, Jr., ed. *From Pearl Harbor to Vietnam: The Memoirs of Admiral Arthur W. Radford* 326 (Stanford, Calif.: Hoover Institution Press). Also see *The New York Times,* December 15, 1953.
26. John Foster Dulles, "Evolution of Foreign Policy," speech to the Council of Foreign Relations, January 12, 1954, Department of State Press Release 8, 1954. For Eisenhower's role in writing the speech, see Bowie and Immerman, *Waging Peace* 199.

27. Press Conference, January 13, 1954, *Public Papers, 1954* 58.

28. Quoted in Robert Gilpin, *American Scientists and Nuclear Weapons Policy* 123, 130 (Princeton, N.J.: Princeton University Press, 1962).

29. Perret, *Eisenhower* 460. Also see *The New York Times,* November 11, 1953.

30. *The Diary of James C. Hagerty: Eisenhower in Mid-Course, 1954–1955* 181–84, Robert H. Ferrell, ed. (Bloomington: Indiana University Press, 1983). Cited subsequently as *Hagerty Diary.*

31. Memorandum of Conference with the President, February 24, 1955, EL.

32. Memorandum of Conference with the President, March 30, May 24, 1956, EL.

33. In 1960, Maxwell Taylor published *The Uncertain Trumpet,* which was highly critical of Eisenhower's defense policy. The book was cited frequently by Democratic candidates during the campaign. Maxwell D. Taylor, *The Uncertain Trumpet* (New York: Harper and Brothers, 1960).

34. Henry Kissinger, *Nuclear Weapons and Foreign Policy* (New York: Harper and Brothers, 1957). The book grew out of a study under the auspices of the Council on Foreign Relations, for which Kissinger was the director. His 1961 book, *The Necessity for Choice: Prospects of American Foreign Policy* (New York: Harper and Brothers, 1961), makes the same argument more concisely.

35. Quoted in Colin L. Powell and Joseph E. Persico, *My American Journey* 576 (New York: Random House, 1995). Secretary Albright expressed the view during a National Security Council discussion of U.S. policy in Bosnia. "I thought I would have an aneurysm," said Powell.

36. DDE, *Mandate for Change* 491–92.

37. Special Message to the Congress on Education, January 27, 1958, *Public Papers, 1958* 127–32.

38. In the Senate, Richard Neuberger picked up the seat in Oregon held by Republican Guy Cordon.

39. Caro, *Master of the Senate.*

40. Adams, *Firsthand Report* 86.

41. Caro, *Master of the Senate* 521.

42. D. B. Hardeman and Donald C. Bacon, *Rayburn: A Biography* 377 (Austin: Texas Monthly Press, 1987). Also see Donovan, *Eisenhower* 312.

43. Hardeman and Bacon, *Rayburn* 378.

44. *The Dallas Morning News,* January 3, 1953.

45. Quoted in Richard Rovere, *The Eisenhower Years: Affairs of State* 203–4 (New York: Farrar, Straus, and Cudahy, 1956).

46. Ann Whitman diary, July 1, 1960, EL.

47. DDE, *Mandate for Change* 493.

48. Quoted in Donovan, *Eisenhower* 312. Cf. Ewald, *Eisenhower the President* 28–29.

49. Ewald, *Eisenhower the President* 189; Milton Eisenhower, *The President Is Calling* 338.

50. *Public Papers, 1954* 479.

51. *Hagerty Diary* 14 (February 5, 1954).

52. DDE, *At Ease* 166–67.

53. Jean Edward Smith, *Lucius D. Clay* 618–19.

54. *Hagerty Diary* 193–95 (February 16, 1955).

55. Special Message to Congress Regarding a National Highway Program, February 22, 1955, *Public Papers, 1955* 275–80.

56. DDE, speech in Wheeling, W.Va., September 24, 1952, quoted in Steven Wagner, *Eisenhower Republicanism: Pursuing the Middle Way* 5 (DeKalb: Northern Illinois University Press, 2006).

57. Blanche Wiesen Cook private papers.

58. DDE, *Mandate for Change* 459–62.

59. Ibid. 464.

60. DDE to Gruenther, July 2, 1954, 16 *The Presidency* 422–23.

61. DDE, *Mandate for Change* 465.

62. Special Message to the Congress Regarding United States Policy for the Defense of Formosa, *Public Papers, 1955* 207–11.

63. The operative portion of the Formosa Resolution (84th Cong., 1st sess., H.J. Res. 159) reads as follows:

> *Resolved by the Senate and House of Representatives of the United States of America in Congress assembled, That:*
>
> The President of the United States be and he hereby is authorized to employ the Armed Forces of the United States as he deems necessary for the specific purpose of securing and protecting Formosa and the Pescadores against armed attack, this authority to include the securing and protection of such related positions and territories of that area now in friendly hands and the taking of such other measures as he judges to be required or appropriate in assuring the defense of Formosa and the Pescadores.
>
> This resolution shall expire when the President shall determine that the peace and security of the area is reasonably assured by international conditions created by action of the United Nations or otherwise, and shall so report to the Congress.

64. *Hagerty Diary* 197.

65. DDE, *Mandate for Change* 477–78.

66. Press Conference, March 23, 1955, *Public Papers, 1955* 358.

67. DDE, *Mandate for Change* 478–79. Also see 15 *Facts on File* 98.

68. DDE diary, March 26, 1955, *Eisenhower Diaries* 296.

69. DDE, *Mandate for Change* 480.

70. 15 *Facts on File* 137.

71. Press Conference, April 27, 1955, *Public Papers, 1955* 425–26.

72. Ambrose, *Eisenhower: Soldier and President* 384.

73. DDE, *Mandate for Change* 483.

74. Robert Divine, *Eisenhower and the Cold War* 65–66 (New York: Oxford University Press, 1981).

## CHAPTER TWENTY-FOUR: HEART ATTACK

The epigraph is from Eisenhower's statement to the staff at Fitzsimmons Army Hospital in Denver upon his release, November 11, 1955. *Public Papers, 1955* 840–41.

1. Quoted in Rovere, *Eisenhower Years* 276.
2. Harold Macmillan, *Tides of Fortune, 1945–1955* 586–87 (New York: Harper and Row, 1969).
3. DDE, *Mandate for Change* 506.
4. Quoted in Lyon, *Eisenhower* 650.
5. Quoted in Parmet, *Eisenhower and the American Crusades* 404.
6. Ibid.
7. Adams, *Firsthand Report* 176.
8. DDE to Hazlett, June 4, 1955, *Ike's Letters to a Friend* 146.
9. Radio and Television Address to the American People Prior to Departure for the Big Four Conference at Geneva, July 15, 1955, *Public Papers, 1955* 701–5.
10. Richard H. Rovere, *The Eisenhower Years: Affairs of State* 276–77 (New York: Farrar, Straus, and Ludahy, 1956).
11. Ibid. 291.
12. Eden, *Full Circle* 345.
13. Quoted in Rovere, *Affairs of State* 283.
14. DDE, *Mandate for Change* 525. Eisenhower's memoirs differ significantly from the obvious pleasure he exuded at his press conference on July 27, 1955, pertaining to his lunch with Zhukov. *Public Papers, 1955* 742.
15. Charles Bohlen notes, luncheon meeting of Eisenhower and Zhukov, July 20, 1955, EL.
16. Statement on Disarmament Presented at the Geneva Conference, July 21, 1955, *Public Papers, 1955* 713–16. (Eisenhower's emphasis.)
17. DDE, *Mandate for Change* 521.
18. Donovan, *Eisenhower* 350; Townsend Hoopes, *The Devil and John Foster Dulles* 297 (Boston: Little, Brown, 1973); *The New Yorker,* July 27, 1955.
19. Closing Statement at the Final Meeting of the Heads of Government Conference, July 23, 1955, *Public Papers, 1955* 721–23.
20. DDE to Milton Eisenhower, July 25, 1955, 16 *The Presidency* 1792–93. One of the most perceptive treatments of the impact of the Reagan-Gorbachev meeting in Geneva is presented by Beth Fischer in *The Reagan Reversal: Foreign Policy at the End of the Cold War* 46–50 (Columbia: University of Missouri Press, 1997).
21. Gallup poll, August 6, 1955.
22. *The New York Times,* August 29, 1955. Also see James Reston, *Sketches in the Sand* 420 (New York: Knopf, 1967).
23. DDE to Nikolai Aleksandrovich Bulganin, July 27, 1955, 16 *The Presidency* 1794–95.
24. Macmillan, *Tides of Fortune.*

25. *The New York Times,* March 20, 1956.

26. Rovere, *Affairs of State* 309.

27. DDE, *Eisenhower Diaries* 288.

28. Ibid. 288–91.

29. DDE to Milton Eisenhower, December 11, 1953, 15 *The Presidency* 759–60.

30. DDE to Hazlett, December 8, 1954, ibid. 1434–38.

31. Remarks to the Bull Elephants Club, August 2, 1955, *Public Papers, 1955* 748–53. The request of the Bull Elephants is on page 753.

32. Press Conference, August 4, 1955, ibid. 760.

33. Ann Whitman diary, September 23, 1955, EL.

34. DDE to LBJ, September 23, 1955, Johnson Library, Austin, Tex.

35. Quoted in Clarence G. Lasby, *Eisenhower's Heart Attack: How Ike Beat Heart Disease and Held On to the Presidency* 71 (Lawrence: University Press of Kansas, 1997).

36. DDE, *Mandate for Change* 536.

37. The comment is that of General Leonard Heaton, Oral History, EL.

38. DDE diary, November 20, 1954, *Eisenhower Diaries* 288.

39. DDE to the Adjutant General, June 8, 1955, EL.

40. A verbatim transcript of the September 24 news conference is reprinted in *U.S. News and World Report* 66, October 7, 1955.

41. *The New York Times,* September 25, 1955. Also see *U.S. News and World Report,* October 7, 1955.

42. James Rowley to Chief U.S. Secret Service, September 26, 1955, EL.

43. Paul Dudley White, *My Life and Medicine: An Autobiographical Memoir* 175–94 (Boston: Gambit, 1971).

44. Quoted in Donovan, *Eisenhower* 373.

45. Remarks on Leaving Denver, November 11, 1955, *Public Papers, 1955* 840–41.

46. Remarks Upon Arrival at the Washington National Airport, November 11, 1955, ibid. 481.

47. *Hagerty Diary* 240–46. Eisenhower, who had developed something of a father-son relationship with Hagerty, admired his press secretary's political acumen and discussed presidential possibilities freely with him. These discussions are reported at length in Hagerty's diary entries of December 10, 11, 12, and 14, 1955, and are the basis for the paragraphs above.

48. Leonard Hall, interview by Jean Edward Smith, Garden City, N.Y., April 4, 1971.

49. Lucius D. Clay, interview, COHP.

50. *The New York Times,* February 15, 1956. Also see Donovan, *Eisenhower* 402–3; Lasby, *Eisenhower's Heart Attack* 188–89.

51. Jean Edward Smith, *Lucius D. Clay* 626–27.

52. Press Conference, February 29, 1956, *Public Papers, 1956* 263–73.

53. Ibid. 266.

54. Richard M. Nixon, *Six Crises* 160–61 (Garden City, N.Y.: Doubleday, 1962). "I could not be certain whether the President really preferred me off the

ticket," Nixon wrote, "or sincerely believed a Cabinet post would better further my career. It probably was a little of both."

55. Ambrose, *Eisenhower: Soldier and President* 402.
56. Ann Whitman diary, March 13, 1956, EL.
57. Quoted in Hughes, *Ordeal of Power* 173. (Eisenhower's emphasis.)
58. Press Conference, April 25, 1956, *Public Papers, 1956* 431–32.
59. Nixon, *RN* 172.
60. Ibid. 172–73.

## CHAPTER TWENTY-FIVE: SUEZ

The epigraph is Eisenhower's instruction to Dulles after learning that Israel had invaded Egypt in concert with Britain and France to capture the Suez Canal. David A. Nichols, *Eisenhower 1956: The President's Year of Crisis: Suez and the Brink of War* 275 (New York: Simon and Schuster, 2011).

1. 279th Meeting of the NSC, March 8, 1956, EL.
2. Eisenhower diary, March 8, 1956, 16 *The Presidency* 2053–55.
3. Tripartite Declaration, May 25, 1950. United States Department of State, 5 *Foreign Relations of the United States, 1950: The Near East, South Asia, and Africa* 167–68 (Washington, D.C.: U.S. Government Printing Office, 1978).
4. Kennett Love, *Suez: The Twice-Fought War* 84 (New York: McGraw-Hill, 1969).
5. Patrick Seale, *The Struggle for Syria: A Study of Post-War Arab Politics, 1945–1958* 265 (New York: Oxford University Press, 1965).
6. Love, *Suez* 88.
7. Hoopes, *Devil and John Foster Dulles* 323–24; Dwight D. Eisenhower, *Waging Peace, 1956–1961: The White House Years* 24 (Garden City, N.Y.: Doubleday, 1965).
8. Love, *Suez* 289.
9. DDE, *Waging Peace* 25. The Soviets offered to provide weapons for Israel, which the Israelis declined.
10. Eugene R. Black interview, Dulles Oral History Collection, Princeton University.
11. Dulles-Macmillan conversation, November 9, 1955, United States Department of State, 14 *Foreign Relations of the United States: 1955–1957: Middle East* 720–23 (Washington, D.C.: U.S. Government Printing Office, 1989). Cited subsequently as *FRUS 1955–57*.
12. Telecom, DDE-JFD (John Foster Dulles), November 29, 1955, White House log, EL.
13. 268th Meeting, NSC, December 1, 1955, EL.
14. Eugene R. Black interview, Dulles Oral History, Princeton University.
15. Adams, *Firsthand Report* 247–48.
16. House majority leader John McCormack wanted to throw the fear of America into Nasser; Senator Estes Kefauver said the arms deal brought the Cold War into the Middle East; Hubert Humphrey assailed the administration for

not providing arms to Israel to offset Nasser's Soviet purchase. Ordinarily such Democrats would have lined up behind the administration. See *The Washington Post,* January 4, 5, 8, 1955.

17. Hoopes, *Devil and John Foster Dulles* 337.

18. Press Conference, May 23, 1956, *Public Papers, 1956* 522.

19. Press Conference, June 6, 1956, ibid. 554–55.

20. Ibid. 556–57.

21. Nichols, *Eisenhower 1956* 154.

22. Lasby, *Eisenhower's Heart Attack* 213.

23. Nixon, *Six Crises* 168.

24. Nichols, *Eisenhower 1956* 160.

25. Eugene Black, interview, Dulles Oral History, Princeton University.

26. *The New York Times,* July 9, 1956.

27. Nichols, *Eisenhower 1956* 170.

28. Conversation, DDE and JFD, July 19, 1956, 15 *FRUS 1955–57* 861–62.

29. Conversation, JFD and Egyptian ambassador, July 19, 1956, ibid. 867–73.

30. DDE, *Waging Peace* 34.

31. Minutes, Cabinet Meeting, July 27, 1956, EL.

32. Ann Whitman diary, July 28, 1956, EL.

33. DDE to Anthony Eden, July 31, 1956, *The Papers of Dwight David Eisenhower,* vol. 17, *The Presidency* 2222–25. Cited subsequently as 17 *The Presidency.* (Emphasis added.) "I realize that the message from both you and Harold [Macmillan] stressed that the decision [to intervene] was already approved by the government and was firm and irrevocable," Eisenhower wrote. "I personally feel sure that the American reaction would be severe and that great areas of the world would share that reaction."

34. Conversation, DDE and JFD, August 14, 1956, United States Department of State, 15 *Foreign Relations of the United States, 1955–1957: Arab-Israeli Dispute January 1–July 26, 1956* 198–99 (Washington, D.C.: U.S. Government Printing Office, 1989).

35. White House Conference, July 31, 1956, EL.

36. Charles A. Thomson, Alexander Holmes, and Frances M. Shattuck, *The 1956 Presidential Campaign* 81–87 (Washington, D.C.: Brookings Institution, 1960).

37. Address Accepting the Nomination of the Republican National Convention, August 23, 1956, *Public Papers, 1956* 702–16.

38. DDE, interview with Kenneth Love, November 25, 1964, EL, quoted in Love, *Suez* 503. Also see Nichols, *Eisenhower 1956* 275.

39. Conference with the President, 7:10 p.m., October 29, 1956, EL.

40. Conference with the President, October 30, 1956, 16 *FRUS 1955–1957* 851–55.

41. Conference with the President, October 31, 1956, ibid. 873–74.

42. Eisenhower, *Waging Peace* 92n.

43. Telephone conversation, DDE and JFD, October 30, 1956, EL.

44. *The New York Times,* October 31, 1956.

45. Radio and Television Report to the American People, October 31, 1956, *Public Papers, 1956* 1060–66.

46. *New York Herald Tribune,* November 2, 1956.

47. Quoted in Nichols, *Eisenhower 1956* 297–98.

48. *The New York Times,* November 1, 1956.

49. Address in Convention Hall, Philadelphia, November 1, 1956, *Public Papers, 1956* 1066–74.

50. Medical diary, November 1, 1956, Snyder Papers, EL.

51. DDE to Alfred Gruenther, November 2, 1956, 16 *The Presidency* 2357–59.

52. DDE to Hazlett, November 2, 1956, ibid. 2353–57.

53. Quoted in Donald Neff, *Warriors at Suez: Eisenhower Takes America into the Middle East* 404 (New York: Simon and Schuster, 1981).

54. Eisenhower, *Waging Peace* 95.

55. Press Conference, November 14, 1956, *Public Papers, 1956* 1100–1.

56. DDE to Bulganin, November 4, 1956, 16 *The Presidency* 2361–62.

57. DDE to Eden, November 5, 1956, ibid. 2363–64.

58. Neff, *Warriors at Suez* 410. Also see Diane B. Kunz, *The Economic Diplomacy of the Suez Crisis* (Chapel Hill: University of North Carolina Press, 1991).

59. Bulganin to Eden, November 5, 1956, EL.

60. Bulganin to DDE, November 5, 1956, 16 *FRUS 1955–1957* 993–94.

61. Hughes, *Ordeal of Power* 223. (Eisenhower's emphasis.)

62. Memorandum of Conversation, November 5, 1956, EL.

63. Telephone conversation, DDE and Eden, November 6, 1956, EL.

64. Eisenhower's statement was repeated by Eden to Guy Mollet immediately afterward. Mollet relayed it to his foreign minister, Christian Pineau, who made it public. See *The Eisenhower Legacy: Dwight D. Eisenhower's Military and Political Crusades,* Part 4: "Commander in Chief," video interview, Starbright Media. Also see Nichols, *Eisenhower 1956* 355.

65. Moses Rischin, *Our Own Kind: Voting by Race, Creed, or National Origin* 28–37 (Santa Barbara, Calif.: Center for the Study of Democratic Institutions, 1960).

## CHAPTER TWENTY-SIX: LITTLE ROCK

The epigraph is from Robert Welch's *Politician,* a book-length attack on Eisenhower as a knowing tool of the Communist conspiracy. According to Welch, "He [Eisenhower] has been sympathetic to ultimate Communist aims, realistically and even mercilessly willing to help them achieve their goals, knowingly receiving and abiding by Communist orders, and consciously serving the Communist conspiracy, for all of his adult life." *The Politician* 267, 278 (Belmont, Mass.: Belmont Publishing, 1964).

1. Lodge to DDE, October 31, 1956, EL.

2. DDE, *Waging Peace* 58.

3. *Plessy v. Ferguson,* 163 U.S. 537 (1896).

4. Ibid., at 544.

5. *Missouri ex rel Gaines v. Canada,* 305 U.S. 337 (1938), ordering Gaines, an African American student, to be admitted to the University of Missouri Law School; *Sipuel v. Board of Regents of the University of Oklahoma,* 332 U.S. 631 (1948), requiring admission of a qualified black applicant to the state's only law school; *Sweatt v. Painter,* 339 U.S. 629 (1950), overturning a Texas ban on admission of black students to the University of Texas law school when the alternative black law school was manifestly inferior; and *McLaurin v. Oklahoma Regents,* 339 U.S. 637 (1950), overturning Oklahoma's effort to segregate graduate students at the University of Oklahoma. All of these cases pertained to professional and graduate study only.

6. *Brown v. Board of Education,* 347 U.S. 483 (1954).

7. *Marbury v. Madison,* 1 Cranch 137 (1803); *McCulloch v. Maryland,* 4 Wheat. 316 (1819); *Gibbons v. Ogden,* 9 Wheat. 1 (1824).

8. Brownell, *Advising Ike* 193–94.

9. State of the Union Address, February 2, 1953, *Public Papers, 1953* 30–31.

10. Press Conference, March 19, 1953, ibid. 108.

11. *The New York Times,* October 31, 1954.

12. Anderson to General Wilton "Jerry" Persons, May 28, 1953, Maxwell D. Rabb Papers, EL.

13. DDE to Powell, June 6, 1953, EL.

14. Byrnes to DDE, August 27, 1953, EL.

15. Morris J. MacGregor, *Integration of the Armed Forces, 1939–1945* 487 (New York: Harper and Row, 1968).

16. Adam Clayton Powell, speech, February 28, 1954, in *The New York Times,* March 1, 1954.

17. Because the District of Columbia is a federal jurisdiction, not a state, the Supreme Court rendered a separate decision (*Bolling v. Sharpe,* 347 U.S. 497 {1954}) pertaining to Washington's schools based on the Fifth, not the Fourteenth, Amendment.

18. Quoted in David A. Nichols, *A Matter of Justice: Eisenhower and the Beginning of the Civil Rights Movement* 66 (New York: Simon and Schuster, 2007).

19. *Brown v. Board of Education* (II), 349 U.S. 294 (1955).

20. For Harlan's exceptional credentials, see Tinsley E. Yarbrough, *John Marshall Harlan: Great Dissenter of the Warren Court* 71–113 (New York: Oxford University Press, 1992).

21. David Halberstam, *Fifties* 661.

22. For the text of the "Southern Manifesto," see *The New York Times,* March 11, 1956. Also see Brownell, *Advising Ike,* Appendix C 359–63.

23. Press Conference, March 14, 1956, *Public Papers, 1956* 303–6.

24. William Martin, *A Prophet with Honor: The Billy Graham Story* 170–72 (New York: William Morrow, 1991).

25. DDE to Graham, March 22, 1956, 16 *The Presidency* 2086–88.

26. *NAACP Annual Report, 1955* 7–10 (New York: NAACP, 1955).

27. Brownell, *Advising Ike* 205.

28. Juan Williams, *Eyes on the Prize: America's Civil Right Years, 1954–1965* 100 (New York: Penguin Books, 1987).

29. Kasey S. Pipes, *Ike's Final Battle: The Road to Little Rock and the Challenge of Equality* 217 (New York: World Ahead Media, 2007).

30. Faubus to DDE, September 5, 1957; DDE to Faubus, September 5, 1957, EL. These letters are not reprinted in *The Papers of Dwight D. Eisenhower.*

31. Nichols, *Matter of Justice* 174.

32. DDE, *Waging Peace* 165.

33. Brownell, *Advising Ike* 208.

34. Ibid.

35. Telephone message, DDE to Brownell, September 11, 1957, quoted in Nichols, *Matter of Justice* 176–77. Brooks Hays was defeated for reelection in 1958 because of his role in attempting to work out a compromise.

36. DDE, *Waging Peace* 166.

37. Ibid.

38. Brownell, *Advising Ike* 210.

39. Ibid.

40. DDE, *Waging Peace* 167.

41. *Public Papers, 1957* 678–79.

42. Woodrow Wilson Mann to DDE, September 23, 1957, EL.

43. Brownell, *Advising Ike* 211.

44. *Public Papers, 1957* 689.

45. *The New York Times,* September 24, 1957.

46. Section 334, Title 10, U.S. Code.

47. DDE, *Waging Peace* 170.

48. Woodrow Wilson Mann to DDE, September 24, 1957, EL.

49. Halberstam, *Fifties* 687.

50. Brownell, *Advising Ike* 211.

51. Radio and Television Address to the American People on the Situation in Little Rock, September 24, 1957, *Public Papers, 1957* 689–94.

52. Halberstam, *Fifties* 687–88.

53. John L. Steele memorandum, September 25, 1957, EL.

54. Gallup poll, October 4, 1957; Nichols, *Matter of Justice* 200.

55. Ashmore to DDE, September 24, 1957, EL.

56. Louis Armstrong to DDE, September 24, 1957, EL.

57. Jackie Robinson to DDE, September 24, 1957, EL.

58. Moncrief to DDE, September 25, 1957, EL.

59. King to DDE, September 25, 1957, EL. Eisenhower replied to King on October 7. "I appreciated your thoughtful expression of the basic and compelling factors involved," said the president. "I share your confidence that Americans everywhere remained devoted to our tradition of adherence to orderly processes of law." *The Papers of Dwight D. Eisenhower,* vol. 18, *The Presidency* 479. Cited subsequently as 18 *The Presidency.*

60. DDE, *Waging Peace* 173. For DDE's September 27 reply to Brown, see 18 *The Presidency* 465–66.

61. DDE to William M. Sheppard, October 3, 1957, ibid. 476.

62. Elliott to DDE, October 2, 1957, EL.

63. Russell to DDE, September 27, 1957, EL.

64. DDE to Russell, September 27, 1957, 18 *The Presidency* 462–64.

65. Statement by the President Concerning the Removal of the Soldiers Stationed at Little Rock, May 8, 1958, *Public Papers, 1958* 387.

66. DDE to Hazlett, July 22, 1957, 18 *The Presidency* 319–25.

## CHAPTER TWENTY-SEVEN:
## MILITARY-INDUSTRIAL COMPLEX

The epigraph is from Eisenhower's farewell address to the American people, January 17, 1961. *Public Papers, 1960–61* 1035–40.

1. Press Conference, October 9, 1957, *Public Papers, 1957* 719–32.

2. Halberstam, *Fifties* 617–18.

3. DDE, *Waging Peace* 545.

4. Quoted in Halberstam, *Fifties* 617–18.

5. Perret, *Eisenhower* 580.

6. Halberstam, *Fifties* 621.

7. Richard Bissell interview, COHP.

8. DDE, *Waging Peace* 227.

9. Ibid. 228.

10. Ibid.

11. Ibid.

12. Ibid. 230.

13. Ibid. 232.

14. Ibid. 233.

15. DDE to Nixon, February 5, 1958; Nixon to DDE, February 10, 1958. Ibid. 233–35.

16. General Lucius D. Clay, interview by Jean Edward Smith, COHP.

17. Press Conference, June 18, 1958, *Public Papers, 1958* 478–81.

18. DDE, *Waging Peace* 315.

19. Ann Whitman diary, September 16, 1958, EL.

20. For Sherman Adams's version of events, see Adams, *Firsthand Report* 435–51.

21. *Joint Resolution to Promote Peace and Stability in the Middle East,* 85th Cong., 1st sess., H.J. Res. 117.

22. DDE, *Waging Peace* 178.

23. Lyon, *Eisenhower* 766.

24. Telephone conversation, DDE and Macmillan, July 15, 1958, EL.

25. DDE, *Waging Peace* 290.

26. Memo of Conference, August 25, 1958, EL.

27. Ibid., September 6, 1958.

28. For the text, see DDE, *Waging Peace* 299–300.

29. *Public Papers, 1958* 694–70.

30. DDE, *Waging Peace* 304.

31. United Nations Statistical Office, *Demographic Yearbook: 1960* 146–47 (New York: UN Department of Economic and Social Affairs, 1960).

32. *The New York Times,* October 30, 1958.

33. For the text of the Soviet note, see Jean Edward Smith, *The Defense of Berlin* 166–78 (Baltimore: Johns Hopkins Press, 1964).

34. *The New York Times,* November 28, 1958.

35. Ibid., December 4, 1958.

36. United States Department of State, *The Soviet Note on Berlin: An Analysis* (Washington: Department of State, 1959).

37. The Allied response, December 31, 1958, is in ibid. 32–36.

38. Quoted in Jean Edward Smith, *Defense of Berlin* 199. A detailed chronology of the 1958–59 Berlin crisis is at pages 181–206.

39. DDE to Macmillan, July 28, 1959, EL.

40. DDE, *Mandate for Change* 424.

41. Walters, *Silent Missions* 489.

42. Ibid.

43. Ibid. 491.

44. Nikita Sergeevich Khrushchev, *Khrushchev Remembers: The Last Testament* 372, Strobe Talbott, ed. and trans. (Boston: Little, Brown, 1974).

45. Ibid. 380.

46. Ibid. 412.

47. United States Department of State, *Foreign Relations of the United States 1958–1960,* vol. 10, *Eastern Europe Region, Soviet Union, Cyprus,* part 1, 462–67 (Washington, D.C.: U.S. Government Printing Office, 1993). Cited subsequently as 10 *FRUS, 1958–1960.* The complete State Department record of Khrushchev's trip is at pages 388–495.

48. DDE, *Waging Peace* 448.

49. Ambrose, *Eisenhower* 567.

50. White House Memo for Record, February 8, 1960, EL.

51. Goodpaster memo, April 25, 1960, EL.

52. *Khrushchev Remembers: The Last Testament* 447. Also see *The New York Times,* May 6, 1960; 10 *FRUS, 1958–1960,* part 1, 510–11.

53. For the text of both the NASA and State Department statements of May 5, 1960, see Department of State *Bulletin* 817–18, May 23, 1960.

54. *Current Digest of the Soviet Press* 3–7, June 8, 1960.

55. Department of State *Bulletin* 818–19, May 23, 1960.

56. Michael Beschloss, *Mayday: Eisenhower, Khrushchev, and the U-2 Affair* 253 (New York: Harper and Row, 1986). Secretary Herter's statement is on pages 257–58.

57. Milton Eisenhower, interview, and John Eisenhower, interview, both in oral histories, EL. Also see Milton S. Eisenhower, *President Is Calling* 335.

58. DDE, *Waging Peace* 552.

59. Virgil Pinkley and James F. Scheer, *Eisenhower Declassified* 373 (Old Tappan, N.J.: Fleming H. Revell, 1979).

60. Quoted in Beschloss, *Mayday* 252.

61. Ibid. 284.

62. Walters, *Silent Missions* 344.

63. Beschloss, *Mayday* 289.

64. *Public Papers, 1960–1961* 427–28.
65. Walters, *Silent Missions* 346.
66. Ibid.
67. Address to the Republican National Convention, July 26, 1960, *Public Papers, 1960–1961* 589–601.
68. Press Conference, August 10, 1960, ibid. 619–29.
69. Press Conference, August 24, 1960, ibid. 646–58.
70. Ann Whitman diary, August 30, 1960, EL.
71. Halberstam, *Fifties* 732.
72. *Congressional Quarterly's Guide to U.S. Elections* 257, 298.
73. For Norman Cousins's influence on Eisenhower, see James Ledbetter, *Unwarranted Influence: Dwight D. Eisenhower and the Military-Industrial Complex* 75–87 (New Haven, Conn.: Yale University Press, 2011).
74. Farewell Radio and Television Address, January 17, 1966, *Public Papers, 1960–1961* 1035–40.

## CHAPTER TWENTY-EIGHT: TAPS

The epigraph contains Ike's last words, spoken to his son John, March 28, 1969. John S. D. Eisenhower, *Strictly Personal* 336.

1. General Ted Clifton interview, cited in David Eisenhower and Julie Nixon Eisenhower, *Going Home to Glory* 16.
2. Speaking in Pittsburgh on October 25, 1962, Eisenhower told a Republican rally, "We are, one and all, deeply concerned with recent events occurring off our southeastern coast. . . . Until this urgent problem is solved to the satisfaction of our nation, every loyal American will without hesitation carry out and conform to any instructions pertaining to it proclaimed by the Commander-in-Chief." EL.
3. Quoted in David Eisenhower and Julie Nixon Eisenhower, *Going Home to Glory* 122.
4. DDE to John Eisenhower, June 16, 1953, 14 *The Presidency* 298–99.
5. Gallup poll, *Los Angeles Times,* January 10, 1968. Eisenhower would win the honor again the following year.
6. I am indebted to David and Julie Nixon Eisenhower for their careful and loving description of Eisenhower's last days. For the golf, see *Going Home to Glory* 239–44.
7. Ibid. 273.
8. According to official filings with the Department of Revenue of the Commonwealth of Pennsylvania, Eisenhower left an estate valued at $2,870,004.90 (roughly $16.4 million in today's dollars). Mamie was awarded a life interest in the estate, with the remainder passing to John and his descendants. Probate Records, Adams County Courthouse, Gettysburg, Pa.
9. David Eisenhower and Julie Nixon Eisenhower, *Going Home to Glory* 65.

# Bibliography

Abels, Jules. *Out of the Jaws of Victory.* New York: Henry Holt, 1959.

Acheson, Dean. *Present at the Creation: My Years in the State Department.* New York: Norton, 1969.

Adams, Sherman. *Firsthand Report: The Story of the Eisenhower Administration.* New York: Harper and Brothers, 1961.

Adjutant General's Office. *Official Army Registers: January 1, 1939–January 1, 1945.* Published by order of the Secretary of War. Washington, D.C.: Government Printing Office, 1939–1945.

Alanbrooke, Field Marshal Lord. *War Diaries, 1939–1945.* Alex Danchev and Daniel Todman, eds. Berkeley and Los Angeles: University of California Press, 2001.

Alexander, Charles C. *Holding the Line: The Eisenhower Era, 1952–1961.* Bloomington: Indiana University Press, 1975.

Alexander, Yonah, and Allan Nanes, eds. *The United States and Iran: A Documentary History.* Frederick, Md.: University Publications of America, 1980.

Aliano, Richard A. *American Defense Policy from Eisenhower to Kennedy: The Politics of Changing Military Requirements, 1947–1961.* Athens: Ohio University Press, 1975.

Allen, Charles. *The Search for Shangri-La: A Journey into Tibetan History.* London: Little, Brown, 1999.

Allen, Craig. *Eisenhower and the Mass Media: Peace, Prosperity, and Prime-Time TV.* Chapel Hill: University of North Carolina Press, 1993.

Allen, Thomas B., and Norman Polmar. *Code-Name Downfall.* New York: Simon and Schuster, 1995.

Alsop, Joseph, and Adam Platt. *I've Seen the Best of It.* New York: Norton, 1992.

Alsop, Stewart. *Nixon and Rockefeller: A Double Portrait.* Garden City, N.Y.: Doubleday, 1960.

Alteras, Isaac. *Eisenhower and Israel: U.S.-Israeli Relations, 1953–1960.* Gainesville: University Press of Florida, 1993.

Ambrose, Stephen E. *Duty, Honor, Country: A History of West Point.* Baltimore: Johns Hopkins Press, 1966.

———. *Eisenhower.* 2 vols. New York: Simon and Schuster, 1983–84.

———. *Eisenhower and Berlin, 1945: The Decision to Halt at the Elbe.* New York: Norton, 1967.

———. *Eisenhower: Soldier and President.* New York: Simon and Schuster, 1990.

———. *Ike: Abilene to Berlin; the Life of Dwight D. Eisenhower from His Childhood in Abilene, Kansas, Through His Command of the Allied Forces in Europe in World War II.* New York: Harper and Row, 1973.

———. *Nixon: The Education of a Politician, 1913–1962.* New York: Simon and Schuster, 1987.

———. *The Supreme Commander: The War Years of General Dwight D. Eisenhower.* Garden City, N.Y.: Doubleday, 1970.

———. *The Victors: Eisenhower and His Boys: The Men of World War II.* New York: Simon and Schuster, 1998.

Ambrose, Stephen E., and Richard H. Immerman. *Ike's Spies: Eisenhower and the Intelligence Community.* Garden City, N.Y.: Doubleday, 1981.

American Battle Monuments Commission. *A Guide to the American Battle Fields in Europe.* Washington, D.C.: Government Printing Office, 1927.

Ancell, R. Manning, and Christine M. Miller. *The Biographical Dictionary of World War II Generals and Flag Officers: The U.S. Armed Forces.* Westport, Conn.: Greenwood Press, 1996.

Anderson, David L. *Trapped by Success: The Eisenhower Administration and Vietnam, 1953–1961.* New York: Columbia University Press, 1991.

Anderson, J. W. *Eisenhower, Brownell, and the Congress: The Tangled Origins of the Civil Rights Bill of 1956–1957.* Tuscaloosa: University of Alabama Press, 1964.

Andreas, A. T. *History of the State of Kansas Containing a Full Account of Its Growth from an Uninhabited Territory to a Wealthy and Important State.* Chicago: A. T. Andreas, 1883.

Appleman, Roy Edgar. *South to the Naktong, North to the Yalu.* Washington, D.C.: Center of Military History, United States Army, 1992.

Arnold, Henry Harley. *Global Mission.* New York: Harper, 1949.

Arnold, James. *The First Domino: Eisenhower, the Military, and America's Intervention in Vietnam.* New York: W. Morrow, 1991.

Aron, Robert. *Histoire de la libération de la France, juin 1944–mai 1945.* Paris: A. Fayard, 1959.

Arthur, Max. *Forgotten Voices of World War II.* Guilford, Conn.: Lyons Press, 2004.

Atkinson, Rick. *An Army at Dawn: The War in North Africa, 1942–1943.* New York: Henry Holt, 2002.

———. *The Day of Battle: The War in Sicily and Italy, 1943–1944.* New York: Henry Holt, 2007.

Attlee, Clement R. *As It Happened.* New York: Viking, 1954.

Badoglio, Pietro. *Italy in the Second World War: Memories and Documents.* Westport, Conn.: Greenwood Press, 1976.

Baker, R. S. *Woodrow Wilson: Life and Letters.* 8 vols. Garden City, N.Y.: Doubleday, 1927–39.

Baldwin, Hanson. *Battles Lost and Won: Great Campaigns of World War II.* New York: Harper and Row, 1966.

Ball, Simon. *The Guardsmen.* London: Harper Perennial, 2002.

Barkow, Al. *The Golden Era of Golf: How America Rose to Dominate the Old Scots Game.* New York: St. Martin's Press, 2000.

Barzum, Jacques, and Henry Graff. *The Modern Researcher.* 6th ed. Belmont, Calif.: Wadsworth, 2004.

Bates, Daisy. *The Long Shadow of Little Rock: A Memoir.* Fayetteville: University of Arkansas Press, 1987.

Beals, Melba Patillo. *Warriors Don't Cry.* New York: Pocket Books, 1994.

Beevor, Antony. *D-Day: The Battle for Normandy.* New York: Viking, 2009.

———. *The Fall of Berlin, 1945.* New York: Viking Press, 2002.

Bendersky, Joseph W. *The "Jewish Threat": Anti-Semitic Politics of the U.S. Army.* New York: Basic Books, 2000.

Bennett, Ralph. *ULTRA and the Mediterranean Strategy.* New York: William Morrow, 1989.

Benson, Ezra T. *Cross Fire: The Eight Years with Eisenhower.* Garden City, N.Y.: Doubleday, 1962.

Ben-Zvi, Abraham. *Decade of Transition: Eisenhower, Kennedy, and the Origins of the American-Israeli Alliance.* New York: Columbia University Press, 1998.

Bernstein, Barton J. *Politics and Policies of the Truman Administration.* Chicago: Quadrangle Books, 1970.

Beschloss, Michael R. *The Conquerors: Roosevelt, Truman, and the Destruction of Hitler's Germany, 1941–45* New York: Simon and Schuster, 2002.

———. *Eisenhower: A Centennial Life.* New York: Harper and Row, 1990.

———. *Mayday: Eisenhower, Khrushchev, and the U-2 Affair.* New York: Harper and Row, 1986.

Billings-Yun, Melanie. *Decision Against War: Eisenhower and Dien Bien Phu, 1954.* New York: Columbia University Press, 1988.

Bird, Kai. *The Chairman: John J. McCloy: The Making of the American Establishment.* New York: Simon and Schuster, 1992.

Bischof, Gunter, and Stephen Ambrose. *Eisenhower: A Centenary Assessment.* Baton Rouge: Louisiana State University Press, 1992.

Bissell, Richard M., Jr. *Reflections of a Cold Warrior: From Yalta to the Bay of Pigs.* New Haven, Conn.: Yale University Press, 1996.

Blood, Thomas. *Madam Secretary: A Biography of Madeleine Albright.* New York: St. Martin's Press, 1997.

Blumenson, Martin. *The Battle of the Generals.* New York: Morrow, 1993.

———. *Breakout and Pursuit.* Washington, D.C.: Office of the Chief of Military History, Department of the Army, 1961.

———. *Eisenhower.* New York: Ballantine Books, 1972.

————. *Mark Clark.* New York: Congdon and Weed, 1984.

————, ed. *The Patton Papers.* 2 vols. Boston: Houghton Mifflin, 1972–74.

————. *Salerno to Cassino.* Washington, D.C.: Office of the Chief of Military History, U.S. Army, 1969.

Blumentritt, Günther. *Von Rundstedt: The Soldier and the Man.* London: Odhams Press, 1952.

Boehm, Randolph, ed. *U.S. Military Intelligence Reports: Surveillance of Radicals in the United States, 1917–1941.* Frederick, Md.: University Publications of America, 1984.

Bogart, Leo. *Social Research and the Desegregation of the United States Army.* Chicago: Markham Publishing, 1969.

Bohlen, Charles E. *Witness to History, 1929–1969.* New York: Norton, 1973.

Botti, Timothy J. *Ace in the Hole: Why the United States Did Not Use Nuclear Weapons in the Cold War, 1945 to 1965.* Westport, Conn.: Greenwood Press, 1996.

Bowers, William T., William M. Hammond, and George L. MacGarrigle. *Black Soldier, White Army: The 24th Army Infantry Regiment in Korea.* Washington, D.C.: Center of Military History, U.S. Army, 1996.

Bowie, Robert R., and Richard H. Immerman. *Waging Peace: How Eisenhower Shaped an Enduring Cold War Strategy.* New York: Oxford University Press, 1998.

Boyle, Peter. *Eisenhower.* New York: Pearson/Longman, 2005.

Bradley, Omar N. *A Soldier's Story.* New York: Henry Holt, 1951.

Bradley, Omar N., and Clay Blair. *A General's Life: An Autobiography.* New York: Simon and Schuster, 1983.

Brandon, Dorothy Barrett. *Mamie Doud Eisenhower: A Portrait of a First Lady.* New York: Scribner, 1954.

Brands, H. W. *Cold Warriors: Eisenhower's Generation and American Foreign Policy.* New York: Columbia University Press, 1988.

Branyan, Robert L., and Lawrence H. Larsen. *The Eisenhower Administration, 1953–1961: A Documentary History.* 2 vols. New York: Random House, 1971.

Brauer, Carl M. *Presidential Transitions: Eisenhower Through Reagan.* New York: Oxford University Press, 1986.

Brechbill, Laban T. *Doctrine of the Old Order River Brethren.* Lancaster, Pa.: Brechbill and Strickler, 1967.

————. *History of the Old Order River Brethren.* Lancaster, Pa.: Brechbill and Strickler, 1972.

Brendon, Piers. *Ike: His Life and Times.* New York: Harper and Row, 1986.

Brinkley, Douglas, and Ronald J. Drez. *Voices of Valor: D-Day, June 6, 1944.* New York: Bulfinch Press, 2004.

Broadwater, Jeff. *Adlai Stevenson and American Politics: The Odyssey of a Cold War Liberal.* New York: Twayne Publishers, 1994.

————. *Eisenhower and the Anti-Communist Crusade.* Chapel Hill: University of North Carolina Press, 1992.

Brodie, Fawn. *Thomas Jefferson: An Intimate History.* New York: W. W. Norton, 1974.

Brownell, Herbert, and John P. Burke. *Advising Ike: The Memoirs of Attorney General Herbert Brownell.* Lawrence: University Press of Kansas, 1993.

Brownstein, Ronald. *The Second Civil War: How Extreme Partisanship Has Paralyzed Washington and Polarized America.* New York: Penguin Press, 2007.

Bryant, Arthur. *Triumph in the West: A History of the War Years Based on the Diaries of Field-Marshal Lord Alanbrooke, Chief of the Imperial General Staff.* Garden City, N.Y.: Doubleday, 1959.

———. *The Turn of the Tide: A History of the War Years Based on the Diaries of Field-Marshal Lord Alanbrooke, Chief of the Imperial General Staff.* Garden City, N.Y.: Doubleday, 1957.

Buhite, Russell D. *Patrick J. Hurley and American Foreign Policy.* Ithaca, N.Y.: Cornell University Press, 1973.

Buhite, Russell D., and David W. Levy, eds. *FDR's Fireside Chats.* New York: Penguin Books, 1993.

Burk, Robert Frederick. *Dwight D. Eisenhower: Hero and Politician.* Boston: Twayne Publishers, 1986.

———. *The Eisenhower Administration and Black Civil Rights.* Knoxville: University of Tennessee Press, 1984.

Busch, Noel F. *Adlai E. Stevenson of Illinois.* New York: Farrar, Straus, and Young, 1952.

Butcher, Harry. *My Three Years with Eisenhower: The Personal Diary of Captain Harry C. Butcher, USNR, Naval Aide to General Eisenhower, 1942 to 1945.* New York: Simon and Schuster, 1946.

Byrnes, James F. *All in One Lifetime.* New York: Harper, 1958.

Caldes, A. *The People's War.* London: Cape, 1969.

Caro, Robert A. *Master of the Senate.* New York: Knopf, 2002.

Caute, David. *The Great Fear: The Anti-Communist Purge Under Truman and Eisenhower.* New York: Simon and Schuster, 1978.

Center of Military History. "*Chronology, 1941–1945,*" *The U.S. Army in World War II.* Washington, D.C., 1994.

Chace, James. *Acheson: The Secretary of State Who Created the American World.* New York: Simon and Schuster, 1998.

Charmley, John. *Churchill: The End of Glory, a Political Biography.* New York: Harcourt Brace, 1993.

Chernus, Ira. *Eisenhower's Atoms for Peace.* College Station: Texas A&M University Press, 2002.

———. *General Eisenhower: Ideology and Discourse.* East Lansing: Michigan State University Press, 2002.

Childs, Marquis William. *Eisenhower: Captive Hero.* New York: Harcourt, Brace, 1958.

———. *Witness to Power.* New York: McGraw-Hill, 1975.

Churchill, Randolph S. *The Rise and Fall of Sir Anthony Eden.* New York: G. P. Putnam's Sons, 1959.

Churchill, Winston S. *The Churchill-Eisenhower Correspondence, 1953–1955.* Chapel Hill: University of North Carolina Press, 1990.

———. *The Churchill War Papers.* See under Gilbert, Martin, ed.

———. *Closing the Ring.* Boston: Houghton Mifflin, 1951.

———. *The Hinge of Fate.* Boston: Houghton Mifflin, 1950.

———. *A History of the English-Speaking Peoples.* Vol. 3, *The Age of Revolution.* London: Cassell, 1957.

———. *Painting as a Pastime.* Delray Beach, Fla.: Levenger, 2002.

———. *The Second World War.* 6 vols. Boston: Houghton Mifflin, 1948–1954.

———. *Triumph and Tragedy.* Boston: Houghton Mifflin, 1953.

Chynoweth, Bradford Grethen. *Bellamy Park: Memoirs.* Hicksville, N.Y.: Exposition Press, 1975.

Clark, Mark W. *Calculated Risk.* New York: Harper, 1950.

———. *From the Danube to the Yalu.* New York: Harper, 1954.

Clark, Maureen. *Captain's Bride, General's Lady.* New York: McGraw-Hill, 1956.

Clay, Lucius D. *The Papers of General Lucius D. Clay: Germany, 1945–1949.* Jean Edward Smith, ed. 2 vols. Bloomington: Indiana University Press, 1974.

Clayton, Anthony. *Three Marshals of France: Leadership After Trauma.* London: Brassey's, 1992.

Clemens, Samuel. *Mark Twain's Autobiography.* 2 vols. New York: Harper and Brothers, 1924.

Clifford, Clark, and Richard Holbrooke. *Counsel to the President.* New York: Random House, 1991.

Cline, Ray S. *Washington Command Post: The Operations Division.* Washington, D.C.: Center of Military History, U.S. Army, 2003.

Clodfelter, Michael. *Warfare and Armed Conflict: A Statistical Reference to Casualty and Other Figures.* Jefferson, N.C.: McFarland, 1992.

Clugston, William George. *Eisenhower for President? Or, Who Will Get Us Out of the Messes We Are In?* New York: Exposition Press, 1951.

Coffman, Edward M. *The Hilt of the Sword: The Career of Peyton C. March.* Madison: University of Wisconsin Press, 1966.

Cohn, Roy M. *McCarthy.* New York: New American Library, 1968.

Coles, Harry L., and Albert K. Weinberg. *Civil Affairs: Soldiers Become Governors.* Washington, D.C.: Center of Military History, U.S. Army, 2004.

Colley, David P. *Decision at Strasbourg: Ike's Strategic Mistake to Halt the Sixth Army Group at the Rhine in 1944.* Annapolis, Md.: Naval Institute Press, 2008.

Collins, J. Lawton. *War in Peacetime: The History and Lessons of Korea.* Boston: Houghton Mifflin, 1969.

Collins, Larry, and Dominique Lapierre. *Is Paris Burning?* New York: Simon and Schuster, 1965.

Colville, John. *Fringes of Power.* New York: Norton, 1985.

*Congressional Quarterly's Guide to U.S. Elections.* Washington, D.C.: Congressional Quarterly Press, 1975.

Conner, Virginia. *What Father Forbad.* Philadelphia: Dorrance, 1951.

Cook, Blanche Wiesen. *The Declassified Eisenhower: A Divided Legacy of Peace and Political Warfare.* Garden City, N.Y.: Doubleday, 1981.

Cooke, James J. *Pershing and His Generals: Command and Staff in the AEF.* Westport, Conn.: Praeger, 1997.

Coon, Carleton S. *A North Africa Story: The Anthropologist as OSS Agent, 1941–1943*. Ipswich, Mass.: Gambit, 1980.

Cooper, Chester L. *The Lost Crusade: America in Vietnam*. New York: Dodd, Mead, 1970.

Craven, Wesley Frank, and James Lea Cate, eds. *The Army Air Forces in World War II*. Vol. 2. Chicago: University of Chicago Press, 1949.

Cray, Ed. *Chief Justice: A Biography of Earl Warren*. New York: Simon and Schuster, 1997.

———. *General of the Army: George C. Marshall, Soldier and Statesman*. New York: Norton, 1990.

Crosswell, D. K. R. *The Chief of Staff: The Military Career of General Walter Bedell Smith*. Westport, Conn.: Greenwood Press, 1991.

Crozier, Brian. *De Gaulle*. New York: Charles Scribner's Sons, 1973.

Cunningham, Andrew Browne. *A Sailor's Odyssey: The Autobiography of Admiral of the Fleet, Viscount Cunningham of Hyndhope*. London: Hutchinson, 1951.

Cutler, Robert. *Louisburg Square*. New York: Macmillan, 1917.

———. *No Time for Rest*. Boston: Little, Brown, 1966.

———. *The Speckled Bird*. New York: Macmillan, 1923.

Dallek, Robert. *Flawed Giant: Lyndon Johnson and His Times 1961–1973*. New York: Oxford University Press, 1998.

———. *Lone Star Rising: Lyndon Johnson and His Times, 1908–1960*. New York: Oxford University Press, 1991.

Damms, Richard. *The Eisenhower Presidency, 1953–1961*. London: Longman, 2002.

David, Lester, and Irene David. *Ike and Mamie: The Story of the General and His Lady*. New York: G. P. Putnam's Sons, 1981.

David, Paul, ed. *Presidential Nominating Politics in 1952*. 5 vols. Baltimore: Johns Hopkins University Press, 1954.

Davis, Kenneth S. *Eisenhower, American Hero: The Historical Record of His Life*. New York: American Heritage, 1969.

———. *The Politics of Honor: A Biography of Adlai E. Stevenson*. New York: G. P. Putnam's Sons, 1967.

———. *Soldier of Democracy: A Biography of Dwight Eisenhower*. Garden City, N.Y.: Doubleday, 1945.

Davis, Richard G. *Carl A. Spaatz and the Air War in Europe*. Washington, D.C.: Center for Air Force History, 1993.

Dear, I. C. B., ed. *The Oxford Companion to World War II*. New York: Oxford University Press, 1995.

De Gaulle, Charles. *Mémoires de Guerre: L'Appel, l'Unité, le Salut*. Paris: Plon, 1994.

———. *Memoirs of Hope: Renewal and Endeavor*. New York: Simon and Schuster, 1972.

———. *War Memoirs*. 3 vols. New York: Simon and Schuster, 1955–60.

Derks, Scott. *The Value of a Dollar: Prices and Incomes in the United States, 1860–2004*. Millerton, N.Y.: Universal Reference Publications, 2004.

D'Este, Carlo. *Decision in Normandy*. New York: Dutton, 1983.

———. *Eisenhower: A Soldier's Life*. New York: Henry Holt, 2002.

———. *Patton: A Genius for War*. New York: HarperCollins, 1995.

Dickson, Paul, and Thomas B. Allen. *The Bonus Army: An American Epic.* New York: Walker, 2004.

Divine, Robert A. *Eisenhower and the Cold War.* New York: Oxford University Press, 1981.

———. *Foreign Policy and U.S. Presidential Elections, 1952–1960.* New York: New Viewpoints, 1974.

Doherty, Richard. *Irish Generals: Irish Generals in the British Army in the Second World War.* Belfast: Appletree, 1993.

Donovan, Robert J. *Confidential Secretary: Ann Whitman's Twenty Years with Eisenhower and Rockefeller.* New York: E. P. Dutton, 1988.

———. *Eisenhower: The Inside Story.* New York: Harper and Brothers, 1956.

Doyle, Edward P., ed. *As We Knew Adlai: The Stevenson Story by Twenty-two Friends.* New York: Harper and Row, 1966.

Dupuy, R. Ernest. *The Compact History of the United States Army.* New York: Hawthorn Books, 1961.

Dupuy, Trevor N. *The Harper Encyclopedia of American Military Biography.* New York: HarperCollins, 1992.

———. *Hitler's Last Gamble: The Battle of the Bulge, December 1944–January 1945.* New York: HarperCollins, 1994.

Duram, James. *A Moderate Among Extremists: Dwight D. Eisenhower and the School Desegregation Crisis.* Chicago: Nelson-Hall, 1981.

Dyreson, Mark. *Making the American Team: Sport, Culture, and the Olympic Experience.* Chicago: University of Illinois Press, 1998.

Eden, Anthony. *The Eden-Eisenhower Correspondence, 1955–1957.* Peter G. Boyle, ed. Chapel Hill: University of North Carolina Press, 2005.

———. *Facing the Dictators: The Memoirs of Anthony Eden.* Boston: Houghton Mifflin, 1962.

———. *Freedom and Order: Selected Speeches, 1939–1946.* Boston: Houghton Mifflin, 1948.

———. *Full Circle: The Memoirs of Anthony Eden.* Boston: Houghton Mifflin, 1960.

———. *The Reckoning: The Memoirs of Anthony Eden, Earl of Avon.* Boston: Houghton Mifflin, 1965.

Edwards, Paul M., comp. *General Matthew B. Ridgway: An Annotated Bibliography.* Westport, Conn.: Greenwood Press, 1993.

Ehrman, John. *Grand Strategy.* Vol. 5, *August 1943–September1944.* London: Her Majesty's Stationery Office, 1956.

Eisenhower, David. *Eisenhower at War, 1943–1945.* New York: Random House, 1986.

Eisenhower, David, and Julie Nixon Eisenhower. *Going Home to Glory.* New York: Simon and Schuster, 2010.

Eisenhower, Dwight David. *At Ease: Stories I Tell to Friends.* Garden City, N.Y.: Doubleday, 1967.

———. *Crusade in Europe.* Garden City, N.Y.: Doubleday, 1948.

———. *Dear General: Eisenhower's Wartime Letters to Marshall.* Joseph P. Hobbs, ed. Baltimore: Johns Hopkins Press, 1971.

————. *The Diaries of Dwight D. Eisenhower, 1953–1969: Microfilmed from the Holdings of the Dwight D. Eisenhower Library.* Frederick, Md.: University Publications of America, 1986.

————. *Dwight D. Eisenhower, 1890–1969: Chronology, Documents, Bibliographical Aids.* Robert I. Vexler, ed. Dobbs Ferry, N.Y.: Oceana Publications, 1970.

————. *The Eisenhower Diaries.* Robert H. Ferrell, ed. New York: Norton, 1981.

————. *Eisenhower's Legacy: The General, the President, the Public Servant: The Report of the Legacy Committee on Dwight David Eisenhower's Military Achievements, Presidential Accomplishments, and Lifetime of Public Service.* Washington, D.C.: Dwight David Eisenhower Memorial Commission, 2003.

————. *Eisenhower's Own Story of the War: The Complete Report by the Supreme Commander on the War in Europe from the Day of Invasion to the Day of Victory.* New York: Arco, 1946.

————. *Eisenhower Speaks: Dwight D. Eisenhower in His Messages and Speeches.* Rudolph L. Treuenfels, ed. New York: Farrar, Straus, 1948.

————. *Eisenhower: The Prewar Diaries and Selected Papers, 1905–1941.* Daniel D. Holt and James W. Leyerzapf, eds. Baltimore: Johns Hopkins University Press, 1998.

————. *General Eisenhower and the Military Churchill: A Conversation with Alistair Cooke.* New York: Norton, 1970.

————. *Ike, A Great American.* Don Ramsey, ed. Kansas City, Mo.: Hallmark, 1972.

————. *Ike's Letters to a Friend, 1941–1958.* Robert Griffith, ed. Lawrence: University Press of Kansas, 1984.

————. *In Review: Pictures I've Kept; A Concise Pictorial "Autobiography."* Garden City, N.Y.: Doubleday, 1968.

————. *Letters to Mamie.* John S. D. Eisenhower, ed. Garden City, N.Y.: Doubleday, 1978.

————. *The Macmillan-Eisenhower Correspondence, 1957–1969.* New York: Palgrave Macmillan, 2005.

————. *Mandate for Change, 1953–1956: The White House Years.* Garden City, N.Y.: Doubleday, 1963.

————. *The Papers of Dwight David Eisenhower.* 21 vols. Alfred D. Chandler, Jr., et al., eds. Baltimore: Johns Hopkins University Press, 1970–2001.

————. *Peace with Justice: Selected Addresses.* New York: Columbia University Press, 1961.

————. *Public Papers of the Presidents of the United States, Dwight D. Eisenhower; Containing the Public Messages, Speeches, and Statements of the President: 1953–1961.* 8 vols. Washington, D.C.: National Archives and Records Service, 1953–61.

————. *The Quotable Dwight D. Eisenhower.* Elsie Gollagher, ed. Anderson, S.C.: Droke House, 1967.

————. *Report by the Supreme Commander to the Combined Chiefs of Staff on the Operations in Europe of the Allied Expeditionary Force, 6 June 1944 to 8 May 1945.* London: HMSO, 1946.

————. *Waging Peace, 1956–1961: The White House Years.* Garden City, N.Y.: Doubleday, 1965.

———. *Yanks.* New York: Touchstone, 2001.

Eisenhower, Edgar Newton, and John McCallum. *Six Roads from Abilene: Some Personal Recollections of Edgar Eisenhower.* Seattle: Wood and Reber, 1960.

Eisenhower, John S. D. *Allies: Pearl Harbor to D-Day.* Garden City, N.Y.: Doubleday, 1982.

———. *The Bitter Woods: The Battle of the Bulge.* New York: G. P. Putnam's Sons, 1969.

———. *General Ike: A Personal Reminiscence.* New York: Free Press, 2003.

———. *Intervention! The United States Involvement in the Mexican Revolution, 1913–1917.* New York: W. W. Norton, 1993.

———. *So Far from God: The United States War with Mexico, 1846–1848.* New York: Random House, 1989.

———. *Strictly Personal.* Garden City, N.Y.: Doubleday, 1974.

Eisenhower, Julie Nixon. *Special People.* New York: Simon and Schuster, 1977.

Eisenhower, Milton S. *The President Is Calling.* Garden City, N.Y.: Doubleday, 1974.

Eisenhower, Susan. *Mrs. Ike: Memories and Reflections on the Life of Mamie Eisenhower.* New York: Farrar, Straus and Giroux, 1996.

The Eisenhower Foundation. *D-Day: The Normandy Invasion in Retrospect.* Lawrence: University Press of Kansas, 1972.

Ellis, John. *Brute Force: Allied Strategy and Tactics in the Second World War.* New York: Viking, 1990.

Ellis, L. F. *Victory in the West.* 2 vols. London: HMSO, 1962–68.

Elm, Mostafa. *Oil, Power, and Principle: Iran's Oil Nationalization and Its Aftermath.* Syracuse, N.Y.: Syracuse University Press, 1992.

Ephraim, Frank. *Escape to Manila: From Nazi Tyranny to Japanese Terror.* Chicago: University of Illinois Press, 2003.

Esposito, Vincent J., ed. *The West Point Atlas of American Wars,* Vol. 2, *1900–1953.* New York: Praeger, 1967.

Eulau, Heinz. *Class and Party in the Eisenhower Years: Class Roles and Perspectives in the 1952 and 1956 Elections.* New York: Free Press of Glencoe, 1962.

Ewald, William Bragg, Jr. *Eisenhower the President: Crucial Days, 1951–1960.* Englewood Cliffs, N.J.: Prentice Hall, 1981.

Fall, Bernard B. *Hell in a Very Small Place: The Siege of Dien Bien Phu.* Philadelphia: Lippincott, 1967.

Farago, Ladislas. *The Last Days of Patton.* New York: McGraw-Hill, 1981.

———. *Patton: Ordeal and Triumph.* New York: Ivan Obolensky, 1963.

Farley, James A. *Jim Farley's Story: The Roosevelt Years.* New York: Whittlesey House, 1948.

Feis, Herbert. *Between War and Peace: The Potsdam Conference.* Princeton, N.J.: Princeton University Press, 1960.

———. *Churchill, Roosevelt, Stalin: The War They Waged and the Peace They Sought.* Princeton, N.J.: Princeton University Press, 1957.

Feldman, Ellen. *Lucy: A Novel.* New York: W. W. Norton, 2003.

Fergusson, Bernard. *The Watery Maze: The Story of Combined Operation.* New York: McGraw-Hill, 1981.

Ferrell, Robert H. *Ill-Advised: Presidential Health and Public Trust.* Columbia: University of Missouri Press, 1992.

Field, Rudolph. *Ike, Man of the Hour.* New York: Universal, 1952.

Findlay, James F. *Dwight L. Moody, American Evangelist, 1837–1899.* Chicago: University of Chicago Press, 1969.

Finer, Herman. *Dulles over Suez: The Theory and Practice of His Diplomacy.* Chicago: Quadrangle Books, 1964.

Fischer, Beth A. *The Reagan Reversal: Foreign Policy and the End of the Cold War.* Columbia: University of Missouri Press, 1997.

Fitzgerald, F. Scott. *The Letters of F. Scott Fitzgerald.* Andrew Turnbull, ed. New York: Scribner, 1963.

Flanner, Janet. *Paris Was Yesterday.* New York: Viking Press, 1972.

Freidel, Frank. *Franklin D. Roosevelt.* Vol. 1, *The Apprenticeship.* Boston: Little, Brown, 1952.

Friend, Theodore. *Between Two Empires: The Ordeal of the Philippines, 1929–1946.* New Haven, Conn.: Yale University Press, 1965.

Frier, David A. *Conflict of Interest in the Eisenhower Administration.* Ames: Iowa State University Press, 1969.

Fromkin, David. *In the Time of the Americans.* New York: Vintage, 1995.

Funk, Arthur Layton. *Charles de Gaulle: The Crucial Years, 1943–1944.* Norman: University of Oklahoma Press, 1959.

————. *The Politics of TORCH: The Allied Landings and the Algiers Putsch, 1942.* Lawrence: University Press of Kansas, 1974.

Gabel, Christopher R. *The U.S. Army GHQ Maneuvers of 1941.* Washington, D.C.: Center of Military History, U.S. Army, 1992.

Ganoe, William Addleman. *The History of the United States Army.* Ashton, Md.: Eric Lundberg, 1964.

Garland, Albert N., and Howard McGaw Smyth. *Sicily and the Surrender of Italy.* Washington, D.C.: Office of the Chief of Military History, Department of the Army, 1965.

Gavin, James M. *On to Berlin: Battles of an Airborne Commander, 1943–1946.* New York: Viking, 1978.

Gelb, Norman. *Ike and Monty, Generals at War.* New York: Quill, 1994.

Gentry, Curt. *J. Edgar Hoover: The Man and the Secrets.* New York: Norton, 1991.

Gilbert, Martin. *Churchill and America.* New York: Free Press, 2005.

————, ed. *The Churchill War Papers.* Vols. 1–3, 1939–May 1941. New York: Norton, 1995–2001.

————. *D-Day.* Hoboken, N.J.: John Wiley & Sons, 2004.

————. *The First World War.* New York: Henry Holt, 1994.

————. *The Second World War: A Complete History.* New York: Henry Holt, 1989.

————. *Winston S. Churchill.* Vol. 7, *Road to Victory, 1941–1945.* London: Heinemann, 1986.

Gilpin, Robert. *American Scientists and Nuclear Weapons Policy.* Princeton, N.J.: Princeton University Press, 1962.

Goebbels, Joseph. *Final Entries, 1945: The Diaries of Joseph Goebbels.* Hugh Trevor-Roper, ed. Richard Barry, trans. New York: G. P. Putnam's Sons, 1978.

Gole, Henry G. *The Road to Rainbow: Army Planning for Global War, 1934–1940.* Annapolis, Md.: Naval Institute Press, 2003.

Goode, James F. *The United States and Iran: In the Shadow of Musaddiq.* New York: St. Martin's Press, 1997.

Gopnik, Adam, ed. *Americans in Paris: A Literary Anthology.* New York: Library of America, 2004.

Goulden, Joseph C. *Korea: The Untold Story of the War.* New York: Times Books, 1982.

Grant, Ulysses S. *Personal Memoirs of U. S. Grant.* 2 vols. New York: Charles L. Webster, 1885–86.

Greeley, Horace. *The American Conflict: A History of the Great Rebellion in the United States of America, 1860–64.* 2 vols. Hartford, Conn.: O. D. Case, 1864.

Greene, John Robert. *The Crusade: The Presidential Election of 1952.* Lanham, Md.: Rowman and Littlefield, 1985.

Greenfield, Kent Roberts, ed. *Command Decisions.* Washington, D.C.: Office of the Chief of Military History, Department of the Army, 1960.

Greenfield, Kent Roberts, Robert R. Palmer, and Bell I. Wiley. *The Organization of Ground Combat Troops.* Washington, D.C.: Center of Military History, U.S. Army, 2004.

Greenstein, Fred I. *The Hidden-Hand Presidency: Eisenhower as Leader.* New York: Basic Books, 1982.

Griffin, Peter. *Less Than a Treason: Hemingway in Paris.* New York: Oxford University Press, 1990.

Gunther, John. *Eisenhower: The Man and the Symbol.* New York: Harper and Row, 1952.

Hagerty, James C. *The Diary of James C. Hagerty: Eisenhower in Mid-Course, 1954–1955.* Robert H. Ferrell, ed. Bloomington: Indiana University Press, 1983.

Halberstam, David. *The Coldest Winter: America and the Korean War.* New York: Hyperion, 2007.

———. *The Fifties.* New York: Villard Books, 1993.

———. *The Powers That Be.* New York: Knopf, 1979.

Hamilton, Charles V. *Adam Clayton Powell, Jr.: The Political Biography of an American Dilemma.* New York: Atheneum Macmillan, 1991.

Hamilton, Nigel. *Master of the Battlefield: Monty's War Years, 1942–1944.* London: Hamish Hamilton, 1983.

———. *Monty: Final Years of the Field-Marshal, 1944–1976.* New York: McGraw-Hill, 1987.

Hardeman, D. B., and Donald C. Bacon. *Rayburn: A Biography.* Austin: Texas Monthly Press, 1987.

Harmon, Ernest N. *Combat Commander: Autobiography of a Soldier.* Garden City, N.Y.: Doubleday, 1970.

Harris, Kenneth. *Attlee.* London: Weidenfeld and Nicolson, 1983.

Harrison, Gordon A. *Cross-Channel Attack.* Washington, D.C.: Center of Military History, U.S. Army, 2002.

Hart, George L., Official Reporter. *Official Report of the Proceedings of the Twenty-fifth Republican National Convention Held in Chicago, Illinois July 7, 8, 9, 10 and 11,*

*1952, Resulting in the Nomination of Dwight D. Eisenhower, of New York, for President and the Nomination of Richard M. Nixon, of California, for Vice President.* Washington, D.C.: Republican National Committee, 1952.

Hastings, Max. *Armageddon: The Battle for Germany, 1944–1945.* New York: Knopf, 2004.

———. *Overlord: D-Day and the Battle for Normandy.* New York: Simon and Schuster, 1984.

Hatch, Alden. *General Ike: A Biography of Dwight D. Eisenhower.* New York: Henry Holt, 1944.

———. *Red Carpet for Mamie.* New York: Henry Holt, 1954.

Heiss, Mary Ann. *Empire and Nationhood: The United States, Great Britain, and Iranian Oil, 1950–1954.* New York: Columbia University Press, 1997.

Hemingway, Ernest. *Dateline, Toronto: The Complete Toronto Star Dispatches, 1920–1924.* William White, ed. New York: Scribner's, 1985.

Hesketh, Roger. *Fortitude: The D-Day Deception Campaign.* Woodstock, N.Y.: Overlook, 2000.

Hewlett, Richard G., and Jack M. Holl. *Atoms for Peace and War, 1953–1961: Eisenhower and the Atomic Energy Commission.* Berkeley: University of California Press, 1989.

Hicks, Wilson, ed. *This Is Ike: The Picture Story of the Man.* New York: Henry Holt, 1952.

Higgins, Trumbull. *The Perfect Failure: Kennedy, Eisenhower, and the CIA at the Bay of Pigs.* New York: Norton, 1987.

Hilton, James. *Lost Horizon.* London: Macmillan, 1933.

Hinsley, F. H. *British Intelligence in the Second World War: Its Influence on Strategy and Operations.* 3 vols. New York: Cambridge University Press, 1979–88.

Hirshson, Stanley P. *General Patton: A Soldier's Life.* New York: HarperCollins, 2002.

Hogan, David W., Jr. *A Command Post at War: First Army Headquarters in Europe, 1944–1945.* Washington, D.C.: Center of Military History, U.S. Army, 2000.

Holbo, Paul, and Robert Sellen, eds. *The Eisenhower Era: The Age of Consensus.* Hinsdale, Ill.: Dryden Press, 1974.

Holland, Matthew. *Eisenhower Between the Wars: The Making of a General and Statesman.* Westport, Conn.: Praeger, 2001.

Holt, Daniel D., and James W. Leyerzapf, eds. *Eisenhower: The Prewar Diaries and Selected Papers, 1905–1941.* Baltimore: Johns Hopkins University Press, 1998.

Holt, Marilyn Irvin. *Mamie Doud Eisenhower: The General's First Lady.* Lawrence: University Press of Kansas, 2007.

Holzimmer, Kevin C. *General Walter Krueger: Unsung Hero of the Pacific War.* Lawrence: University Press of Kansas, 2007.

Hoopes, Townsend. *The Devil and John Foster Dulles.* Boston: Little, Brown, 1973.

Hoover, Herbert. *Memoirs.* 3 vols. New York: Macmillan, 1951–52.

Horne, Alistair. *Harold Macmillan.* 2 vols. New York: Penguin, 1988–89.

———. *Monty: The Lonely Leader, 1944–1945.* New York: HarperCollins, 1994.

Howe, George F. *Northwest Africa: Seizing the Initiative in the West.* Washington, D.C.: Center of Military History, U.S. Army, 1957.

Huff, Sid, and Joe Alex Morris. *My Fifteen Years with General MacArthur.* New York: Paperback Library, 1964.

Hughes, Emmet John. *America, the Vincible.* Garden City, N.Y.: Doubleday, 1959.

———. *The Ordeal of Power: A Political Memoir of the Eisenhower Years.* New York: Atheneum, 1963.

Humes, James. *Eisenhower and Churchill: The Partnership That Saved the World.* Roseville, Calif.: Forum, 2001.

Hunt, E. Howard. *Undercover: Memoirs of an American Secret Agent.* New York: Berkley Publishing, 1974.

Hunt, Frazier. *MacArthur and the War Against Japan.* New York: Charles Scribner's Sons, 1944.

———. *The Untold Story of Douglas MacArthur.* New York: Manor Books, 1954.

Ickes, Harold L. *The Secret Diaries of Harold L. Ickes.* 3 vols. New York: Simon and Schuster, 1953–55.

Immerman, Richard H. *The CIA in Guatemala: The Foreign Policy of Intervention.* Austin: University of Texas Press, 1982.

———. *John Foster Dulles: Piety, Pragmatism, and Power in U.S. Foreign Policy.* Wilmington, Del.: SR Books, 1999.

Ingersoll, Joshena M. *Golden Years in the Philippines.* Palo Alto, Calif.: Pacific Books, Publishers, 1971.

International Military Tribunal. *The Trial of German Major War Criminals: Proceedings of the International Military Tribunal Sitting at Nuremberg, Germany.* 23 vols. London: HMSO, 1946–51.

Irving, David. *The War Between the Generals.* New York: Congdon and Lattes, 1981.

Isaacson, Walter, and Evan Thomas. *The Wise Men: Six Friends and the World They Made.* New York: Simon and Schuster, 1986.

Ismay, General Lord. *The Memoirs of General Lord Ismay.* New York: Viking, 1960.

Ives, Elizabeth Stevenson, and Hildegarde Dolson. *My Brother Adlai.* New York: William Morrow, 1956.

Jacobs, Travis Beal. *Eisenhower at Columbia.* New Brunswick, N.J.: Transaction Publishers, 2001.

Jacobsen, Hans-Adolf, and Jürgen Rohwer, eds. *Decisive Battles of World War II: The German View.* New York: G. P. Putnam's Sons, 1965.

James, D. Clayton. *The Years of MacArthur.* 3 vols. Boston: Houghton Mifflin, 1970–85.

James, D. Clayton, and Anne Sharp Wells. *A Time for Giants: Politics of the American High Command in World War II.* New York: Franklin Watts, 1987.

Jameson, Henry B. *They Still Call Him Ike.* New York: Vantage Press, 1972.

Jenkins, Roy. *Churchill.* New York: Farrar, Straus and Giroux, 2001.

Jensen, Joan M. *Army Surveillance in America, 1775–1980.* New Haven, Conn.: Yale University Press, 1991.

Johnson, David K. *The Lavender Scare: The Cold War Persecution of Gays and Lesbians in the Federal Government.* Chicago: University of Chicago Press, 2004.

Jones, Colin. *The Cambridge Illustrated History of France.* New York: Cambridge University Press, 1994.

———. *Paris: The Biography of a City.* New York: Viking, 2005.

Jones, Ken, and Hubert Kelley, Jr. *Admiral Arleigh (31-Knot) Burke: The Story of a Fighting Sailor.* Philadelphia: Chilton Books, 1962.

Jurika, Stephen, Jr., ed. *From Pearl Harbor to Vietnam: The Memoirs of Admiral Arthur W. Radford.* Stanford, Calif.: Hoover Institution Press, 1980.

Katouzian, Homa. *Musaddiq and the Struggle for Power in Iran.* New York: I. B. Tauris, 1999.

Kaufman, Burton Ira. *Trade and Aid: Eisenhower's Foreign Economic Policy, 1953–1961.* Baltimore: Johns Hopkins University Press, 1981.

Keddie, Nikki R. *Modern Iran: Roots and Results of Revolution.* New Haven, Conn.: Yale University Press, 2003.

Keegan, John. *The Second World War.* New York: Viking Press, 1989.

———. *Six Armies in Normandy: From D-Day to the Liberation of Paris, June 6th–August 25th, 1944.* New York: Viking, 1982.

———, ed. *The Times Atlas of the Second World War.* New York: Harper and Row, 1989.

Kennedy, David. *Freedom from Fear.* New York: Oxford University Press, 1999.

Kennedy, T. Gerald. *Imagining Paris: Exile, Writing, and American Identity.* New Haven, Conn.: Yale University Press, 1993.

Kenney, George C. *General Kenney Reports.* New York: Duell, Sloan, and Pearce, 1949.

Kesselring, Albert. *Kesselring: A Soldier's Record.* Westport, Conn.: Greenwood Press, 1970.

Khrushchev, Nikita Sergeevich. *Khrushchev Remembers.* Strobe Talbott, ed. and trans. Boston: Little, Brown, 1970.

———. *Khrushchev Remembers: The Last Testament.* Strobe Talbott, ed. and trans. Boston: Little, Brown, 1974.

Killian, James. *Sputnik, Scientists, and Eisenhower: A Memoir of the First Special Assistant to the President for Science and Technology.* Cambridge: MIT Press, 1977.

Kimball, Warren F., ed. *Churchill and Roosevelt: The Complete Correspondence.* 3 vols. Princeton, N.J.: Princeton University Press, 1984.

———. *Forged in War.* New York: Morrow, 1997.

Kingseed, Cole C. *Eisenhower and the Suez Crisis of 1956.* Baton Rouge: Louisiana State University Press, 1995.

Kinnard, Douglas. *Eisenhower: Soldier-Statesman of the American Century.* Washington, D.C.: Brassey's, 2002.

———. *Ike, 1890–1990: A Pictorial History.* Washington, D.C.: Brassey's, 1990.

———. *President Eisenhower and Strategy Management: A Study in Defense Politics.* Lexington: University Press of Kentucky, 1977.

Kinzer, Stephen. *All the Shah's Men: An American Coup and the Roots of Middle East Terror.* Hoboken, N.J.: John Wiley and Sons, 2003.

Kissinger, Henry. *The Necessity for Choice: Prospects of American Foreign Policy.* New York: Harper and Brothers, 1961.

———. *Nuclear Weapons and Foreign Policy.* New York: Harper and Brothers, 1957.

Kistiakowsky, George B. *A Scientist at the White House: The Private Diary of President Eisenhower's Special Assistant for Science and Technology.* Cambridge: Harvard University Press, 1976.

Kolata, Gina. *Flu: The Story of the Great Influenza Pandemic of 1918 and the Search for the Virus That Caused It.* New York: Farrar, Straus and Giroux, 1999.

Korda, Michael. *Ike: An American Hero.* New York: HarperCollins, 2007.

Kornitzer, Bela. *The Great American Heritage: The Story of the Five Eisenhower Brothers.* New York: Farrar, Straus, and Cudahy, 1955.

Krieg, Joann P., ed. *Dwight D. Eisenhower: Soldier, President, and Statesman.* Westport, Conn.: Greenwood Press, 1987.

Krock, Arthur. *Memoirs: Sixty Years on the Firing Line.* New York: Funk and Wagnalls, 1968.

Krueger, General Walter. *From Down Under to Nippon: The Story of Sixth Army in World War II.* Washington, D.C.: Combat Forces Press, 1953.

Kunz, Diane B. *The Economic Diplomacy of the Suez Crisis.* Chapel Hill: University of North Carolina Press, 1991.

Lacouture, Jean. *De Gaulle: The Rebel, 1890–1944.* Patrick O. Brian, trans. New York: Norton, 1990.

———. *De Gaulle: The Ruler, 1945–1970.* Alan Sheridan, trans. New York: Norton, 1991.

Ladino, Robyn Duff. *Desegregating Texas Schools: Eisenhower, Shivers, and the Crisis at Mansfield High.* Austin: University of Texas Press, 1996.

Lakoff, Sanford A., ed. *Knowledge and Power: Essays on Science and Government.* New York: Free Press, 1966.

Lamb, Richard. *Churchill as War Leader.* New York: Carroll and Graf, 1993.

Langer, William L. *Our Vichy Gamble.* New York: Knopf, 1947.

Lardner, Ring. *Treat 'em Rough: Letters from Jack the Kaiser Killer.* Indianapolis: Bobbs-Merrill Company, 1918.

Larrabee, Eric. *Commander in Chief.* Annapolis, Md.: Naval Institute Press, 1987.

Larson, Arthur. *Eisenhower: The President Nobody Knew.* New York: Charles Scribner's Sons, 1968.

Lasby, Clarence G. *Eisenhower's Heart Attack: How Ike Beat Heart Disease and Held On to the Presidency.* Lawrence: University Press of Kansas, 1997.

Lash, Joseph P. *A World of Love: Eleanor Roosevelt and Her Friends, 1943–1962.* Garden City, N.Y.: Doubleday, 1984.

Leahy, William D. *I Was There: The Personal Story of the Chief of Staff to Presidents Roosevelt and Truman, Based on His Notes and Diaries Made at the Time.* New York: Whittlesey House, 1950.

Leary, William M., ed. *MacArthur and the American Century: A Reader.* Lincoln: University of Nebraska Press, 2001.

Ledbetter, James. *Unwarranted Influence: Dwight D. Eisenhower and the Military-Industrial Complex.* New Haven, Conn.: Yale University Press, 2011.

Ledwidge, Bernard. *De Gaulle.* New York: St. Martin's Press, 1982.

Lee, R. Alton. *Dwight D. Eisenhower, Soldier and Statesman.* Chicago: Nelson-Hall, 1981.

———. *Eisenhower and Landrum-Griffin: A Study in Labor-Management Politics.* Lexington: University Press of Kentucky, 1989.

Lee, Ulysses. *The Employment of Negro Troops: Special Studies; United States Army in World War II.* Washington, D.C.: Office of the Chief of Military History, 1966.

Leighton, Richard M., and Robert W. Coakley. *Global Logistics and Strategy.* Washington, D.C.: Office of the Chief of Military History, Department of the Army, 1955.

———. *Global Logistics and Strategy, 1940–1943.* Washington, D.C.: Center of Military History, U.S. Army, 1995.

Leuchtenburg, William E. *In the Shadow of FDR: From Harry Truman to Bill Clinton.* Ithaca, N.Y.: Cornell University Press, 1993.

Lewis, Adrian R. *Omaha Beach: A Flawed Victory.* Chapel Hill: University of North Carolina Press, 2001.

Liddell Hart, B. H. *History of the Second World War.* London: Cassell, 1970.

———. *The Other Side of the Hill: Germany's Generals, Their Rise and Fall, with Their Own Account of Military Events, 1939–1945.* London: Cassell, 1951.

Lincoln, Abraham. *The Collected Works of Abraham Lincoln.* Vol. 7. Roy P. Basler, ed. New Brunswick, N.J.: Rutgers University Press, 1955.

Lindley, Ernest K. *The Roosevelt Revolution: First Phase.* New York: Viking, 1933.

Linn, Brian McAllister. *Guardians of Empire: The U.S. Army and the Pacific, 1902–1940.* Chapel Hill: University of North Carolina Press, 1997.

Lisio, Donald J. *The President and Protest: Hoover, MacArthur, and the Bonus Riot.* New York: Fordham University Press, 1994.

Lodge, Henry Cabot, Jr. *As It Was: An Inside View of Politics and Power in the '50s and '60s.* New York: Norton, 1976.

Love, Kennett. *Suez: The Twice-Fought War.* New York: McGraw-Hill, 1969.

Love, Spencie. *One Blood: The Death and Resurrection of Charles R. Drew.* Chapel Hill: University of North Carolina Press, 1996.

Lubell, Samuel. *Revolt of the Moderates.* New York: Harper and Brothers, 1956.

Lyon, Peter. *Eisenhower: Portrait of the Hero.* Boston: Little, Brown, 1974.

———. *The Wild, Wild West for the Discriminating Reader.* New York: Funk and Wagnalls, 1969.

MacArthur, Douglas. *Reminiscences.* New York: McGraw-Hill, 1964.

———. *Revitalizing a Nation: A Statement of Beliefs, Opinions and Policies Embodied in the Public Pronouncements of General of the Army Douglas MacArthur.* Chicago: Heritage Foundation, 1952.

———. *A Soldier Speaks: Public Papers and Speeches of General of the Army Douglas MacArthur.* New York: Praeger, 1965.

MacDonald, Charles B. *The Mighty Endeavor.* New York: Oxford University Press, 1969.

MacGregor, Morris J. *Integration of the Armed Forces, 1940–1965.* Washington, D.C.: Center of Military History, U.S. Army, 1981.

Macksey, Kenneth. *Crucible of Power: The Fight for Tunisia, 1942–1943.* London: Hutchinson, 1969.

Macmillan, Harold. *The Blast of War, 1939–1945.* New York: Harper and Row, 1968.

———. *Riding the Storm, 1956–1959.* New York: Harper and Row, 1971.

———. *Tides of Fortune, 1945–1955.* New York: Harper and Row, 1969.

———. *War Diaries: Politics and War in the Mediterranean.* New York: St. Martin's Press, 1984.

Maddox, Robert F. *The Senatorial Career of Harley Martin Kilgore.* New York: Garland, 1981.

Maher, Marty. *Bringing Up the Brass.* New York: McKay, 1951.

Mallon, Bill, and Ian Buchanan. *The 1908 Olympic Games: Results for All Competitors in All Events, with Commentary.* Jefferson, N.C.: McFarland, 2000.

Manchester, William. *American Caesar: Douglas MacArthur, 1880–1964.* Boston: Little, Brown, 1978.

Manstein, Erich von. *Lost Victories.* Anthony G. Powell, ed. and trans. 1958. Reprint, Novato, Calif.: Presidio Press, 1982.

Marrus, Michael R., and Robert O. Paxton. *Vichy France and the Jews.* New York: Basic Books, 1981.

Marshall, George C. *The Papers of George Catlett Marshall.* Vols. 2–5. Larry I. Bland, ed. Baltimore: Johns Hopkins University Press, 1986–2003.

Marshall, Katherine Tupper. *Together: Annals of an Army Wife.* New York: Tupper and Love, 1946.

Marshall, S. L. A. *Night Drop: The American Airborne Invasion of Normandy.* Boston: Little, Brown, 1962.

Martienssen, Anthony K. *Hitler and His Admirals.* New York, E. P. Dutton, 1949.

Martin, John Bartlow. *Adlai Stevenson.* New York: Harper and Brothers, 1952.

———. *Adlai Stevenson and the World: The Life of Adlai E. Stevenson.* Garden City, N.Y.: Doubleday, 1977.

———. *Adlai Stevenson of Illinois: The Life of Adlai E. Stevenson.* Garden City, N.Y.: Doubleday, 1976.

Martin, William C. *A Prophet with Honor: The Billy Graham Story.* New York: William Morrow, 1991.

Matloff, Maurice. *Strategic Planning for Coalition Warfare, 1943–1944.* Washington, D.C.: Office of the Chief of Military History, Department of the Army, 1959.

Matloff, Maurice, and Edwin M. Snell. *Strategic Planning for Coalition Warfare, 1941–1942.* Washington, D.C.: Office of the Chief of Military History, Department of the Army, 1953.

Mauriac, Claude. *The Other de Gaulle: Diaries, 1944–1945.* Moura Budberg and Gordon Latta, trans. New York: John Day, 1973.

Mauriac, François. *De Gaulle.* Richard Howard, trans. Garden City, N.Y.: Doubleday, 1966.

Mazo, Earl. *Richard Nixon: A Political and Personal Portrait.* New York: Harper and Brothers, 1959.

McCann, Kevin. *Man from Abilene.* Garden City, N.Y.: Doubleday, 1952.

McCann, Thomas P. *An American Company: The Tragedy of United Fruit.* Henry Scammell, ed. New York: Crown Publishers, 1976.

McCullough, David. *Truman.* New York: Simon and Schuster, 1992.

McDougall, Walter A. . . . *The Heavens and the Earth: A Political History of the Space Age.* New York: Basic Books, 1985.

McKeogh, Michael, and Richard Lockridge. *Sgt. Mickey and General Ike.* New York: G. P. Putnam's Sons, 1946.

McPherson, James M. *Battle Cry of Freedom: The Civil War Era.* New York: Oxford University Press, 1988.

Medhurst, Martin. *Dwight D. Eisenhower: Strategic Communicator.* Westport, Conn.: Greenwood Press, 1993.

————, ed. *Eisenhower's War of Words: Rhetoric and Leadership.* East Lansing: Michigan State University, 1994.

Melanson, Richard A., and David Mayers, eds. *Reevaluating Eisenhower: American Foreign Policy in the 1950s.* Urbana: University of Illinois Press, 1987.

Messenger, Charles. *The D-Day Atlas.* New York: Thames and Hudson, 2004.

————. *The Last Prussian: A Biography of Field Marshal Gerd von Rundstedt, 1875–1953.* London: Brassey's, 1991.

Miles, Perry L. *Fallen Leaves: Memories of an Old Soldier.* Berkeley, Calif.: Wuerth, 1961.

Miller, Donald E. *The Story of World War II.* New York: Simon and Schuster, 2001.

Miller, Francis T. *Eisenhower: Man and Soldier.* Philadelphia: John C. Winston, 1944.

Miller, Merle. *Ike the Soldier: As They Knew Him.* New York: G. P. Putnam's Sons, 1987.

————. *Plain Speaking: An Oral Biography of Harry S. Truman.* New York: Berkley, 1974.

Miller, William Lee. *Piety Along the Potomac: Notes on Politics and Morals in the Fifties.* Boston: Houghton Mifflin, 1964.

Miner, Craig. *West of Wichita: Settling the High Plains of Kansas, 1865–1890.* Lawrence: University Press of Kansas, 1986.

Mizener, Arthur. *The Far Side of Paradise: A Biography of F. Scott Fitzgerald.* Boston: Houghton Mifflin, 1965.

Moenk, Jean R. *A History of Large-Scale Army Maneuvers in the United States, 1935–1964.* Fort Monroe, Va.: Continental Army Command, 1969.

Mollenhoff, Clark R. *The Pentagon: Politics, Profits, and Plunder.* New York: G. P. Putnam's Sons, 1967.

Montgomery, Bernard Law. *The Memoirs of Field-Marshal the Viscount Montgomery of Alamein.* Cleveland: World Publishing, 1958.

Moos, Malcolm. *Dwight D. Eisenhower.* New York: Random House, 1964.

Moran, Charles McMoran Wilson. *Churchill: The Struggle for Survival, 1940–1965, Taken from the Diaries of Lord Moran.* Boston: Houghton Mifflin, 1966.

Morelock, J. D. *Generals of Ardennes: American Leadership in the Battle of the Bulge.* Washington, D.C.: National Defense University Press, 1994.

Morgan, Sir Frederick. *Overture to Overlord.* Garden City, N.Y.: Doubleday, 1950.

Morgan, Kay Summersby. *Past Forgetting: My Love Affair with Dwight D. Eisenhower.* New York: Simon and Schuster, 1976.

Morgan, Ted. *Valley of Death: The Tragedy at Dien Bien Phu That Led America into the Vietnam War.* New York: Random House, 2010.

Morin, Relman. *Dwight D. Eisenhower: A Gauge of Greatness.* New York: Simon and Schuster, 1969.

Morison, Samuel Eliot. *History of United States Naval Operations in World War II.* 12 vols. Boston: Little, Brown, 1947–60.

———. *The Oxford History of the American People.* New York: Oxford University Press, 1965.

———. *The Two Ocean War: A Short History of the United States Navy in the Second World War.* Boston: Little, Brown, 1963.

Morris, Roger. *Richard Milhous Nixon: The Rise of an American Politician.* New York: Henry Holt, 1990.

Morrow, Everett Frederic. *Black Man in the White House: A Diary of the Eisenhower Years by the Administrative Officer for Special Projects, the White House, 1955–1961.* New York: Coward-McCann, 1963.

Morton, Louis. *The Fall of the Philippines.* Washington, D.C.: Office of the Chief of Military History, Department of the Army, 1953.

———. *Strategy and Command: The First Two Years.* Washington, D.C.: Office of the Chief of Military History, Department of the Army, 1962.

Moseley, George Van Horn. "One Soldier's Journey." Unpublished manuscript. 4 vols. Moseley Papers. Library of Congress.

Muller, Herbert J. *Adlai Stevenson: A Study in Values.* New York: Harper and Row, 1967.

Murphy, Robert. *Diplomat Among Warriors.* Garden City, N.Y.: Doubleday, 1964.

Murray, Williamson, and Allan R. Millett. *A War to Be Won: Fighting the Second World War, 1937–1945.* Cambridge, Mass.: Belknap Press of Harvard University Press, 2000.

Murrow, Edward R. *In Search of Light: The Broadcasts of Edward R. Murrow, 1938–1961.* Edward Bliss, Jr., ed. New York: Knopf, 1967.

Musaddiq, Mohammad. *Musaddiq's Memoirs.* Homa Katouzian, ed. London: JEBHE, 1988.

Nadich, Judah. *Eisenhower and the Jews.* New York: Twayne Publishers, 1953.

Neal, Steve. *The Eisenhowers.* Lawrence: University Press of Kansas, 1984.

———. *The Eisenhowers: Reluctant Dynasty.* Garden City, N.Y.: Doubleday, 1978.

———. *Harry and Ike: The Partnership That Remade the Postwar World.* New York: Simon and Schuster, 2001.

Neff, Donald. *Warriors at Suez: Eisenhower Takes America into the Middle East.* New York: Simon and Schuster, 1981.

Nelson, James. *General Eisenhower on the Military Churchill: A Conversation with Alistair Cooke.* New York: Norton, 1970.

Nevins, Arthur S. *Gettysburg's Five-Star Farmer.* New York: Carlton Press, 1977.

Newton, Michael. *The FBI Encyclopedia.* Jefferson, N.C.: McFarland, 2003.

Nichols, David A. *Eisenhower 1956: The President's Year of Crisis: Suez and the Brink of War.* New York: Simon and Schuster, 2011.

———. *A Matter of Justice: Eisenhower and the Beginning of the Civil Rights Revolution.* New York: Simon and Schuster, 2007.

Nixon, Richard. *RN: The Memoirs of Richard Nixon.* New York: Grosset and Dunlap, 1978.

———. *Six Crises.* Garden City, N.Y.: Doubleday, 1962.

Nordell, John R., Jr. *The Undetected Enemy: French and American Miscalculations at Dien Bien Phu, 1953.* College Station: Texas A&M University Press, 1995.

Nutting, Anthony. *No End of a Lesson: The Story of Suez.* New York: Clarkson N. Potter, 1967.

Odom, Charles B., M.D. *General George S. Patton and Eisenhower.* New Orleans: Word Picture Productions, 1985.

Orange, Vincent. *Tedder: Quietly in Command.* London: Frank Cass, 2004.

Osgood, Kenneth. *Total Cold War: Eisenhower's Secret Propaganda Battle at Home and Abroad.* Lawrence: University of Kansas Press, 2006.

Oshinsky, David M. *A Conspiracy So Immense: The World of Joe McCarthy.* New York: Free Press, 1983.

Owen, David. *The Making of the Masters: Clifford Roberts, Augusta National, and Golf's Most Prestigious Tournament.* New York: Simon and Schuster, 1999.

Pach, Chester J., Jr., and Elmo Richardson. *The Presidency of Dwight D. Eisenhower.* Lawrence: University Press of Kansas, 1991.

Parmet, Herbert S. *Eisenhower and the American Crusades.* New York: Macmillan, 1972.

Parrish, Thomas. *Roosevelt and Marshall: Partners in Politics and War.* New York: William Morrow, 1989.

Patterson, James T. *Mr. Republican: A Biography of Robert A. Taft.* Boston: Houghton Mifflin, 1972.

Patton, George S., Jr. *War as I Knew It.* Boston: Houghton Mifflin, 1947.

Paxton, Robert O. *Parades and Politics at Vichy : The French Officer Corps Under Marshal Pétain.* Princeton, N.J.: Princeton University Press, 1966.

———. *Vichy France: Old Guard and New Order, 1940–1944.* New York: Knopf, 1972.

Pendar, Kenneth. *Adventure in Diplomacy: The Emergence of General de Gaulle in North Africa.* London: Cassell, 1966.

Perret, Geoffrey. *Eisenhower.* New York: Random House, 1999.

———. *Old Soldiers Never Die: The Life of Douglas MacArthur.* New York: Random House, 1996.

———. *There's a War to Be Won: The United States Army in World War II.* New York: Ballantine Books, 1991.

Perry, Mark. *Four Stars.* Boston: Houghton Mifflin, 1989.

———. *Partners in Command: George Marshall and Dwight Eisenhower in War and Peace.* New York: Penguin Press, 2007.

Pershing, John J. *My Experiences in the World War.* 2 vols. New York: Frederick A. Stokes, 1931.

Peters, Charles. *Five Days in Philadelphia.* New York: PublicAffairs, 2005.

Petillo, Carol Morris. *Douglas MacArthur: The Philippine Years.* Bloomington: Indiana University Press, 1981.

Pickett, William. *Eisenhower Decides to Run: Presidential Politics and Cold War Strategy.* Chicago: Ivan R. Dee, 2000.

Pinkley, Virgil, and James F. Scheer. *Eisenhower Declassified.* Old Tappan, N.J.: Fleming H. Revell, 1979.

Pipes, Kasey S. *Ike's Final Battle: The Road to Little Rock and the Challenge of Equality.* New York: World Ahead Media, 2007.

Pogue, Forrest C. *George C. Marshall.* 4 vols. New York: Viking, 1963–87.

———. *The Supreme Command.* Washington, D.C.: Office of the Chief of Military History, Department of the Army, 1954.

Pollack, Jack Harrison. *Earl Warren: The Judge Who Changed America.* Englewood Cliffs, N.J.: Prentice Hall, 1979.

Pond, Hugh. *Sicily.* London: W. Kimber, 1962.

Porter, Horace. *Campaigning with Grant.* New York: Century, 1897.

Powell, Colin L., and Joseph E. Persico. *My American Journey.* New York: Random House, 1995.

Prados, John. *Presidents' Secret Wars: CIA and Pentagon Covert Operations Since World War II.* New York: William Morrow, 1986.

———. *The Sky Would Fall: Operation Vulture, the U.S. Bombing Mission in Indochina, 1954.* New York: Dial Press, 1983.

Pratt, Fletcher. *Eleven Generals: Studies in American Command.* New York: William Sloane Associates, 1949.

Pusey, Merlo J. *Eisenhower, the President.* New York: Macmillan, 1956.

Pyle, Ernie. *Brave Men.* New York: Henry Holt, 1944.

Rabe, Stephen G. *Eisenhower and Latin America: The Foreign Policy of Anti-Communism.* Chapel Hill: University of North Carolina Press, 1988.

Radford, Arthur W. *From Pearl Harbor to Vietnam: The Memoirs of Admiral Arthur W. Radford.* Stephen Jurika, Jr., ed. Stanford, Calif.: Hoover Institution Press, 1980.

Reed, Roy. *Faubus: The Life and Times of an American Prodigal.* Fayetteville: University of Arkansas Press, 1997.

Reeves, Thomas C. *The Life and Times of Joe McCarthy.* New York: Stein and Day, 1982.

Reichard, Gary W. *Politics as Usual: The Age of Truman and Eisenhower.* Arlington Heights, Ill.: Harlan Davidson, 1988.

———. *The Reaffirmation of Republicanism: Eisenhower and the Eighty-third Congress.* Knoxville: University of Tennessee Press, 1975.

Reston, James. *Sketches in the Sand.* New York: Knopf, 1967.

Reynolds, David. *In Command of History: Churchill Fighting and Writing the Second World War.* New York: Random House, 2005.

———. *Summits: Six Meetings That Shaped the Twentieth Century.* New York: Basic Books, 2007.

Reynolds, Michael S. *Hemingway: The Paris Years.* Oxford: Blackwell, 1989.

Richardson, Elmo. *The Presidency of Dwight D. Eisenhower.* Lawrence: Regents Press of Kansas, 1979.

Ridgway, Matthew. *The Korean War: How We Met the Challenge.* Garden City, N.Y.: Doubleday, 1967.

———. *Soldier: The Memoirs of Matthew B. Ridgway as Told to Harold H. Martin.* New York: Harper, 1956.

Riley, Charles A. *The Jazz Age in France.* New York: H. N. Abrams, 2004.

Rischin, Moses. *Our Own Kind: Voting by Race, Creed, or National Origin.* Santa Barbara, Calif.: Center for the Study of Democratic Institutions, 1960.

Roberts, Andrew. *Masters and Commanders.* New York: HarperCollins, 2009.

Robertson, David. *Sly and Able: A Political Biography of James F. Byrnes.* New York: Norton, 1997.

Robinson, Greg. *By Order of the President: FDR and the Internment of Japanese Americans.* Cambridge, Mass.: Harvard University Press, 2001.

Rodenbough, Theo. F., and William L. Haskin, eds. *The Army of the United States: Historical Sketches of Staff and Line with Portraits of Generals-in-Chief.* New York: Argonaut Press, 1966.

Rommel, Erwin. *The Rommel Papers.* B. H. Liddell Hart, ed. New York: Harcourt, Brace, 1953.

Roosevelt, Elliott. *As He Saw It.* New York: Duell, Sloan, and Pearce, 1946.

Roosevelt, Franklin D. *Complete Presidential Press Conferences of Franklin D. Roosevelt.* New York: Da Capo Press, 1972.

————. *The Public Papers and Addresses of Franklin D. Roosevelt Compiled with Special Material and Explanatory Notes by President Roosevelt.* Vol. 2, *The Year of Crisis, 1933.* New York: Random House, 1938.

————. *The Public Papers and Addresses of Franklin D. Roosevelt with Special Material and Explanatory Notes by Samuel I. Rosenman.* Vol. 12, *The Tide Turns, 1943,* and vol. 13, *Victory and the Threshold of Peace, 1944–45.* New York: Harper and Brothers, 1950.

Roosevelt, Kermit. *Countercoup: The Struggle for the Control of Iran.* New York: McGraw-Hill, 1979.

Rosenthal, Michael. *Nicholas Miraculous: The Amazing Career of the Redoubtable Dr. Nicholas Murray Butler.* New York: Farrar, Straus and Giroux, 2006.

Ross, Lillian. *Adlai Stevenson.* New York: J. B. Lippincott Company, 1966.

Rostow, W. W. *Eisenhower, Kennedy, and Foreign Aid.* Austin: University of Texas Press, 1985.

————. *Europe After Stalin: Eisenhower's Three Decisions of March 11, 1953.* Austin: University of Texas Press, 1982.

————. *Open Skies: Eisenhower's Proposal of July 21, 1955.* Austin: University of Texas Press, 1983.

————. *Pre-Invasion Bombing Strategy: General Eisenhower's Decision of March 25, 1944.* Austin: University of Texas Press, 1981.

Rovere, Richard H. *The Eisenhower Years: Affairs of State.* New York: Farrar, Straus, and Cudahy, 1956.

Rowse, Arthur Edward. *Slanted News: A Case Study of the Nixon and Stevenson Fund Stories.* Boston: Beacon Press, 1957.

Roy, Jules. *The Battle of Dienbienphu.* Robert Baldick, trans. New York: Harper and Row, 1965.

Ruhm von Oppen, Beate, ed. *Documents on Germany Under Occupation, 1945–1954.* London: Oxford University Press, 1955.

Rumsfeld, Donald. *Known and Unknown: A Memoir.* New York: Sentinel, 2011.

Russell, Donald Bert. *Invincible Ike: The Inspiring Life Story of Dwight D. Eisenhower.* Chicago: Successful Living Publications, 1952.

Russoli, Edward. *Dwight D. Eisenhower: General, President, and Cook.* Allentown, Pa.: Benedettini Books, 1990.

Ryan, Cornelius. *A Bridge Too Far.* New York: Simon and Schuster, 1974.

————. *The Last Battle.* New York: Simon and Schuster, 1966.

————. *The Longest Day.* New York: Simon and Schuster, 1959.

Schlesinger, Arthur M., Jr. *The Imperial Presidency.* Boston: Houghton Mifflin, 1973.

Schnabel, James F., and Robert J. Watson. *The History of the Joint Chiefs of Staff.* Vol. 3, *The Korean War.* Wilmington, Del.: Glazier, 1979.

Schwartz, Bernard. *Super Chief: Earl Warren and His Supreme Court.* New York: New York University Press, 1983.

Schwarzkopf, H. Norman, [Jr.]. *It Doesn't Take a Hero: General H. Norman Schwarzkopf, the Autobiography.* New York: Bantam Books, 1992.

Scott, General Hugh. *Some Memories of a Soldier.* New York: Century, 1928.

Seale, Patrick. *The Struggle for Syria: A Study of Post-War Arab Politics, 1945–1958.* New York: Oxford University Press, 1965.

Shank, William H. *History of the York Pullman Automobile, 1903–1917.* York, Pa.: Historical Society of York County, 1985.

Sherwood, Robert E. *Roosevelt and Hopkins: An Intimate History.* New York: Harper, 1948.

Shulman, Milton. *Defeat in the West.* New York: E. P. Dutton, 1948.

Shultz, George P. *Turmoil and Triumph: My Years as Secretary of State.* New York: Charles Scribner's Sons, 1993.

Sinclair, Barbara. *Party Wars: Polarization and the Politics of National Policy Making.* Oklahoma City: University of Oklahoma Press, 2006.

Sixsmith, E. K. G. *Eisenhower as Military Commander.* New York: Stein and Day, 1973.

Slater, Ellis D. *The Ike I Knew.* Ellis D. Slater Trust, 1980.

Smith, A. Merriman. *Meet Mister Eisenhower.* New York: Harper and Brothers, 1955.

————. *A President's Odyssey.* New York: Harper and Brothers, 1961.

Smith, Gene. *Until the Last Trumpet Sounds: The Life of General of the Armies John J. Pershing.* New York: Wiley, 1998.

Smith, Jean Edward. *The Defense of Berlin.* Baltimore: Johns Hopkins Press, 1964.

————. *FDR.* New York: Random House, 2007.

————. *Grant.* New York: Simon and Schuster, 2001.

————. *John Marshall: Definer of a Nation.* New York: Henry Holt, 1996.

————. *Lucius D. Clay: An American Life.* New York: Henry Holt, 1990.

Smith, Richard Norton. *Thomas E. Dewey and His Times.* New York: Simon and Schuster, 1982.

Smith, Walter Bedell. *Eisenhower's Six Great Decisions: Europe, 1944–1945.* New York: Longmans, Green, 1956.

Smythe, Donald. *Guerrilla Warrior: The Early Life of John J. Pershing.* New York: Scribner, 1973.

————. *Pershing: General of the Armies.* Bloomington: Indiana University Press, 1986.

Snow, Edgar. *Journey to the Beginning.* New York: Random House, 1958.

Snyder, Marty, and Glenn D. Kittler. *My Friend Ike.* New York: Frederick Fell, 1956.

Soviet Union. Komissiia po izdaniiu diplomaticheskikh dokumentov. *Stalin's Correspondence with Churchill, Attlee, Roosevelt, and Truman: 1941–1945.* New York: E. P. Dutton, 1958.

Speidel, Hans. *We Defended Normandy.* Ian Colvin, trans. London: Herbert Jenkins, 1951.

Starling, Edmund William. *Starling of the White House: The Story of the Man Whose Secret Service Detail Guarded Five Presidents from Woodrow Wilson to Franklin D. Roosevelt, as Told to Thomas Sugrue by Colonel Edmund W. Starling.* New York: Simon and Schuster, 1946.

Stassen, Harold, and Marshall Houts. *Eisenhower: Turning the World Toward Peace.* St. Paul, Minn.: Merrill/Magnus, 1990.

Statler, Kathryn, and Andrew Johns. *The Eisenhower Administration, the Third World, and the Globalization of the Cold War.* Lanham, Md.: Rowman and Littlefield, 2006.

Stevenson, Adlai E. *Call to Greatness.* New York: Atheneum, 1966.

———. *What I Think.* New York: Harper and Brothers, 1956.

Stimson, Henry L., and McGeorge Bundy. *On Active Service in Peace and War.* New York: Harper and Brothers, 1948.

Stoler, Mark A. *The Politics of the Second Front: American Military Planning and Diplomacy in Coalition Warfare, 1941–1943.* Westport, Conn.: Greenwood Press, 1977.

Stone, David. *War Summits.* Washington, D.C.: Potomac Books, 2005.

Sulzberger, C. L. *The Last of the Giants.* New York: Macmillan, 1970.

———. *A Long Row of Candles: Memories and Diaries, 1934–1954.* New York: Macmillan, 1969.

Summers, Anthony. *Official and Confidential: The Secret Life of J. Edgar Hoover.* New York: G. P. Putnam's Sons, 1993.

Summersby, Kay. *Eisenhower Was My Boss.* New York: Prentice Hall, 1948.

Sundquist, James. *Politics and Policy: The Eisenhower, Kennedy, and Johnson Years.* Washington, D.C.: Brookings Institution, 1968.

Takeyh, Ray. *The Origins of the Eisenhower Doctrine: the US, Britain, and Nasser's Egypt, 1953–57.* New York: St. Martin's Press, 2000.

Tananbaum, Duane. *The Bricker Amendment Controversy: A Test of Eisenhower's Political Leadership.* Ithaca, N.Y.: Cornell University Press, 1988.

Taubman, Philip. *Secret Empire: Eisenhower, the CIA, and the Hidden Story of America's Space Espionage.* New York: Simon and Schuster, 2003.

Taylor, Allan, ed. *What Eisenhower Thinks.* New York: Thomas Y. Crowell, 1952.

Taylor, John M. *General Maxwell Taylor: The Sword and the Pen.* Garden City, N.Y.: Doubleday, 1989.

Taylor, Maxwell D. *Swords and Plowshares.* New York: Norton, 1972.

———. *The Uncertain Trumpet.* New York: Harper and Brothers, 1960.

Tedder, Arthur William. *With Prejudice: The War Memoirs of Marshal of the Royal Air Force, Lord Tedder.* London: Cassell, 1966.

Terraine, John, ed. *The Life and Times of Lord Mountbatten.* London: Hutchinson, 1969.

Theoharis, Athan, ed. *From the Secret Files of J. Edgar Hoover.* Chicago: Ivan R. Dee, 1991.

Thompson, Kenneth W., ed. *The Eisenhower Presidency: Eleven Intimate Perspectives of Dwight D. Eisenhower.* Lanham, Md.: University Press of America, 1984.

Thomson, Charles, Alexander Holmes, and Frances M. Shattuck. *The 1956 Presidential Campaign.* Washington, D.C.: Brookings Institution, 1960.

Thomson, David. *Democracy in France Since 1870.* New York: Oxford University Press, 1964.

Tillotson, Lee S., ed. *The Articles of War, Annotated by Lee S. Tillotson.* Harrisburg, Pa.: Military Service Publishing, 1943.

Tompkins, Peter. *Italy Betrayed.* New York: Simon and Schuster, 1966.

———. *The Murder of Admiral Darlan: A Study in Conspiracy.* New York: Simon and Schuster, 1965.

Truman, Harry S. *Memoirs.* 2 vols. Garden City, N.Y.: Doubleday, 1955–56.

Truscott, Lucian K., Jr. *The Twilight of the U.S. Cavalry: Life in the Old Army, 1917–1942.* Colonel Lucian K. Truscott III, ed. Lawrence: University Press of Kansas, 1989.

Tudda, Chris. *The Truth Is Our Weapon: The Rhetorical Diplomacy of Dwight D. Eisenhower and John Foster Dulles.* Baton Rouge: Louisiana State University Press, 2006.

Underwood, Larry D. *Abilene Lawmen: The Smith-Hickok Years.* Lincoln, Neb.: Dageforde Publishing, 1999.

Union of Soviet Socialist Republics Ministry of Foreign Affairs. *Correspondence Between the Chairman of the Council of Ministers of the USSR and the Presidents of the U.S.A. and the Prime Ministers of Great Britain During the Great Patriotic War of 1941–1945.* New York: E. P. Dutton, 1958.

United Nations Statistical Office. *Demographic Yearbook: 1960.* New York: UN Department of Economic and Social Affairs, 1960.

United States Army, Center of Military History. *American Armies and the Battlefields of Europe.* Washington, D.C.: U.S. Government Printing Office, 1992.

———. *Dwight David Eisenhower.* Washington, D.C.: U.S. Army Center of Military History, 1990.

United States Bureau of the Census. *The Statistical History of the United States from Colonial Times to the Present.* Stamford, Conn.: Fairfield Publishers, 1965.

United States Congress. *Official Congressional Directory. 77th Cong.–86th Cong., 1942–1959.* Washington, D.C.: U.S. Government Printing Office, 1942–59.

United States Department of Defense. *Journey to Victory: Dwight David Eisenhower, 1890–1990.* Washington, D.C.: Department of Defense, 1990.

United States Department of State. *The Conference of Berlin: The Potsdam Conference, 1945.* Washington, D.C.: U.S. Government Printing Office, 1960.

———. *Foreign Relations of the United States, 1942.* Vol. 2, *Europe.* Washington, D.C.: U.S. Government Printing Office, 1962.

———. *Foreign Relations of the United States, 1943.* Vol. 2, *Europe.* Washington, D.C.: U.S. Government Printing Office, 1964.

———. *Foreign Relations of the United States, 1945.* Vol. 3. Washington, D.C.: U.S. Government Printing Office, 1964.

———. *Foreign Relations of the United States, 1950.* Vol. 3, *Western Europe.* Washington, D.C.: U.S. Government Printing Office, 1977.

———. *Foreign Relations of the United States, 1950.* Vol. 5, *The Near East, South Asia, and Africa.* Washington, D.C.: U.S. Government Printing Office, 1978.

———. *Foreign Relations of the United States, 1952–1954.* Vol. 1, *General: Economic and Political Matters.* 2 parts. Washington, D.C.: U.S. Government Printing Office, 1983.

———. *Foreign Relations of the United States, 1952–1954, Guatemala.* Washington, D.C.: U.S. Government Printing Office, 2003.

———. *Foreign Relations of the United States, 1952–1954.* Vol. 10, *Iran 1951–1954.* Washington, D.C.: U.S. Government Printing Office, 1989.

———. *Foreign Relations of the United States, 1952–1954.* Vol. 13, *Indochina.* 2 parts. Washington, D.C.: U.S. Government Printing Office, 1982.

———. *Foreign Relations of the United States, 1955–1957.* Vol. 14, *Middle East.* Washington, D.C.: U.S. Government Printing Office, 1989.

———. *Foreign Relations of the United States, 1955–1957.* Vol. 15, *Arab-Israeli Dispute, January 1–July 26, 1956.* Washington, D.C.: U.S. Government Printing Office, 1989.

———. *Foreign Relations of the United States, 1955–1957.* Vol. 16, *Suez Crisis, July 26–December 31, 1956.* Washington, D.C.: U.S. Government Printing Office, 1990.

———. *Foreign Relations of the United States, 1958–1960.* Vol. 10, part 1, *Eastern Europe Region, Soviet Union, Cyprus.* Washington, D.C.: U.S. Government Printing Office, 1993.

———. *Foreign Relations of the United States, Conferences at Cairo and Tehran, 1943.* Washington, D.C.: U.S. Government Printing Office, 1961.

———. *Foreign Relations of the United States, Conferences at Washington, 1941–1942, and Casablanca, 1943.* Washington, D.C.: U.S. Government Printing Office, 1968.

———. *Foreign Relations of the United States, Conferences at Washington and Quebec, 1943.* Washington, D.C.: U.S. Government Printing Office, 1970.

———. *The Soviet Note on Berlin: An Analysis.* Washington, D.C.: Department of State, 1959.

United States Department of the Army. *The Army Almanac.* Washington, D.C.: U.S. Government Printing Office, 1950.

———. *Army Lineage Book.* Vol. 2, *Infantry.* Washington, D.C.: U.S. Government Printing Office, 1953.

Van Creveld, Martin. *Fighting Power: German and U.S. Army Performance, 1939–1945.* Westport, Conn.: Greenwood Press, 1982.

———. *Supplying War: Logistics from Wallenstein to Patton.* Cambridge: Cambridge University Press, 1977.

Vandenberg, Arthur H. *The Private Papers of Senator Vandenberg.* New York: Greenwood Press, 1974.

Vandiver, Frank E. *Black Jack: The Life and Times of John J. Pershing.* 2 vols. College Station: Texas A&M University Press, 1977.

Van Gelder, Lawrence. *Ike: A Soldier's Crusade.* New York: Universal Publishing and Distribution, 1969.

Van Natta, Don, Jr. *First Off the Tee: The Presidential Hackers, Duffers, and Cheaters from Taft to Bush.* New York: PublicAffairs, 2003.

Varney, Carleton. *The Draper Touch: The High Life and High Style of Dorothy Draper.* New York: Prentice Hall, 1988.

Verckler, Stewart. *Cowtown-Abilene: The Story of Abilene, Kansas, 1867–1875.* New York: Carlton Press, 1961.

Verrier, Anthony. *Assassination in Algiers: Churchill, Roosevelt, de Gaulle, and the Murder of Admiral Darlan.* New York: Norton, 1990.

Vidal, Gore. *United States: Essays, 1952–1992.* New York: Broadway Books, 1993.

Vigneras, Marcel. *Rearming the French.* Washington, D.C.: Office of the Chief of Military History, Department of the Army, 1957.

Vogel, Steve. *The Pentagon: A History.* New York: Random House, 2007.

Wagner, Steven. *Eisenhower Republicanism: Pursuing the Middle Way.* DeKalb: Northern Illinois University Press, 2006.

Waldman, Seymour. *Death and Profits: A Study of the War Policies Commission.* New York: Brewer, Warren, and Putnam, 1932.

Walsh, Kenneth T. *Air Force One: A History of the Presidents and Their Planes.* New York: Hyperion, 2003.

———. *From Mount Vernon to Crawford: A History of the Presidents and Their Retreats.* New York: Hyperion, 2005.

Walters, Vernon A. *Silent Missions.* Garden City, N.Y.: Doubleday, 1978.

Ward, Geoffrey, C. *Baseball: An Illustrated History.* New York: Alfred A. Knopf, 1994.

Warren, Earl. *The Memoirs of Earl Warren.* Garden City, N.Y.: Doubleday, 1977.

Warshaw, Shirley. *Reexamining the Eisenhower Presidency.* Westport, Conn.: Greenwood Press, 1993.

Watson, Mark Skinner. *Chief of Staff: Prewar Plans and Preparations.* Washington, D.C.: Historical Division, Department of the Army, 1950.

Wawro, Gregory J., and Eric Schickler. *Filibuster: Obstruction and Lawmaking in the U.S. Senate.* Princeton, N.J.: Princeton University Press, 2006.

Wedemeyer, Albert C. *Wedemeyer Reports!* New York: Henry Holt, 1958.

Weigley, Russell F. *The American Way of War: A History of United States Military Strategy and Policy.* Bloomington: Indiana University Press, 1977.

———. *Eisenhower's Lieutenants: The Campaign of France and Germany, 1944–1945.* Bloomington: Indiana University Press, 1981.

Weinberg, Gerhard L. *A World at Arms: A Global History of World War II.* Cambridge: Cambridge University Press, 1994.

Weintraub, Stanley. *15 Stars: Eisenhower, MacArthur, Marshall: Three Generals Who Saved the American Century.* New York: Free Press, 2007.

Welch, Robert. *The Politician.* Belmont, Mass.: Belmont Publishing, 1964.

Werth, Alexander. *De Gaulle: A Political Biography.* New York: Simon and Schuster, 1966.

West, J. B., and Mary Lynn Kotz. *Upstairs at the White House: My Life with the First Ladies.* New York: Coward, McCann, and Geoghegan, 1973.

Westphal, Siegfried. *The German Army in the West.* London: Cassell, 1951.

Wheeler-Bennett, Sir John W. *The Nemesis of Power: The German Army in Politics, 1918–1945.* London: Macmillan, 1964.

White, G. Edward. *Earl Warren: A Public Life.* New York: Oxford University Press, 1982.

White, Paul Dudley. *My Life and Medicine: An Autobiographical Memoir.* Boston: Gambit, 1971.

White, Theodore H. *In Search of History: A Personal Adventure.* New York: Warner Books, 1978.

Whitman, Alden, and *The New York Times. Portrait: Adlai E. Stevenson: Politician, Diplomat, Friend.* New York: Harper and Row, 1965.

Whitney, Courtney. *MacArthur: His Rendezvous with History.* New York: Knopf, 1955.

Wicker, Tom. *Dwight D. Eisenhower.* New York: Times Books, 2002.

Wieviorka, Oliver. *Normandy: The Landings to the Liberation of Paris.* Cambridge, Mass.: Belknap Press of Harvard University Press, 2008.

Wilber, Donald N. *Adventures in the Middle East: Excursions and Incursions.* Pennington, N.J.: Darwin Press, 1986.

Williams, Juan. *Eyes on the Prize: America's Civil Rights Years, 1954–1965.* New York: Penguin Books, 1987.

Williams, Mary H. *Chronology 1941–1945.* Washington, D.C.: Office of the Chief of Military History, Department of the Army, 1960.

———, comp. *United States Army in World War II: Special Studies: Chronology 1941–1945.* Washington, D.C.: Office of the Chief of Military History, Department of the Army, 1960.

Willoughly, Charles A., and John Chamberlain. *MacArthur: 1941–1951.* New York: McGraw-Hill, 1954.

Wills, Garry. *Nixon Agonistes: The Crisis of the Self-Made Man.* Boston: Houghton Mifflin, 1970.

Wilmot, Chester. *The Struggle for Europe.* New York: Harper and Row, 1952.

Wind, Herbert Warren. *The Story of American Golf, Its Champions and Its Championships.* New York: Farrar, Straus, 1962.

Winks, Robin W. *Cloak and Gown: Scholars in the Secret War, 1939–1961.* New York: William Morrow, 1987.

Winterbotham, Frederick William. *The Ultra Secret.* New York: Harper and Row, 1974.

Wise, David, and Thomas B. Ross. *The Invisible Government.* New York: Random House, 1964.

Wolf, Stanley R., and Audrey (Wolf) Weiland. *Ike: Gettysburg's Gentleman Farmer.* Privately published, 2008.

Wolf, Thomas P., William D. Pederson, and Byron W. Daynes, eds. *Franklin D. Roosevelt and Congress: The New Deal and Its Aftermath.* Armonk, N.Y.: M. E. Sharpe, 2001.

Wolk, Allan. *The Presidency and Black Civil Rights: Eisenhower to Nixon.* Rutherford, N.J.: Fairleigh Dickinson University Press, 1971.

Woodhouse, C. M. *Something Ventured.* London: Granada, 1982.

Woodward, C. Vann. *The Strange Career of Jim Crow.* Oxford: Oxford University Press, 2002.

Wukovitz, John F. *Eisenhower.* New York: Palgrave Macmillan, 2006.

Yarbrough, Tinsley E. *John Marshall Harlan: Great Dissenter of the Warren Court.* New York: Oxford University Press, 1992.

York, Herbert F. *Making Weapons, Talking Peace: A Physicist's Odyssey from Hiroshima to Geneva.* New York: Basic Books, 1987.

Young, Andrew. *An Easy Burden: The Civil Rights Movement and the Transformation of America.* New York: HarperCollins, 1996.

Young, John Russell. *Around the World with General Grant.* New York: American News Company, 1879.

# Illustration Credits

Images on the following pages are reproduced courtesy of:
Columbia University Archives: 476, 478
Dwight D. Eisenhower Presidential Library: frontispiece, 6, 9, 13,
15, 24, 31, 35, 45, 52, 58, 70, 85, 89, 112, 114, 124, 131, 133, 160,
205, 219, 249, 274, 308, 314, 327, 340, 347, 353, 367, 370, 389,
390, 391, 414, 420, 421, 422, 423, 430, 434, 437, 445, 446, 449,
456, 494, 500, 558, 562, 616, 628, 635, 640, 651, 679, 696, 725,
737, 763, 766
Harold Ober Associates on behalf of the estate of Kay Summersby
Morgan: 195, 424
Library of Congress: 61, 94, 179, 207, 257, 262, 504, 580
National Archives and Records Administration: 244, 361, 431, 440,
521
Raleigh DeGeer Amyx Collection: 217
Susan Eisenhower: 33
The Herb Block Foundation: 543, 586, 668, 749, 758
United States Army Signal Corps, Department of the Army: 163

# Index

JEAN EDWARD SMITH is a senior scholar in the history department at Columbia University, and the author of *FDR,* winner of the 2008 Francis Parkman Prize of the Society of American Historians. His other highly regarded biographies include *Grant,* a 2002 Pulitzer Prize finalist; *John Marshall: Definer of a Nation;* and *Lucius D. Clay: An American Life.*